AMERICAN INTERGOVERNMENTAL RELATIONS

AMERICAN INTERGOVERNMENTAL RELATIONS

THEIR ORIGINS, HISTORICAL DEVELOPMENT, AND CURRENT STATUS

by W. Brooke Graves

ADJUNCT PROFESSOR OF POLITICAL SCIENCE

THE AMERICAN UNIVERSITY

CHARLES SCRIBNER'S SONS, NEW YORK

Picture Acknowledgments

PRESIDENT KENNEDY MOVES AGAINST DISCRIMINATION IN FEDERAL EMPLOYMENT, *The New York Times*, April 12, 1961. United Press International Photo. (P. 181.)

THE CONFERENCE OF CHIEF JUSTICES. Courtesy Council of State Governments. (P. 592.)

PRESIDENT KENNEDY SIGNS THE DEPRESSED AREAS BILL, *The New York Times*, May 1, 1961. Courtesy The White House (By Abbie Rowe). (P. 672.)

DETROIT-WAYNE COUNTY BUILDING. Courtesy City of Detroit, Department Report and Information Committee. (P. 759.)

PIONEERS IN THE MOVEMENT FOR COOPERATIVE FEDERALISM. (P. 819.)
HENRY W. TOLL. Courtesy Council of State Governments.
FRANK BANE. Courtesy Council of State Governments.
WILLIAM ANDERSON. Courtesy University of Minnesota.
LAWRENCE H. FOUNTAIN. Courtesy of Representative Fountain.
ROBERT F. WAGNER. Courtesy Office of the Mayor, City of New York.
EDMUND S. MUSKIE. Courtesy of Senator Muskie.

ACKNOWLEDGMENTS

Grateful acknowledgment is made to the following authors and publishers to quote material from their books and articles.

WILLIAM ANDERSON, *Intergovernmental Relations in Review* (Minneapolis: University of Minnesota Press, 1960). Reprinted with permission of the author.

EDWARD CHANNING, *History of the United States,* 6 vols. (New York: The Macmillan Company, 1905–1925). Copyright 1908 by The Macmillan Company; renewed 1936 by Alice Channing and Elizabeth C. Fuller. Reprinted with permission of the publisher.

EDWARD S. CORWIN, *National Supremacy* (New York: Holt, Rinehart and Winston, Inc., 1913). Copyright 1913, Holt, Rinehart and Winston, Inc.; reprinted with permission of the publisher.

FREDERICK L. ZIMMERMANN AND MITCHELL WENDELL, "Congress: A Second Empire of the Federal System," *Georgetown Law Journal,* May, 1952. Reprinted with permission of the authors and the *Georgetown Law Journal.*

HENRY M. HART, JR. AND HERBERT WECHSLER, *The Federal Courts and the Federal System* (New York: The Foundation Press, 1953). Reprinted with permission of the authors and the publisher.

MORTON GRODZINS, "The Federal System," *Goals for Americans, The Report of the President's Commission on National Goals,* the American Assembly (Englewood Cliffs, N.J.: Prentice-Hall, Inc. 1960). Copyright © 1960 by Prentice-Hall, Inc.; reprinted with permission of the author and the publisher.

EARL MAZO, [Alleged Voting Irregularities in the 1960 Presidential Election], New York *Herald Tribune,* December 4–7, 1960. Reprinted with permission of the author.

LEO EGAN, "Kennedy and New York: He Aids Anti-Prendergast Group," *The New York Times,* January 8, 1961. Copyright by the New York Times; reprinted with permission of the New York Times.

RICHARD P. LONGAKER, *The Presidency And Individual Liberties* (Ithaca: Cornell University Press, 1961). Reprinted with permission of the author and publisher.

RALPH McGILL, "Blame for the Civil Rights Issue," Washington *Evening Star,* March 24, April 17, and April 18, 1962. Reprinted by special permission of the Hall Syndicate, Inc. All Rights Reserved.

"Barnett Pledges Mississippi Aid for Alabama," Washington *Evening Star,* May 22, 1961. Reprinted with permission of The *Evening Star.*

MARTIN LUTHER KING, "Equality Now," *The Nation,* February 4, 1961. Reprinted with permission of *The Nation.*

JOSEPH E. KALLENBACH, *Federal Cooperation with the States Under the Commerce Clause* (Ann Arbor: The University of Michigan Press, 1942). Copyright by the University of Michigan Press; reprinted with permission of the author and publisher.

GLENN E. BROOKS, *When Governors Convene* (Baltimore: The Johns Hopkins Press, 1961). Reprinted with permission of the publisher.

v

27250

LLOYD BLAUCH, in *American Universities and Colleges,* ed. Mary Irwin (Washington: American Council on Education, 1956). Reprinted with permission of the publisher.

WILLIAM B. DALE AND DAVID C. FULTON, *Do the States Have a Role to Play in Foreign Aid?* (Menlo Park, Calif.: Stanford Research Institute, January, 1961). Reprinted with permission of the authors.

WILLIAM H. RIKER, *Soldiers of the States: the Role of the National Guard in American Democracy* (Washington: Public Affairs Press, 1957). Reprinted with permission of the author and publisher.

WILLIAM ANDERSON, *Intergovernmental Fiscal Relations* (Minneapolis: University of Minnesota Press, 1957). Reprinted with permission of the author.

ALBERT LEPAWSKY, "America's Tax Dollar—A Key Problem in Governmental Reconstruction," *The Annals of the American Academy of Political and Social Science,* January, 1940. Reprinted with permission of the author and *The Annals.*

JOSEPH P. HARRIS, "The Future of Federal Grants-in-Aid," *The Annals of the American Academy of Political and Social Science,* January, 1940. Reprinted with permission of the author and *The Annals.*

Federal Grants-in-Aid (Chicago: Council of State Governments, 1949). Reprinted with permission of the Council of State Governments.

BRAESTRUPE, PETER, "Widened Inquiry on Roads Sought," *The New York Times,* December 11, 1960. Copyright by the New York Times; reprinted with permission of the New York Times.

ROSCOE C. MARTIN, "Federalism and Regionalism," *The Rice Institute Lectures on Local Government* (Houston, Tex., 1958). Reprinted with permission of the author and Rice University.

DAMON STETSON, "Schools Merged to End a Dispute," *The New York Times,* November 13, 1960. Copyright by the New York Times; reprinted with permission of the New York Times.

LUTHER H. GULICK, "Reorganization of the State," *Civil Engineering,* August, 1933.

JAMES M. BURNS AND JACK E. PELTASON, *Government by the People: the Dynamics of American National Government,* 4th ed. (Englewood Cliffs, N.J.: Prentice-Hall, Inc., 1960). Copyright © 1960. Reprinted with permission of the publisher.

To Jenifer Ruth and William Blake

This survey of intergovernmental relationships in the United States might be described as the history of a principle of governmental organization, that has been a major characteristic of American government for a period of nearly two hundred years. It attempts to show the origins of the American federal system, and to describe and analyze the many facets of its development as in turn it affected and was affected by other significant aspects of American life. In other words, it attempts to show how we got where we are, governmentally speaking, and to point out some of the major problems of federalism, as our nation enters the closing decades of the twentieth century.

This historical approach has seemed to be desirable because so many of the things that are done or recommended in the field of intergovernmental relations suffer from a lack of historical perspective. In fact, far too many of the studies that have been made have failed, largely to provide either an accurate diagnosis or adequate solution for the problems discussed. No one has stated this inadequacy better than the late Professor Paul Studenski who wrote in October, 1960:

> Far too often they treat old problems as if they were new and prescribe solutions which have been tried in similar situations and found ineffective. Far too often, too, these studies treat problems separately as if they are wholly unrelated to each other, whereas they have common roots and should be jointly treated as different manifestations of the difficulty.

Historical analysis of the problems of intergovernmental relations, he goes on to say, can do much to clarify their nature and create a better understanding of the basic issues involved. Similarly, John E. Bebout observes that "if people can learn to view intergovernmental relations in terms of real history rather than in terms of the clichés derived from political myth-makers, we may be able to deal more rationally with emerging problems."

As work on this project progressed, the character of the treatment was somewhat modified. While the original purpose of describing the origins, growth, and development of intergovernmental relations in this country has been consistently adhered to, it has been supplemented by a fuller treatment of the current situation and possible future trends than was originally contemplated. This change developed gradually, as more and more frequently it appeared to be necessary to elaborate on the existing situation to complete the story and make it meaningful.

The two most difficult problems encountered in the preparation of this volume have arisen from the overwhelming quantities of pertinent materials, past and present, that had to be examined, considered, and

ix

used or rejected, and the problem of organization in an enormously complicated field in which few precedents exist. The problems involving intergovernmental relations in a major national state are so numerous, so intricate, and so far-reaching in their effects as to almost defy classification. This is so because almost every topic one considers affects or is affected by nearly every other topic. One single program or event may have significance in as many as half-a-dozen chapters. One commentator observed—some what facetiously, to be sure—that everything should be discussed in one chapter! Since this is scarcely practical, many, sometimes arbitrary, decisions—have had to be made, even at the risk of some duplication and a great many cross references.

A straight chronological presentation could produce little more than a mere listing of items or incidents bearing little or no relation to one another. A presentation constructed solely around units or levels of government would serve only to perpetuate some unfortunate past assumptions on compartmentalization. An analysis based upon relations existing in individual functional fields could present no more than selected and more or less unrelated pieces or segments of the overall problem. No one of these approaches could, by itself, convey any clear picture of American intergovernmental relations as a whole. Yet, any adequate and reasonably satisfactory presentation must succeed in accomplishing all of these purposes simultaneously. Such is the purpose of the chapters which follow; in order that the reader may have some idea of the route to be followed by this "guided tour," a short summary appears at the beginning of each Part.

Since the scope of intergovernmental relations is so broad, it has been necessary to discuss problems in a tremendous number of subject matter areas, in more than any one student can rightly claim to have a high degree of professional competence. The effort has been made to obtain and present the facts, but reasonable limits of space have precluded any extensive discussion of many of the problems mentioned. Such interpretations of the facts and opinions as may be expressed regarding them are those of the author, not of other persons, agencies, or institutions.

As usual in an undertaking of such magnitude, the author's indebtedness extends to far more people than can possibly be recorded here. At the risk of omitting some who should be included, I must mention a few who have been particularly helpful. Professor Herman E. Slotnick, Chairman of the Department of History and Political Science at the University of Alaska was most helpful and cooperative during a brief but very pleasant visit as a member of his department in 1959–1960. Professors William Anderson (Emeritus) of the University of Minnesota and C. Harold King of the University of Miami (Florida) were generous with their counsel, in ways that were exceedingly helpful, when the book was being planned. Professor William O. Farber of the University of South Dakota contributed much in a series of stimulating discussions that took place during an all too brief service in Washington as a member of a Senate Committee staff.

All of the following have critically read late drafts of one or more chapters, and made constructive comments and suggestions for which I am deeply grateful: Professor Francis R. Aumann, Ohio State University; Dr. William C. Beyer, Moorestown, N.J.; Professor Arthur W. Bromage, University of Michigan; Loren Carlson, formerly Administrative Assistant to Senator Francis Case of South Dakota; Dr. Hugh L. Elsbree, Director, Legislative Reference Service, Library of Congress; Professor Royce Hanson, The American University; Dr. Samuel Humes, Executive Director, Metropolitan Washington Council of Governments; Charles W. Lee, Professional Staff Member, Senate Labor and Public Welfare Committee; Professor Roscoe C. Martin, Syracuse University; Professor William F. Murphy, University of Missouri; Dr. Dorothy Schaffter, Legislative Reference Service, Library of Congress; Edward Staples, Missouri Public Expenditure Council; and Professor John E. Stoner, Indiana University.

Countless others have provided current information, published reports or other materials on many of the topics discussed. To all of them, I am grateful, as I am to the National Municipal League for the release of the substance of the material in Chapters XXV and XXVI which in slightly different form appeared under the title, "Maze of Governments," in the May, June, and July 1960 issues of the *National Civic Review;* to the National Association of County Officials for its permission to reprint here an article on "Interlocal Relations" which was presented in a somewhat abridged form in the January 1963 issue of its journal, *The County Officer;* to the Council of State Governments for its permission to make liberal use of information contained in the author's *Intergovernmental Relations in the United States: An Annotated Chronology,* published in 1958; and finally, to the numerous publishers who have very graciously given their permission to reprint the quoted excerpts from their publications which appear at the beginning of the several chapters of this volume. Henry D. Kass, Miss Yvonne Reed, and Mark H. Freeman, graduate students at The American University have, in successive years, given generously of their time and effort in gathering and analyzing information on many difficult questions. Most of all, I am indebted to my wife, Hazel Wallace Graves, for her continued interest and helpfulness in the always tedious task of completing a manuscript and seeing it through the press.

W. Brooke Graves

Washington, D.C.
November 1, 1963

CONTENTS

xiii

Contents

PART VI ADJUSTMENT AND CHANGE IN
A FEDERAL SYSTEM

TABLES, DIAGRAMS, AND MAPS

AMERICAN INTERGOVERNMENTAL RELATIONS

PART I

HISTORICAL BACKGROUND

Intergovernmental relations, not always recognized as such and certainly not so denominated, have been a matter of concern to man living in organized society throughout the ages, regardless of race, creed, or color, or of time, place, or circumstance. In Chapter I, brief comment on intergovernmental relations in other lands and times is followed by analysis of the origin and development of such relationships in the United States, especially as manifested in some of the outstanding characteristics of American federalism.

Chapter II discusses the origins of American federalism as observed in the relations of the colonies with Great Britain. The deep consciousness of classical civilization in nearly every phase of eighteenth century life cannot be forgotten. Too-strong legislatures and too-weak governors were problems which were at least partially corrected later on. As one writer has expressed it, the tradition of a more balanced relationship between the Executive and Legislative Branches was older than "being temporarily mad and scared at King George."

After independence was achieved, American institutions evolved rapidly. Chapter III considers the first State constitutions, the Articles of Confederation, the unsuccessful convention at Annapolis, and the Constitutional Convention in Philadelphia in 1787, where the American Constitution was framed and submitted to the States for adoption.

1

CHAPTER I

Intergovernmental Relations:
A Universal Problem

A federation is a permanent union of communities so distinct that they might have been sovereign states, so linked by common interest that they have surrendered absolute sovereignty, but so conscious of their distinctness that they have made the surrender in a form which protects those separate rights and these forms of protection may differ in detail from one federation to another; but the making of federations is a difficult feat of political engineering. . . .

A federation requires a written constitution. . . . it is a straightforward enough task to set out in the constitution lists of topics which are to be, respectively, the subject of federal, unit, and concurrent legislation. . . . , in the nature of things, the federation must control defense, foreign affairs and a few essential economic matters. The units—if the status of a unit in a federation is to be worth having—must at least be able to deal with their own local government and education, and—subject perhaps to some federal control—their own police and law courts. In between is a wide range of subjects—the criminal law, marriage and divorce, labour questions, etc., which are sometimes given to the federation, sometimes to the units, and most frequently made subject to concurrent legislative action.[1]

[1] Stewart, Michael, *Modern Forms of Government: A Comparative Study* (New York: Holt, Rinehart and Winston, Inc., 1959; reprinted, New York: Frederick A. Praeger, Inc., 1961), pp. 145–149.

There is little about government that is more important than the interrelationships between the several levels and units through which it operates. How well these units are working together at any given time, in their day-to-day operations, almost provides an index to how well government as a whole is functioning. Good intergovernmental relations may be regarded as an indicator of governmental health in the same way that normal temperature, pulse, and blood pressure are regarded as indicators of normality in the functioning of the human body. Since abundant evidence can be amassed to support the truth of this view, any serious student who examines the record is likely to be more than a little astonished at the casual indifference with which questions of interrelationships have frequently been handled.

Interrelationships in government are of many types. They may involve relations of different branches within a particular government, as in the separation of powers, checks and balances, and the important concept of executive-legislative relations. They may include relations between departments or agencies within the same branch of government, or between the central office of such a department or agency and its field office. Or they may involve relations between governments at different levels within the same national state, such as Federal-State, interstate, regional, Federal-local, State-local, or inter-local.

This chapter and this book as a whole are concerned primarily with intergovernmental relations in the United States. Since the American system of government is federally organized, it follows that much of the discussion deals with American intergovernmental relations in their federal setting. The same or similar problems exist in other governments, whether federally organized or not, but the manifestations of these problems are often quite different from what they are in the United States.

WHAT FEDERALISM IS

The Concept of Federalism

Federalism has been defined by one writer as a principle of political organization which permits erstwhile independent states to combine under a common central government while retaining some portion of their former power and identity.[2] Another writer defines the term as "an association of states which have been founded for certain purposes, but in which the member states retain a large measure of their original inde-

[2] Zurcher, Arnold J., "Federalism," in Smith, Edward C. and Zurcher, Arnold J., eds., *A Dictionary of American Politics* (New York: Barnes & Noble, Inc., 1944), p. 126.

pendence. . . . By the federal principle I mean the method of dividing power so that the general and regional governments are each, within a sphere, coordinate and independent." [3] Still another states simply that "Federalism is a device for dividing decisions and functions of government." [4]

This idea of the division of powers is of paramount importance. "If I were asked," writes Professor William Anderson, "to point out the common features that characterize federal systems, I would mention the constitutional division of the powers and functions of government between two autonomous and constitutionally recognized levels of government, the central and the regional. No strictly unitary system of government . . . has any such arrangement." [5] Questions immediately arise as to the nature of this relationship. One might take issue with the Wheare definition on the ground of internal inconsistencies, as Professor Anderson has done. Two levels of government, he says, are coordinate or not coordinate, independent or not independent. They cannot, in either case, be both. The assumption that governmental powers can and must be divided into separate spheres lies near the center of the Wheare analysis, but how shall these powers be divided? Some students of government maintain that federalism exists as long as even one important power is definitely held at each level. Others take the position that under present conditions no such clear-cut division of powers between different levels and units of government is possible.

In a unitary state, by contrast, territorial subdivisions exist as agents of the central state by which they were created and to which they owe their continued existence. Subdivisions may be abolished, their boundaries may be changed, and their powers may be extended, diminished, or withdrawn. In a federal state, territorial subdivisions exist in their own right. However, this neat contrast is somewhat complicated when home rule powers are granted by the central government of a unitary state to some of its subdivisions, or withheld from a subdivision by the central government of a federal state. In some American States, for example, municipalities and counties have been granted home rule charters in a manner typical of the unitary state system, while provinces in such unitary states as France and Sweden receive the right to elect their own

[3] Wheare, Kenneth C., *Federal Government* (New York: Oxford University Press, 1947), p. 1.

[4] Grodzins, Morton, "The Federal System," *Report* of the President's Commission on National Goals, *Goals for Americans* (New York: American Assembly, Columbia University, Prentice-Hall, Inc., 1960), p. 265.

[5] Anderson, William, *Intergovernmental Relations in Review* (Minneapolis: University of Minnesota Press, 1960), p. 5; see also pp. 142 and 145.

provincial legislatures, although neither home rule nor elected provincial legislatures changes the essential nature of a system in which the territorial subdivisions owe their existence and their powers to the central government.

There are two corresponding—and opposing—forces in government, centripetal and centrifugal. In an over-simplification of the problem, it has been said that the former tends toward organization, order, and even despotism, while the latter tends toward disintegration, chaos, and possibly, anarchy. A federal state may develop as a result of the operation of either of these forces, or as a compromise between either extreme position. Several existent states, for example, may decide to join together and form a federation. It was in this centripetal way that federalism developed in the United States, Switzerland, and Canada. By the centrifugal method, a state decides to adopt federalism and divides its territory into units. Generally speaking, this was how federalism was introduced into such Latin-American states as Mexico and Brazil.[6] Lack of unity is a substantial danger in this method.

The division of powers in a federal state may take either of two forms. It may follow the pattern of the United States and list all of the powers of the central government, leaving the remainder to the regional governments; or, as in Canada, it may list all the powers of the regional governments, leaving the remainder to the central government. Theoretically, the American plan makes it more difficult for the central government to acquire new powers than does the Canadian plan. Harold W. Stoke, however, found in 1933 that the tendencies toward centralization were as strong or stronger in Canada than in the United States.[7] In both of these countries federalism is established on a permanent basis, in contrast with the so-called quasi-federalism that exists in Argentina and the Union of South Africa. In the former, federal supervisors are sent to rule some provinces, while the central government of the Union has in some instances so restricted the powers of the provinces that some writers have argued that the Union has never been a true federal state.

No one has stated more clearly and succinctly the complexities involved in an effort to define federalism than Professor Anderson when he wrote:

> It seems to me that the term *federal system* is a sort of collective name for a vast mass of different and yet interconnected phenomena that are too numerous and too continuously interacting with each other, too fluid and too changing, ever to be reduced to a written record or

[6] Wheare, p. 11.

[7] Stoke, Harold W., "Some Problems of Canadian Federalism," *American Political Science Review*, October, 1933, pp. 804–814.

description at any one time. One slight evidence of this generalization is the continuance of disagreements among well informed persons as to what the system is. In its immensity, its complexity, its ever-changingness, it seems to me the federal system is comparable to such widespread institutions as private property, marriage, religion, and civil liberties. Who can understand all the ramifications of any of these ubiquitous institutions? I, for one, claim to have considerable knowledge of the federal system of government, but I often feel appalled at what I do not know.[8]

People whose governments are organized on a federal rather than a unitary basis, however, have no monopoly on what Americans regard as problems peculiar to a federal system. It is true that the federal form of organization tends to spotlight relations between the center and the outlying areas, but even in a unitary state there must of necessity be relations between the center and the parts, and the people may become quite as aroused over these interrelationships as they do in a federal state.

The point is that relations between the center and the provinces are inevitable, and that periodic outbursts of dissatisfaction with the manner in which these relationships are handled are almost as inevitable. These relationships, in fact, involve fundamental aspects of the political process, and the problems that arise are not only universal as to time and place, but also are perennial within any given society. Each generation, faced with new problems, has to work out its own version of federalism, often after bitter argument and dispute. Of course, it is not the abstract definition of federalism about which men disagree. The dispute arises when one party controls the central government and another some of the provinces, and each uses its own base of operations to attack or resist the other.

Variations in Federal Systems

There are, indeed, as many types of federalism as there are federal states, no two of them exactly alike. Although the federal form has been utilized for centuries in many parts of the world, no single federal system has endured for any extended period of time without change. It is, in fact, one of the most important attributes of federalism that it lends itself to those modifications in function and in the distribution of responsibility called for by the constantly changing social, political, and economic conditions found in a dynamic society.

It thus becomes apparent that one of the major characteristics of federalism is difference and variation, as between one federal system and

[8] Anderson, p. 145.

another. This is true for a number of reasons: differences in time and place; differences in the purposes for which the several systems were originally established; differences in the background and experience of the people who set them up and who later operate them; and differences in the basic attitudes and aspirations of the people who maintain them. Professor Anderson can be quoted again from the summary volume for the Minnesota studies:

> I do not think there is any one constitutional principle of the relations between the central government and the states that applies in all federal systems of government. The constitutional systems that prevail at any one time in Canada, Australia, the Federal Republic of Germany, and the United States, for example, are all unique, *sui generis,* even though they display certain general similarities. The reason for these constitutional diversities need only be suggested to be understood. Each federal-type constitution was drawn up at a different time from every other one, under different circumstances, by different leaders, under the influence of different ideas, to serve the special as well as the general needs of a different people. But this is not all. Each one has continued to change and to be developed over the years to meet the diverse alterations in the needs, conditions, and prevalent ideas of the country concerned. This process of continuous modification and development goes on in every country separately. Thus the legal rules of the Constitution of the United States are not what they were when Minnesota entered the Union a hundred years ago, or even what they were twenty or even ten years ago. That is a major reason why it is necessary to discuss the constitutional rules and principles of the American federal system in their historical development. The constitutional relations of the nation and the states are not fixed but ever changing.[9]

Why Federalism Is Important in America

Federalism is a basic concept in American government. It inspires a sentimental reaction, to be sure, in the minds of many people, but its importance rests upon considerations far more substantial. No one can reasonably argue that the continuance of federalism is indispensable, either to good government in the United States or to our national existence. Experience in other major countries provides abundant proof to the contrary. But there are important arguments in support of the continuance of a federal system of government in this country.

First, federalism was a necessity in the days of the founding. It repre-

[9] Anderson, p. 17.

sented the only means by which a group of independent States, each highly jealous of the others, could be bound together into a nation. The ties were not strong to begin with, but fortunately they were strong enough. In the meantime, the number of States has increased fourfold, and the United States has become a nation, not merely in name but in fact. As a nation, it has grown and prospered as no other nation in history. It has faults, to be sure, which foreigners are quick to recognize, but its accomplishments have been the envy of peoples everywhere, and foreign governments have often paid us the compliment of borrowing American government concepts and adapting them to their own needs.

No reasonable person is going to contend that these accomplishments have been due to the fact that ours is a federal system of government. The achievements were due to the character and industry of the people, to the vast resources of a major portion of a continent, and sometimes to fortuitous circumstances. But, whatever the reasons, progress *was* made in the development of a great civilization, and a federal system of government was and still is an important characteristic of that civilization. For nearly 200 years, federalism has served the nation well. Ordinary prudence would indicate that in the absence of compelling reasons to the contrary, it should be retained, that it should be neither lightly discarded nor permitted to disintegrate through failure to make the adjustments necessitated by new and changed conditions in the economic and social life of the nation.

Some writers take the position that ours is one national government and that there is no reason to be concerned about the national government moving into every field of activity. They would like to see State and local government survive, but are not concerned about the degree of State and local responsibility and autonomy. If ours is to become a unitary state this view may be acceptable, but not if the traditional form of American federalism is to be preserved.

A second major consideration involves the importance of strong, effective institutions of local government. The Anglo-Saxon system of government and law is one of the great systems of the Western world. It is the basis of the American system, and one of its main tenets is an emphasis on strong local government. Local government exists in some form in all countries, but local government in the Anglo-Saxon countries is different from that found in unitary states. It rests upon a philosophy of vigor, independent action, and citizen responsibility in the solution of local problems. It requires a citizenry that is intelligent, informed, and alert. It has given this country the New England town meeting and county government in the South and West. Both were appropriate and effective in the time and environment in which they functioned, and under certain conditions they may still be.

Local government under modern conditions is, of course, something vastly different from a town meeting or the government of an old-fashioned county. States now perform many functions once regarded as strictly local. The system should be different if it is to serve the needs of people in present-day urban life, although the basic concept is still sound. Each unit or level of government should perform as large a portion of the total governmental job as it can perform efficiently and economically. Only in this way can the citizen participate effectively in decisions about what is to be done by government and about how the bill is to be paid; only in this way, it has been said, can one be sure that the hand that collects the tax revenues and the hand that spends the money are attached to the same body. It is difficult, and it may even be impossible, to utilize long-distance financing without having remote control, and often, unfortunately, remote control means no control at all, from the citizen's point of view.

Universal Aspects of Federalism

Although problems involving relationships between different levels and units of government assume a particular importance in federally organized states, such states have no monopoly on them. For more than a decade, it has been the good fortune of the author to discuss governmental problems with considerable numbers of visitors to the United States from countries in all parts of the world. Many of them have been distinguished visitors, important officials in their home governments. Two impressions stand out clearly from these contacts. First, these visitors have almost without exception been deeply interested in the organization and functioning of American governmental institutions. Specifically, they have wanted to know how a difficult problem with which they were confronted in their official capacity is handled here in the United States. Secondly, there is almost invariably some question of interlevel and inter-jurisdictional relations involved in these conversations, whether the visitor's home government is federal or unitary in organization.

Other illustrations of the universality of these problems may be found in press reports of the World Conference of Local Governments which was held in Washington in June, 1961, when more than 800 officials from fifty-one countries met to exchange views and information on problems of local government. The problems discussed could apply to almost any American city, and frequently involved relations of the city with the central government and with intermediate level governments. The Mayor of Freetown, Sierra Leone, Africa, was quoted as saying, "I came here to find out how American cities raise money without raising taxes. . . . The central government," he said, "gives us 60 per cent of the cost of a school, then we have to find the other 40 per cent." Freetown pays about one-third of the cost of its roads, he reported.

The Mayor of Jequie, Bahia, Brazil, observed that like Washington, D.C., Brazilian cities have slums. "Brazilian cities want to get more money back from the Federal government. The payments are very low now. Only about 5.3 per cent of our taxes come back to us. . . . Our biggest problem," he continued, "is finances. We make every effort to get subsidies from the prefectural and central governments, but now I am afraid of centralization from this." [10] All this, and much else that was said at the conference, had a strangely familiar sound.

FEDERALISM IN OTHER LANDS AND TIMES

Experiments With Federalism

The concept of federalism has been closely identified with the history and development of the American nation. It is well to remember, nevertheless, that Americans did not invent the federal idea, nor were they the first to put it into practical operation. Numerous ancient and medieval precedents, even if not specifically involving federalism, raised questions of centralization. Probably the most potent factor in the evolution of the highly centralized kingship in Egypt was the urgent need to make the best use of the Nile, a river which was no more a respecter of States' rights than is the Mississippi. The Greeks, who left few original ideas to be discovered by others, discovered and used the federal idea long before it was adopted here. The Roman Empire in the second century B.C. and the Empire in the first century A.D. always maintained a careful balance between matters which were imperially controlled and those which were scrupulously left to subdivisions (municipalities or provinces). The Romans deferred to the concept of States' rights, until the third century decline began to make the Romans "un-Roman." In more recent times, other peoples—the Dutch and the Swiss, for example—adopted the idea of federalism long before American federalism was born, and Great Britain made use of concepts closely associated with the idea of federalism.

Thus it appears that the problems of central-local relations are age-old and universal in their application. They are not peculiar to the federal form of organization, although they may be more numerous and perhaps more difficult to cope with under such a system. Even in unitary

[10] Clew, Harvey, "World Mayors Face Same Problems," Washington *Evening Star*, June 15, 1961.

governments, particularly in modern times when people are demanding recognition of their rights as individuals, citizens in local units that have never exercised control over their local affairs are insisting upon their right to do so. This change has taken place in one country after another, especially in the years since World War II, and in a highly centralized and authoritarian organization, the process of decentralization—even partial decentralization—raises many difficult questions, both for government officials and for citizens.

It is not essential for the present purpose to review in detail all of the early experiences with federalism. The closeness of the relationship between the legal and political institutions of Great Britain and the United States makes it desirable, however, to note briefly some characteristics of the British experience. Britain, to be sure, is not now and never has been a federal state; yet in the years preceding the Revolutionary War, Britain had problems closely analogous to those of a federal state, problems which surely might be called intergovernmental. Although the federal idea had been invented long before, there was much experimenting to be done under unforeseen circumstances. Britain was groping then, as the United States was to do for long years to come, for solutions to these problems. In the end, Britain almost begged the Americans to suggest an acceptable tax that would be possible to collect.

The British Parliament has often been referred to as the mother of Parliaments. Similarly, it might be said that while the United Kingdom has never itself been federally organized, it has been a mother of federal systems, first in the United States, then in the Dominions of Canada, Australia, New Zealand, and South Africa, and in the newly established republics of India and Pakistan. There are now sixteen national states that are federal in form, though not invariably so in practice.

No two of the Commonwealth constitutions are exactly alike, though all of them reflect basic human concepts of justice, order, and liberty. Michael Stewart observes that "Although the constitutional differences are important, the general similarity of pattern is far more impressive." These constitutions, he continues, "attempt to apply to widely different nations ideas first formulated in Britain." Since British constitutional forms have never been static, one may go on to note that each new constitution, beginning with that of Canada in 1867 and continuing to the recent establishment of the Asian republics, has developed "those forms in such a manner as to make democracy more complete, and to encourage the promotion of social welfare and economic justice." [11]

Australia has an "indissoluble Federal Commonwealth" in which,

[11] Stewart, p. 82.

as in the United States Constitution, all powers not expressly granted to the Commonwealth are reserved for the States. As in the United States, the Commonwealth has exclusive control over foreign affairs, the armed forces, the postal system, customs and excises, the coining of money, and matters relating to the federal capital district. In Canada, the principle governing the division of powers between the provinces and the central government is opposite from that which prevails in Australia and the United States. The central government has general responsibility for the "peace, order and good government" of the country, and all powers not expressly given to the provinces belong to the realm. The very use of the term "provinces" rather than "states" suggests that although the constitution is federal in character, the rights which it guarantees to the provinces are strictly limited.

One finds some unique forms of federalism in the Republics of India and Pakistan. Although the framers of the Indian constitution avoided using the word "federalism," they provided for a hybrid form between a federal and a unitary state. The form of government in the states and the distribution of powers between them and the union are prescribed in the constitution and may be altered only by a special procedure which requires the consent of at least half the states. Although the central Parliament is constructed to represent both the people as a whole and the separate states, it is empowered by the ordinary processes of law-making to alter state boundaries and to create new states. The only restrictions are that such a proposal must be originally recommended by the president and that he must have ascertained—although he need not necessarily comply with—the wishes of the states concerned. On the basis of this and similar provisions of the Indian constitution, it has been argued that the framers managed to express both the need for a federal form of government and a desire that the government should develop in a unitary direction.

The situation in Pakistan is even more unusual. There are only two provinces, each quite different and widely separated from the other, but equally represented in a 300-member unicameral National Assembly. A new constitution, which was adopted in 1956, provides for an allocation of powers which is in many respects similar to our own. The National Assembly has sole power to pass laws concerning defense, foreign affairs, rights of citizenship, foreign and inter-provincial trade and commerce, banking and currency, postal service, and certain phases of taxation. Both national and provincial assemblies may legislate on civil and criminal law, and on social and economic planning, while provincial assemblies alone have authority over local government, education, police, and other phases of taxation not assigned to the National Assembly. Pakistan has a dual system of courts, like that in the United States, with the right of appeal extending from the provincial courts to the national supreme court.

Expansion of Federalism Since World War II

What Americans regard as the problems of federalism are mainly problems in the relations between the center and the outlying areas. Our outlying areas are, of course, States. In Canada and Australia they are called provinces; in Switzerland, cantons; and other names are used in other jurisdictions. While problems in the relations of the center to the provinces may be more characteristic of federal than unitary systems of government, they are common in both types of organization, as illustrated by developments in the years following World War II. These years were characterized, in the first place, by a significantly extended use of the federal form as new governments were established in India, Pakistan, Burma, Libya, Yugoslavia, Western Germany, and Indonesia, although Indonesia subsequently became a unitary state, and the Indian and Pakistani forms of federalism were, as already noted, unusual ones. The British experimented with federalism in Rhodesia, Nigeria, and the West Indies, while developments in other countries and in the overseas possessions of France provide additional examples of a growing trend toward federalism.

Distinguished foreign visitors came to this country during the postwar years, some of them to gain a better understanding of how American federalism is organized and how it functions, others to learn how even with a unitary organization the people might take part in local determination of policies and local administration of law.

The growing trend toward federalism was especially conspicuous in Italy, Greece, and Turkey, among other countries whose people had never, certainly not in modern times, been permitted to exercise any local autonomy whatsoever. It appeared to be a uniquely modern phenomenon that people of all races and nations were demanding the privilege or the right to participate in local self-government, an unfamiliar and previously unknown governmental experience.

FEDERALISM IN THE UNITED STATES

One must, of course, remember that the American experiment was not the first example of a federal state, nor was it even the first republic.

Federalism here was both the means and the price of the formation of the Union,[12] but the scale on which federalism and representative government were attempted was sufficiently new to excite first the curiosity and then the admiration of European observers.

By way of supplement to an earlier word on the nature of federalism in general, it may be appropriate at this point to try to define more exactly the American concept of federalism. The late Professor Frederic A. Ogg once defined a federal government as one in which "the political sovereign has made a distribution of the powers of government among certain agencies, central and divisional, and has done so through the medium of constitutional provisions which neither the central nor the divisional government has made, and which are beyond the power of either to alter or rescind." [13] Restated in terms of American conditions, one might say that "We, the people" have in the Federal Constitution divided the powers of government between the central government in Washington and the governments of the several States. The prescribed division of powers was not devised by either the previously existing central government or by the States acting alone, nor can it be amended or abrogated by the unilateral action of either type of governmental agency. The seemingly clear and simple formula for the allocation of powers between the Federal government and the States is given in the Tenth Amendment to the Federal Constitution:

> The powers not delegated to the United States by the Constitution, nor prohibited by it to the States, are reserved to the States respectively, or to the people.

Following this formula, the central government is one of delegated, enumerated, or expressed powers, a government which may do only those things which it is specifically authorized to do, or which by judicial interpretation may reasonably be implied. The powers involved are chiefly those which experience under the Articles of Confederation had demonstrated that States could not perform properly for themselves. In this category were included the powers of defense, conduct of foreign relations, and domestic matters which involve a national interest or transcend the boundary lines of individual States.

Theoretically, the States were governments possessing only residual powers which could be determined by a process of elimination. If a given

[12] Wechsler, Herbert, "The Political Safeguards of Federalism," *Columbia Law Review*, April, 1954, pp. 543–560.

[13] Zink, Harold, *Governments of Europe* (New York: The Macmillan Co., 1924), p. 53. See also Ogg, Frederick A. and Zink, Harold, *Governments of Europe*, rev. ed. (New York: The Macmillan Co., 1950), p. 37.

power, such as the conduct of public schools, the building of roads, the preservation of public peace, and the protection of life and property were neither granted to the Federal government (Article I, Section 8, and elsewhere) nor denied to the States (Article I, Section 10), it was assumed that these powers belonged to the States.

Although the original concepts of the Founders have not been officially modified since the early amendments (particularly the anti-national Eleventh), the kind of federalism functioning in the United States today is considerably different from that established in 1789. Yet it may well be that if the leading Framers could return, they would be largely satisfied with the system as it exists today, and would feel that it has generally followed its intended lines of development. In other words, careful study of the records of the founding tends to support the historical legitimacy of the present system, and to deny the claims of those who see in this system an alarming departure from its ancient moorings.[14]

Changes have been necessary, of course, in a rapidly changing society. The absence of formal mandates for them may presumably be attributed to the demonstrated reluctance of Americans to use formal and established procedures to accomplish adjustments which they realize must be made. Americans seldom refuse to accept changes, but with a convenient bit of intellectual legerdemain, they can believe that they are preserving the Constitution at the same time that they accept the modifications necessitated by developments in a scientific and technological age.

It is a popular indoor sport to attribute the centralizing tendencies of modern times to the power-grabbing propensities of "bureaucrats." This accusation is not only unfair to the great majority of Federal officers and employees, but it is wholly at variance with the known facts as they have developed during the last century of industrial growth and scientific discovery. Most of the centralization in government which has taken place, in this country and throughout the world, has not been due to the diabolical scheming of the bureaucracy but to developments in science and the useful arts which have so diminished the significance of distance and enhanced the importance of the time factor that government at every level is virtually compelled to function in larger units if it is to be at all effective.

To a considerable extent, therefore, centralization in government is a world-wide phenomenon which cannot be avoided. Local functions have passed to the county and the State, State functions to the central govern-

[14] In this connection, see a significant series of articles by Professor William P. Murphy, "State Sovereignty Prior to the Constitution," *Mississippi Law Journal*, March, 1958, pp. 115–157. See also "State Sovereignty and the Drafting of the Constitution," *ibid.:* I, May, 1960, pp. 203–262; II, December, 1960, pp. 1–23; III, March, 1961, pp. 155–172; IV, May, 1961, pp. 227–242.

ment. Small village problems have become metropolitan area problems, and pressures of economic consolidation have made former State functions the concern of the whole nation. Federal intervention in these areas can be viewed as a working adaptation of the federal principle to modern conditions. And, as mankind seeks to develop effective means for the handling of world problems through the United Nations and its affiliated organizations, national governments are slowly entrusting various responsibilities to international organizations.

Nevertheless, many Americans still assume that intergovernmental relations is a new malady suddenly arisen to plague our otherwise peaceful existence. Nothing could be further from the truth. Intergovernmental relations in America did not, by any means, begin forty years ago when the first large Federal grant-in-aid program for highways became effective, or even fifty years ago when the first Governors' Conference was called by President Theodore Roosevelt. They began in the days of the founding of the Republic, if not before, and have been continuously the subject of various degrees of interest and controversy.

Although the term "intergovernmental relations" is of relatively recent origin (it has not been in use for much more than twenty years), the American concept is a very broad one and, as Professor William Anderson has said, almost as old as British colonization in America.[15] In earlier days, the relations of the colonies with the central government in London were followed by the war for independence, the signing of the Declaration of Independence, the adoption of the Articles of Confederation, the establishment of the first national government, and still later by the formation of the Federal Constitution and the establishment of the present form of government. The discussion which took place in connection with all of these events brought out concepts and ideas pertaining to intergovernmental relations without using that term. The *Federalist Papers* contain some of the best early discussions of related problems to be found in this country, or for that matter, any country.

On the scope and complexity of the problem of intergovernmental relations, Professor Anderson observes that:

> Underlying the concept of intergovernmental relations is the fact that the nation as a whole, each one of the States, and every county, town, city, village, school district, and other special district or local unit is a territorial and corporate or quasi-corporate entity that has a legal existence, rights, functions, powers, and duties within its territory, distinct from those of every other such unit. This is true even though the similar units are generally embraced geographically within the larger ones. Being all separate legal entities, they are all capable of legal and other relations with each other.[16]

[15] Anderson, p. 3.   [16] Anderson, p. 3.

Although the nation's leaders in times past may have been less keenly aware of the importance of intergovernmental relations in the day-to-day operations of government than they are today, the men who governed learned relatively early that expansion, development, and national growth necessitated either cooperation between the Federal government and the States, or Federal control. In the middle of the twentieth century, contacts between the different units and levels of government have become so numerous and so varied that one is at a loss to find a single important function of government that does not involve the cooperative relations of at least two, and often all three, levels of government.

Types of Intergovernmental Relations

Interrelationships in government are of many types. Two important categories, relations within a single unit and relationships involving two or more units, are next to be considered. In the first category, intra-unit relationships, such concepts as separation of powers, checks and balances, and executive-legislative relations are involved; in the second category, such inter-unit relationships as Federal-State, interstate, regional, Federal-local, State-local, or inter-local will be discussed.

Relations Within a Single Unit. The separation of powers concept was neither new nor original with the Founding Fathers. The idea of three distinct functions of government was introduced in Aristotle's *Politics* and was further developed and enlarged by Montesquieu. The interest of the Founders may be attributed largely to two considerations: since they had clearly in mind their recent unhappy experiences with the British Crown and the Royal Governors, they were deeply concerned about preventing, if possible, future abuses arising from too great a concentration of power in the hands of one individual or group of individuals. Secondly, their thinking was oriented to the British system by education and experience. They wanted to retain all that was good in that system, while avoiding certain undesirable features. Their thoughts on the separation of powers were greatly influenced by the writings of Montesquieu. The Founding Fathers read what he wrote, accepted it, and acted upon it, although his analysis is now known to have been somewhat mistaken in that the separation of powers in the British government was actually less extensive and significant than he believed.

No one has surpassed the whimsical analysis of Montesquieu's influence made by the late Senator George Woodward of Pennsylvania, who wrote:

> We all know that it was Thomas Jefferson or some one of the Fathers who could read French who read M. Montesquieu's essay on three com-

partments of government. The Fathers thought it over in English and put it in all our constitutions. It is therefore customary for the legislative, executive and judicial compartments to abstain from one another's society and to try to misunderstand one another as far as possible. This promotes business in the art of government and adds zest to elections.[17]

At any rate, the Founding Fathers established three branches of government, making them as distinct from each other as the organization of the material into three separate articles of the Constitution and a precise use of the English language could make them. The first sentence of Article I states, "The legislative power of the United States shall be vested in a Congress . . ."; Article II begins, "The executive power of the United States shall be vested in a President"; and the opening sentence of Article III provides, "The judicial power of the United States shall be vested in a Supreme Court and such inferior courts as the Congress may from time to time ordain and establish."

The governmental concept may be summarized in the following propositions: (1) there are three intrinsically distinct functions of government—the legislative, the executive, and the judicial; (2) these distinct functions ought to be exercised by three separate departments (or branches) of government; (3) these departments should be constitutionally equal and mutually independent; (4) the legislature may not delegate its own powers. The last is a corollary doctrine derived from the writings of Locke.[18]

The effects of what the Founders did are still very much in evidence. The separation of powers idea has become part of the national political theology and is often a subject in patriotic addresses. Although Americans continue to give lip service to the idea of separation, the concept is not nearly as appealing either in theory or in practice as it once was. An attempt to segment governmental power is bound to be impractical and unrealistic in many situations, particularly in emergencies when prompt and decisive action is essential. In practice the concept is so often a barrier to effective action that government practitioners are obliged to spend much time and energy in a constant effort to find ways of circumventing or bypassing the separation of powers.

As the Founding Fathers established the three separate branches of government, they sought to strengthen the separation by a judicious use of checks and balances. For example, Article I of the Constitution provides that laws may be passed only when the two houses of Congress

---

[17] Woodward, George, *The Pennsylvania Legislator* (Philadelphia: Harris & Partridge, Inc., 1936), III, 67.

[18] Corwin, Edward S., ed., *The Constitution of the United States of America: Analysis and Interpretation* (Washington: Senate Document No. 170, 82nd Cong., 2nd Sess., 1953), p. xvi.

approve identical provisions, and when these provisions are acceptable to and signed by the President. Even then a measure may be declared invalid if the Supreme Court finds all or part of its provisions contrary to the Constitution. Article II directs that the President may appoint "ambassadors, other public ministers and consuls, by and with the advice and consent of the Senate," and he may make treaties "provided two-thirds of the Senators present concur."

At the same time, it is well to remember that checks and balances can be overworked or misinterpreted, as when Montesquieu misread the British system, thinking it was "balanced" when it was not. But the American system of checks and balances was not thus founded upon a fallacy, because the Framers also surveyed the works of contemporary thinkers and in many instances derived their inspiration from the Roman Republic which had incorporated checks and balances among its various magistrates. While an excessive use of checks and balances might have undermined or even completely destroyed the system of the separation of powers, the Founders were shrewd and farseeing enough to stop at the precise point that would best serve their purpose.

Executive-legislative relations may be regarded as analogous to intergovernmental relations, and may be illustrated by reference to the early King-Parliament and Royal Governor–colonial legislature experiences or to the modern President-Congress and Governor–State legislature relations. To say that the colonies all developed executive-legislative-judicial relations is to say very little because, as evidence dating back to prehistoric villages clearly shows, such relations would have been difficult to avoid. The fundamental character of the English and American experience may be found in the relations existing between the three branches of government except, perhaps, when George III tried to reverse the processes of evolution by ignoring the British cabinet system which limited the power of the King.

Current executive-legislative relationships are complicated by many factors. American Presidents and Governors have become popular leaders, party leaders, and legislative leaders, as well as chiefs of state and chief executives. The leadership methods employed may vary in detail according to the history and practices of the jurisdiction involved, the personality and work habits of the executive, and the balance existing between the parties. Some executives are bolder and more aggressive than others in asserting their authority, and some legislatures and legislative leaders tend to be more sensitive than others in defending the legislative prerogative against executive domination or "usurpation"— either real or imagined.

Still another aspect of interjurisdictional relations involves the coordination of policies and programs of the several departments and agencies of a given branch of government. Coordination is essential if one agency is to be prevented from pursuing policies that tend to nullify the efforts of another when both operate in related functional areas. But coordination is a difficult problem in the Executive Branch at all three levels of government, particularly in those programs which involve relationships with other units or levels of government. Nowhere is this better illustrated than in the case of Federal agencies administering programs which affect urban and metropolitan areas.

Almost any Mayor can recite the consequences of uncoordinated Federal activity. Senator Joseph S. Clark of Pennsylvania, testifying on behalf of his bill to establish a Federal department of urban affairs, pointed out several specific instances: "His urban renewal program, supervised by one Federal agency, may be disrupted by the highway plan thrust upon him by another Federal agency. Federal money poured into highways hastens the bankruptcy of the mass transit upon which many a city's life depends. Federal tax policy singles out rail passenger transportation, including commuter traffic, as something to discourage. While one Federal agency seeks to stimulate home-building, another may pursue a credit policy which has the opposite effect. The Defense Department can disrupt all local planning by the manner in which it locates installations." [19]

Coordination is difficult to achieve at the national level because the programs are so numerous and the departments and agencies so large, and at the State level because so many agencies are headed by boards or commissions, or if they have a single head, by a person elected by the voters. Such an official, like the Attorney General, is responsible to the people who elected him and has little incentive for cooperating with the Governor who, though the theoretical head of the State administration, may be a political opponent.[20] Coordination is virtually impossible at the county level because the typical county government lacks a single executive head. It is difficult in cities for much the same reasons as in States, though city charter provisions rather than constitutional requirements stand in the way.

Relationships Involving Two or More Units. There are several different types of interlevel and interjurisdictional relationships in the American federal system, each with its own constitutional and legal

[19] Clark, Joseph S., *Establish a Department of Urban Affairs and Housing*, Hearings before the Senate Subcommittee on Reorganization and International Organizations, on S. 1633 and other bills (Washington: 87th Cong., 1st Sess., 1961), p. 25.

[20] See Heady, Ferrel, *Salient Features of Constitutional Reform in Administrative Integration* (New York: National Municipal League, 1960), pp. 16–18. This report was published in its final form in 1961 under the title, *State Constitutions: The Structure of Administration.*

basis, and each with its own practical and political considerations. They include Federal-State relations; interstate relations; regional relations, both subnational and metropolitan; Federal-local relations; State-local relations; and inter-local relations. Some of them, such as Federal-State, Federal-local, and State-local, involve vertical relationships; others such as interstate and inter-local involve horizontal relationships; and regional relationships may be vertical, horizontal, or both. Although separate chapters are devoted to these several types later in this volume, it is desirable as a means of mapping out the field to define each here and to indicate for each something of its constitutional and legal basis and significance.

Federal-State relations are obviously based upon the relations of the States with the central government. A major part of this volume is directly concerned with these relationships, which also become evident, directly and indirectly, where other topics are under consideration. Federal-State relations inevitably arise under our federal form of government, and they constitute, as Woodrow Wilson pointed out half a century ago, "the cardinal question of our constitutional system." [21] They are based on constitutional provisions, statutes, court decisions, and on the frequent practical need for an administrative unit smaller than the nation but larger than a local area.

Constitutional questions arise from the nature of the Union and from the position and powers of the States as members of it. If the Union were a compact between States, as many have contended, then the States might be regarded as having voluntarily surrendered some portion of their sovereignty, a surrender which they would be free to recall at a later date. If, on the other hand, the States actually surrendered substantial portions of their sovereignty to form an indivisible nation when they entered the Union, then they may properly claim only such rights and powers as were specifically safeguarded under the terms of the Constitution when it was signed, or as it may since have been amended.

Under the first condition, the term "States' rights" means one thing, while under the other, it means something quite different. At any rate, the States' rights argument has been used over and over again by all parties and in relation to just about every important public issue in the history of the nation, most frequently by those who were "out" and desired to get "in." Throughout American history, as one writer has observed, the States' rights argument has had one enduring characteristic, expediency, and "to the problems of federalism, the states' rights doctrine makes no useful contribution. Its function, instead, always has been to afford an emotionally appealing philosophical justification for

[21] Wilson, Woodrow, *Constitutional Government in the United States* (New York: Columbia University Press, 1917), p. 173.

the advance of some mundane and usually ignoble special interest. And so it is today." [22]

When one considers the constitutional basis of the States' rights doctrine, it is well to remember that this doctrine had been tried, and that it had failed rather dismally in the government under the Articles of Confederation. Under the present system, the powers of the central government are delegated and those of the States are residual. The Tenth Amendment thus becomes the crucial constitutional provision for determining the relative position of the two levels of government. The States' rights sympathizers, who were chiefly but not wholly Southern, tried again and again to bring about an acceptance of their point of view within the framework of the present government. Failing that, they ultimately attempted to sever their connections with the Union and to establish a government of their own in which States' rights would reign supreme. This ended, according to a distinguished Southern historian, Frank L. Owsley, as follows:

> There is an old saying that the seeds of death are sown at our birth. This was true of the Southern Confederacy, and the seeds of death were state rights. The principle on which the South based its actions before 1861 and on which it hoped to base its future government was its chief weakness. If a monument is ever erected as a symbolical gravestone over the "lost cause" it should have engraved upon it these words: "Died of State Rights." [23]

The Founding Fathers anticipated interstate relations as well and, in fact, made more constitutional provision for them than they did for the relations of the States with the Federal Government. The erection of trade barriers between the States, in the form of import and export duties or both, was supposedly prohibited in Article I, Section 10. The Supreme Court was given original jurisdiction, in Article III, Section 2, over cases in which a State is a party. Most of the provisions bearing on interstate relations are, however, in Article IV: the full faith and credit clause, one of the guarantees of the privileges and immunities of citizens (the other being in Amendment XIV); the provision for rendition of fugitives from justice; and the provision for the admission of new States. The interstate compact clause is found in Article I, Section 10.

In the early days of the Republic, the hostility between some of the States was intense and exceedingly bitter. In later years, aside from minor outbursts usually caused by differences in temperament of the

[22] Murphy, William P., [book review], *Journal of Public Law*, VIII, No. 1 (1959), pp. 294–295.
[23] Owsley, Frank L., *State Rights in the Confederacy* (Chicago: University of Chicago Press, 1931), p. 1.

personalities involved, the trend has been toward greater interstate cooperation in an ever-increasing number of functional fields. This has been achieved through widespread use of interstate compacts, through administrative cooperation, and through cooperation in the drafting of legislation and the adoption of uniform state laws.

The Constitution makes no mention of or provision for regionalism in the United States. Although there has been considerable sectionalism, the concept of regionalism is relatively new, and official regional arrangements have become increasingly common only during the past few years. As government undertakes to provide more services for individual citizens, the need for a unit of administration that is smaller than the nation but larger than the State becomes more and more apparent. This need led to the establishment of an extensive array of zones, districts, areas, and offices for purposes of field administration.

Subnational regionalism for river valley development has evolved from the increasingly urgent problems of water supply and water conservation. It is obviously desirable to deal with a river valley as a whole, not on a State by State basis, and this can be accomplished if the concept of regionalism is utilized. Under the compulsory type of regionalism, a valley authority is established by act of Congress, as in the case of the Tennessee Valley Authority. This type has also been adopted in part in the Columbia River Basin, and has often been proposed for the Missouri River Basin. The voluntary type of regionalism comes into being by means of an interstate compact drawn up and entered into through the cooperative efforts of the States themselves. This form was first adopted in the Delaware River Valley in 1936 (Delaware River Compact, revised 1962), and later in the Ohio and Potomac River valleys. Two questions are involved here: namely, the extent to which this device is capable of doing the whole job; and the more delicate question of compelling a group of States to do what, theoretically, they ought to do voluntarily.

Metropolitan regionalism represents a still different type. A metropolitan area may be defined as a central or core city together with its surrounding or satellite communities. This type of region has been developing in ever-increasing numbers and size since 1920. In the Federal census of that year, it was reported for the first time that more than 50 per cent of the American people were living in communities officially classified as "urban." The percentage has continued to rise in each succeeding census, and population experts assure us that within a few years, three-fourths of our population will be concentrated in urban areas. The number of Standard Metropolitan Areas (SMA) had increased to 212 in 1962; not only will this number continue to grow, but new areas will be developed to such an extent that the whole East coast from

Portsmouth to Norfolk will become one vast and continuous metropolitan development. Already many signs within this area point toward such a condition.

For well over a century under the present system of government, there were no direct relations between the Federal government and the cities. It is probably no exaggeration to say that such relationships were neither contemplated nor desired. In the interval between World War I and the Great Depression, a considerable number of indirect relationships, in which Federal departments and agencies provided services for municipalities, developed in various fields. Professor Arthur W. Bromage, an authority in the municipal field, has pointed out that "as late as 1932, the delegation of the United States at the International Congress of Cities in London was the only one of more than forty countries represented to report no direct administrative relationships between the central or national government and its cities."[24]

A change in this situation began in the Roosevelt era, and has continued since that time without interruption. The urgent need for distribution of relief funds during the Depression was used as an excuse for short-circuiting the States and for establishing direct Federal-municipal relations. Not long after the Depression came World War II, when the cities, like all governmental units and all citizens, bore a heavy responsibility in the war effort. In the postwar years came a host of new Federal grant-in-aid programs in airport development, health, highways, hospital construction, housing, slum clearance, and urban renewal, all of which provided opportunity for important new Federal-municipal relationships. Thus there has been established during the last quarter of a century a pattern of ever-broadening Federal-municipal relations. In view of the strong national trend toward urbanization, there is no reason to expect that the number and scope of these relationships will decline; on the contrary, there are many reasons for expecting them to increase.

There is no part of our system that is more difficult for citizens of foreign lands to understand than this relationship between Federal and municipal governments. They listen patiently and politely while it is explained to them that local governing bodies are largely free to select among alternative policies on a given matter, or to take no action at all. Still unconvinced, they inquire, "Exactly at what point does the central government intervene to tell them what to do?" While one hesitates a moment, trying to figure out how to answer, the next question comes, "Well, don't you know?"

[24] Bromage, Arthur W., *Introduction to Municipal Government and Administration*, 2nd ed. (New York: Appleton-Century-Crofts, Inc., 1950), p. 182.

There are no provisions in the Federal Constitution which have any bearing on State-local relations, but the State constitutions are replete with such provisions. Just as a State under the Federal Constitution cannot have its representation in the Senate reduced without state consent (which means that for all practical purposes, it will never be done), so in the States no established county can be abolished or its boundaries modified without the consent of the voters. The fact that there are too many counties and that many of them are far too small makes no difference. Not only are counties written into the majority of State constitutions, but these documents contain a variety of restrictive provisions which impair and impede county effectiveness in the discharge of their ordinary governmental activities and responsibilities. Of these numerous provisions, three types are readily distinguishable and worthy of mention.

One type of provision operates to prevent local control over local affairs. It used to be true in many jurisdictions, and it still is in some, that in deciding even the simplest local question, the answer must be determined by the State legislature. This state of affairs became so wasteful of the time of the legislature and so annoying, if not actually humiliating, to the local citizens that a move for home rule was organized. At first it made some progress, then it lagged for many years. Recently there has been evidence of a renewed interest in home rule, not only for cities but also for counties.

A second type of provision concerns the establishment and enforcement of minimum standards. Virtually every aspect of fiscal administration is affected, from levy to final accounting and auditing. In important functional fields also, in education, health, highways, welfare, and many more, states establish minimum standards, impose rules and regulations, and in general regulate the organization and administrative work of various local government agencies. Yet a third type of relationship exists in those jurisdictions in which there is a State department of local government. Such a department is recommended in the National Municipal Leagues' *Model State Constitution;* similar agencies have been established to supervise and assist local governments in at least half a dozen States—Alaska, New Hampshire, New Jersey, New York, North Carolina, and Pennsylvania. In all probability the number will increase during the next few years, as it should.

Although interlocal relations is the most recent form of interjurisdictional relation to develop, it may well prove to be the most common form. In the 1920's and 1930's, several adjacent governmental units in a few states began limited and cautious experiments in cooperation, in the form of cooperative purchasing, or in the construction of costly public works projects such as water works and sewage treatment plants. Such arrangements rested almost wholly on financial considerations. Like the farmer who felt that he could not afford to buy an expensive piece of equipment for his own use, but found that he could do so in cooperation with his neighbors, these communities learned that through cooperation they could provide more and better governmental services for their residents at moderate cost.

As efforts at cooperation proved successful, they drew the attention of legislators, with the result that State statutes giving blanket authorization to their local units to enter into such agreements began to make their appearance; today they are fairly frequent. Another type of usefulness for interlocal agreements has developed in connection with efforts to solve problems of metropolitan area government.

Some Characteristics of American Federalism

Like the society which it serves, government is a changing, developing, dynamic thing, always in the process of adjustment to new conditions and new needs. Adjustments in a federal system may be no greater or more important than those which occur in unitary governments, but they are more conspicuous and perhaps more interesting.

The idea that the central government in the American federal system is not a strong one may come as something of a surprise to most Americans. It may seem strong to them, and to have powers quite adequate to its needs and the needs of the people, but it does not appear so to outsiders. An interesting illustration is found in a publicity pamphlet issued by the Chief Electoral Officer for the Commonwealth of Australia in 1913. He noted, as Americans have often done, that "the Federal Constitution is not a sacred thing. It is an agreement made by the people of the different States in order more effectively to protect their interests, by enlarging their self-governing powers." He goes on to characterize Australian and American federalism as "the weakest in the world":

> There are several countries in which a federal system of government exists. The United States of America, Canada, Germany, and Switzerland are instances. But although they are all Federations, they differ from one another and from our own considerably. In some the Federal Government is strong; in others it is weak. Canada, Germany, and Switzerland are instances of strong federations. Canada has all the powers sought for in these Amendments. So have Germany and Switzerland. America and Australia are instances of weak federal government. Our Constitution is, as Mr. Irvine has pointed out, "one of the weakest in the world." Those who framed it took the United States Constitution as their model. It was a great mistake, and one which the Canadians

living alongside the Americans did not make. . . . It was drafted along wrong lines, and its interpretation by the High Court has shown that the Commonwealth does not possess many powers with which the electors understood it was clothed.[25]

Evolutionary Character. One of the most striking characteristics of American federalism is the evolutionary character of the relationships involved. This statement is not made on the basis of a belief that there must be evolution in everything, any more than multi-causation is necessary to explain every simple action that takes place. Certainly there has been development, or at least significant if not drastic change, in intergovernmental relations.

Fundamentally, this change has been from relative simplicity to great complexity. In the early days of the Republic, specific functions of government could be assigned to specific units or levels. National defense, the conduct of foreign relations, and the regulation of interstate commerce were functions of the national government. State budgets were small, and State functions few in number. Schools and highways were primarily local functions, as were the preservation of peace and the protection of life and property. In the shift from a rural and agricultural society to a basically urban and industrial one, however, government at all levels has increased in size and scope of operations until today in virtually all important functions of government two if not all three of the levels of government are involved. Thus has the simple structure of early American federalism given way to the modern concept of cooperative federalism in which, in patterns varying according to the nature of the function, all levels of government are involved.

Complexity. All large organizations, public or private, are structurally and procedurally complicated, but a federal system of government reaches a maximum of complexity. Whether one regards this as good or bad, it is probably inevitable and unavoidable. The result is that the study of intergovernmental relations in this country involves much more than an analysis of the relationships between one large entity like the United States with another large entity such as one of the fifty States or even one of the larger cities. On the contrary, there are not two governmental entities but many, each of which, with the possible exception of the smallest and simplest uni-functional local units, is composed of at least three branches of government, an undetermined number of departments, agencies, offices, and bureaus, and the individual officers and employees associated with each.

Many of the relationships are between one agency and another, or between one officer and another. The lines, as one writer expresses it,

[25] Chief Electoral Officer, *In re Referendum (Constitution Alteration) Act, 1906–1912* (Melbourne), February, 1913, pp. 9–10.

crisscross, parallel, by-pass, or conflict with each other, pierce through levels from highest to lowest, and cut across geographic and jurisdictional boundaries. . . . As a result, they form ever-changing and indescribably complex patterns when one attempts to view them as a whole. Some of the *intra*governmental relations, such as those between the State governor and the heads of State administrative agencies, are seriously affected by the *inter*governmental relations that each agency has with authorities in other governments. Conversely the intergovernmental relations are affected by the intragovernmental.

These interrelations, in every situation, are a factor that those who deal with politics and government can never afford to forget. Citizen reform groups, pressure groups, and party leaders are well aware of this fact. It enters into the thinking and the actions also of government officials at all three levels and in all three branches, legislative, executive, and judicial.[26]

Constant Adjustment and Change. One of the most important characteristics of American federalism has been its ability to adapt to changing conditions. Over the years, American federalism has changed greatly, and the end has not yet been reached. The study of federalism in other lands and conversation with visitors from many countries convinces the writer that problems which now confront the American people have existed and do exist in federal systems everywhere. They reflect not the peculiarities of Americans, but the characteristics of human beings everywhere in the struggle for power.

The changes in the federal pattern have resulted from legislative actions, executive actions, court decisions, constitutional amendments, and exercise of the treaty power. Yet changes that have resulted from causes other than legislative action have been relatively insignificant. Executive departments and agencies have established standards, influenced State legislation indirectly if not directly, and taken the lead in organizing State and Federal officials for the more effective performance of their duties. The Federal courts have made a conscientious effort to be fair when deciding questions involving Federal-State relationships, but Federal judges are Federal officers. "The Supreme Court of the United States has been as impartial an umpire in national-state disputes as one of the members of the two contending teams could be expected to be." The net result has been, in many instances, "to impair the prestige if not the powers of the states." [27]

Only one serious attempt has been made to modify the allocation of powers between the two levels of government by use of the amending process. This was the unhappy experiment with the Prohibition

[26] Anderson, p. 53.
[27] Field, Oliver P., "State Versus Nation, and the Supreme Court," *American Political Science Review*, April, 1934, pp. 232–245 on p. 233.

Amendment, an experiment that is not likely to be repeated soon. While it is possible to make changes in the allocation of powers through the exercise of the treaty power, the complicated nature of the procedure and its rather limited application to purely domestic problems makes it obvious that it is not now and is most unlikely ever to become a really significant factor in the field of Federal-State relations—former Senator Bricker to the contrary notwithstanding.

Conflict and Compromise. Conflict between the center and the parts is perhaps the most obvious problem of federalism, but it is by no means the only one. Within a federal system, certainly within the American one, a series of adjustments is constantly going on. Some of these involve shifts of powers, sometimes from the center, more often toward the center. They are frequently made quite amicably, in response to changed social, political, or economic conditions. The ebb and flow of power, first in one direction and later in another, is one of the most striking aspects of the history of American federalism and is probably best illustrated by the regulation of commerce.

Equally interesting is the fact that shifts which result in a loss of power by one unit are often offset or compensated by the development of new programs and activities, or by shifts from other units of government. The growth in the number, scope, and effectiveness of governmental services has been one of the most noticeable characteristics of American government during the past century, and it has taken place at all levels, National, State, and local. If the States have frequently lost powers to the central government, these powers have often been replaced by the development of new fields of activity or by State assumption of activities formerly carried on at the local level. Losses of power at the local level have in similar fashion been offset by the establishment of new local functions or by greater local responsibilities in programs involving interlevel cooperation.

BIBLIOGRAPHICAL NOTES

Probably the most useful general works on federalism are Kenneth C. Wheare, *Federal Government,* 3rd ed. (New York: Oxford University Press, 1953); Arthur W. Macmahon, *Federalism: Mature and Emergent* (New York: Doubleday & Co., Inc., 1955); Arthur Maass, *Area and Power: A Theory of Local Government* (Glencoe, Ill.: Free Press of Glencoe, 1959); Michael Stewart, *Modern Forms of Government: A Comparative Study* (New York: Holt, Rinehart and Winston, Inc., 1959), which stresses central-local relationships in the governments of about a dozen countries; and M. J. C. Vile, *The Structure of American Federalism* (New York: Oxford University Press, 1961), an English view. For basic information on the establishment of federalism in the United States in addition to *The Federalist Papers,* see Max Farrand, ed., *Records of the Federal Convention of 1787,* 2nd ed., 4 vols. (New Haven: Yale University Press, 1938) and Jonathan Elliott, ed., *Debates in the Several State Conventions on the Adoption of the Federal Constitution,* 2nd ed., 5 vols. (Washington: printed by the editor, 1836–1845). See also Charles H. McIlwain, *The American Revolution: A Constitutional Interpretation* (Ithaca: Cornell University Press, 1923).

The current widespread interest in federalism has resulted in a sizable amount of new literature, from which selected items are listed below on a country-by-country basis:

Africa. Donald S. Rothchild, *Toward Unity in Africa: A Study of Federalism in British Africa* (Washington: Public Affairs Press, 1960).

Australia. Zelman Cowen, *Federal Jurisdiction in Australia* (New York: Oxford University Press, 1959); Alan F. Davies, *Australian Democracy: An Introduction to the Political System* (New York: Longmans, Green & Co., Inc., 1958); and Geoffrey Sawer, *Australian Federal Politics and Law, 1901–1929* (New York: Cambridge University Press, 1956).

Canada. A. H. Birch, *Federalism, Finance, and Social Legislation in Canada, Australia, and the United States* (New York: Oxford University Press, 1955) and A. R. M. Lower *et al., Evolving Canadian Federalism* (Durham: Duke University Press, 1958).

Central America. Thomas L. Karnes, *The Failure of Union: Central America, 1824–1960* (Chapel Hill: University of North Carolina Press, 1960).

Germany. Elmer Plischke, *Contemporary Government of Germany* (Boston: Houghton Mifflin Co., 1961) and Roger H. Wells, *The States in West German Federalism: A Study of Federal-State Relations, 1949–1960* (New York: Bookman Associates, 1961).

India and Pakistan. Muhammad Asad, *The Principles of State and Government in Islam* (Berkeley: University of California Press, 1961); Joan V. Bondurant, *Regionalism Versus Provincialism: A Study in Problems of Indian National Unity* (Berkeley: Center for South Asia Studies, University of California, 1958); Norman D. Palmer, *The Indian Political System* (Boston: Houghton Mifflin Co., 1961); Moolamattom V. Pylee, *Constitutional Government in India* (London: Asia Publishing House, 1960); and Benjamin N. Schoenfeld, *Federalism in India* (Washington: Public Affairs Press, 1960).

Indonesia. J. D. Legge, *Central Authority and Regional Autonomy in Indonesia: A Study in Local Administration, 1950–1960* (Ithaca: Cornell University Press, 1961) and Gerald S. Maryanov, *Decentralization in Indonesia: Legislative Aspects* (Ithaca: Department of Far Eastern Studies, Cornell University, 1957).

Russia. Vernon V. Aspaturian, *The Union Republics in Soviet Diplomacy: A Study of Soviet Federalism in the Service of Soviet Foreign Policy* (Geneva: E. Droz, 1960); John N. Hazard, *The Soviet System of Government* (Chicago: University of Chicago Press, 1960); Derek J. R. Scott, *Russian Political Institutions,* 2nd ed. (New York: Frederick A. Praeger, Inc., 1961); and Warren B. Walsh, *Russia and the Soviet Union* (Ann Arbor: University of Michigan Press, 1961).

Switzerland. George A. Codding, *The Federal Government of Switzerland* (Boston: Houghton Mifflin Co., 1961).

Underdeveloped Countries. Ursula K. Hicks *et al., Federalism and Economic Growth in Underdeveloped Countries: A Symposium* (New York: Oxford University Press, 1961).

West Indies. David Lowenthal, *The West Indies Federation: Perspectives of a New Nation* (New York: Columbia University Press, 1961).

CHAPTER II

Colonial *Backgrounds* of
American Federalism

We, therefore, the Representatives of the United
States of America, in General Congress, Assembled, appealing
to the Supreme Judge of the World for the Rectitude of our
Intentions, do, in the Name, and by Authority of the good
People of these Colonies, solemnly Publish and Declare, That
these United Colonies are, and of Right ought to be, Free and
Independent States; that they are absolved from all Allegiance
to the British Crown, and that all political Connection between them and the State of Great-Britain, is and ought to be
totally dissolved; and that as Free and Independent States,
they have full Power to levy War, conclude Peace, contract
Alliances, establish Commerce, and to do all other Acts and
Things which Independent States may of right do. And for the
support of this Declaration, with a firm Reliance on the
Protection of divine Providence, we mutually pledge to each
other our Lives, our Fortunes, and our sacred Honor.[1]

[1] From the Declaration of Independence.

THE COLONIES AND THE CROWN

The United States is often spoken of as a new nation. Comparatively
speaking it may be, but even so, its history from 1492 until the present
date spans a period of almost five centuries. Americans, frequently con-
centrating their attention on the period under the present form of government, tend to forget that the colonial period from 1609 is approxi-

32

mately equal in length to the lifetime of the present Constitution and of the Republic which it established.

When one considers that much of the form and substance of American legal and governmental institutions was firmly established during the long colonial period, any casual treatment of it, any disposition to minimize its importance is highly unfortunate. It was during the colonial era that the Anglo-Saxon tradition of government and law was established, with its emphasis on a government of laws, the rights of man, the ideals of peace and freedom, and the development of strong and effective institutions of local government. Circumstances during much of this period were such as to develop patterns of thought which found expression in the structure of the new government that the colonists were eventually to establish.

Controversy Over Governmental Powers

Controversies over governmental powers began to develop at an early date. Pennsylvania provides an excellent illustration. Under the Royal letters patent, Pennsylvania became a province with powers similar to those enjoyed by the Proprietor of Maryland. Channing reports, however, that there were some important limitations on the powers of the Pennsylvania Proprietorship which do not appear in any earlier grant.[2] The legislative supremacy of the Parliament was distinctly recognized in the Pennsylvania Charter, and obedience to the navigation laws was expressly required. The laws of Pennsylvania were to be submitted to the King within five years of their passage, and the King had six months in which to confirm or reject them. There is no evidence that any of the frames of government were laid before the Royal authority, and Penn appears to have felt entirely at liberty to disregard any or all of the Charter's provisions. Therefore, only the actual Charter and the Act of Union were approved by the King. Thus did the peace-loving Quakers develop at an early date—whether by deliberate intent or through a careless oversight in the observance of formal requirements—a variety of nullification.

"The bane of English colonial management," observes Channing, "has always been the tendency to apply principles of law and methods of legal procedure which had been developed in England to its colonies, with a sublime disregard of the wishes of the colonists and of conditions which necessarily prevail in frontier settlements."[3] This policy was in

[2] Channing, Edward, *History of the United States*, 6 vols. (New York: The Macmillan Co., 1905–1925), II, 117.

[3] Channing, II, 164.

evidence under the Stuarts, and continued after the Revolution of 1688–1689 which has been described as "a Whig-Dutch conquest of the English empire carefully concealed under constitutional contrivances." While such a policy confirmed to Englishmen rights and liberties for which the Puritans had struggled in vain, for the colonists it meant nothing of the kind. "Their consent to the change of dynasty was not asked, their interests were not considered; they were simply ordered to proclaim the new monarchs. The effect of the Revolution was to hand them over to the English landowning oligarchy to be exploited for the benefit of English industry." [4] When these considerations did not require intervention in their affairs, they were more or less ignored.

The Glorious Revolution and attendant legislation greatly limited royal power in England, but in the colonies, the King's prerogative remained as great as ever, since the Habeas Corpus Act and other important pieces of legislation did not extend to the colonies. After 1689, the colonists claimed those rights which Englishmen in England had secured in the Bill of Rights and the Act of Settlement, but royal authorities refused to acknowledge that colonial rights had in any way increased. The Revolution government was very destructive of the chartered rights of a number of the colonies, notably those of Maryland and Pennsylvania. Although some efforts were made to reform colonial administration, the system still remained weak and the caliber of the personnel appointed to the colonial service generally inferior. Channing thus summarizes the developments in the century prior to the American Revolution:

> From the English Revolution in 1688–1689 to the American Revolution in 1775–1783, the constitutional development in all royal and proprietary provinces was substantially the same. Everywhere the Assembly claimed for itself the powers and privileges of the House of Commons, and everywhere it denied that the Council bore any resemblance to the House of Lords. Everywhere the Assembly used its control of the purse to compel the representatives of English authority to disobey his instructions, or, at all events, to pay no regard to them.
>
> The mode of compulsion varied slightly in the several colonies, owing to the different constitutional arrangements that prevailed in them: in Massachusetts the salary of the governor was the matter about which the contest was waged; in New York the levying of taxes in general; in Pennsylvania the paying of tribute to the proprietary. It made little difference whether the governor represented the king or proprietor; everywhere the colonists demanded greater control of their affairs than the governors' instructions permitted.
>
> How strenuously the authorities in England would have insisted on their constitutional rights may well be doubted had not the enforcement

[4] Channing, II, 190.

of the imperial commercial system been more or less involved in the control of the colonial government. The phrase "more or less involved" in the preceding sentence is used because under the circumstances of the time it would probably have been impossible to carry out the navigation laws and acts of trade with the means at the command of William, Anne, or the first two Georges.[5]

Thus, one may conclude that the Parliament and the King virtually thrust the colonists out of the protection of the British constitution by denying them basic rights belonging to all Englishmen, whether at home or abroad. It was out of their many unhappy experiences with the Crown and the Royal Governors that the colonists developed that deep distrust of executive power that was to be a characteristic of American political institutions for generations to come. Because time and time again the elected representatives of the people rose courageously to stand between them and oppression (or what, in some instances, they chose to regard as oppression) by drafting resolutions of protest and levying taxes for the arming and training of the militia, the colonists developed an almost naive and unquestioning faith in the integrity of popularly elected legislative bodies.

At the same time, the colonists became familiar with and accepted the idea of judicial supremacy. Their acceptance was so widespread and complete that they did not regard it necessary to write this concept into their basic laws, assuming that it could be taken for granted and that the courts would continue to operate in the future as they had in the past, nullifying enactments that were regarded as violating the spirit of "the law of the land."

Mid-Eighteenth Century Colonial Financing

As has been noted, instances of disagreement, even of conflict, began to appear in the relations between the colonies and the homeland at a very early date. In some cases, it was the colonists who protested against what they regarded as unfair or unjust treatment—treatment which, if their contentions were correct, violated their rights as Englishmen. Sometimes it was the Royal Governors who were involved in controversy with their British superiors. In either case, a pattern of dissension and conflict between the center and the parts was being established, a pattern that was to continue for several centuries.

An illustration in point may be found in the colony of New York at a very early date, and there were many more in the years to follow

[5] Channing, II, 248–249.

in other colonies as well. New York in the latter part of the seventeenth century was very prosperous. Governor Andros informed the Lords of Trade in 1678 that there were twenty-four settlements in the colony, that the militia numbered 2,000, and that the province might be valued at 150,000 pounds.[6] In spite of its wealth, however, its returns to the Crown were small. There were many complaints regarding the Governor and suggestions of peculation and extravagance on the part of New York officials. Channing reports that:

> In 1680 James sent an agent to New York to investigate these charges and directed Andros to return to England to render an account of his stewardship. In the confusion attendant upon his sudden departure, Andros forgot to renew the custom duties, which expired by limitation in that year. Discovering this, the merchants refused to pay the imposts which William Dyer, the Duke's collector, continued to levy. Seizing a vessel with its cargo, Dyer was sued by the owner for unlawfully detaining property which was not his own. He was cast in damages, was indicted on a charge of high treason, and appealing his case to England was sent home to stand trial.
>
> The indictment charged Dyer with having "contrived innovations in government and the subversion and change of the known, ancient, and fundamental laws of the Realm of England . . . contrary to the great Charter of Liberties, contrary to the Petition of Right, and contrary to other statutes in these cases made and provided." Dyer and Andros easily cleared themselves in England; but the New Yorkers continued to act independently of the Duke's officers, refusing to pay duties levied by his command. This movement was the first colonial rebellion against taxation from England, and the words of Dyer's indictment carry one backward to the times of the Puritan Rebellion in England and forward to the days of Otis, Henry, and Dickinson in America.[7]

The defense of the colonies, involving problems both military and fiscal, was no simple task. The colonies were spread over a vast area and little money had been allocated for purposes of defense, with the re-sult that some of them were in a very vulnerable position. Many colonists lost their lives and many settlements were destroyed by Indian attacks before proper measures of defense could be developed and placed in operation. In addition to the long existing points of difference, there was friction between the colonies and Great Britain in an effort to ob-

---

[6] *New York Colonial Documents,* III, 260; quoted by Channing, II, 60, upon which this summary is largely based.

[7] Channing, II, 116-126.

tain men, money, and materials for defense, and friction between colonies which were jealous of each other and were each fearful lest a neighbor colony receive more assistance or be subject to fewer assessments for defense than itself.

Early in the eighteenth century, English expenditures for the colonies caused the Treasury comparatively little concern; the colonial assemblies supplied funds to cover local needs. As defense needs for the colonies increased, the Treasury tried to avoid using the English civil list for colonial purposes; at the same time, it opposed Parliamentary grants (which had gradually been substituted for Orders in Council, in the hope of strengthening colonial administration) because they were a burden on the English taxpayers. In this situation, the Treasury was clearly in the middle.

In 1761, public opinion in America was aroused against England by the eloquent argument of James Otis in opposition to the use of the odious "writs of assistance" as a means of suppressing smuggling in Massachusetts. Otis declared that an act of Parliament contrary to natural right was unconstitutional and void. At the close of the Seven Years' War in 1763, French power had been eliminated in America and England had acquired a heavy debt, largely as a result of its efforts to defend the colonies. At this point, several things happened. George III issued a proclamation in October, 1763, prohibiting settlement west of the Ohio River; by doing so, the British government was seeking to thwart one of the strongest forces in American life—the urge for western settlement and expansion.

The defeat of France had removed the colonists' fears of a hostile neighbor, and it had also lessened their sense of need for British protection. Their own military successes in the course of the war had served to strengthen their self-reliance and confidence in their ability to defend themselves. Americans, though prosperous, contributed very little revenue for the defense provided for them by the British or for the support of civil government. Lord Grenville was under pressure to do something to relieve the heavy burden of taxation in England. While his first thought was to improve the administration of existing customs legislation, he realized that the levy of some new taxes would be necessary. Accordingly, the cabinet in March, 1765 approved the Stamp Act, a measure which provoked a storm of opposition in America. From the point of view of the cabinet and of the British generally, this solution appeared to be eminently fair and reasonable, but the colonists were less and less in a mood to be reasonable. In reality, they wanted the benefits of the protection of the Empire without bearing their share of the costs.

Colonial opposition to the Stamp Act was so effective that the Treasury brought about its repeal, even though Parliament continued to assert its right "to bind the colonies in all cases whatsoever," and to make the trade laws increasingly restrictive.[8]

Effect of European Wars and Trade Rivalries

The conflict which began in America in 1754, where it came to be known as the French and Indian War, spread to Europe and became merged in the world-wide struggle for existence and power known as the Seven Years' War (1756–1763). It was waged against Frederick the Great of Prussia by an alliance whose chief members were Austria, France, and Russia. Great Britain sided with Prussia because France was not only hostile to English interests in America but was trying to drive the English out of India. This war, which resulted in a victory for Prussia, had a tremendous significance for both France and Great Britain. It ruined France on two continents, and England gained control of the seas, mastery of both North America and India, and a position of primacy as a commercial nation.

These European wars, trade rivalries in Europe and America, and the struggle for the expulsion of the French as an influence to be reckoned with on the North American continent all served as complicating factors in the already complex and troubled relations between the colonies and the Crown. Under such circumstances, it was to the advantage of the British to promote union among the colonies as a means of strengthening her own position in the trade rivalry. It was even suggested that Britain should permit France to retain considerable power in America—a zone of influence, so to speak—in order to keep the colonies in subjection. There were suspicions that this was, in fact, being done. Thus the struggle became not merely a fight between England and America but a civil war between opposing factions within the British Empire.[9]

---

[8] This analysis follows Clark, Dora Mae, *The Rise of the British Treasury: Colonial Administration in the Eighteenth Century* (New Haven: Yale University Press, 1960), pp. 198–201; see also Dickerson, Oliver M., *American Colonial Government, 1696–1765*, rev. ed. (New York: Russell & Russell, Inc., 1962).

[9] This phrase is used by Van Tyne, Claude H., *The American Revolution, 1776–1783* (New York: Harper & Brothers, 1907), p. xvii.

The Inter-colonial Wars

The struggle in America developed along three lines: friction between the colonies and Great Britain, friction among the colonies themselves, and the contest of the two against a common enemy. All three involved intergovernmental relationships, although at the time they were not thought of in those terms. Our concern at this point involves inter-colonial rivalries in general and the three inter-colonial wars in particular—begun in 1690 and carried on intermittently until 1748, as follows:

1690–1697—First Inter-colonial War: King William's War
1702–1713—Second Inter-colonial War: Queen Anne's War
1744–1748—Third Inter-colonial War: King George's War

While each war involved rivalries between some colonies, all tended to encourage cooperation between others. This was conspicuously true in the case of the first and third wars. War between England and France had been declared in 1689. As one aspect of their strategy, the French in Canada planned an attack on Boston and New York. With the aid of their Indian allies, they came down from Canada and attacked Schenectady and other New York settlements. The massacres were so horrible that the English colonies became thoroughly aroused. The General Court in Massachusetts proposed a conference at which measures for mutual protection should be considered and arranged. The several colonial legislative bodies were notified. Representatives from Massachusetts, Plymouth, Connecticut, and New York met in New York, and on May 1, only three months after the massacres, they signed an agreement to send 855 men for the purposes of defending Albany and "by the help of Almighty God, subduing the French and Indian Enemies." Attempts to move on Quebec and Montreal failed and were abandoned.

The second war consisted mainly of action in the maritime provinces which were attacked by forces sent out from Boston. Varying degrees of Indian hostility were reported along the coast to the Kennebec River until 1713 when peace was restored. The third war was also centered in the provinces. No less than half a dozen colonies—Connecticut, New Hampshire, New Jersey, New York, Pennsylvania, and Rhode Island—cooperated in furnishing men, money, and supplies, although the heaviest burden fell upon Massachusetts. Successful operations involving some 4,000 men took place in 1745, and in the following year an unsuccessful expedition resulted in the return of Louisburg to the French by the Treaty of Aix-la-Chapelle, October 7, 1748.

THE STRUGGLE FOR INDEPENDENCE

Serious discord between the colonies and the home government began soon after George III became King in 1760. At the beginning of the struggle, there were many colonists who did not want independence. Some, who were predominately English by birth, training, and heritage, never did. They regarded themselves as Englishmen, believed in English institutions, and wished for nothing better, as Professor Carl Becker observed,

> than to fashion their clothes, their houses, their minds, and their manners on the best English models. . . . They opposed parliamentary taxation because they wanted to manage their own affairs in miniature parliaments, where they could carry on miniature contests with the governors for control of the purse, after the manner of the English Parliament in the Seventeenth Century. In no sense were they democrats; and they were as much afraid of radical movements in the Colonies as they were of British oppression. They wanted to preserve their *liberties* against Parliament, without sharing their *privileges* with the people in the colonies. They wanted home rule, but they wanted to rule at home. Left to themselves, the governing classes in America would never have carried the contest to the point of rebellion, would never have created an independent state.[10]

According to this interpretation, the colonists would have been quite contented if only the British had been willing to recognize their rights as Englishmen and to treat them as they thought they were entitled to be treated.

Events conspired to prevent such an obvious and relatively easy solution to their problems, however. Colonial differences with Great Britain were compounded by differences among themselves. At the time of the Revolution, the colonies were held together by little more than a common determination to end British rule.

> A common hate can bring temporary unity and cooperation but it offers no guarantee of survival of togetherness. Our pattern of federal relations was the product of a forging process; it was to be forged not merely by the traumatic experience of the Revolution but also in the crucible

[10] Becker, Carl, *The United States: An Experiment in Democracy* (New York: Harper & Brothers, 1920), pp. 45–46.

of continuing struggle after the adoption of the Constitution, with the Supreme Court as one of the major instruments of the forging process.[11]

The Albany Congress and Plan of Union

Early in the struggle for independence there was serious discussion of the need for union. As a matter of fact, the unity of the colonies had long been a dream of both the imperial administrators and of the political philosophers. Numerous plans had been presented, at one time or another, to bring this about. The New England Confederation had served a useful purpose in its time and remained a valuable precedent; but in the later colonial period the interests of the colonies had become so diverse, even conflicting, that nothing by way of union had actually been accomplished. In 1754, when Benjamin Franklin's famous plan of union was presented to the Albany Congress, interest in union was widespread on both sides of the Atlantic, but for quite different reasons.

The colonies were interested in the project for their own safety. Although Franklin's plan of union for the defense and security of the colonies was but one of four plans that had been outlined in writing at the time, and although it signally failed to stir popular enthusiasm when it was presented, it came to be the plan most in the minds of the radical leaders when the pressure of war made union imperative. Franklin's plan contemplated a union with an executive appointed by the Crown and a legislative branch selected by the assemblies—seven members each from Massachusetts and Virginia, and smaller numbers from the other colonies. No provision at all was made for representation from Delaware and Georgia. After the new council was organized, its members were to be apportioned according to the contributions of the several colonies to the general treasury.

The powers of this general government extended to the defense of the colonies by land and water, to the making of new settlements, and to the management of Indian affairs. For these purposes they might make laws, and lay and levy whatever taxes were most equal and just, "rather discouraging luxury than loading industry with unnecessary burdens." They could appoint whatever officers were necessary to carry out these functions. The plan received the unanimous consent of the delegates at Albany, but seemed to have no appeal whatever to the colonists themselves.

At the same time, the Lords of Trade had a plan of their own, proposing that a circular of instruction be sent to all the Governors of the

[11] Swisher, Carl B., "The Supreme Court and the Forging of Federalism, 1789–1864," *Nebraska Law Review*, December, 1960. p. 4.

continental colonies, setting forth the necessity for union for military purposes. This plan was just one aspect of the trade war, of which the colonies were the center. England wanted to defend the colonies chiefly because of their value to British trade, while the colonies wanted to be in as strong a position as possible to defend themselves against British practices which they regarded unfair or unjust. After the French had been driven from their position of power in North America, there arose a fear in England that the colonies might become too self-sufficient and independent. To control the colonies, it was actually proposed as a matter of policy that Great Britain permit France to retain considerable power in North America. As mentioned earlier, this proposal was much discussed in the colonies, and some of the colonists, strangely enough, reacted favorably to it.

The French and Indian War

In the French and Indian War, it was England and not the colonies that offered determined and ultimately successful resistance to the French. The English government in 1755 sent General Braddock to Virginia with a force intended to drive the French out of the Ohio Valley. At Alexandria, Braddock held a conference with several colonial Governors, and they agreed upon a plan of campaign. Two regiments of British regulars were to be used in four expeditions against the French. One was to proceed from Fort Cumberland in Maryland against Fort Duquesne; another was to proceed by water from New England against Acadia and Louisburg; a third was to move from Albany against the French fort at Niagara; and a fourth was to march against Forts Ticonderoga and Crown Point, and thence against Quebec.

The strategy originally designed was followed quite faithfully until the end of the struggle. It was planned that the first expedition would give the English access to the Ohio Valley; the second would give them mastery of the sea; the third would win them control of the water routes between Canada and the Mississippi Valley; and the fourth would lead to the complete conquest of Canada. The first expedition, however, ended in complete disaster. Untrained in the methods of frontier warfare and unwilling to listen to the advice of those who were, Braddock and the British regulars who made up the bulk of his staff scoffed at the employment of scouts as they approached the immediate vicinity of the enemy. During a long and tedious march (April 2 to July 9), they had seen no enemy, but as they neared Fort Duquesne, they were attacked and completely defeated.

Half of Braddock's 1,600 men were killed or wounded, and he himself died from a wound received in the onslaught. When Braddock fell, Washington took charge of the troops and led them out of the trap into which they had marched, but he did not proceed further against the French. Not only was the first expedition a military failure which left the French stronger than ever in their position at the forks of the Ohio, but Braddock's papers were captured by the French who thereby acquired full information about the plans of the British.

The other portions of the plan were more successful. The second expedition resulted in English control of Acadia. After 1758, when William Pitt assumed the leadership of the government, British policy toward American affairs changed. Instead of merely trying to prevent the French from encroaching on British territory, the new policy was to drive the French from the American continent. In the execution of this bold new policy, Pitt did not depart greatly from the military plan that had already been devised. He completed the expedition along the sea coast, and in a few months the great fortress of Louisburg was in the hands of the English and the gateway to the St. Lawrence was closed to the French.

The expedition against Fort Duquesne was renewed, and on Christmas Day, 1758, that stronghold also fell into the hands of the English who changed its name to Fort Pitt. In July of the next year, Sir William Johnson captured the fort at Niagara, thus cutting off the French in Canada from the Ohio Valley. The purposes of three of the expeditions had been accomplished. The fourth expedition was begun by General Amherst who captured Crown Point, and was finished by General Wolfe who met Montcalm on the Plains of Abraham and precipitated the unconditional surrender of Quebec to the English in September, 1759. About a year after the fall of Quebec, Montreal was captured and the war ended. Canada was completely under English control. In the Treaty of Paris, concluded in February, 1763, it was agreed that all French possessions east of the Mississippi except the city of New Orleans and the island on which it stood, should be given to England. Thus the French and Indian War gave England not only Canada but also the eastern portion of the Mississippi Valley.

The Stamp Act and the Stamp Act Congress

At the close of the French and Indian War, the British Treasury was running low. Although taxes had already been increased, steadily increasing expenditures and a mounting debt, both at home and in the colonies, pointed to the need for further tax increases and greater revenues. Some reduction in the home debt was deemed necessary, and some payments had been made to reimburse the colonies for expenditures incurred in connection with the war. Furthermore, it was felt that there was urgent need for some 10,000 troops to be permanently maintained in the colonies for their defense. Although there were a number of advantages to the government in such an arrangement, it was still thought desirable to provide for the quartering of these troops in the colonies. If, in addition, existing tax measures could be more strictly enforced and some new sources of revenue found, the problem could be solved. It even appeared possible that the troops might be provided, not only without cost to the Treasury, but with some moderate net gain.

The Stamp Tax, already a familiar tax form on both sides of the Atlantic, was the new tax decided upon. It had previously been accepted without protest, and it had been proved to be a productive source of revenue. It appears that at the time of its passage in 1765 no one in London had the slightest idea that it would be opposed in America, nor did even the colonial leaders (such as Benjamin Franklin) foresee the disturbances that would presently appear throughout the colonies. Sometimes in the past the colonists had protested against proposed acts of Parliament, but after these had been passed, they had either obeyed or silently disregarded them. It was generally assumed that the same thing would happen in this instance.

As a revenue measure, the Stamp Act was eminently fair and well constructed. The difficulty arose out of two circumstances: the mode of its passage and the failure to provide adequate machinery for its enforcement. The colonists had freely recognized the right of the imperial government to regulate trade and navigation. Not much attention had been given to this matter, to be sure, and at best it was difficult to separate the regulation of trade from the collection of duties for revenue. The situation had been accepted, but when in addition it was proposed to extend the British stamp taxes to America, there was no possibility of disguise. These were direct taxes to be collected not only at the seaports but in the interior parts of the country. One writer summarizes the situation in these words:

> It was one of the cardinal principles of political action that no Englishman could be "taxed" without his consent being given at least constructively; besides, the colonists were paying enough taxes as it was. To ask them to submit to new levies imposed upon them in what they regarded as an illegal manner at the precise moment when their trade was being restrained, was asking altogether too much. Instead of suggesting alternative modes of taxation, as Grenville had requested, they presented petitions against being taxed at all, in any manner whatsoever, except by vote of their own assemblies.[12]

[12] Channing, III, 47.

Quite understandably, this position was not favorably received in London. Then, after passage of the act, ships were detained repeatedly and unnecessarily because the proper papers for their clearance were unavailable, and courts were not available to adjudicate promptly the disputes which arose. The situation served greatly to strengthen the already latent determination to resist any attempt to enforce the law and collect the tax.

The new system brought about commercial distress in the colonies on a broad scale. Merchants could not collect the monies due them, pay for goods on hand, or place orders for more. Exports to America were reported to have fallen off as much as 50 per cent within a year. Thousands of people were thrown out of work in the English manufacturing towns. Shipping became paralyzed, while in America there developed one of those wars of pamphleteering so characteristic of this stage in the nation's development. The colonists sent delegates to a congress which met in New York and adopted resolutions on October 19, 1765, declaring that such an imposition was unconstitutional and petitioning for its repeal; similar sentiments were expressed in Virginia. Although only nine colonies were represented in the Stamp Act Congress, that body was a forerunner of the Continental Congress which met in 1774 and in succeeding years, and constituted the first Federal government in the emerging nation.

American views set off a heated debate in Parliament, as a result of which the Stamp Act was repealed on March 18, 1766, on the ground that its continuance "would be attended with many inconveniences, and may be productive of consequences greatly detrimental to the commercial interests of these kingdoms." While the news of the repeal was joyfully received in the colonies, whatever advantages the repeal might have provided were more than offset by the passage of the Declaratory Act which continued to assert the supremacy of Parliament and its unlimited power to legislate for America in all cases whatsoever, as the Revenue Act of 1764 had similarly asserted the right of Parliament to levy both internal and external duties throughout the realm.

Years of Controversy

The years immediately following were a period of intense controversy, although controversy between the colonists and representatives of the British government was certainly nothing new in the annals of the new nation. In the 169 years which elapsed between the founding of Jamestown and the Declaration of Independence, there were almost incessant disputes, particularly with the Royal Governors. Many of the disputes were local and personal, but the quarrels became far more serious when England enacted legislation which monopolized trade with the colonies, restricted the production and exportation of certain products in order to protect English manufacturers, and taxed the colonists for the general support of colonial administration.

So it is not surprising that the decade which followed the passage of the Stamp Act, the Stamp Act Congress, and the organization of the movement for resistance were years during which there was a notable outpouring of controversial tracts, setting forth in clear and often forceful language the position of the colonies. Notable among these was Stephen Hopkins' *Rights of Colonies Examined,* and nearly a decade later, Thomas Paine's *Common Sense* and Thomas Jefferson's *Summary View.* The latter paper may be regarded as an earlier and very preliminary version of what was later, under the skillful pen of its author, to be transformed into the Declaration of Independence. At this early stage, when even the idea of independence was still to be evolved, it was a plea directed to the British authorities for relief from what was referred to as "the unwarrantable encroachments and usurpations which the legislature of one part of the empire" has inflicted upon the people in another part—thus completely denying the idea of parliamentary supremacy.

Another very important characteristic of this period was the organization and effective operation of a colonial network of committees of correspondence. The leaders of the individual colonies had long kept in touch with each other by correspondence. The first such committee had been organized by Samuel Adams in Boston in 1772. Within a year almost every town in Massachusetts had formed a similar committee and, encouraged by such events as the Boston Tea Party, which John Adams regarded as "an Epocha in History," [13] they quickly spread to other colonies. By the end of 1773, a complete network of committees had been established, organized somewhat like modern political parties and performing many of the same functions. They not only exchanged ideas and information but took over the management of local affairs.

Later they elected the Continental Congress and provided an agency through which the decisions of that body were enforced, an outstanding illustration being their work in connection with the drastic trade re-

---

[13] He wrote in his diary the next day that this was "the most magnificent Movement of all. There is a Dignity, a Majesty, a Sublimity in this last Effort of the Patriots that I greatly admire. . . . This Destruction of the Tea is so bold, so daring, so firm, intrepid, and inflexible, and it must have so important Consequences, and so lasting, that I cannot but consider it as an Epocha in History." *Proceedings of the Massachusetts Historical Society, 1873–1875,* p. 191, and quoted here from Channing, III, 133.

striction program adopted by the First Continental Congress.[14] Although the regularly constituted, British-controlled governmental machinery still remained, there grew up beside it an extra-legal system which sapped the old machinery of its authority and which in fact became what a contemporary characterized as "the source of the rebellion." The committees had great influence throughout the country through their widespread exchange of information and ideas.

The Continental Congresses

The First Continental Congress met in Philadelphia in September, 1774, the Second in the same city in May of the following year. They were created to function in emergency situations, and were looked upon merely as temporary agencies. Both were composed of able and experienced men, outstanding leaders of the colonies which they represented. At the First Congress, Georgia alone was unrepresented. Although attempts on the part of Great Britain to punish the people of Massachusetts, who were more rebellious than the others, had served to unite the colonists, the sentiment of the members has been described as more conservative in tone than the resolutions of the counties and towns, for the simple reason that only the more radical members felt it necessary to take action. The First Congress was assembled in response to a call issued from Massachusetts proposing that each of the colonies appoint delegates to attend a conference to consider relations with England. Obviously, delegates to such a meeting could not be selected by the established colonial governments which were still under the domination of the British. Instead, they were elected or appointed by local committees, state conventions called by the local committees, or by the state legislatures in which revolutionary elements were dominant.

The Congress, when it assembled, considered a plan of union presented by Joseph Galloway of Pennsylvania, but turned to and entered in the journal the so-called Suffolk Resolves presented by Joseph Warren of Massachusetts. The Suffolk Resolves asserted that no obedience was due to the Intolerable Acts of 1774, and that no public money ought to be paid into the provincial treasuries until the government should be placed on a constitutional foundation or until the Congress should direct otherwise. Sentiment then shifted to a Declaration of Rights which was

[14] In this connection, one of their chief duties was to be the publication of the names of all delinquents in the trade restriction program. They had great power locally in dealing with cases of violation or suspected violation of the trade restriction rules, but the program met with such universal acceptance among the people that they actually had little to do.

adopted on October 14, 1774. This Declaration took the position that the rights of the colonists rested upon the immutable laws of nature, the principles of the British constitution, and the charters or compacts, and that the colonists were entitled to the rights of life, liberty, and property regardless of their migration from the mother country. An extended statement of the grievances of the colonists was included.

The most significant work of the First Continental Congress, however, was its adoption on October 20, 1774, of an agreement or association under the terms of which the delegates from the several colonies bound themselves and the inhabitants of the colonies whom they represented to attack England on the trade and industrial side. This program was to be carried out through the enforcement of a stringent non-importation, non-exportation, non-consumption agreement extending throughout the colonies, the enforcing agency being the committees of correspondence previously referred to. Penalties for violation were provided, but actually they were unnecessary, so solidly was public sentiment behind the program.

The delegates to the Second Continental Congress were assembling in Philadelphia to begin their deliberations as the news of Lexington and Concord was being carried southward and westward to the outermost confines of the colonies. The Ministry in England had addressed a circular letter to the colonial Governors, directing them to prevent the choice of delegates to the Congress. This meant, therefore, that the members of the Congress were chosen by irregular revolutionary conventions or congresses in the several colonies, rather than by the regular assemblies, and that they were more representative of the radical elements in the colonies than might otherwise have been the case. Channing, in fact, characterizes the new Congress as a revolutionary body, in no sense a representative or constitutional authority.[15]

Some of the moderates who had attended the First Continental Congress were also present at the Second, but there were a number of radical members also. Among the moderates were Benjamin Franklin and George Washington. Franklin was a new member, as was Thomas Jefferson, who succeeded Washington when the latter left Philadelphia to take command of the Continental Army at Cambridge. While there were influential men in every colony who had no interest in and no desire for separation from the British Empire, there were many others who did, and these brought with them many resolutions, both for sustaining Massachusetts and for the formation of local revolutionary governments. Independence was still a distant and seemingly impossible goal, but defense of the rights of the colonists and resistance to the minis-

[15] Channing, II, 189–190.

terial army were quite another thing. These were objectives to which the Congress could and did seriously apply itself.

THE DECLARATION OF INDEPENDENCE

The idea of a complete severance of ties with the British Empire involved consequences so serious and far-reaching as not to be taken lightly. Prior to 1775, independence was outside the realm of the practical in American politics and, as of that time, there were few even among the radical leaders who believed separation from England to be either desirable or possible. Events moved so swiftly, however, and developed in such a course as to bring about a virtually complete change of view, first among the radical leaders and a little later among the people generally.

As the war progressed, there was much talk of conciliation on both sides of the Atlantic, but this talk was destined to be fruitless. English views on Parliamentary supremacy, on the one hand, and the views of the colonists on their basic rights as Englishmen on the other, were so far apart as to be virtually irreconcilable. Furthermore, the views of both groups had been expressed so forcefully and unequivocally that neither side was in a position to make concessions that might have been acceptable to the other without completely "losing face."

The King had declared in November, 1774, that "the New England Colonies are in a state of rebellion, blows must decide whether they are to be subject to this country or independent." [16] In 1775, after the first accounts of Lexington and Concord had reached him, he is reported to have written, "America must be a colony of England or treated as an enemy. Distant possessions standing upon an equality with the superior State is more dangerous than being deprived of such connections." [17] While the Crown was talking thus of taking a firm stand, even at a possible cost of losing the colonies altogether, Lexington and Concord had aroused the fighting spirit of America.

The die was cast for the move toward independence. On June 7, 1776, Richard Henry Lee of Virginia introduced in the Continental Congress his famous resolution declaring that "these United Colonies are, and of right ought to be, free and independent States, that they are absolved from all allegiance to the British Crown, and that all political connection between them and the State of Great Britain is, and ought

---

[16] Channing, III, 150.   [17] Channing, III, 159–160.

to be, totally dissolved." This resolution, which Professor Becker has called the Resolution of Independence, was finally voted by the Continental Congress on July 2, 1776. Strictly speaking, this was the official declaration of independence, and Becker continues, "if we were a nation of antiquaries, we should no doubt find an incongruity in celebrating the anniversary of our independence on the 4th of July." [18]

In the meantime, two other important things were happening. On June 10, three days after Lee had introduced his Resolution of Independence, the Congress voted to appoint a committee "to prepare a declaration to the effect of the said first resolution." This committee, which consisted of Thomas Jefferson, John Adams, Benjamin Franklin, Roger Sherman, and Robert R. Livingston, reported a draft of the declaration on June 28, and, with modifications, this became the document popularly known as the Declaration of Independence, which was accepted by the Congress on July 4. At the same time that Lee presented the original Resolution for Independence, he moved the appointment of a committee to draw up "articles of confederation." Scattered proposals looking toward both of these objectives had been presented in the past, but had never received any substantial amount of support. Now the time had arrived when it was no longer possible to evade or postpone either issue. On June 11, the committee that had been appointed on the preceding day to draft a declaration of independence reported, and on the following day, another to draw up a plan for a more substantial union was appointed. The result in the one case was the Declaration of Independence; in the other, the drafting of the Articles of Confederation, the first constitution for a united America, adopted on November 17—for the plan was debated, on and off, for a period of approximately five months before it was approved by the Congress.

Thus it was that the drastic and irrevocable step of proclaiming complete separation from the mother country was not taken either casually or inadvisedly, but rather as the culmination of a long series of events which had convinced a majority of Americans that their freedom and happiness were unattainable under British rule. The Declaration has been so greatly praised that its words have come to be regarded almost with awe and reverence and to be read with a sort of sacred inattention. Being important, the Declaration has been so much analyzed and commented upon that it is difficult to say anything new about it. Even so, it may be noted that it states many of the basic concepts of human liberty in language that has never been surpassed for clarity and effectiveness. In this sense, the Declaration is a document of enduring significance, not only to Americans but to all mankind.

In the second place, the Declaration was important to Americans and

[18] Becker, Carl, *The Declaration of Independence* (New York: Peter Smith, Publisher, 1933), p. 3. See also *Journals of Congress* (Ford ed.), V, 424–429.

to the British because it severed the ties of the American colonies with Britain and established a new nation when it declared "that these United Colonies are, and of right ought to be, free and independent states; that they are absolved from all allegiance to the British Crown, and that all political connection between them and the state of Great Britain, is and ought to be totally dissolved." It was the American view that the Declaration made the colonies independent and sovereign, both internally and externally, so that all steps taken by the Congress subsequent to that date had the sanction of law.

Professor James Bradley Thayer stated the matter in these words: "The Revolution came and what happened then? There was no longer an external sovereign. . . . the people took his place; that is to say, our own home population in the several States were now their own sovereign." [19] The Supreme Court, in 1808, confirmed this view—namely, that the several States from the time when they declared themselves independent were entitled to all the rights and powers of sovereign states and that their laws were obligatory upon the people from the time of their enactment.[20]

In the third place, the Declaration has significance in relation to the main topic with which this volume is concerned—intergovernmental relations. As a question of constitutional law, did the Declaration bring into existence one nation or thirteen of them? If one, then only the central government had authority to levy war, make treaties, and send and receive ambassadors, ministers, and consuls. If thirteen, then all were permitted to enjoy this authority. The words of the Declaration were so ambiguous as to permit either of two interpretations. While States' rights advocates called attention to certain selected phrases, the nationalists directed attention to others:

States' Rights	*Nationalist*
". . . These United Colonies are, and of right ought to be free and independent states . . and that as free and independent states . . . they have full power to levy war, conclude peace, and contract alliances, establish commerce, and do all other acts and things which independent states may of right do."	Stressed the statement that the Declaration was made "in the name and by the authority of the good people of these colonies" by "the representatives of the United States of America, in general Congress assembled."

[19] Thayer, James Bradley, *The Origin and Scope of the American Doctrine of Constitutional Law* (Boston: Little, Brown and Co., 1893), p. 5. This point is also discussed in Story, Joseph, *Commentaries on the Constitution of the United States* (Boston: Little, Brown and Co., 1873), I, 149–150.

[20] *M'Ilvaine v. Coxe's Lessee*, 4 Cranch 207 (1808).

The nationalists seem to have had the better of this argument; if not, at least they had the benefit of having a highly respected and influential spokesman on their side:

> It [the Declaration of Independence] was not an act done by the State governments then organized, nor by persons chosen by them. It was emphatically the act of the whole *people* of the united colonies, by the instrumentality of their representatives, chosen for that among other purposes. . . . It was an act of original, inherent sovereignty by the people themselves, resulting from their right to change the form of government, and to institute a new one, whenever necessary for their safety and happiness. . . . It was, therefore, the achievement of the whole for the benefit of the whole.[21]

In still another way, "this most subversive document," as Henry S. Commager has characterized it, has taken on a new and greater significance for Americans in the 1960's. Though born of revolution, the United States has of late tended to frown upon revolution as something contemptible and unworthy. Meantime, oppressed and downtrodden people in at least three different continents have seized upon the American precedent as a justification for their own revolts against colonialism.

The Revolution made possible the creation of a nation out of thirteen discordant states. The Declaration of Independence gave to us and to all mankind a challenging statement of the concepts of freedom, individual liberty, and equality. A society in which these ideals were realized, at least in part, made possible remarkable developments in science and technology. Now, the emerging countries have appropriated these ideas and procedures and are, to some extent, using them against us. In the words of Professor Commager:

> The methods of this global revolution are familiar enough. For it is one of the paradoxes of history that the revolt of Asia and Africa against the West is being carried on with the tools and techniques devised by the West. The political instrument is Western nationalism; the social instrument is Western equality; the economic instrument is Western science and technology. . . .
>
> The Declaration of Independence is not merely a museum piece. It is not a parchment to take out once a year, celebrate with ceremonial reverence, and then return to the sterility of a glass case. It is not merely a historical document, something to learn in school as we learn so many things that we promptly forget. It is vital and immediate. It argues a case that is still valid and announces principles that are still true. It still calls upon us to pledge our lives, our fortunes, and our honor to their vindication.[22]

[21] *Ibid.*, p. 149.
[22] Commager, Henry Steele, "Our Declaration Is Still a Rallying Cry," *The New York Times Magazine*, July 2, 1961, pp. 1–30.

BIBLIOGRAPHICAL NOTES

The Colonies and the Crown. There are three monumental histories of colonial America, each in four volumes, each in keeping with the highest standards of scholarship and historical writing: Charles M. Andrews, *The Colonial Period in American History* (New Haven: Yale University Press, 1934–1938); Herbert L. Osgood, *The American Colonies in the Eighteenth Century* (New York: Columbia University Press, 1924); and the Thomas J. Wertenbaker volumes which were not conceived, or at least were not published, as a series. Professor Wertenbaker covered the story of the founding of American civilization in four volumes: *The Planters of Colonial Virginia* (Princeton: Princeton University Press, 1922); *The Middle Colonies* (New York: Charles Scribner's Sons, 1938); *The Old South* (New York: Charles Scribner's Sons, 1942); and *The Puritan Oligarchy* (New York: Charles Scribner's Sons, 1947). The first volume of the Cambridge History of the British Empire, *The Old Empire From the Beginnings to 1783* (New York: The Macmillan Co., 1929), presents a balanced picture of the early development of the Empire, thus setting the story of America in a larger framework. See also Herbert L. Osgood, *The American Colonies in the Seventeenth Century*, 3 vols. (New York: Columbia University Press, 1930). Evarts B. Greene, *The Foundation of American Nationality*, rev. ed. (New York: American Book Co., 1935) is a summary of the work of other writers, notably Andrews, Osgood, and Turner, and carries the story to the adoption of the Federal Constitution in 1789; see also Evarts B. Greene, *Provincial America, 1690–1740* (New York: Harper & Brothers, 1905) in the American Nation Series. Volumes by Charles M. Andrews and Leonard W. Labaree emphasize governmental matters, the former in *Colonial Self-Government, 1652–1689* (New York: Harper & Brothers, 1904), which appeared as the fifth volume in the American Nation Series; the latter, in *Royal Government in America: A Study of the British Colonial System before 1783* (New Haven: Yale University Press, 1930), describes the system of royal government in colonial America prior to the end of the Revolution. For the fiscal aspects of this story, see Dora Mae Clark, *The Rise of the British Treasury: Colonial Administration in the Eighteenth Century* (New Haven: Yale University Press, 1960); for the political, industrial, and administrative aspects, see Oliver M. Dickerson, *American Colonial Government, 1696–1765*, rev. ed. (New York: Russell & Russell, Inc., 1962).

The Struggle for Independence. Charles M. Andrews, *The Colonial Background of the American Revolution*, rev. ed. (New Haven: Yale University Press, 1931) is regarded by many as the most satisfactory explanation of the Revolution. Charles H. McIlwain, *The American Revolution: A Constitutional Interpretation* (Ithaca: Cornell University Press, 1923) presents a constitutional analysis. Other standard works deal with the origins theme: Bernhard Knollenberg, *Origin of the American Revolution, 1759–1766*, rev. ed. (New York: Crowell-Collier Publishing Co., 1961); John C. Miller, *The Origins of the American Revolution* (Boston: Little, Brown and Co., 1943); Richard B. Morris and James Woodress, eds., *The Times That Tried Men's Souls, 1770–1783* (St. Louis: Webster Publishing Co., 1961); Laurence H. Gipson, *The Coming of the Revolution* (New York: Harper & Brothers, 1954); and Claude H. Van Tyne, *The Causes of the War of Independence* (Boston: Houghton Mifflin Co., 1922). Gipson contends that the Revolution stemmed from two causes: the efforts of the British government to administer its much enlarged Empire efficiently, and the simultaneous effort on the part of the colonists to achieve a greater measure of autonomy. John C. Miller, *Triumph of Freedom, 1775–1783* (Boston: Little, Brown and Co., 1948) provides a comprehensive history of the Revolution. Allan Nevins, *The American States During and After the Revolution* (New York: The Macmillan Co., 1924) clearly presents the conservative role of the States—their function as the custodian of the political and institutional experience of the colonies. Other standard treatises include John R. Allen, *The American Revolution, 1775–1783* (New York: Harper & Brothers, 1954) and Claude H. Van Tyne, *The War of Independence: American Phase* . . . (Boston: Houghton Mifflin Co., 1929).

The Declaration of Independence. For a textual analysis of the various drafts, see Julian P. Boyd, *The Declaration of Independence: The Evolution of the Text Shown in Facsimilies of Various Drafts by Its Author, Thomas Jefferson* (Princeton: Princeton University Press, 1945) and Earl Latham, ed., *The Declaration of Independence and the Constitution,* rev. ed. (Boston: D. C. Heath and Co., 1956). For two excellent commentaries on the content and significance of this document, see Carl L. Becker, *The Declaration of Independence: A Study in the History of Political Ideas* (New York: Peter Smith, Publisher, 1933) and Edward Dumbauld, *The Declaration of Independence and What It Means Today* (Norman: University of Oklahoma Press, 1950). Both of these works emphasize the permanent value of the Declaration's philosophy of government as a man-made device for promoting human welfare.

CHAPTER III

The Formative
Period

When at length independence came, when the colonies were States, and especially when the war was over, what was America to do? Could the Americans, who had scolded England so roundly and broken away from her control, find imperial organization themselves without giving up all they had contended for? Could they reconcile local liberty with central authority and real unity? . . . To such a people, then, thus distracted and thus divided, came the problem of imperial organization. . . . The work was a momentous one, of great significance to mankind, and it must be done, if at all, by a distracted country emerging from civil war. . . .[1]

[1] McLaughlin, Andrew C., *The Confederation and the Constitution, 1783-1789* (New York: Harper & Brothers, 1907), American Nation Series, X, 39-40, 42-43, 46.

The phrase "The Formative Period" has often been used to describe or characterize the years from 1776 when independence was declared, until 1789 when the government under the present Constitution was established. The significant events of this period include the formation and adoption of the first State constitutions; the formation and adoption of the Articles of Confederation (the first national constitution) and the experience of the government under the Articles; the Annapolis Convention; and finally, the Constitutional Convention of 1787 which met in Philadelphia to frame the present instrument of government.

THE FIRST STATE CONSTITUTIONS

After independence was achieved in 1776, the flight of most of the Royal Governors and other British officials left the people of the former colonies without any official government. In other instances, as in Massachusetts, resistance to the British authorities made new arrangements immediately necessary. When consulted for advice, Congress recommended that the States adopt "such governments as will, in the opinion of the representatives of the people, best conduce to the happiness and safety of their constituents." Since no machinery existed with which to make the transition, Congress recommended that the new governments be established by "assemblies or conventions" in the several States. These terms were, in fact, applied loosely and more or less interchangeably to revolutionary bodies which performed all the functions of government—executive, legislative, judicial, and constituent.

On this basis, most of the States promptly proceeded to revise their colonial charters, transforming them into State constitutions, some with many changes, others with relatively few. Fully half of the States completed the task in 1776 and 1777, and within a decade all but two had done so. The constitutions of six States—Delaware, Maryland, New Jersey, North Carolina, Pennsylvania, and Virginia—bear the date of 1776, Georgia's the date of 1777. The vicissitudes of war delayed the adoption of an organic law in New York and South Carolina until 1779. Massachusetts returned temporarily to the use of her charter of 1691, until a new constitution was adopted in 1780; this constitution is notable not only for its length of life but because it was the first such document to be framed by a convention elected solely for this purpose. It is the oldest constitution in point of continuous service, having remained in effect until the present day. New Hampshire adopted its new constitution in 1784. Two States continued to use their colonial charters for many years—Connecticut, its charter of 1662 until 1819 and Rhode Island, its charter of 1663 until 1842. In view of this record, it is clear that the process of transition from colonial status to statehood was accomplished rather gradually over a period of nearly three-quarters of a century.[2]

Thus in the new constitutions there was no sharp break with the past. Nor did the idea of a written constitution present any problem so far as the inhabitants of the new States were concerned. As long as they

[2] See Dodd, Walter F., "The First State Constitutional Conventions, 1776–1783," *American Political Science Review*, November, 1908, pp. 545–561.

had remained in a colonial status, their laws and the decisions of their courts had been reviewed in England and often annulled or reversed as contrary to acts of Parliament or against the customs and usages of the realm. When, after independence, it was no longer possible to appeal to England and there was no superior American authority, their own judges found themselves obliged to review the acts of State legislatures in the light of State constitutions as interpreted in accordance with the underlying fundamental law.[3] In Virginia, a Court of Appeals was established for the express purpose of deciding on the constitutionality of laws, as well as to hear appeals from other courts.

The new constitutions followed, in the main, the outlines of the colonial governments and established the governmental framework of the present States. They were relatively brief and concise documents providing for the organization and powers of government. The basic ideas of government which they contained were very similar. All of them recognized the doctrine of the rights of man. All were based upon a concept of a government whose powers were vested in and derived from the people, and most of them contained expressed provisions to that effect. By the constitutions, the people both conferred upon and limited the authority of Governors, legislatures, and the judiciary. Eight of the constitutions contained bills of rights, patterned in general after the one drafted by George Mason and included in the Virginia constitution of 1776. All of them severely restricted suffrage. All were based upon the principle of the separation of powers, with a system of checks and balances. All provided for three branches of government, each independent of the other two; yet, in practice, all recognized the principle of legislative supremacy while providing guarantees to the people against legislative abuses. Provisions for amendment were included in eight constitutions, but were omitted in five.

The new constitutions reflected the deep distrust of the executive authority acquired during the colonial period, by depriving Governors of many powers held by the colonial executives. In most of the States, executive powers were vested in the Governor and an executive council. Gov-

---

[3] Channing, Edward, *History of the United States*, 6 vols. (New York: The Macmillan Co., 1905–1925), III, 435, contends that there thus came into being four distinct laws: the political theory as the basis of human society, the fundamental law which was none other than the Common Law of England, the written State constitution, and the laws made by the legislature. Their authority, Channing concludes, was in precisely that order. It may be noted, however, that little attention was paid to the Common Law in the early days, it being regarded as too complicated a system and not particularly suited to American conditions. It was not until the early years of the nineteenth century that serious attention was paid to it in the American States.

ernors were elected by the people in four States and by the legislatures in others, usually for terms of one year but with an unlimited re-eligibility. Only in Massachusetts was the Governor given the veto power, but the veto could be overridden by a two-thirds vote. By the twentieth century North Carolina was the only State still denying its Governor the veto power, and in many States the item veto with respect to appropriation measures had been conferred. Even for the performance of clearly executive functions, the advice and consent of the council was often required.

The legislatures of Georgia, Pennsylvania, and Vermont were unicameral, but only in Vermont was this system retained for any considerable time. The other States followed the colonial practice of having two houses. The lower house, variously designated as the house of burgesses, house of commons, or house of representatives, was almost exactly like that of colonial times; members were elected by the voters and served for one-year terms. They retained the treasured prerogative of originating tax measures. The upper house, called the legislative council in Delaware and New Jersey, and senate or council elsewhere, was usually elected by the voters or by the lower house for terms varying from one to five years. The senate was a smaller body than the house, its members were chosen for longer terms, and the qualifications of its members were more exacting. The senate came to be recognized as representing propertied interests, while the house represented the people of the State.

Even the provisions relating to the judiciary reflected Revolutionary ideas. The judiciary was not, as a rule, fully provided for in the original State constitutions which left the completion of the court plan to the legislatures. The method of selecting judges was changed from appointment by aristocratic colonial Governors to election by State legislatures or appointment by popularly controlled executives. Georgia went so far as to provide for popular election—a method which became generally popular after the Jacksonian era, and is the method now used in all but a very few States. The term of judges was usually during good behavior, but judges were almost without exception subject to removal by the legislature. The court system and procedures, however, remained about as they had been in the past. There were local peace magistrates and local inferior courts for the trial of minor civil cases and offenses. Above them stood a central court, generally similar to our county or district trial courts, with civil and criminal jurisdiction over more serious cases. As the capstone of the judicial system stood the State supreme court with limited original jurisdiction and broad appellate jurisdiction.

While basic principles have remained essentially the same, State constitutions have become much longer, more verbose, and weighted down with further legislative restrictions and provisions.

THE ARTICLES OF CONFEDERATION

In July, 1775, Benjamin Franklin read to the Second Continental Congress a draft of a confederative constitution which he had prepared; the submission of this draft led to the appointment of a committee on June 11, 1776, which drafted the Articles of Confederation, providing the framework of a "perpetual union." The Articles were approved by Congress on November 15, 1777, and became effective after ratification by all of the States on March 1, 1781. Considerable time was consumed in the drafting, and even more before the approval of all the States could be obtained. Until this could be done, the Second Continental Congress continued to serve as the official organization of government for the united colonies.

The Government Under the Articles

Organization of Government. Under the Articles, the country had at last achieved a government resting on a written constitution with powers and duties defined therein. It was a government which marked a considerable improvement over the extra-legal Continental Congress, even though it in turn proved to be inadequate and eventually had to be replaced. The intention of the Framers was to preserve, rather cautiously, the national framework—such as it was—that they already had. Not only was the new governmental machinery simple in form and meager in extent, but its powers and functions were few and relatively restricted. All national powers were vested in a Congress of one house, which was the sole organ of government.

This body, composed of members selected by the State legislatures for a single term, met annually. No person could serve as a delegate for more than three years in any term of six years. Each State paid its own delegates (if they were paid) and could recall them and appoint others at any time. Each State was entitled to not less than two nor more than seven delegates. The delegates voted by State, each State having but a single vote, a provision that was from the beginning the subject of severe criticism. Sessions were poorly attended, and as few as one-eighth of the entire body could veto resolutions. Great difficulty was experienced in securing the attendance of a sufficient number of members to provide a quorum of nine States, without which no important business could be transacted.

Committees were set up; the Congress was authorized to appoint such civil officers as the executive business might require, and these officers performed their duties under Congressional direction. Standing committees were created to handle foreign, financial, and military and naval affairs, and the committees proved to be the forerunners of the corresponding departments in the government under the present Constitution. There was no national judiciary, however, and no Executive Branch. Since the functions of the Congress were, in fact, almost wholly executive, one writer has observed somewhat facetiously that it might be more accurate to say that there was no *Legislative* Branch.

Powers of Government. In constructing the Articles, the central government was given many of the powers that had been exercised by the British government during the colonial period. Congress had only those powers expressly granted; there were no implied powers. Specifically, some of the powers were: to declare war and conclude peace; to conduct foreign relations, including the sending of ambassadors and the making of treaties; to requisition revenue from the States in proportion to the value of the land within each State; to requisition soldiers in proportion to the number of white inhabitants in each State and to build and equip a navy; to borrow money, emit bills of credit, and coin money; to settle disputes, usually boundary disputes, between the States; to establish a postal system; to regulate weights and measures; to create courts for limited purposes; and to appoint committees and officers. The most important of these powers, including the adoption of amendments to the Articles, could be exercised only with the concurrence of all the States, while the other powers required the approval of at least nine State delegations. These restrictive provisions proved to be a major cause of weakness and led to the ultimate collapse of the government under the Articles.

Position of the States. The third important aspect of government under the Articles was the pre-eminent position of the States. This is a consideration of particular importance in its relation to the scope and purpose of the present volume. For generations, the inhabitants of each of the thirteen original colonies or States had regarded themselves as belonging to a distinct governmental entity. They were New Yorkers, Virginians, or Carolinians, as the case might be, but otherwise they were Englishmen. After Parliament and the King had virtually thrust them out of the protection of the British constitution, their sense of allegiance to the State was greatly strengthened. Although there was much talk of the need for unity, most people felt that the States had been in existence long before the Congress, and that the States were sovereign, free, and independent, "retaining all the rights of sovereign, free and independent states, except what they voluntarily gave to Congress by the Confederation."

The sovereignty of the States was, therefore, continued under the Articles, being specifically stated in the second article:

> Each State retains its sovereignty, freedom and independence, and every power, jurisdiction and right, which is not by this confederation expressly delegated to the United States, in Congress assembled.

Although the States relinquished important powers to the national government, these powers were not sufficient to form a strong national government. The result was that the Union remained merely a loose confederation or league of States; although the Articles referred three times to the Union as "perpetual," the States plainly regarded themselves as entitled to withdraw if and when they chose. The States were not only jealous of the central government; they were intensely jealous of each other. In these present days of widespread interstate cooperation in scores of different fields, it is difficult to realize the hostile feelings with which the people of some States looked upon their neighbors.

The States pledged themselves, however, to observe their obligations and the orders of the Congress, but many of them subsequently failed to do so. The States were to extend full rights to one another's citizens; to give full faith and credit to the records, acts, and judicial proceedings of every other State; to deliver up fugitives from justice to each other; to submit their disputes to the Congress for settlement; and to allow open intercourse and commerce between each other. Retaining all powers not granted to the Congress, the States were left with primary responsibility for protecting life and property and promoting the general welfare.

Weaknesses of the Articles

Although it has been said that the Articles were obsolete when they were written and antiquated by the time the last ratification, that of Maryland, was received, there was momentary improvement when they went into effect on March 1, 1781. The new Congress, while not a distinguished one, was superior to its predecessor, but despite efforts which resulted in some notable achievements, the inherent defects of the new plan of government quickly produced some disastrous results. Lengthy lists have been compiled of the defects of the Articles, but these defects can all be classified in one of four groups: basic structural defects, critical weaknesses in fiscal powers, a wholly inadequate power structure, and a faulty Federal-State relations structure.

Structural Defects. The basic structural defects of the Articles seem obvious enough now, but the reasons why they were not obvious then, and why steps were not taken to correct them, are not difficult to discover. It may well be that they were realized but that leaders were even more conscious of the limitations within which public sentiment compelled them to move. The lack of a responsible executive was a concession made to the prevailing distrust of executive power, based upon the recent unhappy experience with George III and the Royal Governors. It may seem naive to us to believe a government could function effectively without an executive; however, there are still, nearly 200 years later, a number of States so bound by tradition that they refuse to give their Governors the power that is commensurate with the duties and responsibilities imposed upon them.

The absence of a national judiciary is somewhat easier to excuse. The judiciary as a separate and distinct branch of government was then a recent development, and even after the experience under the Articles, the delegates to the Constitutional Convention took a long and hopeful look at the possibility of relying upon State courts to interpret the Federal Constitution and laws before deciding that a separate system of Federal courts would be essential. Most perplexing was the requirement of unanimity for approval of amendments, for unanimity on any controversial subject is always difficult and often impossible to achieve.

Fiscal Weaknesses. The critical weaknesses of the fiscal powers grew out of a number of considerations, each of which contributed to the paralyzing lack of funds. The financial needs of the Congress under the Articles seem modest enough today, but the necessary expenditures must have appeared as formidable then as do the billions now expended annually. The tragedy of the situation lay in the sheer inability of the Congress, under the terms of the Articles, to raise money. Interest payments on the Revolutionary War debt were in arrears; State governments which owed most of this debt were unable to retire it and were either unable or unwilling to pay the interest. Officers and soldiers who in many cases had received nothing for their services except certificates of indebtedness were clamoring for their pay, while a new army was needed to repel possible British or Spanish attacks and to hold the Indians in check, and a navy was needed to protect commerce from the depredations of the Barbary pirates. In addition, funds were required to meet the current operating expenses of the new government.

The Congress, which had no authority to tax, had only two ways of obtaining funds, by borrowing and by making requisitions upon the States. The authorization for borrowing was quite ineffective, and although optimistic Dutch bankers continued to extend small loans which quite possibly saved the country from utter bankruptcy, the possibilities of increased borrowing had already been pretty well exhausted. The States could honor Congressional requisitions or not as they pleased, and usually they did not. The Congress could apportion sums and request remittances, but it had no means whatever of compelling a State to turn over a penny. There was widespread objection to the practice of employing land values as a basis of apportionment; actually, the Congress was unable to apportion the requisitions for public contributions in this manner, because there was no money with which to pay for the necessary appraisal of houses and lands. In fact, New Jersey seized upon this condition as a pretext for refusing to contribute at all.

Similarly, there was objection, on the part of the Southern States, at least, to the use of population as a basis for apportionment of requisitions, especially if Negroes as well as whites were included, since in the South Negroes were regarded as property. Furthermore, people disliked sending off the proceeds of local taxation to a distant government, and one State naturally hesitated to meet its obligations in full while others were shirking theirs. The result was that after a brief period some States contributed little or nothing, some paid irregularly, and only two or three, notably New York and Pennsylvania, made genuine efforts to comply with all requests for funds.

Inadequate Power Structure. Evidence of the wholly inadequate power structure for which the Articles provided was of two sorts. First, the Congress was not established primarily as a lawmaking body, for it had more executive than legislative powers. It has even been said that it was, in effect, a grand committee of the States charged with executive and managerial functions of the several different types listed previously. But the terms under which these powers were granted were such as to preclude even the possibility of effective operation. When the Congress proved itself incapable of regulating interstate commerce, the States surrounded themselves with trade barriers which hampered the free flow of commerce at home.[4] When the Congress was unable to regulate foreign commerce, European rivals effectively discriminated against American trade.

Secondly, when the Congressional failures in the area of commerce were coupled with the complete failure of all efforts to strengthen the hand of the Congress through amendment of the Articles, the collapse of the government became a virtual certainty. In its effort to provide for the national defense the Congress was, as in its efforts to raise revenue, completely at the mercy of the States. It could requisition men for service in the armed forces, but could not compel a State to provide a single

---

[4] One contemporary compared North Carolina, situated between Virginia and South Carolina, to a cask tapped at both ends, while another likened New Jersey, situated between New York and Pennsylvania, to a man bleeding at both arms. Connecticut and New Jersey were each described as being "between the hawk and the buzzard."

man. It had power to coin money, but was prevented from establishing a uniform currency. It likewise found itself unable to control the Western lands, or to enforce its treaty obligations.

Federal-State Relations. The faulty Federal-State relations structure is exemplified in a dozen ways. In all of its operations the Congress was dependent upon its ability to retain the good will of the States; so dependent was the Congress that one writer observed that the government under the Articles was a government of States and not of men. Hamilton expressed this idea in the following words:

> The great and radical vice in the construction of the existing Confederation is the principle of legislation for states or governments, in their corporate or collective capacities, and as contradistinguished from the individuals of which they consist.[5]

When States were in trouble and needed assistance in dealing with domestic violence beyond their control, there was no adequate provision for the furnishing of national aid. Balanced against the characteristic over-emphasis of the Articles upon States' rights was a weakness of a quite different type. There was an absolute neglect of population as a basis for representation, and the Congress had no authority whatsoever to act directly upon individuals to enforce laws, collect taxes, or provide for the common defense.

Thus it was that the government under the Articles was described by a contemporary as one which had the power to ask for anything but which lacked the authority to compel the performance of anything. During the years while the Articles were in effect, there was extensive public discussion of their defects, the weaknesses of the Union and of the government under the Articles, and of possible means of correction. When all corrective efforts failed, due to the requirement of unanimity in the amending procedure, the search for means of correction had to be extended into other areas.

An Evaluation

In recent years, it has been customary to heap opprobrium upon the Articles. It is certainly true that they had many weaknesses, weaknesses so serious that it was impossible for the government to continue to function under them for any prolonged period of time. Merrill Jensen strenu-

[5] *The Federalist Papers*, No. 15.

ously objects to the commonly accepted interpretation of the decade of the 1780's, as being too much influenced by the Fiske approach. "Nothing is to be gained," he writes, by following what he calls a "chaos and patriots to the rescue" interpretation of this period. He points out that there were patriots on both sides and that there were honest differences of opinion as to the desirable goals for the new nation. Many did not regard the existing situation as chaotic, nor did they regard without suspicion those who contended that the only solution to such problems as might exist was to substitute a "nationalist" for a "federalist" government.

One does not have to be a partisan for either side to recognize that serious problems did, in fact, exist. One does not have to contend that all was well when it was not, to recognize the validity of the point made so well by Professor Herman V. Ames that the Articles of Confederation served as a bridge, as a means of transition in the history of the new nation. From the long range point of view, the very weaknesses of the Articles may have been a blessing, though they certainly did not appear so to those who were trying to make the government function at the time. They bridged the gap between the achievement of independence and the time when the people were willing to agree to the establishment of a government with adequate powers. It took three and a half years to obtain the unanimous consent of the States which was necessary for the approval of the Articles.

If the present Constitution had been framed and submitted to the people at that time, it would not have been approved. People were not ready for so advanced a step. More than that, if it had been possible to make the amending procedure under the Articles actually work, so that some of the more serious defects could have been corrected at least in part, the amended Articles would probably have continued in effect for many years, in which case the present Constitution might never have been framed at all. That, certainly, would have been a tremendous loss to the nation, and to the evolution of the institutions of democratic government in the modern world as well. If the Articles accomplished nothing more, they preserved the idea of union until the present Constitution could be framed and adopted.

THE ANNAPOLIS CONVENTION

Even before the Articles of Confederation had taken effect, men like Washington, Hamilton, Madison, and Jay, among others, had felt that a government so weak could not succeed. They were inclined to believe that after a brief period of trial the people would be convinced of the futility of such half-way measures and would consent to the stronger system from which they as yet drew back. A few years of experience confirmed their worst fears, and suggestions for amending the Articles gradually grew both in number and in favor. After all suggestions had failed, attention was turned to alternative procedures.

The year 1786 was a critical one. There was economic chaos in New England and political chaos throughout the country as the leaders sought unsuccessfully to meet in Annapolis either to strengthen the existing government or to form a new one. A "little rebellion" named after Captain Daniel Shays of Pelham, Massachusetts, took place in the winter of 1786–1787 with few killings and no hangings, but with great consequences to the movement for a more perfect Union. It was but one indication of a widely prevalent spirit of unrest and lawlessness, but more specifically it was an expression of protest against certain conditions existing in Massachusetts—the seemingly excessive costs of litigation, the high salaries attached to public offices, and the heavy burden of taxation on land.

The measures taken by Governor Bowdoin, in an effort to sustain the credit of the Commonwealth and to diminish the debt, caused further heavy burdens to fall upon the poorer citizens who were already hard hit and bitter in a period of depression. The lower courts were kept very busy, while Shays and his cohorts, some 500 or 600 malcontents, succeeded in preventing the higher courts from sitting in Springfield and Worcester. Washington, deeply alarmed at reports of the early successes of the insurgents, commented, "It was only the other day that we were shedding our blood to obtain the constitutions under which we live—constitutions of our own choice and making—and now we are unsheathing the sword to overturn them."

Governor Bowdoin found it necessary to raise a small army to cope with this threat to peace and order; the funds for equipment and munitions were raised by loans from wealthy citizens and from the recently established Bank of Massachusetts. The Federal interest—if at this time, it may be so described—became very much involved when on December 25, 1787, Shays with 1,100 troops attacked the Springfield arsenal. The attackers were routed in confusion, and though small groups of rebels continued to gather for some months, no large force again appeared. Although the rebellion was over for the time being, it had two important effects: it frightened the conservatives in all the States; and it served as a warning of other protest movements yet to come.

Although one might support Jefferson's theory that "a little rebellion now and then is a good thing, and as necessary in the political world as storms in the physical . . . ," the agitation did not end with the "little rebellion" of Daniel Shays. A few years later the resistance of the farmers of western Pennsylvania to the Excise Act of 1791 resulted in the Whiskey Rebellion. In time came the agrarian movement in the West, with further protests against taxes, a cry for paper money, and a resurgence of old resentments against the bankers and merchants of the East. There were "the Greenback Party, the Grangers, the Populists, Bryan's Cross-of-Gold Speech, the Farmers' Holiday, the rise of the [movement for] cooperatives." [6]

Meanwhile, in another quarter, the movement to improve conditions prevailing under the Articles continued. As far back as 1777, Virginia and Maryland had been trying to arrive at an understanding concerning the navigation of the Potomac River which formed their common boundary. Washington and Madison were especially interested in the matter, and at their suggestion Virginia appointed commissioners in 1784 to renew negotiations. Maryland took similar action in 1785, and at length, at a conference held first in Alexandria and then upon Washington's invitation at Mount Vernon, the desired agreement was reached. Maryland thereupon suggested that other issues between the two States be discussed, on the ground that if questions of navigation could be settled by conference, why not other questions? If two States could confer successfully, why not four—especially in view of the fact that Pennsylvania and Delaware were vitally concerned with some of the same problems?

The result was that early in 1786, Madison piloted through the Virginia General Assembly a resolution appointing commissioners to meet with such representatives as might be named by other States to survey the trade of the country and to "consider how far a uniform system in their [the States'] commercial regulations may be necessary to their permanent harmony." A formal invitation was thereupon issued by the Congress to all of the States to send delegates to a convention in Annapolis the following September. The meeting was attended by twelve delegates from five States; four others had appointed delegates who failed to attend; and four had taken no action at all. Pennsylvania was represented by one delegate only, Maryland not at all. Virginia, sponsor of the meeting, sent the largest delegation, headed by Madison. Delegates from New Hampshire and Massachusetts did not reach Annapolis before the convention adjourned. Because of such a discouraging showing, those present considered it useless to proceed with the contemplated discussions. Some even concluded that the project might as well be dropped. Madison and Hamilton felt otherwise, and before disbanding the delegates unanimously adopted a report prepared by Hamilton which again called attention to the critical situation in the country and proposed that

[6] Starkey, Marion L., *A Little Rebellion* (New York: Alfred A. Knopf, Inc., 1955), Chapter 20.

delegates from all the States meet at Philadelphia on the second Monday of May, 1787.

The purpose was no longer merely to promote agreement on commercial regulations, but "to take into consideration the situation of the United States," with a view to recommending to the Congress changes in the Articles calculated to make them genuinely effective. By this time, the Congress was deeply concerned about the situation, and on February 21, 1787, formally called the proposed convention, specifying that it be held "for the sole and express purpose of revising the Articles of Confederation, and reporting to Congress and the several legislatures such alterations and provisions therein as shall, when agreed to in Congress and confirmed by the States, render the federal constitution adequate to the exigencies of government and the preservation of the Union." Although the Congress had fallen into disrepute, the prestige of its supporters—Washington, Hamilton, Franklin, and others—gave weight to the plan, so that all of the States except Rhode Island eventually followed Virginia's leadership and named delegates. New Hampshire failed to act, however, until the convention was well under way.

THE FEDERAL CONVENTION DRAFTS A NEW CONSTITUTION

Background of the Convention

Numerous attempts to amend the Articles and strengthen the central government had ended in failure. The Alexandria Conference had met with some success in solving specific problems involving a limited number of States, but the effort to extend the use of this procedure by including other States and other subject matter at the Annapolis Convention had ended in dismal failure. There was also the problem of conflict between the States themselves. In fact, one of the major reasons for holding the Philadelphia Convention had been the need to find a remedy for evils arising from State legislation which injured or interfered with the interests of other States, infringed treaties, oppressed individuals, or invaded the sphere of authority of the central government.

Thoughtful men were deeply concerned about the situation. Those who were actively engaged in public life were trying to do something about it. Some, like Peletiah Webster of Philadelphia and James Madison of Virginia, were trying to exert their influence through their writings. Although students of the period tend to minimize the influence of Webster upon the form and content of the new Constitution, some of his ideas are significant in the overall development of intergovernmental relations in the United States. In 1785, he published an essay entitled *A Dissertation on the Political Union and Constitution of the Thirteen United States, of North America.* His first premise was the very sound proposition that "the supreme authority of any state must have sufficient power to effect the ends of its appointment." Recognizing that power is subject to abuse, he took the position that this supreme power should be limited, but not so far as to render it ineffective or to prevent it from accomplishing desirable ends. Abuses are inevitable in any government, strong or weak, but Webster was not willing to forego attempts to establish a stable government with adequate powers for that reason.

On the position of States in a federal system Webster said, "A number of sovereign states uniting into one commonwealth, and appointing a supreme power to manage the affairs of the union do necessarily part with and transfer over to such supreme power so much of their own sovereignty, as is necessary to render the ends of the union effectual." He regarded it as irrational to give a single State the power to destroy the property of the country, or to prevent the central government from taking necessary and desired action. Under his plan, a State might petition Congress for repeal of an act to which it objected, and if more than half of the States joined in such a petition, the repeal should be regarded as mandatory. An exception to this general rule would be necessary in the case of revenue measures, because it would be destructive of the credit of the nation and its financial stability if acts of Congress levying taxes could be repealed or recalled unless other equally effective measures were adopted in their place. If any State were to obstruct or oppose the execution of any act ordered by the supreme authority, the Congress might send troops into that State to enforce the act. Webster sought to soften the consequences of such action by emphasizing the obligation of every citizen to obey the supreme authority.

Webster's idea that sovereignty could be distributed was somewhat new in 1783, and his distinction between sovereignty and supremacy was highly significant. His proposal that the supreme authority should operate directly upon the individual citizen aroused ire in some quarters, and even inspired the fear that a member of a State legislature might be "dragged down to Congress" and subjected to fine, imprisonment, and possibly even corporal punishment.

James Madison was a unique figure in American history, being an unusual combination of scholar and statesman. If it be true, as is often said, that Gouverneur Morris (as chairman of the Committee on Style and Arrangement) wrote the Constitution, James Madison had more to do with determining what he wrote than any other human being. He has been described as a constructive statesman "who stands almost alone by reason of the acumen by which he judged the possible and impossible, conjoined to a knowledge of the present and past." [7]

As the time for the Constitutional Convention approached, Madison applied himself to the study of federations, ancient and modern, including the one then existing in this country. He drew up papers presenting the results of his studies of the Achaean League and other federations of the past. He enumerated the essentials of a strong central government and the weaknesses of the government under the Articles of Confederation. These papers he made available to some of the leaders of the time, notably to Edmund Randolph, then Governor of Virginia, and later to Washington. As a kind of unofficial secretary of the Convention, he became responsible for what is by far the best record of the Convention proceedings, in which he played a leading role.[8] Still later, he contributed twenty-nine papers to the distinguished series of eighty-five known as *The Federalist Papers*.

Madison proposed to change the principle of representation by eliminating the equality of States in Congress. He suggested the division of the national legislature into two houses, with a longer term in one house than in the other, and with a system of staggered terms so that all would not go out of office at the same time. He believed that a central executive ought to be provided, although up to the time of his departure for Philadelphia, he had not committed himself on the question of how it should be constituted. He believed, also, that the national judiciary should be supreme.

Madison also regarded the independence of States as quite irreconcilable with their aggregate sovereignty, but at the same time he viewed the consolidation of all of them into one "simple republic" equally inexpedient and unattainable. His objective was to establish a middle

---

[7] Channing, III, 477.

[8] The official secretary was woefully incompetent; the record which he kept was fragmentary and hopelessly inadequate. Apparently Madison knew this or suspected it, and he also realized the importance of the gathering and the importance which would, in all probability, be attached to its proceedings. He set about his self-imposed task of keeping the record in his usual methodical way, which can best be described in his own words:

I chose a seat in front of the presiding member, with the other members on my right and left hand. In this favorable position for hearing all that passed, I noted in terms legible and in abbreviations and marks intelligible to myself, what was read from the Chair or spoken by the members; and losing not a moment unnecessarily between the adjournment and reassembling of the Convention, I was enabled to write out my daily notes during the session, or within a few finishing days after its close. Farrand, Max, *The Framing of the Constitution* (New Haven: Yale University Press, 1913), pp. 59–60.

ground which would make the national administration supreme without excluding the functioning of the local authorities whenever they could be useful. He thought that national supremacy should include power to negative State legislative acts, and considered anything less than this an inadequate means of assuring his objective. He preferred, and advocated steadily throughout the Convention, a Congressional negative over State laws. The majority of the delegates, however, felt that the Congressional negative would be offensive to the States and impracticable from Congress' point of view. By correlating the language of Article III, Section 2 with the supremacy clause, they provided for judicial enforcement of the desired national supremacy. This was not, however, Madison's original conception.

Madison further thought the central government, in addition to the powers possessed under the Articles, should have positive and complete authority in all cases in which the national interest was involved, or in which uniformity was required, as in the regulation of commerce. He thought well of the New York plan of the Council of Revision, to have a suspensive veto of the acts of the national legislature, but he did not regard this as necessary. Neither he nor Webster suggested that one branch of the national legislature should represent the States in their corporate capacities, and neither of them appear to have anticipated the difficulties which later arose in the attempt to adjust representation and taxation between slave States and non-slave States.

The Convention Meets in Philadelphia

The Constitutional Convention of 1787 met in Philadelphia in the summer and early fall to draft for the United States a charter of government stronger than the loose association existing under the Articles of Confederation. In marked contrast with earlier attempts to assemble such a gathering, this one met under rather favorable circumstances; the sudden change of attitude on the part of the States and of the people is attributable to three principal causes: internal disorders in different parts of the country (as, for example, Shays' Rebellion in Massachusetts); a threatened secession of the southwestern settlements; and the inability of the existing government to provide for the colonization of lands northwest of the Ohio River.

The members of the Convention were a remarkable group of men, fifty-five in number, rather young in years (average age, forty-two or forty-three) but mature when measured in terms of experience and wisdom. They were well-educated (mostly, of course, in Europe), and had read widely in the fields of history and political philosophy. Most of them had played important roles in the Revolution. "A large majority, approximately three-fourths, had served in Congress, and practically all of them were persons of note in their respective States and had held important public positions. In a time before manhood suffrage had been accepted, when social distinctions were taken for granted, and when privilege was the order of the day, it was natural that men of the ruling class should be sent to this important convention." [9]

The delegates were confronted early with the question of whether to abide by their instructions and try to draft amendments which, if adopted, would make the Articles reasonably effective, or to disregard their instructions and proceed to draft a wholly new constitution. Fortunately, they decided upon the latter course, reasoning that whatever they did would have to be approved by the people and that they would be in a singularly weak position, in such a situation, if they were to submit proposals in which they themselves had no confidence.

Although there was agreement among the delegates on some questions, they were from the beginning beset by problems so numerous and so serious, by differences of opinion so deep and so seemingly irreconcilable, that the Convention was more than once on the verge of breaking up without accomplishing its purpose. Through the summer, in closed sessions, the delegates debated, drafted, and redrafted the provisions of the new Constitution. Foremost among its problems were the position of the States in the federal system, the relative position of large States and small ones, the question of representation, and the basis for the allocation of powers between the central government and the States.

While this is neither the appropriate time nor the place to engage in any extended discussion of the work of the Convention, it is pertinent to mention the major proposals presented for the consideration of the delegates, and to suggest the significance of each of the proposals as they affected Federal-State relations. Four plans were presented, two initially —the familiar Randolph or Virginia Plan and the Paterson or New Jersey Plan, two more slightly later—the Pinckney or South Carolina Plan and the Hamilton or New York Plan. The first named plans represented, in general, the views of the large States who wanted representation based on population and a strong central government, while the latter two reflected, in general, the views of the smaller States who wanted equality in representation and a relatively weak central government. The Hamilton and Pinckney Plans exercised little influence upon the final form of the new Constitution.

Randolph Plan (Virginia). While waiting for a quorum to arrive, the Virginia delegation, under the leadership of James Madison, decided to

[9] Farrand, p. 39.

draft a plan of government to be submitted as a basis for discussion when the Convention should finally become organized. Although mainly the work of Madison, the Convention's ablest student of political—and especially federal—institutions, the plan was presented by Governor Edmund Randolph, by whose name it is known, because he was the chairman of the Virginia delegation. The plan did not specifically repudiate the Articles, but it looked toward a general reconstruction of the government under them. It did not envision a real democracy as that term is now generally understood, but it did provide for three branches of a national government, and included the guarantee of a republican form of government for each State.

It was proposed that the Legislative Branch should consist of two houses in which members should be "proportioned to the quotas of contribution, or to the number of free inhabitants" and the members of the lower house should be elected by the people of the several States. The members of the upper house, however, should be elected by members of the lower house "out of a proper number of persons nominated by the individual (State) legislatures." Each house should have the right to originate measures and pass laws. The powers of the Congress were broad. The national executive was to be chosen by the Federal legislature for a fixed term, to be eligible for a second term, and to be granted ample authority to execute all Federal laws. It would exercise a number of executive powers formerly vested in the Confederate Congress.

The Federal judiciary was to consist of one or more supreme tribunals, "and of inferior tribunals to be chosen by the National legislature, to hold their offices during good behavior," with the right to appeal from the inferior tribunals to the higher courts. A council of revision was to exercise a suspensive veto over acts of both the National and State legislatures, and the courts would also have the power of impeachment.

From the point of view of Federal-State relations, it is significant that the Federal legislature was to have the power "to negative" all State laws contravening the national Constitution, and to use force, if necessary, against any State failing to fulfill its duty under the Constitution. The Federal government would admit new States and would guarantee a republican form of government.

Paterson Plan (New Jersey). One feature of the Randolph Plan strongly objected to by members who were particularly sensitive about States' rights was the proposal to substitute for the existing equal voting power of the States in Congress an arrangement under which the voting power in both houses would be apportioned in accordance with the number of free inhabitants or in some similar manner. In order to forestall such a change, certain interested members decided to present a counter proposal based upon a "purely federal" principle. Cast in the form of nine resolutions, this alternative proposal was laid before the Convention by William Paterson of New Jersey.

Paterson wanted to amend the articles extensively in order to make the Federal Constitution "adequate to the exigencies of Government, & the preservation of the Union.' He did not call for a really weak national government; in fact, the general effect of his plan was to increase considerably the powers of Congress, permitting it to exercise all the powers granted to it under the Articles, and granting it in addition the power to levy tariffs and internal taxes. It could continue to requisition the States for revenue, could compel payment thereof if a specified number of States assented, and would have control over interstate and foreign commerce as well.

Under the Paterson plan, Congress would be composed of one house with each State equally represented regardless of size; delegates would be chosen by the State legislature in each case. This was the only one of the four plans presented to propose a unicameral legislature. Provision was made for an executive department in the form of a council, the members of which would be chosen by the Congress and would be ineligible for a second term. They could be removed by the Congress "on application by a majority of the Executives of the several States," through impeachment and conviction for malpractice and neglect of duty. The executive would have ample power to execute laws, to appoint all major Federal officers, and to direct all military operations without taking field command of the troops. Furthermore, there was to be a supreme Federal tribunal, the judges of which were to be appointed by the executive and would continue to hold their offices during good behavior.

Provision was made for the control of intergovernmental relations. All acts of the Congress and all ratified treaties were to be "the supreme law of the respective States," and the government would have power to compel the obedience of non-cooperative States, even to the extent of using force. State laws which conflicted with the "supreme law" were forbidden.

Pinckney Plan (South Carolina). After Randolph had completed his report to the Convention and had urged the adoption of a strong central government, the Virginia Plan was referred to the Committee of the Whole. On the same day, Charles Pinckney's written plan for the creation of a Federal government was likewise referred to this Committee. Due to inadequate records, students have disagreed as to its significance. When John Quincy Adams edited the *Journal* of the Convention, the elderly Pinckney supplied a document so strikingly similar to the finished Constitution that it is inconceivable that he presented his ideas in such a form at the beginning of the Convention.

The Pinckney Plan apparently provided that the legislature was to be bicameral, consisting of a house of delegates and a senate. The members of the former were to be chosen on the basis of population (Negroes counting three-fifths), the latter to be selected by the house of delegates from four districts. Each delegate and each senator would have one vote. The powers of the Congress were broad, and this body was to elect the President annually. There would be a Federal court, with judges appointed for life, and admiralty courts might be established by the Congress in each State. The Federal government would have power to admit new States. In the field of Federal-State relations, the following provisions were significant: States were prohibited from keeping troops of war, or from entering into compacts; and State laws were to be approved by the Congress before becoming effective. One shudders to think what a burden this latter requirement would have become to the Congress, had it been adopted.

Hamilton Plan (New York). In the discussion of the various proposals before the Convention, Alexander Hamilton, though he never presented any formal plan of his own, disagreed with both the Randolph and Paterson Plans. He offered for consideration a form of government that would have a bicameral legislature, one branch to be called the Assembly and the other the Senate. Members of the former were to be elected by the people to hold office for a term of three years, and the latter were to be chosen by electors to serve during good behavior. Congress was to have power to pass all laws deemed necessary to the common defense and general welfare, but the Senate alone would declare war and approve treaties and appointments.

The supreme executive authority would be vested in a President chosen by electors for life or during good behavior. He would be authorized to make appointments and to negotiate treaties, in both cases with the advice and consent of the Senate. He would have veto power, responsibility for execution of the laws, and power to pardon "all offences but treason." Hamilton recommended the creation of a supreme court, with both original and appellate jurisdiction, composed of twelve judges appointed by the President who would hold office during good behavior. A special court might be provided to hear controversies arising between the United States and particular States over territories. Federal officeholders, whether elected or appointed, would be subject to impeachment and conviction.

In the field of Federal-State relations, it was provided that laws contrary to the Constitution would be void. State Governors were to be appointed by the Federal government, and were to have veto power over State legislation.

Many of the provisions of the new Constitution, especially those relating to the obligations of the States and the powers of the Congress, were carried over from the Articles of Confederation. Some provisions were redrafted, where necessary, and new provisions were designed specifically to remedy the serious weaknesses that had developed in the government under the Articles.

Submission and Adoption

On September 17, 1787, the new Constitution was signed and sent to the Congress, which soon forwarded copies to the State legislatures. Then began the great debate. Madison, Hamilton, and Jay wrote the brilliant *Federalist Papers* which defended the new plan and were designed to encourage its adoption in the conventions held in New York and other States. Other men joined in the argument with pamphlets, articles, letters, and speeches; there were discussions in taverns, coffee houses, churches, and homes.

RATIFICATION OF THE CONSTITUTION

Year	State	Date	Vote
1787	1. Delaware *	December 7, 1787	unanimous
	2. Pennsylvania	December 12, 1787	43-23
	3. New Jersey	December 18, 1787	unanimous
1788	4. Georgia	January 2, 1788	unanimous
	5. Connecticut	January 9, 1788	128-40
	6. Massachusetts	February 6, 1788	187-168
	7. Maryland	April 28, 1788	63-11
	8. South Carolina	May 23, 1788	149-73
	9. New Hampshire †	June 21, 1788	57-46
	10. Virginia	June 26, 1788	89-79
	11. New York	July 26, 1788	30-27
1789	12. North Carolina	November 21, 1789	197-77
1790	13. Rhode Island	May 29, 1790	34-32
	14. Vermont ‡	January 10, 1790	

* Since known as the first State.

† Nine States were needed to establish the operation of the new Constitution, and New Hampshire was the ninth State.

‡ Admitted to the Union by Act of Congress approved February 9, 1791, as the fourteenth State.

Ratifying conventions were held in all States except Rhode Island, which remained persistently aloof. The delegates to the conventions were usually chosen by those electors eligible to vote for members of the lower house of the State legislature, and the apportionment was the same. Public opinion generally followed the lead of Virginia and Massachusetts; when the smaller States began to realize that they had probably fared better in this Convention than they might reasonably expect to fare in another, they hastened to ratify the Constitution. The contests in Virginia, Pennsylvania, and New York were exceedingly bitter.

By June 21, 1788, conventions in nine States, the requisite number, had ratified the Constitution so that it might become effective. There was some question about the capacity of the State legislatures to ratify the new Constitution, and about what would happen to the Articles if and when the ratification was completed. While there was no question regarding the ratifying power of the States under the terms of the Articles, the nature of the government created by the Constitution was quite different. It was to be a national government, exercising its powers directly upon individuals without State intervention. As Professor Murphy has stated:

> Its laws were to apply to the individual inhabitants of a State, even though that State's representatives might have opposed such laws. And the new Constitution itself was subject to being amended by Congress and three-fourths of the States, any new amendments being binding upon all dissident States and their inhabitants. Was it within the competence of the State governments to create such power over their constituents, or was it necessary that such power be created by the people themselves? [10]

Both Hamilton and Madison answered the question in the negative. The consensus was, however, that "although the State governments might not be competent to create a national government acting directly upon the people, there was no doubt of the power of the people themselves to create such a government." As for the fate of the Articles, which could be changed only by unanimous vote, whereas the Constitution had been adopted by nine of the thirteen states without such legal authorization, the States took the practical view that the establishment of the new Union was tantamount to secession from the old. This step having been taken by nine States, there was little for the remaining four to do but to acquiesce.

[10] Murphy, William P., "State Sovereignty and the Drafting of the Constitution," Part IV, *Mississippi Law Journal*, May, 1961, pp. 227–242 on pp. 232–233.

The debate in the Congress of the Confederation, though animated, did not turn at all on such vital questions as the legality of the transition from the old government to the new, and the obligations of the States under the Articles to the two remaining members, North Carolina and Rhode Island. Rather, it focused on the question of the location of the capital, and for reasons of expense it was decided to leave the capital in New York. Thus did the States which had so recently won their independence embark upon a new governmental venture "in order to form a more perfect Union."

No idea is more deeply ingrained in the thinking of those who adhere to the Anglo-Saxon system of government and law than that of the importance of a strong and effective local self-government. The English have long believed, and certainly Americans have believed since the establishment of the present form of government late in the eighteenth century, that local government from State and township is more democratic than national government because it is geographically closer to the people. There have been in late years a few who have questioned the sanctity of this attitude toward local government,[11] but even some of those whose influence has been to strengthen nationalism have been philosophically disposed to favor State and local government. Rexford G. Tugwell, for instance, writes that Franklin D. Roosevelt, when President, was really

> against the development of a strong central government. . . . [He wanted] most governmental functions to be decentralized—carried on by the States and municipalities. . . . And when a permanent social security system came to be worked out, he settled an internal argument in his official family by coming down on the side of State rather than Federal administration. This was a momentous and revealing choice; it showed what side he would like to be on if he could.[12]

Federalism in 1787 was a necessity if there was to be an adequate central government at all. As Herbert Wechsler has expressed it, "Federalism was the means and price of the formation of the Union." [13] While many believed in the federal idea, federalism was a political expedient to foster unity among a people who wanted or thought they wanted

[11] See, for instance, Martin, Roscoe C., *Government at the Grass Roots* (University: University of Alabama Press, 1957).

[12] Tugwell, Rexford G., "The Experimental Roosevelt," *Political Quarterly*, July–September, 1950, pp. 239–270.

[13] Wechsler, Herbert, "The Political Safeguards of Federalism," in *Columbia Law Review*, April, 1954, pp. 552–569, and in Macmahon, Arthur W., ed., *Federalism Mature and Emergent* (Garden City: Doubleday & Co., Inc., 1955), pp. 97–114.

diversity. Because of its compromise character, the relationship established between the State governments to which the believers in democracy were so strongly attached and the central government was—and still is—somewhat unstable. The Founding Fathers, perhaps deliberately, left many aspects of the relationship vague.

Much subsequent constitutional history may be viewed in terms of this unstable relationship, that is, in terms of the struggle between two levels of government for the allegiance of and control over citizens to whom both are responsible and over whom both exercise authority. Hence it is that each generation, faced with new problems, has had to work out its own version of federalism. Through all these years of controversy, a system of political safeguards has been developed in which each level of government has an important influence upon the other. States play a significant role in the composition and selection of national government personnel, and the national government, in turn, has no small influence upon the organization, policies, and administrative efficiency of the States.

What then was the basic nature of the American brand of federalism? If the point made in the preceding paragraph is true, it is obviously difficult to formulate a precise definition. Yet, after years of controversy and the struggles and strains of a terrible civil war, some sound basis for a characterization of the system became possible. Nowhere have these basic doctrines been better expressed than in the opinion of Chief Justice Chase in *Texas* v. *White:*

> The union of the States never was a purely artificial and arbitrary relation. It began with the colonies and grew out of common origins, mutual sympathies, kindred principles, similar interests, and geographical relations. It was confirmed . . . by the necessities of war and received definite form . . . from the Articles of Confederation. By these the Union was solemnly declared to be "perpetual." And when these Articles were found to be inadequate to the exigencies of the country, the Constitution was ordained "to form a more perfect Union." It is difficult to convey the idea of indissoluble unity more clearly than by these words. What can be indissoluble if a perpetual Union, made more perfect, is not? But the perpetuity and indissolubility of the Union by no means implies the loss of distinct and individual existence, or of the right of self-government by the States. . . . "Without the States in union, there could be no such political body as the United States." Not only therefore can there be no loss of separate and independent autonomy to the States through their union and under the Constitution, but it may be not unreasonably said that the preservation of the States and the maintenance of their governments, are as much within the design and care of the Constitution as the preservation of the Union and the maintenance of the National Government. The Constitution in

all of its provisions looks to an indestructible Union, composed of indestructible States.[14]

BIBLIOGRAPHICAL NOTES

Several specific topics or periods are discussed in the preceding chapter—the early State constitutions, the Articles of Confederation, the Constitutional Convention, the transitional period, and the period during which the foundations of the present system of government under the Constitution were established. In a literature that is quite voluminous, the selection of a small number of titles is no easy task.

State Constitutions. Walter F. Dodd, life-long student of State constitutions and State government, wrote an article entitled "The First State Constitutional Conventions, 1776–1783," *American Political Science Review*, November, 1908, pp. 545–561; see also his *The Revision and Amendment of State Constitutions* (Baltimore: Johns Hopkins Press, 1910), James Q. Dealey, *The Growth of American State Constitutions* (Boston: Ginn & Co., 1915) is also a good study. W. Brooke Graves' *Selected Bibliography in Major Problems in State Constitutional Revision* (Chicago: Public Administration Service, 1960) provides many additional references.

The Period of the Confederation. There are several older titles dealing with the troubled years from 1775 to 1789. John Fiske, *The Critical Period* (Boston: Houghton Mifflin Co., 1888) was for a long time tremendously popular; although it may not have been completely accurate, the book was well written. The following year, John F. Jameson, *Essays in the Constitutional History of the United States in the Formative Period, 1775–1789* (Boston: Houghton Mifflin Co., 1889) was published. Two decades later, a doctoral dissertation by Frank F. Stephens, *The Transitional Period, 1788–1789, in the Government of the United States* (Columbia: University of Missouri, 1909) appeared; this publication still remains an important study of the period, and contains chapters on elections and the adjustment of National and State relations.

Other significant works include Richard Frothingham, *Rise of the Republic of the United States*, 10th ed. (Boston: Little, Brown and Co., 1910), a standard and useful work, and Edmund S. Morgan, *The Birth of the Republic, 1763–1789* (Chicago: University of Chicago Press, 1956). Jackson T. Main, *The Antifederalists: Critics of the Constitution, 1781–1788* (Chapel Hill: University of North Carolina Press, 1961) develops the thesis that the Constitution was the work of the social elite. Marion L. Starkey, *A Little Revolution* (New York: Alfred A. Knopf, Inc., 1955) describes the famous episode of Shays' Rebellion in terms of human experience and with dramatic effect, without ascribing wickedness to either side.

For discussion of the Continental Congress, see Edmund C. Burnett, *Letters of Members of the Continental Congress*, 8 vols. (Washington: Carnegie Institution of Washington, 1921–1936) and Worthington C. Ford *et al.*, eds., *Journals of the Continental Congress, 1774–1789*, 34 vols. (Washington, 1904–1937). Three titles deal specifically with the Articles and the government which functioned under them: Merrill Jensen, *The Articles of Confederation: An Interpretation of the Social-Constitutional History of the American Revolution, 1774–1781* (Madison: University of Wisconsin Press, 1940), and *The New Nation: A History of the United States During the Confederation, 1781–1789* (New York: Alfred A. Knopf, Inc., 1951); and Andrew C. Mc-

[14] 7 Wallace 700 (1868).

Laughlin, *Confederation and Constitution* (New York: Harper & Brothers, 1905), a standard treatise in the original American Nation Series.

The Constitutional Convention. The essential facts in the story can be found in any good text in American history or American government. Two basic primary sources are Max Farrand, ed., *The Records of the Federal Convention*, 4 vols. (New Haven: Yale University Press, 1937) and Hamilton, Madison, and Jay, *The Federalist Papers.* There are almost innumerable editions of these papers, at least four having been published in 1961: Jacob E. Cooke, ed. (Middletown, Conn.: Wesleyan University Press); Roy P. Fairfield, ed. (Garden City: Doubleday & Co., Inc.); Clinton L. Rossiter, ed. (New York: New American Library of World Literature, Inc.); Benjamin F. Wright, ed. (Cambridge, Mass.: Belknap Press). Three of these are reviewed by Irving Brant, "Settling the Authorship of *The Federalist,*" *American Historical Review,* October, 1961, pp. 71–75. Gottfried Dietze made a study of these papers under the title *The Federalist: A Classic in Federalism and Free Government* (Baltimore: Johns Hopkins Press, 1960). Among the compilations of materials relating to the Convention are Arthur T. Prescott, *Drafting the Federal Constitution* (Baton Rouge: Louisiana State University Press, 1941) and Winton U. Solberg, *The Federal Constitution and the Formation of the Union of the American States* (New York: Liberal Arts Press, Bobbs-Merrill Co., Inc., 1958). Jane Butzner has gathered together the rejected suggestions presented to the Convention in *Constitutional Chaff* (New York: Columbia University Press, 1941); see also Jonathan Eliot, ed., *The Debates in the Several State Conventions on the Adoption of the Federal Constitution*, 5 vols. (Washington: 1836–1845). Professor Robert E. Cushman is editing a compilation of all existing materials on the ratifying conventions which will be published soon by the Government Printing Office, Washington.

The following are reliable secondary works on the Constitutional Convention: Max Farrand, *The Framing of the Constitution* (New Haven: Yale University Press, 1913); S. G. Fisher, *The Evolution of the Constitution of the United States* (Philadelphia: J. B. Lippincott Co., 1900); Robert L. Schuyler, *The Constitution of the United States: An Historical Survey of Its Formation* (New York: The Macmillan Co., 1923); Adrienne Koch, *Power, Morals, and the Founding Fathers* (Ithaca: Cornell University Press, 1961), which contains essays on five leaders "in the interpretation of the American enlightenment"; Saul K. Padover, *The World of the Founding Fathers: Their Basic Ideas on Freedom and Self-Government* (New York: Thomas Yoseloff, Inc., 1960); Kenneth B. Umbreit, *Founding Fathers: Men Who Shaped Our Tradition* (New York: Harper & Brothers, 1941); Carl Van Doren, *The Great Rehearsal: The Story of the Making and Ratification of the Constitution of the United States* (New York: Viking Press, 1948); and Charles Warren, *The Making of the Constitution*, rev. ed. (Boston: Little, Brown and Co., 1937).

Much has been written about the origins of the Constitution, economic and otherwise. The most useful titles in this area are: Charles A. Beard, *An Economic Interpretation of the Constitution of the United States* (New York: The Macmillan Co., 1913), and for a commentary on Beard, Robert E. Brown, *Charles Beard and the Constitution: A Critical Analysis of "An Economic Interpretation of the Constitution"* (Princeton: Princeton University Press, 1956); Breckenridge Long, *Genesis of the Constitution of the United States of America* (New York: The Macmillan Co., 1894); and Burleigh C. Rodick, *American Constitutional Custom: A Forgotten Factor in the Founding* (New York: Philosophical Library, 1953). For an excellent summary of changing evaluations of the Founding Fathers and their work, see Stanley Elkins and Eric McKitrick, "The Founding Fathers: Young Men of the Revolution," *Political Science Quarterly,* June, 1961, pp. 181–216.

Of particular significance to the subject matter of this volume is a series of articles on state sovereignty in the formative period by Professor William P. Murphy which appeared in the *Mississippi Law Journal* as follows: "State Sovereignty Prior to the Constitution," March, 1958, pp. 115–157. "State Sovereignty and the Founding Fathers," in three parts: I, March, 1959, pp. 135–164; II, May, 1959, pp. 261–292; III, December, 1959, pp. 50–82. "State Sovereignty and the Drafting of the Constitution," in four parts: I, May, 1960, pp. 203–262; II, December, 1960, pp. 1–23; III, March, 1961 pp. 155–172; IV, May, 1961, pp. 227–242.

The Early Republic. For discussion of the period when the new government was being organized and established and the Federalists were in control, see Keith B. Berwick, *The Federal Age, 1789–1829: America in the Process of Becoming* (Washington: Service Center for Teachers of History, 1961); Marcus Cunliffe, *The Nation Takes Shape: 1789–1837* (Chicago: University of Chicago Press, 1959); John C. Miller, *The Federalist Era, 1789–1801* (New York: Harper & Brothers, 1960); and Charles M. Wiltse, *The New Nation, 1800–1845* (New York: Hill & Wang, Inc., 1961).

Standard constitutional histories of the United States deal extensively with the problems encountered in the establishment of the new government: Homer C. Hockett, *The Constitutional History of the United States,* 2 vols. (New York: The Macmillan Co., 1939); Alfred H. Kelly and Winifred A. Harbison, *The American Constitution* (New York: W. W. Norton & Co., Inc., 1948); Andrew C. McLaughlin, *A Constitutional History of the United States* (New York: The Appleton-Century Company, 1935); Carl B. Swisher, *American Constitutional Development,* 2nd ed. (Boston: Houghton Mifflin Co., 1954); and Charles C. Tansill, ed., *Documents Illustrative of the Formation of the Union of American States* (Washington: House Document No. 398, 69th Cong., 1st Sess., 1927).

PART II

The new government having been organized and established, the next question that naturally presents itself is: How and by whom is policy determined? The major influences in determining policy on inter-governmental relations, as on other important matters, are to be found in the provisions of the constitutions, both Federal and State, and in the three branches of government—executive, legislative, and judicial—for which these constitutions provide. This is the structure of the machinery for policy determination.

The following chapters discuss the effect of the constitutional provisions bearing on intergovernmental relations and the role of each branch of government, at both levels in determining what policy shall be on any given matter. Since political parties, though not provided for in the fundamental law, are so vital a part of the process of decision-making and policy determination, a chapter is also devoted to their role.

CHAPTER IV

Constitutional
Provisions

Federalism in the United States embraces [a number of] elements [among which these two] salient features: (1) the direct operation, for the most part, of each of these centers of government [National and State] within its assigned sphere, upon all persons and property within its territorial limits; (2) the provision of each center with the complete apparatus of law enforcement, both executive and judicial . . . are the ones which at the outset marked it off most sharply from all preceding systems, in which the member states generally agreed to obey the mandates of a common government for certain stipulated purposes, but retained to themselves the right of ordaining and enforcing the laws of the Union. This, indeed, was the system provided in the Articles of Confederation.

The Convention of 1787 was well aware that, if the inanities and futilities of the Confederation were to be avoided in the new system, the latter must incorporate "a coercive principle" . . . , the only question being whether it should be "a coercion of law, or a coercion of arms," that "coercion which acts only upon delinquent individuals" or that which is applicable to "sovereign bodies, states, in their political capacity."

In Judicial Review, the former principle was established, albeit without entirely discarding the latter, as the War Between the States was to demonstrate. The sheer fact of federalism enters the purview of Constitutional law, that is, becomes a judicial concept, in consequence of the conflicts which have at times arisen between the idea of State autonomy ("State sovereignty") and the principle of national supremacy.[1]

[1] Corwin, Edward S., ed., *The Constitution of the United States of America: Analysis and Interpretation* (Washington: Senate Document No. 170, 82nd Cong., 2nd Sess., 1953), pp. xi–xii.

It is difficult to determine what constitutional provisions were most important or what the major influences shaping Federal policy were unless one has a fairly clear idea of what the Founding Fathers intended and what the people themselves really wanted. Actually, these things are not easy to ascertain. It appears that in the years after the Revolution there was little thought of forming a new "nation." The Framers refrained from using this word in the Constitution, although it was the purpose of some of them to establish a consolidated government. The first amendment after the Bill of Rights took away from the Supreme Court the power to adjudicate disputes between a State and citizens of another State. For years after the present government was established, the controversy over the nature of the constitutional system continued.

Few in the early days recognized any obligation of loyalty to the new government. Discussion of whether or not it was desirable to maintain it, and threats to break it up were heard on every hand. A decade after the system was established, the States were almost at the point of "flying at each other's throats." [2] The question of nullification was raised in 1798 and in 1832. In 1803 and again in 1808, the spirit of disunion had been rife in New York and in New England, even during the perilous years of the War of 1812. Although with the coming of peace in 1815 a tendency toward greater unity appeared, there was not in the first century, nor for long years thereafter, anything that might be described as true nationalism. Differences in race, language, religion, and national origin were barriers to nationalism. As one views the excesses for which nationalism has been responsible in world politics, it may even be that the tardy development of nationalism in the United States was no great misfortune.

There are, however, many questions of a general nature arising in the conduct of a federal system that affect all the States, though some States have been much more prone to raise questions challenging the exercise of Federal power than others. Some of these questions, which will be discussed in this chapter, are not necessarily the subject of controversy, but are merely questions involving relationships between the central government and the political subdivisions. They must be answered in some manner if the regular day-to-day operations of government are to function smoothly or, if indeed they are to function at all. At the same time, there are numerous agencies or influences in a government as large and complex as ours that have a role in determining Federal policy. Among these are the provisions of the Constitution and the role of the three branches of government.

[2] For an account of the early separatist movements, see Powell, Edward P., *Nullification and Secession in the United States: A History of Six Attempts During the First Century of the Republic* (New York: G. P. Putnam's Sons, 1898), p. 461.

The constitutional provisions pertinent to this discussion include certain aspects of both State and Federal constitutions. In the case of the former, concern is with such questions as intergovernmental cooperation and continuity of government, both of recent origin, and in the latter case with various provisions affecting Federal-State and interstate relations. What, for instance, is a republican form of government, and how and by whom shall the determination of its existence or non-existence be undertaken? What is the significance of the various constitutional changes on Federal-State relationships, particularly the War Amendments? What of the obligation of contract clause and other provisions which have a bearing on property rights? It is to the consideration of questions such as these, and to the role of the three branches of government in the determination of Federal policy in this important area, that attention is now directed in this chapter and the three which immediately follow.

It is important to emphasize once again the point that constitutional principles relating to federalism are not static, any more than they are with regard to other important aspects of government. Constitutional requirements do change, and should change, in response to the needs of people in the changing social, political, and economic environment in which they live. Thus the legal rules of the Constitution of the United States governing Federal-State relations or any other important subject are not today what they were 100 years ago, what they were at the turn of the century or even a decade ago. And by the end of this century, they will have changed still further.

STATE CONSTITUTIONS

If some years ago a student of American government had included State constitutions as an important factor in the functioning of American federalism, many people might have wondered why; now, they might properly wonder why if he did not. Although most of the original State constitutions preceded the Federal one, their contents were of little concern to the central government. Their framers did not, as a matter of fact, have to reckon with federalism. In a day when transportation and communication were slow and uncertain, individual States were more or less self-sufficient and it made little difference what they put into their constitutions or what they left out. The States were in theory, and almost in fact, sovereign and more or less independent entities. They could solemnly declare just about anything that struck their fancy.

Now, in our highly urbanized and industrialized society, conditions are vastly different. New conditions demand the recognition of new rights

—rights of organization and protection from discrimination in employment or in the use of public facilities based upon race, color, creed, or national origins. If, by too lengthy residence requirements, the State constitutions exclude many citizens from voting, or by discriminatory practices prevent qualified electors from registering to vote at elections in which Federal officials are to be chosen, these facts are of immediate interest and concern to the Federal authorities. And, again, it may be that the Federal government is concerned with what is omitted as well as what is included. When the States fail to protect rights that are a part of "the Supreme Law of the Land," or to perform adequately the duties assigned to them, these matters are of concern to the Federal government.

Intergovernmental Cooperation

From the point of view of intergovernmental relations, those provisions which either facilitate or impede cooperative relationships are of special significance. While it has been shown that there are few actual barriers to cooperation in the State constitutions,[3] this author has long contended that a mere absence of impediments is not good enough, that effective cooperation is so important as to justify some more positive effort to promote it.[4] On the basis of this reasoning, there was included in the more recent editions of the *Model State Constitution* a separate article which seeks to facilitate Federal-State, interstate, and interlocal consolidation and cooperation. While the purpose is sound, this particular method of achieving it has been justifiably criticized as "carrying over to a large extent some of the unfortunate assumptions of compartmentalization," and thereby itself providing "an inadequate enablement" for some new forms of cooperative relationship across interstate and international boundary lines that have since been developed. Wiltsee and Wendell take the position that while the absence of constitutional authorizations has not, of itself, been a major factor in retarding desired cooperation in the past, "much can be said for incorporating express provisions on intergovernmental cooperation in the State constitutions of the future."[5]

[3] See Zimmermann, Frederick L., and Wendell, Mitchell, "No Positive Barriers," *National Civic Review*, November, 1959, pp. 522–524, 554.

[4] See "State Constitutional Provisions for Federal-State Cooperation," *Annals of the American Academy of Political and Social Science*, September, 1935, pp. 142–148.

[5] Wiltsee, Herbert L., and Wendell, Mitchell, "Intergovernmental Relations," in Graves, W. Brooke, ed., *Major Problems in State Constitutional Revision* (Chicago: Public Administration Service, 1960), Chapter 16.

Continuity in Government

The emergence of a new age of science and technology poses new questions, not only for the national government, but for State and local governments as well. The fact that thermonuclear weapons exist, and that their use is an ever-present possibility, imposes upon governments the necessity for planning effective operation under emergency conditions. Such planning is an essential part of non-military defense. The Committee of State Officials on Suggested State Legislation notes that:

> . . . In the event of such a catastrophe State and local governments could be isolated for days or weeks and would have to assume responsibility for all governmental functions, including some normally performed by the national government. The maintenance of effective civilian government would depend in large measure on the extent to which States and local governments would be prepared to operate in such an emergency.[6]

The Committee studied the question of the governmental needs that would confront the States after such an attack, which would presumably result in large numbers of casualties, and a serious disruption of transportation, communication, production, and economic systems. The Committee developed a series of five proposals providing a basic framework of government in an emergency period—proposals which would change existing procedures as little as possible but still permit the establishment of machinery which could operate efficiently under difficult and unusual circumstances. Most States already had provisions for succession to the office of Governor, but the number of designated successors varied and was often limited to two or three. There was no provision for succession in the legislative and judicial branches, or for an emergency local or State government. The proposed program included these essential items:

1. Emergency Interim Executive and Judicial Succession
2. Emergency Interim Legislative Succession
3. Emergency Location of Governments for State Political Subdivisions
4. Emergency Location of State Government
5. Constitutional Amendment—Authorizing State Legislation to Provide for Continuity of Government

[6] *Continuity of Government* (Chicago: Council of State Governments, 1959), p. 29.

California in 1958 and Michigan in 1959 ratified constitutional amendments relating to continuity of government, and in 1960 fourteen more States approved the constitutional amendment. By the end of 1961, thirty-four States had enacted all or portions of this program. In the 1961 legislative sessions, seven States approved measures pertaining to succession in the office of Governor, and seven others for succession in other executive offices. Legislative succession was a subject of legislation in six States, for the judiciary in six, for local offices in eight, for the relocation of State and local governments in ten.[7]

THE UNITED STATES CONSTITUTION

The Supreme Law of the Land

It appears from the record that the members of the Federal Convention were clearly in favor of the principle of national supremacy. Their views on this basic problem of effecting national supremacy were expressed in Article VI, Section 2, of the Constitution:

> This Constitution, and the laws of the United States which shall be made in pursuance thereof, and all treaties made, or which shall be made, under the authority of the United States, shall be the supreme law of the land; and the judges of every State shall be bound thereby, anything in the Constitution or laws of any State to the contrary notwithstanding.

The Convention had first considered a Congressional negative on State laws; this would have made national supremacy a political issue to be dealt with by Congress, whereas the solution adopted made it a legal principle enforceable in the courts. This solution, as Professor Murphy has pointed out, was more consistent with the concept of a national government operating upon individuals.[8]

Guarantee of a Republican Form of Government

The Constitution specifices in Article IV, Section 3, that it shall be the duty of the United States to guarantee to every State "a republican form of government." The Federal courts have consistently refused to

[7] *Book of the States, 1960–1961*, p. 404; see also *State Government News*, May, 1961.

[8] Murphy, William P., "State Sovereignty and the Drafting of the Constitution," Part II, *Mississippi Law Journal*, December, 1960, pp. 15–17.

give meaning to this clause, declaring it to be a "political" question not susceptible to judicial interpretation. In *Luther* v. *Borden,* the Supreme Court said that "it rests with Congress to decide what government is the established one in a State . . . as well as its republican character." [9] Thus, if Congress seats the Congressional delegation from a given State, that State may be said to have a "republican" form of government.

A further interpretation of this clause in 1911, in a case involving the initiative and referendum, held that the use of these devices in a manner supplementing the ordinary legislative processes did not contravene the guarantee of a republican form of government.[10] It may be noted that many of the bills introduced in Congress calling for the admission of Alaska and Hawaii as States specified that their constitutions "shall be republican in form"—which makes Congress the arbiter of the point and presumes that a constitution which Congress accepts may automatically be deemed to be "republican in form."

Distribution of Powers

There is no more important matter in any system of government than the method provided for determining its powers and the method of their distribution. There are two basic methods available for both of these purposes. All the powers of a government may be centralized in a form of organization known as a unitary state. Under this system, no powers of right belong to the local units which may do only those things which they have been authorized or directed to do. Under the alternative, the federal form of organization, governmental powers are divided between the central government and its political subdivisions, variously designated as states, provinces, cantons, or otherwise.

A federal system normally provides that delegated powers be vested in one unit or level of government, residual powers in the other. The Tenth Amendment delegates powers to the central government of the United States, and grants residual powers to the States: "The powers not delegated to the United States by the Constitution, nor prohibited by it to the States, are reserved to the States respectively, or to the people." On the other hand, the Canadians, who had the horrible example of the American Civil War fresh in their memory, provided for exactly the opposite arrangement in the British North America Act of 1867, which serves as their constitution. In Canada, the government of the Dominion is the government of residuary powers, while the provinces have delegated powers.

[9] 7 Howard 1 (1849).
[10] *Pacific States Telephone & Telegraph Company* v. *Oregon,* 233 U.S. 118 (1912).

It is probably impossible for anyone to determine which system is better. Each has its advantages and its disadvantages, but the records of the two countries show that both can be made to work.[11] As time passes and the problems of government and the needs of the people change, the specific characteristics of any given brand of federalism will change also. Certainly this has been true in both the United States and Canada.

The distribution of powers in the American federal system did not turn out to be what its principal draftsmen hoped that it would be. The system that was adopted by the Convention was, in turn, soon modified, and it has been in a continuous process of change ever since, sometimes by constitutional amendment, statute, executive action, judicial interpretation, or very often by the rather informal procedures of custom and usage. Two aspects of the original plan should be mentioned here; the various methods of change, and their effects, will be considered at appropriate points in later chapters.

The first question involves the manner in which the original plan was modified in the course of the deliberations of the Convention, the second the limitations imposed by the Convention upon the States. The original Virginia Plan called for unlimited legislative power to be vested in Congress, as well as power to negative or veto any State laws which, in its opinion, contravened the provisions of the Constitution. By the time these proposals had gone through the process of Convention consideration, the solution—a long list of delegated powers, minus the veto—bore little resemblance to the original proposal.

Under the original proposal, there would have been no necessity for any specific limitations on State powers. After the proposal had been modified and stripped of the veto, however, "it was deemed necessary as a means of protecting the national government against intrusions by the States to expressly prohibit or limit the exercise of State power in certain areas." [12] In addition to the fact that the Founders were fearful not of the expansion of Federal power but of State power, there was ample historical precedent for imposing limitations upon the States. Such limitations had been listed in Article VI of the Articles of Confederation, although a notoriously weak government had not been able to enforce them. All of these restrictions were carried forward and many new ones were added, the States losing considerably in the process. As Professor Murphy has expressed it, "the Constitution placed substantial restrictions upon the political powers of the States which still further reduced the area of what had previously been unlimited sovereignty."

[11] Stoke, Harold W., "Some Problems of Canadian Federalism," *American Political Science Review*, October, 1933, pp. 804–814.
[12] For a full analysis of the problem, see Murphy, Part II, December, 1960, pp. 1–23.

This was, in fact, only the beginning. The Virginia Plan, considerably modified in the Convention to the disadvantage of the States, was further modified in the future. The Bill of Rights was adopted as a series of limitations on the power of the central government, but over the years, by the process of judicial interpretation, they became limitations upon the States as well—limitations effective to such an extent that many now argue that the bills of rights in State constitutions are largely superfluous.

The Tenth Amendment did, however, attempt to clarify the line of demarcation between the authority of the central government and that of the States. With the passage of time this rule has been extensively modified, though rarely formally, by one technique of modification or another. These modifications constitute, in fact, both the subject matter of the chapters which follow, and the justification for attempting to present the story which they contain.

Admission of New States

The constitutional authorization in Article IV, Section 3, that "New States may be admitted by the Congress into this Union," is subject to only two restrictions, namely that "No new State shall be formed or erected within the jurisdiction of any other State," and that "No State shall be formed by the Junction of two or more States, without the Consent of the Legislatures of the States concerned as well as of the Congress." Since the conditions of admission are not specified in the Constitution, Congress has the power to determine them, although the courts discouraged conditions of admission that would cause continuing limitations on the control of the new State over its own affairs. In practice, there was little uniformity with respect to either the organization of territories or the requisites of statehood.

Territorial Organization. An "organized territory," whether incorporated or not, is one in which Congress, through legislation establishing a systematic government in the area, conferred upon the inhabitants some measure of local self-government. The distinction between incorporated and unincorporated territories was never very clearly drawn. The Supreme Court, in the absence of a specific declaration, held that certain territories were incorporated simply because Congress, in practice, dealt with them as though they were, setting up organized governments and extending to them all of the provisions of the Constitution, with the apparent intention that they should be so regarded. Not all provisions of the Constitution apply to unincorporated territories.

"Normal" Process of Admission. There were never absolute standards

regarding area, population, or other characteristics required of territories desiring statehood. In some instances, current political conditions counted heavily in determining eligibility. Several different admission procedures were followed by the fifty existing States. The original thirteen States were never territories, and became "charter members" of the Union at the time of its establishment. In twenty instances, incorporated territories were admitted after Congress passed enabling acts. Seventeen unincorporated territories were admitted under other procedures. The traditional standards for statehood which Congress required have been summarized as follows:

> 1. That the inhabitants of the proposed new State are imbued with and are sympathetic toward the principles of democracy as exemplified in the American form of government;
> 2. That a majority of the electorate desire statehood;
> 3. That the proposed new State has sufficient population and resources to support State government and to provide its share of the cost of the Federal government.

When the resolution was signed by the President, the process was complete.

This procedure was an outgrowth of the administration of the Northwest Territory. The celebrated Ordinance of 1787 provided for the future division of that territory into not less than three nor more than five States. A further qualification for statehood contained in the Ordinance was a population minimum of 50,000. This stipulation was observed rather closely for some time, but Kansas adopted another rule which required a population equal to the current unit of representation in the House of Representatives. The latter policy was not invariably complied with in later admissions.

Incorporation was normally considered a preferred status, but it was never regarded as essential to statehood. Nor did it offer assurance that a territory would not encounter serious obstacles on the road to statehood, a status which was never even relatively easy to attain. For the thirty-one States having previous territorial status, the waiting period ranged from two or three years for Alabama (1817–1819) and Nevada (1861–1864) to as much as sixty-two years for New Mexico (1850–1912). Similarly, Arizona waited forty-nine years (1863–1912), and our two most recently admitted States, Alaska (1912–1959) and Hawaii (1900–1959), waited for forty-seven and fifty-nine years respectively.

The process of admission for each of the unincorporated territories began when the people of that territory expressed substantial pro-statehood sentiment (usually through a plebiscite) and sent a petition to Congress, either through the territorial legislature or its delegate in Congress or both, requesting the admission of the territory into the Union. Congress then considered the petition, and if favorably disposed, passed an enabling act, authorizing the people, through a constitutional convention, to draw up a State constitution. The new constitution had to be submitted both to the electorate and to Congress for approval or rejection. Then a joint resolution was passed by Congress declaring the territory a State.

Other Admission Procedures. Seventeen unincorporated territories have been successful in gaining admission to the Union. For these territories, the road to statehood was normally even longer and more difficult than for those which were incorporated, although many States have been admitted without following the "normal" procedure. All seventeen of these territories entered the Union without benefit of enabling acts. Eleven of them were organized and incorporated: Alaska, Arkansas, Florida, Hawaii, Idaho, Iowa, Kansas, Michigan, Oregon, Tennessee, and Wyoming. Four other areas (not incorporated territories) had been parts of other States and were admitted as separate entities by simple acts of admission; thus Kentucky was fashioned from territory formerly within the jurisdiction of Virginia; Maine from Massachusetts; Vermont from New York; and West Virginia from Virginia. Texas, which had been independent prior to its annexation by the United States, had its enabling act incorporated in the joint resolution of annexation. Still another unit, California, was an unorganized area subject to the hegemony of a United States Army general who served as *de facto* Governor.

In seven of these jurisdictions—Alaska, California, Iowa, Kansas, Michigan, Oregon, and Tennessee—"Senators" and "Representatives" were elected to Congress before they were admitted to statehood. These States are popularly known as "Tennessee Plan States," after the procedure initiated by the people of Tennessee in 1796, whereby they induced the territorial governor to call a constitutional convention, formulate a State constitution, and elect their representatives to Congress, all without Congressional authorization. The other four jurisdictions—Arkansas, Florida, Hawaii, and Wyoming—drafted State constitutions without prior Congressional authority, but did not elect Congressional representatives until after admission to the Union. Two other jurisdictions—Minnesota and New Mexico—which are not included in the seventeen which entered the Union without enabling acts, had peculiar admission histories.[13]

[13] This summary is based on Tansill, William R., *Admission of States into the Union: A Brief Summary of Procedure* (Washington, 1960), and Graves, W. Brooke, *Federal Assistance to New States During the Period of Transition and Adjustment* (Washington, 1960). Since Legislative Reference Service reports are generally available only when published as Congressional documents, they are cited only when they have been used.

Political Considerations. The admission of new States into the Union has often occasioned a great deal of jockeying for position between rival factions, sometimes political, sometimes centered around differing views in regard to an issue considered to be of supreme importance. Two cases are cited here, but there are many others.

One involved the organization of Kansas and Nebraska as territories and later their admission as States. Scattered residents in these areas had long desired a territorial form of government so that free lands might be opened to settlers from the East. When a variety of pressures brought about the introduction of a bill for this purpose, a controversy immediately arose as to whether these areas would become slave territory or free. The Southern group wanted to preserve the Missouri Compromise of 1820, the Northern group to repeal it. When Senator Douglas realized that there was little chance of passing his bill in its original form, he promptly proposed a division of the territory on the fortieth parallel, leaving the question of slavery upon admission to the Union to the wishes of the respective States (popular sovereignty). It was apparently assumed—without any basis in fact that can be documented —that Nebraska would become a slave State and Kansas a free State. The final solution was not achieved without a good deal of disorder, bloodshed bordering on civil war and some of the bitterest controversy in Kansas and in Washington in the history of American politics.

The second illustration is of an entirely different sort, involving party rivalry but no momentous issue. Party leaders are always mindful of factors affecting their voting strength. They have to be. From 1900 on, when the question of admitting Hawaii to the Union was presented with increasing frequency, Democrats delayed lest there be two more Republican Senators and a Republican Representative. It was not until the 1950's that this party rivalry was settled by a compromise, when a Republican President and a Democratic Congress supported the admission of Alaska which had normally been strongly Democratic, and Hawaii which had equally strong Republican leanings. Thus was the existing balance of power preserved.

CONSTITUTIONAL AMENDMENTS
OF INTERGOVERNMENTAL SIGNIFICANCE

The Amending Procedure

When amendments to the Federal Constitution are under consideration, the States have a vital role to play. Article V provides two methods by which amendments may be proposed, and two, either of which may be designated by Congress, for their ratification. While the normal method of proposal has been a two-thirds vote of both houses of Congress, the alternative method permits proposal by a convention called by Congress at the request of the legislatures of two-thirds of the States. Affirmative action by three-fourths of the States is necessary for ratification, either legislative action by three-fourths of the States or, if Congress so specifies, conventions called in at least three-fourths of the States for the purpose of considering the proposed amendment. Thus "the Convention repudiated State sovereignty by adopting an amending process under which a State could be bound without its consent, either in the proposal or in the ratification of an amendment." [14]

It may be worth noting that while the amending procedure has often been criticized as slow and excessively cumbersome, the speed with which the Eighteenth, Twenty-first, and Twenty-third Amendments were ratified clearly shows that it can be made to work efficiently.

In its lifetime of nearly 200 years, the Constitution has been amended twenty-three times, though Congress has considered a tremendous number of proposals for change. In their eagerness to secure ratification of the Constitution itself, Washington and Madison practically pledged themselves to work for the passage of amendments that would make the document more acceptable, and Washington, in his first inaugural address, earnestly set forth the need for attending to the matter at once. After the new governmental machinery began to operate, the pressure for amendments completely faded away. Even so, Madison presented twelve proposals for amendment based upon those that had been suggested by the ratifying conventions. Of these, ten were approved and became the Bill of Rights; two, dealing with matters of detail, were not approved. In view of their great importance, it is strange indeed that so little information is available about the proposals either in documentary sources or in the writings of those who secured their consideration and adoption.[15] (See the table on page 98.)

A number of the twenty-three amendments have significantly affected the position of the States, notably the Ninth, Tenth, and Eleventh Amendments, adopted within ten years of Washington's inauguration; the Thirteenth, Fourteenth, and Fifteenth—the so-called War Amendments—adopted during the Civil War; and more recently, the Eighteenth Amendment which federalized control of liquor traffic, and the Twenty-first which returned control to the States.

The adoption of the first Ten Amendments postponed attempts to

---

[14] Murphy, Part III, March, 1961, p. 172.

[15] This need is currently being met by a project under the direction of Professor Robert E. Cushman, for the publication of all pertinent materials.

divide the Union into two or three parts, and the last two of these amendments plus the Eleventh went far toward changing the basic character of the Constitution as it came from the Convention and as it was ratified by the States, by modifying many of its attributes of federal organization and limiting its strong nationalistic tendencies. The Ninth Amendment prohibited, or seemed to prohibit, a "broad construction" of the organic law, while the Tenth expressly declared that undelegated powers were reserved to the States respectively, or to the people. Under the terms of the Eleventh Amendment, "the people" recalled, to some extent at least, their earlier commitment to a strong federal form of or-

CONSTITUTIONAL AMENDMENTS

Period	Amendments	Subject Matter	Discussed
1791–1804	I–X	Bill of Rights	Chapter XI
	XI	Limiting Power of Federal Courts	Chapter VII
	XII	Election of the President	Chapter VIII
1861–1870	XIII–XV	War Amendments	Chapter IV
1913–1933	XVI	Income Tax	Chapter XIII
	XVII	Direct Election of Senators	
	XVIII, XXI	Liquor Control	Chapter X
	XIX	Woman Suffrage	
	XX	Lame Duck Amendment	
1951–1961	XXII	Two-term Limitation for President	
	XXIII	District of Columbia Suffrage	

ganization, and modified the organic law so that the question of its national character now became a matter for judicial determination and legislative conflict.

The Problem of Immunity From Suit

In every organization, large or small, there must be an established procedure for decision-making and a means for resolving conflicts. In a federally organized democracy such as ours, decisions are made by responsible elected officials within the framework of the government and the political structure that has developed around it. In a governmental system in which the doctrine of the separation of powers prevails, as it does in the United States, there are obviously three possible repositories for the power to resolve conflicts and settle disputes—the Executive, Legislative, and Judicial Branches.

Because of their recent unpleasant experience with George III and the Royal Governors, the Founding Fathers ruled out the possible use of the executive as final arbiter. Though the concept of parliamentary supremacy was a basic part of the Anglo-Saxon heritage, most of which they found quite acceptable, they chose not to confer this power upon the Legislative Branch. No choice remained except to use the third, the judiciary, as final arbiter. While this was eventually done, it required a far-reaching decision by Chief Justice John Marshall in an important case and also a constitutional amendment to fully establish the American doctrine of judicial supremacy. The American practice served as a prototype for such other major federal systems as those in Australia, Canada, and West Germany, but none of these found the doctrine of judicial supremacy acceptable.

Obviously, it would be impossible for the judiciary to discharge its function as arbiter in the federal system if suits could not be instituted against that government when someone had a grievance. The Eleventh Amendment grew out of a case involving precisely this question. According to Article III, Section 2 of the Constitution, suits brought by a State against citizens of another State are heard in Federal courts, as are those "between a State, or the citizens thereof, and foreign States, citizens, or subjects." This phrase, which obviously raises a question with regard to distribution of power, appears to have been inserted into the text of the Constitution somewhat suddenly, on its emergence from one of the committees to which it had been referred. It was not long before several suits had been entered under it. Patrick Henry and the Virginia Yazooites had thought of using the clause in suing Georgia for its cavalier treatment of their claims. Also under this clause, George Mason had taken steps toward testing the right of Virginia to repudiate her contract with the Indiana claimants, and suits had actually been entered against Massachusetts, New Jersey, and Georgia.

In the last of these, some citizens of North Carolina, the heirs of Alexander Chisholm, had brought suit against Georgia to enforce the payment of certain claims for property that had been confiscated during the Revolution. A general outcry was heard over the indignity of a sovereign State being sued without its consent. Georgia refused to appear. The Supreme Court ordered judgment by default to be entered against the State at the next term, unless Georgia should appear and show cause to the contrary. As Georgia showed no sign of yielding, judgment was entered for Chisholm in February, 1794.[16]

---

[16] *Chisholm* v. *Georgia*, 2 Dallas 419 (1793).

No actual writ of execution was ever issued, probably because the State legislature by law declared it to be a felony to proceed any further in the matter, thus nullifying the decision of the Supreme Court, the Judiciary Act passed by Congress, and the provision of the Constitution itself. A large segment of the public was very much aroused. Congress promptly proceeded to adopt and submit to the States for their approval or rejection the text of an Eleventh Amendment assuring that, in future, no State would be sued by anyone without its consent. At present, when both the Federal government and the States have long provided a blanket authorization, given in the form of legislation and through the operation of State courts, and when both jurisdictions have in addition provided for such suits by creating special courts of claims, this issue, deemed so important a century and a half ago, seems a good deal like a tempest in a teapot.

Significance of the War Amendments

The three War Amendments, the Thirteenth, Fourteenth, and Fifteenth, were adopted between 1865 and 1870. The three key words in these amendments may be said to be: "Free," "Citizen," and "Vote." These amendments were framed and adopted solely and exclusively with the problems of the American Negro in mind, although in the years since their adoption they have been applied to many other things. The Thirteenth Amendment abolished the institution of slavery, making the Negro free; the Fourteenth defined citizenship for the first time in the Constitution, in such terms as to confer citizenship upon the Negro; and the Fifteenth, as much as is possible by provision in the basic law, assured the Negro that he would in the future enjoy the privilege of voting.[17]

For present purposes, probably the most significant things about these amendments—Amendment Fourteen in particular—is the great change accomplished with respect to citizenship, and the enormous amount of litigation which was engendered. The background of the citizenship problem begins in colonial times. All of the colonial charters except that given to William Penn contained a provision to the effect that the inhabitants and their children should be deemed British subjects. British citizenship was terminated by the Declaration of Independence, and citizenship in the individual colonies established. Since the colonies, which now became States, were sovereign under the Articles of Confederation, there was no national citizenship during that

[17] See U.S. Commission on Civil Rights, *Freedom to the Free: Century of Emancipation, 1863–1963* (Washington, 1963).

period. All inhabitants were citizens of their respective States. When the new Constitution was adopted, persons recognized as citizens of the several States became citizens of the United States also. Since the Constitution did not specify which form of citizenship had priority, or which was dependent upon the other, it appears to have been generally assumed, prior to the adoption of the Fourteenth Amendment, that United States citizenship, except in cases involving naturalization, was subordinate to and derived from State citizenship.

The Supreme Court had ruled in 1857 that neither a State nor the Federal government could confer Federal citizenship upon native-born Negroes, whether slave or free.[18] This decision, followed by the War Between the States, led to the adoption of the War Amendments, the second of which defined citizenship for the first time in these words: "All persons born or naturalized in the United States, and subject to the jurisdiction thereof, are citizens of the United States and of the State in which they reside." While this statement, creating dual citizenship, had a clarifying effect and was to that extent beneficial, it left unchanged the concurrent jurisdiction of State and Federal courts in conferring citizenship upon those who had completed the requirements for naturalization.

Among the many cases which arose under this amendment, one of the earliest and certainly one of the most important decisions was made on the Slaughter House Cases, a decision which involved several cases in which New Orleans butchers appealed for the protection of the amendment against a police power regulation enacted by the Louisiana legislature.[19] The Supreme Court held that though the amendment created national citizenship, the rights guaranteed against impairment were rights of national, not State citizenship; furthermore, its adoption did not indicate any purpose on the part of Congress which proposed it or the State legislatures which ratified it to destroy or modify the essential features of the federal system, as previously existing. The Federal government gained no new powers under the amendment, and the States lost none.

A second significant effect of the amendment was indirect, and probably quite unanticipated by its framers. Conceived and adopted for the sole purpose of protecting Negro rights, the amendment was presently seized upon and used—all too often successfully—as a means of attacking the validity of virtually every progressive and forward-looking piece of legislation enacted by any State, and the courts unfortunately sympathized with this point of view to such an extent that Charles A. Beard

[18] *Dred Scott* v. *Sandford,* 19 Howard 393 (1857).
[19] *Butchers' Benevolent Association of New Orleans* v. *Crescent City Livestock Landing and Slaughter House Company,* 16 Wallace 36 (1873).

was later to describe the Fourteenth Amendment as the Magna Charta of American business. Thus an effort to guarantee the rights of a minority group (and of all citizens as well) was distorted and twisted into a device for restricting the powers of the States in dealing—or even attempting to deal—with pressing social and economic problems.

Important as these considerations have been, it should be added that the general impact on Federal-State relations of the due process and equal protection clauses of the Fourteenth Amendment has been immense. There have, in fact, been many centralizing effects of the amendment. Over the years, a whole battery of protections against State and local action, covering virtually the entire Bill of Rights, has been read into these clauses. After two generations of construing the amendment so narrowly that no great changes resulted, the Supreme Court began in the 1920's to make its full impact upon the States felt, first with respect to questions involving freedom of speech, press, religion, and assembly, later in regard to matters in the fields of labor, price fixing, utility regulation, and many more.

By interpreting the Fourteenth Amendment as making the First Amendment applicable in Federal and State spheres alike, the Supreme Court began to develop "what to all intents and purposes is a single (and nationalized) system of rights," at least in the major areas mentioned. Not all liberties have as yet undergone such assimilation, although others may do so in the future. In some fields, such as judicial procedure, important differences between Federal and States' rights still exist, but the characteristic complexity of the federal system has been materially reduced in those areas in which the Supreme Court has extended the application of the Fourteenth Amendment to include the protections contained in the First.

Twentieth Century Amendments

Of the seven amendments adopted in the twentieth century, there are only two, the Twentieth and the Twenty-second, that do not in any direct way affect the balance of power between the Federal government and the States. Both are concerned with the presidential office. The Sixteenth or Income Tax Amendment has had an effect quite different from what was anticipated by those responsible for framing and adopting it. This was the third attempt to establish the income tax as a major source of national revenue. The first, in Civil War times, had been upheld by the Supreme Court.[20] The second, passed some years later,

[20] *Springer* v. *United States,* 102 U.S. 586 (1881).

was declared unconstitutional in 1895.[21] Though nowhere specifically required, it was assumed when the amendment was proposed that, in keeping with the long-established practice of assigning particular tax sources to particular levels or units of government, if the amendment was approved, the States would not enter the income tax field. This, obviously, has not been the case; not only are there personal income tax laws in more than half of the States and corporate income tax laws in approximately three-fourths of them, but in some thirty cities as well, beginning with Philadelphia in 1944.

A second development was no more anticipated than the first. The adoption of the Sixteenth Amendment assured the Federal government, for the first time, a continuing source of revenue in substantial amounts. This revenue provided a basis for initiating and developing the extensive program of grants-in-aid that has now been established. (See Chapters XIV, XV, and XVI.)

The Seventeenth Amendment, providing for direct election of Senators, obviously affected the States. Though it neither increased nor decreased the scope of State powers, it directed that States abandon legislative selection of United States Senators, and utilize instead the method of election by popular vote. Though the legislatures themselves lost an important power, popular sentiment in favor of the change was strong enough so that they voted to ratify the amendment.

Although woman suffrage was still a highly controversial subject at the time of its adoption, there was overwhelming public sentiment for the Nineteenth Amendment, as there had been for the Seventeenth. While this sentiment did not modify existing arrangements respecting the distribution of powers in our federal system, it did, by doubling the number of qualified voters with one stroke, have a profound effect upon the development of democratic institutions in America.

The Liquor Control Amendments, Eighteen and Twenty-one, were unique in American history. They constitute the only serious attempt made in modern times to modify the pattern of the allocation of powers between the Federal government and the States by the amending procedure. The unhappy experiment with the Prohibition Amendment is not likely to be repeated soon. A Federal child labor amendment was proposed during the prohibition era and its adoption strongly urged. This amendment, like the Eighteenth, would have provided for a formal shift of power from the States to the nation, but the proposal made little headway and was soon abandoned. After the Fair Labor Standards Act of 1938 was enacted (see Chapter X), there was no real need for it.

The most recent constitutional amendment, the Twenty-third, also

[21] *Pollock* v. *Farmers Loan and Trust Company*, 157 U.S. 429 (1895) and 158 U.S. 601 (1895).

has significance here. After 161 years, it allowed the erstwhile voteless residents of the District of Columbia to vote in presidential elections. With amazing alacrity, the legislatures of the States responded favorably; only Arkansas rejected the proposal, and it is rumored that some members of the General Assembly in that State had heard that there was a considerable number of Negroes living in the District of Columbia. Actually, the requisite number of ratifications was given in record time, well in advance of the time necessary to insure participation of District residents in the 1964 presidential election. The amendment was only one step, though an important one, toward recognition of the fact that District residents *are* citizens of the United States.

CONFLICT OVER PROPERTY RIGHTS

It has been observed that the financial nerve is the most sensitive one in the whole human organism. If people as individuals are sensitive regarding money matters and the ownership and control of property, so are governments and the people who operate them. This truth is abundantly illustrated in the annals of history, but for present purposes, a few instances will suffice: the Supreme Court's interpretation of the obligation of contract clause, and the effect of this interpretation; the tidelands controversy of recent years; and the problems raised by Federal property ownership within the borders of the several States.

The Obligation of Contract Clause

In Article I, Section 10, the Federal Constitution imposes upon the States a restriction that "no State shall impair the obligation of contract." This provision has a long and interesting history. Although no such provision had been contained in the Articles of Confederation or in the draft submitted by the Constitutional Convention's Committee on Detail, there had been in the Northwest Ordinance a prohibition against laws which interfered with or affected private contracts. There was much discussion of this proposal during the Convention, opinion being divided between those who believed it necessary to include such a provision in the new Constitution and those who believed that the courts could and would provide adequate protection against the impairment of such rights.[22]

[22] Murphy, Part II, December, 1960, pp. 4–5.

Although the final decision was in favor of a constitutional restriction, experience has shown that the courts have been keenly aware of the problem and have been diligent in protecting the rights of individuals arising under contract. This constitutional provision has been a special favorite of lawyers over the years, because its strict enforcement promotes stability in the business and economic life of the nation. From the beginning, there were difficult questions regarding the application of this provision, and various recent developments have raised others. The trouble began with the interpretation given by the Supreme Court in the Dartmouth College Case, which grew out of a bitter personal, political, and religious feud between the president and a majority of the trustees of the College.[23] It is an important case because of the interpretation it gave to the contract clause of the Constitution, and an interesting one because of the manner in which it was handled. In 1769, King George III gave to the Reverend Eleazer Wheelock, who had previously established a charity school for Indians, a charter authorizing him to establish a school for "the education and instruction of Youth of the Indian Tribes in this land, in reading, writing . . . as well as in all liberal arts and sciences, and also of English youth and any others." The school was established at Hanover, New Hampshire.

After some years of emphasis on training for the clergy, there came to the presidency of the college a man with progressive ideas on higher education, who saw the need for expanding the program of the college and extending its opportunities to more people. When his plan was submitted to the trustees, it was strongly opposed. At the instigation of the president and his friends, the New Hampshire legislature passed an act bringing the college under State control. It also increased the number of trustees from twelve to twenty-one, the new trustees to be appointed by the Governor and Council. The old trustees dismissed the secretary, Woodward, who had aligned himself with the opposing faction. When he refused to turn over the college seal and other property, suit was instituted to recover them. Plaintiffs claimed that the New Hampshire statute was invalid. The State court gave judgment for the defendant, but the Supreme Court reversed that decision on the ground that the college charter was a contract within the meaning of the Federal Constitution and that the State law constituted an invalid impairment of it.

The case was argued on March 10 and 11, 1819, Daniel Webster appearing as counsel on behalf of the trustees. Although he was not at the time a Member of Congress, his appearance in the case and the manner in

[23] *Dartmouth College* v. *Woodward*, 4 Wheaton 518 (1819). See also Ellsworth, Clayton S., "Ohio's Attack Upon Abolition Schools," *Mississippi Valley Historical Review*, December, 1934, pp. 379–386.

which he presented his argument suggest interesting questions in a day in which there is so much public discussion of civil ethics. Because the case had been inadequately presented by Woodward's counsel, it was reported that he had engaged another counsel who intended to ask for a reargument at the next term (but no motion for reargument was made). Upon completion of the argument, but before the Court adjourned on March 14, Chief Justice John Marshall polled the Court. Finding himself in the minority, he postponed announcing the decision until the opening of the Fall Term.[24] It is interesting and may be significant to note that the college trustees had lavishly entertained the members of the Court in the interval; it is inconceivable today that any party to a case before the Supreme Court would attempt to use such tactics, or that the members of the Court would for a moment permit themselves to be subjected to such influence.

The Dartmouth College decision has often been praised as a step toward the stabilization of the economic order. Against its advantages in this connection, however, must be weighed its unfortunate effects upon the States, which were placed in a very difficult and embarrassing position. Not many years after the decision was handed down, current changes in the economic life of the nation led to a widespread substitution of corporate business organization for the individual entrepreneur and the partnership. In the early days of the corporate form, every corporate charter was conferred by a separate legislative act, and under the terms of such an act, each charter became an irrevocable, unmodifiable contract between the State and the persons to whom it was granted. If the legislatures had always been careful and honest in the granting of charters, the situation would have been bad enough. Unfortunately, they were often neither careful nor honest. Vast portions of the public domain were given away under such grants, without any consideration whatever to the State, then or in the future. Rights, privileges, and benefits of incalculable value were conferred for all time without limitation, compensation, or any hope of compensation to the State.

[24] Warren, Charles, *The Supreme Court in United States History* (Boston: Little, Brown and Co., 1922), I, 480, 483. The Chief Justice dominated the Court during his long tenure in a most extraordinary manner. In those thirty-four years, the Court decided 1,106 cases, of which Marshall himself wrote the opinion for 519. In all these years, he dissented from the majority in only eight cases, and wrote only one dissenting opinion—that in *Ogden* v. *Saunders,* 12 Wheaton 213 (1827). This is the more remarkable when one considers the number of dissenting opinions filed by members of the present Court. Many of Marshall's contemporaries have testified to his extraordinary influence over his colleagues; brilliant young followers of the Jeffersonian philosophy were transformed into arch-conservatives under his influence, much to the dismay of the Anti-Federalist leaders. See Hall, James P., *Cases on Constitutional Law* (St. Paul: West Publishing Company, 1926), p. 800.

The situation thus created was highly complex, and from the point of view of the States, critical. Most of the basic facts are well established. State legislatures did make grants and confer tax exemptions and other benefits which aroused many citizens. When later legislatures sought to revoke or modify these enactments, they were thwarted in their efforts by the contract clause which the Supreme Court had to enforce. In this situation, States were forced to invent methods of evading and circumventing the Court decision if they were to establish control over their corporations. They were obliged to insert in corporate charters, as a condition of their acceptance, arbitrary limitations on the life of the charter and clauses reserving the right to modify or abrogate the charter if the public interest might require it. By such roundabout methods, States eventually regained a limited measure of control over the corporations that they themselves had created.

One view is that the Supreme Court did not have to interpret the contract clause as it did; it might, for example, have sought to develop a more fluid system of legislative supremacy. At any rate, the course adopted tended to give the impression that the Court was the special friend of corporations and the enemy of the sovereign States. It is still true, however, as Professor Swisher has pointed out, that much of the popular resentment which the Court had to bear might more properly have been directed toward the legislatures:

> The Court was often blamed in situations wherein the fault lay not with the Court but with the legislatures, which, corrupt or not, had made the initial grants. In such situations, the Court [under Taney] began to build the same reputation as a friend of property which had characterized the Marshall Court.[25]

In later years, to be sure, the Court has held that every contract is made subject to the implied condition that its fulfillment may be frustrated by proper exercise of the police power.[26]

[25] Swisher, Carl B., "The Supreme Court and the Forging of Federalism: 1789–1864," *Nebraska Law Review*, December, 1960, pp. 2–15; see also his *Historic Decisions of the Supreme Court* (Princeton: D. Van Nostrand Co., Inc., 1958).

[26] For further discussion, see Orton, Jesse F., "Confusion of Property with Privilege: Dartmouth College Case," *Independent*, August 19 and 26, 1909, reprinted in Orth, Samuel P., *Readings on the Relation of Government to Property and Industry* (Boston: Ginn & Co., 1915), pp. 7–24. See also Lodge, Henry C., *Daniel Webster*, American Statesman Series (Boston: Houghton Mifflin Co., 1889); Mott, Rodney L., *Due Process of Law* (Indianapolis: Bobbs-Merrill Co., Inc., 1926), Chapter 19; and Hervey, John G., "The Impairment of the Obligation of Contract," *Annals of the American Academy of Political and Social Science*, January, 1938, Supplement, pp. 87–120.

The Tidelands Controversy

A controversy over the determination of the coastal boundaries of the States was precipitated by the discovery of tidelands oil. The question at issue was whether title to the tidelands oil deposits, located between low-water mark and the limit of American jurisdiction along the coasts of California, Alabama, Florida, Louisiana, Mississippi, and Texas, was vested in the national government or in the governments of the States concerned. It is interesting to note that even in the early stages the controversy involved not only a number of States but all three branches of the Federal government as well.

Prior to the 1930's, there was no dispute over the ownership of offshore lands. The States assumed that they owned them—insofar as the question was considered at all—and the Federal government gave no indication of challenging this assumption until, in 1937, Senator Gerald P. Nye of North Dakota introduced a bill which brought the matter to the attention of Congress. A historical study of Congressional action shows that prior to that time the Federal government had never asserted claim to ownership.[27] Although Congress tended to favor State ownership of the submerged lands, it did not act during the early period of the dispute, a fact which gave the Department of Justice an opportunity to engage in a preliminary skirmish in the form of a suit filed against the Pacific Western Oil Corporation[28] which leased lands situated beneath the marginal sea from California. By determining the rights of the lessee, the United States would, in effect, also determine California's title to these lands, because the rights of the lessee would be dependent upon the validity of California's title. Before this suit was disposed of, it was dropped, and a new one was instituted against the State of California. At approximately this time, 1945, President Truman issued a proclamation stating that the continental shelf was subject to the jurisdiction and control of the United States. In 1946, Congress passed and the President vetoed a bill which recognized the States as having a clear title to these lands. In 1947, when the suit against California had been appealed to the Supreme Court,[29] the Court ruled against California without expressly stating that the Federal government owned the tidelands. After rather cursorily dismissing questions regarding the Court's jurisdiction where no controversy existed, and the authority of the At-

[27] *Dorr* v. *United States,* 195 U.S. 138 (1903).
[28] *United States* v. *Pacific Western Oil Corporation,* U.S. District Court for Southern District of California (1945).
[29] *United States* v. *California,* 332 U.S. 19 (1947).

torney General to institute this particular suit, the Court proceeded to demolish, one by one, the arguments presented in behalf of California, thereby creating a legal setting and psychological atmosphere in which it would be easier for the individual States to win in the next round. California had contended that:

1. The original constitution adopted by California prior to its admission into the Union placed its boundaries three English miles from the shore;
2. The enabling statute which admitted California into the Union ratified the boundary thus established;
3. California was admitted on an equal footing with the original states in all respects.

Thus the United States rather than individual States possessed paramount rights to the soil beneath the open sea adjacent to the coast and to the mineral resources thereunder, as distinguished from rights to the soil and mineral resources under inland waters. California sought to establish its title as owner of the marginal sea on the basis of the long established "equal footing" rule announced in *Pollard's Lessee* v. *Hagen*.[30] In 1950, cases involving the rights of Louisiana and Texas to tidal oil deposits computed to be worth $27 billion reached the Supreme Court, whose decision followed the lines established in the California case.[31] But the controversy, still far from settled, continued on through the Eisenhower administration. Fulfilling a campaign promise, this administration recommended and Congress passed in 1953 the Outer Continental Shelf Lands Act, similar to the one that had been vetoed by President Truman. This legislation, designed to "correct" the Supreme Court decision, vested title to oil resources in lands out to the three-mile limit in the coastal States.[32] Long-time conservationists and friends of education, who saw in Federal control of the tidelands a means of financing Federal aid for education, alike regarded the enactment of this legislation with dismay. To the former it represented another victory for the exploiters of the nation's resources, while to the latter it appeared that the property of all the people in all the States had, as the result of a well-organized and well-financed campaign on the part of the large oil companies, been handed over to a few States which happened to be strategically located. Senator Joseph C. O'Mahoney, in a speech in the Senate on September 20, 1951, stated the matter well when he said,

[30] 44 U.S. (3 Howard) 212 (1845).
[31] *United States* v. *Louisiana*, 339 U.S. 679 (1950); and *United States* v. *Texas*, 339 U.S. 707 (1950).
[32] Outer Continental Shelf Lands Act, 43 U.S.C.A. Sec. 1301 (Supp. 1959).

"The record clearly shows that what is represented as a raid by the Federal Government on State property is in fact a raid by the coastal States upon lands which are not only within the Federal jurisdiction, but the wealth of which belongs to the people of all the interior States as well as to those of the coastal States."

Title to all deposits under waters beyond the three-mile limit was apparently retained by the national government, insofar as national jurisdiction could be established. This interpretation of the act was promptly challenged by Louisiana, which claimed title beyond the three-mile boundary, and the case was decided by the Supreme Court in the spring of 1960.[33] Although the suit was instituted by the government against Louisiana, the government ordered it to be broadened to include all four of the Gulf States. Separate opinions were prepared for Florida and Texas, but because of the similarity of their claims, the other four were considered together. The boundaries of these States, finally determined more than 180 years after the establishment of the present government, were established at three geographical miles from the coastal line, with the exception of Florida. In this State, where the situation was somewhat different, the coastal boundary extended three marine leagues into the sea from low-water mark.

Federal Property Ownership Within States

In days of old, except within the thirteen original States, the Federal government owned the land. For well over a century this government worked diligently to divest itself of an enormous portion of its land holdings. This was done through grants to new States upon admission to the Union, and later by opening public lands for homesteads, for railroads, for higher education, for agricultural development and promotion, and for various other purposes. In time, the supply of desirable lands approached the point of exhaustion. In the twentieth century, beginning with the period of World War I, a counter trend has been in evidence.

The bulk of the lands acquired by the Federal government in recent decades has been taken in connection with the needs of national defense as sites for training camps, supply depots, or industrial establishments.

---

[33] *United States* v. *Louisiana, Texas, Mississippi, Alabama, and Florida,* 80 Sup. Ct. 961 (1960). Out of a rather voluminous literature, especially in the law reviews, see Bartley, Ernest R., *The Tidelands Controversy: A Legal and Historical Analysis* (Austin: University of Texas Press, 1953) and Harder, Marvin A., *The Tidelands Controversy,* University of Wichita Bulletin, November, 1949, entire issue.

Some of these military installations and shore establishments require extensive areas of land which, when purchased or taken under eminent domain, are removed from the local tax rolls. The resulting loss of revenue can be serious for the local units concerned. Every effort of a State (or local unit thereof) to tax real estate or other property belonging directly to the national government had met with defeat, and with a Supreme Court decision in 1939 [34] the situation became acute. An early move to provide some relief was initiated by President Roosevelt on January 14, 1939, when by Executive Order he established a Federal Real Estate Board charged with making a study of the effect of Federal ownership of real property on State and local finance.[35]

The report of this Committee presented three recommendations: (1) that a complete inventory be undertaken of all surplus land and improvements, in order that a prudent use might be found for such properties or that they might be offered for sale; (2) that, once compiled, this record be maintained on a current and up-to-date basis; (3) that a Federal Real Estate Board be established to study and make recommendations regarding the situation existing in individual communities adversely affected by expanded Federal holdings. Thus a problem that was beginning to be serious before World War II became very serious during and after the war as Federal holdings continued to increase. In the meantime, three more studies have been prepared,[36] all looking toward solutions of the problems involved.

The Interdepartmental Committee found four categories of legislative jurisdiction over the government's land holdings: exclusive, concurrent, partial, and proprietorial. Of these, the last is by far the largest. Each tends to immunize, in whole or in part, the income, transactions,

---

[34] In *City of Springfield* v. *United States*, 306 U.S. 650 (1939), it was held that not only Federal property in general, but such property when leased to private users, is tax exempt. *United States and Mesta Machine Company* v. *County of Allegheny*, 322 U.S. 174 (1944), involving an attempt in Pennsylvania to tax gun-making machinery belonging to the Federal government but leased to a private manufacturer of munitions, said the same thing. The decisions have not always been consistent, however.

[35] *Federal Ownership of Real Estate and Its Bearing on State and Local Taxation* (Washington: House Document No. 111, 76th Cong., 1st Sess., 1939). The report came to Congress as a message from the President, and was referred to the Committee on Public Buildings and Grounds.

[36] Another inventory study, twenty years later, was completed by the General Services Administration, *Inventory Report on Jurisdictional Status of Federal Areas Within the States* (Washington, 1957). An Interdepartmental Committee, headed by the Department of Justice, subsequently produced a *Report,* and the Advisory Commission on Intergovernmental Relations put out *State and Local Taxation of Privately Owned Property Located on Federal Areas* (Washington, June, 1961).

activities, and properties of private persons located in areas subject to such jurisdiction from State and local taxation. In order to ameliorate the consequences of this immunity and to preserve something approaching equality of tax treatment for the private interests involved, Congress has established suitable procedures, so far as individuals are concerned, but leaves untouched the immunity enjoyed by the Federal government itself.

While it is neither necessary nor possible within the limits of available space to explore in detail the highly complicated questions involved, it may be noted that two procedures have been developed by which the Federal government does provide some relief to adversely affected communities. One is the in-lieu payments device by which one government agrees to make a payment to another in lieu of taxes in situations in which it has no legal obligation but where a moral obligation exists that may not properly be ignored. This may be regarded as a sort of service charge, in recognition of benefits received from fire and police protection, street maintenance, etc. For years now, Congress has authorized and appropriated such payments.

The other device is the making of payments to federally impacted areas. These are areas in which the opening of a Federal establishment or installation causes a large influx of workers and their families who make demands upon the resources of the community in housing, schools, etc., far in excess of the normal needs of the community or of its ability to handle them. Congress has provided funds to take care of such cases since 1950, and formulas have been developed under which a reasonably equitable financial adjustment is possible. Such payments are not to be confused with those under the depressed areas program. The two have no relation to each other, but in fact relate to situations of exactly opposite types. In one case, the problem is that of providing accommodations for more employed workers and their families than the community is prepared to care for; in the other, the problem arises from a very high level of unemployment, with few if any employment opportunities in sight.

STATES' RIGHTS AND FORMS OF REMONSTRANCE

The Nature of the Union

In *Texas* v. *White,* the Supreme Court told us that ours was "an indestructible union of indestructible States," [37] but it was not always so.

---

[37] *Texas* v. *White, 7 Wallace* 700 (1868); see quotation on pp. 79–80.

Words like "secession" and "disunion" may have a dreadful sound to us, but in the early days of the Republic these ideas were freely discussed and were quite generally the subject of correspondence. The Union was new then, and was justified only on the basis of current need or advantage. It had yet to become, as it is today, the symbol of a great and powerful nation, a symbol which in itself could arouse sentiments of loyalty and devotion on the part of the people.

The people, as a matter of fact, were still not entirely sure whether it was better for all to work together as a nation, or to break up the existing constitutional arrangements and divide into two or three groups. The advantages and disadvantages of these alternatives were brought forward for discussion in various ways. It had been recognized in 1790, for instance, that the question of the assumption of State debts involved the continuation or the dissolution of the federal system. In 1792, the possibility of terminating the Union was constantly mentioned in letters, and it is reported by George Carroll of Georgetown, one of the commissioners of the new Federal city, that Congress was unwilling to vote money for executing the plans for laying out a city because there was so strong a disposition to dissolve the government.

Oliver Wolcott, writing to his father on February 3, 1793, used language suggestive of Horace Greeley's phrase, "Let the erring sisters depart in peace," which was to become famous more than half a century later. Noting that the pressure of debts made the Virginia farmers uneasy, he said that if Union with the Southerners should prove to be unsuccessful, the two sections ought to part like good friends, but that "the separation ought to be eternal." [38] In 1795, the Reverend John Pierce, noting the sumptuousness of the new State capitol at Hartford, wrote that it "excites the suspicion . . . that it is contemplated by some to make this a Capitol, should there be a division of the Northern from the Southern States."

The next year, Washington devoted a portion of his Farewell Address to urging "Unity of Government." It is reported that in his original draft he made considerable reference to sectional jealousies and threats of dissolution, but on reflection decided that this was the wrong approach to the problem and deleted these comments from the Address in its final form. In 1798, Jefferson, a strong supporter of the Union, discussed the threats of dissolution in a letter to John Taylor of Caroline. He observed that if the New England States were cut off, Pennsylvania

[38] Gibbs, George, ed., *Memoirs of the Administrations of Washington and John Adams* (New York: Van Norden, 1846), I, 86, and quoted here from Channing, Edward, *History of the United States*, 6 vols. (New York: The Macmillan Co., 1905–1925), IV, 155. This summary is based largely on Channing's discussion.

and Virginia would rise to control what remained of the Union, that it was convenient to have someone to quarrel with, and that the New Englanders were good for that purpose. "A little patience and we shall see the reign of witches pass over" and the South will come into its own.

The Hartford Convention

On October 17, 1814, a circular letter was issued by the Massachusetts General Court, summoning a convention of all the New England States to meet in Hartford to consider the existing situation and to suggest remedies. President Madison had just sent Congress the report from the commissioners at Ghent, which stated that the British negotiators were demanding extensive sessions of lands and the formation of an Indian state as a price of peace. These demands were so distasteful that, at long last, public attention was concentrated on the war. Publication of these documents, together with the serious financial condition of the central government, served to raise questions regarding the possible dissolution of the Union.

Much of the discontent in New England was, of course, due to the trade restrictions that had all but stopped commerce during the preceding winter and spring. The acquisition of Louisiana was regarded as a blow to the prestige of New England, since representation in Congress from this region would inevitably reduce the influence of the New England States. The situation was, in fact, widely regarded as justification for secession from the Union. So, on one pretext or another, reports, resolutions, and letters to the press were used to fan the flames of discontent. Newspapers in Boston and other cities declared that "the Federal Constitution is nothing more than a treaty between independent sovereign States." It was argued that the States had entered into the compact and that it was up to them to decide whether the conditions stipulated therein were being observed; if not, they should leave amicably if they could, violently if they must.

There had been some sentiment in earlier years for the calling of a convention to consider Northern grievances. A convention was a long recognized English and American method of political procedure; although no action was assured, a convention provided a safety valve. The Massachusetts House of Representatives had adopted a report advocating passage of laws nullifying the existing embargo and advocating a convention to propose amendments to the Constitution for the protection of the people from future abuses of power.

When the convention met, the New England States were well represented. A report was adopted, holding that acts of Congress in violation of the Constitution were void, but that it was not necessary for a State to resort to open resistance upon every infraction of the Constitution. Seven amendments to the Constitution were proposed, including one to do away with the Federal ratio. Another would have required a two-thirds majority to admit new States into the Union, pass non-intercourse laws, and declare war. A third proposed to bar naturalized citizens from holding Federal office.

Connecticut and Massachusetts sent commissioners to Washington to make arrangements with the national government for the separate defense of these States. The commissioners had proceeded as far as Baltimore, on their way to Washington, when word of peace was received. Then, as a burst of happiness and hope for the future swept over the country, past grievances were forgiven and forgotten.

Interposition

Interposition is probably the oldest and certainly the mildest means of achieving the objectives of its proponents. The Third Edition of Webster's New International Dictionary defines it as the "act of interposing, or state of being interposed; a being, placing, or coming between, mediation; intervention; something that is interposed." An estimate of its effectiveness appears to depend largely upon one's point of view. While interposition is commonly regarded by students as the least effective means of accomplishing its objectives, one proponent who defines it as "the right of a State to interpose its sovereign authority against a violation of the Constitution by the Federal Government," asserts that it has never failed: "From its early history to this date, interposition has always succeeded in the hands of a Governor or a State court that has had the desire and the courage to use it with determination." [39] Constitutional or not, much interposition by State governments against the 1954 desegregation decision still continues.

Interposition was first advocated as a means of obtaining redress from the Alien and Sedition Laws, in the Kentucky and Virginia Resolutions. The word "sovereign," as applied to the States, appeared in Article II of the Articles of Confederation; although it is nowhere to be found in the Declaration of Independence, the Constitution, or the Bill of Rights, some of the early writers, nevertheless, contended that the States were "sovereign," and according to the common understanding at

[39] Smith, Drew L., *Interposition: the Neglected Weapon* (New Orleans: Federation for Constitutional Government, 1959) and reprinted in *Congressional Record*, April 23, 1959, pp. A3365–A3367. See also Franklin, Mitchell, "Interposition Interposed," *Law in Transition*, Spring, 1961, pp. 1–22.

the time, the organ of sovereignty was the legislature. If the States were opposed to some action taken by the central government, it was the duty of the State legislatures to record their disapproval. Madison clearly stated this position in the Third Virginia Resolution, the essence of which may be summarized as follows:

> Resolved . . . that this assembly doth explicitly and peremptorily declare that it views the powers of the Federal Government as resulting from the compact to which the States are parties. . . . That in the case of a deliberate, palpable, and dangerous exercise of other powers not granted by the said compact, the States who are parties thereto, have the right and are in duty bound to interpose for arresting the progress of the evil and for maintaining within their *respective* limits the authorities, rights, and liberties appertaining to them.

Two distinct propositions are included here: (1) that the Constitution is a compact among the States, and (2) that the States have a right to judge, each for itself, whether a dangerous breach of the Constitution has been committed. The latter proposition, brought forward again in New England in 1814 and by Calhoun in 1832, was, in the words of Professor Edward S. Corwin, "soon discretely shelved." Submitted to the other States in hopes of support, the Kentucky and Virginia Resolutions invariably drew responses from the Northern legislatures which were condemnatory in tone and which frequently asserted the authority of the national judiciary as the final interpreter of the Constitution. As noted previously, in the discussion of these Resolutions, Madison himself retreated in a second set of resolutions from what he must have fully realized was an untenable position. Corwin finds little of substance in the whole argument and concludes that "the boasted faculty of *Interposition* of the State legislature, its right to insert the aegis of its sovereignty between the National Government and such portion of the national citizenship as might chance to reside within the State boundaries, amounts in the last analysis, so far as legal force is concerned, to no more than the fulminations of garrulous hangers-on at a cross-roads post office." [40]

This ancient doctrine was, nevertheless, resurrected and widely advocated throughout the South by opponents of the Supreme Court's desegregation decision of 1954. Recalling that the Northern States had used it with some degree of effectiveness on the issue of slavery, the South now tried to convince itself that this might be the answer to its problem of desegregation. Consequently, one State after another passed resolutions

[40] Corwin, Edward S., *National Supremacy* (New York: Henry Holt & Co., 1913), p. 106.

or acts of interposition until, of the eleven Southeastern States, North Carolina stood alone as the only one whose legislature had refrained from providing for interposition.[41] When one reviews the use made of the authorization, four cases come to light, in each of which it is claimed that interposition was used "successfully," [42]—depending, of course, upon one's idea of success.

In the first of these cases, Governor Allen Shivers of Texas, following a decision of the United States District Court for the Northern District of Texas,[43] issued an Executive Order to the local authorities in Mansfield based upon the general powers of the Governor to enforce the laws and see that order is maintained within the State, as a result of which it is claimed that "no Negro children have entered the Mansfield High School." The second instance involved the constitutionality of a Virginia miscegenation statute, a case dealt with in Chapter VII where other instances of State court defiance of Supreme Court decisions are considered. The third case involved the admission of a Negro to the University of Florida law school; this particular Negro was not admitted for the time being—again demonstrating the effectiveness of interposition as a form of delaying action and as a tactic of harassment. In 1960, interposition was tried in Louisiana on a broad scale in the row over school integration—both official and unofficial interposition, as *The New York Times* noted editorially:

> There has been "interposition" by mobs who have threatened and insulted school children and their parents—including at least one white child and her parents. There has been "interposition" by adolescents in calendar years, or in intellect, who sneered at and reviled ministers of the Gospel.[44]

[41] The provisions were: Alabama: Act No. 42, Special Session, 1956; Arkansas: Constitutional Amendment No. 47, 1957; Florida: House Concurrent Resolution No. 174, May 2, 1957; Georgia: House Resolution No. 185, 1956; Louisiana: House Concurrent Resolution No. 10, 1956; Mississippi: Resolution No. 125, 1956; South Carolina: Resolution of February 14, 1956; Tennessee: House Resolution No. 1, January 17, 1957; Texas: House Concurrent Resolution No. 23, 1957; Virginia: Senate Joint Resolution No. 3, February 1, 1956.

[42] Smith, *Interposition;* see also Kilpatrick, James J., *The Sovereign States: Notes of a Citizen of Virginia* (Chicago: Henry Regnery Co., 1957).

[43] *Jackson* v. *Rawdon*, 235 F. 2d 93 (1956).

[44] *The New York Times,* December 2, 1960; for a summary of the actions taken by the legislature and by various school officials, see *Race Relations Law Reporter,* Fall, 1960, p. 599, and for the text of the several acts adopted by the legislature, *ibid.,* pp. 857–868. For able discussions of the constitutional issues involved, see Corwin, Edward S., "National Power and State Interposition, 1787–1861," *Michigan Law Review,* May, 1912, pp. 535–551 and Franklin, Mitchell, "The Unconstitutionality of Interposition," *Lawyers Guild Review,* Summer, 1956, pp. 45–60.

The three Federal judges, all of Southern birth and training, who held interposition contrary to the Constitution pointed out that the State legislature was not legislating when it "seeks to act as executor of its own laws," that the doctrine of interposition may have had validity 171 years ago, but that it had no validity now. They cited a Virginian named John Marshall, once Chief Justice of the United States; they reaffirmed the doctrine that the Supreme Court system is "the only solution short of anarchy"; and having thus disposed of "interposition" as "a patent subterfuge," they proceeded to eliminate the whole package of laws by which the State government of Louisiana, with the aid of some disturbers of the peace in New Orleans, had attempted to prevent integration.

Nullification

Nullification has been defined as the alleged right of a State in the American Union, acting in a sovereign capacity through a convention of the people, to declare an act of Congress "null, void, and no law, not binding upon the State, its officers or citizens." While the various forms of remonstrance have been most frequently associated with questions involving civil rights and race relations, nullification was proposed in New England in 1812–1814, and was first seriously attempted in South Carolina in opposition to the tariff acts of 1828 and 1832. In this connection the General Assembly met in special session and provided for a convention which on November 23, 1832, resolved that the duties and imposts established by Congress were null and void, and that no "constituted authorities, whether of this State or of the United States," shall enforce them, and that "all persons holding any office" of South Carolina (members of the legislature excepted) shall take an oath to obey and execute the ordinance.

Southerners did not object to government regulations, or even to government ownership and operation of business or industry (South Carolina and Virginia both successfully operated state-owned banks), but they did object to trade and tariff policies that tended to siphon off their money to the North and that resulted in higher prices for the necessities they had to buy. If the tariff did not actually have this effect, they believed it did, so the result was the same. Not only South Carolina, but North Carolina and Georgia as well, had protested against the protective system. There is some reason for suspecting, therefore, that the opposition to these particular tariff acts may have been based at least as much on political considerations as upon conviction.

Both South Carolina Senators expounded their views on the nature of the Union at length, Hayne in his debate with Webster in 1830, Calhoun in his able statement of the doctrine of nullification in the "Exposition" in 1828, and in his speech on the Force Bill in 1833. While speaking in the Senate on the Foot Resolution on the sale of public lands, January 21, 1830, Hayne recalled that those who favored a "national union" were known as Federalists and as "devoted advocates of power" and that the Anti-Federalists preferred a "federal union," being "lovers of freedom."

He identified as "true friends of the Union those who would confine the federal government strictly within the limits prescribed by the Constitution" and its enemies as "those who are in favor of consolidation, who are constantly stealing power from the States." Webster replied on January 26 that his concern was "to preserve, not to enlarge" the powers of the central government, and not for "consolidation in that odious sense in which it means an accumulation, in the Federal government, of the powers properly belonging to the States." He emphatically rejected "the proposition that, in case of a supposed violation of the Constitution by Congress, the States have a constitutional right to interfere and annul the law of Congress."

Calhoun's views on these matters seem to have undergone a significant change. His basic assumption was that the people of each State were sovereign when the Constitution was ratified. In ratifying that instrument, each acted in its separate or sovereign capacity. The Constitution thus became a compact to which each State was a party, and each State had a right to judge its own infractions and to take appropriate steps within the limits of its capacity when such infractions occurred, even to the extent of declaring an act of the Federal government null and void and not binding upon it.

As Calhoun held the center of the stage in this controversy in his native South Carolina, President Jackson held it in Washington. Jackson's background and orientation were decidedly Southern; he believed in States' rights, like most Southerners, but he had a deep and abiding love for the Union. He had saved the Union once at New Orleans, and he had no disposition now to permit the use of a dogma on States' rights to justify action threatening its very existence. He took steps to organize and equip Federal forces, in the event that their use might become necessary. These considerations tend to explain both his course of action and the reasoning that impelled him to adopt it.

Promptly after the adoption of the South Carolina Ordinance of Nullification, President Jackson declared "the power to annul a law of the United States, assumed by one State" to be "incompatible with the existence of the Union" and announced his intention to enforce the

Federal laws. The controversy subsided after some further forensics on both sides when it became apparent that the President would use the Army and Navy, if need be.

The evidence appears quite conclusive, however, that at least from the time of Jackson's election the compact view of the Constitution had come to be the dominant one in all parts of the country. Indeed, it sometimes found expression in strange places. At the very time that Jackson was assailing the doctrine of nullification in his famous Proclamation to the People of South Carolina, he accepted the theory of the Union from which the right of nullification was deduced, and less than a decade later the chief apostle of nullification brought the Senate of the United States to declare by a vote of 31-13 that the Constitution was a compact among sovereign States—a doctrine that might have had a far greater impact in the field of constitutional law than it did, had the Supreme Court ever accepted it.

Secession

Secession is defined as voluntary withdrawal from an organization. The earliest attempts at secession in the American federal system took place early in the nineteenth century—the plot to form a Northern Confederation in 1803–1804, and Aaron Burr's famous attempts to break up the Union, a series of plottings in the Southwest which brought him to an ignoble end when in March, 1807, he was forwarded from New Orleans to Richmond for trial.[45] Next, of course, came the action of eleven Southern States which, between December 20, 1860, and June 8, 1861, attempted to withdraw from the Union. If the arguments for interposition were weak and easily disposed of, the fundamental assumptions on which interposition was based were not. On the contrary, as expressed by Professor Corwin, "it was still wrapped around the whole brood of secession and civil war." From the moment the idea was formulated, the doctrine that the Constitution was a compact between sovereign States moved steadily into the realm of the axiomatic in the popular consciousness. There was vigorous protest regarding this development from many quarters, to be sure; able spokesmen for the older view were to be found, for example, in the Virginia legislature. The older view was stated and restated in the decisions of Marshall and Story, in the *Commentaries* of Story and Kent, and finally with very great force in the orations of Webster.

The dominant theory of pre-Civil War days looked neither to se-

[45] Powell, Chapters II and III.

cession nor to making the national government the mere agent of the individual States. On the contrary, it spoke of the national government as being itself sovereign within the sphere assigned to it. The disagreement seemed to arise chiefly regarding what actually was assigned to it, and the answer to this question depended largely upon one's point of view. Corwin summarizes the theory that was dominant with the judiciary, and particularly with the Supreme Court from 1837 on, as follows:

(1) The Constitution of the United States rested in each State upon the same basis as the State constitution itself and owed its existence, therefore, as part and parcel of the laws of a particular State to an exertion of the sovereign right of self-government by the people of that State, exercised, however, in this instance, once for all time. From the point of view of constitutional origin, therefore, the government of a State was of equal dignity with that of the United States.

(2) Sovereignty in the United States was divided between two centers, the States and the National Government, both of which operated over a common territory and a common citizenship for distinct purposes; each of which was completely equipped with the organs necessary for the discharge of its functions and neither of which was dependent upon or subordinate to the other, save in one particular which did not alter the theory of the system. For while an organ of the National Government, the Supreme Court, construed the Constitution finally, yet it did so under the Constitution which recognized the sovereignty and independence of the States within the range of their powers.

(3) The Constitution, in other words, contemplated the co-existence of these two centers of authority, these twin depositories of sovereignty, whence it followed that neither could assume to control the other to any extent or assume to exercise any power, which, if abused, would hamper or menace the independence and efficiency of the other. In *McCulloch* v. *Maryland,* Marshall had established the rule, upon the basis of the doctrine of national supremacy, that a State could not tax an agency of the National Government. The Court after Taney established the converse rule upon the basis of the doctrine just stated, namely, of the duality of the federal system, and the general principle inferred therefrom, that each of the two centers must live and let live. In the last analysis the two rules are contradictory, for if the National Government's implied power to charter banks is paramount to the State's power of taxation, why, then, should not its express power of taxation be paramount to any State power whatever?

(4) In apportioning the sum total of governmental power between the two centers, the guiding principle of the Constitution was to make the National Government sovereign in the field of internal relations, when it followed that any attempt on the part of the National Government to exercise the powers delegated to it in a fashion to involve disturbance

with the internal relations established by the States was to be regarded as at best suspicionable. The branch of national power most likely to conduct the General Government into the interior of the States, so to say, was its power to regulate interstate commerce. The clause of the Constitution, therefore, which bestows this power, though part and parcel with the clause respecting the regulation of foreign commerce, was held to intend "a negative and preventive provision against injustice among the States themselves, rather than as a power to be used for the positive purposes of the General Government." Similarly, the power of the National Government to construct roads and canals, under warrant of this clause, though originally conceded without qualification of any sort, came, as early as Jefferson's administration, to be subject to the necessity of the National Government's obtaining the consent of the States wherein such roads or canals were to lie. More generally, as, of course, goes without saying, the doctrine of implied powers are pared down to every angle where it projected into the sphere of power theoretically belonging to the States.[46]

On the basis of such a foundation, how does one explain the growth and development of the States' rights doctrine to the point where it was actually in the ascendency? An explanation, or at least part of an explanation, is found in the peculiar position of the South—in the special necessities of its "peculiar institution" and in its awareness of its position, after the Compromise of 1820, as a minority section. On the other hand, the doctrine of State sovereignty was not by any means regarded as the exclusive property of any one section of the country, but of all sections. The police power of the State came to exemplify the vital substance of State power in actual and beneficial use. In time, it became a leading concept of constitutional law, and though it arose quite independently of the concept of State sovereignty, it became safely ensconced behind that concept.

Certain it is that the Constitution contains no provisions granting a State the right to withdraw from the Union, yet the Southern leaders advocated such a course as a means of preserving their economic life and their social institutions. Jefferson Davis pointed to the reservations with which New York, Rhode Island, and Virginia had ratified the Constitution in support of the theory of secession, asserting that the powers granted to the Federal government might be resumed by the people at will. He concluded that "The right of the people of the several States to resume the powers delegated by them to the common agency, was not left without positive and simple assertion, even at a period when it had never been denied." [47] John C. Calhoun advocated secession and justified

[46] Corwin, *National Supremacy*, pp. 108–110.

[47] Davis, Jefferson, *The Rise and Fall of the Confederate Government* (New York: 1881), I, 173.

it as a final remedy to preserve States' rights, his theory being that in such a case the Federal government could appeal to the amending process, and that if three-fourths of the remaining States upheld the Federal claim, the matter would be settled as far as those States were concerned.[48]

What appear to have been the first specific moves in the direction of secession occurred in the decade of the 1850's, first in the South for one set of reasons, a little later in the North for other reasons; both cases centered around the slavery issue. The Southern States had been nursing an accumulation of grievances over the treatment accorded them by the Northern States ever since South Carolina's struggle over the tariff. Their difficulties in obtaining the return of fugitive slaves were at their height, prior to the enactment of the Fugitive Slave Law of 1850. Calhoun thought that the only thing that could save the Union would be for a united South to threaten secession, and that such a united South would be achieved only by a convention of the Southern States.

Thus, on March 6, 1850, the Mississippi legislature, following the action of a convention that had been held in Jackson the preceding October to consider Southern grievances, passed thirteen resolutions summoning a convention of the slaveholding States to be held in Nashville on the first Monday in June, 1850, to "devise and adopt such mode of resistance to these aggressions," and to pledge Mississippi to "stand by and sustain her sister States of the South" in whatever action the convention might decide upon. This convention was held, as was another in November; neither amounted to much because by the time they met, sentiment for radical action had almost entirely subsided.[49]

Just as some of the extremists in the South regarded the preservation of slavery as more important than the preservation of the Union, their Northern counterparts were willing to give up the Union, if necessary, in their anxiety to abolish the institution of slavery. Thus it was that the Phillips-Garrison-Higginson abolitionist group in Massachusetts called for a State convention to be held in Worcester in 1857 to start a movement for secession. Senator Henry Wilson, who counseled moderation, was regarded as a traitor to the cause and no fit leader for the antislavery forces. Theodore Parker took an uncompromising position against any union with slaveholders, and bemoaned the fact that whereas the country had had great leaders like Washington before the present government was established, it had had none since. Phillips maintained that "the sin of the Union is that it manufactured Webster."

The call for the convention met with a tremendous response; by mid-September more than 6,000 persons had sent in their signatures to a

[48] Cralle, Richard K., ed., *The Works of John C. Calhoun,* 6 vols. (New York: The Century Company, 1851–1855).

[49] Channing, VI, 71–72 and 79–80.

petition for the call. But even so, the convention was never held, due, according to Channing, to "the sudden and terrific pecuniary pressure of the panic that struck the country, making it impossible for any large number of persons to leave their business or to spend what little available money they had in railroad fares and lodging expenses."

The election of Lincoln seems to have been the single event which actually triggered secession. Dissatisfaction and discontent had been mounting for some years on both sides, but particularly in the South, where Lincoln's election was interpreted as an indication of a clear and unmistakable intention to "crack down" on the South, to destroy slavery, and to destroy the South itself in the process. The idea that the abolitionists were behind Lincoln was widely prevalent; as one writer expressed it, "When Lincoln is in place, Garrison will be in power."[50] Opposition to slavery was believed to be the chief if not the sole cohesive element in the new Republican party. They imagined and professed to believe that the great majority of those who had voted for the "Black Republican" President wished to annihilate the South. The *Richmond Examiner,* for example, maintained that "every Yankee had hated every Southern citizen from the day of his birth."

Thus the situation was one of great emotional conflict for all concerned. Horace Greeley urged that the erring sisters be permitted to depart in peace, as most certainly they hoped they might. Many of them seem to have believed that they could,[51] and there is reason for questioning whether they really meant to leave at all. At the beginning, the act of secession was much more a political maneuver than a really warlike gesture. It was, as Bruce Catton has said, "a means of putting on the political heat." There was still talk of compromise, and efforts in this direction might have succeeded had not the gesture had the unfortunate effect of evoking a defiant reaction in the North. The issue was now changed from slavery to the Union. Neither side was ready to fight about slavery, but there were many on both sides who were ready to fight about the Union.

Even so, when the time came, withdrawal from the Union was a sad and unpleasant experience, but it was felt to be necessary. As the Southern States withdrew one by one, their representatives in Congress and

[50] Holcombe, William H., *The Alternative: A Separate Nationality or the Africanization of the South* (New Orleans: Delta Mannouth Job Office, 1860), pp. 256–269, quoted by Channing, VI, 259. Holcombe presents an excellent summary of sentiment at the time.

[51] For instance, commissioners were at once appointed to go to Washington and arrange for disposition of the public property within the limits of the seceded States; if this seems strange, it may be noted that there was considerable basis for the idea of peaceful separation, in the North as well as in the South.

their Governors expounded at length on their motivation and reasons; there is no better source of information on these matters than their speeches in the *Congressional Globe*. Most of them warmed to the occasion, only a few like Alexander H. Stephens of Georgia counseling moderation, and declared that the extreme step should be taken only after "some positive aggression upon our rights by the general government." Even at this late date, serious efforts were made at the Peace Conference in Washington in December, 1860, and through the Crittenden Compromise amendment proposal in 1861, to save the Union.

One of the differing views that separated North and South concerned the nature of the Union and the constitutional position of the States within it. Although in the days of the Hartford Convention many Northerners had believed that they were entitled at any time to withdraw powers that they had delegated to the central government, they now tended to regard the Union as sovereign, and the States as a part of it. It was the South that now believed that delegated powers could be withdrawn, and even that States themselves might withdraw from the Union at will. As one examines the constitution of the Confederacy now, he is bound to wonder how firmly the Southerners actually held the views they expressed.

No attempt was made to adjust the new fundamental law to the condition created by a governmental organization in which each State was sovereign when it went in and remained sovereign after the government—which necessarily possessed some elements of sovereignty itself—was established. The old Federal ratio was preserved, insuring the continued influence of States that had a large slave population in proportion to their white population. The most notable differences between the Constitution of 1789 and the Confederate constitution were the lack of any adequate provision for a Supreme Court, and the introduction of an item veto on appropriation bills for the President.

The conclusion of the War Between the States closed this chapter of the debate over the nature of the Union and the legality of secession. The position taken by a majority of the States was that the Constitution was not a mere compact between States, but that it created a consolidated government of all the people, and that consequently no State had the right to secede from the Union. Shortly after the war, in the familiar case of *Texas* v. *White,* the Supreme Court had before it the question of whether or not Texas had ever left the Union. The Court held that when Texas became one of the United States, she entered into an indissoluble relationship. The union between Texas and the other States was as complete, as perpetual, and as indissoluble as the union between the original States. There was no place for reconsideration or revocation, except through revolution or through consent of the States. The ordinance of secession, adopted by the Texas convention and ratified by a majority of her citizens, and all the acts of her legislature intended to give effect to that ordinance, were absolutely null and void and without legal basis. Texas had never ceased to be a State, nor her citizens to be citizens of the Union.[52]

Although in subsequent cases the Court has consistently supported the view expressed in *Texas* v. *White,* arguments are still occasionally advanced to the effect that a State does have reserved powers under the Tenth Amendment to withdraw from the Union whenever its people think it necessary for their welfare.[53] The Supreme Court has not had this subject before it in recent years, but in view of the decisions noted here it would seem clear that a State has no right, under any circumstances, to withdraw from the Union.

BIBLIOGRAPHICAL NOTES

All of the subjects considered in this chapter as examples of problems arising in Federal-State relations are dealt with in standard works on the American Constitution and constitutional law, such as Charles K. Burdick, *The Law of the American Constitution* (New York: G. P. Putnam's Sons, 1922); Edward S. Corwin, ed., *The Constitution of the United States of America: Analysis and Interpretation* (Washington: Senate Document No. 170, 82nd Cong., 2nd Sess., 1953); and Westel W. Willoughby, *Constitutional Law of the United States,* 3 vols., 2nd ed. (New York: Baker, Voorhees, 1929), Chapter XII of which deals with civil rights and security legislation. Major works on the tidelands oil controversy are Ernest R. Bartley, *The Tidelands Oil Controversy: A Legal and Historical Analysis* (Austin: University of Texas Press, 1953); Marvin A. Harder, "The Tidelands Controversy," *University of Wichita Bulletin,* November, 1949; and symposium, "Texas Tidelands Case," *Baylor Law Review,* Winter, 1951, entire issue.

Interposition. For particularly helpful works on the forms of remonstrance adopted by the States at various times, in addition to the major general works on American history, see Edward S. Corwin, *National Supremacy* (New York: Henry Holt & Co.,

[52] *Texas* v. *White,* 74 U.S. 700 (1869); this judicial position has been uniformly adhered to in the following subsequent cases: *White* v. *Hart,* 80 U.S. 646 (1871); *Horn* v. *Lockhart,* 84 U.S. 670 (1873); and *Keith* v. *Clark,* 97 U.S. 457 (1878).

[53] The more recent arguments in the law reviews presenting this point of view are: Holifield, M. B., "Secession: A Right Reserved to the States," *Kentucky State Bar Journal,* September, 1954, pp. 160–173, and "The Secession of Southern States Did Not Constitute Rebellion or Insurrection Against the United States Because They Legally Exercised Their Reserve Powers," *Alabama Lawyer,* January, 1955, pp. 75–90. Also Morse, H. N., "Study in Legality of Doctrines of Nullification and Secession," *Journal of the Bar Association of the District of Columbia,* March, 1950, pp. 130–142, and April, 1950, pp. 182–193.

1913), which centers around the relation between the treaty power and State power, but includes an excellent discussion of interposition in Chapter 5, and James J. Kilpatrick, *The Sovereign States: Notes of a Citizen of Virginia* (Chicago: Henry Regnery Co., 1957), which grew out of the controversy over school desegregation and presents a Southern point of view, as does Senate Committee for Courts of Justice, *The Doctrine of Interposition, Its History and Application* (Richmond: Virginia General Assembly Report, 1957). Most worthy of attention among the many articles in the journals and law reviews are "The Doctrine of Interposition," *Journal of Public Law*, Spring, 1956, pp. 1–109, a round table presenting an historical and constitutional basis of the doctrine; "Interposition vs. Judicial Power: A Study of Ultimate Authority in Constitutional Questions," *Race Relations Law Reporter*, April, 1956, pp. 465–499, including bibliography; "Judge Spencer Roane of Virginia: Champion of States' Rights, Foe of John Marshall," *Harvard Law Review*, May, 1953, pp. 1242–1259; Lloyd M. Wells, "Interposition and the Supreme Court," *Southwest Review*, Autumn, 1956, pp. 305–313, a highly critical essay; and R. L. Woodward, Jr., an address on interposition citing historical examples of the successful use of the doctrine, in *Congressional Record*, May 16, 1956, pp. A3995–A3997.

Nullification. While sentiment for union evolved rather slowly, separatist sentiment was easily stimulated. For a history of six attempts during the first century of the Republic, see Edward P. Powell, *Nullification and Secession in the United States* (New York: G. P. Putnam's Sons, 1898) and Massachusetts General Court, *State Papers on Nullification* (Boston, 1834). Although the concept of nullification has long been known and discussed, the best sources of information on it are the writings and biographies of its advocates, most notably Calhoun: Margaret L. Coit, *John C. Calhoun, American Patriot* (Boston: Houghton Mifflin Co., 1950); Charles M. Wiltse, *John C. Calhoun*, 3 vols. (Indianapolis: Bobbs-Merrill Co., Inc., 1944–1951), vol. II of which deals with Calhoun's activities in nullification, 1829–1839; and John M. Anderson, ed., *Calhoun, Basic Documents* (State College, Pa.: Bald Eagle Press Books, 1952), which emphasizes Calhoun's views on dual sovereignty. See also Dumas Malone, *The Public Life of Thomas Cooper, 1783–1839* (New Haven: Yale University Press, 1926), which deals with the life of a Jeffersonian pamphleteer, a defender of slavery and nullification, and two articles by H. N. Morse, "Doctrines of Nullification and Secession: An Historical Study," *South Carolina Law Quarterly*, March, 1950, pp. 245–264, and "Study of the Legality of the Doctrines of Nullification and Secession," *Bar Association of the District of Columbia Journal*, March, 1950, pp. 130–142, and April, 1950, pp. 182–193.

Secession. There is somewhat more material, of several different types, on secession. Powell, *Nullification and Secession*, reports on six early attempts. First among the items relating to the Civil War period are such contemporary-participant accounts as William G. Brownlow, *Sketches of the Rise, Progress, and Decline of Secession . . .* (Philadelphia: G. W. Childs, 1862) and Alexander H. Stephens, *Constitutional View of the Late War Between the States*, 2 vols. (Philadelphia: National Publishing Company, 1868–1870). Some half dozen general works give considerable attention to secession: James T. Carpenter, *The South as a Conscious Minority, 1789–1861* (New York: New York University Press, 1930); Dwight L. Dumond, *Antislavery Origins of the Civil War in the United States* (Ann Arbor: University of Michigan Press, 1939), and *The Secession Movement, 1860–1861* (New York: The Macmillan Co., 1933); Ulrich B. Phillips, *The Course of the South to Secession: An Interpretation* (New York: The Appleton-Century Company, 1939); and Kenneth M. Stampp, *And the War Came: The North and the Secession Crisis, 1860–1861* (Baton Rouge: Louisiana State University Press, 1950).

Two volumes containing good chapters on secession are Arthur M. Schlesinger,

New Viewpoints in American History (New York: The Macmillan Co., 1922), pp. 220–244 on the States' rights fetish, and Wilfred B. Yearns, *Confederate Congress* (Athens: University of Georgia Press, 1960). The following biographies of persons prominent in the secession movement are of interest: Wirt A. Cate, *Lucius Q. C. Lamar, Secession and Reunion* (Chapel Hill: University of North Carolina Press, 1955); Avery O. Craven, *Edmund Ruffin, Southerner: A Study in Secession* (New York: The Appleton-Century Company, 1932); Ulrich B. Phillips, *The Life of Robert Toombs* (New York: The Macmillan Co., 1913). Two compilations of contemporary editorial comment (New York: The Appleton-Century Company, 1942) are Dwight L. Dumond, ed., *Southern Editorials on Secession* and Howard C. Perkins, ed., *Northern Editorials on Secession,* 2 vols.

Of the tremendous literature produced by the Civil War Centennial, the following titles are pertinent: Norman A. Graebner, ed., *Politics and the Crisis of 1860* (Urbana: University of Illinois Press, 1961); Robert G. Gunderson, *Old Gentlemen's Convention: The Washington Peace Conference of 1861* (Madison: University of Wisconsin Press, 1961); and Ralph A. Wooster, *The Secession Conventions of the South* (Princeton: Princeton University Press, 1962). For a standard account of the whole period, see James G. Randall and David Donald, *The Civil War and Reconstruction,* rev. ed. (Boston: D. C. Heath and Co., 1961).

CHAPTER V

The Role
of the Legislature

The character of National-State relations has altered markedly since Chief Justice Marshall began building his bench into the "umpire of the federal system." For a long time the principal task seemed to be that of making sure that none of the governments in the American federalism operated beyond their constitutionally defined jurisdiction. This was a problem of containment and was business almost exclusively for the courts. But as government began to grow more extensive and positive in character, more was needed than a guardian of the boundary lines between National and State power.

Congress began to recognize this fact at least as early as 1862 when the Morrill Act started the conversion of sporadic outright grants into a complex structure of grants-in-aid. In time, other milestones along the road of developing National-State cooperation followed with the passage of the now familiar divestment statutes. . . . These and similar events have made Congress a second "umpire of the federal system." . . .

To date Congress has chosen to force the hand of the States in only a limited number of circumstances. The most notable example is compulsory assumption of jurisdiction over causes of action arising under Federal statutes. Were Congress to require State courts to enforce federally created rights on a wholesale basis, overburdening of already severely taxed judicial facilities would probably result. But as long as Congress remains highly selective in its imposition of these burdens, the advantages of the system may outweigh its difficulties. . . .[1]

[1] Zimmermann, Frederick L., and Wendell, Mitchell, "Congress: A Second Umpire of the Federal System," *Georgetown Law Journal*, May, 1952, pp. 499–522.

RESOLVING QUESTIONS OF JURISDICTION

Legislative jurisdiction in a federal system is determined, in the first place, by Federal and State constitutional provisions. Although the nature of these powers is indicated, either through enumeration or the establishment of general principles by which they may be determined, their scope and application has to be determined by usage in the legislative bodies and by judicial interpretation.

Constitutional Provisions

Under the provisions of the Federal Constitution bearing on legislative powers, these powers may be exercised exclusively and/or concurrently; with respect to certain subjects, they may be prohibited. Since the Federal government is one of delegated, enumerated, or expressed powers, the powers of Congress are those specifically set forth in the Constitution, chiefly in the eighteen paragraphs of Article I, Section 8. In practice, jurisdiction in many of these areas is not exclusive. For example, many State laws affecting interstate commerce would have been upheld if Congress had not acted, and if the law was not of such a nature as to interfere with such commerce. While Congress has a very broad, in fact a virtually unlimited power to tax, State and local governments also have the power to tax.

Although the Founders found it difficult to reconcile the idea of imposing prohibitions upon Congress with the principle of delegation, they nevertheless believed it important that certain limitations be imposed, if abuses that had been experienced in the past were to be prevented in the future. These limitations are set forth in Article I, Section 9; some of the same items are repeated in the following section, which applies to the States.

In the federal system, the State governments are governments of residuary powers, in accordance with the principle established in the Tenth Amendment. Although there could be, on this basis, no enumeration of State powers in the Federal Constitution, a few State constitutions have attempted some enumeration of legislative powers.[2] The general theory is, however, that the State legislatures are free to act with respect to all matters not exclusively reserved to the Federal government, or denied to

[2] For example, see Massachusetts whose constitution is the oldest in continuous existence, Chapter I, Section I, IV (Powers of the General Court).

them under the terms of either the Federal Constitution in Article I, Section 10, or in the State constitution.

The earliest draft of the Federal Constitution contained a Congressional negative on State legislation (Madison's idea). After this was rejected by the Convention, the Committee on Detail substituted an extensive enumeration of express powers; this, too, was rejected by the Convention. Then, "with the Congressional negative and a general legislative power both eliminated, it was deemed necessary as a means of protecting the national government against intrusions by the States expressly to prohibit or limit the exercise of State power in certain areas." [3]

Congressional Determination

Any legislative body has a large measure of responsibility for the nature and scope of its own powers, within the limits established in the constitution, and in a federal system, the national legislature has a profound influence in determining what the legislatures of its component parts can or cannot do. Congress has no specific authority to define State legislative powers, but the use which it makes (or, in some instances, fails to make) of its own powers has the effect of either expanding or limiting the area within which State legislatures are free to act on many subjects. If the question of the limits of Federal and State powers over any given subject were exclusively a judicial matter, it would then appear that neither action nor inaction on the part of Congress could change the extent of State powers with respect to legislative action in a given subject matter. The question, however, is not an exclusively judicial one.

Congress can and does exert its influence in a variety of ways. If it acts in a given field, it may be assumed that it has taken over this field; this is known as the doctrine of preemption.[4] A failure on its part to act in a given field may be interpreted to mean that, not having taken possession of the field, the States are free to act. Or it may be interpreted as indicating a decision on the part of Congress that no action is necessary, or a desire that none be taken. Questions of legislative intent in such situations are difficult, and are frequently susceptible to several quite diver-

[3] Murphy, William P., "State Sovereignty and the Drafting of the Constitution," Part II, *Mississippi Law Journal*, December, 1960, pp. 1–23. The prohibitions upon the States are discussed *seriatim*, pp. 1–8, the Congressional negative, pp. 10–15.

[4] This problem was a matter of some interest in the 85th and the 86th Congresses, when several bills were introduced designed to clarify the situation. See American Enterprise Association, *Bill Analysis; Preemption: Proposals to Establish Rules of Interpretation Governing Questions of the Effect of Acts of Congress on State Laws* (Washington, June, 1959).

gent, yet acceptable and logical interpretations. In other instances, Congress has made known its wishes in a positive way. It may authorize State action, under the divestment theory illustrated by the Wilson Act of 1890, which established the original package doctrine with respect to the liquor traffic.

Immediately after the decision of the Supreme Court in *Leisy* v. *Hardin*,[5] denying to the States the right to enforce prohibition laws which interfered with interstate commerce on the ground that the silence of Congress was an expression of its will that such commerce, national in scope, should be free of State regulation, Congress passed the Wilson Act of August 8, 1890; the validity of this act was upheld by the Supreme Court in *In re Rahrer*.[6] Some years later, the Webb-Kenyon Act of 1917 provided that "all fermented, distilled, or other intoxicating liquors or liquids transported into any State or Territory or remaining therein for use, consumption, sale or storage therein, shall upon arrival in such State or Territory be subject to the operation and effect of the laws of such State or Territory enacted in exercise of its police powers, to the same extent and in the same manner as though such liquid or liquors had been produced in such State or Territory and shall not be exempt therefrom by reason of being introduced therein in original packages or otherwise."

The Wilson Act formula for the confirmation of State power has since been applied in a number of different ways and to many other aspects of interstate commerce, including control over game animals and birds, oleomargarine and butter products, misbranded articles of gold and silver, and plant quarantines. In some instances, State powers have been extended under the same formula, as under the Hawes-Cooper Act applying to prison-made articles, and with respect to prizefight films and other items. The famous Webb-Kenyon Act illustrates divestment by legislative prohibition.[7]

As has been noted, the divestment technique has been used in a number of different ways: in some instances to clear the way for more effective State legislation, or in the effort to stimulate such action, as in the case of rent control. Until the Taft-Hartley Act was passed in 1947, Congressional consent was commonly thought to exist in areas in which there was little or no positive Federal legislation. In this important legislation in the labor field, Congress acted, but it also simultaneously defined an area in which the States might act.

---

[5] 135 U.S. 100 (1890).   [6] 140 U.S. 545 (1891).

[7] See the Lacey Act on game birds and animals, 31 Stat. 188 (1900); Dyer Motor Vehicle Theft Act, 41 Stat. 324 (1919); Hawes-Cooper Act on prison-made goods, 45 Stat. 1084 (1929). For discussion of divestment legislation, see Kallenbach, Joseph E., *Federal Cooperation With the States Under the Commerce Clause* (Ann Arbor: University of Michigan Press, 1942), Chapters 3–7.

Judicial Decision

People have often repeated the remark of the late Chief Justice Hughes to the effect that the Constitution is what the Supreme Court says it is. Over the years, the Court has, in determining questions involving Federal-State relations, based its decisions on a number of different theories. One, the theory of exclusiveness, has been applied particularly to the commerce power, but is quite as applicable to many of the other powers specifically granted to Congress by the Constitution. This theory has been applied in a number of different ways, making the commerce power conditionally exclusive, concurrent, exclusive, or local-concurrent. In dealing with the commerce power, the Court has also made considerable use of the doctrine of preemption, and the divestment theory, both of which can, of course, be applied to other subjects as well as to commerce.

If, as time passes, the Court tends to modify its position, what the Court says the Constitution is may not be too clear. This happened with respect to the interpretation of the commerce clause. Having established the principle of exclusiveness in the early cases, notably in *Gibbons* v. *Ogden*,[8] the Court heard more than 100 cases in the next sixty years. Having accepted the idea that a uniform system of regulation was essential, it began in 1873 to annul State legislation when it seemed to interfere with an exclusive power of Congress over commerce, whether or not that power had actually been exercised. As the number of cases increased, the commerce clause rapidly acquired an important position as a limitation on State power.

This evolutionary process is mentioned here merely as an illustration of the manner in which and the extent to which the courts do, in practice, define the nature and scope of the legislative power. What is stated in the Constitution is important. What the legislature interprets this to mean is also important, but what the courts say with respect to both is quite final and conclusive in determining legislative powers—unless the Court later changes its mind, or unless at some future time, the Constitution is amended to provide otherwise.[9]

[8] 9 Wheaton 189 (1824).
[9] The most helpful references here are Kallenbach, *Federal Cooperation* and Hart, Henry M., Jr., and Wechsler, Herbert, *The Federal Courts and the Federal System* (Brooklyn: Foundation Press, 1953).

THE CONGRESS OF THE UNITED STATES

The Congress of the United States, with representation in one chamber based upon population, and representation in the other based upon the individual States, was purposely constructed as an instrument of federalism. Indeed, it has been said that the Senate is a living symbol of the Union of the States. Whatever the intentions of the Founders may have been with respect to the Legislative Branch, the record shows that not only was the structure of Congress influenced by the federal concept, but that its actions have since had a profound influence upon the evolving pattern of American federalism. It may well be that the actions of Congress have been the most important single source of change in the character of American federalism.

As in the States, problems of apportionment and districting loom large. While the system of apportionment of representation in the States is frequently unsatisfactory from the national point of view, and even contrary to the national interest, it is also true that the system of apportionment in Congress is something less than satisfactory to many of the States. The manner in which Congressional districts are laid out influences the representative character of the State delegation, both politically and in regard to population, even where there is no evidence of unfairness or discrimination. The current New York delegation of forty-three, for example, is evenly divided politically, with a little more than half from the New York metropolitan area, a little less than half from upstate. One Member, John R. Pillion, complains in effect that the delegation is so representative in character that, as a group, it lacks both the political unity that might flow from a common philosophy, or political effectiveness. He states his views in rather dramatic language:

In the House of Representatives, the forty-three Representatives are almost equally divided in their political philosophy. They usually cancel each other out. They lack political unity and political effectiveness.

As a partial result of our political anemia, New York's taxpayers pay approximately $10 billion of taxes annually into the Federal Treasury. We receive back approximately $7.5 billion in total payments and benefits. A $2.5 billion annual deficit balance of payments between the State of New York and the U.S. Government is a severe handicap to our economy, to our welfare, to our future.

We must face Federal-aid programs that are political subsidies to other States. These 100-odd programs return $1 to New York for each $2.50 paid in. These subsidies enable other States to offer lower State taxes to attract industry and business. Agricultural, reclamation and irrigation subsidies are politically tailored to favor other areas of the Nation at the expense of the Northeastern States. . . .[10]

These actions, and others that have affected the course of intergovernmental relations, have occurred to a large extent in the normal course of the transaction of Congressional business, as new States have been admitted to the Union, as the Senate has used (or abused) its right of unlimited debate, or to such specific types of legislative action as have been taken under the commerce power, the tax power, or the steady extension of the grant-in-aid system. In most of these situations, the intergovernmental relations aspects of what took place were largely incidental, if not accidental. Although there have been important intergovernmental relationships involved in filibustering, and in the consent of Congress idea—both of which are discussed here—little thought was ever given specifically to the consequences of the actions taken on intergovernmental relationships.

An interesting and possibly significant exception to this generalization may be noted in a provision written into the Legislative Reorganization Act of 1946, charging both the Senate and House Committees on Government Operations (then designated as the Committees on Expenditures in the Executive Departments) to study "intergovernmental relationships between the United States and the States and municipalities." Acting pursuant to this provision, the Senate Committee established a subcommittee in 1947; a couple of years later, acting under the same mandate, the House followed suit. The House Subcommittee on Intergovernmental Relations has continued to function constructively and well, but the Senate Subcommittee was permitted to lapse when its funds ran out in 1950, and the full Committee took over responsibility for the work in this field. This Subcommittee was reestablished in 1962. The problem of Congressional organization for the handling of intergovernmental matters is considered further in Chapter XXVI.

Federal Leadership in State Legislation

For a long time, the principal task in umpiring the American federal system was, as has been pointed out, one of making certain that none of the governments in the system operated beyond their constitutionally defined jurisdiction. This was largely a problem of containment, and one that was almost exclusively the business of the courts. As the need developed for something more than a mere guardian of the boundary lines

---

[10] *Congressional Record,* July 12, 1961, pp. A5187–A5188.

between one level of government and another, Congress began to adjust to this need. As early as 1862, the passage of the Morrill Act started the conversion of sporadic outright grants into a complex structure of Federal grants-in-aid. Next to develop was the consent of Congress idea, the first instance of its use occurring in the Wilson Act of 1890.

There are, as a matter of fact, several ways in which Congress can, by legislative provisions, affect the course of legislative action. It can move to strengthen State legislative power by prohibiting certain types of commerce for the protection of either the receiving or the sending State, or through accepting and adopting State laws or regulations as its own. It can or at least the Federal government frequently has exerted pressure upon the States to induce them to adopt legislative provisions desired by the Federal authorities. These practices, as will be made clear, may operate in both directions; just as there is Federal pressure upon the State legislatures, there are also State pressures upon Congress.

Illustrations of the protection of State authority through Federal action may be noted in several familiar areas. Early in the controversy over the slave trade, provision was made for respecting the wishes of those States in which this trade had been outlawed. The first statute in this area was passed in 1803, but others were to follow. Nearly a century later, as is noted at some length in Chapter XII, a similar consideration was given by the "dry" States with respect to the liquor traffic, and later with respect to the shipment of prison-made goods. The first section of the Ashurst-Sumners Act of 1935 (amending the Hawes-Cooper Act of 1929) made unlawful the transportation of goods manufactured, produced, or mined wholly or in part by convict labor into any State when they were intended to be "received, possessed, sold or in any manner used in violation of State law."

Where the purpose is to aid in the enforcement of the laws of the sending State, one may cite Federal acts prohibiting the shipment of illegally killed game, or "hot" oil. Both types of legislation seek to place the power of the Federal government squarely in support of State authority. While the principles involved in the two types of legislation are essentially the same, each type presents its own legal problems, due largely to the difference of the subject matter involved.[11]

The practice of exerting Congressional pressure upon the State legislatures has grown and developed as the grant-in-aid system has grown. So far as is known, pressures upon the legislatures from the Federal administrative departments and agencies were greatly expanded, if not originated, during the Roosevelt era. While these techniques were being perfected and refined, and used with increasing effectiveness, the depart-

[11] Kallenbach, Chapters 8 and 9.

ments and agencies using them piously asserted that they would never even consider doing such a thing, and that nothing could be farther from their minds than a desire to coerce or even to influence the actions of the State legislatures.[12]

There are many ways in which action taken by the Federal government can and does exert pressure upon the States in ways that are entirely proper and constitutionally correct. Within the sphere of Congressional action, numerous illustrations could be cited. In many a piece of grant-in-aid legislation, for instance, the Congress gently nudges the States, sometimes in influencing policy, sometimes in the way in which they spend their money, or in the procedures they employ in administering federally aided programs. These pressures have become so common that they are now generally accepted, and relatively little adverse comment or criticism is heard regarding them. Sometimes the influence aimed at federally aided programs spills over into other State departments and programs as well.

Thus Federal insistence upon the merit principle as applied in personnel administration in health and welfare programs has had an enormous influence in the improvement of State personnel administration generally. All States now have merit systems at least for those departments and agencies that are administering federally aided programs. Some States have enlarged the coverage and improved the administration of their civil service programs under Federal influence.

The pressure for merit systems originally came from the executive, when the Social Security Board prescribed it as an eligibility requirement in its regulations for the administration of the Social Security Act. When a few States questioned its authority or complained about this requirement, Congress gave its support to the Board and a basic concept of good administration by writing it into the law. The effect has been an important one in improving the tone and quality of all State administration; its effects are sometimes curious, even slightly absurd. In those States where political assessment of public employees is still tolerated, those employees in federally aided programs are exempt. The collectors may go into the offices of a few small agencies, but they have no right to enter the offices of the health and welfare agencies, where large numbers of personnel are employed.

Particularly significant here is the influence of the Hatch Act, now so familiar as to be almost a byword in America. The Federal law had

[12] The author explored these techniques at the time, reporting his findings in several articles: "Stroke Oar," *State Government*, December, 1934, pp. 259–262; "Federal Leadership in State Legislation," *Temple Law Quarterly*, July, 1936, pp. 385–405; "The Influence of Congressional Legislation on Legislation in the States," *Iowa Law Review*, May, 1938, pp. 519–538.

long prohibited persons in the Federal civil service from engaging in partisan political activities, but these provisions naturally did not apply to State employees and there was serious question as to whether they could be applied even to those engaged in federally aided programs. The Civil Service Commission had long complained that its findings in cases involving political abuse were frequently ignored by the authorities having power to remove, and that such abuses emanated chiefly from that portion of the service remaining on a political or patronage basis. To meet this situation, the Hatch Political Activities Act was passed in 1939 and amended in 1940.

When approving the first Act, President Roosevelt called attention to the fact that it applied to officers and employees of the Federal government only, and recommended that it be extended to cover "State and local government employees participating actively in Federal elections." Consequently, the second Hatch Act was passed in 1940: (1) forbidding employees of State and local government, if engaged in fulltime activities financed wholly or in part by Federal funds, to use their official authority in such ways as to "interfere with" any presidential or Congressional nomination or election; and (2) forbidding any persons whose *principal* employment is in a federally aided activity (a) to use their official authority or influence for the purpose of interfering with any nomination or election, (b) to coerce, command, or advise any other such employee to make political contributions or loans, and (c) to take any active part in political management or a political campaign. Not too long ago, the number of persons affected by legislation along these lines would not have been large, but the enormously increased interlocking personnel of Federal, State, and local governments as developed in recent years has brought hundreds of thousands of State and municipal employees into a position to feel the force of these restrictions.

The Filibuster and States' Rights

The filibuster may be defined as the exercise of unrestrained garrulity by a minority member or group for the purpose of preventing some action by the majority which they regard as improper or distasteful. In its effort to prevent action, the minority holds the floor, talking on and on, hour upon hour, for days at a time, on any subject, whether or not it has any bearing on the subject of the controversy. Theoretically, at least, its use can be justified if some important principle is involved, or some great injustice is about to be perpetrated. To most present-day Americans, however, the filibuster is an anachronism in modern democracy, a parliamentary maneuver in the never-ending struggle for power between parties, factions or regions. Thus, it rarely becomes an issue, being regarded as a more or less infrequent, though unfortunate, occurrence, still possible under the Senate rules under which cloture is well nigh impossible.

Strangely enough, the filibuster has sometimes been utilized in struggles involving Federal-State relations, and these are of present concern. In the famous civil rights filibuster of 1960—a filibuster which shattered all previously existing records—many comments were made and vast numbers of words were written about this strange and curious procedure. One such comment came from Senator Barry Goldwater of Arizona who termed the filibuster "a very valuable tool of our Republic," and added that when he came to the Senate, he was "dead set against it." He changed his mind when he realized "what it had done for his State," noting that his State now receives power and revenues from the Hoover Dam "which we got due to the filibustering of Senator Henry F. Ashurst and Senator Carl Hayden." He concluded that he did not care how long the Southern Senators talk "as long as they feel they are protecting the rights of the people in their States." [13]

Compilations of significant filibusters during the past century reveal an amazing number of instances (approximately one-third of the total number) in which issues of the type here under consideration were involved.[14] Some of these are listed by year and by subject, with brief notations in the following table.

LEGISLATION INVOLVING ISSUES OF STATES' RIGHTS OR
FEDERAL-STATE RELATIONS, DELAYED OR
DEFEATED BY FILIBUSTERS, 1846–1961

1846 — The Oregon Statehood Bill
        This bill was filibustered for two months.

1865 — Reconstruction in Louisiana

1879 — Repeal of Election Laws

1890 — The Blair Education Bill

1890– — The "Force Bill"
1891   This measure, providing for Federal supervision of elections, was successfully filibustered for twenty-nine days; cloture resolution introduced by Senator Aldrich of Rhode Island was also filibustered, and it failed of passage.

[13] *Washington Post*, March 9, 1960.
[14] Galloway, George B., *Limitation of Debate in the United States Senate* (Washington, 1960) and Saylor, James A., *Outstanding Senate Filibusters from 1920 to 1961* (Washington, 1961).

1902 — The Tri-State Bill
A successful filibuster against this bill to admit Arizona, New Mexico, and Oklahoma to statehood was conducted because all of Indian Territory, according to the original boundaries, was not included.

1903 — Deficiency Appropriation Bill
Senator Tillman of South Carolina filibustered against this bill because it failed to include an item paying his State a war claim; the item was finally restored.

1911 — Admission of Arizona and New Mexico to Statehood
Senator Owen of Oklahoma filibustered against Senate passage of a House bill admitting New Mexico but omitting Arizona because of her proposed constitution. The Senator continued his filibuster until Arizona was restored.

1922 The Dyer Anti-Lynching Bill
This measure was successfully filibustered by a group of Southern Senators.

1926 — Migratory Bird Refuge Bill
This bill was talked to death by a group of States' rights advocates, again mostly from the South. A motion for cloture failed by a vote of 46-33.

1927 — Swing-Johnson Bill on Lower Colorado River Basin
A motion for cloture was rejected by a vote of 59-32, as a means of ending obstruction to this proposal to provide flood protection, power, and reclamation facilities for this area through construction of Boulder Dam. Participants included both Senators from Arizona, one from Colorado.

1927 — Reed Special Campaign Investigating Committee
One of the fiercest filibusters in recent decades succeeded in preventing, despite the wishes of a clear majority of the Senate, an extension of the life of the Reed Committee, whose exposé of corruption in the 1926 election victories of Smith in Illinois and Vare in Pennsylvania had aroused the ire of a few Senators.

1935 — Work Relief Bill (prevailing wage amendment)

1937-— Federal Anti-Lynching Bill
1938 Although an overwhelming majority of the Senate favored this bill, its passage was prevented by an intermittent filibuster, extending from August 11, 1937 to February 21, 1938, carried on by Southern Senators.

1942-— Federal Anti-poll Tax Legislation
1944 Four organized filibusters by Southern Senators on the perennial question of
1946 anti-poll tax legislation were successful in these years. The first lasted ten days,
1948 November 13 to 23, 1942; the second was a little longer, extending from May 9 to 15, 1944; the third, from July 29 to August 2, 1946; the last from July 29 to August 4, 1948.

1946– — Fair Employment Practice Legislation
1950   An attempt to pass fair employment practice legislation was killed by a Southern filibuster lasting from January 17 to February 9, eight Senators participating. In 1950, five Southern Senators filibustered on the same question from May 8 to 19, consuming some 3,414 inches of the *Congressional Record* in the nine days.

1949 — Liberalization of the Senate Cloture Rule (Rule 22)
     Thirteen Southern Senators carried on an intermittent filibuster on liberalizing the cloture rule, from February 28 to March 17.

1950 — Tideland Offshore Oil Bill
     Prolonged debate on the tidelands, one of the longest on record, lasted thirty-five days, from April 1 to May 5. Nine Northern and Western Senators participated; Senator Morse of Oregon established a new record for the longest single speech—twenty-two hours and twenty-six minutes—on April 24-25.

1954 — Amendment of Atomic Energy Act of 1946 (Dixon-Yates Controversy)
     During a debate lasting thirteen days, a motion to invoke cloture was defeated by a vote of 44-42. There were twelve participants from ten States, including many of the same Senators who had taken part in the tidelands controversy, with, however, a heavier representation from the South.

1957– — Civil Rights Legislation
1960   In August 28–29, 1957, during the civil rights debate, Senator Thurmond of South Carolina made a speech lasting twenty-four hours and eighteen minutes, the longest in Senate history. The debate from February 15 to April 11 consumed thirty-seven days, during which forty-five roll calls were taken. In an effort to break the systematic filibuster conducted by eighteen Southern Senators, around-the-clock sessions were held from February 29 through March 8. The Senate was in continuous session for nine days, a total of 157 hours and twenty-six minutes, with two breaks.

Whether or not one approves of filibustering as a parliamentary device in a democratic system, the record seems to provide some support for the position taken by Senator Goldwater. Filibusters have successfully prevented the passage of bills lacking provisions that particular Senators desired for the benefit of their States, or including provisions to which they objected. They have sometimes succeeded in modifying the terms of legislation, forcing a compromise, delaying passage, delaying the adjournment of Congress, forcing special sessions, adopting or rejecting conference reports, or postponing consideration of legislation. Legislative proposals have been defeated or modified by the mere threat of a filibuster. Truly the filibuster is a potent weapon in the hands of any "little group of willful men" who are disposed to utilize it.

THE STATE LEGISLATURES

The Federal Interest in the State Legislatures

It has never been commonly realized in the past, and may not be even today, that there is a strong Federal interest in the State legislatures and in the question of whether or not their organization and procedures are such as to enable them to discharge their responsibilities effectively. What the States and their legislatures do or do not do is a matter of vital concern to Congress, to the nation, and possibly even to the world. Although, for nearly half a century, the legislatures have not chosen the members of the United States Senate, they do—in all instances in which the normal procedure is used—pass upon proposed constitutional amendments, and they must enact cooperative legislation for their States to qualify for Federal grants-in-aid. Their functioning (or non-functioning) and the quality of their work is, in many fields, a matter of vital concern to the national government.

The central government is concerned that all citizens shall be fairly treated in the matter of representation, that the principle of "one man, one vote" shall be everywhere observed. This principle should be a matter of concern to the States themselves, but it should also be a legitimate matter of Federal interest, in our position of world leadership, to prevent abuses and violations of democratic practices and procedures. At present, American democracy has to be carried on in a gold fish bowl. Everything that is done wrong, everything that should be done that is not accomplished reflects upon the nation, impairs its "image," and diminishes its influence as the leader of the free world. When new and underdeveloped countries are looking to the United States for example and leadership, the nation can ill afford to permit the continuance of practices which, however old and well established, violate the basic principles of democracy.

The State legislatures are the constitutionally designated bodies charged with apportionment of representation and the establishment of legislative districts—a function that has much to do with determining who gets what, when, and how. No apportionment is possible that does not, in one way or another, affect the locus of power and the power structure within the State. Not only does the State legislature control the allocation of representation at the State level, but it has the power and the duty to establish legislative districts for both the State legislature and for Representatives in Congress. The apportionment and the established district system affect the character of representation—politically, socially, economically, and in other ways. It determines, to a large extent, the quality, tone, and outlook of the majority in the legislature, and these factors are of the utmost importance to Congress.

"As Your Representative, I Promise to Continue Our Fight Against Redistricting"

Herblock in the Washington *Post*, August 11, 1961.

Hence it is that the composition of the State legislature affects the problems of the nation, not only legislatively, but in many other ways as well. Serious malapportionment of the State legislatures has been undermining the strength of State government, causing it to lose public confidence, and being largely responsible for the failure of the States to meet pressing State and local needs. Just as a legislature whose orientation is rural may ignore the needs of cities, the rural outlook of a majority of the members may in other ways affect the course of national policy. The States are responsible for passing upon proposed constitutional amendments, and so far with one exception, it has been the legislatures that have done this. It is, to a large extent, the legislatures that are responsible for seeing to it that their respective States maintain a republican (*i.e.,* representative) form of government. They participate in the selection of presidential candidates and indirectly in the election of the President. It is the legislatures that determine the qualifications for voting in national as well as in State and local elections, and they are responsible for the legislation under which elections are administered.

Most important of all, from the national point of view, is their influence upon the political complexion and basic attitudes of the House of Representatives in the Congress of the United States. Just as malapportionment tends to make a mockery of the principle of equality at the State level, it has the same effect upon the national House of Representatives. The same State legislatures that are responsible for maintaining the malapportionment characteristic of so many of them also have responsibility for creating the districts from which Members of the House of Representatives are elected. By precisely the same type of favoritism toward rural areas at the expense of urban voters, they have in effect already— in the opinion of many well-informed persons—changed the complexion of the House. Long regarded as the more popular body, it has in recent years surrendered its popular leadership to the Senate. This type of thing is difficult to document, but the record speaks for itself. When bills are under consideration for aid to education, medical care for the aged, a department of urban affairs, depressed areas, and other social welfare legislation, the support comes from the Senate, the bitter-end opposition from the House. This transformation is very significant in any consideration of the national interest.

The Struggle Over Apportionment

Practically all of the State constitutions require reapportionment following each decennial Federal census. Prior to 1920, these apportionments were ordinarily made when due, or soon after; following that date, apportionments in many jurisdictions were rare, perfunctory, or nonexistent. The reason for this is clear; the returns from the 1920 census revealed that, for the first time, more than half of the population lived in communities classified as urban. As long as most of the people were residents of rural communities, rural dominated legislatures could—and did—make adjustments in representation without fear of losing control. Since 1920, however, the percentage of urban dwellers has been steadily increasing until, in 1963, this nation had definitely become urban— seven out of ten Americans living in cities or in metropolitan areas.

This transition from a rural and agrarian society to one largely urban and industrial has had important effects upon our political and governmental institutions, not the least of which has been the effect upon the representative character of the State legislatures. For many years, and properly so, these legislatures were dominated by rural members. With the steady shift of the people from rural to urban areas, reapportionment on the basis of population was certain to involve a shift in control, and loss of power, so far as the existing rural majorities were concerned. The shift might well mean a change in party control, and would most certainly involve readjustments among the various interest and pressure groups within the State. Although apportionments are constitutionally mandatory, the effectiveness of these mandates in securing reapportionments has been steadily declining as this dramatic shift in population has continued.

Gross under-representation of urban areas, accompanied by gross over-representation of rural areas, made constructive legislative action on current urban problems virtually impossible in many jurisdictions. By making appropriate changes in place names, the colorful statement made by Mayor Ben West of Nashville, in testifying before a Congressional Subcommittee on the department of urban affairs bill in 1961, would apply as well to almost any one of the other forty-nine States: "In Tennessee, the pigs and cows in rural Moore County are better represented in the Legislature than the people of my City of Nashville." This rural over-representation did not mean the rule of honest farmers and rural folk; in practice, "it means rule by rural politicos and county rings in cahoots with big landowners and corporate businesses located in cities of the North and South. It means the financial starving of urban constituencies. . . ." It meant that the disparity between the value of a rural vote on the one hand, and an urban vote on the other, has continued to increase.

Under these circumstances, one rural vote might weigh as heavily as half a dozen of the votes of urban dwellers. The situation developed into a power struggle of a rather ominous and cynical sort, a struggle that has been going on for three or four decades, with little progress being made toward achieving the democratic ideal of representation on the basis of population. Stupendous efforts have many times been blocked by built-in barriers to the achievement of such a system—guarantees of at least one representative to each town or to each county in the State or limitations upon the percentage of representation that might be apportioned to any city or county. Where such constitutional barriers have not prevented the making of a fair apportionment, apathy on the part of some voters and obstructive tactics on the part of others has.

There are many reasons why, over a period of years, this problem developed into a major one, perhaps *the* major problem in current American government. Seldom, indeed, do those who hold power relinquish it willingly and voluntarily. In this case, their reluctance was strengthened and in a sense justified by an ancient and almost inherent distrust which country people feel toward cities and city dwellers. And the urbanites did nothing to allay these suspicions and fears when, in so many instances, they permitted corrupt city machines to continue in power and when they sent to the State Capitols delegations often of mediocre ability, or still worse, including persons of dubious character and integrity. The ruralites feared, too, that if they relinquished control, their interests would be treated with the same indifference and lack of understanding that had so frequently characterized their own handling of the problems of the cities.

Legislative Failures. Under these circumstances, apportionment developed into an enduring problem of such difficulty and complexity as, seemingly, to defy solution. The responsibility was, and still is, primarily that of the State legislatures, but as the Maryland Committee on Fair Representation expressed it, efforts to get action from the legislature "is demonstrably almost shockingly futile." As of 1960, it was reported among the three-fourths of the States relying upon legislative apportionment (all but one of them exclusively), eighteen had had their most recent apportionment in the 1950's, eight in the 1940's, and three each in each of these earlier periods: the 1930's, the 1920's, and 1900 to 1920. Two had had their last apportionment prior to 1900. This was the current situation with respect to this national problem—and a national problem it most certainly was.

When, decade after decade, the legislatures failed to discharge their responsibility adequately, or even to discharge it at all, the people began to search for some effective means of accomplishing what the legislatures were unable or unwilling to do. Since the legislature cannot be mandamused, the people established, in many jurisdictions, so-called automatic apportionment procedures which either took the problem completely out of the hands of the legislature or became operative when the legislature failed to act. While these devices were reasonably effective in securing reapportionment in the States adopting them, and while popular pressure upon the legislature produced reapportionment statutes in others, the basis of representation in many States still remained grossly unfair and inequitable to a constantly increasing urban population.

Efforts to Obtain Judicial Intervention. By 1960, a new concept of a Federal interest in the fairness and equitableness of State legislative representation began to emerge. It expressed itself in a number of different ways, one of them in numerous suits filed in Federal courts, chiefly in the rapidly expanding and grossly under-represented metropolitan

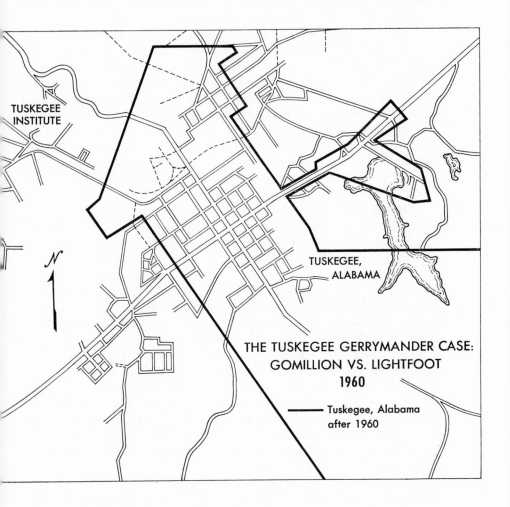

TUSKEGEE
INSTITUTE

N

TUSKEGEE,
ALABAMA

THE TUSKEGEE GERRYMANDER CASE:
GOMILLION VS. LIGHTFOOT
1960

——— Tuskegee, Alabama
after 1960

areas. Since the end of World War II, a score or more of such cases have come before Federal courts, involving about twelve States. The courts had formerly refused to consider such cases on the ground that the questions involved were political, not justiciable.[15] In 1959 and 1960, suits

[15] *Colegrove* v. *Green*, 328 U.S. 549 (1946); see Taylor, William L., "Legal Action to Enjoin Legislative Malapportionment: The Political Question

were brought in Alabama, Massachusetts, Tennessee, Vermont, and Maryland—the latter in a State court, with the idea of filing in a Federal court if and when the suit in the State court was thrown out. All of these actions sought to invoke the power of the Federal judiciary in bringing sufficient pressure to bear in these States to achieve a fair and equitable apportionment, in the belief that this was the only realistic means of attacking the problem of malapportionment.

The situation is equally startling in many States. In Maryland, suit was filed in the State Circuit Court in Anne Arundel County by the Maryland Committee for Fair Representation against the Governor of the State and other officials. Similarly, also, this suit was rejected, and an appeal taken. These facts were cited in the complaint: on the basis of the 1960 census, four populous counties and the City of Baltimore, with 76 per cent of the State's population, had only 34 per cent (10 out of 39) of the State Senate members, and 49 per cent (60 out of 123) of the members of the House of Delegates. These five areas contribute from 70 to 84 per cent of the major taxes, but only a minor fraction of these funds are returned to them in benefits.

On the basis of population, these areas are entitled to twenty-two State senators and ninety-two delegates. However, sections of the State constitution governing apportionment discriminate in favor of the rural minority; the complaint alleged that these sections are in violation of the Fourteenth Amendment of the Federal Constitution as well as of the Maryland Declaration of Rights, which is a part of the State constitution. That the plaintiffs had exhausted all other remedies is demonstrated by the story of ten years of unsuccessful introduction of bills in the General Assembly designed to correct this situation, and a parallel ten years of experience in seeking a constitutional convention which could have dealt with the subject. The outstanding incident in the latter effort was the approval given in 1950, by a vote of 200,439 to 56,998, on a referendum proposal to call a constitutional convention. The two houses of the legislature failed to agree at the next session on legislation designed to implement this mandate, and during the decade which has followed, they have ignored or failed to implement it, despite repeated and insistent demands from the people to do so.

The Committee which filed the suit demanded that the election authorities be restrained from certifying candidates to the General Assembly in November, 1962 unless, in the meantime, the situation had been cor-

Doctrine," *Southern California Law Review,* Winter, 1961, pp. 179–189. The author contends that the question is justiciable, and that the courts should require fair apportionment. A recent case, *Gomillion* v. *Lightfoot,* 364 U.S. 339 (1960), which arose in Alabama, dealt with redistricting rather than reapportionment.

rected. The only alternative would be to elect all members of the General Assembly at large—a situation too horrible to contemplate. Nevertheless, the legislature adjourned its 1962 session without taking any action. The Governor, a candidate for renomination in the spring primary, was urged to call a special session. This he refused to do, pending the decision of the court in the reapportionment suit. After the primary, the court de-

Shore Dinner
Source: Washington *Evening Star*, May 28, 1962.

cided that the 1943 apportionment of the House of Delegates was unrepresentative and unconstitutional, but that it was proper for the State Senate to be apportioned (as is the Congress) on an area basis. The decision came after and was probably influenced by *Baker* v. *Carr*. The Governor then called a special session which met during the last week in May.

The Governor presented to the General Assembly a reasonably acceptable plan designed to provide a partial correction of existing inequities immediately, with apportionment on a purely population basis in four years. The House, at the end of a thirteen-hour session of bitter argument and debate, passed a sadly mutilated version of the Governor's bill; the Senate Judiciary Committee on the following day added amendments carrying the process of emasculation to the point that the Chairman of the Maryland Committee for Fair Representation characterized the bill as "practically worthless," as, in fact, it was. Then the Governor intervened to rescue his bill. As passed on May 31, it became the first State apportionment legislation enacted following and because of the Supreme Court decision.

The Tennessee case, *Charles W. Baker et al.* v. *Joe C. Carr et al.*, was dismissed by a three-judge District Court for the Middle District of Tennessee in December, 1960. The plaintiff's brief pointed out, for example, that the legislative districts in that State had not been reorganized since 1901, despite sizable shifts in population and a clause in the State constitution requiring redistricting every ten years. These districts are even more inequitably apportioned in many States than the Congressional districts, which are certainly bad enough. A voter in Moore County, Tennessee, population 2,340, has twenty-three times as much representation in the lower house of the State legislature as does a voter in Shelby County, population 312,345, including the city of Memphis. One result of this malapportionment, it is pointed out, is that Moore County receives seventeen times the apportionment of State gasoline and motor vehicle taxes as does Shelby County.[16]

The court was impressed, but not sufficiently to do anything about it. "With the plaintiff's argument that the legislature of Tennessee is guilty of clear violation of the State Constitution and the rights of the plaintiffs the court entirely agrees"; but it then proceeded to dismiss the complaint, in accordance with prior decisions, on the ground that the court ". . . has no right to intervene or to grant the relief prayed for. . . ."[17] An appeal to the Supreme Court was promptly filed, and in late 1960, the case was heard and docketed for re-argument during the Term beginning in October, 1961.

The situations existing in Maryland and Tennessee have been discussed at some length because they are so typical. They could be duplicated in a dozen other States with illustrations equally useful for our purpose. Promise of improvement came suddenly when, on March 16, 1962, the Supreme Court handed down its decision in the Tennessee case,

[16] See West, Ben, *Legislative Apportionment in Tennessee, 1901–1961* (Nashville: August, 1961), a pamphlet prepared by the Mayor of Nashville.

[17] *Book of the States, 1960–1961* (Chicago: Council of State Governments, 1960), pp. 34–35.

Baker v. *Carr.*[18] This decision was the most important decision of the Court since the school desegregation case in 1954. It was undoubtedly one of the most important decisions of the Court in the twentieth century, and possibly in the entire history of the Court.[19] It was a decision that, observers have agreed—whether they liked it or not—"could change the political face of America." The realization of its importance has been widespread. By many, it has been greeted with enthusiastic approval, but there are some who regard it with great misgivings, and who have expressed dire warnings regarding its future consequences.

Under these circumstances, it seems appropriate to attempt to state briefly what the Court decided and what it did not decide, what the immediate consequences have been, and what long-range consequences may reasonably be anticipated. For sixty years since 1901, the Tennessee General Assembly had consistently refused to carry out the constitutional mandate requiring reapportionment every ten years. The plaintiffs, Tennessee citizens, having at their disposal no legal remedy within the State by which the legislature could be compelled to honor this mandate, sought relief through a suit in the Federal District Court, alleging that they "and others similarly situated, are denied the equal protection of the laws accorded them by the Fourteenth Amendment to the Constitution of the United States by virtue of the debasement of their votes." The District Court dismissed the suit for lack of jurisdiction. Mr. J. Brennan, speaking for the Supreme Court majority, held the action of the District Court to have been in error, finding in the situation none of the inhibiting factors that had deterred the Court from taking jurisdiction in comparable earlier cases. In a concurring opinion, Mr. J. Stewart took occasion to summarize what he deemed to have been decided, namely: (1) that the Supreme Court has jurisdiction over Tennessee's apportionment system; (2) that a justiciable cause of action is stated; (3) that the appellants have standing to challenge the Tennessee apportionment statutes.

It is significant that the Court did not—and presumably will not in the future—decide what or how a given apportionment should be made; that is the responsibility of the duly constituted authority within the State. Were it to decide such questions, the Federal courts would immediately become involved in the "constitutional thicket," the fear of which

[18] 369 U.S. 186 (1962).

[19] Professor Ruth C. Silva has called it the most important decision since *Marbury* v. *Madison.* Other significant decisions have affected social relations, but *Baker* v. *Carr* "will affect the governmental power structure by shifting the balance of State legislative power from rural conservatives to city and suburban voters who tend to be sympathetic toward social change and governmental intervention." "Apportionment in New York," *Fordham Law Review,* April, 1962, pp. 581–650 on p. 581.

was so eloquently expressed in Mr. J. Frankfurter's dissent. The effect of the decision is to establish the principle that the Federal courts have the authority to decide whether a given scheme of apportionment is or is not in harmony with constitutional requirements. Thus are the long under-represented urban majorities provided with a new weapon which may enable them to obtain some relief. The response of the people to the decision was immediate and impressive.

The decision spurred the authorities in some States into taking appropriate corrective action before they were forced to do so. On March 26, 1962, ten days after the decision had been handed down, Senator Jack R. Miller of Iowa stated on the floor of the Senate:

> Mr. President, I am pleased to point out that the Iowa Legislature has, of its own volition, taken positive steps to amend the State constitution in such a manner as to provide for control of one house of the legislature by a majority of the people and to insure prompt reapportionment if the legislature itself fails to act. This action has come about only after much debate, public information programs of civic and farm organizations and of the press, and the hard work of legislators who were statesmen enough to surrender the power which they possessed. I hope that other legislatures will take similar action in the near future, so that the power of the Federal courts will not have to be invoked, and so that the increasing trend toward centralized Federal Government will be reversed.

Mention has been made of the action taken by the Maryland General Assembly; this, however, was rejected by the voters in a referendum in November.

A host of judicial proceedings—much more than the flurry of litigation that had been anticipated—was soon instituted. When, a little more than a month after the decision, eight suits had been filed, Roscoe Drummond observed that "A great political reform has never moved so rapidly." By the end of May, in a little more than two months, suits had been filed in seventeen States. By June 30, seventy suits had been brought in thirty-three States.[20] It is already clear that forces have been set in motion that may, very likely within a decade, transform the State legislatures into bodies that are truly representative in character. One observer who regards the decision "as a giant step forward" concludes that it "cannot help but have far-reaching consequences."

[20] See *Legislative Reapportionment in the States* (Chicago: Council of State Governments, September, 1962); this summary is to be kept up to date by periodic supplements. See also David, Paul T. and Eisenberg, Ralph, *State Legislative Redistricting: Major Issues in the Wake of Judicial Decision* (Chicago: Public Administration Service, 1962).

Charles S. Rhyne, the attorney who argued the case before the Supreme Court, foresees in the expected "removal of this cancerous growth of malapportionment of the State legislatures" a possibility that the State governments may be restored to health, but this would be only the beginning of the changes that he envisions. In an address before the United States Conference of Mayors, he discusses these possible effects of the decision:

1. Making the State governments actors, rather than bystanders, in solving current problems.
2. Causing State legislatures to delegate more powers to cities, so that more municipal problems can be dealt with on the local level.
3. Arresting the flow of political power to Washington through better exercise of political power by States and cities.
4. Modernizing the structure of State and local government.
5. Reversing the trend toward a search for a Federal cure for many city ills, thus affecting an important change in Federal-city relations.

"In this decision and in the consequences flowing from it," he concludes, "the Supreme Court made itself not an enemy but an ally of effective State government."

Proposals for Constitutional Amendment. An issue as important as apportionment is almost certain to produce, sooner or later, proposals for constitutional amendment. Such proposals have been advanced by both proponents and opponents of reform in apportioning procedures. The Federal Constitution provides that the States shall maintain a republican form of government. Thus, there is a national interest in the extent to which the States do or do not maintain representative institutions that are truly representative.

Acting on this premise, Senator Joseph S. Clark of Pennsylvania introduced three measures into the Senate on June 29, 1960, as follows:

S.J. Res. 215. Joint resolution proposing an amendment to the Constitution of the United States to assure equitable representation of the people in the legislatures of the several States.

S. 3781. A bill to make further provision concerning the ratification of proposed amendments to the Constitution of the United States by conventions in the several States.

S. 3782. A bill to provide for the equitable representation of the people in the legislatures of the several States in conformity with the requirements of the Constitution of the United States.[21]

[21] For Senator Clark's statement, containing extensive supporting data, see *Congressional Record*, June 29, 1960, pp. 13827–13842. Reprints are available at the Senator's office. The same measures were introduction in the 87th Congress, September 19, 1961.

Obviously, the purpose of these proposals is to assure equitable representation of the people in the State legislatures. Such reapportionment and redistricting as might be required to attain this purpose would be made when the amendment was ratified and thereafter when the results of each decennial census are announced. The two supporting bills were designed to facilitate ratification of the amendment and to establish standards of fair representation and methods of enforcement. Congress would prescribe by law the standards and manner of such reapportionment and redistricting.

Since it is highly improbable that State legislatures which have failed to perform their duty fairly and properly to reapportion representation in their respective States would vote to ratify this amendment, Senator Clark proposes ratification by conventions called in the States for the purpose. And, inasmuch as Congress is granted constitutional authority to provide directly for such conventions, one of the bills would clarify the convention procedure. State conventions called to ratify or reject proposed constitutional amendments would—it is proposed—be composed of delegates elected at large, and chosen at the next general election for Members of the House of Representatives. They would meet following their election and continue in session until the proposed amendment shall have been ratified or rejected by a majority. Suggested standards of representation, proposed in the second bill, would take into consideration problems of physical topography, natural community boundaries, and political boundaries that may exist for other purposes. Enforcement procedures are left to the State authorities.

Whether or not this proposal is ever submitted to the States and ratified by them, the mere fact that it was made served to reflect, in the words of the *Washington Post,* "the rising tide of disgust over the repudiation of the principle of equal representation by the legislatures of most of the States." By dramatizing the growing public dissatisfaction with the existing situation, it may serve to prod the States to set their houses in order. It also serves to illustrate the way in which a Federal interest in many problems formerly regarded solely as the responsibilities of State and local government are helping to create new patterns in the field of intergovernmental relations. If adopted, "cow-county majorities in the legislatures could doubtless be forced to yield equal representation to their disadvantaged urban neighbors." [22]

On the other side of the controversy, the *Baker* v. *Carr* decision stirred up the opposition of the Council of State Governments, or at least of some of its affiliated groups and organizations. One of these, the National Legislative Conference, meeting in Phoenix in the fall of 1962,

[22] Editorial, "Rotten Boroughs," *Washington Post,* July 5, 1960.

"Just Dead Wood, Fellers."

Courtesy of Scripps-Howard Newspapers, June 3, 1963.

adopted a resolution directing its Federal-State Relations Committee to prepare a report exploring the possibility of an amendment to the United States Constitution through initiation by the States of a constitutional convention and, in addition, possible and feasible areas in which the Tenth Amendment to the Constitution might be strengthened. The Council was requested to include this subject as a major item on the program of the General Assembly of the States in December, which was done.

The three highly controversial proposals emanating from this meeting had the dual purpose of providing an effective curb on Federal authority in matters involving Federal-State relationships, and of restoring and perpetuating the inequities against which urban dwellers and believers in democratic government have struggled for so long:

1. Revise Article V of the Constitution by giving the State legislatures the primary responsibility heretofore held by the Congress to
propose constitutional amendments;

2. Deny to the Federal courts jurisdiction over State reapportionment cases;

3. Establish a "Court of Union" composed of the chief justices of
the fifty States with authority to overrule the Supreme Court on matters
affecting Federal-State relationships.

When these proposals were transmitted to the States, they attracted little
attention. By March 1, however, twenty-nine of the forty-two legislatures
in regular session had given consideration to one or more of them. Of
these twenty-nine, one or both houses of twelve legislatures had approved the first proposal, sixteen legislatures the second, and six legislatures the third. When the press began to publicize the absurd nature
of these proposals and the drastic effects their adoption would certainly
have on the long-established pattern of American federalism, their progress was temporarily, or—one may hope—permanently halted. *The New
York Times* characterized them as "a States' rights nightmare," while the
Washington Post commented on them under the heading, "Three Non-
sensical Amendments." Both characterizations are appropriate and well-
deserved.

State Legislative Influence on Federal Action

From the earliest times, the States have influenced, or attempted to
influence the course of Congressional action. Once within the Union—
there has often been bitter controversy or long delay, as noted in the
preceding chapter, over new admissions—they have resorted to a variety
of methods and procedures to get what they wanted. Some States, to be
sure, have been more interested in, and far more aggressive in defending
their point of view, than have others. Some have utilized the members
of their Congressional delegations as their spokesmen, and through resort
to the filibuster, made the floor of the United States Senate a battleground for the protection of their rights against the terrible monster
that the central government is sometimes assumed to be. Other States
have registered their protest over Federal action through memorials,
sometimes strongly worded memorials, adopted by their State legislatures.
On the positive side, they have frequently sought to influence Congress
to adopt some particular measure or course of action on a matter in
which the State was interested. Others have, under varying degrees of
Federal persuasion, enacted legislation designed to facilitate direct Federal administrative action affecting individuals, corporations or political
subdivisions within the State.

The earliest instances of vigorous State protest against Congressional action occurred with respect to the Alien and Sedition Acts (discussed in Chapter IX) and the Embargo Act of 1807, a measure which led to much discontent in the New England States. Many memorials against the Act were passed, but Congress ignored the protests and in 1809 passed a stringent enforcement act. Connecticut adopted a policy of non-cooperation, refusing to enforce the Act. Its General Assembly, meeting in special session, resolved "That to preserve the Union, and support the Constitution of the United States, it becomes the duty of the legislatures of the States, in such a crisis of affairs, vigilantly to watch over, and vigorously to maintain, the powers not delegated to the United States, but reserved to the States respectively, or to the people; and that a due regard to this duty, will not permit this Assembly to assist, or concur in giving effect to this unconstitutional act, passed, to enforce the Embargo." [23]

This language strongly suggested interposition, if not nullification. From that day to this, the State legislatures have been passing resolutions memorializing Congress to take all kinds of actions on all manner of subjects. Some are resolutions of protest, not necessarily as strong as the one from Connecticut; others request that some specific action be taken regarding some pressing problem at the time. A glance through the front pages of almost any daily edition of the *Congressional Record* during the first few months of an odd-numbered year will disclose a number of illustrations of the memorializing practices of present-day State legislatures. No one has ever made a study of these resolutions to determine their number, the nature of the subject matter with which they deal, or their possible influence, as reflected in subsequent legislative action on the part of the Congress.

The third type of relationship mentioned previously was State legislation facilitative of Federal action—in this case administrative action. Such legislation may be essential for the conduct of the Federal activity, or it may merely make Federal administrative action simpler or easier. Among the various possible incentives for such laws may be the desire to meet some condition precedent to the enjoyment of particular Federal services by the citizens of the State. This type of qualifying legislation, now fairly common, first appeared in quantity in the Roosevelt era with the sudden multiplication of Federal grant-in-aid programs.[24]

For example, the Federal mortgage insurance program, inaugurated in 1934, immediately encountered the obstacle of State legislation that

[23] Quoted from Ames, Herman V., ed., *State Documents on Federal Relations: the States and the United States* (Philadelphia: University of Pennsylvania, 1906).

[24] See, for example, American Legislators' Association, *State Legislation to Aid National Recovery: a Survey of Types of State Statutes Which Might Be Enacted to Supplement Recent Federal Acts* (Chicago, July, 1933).

prevented State-chartered lending agencies from taking advantage of mortgage insurance. After the President transmitted letters to the Governors calling attention to the need for facilitative legislation, the States responded promptly. All legislatures in session in 1935 except one enacted the necessary legislation. During the 1937 sessions, it was reported that a total of 105 laws to aid the Federal Housing Administration were enacted in the legislatures of forty-two States.

Other areas in which similar cooperative effort on the part of the State legislatures occurred were the programs of the Farm Credit Administration, the Federal Home Loan Bank Board, Federal Deposit Insurance Corporation, Public Works Administration, Rural Electrification Administration—to mention only a few. The speed with which this legislation was enacted by most States to facilitate Federal programs may be attributed in part to the general concern over the Depression and to the fact that most of the Governors were in sympathy with the national administration. Party forces tended to amalgamate Federal and State powers and to create, at least for the time being, a new and quite different kind of federalism—a kind that has continued to develop during succeeding years.[25]

A fourth method is through Congressional adoption of State legislation. Professor Kallenbach, who made a thorough study of Federal-State relations in the field of the regulation of commerce, devotes a full chapter to the uses made of this device, finding no less than five important areas in which, from the days of the framing of the Constitution, Congress has taken over the provisions of previously enacted State laws.[26] These fields include quarantine and health laws, the slave trade, pilotage regulations, workmen's compensation in maritime employment, and laws relating to the interstate shipment of intoxicating liquors.

Perhaps the quarantine and health laws, which are the oldest form, will serve for illustrative purposes here. In 1795, the health authorities of New York City were confronted with a serious yellow fever epidemic. Kallenbach reports that it soon developed, by reason of provisions in the Federal customs laws and regulations, that vessels arriving from foreign ports were unable to comply with the local quarantine regulations adopted to cope with the situation. Governor Jay appealed to the President, and the matter was considered in Congress, where doubts were expressed regarding the Federal authority to adopt regulations which might be contrary to the laws of some of the States. Consequently, al-

[25] Summary based on Key, V. O., Jr., "State Legislation Facilitative of Federal Action," *Annals of the American Academy of Political and Social Science,* January, 1940, pp. 7–11; see also Corwin, Edward S., "National-State Cooperation: Its Present Possibilities," *Yale Law Review,* February, 1937, pp. 499–523.

[26] Kallenbach, Chapter 10.

though legislation was passed, its provisions were weak. Then, a reappearance of yellow fever in other Atlantic ports led in 1799 to the enactment of a more comprehensive statute—the essential provisions of which have been carried forward and are still in effect. This measure repealed the earlier act, and contemplated a closer Federal-State cooperation. The first section of the new act made compliance with State quarantine laws obligatory upon Federal revenue officers, leaving no leeway for administrative discretion on their part.

State Adoption of Federal Legislation

During the many years since the Federal Constitution has been in effect, Congress and the State legislatures have developed legislative forms and practices for various situations in which each recognizes the other's legislative powers, or adjusts its respective legislative actions to those of the other governmental level. There is, in fact, a good deal of evidence of a general tendency on the part of both national and State legislatures to recognize and depend upon each other's laws and services in various situations. It has been said that the common law and even the basic statute laws of the States form an essential substratum for most Federal legislation.

In many instances, the underlying purpose is to achieve some semblance of uniformity in the provisions of the law, a purpose which can be accomplished either through State adoption of Federal laws, Federal adoption of State laws, or State adoption of uniform statutes. In some instances, the States are forced to rely upon Federal law because of the inadequacies of their own constitutions or laws. Attorney General William G. Clark of Illinois clearly stated this problem in an address before a state-wide conference of the League of Women Voters in Chicago on November 2, 1961.

> As the Attorney General of Illinois, I can tell you that Illinois, like all of the fifty States, is often compelled to rely upon Federal legislation, such as Federal grants of funds for highways, because some provision of the State's Constitution of 1870, wisely as that document was written in its day, prohibits an enlightened and modern solution of problems that, simple under a modern Constitution, are grave indeed under the archaic Constitution.

All of these devices have been used more or less frequently, but the purpose of achieving some semblance of uniformity is especially pertinent to the discussion at this point. Obviously, this type of cooperation is more likely to take place in functional fields in which the two levels of government have overlapping or concurrent jurisdiction, as in the regulation of commerce. Various technical problems present themselves in the process, such as adoption by reference—a very lax procedure from the legislative point of view, but one which is nevertheless widely used, or the extent to which State enactment of a statute carries with it the supplementary rules and regulations established by the enforcing agency.[27]

COOPERATIVE RELATIONSHIPS

There are many ways in which Congress and the State legislatures have taken action designed to facilitate interlevel and interjurisdictional relations in our federal system. There are many instances in which the laws of one level have been adopted, either formally or by implication, by the other. The Federal government and the States have developed cooperative machinery to aid in the drafting of legislation on subjects of mutual interest, and Congress has for more than a decade maintained, at least in the House of Representatives, a Subcommittee on Intergovernmental Relations. After a lapse of more than ten years, a Senate subcommittee was reestablished in 1962.

Instead of making its laws cover every aspect of the subject upon which it is legislating, the Congress has in many instances simply taken over and in effect adopted for Federal purposes the pertinent legislation and common law of the States. Specific examples are to be noted in the property laws and the registration of property deeds and titles, marriage and dependency laws, and the laws of wills and estates, to mention only a few of the State laws which have been recognized by Congress as binding upon the national authorities when pertinent.

Historical Background

Some of the historical background of this problem has been discussed in the preceding pages. In enacting legislation concerning many

[27] These questions are discussed in: Brabner-Smith, John W., "Incorporation by Reference and Delegation of Power," *George Washington Law Review*, January, 1937, pp. 198–222; Kauper, Paul G., "Validity of State Recovery Acts Adopting Federal Codes," *Michigan Law Review*, February, 1935, pp. 597–604; King, Elwyn A., "State Constitutions Forbidding Incorporation by Reference," *Brooklyn Law Review*, June, 1936, pp. 625–634; and Tilden, Richard A., "Incorporation by Reference of Federal Recovery Laws and Administrative Regulations in State Acts," *George Washington Law Review*, May, 1935, pp. 482–494. See also the cases cited in these articles.

aspects of foreign and interstate commerce, for instance, Congress has recognized the laws of the several States. As early as 1790, in legislating upon matters affecting ships, Congress adopted the provisions of State law on matters relating to pilotage. Similarly, Congress has in effect adopted for purposes of Federal elections the election laws and procedures of the several States, instead of enacting a complete and uniform code of Federal election laws—as it has the unquestioned power to do and might do at any time.

These instances and many others that might be cited serve well to illustrate the point argued by Hart and Wechsler, that "Federal law is generally interstitial in its nature." It is their contention that Congress

> rarely occupies a legal field completely, totally excluding all participation by the legal systems of the States. This was plainly true in the beginning when the Federal legislative product (including the Constitution) was extremely small. It is significantly true today, despite the volume of Congressional enactments, and even within areas where Congress has been very active. Federal legislation, on the whole, has been conceived and drafted on an *ad hoc* basis to accomplish limited objectives. It builds upon legal relationships established by the States, altering or supplanting them only so far as necessary for the special purpose. Congress acts, in short, against the background of the total *corpus juris* of the States in much the same way that a State legislature acts against the background of the common law, assumed to govern unless changed by legislation.[28]

This interstitial nature of Federal law, a fact so fundamental to an understanding of Federal-State relations, has been true from the very beginning, having been incorporated in the Judiciary Act of 1789. Indeed, Hart and Wechsler continue:

> The strength of the conception of the central government as one of delegated, limited authority is most significantly manifested on this mundane plane of working, legislative practice. . . . It explains why Federal law often embodies concepts that derive their content, or some portion of their content, from the States. It makes it less anomalous, at least, that substantive rights may be defined by Congress but the remedies for their enforcement left undefined or relegated wholly to the States; or that *per contra* national law may do no more than formulate remedies for vindicating rights that have their source and definition in State law.

The States, on the other hand, have recognized and made use of Federal laws in a great variety of ways. The Federal census has been

[28] Hart, Henry M., Jr., and Wechsler, Herbert, *The Federal Courts and the Federal System* (Brooklyn: Foundation Press, 1953), p. 435n.

accepted in all States for many purposes in State legislation, sometimes with rather curious effects. In 1960, for example, New York City, like other large cities, was shown to have lost population. Its officials thereupon proposed to conduct a census of their own, in order to demonstrate the error in the Federal figures, thereby to retain some $15 million of State aid for schools which would otherwise be lost. Similarly, Federal standards in many fields such as weights and measures, milk pasteurization, and food and drugs have generally been accepted and woven into the legislation of the States. Lacking their own postal services, the States have made the mailing of legal notices, documents and remittances by United States mail sufficient to satisfy the legal requirements for a number of State and local purposes. In this connection, they have given registered mail an especially high priority.

A great many of the illustrations which might be cited here involve the use of powers which are discussed at some length in other chapters. Hence mere mention at this point may be sufficient. The free movement of goods and persons in interstate commerce created many difficult problems for the States in the field of law enforcement. The remedy with respect to a criminal crossing State lines might involve interstate rendition, an interstate compact, or Federal legislation under the commerce clause. A problem involving interstate transportation for immoral purposes might similarly be dealt with by Federal legislation under the commerce clause. Crime committed by mail or the shipment of pornographic literature might be handled under the laws and regulations governing the Post Office Department. Other comparable problems have been dealt with by legislation based upon the national taxing power, the monetary and banking power, the war power, and others. But the commerce power and the national police power have been relied upon most frequently.

In this connection, one may note the Federal laws on narcotics, including a strict code on illegal possession, use, and sale based upon a Federal license tax; the Federal gambling tax and license tax, the firearms act, and laws on the robbery of the mails, of national banks and banks with nationally insured deposits. All of these laws call for national enforcing action, and bring Federal officials into cooperation with State and local officers.

Another type of Federal-State cooperation in the field of legislation is to be found in legislative drafting. The drafting of legislation is probably one of the oldest activities of government, but prior to World War II, no one ever considered the possibility of Federal-State cooperation in this field. The laws enacted by Congress were drafted in Washington with little or no concern about their effects upon the States. Similarly, the State legislatures drafted and passed whatever legislation they chose without much consideration of its effects upon other States or their own

cil of State Governments collaborate with the House Committee in developing a program which would provide substantially uniform Federal and State laws and regulations and enforcement procedures.

In response to this proposal, a special subcommittee was created to work with Federal legislative and administrative officials in drafting generally uniform or coordinated Federal and State regulatory legislation relating to recreational boating safety. The Federal-State group met in a number of conferences in late 1957 and early in 1958, ultimately agreeing to certain amendments to the bill then pending in the House Committee. In April, 1958, the House Committee reported a clean bill conforming closely to the draft approved by the Federal-State conferees. This joint effort made possible the necessary degree of coordination between Federal and State laws in this field. Without such cooperation, either the Federal government would have preempted this area completely or the States would have been faced with the necessity of enacting legislation to fit a Federal statute developed without consideration of State interests and possibly one to which many States could not conform. Such successes in Federal-State cooperation may well prove to mark a new advance in cooperative bill drafting relationships.[31]

The insurance field provides another illustration; here, in recent years, the use of the consent doctrine has been considerably expanded. After the Supreme Court had belatedly decided that insurance is commerce, thereby bringing it within the regulatory powers of Congress under the commerce clause, Congress stepped aside in favor of the States, providing that each State submitted proof that it had suitable laws and a satisfactory regulatory system. This arrangement appears to have been designed to extend indefinitely into the future.[32] This was the first broad application of the consent doctrine to an entire field of economic enterprise affecting all States in the same manner.

A new and novel technique was developed in the field of rent control—a field that had been occupied by Federal legislation, but one from which the Federal government wanted to be relieved of responsibility. Rent control had been established during World War II, as one phase

[31] See Bonner, Herbert C., "An Exercise in Federal-State Relations," *State Government*, Winter, 1959, pp. 50–54; Waite, G. Graham, "Pleasure Boating in a Federal Union," *Buffalo Law Review*, Spring, 1961, pp. 427–447.

[32] See Ferguson-McCarran Act of 1945, 59 Stat. 33, upheld in *Prudential Insurance Company* v. *Benjamin*, 328 U.S. 408 (1946). The earlier pertinent cases were *Paul* v. *Virginia*, 8 Wallace 168 (1868), overruled in *United States* v. *Southeastern Underwriters' Association*, 322 U.S. 533 (1944). It may be noted that the Lynch Act of 1946, 60 Stat. 981, which approved the coverage of maritime workers by State unemployment compensation laws, is another recent example of the use of the consent of Congress idea in the fields of labor and insurance.

of the overall effort to control prices. While at the end of the war, price controls had been hastily abandoned—too hastily, to be sure—the need for rent control was so great and so obvious in the face of a continuing housing shortage, that this type of control was temporarily retained. In 1947, Congress gave the States and the local communities some authority in the matter; when this did not promptly result in decontrol, Congress in 1949 established an ingenious scheme for shifting responsibility in this area from the Federal government to the States and their political subdivisions. Three methods were provided by which these units could displace Federal action:

1. A State could pass its own rent control legislation in which event the Federal law became inoperative within that State.
2. A State legislature could declare that rent control was no longer necessary within its borders, in which event rental units throughout the State would be decontrolled.
3. The city council or equivalent organ of a local government might, after public hearing, pass a resolution declaring that rent control was no longer necessary. If the resolution received the approval of the Governor of the State, the locality would be decontrolled.

While the three methods were different, each from the others, all of them opened the way for State (or local) action to supersede national action. Shortly thereafter, these local option features were struck down by the courts.[33] Nevertheless, as Zimmermann and Wendell observe, a new element had been introduced into this type of legislation. Congress still had responsibility for establishing the pattern, but means for the elimination of unneeded or unwanted national action was a part of the pattern. These flexible methods of control have been most effective when the constitutional power of Congress is clearly plenary. In other areas, where it is not, coercive measures may be applied, as through the conditions attached to grants-in-aid.

These illustrations serve amply to support the assertion that the United States Statutes at Large contain evidence that Congress is becoming "ever more inventive" in the quest for new ways of integrating national and State action. This has been illustrated many times and in many fields. The total number of instances, which indicate a desire on the part of Congress to establish conditions under which a "gearing-in"

[33] In *United States* v. *Bize,* 86 F. Supp. 939 (D. Neb. 1949), the statute was upheld. In *Woods* v. *Shoreline Cooperative Apartments,* 84 F. Supp. 660 (N.D. Ill. 1949), it was struck down. The Supreme Court reversed the Shoreline decision, but did not write an opinion, relying upon an earlier opinion in which a recent control statute had been upheld; 338 U.S. 897 (1949) and *Woods* v. *Miller Company,* 333 U.S. 138 (1948).

of Federal and State governmental machinery is possible, is impressive. Zimmermann and Wendell have analyzed the methods employed, while Professor Anderson has supplied some statistical data regarding the number of instances involved—instances in which the statutes of one State were specifically related to Federal statutes in the same field.

The discovery that Congress could govern many intergovernmental situations by statute was one of the most important contributions to the successful functioning of our highly intricate modern federal system. Like most other legal discoveries, it was not made all at once. In fact, Congress is constantly refining and adding to its stock of statutory devices. Taken by itself, the first divestment statute counted for relatively little. But as other and more varied divestment techniques were developed and as Congress invented other means of providing for State initiative with a national pattern of action, the national legislature established itself as a second umpire of the federal system. There is every evidence that its importance as an umpire will continue to grow.[34]

BIBLIOGRAPHICAL NOTES

State Apportionment Studies. For the overall picture, see Gordon E. Baker, *State Constitutions: Reapportionment* (New York: National Municipal League, 1960); Malcolm E. Jewell, ed., *The Politics of Reapportionment* (New York: Atherton Press, 1962), case studies of both State and Congressional apportionment; and studies and articles by Charles W. Shull and Ruth C. Silva. Two national organizations have published compilations which are to be kept up-to-date by periodic revisions: Richard S. Childs, ed., *Compendium on Legislative Apportionment*, rev. ed. (New York: National Municipal League, 1962), a collection of statistics and appraisals of inequalities in the legislative and Congressional representation of voters in the fifty States, and Council of State Governments, *Legislative Reapportionment in the States: A Summary of Action Since June 1960* (Chicago, September, 1962). Paul T. David and Ralph Eisenberg present the results of a statistical investigation of long-term trends in *State Legislative Representation in Devaluation of the Urban and Suburban Vote*, 2 vols. (Charlottesville: Bureau of Public Administration, University of Virginia, 1961 and 1962). For a statement of basic principles of legislative apportionment as agreed

[34] Anderson, William, *Intergovernmental Relations in Review* (Minneapolis: University of Minnesota Press, 1960), p. 57. In a two-volume edition of the *Minnesota Statutes* published in 1949, Professor Anderson found no less than 273 distinct passages that clearly referred to laws, services, grants-in-aid, property, and activities of the United States, or to the State's relation to the nation and its government. In the *Session Laws of 1951*, he found forty-four statutes and eleven resolutions touching on National-State relations or making recommendations to Congress for action on issues of national policy and legislation.

upon at a conference of research scholars and political scientists held by the Twentieth Century Fund, see *One Man-One Vote* (New York: Twentieth Century Fund, 1962).

Apportionment has been a major concern for so many years that there are few States that do not have at least one reasonably good study of the problem; some States, like Michigan and New York, have several. Among the more recent and significant of these studies are: William C. Havard and Loren P. Beth, *The Politics of Misrepresentation: Urban-rural Conflict in the Florida Legislature* (Baton Rouge: Louisiana State University Press, 1962); Edward H. Hobbs, *Legislative Apportionment in Mississippi* (University: Bureau of Public Administration, University of Mississippi, 1956); Joseph C. Pray and George J. Mauer, *The New Perspective of Legislative Apportionment in Oklahoma* (Norman: Bureau of Government, University of Oklahoma, July, 1962); and articles on apportionment in New York by Ruth C. Silva in the March and April, 1962, issues of the *Fordham Law Review*.

The Courts and Reapportionment. Among the numerous titles now available, see David and Eisenberg, *State Legislative Redistricting: Major Issues in the Wake of Judicial Decision* (Chicago: Public Administration Service, 1962); James E. Larson, *Reapportionment and the Courts* (University: Bureau of Public Administration, University of Alabama, 1962); and Bernard Taper, *Gomillion Versus Lightfoot* (New York: McGraw-Hill Book Co., Inc., 1962). The first deals with the problems presented by *Baker* v. *Carr* and other decisions; the second is a survey of recent cases, both Federal and State; and the third is an excellent case study of the Tuskegee Gerrymander Case. The *Yale Law Journal* devoted its November, 1962, issue to a symposium on *Baker* v. *Carr*, and the National Municipal League published *Court Decisions on Legislative Apportionment*, 2 vols. (New York, 1962) and has indicated its intention of keeping the compilation up-to-date by annual volumes.

Congressional Apportionment. The standard work on Congressional apportionment is Laurence F. Schmeckebier, *Congressional Apportionment* (Washington: Brookings Institution, 1941). Alan Rosenthal, *Toward Majority Rule in the United States Senate* (New York: McGraw-Hill Book Co., Inc., 1962), an Eagleton Institute case study in practical politics, shows why the Democratic liberals who predominate in numbers are relatively powerless to enact legislation reflecting their point of view. Just as there are numerous studies of apportionment and redistricting with respect to the legislatures of individual States, there are studies of the Congressional districting problem in a few States. Two recent examples are Citizens Research Council of Michigan, *Congressional Reapportionment in 1961: A Puzzle for Michigan* (Detroit, 1960) and Claude J. Davis, *Congressional Redistricting in West Virginia for the 'Sixties* (Morgantown: Bureau for Government Research, West Virginia University, 1960).

CHAPTER VI

The Role of
the Executive

Governmental activities [in the eighteenth century] were not extensive. But relative to what governments did, intergovernmental cooperation during the last century was comparable with that existing today. Administrative contacts were voluminous, and the whole process was lubricated, then as today, by constituent-minded members of Congress. Occasional Presidential vetoes of cash and land grants, [though they are] evidence of constitutional and ideological apprehensions about the extensive expansion of Federal activities . . . , are a more important evidence of the continuous search . . . for ways and means to involve the central government in a wide variety of joint programs. The search was successful.

. . . The Federal Government, theoretically in exclusive control of the Indian population, relied continuously . . . on the experience and resources of State and local governments. State militias were an all-important ingredient in the nation's armed forces. State governments became unofficial but real partners in Federal programs for homesteading, reclamation, tree culture, law enforcement, inland waterways, the nation's internal communications system . . . and veterans' aid of various sorts.[1]

[1] Grodzins, Morton, "The Federal System," Report of the President's Commission of National Goals, *Goals for Americans*, American Assembly, Columbia University (Englewood Cliffs, N.J.: Prentice-Hall, Inc., 1960), pp. 265–282, at 270.

The President of the United States is, to use Merriman Smith's phrase, many men.[2] This, in fact, is true in two different senses. The President is the Chief of State, the ceremonial head of the nation. He is the Chief Executive, responsible for much in the formulation of policy and in the administration of the government. He is the political leader of his party.[3] He is Commander-in-Chief of the Armed Forces,[4] head and chief spokesman for the nation in matters of foreign policy,[5] and he is chief legislator, proposing legislation, prodding Congress to get his program enacted, and exercising (or threatening to exercise) his veto power when the legislative product is not to his liking.[6] And, in addition, since the President is the only official elected by all the people, he is in a unique sense their leader. He can never stop being any of these things and still be a successful President, for his effectiveness in any one role has its bearing on his effectiveness in each of the others.

The Presidency in the 1960's is something quite different from what it was a generation or two ago. President Wilson and the two Roosevelts established new precedents, creating a "new image" of the office, and present conditions virtually require a President to conform with this new pattern. In the past, Presidents whose constitutional scruples or personal inclination restrained them were able to follow their own preferences. Now the requirements of the office compel even a weak President to become involved in many matters from which he might once have been able to abstain. Professor Neustadt presents some significant illustrations: "Once, TR daringly assumed the 'steward's' role in the emergency created by the great coal strike of 1902; the Railway Labor Act

[2] Smith, A. Merriman, *A President Is Many Men* (New York: Harper & Brothers, 1948). See also Rossiter, Clinton L., *The American Presidency* (New York: Harcourt, Brace and Co., Inc., 1956), pp. 3–37.

[3] See Odegard, Peter H., "Presidential Leadership and Party Responsibility," *Annals of the American Academy of Political and Social Science,* September, 1956, pp. 66–81, and Seligman, Lester G., "The Presidential Office and the President as Party Leader," *Law and Contemporary Problems,* Autumn, 1956, pp. 724–734.

[4] See May, Ernest R., ed., "The President as Commander-in-Chief," *The Ultimate Decision* (New York: George Braziller, Inc., 1960).

[5] See Corwin, Edward S., *The President's Control of Foreign Relations* (Princeton: Princeton University Press, 1917); Longaker, Richard P., "The President as International Leader," *Law and Contemporary Problems,* Autumn, 1956, pp. 735–752; and Nitze, Paul H., "The Modern President as a World Figure," *Annals of the American Academy of Political and Social Science,* September, 1956, pp. 114–123.

[6] See Herring, E. Pendleton, *Presidential Leadership: The Political Relations of Congress and the Chief Executive* (New York: Farrar, Straus and Young, Inc., 1940) and Binkley, William E., "The President as Chief Legislator," *Annals of the American Academy of Political and Social Science,* September, 1956, pp. 92–105.

and the Taft-Hartley Act now make such intervention mandatory upon Presidents. Once, FDR dramatically asserted personal responsibility for gauging and guiding the American economy; now, the Employment Act binds his successors to that task. Wilson and FDR became chief spokesmen, leading actors on a world stage at the height of war; now UN membership, far-flung alliances, the facts of power, prescribe that role continuously in times termed 'peace.' " [7]

Now, to return to the concept of the Presidency as many men: while the man who bears the title of President must do many different kinds of things, the individual human being who holds the title is at the same time a symbol of an institution. Although the Constitution vests the executive power in the President, the President is aided by the White House staff, the staff of the Executive Office of the President (with all its many subdivisions), the several executive departments of the government, the numerous offices, boards, administrations, and other independent agencies, and the group of independent regulatory commissions established by Congress.

The significant point is that while the activities of the Federal government are far too extensive for any one man to keep in touch with more than a small portion of them, yet one man is largely responsible for what the government does. It is the President only—theoretically, at least—whose motive power puts the government into action, and it is he who has the final and awesome power of decision. (Although it may have other implications as well, Mr. Truman used to have a sign on his desk, "The buck stops here.") The President must accept full responsibility for the decisions he makes, and he must accept as well the responsibility for the activities of those he has appointed—even when it is embarrassing for him to do so (as it was for Mr. Kennedy after the Cuban invasion fiasco).

For these reasons, the organization of a discussion of the role of the Executive Branch in the determination of policy on matters affecting intergovernmental relations presents many formidable difficulties. In the organization adopted here, the first two sections deal specifically with the Presidency, its historical background and the more recent developments affecting its role; the third section deals with the Governors; and the concluding section is concerned with changing patterns in executive cooperation between the Federal government and the States. The discussion is more concerned with programs than with powers, and the existence of the programs rests primarily on legislative provisions, Federal and State, not upon the powers of either the President or the Governors.

[7] Neustadt, Richard E., "The Presidency at Mid-Century," *Law and Contemporary Problems*, Autumn, 1956, pp. 609–645.

HISTORICAL BACKGROUND

The federal system is, as Clinton L. Rossiter has so well stated, "an involved network of fifty separate and independent governments and their countless subdivisions, all of which possess powers whose use or disuse can seriously embarrass the President and his policies. Although the States no longer have the restraining influence of the days when they defied Jefferson, ignored Madison, and heckled Lincoln, they remain an obstacle to the determined President, especially to one who is eager to push ahead boldly with experiments in education and social justice." [8]

The executive contacts between the Federal government and the States are so numerous and so varied that it is not easy to identify or classify all of them. Some go very far back in the history of the nation. Their effects upon the States are likewise many and varied. In considering the role of the executive in policy determination, one should not assume, however, that such influences travel only in one direction, for while presidential action does influence the States, executive action at the State level in turn sometimes influences national policy.

Many, but by no means all, of these contacts involve grant-in-aid programs, no two studies of which arrive at the same number. A tabulation undertaken by the author and reproduced in Appendix A to this volume enumerates fifty major programs. In Minnesota, in 1958, a Special Committee on Intergovernmental Relations appointed by the Governor produced a list of eighty-one "separate identifiable programs involving about $75 million of Federal funds per year. This does not include additional amounts reported by State departments as expended [by the national agencies] in programs paralleling theirs," [9] nor did it include cases of informal cooperation between Federal and State authorities in which no money was granted or received. More than $65 million of the total amount received by Minnesota in 1957 came to the State from Federal grants-in-aid and closely related programs such as employment security. The effects of these programs upon the States is considered in Chapter XXIII.

Important among programs of a non-grant-in-aid nature, the following may be mentioned: (1) cooperation in law enforcement activities, including police training, criminal identification, etc.; (2) services of the Post Office Department to State agencies enforcing laws prohibiting ship-

[8] Rossiter, p. 45.
[9] Anderson, William, *Intergovernmental Relations in Review* (Minneapolis: University of Minnesota Press, 1960), p. 60.

ment into the State of uninspected seeds, noxious plants, and other objectionable materials; (3) the extension of Federal OASI (Old Age and Survivors' Insurance) to State officers and employees as a supplement to their retirement allowances; (4) cooperation between the Interstate Commerce Commission and State public untility commissions in certain phases of railroad regulation, grain inspection, etc.

In some instances, though the program was initiated with the aid of a Federal grant, the grant has long since ceased to be the dominant characteristic of the program. The 4-H Club work affords a good example. While grants are still given for 4-H work, the program long ago outgrew its modest beginnings. From what was characterised as "an inauspicious beginning" around the turn of the century, the extensive system of 4-H Clubs now encircles the globe, more than forty countries having adopted all or part of the plan. This tremendous growth has been due in part to the appeal of the program itself, but also to the fine guidance it has had from three major groups which direct its activities. These groups are the National 4-H Club Foundation, the Cooperative Extension Service of the Department of Agriculture, and the National 4-H Service Committee. These groups, governmental and private, join together in their common endeavor to assist 4-H members to make the most of their abilities, to utilize scientific advances in farming and homemaking, and to render more efficient service to their community, State, and nation. At the local level, instruction and direction are provided by county agents, home demonstration agents, parents, businessmen, teachers, and older 4-H'ers who give generously of their time and talent to insure the success of the work.

The Olmstead Case

In 1778, Gideon Olmstead, a Connecticut-born seafarer, with three companions had captured a British sloop, the *Active,* with thirteen seamen aboard. Before he could get his prize into a New Jersey harbor, two Pennsylvania vessels—one of them a State ship—took her away from him. After a Pennsylvania jury decided that the Commonwealth and not Olmstead had captured the vessel, Olmstead appealed to the Continental Congress. Commissioners appointed by the Congress reversed the judgment of the Pennsylvania court, but the prize money had already been paid over to the State Treasurer.

Year after year and decade after decade, Gideon Olmstead fought on. In 1808, when he was over eighty years of age, he secured a mandamus from the Supreme Court directing the marshal of the Pennsylvania Federal court to take possession of the prize funds and turn them over to Olmstead. When the marshal attempted to serve process on the State Treasurer, he found the way barred by State militia commanded by the Adjutant General of Pennsylvania. He then declared his intention to call out a posse in order to enforce his authority. A little later, the marshal tried again, and this time he secured the persons of the custodians of the money. Next came a writ of habeas corpus, but the Chief Justice of Pennsylvania realized that the time had come to yield and returned the prisoners to the marshal. The State backed down; the process was served, and the General Assembly appropriated $18,000 to be expended at the discretion of the Governor. Upon receiving this money, the marshal released his prisoners and paid it over to Olmstead.

As a final humiliation, the Adjutant General had been charged and tried for obstructing Federal processes and had been sentenced to fine and imprisonment, as had some of his men. It was during the course of these later events that the Pennsylvania legislature resolved that "as the guardians of the State rights," they could not permit an infringement of these rights by an unconstitutional exercise of power—a position that they took some five paragraphs to expound. Governor Snyder sent these resolutions to President Madison, expressing the hope that he would "adjust" the present "unhappy collision of the two governments in such a manner as will be equally honorable to them both," and told him of the $18,000. The President replied on April 13, 1809, that the Chief Executive of the United States is not only unauthorized to prevent the execution of a decree of the Federal court "but is expressly enjoined, by statute, to carry into effect any such decree where opposition may be made to it." He felt that it was a propitious circumstance that the legislature had made adequate provision for the removal of the existing difficulty, and he said that he felt "great pleasure" in assuring himself that the authority given in the legislation would be exercised in a patriotic spirit. Almost immediately, the President pardoned Adjutant General Bright and his militiamen on the ground that they had acted under a mistaken sense of duty.[10]

Developments in the Twentieth Century

In other chapters, emphasis has been placed upon the role of executive leadership, particularly in periods of national emergency such as war (Chapter XII) or depression (Chapters XV and XVI). But since the begin-

[10] For a full account, see Carson, Hampton L., "The Case of the Sloop 'Active,'" *Pennsylvania Magazine of History and Biography* (1892), IV, 385–398. See also Warren, Charles, *The Supreme Court in American History*, 2 vols. (Boston: Little, Brown and Co., 1926), I, 374–387.

ning of the twentieth century, the role of the executive in American government has been largely transformed, and strong executive leadership has come to be a daily requirement for efficient governmental action. This transformation has been due to the changed conditions of modern life and to the emergence of a group of strong and able executives in American public life. Notable among the members of this group have been Woodrow Wilson and the two Roosevelts. These leaders capitalized on a wave of democratic sentiment, popular resentment against "bossism," the desire for social legislation, and the general distrust of legislative bodies. These factors, together with effective leadership on the part of both Governors and Presidents, served to give to the executive a new popular appeal and a new prestige.

Ever since President Jefferson wrote in 1807 to the Governor of Massachusetts concerning the desirability of "a more intimate correspondence between the executives of the several States, and that of the Union," the need for informal machinery of communication between the President of the United States and the Governors had been recognized. Theodore Roosevelt, with his calling of the first Governors' Conference in 1908, initiated an era of Federal-State cooperation of tremendous significance. The pattern which he established in the field of conservation has spread to many other fields and has been utilized, to some degree at least, by many of his successors in the office of the Presidency. Through informal personal contacts with Governors and Mayors, Presidents have frequently been able both to influence State policy and to increase the efficiency of Federal operations.

President Taft faced a problem of an entirely different nature in 1913 —a problem that was to occupy a prominent place in American politics for the next two decades. The President considered the Webb-Kenyon Act, prohibiting the shipment of liquor into dry States, unconstitutional. Failure on his part to enforce the law in dry States or any vigorous attempt to enforce it in wet States would be equally unpopular, especially when the subject was theoretically within the limits of State responsibility. If this situation was acute in the earlier days, it became far more so later on under the Eighteenth Amendment and the Volstead Act of 1920.

In 1919, President Wilson summoned a White House Conference of Governors and Mayors to consider problems of re-employment at the end of World War I. The Governors met with President Coolidge once, and years later with President Franklin D. Roosevelt once. Among more recent developments, President Eisenhower maintained a close working relationship with the Governors, addressing their annual Conference twice, and meeting with them three times to consider questions relating to national security, intergovernmental relations, and employment security. He also used these contacts in his effort to establish the Federal-State Joint Action Committee, whose organization and work is discussed in Chapter XXV. President Truman considered the Labor-Management Relations Act of 1947 (Taft-Hartley) not only undesirable but even unconstitutional. Vigorous enforcement efforts would offend organized labor in the large cities, he felt, while failure to enforce it would offend business leaders in all parts of the country.

Sometimes Governors are indifferent, non-cooperative, and even opposed to vigorous enforcement action on the part of the President to maintain law and order and preserve the peace, although Congress has passed numerous laws authorizing the use of both national and State forces for the purpose. Such an instance occurred in 1894 when President Cleveland resorted to the use of troops in an effort to keep the mails moving and prevent interruption in the flow of interstate commerce. Governor Altgeld of Illinois, who had hoped to settle the strike and was confident of his ability to maintain order, vehemently protested against the use of Federal troops within the State unless he or the legislature requested them.[11]

Governor Patterson of Alabama likewise protested vigorously in 1961, at a far milder form of Federal "interference," when President Kennedy sent in a sizable force of United States Marshals to maintain the public peace and protect the free flow of interstate commerce. There have been instances, of course, in which the Governor has requested such assistance, as did Governor Cornwall of West Virginia in 1921 when his State was in the grip of a serious coal strike. In either case, whether the Governor likes it or not, the President has both the right and the duty to execute the national laws with all the force at his command, and the courts have fully sustained his action.

It is natural that such incidents should stir up a considerable amount of controversy; no one is likely to be entirely happy in what is admittedly a bad situation. Nevertheless, the responsibility of the President to preserve and protect the peace is now universally recognized. According to Rossiter's analysis, the President's powers in this area fall under three headings: (1) the power literally to "keep the peace of the United States"

[11] For President Cleveland's own account of this episode, see his *Presidential Problems* (New York: The Century Company, 1904), Chapter 2; Rich, Bennett M., *The Presidents and Civil Disorder* (Washington: Public Affairs Press, 1941), Chapter 6; Lindsey, Almot, *The Pullman Strike* (Chicago: University of Chicago Press, 1942); Browne, Waldo R., *Altgeld of Illinois* (New York: B. W. Heubsch, 1924), Chapters 11–16; Nevins, Allan, *Grover Cleveland: A Study in Courage* (New York: Dodd, Mead & Co., 1932), Chapter 33; and Christman, Henry M., ed., *The Mind and Spirit of John Peter Altgeld* (Urbana: University of Illinois Press, 1961).

by instituting military action in strikes attended by violence and public disorder; (2) the power to remove obstructions to the flow of industrial production in time of war, or just before or after a war; (3) the power to intervene in disputes that constitute economic national emergencies.[12]

PRESIDENTIAL POWERS AND ACTIONS

There has been a great deal of writing of late about the powers of the President. One able columnist reports that one "Kennedy quality is an unabashed love of power." [13] This is probably true of most Presidents, though their reasons may be different, and some may be far more skillful in their use of power than others. Alsop continues, "Self-confidence and a love of power are vast assets in the Presidency." Certainly Wilson and both Roosevelts, as well as Kennedy, thoroughly enjoyed the exercise of power.

While the powers of the President are important, the use that is made of these powers is even more important. In a given situation, of course, the President may decide not to use his powers at all, in which case his silence or inaction may in itself be significant. What he does (or does not do) depends to a large extent both upon his personal characteristics and upon existing circumstances. He may decide, as a matter of strategy, to move on a given subject using his executive powers, rather than to risk a losing battle in Congress. Or, if he thinks that he can win in Congress, he may prefer to have Congress responsible for the action taken.

The powers of the President in the field of intergovernmental relations, as in any other, are based upon the provisions of the Constitution, the precedents that have been established, the statutes, and the decisions of the Supreme Court interpreting presidential powers. Although the nature and scope of these powers are important, it is significant that in practice the orderly development of intergovernmental relations has suffered because so few Presidents have given any serious or sustained attention to them, and then usually only in periods of crisis. The rest of the time, vital decisions on many problems affecting intergovernmental relationships have been made with little or no consideration being given to their probable effects on the relations between the Nation and the States.

[12] Rossiter, pp. 91–92.

[13] Alsop, Stewart, "The President of the United States," *Washington Post,* May 1, 1961.

Presidential Leadership

President Lincoln in the dark days of the Civil War needed the assistance and support of the Governors of the Northern States; consequently, he took pains to inform them and to cultivate their understanding and cooperation.[14] President Theodore Roosevelt, as noted above, having in mind the urgent need for conservation and the more intelligent utilization of the nation's natural resources, called the Governors together in 1908 to discuss the matter, thereby providing the initiative for the establishment of the Governors' Conference, now more than half a century old. President Eisenhower, during his eight years in the White House, took a more active and sustained interest in intergovernmental relations than any of his predecessors, having been largely responsible for at least three major projects designed to improve interlevel and interjurisdictional relations; [15] in fact, at one time, he expressed the hope that his administration would be remembered in the years to come for its contribution to the solution of problems in the intergovernmental field.

While some Presidents have used their official position to encourage cooperative relationships by formal methods, others have made effective use of quasi-official or even informal methods. Although the Presidency is a continuing institution, the fact that individual Presidents change may affect the course of events. President Roosevelt, during World War II, believed that it was essential for the Federal government to take over the public employment offices from the States, in order to establish uniform wartime controls over manpower. To accomplish this, he made a commitment that when the emergency was over these offices would be returned to the States. When the time came to fulfill the pledge, there was a different President in office (Truman) who felt that these offices should remain under Federal control, and who also felt no special obligation to carry out an informal agreement made during a previous administration.

In some instances, even what the President says or does informally, what he writes, or the places he goes [16] may have influence as great or

[14] See Hesseltine, William, *Lincoln and the War Governors* (New York: Alfred A. Knopf, Inc., 1948).

[15] These were, in addition to two addresses before the Governors' Conference and reference to these problems in many of his public papers and addresses: (1) the Commission on Intergovernmental Relations, a national study commission (1953–1955) commonly referred to from the name of its chairman as the Kestnbaum Commission; (2) the Federal-State Joint Action Committee (1957–1959); (3) the National Advisory Commission on Intergovernmental Relations, established in 1959, with Frank Bane as chairman.

[16] For illustration, see Longaker, Richard P., *The Presidency and Individual Liberties* (Ithaca: Cornell University Press, 1961), Chapter 5.

greater than his official acts. When the first President Roosevelt invited Booker T. Washington to the White House, he accomplished more by way of recognition of the achievement of members of the Negro group than he might have accomplished by several Executive Proclamations, Executive Orders, or pieces of legislation—had such procedures been applicable. When the President addresses the annual meeting of the Governors' Conference—sometimes traveling way across the continent to do so—he effectively emphasizes to all Americans the importance of intergovernmental cooperation.

When Harold D. Smith, Director of the Budget under President Franklin D. Roosevelt, participated in the formation and administration of the Council on Intergovernmental Relations, the President's sanction of the activities of a member of his immediate staff gave at least implied approval to the goals of the Council. Similarly, when the field offices of the Budget Bureau were established, the efforts of the head of one of these offices brought about the establishment of the interesting and productive work of the Pacific Coast Board of Intergovernmental Relations. This important experiment in intergovernmental cooperation would not have been undertaken without the President's knowledge, nor would it have succeeded without his support.

Law Enforcing Powers

While the Constitution imposes upon the President a solemn obligation to "take care that the laws be faithfully executed" (Article II, Section 3), the degree to which he succeeds in doing this depends upon many things. He is supposed to enforce *all* the laws impartially; nowhere is he authorized to choose to enforce some or to ignore others. But most laws are not self-enforcing. Before action is taken for their enforcement, they have to be interpreted. The enforcing officer—in this case, the President—has to decide (subject to review by the courts) what the law means and the extent to which it is applicable to the situation at hand. Very often the subject matter of the dispute leads him into direct contact—if not conflict—with State officials.

In addition to giving "moral and persuasive leadership," the President is under obligation both to create conditions under which compliance with constitutional and statutory requirements may be met, and to use his authority to insure that they will be met. This involves, in the first place, using his own powers to the fullest; since, however, ours is a democratic, not a totalitarian, society, there is no assurance that his wishes will be complied with. The President in most cases cannot order; he can only attempt to persuade. President Truman once said that he spent a great deal of his time trying to persuade people to do things that they ought to do anyway. Dean Stephen K. Bailey alludes to the fact that Nicholas I, the "Iron Czar" of Russia, was reputed to have said shortly before his death, "I do not rule Russia; ten thousand clerks do." Then, Bailey continues: "Nicholas, unfortunately, was silent on the extent to which he ruled the ten thousand clerks. For if the ten thousand clerks were *his* clerks, then *he* ruled Russia. If they were not *his* clerks, he did not." [17] Of course, the President's ability to persuade is measured at least in part by the sanctions that he might be in a position to apply then or later.

Presidents have made extensive use of both formal and informal procedures, sometimes in an effort to persuade, sometimes actually to establish public policy. When, for example, the Civil War Centennial Commission planned to hold a meeting in Charleston in March, 1961, and it became known that a Negro member of the Commission was unable to obtain hotel accommodations there, President Kennedy requested that the meeting be held elsewhere and made it very plain at a press conference that he had no intention of yielding on this point. When the Commission resisted changing the meeting place, the President ordered that no segregated meeting be held. This time the meeting place was changed, not from Charleston but to government-owned property in the Charleston area.[18]

The Centennial celebration of President Lincoln's signing of the Emancipation Proclamation served to remind Americans of the great power the President has in the use of Proclamations and Executive Orders, when and if he chooses to utilize it.[19] In his campaign in 1960, Mr. Kennedy had said that the President could "by a stroke of the pen" put an end to discrimination in federally aided housing. Still of the opinion, after he became President, that a great deal could be accomplished in the field of civil rights by using Executive Orders and other powers of the

[17] Stephen K. Bailey, "The President and His Political Executives," *Annals of the American Academy of Political and Social Science*, September, 1956, pp. 24-36.

[18] See two articles by Alvin Shuster in *The New York Times:* "Civil War Centennial Commission Rebuffs Kennedy's Desegregation Plea," March 22, 1961, and "President Tells Civil War Unit Not to Hold Segregated Meeting," March 24, 1961.

[19] See *Emancipation Centennial, 1962: A Brief Anthology of the Preliminary Proclamation* (Washington: Civil War Centennial Commission, 1962). For comment, see Franklin, John H., *The Emancipation Proclamation* (Garden City: Doubleday & Co., Inc., 1963); Quarles, Benjamin, *Lincoln and the Negro* (New York: Oxford University Press, 1962); and an excellent symposium, "A Century of Struggle: Emancipation Proclamation, 1863-1963," *The Progressive*, December, 1962, a special issue.

Presidency, he sought to postpone a struggle in Congress over civil rights legislation during the early months of his administration.

Meanwhile, he issued Executive Orders designed to put an end to discriminatory hiring practices on the part of government contractors,

PRESIDENT KENNEDY MOVES AGAINST DISCRIMINATION
IN FEDERAL EMPLOYMENT

President Kennedy confers at the White House with members of Committee on Equal Employment Opportunity, whose chairman is Vice President Johnson, far right. In first row are, from left: Luther H. Hodges, Secretary of Commerce; Arthur J. Goldberg, Secretary of Labor; the President; Mrs. Mary Lasker and the Vice President.

or within the government itself.[20] Vice-President Johnson was asked to serve as chairman of the President's Committee on Equal Employment Opportunity. On November 20, 1962, the President issued an Executive

[20] For a summary of actions taken during the first year, see a report of the Attorney General issued December 29, 1961, in the form of a press release; many civil rights advocates were disappointed that the administration was not moving faster, or trying to do more.

Order to end discrimination in all Federal housing programs, and soon after he appointed former Governor David L. Lawrence of Pennsylvania as chairman of an enforcing board. As might be expected, there were widely divergent views as to the probable effects of the order. Informed opinion anticipated a reduction in the number of housing starts as a short-term effect, with no adverse effect upon the industry in the long run. It was also assumed that the beginnings in the elimination of discriminatory practices made possible under the terms of this Order would gradually be extended in the future to non-Federal types of housing.

The full exercise of the powers of the Presidency may include invoking the assistance of the other branches of government, in initiating —or having the Department of Justice initiate for him—judicial proceedings, by starting suit or seeking an injunction to put an end to some action regarded as improper or undesirable, or by urging Congress to enact additional legislation if necessary. Cases requiring such action have a way of arising suddenly without warning. In May, 1961, a bi-racial group of "Freedom Riders" on a pilgrimage from Washington, D.C. to New Orleans to test the use of interstate travel facilities by the two races was violently attacked in a Birmingham bus station, apparently with the full knowledge and support of the Governor of the State. In the melee, involving injuries to persons and destruction of property, one member of the group had to have fifty-seven stitches taken in his head, and an interstate bus was burned. At this point, the Attorney General stepped into the situation in an effort to make certain that, if the State of Alabama was unable or unwilling to protect life and property, steps should be taken to enforce the laws of the United States.[21]

In this instance, President Kennedy combined in an unusual manner the use of both formal and informal procedures. Being extremely anxious to avoid the necessity for using Federal troops in a "second Little Rock," he and his staff went to great lengths to prevent trouble in Montgomery. When State and local officials, though they had abundant warning, made no effort to prevent disorder or to combat it when started, the President had no choice but to use the authority of the Federal government to protect citizens lawfully moving in interstate commerce. The Governor protested that he had not asked for, did not want, and did not need Federal assistance—though the third contention was obviously untrue. The President made it clear that the Federal government could and would protect citizens in interstate commerce and the movement of interstate commerce. While he urged all citizens to abide by the laws, and State and local officers to enforce the law, the Attorney General with the approval of the President dispatched 200 (and later two to three

---

[21] See current newspaper accounts, and Senator Jacob Javits of New York, *Congressional Record*, May 16, 1961, p. 7483.

times that number) United States Marshals to the strife-torn area. Although United States Marshals are not military personnel but officers of the civil courts, even their presence was resented in Alabama, largely because the legal basis for their dispatch was found in an 1871 law of Reconstruction days, used by Presidents Grant and Cleveland.

All this serves strongly to underscore the highly emotional character of the situation in the South today. The questions are not merely questions of race relations. Federal action to enforce the law, no matter how justified, conjures up visions of a return of the abuses of Reconstruction days—a psychological reaction that the President had very earnestly sought to avoid.

Advances in the legal protection of any important concept, such as equality of opportunity, need not be limited to legislation or litigation, or in the Executive Branch to action by the Chief Executive at any level of government. In the civil rights field, for instance, progress is constantly being made by the determinations of administrative officers and agencies on a wide variety of questions. A summary of such developments over the past two years was recently prepared by Sol Rabkin who reported that in the latter half of 1959, one university in New York and another in Colorado formally adopted policies aimed at requiring non-discrimination in off-campus housing listed by the universities as available to students.[22] The Attorney General of California ruled in 1959 that a public high school may not legally have a swimming team if the only facilities for practice are at a privately-owned pool which refuses to admit members of minority groups. The same official also ruled that a State redevelopment agency is barred by Amendment XIV to the Federal Constitution from including in a listing of available relocation landlords who refuse to accept members of minority groups as tenants, and that real estate brokers and salesmen are public establishments within the law and therefore may not discriminate in offering their services on the basis of race or creed.

Other States provide similar illustrations. The Attorney General of Massachusetts and the Michigan Corporation and Securities Commission both made similar rulings with regard to real estate salesmen. The Attorney General of Pennsylvania ruled it illegal for the State to disburse public funds to institutions founded on covenants and conditions which discriminate on account of race, creed, or color, observing that "use of public funds by a private corporation or institution brings such institution within the ambit of the Fourteenth Amendment, and hence racial

[22] Rabkin, Sol, "Administrative Rulings on Civil Rights: Trends and Developments," *Journal of Intergroup Relations,* Winter, 1960–1961, pp. 82–84; for further information on housing, see Rutledge, Edward, "Campus Housing," *ibid.,* Autumn, 1960, pp. 30–39.

or religious discrimination is prohibited." The New York Commission Against Discrimination protected the right of a young Negro woman who had been trained as an airline stewardess to be appointed to a position of this type. In Baltimore, all department and agency heads are required to include in all contracts let by the City a general provision which bars racial and religious discrimination in employment under such contracts.

These specific cases serve to illustrate the progress that can be made in carrying out a given policy determination by means of administrative rulings at any or all levels of government. Such rulings often serve to clear up ambiguities in existing law, and unless they are successfully challenged in the courts, they may well bring about new patterns of procedure on the subject to which they relate. They may be quite as effective as statutory enactments or judicial decisions.

THE ROLE OF THE GOVERNORS

American Governors have always been important public figures, but in the last half century there have been tremendous changes in the characteristics of the office. In the early days, the Governorship suffered from the limited powers which were a direct result of the deep-seated fears of the executive power engendered by colonial experience with the British Crown and the Royal Governors. The Founding Fathers were determined to prevent, if possible, the recurrence of abuses which they had suffered in the past. In some States, the gubernatorial office is still pitifully weak and inadequate, but the general trend has been to strengthen both the powers and the prestige of the office.

The changes that have taken place in the Governorship have been similar to, and more or less parallel with, those that have occurred in the presidential office, and in many cases for precisely the same reasons. As Woodrow Wilson once remarked, a Governorship might be characterized as "a little Presidency." In the last half century, the Governor has become, like the President, a popular leader, party leader, and legislative leader, as well as the chief executive of his State. Whereas in former times his time was so fully occupied with State and local affairs that he rarely left the State on official business, the modern Governor has come to be an important personage in the determination of national policy questions, making frequent trips to Washington in the process. He has come to have important administrative relationships with Federal departments and agencies which require an estimated one-fifth or one-fourth of his working time.

The nature and scope of these changes have been clearly described and analyzed by Glenn E. Brooks in a small volume which, though centered upon the Governors' Conference and its role in national politics, sheds much light on the role and influence of the individual Governors.[23] The change has been so great that the concern of the Governors now extends, not only to important questions of national policy, but to foreign and international affairs as well. The latter are considered in Chapter XI.

When at the turn of the century the governorship was at a low ebb, "a new breed of governors," to use Brooks' phrase, came upon the scene. Since then, he writes, these "modern governors have become key figures in the swiftly changing political system. . . . They are key figures not only in the quadrennial tug of war for the Presidency, but also in the arduous day to day political struggle that shapes government policies and puts them into action." The political aspects of the gubernatorial office are considered in Chapter VIII.

The Governors and Congress

"The concerted influence of the State governors is clearly evident" in many of the important issues that have come before Congress, for following World War II, when:

> the activist techniques of the Governors' Conference matured to a point of effectiveness, gubernatorial influence in Congress has grown until it is worthy of special note.
>
> A glance at the resolutions passed by the Governors' Conference in recent years reveals how the governors have become absorbed in Congressional policy issues. Between 1943 and 1959, 60 per cent of all resolutions passed by the Conference were addressed entirely or in part to the national government. Of these national policy resolutions, over two-thirds were aimed at Capitol Hill. In marked contrast, only 17 per cent of Conference resolutions were directed to State governments.
>
> The subjects of greatest concern to the governors during this period, judging from the contents of their resolutions, were national military and civil defense policy and general Federal-State relations.[24]

The former Governors in the Senate, sometimes referred to as the Governors' Bloc, frequently show a high degree of unanimity, regardless of party affiliation. In sheer numbers, the size of the Bloc is sufficient to

[23] Brooks, Glenn E., *When Governors Convene: The Governors' Conference and National Politics* (Baltimore: Johns Hopkins Press, 1961).
[24] Brooks, pp. 53–54.

be significant, ranging from fifteen or sixteen to as many as thirty or thirty-five. Many more Governors aspire to Senate seats, but often their path is blocked by incumbents (who may also be former Governors), especially in States in which there is an established pattern of re-electing incumbent Senators, in part to retain their seniority and committee chairmanships.

The Governors and the President

"Relations between the governors and the White House have been erratic and sometimes discordant," Brooks reports, "but the record is rather clear on one central matter: in their dealings with the President, as with Congress, the governors have often encouraged the national government to preserve or expand its programs, even, on occasion, at the expense of State power. While the governors have been prompt to argue with Presidents over programs which they felt belonged to the States, they have also urged Presidents to keep other responsibilities off the shoulders of the States." [25]

In the last half century, most Presidents and presidential candidates have been either Governors or former Governors. Consequently, the Governors of New York and, more recently, California are almost automatically regarded as presidential possibilities, and the Governors of many other States may be—Illinois, Michigan, New Jersey, Ohio, or Kansas, though Kansas does not have a large number of electoral votes. The relationship between the Governorship and eligibility for presidential candidacy is discussed in Chapter VIII.

Brooks reports that three Presidents have personally addressed the Governors' Conference in regular sessions: Theodore Roosevelt in 1908, Taft in 1912, and Eisenhower in 1953 and 1957. President Truman twice accepted invitations to address the Conference, but on both occasions he was forced to cancel his appearance. The same thing happened to President Kennedy in 1961, but Vice-President Johnson appeared in his place. Informal (sometimes social) contacts between Presidents and Governors have been much more numerous. "On eleven occasions the Governors' Conference has been asked by the President to a special White House meeting." Since its initial meeting in 1908 with President Roosevelt to discuss conservation, the Conference has met at the White House on numerous occasions: with President Taft to discuss rural credits, without achieving any significant result; with President Wilson in 1919 to discuss problems of postwar reconstruction; with President

[25] Brooks, p. 88.

Harding in 1922; with President Coolidge in 1923; several times with President Roosevelt; and several times with President Eisenhower.[26]

The Brooks study considers other aspects of the Governorship—its international dimension, its partisan role, and its position at mid-century. Each of these aspects will be discussed later at appropriate places. Suffice it to note at this point that the rigid separatism that for so long characterized much of the thinking on problems of American federalism has, in the opinion of this writer, fortunately given way to the more practical and workable concept of cooperative federalism.

CHANGING PATTERNS OF EXECUTIVE COOPERATION

There are many ways in which, in the normal course of operations, the administrative departments and agencies of the Executive Branch of the Federal government can and do influence State and local government. Some of these actions are specifically designed to exert pressure on the States to raise standards or to improve administration, while others only incidentally have this effect. Perhaps most significant have been the budgetary lever and the Federal pressure upon the States to establish and properly administer merit systems for personnel engaged in federally aided programs in health and welfare. Federal agencies also influence State administrations by setting standards and by using various other administrative techniques.

There are encouraging signs that Federal-State cooperation at the highest levels is becoming the common procedure in dealing with difficult problems. Daily papers provide frequent illustrations. For example, on May 9, 1961, it was reported that President Kennedy had held a conference with the Governors of eight States in the Appalachian area for the purpose of focusing attention upon the economic problems of that depressed area, including the financing of highways and education and the conservation of water and timber resources. An Area Redevelopment Administration was organized to deal with the problems of the area, the first such body to be established under the Depressed Area Act of 1961. At the conclusion of the meeting, the President's statement emphasized the importance of the innovation, and urged expansion of the program for retraining unemployed workers and reviewing Defense Department policies in placing contracts in areas of substantial unemployment. An advisory group of the Appalachian Governors' Conference was organized

---

[26] Brooks, Chapter 5.

to work closely with the new Federal agency. These cooperative executive arrangements provide a basis for hoping that the benefits envisioned by Congress when it enacted the Depressed Area Act may be realized.

IOWA STATE DEPARTMENT OF HEALTH
UNIFORM STAMP FOR VACCINATION CERTIFICATE *

On June 22, 1961, the United States Public Health Service notified all state and territorial health officers that a uniform type of stamp for authenticating International Certificates of Vaccination against smallpox and cholera was to be adopted throughout the fifty states of the union. This newly approved stamp is to replace all stamps now in use. The stamp illustrated here is the stamp to be used in Creston, Union County, Iowa:

Official Vaccination

Iowa

14   175   240

U.S.A.

Throughout the fifty states, the first and last lines of the stamp will be the same. The second line in all instances bears the name of the state. The third line will vary, based upon the National Numerical Code for states, counties and cities of the United States. According to this Code, Iowa is 14, Union County is 175 and the city of Creston 240.

The new stamp is to be used by the local health officer who must be a licensed physician. It is to be prepared and issued to the local health officer by the State Department of Health. All stamps antedating this new stamp are to become void.

Copies of this notification are being sent to all county medical societies and all health officers. The new stamp will be issued to the local health officer upon his request to the Iowa State Department of Health. Upon receipt of such application, together with a remittance of $2.00 (to cover costs of the stamp), the stamp with the proper identifying data will be sent.

* Iowa State Department of Health.

All of the larger Federal departments and agencies have field establishments; some of them are so extensive as to form a network of field offices that literally blankets the country. The presence of numerous field officers and installations affects State and local government in many ways. The numerous contacts with State personnel and State agencies which their presence makes possible can be utilized for cooperative effort, may be wasted through non-use, or may be permitted to degenerate into an attitude of suspicion or friction. For instance, every State has its own agency and program for industrial development. Similarly, every city, and many counties as well, are organized to attract new industry and to get their share of tourist trade profit. What happens, then, when the Small Business Administration establishes a field office in a small city in which, presumably, State and local programs are already functioning in the same field?

To answer this question, numerous illustrations of cooperation might be cited from the Department of Agriculture, pioneer in the field, and from all three functional areas within the Department of Health, Education, and Welfare. Only three are selected for discussion here. Agencies like the Veterans Administration and the Bureau of Employment Security have recently shown an awareness of the possibilities of using field contacts as a means of fostering cooperation and integrating the efforts of Federal and State people administering parallel or related programs in the same geographical area. Both of these Agencies recently included intergovernmental relations in their management training programs for supervisory personnel. In addition, agencies like the Food and Drug Administration and the Public Health Service (see illustration page 188) in the Department of Health, Education, and Welfare, and the Bureau of Labor Statistics in the Department of Labor are both continuing to utilize close working relationships with State personnel that have been built up over a period of many years.

Food and Drug Administration

The high degree of Federal-State cooperation in the field of food and drug administration has long been recognized and discussed.[27] The matter is considered here partly because of the pioneer work done in this field, and partly because it offers an exceptionally good illustration of the mechanics of effective cooperative effort. Both levels of government were alerted to the seriousness of the problem of food and drug regulation by the Department of Agriculture exhibit at the World's Fair in St.

[27] See Conover, Milton, "National, State, and Local Cooperation in Food and Drug Control," *American Political Science Review*, November, 1928, pp. 910–928. See also Christopher, Thomas W., "Conflicts Between State and Federal Food and Drug Laws," *Food Drug Cosmetic Law Journal*, March, 1961, pp. 164–168; Harper, Harold, "The Impact of Federal Law Upon State Law in the Field of Food and Drugs," *ibid.*, May, 1957, pp. 263–270; Laschever, Richard, "Commerce Clause," *ibid.*, March, 1956, pp. 163–173; and W. Brooke Graves, *Uniform State Action* (Chapel Hill: University of North Carolina Press, 1934), pp. 99–105.

Louis in 1904.[28] Several States already had official agencies for this purpose when the Federal law was enacted on June 30, 1906.

Cooperation between State and Nation began very early, for the Department of Agriculture was emphasizing this aspect of its work half a century ago.

> The Food and Drug Administration maintains close cooperation with State and municipal officials, who enforce laws regulating, within their respective jurisdictions, the manufacture and sale of foods, feeding stuffs, drugs, insecticides, fungicides, and caustic poisons. The Federal officials have jurisdiction over only such of these commodities as enter interstate or foreign commerce or are made, sold, or offered for sale in the District of Columbia or the Territories of the United States. They have no jurisdiction over those articles which are produced and sold within the confines of a single State. Most or all of the States, however, have laws covering some or all of these products, similar in many respects to the Federal Acts and designed to afford the same protection to the several States that the Federal Acts do to the Nation at large.
>
> The Office of Cooperation, established in 1913, is designed to promote effective cooperation and seeks to afford a ready means for the interchange of information among all concerned and to render cooperating officials all possible assistance of a technical or administrative character. In an endeavor to keep in close touch with State and city officials, it has established very definite cooperative relationships with over a hundred departments throughout the United States and in the Dominion of Canada, Puerto Rico, and Hawaii. Through these contacts the administration continually receives advice as to adulteration and misbranding, and through the prompt assistance offered by State and city officials in the collection of official samples and otherwise, it is able more effectively to check adulteration and misbranding than would be possible by acting solely through its own personnel.[29]

In connection with these cooperative efforts, the Department was even then holding national, sectional, regional, and local conferences of dairy, food, and drug officials, and was lending encouragement and assistance to sectional associations of such officials. Numerous small conferences with local officials were held on a quarterly basis for the exchange of information and the discussion of common problems. The cooperative efforts of administrative officers were facilitated in many instances by legislative cooperation. Often the States passed either regulatory acts which were verbatim copies of Federal laws, or put the provi-

---

[28] See Sullivan, Mark, *Our Times*, 5 vols. (New York: Charles Scribner's Sons, 1927), II, 522–525, and Ross, Edward A., *Sin and Society* (New York: The Macmillan Co., 1907) on "long-distance sinning."

[29] Miscellaneous Publication No. 48, Washington, January, 1931, pp. 18–19.

sions of such laws into effect by reference. Occasionally the process was reversed, State legislation influencing that of the Federal government.

In similar fashion, the cooperation of marketing officials was useful in the development of uniform standards for grades, containers, etc., standards which could be accepted and enforced by all levels of government. The very close cooperation of the members of this group enabled them to establish control over the marketing of poultry and poultry products in the New York area, and over the interstate marketing of cheese, honey, grapes, tobacco, and other products. As early as 1914, definite policies for cooperation had been developed by the National Association of Dairy, Food, and Drug Officials for both the Federal government and the States, along the lines indicated in the table on page 192.

Bureau of Labor Statistics

The Employment Statistics Program of the Bureau of Labor Statistics provides an interesting illustration of successful Federal-State cooperation on a fairly long-range basis. Under a basic statute, the Secretary of Labor is authorized to enter into agreements with the several States for the collection of statistical data. Although the program could have been developed on a highly centralized basis, this authorization has been extensively used, the primary purpose being the development of a national system providing at all governmental levels comparable statistics in terms of common concepts, schedules, and sampling and estimating techniques. The cooperative program was initiated and has been encouraged and developed on the theory that the States are closer to the scene and are thus in a better position to maintain samples that are adequate in size and representative of the condition of the business life of the community at any given time. The program immediately increased the technical resources of the Bureau, since each of the State agencies has a technical staff of trained economists and statisticians engaged in operating a research program in connection with their administrative responsibilities. Each has tabulating and other equipment necessary for the handling of the State program. Another very important reason for cooperative effort has been to reduce the demands made upon employers for the reporting of employment information; under the present arrangement, one schedule filed by an employer simultaneously serves the needs of the State, the area, and the national program, the same figures being used at all levels as a basis for estimates.

Nevertheless, the program has developed very slowly, and it has even had some set-backs, due for the most part to fluctuations in appropriations. While the Bureau has been dealing with the States for many years,

FUNCTIONS OF STATE AND NATION IN DAIRY, FOOD, AND DRUG
ADMINISTRATION PROPOSED BY THE ASSOCIATION OF
DAIRY, FOOD, AND DRUG OFFICIALS *

Federal Functions	State Functions
1. That the guaranty legend be abolished.	1. That State officials give to the Federal government information concerning violations of the Food and Drug Act.
2. That a clearing house office be established to make effective policies of cooperation.	2. That State officials give to the Federal government information with respect to official work and investigations.
3. That the USDA offer its information and advice to State officials when needed in their law enforcement work.	3. That State officials make factory inspections and other investigations for Federal agencies when requested.
4. That the Secretary of Agriculture arrange to cooperate fully with the Association of Dairy, Food and Drug Officials.	4. That State officials place their inspection forces at the service of the Federal enforcing agency whenever it may be desirable.
5. That a joint committee be established to formulate and adopt suitable definitions and standards for food and drug products.	5. That State officials prepare circulars of confidential information concerning illegal drug preparations and send them to other State officials and to the Federal officials.
6. That the USDA supply State officials with new methods of analysis which have been approved by the Secretary of Agriculture.	

7. That the USDA furnish State officials with information on violations of the Federal law originating in their respective jurisdictions.

8. That the USDA inspectors report to the proper State officials the violations of State laws coming under their observation.

9. That the USDA give to the proper State officials full information concerning perishable food or drug products shipped from their States in interstate commerce. . . .

10. That the USDA inspectors, at the request of State officials, be instructed to collect samples of intrastate shipments of food and drug products which appear to be illegal and to send them to the State officials concerned.

* Adapted from a bulletin of the Department of Agriculture.

some of them had employment statistics prior to their agreements with the Bureau, and one had a program in operation before the Bureau was created. The first State agreement was made in 1922, approximately forty years ago. By World War II, there were ten such agreements. The early agreements were limited largely to State collection and editing of schedules, and sending the material to Washington. Late in the 1930's, the Bureau began to make some estimates on a percentage basis in its

Washington office, but it was not until 1940 that aggregates, *i.e.,* estimates of total employment, were issued for each State and the District of Columbia. Later, this work was transferred to the regional offices of the Bureau, still using Federal personnel.

Gradually this work was turned over to the States, so that by 1946 there were fifteen cooperating States. From that point on, the program developed rather rapidly until all States and the District of Columbia were included. Probably the most important factor leading to the growth of the program was the establishment in 1935 of the social security system, including both a national system of old age pensions and a Federal-State system of unemployment insurance. A tax deduction (up to 90 per cent of the Federal levy) was permitted upon tax payments under approved State laws. With this inducement, all of the States enacted unemployment insurance laws, so that by the late 1930's every State had such a program. The development of this system, basically designed to pay benefits to unemployed persons, created a source of statistics which had never before existed.

As employers file their tax reports, they are required to report on the number of employees engaged and wages paid. Generally, they file a report every three months showing the total amount of wages paid for the three-month period, the amount of tax, and the number of workers employed during one payroll period of each month. The Bureau believed that this new source of data would provide an excellent basis for bench marks for the national employment series, as well as for the State and local series.

As of 1952, the cost of the program to the Federal government was approximately $1 million a year, but it is doubtless much higher now.[30] The financing arrangements are somewhat complicated. The Federal portion of the cost is borne equally by the Bureau of Labor Statistics and the Bureau of Employment Security. Since the statistics are needed by both, they are able to share the cost. As of 1952, the Federal agreement was with the employment security agency in thirty-nine States. The remaining States each pay part of the cost under negotiated agreements, and the remainder of the cost is paid from BLS funds. Direct cash payments are made to most States, although in some instances, BLS actually assigns Federal employees to the State.

Technical guidance given to the States takes several forms, but all relationships have been formed on a partnership basis. It is the intention of the Bureau to lead the States, not to direct them. Each is provided with a very detailed manual of operations which is revised and supple-

[30] Data supplied by Dudley E. Young of the BLS staff, including technical paper by Robert O. Dorman, *Federal-State Cooperation in the Employment Security Program* (Washington, 1952).

mented from time to time. This is a basic document telling the cooperating States what to do and how to do it. Actual schedules for the collection of data from employers are also provided, and these are revised annually on the basis of extensive consultation with the cooperating State agencies. When the schedules have been developed in final form, BLS prints them for most of the States, and furnishes the States with their supplies for the year.

Perhaps the most important method used in assisting the States and in getting them to prepare valid State and area statistics is through the cooperation of the five regional offices, in each of which there is a small staff of employment analysts who go out and personally visit the State agencies for several days at a time, going over their work, suggesting work sheets to be set up, recommending methods of tabulation, revising samples by the inclusion of new plants [31] to keep them up to date, etc. These men are the Bureau's most important links in dealing with the State agencies, and to them belongs a large portion of the credit for the success of the program. A third method of assistance to the State agencies is through conferences held in Washington and in the regional offices for the discussion of program problems.

All of the States do essentially the same things, yet the problems (and the results) of the program are bound to be quite different in large industrial States from what they are in sparsely settled agricultural States. It takes forty people to do the job in New York, while two can do it in Nevada. In every State, however, large or small, the staff collects schedules from employers every month and edits them to see that the reported data are internally consistent and comparable to that reported for the previous month, thus insuring that the employer has not changed his basis for reporting. In some instances, problems found in the editing process require further inquiry to the employer. From their unemployment insurance records, the States find most of the bench mark materials used in the preparation of State and area estimates.[32]

Although this discussion has, thus far, been confined to the Bureau of Labor Statistics, it is well to remember that cooperative arrangements between the Department of Labor and the States are by no means confined to this one Bureau. A Virginia State reorganization survey, completed in 1961, reports that the State Division of Factory, Institution, and Mercantile Inspection works in close cooperation with Federal Wage-

---

[31] New plants may be spotted from State and local sources, from registration in Washington to pay the unemployment insurance tax, and from the 1800 or more local employment offices.

[32] For current information, see *Major BLS Programs for 1961; A Summary of Their Characteristics* (Washington: Bureau of Labor Statistics, August, 1960).

Hour officials. "The Federal inspectors send reports to the Division of establishments inspected and the Division then inspects the establishments for health and safety and reports its findings to the Wage-Hour Division. The Federal law makes provision for payment of any expenses incurred by the State agency in making the follow-up inspection. The Division, however, has never billed the Federal agency for its services, such inspections being a part of its duties under Virginia law." [33]

Personnel Administration

The response of the State political organizations to the urgent need for sound systems of public personnel administration in modern government has been pitifully slow and inadequate. Although the Federal civil service system is three-quarters of a century old, the record shows that only six States had adopted civil service by 1910, seventeen by 1940, twenty-six by 1950, and thirty-three by 1962. In a few instances, early laws were repealed, later to be replaced by new legislation (as in Arkansas, New Mexico, and Connecticut), or were weakened through the adoption of crippling amendments (as in Michigan) or by judicial interpretation (as in Arizona). Kansas adopted a statute in 1916 that remained inoperative until 1941, when the present constitutional amendment became effective. More progress has been made in the last two decades than in the previous half century, largely due to the exertion of continuing pressure upon the States by the Federal government, through both the Executive and Legislative Branches.

The Social Security Board initially prescribed a civil service requirement as a means of establishing eligibility for State participation in the program. When this aroused criticism in some quarters, Congress was asked to amend, and did amend, the Social Security Act in 1940 to require a merit system in all departments administering federally aided health and welfare programs in all participating States. As a result, all States established a merit system with at least partial coverage of State employees, including at least the large agencies administering federally aided health and welfare programs. Not only has a merit system been in existence in many States for many years, but the processes of administration have been continuously improved and coverage has gradually been extended in many jurisdictions to more employees and more agencies.

Pennsylvania is a case in point. Civil service began in Pennsylvania

[33] Governor's Committee on Organization of the State Government, *Report of the Committee to Study Stimulation and Development of the State's Economy* (Richmond: State Inspection Activities, 1961), Chapter 6.

when, under the insistence of Governor Gifford Pinchot, State Liquor Control Board employees were placed under a merit system in 1933. The State Police were operating under a voluntary merit system of their own. Next, in accordance with Federal requirements, civil service was established in the Unemployment Compensation Division of the Department of Labor and Industry, in the Department of Public Assistance, and in parts of the Department of Health. By executive action in 1956, Governor George M. Leader extended merit system coverage to some 10,000 professional and technical positions. This action caused bitter resentment on the part of many party leaders in the State, although they were unable to supply qualified candidates for a great many of the positions. Over a period of years, approximately one-third of the employees in Pennsylvania have been brought under civil service.

The same type of development has taken place in other States. In Kentucky, Governor Bert T. Combs signed into law in 1960 a measure covering a large part of the State employees, in keeping with an election pledge.[34] The same thing happened in Oklahoma under the leadership of Governor J. Howard Edmondson, when "a fifty-year era of political patronage and over-loaded payrolls" came to an end.[35]

A quarter of a century ago, Dr. Leonard D. White, serving as a member of the Civil Service Commission, suggested the possibility and desirability of Federal-State cooperation in the field of personnel administration. There is much that could be done, though little has actually been accomplished thus far, by way of cooperation in this field. Why should Federal, State, and local agencies, all recruiting, examining, and hiring new employees for necessary common types of work, all in the same geographical area, compete with one another and duplicate one another's efforts? Tests for clerical and stenographic work, for instance, are fairly well standardized. Why shouldn't there be *one* place in St. Louis, for example, where tests are given and scored, eligible lists compiled, and eligibles certified therefrom to *any* government appointing officer in the area—Federal, State, or local—having clerical-secretarial vacancies to be filled? The costs would be greatly reduced because overlapping and duplication of effort would be eliminated. There are many common types of employment for which such cooperation should now be possible, and probably others that could be added after satisfactory working arrangements had been established.

Wendell Willkie reminded Americans in the 1940's that this is "one world"; perhaps they need to be reminded in the 1960's that the United

[34] See Schten, Edward V., "Forward in Kentucky," *National Civic Review*, June, 1960, pp. 302–307.

[35] Stahl, Steve, "A Half-Century of Patronage Ends," *Good Government*, September, 1960, pp. 1–2.

States is "one country." This concept was admirably expressed in the report of the Sixth American Assembly on the Federal Service in 1954:

> The Federal Service should provide both for promotion from within and for the lateral entry of personnel, particularly in the middle and higher grades. It should be open to interchange with the other fields of American life—business, trade unions, universities, the professions, State and local government. Such exchanges benefit both the Federal Service and these groups, and our society is the richer. Efforts to close the door on such interchange should be vigorously resisted.

While the interchange of personnel has great and obvious advantages, there are several obstacles that will have to be overcome. One is the utter lack of uniformity in the requirements for positions and the fact that, in many jurisdictions, there is still no merit system applicable to personnel in executive agencies, other than those administering federally aided health and welfare programs. Low salary schedules in many States—very often the ones that would profit most from such a program—are another factor. The multiplicity of public employee retirement systems and the lack of even a semblance of uniformity among them, even within a single State, is a major obstacle to interchange, to which may be added the probable opposition of the poorer, low salary States which might expect to lose such outstanding employees as they happen to have.

The well-known shortage of qualified professional personnel, on the other hand, is in itself a strong argument for interchange. Often one agency or unit of government has need for a high grade professional man in a given field only occasionally, or only on a part-time basis. It should be possible for such an agency to arrange to borrow a specialist for a limited time, and this without prejudice to the specialist—his status, pay, retirement, or other benefits relating to his regular employment.[36] The agency regularly employing the specialist would be deprived of his services only temporarily, the agency which borrowed him would be greatly benefited, and the specialist himself would have gained additional experience in his field in another work situation. Interchange procedures might first be worked out purely on a loan basis, but they might later be extended to permanent transfer, of course without prejudice to the employment rights of the transferee, after suitable procedures had been developed and perfected.

A small beginning was made under a provision contained in the

[36] For a presentation of many points of view, see a symposium, "What Is Desirable Policy on the Interchange of Personnel?" *Public Personnel Review,* October, 1961, pp. 269–277.

amended Public Health Service Act of 1944,[37] under which the Secretary of Health, Education, and Welfare has authority to place officers in an LWOP status for periods up to two years, and the Surgeon General under contract on a reimbursible basis for an extendable period of one year. Placements may be made upon the request of any State or local health or mental health authority, the detail being authorized for the purpose of assisting such State or political subdivision thereof in work relating to the functions of the Public Health Service. Such personnel are paid from applicable appropriations for the Service, except that in accordance with regulations they may be placed on leave without pay and paid by the State, subdivision, or institution to which they are detailed. The status and personal rights of the detailed officers are specifically protected by the statute: "The services of personnel while detailed pursuant to this section shall be considered as having been performed in the Service (U.S.P.H.S.) for purposes of computation of basic pay, promotion, retirement, compensation for injury or death" and other benefits as provided by law. Although no very extensive use has been made of this authorization,[38] the mere fact that it exists constitutes a precedent for the development of similar arrangements applicable to specialists in other fields.

A further step in the direction of such cooperation was made in 1956 when Congress conferred a similarly limited authority upon the Department of Agriculture, providing for the exchange of employees of the Department and employees of States, their political subdivisions, or educational institutions, for the purpose of aiding the dissemination of information on agricultural subjects, and providing a means for more effective working relationships in agricultural administration.[39] In 1959, the Department proposed to the Committee of State Officials on Suggested State Legislation that this Congressional legislation be implemented and supported by appropriate State legislation.

The Committee of State Officials supported the theory of the Department proposal, but thought that authorization for a more comprehensive employee interchange program would better serve the needs of the States. The Civil Service Commission similarly suggested that the scope of the Act be broadened. The present suggested legislation, the State Employee Interchange Act, is designed to permit departments and agencies of State and local governments to participate in employee interchange programs with the Federal government, as well as with the departments or agencies

[37] 42 U.S.C. 215 (1944).

[38] As of mid-1961, four officers were on LWOP and several more on reimbursible detail. The men on leave were serving with the Pan-American Union, city health departments in Boston and Kansas City, Mo., and the county health department of Allegheny County (Pittsburgh), Pa.

[39] Public Law 918, 84th Cong., 2nd Sess., August 2, 1956; two years later, the Department Office of Personnel issued a brief report on its interchange program.

of other State and local governments within the State or in other States.[40] If any appreciable number of State legislatures react favorably to this proposal and enact it into law, the obvious next step would be a Congressional act extending the HEW-USDA type of authorization to all executive departments and agencies of the Federal government, and facilitating interchanges along the lines provided for in the proposed State statute.

Training is another area in which the possibilities of cooperation are great. The Federal government does have extensive cooperation in this area among its own departments and agencies,[41] and there is some cooperation in some States between the States and their local political subdivisions, but the barriers to Federal-State-local cooperation in this area have as yet been scarcely cracked. The Federal Bureau of Investigation does train law enforcement officers, and the Food and Drug Administration trains enforcement officers in its field, but there are few others.

Some progress in cooperative training was made over two decades ago, under the George-Deen Act of 1936, a vocational training act under which grant-in-aid funds were provided for a number of types of training. By administrative determination, funds were made available to the States from 1937 to 1945 for the training of local government personnel. During these years, great progress was made in many States, until in 1945, suddenly and without cause or justification, the funds were cut off by an adverse ruling of the general counsel of the administering agency.[42] In an effort to restore this type of program on a permanent basis, a bill was introduced in the 87th Congress by Representative Gonzalez of Texas (H.R. 13305) and again in the 88th Congress (H.R. 4561).

BIBLIOGRAPHICAL NOTES

Three very old treatises on the American executive, long standard and still useful, are Charles C. Thatch, Jr., *The Creation of the Presidency, 1775–1789: A Study*

[40] *Program of Suggested State Legislation, 1962* (Chicago: Council of State Governments, November, 1961), pp. 46–51.

[41] U.S. Civil Service Commission, *Interagency Training Programs, Spring, 1961—February–July* (Washington, 1961).

[42] For the full story of this interesting episode, see W. Brooke Graves, "Public Service Training for Local Government Personnel," *The County Officer*, February, 1960, pp. 53–56. For a summary of a fairly recent survey of State activity in this field, see Graves, "An Intergovernmental Attack on Local Training Needs," *Personnel Administration*, May–June, 1959, pp. 30–38.

in Constitutional History (Baltimore: Johns Hopkins Press, 1922); John H. Finley and John S. Sanderson, *The American Executive and Executive Methods* (New York: The Century Company, 1908); and John A. Fairlie, *The National Executive in the United States of America* (New York: The Macmillan Co., 1920).

The Presidency. Out of an enormous and constantly increasing literature on the Presidency, the following titles are most helpful on questions discussed in this chapter: Wilfred E. Binkley, *Powers of the President* (New York: Alfred A. Knopf, Inc., 1937); Edward S. Corwin, *The President: Office and Powers* (New York: New York University Press, 1948, rev. ed. with Louis W. Koenig, 1956); Sidney Hyman, *The American President* (New York: Harper & Brothers, 1954); Clinton L. Rossiter, *The American Presidency* (New York: Harcourt, Brace & Co., Inc., 1956); and A. Merriman Smith, *A President Is Many Men* (New York: Harper & Brothers, 1948). Three significant symposia on the Presidency are available in professional journals: Sidney Hyman, ed., "The Office of the Presidency," *Annals of the American Academy of Political and Social Science,* September, 1956; J. Francis Pachal, ed., "The Presidential Office," *Law and Contemporary Problems,* Autumn, 1956; and Robert S. Rankin, "The Presidency in Transition," *Journal of Politics,* February, 1948 (and in book form, Gainesville: Kallam Publishing Company, 1949).

Richard E. Neustadt, *Presidential Power: The Politics of Leadership* (New York: John Wiley & Sons, Inc., 1960) is concerned, not with the President's powers as such, but with the ways in which the occupant of the White House at any given time goes about the task of making his influence effective. Although Richard P. Longaker, *The Presidency and Civil Liberties* (Ithaca: Cornell University Press, 1961) centers attention on civil liberties (discussed in this volume in Chapter IX), there is much discussion of the role and responsibility of the President in policy determination.

The Governorship. Four general works give a clear picture of the evolution of the office: Leslie Lipson, *The American Governor: From Figurehead to Leader* (Chicago: University of Chicago Press, 1939); Coleman B. Ransone, Jr., *The Office of the Governor in the South* (University: Bureau of Public Administration, University of Alabama, 1951) and *The Office of Governor in the United States* (University: University of Alabama Press, 1956); and Glenn E. Brooks, *When Governors Convene: The Governors' Conference and National Politics* (Baltimore: Johns Hopkins Press, 1961).

There appears to be a stronger tendency to think about Federal-State executive relations in wartime than in peacetime. There is a good study of wartime relationships in William Hesseltine, *Lincoln and the War Governors* (New York: Alfred A. Knopf, Inc., 1948). For a brief sketch of executive relationships during World War II, see W. Brooke Graves, *American State Government,* 3rd ed. (Boston: D. C. Heath and Co., 1946), Chapter 24. On executive relationships in peacetime, there are a few books and numerous articles on cooperation in individual functional fields: Carleton R. Ball, *Federal, State, and Local Relationships in Agriculture,* 2 vols. (Berkeley: University of California Press, 1938); Gladys Baker, *The County Agent* (Chicago: University of Chicago Press, 1938); and Jane Perry Clark (Carey), *The Rise of a New Federalism: Federal-State Cooperation in the United States* (New York: Columbia University Press, 1938).

CHAPTER VII

Judicial Relations
in Federalism

The outstanding development in Federal-State relations since the adoption of the national Constitution has been the expansion of the power of the national government and the relative contraction of the powers of the State governments. . . . Second only to the increasing dominance of the national government has been the development of the immense power of the Supreme Court in both state and national affairs.

The Conference of Chief Justices, in December 1957, appointed a committee to consider Federal-State relationships as affected by judicial decisions (specifically, decisions of the Supreme Court). The Committee concluded that "the overall tendency of decisions of the Supreme Court over the last twenty-five years or more has been to press the extension of Federal power and to press it rapidly"; that the Court has "exercised policymaking powers going far beyond those involved in making a selection between competing rules of law"; and "too often has tended to adopt the role of policy-maker without proper judicial restraint" particularly in "the extent and extension of the Federal power and the supervision of State action by the Supreme Court in virtue of the Fourteenth Amendment." [1]

[1] Conference of Chief Justices, *Report of the Committee on Federal-State Relationships as Affected by Judicial Decisions* (Chicago: Council of State Governments, August, 1958). Reprinted, *Congressional Record*, August 25, 1958, pp. A7782–A7788.

JUDICIAL STRUCTURE AND PROCEDURE

Separate Federal and State Courts

It will be recalled that no separate national judiciary had been provided for under the Articles of Confederation, an omission which is usually counted among the serious weaknesses of that document. This may be accounted for partly by the fact that the judiciary as a separate branch of government had not at that time become as firmly established as the Executive and Legislative Branches, and partly by the fact that it was generally believed that a separate system of national courts would involve needless duplication as long as State courts were available to interpret and enforce the Federal law.

Although this method of handling the problem left much to be desired, the case for a separate system of national courts was by no means clear cut. The delegates to the Constitutional Convention in Philadelphia were still seriously tempted to continue the same arrangements in the new constitution. The fundamental question was, Should the State courts be relied upon to do the whole job, for original jurisdiction, with appeal to a national supreme court, or should a completely independent national judiciary be established?

It was only after serious consideration and prolonged debate that the delegates concluded that, for several reasons, a separate system of national courts was necessary. Without such a system, it would be virtually impossible to obtain a uniform interpretation of the Federal Constitution, laws, and treaties from the courts of the several States. National courts would be essential to consider cases involving citizens of different States, cases in which neither party would be willing to entrust enforcement of his rights to the courts of his opponent's State. National courts were deemed necessary to maintain national control over national affairs, and there was the fear that the State courts, given the opportunity, would do what, in fact, the Federal courts have done, *i.e.*, show favoritism toward their own unit or level of government as against the other. Furthermore, there was a need for national courts to handle land claims and Indian questions.[2] Channing adds the thought that the Federal judiciary had been established, at least in part, to compel the payment of debts by the people in one part of the country to creditors living in other parts or in other countries.

Thus, the decision was made to establish a separate system of Federal

[2] Young, James T., *The New American Government and Its Work*, 3rd ed. (New York: The Macmillan Co., 1933), p. 162.

courts, with the result that there are in the country two complete and parallel judicial systems, each exercising jurisdiction simultaneously over the same territory and the same people, normally without conflict, certainly without any serious conflict. Unlike Congress and the various executive offices which had existed in some form before the Constitution was drafted, the judiciary was the creation of the members of the Constitutional Convention and of the Constitution which they framed. The language of the Constitution, however, provides only for a Supreme Court and "such inferior courts as the Congress may from time to time ordain and establish," thereby leaving to the discretion of Congress the whole question of the organization of the judiciary. This language did not require Congress to establish, nor does it require Congress now to retain, any Federal tribunals in addition to the Supreme Court. If Congress were to abolish the United States District Courts and Circuit Courts of Appeal —which under present conditions is scarcely conceivable—the remaining judicial structure would, in formal outline, resemble that of Brazil.

The framework of the Federal judicial system was established in the Judiciary Act of 1789, which remained in effect in substantially its original form until 1911, when it was thoroughly revised and rewritten. The only significant exception was the creation in 1891 of an additional level of circuit courts; these were abolished twenty years later, in the interest of simplification, leaving the Circuit Courts of Appeal, as they are today, the only Federal courts of intermediate status. The decisions made by the Convention and the first Congress to provide for a strong Federal judiciary were of immense importance in the development of American nationalism, and under the Federalists, rapid extension of the activity and jurisdiction of the United States courts continued.

Jurisdictional Problems

As Leland G. Tolman has pointed out, the American system of law and the administration of justice is probably the most complicated in the world. There are complete and completely separate systems of courts exercising jurisdiction over all citizens simultaneously, wherever they may happen to live. Although there are areas of concurrent or overlapping jurisdiction and frequent questions with respect to jurisdiction in diversity of citizenship and other types of cases, the two systems ordinarily function side by side with a good deal of cooperation and a minimum amount of friction and misunderstanding.

The successful operation of a federal system requires coordinated action by the central and divisional governments, and this coordination is quite as important in the judicial field as it is in other areas of government. Where it is possible to assign sole responsibility for a given activity to one unit or level of government, the assignment must be made according to accepted standards. Where it is necessary for Nation and State to operate concurrently, care must be taken to minimize the possibilities of conflict. The administration of justice is a function of all courts, but as one writer has observed, "Our judiciaries cannot accomplish their assigned tasks unless they are sure of the extent of their jurisdiction and of the ways in which they are to exercise it. Moreover, the people who rely on the courts for the protection of their rights must know which judicial system—State or Federal—is equipped to hear each grievance as it arises and to make a generalized law come alive by applying it to specific situations." [3]

Not only is the judicial structure complicated, but the system of laws which these courts are obliged to enforce is even more intricate. The Federal Constitution, laws, and treaties are "the supreme law of the land." In addition, there are court decisions and the writings of legal scholars which frequently have influence if not authority. At the State level there are constitutions, laws, and court decisions, and at the local level charters, ordinances, and more court decisions, not to mention books and articles on the law. As Mr. Tolman observes:

> . . . It is a system where constitutionally independent courts of the Nation operate side by side—and often in identical matters—with the separate court system of each of the sovereign forty-eight [now fifty] States; where Federal courts administer State Law and State courts administer Federal law; where the very essence of federalism, the areas where Federal and State law touch and overlap, is made integral in the national judicial structure to a degree greater than in any other federated government.[4]

The Federal courts in general, and the Supreme Court in particular, have to deal with difficult questions in a wide variety of highly controversial fields, such as loyalty regulations, the right to restrict passports, interpretation of voting rights, and some aspects of the labor laws. One area that greatly interests the general public is the drawing of boundaries between Federal and State authority. Another often related area involves boundaries between the rights of individuals and the rights of the government. The extent to which Supreme Court decisions may affect local and domestic policies within the States is well illustrated by

[3] Wendell, Mitchell, *Relations Between the Federal and State Courts* (New York: Columbia University Press, 1949), pp. 22–23.

[4] Tolman, Leland G., *Columbia Law Review*, April, 1954, pp. 650–657, a book review.

the school desegregation decision handed down on May 17, 1954.[5] About a year later, on May 31, 1955, the Court's decree ordered Federal courts to determine in each case how best to end segregation.

At this point, one may observe a very interesting coincidence. On May 17, 1954, on the same day that the Brown Case was decided, the Court decided another somewhat similar case.[6] Both involved school segregation, and both ordered integration. The differences, however, are quite as interesting as the similarities and for present purposes, more significant. In the Brown Case, the problem was a State one, the decision involving equal protection—or the denial thereof—under Section 1 of the Fourteenth Amendment; in the Bolling Case, the jurisdiction was Federal and the decision hinged upon the application of the Fifth Amendment. The difference is clearly stated in the following paragraph from the opinion written by Chief Justice Warren:

> We have this day held that the Equal Protection Clause of the Fourteenth Amendment prohibits the States from maintaining racially segregated public schools. The legal problem in the District of Columbia is somewhat different, however. The Fifth Amendment, which is applicable in the District of Columbia, does not contain an equal protection clause as does the Fourteenth Amendment which applies only to the States. But the concepts of equal protection and due process, both stemming from our American ideal of fairness, are not mutually exclusive. The "equal protection of the laws" is a more explicit safeguard of prohibited unfairness than "due process of law," and, therefore, we do not imply that the two are always interchangeable phrases. But, as this Court has recognized, discrimination may be so unjustifiable as to be violative of due process.

Concurrent Jurisdiction. Concurrent jurisdiction exists when a given case may with equal propriety be heard in either a Federal or a State court. There are actually a good many such cases. During the life of the Eighteenth Amendment, there were large numbers of cases in which the same individual could be prosecuted, convicted, and sentenced for the same acts, separately and independently, in both the Federal and State courts. In such situations, it became a matter of practice for the Federal government to take precedence over the State, although if the Federal government failed to secure a conviction, it was still possible for the State concerned to attempt to do so. Control over citizenship illustrates concurrent jurisdiction in the civil field. Federal law provides that citizenship may be granted either by the Federal courts or by a State

---

[5] *Brown v. Board of Education of Topeka*, 347 U.S. 483 (1954).

[6] *Bolling v. Sharpe*, 347 U.S. 497 (1954).

court of record. Although the Federal government possesses full power to control this subject, the greatest diversity is permitted with respect to the conditions under which citizenship is conferred.

If the case hinges on a question involving the Federal Constitution or a Federal statute, either court will be guided by these provisions in making a decision, or by court decisions relating to the matter. The question arises as to whether the State courts will follow their own normal procedures, or whether they must adapt their procedure to meet Federal requirements. If the case hinges on a provision of State law and is tried in a State court, the court will similarly be guided by the provisions of the law as interpreted by the courts. These observations are rather obvious, but suppose the case hinges on a provision of State law and is tried in a Federal court. Will the Federal court, in making its decision, be guided by "the rule of law that would be applied by the courts of the State in which the Federal court is sitting, or by some other rule of law that the Federal court thinks preferable"?

This is a difficult question to answer, and one can only recite briefly what the history has been. Section 34 of the Judiciary Act of 1789 provides that, in diversity cases at common law, the laws of the several States should be the rules of decision in the Federal courts. However, in *Swift* v. *Tyson*,[7] the Supreme Court refused to apply this section on the ground that it did not extend to contracts or instruments of a commercial nature, the interpretation of which ought to be in accordance with "the general principles and doctrine of jurisprudence"; and while the decisions of the State courts on such subjects were entitled to and would receive attention and respect, they could not be conclusive or binding upon the Federal courts.

Originally limited to questions of general commercial law, this doctrine was gradually expanded to cover almost the entire subject matter of the common law. As viewed in the perspective of time, as Justice Schaefer has observed, this "experiment in nation-wide uniformity [had] a long and lusty life"[8] of almost a century, until in 1938 it was overruled in *Erie Railroad* v. *Tompkins*.[9] In this case, which laid a legal basis for "a more modest uniformity," it was held that a Federal court must decide diversity cases in accordance with those rules of substantive law that

[7] *Swift* v. *Tyson*, 16 Peters 1 (1842); for a good discussion, see Frank, John P., "Historical Bases of the Federal Judicial System," *Law and Contemporary Problems*, Winter, 1948, pp. 3–28.

[8] Schaefer, Walter V., *Courts and the Commonplaces of Federalism* (Urbana: University of Illinois Bulletin, 1959), p. 6; this excellent paper was the 1959 Edmund J. James Lecture on Government. See also Wendell, Chapters 6–8.

[9] *Erie Railroad* v. *Tompkins*, 304 U.S. 64 (1938); see Wendell, Chapters 9–11.

would be applied by the courts of the State in which the Federal court was sitting. This represented a major change in American law, as well as *"a major shift of power from the Federal courts to the State courts"* (italics supplied).

Jurisdiction in Diversity Cases. So-called diversity cases arise under the constitutional provision extending jurisdiction of the Federal courts to controversies between citizens of different States, or where cases arising under Federal law are tried in State courts. In all such cases, as well as in those arising under the Federal Employers' Liability Act (which governs the rights of injured railroad men, instead of the workmen's compensation act of the State concerned), the goal of the Supreme Court is to attain uniformity of result whether the case is tried in a State court or a Federal court. This objective would be relatively easy to accomplish if all cases could be tried in the courts of the sovereignty that established the governing principles of substantive law, but in a federal system such as ours this is not practical. It may not even be possible. While the main question at the Federal level is one of uniformity, that at the State level involves the right of the State to maintain its own rules and to render judgment against a citizen or a corporation of another State.[10]

The effects of the *Erie Railroad* v. *Tompkins* decision were immediate and widespread, and productive of a vast amount of confusion which, nearly a quarter of a century later, has not been entirely dissipated. In fact, it is asserted that "perplexing problems of Federal-State relations continue to stem from it." [11] The decision did much more than merely overrule *Swift* v. *Tyson*. It swept away a tremendous mass of precedents which the Federal courts had developed in the decision of cases at common law, greatly limiting the scope of that law and resulting in the application of the rules of substantive law of the States to many matters. In spite of the inconvenience and annoyance involved in adjustment to change, it was estimated ten years later that there was "general agreement with the aim of *Erie Railroad* v. *Tompkins*." All would agree that "the exercise of legislative power by the States is an essential feature of our federal system. In order to make this State power meaningful, it would seem only natural that the States should exert control over the content of their own laws." [12]

[10] See Phillips, Orie L., and Christenson, A. Sherman, "The Historical and Legal Background of the Diversity Jurisdiction," *American Bar Association Journal,* September, 1960, pp. 959–965.

[11] Friedelbaum, Stanley H., "The Warren Court and American Federalism: A Preliminary Appraisal," *University of Chicago Law Review,* Autumn, 1960, pp. 53–87.

[12] Wendell, Chapter 11, p. 224; that this is still a "touchy" subject is attested by the comment of a friend who read this chapter. He notes that the late Justice Arthur H. Vanderbilt regarded the Erie Case as a setback to the

Removals From State to Federal Courts. The determination of jurisdiction through the normal operation of the provisions of the Constitution may be modified when the provisions of certain acts of Congress, notably the Removal Act of 1875, are invoked. Under the terms of this legislation, defendants have the right in nearly all civil cases within the original jurisdiction of a United States District Court to remove their cases from State to Federal courts. With the specific exception of certain types of cases, such as diversity cases, claims cases arising under the Federal Employers' Liability Act, or for damages resulting from delay or loss or injury to goods shipped by rail, the present law provides that any civil action brought in a State court over which the District Courts of the United States have original jurisdiction may be so removed. There has been much uncertainty as to the removability of cases under the Fair Labor Standards Act. Actually, the number of cases involved in a single State is not very great; a Minnesota study covering the five-year period from 1942 to 1946 inclusive showed that the number of cases annually was less than 100, and that these constituted between one-fourth and one-third of the total number of private civil cases reported.[13]

LAWS OF ONE JURISDICTION IN THE COURTS OF THE OTHER

The States and State Laws in United States Courts

The States as Litigants. Mention has been made of this problem in Chapter IV. The provisions of the Constitution on the judiciary, and the Judiciary Act of 1789, designed to implement them, assumed that when necessary the States would appear as litigants in the Federal courts like other litigants. When in 1793 the Supreme Court proceeded on this basis, its decision in *Chisholm* v. *Georgia* [14] created such a furor that Congress lost no time in proposing, or the States in ratifying, a constitutional amendment providing that no State without its consent should be compelled to appear in court as a defendant. The theory was that requiring a State to appear like an ordinary individual was an inexcusable

movement toward a sort of common law for the United States. He, like Munro Smith with whom he had studied, was greatly impressed with the development of great national systems of law from fragmented, tribal beginnings, and he undoubtedly would have preferred to see development in this country toward one unified system rather than toward a series of disparate systems.

[13] See Talbott, Forrest, *Intergovernmental Relations and the Courts* (Minneapolis: University of Minnesota Press, 1950), Chapter 5 of which considers the nature and scope of the removal problem.

[14] *Chisholm* v. *Georgia*, 2 Dallas 419 (1793).

affront to its dignity and sovereignty. Since then, times and public reactions to the problem have changed greatly. All States and the Federal government as well have passed legislation authorizing suits against them, under specified conditions. If the same question were to arise now, it would create no problem.

The Federal Courts and State Statutes. The overwhelming majority of the cases arising in Federal District Courts have their causes of action in national laws, but State laws may be involved both in cases to which the United States is a party and in private cases in which the primary question is one of State law. In the Minnesota study cited previously, it was found that between 1942 and 1946 inclusive, only twenty-six out of 195 published opinions of Federal District Court judges in the State concerned Minnesota law as the principal question and only thirteen as a secondary question. There were only five cases in which a Minnesota State agency or a subdivision thereof was a party, and two opinions concerned the law of another State. The remaining 148 were exclusively concerned with issues under Federal law, and Federal law was the primary question in twelve.[15]

Although it has long been a part of our system that State statutes may be reviewed by the Supreme Court where questions of constitutionality are involved, this was not true in the early days of the Republic. Warren reports that "Between 1789 and 1860, the courts of seven States denied the constitutional right of the Supreme Court to decide cases on writs of error to State courts—California, Georgia, Kentucky, Ohio, South Carolina, Virginia, and Wisconsin. The Legislatures of all these States (except California), and also of Maryland and Pennsylvania, formally adopted resolutions or statutes against this power of the Supreme Court. Bills were introduced in Congress on at least ten occasions to deprive the Court of its jurisdiction—in 1821, 1822, 1824, 1831, 1846, 1867, 1868, 1871, 1872, and 1882." [16]

In reviewing State statutes, the general attitude of the Supreme Court has been understanding and sympathetic. The Court has assumed that a problem existed, otherwise the legislature would not have acted. If action taken in relation to the problem before them appeared reasonable, justifiably based on fact, every presumption has been in favor of the enactment. In addition, the Federal courts have normally accepted the

---

[15] See Talbott, Chapter 7, for a listing and discussion of the various types of cases considered.

[16] Warren, Charles, "Legislative and Judicial Attacks on the Supreme Court of the United States: A History of the Twenty-Fifth Section of the Judiciary Act," *American Law Review*, January–February, 1913, pp. 3–4, quoted in Hart, Henry M., Jr., and Wechsler, Herbert, *The Federal Courts and the Federal System* (New York: Ziff-Davis Publishing Co., 1953), pp. 418–419.

interpretation of a State statute adopted by the highest State court, the theory being that the States were in a better position to judge the purpose and intent of their own legislatures than the Federal courts could possibly be. The question before the Federal court in cases of this sort is not, therefore, whether the State law as they read it is constitutional, but whether the State law as understood and interpreted by the State court is within the limits of State power, so far as the provisions of the Federal Constitution are concerned.

To state this concept in another way, the Supreme Court will interfere with a decision of a State court only when, in its judgment, the State ruling amounts to mere arbitrary or capricious exercise of power, or is in clear conflict with those fundamental principles which have been established for the protection and enforcement of private rights.[17] Strong objection has been raised, however, to the Supreme Court's "ordering a Federal ruling deferred until the States have spoken," because, if for no other reason, the delay so imposed on many litigants might defeat the ends of justice.[18] In recent years, a considerable number of cases involving various aspects of this question have come before the Supreme Court.

In the discussion of diversity jurisdiction, now claimed to be unnecessary, mention has been made of the *Swift* v. *Tyson* and *Erie Railroad* v. *Tompkins* decisions. Under the new rule, the Federal courts no longer have the authority to make local law. Judicial decisions, like statute law, are now "laws of the several States." The heart of the new doctrine is that the choice of a forum, whether Federal or State, should not be permitted to lead to a substantially different result. The abandonment of the old general law philosophy and the adoption of a new approach imposed upon the Federal courts and ultimately upon the Supreme Court a responsibility for formulating rules and procedures compatible therewith. Although some answers have been supplied in the two decades since the Erie decision was handed down, other questions affecting the federal system still remain to be answered.[19]

[17] See Jacobson, J. Mark, "Federal Interpretation of State Law," *University of Pennsylvania Law Review*, February, 1938, pp. 335–369, and cases therein cited.

[18] For discussion, see Cardozo, Michael H., "Choosing and Declaring State Law: Deference to State Courts Versus Federal Responsibility," *Northwestern University Law Review*, September-October, 1960, pp. 419–436, and Mr. Justice Douglas' dissent in *Clay* v. *Sun Insurance Office Limited*, 363 U.S. 207 (1960).

[19] For discussion, see Corwin, Edward S., ed., *The Constitution of the United States of America*, rev. and annotated (Washington: Senate Document No. 170, 82nd Cong., 2nd Sess., 1952), pp. 605–608; Pritchett, C. Herman, *The American Constitution* (New York: McGraw-Hill Book Co., Inc., 1959), pp. 124–126; and Hill, Alfred, "The Erie Doctrine and the Constitution," *Northwestern University Law Review*, September–October, 1958, pp. 427–456, and November–December, 1958, pp. 541–609.

United States Laws in State and Local Courts

It comes as a surprise to most people when they learn of the extent to which the State courts in the regular course of business not only try civil cases under laws passed by Congress, but render assistance in the administration of many others. Thus, during World War II, State courts handled many cases under the Federal Fair Employment Practices and national rent control regulations, and in more normal times they handle large numbers of cases involving Indians, cases arising under the Federal Employers' Liability Act, naturalization cases, and many more. Further interrelationships develop when State district courts receive and transmit passport applications to the Department of State, and when they probate wills of veterans and participate in the settling of the estates of veterans and their dependents for the Veterans Administration.

In his survey of Federal-State judicial relations in Minnesota a number of years ago, Talbott pointed out that few of these types of cases are simple, common law adversary proceedings in which the government merely provides the forum, but that many cases involve problems of administration as well as adjudication. In the latter instance, he explains, the Federal government is definitely interested in the outcome and in the manner in which the cases are handled:

> The Immigration and Naturalization Service practically directs the naturalization process; the Veterans Administration keeps a close watch on guardianships and commitments for incompetent veterans; the rent control officials go so far as to call the local judges together to instruct them concerning new rent laws and regulations. This sounds like the administration process, not the judicial. And when we realize that the national administration in all its might is the promoter and director of the service, we are not surprised to see it selecting the courts that it wishes to use for its own convenience, as in the naturalization process, and instructing them in their work, as in rent control, although it cannot control their decisions. In some fields the national government is, of course, paying at least in part for the services it is getting from the State courts, as in naturalization proceedings, but mostly it is merely using these local tribunals for its own purposes.[20]

Normal Appeals Procedures

Basically, there are only two types of cases in which appeals from State to Federal courts may be regarded as a matter of right. These are

[20] Talbott, Chapter 8.

when the highest State court, in cases involving a Federal question, has declared either a challenged State statute valid or a challenged Federal statute invalid. Since no appeal lies from a lower State court under any circumstances, it is necessary to delay an appeal until the highest State court has spoken. Then the appeal goes directly to the Supreme Court, because an appeal to any lower Federal court would not be in keeping with the sovereign dignity of a State.

Since there are so few cases in which appeal is a matter of right, a litigant seeking Supreme Court review of a State case usually invokes the Court's discretionary certiorari jurisdiction.[21] Moreover, relatively few of these cases are accepted by the Court, as Mr. Justice Brennan has explained:

> Crucial to the exercise of our certiorari jurisdiction is whether the controlling issue in the State court case is a Federal issue, that is, an issue arising under the United States Constitution or under Federal laws or treaties. But the fact that a Federal question lurks in the case doesn't mean, standing alone, that a State decision will be reviewed. *First,* the Federal question must be a substantial question. *Second,* the Federal question must have been properly raised in the State courts. This is required because the State courts must first be afforded an opportunity to consider and decide the Federal question. *Third,* even then we may not take the case if the State court's judgment can be sustained on an independent ground of State law. . . .[22]

In the 1958–1959 Term of the Court, 792 cases were presented for review and were acted upon by the Court. Nine out of ten cases were rejected—734 or 93 per cent—meaning that the Court was able to find only fifty-eight State court decisions on Federal questions which seemed to justify its inquiry into the merits of their disposition by the State courts. The Supreme Court heard and decided thirty of these cases from seventeen States, affirming the State judgments in thirteen and reversing them in seventeen. The highest number from any one State court was six; only a single case came from each of ten States. Although a minimum of five votes is necessary to constitute a majority in deciding a case, four votes are sufficient to assure a review of the merits in a case on certiorari.

[21] In Minnesota, for example, between 1933 and 1948, there were twenty-five petitions for writs of certiorari, of which six were granted (four affirmed, two reversed) and nineteen denied; sixteen appeals, of which eight were accepted (seven affirmed, one reversed) and eight dismissed. These cases may be classified as Fourteenth Amendment cases, interpretation of national statutes, tax immunity, domicile for tax purposes, obligation of contracts, interstate commerce, and miscellaneous. See Talbott, Chapter 6.

[22] Brennan, William J., Jr., "State Court Decisions and the Supreme Court," *Pennsylvania Bar Association Quarterly,* June, 1960, pp. 393-407.

Denial of certiorari is not to be interpreted, however, as affirmation of the State court, or as an indication that the Supreme Court agrees with the result. An application is frequently denied even though the Court believes that the State court's result was quite wrong.

SUPREMACY OF THE FEDERAL COURTS

Early Developments

The concept of a powerful judicial body maintaining a division of powers in a federal system did not appear miraculously to the justices of the Supreme Court after the adoption of the Constitution. On the contrary, it had been clearly understood and partially applied during the long colonial period. The British Empire maintained the fiction that it was a unitary system until after the Revolution, "but its relations with the colonies had, in reality, become essentially federal. . . . After the colonies broke with Great Britain, a temporary solution was found in the creation of a confederate system." [23] For some time after the present government was established, there were few cases and little work for the Supreme Court justices to do. Though well paid, the positions were difficult to fill, due to the circuit riding required in a day when travel was uncomfortable, exhausting, and even dangerous.

The question of who should serve as final arbiter in the new federal system was much considered in the Constitutional Convention. The Federalists believed that the chief danger in such a system lay, not in the possibility of encroachment by the central government upon the States, but in the divisive tendencies of the States themselves. Hamilton stressed this point in his discussion of the relation of Federal and State courts in No. 82 of *The Federalist Papers*. The Anti-Federalists took the opposite view, but both groups agreed upon the necessity of having some organ of the national government empowered to act impartially in settling conflicts between the central government and the States. The Federalists preferred a legislative veto of State laws, as proposed in the Randolph Plan, but after this proposition was rejected a number of times in the Convention, they were more or less obliged to accept the judicial arbiter idea.

[23] Schmidhauser, John R., *The Supreme Court as Final Arbiter in Federal-State Relations, 1789–1957* (Chapel Hill: University of North Carolina Press, 1958), Chapter 1. See also Swisher, Carl B., "The Supreme Court and the Forging of Federalism, 1789–1864," *Nebraska Law Review*, December, 1960, pp. 3–15.

One of the last acts passed by the Federalist Congress and approved by President Adams materially extended and improved the judicial system. Then, for a period of thirty-five years, the Supreme Court was dominated by the powerful personality of John Marshall, who remained a staunch Federalist throughout. Moreover, as one after another of the old Federalist justices died and their places were taken by Republican justices appointed by one of the Virginia Republican Presidents, they fell immediately under the influence of the Chief Justice—as other Republicans noted with some dismay. In seven leading cases during the twenty-one years from 1803 to 1824, Marshall and his colleagues announced the supremacy of the Federal government over the States, as regards powers delegated to it by the people under the terms of the Constitution. The cases were:

Marbury v. Madison, 1 Cranch 137 1803
Fletcher v. Peck, 6 Cranch 87 1810
Martin v. Hunter's Lessee, 1 Wheaton 304 1816
McCulloch v. Maryland, 4 Wheaton 316 1819
Cohens v. Virginia, 6 Wheaton 264 1821
Osborn v. Bank of the United States, 9 Wheaton 739 1824
Gibbons v. Ogden, 9 Wheaton 1 1824

In Marbury v. Madison, the supremacy of the Supreme Court over Congress was enunciated. In Fletcher v. Peck, a State legislature was denied the right to correct a previous mistake, on the ground that it could not violate the obligation of contract clause of the Constitution. In Cohens v. Virginia and Martin v. Hunter's Lessee, the Court had the temerity to issue orders to Virginia State courts; the effect of these decisions was to increase the powers of the Federal judiciary in its interstitial relations with the State courts. In McCulloch v. Maryland and Osborn v. Bank, the power of the central government to regulate the financial concerns of the several States and of practically every citizen was laid down with clarity and distinctness. In the last of these cases, Gibbons v. Ogden, the supremacy of the Constitution over State constitutions and laws was set forth by the decision that navigation, so far as it could be included within the phrase "regulate commerce between the States," was within Federal control. The persons and powers directly affected by some of these decisions paid little attention to them, but the orders, principles, and reasoning upon which they were based have remained to this day as a part of the law of the land.

These developments were all a matter of deep concern to Jefferson and his followers. Spencer Roane and John Taylor of Caroline, both Virginians, took up the cudgels against these decisions and against the Court that made them, denying the supremacy of the Federal Supreme

Court, exalting the constitutional rights of the State courts, and through them the rights of the States. This controversy over the courts illustrates two things: the basic differences in the philosophy of the two parties, and the considerable similarity between the philosophy of the Southern region then and now, almost a century and a half later.

As regards party differences, it may be noted that the Federalists had their strength mainly in the large States; they wanted a strong central government and a loose construction of the Constitution as a means of developing it. The Republicans, on the other hand, were chiefly small-State people who believed that individual States were the most important political entities and who tolerated the Union only as a painful necessity. They wanted a weak central government and a strict interpretation of the Constitution to make sure that it remained weak. To realize the similarity in past and present Southern attitudes, one need only compare the abuse heaped upon Chief Justice Marshall in the early nineteenth century with that heaped upon Chief Justice Warren since the desegregation decision of 1954.

The adoption of the Fourteenth Amendment in 1868 served to accentuate the importance of the Supreme Court as the final arbiter in the federal system. The concluding sentence of the opinion of the majority in the Slaughter House Cases, written by Mr. Justice Miller, attests to the fact that the Court took its role most seriously:

> But whatever fluctuations may be seen in the history of public opinion on this subject during the period of our national existence, we think it will be found that this Court, so far as its functions require, has always held with a steady and an even hand the balance between State and Federal power, and we trust that such may continue to be the history of its relation to that subject so long as it shall have duties to perform which demand of it a construction of the Constitution, or of any of its parts.

Most of the State court decisions turning on constitutional or other Federal questions upon which the Supreme Court must pass, involved challenges to State action under the Fourteenth Amendment. Mr. Justice Brennan summed up the situation in these words:

> For some ninety years, in consequence of the adoption of that Amendment, every enactment of every State, every action by the Governor of a State, any governmental act of any of the States, or of the instrumentalities thereof, including judicial actions, may in a proper case be challenged at the Bar of the Supreme Court on the ground that such action, such legislation, such State court decision, is a deprivation of liberty without due process of law, or denies the equal protection of the laws.

I don't mean that the enforcement of constitutional limitations and guarantees is not also a responsibility of the State courts. To the contrary, the obligation rests upon the State courts, equally with the Federal courts, to guard, enforce, and protect every right granted or secured by the Federal Constitution. The point is that the Supreme Court is concerned with State judicial determinations only because the distribution of judicial power under our federal system assigns the responsibility for ultimate constitutional interpretation as well as final decision of other Federal questions to the Supreme Court.[24]

Though the decisions of the Supreme Court have from time to time been the cause of friction, the Court itself has frequently been and is widely regarded as a staunch defender of the federal system and the powers of the States. Probably no one has ever expressed this view better than Daniel Webster in his famous Reply to Hayne, in which he declared that the Constitution and the government established under it were both made by and for the people, and that the government was answerable to the people. "The general government and the State governments derived their authority from the same source." In cases of conflict, he pointed out, several methods of relief are provided—frequent elections, the power of amendment, and most significantly for purposes of the present discussion, the Federal judiciary. He maintained that the government could be neither overthrown by direct assault nor "evaded, undermined, nullified" if the representatives of the people conscientiously discharge the public trust committed to them.

Uniform Rules and Minimal Procedural Standards

The Federal courts have rendered a significant service to the nation as a stabilizing force. Although such things are difficult to measure accurately, there have probably been many more miscarriages of justice in State than in Federal courts, and there doubtless would have been even more had it not been for the due process and equal protection clauses of the Fourteenth Amendment, and for judicial review in the Federal courts by Federal judges who were removed from local prejudice and sustained by a broad national opinion and who thus took the larger and longer view of each question.

It is true that there was a notable disregard of civil liberties during the Civil War, during the A. Mitchell Palmer abuses during World War I, and during the Japanese detention program during World War II, but in recent years the most frequent violations of constitutional processes

[24] Brennan, p. 395.

and civil liberties in this country have been in the States and localities. Illustrations are not hard to find:

> . . . the shoddy treatment of Negroes, aliens and migratory workers in many States; the Lusk gag laws of 1919 in New York State and the expulsion of the Socialist Assemblymen from the New York State legislature in the same year; the control of Indiana by the Ku Klux Klan in the mid-1920's; the Huey Long dictatorship in Louisiana; the existence of prohibition in many States long before and long after prohibition on the national scene. Traditional decentralizers are in the habit of saying that prohibition in Kansas is all right because it is an adjustment to a local variation, but that prohibition on the national scene is a mistake. Are not a person's liberties as much impaired by prohibition from Topeka as by prohibition from Washington? [25]

In some instances at least, Supreme Court decisions put brakes on some of the most objectionable practices. It would, in fact, be difficult to exaggerate the importance of the services rendered by the Federal courts in checking abuses and placing their influence definitely behind a uniform national observance of minimum standards of equity and fairness in the treatment of individuals and groups.

There are several procedures by which the Federal courts have been able to establish and maintain their supremacy. By their decisions and through their influence, they have sought to achieve uniform rules and procedures, and they have also sought to establish and maintain minimum procedural requirements, particularly with respect to criminal cases. As Judge Charles E. Clark has pointed out, they have provided leadership in the movement for improvement in the administration of justice. Furthermore, they have recently been evolving new techniques for compelling compliance with the school desegregation rulings.

Establishing Uniform Rules. During the century when the *Swift* v. *Tyson* doctrine was in the ascendency, the Federal courts felt free to follow their own ideas about substantive law, but the procedure used in the Federal courts in law cases was basically that used in the courts of the State in which the Federal court was sitting. In 1938, the year in which *Swift* v. *Tyson* was overthrown, the Supreme Court adopted uniform rules of civil procedure for the Federal District Courts, largely as a means of assuring that the outcome of a case did not depend on whether it was tried in a Federal or a State court. Due to the blurred line between what constitutes substance and what procedure, doubts have arisen as to the validity of many of the provisions contained in these rules.

Minimum Procedural Standards. The maintenance of minimum pro-

---

[25] These matters are discussed by Carleton, William G., "Centralization and the Open Society," *Political Science Quarterly*, June, 1960, pp. 244-259.

cedural standards, chiefly in connection with criminal proceedings, is a second control device. It is largely a policing operation designed to make certain that no defendant in any State shall be denied his right to counsel or to a fair trial, or be placed in double jeopardy. Similarly, an effort is made to prevent such police abuses as cruel and inhuman treatment of accused or suspected persons, too prolonged periods of questioning, forced confessions, and the use of improper methods in acquiring evidence during the period of investigation.[26]

Techniques for Compelling Compliance

Although it used to be said that courts were without means for enforcing their decisions, some recent developments indicate that this is not entirely accurate. In the words of the late Senator Warren R. Austin, "The Supreme Court is a unique instrument of popular sovereignty. Without power to enforce its judgments, uncrowned, unsceptered, devoid of sword, or purse, the Supreme Court of the United States for 150 years has successfully guarded the institutions which expel autocracy and animate free government." [27] Nevertheless, since the school desegregation decisions, the Court has found that it is not entirely without means of exerting pressure on recalcitrant States or communities, or upon those resorting to dilatory tactics.

Once a precedent-setting decision has been handed down by the Court, there are forces which operate to bind the State courts to that decision—even though it be against the prevailing sentiment of a community—to the extent of carrying out the order or of following the decision in analogous cases subsequently arising. Actually, the State courts have no legitimate right to do otherwise. The claim that the Supreme Court usurped its authority over State courts of last resort has long been recognized as invalid. A study of the proceedings of the Constitutional Convention and of the State ratifying conventions clearly indicates that the grant of authority was intentional. The restraint brought about by the absence of a legal justification for defiance can be very real indeed in a country where a long tradition of respect for the law exists.

[26] For example, see law review note, "Illegal Search and Seizure: Evidence Illegally Obtained by State Officers Inadmissible in Federal Courts," *Rutgers Law Review*, Fall, 1960, pp. 116–128. The intergovernmental relations aspects of these problems are discussed briefly in Schaefer, pp. 13–17.

[27] Bloom, Sol, "Address in Celebration of the Constitution Sesquicentennial," *Formation of the Union Under the Constitution* (Washington: U.S. Constitution Sesquicentennial Commission, 1943), pp. 730–731.

A second restraint is found in the tradition of the judges themselves. Judges have a habit of adhering to precedent, and it is to the Supreme Court that judges look for precedent when the Court's rulings are applicable. A judge tends to be extremely conscious of his responsibility as impartial interpreter and administrator of the law, and he is therefore likely to find it difficult to disregard the principle of *stare decisis*. Thus, while an individual judge may seek to ignore a particular Supreme Court ruling, it will prove difficult for him to continue to render decisions which he knows may be overturned by a higher court—perhaps eventually by the highest court in the land.

STATE DEFIANCE OF THE FEDERAL COURTS

Whatever may be the theory of Federal judicial supremacy, the early history of the Republic is punctuated with examples of protest by the States against Federal action. In a number of these controversies, the courts were involved. At least half a dozen widely separated States have, over an extended period of time, defied the judgments of the Federal courts. These States, including Connecticut, Georgia, Ohio, Pennsylvania, Virginia, and Wisconsin, have not stopped with disrespect and disobedience, but some of them have resorted to "massive resistance." In two of these States, such tactics have been repeated a second time, or a third, after an interval of several years.[28] In point of time, the incidents range from the early days of the government under the Constitution to the present.

Georgia, the State Lands, and the Cherokee Indians

The State of Georgia has been involved in at least three important challenges to the power and authority of the Supreme Court. The issue in the case of *Chisholm* v. *Georgia,* mentioned earlier, was the right of the Supreme Court to hear cases in which a State was being sued by a citizen of another State. Chisholm, a citizen of South Carolina, sued Georgia to recover some lands confiscated during the Revolutionary War. Georgia refused to recognize the competence of the Court to hear the

[28] For fuller comment on some of these instances, see Demet, Francis J., "A Trilogy of Massive Resistance," *American Bar Association Journal*, March, 1960, pp. 294–296.

case and, when the case was called in 1792, declined to enter an appearance, merely submitting a written remonstrance against the jurisdiction of the Court. The following year, the Court ordered Georgia to appear under penalty of a judgment by default for Chisholm. Georgia maintained its defiance and a writ of inquiry was awarded for Chisholm.

The writ was never executed, and Georgia succeeded in its defiance of the Court.[29] Opposition to the Court's assumption of jurisdiction was intense in Georgia and widespread in the other States. The Georgia House of Representatives passed a bill declaring it a felony punishable by death for anyone to attempt to execute any compulsory process issuing from the Supreme Court in this case.[30] On the day after the Court's decision was announced, a constitutional amendment was introduced in Congress to prevent a State from being sued in the Federal courts. The Eleventh Amendment which reversed the decision in *Chisholm* v. *Georgia* was finally ratified in 1798; this matter is discussed further in Chapter IV.

In the 1820's, Georgia became dissatisfied with the slowness of the Federal government's removal of the Creek Indians from Georgia territory. Governor Troup charged the government with failure to carry out its promises and ordered a State survey of the lands. President Adams threatened to use the Army to stop the Georgia surveyors, but Governor Troup successfully defied him. The issue was settled by withdrawal of the Creeks beyond the Mississippi. At the same time as the Creek controversy, Georgia also took over the lands of the Cherokees within its borders. The Cherokee laws were annulled and Georgia statutes enforced in the territory. This controversy went to the Supreme Court when a Cherokee named Corn Tassel was convicted under Georgia law and sentenced to death for the murder of another member of his tribe.

It was in connection with this famous case that President Jackson is reputed to have made the oft-quoted remark, "John Marshall has made his decision; now let him enforce it!" The Court had granted a writ of error, but this was ignored and the Cherokee was executed for murder on the date originally set, contrary to his rights under Federal law under which a writ of error supersedes sentence until the appeal is decided. This defiance and disobedience of process issued by the Supreme Court took place because the Governor had, with legislative approval, adopted an outspoken policy that the judicial process of the State of Georgia would not be interfered with by orders and writs of the Federal Court

---

[29] See Haines, Charles G., *The Role of the Supreme Court in American Government and Politics, 1789–1835* (Berkeley: University of California Press, 1944), p. 135.

[30] For the text of the bill, see Ames, Herman V., *State Documents on Federal Relations* (Philadelphia: University of Pennsylvania Press, 1906), pp. 9–11.

and that the State would resist by force any attempt to enforce Court orders with all the forces at his command.[31]

Two years later, in an equally spectacular case, Georgia again defied the Supreme Court. Two missionaries, Worcester and Butler, were convicted of residing among the Indians without a license. The Supreme Court reversed the convictions on jurisdictional grounds, holding that the Georgia court had no authority within an Indian reservation. The trial court, ordered to release Worcester, ignored the mandate with the support of the Governor who again declared that he would resist enforcement of the mandate with force, if necessary. The two defendants remained in a Georgia jail until they agreed to abandon further attempts to secure a writ of error from the Supreme Court, whereupon they were pardoned by the Governor on the strength of their further agreement to leave the State.[32]

Pennsylvania and the Case of the Sloop Active

This conflict between Pennsylvania and the Federal government originated during the Revolutionary War when the sloop *Active* was captured and sold. The Pennsylvania Court of Admiralty ruled that the proceeds belonged to the captors, but the owners of the ship appealed to the Continental Congress which, through its Committee on Appeals, reversed the State court. The ruling of the Committee on Appeals was ignored.[33] Almost twenty years later, Olmstead, the owner, applied to the Federal District Court for a process to enforce the ruling of the Committee on Appeals. In 1803 Federal District Judge Peters ruled that the money be paid to Olmstead, but he was defied by the State and his decree was not enforced. Olmstead applied to the Supreme Court which in 1809 issued a writ of mandamus directing the enforcement of the District

[31] *Cherokee Nation* v. *Georgia*, 5 Peters 1 (1831). This case is discussed at length in Warren, Charles, *Supreme Court in United States History*, 2 vols. (Boston: Little, Brown and Co., 1922), II, 193–94. See also Baldwin, Simeon E., *The American Judiciary* (New York: The Century Company, 1905), p. 163. At least two other cases arising out of Georgia statutes regulating the Cherokee lands were appealed to the Supreme Court, in both of which the Court ruled against the State, the State authorities ignored all communications from the Court, and the criminal penalties awarded by the Georgia courts were carried out. The cases were *Corn Tassel* v. *Georgia* (no report), *Worcester* v. *Georgia*, 6 Peters 515 (1832), and *In re James Grave* (no report). They are discussed and newspaper citations given in Haines, pp. 597–605.

[32] *Worcester* v. *Georgia*, *supra*.

[33] For a history of the controversy, see Dunaway, Wayland F., *A History of Pennsylvania* (New York: Prentice-Hall, Inc., 1935), pp. 436 ff.

Court's decree.[34] When the Supreme Court's decision was announced, the Governor notified the legislature that he proposed to call out the State militia to prevent the enforcement of the Court's decree. Other aspects of this case have been considered in Chapter VI.

Virginia and the Federal Courts

A conflict between Federal and State authorities in Virginia arose out of litigation to determine the title to certain lands in Virginia.[35] The history of the litigation and the issues of law involved are very complex. The case originated in an ejectment action in the Winchester County District Court, in which Hunter sued Martin to recover possession of certain Virginia land. Martin based his right and title to the land upon the construction of the Treaty of 1783 between the United States and Great Britain and upon the fact that he was an heir of Lord Fairfax. The trial court held for the defendant, and the State Court of Appeals for the plaintiff. Martin appealed to the Supreme Court under Section 25 of the Judiciary Act of 1789, which gave that Court appellate jurisdiction over State courts in certain cases arising under the Federal Constitution.

In 1810, the Virginia Court of Appeals held that Martin's claim to the lands in issue was not valid because of Virginia statutes restricting the rights of aliens to inherit land within the Commonwealth. A writ of error to the Supreme Court was allowed, however, and that Court reversed the Virginia decision and entered an order requiring the Virginia Court of Appeals to enter judgment for Martin. The opinion reversing the Virginia Court was written by Mr. Justice Story, then thirty-seven years of age, and held that in a proper case the Supreme Court has appellate jurisdiction over State courts of last resort. The Virginia Court refused to comply with the mandamus on the ground that Congress had no power to give the Court appellate jurisdiction over the State courts and that Section 25 of the Judiciary Act of 1789 was unconstitutional. The Virginia Court acknowledged the supremacy clause of the Constitution, denied that this involved the supremacy of the Federal courts, and refused to implement the Supreme Court's decision, after which the case went back to the Supreme Court on the sole issue of the latter Court's power to secure compliance with its decisions. Because of the delicate situation that had developed, the second mandate was issued not to the Virginia Court of Appeals but to the District Court of the county in which the land was situated and in which the suit had originated. Com-

[34] *United States* v. *Peters,* 5 Cranch 115 (1809).
[35] *Martin* v. *Hunter's Lessee,* 1 Wheaton 304 (1816).

pliance was secured when the District Court enforced the Supreme Court's decision.

Significantly, as recently as 1956, the Virginia Supreme Court took a similar position on an entirely different matter. The court held that under the Virginia statutes and its rules of practice and procedure, it was without power to obey the mandate of the Supreme Court in a divorce case. In a *per curiam* opinion, the Federal Supreme Court had ordered the Virginia Supreme Court to return a divorce case based on the miscegenation statute to the trial court for further findings, and vacated the judgment of divorce. When the case was returned to the Federal Supreme Court by motion to recall the mandate and to set the case for oral argument upon the merits, or to recall and amend the mandate, the motion was denied on the ground that the action of the Virginia Court of Appeals in response to the Supreme Court's mandate left the case devoid of a properly presented Federal question.[36]

Ohio and the National Bank

In 1819 Ohio placed a tax of $50,000 on every branch of the Bank of the United States within its borders in order to drive it from the State. Despite the Supreme Court decision in *McCulloch* v. *Maryland*,[37] which had declared such a tax to be unconstitutional, Osborn, the State Auditor, was determined to collect the tax. He was enjoined from so doing by the Circuit Court, but proceeded nevertheless to take the tax money by force from one of the branches of the Bank. The Ohio legislature supported Osborn in a series of resolutions objecting to the doctrine that the States are bound on questions of constitutionality by Supreme Court decisions. It also passed an "Act to withdraw from the Bank of the United States the protection of the laws of this State" as a further means of seeking to expel the Bank which had been supported by the Supreme Court. The Bank instituted proceedings against Osborn, and in 1824 the Supreme Court affirmed a lower court decision against him. The tax money was refunded to the Bank.[38]

Wisconsin, Fugitive Slaves, and Personal Liberty Laws

The Federal Fugitive Slave Act of 1793 caused opposition from States in which abolitionist sentiment was strong. The act relied on State

[36] *Naim* v. *Naim*, 197 Va. 734, 90 S.E. (2d) 849; 350 U.S. 891 (1956).
[37] 4 Wheaton 316 (1819).
[38] *Osborn* v. *Bank of the United States*, 9 Wheaton 738 (1824); see also Warren, Charles, "Legislative and Judicial Attacks," *American Law Review*.

officers to enforce its provisions, and several States passed laws extending to suspected fugitive slaves the right to jury trial: Indiana (1824), Connecticut (1838), New York and Vermont (1840).[39] Although these laws were not direct challenges to Federal authority, they undoubtedly were designed to hinder the operation of the Federal statute.

The situation was altered by the Supreme Court decision in the case of *Prigg* v. *Pennsylvania*.[40] The significant portion of that decision was the ruling that State officers could not be compelled to enforce a Federal statute. As a direct result, four States (Massachusetts, Pennsylvania, Rhode Island, and Vermont) passed laws prohibiting State officers from performing the duties assigned to them under the law of 1793 and forbidding the use of State jails for fugitive slaves.[41]

The most positive defiance of the Federal government on the fugitive slave issue occurred in Wisconsin in the 1850's. Congress had enacted a new Fugitive Slave Law as a part of the famous Compromise of 1850. Its effect was to retain the institution of slavery and the status of slaves as personal property, the owner of a runaway slave being authorized to use Federal process for the recapture of the slave. Although punishment was prescribed for those who aided or abetted runaways, local sentiment against slavery (and against this legislation) was so strong in some States, including Wisconsin, as to encourage widespread violation of the law.

In the famous case of *Abelman* v. *Booth*,[42] Sherman Booth, an abolitionist editor, was arrested and held in custody by Abelman, the United States Marshal in Milwaukee County, on the charge of having forcibly aided and abetted the escape of a fugitive slave in March, 1854. On a writ of habeas corpus, the State Supreme Court discharged Booth from custody and at the same time held the Federal Fugitive Slave Law unconstitutional. However, Booth was later indicted, tried, convicted, and sentenced to fine and imprisonment by the United States District Court, only to have the State Supreme Court release him again on a new writ of habeas corpus. In 1855, the case was brought to the Supreme Court on a writ of error; here the verdict was reversed, Chief Justice Taney speaking for the Court. The decision and the events which followed it were noteworthy for several reasons.

Although the Chief Justice, then eighty-two years old, had long been an ardent supporter of States' rights, he held that in a sphere of action

[39] See McDougall, Marion G., *Fugitive Slaves* (Boston: Ginn & Co., 1891), pp. 65–66.

[40] 16 Peters 539 (1842).   [41] McDougall, p. 66.

[42] 21 Howard 506 (1859). A history of the whole controversy is given in Warren, II, 332–349.

appropriate to the Federal courts, the action of Wisconsin in this instance went far beyond the reach of the judicial process for a State judge or a State court. Wisconsin's action was, therefore, reversible error. The Fugitive Slave Law was thus upheld, although the case was never technically closed. One show of disobedience followed another. First the State Supreme Court ignored the writ of error issued by the Supreme Court and refused to comply with it. The Supreme Court, however, managed to procure a copy of the record in 1857 and reversed the judgment of the Wisconsin court the following year. The State courts refused to enforce the verdict.

A motion to file the remittitur was denied by the State court through Justice Cole, without a written opinion. Chief Justice Dixon wrote a minority opinion on the motion, urging that the remittitur should be filed and honored.[43] Although the Chief Justice was correct, the opinion was later used successfully against him in a campaign for re-election, after which he was overwhelmingly defeated. Demet asserts that to the best of his knowledge, the remittitur has not been filed to this day in the office of the Clerk of the State Supreme Court.[44] In subsequent litigation in Federal and State courts, the Marshal was allowed to replevy the slave and to recover a money judgment for the unlawful detention. Booth was arrested by a United States Marshal in 1860; he was rescued, rearrested, and finally pardoned by President Buchanan the same year.

Nor was this the end of the judicial rebellion in Wisconsin. In spite of the final outcome of the Booth Case, the State Supreme Court, thirteen years later, ordered the release of an enlisted man held in the custody of a recruiting officer of the Army. Again the Supreme Court denied the authority of a State court to issue a writ of habeas corpus for the release of persons held under the authority of the Federal government. Justice Field ruled that neither sovereign "can intrude with its jurisdictional process into the domain of the other, except so far as such intrusion may be necessary on the part of the National Government to preserve its rightful supremacy in cases of conflict."[45]

The School Desegregation Cases

The school desegregation decisions of 1954 and 1955 aroused a storm of protest, particularly in the Southern region. Although it is well established that the Constitution is at any given time what the Supreme Court

[43] *Ableman* v. *Booth,* 11 Wis. 517 (1859).
[44] Demet, "A Trilogy," *American Bar Association Journal,* pp. 294–296.
[45] *United States* v. *Tarble,* 13 Wallace 397 (1872).

says it is, there were extremists and irreconcilables who determined to utilize every known means short of war to resist these decisions and prevent them from being put into effect.

The chief arguments of the opponents were that the Supreme Court had exceeded its powers, that it was legislating rather than interpreting the Constitution, and that these decisions were violative of States' rights. None of these contentions could be taken very seriously, and it may even be that no one really expected that they would be. It is the business of the Court to interpret the Constitution, and it is impossible to do this without "making law." As for the States' rights argument, it has been pointed out that

> . . . the states do not have the "right" to deny the constitutional rights of individual Americans; they have no "right" to discriminate unfairly against some of their residents. . . . The Supreme Court may be said to have recognized "states' rights" when it invited the State and local governments to devise their own desegregation procedures, instead of imposing a national plan. Education has traditionally been regarded as primarily a State and local responsibility. The Supreme Court has not changed that; it has only required that the schools be operated without discrimination, in accord with the principles of the Constitution.[46]

In this situation, obstructive tactics came not from the courts, but primarily from legislatures spurred on by political leaders who believed that the preservation of their political lives made it essential that they make at least a show of resistance to the mandate for school desegregation. There were hurriedly convened constitutional conventions in some States, and legislation was enacted which provided for pupil assignment systems. In spite of determined efforts on the part of citizens groups to keep the schools open, the schools in a few scattered communities were actually closed, apparently on the basis of the theory that it was better for children to receive no training than to run the risk of white children becoming contaminated by being in the same classroom with children of a different color—children with whom they could and probably often did play outside of school.[47]

[46] Southern Regional Council, *School Desegregation: The First Six Years* (Atlanta, May, 1960), p. 3.

[47] Although a few privately financed, segregated schools were hurriedly established in some communities, it was the pupils in these areas who were victimized. As Secretary of Health, Education, and Welfare, Arthur S. Flemming pointed out in a statement released June 22, 1959, the closing of thirteen schools in Virginia and Arkansas represented a loss of about 1,800,000 pupil-days, and approximately 14,500 of the 16,300 pupils affected by the shutdowns were exposed to schooling of one kind or another during the years.

As a result of an unfortunate combination of circumstances, the most serious crisis developed in Little Rock. On September 2, 1957, after several futile attempts to postpone the school board's plan for integration, the Governor of Arkansas ordered the National Guard to surround Little Rock's Central High School the day before integration was to begin. The following day, the Federal District Judge directed the school board to disregard the troops and to permit Negroes to attend classes, but on September 4, the National Guardsmen and State troopers refused to allow nine Negro students to enter Central High School.

The State courts in general did not actually obstruct integration, though they did not assist it. Federal courts, for the most part, as in Little Rock, supported integration, gently prodding local school authorities and setting target dates in accordance with which partial if not complete school integration should be undertaken.

APPRAISAL OF FEDERAL-STATE JUDICIAL RELATIONSHIPS

It is not easy to generalize on Federal-State relationships in the judiciary. Evidence accumulated over a period of many years, however, shows that when a dispute arises between State and Federal courts, the latter almost invariably wins its point. The late Professor Oliver P. Field pointed out that the Federal courts may release a person who is in the custody of a State officer if a proper showing justifies the issuance of the writ of habeas corpus,[48] but the State courts may not interfere by habeas corpus with the work of Federal officers or courts.[49] The Federal courts are careful to say that they will interfere only upon great provocation, but the fact remains that they do interfere in a manner not permitted to the State courts in dealing with Federal officers. Such officers may surrender a person in their custody to the State courts if they wish, as a matter of comity, but they have no legal obligation to do so.[50]

"The Federal courts may enjoin State courts from proceeding with a case, and have done so occasionally, but the State courts, are not permitted to enjoin the Federal courts in their work." [51] Federal courts con-

[48] Field, Oliver P., "State Versus Nation and the Supreme Court," *American Political Science Review*, April, 1934, pp. 233–245, and *Moore* v. *Dempsey*, 261 U.S. 86 (1923). The constitutionality of the Federal statute permitting such release was sustained in *Frank* v. *Mangum*, 237 U.S. 209 (1914).

[49] *Tarble's Case*, 13 Wallace 397 (1872). State courts may not issue the writ to a Federal military officer to test legality of enlistment.

[50] *Pomi* v. *Fessenden*, 258 U.S. 254 (1922).

[51] *Rigg* v. *Johnson County*, 6 Wallace 166 (1867).

stantly interfere with State administrative officers by injunction, particularly in the field of public utility regulation and in taxation, but State courts rarely if ever step in to halt Federal administrative action. Congressional attempts to curtail Federal injunctive interference with State administration have been so restricted in application by the courts that they have been relatively ineffective.[52] Mention has been made previously of the rules governing removal of cases from State to Federal courts.

Professor Field summarized the whole situation clearly and succinctly as follows:

> . . . The only consolation left to the States in the relations between the two judicial systems is that arising from the permission granted them by Congressional statute to try cases involving Federal questions, and that they not only decide questions arising under the Constitution of the United States in some instances, but may decide them as matters of first impression if no Federal precedent exists, and may even ignore such precedent when it exists, and evade compliance with the known rule of law for several years at a time.* But of course Supreme Court review substantially restricts the States in the long view, because of Congressional statutes permitting that Court to override State decisions upon Federal constitutional questions.† But here also, such questions are commonly brought to the Supreme Court at the initiative of the aggrieved individual rather than at the instance of the governments involved.[53]
>
> * It often takes several years before State practice is really changed to conform to Supreme Court decisions on State powers, partly because a decision that a statute in one State is invalid does not automatically or immediately strike down similar statutes in other States.
>
> † It is commonly overlooked that a statute now provides for the appellate jurisdiction of the Supreme Court, and that a repeal of the statute would leave to the State courts final jurisdiction over questions of Federal constitutional law arising in the State courts and not removed under the removal statutes. Appellate jurisdiction on this head is subject to "regulation" by Congress. [Important early cases are *Cohens* v. *Virginia* and *Martin* v. *Hunter's Lessee*.]

Elsewhere in the same paper, Field observes that although the States as members of the federal system have had to play against the umpire as well as against the national government, "the Supreme Court of the United States has been as impartial an umpire in national-state disputes as one of the members of two contending teams could be expected to be." [54]

---

[52] See the fate of the "Three Judge Rule" in *U.S. Code*, Title 28, Sections 380–389, as described in *Yale Law Journal*, May, 1929, pp. 955–983.

[53] Field, p. 239. [54] Field, p. 233.

The position of the Court itself is not an easy one. It must function as the final arbiter in the maintenance of a system in which the allocation of powers between the two levels of government has never been specifically defined. Although there has been and is now much cooperation between the two, the Federal government tends to be the dominant partner, and it could be even more so if it chose. It is in a position to preempt certain areas of responsibility by use of both delegated and implied powers, though it has not always done so. Federal control over commerce, which could be made complete, is shared with the States. Federal control over banking, currency, and immigration (formerly shared) is now complete or relatively so. Federal control over insurance, finally established by judicial decision, was soon largely abrogated to the States by act of Congress. Federal control over the militia, once very limited, has been considerably extended, and if Congress so chose, it could be taken over completely. In all of these matters and many more, it is the Supreme Court that is the final arbiter; its job is to rationalize the federal system, but it does this as an agency of the Federal government.[55]

The questions that are raised here are not simple ones to which it is possible to give short, "right" answers. The Court does the best it can at any given time under the existing circumstances. Its decisions must, in the long run though not necessarily at the moment, have the support of public opinion, and its judgments must be carried out in such an atmosphere as may be provided by the current political situation. As scientific and technological advances literally shrink the size of the world and transform the environment in which people live, making them aware of the need for uniformity and willing to pay the price of achieving it, the question arises as to whose responsibility it should be to engineer change in the governmental arrangements. Certainly the courts will play a part, but primary responsibility should perhaps be assumed not by the courts, but by the popularly elected representatives of the people—Congress.

Professor Stanley H. Friedelbaum has published an excellent analysis of the role of the Supreme Court in American federalism since 1938, with special emphasis on the Warren Court.[56] Five important areas are covered: preemption, non-economic due process, Federal enforcement of State-created rights, intergovernmental immunities, and State taxing

---

[55] One must remember that the authorities frequently disagree; see Mr. Justice Frankfurter in *Polish National Alliance* v. *National Labor Relations Board*, 322 U.S. 650 (1944).

[56] Friedelbaum, Stanley H., "The Warren Court and American Federalism: A Preliminary Appraisal," *University of Chicago Law Review*, Autumn, 1960, pp. 53–87.

powers and the commerce clause. Briefly, these are his conclusions: The Warren Court has not been an innovator of the preemption or "new" due process doctrines, but there has been some shift in emphasis as the doctrines have been applied in new areas. The Court has continued, if not expanded, a policy of deference to State legislation. Intergovernmental tax immunities have been still further restricted, and a new permissive pattern has emerged from cases defining the scope of State tax powers. Deference to State decisional law has developed in some types of Federal question cases. A majority of the Court has tended toward a vigorous defense of civil rights, a defense which in some instances has had the effect of restricting State powers. Professor Friedelbaum finds the Court "on stronger ground today than it was during the constitutional crisis of the 1930's," its position as umpire in Federal-State relations remaining secure.

BIBLIOGRAPHICAL NOTES

Although there is an enormous literature dealing with the judiciary as a whole, relatively little attention has been given to the relations between Federal and State courts. For the formative period and Marshall's influence on the Supreme Court, one cannot do better than to consult Albert J. Beveridge, *Life of John Marshall*, 4 vols. (Boston: Houghton Mifflin Co., 1911–1916), a monumental history of Marshall's life and times and of the Court over which he presided for so many years. Also important are two volumes by Charles Grove Haines, able critic of the doctrine of judicial review, *The Role of the Supreme Court in American Government and Politics, 1789–1835* (Berkeley: University of California Press, 1944) and *The Role of the Supreme Court in American Government and Politics, 1835–1864* (Berkeley: University of California Press, 1957), published posthumously with Foster H. Sherwood; a third volume was projected to complete the story. Probably the best general history of the Court is Charles Warren, *The Supreme Court in United States History*, rev. ed. (Boston: Little, Brown & Co., 1947).

Several books have been devoted to Federal-State relations in this area. The oldest, George Wharton Pepper, *The Borderland of Federal and State Decisions* (Philadelphia: T. and J. W. Johnson & Co., 1889), was a prize essay written by this one-time Senator and long-time dean of the Philadelphia Bar; see also Charles Warren, *The Supreme Court and Sovereign States* (Princeton: Princeton University Press, 1924). The most recent works include Mitchell Wendell, *Relations Between the Federal and State Courts* (New York: Columbia University Press, 1949) and John R. Schmidheiser, *The Supreme Court as Final Arbiter in Federal-State Relations, 1789–1957* (Chapel Hill: University of North Carolina Press, 1958). Schmidheiser deals with two aspects of the problem, the origins of the Supreme Court's power, and the manner in which this responsibility has been discharged by each Chief Justice from Marshall to Warren during their respective leadership periods. Forrest Talbott, *Intergovernmental Relations and the Courts* (Minneapolis: University of Minnesota Press, 1950), deals particularly with the problem in Minnesota, but includes much material of general application.

Dean Alfange, *The Supreme Court and the National Will* (New York: Doubleday, Doran & Co., Inc., 1937), Chapter 4, discusses some problems of national power and States' rights as they appeared at the time of the controversy over the Court; for a later, different view, see Owen J. Roberts, *The Court and the Constitution* (Cambridge: Harvard University Press, 1951).

Three quarters of a century ago appeared George C. Holt, *The Concurrent Jurisdiction of the Federal and State Courts* (New York: Baker, Voorhis & Co., 1888). The leading cases on this and other aspects of Federal-State jurisdictional problems have been brought together in two excellent compilations: Felix Frankfurter and Harry Shulman, *Cases on Federal Jurisdiction and Procedure*, rev. ed. (Chicago: Callaghan, 1937) and Henry M. Hart, Jr. and Herbert Wechsler, *The Federal Courts and the Federal System* (New York: Foundation Press, 1953). William G. Rice, *Law Among States in Federacy* (Appleton, Wisc.: C. C. Nelson, Publishing Co., 1959) presents some comparative information, particularly relating to Switzerland. See also Justice Walter V. Schaefer, *Courts and the Commonplaces of Federalism* (Institute of Government and Public Affairs, Urbana: University of Illinois, 1959) a lecture which presents a penetrating analysis of some of these problems in the United States.

Periodically throughout our history, there have been outbursts of bitter criticism of the Supreme Court, its members, and their decisions. An interesting example of the current wave of this type of literature is found in Thomas Wilcox, *States' Rights vs. the Supreme Court* (Boston: Forum Publishing Co., 1960), of which the publishers proclaim, "This book reads like a prosecuting attorney's indictment of a malefactor. The plaintiff is the fifty States, the defendant is the Supreme Court, the jury is the great American Public and the prosecutor is the author."

CHAPTER VIII

Political Parties in a Federal System

Government is a complicated affair. There is a visible mechanism which functions in plain view. But behind it, providing it with momentum, keeping it lubricated, with hands on the throttle, stands a great array of forces which are only half visible, but are always at work. When people find the study of government a simple affair (as some of them say they do), it is because they see the husk and miss the kernel. They look at Congress in session and imagine that they are viewing the entire process of lawmaking. They read that the President has sent some names to the Senate for confirmation and assume that this constitutes the whole process of appointment. . . . To master the superficial anatomy of government is not difficult. Its physical contour, its shape and mass, are easily described. All this is very simple political biology. But the physiology of government, its bones and muscles, its heart and brain, its temper and idiosyncrasies—to master these things is a task that requires intelligence, industry, discrimination, and tolerance. Political parties have helped to make it so.[1]

[1] Munro, William B., *The Government of the United States*, 5th ed. (New York: The Macmillan Co., 1946), pp. 127-128.

How have they helped? To any alert observer, there are abundant illustrations. Here are a few. A Senator from a Midwestern State learned that he could not replace the able and qualified Director of Extention at the State College of Agriculture (whose removal he had engineered) with a wholly unqualified political lieutenant. The Department of Agriculture objected, and the original Director was reinstated. The same

Senator found out that his "2 Per Cent Club" could not shake down the employees of the Unemployment Compensation program, the administrative expenses of which are borne by the Federal government. The Department of Labor informed him that such assessments are illegal. A Governor of a large Eastern State, and a political doctor he had appointed as Secretary of Health, proceeded to make a shambles of the Department, replacing professionally competent personnel with political hacks, who were assessed for a "2 Per Cent Club." They discovered that the Public Health Service would withhold Federal funds if they persisted, since these employees administer federally aided programs as well as State-supported programs. These incidents illustrate —in fact, they are the politics of federalism in action.

If one were to search diligently through the Constitution from beginning to end for some mention of or reference to political parties, he would not find it for the simple reason that it is not there. Nor would he be more successful if he were to extend his search to the many State constitutions, which have provisions on suffrage and elections, but none on parties. When one considers how vital political parties have become in the functioning of American government, the lack of any constitutional provision for them seems more than passing strange. But there is good historical reason for it.

The writings of the Founding Fathers are replete with critical references to and denunciations of what Washington characterized as "the baleful effects of party spirit." The basic reason for this attitude may be attributed to the fact that the Founding Fathers' concept of party was vastly different from our own. The parties that they knew had been proponents of different forms or types of government, so that the triumph of one party over another was likely to warn of pending change in the form of government. The Founders did not dignify political parties by constitutional or other recognition because they hoped that there would be no parties.

How widely this concept of party is at variance with the major parties now existing in the United States is illustrated by the fact that today virtually all Americans and both major parties are dedicated to the support of the Constitution and to the government which functions under it. Individuals can and do have strong preferences for certain candidates and parties during a political campaign, but no informed person really fears that the American Constitution or system of government will be overthrown or seriously endangered, whatever the outcome of the voting.

On the contrary, political parties have become so deeply imbedded in the unwritten portions of the Constitution that they have, in fact, become essential to its successful operation. It is no exaggeration to say that if by some stroke of magic the whole party system could suddenly be wiped out of existence, it would either have to be reconstructed or the governmental system itself would soon cease to function effectively.

The national parties reflect the decentralizing tendencies derived from constitutional provisions and governmental structure, and add others of their own. Organizationally, they parallel the three-layer structure of government. Functionally, they produce in legislation the same basic division of responsibility between the several levels and units of government. The parties have often been criticized as being undisciplined—which, to a large extent, they are—and this very characteristic goes far toward explaining the tremendous amount of time and energy that Members of Congress and their staffs devote to local problems and the problems of individual constituents. This, of course, is a form of legislative (and political) interference with administration, having the effect of compelling the administration to concern itself with political matters. The lack of discipline and the openness of the system make it possible for individuals, groups, and institutions (including State and local governments) to attempt to influence national policy at every step of the legislative-administrative process.[2]

The party system has achieved its position of indispensability by reason of a number of factors. The State and local party organizations play a vital role in the process of nominating and electing a President of the United States, and in addition they are deeply involved in the men, money, and issues aspects of what is now frequently referred to as political dynamics. It is with these matters that this chapter is concerned.

THE ROLE OF THE STATES IN THE NOMINATING PROCESS

Political parties in the United States are organized on a State and local, not a national basis. The national party organization can best be described as a loose confederation of State party organizations, which at intervals of four years, during each presidential campaign, emerges with a tremendous show of activity, but remains largely dormant at other times. Under these circumstances, it is easy to understand why the

[2] These matters are discussed in Grodzins, Morton, "The Federal System," *Report* of the President's Commission on National Goals, *Goals for Americans* (New York: American Assembly, Columbia University, Prentice-Hall, Inc., 1960), pp. 265–282 on pp. 272–275.

role of the States and their Governors in the nominating process is the vitally important role that it is. The State and local party organizations are thriving concerns of more or less continuous activity. Months, if not years, in advance of the date at which the party nominating convention will meet, the candidates themselves and their pre-convention managers begin contacting the Governors and key political leaders of the States, particularly of those States with large delegations, in the hope of obtaining their support. Both Roosevelt in 1932 and Kennedy in 1960 did this with notable success.

Thus a winning candidate for the nomination of his party must do three things simultaneously. He must demonstrate a capacity for national leadership by "projecting an image" that has wide popular appeal; he must strengthen his position with the State organizations of his party, particularly in the States with large delegations; and he must demonstrate his ability to win votes by entering all or nearly all of the State presidential primaries, in the effort to solidify his delegate support in the approaching national convention.

Projecting a Presidential Image

The idea of "projecting an image," scoffed at by some as a product of the Madison Avenue approach to politics, nevertheless has some validity. It *is* important that a candidate not only announce his candidacy but that, at proper times and in appropriate places, he convey the impression that he is of the caliber associated with the presidential office and has some grasp of national issues and problems—in other words, that he looks and acts like a President. Such an image can be projected in various ways, such as by making major addresses before influential groups, thereby demonstrating his interest in and knowledge of important public questions. He may attend and speak at various State, local, and regional meetings of party leaders. Even the projected image of his wife as a potential first lady may play a part in determining public reaction toward him.

Gaining State Organization Support

The efforts of the leading contenders for the nomination to gain State organization support bring one face to face with the fact that the national arena frequently becomes the battleground for the achievement of State party goals and interests. The delegates, whoever they are, are certain to carry to the convention with them many "local jealousies and favoritisms," as Herring has called them.[3] Their preferences between candidates, and the way they finally vote, will to a large extent be determined by these considerations, most of which have little or no relation to the fitness or qualifications of the several candidates. Professor Sorauf cites an interesting example from Pennsylvania in 1960:

> Governor David L. Lawrence, I am reliably informed, is cool to the ambitions of Senator John Kennedy. One rather substantial explanation goes this way. The Governor wants desperately to work with a Democratic legislature in the final two years of his tenure. In order to capture the State Senate and hold the House, the Democrats will have to win and hold seats outside of the two metropolitan areas. However, these rural and mixed urban-rural areas are the very sections of the State where the resistance to Catholic candidates is the strongest. Hence, the Governor feels that a Catholic—any Catholic—heading the ticket will seriously threaten his chances of carrying the State legislature this fall. If this rationale actually represents the Governor's thinking— and I have no reason to doubt that it does—we have here a classic example of the impact of local political considerations and strategy on the selection of Presidential candidates.[4]

The efforts of the candidate to gain support must capitalize on situations such as this when they are in his favor, and must find ways of overcoming them when they are not. The candidate who gets the firm support of State organizations is rarely defeated in the convention, whether or not he is afterward able to win the election. The support of the State delegations is essential to the candidate, as the control of the delegation is essential to the State party if it is to achieve its goals at the convention. Thus, to some degree, the State organization and a candidate who can win in the convention have much in common.

The many goals of the State party organizations are varied. Those whose States have a major candidate or a favorite son are anxious to advance his interests as a means of advancing their own, but those States that have no candidate may be interested in patronage or in assuring favorable legislative or administrative consideration of some local interest if the party is successful at the polls. Lasswell pointed out long ago that politics is a struggle for power, a struggle to determine who gets

[3] Herring, E. Pendleton, *Politics of Democracy* (New York: W. W. Norton & Co., Inc., 1940), p. 40.

[4] Sorauf, Frank, "The Relationship Between State and Presidential Nominating Politics," *Nominating the President: Commentaries on the Process* (University Park: Institute of Public Administration, Pennsylvania State University, 1960), pp. 23–28. See also David, Paul T., "The Role of Governors at National Party Conventions," *State Government*, Spring, 1960, pp. 103–110.

what, when, and how. The members of State organizations, as loyal Americans, are interested in helping to nominate and elect a good President, but they also want to win. They are anxious, furthermore, to protect and further their own interests and those of their State.

The importance of the role of the States and of the Governors, many of whom are State party leaders, in nominating politics is further illustrated by the vast amount of "politicking" that takes place at the annual Governors' Conference in presidential years. Although it is not reflected in the topics listed on the printed program, pre-convention politics are a major concern of most of the Governors at that time, regardless of party. Their ability to control their delegations, and thus to deliver the vote for a preferred candidate, are greatly affected by the method used in selecting delegates. The Governors' control is likely to be most effective if the delegates are selected by a State convention, less certain if all or a major portion of them are selected by district conventions, still less certain if they are elected unpledged, and least certain of all if they are chosen in a primary and pledged to a candidate.

It is thus in the interest of the candidate to work with the State organizations in the effort to bring about the selection of delegates pledged to or favorably disposed toward him. In the process, he may become involved in intra-party squabbles, as Mr. Kennedy did in New York in 1960. Needed support given at a critical moment may pay off well later. As Professor Sorauf observes, "I presume it is no accident that Arthur Summerfield, head of the 1952 Michigan delegation that moved at a crucial moment for Eisenhower, has sat in the cabinet since 1953. Now one reads that Governor Loveless of Iowa has vice-presidential ambitions and therefore inclines to Kennedy rather than Humphrey or Symington since the Democrats are unlikely to name an all-Midwest ticket. Others say that Governor Brown of California, similarly afflicted, opposes Kennedy on the ground that the party can hardly be expected to nominate two Catholics." [5]

While it is a major concern of the State party organizations to promote the nomination of their favorite candidates, it may be equally or more important for them to exercise a veto power over candidates they do not want. This was done more easily in the Democratic conventions while the two-thirds rule was in effect, but it may still be accomplished by personal conference, thereby avoiding a bitter contest on the convention floor.[6] The two-thirds rule was a made-to-order device to insure

---

[5] Sorauf, p. 26.

[6] President Roosevelt had intended in 1944 to keep Henry A. Wallace as his running mate, and was dissuaded from doing so only under great pressure from several big city bosses who assured him that naming Wallace would cost him millions of votes in the big cities. Frank R. Kent, in *Louisville Courier-*

minority rule, if the minority was well organized and wished to exert its power. But short of this, any observer of recent American politics can name individual candidates for a major party nomination who were able and well qualified, yet failed to gain significant organization support. They were not "politicians' politicians." Without substantial organization support, they had little chance of being nominated, much less elected.

Participating in the Presidential Primaries

While the candidate and his managers are busy contacting State party leaders, the candidate must be campaigning in some if not all of the States which conduct some form of presidential preference primary. Many of the primary laws were enacted between 1911 and 1915, as a phase of the Progressive Movement. After a long period of inactivity, five more (including the model Florida law) were enacted in 1954 and 1955. Altogether, there have been twenty-two original enactments and four re-enactments. Three States that repealed their laws had not, up to 1960, re-enacted them. Laws still on the books were used in sixteen States in 1960; detailed information regarding these developments appears in the table on page 239.

The laws vary considerably in scope and effectiveness. One writer who has studied all of them carefully finds no less than four categories:

1. Ballot *must not* show the delegate's preference among candidates; delegates *must run* on a "no preference" basis so far as the ballot is concerned. In 1956: Alabama, Illinois, Nebraska, New York, Pennsylvania, West Virginia, and District of Columbia.

2. Ballot *may* show delegate's preference *if* the candidate consents; delegates may also run on a "no preference" basis. In 1956: Massachusetts, New Jersey, South Dakota.

3. Ballot *may* show delegate's preference, whether or not the candidate consents; delegates may also run on a "no preference" basis. In 1956: Florida and New Hampshire.

4. Ballot *must* show delegate's preference for a candidate who has given consent; delegates *must not* run on a "no preference" basis. In 1956: California, Minnesota, Ohio, and Wisconsin.[7]

Journal, February 7, 1948, and quoted by Jasper B. Shannon, "Presidential Politics in the South," *Journal of Politics,* August, 1948, pp. 464–489, on p. 486.

[7] David, Paul T. *et al., The Politics of National Party Conventions* (Washington: Brookings Institution, 1960), pp. 120–121. See also David *et al., Specifications for a Model State Primary Law* (Washington: Brookings Institution, 1956).

PRESIDENTIAL PREFERENCE PRIMARY LAWS—
ADOPTIONS, REPEALS, AND DATES OF 1960 VOTING *

Date of Adoption (26 States)		Date of Repeal (7 States)		Date of 1960 Voting (16 States)
1911	California	1921	Vermont	March
	Nebraska			New Hampshire, March 8
	North Dakota	1927	Minnesota	
	Ohio		Re-enacted, 1944	April
	Oregon		Montana	Wisconsin, April 5
	Pennsylvania		Re-enacted, 1954	Illinois, April 12
	Wisconsin		North Carolina	New Jersey, April 19
				Massachusetts, April 26
1912	Massachusetts	1929	Indiana	Pennsylvania, April 26
	Michigan		Re-enacted, 1955	
	New Jersey			May
		1933	Illinois	District of Columbia, May 3
1913	Illinois		Re-enacted, 1955	Indiana, May 3
	Iowa			Ohio, May 3
	Minnesota	1935	North Dakota	Nebraska, May 10
	Montana			West Virginia, May 10
	New Hampshire			Maryland, May 17
				Oregon, May 20
1915	Indiana			Florida, May 24
	Vermont			
	West Virginia			June
				California, June 7
1917	South Dakota			South Dakota, June 7
1919	North Carolina			
1944	Minnesota			
1954	Montana			
1955	Alaska			
	Florida			
	Illinois			
	Indiana			

* Data in first two columns from Richard H. Hansen, "Performance and Potential of Presidential Primary Laws," *Nebraska Law Review*, May, 1960, pp. 473–526. Third column from Richard D. Hupman, comp., *Factual Campaign Information* (Washington: Secretary of the Senate, 1960), p. 7.

On the basis of even a cursory examination, it is obvious that these laws constitute a curious collection of inconsistencies and contradictions. What is specifically required in some jurisdictions is specifically forbidden in others. Not only are the laws poorly drawn, but any advantages they may have been intended to produce in drawing party members actively into the process of selecting the presidential candidates are more than offset by the enormous financial cost of operating the system and the almost inhuman mental and physical strain that they impose upon the major candidates. A glance at the dates of the 1960 primaries in the table on page 239 clearly indicates the reason. There were fifteen primaries in three months, thirteen of them in two months, not more than a few days or a week apart. In several instances, two or three of them in widely separated States occurred on the very same day.

Often when the sound and fury are over, it happens that nothing has been accomplished at all. In some jurisdictions, the elected delegates are not obliged to vote for the winner in the primary. Actually, the names of major candidates frequently do not appear on the ballot out of courtesy to favorite sons, and some candidates do not wish to compete in a particular State for other reasons. Since only about one-third of the States have primaries, it can happen that a major candidate enters and wins in all of them and still fails to receive the nomination of his party. Winning in the primaries does, however, give him a psychological and tactical advantage. In sum, the system as it now exists simply does not make much sense.

If there were uniform primary laws in all the States and a primary were held for both parties in all States throughout the nation on the same day, the system might have some value. Even so, it would still remain an idle exercise unless all of the leading candidates were on the ballot and the voting results were binding upon the convention delegates elected. In addition, some provision should be made to have the public treasury bear a substantial portion of the cost; under the prevailing system, the cost is so great that a candidate must either be very wealthy himself or have very wealthy and generous backers if he is to stand even a chance of winning the nomination. In other words, as one very able Democratic candidate learned to his sorrow in 1960, a man without considerable means is beaten before he starts.

THE STATES IN THE CAMPAIGN

The role of the States is as important during the campaign as it is in the steps leading up to the nominating conventions. The first step for the successful candidate and his advisors following the convention is to plan the campaign and map a strategy. They quickly tabulate the States that they expect to carry, the ones they will almost certainly lose, and the doubtful States in which they have at least a fighting chance. Obviously there is little to be accomplished by spending money and working hard in the sure States in either category, so the campaign centers on the doubtful States, particularly upon those having large numbers of electoral votes.

In less strenuous times, front-porch campaigns were sometimes possible, but the whistle-stop tour with a campaign train has long been and still is probably the most effective means of giving a candidate the maximum public exposure, *i.e.*, of having him seen and heard by the largest possible number of voters. Radio greatly enlarged the possible audience, but radio time is expensive. Television enlarged the possible audience still more, but television time on a national network can be purchased only at costs that are almost prohibitive. These conditions pose great financial difficulties for the national party organizations, neither of which ever admits having much money and one of which is almost constantly in debt.

The result is that campaign strategy usually is to give the candidate maximum public exposure by using as much national radio and television time as the party can collect money to buy, and by whistle-stop touring ten to sixteen hours a day through key States. Modern aviation gives flexibility to a candidate's schedule, permitting him to visit distant States to keep speaking engagements which were planned early in the campaign, or to bolster the efforts of party workers when trouble spots are reported around the country as the campaign develops.

It is ordinarily to the advantage of the State party organizations to put forth their utmost effort in behalf of the national ticket, for winning may mean much to them. For reasons of their own, however, they may occasionally decide to sit out a particular campaign because they do not like the candidate or the platform. In some cases, they may merely "sulk in their tent," although such a procedure offers no hope for the future if the party ticket wins the election without their help.

Reliance upon State and local party organizations for a major portion of the campaign effort rests upon many considerations. The State organization is normally a thriving concern, while, as has been noted, the national organization is a hastily improvised and more or less temporary affair. Moreover, the resources of the national organization may be so limited as to permit no other course. Even if this were not the case, national laws governing campaign expenditures place many theoretical and some actual limitations on the campaign spending of national party organizations. These restrictions do not apply to the State organizations, where there is virtually no limit to the number of special committees that may be organized to collect and expend funds in behalf of the party candidates at all levels. This situation emphasizes once again the dominant role of the States in the process of nominating and electing a President of the United States.

THE STATES IN THE ELECTORAL PROCESS

Nowhere is the influence of the States and the State party organizations greater than in the actual process of electing the President. Under the system prescribed by the Constitution, the Electors vote by States in their respective State capitols, and the party which wins a majority of the popular votes casts the full number of electoral votes to which the State is entitled. There is much to be said in favor of this system of election within a federally organized government such as ours.

The States have an important role in the governmental system, and it seems quite appropriate that they should have a similarly important role in selecting the leadership of the central government. While this view is generally accepted, it has in recent years been criticized. Discussion in this chapter is now directed to the system itself, then to proposals for change, and finally to some of the basic weaknesses in the American system of elections administration.

The Electoral College

Article II, Section 1 of the Constitution provides that the President and Vice-President shall be elected by the members of the Electoral College. They are the only elected Federal officials not chosen by direct popular vote. On presidential election day, the first Tuesday after the first Monday in November of every fourth year, each State elects as many Electors as it has Senators and Representatives in Congress. An Elector cannot be a Member of Congress or hold Federal office. The Electors of the party receiving the highest popular vote meet at the State Capitol on the first Monday after the second Wednesday in December to cast their votes for President and Vice-President. Customarily, they vote for the nominees of their party, although the Constitution does not require them to do so. The only constitutional requirement is that at least one of the men for whom they cast their ballots shall not be an inhabitant of their own State.

There have been few instances in which Electors have ignored the mandate of the voters of their States, but the number has been increasing in recent years. The first instance took place in 1820 when William Plumer, a New Hamphire Elector pledged to Monroe, voted for John Quincy Adams on the patriotic pretext that only George Washington "deserved a unanimous election." No other instance occurred for more than a century, until in 1948 Preston Parks, a Tennessee Elector chosen by both the Democratic and the States' Rights parties, cast his vote for J. Strom Thurmond because of his dislike for President Truman and for Truman's civil rights program. Since then, Democratic Electors in the Southern States have revolted, or threatened to revolt, more or less with impunity. In 1960, there were fourteen "independent" Electors from the South, eight from Mississippi, and six from Alabama.

In the early days, two certified copies of the Electors' votes were forwarded to Washington, one by post and the other by a rider on horseback. Both copies are now mailed to the President of the Senate. On January 6, the Senate and House of Representatives, meeting in joint session, open and count the electoral votes. Although the result of this ceremony is known for weeks in advance, there is no official President-Elect until it has been completed. If no candidate for President has a majority, the House elects a President from among the three highest candidates, each State's Representatives having one vote. If no candidate for Vice-President has a majority, the Senate elects one of the top two, Senators voting as individuals.

Proposals for Change

Every system of election, existing or recommended, represents a compromise between conflicting interests and points of view. No system is or is likely to be perfect, and this one has many weaknesses which are generally recognized and widely admitted. Professor Burns has summarized its faults by saying that the Electoral College system is unfair, inaccurate, uncertain, and undemocratic.[8] It is doubtless true that if a new start were made now, the Electoral College would not be established in its present form, but the fact remains that on the whole it has worked well.

During a period of almost two centuries, there have been only three instances in which the election has been thrown into the House of Repre-

[8] Burns, James M., "A New Course for the Electoral College," *The New York Times Magazine*, December 18, 1960, pp. 10, 22, 25–28.

sentatives,[9] and only five in which a President has been elected who had less than a majority of the popular vote.[10] This appears to do no harm, and the leadership of these Presidents and their authority to govern have seemed to be unaffected by their plurality status.

Nevertheless, there are periodic demands for change—demands which ignore the oft-quoted judgment of Falkland that "When it is not necessary to change, it is necessary not to change." These demands now arise during presidential elections with considerable regularity, and the close popular vote in the 1960 election gave *or* provided temporarily unusual encouragement to the advocates of change. The proposals for change fall into one of two categories: (1) abolish the Electoral College and substitute direct election of the President by the people; [11] (2) modify the unit rule which now governs Electoral College voting in each State. The latter proposal is, in turn, of two types, those which suggest the establishment of a district system and those which would apportion the electoral votes in each State on a proportionate basis in relation to the popular vote.

Although it is difficult for those who believe in democracy to argue *against* direct election by the people, it is easy to argue *for* the continuance of the recognition of the States in a federal system, for which the present system provides. Even the most ardent advocates of direct election do not regard it as possible to achieve, because it would require a constitutional amendment approved by a two-thirds vote of both houses of Congress, neither of which has ever shown any enthusiasm for the idea.

Several plans for changing the Electoral College (Lodge-Gossett, Coudert, and Mundt) have been given serious consideration and have been debated at length in the Senate, in 1950 and again in 1956. The first of these plans proposed to split the electoral vote in each State in exactly the same proportion as the popular vote; with this was a provi-

[9] These were: *1800*, when Thomas Jefferson was chosen by the votes of ten States, with four voting for Aaron Burr and two abstaining; *1824*, when John Quincy Adams was elected—amidst cries of bargain and corruption—receiving the votes of thirteen States, with seven for Andrew Jackson and four for William H. Crawford; *1876*, when following the failure of both the Electoral College and the House of Representatives to elect, a specially constituted electoral commission selected Rutherford B. Hayes over Samuel J. Tilden.

[10] In 1888, Benjamin Harrison was elected with less than 50 per cent of the popular vote and with only 58 per cent of the electoral vote (5,444,337 as compared with 5,540,000 for Grover Cleveland, 233 as compared with 168 for Cleveland); other so-called minority Presidents have been Lincoln, Wilson, Truman, and now Kennedy.

[11] See Lewis, Ted, "Electoral College: Facts and Fallacies," *The Nation*, December 10, 1960, pp. 448–450, which emphasizes abolition and proportionate division of the electoral votes.

sion allowing a President to be elected by 45 per cent of the electoral votes, instead of by the majority of these votes now required by the Constitution. The second provision was added to make popular election of a President more certain, so that the House of Representatives need not be given the final choice.

In arguing for his plan, Senator Lodge listed what he termed the "defects, unhealthy practices and potential evils" of the unit rule system, which gives all of a State's electoral votes to the popular-vote victor:

> One was the possibility that the winner of the popular vote nationally would lose in the Electoral College. [But this rarely happens!] A second was the thesis that the hopelessness of upsetting the majority in one-party States discouraged minority voters from bothering to turn out on Election Day; if they knew that every vote would count in the electoral total, it was reasoned, more would care and one-party rule would be threatened. Third was the argument that under the unit rule all votes cast for the losing candidate in a State are "wasted." [The only trouble with this is that it does not happen to be true.] [12]

The Senate, although it has now become the more popular body, passed the proposal in 1950 by a vote of 64 to 27, but it failed to clear the House Rules Committee. In 1956, two alternative proposals were combined in one resolution, adding to the Lodge-Gossett plan a proposal that the States elect two presidential Electors at large and one in each Congressional district. This proposal was recommitted in the Senate, its supporters frankly admitting that their aim was to minimize the influence of such powerful pressure groups as labor, N.A.A.C.P., and the minority groups in the electorate of the large cities and States.

Thus the question at issue is quite clear. The Republican-conservative-rural coalition now controls most of the State legislatures, which in turn determine the districting and, to a considerable extent, the political complexion of Congress. If this group could re-create the complexion of the Electoral College in its own image, by minimizing the Democratic-liberal-labor-minority-group-urban influence, they would stand a better chance of controlling the Presidency. The conservatives, however, are not united, either on what they want or in their estimate of what its probable result would be. Senator Robert A. Taft had written to every Republican Member of the House in 1950, predicting that if such a proposal were adopted, the G.O.P. would never again elect a President, because the Democrats would always have a huge proportion of the popular vote in the South and, therefore, a heavy proportion of the electoral vote.

[12] Summarized by Lewis, Anthony, "The Case Against Electoral Reform," *The Reporter*, December 8, 1960, pp. 31-33.

This is an old, familiar conflict in American politics. The conflict is not likely to subside, nor is the electoral system likely to be changed in this manner—certainly not so drastically—in a nation that is steadily becoming more highly urbanized. The operation of the present system is familiar, but it would require years of experience to learn how any new system might work. While it is a good maxim in politics not to expend time, money, and energy in an effort to change something that is really not very bad and that probably cannot be changed anyway, it is also good policy to do whatever is politically possible by way of improvement.

A constitutional amendment could perhaps be passed that would end such recent procedural irregularities as: (1) the refusal of a State to put on the ballot the names of the candidates of any party that meets a reasonable set of qualifications, the reasonableness to be subject to judicial review. This would prevent a repetition of what happened in Alabama in 1948, when a dissident-controlled party organization denied the voters of that State an opportunity to vote for the Truman-Barkley ticket; (2) the practice followed in Alabama and Mississippi in 1960, when voters were asked to support uncommitted or "independent" electors; (3) the refusal of an Elector to vote for the candidate who won the popular election in his State. This would remedy cases like that of the confused Oklahoma Elector in 1960 who rejected the idea that the majority vote of his fellow Oklahomans for Nixon meant that he had to support the Vice-President; he thoroughly tangled party lines by voting for Democrat Harry F. Byrd for President and Republican Barry Goldwater for Vice-President.

These proposed changes make sense, and should be possible to accomplish. Probably they should be made, but it is also urgent that steps be taken to insure better supervised elections in many of the States. Attention is now directed to the matter of elections administration.

Weaknesses in Election Administration

Although the vital importance of honest and efficient elections administration in a democracy is universally recognized, Americans have long been remiss in their handling of this problem. Article I, Section 4 of the Constitution delegates responsibility for the whole nominating and electoral process to the States:

> The times, places, and manner of holding elections for Senators and Representatives shall be prescribed in each State by the legislature thereof; but the Congress may at any time by law make or alter such regulations, except as to the places of choosing Senators.

Article I, Section 2 provides that "the electors in each State shall have the qualifications requisite for electors of the more numerous branch of the State Legislature." The same rule has long been followed in practice in the selection of presidential Electors. Commenting on this matter in No. 59 of *The Federalist Papers,* Hamilton observed:

> Suppose an article had been introduced into the Constitution, empowering the United States to regulate the elections for the particular States, would any man have hesitated to condemn it, both as an unwarrantable transposition of power, and as a premeditated engine for the destruction of the State governments? The violation of principle, in this case, would have required no comment; and, to an unbiased observer, it will not be less apparent in the project of subjecting the existence of the national government, in a similar respect, to the pleasure of the State governments. An impartial view of the matter cannot fail to result in a conviction, that each, so far as possible, ought to depend on itself for its own preservation.

So deeply has this line of thought become imbedded in the thinking of most Americans that Congress has never undertaken to exercise such constitutional powers as it actually has to supervise elections, choosing rather to defer to the States. So much has this been the case that early Congressional efforts to regulate primary elections were challenged on the ground that they interfered with the powers of the States, a view which was rejected by the Supreme Court in *Newberry* v. *United States.*[13]

Many questions have arisen with regard to the manner in which the States have met their responsibility. Few States have provided suitable, adequate machinery for the administration of elections; some of them have permitted the continuance of such anomalies as the unit rule and the poll tax, and many of them have authorized and have sought vigorously to enforce various unfair and discriminatory laws designed to prevent qualified citizens from voting.

Poor Electoral Machinery and Inadequate Supervision. American scholars who have studied the electoral process in this country invariably comment on the lack of any suitable administrative machinery and of

[13] 256 U.S. 232 (1921). Since the law in question had been passed prior to the adoption of the Seventeenth Amendment, the Court held that the term "election" must be interpreted in the manner intended by the authors of the Constitution. Party nominating conventions were unknown to them; therefore the selection by the members of a party of a candidate to represent the party was not in their minds when they gave Congress authority to regulate "the manner of holding elections." At the same time, Section 8 of the Act was held unconstitutional as an exercise of power that had not been granted to Congress. The 5-4 decision created such an unfavorable public reaction that after the 1922 election, Senator Newberry resigned his seat in order to relieve his party of embarrassment.

any State attempts at supervision. Foreign observers are quite dumb-founded by the completely decentralized, utterly unsupervised nature of the operation. Nothing similar to it exists in any other major country in the world. No one would object to the unique character of the system if it worked, but that it does not work even moderately well in a great many cases is illustrated every time an election is held. The inadequacy of the system is particularly evident when the election is close.

During close elections, charges of fraud and irregularity are heard so often and from so many quarters that if even a fraction of them were well founded, the integrity of the whole system would be called into question. Yet the United States can and does send specialists in election administration to the far corners of the earth to help new countries establish an electoral system, while here at home Americans remain quite indifferent to the problem of putting their own electoral machinery in order. As implied, the problems involved are of two kinds—organizational and supervisory.

Most States have constitutional provisions for suffrage and elections, but there is in most jurisdictions no single State official whose chief duty is to administer and to supervise the electoral machinery. By custom, this task is assigned as one among a group of miscellaneous and unrelated duties performed by the secretary of state, who receives and files nominating papers in the performance of his duties in the preparation of ballots. Voting results are reported to him, and he compiles and publishes the official election returns and issues certificates of election to the winning candidates.

But the whole vitally important task of actually administering the election is left by law to the local authorities, usually the county boards, who either perform this function themselves or are specially constituted as a county board of elections to discharge the responsibility. Election laws are voluminous, are frequently amended, and may become extremely involved and complicated. The county board members, normally local party politicians with no qualifications for the job, are turned loose to conduct the election and count the ballots with no supervision and very often without instruction. It is no wonder that the results are often such as to stagger the imagination. Instead of recognizing—as is clearly the case—that such a system practically invites irregularities, that they are almost inevitable, Americans usually express surprise and shock when irregularities are reported.

There have been irregularities in the past—numerous, serious, and significant ones—and they still occur. It has been clearly established that there have been districts in which more votes were cast than there were residents; in which citizens who had conscientiously registered went to the polls only to find that their registrations had been "lost"; in which a disproportionate number of Republican ballots have been thrown out in heavily Democratic districts, and vice versa. The literature on parties and elections is replete with illustrations of the chicanery and skulduggery that has all too often characterized the administration of elections in this country. A few of the hoary tricks alleged to have been used as recently as November 8, 1960, in Chicago and Texas, will suffice to illustrate here:

Chicago. A study of incidents being processed for grand jury action and collected as exhibits in the Republican Party's election challenge shows that even these hoary standbys, the cemetery and floater votes, were used.

The cases of the late Ed Myles and his son, Jimmy Powell Myles, typify numerous reports in these categories. The two men lived in an apartment at 4932 Blackstone Street. After the father died a couple of years ago, the son moved—and was not heard from again.

Nevertheless, both "Ed Myles" and "Jimmy Powell Myles" voted, as usual, on November 8 in the solidly Democratic Fourth Ward, 31st Precinct. . . .

Meanwhile, the collection of cases disclosed by State and Federal investigators, civic groups and the Republican organization is growing rapidly as more and more individuals voluntarily report incidents they experienced or witnessed while voting.

For example, a doctor declared that when he entered his polling place he discovered from an election clerk's off-hand remarks that his father and mother were also enrolled and probably had voted.

"Dad died in 1943," wrote the doctor. "Mother . . . has not voted in at least ten years. She moved . . . four years ago and has never registered in this ward to vote."

Many city precincts reported more votes than were actually cast on the basis of the ballots requested. In at least a half dozen precincts, the excess totalled 75 to 100 "votes," all of which were certified on November 23 by the county's Democratic-controlled Election Board. . . .

Among the most common allegations were those against the practice of Democratic precinct captains who ignored the law that forbids electioneering in polling places.

Dan Leavey, Democratic sachem of Precinct 47, Ward 29, allegedly brought along a Spanish interpreter to simplify the problem of instructing Puerto Rican voters as they entered the booth.

"Vote straight Democratic, that's all," they reportedly were told —first in English, then in Spanish.

Texas. Being more eager at the moment to get "a straight, orderly count" than to punish wrongdoers, the Republicans say their immediate concern is to turn up "at least" 100,000 ballots that private surveys convince them were illegally counted. . . . The all-Democratic Board of Canvassers has either put off hearing or has overruled Republican

complaints of "numerous and widespread frauds, irregularities and il-
legalities" in the November 8 election.

But a public airing might also disclose answers to some typical inconsistencies in the Texas election.

Why, for instance, were 6,138 votes cast in Fannin County when
only 4,895 people were on the "poll list" as having paid their poll tax or
gotten exemption certificates? (Fannin, the home bailiwick of House
Speaker Sam Rayburn, went 3-to-1 Democratic.)

Why were 234 ballots thrown out as improperly marked in Eagle
Lake and only two were voided in Precinct 54, Wichita Falls? (Eagle
Lake is considered a representative middle-income community with a
better-than-average percentage of college graduates. Its recorded vote
was 475 for Nixon-Lodge, 357 for Kennedy-Johnson. Precinct 54,
Wichita Falls, like most substandard neighborhoods, has a low literacy
rate. Its vote was six-to-one Democratic.) . . .

The discrepancies in voided votes are laid to the whims of election judges—and the unique practice whereby Texans outside voting
machine areas vote a "negative ballot," striking out all the candidates
they don't want instead of merely checking the ones they favor. . . .

An overwhelmingly Kennedy-Johnson precinct, examined to settle
a contest for a local office, unofficially turned up about 200 Kennedy-
Johnson votes that should have been disqualified. . . .

Typifying the contrast in how election judges handled the "negative ballots" were the returns from Precincts 34 and 35, Wichita
County. These neighbors in a rural area are twins in almost every
respect, yet only 3 per cent of the votes were thrown out for being
illegally marked in one, and 22 per cent in the other.[14]

The records of the Committee of Seventy in Philadelphia, or of
similar election-policing citizen groups in other large cities, would provide abundant illustrations of actual irregularities, as do some of the
published reports of Congressional committees on contested elections. At
the same time, one must admit that there has been entirely too much
hearsay and allegation in the discussion of election irregularities. If one
loses a close election, it is always easy to fall back on the excuse that "the
election was stolen," as was done in 1960 when wholesale fraud was
charged not only in Illinois, Pennsylvania, and Texas, but in large urban
centers generally.

Obviously, alleged irregularities and errors could, if in fact they
occurred, make the difference between victory and defeat for a presidential candidate in a close election. In the 1960 election, however,

[14] Earl Mazo wrote a series of four articles on alleged voting irregularities
in the 1960 Presidential election which appeared in the New York *Herald-
Tribune*, December 4–7, 1960, and in the *Washington Post*, December 11,
1960. The excerpts quoted here follow the text of the former.

unusual precautions against fraud had been taken in many jurisdictions well in advance, with the result that on the whole this election was more than normally free from irregularities of the type charged. Both the observations of informed and experienced individuals and the published findings of investigators have substantiated this fact in several jurisdictions.

A long-time, highly respected student of Texas politics informed the writer that the allegations of fraud and irregularity in that State were "greatly exaggerated." This verbal statement is confirmed by the fact that the published report of his findings with respect to the Texas election makes no mention of the alleged irregularities. Similar conclusions are indicated in the reports of studies of the 1960 elections in Illinois and Pennsylvania. In the former State, three distinguished political scientists at the University of Chicago, stirred by "the charges of wholesale fraud perpetrated in Chicago," undertook a study of the press coverage of the election in that city.[15] Although they were not in a position to attempt "an independent examination of the presence or absence of fraud" in this election—a task which would require "a large-scale official investigation"—they could and did "attempt to examine the evidence put forward by the Republican Party and the Chicago newspapers to support the charges of fraud which they made." They concluded that the charges were "baseless and unsubstantiated."

In somewhat similar circumstances, the Pennsylvania State Senate established, early in 1961, a Committee to Investigate Alleged Election Irregularities, particularly in Philadelphia. In its *Final Report,* this Committee took the position that it "was not established to indict, censure or condemn any public official or agency," but merely to obtain the facts upon which any needed legislation might be developed. Acknowledging as fact that some irregularities had occurred during the recent elections in Philadelphia, the Committee addressed itself to the task of determining the causes and to proposing such remedies as were deemed necessary and proper. After citing, with apparent approval, the Citizens' Charter Committee's view that some of the State statutes on registration and elections "are obsolete, anachronistic, and actually conducive to election irregularities," the *Report* presents some proposed changes in the law that might, to the extent that laws alone can do so, eliminate such irregularities from Philadelphia elections in the course of time.

Since Federal officers are elected under State laws, and under such arrangements for election administration as the States may see fit to

---

[15] On Texas, see Weeks, O. Douglas, *Texas in the 1960 Presidential Election* (Austin: Institute of Public Affairs, University of Texas, 1962); on Illinois, see Finer, Herman *et al., An Analysis of the Press Coverage of the 1960 Election in Chicago* (Chicago: private printing, February, 1961).

provide, the wonder is not that Congress has occasionally become impatient with the serious shortcomings of the States in this field, but that it has for so long refrained from taking positive action, under the authority conferred upon it by the Constitution, to establish standards of election administration and to insist that these standards be adhered to in all elections in which candidates for Federal office appear on the ballot.

Use of the County Unit System. The existence of the county unit system in Georgia primaries has been widely publicized, but a similar system has also existed in Maryland and Mississippi. Section 140 of the Mississippi constitution sets up a comparable system in the general elections in that State. The Maryland system, like that in Georgia, is restricted to primaries. The purpose in either case, whether constitutional or statutory, was to keep control in the hands of the rural counties, and it did precisely that, placing the urban areas of the State in such a disadvantageous position that it was rarely possible for them to win a nomination for state-wide office. This system also worked against the urban areas in the allocation of funds for schools, highways, and other purposes—a matter which may have some bearing upon the distribution of Federal aid funds as well. The Supreme Court invalidated the Georgia system in the spring of 1963, whereupon, after the General Assembly had failed to act, the Maryland State Court of Appeals did likewise.

Unfair and Discriminatory Laws and Procedures. Many States have long enforced statutory laws deliberately designed to prevent certain classes of citizens from registering and voting. Poll tax laws, now gradually disappearing, are in this category, as are certain types of literacy tests, constitution-interpretation tests, and others. Thousands of citizens are disfranchised because of inequitable absentee voting laws and unreasonable residence requirements. Where the results of discriminatory legislation and discriminatory enforcement procedures did not sufficiently restrict the suffrage, intimidation and retaliatory measures bordering on persecution have been invoked in many communities. The work of the Civil Rights Commission and the Civil Rights Division of the Department of Justice is beginning to make some headway, but the problem is still a serious one in many jurisdictions.

As one surveys these weaknesses in State election administration, he may be pardoned for wondering if dissatisfaction with the Electoral College is not based far more on the weaknesses than upon any injustices, either real or alleged, in the Electoral College procedure itself. Clearly needed to assure equal rights and protections for all citizens qualified to vote for President, Vice-President, and Members of Congress are a uniform Federal-State election law, and better enforcement procedures to guarantee against fraud, false count, and irregularity. They are necessary to prevent the spread of a corrosive cynicism which is undermining confidence in the whole electoral process and keeping large numbers of citizens away from the polls.

POLITICAL DYNAMICS: MEN, MONEY, AND ISSUES

The discussion up to this point has emphasized the power and influence of State and local organizations and leaders in presidential politics, but it would be a major error to assume that the influence is only in one direction, that it is confined to presidential years, or that it stops when a presidential election is over. Party politics in a federal system travel on a two-way street. There is a never-ending quest for experienced personnel for national leadership; in connection with this and other matters, national party leaders are in almost constant contact with State leaders and the State party organizations and occasionally exert pressure upon them, while the State leaders exert pressure upon those at the national level in behalf of local needs.

The Quest for Experienced National Leadership

A democratic government rather quickly reflects the quality of its leadership in high positions. If that leadership is progressive, far-sighted, and energetic, society responds by "moving ahead," but if it is indifferent or incompetent, society quickly reflects that also. This is merely another way of saying that competent leadership is essential to the proper functioning of democratic institutions. Where, one may ask, shall such leadership be found? How can potential leaders of ability be identified, and how and where shall they be trained for the highest positions in government?

In the early days of the Republic, able leaders were found among those who had had extensive experience in public affairs, both at home and abroad. After the Virginia dynasty and the Jacksonian era, the quality of leadership declined during most of the nineteenth century—Lincoln and Cleveland excepted—while the nation experimented, not too successfully, with military leaders or run-of-the-mill politicians as Presidents. With the advent of the twentieth century and a considerable transformation of the office of the Governorship, the nation began to rely primarily on Governors and ex-Governors, men with experience in State and local government and politics. This practice gave the nation the leadership of a Wilson, two Roosevelts, and though not elected, a Stevenson.

It has become customary to refer to Ohio as the Mother of Presidents, but in the early days Virginia did very well. Later, Illinois, Indiana, California, and Missouri have produced a considerable number of candidates for the two top offices, but no other State in the last century has nearly equaled the record of New York, whose Democratic Party alone has produced Seymour, Greeley, Tilden, Cleveland (three times), Parker, Davis, Smith, and Franklin Roosevelt (four times). New York's Republican Party has produced Arthur, Theodore Roosevelt (two times), Hughes, Dewey (two times), and half a dozen vice-presidential candidates. Pennsylvania alone, among the larger States, has produced only one President (Buchanan, 1856), one unsuccessful candidate for the Presidency on a major party ticket (Winfield Scott Hancock, 1880), and one unsuccessful candidate for President on a significant third-party ticket (Wharton Barker, a Populist, in 1900).[16]

BACKGROUNDS OF PRESIDENTIAL CANDIDATES, 1900–1960

| Year | Gubernatorial Experience | | Other | |
	Democratic	Republican	Democratic	Republican
1900			Bryan	McKinley *
1904		T. Roosevelt *	Parker	
1908			Bryan	Taft *
1912	Wilson *	T. Roosevelt (Prog.)		Taft
1916	Wilson *	Hughes		
1920	Cox			Harding * †
1924		Coolidge *	Davis	
		LaFollette (Prog.)		
1928	Smith			Hoover *
1932	Roosevelt *			Hoover
1936	Roosevelt *	Landon		
1940	Roosevelt *			Willkie
1944	Roosevelt *	Dewey		
1948		Dewey	Truman *	
1952	Stevenson			Eisenhower *
1956	Stevenson			Eisenhower *
1960			Kennedy *	Nixon

* Indicates elected candidate.

† Had been an unsuccessful candidate for Governor of Ohio.

[16] See Coleman, John M., "The Role of Pennsylvania in Presidential Nominating Conventions," *Nominating the President: Commentaries on the Process*, pp. 1–6.

The preceding table indicates the experience of the major parties in nominating candidates with and without gubernatorial experience in sixteen campaigns from 1900 to 1960 inclusive. During this time, the Democrats nominated a candidate with gubernatorial training in ten elections and won in six (twice with Wilson, four times with Roosevelt), while the Republicans did so in eight elections, winning in two (Roosevelt in 1904, Coolidge in 1924). The Democrats ran six candidates without such experience and won twice (Truman in 1948, Kennedy in 1960), while the Republicans ran such candidates in ten elections and won in six (McKinley, Taft, Harding, Hoover, and twice with Eisenhower). Judging by these statistics, it appears that the Democrats do better with Governors or former Governors as candidates, while the Republicans have been more successful with candidates lacking such experience.

Calvin Coolidge, of course, is the best example of "risen from the ranks" national leadership. Beginning his public career in his home city of Northampton, Massachusetts, he served as a member of the city council, as Mayor, as a member of the General Court, as Lieutenant-Governor, and as Governor before moving on to Washington, first as Vice-President and later as President. What happens with respect to the Presidency, however, is only part of the story. A significant number of those who serve as Members of Congress, in cabinet posts, as members of regulatory agencies, as heads of independent establishments, in the foreign service, or in other high positions in the Federal Service, receive their early training and experience in State and local government posts.

During recent Congresses, approximately one-third of the Members of the Senate have been former Governors of their States, while nearly half of the membership in the House of Representatives has had previous experience in the State legislatures. Included in this number are many former speakers, majority and minority floor leaders, and others with extensive periods of legislative service.[17] Significantly, as the political influence of the cities increases, three Members of the Senate are former Mayors of their home towns (Evansville, Minneapolis, Philadelphia, and in the preceding Congress, Gloucester, Mass., as well). In addition, the Mayor of the nation's largest city made an unsuccessful bid for a Senate seat in 1956.

In view of this rise of the cities, and in spite of the fact that only

---

[17] Three articles by John Mason Brown are of interest here: "184 of Us in Congress," *State Government*, June, 1934, pp. 126–128; "The State Legislatures: The Proving-Grounds of American Statesmanship," *ibid.*, December, 1938, pp. 230–231, 239; and "The State Legislatures as Training for Further Public Service," *Annals of the American Academy of Political and Social Science*, January, 1938, pp. 172–186.

two Senators (Harding and Kennedy) have won nomination and election to the Presidency in the twentieth century, it has been suggested that the Kennedy and Nixon nominations might indicate a coming shift from reliance on State and local training for high national office toward a dependence on experience at the national level with big city support.[18]

The Politics of Party Leadership

The contacts between national leaders and those at the State and local levels include both executive and legislative officers, and they may be either formal, informal, or both. The President is the recognized leader of his party; the national chairman is personally selected by him, but there are many political functions that the President himself must perform. He addresses many meetings of State and local party leaders, both in Washington and in the States, in person where possible, or as in the case of the Lincoln Day and Jackson Day dinners, by closed circuit television. Far more significant, however, are his numerous personal conferences and telephone conversations with State and local party leaders.

Ours is a political society, and political leadership is a part of the President's job. If he neglects it or is personally disinclined to politics, he may both impair the success of his program and encourage the development of difficult political situations for himself and his party at election time. One can afford neither to ignore nor to remain aloof from party squabbles in the States, at least not in the large and important ones; witness Mr. Kennedy's intervention as peacemaker in the troubled situation within his party in New York, both before and after the 1960 election.

For present purposes, this is a particularly good illustration. Kennedy's job before the election was to arrange a truce between the warring factions that would last at least until the election was over. This he did, although friction broke out anew almost before all the votes were counted. Then the President-elect's task became one of restoring unity within the party—a goal in which he might have a considerable personal stake—with a view to helping the party win the Governorship in 1962 and carrying the State in the presidential election of 1964. Apparently convinced that the incumbent state chairman, though he turned in a very respectable margin of victory in the November, 1960 election, was responsible for the schism, and that party unity in the State was impossible as long as he remained in command, the President-elect set about under-

[18] See Baker, Russell, "Best Road to the White House—Which?" *The New York Times Magazine,* November 27, 1960, pp. 22, 123–125.

mining his position, using several tried and proven techniques. A political reporter for *The New York Times* ably analyzed the situation:

> New York's Democratic State Chairman is suffering the cruelest fate that can befall a politician; he is being studiously ignored by the President-elect of his own party. President-elect John F. Kennedy's deliberate avoidance of the nominal head of the Democratic party in the nation's most populous State has been quietly emphasized since the election. Mr. Kennedy has found time to see a great many New York Democrats and the Democratic leaders of other States, but has found none for Mr. Prendergast. . . .
>
> Presumably acting with Mr. Kennedy's approval, his associates in the new Administration have been carefully by-passing New York's Democratic State Chairman in seeking advice and recommendations for personnel to serve in Washington with Mr. Kennedy.
>
> Individual Democratic county chairmen in the State have been encouraged to present suggestions and recommendations directly to Mr. Kennedy's patronage advisors. They likewise have been encouraged to give thought to a successor for Mr. Prendergast. The course of conduct adopted by Mr. Kennedy appears unmistakably calculated to force Mr. Prendergast out of office as state chairman. So long as he is denied access to the President-elect and his top advisors, he is unable to perform one of the major functions as a party state chairman—the function of using the Presidential power of appointment to strengthen the party organization in the State.[19]

These problems of party leadership are by no means limited to the majority party; those of the minority may, in fact, be more acute. After the 1960 election, Senator Case, for example, indicated a willingness to assume the leadership of his party in New Jersey, suggesting former Secretary of Labor James P. Mitchell as a suitable candidate for the Governorship, somewhat to the dismay of several legislative candidates. This move toward winning another Governorship for his party was quite in harmony with the judgment of other party leaders, who concluded that the G.O.P. needed more Governors. In this respect, they were in a bad position, holding only sixteen to their rival's thirty-four. The importance to the party of occupying the Governor's mansion is readily discernible. The Governor controls the State patronage and is in a position to help tremendously in building and maintaining a State political organization

[19] Egan, Leo, "Kennedy and New York: He Aids Anti-Prendergast Group Among Democrats by Ignoring the State Chairman on Patronage," *The New York Times*, January 8, 1961; see also Phillips, Wayne, "Kennedy Confers with Two Sides Here in Party Conflict," *ibid.*, January 9, 1961. Copyright by The New York Times.

By the same token, control of the city halls and county court houses is of tremendous importance to the party, whether it wants to stay in power or return to power.

Just as party leaders in the Executive Branch keep in touch with State constituents, so do Members of Congress by mail, by phone, and through the weekly newsletters sent out from their offices. In fact, failure on their part to maintain contacts in a satisfactory manner may be an almost certain indication of serious difficulty when they next come up for re-election. Usually also, the State delegations as a body attend inaugurations and other important political events at home. The Congressional delegation and the Governor should and frequently do work in close cooperation. After the North Carolina delegation had made such a pilgrimage back to Raleigh in 1961, one of the members reported in the *Congressional Record* on both the outgoing and incoming Governors:

> I would like to point out that Governor Hodges has had the longest tenure as Governor since North Carolina became a State in 1776. Governor Hodges has made us proud. We are proud of his success as a businessman, of his greatness as Governor, and of his integrity as a human being. It was no surprise to North Carolina that Governor Hodges was appointed as Secretary of Commerce for the Cabinet of President-elect John F. Kennedy.
>
> Youthful, but mature, *Terry Sanford is also capable of great leadership. He has the firm backing of* the North Carolina citizenry and of *the North Carolina Congressional delegation that accompanied me yesterday.* Our interest and presence at the inauguration is witness of our support and sincere best wishes for Governor Sanford's tenure in office.[20]

Such contacts as these are most welcome, but the State organizations and the people in the States become exceedingly sensitive when the national party leadership attempts to exert its influence with respect to matters that they regard as solely their own business. A striking group of illustrations was provided in 1938 when President Roosevelt undertook to purge Representative John J. O'Connor in his home State of New York, Senator Walter F. George in his adopted State of Georgia, and Senator Millard F. Tydings of Maryland. In the first instance, Roosevelt succeeded, probably because it was his home State, but in both of the other cases, the candidates that he supported were roundly defeated (although he campaigned actively in their behalf) and those that he opposed were re-elected by substantial majorities. The moral of this story, if it has a moral, is that no national party leader, no matter how

[20] Bonner, Herbert C., *Congressional Record,* January 6, 1961 (emphasis supplied).

great his stature, should ever attempt to influence the voters of a State or district in an effort to unseat a sitting Member of Congress. He may certainly endorse his party's candidates for public office, but there is a good deal of question regarding the effectiveness even of this action. Political allegiance held by one leader is not readily transferable to another.

The Politics of Patronage

Patronage—or the hope of patronage—plays a considerable part in the relations of the party leaders of State and Nation. Job hunters are a plague for every new administration, although civil service has eliminated the vast hoards of job seekers who once literally swarmed on Washington. The State party leaders may be involved in two different ways. Those leaders who were successful in carrying their States in the preceding election are on hand requesting, and exerting pressure to obtain, their share of the spoils. Later, when the jobs have been given out, they come with requests for new post offices, river and harbor improvements, and the like. In other instances, these leaders may find that incumbent office holders—Members of Congress or holders of top jobs in the Executive Branch—have taken such good care of ambitious party leaders in the State (in part, no doubt, to eliminate future competition) that they have a dearth of good material for filling the party ticket.

Patronage still plays a considerable role in politics, more in some jurisdictions than in others. Somewhat paradoxically, however, while the population of the country increases and government grows in size, the extension of the merit system has steadily reduced the number of jobs available for distribution on a patronage basis, and even when openings do exist, minimum job qualifications are as necessary under good party leadership as the proper political clearance. Nevertheless, astute political leadership can still make effective use of such positions as are available, sometimes by withholding them temporarily, sometimes by the manner or the time and circumstances under which they are distributed.

The hope of patronage exerts a restraining influence upon both State and Congressional leaders during the early weeks or months of a new administration, and the judicious use of available positions can do much to advance an administration's legislative program and to keep incipient dissent or revolt from breaking out into the open. Until the jobs are given out, and as long as there is any hope of "getting something," even leaders who have no real enthusiasm for the new administration are likely to behave conservatively and refrain from voicing their reservations publicly; afterward, when they know they have gotten all they can expect to get, their reticence disappears. This is true of Governors and other State party leaders as well as of Members of Congress, who normally maintain close working relationships with the State party organization and leaders.

Some Presidents have deliberately delayed "the shaking of the plum tree" until their legislative programs were well advanced. This procedure causes much grumbling and dissatisfaction among the party leaders, but it works and there is really very little that they can do about it. President Wilson used this method, along with other techniques, to secure the enactment of an extraordinary amount of major legislation during his first two years in office, and President Roosevelt's first 100 days stand out as a remarkable period of accomplishment.[21]

Presidents have always used patronage in this way. A further, striking illustration is noted in its use by President Lincoln to secure votes for the admission of Nevada in 1864, in order that this State might later vote to approve the Thirteenth Amendment.[22] President Wilson was often accused of withholding patronage from Congressmen who disagreed with him, though he denied this. Whether he did so or not, it is certain that other Presidents, including all recent Presidents, have at times appealed to the public for support of their policies, as a means of gaining Congressional support. The filling of a judgeship at a critical moment in the legislative history of an administration-sponsored bill can do wonders in convincing a hostile or wavering Member that it would be best for him to support the bill.

BIBLIOGRAPHICAL NOTES

The problems considered in this chapter are normally discussed in standard textbooks on political parties and elections. For an early discussion, see Henry Jones Ford, "The Influence of State Politics in Expanding Federal Power," *Proceedings of the American Political Science Association, 1909,* pp. 53–63. More recently, David B. Truman has written on "Federalism and the Party System," in Arthur W. Macmahon, ed., *Federalism: Mature and Emergent* (New York: Doubleday & Company, 1955), Chapter 8, and Morton Grodzins, in *Report* of the President's Commission on National Goals, *Goals for Americans* (New York: American Assembly, Columbia University, Prentice-Hall, Inc., 1960), pp. 265–282, emphasizes the effect of "the undisciplined parties" upon the character of the federal system. Especially valuable is the two-volume

[21] See Alsop, Joseph, and Catledge, Turner, *The 168 Days* (New York: Doubleday, Doran & Company, 1938).

[22] Dana, Charles A., *Recollections of the Civil War* (New York: D. Appleton & Company, 1902). pp. 174–177.

symposium on "The Electoral Process," *Law and Contemporary Problems,* Spring and Summer issues, 1962.

V. O. Key, Jr., *Southern Politics in State and Nation* and *American State Politics* (New York: Alfred A. Knopf, Inc., 1949 and 1956 respectively), has done the most distinguished writing on State party systems. In addition, at least three other studies have been made on a regional basis: Thomas C. Donnelly, ed., *Rocky Mountain Politics* (Albuquerque: University of New Mexico Press, 1946); John M. Fenton, *Politics in the Border States: A Study of the Patterns of Political Organization and Political Change Common to the Border States* (New Orleans: Hauser Press, 1957); and W. Duane Lockard, *New England State Politics* (Princeton: Princeton University Press, 1959). The National Center for Education in Politics in New York has sponsored the writing and publication of a series of State manuals on party organization and the electoral process; in this series, the following titles are now available: California: Joseph P. Harris, *California Politics,* 3rd ed. (Stanford: Stanford University Press, 1961); Illinois: Gilbert Y. Steiner and Samuel K. Gove, *Legislative Politics in Illinois* (Urbana: University of Illinois Press, 1960); Massachusetts: Earl Latham and George Goodwin, *Massachusetts Politics,* 2nd ed. (Medford: Tufts University, Civic Education Center, 1960); Michigan: Joseph LaPalombara, *Guide to Michigan Politics,* rev. ed. (East Lansing: Michigan State University, 1960); Minnesota: G. Theodore Mitau, *Politics in Minnesota* (Minneapolis: University of Minnesota Press, 1960); New York: Ralph A. Straetz and Frank Munger, *New York Politics* (New York: New York University Press, 1960); Pennsylvania: Edward F. Cooke and G. Edward Janosik, *Guide to Pennsylvania Politics* (New York: Holt, Rinehart and Winston, Inc., 1957); Washington: Daniel M. Ogden and Hugh A. Bone, *Washington Politics* (New York: New York University Press, 1960); and Wisconsin: Leon Epstein, *Politics in Wisconsin* (Madison: University of Wisconsin Press, 1958). Noteworthy also are James K. Pollock and Samuel J. Eldersveld, *Michigan Politics in Transition* (Ann Arbor: Bureau of Government, University of Michigan, 1943) and Warren Moscow, *Politics in the Empire State* (New York: Alfred A. Knopf, Inc., 1948).

The most significant work on national party conventions has been done by Paul T. David *et al., Presidential Nominating Politics in 1952,* 5 vols. (Baltimore: Johns Hopkins Press, 1954). Continuing their work, this group published *The Politics of Nominating Conventions* (Washington: Brookings Institution, 1960), which is available in both a full and an abridged, paperback edition. Also valuable is a group of papers presented at the Annual Conference of the Pennsylvania Political Science and Public Administration Association held in Harrisburg, April 8–9, 1960, *Nominating the President: Commentaries on the Process* (University Park: Institute of Public Administration, Pennsylvania State University, 1960).

PART III

In the particular brand of federalism that has developed in the United States, certain powers are assigned to the central government on the ground that they are clearly matters of national concern, that the nature of the problem requires a degree of uniformity that can be achieved only through a large measure of central control, or that the subject is one which the States are not in a position to handle effectively.

The chapters of Part III are concerned with a number of these powers —civil rights; commerce, labor, and finance; foreign affairs; and national security. Fiscal relationships, which might fall within this category, are dealt with in Part IV. It has often been assumed that in these areas of major Federal responsibility, the role of the States, if any, was so minor as to be quite unimportant.

These chapters make it unmistakably clear that even in these vital areas, there is no longer any such thing as "exclusive jurisdiction." The States, as well as the Federal government, have responsibilities in these important functional areas—responsibilities which, if met, go far to insure the success of the national effort, but which if ignored or handled ineptly, can create situations that are embarrassing or even dangerous to the well-being of the nation.

CHAPTER IX

Civil Rights and
Human Values

Barnett Pledges Mississippi Aid for Alabama

Jackson, Miss. (AP)—Governor Ross Barnett telegraphed Alabama Governor John Patterson last night that Mississippi "stands ready to lend you any assistance you may need in these troubled days."

"We stand ready to help others of our sister States who refuse to be run over and stomped in their efforts to protect their people from Federal aggression," Governor Barnett said.

Governor Barnett said he was "deeply shocked that the Federal Government has seen fit to send armed marshals into your State for the purpose of meddling in a situation prompted by the unlawful acts of outsiders boastfully violating the laws of your great State."

"If this is an example of how the Federal Government expects to force integration on the people," Governor Barnett said, "then it is more important than ever before that we have solid Southern unity."

"We shall never surrender our rights as a sovereign State and a free people." [1]

[1] Washington *Evening Star*, May 22, 1961, p. A-5.

After World War I, there were race riots in Chicago, Detroit, St. Louis, and Washington, D.C. Controversies over school integration, following the 1954 decision of the Supreme Court, have occurred in many communities, mostly but not exclusively in the Southern region. The Brown Case itself arose in Topeka, Kansas, and a bitter controversy on desegregation raged in New Rochelle, New York. The efforts of the Freedom Riders to test their constitutional right to travel in interstate commerce was the cause—indirectly, if not directly—of serious disorder in three Alabama cities in 1961, and resulted in more than 100 arrests in Jackson, Mississippi, which led to convictions and suspended sentences of $200 fine and sixty days at hard labor for "disturbing the peace." These incidents, and many others which might be cited, tend to create an impression in the minds of many people that civil rights necessarily involve race relations.

Civil rights questions do normally involve minorities, but not necessarily racial minorities. The status of the Negro, in slavery prior to 1863.

PERSONAL AND PROPERTY RIGHTS GUARANTEED AGAINST ENCROACHMENTS BY THE FEDERAL CONSTITUTION *

By Federal Government	By Federal and State Governments	By State Governments
1. Writ of habeas corpus to be suspended only during rebellion or invasion.	1. Bills of attainder forbidden.	1. No laws impairing obligation of contract to be passed.
2. Congress may not enlarge number of treasonable offenses.	2. No ex post facto criminal laws to be passed.	2. Full faith and credit to be granted to acts, records and proceedings of other States and of the United States.
3. Heirs of persons convicted of treason may not be forbidden to inherit property.	3. No class distinctions to be created by granting titles of nobility.	
4. No infringement of the right of the people to bear arms.	4. Slavery and involuntary servitude prohibited.	3. Citizens of other States must be granted same privileges and immunities as are enjoyed by their own.
5. No soldiers to be quartered in private homes in time of peace without owner's consent.	5. Privilege of voting may not be denied because of race, color, sex, or previous condition of servitude.	4. Equal protection of the laws may not be denied.
6. No unreasonable searches and seizures, and no warrants to issue except upon proper cause.	6. No laws respecting an establishment of religion, and none that interfere with the free exercise of religion.†	
	7. No laws abridging freedom of speech or of the press.†	

and as an emerging group in a free society since that date, provides much of the subject matter of this chapter, to be sure, but there are numerous other types of minorities. They may be minorities on the basis of national origin, religious affiliation, or opinion. Those who are non-conformist, whose views or modes of behavior differ from generally accepted patterns of the community, often find themselves the victims of local prejudice if not actual discrimination. Since human nature is what it is, violations of civil rights may occur anywhere and at any time.

While Negroes and Jews are the most numerous minority groups, others in wide variety exist in all parts of the country. As the author once observed elsewhere, "In southern New Jersey, it is the Italians; in Pennsylvania, Nebraska, and Wisconsin, the Germans; in Minnesota and the Dakotas, the Scandinavians; in the New England mill villages, the French-Canadians; in Boston, the Irish; in Chicago and Detroit, the Poles; in

By Federal Government	By Federal and State Governments
7. No criminal prosecution except by indictment or presentation by a grand jury.	8. No interference with the right of peaceful assembly and petition.†
	9. Life, liberty and property may not be taken without due process of law.
8. No double jeopardy (no trial twice for same offense).	10. Right of privacy.

9. No self-incrimination (accused cannot be compelled to testify against himself).

10. Speedy, public, impartial trial by jury of twelve persons whose verdict must be unanimous.

11. Trial by jury assured in civil suits involving more than $20.

12. Procedural rights—accused must be informed of charges, have right to counsel, be present in court during testimony against him, and have right to compel the attendance of witnesses to testify in his own behalf.

13. No excessive bail or fines permitted, and no cruel or unusual punishments.

14. Property may not be taken without just compensation.

---

* Adapted from Ferguson, John H. and McHenry, Dean E., *The American System of Government*, 5th ed. (New York: McGraw-Hill Book Co., 1959), p. 130.

† Have been interpreted as included within the life, liberty and property due process clause of the Fourteenth Amendment.

Texas and the Southwest, the Mexicans; on the Pacific Coast, the Orientals." [2] In addition, there are now many Puerto Ricans in East Coast cities, and Cubans in southern Florida.

Although the problems of civil rights and race relations are interesting and important from many angles—sociologically, economically, constitutionally—the present discussion must necessarily be confined to those aspects which involve intergovernmental relationships. Because many of these problems provoke deep emotional reactions, all too often they have led to disagreement and bitter controversy. Sometimes they have flared up suddenly in an ominous fashion.

It is not easy to generalize about these controversial aspects of federalism. All of them raise questions involving in varying degrees the power and prestige of the Federal government on the one hand, and of the States on the other. They involve a variety of subjects ranging from the control of the slave trade in colonial times to the protection of the rights of members of minority groups or of persons charged with crime in the middle of the twentieth century.

Throughout the years of controversy with Great Britain, great emphasis was laid upon questions pertaining to civil rights. The Declaration of Independence had given the world a statement of the basic rights of the individual that has become a classic, never having been equaled for clarity and cogency of expression. In the period of transition, the States incorporated bills of rights in their constitutions. When the Constitutional Convention submitted the new Constitution without a bill of rights, a number of States ratified it with the specific understanding that Congress should at an early date adopt, and submit to the States for their approval or rejection, a series of amendments including guarantees of the fundamental rights of citizens. Of the twelve resolutions submitted, ten were approved and became the first ten amendments to the Constitution, commonly referred to as the Bill of Rights; to these, in time, were added the War Amendments which have been interpreted as being applicable to the States and of carrying over to the States certain basic concepts contained in the Bill of Rights.

The American system of civil rights, showing major rights protected, and the level of government responsible in each instance, is shown in the table on pages 266–267. Were it not for the fact that freedom can never be taken for granted, it might have been supposed that under a government born of revolution, in an era during which there was an intense devotion to the concept of the rights of man, civil rights would always be diligently protected. Frequently, however, this has not been the case.

[2] Graves, W. Brooke, *Fair Employment Practice Legislation in the United States: Federal, State, Municipal,* Public Affairs Bulletin No. 93 (Washington: Legislative Reference Service, Library of Congress, 1951), p. 16.

On the contrary, our history has from the very beginning been replete with incidents involving the rights of individual persons and of minority groups, and as a result, most of these incidents raised difficult questions in the field of Federal-State relations.

THE ROLE OF CONGRESS IN CIVIL RIGHTS

The role of Congress in such a controversial field as civil rights is bound to be a difficult one. In the nature of things, a representative body is subject to pressure from every prevailing trend of public opinion, whether constructive or not. The legislative record invariably reflects these pressures. Probably the earliest legislation reflecting public opinion involved the slavery issue which plagued the colonies for decades before the Constitutional Convention was confronted with it. This question, including the return of fugitive slaves, was to continue for many years to come. Another issue resulted from the general dissatisfaction engendered by the passage of the Alien and Sedition Acts of 1798. And in the twentieth century, in the enactment of the Smith Act in 1940, Congress committed what many regard as a major blunder in the field of civil rights.

On the constructive side, by an act aimed primarily at the Ku Klux Klan, Congress in 1871 sought to abolish lynchings and mob actions by making it a Federal crime for two or more persons to conspire to deprive others of due process of law. The first major enactment in this field, the Civil Rights Act of 1875, was nullified by the courts a few years later. Although in recent years there has been long and heated controversy over civil rights legislation, including a number of rather lengthy filibusters, no major civil rights legislation was enacted from 1875 to 1957, when the Civil Rights Act of 1957 was passed. This was followed by legislation in 1960, centered primarily on voting rights, and additional legislation in this field appears highly probable in the years ahead.

Fugitive Slave Laws

The institution of slavery in general, and the slave trade in particular, had been subjects of controversy through a major portion of the colonial era. It is not surprising, therefore, that they assumed a prominent place in the deliberations of the Constitutional Convention. In the colonies and under the Confederation, fugitive slaves could be reclaimed only through inter-colonial or inter-state comity; consequently, in framing the Constitution, one of the chief inducements for the South to join the new Union was the inclusion of a fugitive slave clause.

The compromises entered into at the Convention with respect to the Negro and slavery are familiar to all—counting all white persons but only three-fifths of the Negro population for purposes of representation, and authorizing the continuance of the slave trade until 1808. A concession to the slave States was made also in the provision in Article IV, Section 2, designed to facilitate the return of runaway slaves. The language was neither very clear nor very specific, leaving the inference that the return of fugitives would be made to the owner or his agent. Neither the free nor the slave States recognized any responsibility for cooperation in this matter. In 1791, Governor Mifflin of Pennsylvania demanded the surrender of three men charged with kidnapping a Pennsylvania Negro and taking him to Virginia to be sold into slavery. The Virginia Governor refused to comply and Governor Mifflin thereupon appealed to President Washington. It has been generally believed that the friction engendered in this case was responsible for the enactment of the first Federal fugitive slave law, signed by President Washington on February 12, 1793. In succeeding years, this legislation and the Fugitive Slave Laws of 1818 and 1850, to which attention is now directed, became the subject of litigation and bitter controversy between North and South.

The Northern States were as strongly opposed to the institution of slavery as the Southern States were dedicated to it. In the latter case, there was an economic interest involved, which goes far toward explaining their desperate effort to rationalize and justify their position. In 1826, the Pennsylvania General Assembly took the lead in giving statutory expression to the point of view that generally prevailed throughout the North, and other States soon followed suit. The Pennsylvania law, the title of which stated that it was passed to aid in carrying into effect the provisions of the Constitution and Federal laws relating to fugitives from labor, made kidnapping a felony punishable by fine and imprisonment at hard labor for periods ranging from seven to twenty-one years. It was provided that "no alderman or justice of the peace of this commonwealth shall have jurisdiction or take cognizance of the case of any fugitive from labor from any of the United States or territories under a certain act of Congress" of February 12, 1793, or grant any certificate or warrant of removal of any such fugitive under pain of being found guilty of a misdemeanor punishable by a fine of $500 to $1,000. Jurisdiction in such cases was awarded to certain judges whose powers were also somewhat limited.

The Prigg Case arose out of the incursion of one Edward Prigg, a citizen of Maryland, into Pennsylvania in 1837. When he left, he forcibly carried away a Negro woman, Margaret Morgan, who was claimed as a slave by another Marylander. Prigg had obtained a warrant from a Pennsylvania justice of the peace directing him to bring Mrs. Morgan before him; when he did this, the justice refused to take cognizance of the case, and Prigg carried the woman and her children, all of whom had been born in Pennsylvania, with him to Maryland. Being in Pennsylvania again, two years later, he and three other persons were indicted by the grand jury in York County. From this beginning, the case went to the Supreme Court of Pennsylvania, then to the Federal Supreme Court where, in *Prigg* v. *Pennsylvania*,[3] it was decided that the execution of Federal laws could not be imposed on State officials. Chief Justice Taney dissented from that portion of the opinion which denied the right of State authorities to protect the master when he was pursuing a fugitive from his service, and declared that if the States are forbidden to legislate on this subject on the ground that the power belongs exclusively to Congress, the State of Maryland "must soon become an open pathway for fugitives escaping from other States."

From the point of view of the South, the Prigg decision created an intolerable situation. The Northern States seized upon the Taney dissent as a basis for passing "personal liberty laws" to prevent their officials being so employed or their buildings used as places of detention. No Southerner could go into a free State to recover his fugitive slave without danger to life and limb. With the spread of antislavery sentiment, there also developed the so-called underground railroad, a method of assisting runaway slaves by sending them under cover of night from one sympathizer to another. The South, aroused both by the decision and by these practices, began to demand an effective fugitive slave law as the price for remaining in the Union.

The Fugitive Slave Act of 1850, which marked the end of the Whig Party, placed full responsibility for the return of fugitives in the hands of the Federal authorities, including the Courts and the Army, which became part of a new and strengthened system. Marshals were liable to $1,000 fine plus the value of the slave if he escaped or even if he was forcibly rescued, and bystanders were held guilty of treason for refusing to assist. The owner's oath was full evidence, that of the alleged fugitive was not to be received, and habeas corpus was rendered null. Obstruction, rescue, or concealment were punishable by six months' imprisonment and $2,000 in damages and fine. If the claimant "apprehended" a rescue, the marshal was to take the fugitive to the claimant's State himself before surrendering him, and an affidavit and general description made in the claimant's own State was to be valid for a reclamation in any State.

[3] 16 Peters 539 (1842); see Johnson, Allen, "The Constitutionality of the Fugitive Slave Acts," *Yale Law Journal*, November, 1921, pp. 161–182.

This was, indeed, a most extraordinary piece of legislation; one writer has described it as "atrocious." The ink of President Fillmore's signature on September 18 was scarcely dry before test cases involving the rights of free Negroes began to arise. This legislation served to inspire more stringent personal liberty laws, making it difficult for an alleged slaveowner or Federal agent to find any State soil to stand on in executing the writs or holding the fugitive. In 1859, Wisconsin went so far as openly to threaten secession if the mandates of this act were enforced within her borders. Its political results were a boomerang which might have been anticipated, each seizure arousing a storm of indignation which was often inflamed by such specific incidents as riot and bloodshed, a mother's murder of her child to save it from slavery (Garner Case), the prosecution for treason of two Quakers who refused to join the hunt (Christiana Case), and the seizure of long-time free Negro citizens. The Free Soil Party demanded the repeal of this legislation, as did their successors, the Republicans, whose victory in 1860 was interpreted as notice to the South that the next administration would bring about its repeal.

Repealed it was, in 1864, having been in the meantime a leading cause of the secession movement of 1861. In addition, as a symbol of a discredited institution, it was also a leading cause of the inability of the Confederacy to obtain substantial assistance from major European powers.[4] Perhaps the strangest thing was the apathy of the Republican Party in repealing it. In November, 1861, and again in June, 1862, persons were prosecuted for offenses under this law. One of these, the Reverend George Gordon, President of Iberia College in Ohio, was convicted of resisting a deputy marshal in the latter's attempt to arrest a fugitive slave, and was sentenced to six months' imprisonment, a fine of $300, and costs. In April, 1862, President Lincoln pardoned him, after noting the serious nature of his offense, on the ground that he had atoned sufficiently for it. On January 1, 1863, the President issued the definitive Emancipation Proclamation, declaring all persons held as slaves in certain areas to be free. It was not until 1864, and —as Channing notes—"then without any apparent enthusiasm."[5] that Congress repealed the Fugitive Slave Law.[6]

[4] Channing states this vividly: The influence of *Uncle Tom's Cabin* "on the plain people of France and Great Britain was so tremendous that no man possessed of political instinct in either of those countries–no matter what were his wishes and those of his class—no ruler of Great Britain or of France could have recognized the Confederacy whose corner-stone rested on the mutilated body of 'Uncle Tom.'" See Channing, Edward, *History of the United States*, 6 vols. (New York: The Macmillan Co., 1905–1925), VI, 115.

[5] Channing, VI, 536.

[6] For a discussion of the Dred Scott Case and the judicial aspects, see pp. 294–297.

Alien and Sedition Laws

Prior to 1800, there had been an influx of radicals who in their former countries had detested kings and governors, but had been restrained in their utterances by fear of the guillotine, axe, Bastille, or Tower. Finding these restraints non-existent in America, they leveled venomous attacks upon American officeholders by both speech and pen. Probably their attacks were not particularly dangerous, but they were so vexatious and annoying, and in such exceedingly bad taste, that public opinion was aroused against these radicals. In June and July, 1798, a Federalist Congress responded with the enactment of four laws. The first of these laws extended from five to fourteen years the minimum time required for naturalization; although exceptions were made in favor of persons actually in the country in January, 1795, the mass of foreign immigrants would be disfranchised for years to come. Two acts gave the Federal government power to deal with enemy aliens and authorized the President to order deportation of any alien, whether an enemy or not, or to license him to reside within the United States, at whatever place the President might designate. The Sedition Act applied to all persons, citizens and aliens alike, who conspired against the government, or who through writing or printing did anything to bring it or its officers into disrepute. Jurisdiction under these laws was given to the Federal courts, and punishment was limited to five years' imprisonment and $5,000 fine.

When one reviews the circumstances surrounding the adoption of this legislation and, at the time, the slight attention accorded it by the administration, he is apt to be somewhat puzzled by the furor it created. Neither Hamilton nor President Adams was in a bitter or vindictive mood. Hamilton's endorsement of the proposed legislation was, at most, lukewarm, and he commented, "Let us not be cruel or violent." President Adams exhibited slight interest in the legislation, and after it was passed, never made use of the powers which it conferred upon him. True, he did not veto the bills, but he never licensed any alien to restricted residence nor did he compel a single person to leave the country. There were a few prosecutions under the legislation, but not many, but even these few aroused considerable indignation. Some French refugees fled of their own volition while they were still free to do so. Channing concludes that "there was undoubtedly some harshness and some injustice to individuals as a result of the passage of the laws, but it was trifling in comparison with the harm done" to those at whom it was primarily directed.[7]

[7] Channing, IV, 224.

A recent Pennsylvania case had given point to the Federalist contention that the Sedition Act was in reality a mitigation of the law of libel as administered by the State courts, for the defendant in any libel suit brought under it might give in evidence the truth of the matter, and the jury was entrusted with the determination of both law and fact. The legislation modified the State laws as to libel; it extended jurisdiction to the Federal courts, but it was unlikely that the judges of these courts would proceed very far in exercising criminal jurisdiction without direct legislative authorization.[8]

Jefferson, operating quietly from his home at Monticello, appears to have been the real leader of the opposition. He was not afraid of Frenchmen or of French ideas, and furthermore, he was at the time a politician in search of an issue. Possibly this legislation was the answer to his quest. At any rate, the ten Kentucky Resolutions were from his pen. They were adopted by the General Assembly of Kentucky in 1798 and 1799, the first group shortly after the adoption of the legislation, and they were sent to the other States for their consideration. There had been public meetings held in Kentucky, at which resolutions had been adopted, but there appears to be some doubt as to how significant these happenings actually were.

The Virginia Resolutions, drafted by James Madison and adopted by the General Assembly of Virginia in 1798, were briefer in form and considerably milder in tone than the resolutions adopted in Kentucky. The Virginia Resolutions declared that the Constitution was a compact among the States and that they should interpose when the national government attempted to exercise powers not granted in plain terms. As in the case of Kentucky, the Resolutions followed upon the adoption of memorials by voters at meetings held in various parts of the State, and other States were invited to concur in voicing their objections to this legislation and in declaring it unconstitutional. If it was hoped or expected that the spirit of protest might become contagious and spread from State to State, certainly the authors of the Resolutions must have been greatly disappointed, for the other States showed little interest and either took no action or indicated their disapproval of the views expressed.[9]

[8] See Anderson, Frank M., "The Enforcement of the Alien and Sedition Laws," American Historical Association *Reports*, 1912, pp. 113–126; for an excellent recent treatment, see Smith, James M., *Freedom's Fetters: The Alien and Sedition Laws and American Civil Liberties* (Ithaca: Cornell University Press, 1956).

[9] See Ames, Herman V., ed., *State Documents on Federal-State Relations*, Nos. 7–15 (Philadelphia: University of Pennsylvania Press, 1900); Jefferson, Thomas, *Notes on Virginia*, William Peden, ed. (Chapel Hill: University of North Carolina Press, 1955); and Loch, Adrienne, and Ammon, Harry, "The Virginia and Kentucky Resolutions: An Episode in Jefferson's and Madison's

Actually, there is good basis for questioning whether the action taken by these two States was as spontaneous as it appeared on the surface, for these were the two States in which Jefferson's political organization was most fully developed. Both Maryland and North Carolina, adjoining Virginia, were silent, and in New York and Pennsylvania where the Republicans were strong, there was little opposition to the legislation. In Maryland, Massachusetts, and Vermont, the Resolutions were strongly condemned by Federalist supporters; in fact, in every answer that was voted to the Kentucky Resolutions, the idea of State nullification was vigorously denounced.

When the news of these adverse reactions reached Kentucky, the General Assembly passed its second set of Resolutions, which were far milder than those first adopted and merely registered the Assembly's solemn protest against the Alien and Sedition legislation. Under the same circumstances, the General Assembly of Virginia completely shifted its emphasis from the alleged abuses contained in the legislation to questions pertaining to its constitutionality. Madison himself, in his famous Report to the Virginia Legislature in 1800, after reiterating the views expressed in the earlier resolutions, concedes that while the ultimate authority for any decision of the Federal judiciary may be binding upon the other departments of the Federal government, it cannot possibly be enforced "in relation to the rights of the parties to the constitutional compact, from which the judicial as well as the departments hold their delegated trusts." This more moderate view ultimately prevailed. As Patrick Henry pointed out in the last great speech of his career, the life of the legislation was strictly limited by its own provisions, and in the ordinary working of the established constitutional procedures, there were suitable means by which unwanted legislation might be repealed.

Civil Rights Acts of 1875, 1957, and 1960

The War Between the States ended in 1865. In the next five years, Congress passed and the States ratified the Thirteenth, Fourteenth, and Fifteenth Amendments. Between 1866 and 1875, Congress enacted five major civil rights and reconstruction acts, the last of which will be considered here. In the years which followed, these laws were so modified by amendment, or restricted in their application by narrow judicial interpretation that they ceased to have any real effect or significance. One was declared unconstitutional.

The concluding section of the Fourteenth Amendment provides that

Defense of Civil Liberties," *William and Mary Quarterly*, April, 1948, pp. 145–176.

"The Congress shall have power to enforce, by appropriate legislation, the provisions of this article." Proceeding on the basis of this authorization, Congress enacted the Civil Rights Act of March 1, 1875, which declared that all persons (meaning, particularly, the emancipated Negroes) should be "entitled to the full and equal enjoyment of the accommodations, advantages, facilities and privileges of inns, public conveyances on land and water, theaters, and other places of public amusement. . . ." This Act, as will be noted presently in some detail, was the one declared unconstitutional by the Supreme Court.[10]

After a series of repressive measures dealing with internal security matters, Congress turned in 1957 and 1960 to a more constructive approach to the problems of civil rights when, after an interval of three quarters of a century, it enacted new civil rights legislation. The controversy over the nature and scope of Federal responsibility in this field began to build up during World War II. Whereas there had been only fourteen bills on civil rights matters introduced in the 76th Congress, which preceded Pearl Harbor, the number of such bills gradually increased until there were seventy-two in the 81st Congress. The controversy was intensified after the Supreme Court desegregation decision in 1954.

By 1957, the pressure for Congressional action had increased to such a point that something had to be done. While the Federal courts had sought, as best they could, to enforce the 1954 decision without supporting legislation, the champions of civil rights pressed for legislation containing both civil and criminal penalties. Opponents, armed with the filibuster, played a delaying action; but a vote of 279 to 97 in the House and 60 to 15 in the Senate was mustered to pass the Civil Rights Act of 1957.

Although weaker than its advocates desired, the new law strengthened Federal authority to safeguard civil rights, whether violated by State officials or private individuals. Containing a number of important provisions, it:

1. Authorized a six-member Commission on Civil Rights to investigate and report;
2. Provided for the appointment of a new Assistant Attorney General to head a division of civil rights within the Department of Justice;
3. Outlawed interference with voting in primaries or general elections;
4. Empowered the Attorney General to obtain court orders, at public expense, to halt threatened violations of voting rights;
5. Made disobedience to court orders punishable as civil or criminal

[10] Civil Rights Cases, 109 U.S. 3 (1883); see Black, Charles L., Jr., "The Supreme Court and Democracy," *Yale Review*, Winter, 1961, pp. 188–201. Using these cases as an example, the author asks whether the Court's power to strike down acts passed by a popularly elected legislature negates the principles of democracy.

contempt (in the former, compliance is the objective; in the latter, punishment);

6. Provided that criminal contempt proceedings may be tried with or without jury, but if trial is without jury and the judge imposes a fine of over $200 or imprisonment of more than forty-five days, the defendant is entitled to a new trial with jury;

7. Fixed uniform qualifications for Federal jurors as a means of preventing State regulations from keeping Negroes off juries that try civil rights cases.

In 1960, Congress passed additional legislation in the form of the Civil Rights Act of 1960. After much delay and uncertainty as to whether

"NOW HURRY UP, CHILD—YOU'LL BE LATE FOR SCHOOL."
Mauldin in the St. Louis *Post-Dispatch*, November 16, 1960.

additional legislation should be attempted at all, the administration proposed a seven-point program which in time was whittled down to three items, requiring the preservation of voting records, easing the social and economic strain of desegregation by special Federal grants of assistance to communities inaugurating school desegregation plans, and providing for the education of the children of servicemen when State policy closed the schools near military bases.[11] By this legislation, plus the preceding act of 1957, Congress put on the statute books the first civil rights legislation in three quarters of a century.

Both party platforms in the 1960 presidential campaign contained strong pledges in the civil rights field. Many persons adopted a cynical attitude, assuming that these pledges could not and would not be carried out; however, soon after his inauguration, President Kennedy requested legislation designed to translate the Democratic planks into national policy be prepared for introduction in the 87th Congress. While the President made it plain that he wanted first to ascertain how much could be accomplished by executive action under existing laws before an attempt was made to secure additional legislation, a group of liberal-bloc Senators sponsored in the 87th Congress and again in the 88th a group of bills designed to make effective the recommendations contained in the Report of the President's Commission of Civil Rights.[12]

Recent Security Legislation

There was no question regarding the constitutional power of Congress to enact the Smith Act of 1940, the Internal Security Act of 1950 (the McCarran Act), or the Communist Control Act of 1954, but there were many who questioned both the necessity for and the propriety of such legislation. The Smith Act, which sought to provide a means by which the government could prosecute Communist leaders who willfully and knowingly conspired to organize the Party in order to teach and advocate the overthrow and destruction of the American government by force and violence, was upheld in *Dennis* v. *United States*,[13] but there was sharp dissent. The Communist Control Act was aimed at

[11] For an account of the legislative maneuvering, and the weak and indecisive attitude of the administration relating to this legislation, see Longaker, Richard P., *The Presidency and Individual Liberties* (Ithaca: Cornell University Press, 1961), Chapter 2. See also Berman, Daniel M., *A Bill Becomes a Law: The Civil Rights Act of 1960* (New York: The Macmillan Co., 1962).

[12] For complete text of all bills and resolutions, with explanatory comment, see *Congressional Record*, May 8, 1961, pp. 6949–6958.

[13] 341 U.S. 494 (1950); see articles by Alan R. Hunt in Bibliographical Notes on p. 315.

totalitarians in general and the Communists in particular, requiring all such persons and organizations to register within thirty days, and all Communists—though not members of mere Communist-front organizations—to register individually. It barred members of such organizations from employment by the government or any defense plant or installation, empowered the government during war or insurrection to put Communists and other potential spies and saboteurs in detention camps and to keep them there for the duration of the emergency, and tightened provisions for the punishment of spies and saboteurs.

Passed in both houses by substantial majorities, the legislation incurred a strongly worded veto from President Truman on the ground that it would not only prove unworkable (about as practical as requiring thieves to register with the sheriff) and would actually stimulate the very elements at which it was aimed in their efforts to create dissension and confusion in the country, but that it would "put the United States in the thought-control business" leading to official harassment of "all our citizens in the exercise of their right of free speech." Partly for political reasons, but largely in response to the popular hysteria that was sweeping the country at the time, both houses voted to override the veto—the House by 286 to 48 and the Senate, after a dramatic nineteen-hour filibuster, by 57 to 10. Issues were presented which, it was anticipated, would be a subject of litigation in the courts for years to come.

The Communist Control Act purports to outlaw the Communist Party or any successor organization, regardless of the name which it may assume, by declaring that it is not entitled to any of the rights, privileges, and immunities which other political parties enjoy under the laws of the United States or any political subdivisions thereof. Although it strikes at membership in the Party or other organizations advocating overthrow of the government by force and violence, it stops short of making such membership a criminal offense. Instead, it reverts to the disclosure provisions of the McCarran Act. Its constitutionality was upheld by the Supreme Court in 1961.[14]

This legislation served to bring the conflict between Federal and State authority in this field clearly into focus. The Commonwealth of Pennsylvania had in 1955 enacted a State Communist control act, for violation of which Nelson, a long-time Communist, was indicted and brought to trial. The Pennsylvania court declared the State act unconstitutional on the ground that Congress, by its enactment of the Communist Control Act, had pre-empted the field. The Commonwealth appealed the case, and the Supreme Court affirmed the decision of the

[14] *Communist Party of the United States* v. *Subversive Activities Control Board,* 367 U.S. 1 (1961).

Pennsylvania court.[15] When one listens, as from time to time he must, to denunciation of the Supreme Court's doctrine of supersession and Federal pre-emption, it is well to recall that, at least in this particular area, it was first presented, not by the Supreme Court, but by a State court whose judgment was affirmed on appeal.

THE PRESIDENT'S ROLE OF LEADERSHIP

Much of what the President does, and much of what government in general does, in the field of civil rights depends to a considerable extent upon the character of the man in office and upon the politics of the time. When one observes the bitter controversy which confronts the nation in the 1960's, he notes round-the-clock sessions of the Senate during a Southern filibuster, sit-in demonstrations in the South (with sympathizers demonstrating for the demonstrators from Maine to California), and finally, busloads of Freedom Riders moving southward. Why? At the same time, violence breaks out in South Africa and many persons are killed in race riots. Again, why?

It took the white man several hundred years to get himself into this mess, and no one need expect that the problems will be solved either quickly or easily. Yet the reasons for the problems are not hard to find. For generations, indeed for centuries, members of minority groups have been held in a state of subjection. Even after slavery was abolished, Negroes in the United States were treated as second-class citizens, being denied their basic rights and the full protection of the law. The dissemination of education and improved methods of communication have wrought great changes in the United States, as elsewhere. There is today a great demand among downtrodden and oppressed peoples everywhere for recognition of their rights as human beings. The demands of these peoples cannot be met by double-talk, nor can they be ignored. The problems are almost parallel in the United States, South Africa, and elsewhere, though the primary concern here is with the United States.

Historical Background

Presidents, like Congresses, have varied greatly in their interest in the field of civil rights, perhaps for some of the same reasons. John Adams,

[15] *Commonwealth of Pennsylvania* v. *Nelson*, 350 U.S. 497 (1956). For comment, see Cramton, Roger C., *"Pennsylvania* v. *Nelson:* A Case Study in Federal Pre-emption," *University of Chicago Law Review*, Autumn, 1958, pp. 85–108.

eminent constitutionalist, for example, stirred public feeling to bring about the adoption of the Alien and Sedition Acts and spoke feelingly of his political detractors. Jefferson, liberal spokesman for natural rights, pardoned Adams' enemies, to be sure, but is said to have been not without rancor where his own political enemies were concerned. Jackson did not hesitate to use administrative coercion to halt the distribution of abolitionist literature in the South. Lincoln, though he freed the slaves and preserved the Union, "brought the country closer to dictatorship than at any time in the nation's history." [16] But Lincoln was struggling against disloyalty in the North as well as in the South.

It was, however, in the period of Reconstruction that followed the Civil War that civil rights took their worst "beating." For nearly forty years, the standard interpretation of this period followed the Dunning analysis. Twenty years ago, a few writers cautiously began to question the accuracy of this analysis; now a new and quite different interpretation is gradually finding acceptance. The Reconstruction legislatures were corrupt, and in an era when the prestige of elected representative assemblies was at an all-time low, the corruption was nationwide. Radical reconstruction was neither overwhelmingly "black" nor wholly inept; rather, it was a surprisingly brief and incomplete effort to secure some measure of justice for Negroes and whites alike. Due to the failure to carry through wartime promises of racial justice, many of the civil rights problems of the present decade are but the unfinished business of that troubled era. A distinguished Southern journalist, Ralph McGill, whose ability and integrity are recognized throughout the country, has clearly indicated the origin and background of much of the current controversy:

> Newspapers, some gleefully, and some angrily, noted and charged that the rights of the newly made Negro citizens were hypocritically abandoned as a part of the deal [in 1876–1877 to abandon implementation of the relatively new constitutional provisions in exchange for Democratic acceptance of the electoral commission's decision]. They were. And since they were, the issue has been remindful of the legend of the sown dragon's teeth. But meanwhile, the South could, as it did, find reason to believe that the nation, despite the Constitution, officially and permanently had relegated the Negro to a position where he was a citizen in theory, but not in fact.
>
> There is explanation, if not justification, for some of the bewilderment and anger over what seems to many Southerners a reversal and a revival of an issue settled long ago by the Republican administrations which for so long dominated the government and appointed carefully screened men to the courts.
>
> It was, of course, inevitable, as civilization progressed and two

[16] Longaker, pp. 19–20.

world wars dramatized freedom and human rights, that the cynical sell-out of 1877 would be disinterred. There is no way for the Republican Party to escape accountability for this dilemma, and if the Deep South Democrats claim they were assured in 1877 and the years thereafter that the issue was settled, they are right. They were so assured.[17]

Among the Presidents in the twentieth century, none has shown so little interest in and concern for civil rights as Woodrow Wilson; while a war period is not the ideal time to look for tolerance and consideration of the rights of others, the Wilson record is a surprising one for a man with a scholarly background in history, political science, and law. As Longaker points out, Wilson had little concern for the rights of minority groups, and he tolerated in his Cabinet the presence of an Attorney General whose antics in hunting "Bolsheviks" might have appeared ludicrous if the consequences had not so often been tragic. Popular intolerance was carried to such extremes that any reference to or display of German culture was considered unpatriotic. During World War II, with a President who was interested in civil rights and a levelheaded Attorney General, the record was far better, the one serious blemish being the herding of the Japanese, including those who were American citizens, into relocation camps.

The contrast between the Wilson–World War I attitude, on the one hand, and the Lincoln–Civil War—Roosevelt–World War II attitude, on the other, has been admirably summarized by Longaker as follows:

> The Wilsonian reaction lacks the humanity, the self-doubt, and the declarations of necessity associated with the other two comparable periods of crisis. During the Civil War and World War II, invasions of individual liberty, when they came, were severe but were never marked by presidential indifference, nor did they lapse into crusades for ideological conformity. Presidential decisions were made reluctantly with a sense of the competing values at stake. There were, as well, conscious attempts to control the effects of the programs. In a word,

[17] McGill, Ralph, "Blame for the Civil Rights Issue," Washington *Evening Star*, March 24, April 17 and 18, 1960. Similarly, David Lawrence, "Does 'Might Make Right'?" *U.S. News and World Report*, April 17, 1961, generally condemns actions of Northern Congressmen during the Reconstruction period in foisting military government on the defeated South and in requiring the South's consent to postwar constitutional amendments. The conventional view was presented in Dunning, William A., *Reconstruction: Political and Economic, 1865–1877* (New York: Harper & Bros., 1907); for an excellent scholarly analysis of the newer interpretation, see Franklin, John H., *Reconstruction: After the Civil War*, Chicago History of American Civilization (Chicago: University of Chicago Press, 1961).

constitutionalists may find evidence on both sides which may begin to justify the wholesale withdrawal of the writ of habeas corpus by President Lincoln or President Roosevelt's approval of the evacuation of Japanese-Americans from the West Coast in 1942. But the character and extent of prosecutions under the Wilson Administration violate even the most flexible canons of crisis leadership.[18]

President Roosevelt had, by administrative action, set up a civil rights section in the Department of Justice in 1939. Civil rights planks began to appear in the platforms of the major parties in 1944 and have continued to appear regularly since that date. President Truman sent a ten-point civil rights program to Congress in 1948, President Eisenhower made recommendations in this area in 1956, and both Presidents sponsored civil rights study commissions. The major difficulties of the World War II period came, as a matter of fact, not during but after the war, the most serious manifestation being expressed in the wave of hysteria known as McCarthyism—the President seemed to accept this national tragedy, the after-effects of which are still apparent, making only one slight effort to quiet the fears that beset many people in his reference to book burning in a speech at Dartmouth College.

The President and Public Opinion

However dubious some aspects of the past record may have been, the day when the President may remain either aloof or indifferent to civil rights problems is past.[19] The President can and, in late years, often has taken action designed to strengthen the observance of civil rights, either directly as when President Roosevelt during World War II established the Fair Employment Practices Commission, or indirectly through steps taken to inform the public and mobilize public support for civil rights. Presidents Truman and Eisenhower, as noted, both sponsored study commissions charged with surveying the existing situation and recommending measures necessary for its improvement. President Truman's Committee on Civil Rights, established by the President himself, reported in 1947. The Federal Commission on Civil Rights was created by Act of Congress upon recommendation of President Eisenhower. This group was slated to expire in the fall of 1959, when a preliminary report was presented and the Commission's life was extended by Congress for two years so that it might have an opportunity to complete more adequately its fact-finding assignment.[20] There was strong sentiment

[18] Longaker, p. 24.   [19] Longaker, Chapter 1.
[20] The Commission devoted much attention to the denial of voting rights

for establishing this Commission, or a similar one, on a permanent basis. Action to accomplish this was still pending in Congress in 1963.

It is interesting to note how similar these two Commissions were from a number of points of view. Not only were they similar in basic organization, powers, and purpose, but both received strong executive support. At intervals approximately a decade apart, they surveyed conditions in the field of civil rights and found the major problems much the same in 1959 as in 1947. Their recommendations were likewise comparable, if not exactly the same. Specifically, the Truman Committee found the major issues to be the barriers raised to Negro suffrage in the South and discriminatory practices in housing. They recommended Federal and State action to end poll taxes as a voting prerequisite and to eliminate segregation based on race, color, creed, or national origin. As a means of accomplishing this latter objective, they recommended: (1) the conditioning by Congress of all Federal grants-in-aid and other forms of financial assistance to public or private agencies for any purpose on the absence of discrimination and segregation based on race, color, creed, or national origin; (2) the enactment of Federal and State legislation prohibiting all forms of discrimination in private employment, based upon these same factors; (3) the enactment of a Federal mandate against discrimination in government employment and the creation of adequate machinery to enforce this mandate.[21]

The Federal Commission on Civil Rights found, more than ten years later, that obstacles to Negro voting in the South were still a major issue, the chief cause now being discriminatory practices in registration rather than the poll tax. Other major issues were school segregation and discriminatory practices in housing. To cope with these problems, the Commission recommended: (1) Census coverage to include registration and voting statistics, and such records to be made public and to be preserved for a period of five years; (2) Temporary Federal Registrars to be appointed to assure the proper conduct of elections at which Federal officers are elected; (3) as a long-range policy, a constitutional amendment establishing a universal suffrage to be approved by Congress and submitted to the States for their approval or rejection.[22]

In the field of education, the Commission found that segregation

---

in the South and to discriminatory practices in higher education; see its annual reports and *Equal Protection of the Laws in Public Higher Education,* Washington, November, 1960.

[21] *To Secure These Rights: The Report of the President's Committee on Civil Rights* (Washington, 1947).

[22] Civil Rights Commission, *Report and Recommendations* (Washington, 1959); for a summary of this report, see *The New York Times,* September 9, 1959, pp. 44–45.

was widely prevalent, and while the members believed that it should be eliminated, they opposed the recommendation of the Truman Committee that the withholding of grant-in-aid funds be utilized as a sanction in securing compliance. With regard to discriminatory practices in housing, they made several recommendations: (1) that a bi-racial committee or commission on housing be established in all cities and states having a substantial non-white population; (2) that the President issue an Executive Order setting forth the constitutional objective of equal opportunity in housing; (3) that the Federal Housing and Home Finance Agency give a high priority to the attainment of this objective, and that, where necessary, present laws on this subject be strengthened; (4) that in the preparation of overall community "workable programs" for urban renewal, spokesmen for minority groups be included among the required citizens' participation.

Just how important the personal leadership of the President in this field actually is may be illustrated by what appeared at the time to be a minor incident occurring during the 1960 presidential campaign. Dr. Martin Luther King, anti-segregation leader, was arrested in Atlanta on a technical traffic charge and thrown in jail on October 25. King had received a twelve-month suspended sentence for driving with an Alabama license too long after moving to Georgia. That day, Department of Justice officials discussed steps that might be taken to free him. Various legal procedures were considered, but the decision finally made was that the most effective move would be a statement by President Eisenhower. A suitable statement was actually drafted:

> It seems to me fundamentally unjust that a man who has peacefully attempted to establish his right to equal treatment, free from racial discrimination, should be imprisoned on an unrelated charge, in itself insignificant. Accordingly, I have asked the Attorney General to take all proper steps to join with Dr. Martin Luther King in an appropriate application for his release.

For some reason, not now very clear, the statement was not released. On the morning of the following day, Senator Kennedy telephoned Dr. King's wife to express concern about the minister and sympathy for her. Robert Kennedy telephoned the judge to inquire whether there were obstacles to Dr. King's release on bail, pending appeal. He was eventually released on bail. The Democrats publicized the two phone calls, the absence of any statement from the White House, and the contrasting statement of Mr. Nixon's aides that he would have no comment on the case, and they distributed about 2,000,000 pamphlets outlining this incident during the last week of the campaign.

About a month after the election, it was reported that Mr. Eisenhower commented somewhat ruefully on why so large a portion of the Negro vote appeared to have gone to Senator Kennedy, explaining that a statement on the case had been prepared, but that it had never been released. He attributed the vote to the telephone calls made by Senator Kennedy and his brother and to the publicity given these calls.[23] Does one need any better evidence of the important influence of prompt and effective leadership on the part of the President on questions in the field of civil rights?

The President as Administrator

No better example of the power of the President to create policy or to make existing policy effective can be found than in his action or lack of action in the field of civil rights. The Eisenhower administration was frequently criticized, even before the 1960 campaign, for its failure to put its full weight and influence behind the enforcement of civil rights. Mr. Kennedy repeated during the campaign, and affirmed after he became President, his intention of doing precisely that. At his third press conference on February 8, 1961, he stated in reply to a question that the matter was under consideration and that he wanted to act when, where, and in the manner that would do the most good.

This, of course, raises a question as to what, exactly, the President can do, but neither the question nor the answer is new. There is, in fact, much that other Presidents have done, as well as much that needs to be done now and much that the President can do in national leadership, in the formulation of domestic policies—ways of using the influence of his office and exercising the broad powers with which that office is invested. President Roosevelt faced this problem at the time of the race riots in Detroit in June, 1943, when he issued a proclamation calling upon the rioters to "disperse and retire peaceably to their respective abodes"; and when the Governor of the State (who was almost helpless in the situation because the State's National Guard units had been called into wartime Federal service), having imposed a modified form of martial law on the Detroit metropolitan area, requested the aid of Federal troops, some 6,000 were moved in as a means of restoring order.[24]

What the President does or does not do in the field of civil rights de-

[23] See *The New York Times:* Belair, Felix, Jr., "President Rueful on the Negro Vote," December 14, 1960, and Lewis, Anthony, "U.S. Planned Help in Dr. King's Case," December 15, 1960.
[24] See Brown, Everett S., "The Truth About the Detroit Riot," *Harper's Magazine,* November, 1943, pp. 488–498.

pends upon many things. His own personal style and method of work have already been mentioned, and he is also influenced by the existing circumstances, the temper of the time, and to some extent by political considerations.[25] Longaker points out that "The President has been forced into the field by the Cold War and the political power of minorities as well as the inherent limits of the other branches of the national government." His action in any given situation must be within the confines of his constitutional and statutory powers, but what he does may be conditioned by what the legislative and judicial branches of government have (or have not) done. Again, as Longaker has observed, "What the national legislative and the Federal judiciary are unable or unwilling to do may create a hiatus which only the national executive can fill." [26]

The official law enforcement activities of the President are exercised to a large extent, in this field as elsewhere, through the operations of the various departments and agencies of the Federal government which operate under his general supervision and control. For present purposes, chief among these is the Department of Justice, and within that Department, the Federal Bureau of Investigation. The authority of the FBI in the field of civil rights rests chiefly upon two sections of the United States Code.[27] The field is a very sensitive one because investigations frequently touch upon the jealously guarded rights of the States and deal with subjects on which human passions are easily aroused. As a consequence, it is not unusual for the FBI to be subjected to criticism for meddling in State affairs and, at the same time, for not being aggressive enough and plunging more deeply into this field.

At a House Appropriations Subcommittee hearing in 1956, Director J. Edgar Hoover testified that "in civil rights cases, the Bureau is in a situation that if it obtains facts which result in prosecution, it is unpopular, and if it doesn't obtain facts, it is unpopular. Our sole purpose is to do our job effectively." In order that the job may be done effectively, the Attorney General has established definite procedures to be followed by the FBI in all civil rights matters:

1. A preliminary investigation is made whenever a complaint is received alleging a violation of Federal civil rights statutes;

---

[25] Along this line, Longaker observes, "How a President will act when constitutional rights move into his span of authority will depend on circumstances and his personality." Longaker, p. 31.

[26] Longaker, pp. 18 and 12.

[27] Sections 241 and 242 of Title 18; the former deals for the most part with involuntary servitude, peonage, and voting rights; the latter with actions of law enforcement officers who, "under color of law," willfully deny a person the rights guaranteed by the Constitution and by law.

2. The results of the inquiry are given to the Criminal Division of the Department of Justice for study;

3. If the Criminal Division decides that the case is not a violation of Federal law or that Federal action is not warranted, the FBI takes no further action;

4. If the Criminal Division decides there has been a violation, a full investigation is made and all evidence is gathered for use in prosecution;

5. In no case does the FBI recommend what action the Department should take.

One of the greatest barriers encountered in such investigations is local prejudice and/or apathy. Nevertheless, it is the duty of the FBI to investigate, if so instructed by the Criminal Division of the Department, whenever a police officer or an official of a State institution is accused of a possible civil rights violation. The investigation must be made whether or not the State officials have taken action, although it is an established policy of the agency to stand aside if the State indicates that it desires to take action. Civil rights enforcement, in a good many instances, brings the FBI into sharp conflict with police officers and even with the Governors of States. Recent disputes have involved Governors Allen Shivers of Texas, John S. Fine of Pennsylvania, and John S. Battle of Virginia.

Since instances of conflict are numerous and situations involving cooperative relationships are arising continuously, illustrations might be cited at length. For present purposes, perhaps two will suffice. The FBI has found that local police officers are, for the most part, willing to cooperate in civil rights investigations, but there have been exceptions to this rule. In 1953, for example, the Police Commissioner of New York City refused to permit members of his force who had been accused of brutal treatment of prisoners in violation of their rights to cooperate with the FBI, on the ground that FBI investigations were having a bad effect on the morale of his force and that at least one case in which the FBI was interested had already been investigated by his own Department, the officers had cleared the case, and a report had been sent to the Federal Attorney for the Southern District of New York. It developed that the Commissioner had reached an agreement with the Federal Attorney and the Criminal Division of the Department of Justice, under which the latter would refer civil rights complaints to the New York Police Department for investigation. The report would be forwarded to the Department of Justice through the Federal Attorney. If the Department was not satisfied, it could take whatever steps it deemed necessary. The arrangement, made without the knowledge of the FBI, was revoked by the Attorney General when the matter was brought to his attention, although an agreement between the FBI and the New York City Police

Department calling for mutual cooperation in the handling of civil rights cases was subsequently developed.

Another interesting illustration is to be found in the training activities of the FBI, in connection with which it is claimed that a major contribution has been made in protecting civil rights. The FBI has, since 1945, operated its National Academy and some 23,419 police training schools on the local level. As racial tensions mounted, the FBI experimented in late 1955 with a specialized Civil Rights School for police, and then launched a nationwide program in this area early in 1956, when 420 schools were held during the first six months. These schools have been well received and have been supported by State, county, and local authorities; in late 1956, the FBI reported that, of the 21,980 officers attending such schools up to that time, not one had been involved in a civil rights accusation.

A careful analysis of the possible types of presidential action was made by the Southern Regional Council in early 1961, urging that the President speak "forthrightly" on the subject of discrimination and that he "pledge a painstaking effort by all Federal departments and agencies to administer their programs in such ways as to hasten the end of discrimination." [28] Even more impressive is an article by Martin Luther King which clearly specifies individual actions and types of actions which could be taken by the administration, and which should be taken if any really serious attack is to be made to eliminate discriminatory practices. "The new Administration," he writes, "has the opportunity to be the first in 100 years of American history to adopt a radically new approach to the question of civil rights," and he contends that it must recognize that the Federal government already has at its disposal sufficient power to do the job. The distressingly slow progress of civil rights up to this time has been due, he believes, "at least as much to the limits which the Federal Government has imposed upon its own actions as it is to the actions of the segregationist opposition."

If we examine the total of all judicial, executive, and legislative acts of the past three decades and balance them against the sum needed to achieve fundamental change, two startling conclusions are inescapable. The first is the hopeless inadequacy of measures adopted—pitifully insufficient in scope and limited in conception. The second conclusion is even more disturbing. Federal action has been not only inadequate; viewed as a whole, it has also been self-nullifying. In 1954, the Supreme Court declared school segregation to be unconstitutional.

[28] *The Federal Executive and Civil Rights* (Atlanta: Southern Regional Council, January, 1961) and Pollitt, Daniel H., "The President's Powers in Areas of Race Relations: An Exploration," *North Carolina Law Review*, April, 1961, pp. 238–281.

Yet, since then Federal executive agencies and vast Federal legislative programs have given millions of dollars yearly to educational institutions which continue to violate the Supreme Court decision.

Further, the Federal Government collects taxes from all citizens, Negro and white, which it is constitutionally obligated to use for the benefit of all; yet, billions of these tax dollars have gone to support housing programs and hospital and airport construction in which discrimination is an open and notorious practice. Private firms which either totally exclude Negroes from the work force, or place them in discriminatory status, receive billions of dollars annually in Government contracts. The Federal Government permits elections and seats representatives in its legislative chambers in disregard of the fact that millions of Negro citizens have no vote. It directly employs millions in its various agencies and departments; yet its employment practices, especially in Southern States, are rife with discrimination.[29]

On the basis of this recital of facts which are a matter of record, it is obvious that if the President wants to advance the cause of civil rights, the first thing for him to do is to bring these self-defeating policies to an abrupt halt; secondly, he should proceed to make full and effective use of the great powers already vested in the Executive Branch of government. While Dr. King's statement, "It is no exaggeration to say that the President could give segregation a death blow through a stroke of the pen," itself sounds like an exaggeration, it is true that the power inherent in Executive Orders has not been exploited in recent years as it was in the past. Dr. King continues:

Historically, the Executive has promulgated orders of extraordinary range and significance. The Emancipation Proclamation was an Executive Order. The integration of the Armed Forces grew out of President Truman's Executive Order No. 8891. Executive Orders could require the immediate end to all discrimination in any housing accommodations financed with Federal aid. Executive Orders could prohibit any contractor dealing with any Federal agency from practicing discrimination in employment by requiring (a) cancellation of existing contracts; (b) and/or barring violators from bidding; (c) and/or calling in of government loans of Federal funds extended to violators; (d) and/or requiring renegotiation of payment to exact financial penalties where violations appear after performance of contract. With such effective penalties, enforcement of fair employment practices would become self-imposed by those enjoying billions of dollars in contracts with Federal agencies.

It may be noted for the record that President Kennedy issued a strongly worded Executive Order early in his administration, designed

[29] King, Martin Luther, "Equality Now," *The Nation*, February 4, 1961, and *Congressional Record*, May 2, 1961, pp. A3007–A3009.

to end discriminatory hiring practices on the part of government contractors. He also ordered a survey of Federal employment practices on an agency by agency basis, including the grades of all positions filled by Negro employees. In spite of laws and regulations prohibiting discrimination in the Federal service, discrimination is known to exist. There are few Negroes in higher grade positions, and if government is to serve as a yardstick for private employers, such discrimination must be eliminated. And it can be eliminated, to a considerable extent, by presidential action, "just as it was in the military services, by setting up adequately staffed committees with authority to punish those who violate government policy from the inside." Negroes could be valuable assets, if judiciously placed, in the representation of the United States abroad.

There are many Federal programs in which discrimination is commonplace, and from which, with a little determination, it could be almost totally eliminated. Included in this category are education, housing, hospitals, agriculture, and many more. In the field of education, there are a number of things that the President could do. He could, for instance: (1) publicly affirm his full support of the Supreme Court's 1954 decision and his intention to employ his executive powers as needed to insure orderly compliance therewith; (2) publicly affirm his administration's belief that segregation is an intolerable hindrance to the national goal of higher educational standards; (3) direct the Secretary of Health, Education, and Welfare to assemble and disseminate for the use of educators and the instruction of the public educational facts related to the integration process; the Department could give valuable assistance to local school boards without any additional legislative enactments. The President already has full authority to see that the vast Federal outlays for public school education are administered with scrupulous regard for the basic Federal policy against discrimination, and he could also announce that after a certain date, no research funds would be granted by the Federal government to any institution of higher learning (or to its faculty) in which discrimination is practiced.[30]

In all of this there is an important role for the Attorney General who can look closely into the authorizations he has for initiating or intervening in segregation cases, as Attorney General Kennedy did in the Prince

[30] These recommendations have been made by the Southern Regional Council, the Commission on Civil Rights, and other groups; see Goostree, Robert E., "Presidential Power: Spending and Segregation," *American University Law Review,* January, 1962, pp. 32–47, on the power of the President to impound appropriated funds, with special reference to grants-in-aid to segregated activities. The Council's *Desegregation in Higher Education* (Atlanta, 1961) lists formerly all-white colleges in seventeen Southern and border States and the District of Columbia which have desegregated since 1935. For a symposium on Racial Segregation in Education, see *School and Society,* May 7, 1960.

Edward County Case in Virginia early in 1961.[31] Under existing law, he could go into court in many of the current school struggles. Atrophy, it has been pointed out, is not a medical phenomenon alone; it has its counterpart in social and political life as well. Long years of disuse may have had this effect on some of the executive powers.

Discrimination in housing, in many communities, has been so bad that it has been virtually impossible for many families in minority groups to obtain decent accommodations. Many have noted that the President could effect a vast improvement by directing the Housing Administrator to require all participants in Federal housing programs to agree to a policy of open occupancy. The President himself, during the 1960 campaign, said that this could be accomplished "by a stroke of the pen." Such a policy could be enforced either by excluding violators from future participation in federally financed housing programs, or by providing that the entire mortgage debt might be declared due and payable upon breach of the agreement. The President did, by an Executive Order issued on November 20, 1962, use his powers to ban racial discrimination in federally assisted housing. It is now anticipated that, in time, the ban may be extended to much non-Federal housing as well.

A temporary reduction in the number of housing starts may be expected, as well as some dislocations in urban renewal plans, but the desire to qualify for Federal aid is strong enough so that these developments appear unlikely to have any serious long-term effect. Various sanctions are available for enforcement, but there may be political hazards in invoking them.

Another area in which an Executive Order could bring an end to a considerable amount of discrimination is that of health and hospitalization. Under the Hill-Burton Act of 1946, the Federal government makes funds available to the States for the construction of hospitals and health facilities. Since this program began to function, more than $100 million a year has gone to the States in direct grants. Funds are also made available for mental health, maternal and child-care services, and for control of such specific diseases as tuberculosis, cancer, heart disease, etc. Says Dr. King: "In spite of this sizable Federal support, it is a known fact that most of the federally financed and approved health and hospitalization programs in the South are operated on a segregated basis. In many instances, the Southern Negroes are denied access to them altogether." By withholding funds in those jurisdictions in which segregation is practiced, this type of discrimination could be wiped out almost over night.

Similarly, in the Department of Agriculture, the officials probably consider their work far removed from the field of civil rights. Yet it is

[31] See, in this connection, his University of Georgia address, May 6, 1961, in the *Congressional Record*, May 10, 1961, pp. A3263–A3265.

reported that the Department could be of tremendous assistance to Negro farmers who are now denied credit simply because of their desire to exercise their rights of citizenship. Eliminating this kind of discrimination would transform the lives of great numbers of Negro farmers. In doing so, the image of the Department might be transformed from a symbol of hostility and discrimination to one of security and help for struggling farmers.

Much of the current difficulty in the field of race relations arises from attempts on the part of Negro citizens to exercise their right to vote, direct Federal action for the protection of which has been authorized by law. Not only are many farmers denied credit because of this, but others are blacklisted so that they are unable to purchase necessary supplies or services, or are ruthlessly told to "get off the land." [32] During the 1960 presidential campaign, Mr. Kennedy declared that "the executive has full power to provide the right to vote . . . and in my judgment a major effort should be made in 1961 to make sure that there is no subterfuge, that every one has the right to vote." The Council made two recommendations that might help to achieve this objective: (1) that the Civil Rights Division be adequately staffed with able men, and that there be close cooperation between this Division and the Federal District Attorneys; (2) that a national registration drive, under the personal sponsorship of the President, be launched, and that it be supported by publications describing registration and voting qualifications and procedures under the laws of every State.

Commitments made in the platforms of both parties during the 1960 campaign cover a wide range of possibilities for legislative and executive action in the field of civil rights. The President might back civil rights legislation, but the exercise of heretofore unused executive powers would be far less difficult than seeking legislative action, in many instances, for actions which Congress itself has specifically rejected on one or more occasions in the past. Illustrations might include the outlawing of the poll tax, the passage of an anti-lynch law, the establishment of the Commission of Civil Rights on a permanent basis, the guarantee of equal job opportunities in the Federal Service and with government contractors, the ending of discrimination in housing, and the withholding of Federal aid funds, not only from segregated colleges and universities, but from such other facilities as airports, hospitals, vocational programs, and recreational facilities which practice discrimination.

[32] See *Tent City . . . "Home of the Brave"* (Washington: Industrial Union Department, AFL-CIO, 1961). This tells the tragic story of Fayette County, Tennessee.

THE SUPREME COURT AS GUARDIAN OF CIVIL RIGHTS

In the nearly 200 years of its existence, the Supreme Court has on several occasions handed down decisions involving important policy questions in the field of civil rights and race relations. In addition to constitutional restrictions and restraints, the Supreme Court has narrowed the field of its activity by self-imposed limitations. Where time and the nature of the judicial process did not establish limits, the Court has used narrow statutory construction as a means of deterring Congress and the executive, rather than finding unconstitutionality. Nevertheless, some of its decisions have stirred up a vast amount of controversy. The first such decision, *Dred Scott* v. *Sandford*,[33] increased the tension which eventually fulminated in the War Between the States; the other, *Brown* v. *Board of Education of Topeka*,[34] almost exactly 100 years later, gave rise to an ugly situation leading to attempts to revive the ancient doctrine of interposition, and at one time in one State, to a situation so dangerous that the President felt it necessary to resort to the drastic expedient of sending in Federal troops to preserve order.

The Slavery Controversy

The institution of slavery and the slave trade itself were controversial issues for at least a century before the adoption of the Thirteenth Amendment. Slavery existed in all the colonies, but since it was most profitable in the South, where it was regarded as necessary for the cultivation of cotton, it increased and became deeply entrenched as an institution only in that area. Its importance as an issue in the Constitutional Convention resulted in one of the significant compromises embodied in the Constitution. After the new government was established, the slavery issue soon came before Congress.

The discussion of the role of Congress in the area of civil rights began with the Federal Fugitive Slave Law of 1793 and subsequent legislation and efforts on the part of some States (notably Pennsylvania and Wisconsin) to evade their responsibilities under these laws. Many of the earlier settlers in Ohio and Indiana were Southern people who had left their homes to get away from contact with slavery. In Ohio, these new settlers joined the antislavery societies, welcomed fugitives from across the Ohio River, and helped them along on their journey to Canada.

[33] 19 Howard 393 (1857).   [34] 347 U.S. 483 (1954).

Some Ohio men even went into Kentucky and incited slaves to leave their masters. At this time, however (the early 1800's), Pennsylvania was the most hospitable of all the States to fugitive slaves. Its proximity to Maryland and Virginia made it easily accessible, and Philadelphia, because of its size, afforded fairly secure hiding places for those coming overland from neighboring States, as well as for those who came by water from the Carolinas.

Other States offered full cooperation. Because of the inadequacy of the original Federal law, the border States took the matter largely into their own hands. In Kentucky, a 1798 statute was still in force which provided that any person might apprehend a runaway servant or slave, take him to a justice of the peace, and receive ten shillings' reward and one shilling for every mile of his journey with the runaway. In 1842, in the Prigg Case previously referred to, the Supreme Court gave some standing to the idea that State officials could not be required to aid in the enforcement of Federal laws. This decision and the legislation of the Northern States which it inspired, caused deep concern in the South. North Carolina reflected the growing uneasiness of the Southern States by making it a felony to steal a slave for the purpose of sending him out of the State or to aid a slave to escape.

Nevertheless, there were many Southern slaveholders who, in the earlier years of the nineteenth century, had grave doubts regarding the advisability of the slave system, and some attempts were made to abolish it, the last notable one occurring in Virginia in 1832. The bitter attacks of Garrison and the abolitionists served to dispel their doubts and to solidify the slaveholders in defense of slavery, not only as necessary and proper, but also as a positive good. In 1835, a wave of indignation rolled through the Southern States. Public meetings were held and resolutions adopted. Not content to stand on the defensive, Southerners assumed an aggressive pro-slavery, anti-abolitionist attitude. They were, in fact, the more defensive because they were beginning to feel the reproach cast upon them by public opinion outside the United States, while the emancipation of the slaves in the British West Indies in 1833 had excited their apprehensions of interference from outside.

The controversy over fugitive slave laws was outlined earlier in this chapter as a phase of the controversy over civil rights. At this point, however, the concern is mainly with the institution of slavery, the controversy with regard to which came to a head when the Supreme Court attempted —to use the phrase coined by President Buchanan in his Inaugural Address—"speedily and finally" to settle it, as it did in the Dred Scott case.[35] No controversy could be more complicated or long enduring than the

[35] See also Mendelson, Wallace, "The Dred Scott Case—Revisited," *Louisiana Law Review*, March, 1947, pp. 398–405.

one over slavery. Here were presented a variety of social, political, and economic issues over which men had differed almost from the days when the first colonies were established on these shores. Humanitarian concern over the plight of the Negro, on the one hand, was countered on the other by the desire of those Northern manufacturers and businessmen to maintain profitable business relationships with the South. Resentment arose when Northern whites and recently arrived immigrants found free Negroes holding jobs that they themselves wanted. This feeling of antagonism took the form of fights and riots and petitions for action addressed to legislative bodies.

It was in this climate of opinion that the Dred Scott decision was received and the presidential elections of 1856 and 1860 were held. In spite of all that has been written about the decision, the details of the case are somewhat obscure. Dred Scott, born a slave on the Blow estate in Virginia (or in Missouri, according to another authority), was sold to Dr. Emerson, a surgeon in the Army, whom he accompanied as a household servant in various free States and territories north of the Mason-Dixon Line. While at these Northern posts, Scott married a woman purchased by Dr. Emerson, and two children were born to them. Dr. Emerson was then transferred to an Army post at St. Louis in the slave State of Missouri, taking the Scott family with him. Six years later he died, leaving all his property, including the Scott family, in trust to his widow and to John A. Sandford, his brother. From this time on, the family appears to have been a burden to the Emerson estate. One writer characterizes Scott as "a rather inefficient Negro, who may have been a good household servant, but was hardly capable of looking out for himself and his family." Having no use for him or his family, Mrs. Emerson hired him out, but he never seemed to stay long on one job. Since the family was held in trust, they could not be sold or given away. In 1850, Mrs. Emerson married Dr. Calvin C. Chaffee, a Representative in Congress from Massachusetts, who inherited the Scott family upon her death. Dr. Chaffee conveyed them to Taylor Blow of St. Louis for emancipation, and they were emancipated on May 26, 1857.

As far back as 1846, Scott had brought suit against Mrs. Emerson for their freedom in a Missouri State court. There were four suits in all, two brought by Scott, and two by his wife, Harriet. The first of each pair was in the form of a petition to bring suit, for suit was sustainable only if Scott was a free citizen, charging violence from another citizen. The other suits, instigated by attorneys as test cases, were for alleged assault and battery (a beating for disciplinary purposes) on the part of Irene Emerson and illegal imprisonment for twelve hours. The object was to get a decision that the Scott family, all Negroes, were free persons, for the assault and imprisonment alleged could not have been committed on a slave. The jury in the State Circuit Court brought in a verdict to the effect that Dred Scott was a free man. Residence on free soil had made him free, and there was no legal power to re-enslave him. The case was thereupon appealed to the State Supreme Court which ruled that although Scott may have been free in free territory, he had resumed his status as a slave by voluntarily returning to a slave State. The court refused to consider the Illinois Constitution or the Missouri Compromise as relevant and sent the case back to the Circuit Court. After a diversity of citizenship action in the Federal Circuit Court for Missouri, the case went to the Federal Supreme Court.

The importance of the case was realized in advance, as indicated by President Buchanan's reference to it in his Inaugural Address. Chief Justice Taney was induced to prepare the opinion, concurred in by six justices. It was a learned and lengthy argument, extending to some fifty-five printed pages, and one which has been characterized by Professor Edward S. Corwin as a "calamitous" decision. It was in two parts, the decision proper and an extended *obiter dicta*. The decision, that a Negro whose ancestors were imported into this country and sold as slaves could not become a member of the political community, brought into existence under the Constitution, was bad enough, but the *obiter dicta*—which took the position that slaves were not constituent members of our society and could not pretend to any benefit from the maxim that all men are by nature free, equal, and independent—added insult to injury, inflaming the public wrath in the North by what was regarded as still another aggression of the slave power.

Channing observes that the decision "aroused such a storm in the North as the country had seen only on two or three occasions before." Technically, he says:

> . . . the only thing decided was that the Supreme Court of the United States and the Federal Circuit Court of the Missouri district had no jurisdiction because Dred Scott was not and could not be a "citizen" within the meaning of the Constitution, and therefore the suit must be dismissed. As by-products, the majority of the judges in reaching this decision had incidentally rendered other decisions or quasi-decisions— one of these was that mere residence in a Free State did not prevent a Negro from returning to the condition of slavery by returning to a Slave State. Another, a third, was that Congress could not exclude slavery from the national domain by a law and therefore that the Missouri Compromise and probably the law confirming the Ordinance of 1787 was illegal.[36]

[36] Channing, VI, 194–195; for a current view, see Arthur Bestor, *State Sovereignty and Slavery: A Reinterpretation of Proslavery Constitutional Doc-*

In Chapter IV an attempt was made to trace the development of attitudes toward the Federal Union, noting first the widespread uncertainties that were generally prevalent in the early days, the growth of sentiment for disunity in New England which resulted in the famous Hartford Convention, and the ways in which the long drawn-out controversy over the slavery question involved both arguments and actions based upon the concept of the supremacy of the States vis-a-vis the central government under the Constitution.

During this long period of conflict in Federal-State relations, three major methods of remonstrance were threatened, attempted, or actually used—interposition, nullification, and secession. Each has been applied to a variety of subjects; each represents a different degree of intensity of feeling, for the justification of which weighty constitutional and legal arguments have been propounded; and each represents a different approach to the basic question of the nature of the Union and of the respective powers of the Federal government and of the States as members of the Union.

The controversy over slavery ended finally in secession, or at least in a quite determined attempt at secession, which was brought to a close only after four years of internecine strife. Presidents Lincoln and Johnson both maintained that no State had seceded and that attempts to do so had been frustrated. Radical Congressional opinion, however, asserted that secession had been accomplished and that the former States must be readmitted, with penalties for misconduct, before they could resume their membership in the Union. Politically, the argument extended over the Reconstruction Period without being conclusively settled; it was not legally and constitutionally settled until 1869 when the Supreme Court ruled that a State cannot secede from the Union.[37]

From "Separate But Equal" to "Equality"

In the Dred Scott decision, Chief Justice Taney answered in the negative the much discussed question as to whether the term "citizen" could be interpreted to include free Negroes. "Citizens of each State," he wrote, meant citizens of the United States as understood at the time the Constitution was adopted, and Negroes were not then regarded as capable of citizenship. Justice Curtis dissented, denying the assertion that there were no Negro citizens of States in 1789, and arguing that while Congress alone could determine what classes of aliens should be naturalized, the several States retained the right to extend citizenship to

trine, 1846–1860 (Urbana: Illinois State Historical Society, 1961); also in Journal of the Illinois State Historical Society, April, 1961.

[37] Texas v. White, 7 Wallace 700 (1869).

classes of persons born within their borders who had not previously enjoyed citizenship, and that those upon whom State citizenship was thus conferred became citizens of the State in the full sense of the Constitution. So far as persons born within the United States and subject to the jurisdiction thereof are concerned, the question was settled finally and decisively by the Fourteenth Amendment which, for the first time in the Constitution, gave a clear and concise definition of the term "citizenship."

Then in 1883, toward the end of the period of Reconstruction, came the Civil Rights Cases [38] in which the Supreme Court held unconstitutional certain sections of the Civil Rights Act of 1875 which provided punishment for *persons* who should interfere with the rights covered in the Act, for the protection of which action is directed only against action taken by States. "Until some State law has been passed," said the Court, "or some State action through its officers or agents has been taken adverse to the rights of citizens sought to be protected by the Fourteenth Amendment, no legislation of the United States under said Amendment, nor any proceeding under such legislation, can be called into activity." Thus, less than thirty years after its inception, the ambitious program of the Civil War years to outlaw the most serious forms of discrimination against Negroes ended in failure.

This was, in fact, only the first in a series of decisions that drastically narrowed the scope of Federal authority in the civil rights field. In another, in 1896, midway between the Dred Scott decision and the school desegregation cases, the Court handed down an opinion which firmly established in American law for a period of half a century the separate but equal doctrine which served as a basis for the segregation of the races.[39] A Louisiana statute of 1890 imposed a $25 fine on persons of Negro blood who attempted to enter railway train coaches set aside for whites. The statute also required railroads to furnish "separate but equal" accommodations for white and colored people. Plessy was one-eighth Negro, but appeared white. He occupied a vacant seat in a railway coach reserved for white passengers, to which his ticket otherwise entitled him. He was arrested, charged, tried, convicted, and fined as provided in the statute. On appeal, the higher state courts and, in turn, the Supreme Court held the statute constitutional. Speaking for the Court, Mr. Justice Brown said:

[38] 109 U.S. 3; see also *United States* v. *Harris*, 106 U.S. 629 (1882) in which the Court held the criminal conspiracy section of the Civil Rights Act of 1875 void, on the ground that the Fourteenth Amendment restricted the States but did not cover the acts of private individuals. Thus a mob might lynch a victim in violation of every concept of decency and fair play without necessarily violating any Federal law.

[39] *Plessy* v. *Ferguson*, 163 U.S. 537 (1896).

We consider the underlying fallacy of the plaintiff's argument to consist in the assumption that the enforced separation of the two races stamps the colored race with a badge of inferiority. If this be so, it is not by reason of anything found in the act, but solely because the colored race chooses to put that construction upon it.

Mr. Justice Harlan, dissenting, wrote some significant sentences which might with equal propriety have been incorporated in the Court's school desegregation decision half a century later:

The arbitrary separation of citizens on the basis of race, while they are on a public highway, is a badge of servitude wholly inconsistent with the civil freedom and equality before the law established by the Constitution. It cannot be justified upon any legal grounds.

If evils will result from the commingling of the two races upon public highways established for the benefit of all, they will be infinitely less than those that will surely come from State legislation regulating the enjoyment of civil rights upon the basis of race. We boast of the freedom enjoyed by our people above all other peoples. But it is difficult to reconcile this boast with a state of the law which, practically, puts the brand of servitude and degregation upon a large class of our fellow citizens, our equals before the law. The thin disguise of "equal" accommodations for passengers in railroad coaches will not mislead anyone, nor atone for the wrong this day done. . . .

In the years that followed, the Court was guided largely by two considerations in dealing with segregation cases: (1) the assumption that segregation did not imply anything with regard to the superiority or inferiority of either race and (2) the parallel assumption that where segregation was required by law, the facilities provided for the two races would in fact be equal in quality and adequate in quantity. Rare indeed was the case in which either of these assumptions was realized in practice. It was not until the middle of the twentieth century that the Court began to retreat from this position in public accommodation cases and other fields.

In 1914, the Court had held that Pullman accommodations could not be denied to Negroes if they were available to white persons,[40] but it was not until many years later that it consistently refused to tolerate discriminatory practices in this area. In *Mitchell* v. *United States*,[41] it was made clear that the Court would insist that in spite of Southern segregation laws, Negroes receive accommodations and treatment substantially

[40] *McCabe* v. *Atcheson, Topeka & Santa Fe Railroad Company*, 235 U.S. 151 (1916).

[41] 313 U.S. 80 (1941). Mr. Mitchell was a Negro Congressman from Chicago; the case arose under Arkansas law.

equal to those given whites. The test of equality is not met by giving Negroes with first class tickets accommodations equal to those enjoyed by white persons traveling second class, nor by allowing them to buy drawing room space, if available. The Court held that a Virginia statute requiring the segregation of Negroes and whites on interstate buses unduly burdened interstate commerce.[42] Eighteen States, the Court noted, prohibit racial segregation on public carriers, while ten require it on motor carriers. The enforcement of these State laws against carriers engaged in such commerce produces cumulative inconveniences and burdens, among which are the repeated shifting of seats upon reaching State lines, as well as the difficulty of applying the various definitions used to identify white and colored passengers. The Court held the Virginia statute invalid, noting that the protection given to members of minority groups came under the commerce clause of the Constitution, not under the Bill of Rights.

Still later, in 1950, the Supreme Court banned segregation in railway dining cars.[43] Elmer W. Henderson had been refused service in a Southern Railway dining car in 1942 because there were no empty seats at tables reserved for Negroes, although there were seats at tables for whites. Speaking for the Court, Mr. Justice Burton said:

> Where a dining car is available to passengers holding tickets entitling them to use it, each such passenger is equally entitled to its facilities in accordance with reasonable regulations. The denial of dining service to any such passenger by the rules before us subjects him to a prohibited disadvantage.

The Supreme Court also ruled that a State can forbid racial discrimination on an excursion boat, even though the boat goes into foreign waters. By a 7-2 decision, it upheld the conviction of the Bob-Lo Excursion Company of Detroit for putting a Negro high school girl off one of its boats. The Company was found guilty of violating the Michigan civil rights statute and fined $25.[44]

When one considers this long line of decisions, and others in related areas as well, particularly a group that had gradually been whittling away racial barriers in institutions of higher education, the desegregation decision in the Brown Case comes as no great surprise. Segregation of races was by no means an exclusively Southern practice. Negroes were

[42] *Morgan* v. *Virginia*, 328 U.S. 373 (1946); see also *Hall* v. *DeCuir*, 95 U.S. 495 (1878), in which State law forbidding steamboats on the Mississippi to segregate passengers according to race was held unconstitutional under the commerce clause.

[43] *Henderson* v. *United States*, 339 U.S. 816 (1950).

[44] *Bob-Lo Excursion Company* v. *Michigan*, 333 U.S. 28 (1948).

segregated in practice if not by legal requirement in many Northern communities—a sort of *de facto* segregation.[45] Mexicans were segregated in West Texas and in New Mexico, Orientals in the Pacific Coast States, and Indians were segregated in many States in various parts of the country. Ironically enough, the Brown Case developed in the free State of Kansas.[46] In many communities in which the pattern of segregation had been followed in the schools, this decision created tremendous problems of adjustment and change.

Chief Justice Warren, speaking for the Court on the Brown Case, noted that these cases came to the Court from the States of Kansas, South Carolina, Virginia, and Delaware. "They are premised on different facts and different local conditions, but a common legal question justifies their consideration together in this consolidated opinion." He continues:

> In each of the cases, minors of the Negro race, through their legal representatives, seek the aid of the courts in obtaining admission to the public schools of their community on a nonsegregated basis. In each instance, they had been denied admission to schools attended by white children under laws requiring or permitting segregation according to race. This segregation was alleged to deprive the plaintiffs of the equal protection of the laws under the Fourteenth Amendment. In each of the cases other than the Delaware case, a three-judge Federal District Court denied relief to the plaintiffs on the so-called "separate but equal" doctrine announced by this Court in *Plessy* v. *Ferguson*, 163 U.S. 537. Under that doctrine, equality of treatment is accorded when the races are provided substantially equal facilities, even though these facilities be separate. . . .
>
> The plaintiffs contend that segregated public schools are not "equal" and cannot be made "equal," and that hence they are deprived of the equal protection of the laws. . . . The effect of this separation on their educational opportunities was well stated by a finding in the Kansas case by a court which nevertheless felt compelled to rule against the Negro plaintiffs:
>
> Segregation of white and colored children in public schools has a detrimental effect upon the colored children. The impact is greater when it has the sanction of law; for the policy of separating the races is usually interpreted as denoting the inferiority of the Negro group. A sense of inferiority affects the motivation of a child to learn. Segrega-

---

[45] See Maslow, Will, "De Facto Public School Segregation," *Villanova Law Review*, Spring, 1961, pp. 353–376.

[46] *Brown* v. *Board of Education of Topeka*, 347 U.S. 483 (1954). An enormous literature has been developing around this subject, covering all aspects. All governmental actions taken regarding it are recorded in the successive issues of the *Race Relations Reporter*; for other sources, see Bibliographical Notes on p. 315.

tion with the sanction of law, therefore, has a tendency to retard the educational and mental development of Negro children and to deprive them of some of the benefits they would receive in a racially integrated school system.

Whatever may have been the extent of psychological knowledge at the time of *Plessy* v. *Ferguson,* this finding is amply supported by modern authority. Any language in *Plessy* v. *Ferguson* contrary to this finding is rejected.

We conclude that in the field of public education the doctrine of "separate but equal" has no place. Separate education facilities are inherently unequal. Therefore, we hold that the plaintiffs and others similarly situated for whom the actions have been brought are, by reason of the segregation complained of, deprived of the equal protection of the laws guaranteed by the Fourteenth Amendment. This disposition makes unnecessary any discussion whether such segregation violates the due process clause of the Fourteenth Amendment.

Protection of the Right to Vote

The right to vote, at least for such Federal officers as President, Vice-President, Senator, and Representative, is not only a Federal right, but one that is explicitly spelled out in the Constitution, being given fuller treatment, in Articles I and II, and in Amendments XII, XIII, XIV, XV, XVII, XIX, XXII, and XXIII, than any other interest. All of these deal with one aspect or another of the right to vote. Although the suffrage is thus established as a Federal right, there is no affirmative policy to be found in any of these provisions. The substance of all of them is that persons may not be denied the privilege of the suffrage for any one of a number of specified reasons. The right to establish and administer qualifications for voting is left to the States, in Federal as well as in State and local elections.

State and local authorities, operating sometimes through legislation and sometimes by discriminatory administrative action, have demonstrated amazing ingenuity in devising schemes for the disfranchisement of any minority group against which a strong local prejudice exists. The largest such group, of course, has been the Negro. Force and intimidation, once common, have been largely supplanted by literacy tests, constitution interpretation tests, property, residence or character qualifications, the grandfather clause, the poll tax, and the white primary. As soon as one device for disqualification has been ruled out by the courts, another means of achieving the same end has promptly been placed in operation. The Civil Rights Commission reported in 1959 that the prevailing means currently employed might be described as "discriminatory application and administration of apparently non-discriminatory laws" in the process of registration, and of less subtle means involving violence and intimidation,[47] or as in Tennessee in 1960, eviction and reprisal.

For nearly 100 years, efforts have been made to involve the Federal government actively, in one way or another, in the protection of the voting rights of individual citizens. The Supreme Court has been called upon in case after case by persons barred from voting who sought to make their constitutional rights effective.[48] At the same time, Congress was called upon year after year to enact anti-poll tax legislation and other measures designed to prevent discriminatory practices. Efforts to enforce voting rights through judicial action have, with the exception of the decisions in the white primary cases, been notably unsuccessful, the Court consistently taking the position that these questions were political, not justiciable.

In spite of considerable improvement in the situation in recent years, discriminatory practices are still widely prevalent: against Negroes in many parts of the South, against urban dwellers in many States, and against other minority groups elsewhere throughout the country. In 1947, only 12 per cent of the Negroes could vote; by 1956, this percentage had been increased to 25, as compared with 60 per cent for Southern whites of voting age. When in 1960, urban dwellers in three States—Tennessee, Maryland, and Michigan—claimed that they were disfranchised by reason of unfair, discriminatory, and unconstitutional apportionment of representation in the State legislatures and sought relief in the courts, they were given little encouragement. In one New Jersey Supreme Court case, the Frankfurter doctrine set forth in *Colegrove* v. *Green* [49] was rejected; however, a Federal court did trigger legislative action in Minnesota in 1959, when it took jurisdiction in a redistricting case. In most cases, however, the courts have not been helpful.

Congress has, in recent legislation, given consideration to the problem of the right to vote. Existing abuses in this field have also been brought to light by the work of the Civil Rights Commission; the problem now appears to be largely one of effective enforcement of law already on the books. In 1959 and 1960, following the November elections, some amazing cases came to light in two East Tennessee counties, involving economic reprisals against tenant farmers whose families were evicted and dismissed from their jobs and denied supplies, insurance, and credit. These actions on the part of private individuals, acting in cooperation on a county-wide basis, brought forth action by both the Civil Rights

[47] Civil Rights Commission, *Report* (1959), p. 133.

[48] *Nixon* v. *Herndon*, 273 U.S. 536 (1927); *Nixon* v. *Condon*, 286 U.S. 73 (1932); *Grovey* v. *Townsend*, 295 U.S. 45 (1935); *U.S.* v. *Classic*, 313 U.S. 299 (1940).

[49] 66 Sup. Ct. 1198 (1946).

Division of the Department of Justice and the Federal courts. In November, 1959, complaint was filed in the Federal District Court, naming eighty-two defendants, including twenty-five landowners, twenty-four merchants and a bank, charged with the following practices among others:

> Terminating leases and sharecropper arrangements held by Negroes who had registered.
> Dismissing Negro employees involved in the voting campaign.
> Refusing to sell supplies to Negro registrants, even for cash, and refusing other families the credit they had always had.
> Cancelling insurance policies of Negroes who had registered.
> Persuading whites to join in the economic pressure by circulating lists of Negro voters, and refusing to deal with white merchants and others believed to be in sympathy with Negro voting.[50]

In addition to the temporary injunction to stop the evictions, the suit asked a permanent injunction against any efforts to discourage Negro voting. The suit invoked a section of the 1957 Civil Rights Act that prohibits intimidation or coercion to discourage registration or voting because of race. The section applies to State officials and individuals. The significant aspect of the case was the effort to uncover private pressures in the racial field; all previous Department of Justice suits had been directed at official action.

In an excellent law review article, John C. McDonald points out that the process of judicial enforcement of suffrage rights involves a number of inherent defects. He discusses more than half a dozen continuing obstacles to Negro voting. First among them, and certainly one of the most important, is the limited coverage of existing legislation, followed by such other considerations as reluctance to prosecute, difficulty in locating defendants, lack of evidence, presumption of innocence, and limited effect of judgment, if and when obtained.[51]

While it is clear that the existing situation is not encouraging, it is not hopeless. Numerous possible solutions of the problem have been suggested, in Congress and elsewhere. Three may be mentioned here. The local registrars might be replaced by impartial Federal referees; this proposal would doubtless result in improvement, but it is too restricted in scope. A better solution, which could be expected to result in a more uniform and democratic suffrage throughout the nation, would be the adoption of such a constitutional amendment as the following, proposed by the Civil Rights Commission:

[50] "U.S. Fights Abuse of Negro Voters," *The New York Times*, December 13, 1960.
[51] McDonald, John C., "Judicial Protection of Minority Voting Rights: The Case for Constitutional Reform," *Ohio State Law Journal*, Spring, 1961, pp. 390–420.

Section 1. Every citizen of the United States of the age of twenty-one years or older who has resided in any State or Territory six months and in the voting precinct three months, immediately before offering to vote, shall be entitled to vote at any primary election or other election therein, in which candidates for any public office are nominated or elected, except that the privilege of voting shall not extend to persons in confinement for crime nor to persons adjudicated insane of mind.

Section 2. Congress shall have power to enforce this Article by appropriate legislation.[52]

In December, 1960, it was proposed that a long unused remedy should be pressed into service. Gordon Tiffany, retiring executive director of the Civil Rights Commission, proposed that Section 2 of Amendment XIV, which provides that the basis of representation of a State "Shall be reduced in the proportion which the number of disqualified citizens shall bear to the whole number of [male] citizens twenty-one years of age in such State," be invoked with respect to those States that consistently refuse to permit qualified Negroes to register and vote. Dormant for almost 100 years, occasional suggestions that Section 2 be invoked were always rejected, basically on the theory that no State was perfect and that none was in a position to cast the first stone.[53] In May, 1963, the NAACP filed suit in the U.S. District Court for the District of Columbia invoking this provision.

BASIC ATTITUDES TOWARD CIVIL RIGHTS

The world-wide demand for the recognition of basic human rights on the part of suppressed and underprivileged peoples everywhere finds expression in the United States by the attempt to inject civil rights issues into the consideration of many matters that come before Congress—matters with which civil rights were never associated in the past. Examples may be noted in grant-in-aid legislation for education and for public housing, the right of citizens to vote, and Senate confirmation of nominations submitted by the President.

[52] Civil Rights Commission, *Report* (1959), p. 144; see also McDonald, p. 420.

[53] This possibility is discussed in Emerson, Thomas L., and Bonfield, Arthur E., "Forgotten Remedy for the Voteless Negro," *The Nation,* January 21, 1961, pp. 55–59; and in Doyle, Vincent A., *Study of Section Two of the Fourteenth Amendment* (Washington: Legislative Reference Service, Library of Congress, 1960).

The responsibility of Congress for complying with both the letter and the spirit of the law in the area of grants for education has been dramatically presented on a number of occasions in recent years. Several aid-for-education bills have been blocked by the demand that they contain a proviso that no aid will be provided for segregated schools. In late 1960, the controversy over the admission of two Negro students at the University of Georgia, and shortly thereafter, the publication of a Civil Rights Commission report on higher education, presented the same problem. The report pointed out that while the law of the nation is committed to a policy of desegregation, the Federal government has been and is now providing financial assistance to public colleges and universities that exclude Negroes or discriminate against them.

STATISTICAL SUMMARY OF SCHOOL SEGREGATION—DESEGREGATION IN THE SOUTHERN AND BORDER STATES
1954 — 1962

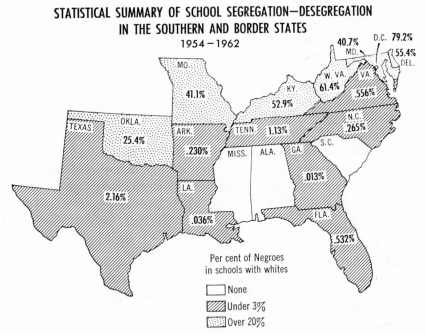

D.C. **79.2%**

40.7% MD.

55.4% DEL.

W. VA. 61.4% VA.

MO.

41.1%

KY.
52.9%

.556%

OKLA.

TEXAS

25.4%

ARK.
.230%

TENN. 1.13%

N.C.
.265%

MISS. ALA. GA.

S.C.

.013%

LA.

2.16%

.036%

FLA.

.532%

Per cent of Negroes
in schools with whites

☐ None
▨ Under 3%
▨ Over 20%

Source: Southern Education Reporting Service, November, 1962

Almost half of the State colleges and universities established for white students in the Southern and border States remain completely segregated. Even where desegregation has occurred, it has usually been of the "token" variety. There are many other findings in the report that indicate very clearly that there is much work yet to be done in this field.[54]

[54] See Lewis, Anthony, "U.S. Urged to End Help to Colleges That Bar Negroes," *The New York Times,* January 16, 1961.

The Commission maintained that conditions must be imposed on Federal aid programs by executive action, or if need be, by act of Congress, to see that the discriminatory practices are ended. In housing, comparable and in many respects parallel problems exist.

The Bill of Rights and the States

The background of this problem may be briefly stated. Each of the States has adopted a bill of rights; in fact, most of them were adopted even before the Federal Constitution was framed. The States regarded these guarantees as important, so important that when the Federal Constitution was submitted minus such a statement, several of them gave their approval only on condition that, at the earliest possible time, Congress should frame and present to the States for their approval, a series of amendments to the Federal Constitution that would remedy this omission. Then, in a case decided by the Supreme Court some years later, it was held that the Federal Bill of Rights operated solely and exclusively as a restriction upon the Federal government, not upon the States.[55]

After the Civil War, a demand arose for national protection against abuses (or alleged abuses) of State power. With this in mind, Congress proposed and the States ratified the War Amendments. The substance of these amendments has been previously stated. Such significant changes in the Constitution were certain to be challenged in the courts, and a test case on the Fourteenth Amendment was not long in arriving. The decision of the Supreme Court in the Slaughter House Cases stated, in effect, that this Amendment really had not changed anything. There had been no intention, the Court said, that the police powers of the States would be disturbed. They were vested now, as they had always been, in the States, not in the Federal government.[56] In later years, the question has been raised repeatedly as to whether the Fourteenth Amendment has "absorbed" the Federal Bill of Rights. Mr. Justice Black has been a leading advocate of the position that it has.

While this view has not yet been accepted by a majority of Justice Black's colleagues, there have been a number of decisions since 1925 that "have extended against State power the First Amendment's protections for religion, speech, press, assembly, and petition." [57] While considerations of federalism have overborne the arguments in favor of ex-

[55] *Barron* v. *Mayor and City Council of Baltimore,* 7 Peters 243 (1833).
[56] 16 Wallace 36 (1873).
[57] This discussion is based upon the findings of Justice William J. Brennan, Jr., in his *The Bill of Rights and the States* (Santa Barbara: Center for the Study of Democratic Institutions, 1961) and in *New York University Law Review,* April, 1961, pp. 761–778. See also Fairman, Charles, "Does the

tension in many cases, the Court has repeatedly held that some of the Federal procedural guarantees were an essential part of due process. And the States themselves have voluntarily and effectively enforced, in many instances, "the counterparts in State constitutions of the specifics of the Bill of Rights. Indeed, some have been applied by States to an extent beyond that required of the national government by the corresponding Federal guarantee. But too many state practices fall far short." [58]

The Supreme Court has, in the past generation, paid more attention than ever before to the basic personal rights set forth in the First Amendment: separation of church and state, equal protection in the processes of law enforcement, access to and use of public schools and all other public facilities, and due process in criminal procedure. It has declared a number of State actions and some actions of the Federal government as well to be unconstitutional, thus narrowing the scope of some of the supposed governmental powers in this field and, in effect, enlarging considerably the rights of individuals against the government. Illustrations are to be found not only in the school desegregation decision, but in decisions in the field of judicial due process in criminal cases in which the Court has in general enforced higher standards in the activities of courts and prosecutors, and even higher standards for the Federal government than for the States.

Even so, one eminent student of civil rights questions, Professor Robert K. Carr, finds the recent record of the Supreme Court in this field uncertain and confusing. In a discussion which appears under the title, *The Seesaw Between Freedom and Power*,[59] he points out that during the past three decades, in the Court's search for a "satisfactory equilibrium between liberty and authority in the area of the so-called First Amendment freedoms," it has taken five basic positions respecting the way in which competing interests of liberty and authority may be reconciled, ranging from the view that such "freedoms are absolute and all governmental encroachments on them, great and small, are *per se* unconstitutional" to "certain social needs as reflected in the exercise of authority are absolute and the liberty of the individual must give way where society chooses to assert these interests." [60]

Fourteenth Amendment Incorporate the Bill of Rights?—The Original Understanding," *Stanford Law Review*, June, 1949, pp. 587–645.

[58] Brennan, p. 20.

[59] (Urbana: University of Illinois Press, 1960); this was the Edmund K. James Lecture on Government, delivered March 17, 1960.

[60] For example, in *Sweezy* v. *New Hampshire*, 354 U.S. 234 (1957), a majority of six justices resolved the balance in favor of academic freedom, while in *Barenblatt* v. *United States*, 360 U.S. 109 (1959), a majority of five justices decided in favor of the legislative power to investigate. Such lack of consistency makes it difficult to discern what the policy really is.

Nowhere is this confusion more complete and more overwhelming than in the field of church-state relations.[61] If it be true, as it appears to be, that the Supreme Court has difficulty in deciding what religious groups may or may not do in relation to the public schools under particular circumstances, the public is left completely confused as is demonstrated by the widespread discussion of Federal aid for education. Most of the discussion has been based upon the erroneous assumption that complete or virtually complete separation of church and state now exists, whereas in practice, there is relatively little separation.

Small wonder that the Supreme Court has difficulty making up its mind, when the people themselves and their elected representatives in the legislatures talk one way and act another. Although the institution of the established church has disappeared, the ancient tradition of associating religion with education and various other aspects of life through governmental action and even through public financial support "dies hard and revives easily." Examples are abundant. Under the G.I. Bill of Rights, the United States expends public funds to train young men for the ministry in the doctrine of their chosen sects, and it expends funds to support a chaplain's corps in each of the armed services. Church-owned property is regularly exempted from taxation by Federal, State, and local governments. By constitutional provision, New York requires that school buses carry Catholic children to parochial schools.[62]

Bible reading has long been practiced in many schools, and required by law in some. Under an 8–1 decision of the Supreme Court, handed down during the summer of 1963, neither Bible reading nor an opening prayer may be required. While the decision does not prohibit such observances, it does hold that for a State to require them violates the basic concept of separation of church and state. While the decision settles some questions, it also raises others. What its ultimate effect may be on such common practices as the invocation by a local minister at commencement

[61] Although it talked of a "wall of separation between church and state," the Court still found it possible to uphold by a 5-4 decision a New Jersey law authorizing reimbursement of patrons of Catholic schools for transportation costs in *Everson* v. *Board of Education*, 330 U.S. 15 (1947); in another two years, it ruled out in an 8-1 decision a released time program for religious instruction in Illinois in *McCollum* v. *Board of Education*, 333 U.S. 203 (1948), and see McCollum, Vashti C., *One Woman's Fight* (New York: Doubleday & Co., Inc., 1951); in 1952, a released time program in New York City, instruction given off the premises, was upheld 6-3 in *Zorach* v. *Clauson*, 343 U.S. 306 (1952).

[62] As of 1960, there were nineteen States transporting non-public school children, and eight more that had formerly done so. See Shanahan, Patrick E., *State Laws Providing for Free Transportation for Nonpublic School Children: Their Nature, Interpretation and Execution* (Washington: doctoral dissertation, Catholic University of America, 1960).

exercises or other public functions, reminders of the Deity and of organized religion appearing on government-issued coins, stamps, and public documents, or Executive Proclamations of the various holidays cannot now be stated with any assurance. As late as 1961, the Court had upheld the validity of the blue laws which still persist in many jurisdictions.[63]

State Laxity vs. Federal Intervention

On the basis of the past record, there have been fewer instances of extremism, hysteria, and flagrant abuse of civil rights at the national level than at the State level. Not only have the national abuses been fewer in number, they have also been relatively short-lived, probably because a McCarthy arouses national indignation whereas a burst of activity on the part of the Ku Klux Klan may be greeted with apathy or even given popular support in individual States. A recent writer has stated some of these points extremely well:

> Witch-hunting on the national scene created a furor and collapsed several years ago, but it continues on the State level, where little McCarthys in some of our State legislatures have set up committees which are currently investigating subversion, un-Americanism, socialism, communism, the NAACP, immorality, and sundry other things. It goes without saying that many of these investigations are being conducted with no nice respect for personal civil liberties. . . .
>
> There are several reasons why liberty is better safeguarded in the nation than in the State. The chances are greater of having independent citizens and newspapers to speak out against passion and injustice. It is harder for a single group or faction to get control of the government. It is more difficult to form a minority, and even more difficult to form an opinionated majority. Within the wide scope of the nation there are many more classes, groups, interests, and values which check, restrain, and counterbalance one another. All of this is stated in *The Federalist,* and it is as true now as when it was written.[64]

In procedural matters, were it not for the insistence of the Federal courts on due process and equal protection, the situation in the States

[63] In Pennsylvania, *Two Guys* v. *McGinley,* 366 U.S. 582 (1961) and in Maryland, *McGowan* v. *Maryland,* 366 U.S. 420 (1961). This comment is based largely on Sutherland, Arthur E., Jr., "Due Process and Disestablishment," *Harvard Law Review,* June, 1949, pp. 1306–1344.

[64] Carleton, William G., "Centralization and the Open Society," *Political Science Quarterly,* June, 1960, pp. 224–259.

would probably be far worse than it is; none will deny that it is bad enough. Mr. Justice Brennan has recently observed that "Far too many cases come from the States to the Supreme Court presenting dismal pictures of official lawlessness, of illegal searches and seizures, illegal detentions attended by prolonged interrogation and coerced admissions of guilt, of the denial of counsel, and of downright brutality." [65]

Professor William Anderson has thus summarized the overall significance of the changes that have taken place in the attitudes of the Court on these important matters:

> In almost every area of governmental action, the constitutional rules of what the States may do and what the national government may do have undergone important if not revolutionary changes in the past three decades. Important old restrictions on both national and state activity in the economic field have been removed by the Supreme Court's reversing some of its earlier doctrines. At the same time, restrictions of new types have been applied to personal and social rights. In general it appears that the old restrictions that have been removed from the activities of the national government are more numerous than the new ones that have recently been imposed. This is true to a great extent also with respect to the States—but precise statements and comparisons are impossible to formulate because the loosening of bonds has been primarily in one field and the imposing of new restrictions in another. In most areas of governmental activity the state and national governments are both more free to move ahead, because the old attachment to laissez-faire and the old suspicions of governmental action are less than they were and are largely ineffective. What is more, the growing trend toward cooperative action between the states and the national governments, though not originated by the Court, has received its approval, and the fears that marked relations between the two levels of government are certainly on the decline.[66]

There is little doubt that the balance in the federal system has swung against the States in most areas where individual liberties are at stake. In dealing with these questions, the Supreme Court is in a difficult and almost impossible position. When it takes a courageous and positive stand in support of civil rights, it is denounced for "interference" in matters which are, in the American brand of federalism, normally regarded as subject to State and/or local control. When it recognizes that this *is* a federal system in which State and local governments are supposed to have important responsibilities, it is criticized for (as one writer expresses it)

---

[65] Brennan, pp. 20–21.

[66] Anderson, William, *Intergovernmental Relations in Review* (Minneapolis: University of Minnesota Press, 1960), p. 33.

"an anachronistic reliance upon the otherwise discredited doctrine of dual federalism."

Behind what Professor Friedelbaum has characterized as "the legal façade of pre-emption and due process," there appears to be a strong predilection on the part of a majority of the Court in favor of a vigorous pro-civil rights approach. These considerations have great significance for every phase of Federal-State relations. The written constitution as interpreted by the three branches of government, and especially by the Supreme Court, defines the channels within which governments may act. "These channels," Professor Anderson has said, "have changed significantly in our time." [67] And from all indications, they are likely to change even more in the years ahead.

BIBLIOGRAPHICAL NOTES

The Negro in America. The three main aspects of this story are probably slavery, the struggle for freedom, and the quest for equality. The better general works are: Anna Bontemps, *100 Years of Negro Freedom* (New York: Dodd, Mead & Co., 1961); John H. Franklin, *From Slavery to Freedom: A History of American Negroes*, 2nd ed. (New York: Alfred A. Knopf, Inc., 1956); Charles S. Logan, *The Negro in American Life and Thought: The Nadir, 1877–1901* (New York: Dial Press, Inc., 1954); and Carter G. Woodson and Charles H. Wesley, *The Negro in Our History*, 10th ed. (Washington: Associated Publishers, 1962). Arthur Bestor, *State Sovereignty and Slavery* (Springfield: Civil War Centennial Commission, 1961) is a reinterpretation of pro-slavery constitutional doctrine, 1846–1860; the political aspects of this problem are covered in Theodore C. Smith, *Parties and Slavery, 1850–1859* (New York: Harper & Bros., 1906). Standard titles on the Fugitive Slave Law and its enforcement are Marion G. McDougall, *Fugitive Slaves, 1619–1865* (Boston: Ginn & Co., 1891) and Wilbur H. Siebert, *The Underground Railroad from Slavery to Freedom* (New York: The Macmillan Co., 1898). The civil rights aspects of the slave era are well presented in Gilman Ostrander, *The Rights of Man in America, 1606–1861* (Columbia: University of Missouri Press, 1960).

In addition to *A Bibliography on Antislavery in America*, Dwight L. Dumond has two books: *Antislavery: The Crusade for Freedom in America* and *Antislavery Origins of the Civil War* (all three, Ann Arbor: University of Michigan Press, 1961). Nineteen sixty-one was a banner year for studies of the antislavery movement; see Lawrence Lader, *The Bold Brahmins: New England's War Against Slavery* (New York: E. P. Dutton & Co., 1961); Leon F. Litwack, *North of Slavery: The Negro in the Free States, 1790–1860* (Chicago: University of Chicago Press, 1961); and O. A. Sherrard, *Freedom From Fear: The Slave and His Emancipation* (New York: St. Martin's Press, Inc., 1961). Also pertinent is Jacobus Ten Broek, *The Antislavery Origins of the Fourteenth Amendment* (Berkeley: University of California Press, 1951).

[67] See, for instance, the report of Stetson, Damon, "Bigger U.S. Role on Rights Urged," *The New York Times*, December 15, 1960, p. 32.

The Bill of Rights. On the historical background of the Bill of Rights, see Zechariah Chafee, Jr., *How Human Rights Got into the Constitution* (Boston: Boston University Press, 1950); Leonard W. Levy, *Legacy of Suppression: Freedom of Speech and Press in Early American History* (Cambridge: Harvard University Press, 1961); Max Savelle, *Seeds of Liberty: The Genesis of the American Mind* (New York: Alfred A. Knopf, Inc., 1948); and Robert A. Rutland, *The Birth of The Bill of Rights, 1776–1791* (Chapel Hill: University of North Carolina Press, 1955). For commentary, see William J. Brennan, *The Bill of Rights and the States* (Santa Barbara: Center for the Study of Democratic Institutions, 1961); Walter Gellhorn, *American Rights: The Constitution in Action* (New York: The Macmillan Co., 1960); Paul G. Kauper, *Civil Liberties and the Constitution* (Ann Arbor: University of Michigan Press, 1961); and Andrew D. Weinberger, *Freedom and Protection: The Bill of Rights* (San Francisco: Chandler Publishing Company, 1962).

Federal Civil Rights. Of particular value is the collection of legal and related materials by Thomas I. Emerson and David Haber, eds., *Political and Civil Rights in the United States,* rev. ed. (Buffalo: Dennis and Company, 1956). Although the volume of published materials on civil rights is overwhelming, relatively few writers have addressed themselves to the intergovernmental relations aspects of the problem. Important exceptions are Robert K. Carr, *Federal Protection of Civil Rights* (Ithaca: Cornell University Press, 1947) and *The Seesaw Between Freedom and Power* (Urbana: University of Illinois Bulletin, 1960); Osmond K. Fraenkel, *The Supreme Court and Civil Liberties* (New York: American Civil Liberties Union, 1941); Robert L. Hale, *Freedom Through Law* (New York: Columbia University Press, 1952); Oscar Handlin, *The Dimensions of Liberty* (Cambridge: Belknap Press, 1961); Robert J. Harris, *The Quest for Equality: The Constitution, Congress and the Supreme Court* (Baton Rouge: Louisiana State University Press, 1960); Milton R. Konvitz, *A Century of Civil Rights* (New York: Columbia University Press, 1961); and Philip B. Yeager and John R. Stark, *Your Inalienable Rights* (Washington: Public Affairs Press, 1960). Felix Morley has written *Freedom and Federalism* (Chicago: Henry Regnery Co., 1959), and for comparative purposes, see Francis R. Scott, *Civil Liberties and Canadian Federalism* (Toronto: University of Toronto Press, 1959). Walter Gellhorn, *The Constitution in Action* (New York: The Macmillan Co., 1960) presents an excellent summary.

Internal Security Legislation. The early Alien and Sedition Laws were conceived of largely as security measures; see: Frank M. Anderson, "The Enforcement of the Alien and Sedition Laws," in American Historical Association, *Annual Report, 1912,* pp. 113–126 (Washington, 1914); James M. Smith, *Freedom's Fetters: The Alien and Sedition Laws and American Civil Liberties* (Ithaca: Cornell University Press, 1956); and Ethelbert D. Warfield, *The Kentucky Resolutions of 1798: An Historical Study,* 2nd ed. (New York: G. P. Putnam's Sons, 1894).

At least two national organizations have compiled basic materials bearing on recent Federal-State relations in this area: American Civil Liberties Union, *The States and Subversion* (New York, 1953) and Council of State Governments, *Digest of State and Local Activities Relating to Internal Security* (Chicago, 1960). The most significant writing in this field has been done for the Cornell Studies in Civil Liberty under the editorship of Robert E. Cushman. Included in the more than fifteen volumes are studies of both Federal and State programs; as an example of the former, see Walter Gellhorn, *Security, Loyalty and Science* (Ithaca: Cornell University Press, 1950) and of the latter, Lawrence H. Chamberlain, cited below. See also Alan Barth, *The Loyalty of Free Men* (New York: Viking Press, 1950). Herbert Aptheker, *Dare We Be Free?* (New York: New Century Publishers, 1961) discusses the meaning of the attempt to outlaw the Communist Party. Harold D. Lasswell, *National Security and Individual Freedom* (New York: McGraw-Hill Book Co., Inc., 1950) is also important.

The following articles should be noted: Roger C. Cramston, "Supersession and Subversion: Limitations on State Power to Deal with Issues of Subversion and Loyalty," *University of Chicago Law School Record,* Autumn, 1958, pp. 24–53; Alan R. Hunt, "Federal Supremacy and State Anti-Subversive Legislation," *Michigan Law Review,* January, 1955, pp. 407–438, and "State Control of Sedition: The Smith Act as the Supreme Law of the Land," *Minnesota Law Review,* February, 1957, pp. 287–332; William B. Prendergast, "State Legislatures and Communism: The Current Scene," *American Political Science Review,* September, 1950, pp. 556–574; and "State Control of Subversion: A Problem of Federalism," *Harvard Law Review,* December, 1952, pp. 327–334.

Civil Rights in the States. Although much of the recent work in this field involves issues of segregation and race relations, the following general titles are available: Richard Barnett, *Where the States Stand on Civil Rights* (New York: Sterling Publishing Company, 1962) and Lawrence H. Chamberlain, *Loyalty and Legislative Action: A Survey of Activity by the New York State Legislature, 1919–1949* (Ithaca: Cornell University Press, 1951). Two articles give some of the historical background of school segregation: Alfred H. Kelly, "The Congressional Controversy Over School Segregation, 1867–1875," *American Historical Review,* April, 1959, pp. 537–563, and John H. Franklin, "Jim Crow Goes to School: The Genesis of Legal Segregation in Southern Schools," *South Atlantic Quarterly,* Spring, 1959, pp. 225–235. The entire story of the desegregation movement since the Supreme Court decision in 1954 has been reported at length in *The New York Times,* and very fully reported, with reprints of essential portions of the documents involved, in the *Race Relations Reporter* and the *Southern School News.* For an able discussion of the problems involved, see Robert J. Harris, *The Quest for Equality.*

For the Virginia story in some detail, see Benjamin Muse, *Virginia's Massive Resistance* (Bloomington: Indiana University Press, 1961); David J. Mays, *A Question of Intent: The States, Their Schools and the Fourteenth Amendment* (Richmond: Virginia Commission on Constitutional Government, 1959); Marvin B. Norfleet, *Forced School Integration in the U.S.A.* (New York: Carlton Press, Inc., 1961); and Roy R. Pearson, *Setting up Private Schools* (Farmville, Va.: Prince Edward School Foundation, 1961). Former Congressman Brooks Hays, deeply involved in the Little Rock controversy, has told the story in a book and two articles: *A Southern Moderate Speaks* (Chapel Hill: University of North Carolina Press, 1959). "The Inside Story of Little Rock," *Look,* March 17, 1959, pp. 23–27, and *U.S. News and World Report,* March 23, 1959, pp. 118–135. A collection of materials for analysis of the Little Rock story is presented in Wilson and Jane Record, *Little Rock, U.S.A.* (San Francisco: Chandler Publishing Company, 1960). For comment on the world impact of such incidents as took place in Little Rock and New Orleans, two good articles are: Charles E. O'Neill, "Europe Reads About New Orleans," *America,* December 17, 1960, pp. 401–403; and Darwin T. Turner, "America and Race Relations," *Journal of Human Relations,* Autumn, 1960, pp. 48–57, which deals with the world reaction to social tension in America and with the implications for America of racial issues in other countries.

The President's Role. The civil rights aspects of this question, which are discussed at length in Chapter IX, are considered in two recent volumes which stress the President's leadership of Congress, in administration, and of public opinion: Richard P. Longaker, *The Presidency and Individual Liberties* (Ithaca: Cornell University Press, one of the Cornell Studies in Civil Liberty, 1961), and Richard E. Neustadt, *Presidential Power: The Politics of Leadership* (New York: John Wiley & Sons, Inc., 1960). For a review of the President's powers to improve race relations and to aid the Negro, see Daniel E. Pollitt, "The President's Powers in Areas of Race Relations: An Exploration," *North Carolina Law Review,* April, 1961, pp. 238–281.

CHAPTER X

Commerce, Labor, and Finance

The phraseology of the Constitution permitted a wide latitude of thought and opinion on the question of the relationship of State and Federal authority in the regulations of commerce, the constitutional theory of which has been primarily a problem of judicial elaboration. Notwithstanding a generally recognized need for concentration of authority over commercial affairs in the national government, the fundamental law as it came from the hands of the Founders was vague on the degree to which the States had been deprived of power in this field. It must have been generally recognized in 1787 that the conveyance of the commerce power to Congress would seriously impair State authority. Nevertheless, in the Convention debates and in contemporary discussions of the new plan of government there was a notable lack of consideration of the implications of this grant of power. . . . The potentialities of the commerce clause as a bar to future State action were generally left unexamined.

What Congress might do under this grant of power, and what the States might not do as a result of it, was the question which gave the Framers concern. [It has continued to be a matter of concern in all the years since.] One writer has observed that "if all the opinions, monographs, treaties and articles which have been written concerning [it] were laid end to end, they would reach from confusion to futility." Another . . . concludes that the Supreme Court cases bearing on this part of the Constitution are "utter confusion. . . ." Their conclusions appear to be well founded. . . . The paths of constitutional construction in this broad field of governmental action are devious, the obscurities profound, the inconsistencies many, and the suppositions and queries practically infinite.[1]

[1] Kallenbach, Joseph E., *Federal Cooperation With the States Under the Commerce Clause* (Ann Arbor: University of Michigan Press, 1942), pp. 8–9 (first paragraph), and page v (second paragraph).

One of the major defects of the government under the Articles of Confederation had been its inability to regulate commerce effectively. With a powerless central government and thirteen separate States each looking out for its own interests, concerted action was impossible. So significant did this failure become that it is considered a decisive factor in the downfall of the Articles and of the government which functioned under them. Mention has been made of the fact that the Annapolis Convention, however unsuccessful, was able to agree on and recommend one thing: that the power of the central government to regulate commerce should be strengthened.

The ravages of war had completely upset the economy of the nation and of the individual States as well. In many areas, there was a serious labor shortage. The British had taken away thousands of Negroes from South Carolina and elsewhere in the South. Throughout the country, it took weeks and months to bring the disbanded soldiers home, even longer to bring home those who had been engaged in the naval service, and longer still to get the members of both groups settled in suitable employment. In many States, the market was already glutted with British goods, and more were arriving at such a rate that the market could not absorb them. Manufacturing was at a standstill. All attempts by the State legislatures to remedy these conditions proved of little avail, and the efforts of the United States Ministers in London and in Paris were not much more effective. The trade situation in the country was critical in the extreme.

Article I, Section 8 of the new Constitution gave Congress the power to regulate five types of commerce—commerce "with foreign nations, among the several States, and with the Indian tribes," and in what is now known as the District of Columbia; in addition, Article IV, Section 3 gave Congress control of commerce in the territories. Most important is the control of interstate commerce—commerce which crosses State lines, including even shipments originating and terminating within the borders of the same State, if in the process of transit they are carried outside the

State and back again. Where actual shipment is not involved, there is the concept of essentiality, which brings almost anything that relates to the conduct of business and industry under Congressional jurisdiction.

The field of economic regulation is so vast that only selected areas can be considered here to serve as significant illustrations rather than as a comprehensive coverage of the field. The discussion of interstate commerce includes brief consideration of such borderline cases as the suppression of lotteries, motor vehicle thefts, control of the shipment of convict-made goods, the liquor traffic, and prohibition. Areas of conflict in the field of labor relations are followed by the national banking system and securities regulation. Although the chapter is a long one, there is still no discussion of the important area of utility regulation, in which Federal-State relationships are numerous. Immigration is included because the history of policy in this field provides an exceptionally good illustration of effective national action after attempts at State control had completely broken down.

THE EBB AND FLOW OF FEDERAL POWER
OVER INTERSTATE COMMERCE

Federal Supremacy Firmly Established

In spite of the broad grant of power to Congress to regulate interstate commerce, it was for a time seriously contended that this power did not penetrate the interior of a State, but that it stopped at the border. Had the supporters of this view had their way, the new government might have been destroyed as was its predecessor under the Articles of Confederation. Denying this contention, the Supreme Court repeatedly rejected the claim that a State had the right to regulate apparently local matters in such a way as to hamper Federal power over interstate commerce. The principles which Marshall had developed in *McCulloch* v. *Maryland* with respect to the taxing powers of the States he applied in *Cohens* v. *Virginia* [2] and in *Gibbons* v. *Ogden* [3] to what is now known as the police powers of the States. The States, he said, "are members of one great empire—for some purposes sovereign, for some purposes subordinate." In his opinion on *Gibbons* v. *Ogden,* Chief Justice Marshall stated:

[2] 6 Wheaton 264 (1821).

[3] 9 Wheaton 1 (1824). See also Abel, A. S., "Commerce Regulation Before *Gibbons* v. *Ogden:* Trade and Traffic," *Brooklyn Law Review,* April, 1948, pp. 215–243, and Mendelson, Wallace, "New Light on *Fletcher* v. *Peck* and *Gibbons* v. *Ogden,*" *Yale Law Journal,* March, 1949, pp. 557–573.

In argument, however, it has been contended that if a law passed by a State, in the exercise of its acknowledged sovereignty, comes into conflict with a law passed by Congress in pursuance of the Constitution, they affect the subject, and each other, like equal opposing powers.

But the Framers of our Constitution foresaw this state of things, and provided for it, by declaring the supremacy not only of itself, but of the laws made in pursuance of it. The nullity of an act, inconsistent with the Constitution, is produced by the declaration that the Constitution is the supreme law. The appropriate application of that part of the clause which confers the same supremacy on laws and treaties, is to such acts of the State. Legislatures do not transcend their powers, but, though enacted in the execution of acknowledged State powers, interfere with, or are contrary to the laws of Congress, made in pursuance of the Constitution, or some treaty made under the authority of the United States. In every such case, the act of Congress, or the treaty, is supreme; and the law of the State, though enacted in the exercise of powers not controverted, must yield to it.

The doctrine of the police power was written into the State constitutions by the State judiciaries in the first half of the nineteenth century; it was the task of the Supreme Court under Chief Justice Taney to write it into the Federal Constitution in the phraseology of State sovereignty. The first decisive step in this direction was taken early in Taney's tenure in *Miln* v. *New York*,[4] a few months after Marshall's death. The question at issue was whether a statute establishing an inspection of immigrants represented an attempt on the part of the enacting State to regulate foreign commerce—an exclusive power of Congress—or whether it was a proper and legitimate exercise of the police power of the State. Justice Barbour, speaking for the Court, took the latter position when he wrote:

A State has the same undeniable and unlimited jurisdiction over all persons and things within its territorial limits as any foreign nation, where that jurisdiction is not surrendered or restrained by the Constitution of the United States. That, by virtue of this, it is not only the right but the bounden and solemn duty of a State to advance the safety, happiness and prosperity of its people, and to provide for its general welfare, by any and every act of legislation which it may deem to be conducive to these ends; where the power over the particular subject or the manner of its exercise is not surrendered or restrained, in the manner just stated. That all these powers which relate to merely municipal legislation, or what may, perhaps, more properly be called internal police, are not thus surrendered or restrained, and that consequently, in relation to these, the authority of a State is complete, unqualified, and exclusive.

[4] 11 Peters 102 (1837).

A concurring opinion by Justice Baldwin emphasized the same point of view:

> By inherent original right, as a single sovereign power, each State has the exclusive and absolute right of regulating its internal police. . . . If it is doubted whether the power (in any particular case) is granted, or prohibited, or reserved, then by the settled rules . . . of this Court its decision must be in favor of the State law.

In the same Term of Court, in the Charles River Bridge Case,[5] Chief Justice Taney expressed the matter in the following words:

> The object and end of all government is to promote the happiness and prosperity of the community by which it is established; and it can never be assumed, that the government intended to diminish its power of accomplishing the end for which it was created. . . . We cannot deal thus with the rights reserved to States and by legal intendments and mere technical reasoning take away from them any portion of that power over their own internal police and improvement, which is so necessary to their well-being and prosperity.

In 1851, the question was presented to the Court in another form. As a safety measure, the Board of Port Wardens of Philadelphia had established regulations under which only licensed pilots were authorized to pilot vessels through the Delaware River channel and to bring them to the Philadelphia docks. Although in the Pilotage Act of 1789 Congress had authorized State legislation on the subject, a Mr. Cooley, who was engaged in the shipping business in Philadelphia, challenged the constitutionality of the regulation on the ground that it constituted an unnecessary and unwarranted interference with the power of Congress to regulate commerce "with foreign nations, among the several States. . . ." The rule that was laid down by a unanimous Court was intended to be equally applicable to both:

> Whatever subjects of this power (to regulate commerce) are in their nature national, or admit only of one uniform system, or plan of regulation, may justly be said to be of such a nature as to require exclusive legislation by Congress.[6]

The corollary of this rule left to the States the regulation of such commerce as could properly be made subject to diversity of treatment. State action would be possible if and only if Congress had not "occupied

[5] 11 Peters 420 (1837).
[6] *Cooley v. Port Wardens of Philadelphia*, 12 Howard 299 (1851).

the field." Since there were many fields which, for one reason or another, Congress might choose not to "occupy," the area of freedom left to the States might be considerable. Nevertheless, the doctrine had two serious limitations. State action was not permissible when the commerce was interstate, and there was no means short of legislative enactment and a test case of ascertaining in advance which commerce could and which could not be permitted to be subject to diverse regulation.

The Definition of Interstate Commerce Narrowed

Early Supreme Court decisions, as has been shown, had established a broad definition of interstate commerce, and had so interpreted the power of Congress to regulate it that for more than half a century virtually all commerce that crossed State lines appeared to be interstate and subject to Federal regulation. This period of Federal supremacy was followed by a longer period of weakness, wavering, and uncertainty, a period which extended roughly from the end of the Civil War to the middle of the Roosevelt era.

This surprising shift of position began with cases like *Peik* v. *Chicago & Northwestern Railway Company* [7] and *Paul* v. *Virginia*.[8] In the former, it was held that the rates on goods destined for points outside the borders of a State were more a State than a National consideration, and that in the absence of positive Congressional legislation to the contrary, were a matter for State determination. This point will be considered further in a later portion of this chapter.

In *Paul* v. *Virginia*, the Court handed down the first of a long series of important decisions that for more than half a century severely restricted the power of Congress to regulate interstate commerce. Beginning with insurance, this restrictive policy was gradually extended to include mining, fishing, lumbering, and the extractive industries generally; manufacturing, advertising, baseball, and many others. The significance of these Court decisions on Federal-State relations was very great, for they excluded the forenamed activities from interstate commerce—activities which would otherwise have been subject to regulation by Congress under the commerce clause. Since they were not to be considered interstate, but local in character, they were subject to regulation by the States. This policy caused a vast amount of confusion in the American business community until, during the Roosevelt era when the Nine Old Men on the Supreme Court were gradually replaced by the Nine Young Men, a contrary tendency appeared.

[7] 94 U.S. 164 (1876).　　　　[8] 8 Wallace 168 (1868).

Thus, in the latter part of the nineteenth century and the early part of the twentieth, a strongly conservative Supreme Court, in an era when government was characterized more by lethargy and inactivity than by diligence in protecting the public welfare, assiduously whittled away at the powers of Congress to regulate interstate commerce. In this whittling process, two techniques appear to have been notably successful and therefore favored: (1) to declare that the industry which Congress was seeking to regulate (insurance, manufacturing, lumbering, mining, fishing, etc.) was not commerce, and therefore not subject to the regulatory powers of Congress under the commerce clause; and (2) to declare that the method used by Congress was either not a proper or even a legitimate method. In either case, Congress lost. The people lost also when they failed to receive the government protection to which they were entitled.

The story of this unhappy chapter in the history of the Supreme Court is a long and complicated one. The broad outlines of one important aspect of it are shown in the following table. In an era when hijacking appears to have been a more or less accepted method of business competition, a large number of abuses developed. Time after time, the States whose legislatures were frequently under the influence of large business interests were either unwilling or totally incapable of protecting the public interest. When Congress attempted to act, it was rebuffed by the Supreme Court. As if this were not enough, Congress also had to exercise the utmost caution in selecting its means of action. Although Chief Justice Marshall had sought to establish the doctrine that any suitable means might be employed toward a proper objective, the Court repeatedly substituted its judgment for that of Congress as to what means were suitable and proper.

TYPES OF BUSINESS ACTIVITY EXCLUDED FROM CONGRESSIONAL REGULATION UNDER THE COMMERCE CLAUSE, BY DECADE
1850–1920

1850 Exchanges, buying and selling bills of exchange
      Nathan v. *Louisiana*, 8 Howard 73 (1850).

1860 Insurance
      Paul v. *Virginia*, 8 Wallace 168 (1869).
      Hooper v. *California*, 155 U.S. 648 (1895).
      New York Life Insurance Company v. *Cravens*, 178 U.S. 389 (1900).
      New York Life Insurance Company v. *Deer Lodge County*, 231 U.S. 495 (1913).

1870 Fishing, including oyster dredging and taking sponges
      McCready v. *Virginia*, 94 U.S. 391 (1876).
      Manchester v. *Massachusetts*, 139 U.S. 240 (1890).
      The Abby Dodge, 223 U.S. 166 (1911).

1880   Agriculture, including intention to export and timber production
      Kidd v. *Pearson*, 128 U.S. 1 (1888).

      Patents and Copyrights
      Missouri v. *Bell Telephone Company*, 23 Fed. 539 (1885).

1890   Manufacturing
      United States v. *E. C. Knight Sugar Refining Company*, 156 U.S. 1 (1895).

      Exchanges
      Hopkins v. *United States*, 171 U.S. 578 (1898).
      Ware & Leland v. *Mobile County*, 209 U.S. 405 (1908).

1900   Employment and contracts of employment
      Williams v. *Fears*, 179 U.S. 270 (1900).
      Adair v. *United States*, 208 U.S. 161 (1908).

1910   Construction
      E. A. Browning v. *City of Waycross*, 233 U.S. 16 (1914).

      Credit Ratings
      U.S. Fidelity & Guaranty Company v. *Kentucky*, 231 U.S. 394 (1913).

1920   Advertising Contracts
      Blumenstock Brothers Advertising Agency v. *Curtis Publishing Company*, 252
      U.S. 436 (1920).

      Banking
      Smith v. *Kansas City Title & Trust Company*, 255 U.S. 180 (1921).

      Leasing
      United States v. *United Shoe Machinery Company*, 258 U.S. 451 (1922).

      Personal and Professional Services, including baseball players, lawyers, lecturers.
      Federal Baseball Club v. *National League*, 42 Sup. Ct. 465 (1922).

      Strikes, if not aimed at blocking interstate commerce
      United Mine Workers v. *Coronado Coal Company*, 259 U.S. 344 (1922).

For example, an act of Congress to penalize the shipment in interstate commerce of goods made by child labor was ruled to be not a regulation of commerce but an unconstitutional attempt under that guise to invade the power of the States to regulate manufacturing. A further attempt to accomplish the same objective through the use of the tax power was held to be unconstitutional because it involved a use of that power not primarily to raise revenue but to accomplish some other objective. After these rebuffs, Congress resorted to the abortive effort to solve the problem by a constitutional amendment. From 1937 on, all such national legislation was upheld, including the power of Congress when regulating commerce to control production, to enforce fair standards with respect to hours of labor and wages, and to control agricultural production. (In this latter connection, a conclusion against the power of Congress was effectively sealed off and bypassed by later decisions.)

The Definition of Interstate Commerce Broadened

The South Eastern Underwriters' Case [9] in effect reversed *Paul v. Virginia*. It can be argued, of course, that Congress always had the power "to regulate interstate commerce." The power is conferred by the Constitution, but its application had been so restricted by exceptions and exclusions established in the process of definition that the new line of decisions which began with the South Eastern Underwriters' decision actually had the effect of restoring to Congress what had previously been denied.

Over a long period of time during the late nineteenth and early twentieth centuries, consistency was not one of the Supreme Court's virtues. While the Court was narrowing the definition of interstate commerce under the Sherman and Clayton Acts for purposes of regulation, it was steadily extending its own authority with relation to common carriers until it appeared that virtually every employee of an interstate carrier was engaged in interstate commerce and subject to regulation by Congress under the commerce clause.

This development came about in a very interesting way. The recovery provisions of the Federal Employers' Liability Law were more lenient with respect to eligibility and more generous with respect to benefits than were those of the States. If, therefore, an employee of an interstate carrier, injured while in line of duty, no matter how minor his position or how menial his duties, could prove that the performance of his duties was essential to the continuing flow of interstate commerce, then he was assured of the larger benefits provided under the terms of the Federal law. The courts were, for a period of several years, virtually inundated with such cases. Even though in some instances the cases arose out of tragedy and death, a whimsical if not slightly humorous aspect crept into many of the decisions.

A few cases will illustrate the point. A member of the crew on a freight train in the Erie Railroad yards in Northern New Jersey, just prior to departure on a regular run, wanted a drink of water. Finding no drinking cup in the caboose, he ran across the tracks to the supply room near the roundhouse. On the way back, he was struck and severely

[9] 322 U.S. 533 (1945); for comment, see Walling, Robert H., "Regulation of Insurance: Another Jurisdictional Battleground," *Journal of Public Law*, Fall, 1956, pp. 494–563.

injured by a backing locomotive. His errand was held to be in line of duty: equipping a train moving interstate traffic.[10]

A track worker named Smith, carrying a sack of bolts along the track, was hit and injured by a passing train. One is reminded by the Court decision of the old doggerel about the house that Jack built. Smith was held to be performing duties essential to the movement of interstate commerce: he was the man who carried the bolts to repair the track that rolled the trains in interstate commerce.[11]

A charwoman cleaning up washrooms in a railroad station was engaged in the performance of duties essential to the movement of interstate commerce if the station handled passengers traveling on interstate journeys, and there were few stations that did not handle at least a few passengers beginning or terminating interstate travel.

If one carries the principle behind these cases to its ultimate limits, there can be few employees of an interstate carrier whose duties are not essential to interstate commerce. The train dispatcher, the man in the signal tower, the accountant and the clerical worker, even the janitors and charwomen all perform duties of benefit to interstate travelers and to those who make interstate shipments of goods. This interpretation may be a good thing, from the "one nation" point of view, but it should be apparent to anyone that if virtually all commerce is interstate, there is little commerce left within the province of the regulatory powers of the States. Nor, apparently, has either Congress or the courts intended that there should be, as one law after another was enacted governing headlights, pneumatic brakes, safety couplers, prohibiting the use of coal stoves as heating devices, and so on. Each new regulation was challenged in the courts, but each in turn was upheld.

Some Borderline Cases

The power of Congress over interstate commerce has repeatedly been used as a means of exercising control over conditions that were judged to be contrary to sound public policy or to the best interests of the welfare of the country. In such situations, the Supreme Court has consistently declared that "the motive and purpose of a regulation of interstate commerce are matters for the legislative judgment upon the exercise of which the Constitution places no restriction and over which the courts are given no control." [12]

Congress has invoked the commerce power as a basis for the estab-

---

[10] *Erie Railroad* v. *Szary*, 253 U.S. 86 (1920).

[11] *P. B. & W. Railroad* v. *Smith*, 248 U.S. 101 (1919).

[12] *United States* v. *Darby Lumber Company*, 312 U.S. 100 (1940), p. 115.

lishment of public policy in numerous areas in which the public interest was being inefficiently or inadequately served by State action, such as the suppression of lotteries and of the white slave traffic, motor vehicle thefts, shipment of convict-made goods, and the maintenance of fair labor standards.

Suppression of Lotteries. An act for the suppression of lottery traffic through national and interstate commerce was adopted March 2, 1895; a few years later in a test case, the Supreme Court upheld the act as follows:

> In legislating upon the subject of the traffic in lottery tickets, as carried on through interstate commerce, Congress only supplemented the action of those States—perhaps all of them—which, for the protection of the public morals, prohibit the drawing of lotteries as well as the sale or circulation of lottery tickets, within their limits. It said, in effect, that it would not permit the declared policy of the States, which sought to protect their people against the mischiefs of the lottery business, to be overthrown or disregarded by the agency of interstate commerce. We should hesitate long before adjudging that an evil of such appalling character, carried on through interstate commerce, cannot be met and crushed by the only power competent to that end. We say competent to that end, because Congress alone has the power to occupy, by legislation, the whole field of interstate commerce. . . . If Congress is of the opinion that an effective regulation for the suppression of lotteries, carried on through such commerce, is to make it a criminal offense to cause lottery tickets to be carried from one State to another, we know of no authority in the courts to hold that the means thus devised are not appropriate and necessary to protect the country at large against a species of interstate commerce which, although in general use and somewhat favored in both national and state legislation in the early history of the country, has grown into disrepute and has become offensive to the entire people of the Nation. It is the kind of traffic which no one can be entitled to pursue as of right.[13]

White Slave Traffic. The so-called White Slave Traffic Act, the Mann Act of June 25, 1910, made it a criminal offense to transport in interstate commerce any woman or girl for the purpose of prostitution or for any other immoral purpose. The Supreme Court upheld the statute as applied in various different situations, such as transporting a woman across State lines for purposes of an immoral practice having no commercial aspect [14] and transporting a woman across State lines for the purpose of

[13] Federal Lottery Law, 28 Stat. 963, c. 191; the case, *Champion* v. *Ames,* 188 U.S. 321 (1903), 357–358.

[14] The act, 36 Stat. 825; the case, *Caminetti* v. *United States,* 242 U.S. 470 (1916).

a polygamous marriage,[15] among others. In the latter case, the Court said, "The fact that the regulation of marriage is a State matter does not, of course, make the Mann Act an unconstitutional interference by Congress with the police powers of the States. The power of Congress over the instrumentalities of interstate commerce is plenary; it may be used to defeat what are deemed to be immoral practices; and the fact that the means used have 'the quality of police regulations' is not consequential."

Motor Vehicle Thefts. The purpose of the National Motor Vehicle Theft Act of October 29, 1919, was to punish the transportation of stolen motor vehicles in interstate or foreign commerce. In upholding this legislation in a test case, the Supreme Court said:

> Congress can certainly regulate interstate commerce to the extent of forbidding and punishing the use of such commerce as an agency to promote immorality, dishonesty or the spread of any evil or harm to the people of other States from the State of origin. In doing this it is merely exercising the police power, for the benefit of the public, within the field of interstate commerce.[16]

A further, most interesting development in this field came many years later. Whereas the Theft Act had been passed in an effort to control interstate crime, the latter was designed to protect the public safety by preventing a State from inadvertently granting an operator's license to any person whose license in another State had been revoked because of drunken driving or for conviction of a violation involving a traffic fatality. The first was a Federal program, the latter a purely voluntary, cooperative Federal-State enterprise established in 1961 on the basis of legislation enacted by Congress. Many States have been exchanging driver records with neighboring States for many years. The National Driver Register Service makes this exchange nationwide and complements the license records of the fifty-five States and territories by establishing a central file where any driver's history may be quickly checked.[17]

Shipment of Convict-Made Goods. The Ashurst-Summers Act of July 24, 1935, makes it unlawful knowingly to transport in interstate or

---

[15] *Cleveland v. United States,* 329 U.S. 14 (1946), p. 19; see note, "Interstate Immorality: The Mann Act and the Supreme Court," *Yale Law Journal,* April, 1947, pp. 718–730.

[16] The act, 41 Stat. 324; the case, *Brooks v. United States,* 267 U.S. 432 (1925), p. 436.

[17] *The National Driver Register Service* (Washington: U.S. Bureau of Public Roads, May, 1961). Hearings were on the bill H.R. 5436 in both houses, and reports issued: House Report No. 1762, Senate Report No. 1826, 86th Cong., 2nd Sess. (Washington, 1960).

foreign commerce goods made by convict labor into any State where the goods are intended to be received, possessed, sold, or used in violation of State laws. In sustaining the validity of this statute, the Supreme Court declared:

> The pertinent point is that where the subject of commerce is one as to which the power of the State may constitutionally be exerted by restriction or prohibition in order to prevent harmful consequences, the Congress may, if it sees fit, put forth its power to regulate interstate commerce so as to prevent that commerce from being used to impede the carrying out of the State policy.[18]

The Liquor Traffic and Prohibition

The intergovernmental relations aspects of the century-long battle over the manufacture, transportation, and sale of intoxicating liquors are both interesting and complicated. In early times, hard liquor was taken for granted and was manufactured and consumed in quantities. The first controls were predicated not upon moral considerations but upon the belief that a tax on liquor was an appropriate revenue source. This was a new concept at the time, one whose execution aroused a considerable amount of public opposition (see Chapter XII) which was quelled only by resort to stern measures. The next regulation was undertaken by local, not national, authorities; the concept of the regulation of the distribution and sale of intoxicating liquors under local option evolved as one phase of the reform movement which swept over the country in the mid-nineteenth century.

A national political party was formed to fight "the demon rum," and as the agitation of the prohibition forces built up opposition to the liquor traffic, public legislative bodies felt obliged to respond to what appeared to be a widespread popular demand for regulatory laws. Beginning in Maine in 1857, a number of States adopted constitutional amendments establishing prohibition on a statewide basis, and late in the century, Congress was induced to legislate on the subject. The immediate cause of Congressional interest was the Supreme Court decision in *Leisy* v. *Hardin*,[19] the original package doctrine case. In this decision, the Court held that liquor shipped in interstate commerce was not sub-

---

[18] The act, 49 Stat. 494; the case, *Kentucky Whip & Collar Company* v. *Illinois Central Railway Company*, 299 U.S. 334 (1937), p. 351; see Rhyne, Charles S., "Constitutionality of Federal Acts Divesting Prison-Made Goods of Interstate Character," *George Washington Law Review*, November, 1936, pp. 100–111.

[19] 135 U.S. 100 (1890).

ject to State regulation or control until it reached its destination, as long as it remained in the original package and as long as the original seal remained unbroken. In later cases, decided even after the passage of the Wilson Act of 1890, which was designed to restore some measure of State control over the interstate liquor traffic, it was held that this rule was applicable even to relatively minute quantities (one or a few bottles), as long as the liquor was carried on, not in, the person of the owner.[20] The Wilson Act introduced a time factor in determining jurisdiction over interstate shipments; under its terms, State control became effective upon the arrival of a shipment within state borders.

Greatly disturbed at the infringement of State police powers indicated in the Leisy decision, and foreseeing a deluge of liquor shipped into dry States in interstate commerce, the prohibitionists prevailed upon Congress to pass the Webb-Kenyon Act of 1917, exempting the liquor traffic from the normal Congressional controls over interstate commerce and guaranteeing jurisdiction over it to the States. As a means of conserving grain for food purposes, the distilling industry had been practically closed down during World War I; lest it be reopened, the Anti-Saloon League, led by Wayne B. Wheeler and the W.C.T.U., succeeded in rushing through Congress and persuading the State legislatures to ratify the Eighteenth or Prohibition Amendment which was proclaimed on January 29, 1919.[21] Supporting legislation was promptly enacted.

Thus, authority for complete control of the liquor traffic was transferred from the States to the Nation at the end of World War I, and thus did the national orgy of prohibition begin.[22] The general outlines of this story are so familiar that it is scarcely necessary to detail them here. Bootlegging, crime, and corruption of both public and private life developed on such a scale as to constitute a national scandal. It only ended after (1) the report of President Hoover's Wickersham Commission had made unmistakably clear the extent of the problem and its danger to the country,[23] and (2) President Roosevelt had assumed active

[20] *United States* v. *Dan Hill,* 248 U.S. 420 (1918) and *United States* v. *Simpson,* 252 U.S. 465 (1919).

[21] For an excellent account of this whole movement, see Odegard, Peter H., *Pressure Politics: The Story of the Anti-Saloon League* (New York: Columbia University Press, 1928); for the constitutional and statutory background, see Kallenbach, Chapters 3–8.

[22] The story is well told in Allen, Frederic L., *Only Yesterday* (New York: Harper & Brothers, 1932), in Sullivan, Mark, *Our Times,* 5 vols. (New York: Charles Scribner's Sons, 1927), VI, and in Alsop, Kenneth, *The Bootleggers and Their Era* (New York: Doubleday & Co., Inc., 1961).

[23] Report of the Commission on Observance and Enforcement of the Law (Washington, 1931); commonly known as the Wickersham Commission for its chairman, George W. Wickersham.

leadership of the drive to secure the adoption of the Twenty-first Amendment and the repeal of the Eighteenth. To a large extent—though not
entirely—this restored the *status quo ante*. Before the Eighteenth Amendment, the Federal government was free to regulate or to ignore the
interstate liquor problem, whereas the Twenty-first Amendment definitely obligates it to protect the dry States against liquor being shipped
into their territory from wet States. The dry States concerned, however,
must enact certain cooperating legislation before Washington will bring
its full energies to bear upon the matter. Because of the peculiar language of the Repeal Amendment, the States have been permitted a much
greater degree of latitude as regards intoxicating liquors in interstate
commerce than they may exercise with respect to other commodities.
These regulations, designed to protect the dry States, have been interpreted by the Supreme Court in such a manner as to enable wet States
to discriminate against the products of other wet States in favor of their
own.[24]

All of the States that had had prohibition abandoned it except
Oklahoma, which did so in 1959. After the Repeal Amendment, the
States (and their local political subdivisions) were once again responsible
for the establishment and enforcement of rules governing the liquor
traffic; some returned to a license system, while a sizable number (about
one-third) established state monopoly systems for the sale of package
goods. In less than a quarter of a century, the Nation and the States had
lived through a dramatic experience involving first, complete centralization, and later, virtually complete decentralization of authority in a field
of governmental activity that is of interest to a great many people, though
few would contend that it is among the most vital of governmental
functions.

An interesting development having intergovernmental implications
occurred in Ohio in late 1960, when State stores were authorized to sell
gift certificates "cashable in any other store in the State within a year."
This was intergovernmentally significant for two reasons: (1) although
Federal law has long prohibited the shipment of liquor by mail, the
Ohio plan is perfectly legal; and (2) the authorization may establish a
precedent which other monopoly States may follow, first within their
own borders and later, by agreement, on an interstate basis.[25]

[24] *Indianapolis Brewing Company* v. *Michigan Liquor Control Commission,* 305 U.S. 391 (1938).
[25] See Nagle, James J., "Ohio Side-Steps Liquor Mail Ban," *The New York
Times,* October 9, 1960, pp. 1, 13.

CONFLICTS IN LABOR RELATIONS

There are probably no better illustrations of the influence of Congressional legislation in the extension of Federal power than are provided by the labor laws, notably the Wages and Hours and Fair Labor Standards Act of 1938, and the Fair Employment Practices law of World War II. Extension of Federal control over interstate carriers took place, as has been shown, during the early years of this century, but its expansion into the field of labor relations is a relatively recent occurrence. The 1938 legislation was designed to accomplish the very worthy purpose of putting a ceiling on hours and a floor under wages, but the accomplishment of this objective, however worthy, was possible only at the price of an extensive invasion of the powers of the States.

An almost incidental effect was to curb the evils of child labor. For a quarter of a century, a determined effort had been made to control this problem. Congress had tried twice, once under the commerce power, once under the tax power, but both attempts were rebuffed by adverse court decisions. The Federal Fair Employment Practices Committee was, to be sure, created by an Executive Order. It was an emergency measure taken during the war for the purpose of achieving maximum utilization of an important segment of the nation's manpower, and was justified chiefly as a wartime necessity. Yet when the emergency was over and the agency was liquidated, there were insistent demands that the Federal government should enter the field of labor relations on a permanent basis. In session after session, pressure was exerted on Congress for the passage of regulatory legislation. The idea that employees should be selected on the basis of their training, experience, and qualifications, rather than on the basis of race or religious affiliation, already had strong appeal.

Child Labor

Questions involving Federal-State relations have arisen a number of times in the field of labor relations, the first being the struggle to establish adequate controls over child labor. Flagrant abuses involving the exploitation of child labor by unscrupulous employers had been widely publicized during the early years of the twentieth century. When the States proved to be either unable or unwilling to deal with the problem effectively, strong pressure began to be exerted on Congress for Federal legislation dealing with the problem. Thus began a series of attempts by Congress to cope with these abuses, first under its power to regulate interstate commerce and later under its taxing powers, both of which were declared unconstitutional.[26] Then the problem was tackled through a proposed constitutional amendment which was first proposed in 1921, then revised in 1927. For various reasons, the amendment won little favor with the States. When it was found that the problem could be controlled under the Wages and Hours Act, the movement in favor of the amendment gradually died out.

Congress' third attempt to deal with this problem, then, was made in the form of the proposed amendment. After the original proposal had been before the States for some time without attracting any appreciable amount of support, it was revised and resubmitted. During the controversy over prohibition (which involved somewhat comparable questions of State powers), action on the proposed amendment bogged down completely. Technically, the proposal is still before the States, for it contained no time-limit clause, although at this late date, it is certain that the proposal is dead. As a matter of fact, the passage of the Fair Labor Standards Act in 1938 made an amendment unnecessary.

Labor Relations Legislation

Prior to 1935, most of the existing labor legislation was State legislation. The enforcement machinery, in most States, was neither very good nor very effective, thanks to the influence of the State manufacturers associations and chambers of commerce. The early labor relations acts were among a number of legislative steps designed to protect the rights of workers to organize and bargain collectively. The Federal Railway Labor Act of 1926 had prohibited railroad employers from interfering with the organizational activities of their employees. In the early 1930's the Norris–La Guardia Act of 1932 and the National Industrial Recovery Act (NIRA) of 1933 were passed, establishing the policy that workers should be free to organize and bargain collectively without employer interference.

Only a few months after NIRA was invalidated, Congress enacted the National Labor Relations Act of 1935, popularly known as the Wagner Act; this Act guaranteed to all workers in interstate commerce the right to join any union they pleased and definitely forbade employers to interfere with such unions in any way. When a given union secured

---

[26] Under the commerce power, *Hammer* v. *Dagenhart*, 247 U.S. 251 (1918); under the taxing power, *Bailey* v. *Drexel Furniture Company*, 259 U.S. 20 (1922).

a majority of the workers of any particular employer, the latter was obligated by law to bargain collectively with its representatives. The original Wagner Act specified five unfair labor practices, forbidding the employer to practice various kinds of discrimination against workers for union activities, and the NLRB was authorized to add others by interpretation. Many regarded the law as one-sided and discriminatory and questioned its constitutionality, although the Supreme Court not only upheld its validity but usually upheld the interpretations of it adopted by the Board as well.[27]

While the Board's interpretation of the Act, and of its own powers, was frequently liberal, the most interesting aspect of the relationship from the point of view of federalism was probably to be found in the way in which the Board (a Federal agency) and the Supreme Court together developed a veritable no man's land in the field of labor law. After the Board refused to act in many cases involving relationships in small business, on the ground that the businesses were too small, the Supreme Court ruled that the States could not take action in many cases, for reasons which the Court took great pains to explain. In other words, when the Board refused to act, or at least refrained from acting in certain types of cases, the Court refused to permit the States to act.

Such was the situation in 1946 when the Republicans interpreted their election victory, which gave them control of the 80th Congress, as in part, a mandate to amend or rewrite the nation's labor laws. This they did in the Taft-Hartley Act of 1947, which added a list of unfair practices on the part of labor which, like the restrictions put upon management by the Wagner Act, could also be punished. The list included such matters as secondary boycotts, jurisdictional strikes, and strikes in violation of contract. This legislation, still on the books, was just as obnoxious to labor as the Wagner Act had been to management.

Both laws gave rise to an enormous number of new problems in the field of Federal-State relations. The original Wagner Act was soon followed by a series of State labor relations acts, thirteen of them as of 1961. They are of two types: ten,[28] the so-called "Little Wagner Acts," affirm the rights of employees to have unions of their own choosing; to bargain collectively if they so desire; to set up agencies—State counterparts to NLRB—to enforce these rights, prevent or remedy unfair labor practices, and provide a method of determining collective bargaining representatives. In three States (Kansas, Michigan, and Minnesota), the acts do not set up enforcement agencies, but leave this function to the courts instead.

---

[27] See *Phelps-Dodge Corporation* v. *National Labor Relations Board*, 313 U.S. 177 (1941).

[28] Colorado, Connecticut, Hawaii, Massachusetts, New York, Pennsylvania, Puerto Rico, Rhode Island, Utah, and Wisconsin.

Since these acts do contain provisions protecting employees' rights to organize and to bargain collectively, and prohibiting unfair practices, they are classified as labor relations acts. For a time, it was exceedingly difficult to determine who had jurisdiction over any given dispute and when jurisdiction was concurrent—as it often was—and how to coordinate the rules and policies of one jurisdiction with those of the other.[29]

Congress, when it passed the Taft-Hartley Act in 1947,[30] had three broad objectives: to encourage the settlement of jurisdictional differences without government intervention; to empower the NLRB to determine disputes not resolved by private arbitration, thus avoiding complaint proceedings; and to outlaw jurisdictional strikes in the interest of neutral employers and the public. Viewed in terms of intergovernmental relations, this legislation contained some controversial provisions designed to clarify existing ambiguities:

> Nothing in this Act shall be construed as authorizing the execution or application of agreements requiring membership in a labor organization as a condition of employment in any State or Territory in which such execution or application is prohibited by State or Territorial law. . . .
>
> The Board is empowered by agreement with any agency of any State or Territory to cede such agency jurisdiction over any cases in any industry (other than mining, manufacturing, communications, and transportation except where predominantly local in character) even though such cases may involve labor disputes affecting commerce, unless the provisions of the State or Territorial statutes applicable to the determination of such cases by such agency is inconsistent with the corresponding provision of this Act or has received a construction inconsistent therewith.

Although these provisions undoubtedly contributed something toward greater clarity and flexibility in Federal-State relations, instances of overlapping and conflict in the provisions of Federal and State labor laws continued to occur in such important areas as representation, unfair employee labor practices, concerted employee activities such as strikes and picketing, and the terms and enforcement of collective bargaining agreements.[31] The persistent problem of a jurisdictional gray zone, of the governmental no man's land in the field of labor law, was moved one

---

[29] See Swankin, David A. et al., *State Labor Relations Acts* (Washington: U.S. Bureau of Labor Standards, January, 1961); for an earlier and more extensive analysis, see Killingsworth, Charles C., *State Labor Relations Acts: A Study in Public Policy* (Chicago: University of Chicago Press, 1948).

[30] 61 Stat. 146.

[31] For a discussion of these problems, see Cox, Archibald, and Seidman, Marshall J., "Federalism and Labor Relations," *Harvard Law Review*, December, 1950, pp. 211–245.

step further toward solution by the passage of the Landrum-Griffin Labor-Management Reporting and Disclosure Act of 1959, under which the maximum area left for State regulation under State law was limited to those employers and employees not subject to Federal law. The States may exercise jurisdiction over cases which involve interstate commerce, but only those cases which the NLRB has refused to accept on grounds of a lack of jurisdiction. The Board, however, is barred from enlarging the categories of cases it declines to handle.[32]

The application of this legislation, though it was primarily concerned with the internal affairs of labor organizations and with labor-management relations, finally established a more precise method of resolving Federal-State jurisdictional conflicts in the labor field. While such an eminent authority in the field as Professor Archibald Cox foresaw "no reason to anticipate difficulty in the administration" of the new law,[33] it still appears to be necessary to make careful, detailed analyses of all available published materials in order to determine the intent of Congress with respect to any single area of the field. One investigator finds that confusion arises mainly when a majority of the Supreme Court changes its views on the scope of Federal and State powers;[34] another, noting that "duets" or joint mediation by Federal and State mediators in the same case are not uncommon, concludes after studying the record that Congress intends to allow concurrent mediation of disputes by Federal and State agencies.[35]

Fair Labor Standards

The Fair Labor Standards Act of 1938 [36] fixed minimum wages and maximum hours for employees engaged in the production of goods for

[32] Swankin, p. 4. Professor Archibald Cox, who served as an advisor to Senator Kennedy on labor legislation, including Landrum-Griffin, has two important articles covering developments in the 1950's, "Federalism in the Law of Labor Relations," *Harvard Law Review*, June, 1954, pp. 1297–1348, and "The Landrum-Griffin Amendments to the National Labor Relations Act," *Minnesota Law Review*, December, 1959, pp. 257–274.

[33] Cox, "The Landrum-Griffin Amendments," *Minnesota Law Review*, p. 262.

[34] McCoid, Allen H., "Notes on a 'G-String': A Study of the 'No Man's Land' of Labor Law," *Minnesota Law Review*, December, 1959, pp. 205–256; see also Cohen, George M., "Congress Clears the Labor No Man's Land: A Long-awaited Solution Spawns a Host of New Problems," *Northwestern University Law Review*, July-August, 1961, pp. 333–389.

[35] See Lazar, Joseph, "Concurrent Jurisdiction of Federal and State Mediation Agencies," *Labor Law Journal*, March, 1962, pp. 254–261; see also a note, "The Agency Shop, Federal Law, and the Right-to-Work States," *Yale Law Journal*, December, 1961, pp. 330–343.

[36] 52 Stat. 1060.

interstate commerce, with increased compensation for overtime. It forbade under penalty of fine and imprisonment: (1) violation by an employer of these wage and hour provisions; (2) shipment in interstate commerce of any goods, the production of which required employment in violation of the provisions; and (3) failure of the employer to keep records of his employees and of their wages and hours, as prescribed by administrative regulations.

In *United States* v. *Darby Lumber Company*,[37] it was argued that this prohibition of the shipment of the prescribed goods in interstate commerce was unconstitutional because it was only nominally a regulation of commerce. The real purpose or motive, it was contended, was regulation of wages and hours of persons engaged in manufacture, the control of which had been reserved to the States and upon which some of the States of destination had placed no restrictions. Furthermore, the effect of the statute was not to exclude the prescribed articles from interstate commerce in aid of State regulation, as in the Kentucky Whip & Collar Company Case.[38] Instead, the Fair Labor Standards Act, supposedly a regulation of interstate commerce, undertakes to regulate wages and hours within the State, contrary to the policy of the State which has elected to leave them unregulated. The Supreme Court declared in answer to these charges:

> Congress, following its own conception of public policy concerning the restrictions which may appropriately be imposed on interstate commerce, is free to exclude from the commerce articles whose use in the States for which they are destined it may conceive to be injurious to the public health, morals or welfare, even though the State has not sought to regulate their use. . . .
>
> Such regulation is not a forbidden invasion of State power merely because either its motive or its consequence is to restrict the use of articles of commerce within the States of destination; and it is not prohibited unless by other constitutional provisions. It is no objection to the assertion of the power to regulate commerce that its exercise is attended by the same incidents which attend the exercise of the police power of the States.
>
> The motive and purpose of the present regulation are plainly to make effective the Congressional conception of public policy that interstate commerce should not be made the instrument of competition in the distribution of goods produced under substandard labor conditions, which competition is injurious to the commerce and to the States from and to which the commerce flows. . . . Whatever their motive and purpose, regulations of commerce which do not infringe some constitutional prohibition are within the plenary power conferred on Congress

[37] 312 U.S. 100 (1940).　　　　[38] 229 U.S. 334 (1937).

by the Commerce Clause. Subject only to that limitation, . . . we conclude that the prohibition of the shipment interstate of goods produced under the forbidden substandard labor conditions is within the constitutional authority of Congress. . . .

Congress, having by the present Act adopted the policy of excluding from interstate commerce all goods produced for the commerce which do not conform to the specified labor standards, it may choose the means reasonably adapted to the attainment of the permitted end, even though they involve control of interstate activities. Such legislation has often been sustained with respect to powers, other than the commerce power granted to the national government, when the means chosen, although not themselves within the granted power, were nevertheless deemed appropriate aids to the accomplishment of some purpose within an admitted power of the national government.[39]

This type of regulation, once enacted and accepted by the courts and by the people, never recedes but, on the contrary, tends gradually to expand into new fields. A good illustration is found in the probable extension, within a few years, of the provisions of this legislation to farm workers. An extensive study of the problem in 1960 reported that "it appears both desirable and feasible to extend the Federal minimum wage legislation to agriculture" in order to establish a wage standard for agriculture and to bring about an improvement in the wage structure of hired farm labor.[40]

Public Employment Offices

Other issues in the field of labor relations appeared at the close of World War II in the controversies over the public employment offices and over the interpretation and application of the Taft-Hartley Act. Shortly after Pearl Harbor, the Governors, at the request of the President, had transferred administration of the public employment offices to the Federal government in order to expedite the nation's industrial mobilization, with the understanding that Federal administration should continue only for the duration of "the war production emergency." When the emergency did come to an end, however, the Federal government developed a reluctance to return the offices to the States.

At its meeting in Hershey, Pennsylvania, in 1944, at Mackinac Is-

---

[39] *Seven Cases* v. *United States*, 239 U.S. 510 (1915), p. 514. The third and fourth paragraphs are from *United States* v. *Darby*, pp. 114–115, 121.

[40] See Kantor, Harry S., *Problems Involved in Applying a Federal Minimum Wage to Agricultural Workers*, 2 vols. (Washington: Department of Labor, 1960).

land, Michigan, in 1945, and at Oklahoma City in 1946, the Governors' Conference urged the transfer to State administration. President Truman agreed with the Governors in principle, but felt that the offices should be returned at the end of the reconversion period. It was agreed that the building of an effective public employment service required cooperation between the Federal government and the States, and that the actual administration of the employment offices was a function appropriate to State government. In November, 1946, the controversy was resolved when the employment offices were returned to State administration by act of Congress.

Status of Workmen's Compensation

The first workmen's compensation law in this country was enacted in Wisconsin more than half a century ago. This system in time completely replaced both the right of the injured employee to sue under common law, and the system of employers' liability which had replaced that right. Although all States now have some kind of workmen's compensation law, there is great diversity in the provisions of these laws. Some are compulsory, while others are optional; some are public, while others are private; some permit self-insurers, and others do not. It is because of these diversities, and the inequities resulting from them, that organized labor is now raising the issue: Workmen's compensation is a national problem!

Workmen's compensation originated in the States, was developed by the States, and has always been financed and administered under State statutes. But it appears that under present conditions, most States are doing the job very inadequately. In 1960, some 1,823,000 workers were temporarily disabled, 85,000 more were permanently impaired, and 14,200 were killed or died as a result of accidents. It appears that today only three out of four employees of private employers are covered by workmen's compensation. Twenty-five, exactly one-half, of the States still permit private employers the privilege of rejecting workmen's compensation coverage of their employees. Assured benefits of employees injured on the job are limited in twenty-seven States by excluding from coverage those employers who have less than a specified number of employees—numbers ranging from two to five in eighteen States to as high as fifteen in South Carolina. Only four States—California, Connecticut, New Jersey, and Ohio—cover agricultural employees, although a few additional States cover selected employees on farms. Two States make no statutory provision for the coverage of occupational diseases, and an additional nineteen cover only those occupational diseases specifically enumerated in the statute. In at least ten States, workmen's compensation applies only to those occupations enumerated in the law as "hazardous" or "extra-hazardous."

Not only are there great gaps in the coverage of workers, but the inadequacy of the benefits provided is often shocking. Reasonably adequate standards do exist. All of the provinces of Canada, for example, provide a weekly benefit of 75 per cent of the injured worker's average weekly wage, whereas organized labor in this country has formally accepted 66⅔ per cent as a standard. But the States fall far short of even this standard; for instance, "For an $80-per-week worker (with a wife and child) who was disabled in 1957 for twenty-nine days three States replaced less than 30 per cent of his lost wages; sixteen States replaced less than 40 per cent of his lost wages; and thirty-nine States replaced less than 50 per cent of his lost wages." [41]

For scheduled permanent partial injuries, the employee is likely to be confronted with benefits which are both inequitable and inadequate, while unscheduled permanent impairments present the most difficult problems of all. Loss of life from on-the-job injuries, in most jurisdictions, is covered in a wholly inadequate manner. State standards in these areas are far, far below those established by law for Federal employees. The maximum compensation for loss of an eye to an employee of the Federal government living in Alabama is six times more than to an employee of a private employer.[42] The foregoing explanation of State inadequacies in the field of workmen's compensation thus further illustrates why time after time the Federal government has assumed responsibilities formerly belonging to the States, but which the States were either unable or unwilling to meet.

CONTROL OVER IMMIGRATION

The United States is, historically, a nation of immigrants. All Americans, except the Indians, either came to this country from foreign lands or are the descendants of those who did so some time after the beginnings of European settlement on American soil.

Attempts to select immigrants date back to the colonial period, when legislation was enacted to prevent the entry of paupers (paupers, vaga-

[41] Berkowitz, Monroe, *Workmen's Compensation: The New Jersey Experience* (New Brunswick: Rutgers University Press, 1960), p. 49.

[42] See Department of Labor Bulletin No. 161, *State Workmen's Compensation Laws*, rev. ed. (Washington, May, 1960); see also Fair, Clinton, "Workmen's Compensation: A National Problem," *Labor's Economic Review*, March-April, 1961, entire issue.

bonds, and sturdy beggars, they were called in the Elizabethan era), criminals, and certain unwanted religious groups such as Catholics and Quakers. This was a real problem in an age when colonies were generally regarded as a proper dumping ground for any troublesome, undesirable, or unwanted group. After the Revolution, the States fell heir to the task of legislation, but in general few restrictions were added prior to 1830.

When one recalls that many of the colonists who came to America were at least partly motivated by the desire to escape from religious persecution, it appears more than a little strange that they should have so soon begun denying to others rights which they had only recently won for themselves. This they did in two ways: they denied asylum to members of dissident groups and, unfortunately in some cases, persecuted such adherents to those groups as were already in their midst. The story of the religious persecution of Roger Williams and Anne Hutchinson in Rhode Island is known to every schoolboy, but efforts to exclude the Quakers from Massachusetts and Maryland and later persecutions of them in both colonies in the late seventeenth century—in which the rulers of both colonies, in the words of one contemporary, "confiscated the Quakers' goods, tortured, imprisoned, whipped and scourged them" are not so well known. Also, the Catholics who had founded Maryland were persecuted in that colony when Protestants came into the majority; further entry of Catholics was restricted, and repressive measures were applied to those who were already there.

During the eighteenth and nineteenth centuries, our fast-growing population was continually fed by immigration streams from the northern European countries—Great Britain, Ireland, Germany, and the Scandinavian countries—and by large numbers of Negroes from Africa. From 1698 to 1707, for instance, it was reported that some 25,000 Negroes were brought to the English colonies annually, in a slave trade that was then very profitable.[43] Later, the stream of immigrants came from southern and eastern Europe—Italy, Greece, and the Slavic countries—and to a lesser extent from Latin America and Canada. The coming of some 40,000,000 immigrants to our shores in little more than a century has no parallel in the history of mankind. By the first decade of the twentieth century, they were arriving at the rate of more than 1,000,000 a year. Whereas in colonial times probably not more than five out of ten children born in this country had native-born American parents, the ratio had increased to nine out of ten by 1930.[44]

[43] Channing, Edward, *History of the United States*, 6 vols. (New York: The Macmillan Co., 1905–1925), II, 512–513.

[44] President's Committee on Social Trends, *Recent Social Trends in the United States*, one vol. ed. (New York: McGraw-Hill Book Co., Inc., 1933), p. 19.

To these immigrants, the United States was a haven of refuge and opportunity; all were welcomed by the young nation, where labor was still in short supply. They comprised the reservoir of human strength and resources required to exploit our vast natural resources, expand our population, and attain great power both at home and abroad. The regulation of this vast influx of new arrivals was long left to the States, for although the Constitution provides that Congress may "establish an uniform rule of naturalization," it says nothing about immigration. Aside from certain legislation of humanitarian import, such as that which forbade the over-crowding of immigrant-carrying vessels, Congress had not entered the field.

State Regulation

As the numbers of immigrants continued to grow and the need for excluding undesirables increased, States like New York and Massachusetts, whose ports placed them in an exposed position, responded to a popular clamor for more stringent control and began after 1830 to impose some restrictions. State control was never entirely satisfactory, since the States were in competition with each other for desirable immigrants, and since they lacked the power to regulate foreign commerce. In order to strengthen their control, several States enacted laws requiring the bonding of ship captains as a guaranty that immigrants would not become public charges and requiring the payment of a head tax by all alien passengers arriving at their ports. The Supreme Court, however, by the narrow margin of five to four, pronounced these statutes null and void on the ground that they placed an unconstitutional burden in foreign commerce.[45] The commerce clause of the Constitution, the acts of Congress passed in pursuance thereof, and certain treaties of the United States were all involved. The treaties had little relevance to the subject at hand, however, because immigrant aliens were under the very terms of the treaties subject to the laws of the country.

These and similar experiences served to demonstrate the incapacity of the States to cope with a problem of such magnitude, a problem which was by no means limited to those States and cities were the initial impact was greatest. The Passenger Cases decision left State inspection laws and programs aimed at paupers and diseased immigrants intact, but since funds were necessary to execute the laws properly, New York made two attempts to modify her head tax legislation to make it appear a legitimate exercise of the State police power. Both of these attempts were declared

[45] The Passenger Cases, 7 Howard 282 (1849).

unconstitutional.[46] The confusion that resulted from the inability of the State governments to deal with the subject made Federal legislation imperative, but it was not until 1882 that Congress recognized and accepted immigration regulation as a Federal responsibility.

Although it has been fully established as an area of Federal responsibility for three quarters of a century, various States have intermittently continued to carry on a sort of rear-guard operation directed toward the members of various unwanted minority groups. A number of States, especially those on the West Coast, have enacted discriminatory legislation of various types designed to limit their power to engage in business, to hold or dispose of property, to attend the public schools, or, in one instance, even to enter the State. All of this legislation was declared unconstitutional when it reached the Supreme Court, and the San Francisco School Case, which developed from discriminatory action by the San Francisco Board of Education, came very close to creating a serious international incident.[47]

The Growth of Federal Regulation

The first Federal law dealing with the subject of immigration was enacted in 1819. This law, the first of a series called "steerage legislation," limited the number of immigrants that could be carried on one ship, prescribed minimum amounts of food and water to alleviate hardships en route, and required ship captains to file lists of passengers with certain information about each of them. Official immigration statistics date from this enactment. Other Federal laws enacted during the next sixty years were largely designed to improve the welfare of the immigrant. These, in general, had the effect of encouraging immigration rather than restricting it as many nativist groups were demanding. The position of Congress when, in 1882, it did assume full responsibility for the regulation of immigration was strengthened by a series of Supreme Court decisions handed down between 1875 and 1894, which first based the function upon the power of Congress to regulate foreign commerce, but later founded it upon the right of any sovereign nation to control its own foreign relations.[48]

Even when the Federal government took over, the national policy was still to encourage and even to stimulate the coming of home-seekers,

---

[46] *Henderson* v. *Mayor of New York,* 92 U.S. 259 (1875) and *People* v. *Compagnie Generale Transatlantique,* 107 U.S. 59 (1883).

[47] See Chinese Exclusion Case, 130 U.S. 581 (1889).

[48] Chinese Exclusion Case, 130 U.S. 581 (1889), and *Fong Yue Ting* v. *United States,* 149 U.S. 698 (1894).

laborers, and political refugees. A new immigration from southern and eastern Europe, however, caused concern in the East, while Pacific Coast sentiment mounted against the admission of Chinese laborers. As a result, the shift to Federal control was characterized by a general tightening and extending of restrictive policies, directed as yet not as much toward reducing numbers as toward screening the newcomers and excluding the undesirable, the unfit, and the unwanted.

The year 1882 saw not only the first effective Chinese Exclusion Act passed, but acts barring entrance to convicts, paupers, insane persons, and undesirables from other countries as well. Three years later, laborers under contract to individuals or corporations were debarred, anarchists and immoral persons were added to the ineligible list in 1903, and by 1917 the laws enumerated no less than thirty different grounds for exclusion. That same year, still another category of ineligibles was established when, after an effort extending over twenty years and over two vetoes by President Wilson, Congress passed a law refusing admission to any migrant over sixteen years of age who could not read English or some other language or dialect of his own choosing. The Act of 1907, terminating immigration from Japan by a "barred-zone" provision, stopped all immigration from Southeast Asia.

Relations with the Chinese on the West Coast became a complicated major problem. Articles V and VI of the Treaty of 1868 between the United States and China had provided for the recognition of full rights for nationals of both countries on a reciprocal basis:

> The United States of America and the Emperor of China cordially recognize the inherent and inalienable right of man to change his home and allegiance, and also the mutual advantage of the free migration and emigration of their citizens and subjects respectively from one country to the other for purposes of curiosity, of trade, or as permanent residents.
>
> Citizens of the United States visiting or residing in China shall enjoy the same privileges, immunities, or exemptions in respect to travel or residence as may be enjoyed by the citizens or subjects of the most favored nation; and reciprocally, Chinese subjects visiting or residing in the United States shall enjoy the same privileges, immunities, and exemptions in respect to travel or residence as may there be enjoyed by the citizens or subjects of the most favored nation.

All went well as long as cheap Chinese labor was needed in the construction of the western railroads, but when the railroads were completed and these same Chinese came in competition in the labor market with native, white Americans, friction began to develop. The aliens had a much lower standard of living and were able to get along, after a fashion, on wages so low that native American workers could not even exist on them. After various unsuccessful State attempts to nullify the Treaty indirectly, if not directly, pressure was turned on Congress. If the economic habits of the Chinese immigrant were good, his social and moral standards, such as habitual gambling, opium smoking, and prostitution, were widely at variance with prevailing American standards. In time, all of these considerations led to exclusion and to long years of diplomatic controversy with respect to the enforcement of the treaty rights of the Chinese in America.

During these years, the Pacific Coast States enacted various discriminatory measures designed to drive the Chinese from the States in which they had settled. Orientals, discriminated against by State laws and prosecuted by the local citizenry, received inadequate protection from either State or Federal authorities. During the period from 1877 through the 1880's, they were frequently the victims of mob violence. Although the courts did withhold approval of the discriminatory legislation, State authorities were lax in enforcing the law against mob violence and the wrongful actions of individuals and local groups.

The government of China protested against these abuses through diplomatic channels, basing its case on the reciprocity Treaty of 1862, only to be informed that the unsatisfactory conditions were State matters and that the Federal government could do nothing about them. Meanwhile, California and the other Western States pressed Congress to enact legislation that would eventually exclude the Chinese. Many restrictive bills were introduced, and in 1882 the famous Chinese Exclusion Act was written into law. The driving force behind the movement for these drastic restrictions had been supplied by organized labor, in the interest of preventing the impairment of wage-levels and the workingman's standard of living by the admission of workers who were willing to accept meager wages and were accustomed to "un-American living conditions."

Although the foregoing account leaves the development of American immigration legislation in mid-stream, so to speak, it is neither necessary nor appropriate for the present purpose to carry the story further. The important point is that responsibility for immigration regulation originally fell to the States; that after the States had failed quite generally to exercise the power effectively, responsibility shifted to the Federal government in 1882; and that in subsequent years a vast and complex system of statutory regulation has been developed at the Federal level.

THE NATIONAL BANKING SYSTEM AND
SECURITIES REGULATION

Historical Background

Although the colonists had never developed a real banking system, the Founding Fathers were apparently of one mind regarding the need for strong national controls of banking and currency. Not only did they include in Article I, Section 8 of the Constitution broad grants of power in this area to the central government, but they imposed very specific prohibitions on State action. Under the Articles of Confederation, the power to coin money had been a concurrent power with only one qualification on State activity, namely, that Congress could regulate the alloy and value of State coins. This supervisory authority was not sufficient to eliminate variations in sizes and weights or to achieve the necessary uniformity of the national currency, however, so the Constitution provided forthrightly that "No State shall coin money."

The Articles had contained no limitations on the issuance of bills of credit (promises to pay designed to circulate either as currency or as legal tender in payment of debts), although such activity by the States was regarded with suspicion, at least by the conservatives. The Constitution minced no words on this matter when it declared, "No State shall . . . emit bills of credit; make anything but gold and silver coin a legal tender in payment of debts." There is no specific mention of banking as such in the Constitution, but the grants of power to the central government and the prohibitions upon the States with respect to integral parts of the banking operation serve to make the intentions of the Framers unmistakably clear.

The question of the proper organization of the banking system of the country had been a subject of controversy from the beginning. Actually, there were few banks in existence because merchants served as bankers on the side. The first real one in the country was the Bank of North America, established in Philadelphia by the "United States in Congress Assembled" on December 31, 1781. By the time the new Constitution became effective, there were still only three banks in the country—in Boston, New York, and Philadelphia, with a fourth on the point of starting in Baltimore. The combined capital of these institutions was about $2,000,000. Hamilton was convinced that a national bank was absolutely essential, and argued that such a bank with branches in the more important centers of population would not only encourage and facilitate business, but that unless or until there was one, there would be no rapid development of the country's resources, no great increase in manufacturing, and no rapid and substantial settlement of the Western lands.

The Banks of the United States. Hamilton signed his report on the national bank on December 13, 1790. Much discussion and debate ensued; though there was some question of the constitutionality of such legislation, Congress generally reacted favorably to the proposal, as it had to the proposal for the assumption of the State debts. Hamilton's arguments convinced Washington of the constitutional propriety of the measure, and Washington approved the bill establishing the First Bank of the United States on February 25, 1791. The entire capital was so quickly subscribed that many who had hoped to take up stock were left out.

The Charter of the First Bank was scheduled to expire in 1811; for several years, one attempt after another was made to prolong its life, but all were in vain since Jefferson had fully aroused the suspicions of the people against a centralized financial power. Far more objectionable than a central bank, however, were the lax and vicious banking practices that developed in other parts of the country. The demise of the old bank was followed by the chartering of innumerable State banks, created without any regulation or supervision whatsoever. They issued paper money practically without limit and made loans on very slight security. By the time the Treaty of Ghent was ratified, the financial condition of the country was actually desperate.

After an interval of five years, in 1816, a Second National Bank was established. It resembled the First National Bank in many ways. The government was to subscribe a portion of the capital stock and appoint five of the twenty-five directors. Government funds were to be deposited in the Bank unless the Secretary of the Treasury should deem it inadvisable to do so, but if he did not so deposit them, he must state his reasons to Congress as soon as possible. The Bank was to transfer the public funds from one part of the country to another without any expense to the government, and it was required to pay interest on public money. Capital stock might be largely composed of government securities; the institution was to perform certain functions in the handling of government loans, and was to pay a bonus to the government of $1,500,-000 in three payments within four years after its organization. The subscription of the stock of the Second Bank moved slowly, and for the first four or five years after it actually opened its doors, it was badly managed.

The new Bank was authorized to establish branches in different parts of the country, and it could issue circulating notes which had to be signed by its president and cashier. Due partly to the conditions existing at the time, partly to the policies pursued by the Bank itself, and partly to the pressure that it put on State and local banks, it engendered an amazing amount of ill will during its first few years of operation.

One of the chief objectives in establishing the Bank had been to make possible a more reliable and more uniform currency. Congress, of course, is authorized to establish and maintain a currency, and to regulate the value thereof, but for a long time the central government had made little effective use of this grant of power. Consequently, the notes of the State and local banks tended to depreciate in value in direct proportion to the distance from their point of origin. The new Bank undertook to deal with this situation by transferring funds from one part of the country to another through its various branches. Having more funds at their command than any other banking institution, the branches were able to put pressure upon almost any State or local bank by collecting and presenting a number of its notes for payment, and by refusing to accept as payment anything but specie.

When the constitutionality of the legislation which established the Bank was challenged in the famous case of *McCulloch* v. *Maryland*,[49] the Supreme Court availed itself of the doctrine of implied powers to put practically beyond question the authority of Congress to create banking corporations. In 1832, President Jackson, following an historic struggle with Congress, vetoed a bill that would have renewed the Bank's charter. The destruction of the Second Bank and the cooperative system that had developed under it marked the beginning of a period of near-chaos, during which piecemeal attempts were made to restore the national role in this field. This was finally accomplished by the creation of the Federal Reserve System.

Private, Local, and State Banks. It appears that Massachusetts had the first State bank in the country. After Congress had created the Bank of North America, the Massachusetts General Court promptly incorporated the same group of founders of the national bank on behalf of the Commonwealth, providing that no other bank should be created within the Commonwealth "during the Continuance of the present war with the Crown of Great Britain." Not long after, in 1784, the State legislature decided that Massachusetts, as a great trading center, should have a bank of its own and proceeded to establish one. It is interesting to note that the Commonwealth borrowed money from this new bank three years later to pay the troops enlisted to suppress Shays' Rebellion. In 1792, the legislature enacted the first of a long series of regulatory measures relating to the bank, a series which culminated in 1829 in the first complete statement of banking principles in Massachusetts, "An Act to Regulate Banks and Banking." [50]

[49] 4 Wheaton 316 (1819).
[50] This summary is based on League of Women Voters of Massachusetts,

State banks, such as those established in Virginia and South Carolina to save the landowners from ruin, were either a part of the State Treasury or were otherwise connected with the State fiscal system. They received and were responsible for the custody of tax receipts and other public moneys, which they paid out on proper warrant. For the convenience of all citizens, these banks often had branches located in different parts of the State, just as modern banks have branches scattered throughout metropolitan areas. State banking flourished for a brief period in all sections of the country, but continued in the Old South only until 1861.[51] Other so-called State banks were then, as now, actually local banks, operated under a State charter and subject to some measure of State supervision. The States at times put various pressures upon these banks to compel them to conform to proper standards.

From the time the Second Bank closed its doors in 1836 until the Civil War, the field was left entirely to banking institutions chartered under widely varying State laws. In this period of turmoil, there were three general types of banks in existence: private, local, and State. The first type, private or "wildcat banks," have been described as consisting of a banker or two, a valise or trunk filled with printed bank notes of their own issue, and a meager office, the whole concern flourishing solely on the credit of the bankers. Some of these succeeded and developed into stable institutions, while others failed and completely disappeared. Local banks, established for the most part in frontier communities, and operated under some degree of State supervision and under the guidance of public opinion, served the needs of areas that would otherwise have been entirely without banking facilities.

Just as Jackson had made a primary political issue out of the Second United States Bank, the State and local banks now competed wholeheartedly for designation as depositories of Federal funds. The Federal government then had no Fort Knox and no vaults for the storage of bullion or paper money, and under these circumstances, its only recourse was to utilize State banks. This expedient, however, presented many problems. The political leaders generally believed that banks should be of political service, and that successful party leaders should be of service to the banks that favored them.

> In the Northeastern States there were fairly sound State banks that were officered and capitalized by Democrats that could be expected to weather storms of ordinary violence. In the South and West, however, most of the banks were organized on perilous foundations and were already trans-

---

Massachusetts State Government (Cambridge: Harvard University Press, 1956), pp. 268–269.

[51] Channing, V, Chapter 14, gives a good summary of these developments.

acting business in a hazardous manner. The government prescribed stringent conditions as the price of receiving public deposits, but the selection of the favorite banks was distinctly a matter of politics, like the appointment of Treasury officials in Washington and financial officers elsewhere. And it was by no means an easy task to differentiate between Democratic banks. The banks selected were as good as could be found, complying with the requirements of "sound politics" and willingness to assume the responsibilities attached to the holding of Government funds; but it was inevitable that these "pet banks," as they came to be called, should make many bad loans and should loan money with a free hand to their friends.[52]

The National Banking Act. These makeshift arrangements, both Federal and State, proved to be quite inadequate for financing the Civil War. The sad experience with the notes issued by inadequately regulated institutions, the urgent need for a currency of uniform value throughout the country, and a desire to facilitate the sale of government bonds on favorable terms during the war led Congress in 1863 and 1864 to establish, not a single bank as previously, but a long-delayed national banking system. In 1913, this in turn gave way to the Federal Reserve System.

Under the Civil War legislation, banks throughout the country were chartered, regulated, and inspected by national authorities, and empowered to issue notes (backed by Federal bonds) designed to circulate as currency. With the notes of State banks almost taxed out of existence— as they were a few years later—the right to issue notes became a monopoly of the new national banks and remained so until the creation of the Federal Reserve System in 1913. State banks continued to exist and to carry on a great deal of business side by side with national banks, as some 10,000 of them still do today. This figure represents a reduction of more than half since 1920, but the number may still be excessive. In some States, the requirements for starting a bank are much too lax.

A State bank might become a national bank by buying a prescribed amount of Federal bonds and holding them as security for the redemption of its paper issues, and, of course, by accepting Federal regulation, or new banks might be established. This provision of the 1913 legislation was significant in that it greatly improved the banking system of the country and clarified the respective roles of State and Nation in the banking business. More than 5,000 national banks now exist; some in large cities have deposits running into the billions and others in county seats or smaller towns have deposits of only a few hundred thousand, but all have capital subscribed by their stockholders which is privately man-

[52] Channing, V, 451.

aged but closely supervised by the Comptroller of the Currency in the Treasury Department,[53] who sends examiners to inspect them at least twice a year and to make full reports of their condition at least three times within the same period.

One other development in this field deserves attention. If, under the terms of the Federal Constitution, the States could not issue paper money designed to circulate as currency, they could charter banks which in turn could issue paper money. In the period following the Civil War, there was an era of wildcat banking which gave encouragement to many abuses and then to a movement for regulation. The amount of paper money issued by the State banks became so great as to threaten the position of the Federal currency and to cause great concern in Congress since it is responsible for establishing, maintaining, and regulating the value of the currency.

To limit the issue of paper money by State banks by making such issue unprofitable, Congress imposed a 10 per cent tax upon all such paper money designed to circulate as currency. In this legislation, Congress was careful not to prohibit the use of paper currency by State banks, which obviously it had no authority to do, and the tax was sustained in 1869 in the case of *Veazie Bank* v. *Fenno*.[54] While this decision took care of paper money, the need for regulations to control other banking activities steadily increased.

The Federal Reserve System

Originally, national banks were completely independent establishments, with no more means of coming to one another's relief in times of stress than railroads or merchandising establishments; hence, embarrassments and failures which might have been prevented resulted from recurring cycles of prosperity and depression. To remedy this situation by linking all national banks in an integrated series and imparting greater elasticity to their operation, Congress in 1913 created an independent agency known as the Federal Reserve System [55] which has been the prin-

[53] This relationship is largely nominal, since the Comptroller is independent and reports to Congress rather than to the Secretary. Reorganization Plan No. 1, submitted by President Truman in 1950, would have subjected him to Treasury control, but the plan was defeated in the Senate.

[54] 8 Wallace 533 (1869); for the story of chaotic conditions at an earlier date, see J. Schoolcraft, "Inflation in Lilliput: Paper Currency in Colonial Rhode Island," *Virginia Quarterly Review*, April, 1936, pp. 220–231.

[55] 38 Stat. 251. President Wilson was the person most responsible for the enactment of this legislation, Senator Carter Glass of Virginia the one most responsible for its form.

cipal controlling agency for our national banking arrangements ever since.

Since our present concern is primarily with the intergovernmental aspects of the banking system, no detailed discussion of the organization, powers and duties, and methods of operation of the Federal Reserve System need be included here. Suffice it to say that its general management is entrusted to a Federal Reserve Board of seven members appointed for fourteen-year terms by the President and Senate, with due regard for both geographical distribution and representation of financial, agricultural, industrial, and commercial interests. This Board, quartered in an imposing building in Washington and endowed with broad supervisory and regulatory powers, bears full responsibility for formulating monetary policies and generally directing the System. The country was divided regionally into twelve Federal Reserve Districts, in each of which is located a main Federal Reserve Bank, usually in the district's principal city, and sometimes branch banks as well. These cities, listed in the following table are well distributed for business purposes. In each case, all or nearly all stock (the minimum is $4,000,000) is subscribed by the member banks within the district, and control is vested in a board of nine directors, three named by the general management of the System in Washington and six by the member banks. These banks, often referred to as "banker's banks," do not carry on a general banking business with individuals and corporations, but instead perform a variety of services for the Federal government and for the member banks in their respective

THE FEDERAL RESERVE SYSTEM *

District	Location of Federal Reserve Bank	Branch(es)
1	Boston	. . . . .
2	New York	Buffalo
3	Philadelphia	. . . . .
4	Cleveland	Cincinnati, Pittsburgh
5	Richmond	Charlotte
6	Atlanta	Birmingham, Jacksonville, Nashville, New Orleans
7	Chicago	Detroit
8	St. Louis	Little Rock, Louisville, Memphis
9	Minneapolis	Helena
10	Kansas City	Denver, Oklahoma City, Omaha
11	Dallas	El Paso, Houston, San Antonio
12	San Francisco	Los Angeles, Portland, Salt Lake City, Seattle

* *The Federal Reserve System: Purposes and Functions* (Washington: Federal Reserve System, 1961), pp. 68–69.

districts. All national banks must belong to and hold stock in the Federal Reserve Bank for their district; State banks may do so if they meet the membership requirements and find membership to their advantage, as many of them do. It is reported that:

> At mid-1960 the Federal Reserve System had 6,217 member banks. Of these, 4,542 were national banks and 1,675 were State-chartered banks. In all fifty States and the District of Columbia, banks with national charters are required to belong to the System. Banks with State charters may join if qualified for membership and if accepted by the Federal Reserve. While somewhat less than one-half of all banks in the United States belonged to the System in mid-1960, this group held nearly three-fourths of the country's total bank deposits. . . . Member banks hold about 85 per cent of the demand deposits of all banks which, along with currency, serve as means of payment.[56]

From the date of its establishment in 1913 until the period of the Great Depression, the System appeared to have solved the major banking problems. Certainly it helped to guide the nation through the financial expansion during the period of contraction following World War I. It failed, however, to curb the over-extension of credit during the late 1920's or to prevent a banking crisis so serious that President Roosevelt, immediately after taking office in 1933, was obliged to declare a bank holiday and temporarily close every bank in the land. There were only a few national banks that failed, but the failures of State banks in many jurisdictions were of catastrophic proportions. These failures were due primarily to laxity in State laws and supervisory procedures. As a result, the States tightened up both their laws and their supervisory procedures, while in addition, large numbers of State banks qualified for membership in the Federal Deposit Insurance Corporation, thereby providing insurance for their depositors against loss (up to $5,000 or $10,000) should some future emergency occur.

FDIC—The Federal Deposit Insurance Corporation

The regulation of the banking business in this country was long a matter of serious concern. Bank charters were too easy to obtain, and in many jurisdictions there was little or no supervision of the establishments to which charters had been issued. Instances of incompetence and dishonesty in bank management were fairly frequent, resulting in loss and distress to depositors. In an effort to cope with this situation during the first quarter of the present century, no less than eleven States adopted

[56] *The Federal Reserve System*, p. 64.

bank deposit guaranty laws; due to lax or at least ineffective administration, none of these laws was regarded as a success. They were, in fact, so unsatisfactory and unworkable that, one by one, they were all repealed.

Yet, after careful study and analysis of this experience, it was possible for Congress, in 1933, to frame and adopt the Federal Deposit Guarantee Act which has functioned satisfactorily ever since. The experience is significant from the point of view of Federal-State relations in two ways. It provides an excellent illustration of the manner in which experience at one level of government can be utilized at another level; and it illustrates how significant Federal legislation can influence both law and administration at the State level.[57]

The chief purpose of the Federal Deposit Insurance Corporation, the agency established to administer the law, is to insure the deposits of all banks which are entitled to the benefits of insurance under the law. All national banks are required by law to meet the conditions for participation in this program, and many State banks also qualify. It is good business for them to participate; the proud assertion that one may note in bank literature or advertisements that all their deposits are insured under FDIC tends to build and maintain public confidence in the institution.

The major functions of the Corporation are to pay the depositors of insured banks which are closed without having made adequate provision to pay the claims of depositors, to act as receiver for all national banks placed in receivership and for State banks when appointed receiver by State authorities, and to prevent the continuance of unsound banking practices. The Corporation functions promptly and effectively; anyone who recalls the anguish that accompanied bank closings during the Great Depression can view such an incident as the following only with wonder and admiration: On August 2, 1960, the State Bank Commissioner of Oklahoma told a Federal District Court that an Oklahoma City bank, chartered by the State, had a shortage of more than $1,500,000. Cash and securities had been removed from the bank without the knowledge and consent of the bank board. The Commissioner closed the bank and appointed the FDIC as receiver, and that very day the Chairman of the Corporation stated that:

> The Corporation will begin payments of their insured claims to depositors of the bank as soon as records can be verified. Each depositor is protected by Federal deposit insurance to a maximum of $10,000. It is expected to take no more than ten days until payments to depositors commence.[58]

[57] See Golembe, Carter H., "The Deposit Insurance Legislation of 1933: An Examination of Its Antecedents and Its Purpose," *Political Science Quarterly*, June, 1960, pp. 180–200.

[58] Millen, William A., "Depositors' Protection by FDIC Illustrated in Closing of Bank," Washington *Evening Star*, August 2, 1960, p. A-18.

There were only three such bank failures for which the FDIC had to make good in 1959.

Although the Corporation appears to function smoothly and in a generally satisfactory manner, there is concern in some quarters lest the system become too highly centralized. Accordingly, the late Senator H. Styles Bridges of New Hampshire, with more than half a dozen co-sponsors including members of both parties and of both liberal and conservative inclinations, introduced two bills in the first session of the 87th Congress that "would assist in the perpetuation of the dual banking system and further improve the banking climate." One proposal was designed to insure the independence of the governing board of the FDIC, the second to give the Board greater power in accepting or rejecting banks and branch banks desiring to participate in the Corporation's insurance program.[59]

Relationships in Securities Regulation

Legislation providing for the regulation of security sales and salesmen is wholly a product of the twentieth century. Prior to that time, the only means of protection was the state's police power to prevent fraud, or civil suit on the part of the unfortunate purchaser of worthless stock to recover damages. In 1903, however, Connecticut adopted a brief statute imposing filing requirements before securities of any oil or mining corporation not having all of its mines in Connecticut could be offered or sold in that State. In 1909, Nevada adopted a statute designed to require full disclosure in the sale of mining stock; certain information filed with the State Attorney General was to be made available to purchasers or prospective purchasers of such stock. Rhode Island adopted the first statute of general application in 1910, and the first blue sky law in 1917. Kansas, with whose name the blue sky law concept is always associated, had in 1911 enacted the first comprehensive licensing system applicable to securities and to those selling securities. Although this early legislation was crude compared with present Federal and State legislation in the field, acceptance of the idea spread so rapidly that by 1917 twenty-seven States had enacted some legislation regulating the securities industry.[60]

It is thus clear that the States had been experimenting and seeking

[59] S. 2301 and S. 2302, sponsored by Senators Bridges, Bush, Clark, Cotton, Jackson, Javits, Keating, and McClellan.

[60] These data, and much of that which follows, is based on Cowett, Edward M., "Federal-State Relations in Securities Regulation," *George Washington Law Review*, October, 1959, pp. 287–305. For further comment on the same subject, see Cook, James M., "National-State Cooperation in Securities Regulation," *State Government*, Winter, 1962, pp. 57–61; Smith, Russell A., "State

to develop such legislation for a quarter of a century prior to Congress' passage of the Securities Act of 1933. This legislation, it will be recalled, and the Commission established to administer it, were products of the Great Depression, during which significant abuses, not covered or at least not being prevented by State law, in the advertising and sale of securities were revealed. After any doubts as to the constitutionality of such legislation had been dispelled,[61] other States followed suit until by 1933, every State except Nevada had some form of blue sky law on its books. A quarter of a century later, in 1959, all but two of the fifty States, Delaware and Nevada, had blue sky laws.

The various State laws differ considerably in both method and effectiveness; the present concern, however, is not with these differences but with the relationships between Federal and State laws and their respective enforcing agencies. Edward M. Cowett, who has done extensive work in this field, reports that while Congress could, within the limits of its powers over interstate commerce, have pre-empted for the Federal government the entire field of regulation of the securities industry, it did not choose to do so. On the contrary, five of the six statutes administered by the Securities and Exchange Commission contain specific provisions reserving to the respective States their power to regulate intrastate activities.[62]

Many persons argued for Federal pre-emption in 1933, and many still feel that it would have been a good thing. Discussion of this point, interesting though it may be, is of no avail; for twenty-five years there have been parallel systems of securities regulation, and there is no present indication of probable change. Cowett has some very pertinent observations on this dual system:

> That such parallel systems are permitted to exist is at once the genius and the curse of our federal system. To the extent that the systems may be accommodated to one another, the curse is removed; to the extent that they are identical, the justification for their separate existence is likewise removed. The problem is not whether the parallel systems of Federal and State securities regulation are advisable, but whether such systems can accomplish their respective objectives without unnecessary duplication and without imposing an undue burden upon legitimate business activities.[63]

Blue Sky Laws and the Federal Securities Acts," *Michigan Law Review,* June, 1936, pp. 1135–1166; "Jurisdiction of States Under Blue Sky Laws," *University of Chicago Law Review,* Winter, 1950, pp. 382–388; and Wright, T. Z., "Correlation of State Blue Sky Laws and the Federal Securities Acts," *Cornell Law Quarterly,* February, 1941, pp. 258–295.

[61] *Hall* v. *Geiger-Jones Company,* 242 U.S. 539 (1917), and other cases often referred to as the Blue Sky Law Cases.

[62] Cowett, p. 289.   [63] Cowett, p. 290.

In practice, it appears that an effective working partnership has been developed, particularly at the administrative level, but that there is considerable opportunity for improvement in coordination between Federal and State securities statutes. While the State legislatures have been hesitant and less than diligent in changing blue sky laws to accommodate them to the provisions of the Federal Securities Act of 1933, the State officers charged with the administration of these laws have overcome whatever fears of Federal encroachment they may once have had, and are voluntarily cooperating fully—in many cases even eagerly—with Federal enforcing officers in Washington and in the field. Cowett concludes:

> By and large, it can be said that on a personal and administrative level, there is substantially better accommodation between Federal and State securities regulators than there is on the statutory level between Federal and State securities regulation.[64]

BIBLIOGRAPHICAL NOTES

Commerce. The following are among the more significant works dealing with Federal-State relations under the commerce clause: Edward S. Corwin, *The Commerce Power Versus States' Rights* (Princeton: Princeton University Press, 1936); Felix Frankfurter, *The Commerce Clause Under Marshall, Taney, and Waite* (Chapel Hill: University of North Carolina Press, 1937); Joseph E. Kallenbach, *Federal Cooperation with the States Under the Commerce Clause* (Ann Arbor: University of Michigan Press, 1942); George G. Reynolds, *The Distribution of Power to Regulate Interstate Carriers Between the Nation and the States* (New York: Columbia University Press, 1928); and Frederick D. G. Ribble, *State and National Power Over Commerce* (New York: Columbia University Press, 1937). There are also a great many articles in the law reviews, covering virtually all aspects of the subject.

Labor. In an abundant literature on labor law and labor relations, there are few books but many articles dealing with the Federal-State relations aspect of the problem. Significant books include: Sanford Cohen, *State Labor Legislation, 1937–1947* (Columbus: Bureau of Business Research, Ohio State University, 1948); Charles C. Killingsworth, *State Labor Relations Acts: A Study of Public Policy* (Chicago: University of Chicago Press, 1948); Gerald D. Reilly, *States' Rights and the Law of Labor Relations* (New York: American Enterprise Association, 1955); and Chamber of Commerce of the United States, *States' Rights in Labor Relations* (Washington, 1954). On labor board jurisdiction and labor standards, the following titles may be helpful: Algernon S. Belcher, *A Study of the Factors Determining the Exercise of Jurisdiction by the National Labor Relations Board in Three Selected Industries* (Washington: Catholic University of America, 1954) and Abraham J. Berman, *State and Federal Minimum Wage Coverage in New York State* (New York: Division of Research and Statistics, State Department of Labor, 1948). Numerous articles are

[64] Cowett, p. 305.

cited in W. Brooke Graves, *Intergovernmental Relations in the United States: A Selected Bibliography* (Washington: Committee Print, House Intergovernmental Relations Subcommittee, 84th Cong., 2nd Sess., November, 1956), pp. 112–113.

The literature on unemployment compensation and employment security is more extensive, including Raymond C. Atkinson, *The Federal Role in Unemployment Compensation Administration* (Washington: Social Science Research Council, 1941); Joseph M. Becker, *Shared Government in Employment Security: A Study of Advisory Councils* (New York: Columbia University Press, 1959); Paul Rausenbush, *Unemployment Compensation:* Federal-State Cooperation (Madison: Industrial Commission of Wisconsin, 1943); Francis E. Rourke, *Intergovernmental Relations in Employment Security* (Minneapolis: University of Minnesota Press, 1952), one of the ten-volume series in the Minnesota survey; and U.S. Commission on Intergovernmental Relations, *A Study Committee Report on Unemployment Compensation and Employment Security* (Washington, June, 1955).

Banking. Probably the standard general work in this field is Davis R. Dewey, *Financial History of the United States* (New York: Longmans, Green & Co., Inc., 1922) which has gone through many editions. There are good books on both of the United States Banks: John T. Holdsworth, *The First Bank of the United States* (Philadelphia: University of Pennsylvania, 1910), a doctoral dissertation, and Ralph C. H. Catterall, *The Second Bank of the United States,* 2nd ed. (Chicago: University of Chicago Press, 1960), though of course the story is told in most historical works covering the Jackson era. John R. Hurd, at the time of the experiment with the independent treasury, wrote a strong plea for *A National Bank: An Appeal to the Common Sense of the People of the United States* (New York: W. E. Dean, 1842). See also Bray Hammond, *Banks and Politics in America From the Revolution to the Civil War* (Princeton: Princeton University Press, 1957).

The Federal Reserve System has been written on extensively. Carter Glass, father of the Act and later Secretary of the Treasury, tells the story of its passage in *An Adventure in Constructive Finance* (New York: Doubleday, Page & Co., 1927). A standard description of the system is found in Edwin W. Kemmerer, *The ABC of the Federal Reserve System,* rev. ed. (Princeton: Princeton University Press, 1950). See also Paul M. Warburg, *The Federal Reserve System: Its Origin and Growth* (New York: The Macmillan Co., 1930), and for its early history, Seymour E. Harris, *Twenty Years of Federal Reserve Policy,* 2 vols. (Cambridge: Harvard University Press, 1943). The intergovernmental relations aspects of the problem are covered in T. J. Anderson, Jr., *Federal and State Control of Banking* (New York: Bankers Publishing Company, 1934), and its politics during the decade of the Great Depression are recorded on microfilm in a doctoral dissertation by Robert H. Meyers, *The Politics of American Banking: The Dual System, 1929–1939* (Chicago: University of Chicago Library, 1955). Federal-State relations are stressed in a new book by Thomas W. Thompson, *Checks and Balances: A Study of the Dual Banking System in America* (Washington: National Association of Supervisors of State Banks, 1962) and in two articles: "State Exclusion of National Banks," *Columbia Law Review,* September, 1954, pp. 760–763, and T. L. Wentling, "National Banks and Protective State Laws," *Dickinson Law Review,* March, 1947, pp. 169–172. For a survey of Federal and State supervisory agencies, see Homer J. Livingston, *Management Policies in American Banks* (New York: Harper & Brothers, 1956).

Insurance. The standard work on State insurance administration is Edwin W. Patterson, *The Insurance Commissioner in the United States* (Cambridge: Harvard University Press, 1927). Three other useful titles are: John W. Cowee, Federal Regulation of Insurance (Madison: University of Wisconsin Press, 1948); National Association of Attorneys General, *Problems in the Regulation of Insurance* (Chicago: Council of State Governments, July, 1961); and Elmer W. Sawyer, *Insurance as Interstate Commerce* (New York: McGraw-Hill Book Co., Inc., 1945). Among the many articles on insurance as interstate commerce, most of them written subsequent to the Supreme Court decision in the South Eastern Underwriters' Case, the following are of general interest: J. W. Clement, "Life Insurance Business and the Federal Government," *Illinois Law Review*, May, 1941, pp. 83–112; S. Launer, "States' Rights and Fire Insurance Regulation," *St. John's Law Review*, November, 1944, pp. 38–45; Edwin W. Patterson, "The Future of State Supervision of Insurance," *Texas Law Review*, December, 1944, pp. 18–38; and E. M. Thore, "Extension of Federal Power and Its Significance to the Insurance Business," *Insurance Counsel Journal*, October, 1949, pp. 287–295.

CHAPTER XI

Foreign Affairs in a Federal System

A few years ago it would have seemed incongruous—if not wholly inappropriate—for State governors to be concerned officially with foreign affairs. Yet in recent years, delegations of governors have conferred with heads of foreign states in Buenos Aires, Rio, and the Kremlin, while a steady flow of foreign policy resolutions has issued from the annual Governors' Conferences. While these actions have had only a minor influence in the international scheme of things, they notably alter the traditional role of the State executives.

In a sense, the addition of this international aspect of the daily concern of governors is merely a reflection of the growing interdependency of all nations in a complex planet. What happens in Leopoldville or Havana may ultimately affect the States as much as what happens in Sacramento or Hartford, and modern governors who ignore international developments do so at their own peril. But in a more particular sense, the governors have discovered that American foreign policies tangibly affect internal State affairs. The economy of a State may be bolstered or hindered by Federal immigration policies, tariffs, and export licensing restrictions. The financial burden of national defense and foreign aid has placed a direct strain on the ability of States to find sources of revenue for their own programs. Governors have felt the pinch of international necessity and they have stepped up their interest in foreign affairs.[1]

[1] Brooks, Glenn E., *When Governors Convene* (Baltimore: Johns Hopkins Press, 1961), pp. 109–110.

FEDERAL-STATE RELATIONS

Under the terms of the Constitution, the Federal government is responsible, and the President is the head and chief spokesman, for the nation in the field of foreign affairs. The primacy of the central government in this field dates back to 1776 or earlier, for even prior to the Declaration of Independence, the colonies were a unit in foreign affairs and acted through a common agency, the Continental Congress, composed of delegates from the thirteen colonies. This body exercised powers of war and peace, raised an army, created a navy, and finally, adopted the Declaration of Independence. As a result of the separation of the colonies from Great Britain, the powers of external sovereignty passed from the British Crown, not to the colonies individually and severally, but to the colonies in their collective and corporate capacity as the United States of America.

Constitutional Provisions

The Constitution provides specifically that "No State shall enter into any treaty, alliance, or confederation. . . ." (Article I, Section 10). Although the parallel provision in the Articles of Confederation and in the draft of the Committee on Detail in the Constitutional Convention was a qualified restriction only, there was no debate and no objection when this absolute prohibition was presented for adoption. "The threat to the national government would be obvious," writes Professor Murphy, "if such a power remained in the States. But the absolute prohibition serves also to make it manifest that the States were to be completely excluded from the areas of foreign affairs, and that the only sovereignty which could deal with other sovereign powers of the world was to be the national government." [2]

Although the Constitutional position of the States in this area is reasonably clear, there has nevertheless been a good deal of disagreement over the role of the States or whether, in fact, they have a role at all in the field of foreign affairs. While a good many writers have contended that they do not, this appears to be a mistaken view. They have long had a considerable influence in foreign affairs, and there is good reason for believing that this influence is likely to increase rather than diminish.

[2] Murphy, William P., "State Sovereignty and the Drafting of the Constitution," II, *Mississippi Law Journal*, December, 1960, pp. 1–23.

The States' influence arises from a number of different sources. They sometimes seriously imperil the peaceful relations of the Federal government with foreign nations by their failure to cooperate in the enforcement of Federal treaty obligations. Their influence has of late increased greatly in new and unexpected ways as a result of obligations arising from the establishment of a considerable number of agencies of world government. It might increase further if a proposal made here to give the States a definite role in the foreign aid program were implemented.

The powers of the President in the field of foreign affairs are very broad. Subject to the Senate's right of confirmation, he appoints all ambassadors and ministers to foreign countries, and all foreign service officers (including consuls) stationed therein, with, of course, the full power of direction and removal which the appointing power entails. Indeed, in the belief that he can sometimes accomplish more by informal contacts than can be achieved through the formal channels of diplomacy, he may employ "special," "secret," or "personal" agents abroad, as many Presidents have done, some more frequently than others. These agents, not technically public officers, require no senatorial confirmation, and receive their pay, if any, from a presidential contingent fund.

In the exercise of his considerable powers in this field, the President may find the cooperation of the Governors very helpful in some instances, the lack of it in others personally irritating if not actually thwarting his policies. Dennis J. Palumbo reminds us that in attempting to enforce the Embargo Act in 1807–1808, President Jefferson relied heavily upon the Governors, especially on Governor Sullivan of Massachusetts whose State was important because, at the time, it carried on about one-third of the nation's commerce.[3] The Governors of New York and Rhode Island were more or less cooperative. In general, however, the Governors promised much and did little, with the result that enforcement of the Embargo, as the President himself soon recognized, was meeting with only moderate success.

Professor Clinton L. Rossiter cites two pertinent illustrations from the experience of Presidents Theodore Roosevelt and Woodrow Wilson. The first occurred in 1906 when Roosevelt's "Japanese policy nearly floundered on the anti-Oriental obstinacy of the San Francisco Board of Education; the Board gave way to the President only after he had promised to see what he could do to reduce the flow of Japanese immigrants into California. . . . In 1913, the Republican-dominated legislature of California made even more trouble for President Wilson by passing an alien land law aimed primarily at the Japanese—despite the earnest pleas of the President, which Secretary of State Bryan delivered personally in

---

[3] Palumbo, Dennis J., *The States and American Foreign Relations* (Chicago: University of Chicago Library Microfilm, 1960), p. 43.

Sacramento, that the Nation might be spared the consequences of this insult to proud Japan." [4]

If a particular problem of importance to the States, which also has repercussions in the field of foreign relations, can be solved by action of a few States, this may be done; if, on the other hand, it can be solved only through national action, the States are likely to exert a powerful political influence to get Congress to act in accordance with their wishes. In doing so, they are more likely than not to succeed. In such a situation, the States are apt to be on one side and the Executive Branch, representing the national interest in a foreign relations question, on the other. Changes in tariff policy are a good example. When the Federal government eases its tariff policies, the States, becoming fearful of foreign competition, break out in a rash of restrictive laws; when Federal restrictions become more stringent, the existing State laws fall into disuse and the States refrain from enacting further restrictive legislation.

The "new Supreme Court" which came into existence in the late 1930's made a sharp distinction between the external or foreign and the internal or domestic powers of the national government. The Court's reasoning with respect to the former, based in part upon some earlier decisions, can be seen by piecing together a number of its statements on the subject, not exactly in the order used by the Court, but in a fairly logical order, as Professor William Anderson has done:

> Sovereignty is never held in suspense. When, therefore, the external sovereignty of Great Britain in respect to the colonies ceased, it immediately passed to the Union. . . .
>
> It results that the investment of the Federal Government with the powers of external sovereignty did not depend upon the affirmative grants of the Constitution. The powers to declare and wage war, to conclude peace, to make treaties, to maintain diplomatic relations with other sovereignties, if they had never been mentioned in the Constitution, would have [been] vested in the Federal Government as necessary concomitants of nationality. . . . As a member of the family of nations, the right and power of the United States in that field [foreign affairs] are equal to the right and power of the other members of the international family. Otherwise, the United States is not completely sovereign.[5]

In developing the distinction between the internal and external powers, the Court held that:

[4] Rossiter, Clinton L., *The American Presidency* (New York: Harcourt, Brace & Company, 1956), p. 45.

[5] Anderson, William, *Intergovernmental Relations in Review* (Minneapolis: University of Minnesota Press, 1960), pp. 27–28.

The two classes of powers are different, both in respect to their origin and their nature. The broad statement that the Federal Government can exercise no powers except those specifically enumerated in the Constitution and such implied powers as are necessary and proper to carry into effect the enumerated powers, is categorically true only in respect to our internal affairs. In that field, the primary purpose of the Constitution was to carve from the general mass of legislative powers *then possessed by the States* such portions as it was thought desirable to vest in the Federal Government, leaving those not included in the enumeration still in the States. . . . That this doctrine applies only to the powers which the States had is self-evident. Since the States severally never possessed international powers, such powers could not have been carved from the mass of State powers, but obviously were transmitted to the United States from some other source.[6]

Sometimes these two types of powers come in contact, if not in conflict, with one another, as in the Michigan water diversion and St. Lawrence Seaway situations.

Lake Michigan Water Diversion

The city of Chicago required considerable quantities of water to flush garbage through a canal into the Mississippi River. The controversy over diversion of water from Lake Michigan arose out of this need. After Chicago had begun diverting some water for this purpose, and attempted to increase the amount, the national government filed a suit to enjoin the city from doing so. In *Sanitary District of Chicago* v. *United States*,[7] it was held that "This is not a controversy among equals." Speaking for a unanimous Court, Mr. Justice Holmes declared: "The United States is asserting its sovereign power to regulate commerce and to control the navigable waters within its jurisdiction. . . . There is no question that this power is superior to that of the States to provide for the welfare or necessities of their inhabitants." The Court further cited the 1909 Treaty between the United States and Canada, which provides for the regulation of boundary levels in Lake Michigan. Illinois thereupon brought pressure to bear upon Congress, and only two vetoes by President Eisenhower in 1954 and 1956, stressing the fact that the water had been diverted without reference to negotiations with the government of Canada, kept Chicago from obtaining the water it so badly wanted.[8]

[6] *Kansas* v. *Colorado,* 206 U.S. 46 (1907).   [7] 266 U.S. 405 (1925).

[8] Senate Committee on Public Works, *Lake Michigan Water Diversion,* Hearings before a Subcommittee on H.R. 3210 and other bills, 84th Cong., 2nd Sess. (Washington, 1956).

In its efforts to prevent the diversion, the State Department contended that lowering the level of Lake Michigan would affect other waterway levels, thus bringing the question within the range of the 1909 Treaty which authorizes investigation of any question involving the use of boundary waters. On this basis, the question would not be one for Congress to decide, but one based on international policy, though the lake itself is wholly within the confines of the United States. There was ground for questioning whether the Treaty was applicable to waters within either country. The whole incident provides an excellent illustration of local versus foreign interests and shows how, regardless of the legal situation, local and State considerations influence the course of the nation's foreign relations.

The St. Lawrence Waterway

From the very beginning, the St. Lawrence Seaway project caused an enormous amount of controversy, and from the power standpoint, it caused friction both between the State of New York and the National government, and between the latter and the government of Canada. The Federal-State friction began in 1929 when Governor Roosevelt wanted the State Public Service Commission to handle the power that would become available when the Seaway was completed, and President Hoover wanted private interests to exploit it. Difficult as were the engineering problems connected with the construction of the Seaway, the "engineering of consent" necessary before actual construction could be undertaken was even more complex.

The jurisdiction squabble continued over a period of many years; it was not resolved until 1953 when two new members of the Federal Power Commission ruled in favor of public power. The problem of disposing of the power to be created was only one of the stumbling blocks which delayed the construction of the Seaway project. As far back as 1948, twenty years after the agitation for the Seaway began, a resolution was introduced in Congress providing that the arrangements made with the government of Canada should become effective "only after approval by the Congress of the United States and the Legislature of the State of New York." [9]

[9] Senate Committee on Foreign Relations. *St. Lawrence Seaway Project*, Hearings before a Subcommittee on S.J. Res. 111, 80th Cong., 1st Sess. (Washington, 1947), Part IV. Out of a voluminous literature, the earliest and the most recent scholarly analyses are Warner, Fayette S., *The Future Movement of Iron Ore and Coal in Relation to the St. Lawrence Seaway* (Philadelphia: University of Pennsylvania Press, 1930) and Willoughby, William R., *The St. Lawrence Waterway: A Study in Politics and Diplomacy* (Madison: University of Wisconsin Press, 1961).

THE STATES AND FEDERAL TREATY OBLIGATIONS

The Constitution in Article II, Section 2, provides that the President "shall have power, by and with the advice and consent of the Senate, to make treaties, provided two-thirds of the Senators present concur." Also, in Article I, Section 10, the States are specifically forbidden to "enter into any treaty, alliance, or confederation," or to "enter into any agreement or compact with another State or with a foreign power, or engage in war, unless actually invaded or in such imminent danger as will not admit of delay." Judging by these provisions, it would appear that the States were expected to have little or no interest or concern about questions relating to the foreign affairs of the nation. The States have, in fact, had more influence on such questions than has been popularly supposed, and the trend indicates a probability that they will have more concern with such matters in the future than in the past.

The States and the Treaty Power

The wording of the treaty clause seems to be clear and to provide for a broad and virtually unlimited delegation of power. Nevertheless, there has been controversy with respect to its meaning and its effect upon the States and their powers from the very beginning. The matter was discussed in the Constitutional Convention, has been the subject of innumerable court decisions over the years, and was the subject of heated Congressional discussion and debate as recently as the proposal of the Bricker amendment. An effort will be made in this section to summarize the major views that have been presented with respect to the meaning of the treaty clause and to note a few of the more significant cases and problems that have been raised involving questions of interpretation. Important among these are the problem of diplomatic immunity and the effect upon the States of decisions relating to such matters as the migratory bird act and the regulation of fisheries in navigable waters.

Nationalist versus *States' Rights Views.* Two fundamentally different views originally existed respecting the meaning of the treaty clause; both have had wide acceptance and periods of ascendency in American law. The Federalists looked upon this clause as a source of national power, while the Anti-Federalists regarded it as a means of protecting States' rights. Neither school of thought was entirely wrong, and neither could foresee how the clause would be interpreted by the Supreme Court or how the Senate would exercise its power—it soon becoming a ratifying rather than a consulting and cooperating body. The nationalist view was prevalent in the Constitutional Convention and was the view first accepted and acted upon after the new government was established, and it continued to be the accepted one as long as the Supreme Court remained under the domination of the point of view of the Founders.

While the Court has held that treaties are of equal dignity with acts of Congress, it has also held that a later act of Congress may override an earlier treaty and has repeatedly upheld the supremacy of treaties over conflicting State laws.[10] During the nationalist era, the leading precedent was *Ware* v. *Hylton* [11] in which the Court held that the Treaty of Peace with Great Britain, even on so sensitive an issue as a pre-Revolutionary War debt owed by a Virginian to a British subject, took precedence over a State statute. In this decision, the Court made the sweeping assertion that the treaty clause inferred "supremacy on the part of the treaty power over State power to the fullest conceivable extent."

During the war, the Virginia debtor had made payments on the loan into the loan office of Virginia according to a State law of December 20, 1777, which sequestered British property and provided that such payment and a receipt therefor should discharge the debt. Although Virginia had had authority to make such an agreement at the time, Article IV of the Treaty of 1783 had nullified the State law, thereby destroying the payments made under the law, reviving the debt, and giving a right of recovery against the principal debtor, notwithstanding the fact that payments had been made under authority of State law. Chief Justice Chase wrote the opinion of the Court, in which he stated that:

> treaties made by Congress according to the Confederation, were superior to the laws of the States; because the Confederation made them obligatory upon the States. . . . But, if doubts could exist before the establishment of the present national government, they must be entirely removed by the sixth article of the Constitution. . . . It is the declared will of the people of the United States that every treaty made, by the authority of the United States, shall be superior to the constitution and laws of any individual State; and their will alone is to decide. . . .
>
> Four things are apparent on a view of this sixth article of the National Constitution. First, that it is retrospective, and is to be considered in the same light as if the Constitution had been established before the making of the Treaty of 1783; second, that the constitution or laws of any of the States so far as either of them shall be found contrary to that

[10] In this respect, executive agreements enjoy the same status as treaties; see *United States* v. *Belmont*, 301 U.S. 324 (1937) and *United States* v. *Pink*, 315 U.S. 203 (1942).

[11] 3 Dallas 199 (1796); in addition, see *Fairfax* v. *Hunter*, 7 Cranch 603 (1813) and *Chirac* v. *Chirac*, 2 Wheaton 259 (1817).

treaty are by force of the said article, prostrated before the treaty; third, that consequently the Treaty of 1783 has superior power to the legislature of any State, because no legislature of any State has any kind of power over the Constitution, which was its creator; fourth, that it is the declared duty of the State judges to determine any constitution or laws of any State contrary to that treaty (or any other) made under the authority of the United States, null and void. National and Federal judges are bound by duty and oath to the same conduct.

Elsewhere, the Supreme Court has recognized this power as extending to "all proper subjects of negotiation between this government and those of other nations." [12] Chief Justice Taney used the following language, which can scarcely be described as particularly forceful and direct:

> It must be assumed that the Framers of the Constitution intended that it [the power to make treaties] should extend to all those objects which in the intercourse of nations had usually been regarded as the proper subjects of negotiation and treaty, if not inconsistent with the nature of our government and the relation between the States and the United States.

Gradually, as nationalist sentiment declined and sentiment for States' rights tended to increase, the alternative view involving a States' rights interpretation of the treaty clause was developed and for a period of half a century enjoyed general acceptance. After the Civil War, with nationalism again triumphant, the nationalistic view regained precedence and has rarely been seriously challenged since that time, probably the most significant challenge being presented by the Bricker amendment of the early 1950's.

The States' rights view of the treaty power may be formulated in three ways, according to Edward S. Corwin, who made one of the earliest and one of the most thorough studies of the relation of the treaty clause to the States. The first formulation identifies the authority of the United States under which treaties are made with the sum total of the enumerated powers of the United States, exclusive of the treaty power, which thus becomes only a method of exercising these powers. The second method states the matter from the point of view of State power; this was the method adopted by Thomas Jefferson in his famous *Manual of Parliamentary Practice* when he argued that the treaty power must have meant to except the rights reserved to the States, "for surely the President and Senate cannot do by treaty what the whole government is interdicted from doing in any way." This approach was so weak that it was soon abandoned; if the legislative power of the States is a barrier

---

[12] *Holmes* v. *Jennison*, 14 Peters 540, 569 (1840).

to the treaty power, then the legislative power of the Congress must be one also, since Congress, within the range of its powers, is constitutionally equal to the State legislatures. The third method rests upon the notion that the States possess certain inalienable rights; because this view restricts the treaty power less rigorously than the others, it may be even more objectionable.

Significant Instances. The first practical application of the States' rights view occurred in South Carolina in 1823 when the legislature, suddenly overtaken by one of its periodic seizures of terror of a slave insurrection, passed an act "the more effectively to prohibit free Negroes and persons of color from entering into" the State; the second section provided that if any vessel arriving in a port of the State from any other State or *foreign port,* should have on board, in its employment, any free Negro, it should be "the duty of the sheriff of the district" immediately to apprehend such person "and to confine him closely in jail" until the departure of the vessel, when upon payment of the expenses of his detention, the Negro would be restored to his captain. The enforcement of this measure against a colored British seaman provoked a protest from Great Britain based upon the Commercial Convention of 1815.

At first an effort seems to have been made by the national government to arrive at some understanding with the State authorities that would remove the basis for the complaint, but in a dispute between the National and State authorities as to what had been agreed upon, an application was entered with a Federal court sitting in Charleston for a writ of habeas corpus in behalf of Henry Elkinson, a British subject who had been imprisoned under the act. In the trial, the States' rights point of view was forcefully presented, but the presentation seems to have made singularly little impression upon Justice Johnson, the able South Carolinian who heard the case. Since this took place some years before Calhoun went over to the States' rights side, the Justice was quite free to deal with the constitutional issues involved solely on their merits. He found himself unauthorized by law to grant a writ of habeas corpus, since the law itself was completely at variance with the provisions of both the Convention and the Constitution:

> A reciprocal liberty of commerce is expressly stipulated for and conceded by that treaty [the Commercial Convention of 1815]. To this the rights of navigating their ships in their own way, and particularly by their own subjects, is necessarily incident. If policy requires any restriction of this right, with regard to a particular class of the subjects of either contracting party, *it must be introduced by treaty.* The opposite party cannot introduce it by a legislative act of his own. Such a law as this could not be passed, even by the General Government, without furnishing a just cause of war.

The Justice found the Court in a very weak position, lacking the necessary power and with both the district attorney and the local Federal officers supporting the position of the State. The futility of further negotiation between the National and State authorities was made clear both by new incidents and by the spread of similar legislation in other States. To add to the confusion, the national government's adherence to the national point of view wavered, with one Attorney General overruling another in rapid succession.

It is interesting to note that while this controversy was going on, Great Britain was obliged to open additional consulates in the South to deal directly with the States concerned, because the Federal government was unable either to obtain the release of imprisoned British Negroes or to induce the States to modify their laws concerning foreign Negroes. It is also interesting, and possibly significant, that eventually the British consuls were able to persuade the States to modify these laws, thereby accomplishing in six years what the national government had been unable to accomplish in twenty-five.

Another controversy with Great Britain, this one over the northeastern boundary and involving the same basic issue, was settled in 1842 by the ratification of the Webster-Ashburton Treaty. The controversy dated from the Treaty of 1783, which contained only weak and ineffective provisions on this boundary matter, but had become a matter of serious concern only during Jackson's administration. One administration after another had negotiated, in a prolonged argument which lasted more than sixty years, always questioning whether the central government had the power to cede by treaty "even an inch of the territory of any State that did not belong to the Central Government." Dealing with the matter in 1840, Justice McLean wrote:

> It is a sound principle of national law, and applies to the treaty-making power of this government, whether exercised with a foreign nation or an Indian tribe, that all questions of disputed boundaries may be settled by the parties to the treaty. And to the exercise of these high functions by the Government within its constitutional powers, neither the rights of a State nor those of an individual can be interposed.[13]

Two years later in the Webster-Ashburton Treaty, Secretary of State Webster apparently accepted—officially, at least, whatever his private views may have been—the Maine-Massachusetts view that the United States could not cede any part of a State's territory without that State's consent. Article V of the Treaty provided that the United States should pay to the States of Maine and Massachusetts certain moneys "in equal

---

[13] *Lattimer* v. *Poteet*, 14 Peters 4 (1840).

moieties, on account of their assent to boundary lines described in the treaty." The States' rights view thus prevailed, and it is doubtless due to this precedent that the doctrine that the nation may not cede the territory lying within a State without the State's consent, still occasionally finds its way into judicial dicta.[14]

The Problem of Diplomatic Immunity. The immunity of duly accredited diplomatic representatives from the provisions of State law has long been a troublesome problem, and it is quite as troublesome today as it has been at any time in the past. During the entire period in which the States' rights doctrine was in the ascendency, treaties continued, as they had from the beginning, to assure for consuls who were not United States citizens their regular immunities from local jurisdiction. Included were exemption from taxation, except upon real estate and personal investments; exemption from the duty of rendering testimony in court in person; the inviolability of their archives from any sort of judicial process whatsoever; the right to assume jurisdiction over disputes between sea captains and members of their crews which did not involve the peace of the port; the right to apply to local authorities for assistance in securing the arrest and detention of deserters; and the right to intervene in the case of death of citizens or subjects of their respective countries, to make inventory of the property of the deceased, and to take other steps necessary to the safe transmission of that property to the rightful heirs.

During the same period, treaties also assured aliens rights of sojourn, travel, residence, and trade, subject to the *ordinary laws* and equal to the rights of citizens of the United States or of citizens or subjects of the most-favored-nation, and guaranteed them freedom of religion and rights of burial, and freedom of access to the courts of justice on an exact equality with citizens. Similarly, they assured aliens unqualified equal rights of acquiring, passing, willing, inheriting, and disposing of personal property. Further, if an alien should inherit real estate, but local laws made alienage a bar to his succeeding, he was guaranteed a reasonable term to dispose of such real estate to whom he chose; in some instances, the earlier type of treaty provision, which guaranteed the right of succession to real estate, recurred. Extradition treaties were common during this era and covered a progressively wider range of offenses.

Fisheries and Migratory Birds. It occasionally happens that the Federal government negotiates and ratifies treaties with regard to subjects that are proper in themselves but which, under the American system of

---

[14] In this connection, Corwin cites J. Field in *Geofroy* v. *Riggs,* 133 U.S. 258 (1890), and J. White in *Downes* v. *Bidwell,* 182 U.S. 244 (1901), but notes that J. White finally substitutes the consent of Congress for State consent.

the allocation of powers, are commonly regarded as State powers. Illustrations are noted in the effort to regulate fisheries in navigable waters and in the protection of migratory birds. Chronologically, the fisheries problem was first to arise. In Articles II and IV of the Treaty of 1854 with Great Britain, reciprocal privileges were agreed upon for the taking "of fish of every kind except shell fish on the eastern sea coasts and shores of the United States." These provisions appeared again, in practically the same form, in the Treaty of 1871. Attorney General Griggs sustained the constitutionality of these provisions in an opinion presented on September 20, 1898:

> The regulation of fisheries in the navigable waters within the territorial limits of the several States, in the absence of Federal treaty, is a subject of State rather than Federal regulation. The fact that a treaty provision annuls and supersedes the law of a particular State upon the same subject is no objection to the validity of the treaty.[15]

A provision contained in Article IV of the Treaty of 1854 provided a basis for questioning the finality if not the legal soundness of this opinion. The Treaty provided, for instance, that "The Government of the United States . . . engages *to urge upon the State governments* to secure for the subjects of Her Britannic Majesty the use of the several State canals on terms of equality with the inhabitants of the United States." The provision was obviously based upon the assumption that the canals, unlike the fisheries, owed their existence not to nature but to the States themselves, and it is inferred, as Corwin points out, that they are not, for this reason, subject to the control of the central government.

> If the use to which the National Government, in the exercise of its treaty-power, should subject State property should amount to a "taking," doubtless the National Government would have to render "due compensation" for it. And that a State would be given a fair opportunity to establish such a claim in a court of equity seems also beyond doubt.[16]

Many years later, these same questions of Federal-State relations in the fisheries and wildlife field were raised after the United States and Great Britain had entered into a Treaty, approved August 16, 1915, for the protection of migratory birds, the constitutionality of which was challenged by the State of Missouri. In an effort to discharge faithfully American obligations under the Treaty, Congress had enacted the Migra-

[15] 22 Opinions 214, citing *Ware* v. *Hylton* and ensuing decisions.

[16] Corwin, Edward S., *National Supremacy* (New York: Henry Holt & Co., 1913), p. 142.

tory Bird Act of July 3, 1918, which provided for the protection of migratory birds passing between the United States and Canada. The act authorized the Secretary of Agriculture to execute the law and to make and proclaim the necessary rules and regulations for its enforcement.

The Missouri authorities objected to the activities of Holland, a Federal Game Warden, who was proceeding under the terms of the Treaty, the Act of Congress, and the regulations of the Secretary of Agriculture. The State contended that the Federal Act was unconstitutional, since the control of wild game was a subject reserved to the States or to the people under the terms of the Tenth Amendment. The Supreme Court fully sustained the Treaty, the Act of Congress, and the regulations on the ground that while control of bird life is, of course, not a power which the Constitution confers upon the Federal government, it is a proper subject for treaty agreement. Furthermore, treaty-making is one of the many Federal powers which Article I, Section 8, Paragraph 18 (the "necessary and proper" clause) authorizes Congress to implement by legislation. It is significant that in order to be the supreme law of the land, acts of Congress must be "made in pursuance" of the Constitution, but that treaties may be made simply and more broadly "under the authority of the United States." This, of course, does not exempt treaties from judicial invalidation on grounds of unconstitutionality, although up to this time, none has ever been overthrown in this way.

Mr. Justice Holmes, at the conclusion of an opinion upholding the Migratory Bird Act and emphasizing the fact that the Federal power to make treaties was broader and covered a wider range of subjects than the lawmaking power, made the following significant statements:

> Here a National interest of very nearly the first magnitude is involved. It can be protected only by national action in concert with that of another power. The subject matter is only transitory within the State and has no permanent habitat therein. But for the treaty and the statute there soon might be no birds for any power to deal with. We see nothing in the Constitution that compels the Government to sit by while a food supply is cut off and the protectors of our forests and our crops are destroyed. It is not sufficient to rely upon the States. The reliance is vain, and were it otherwise, the question is whether the United States is forbidden to act. We are of opinion that the treaty and the statute must be upheld.[17]

[17] *Missouri* v. *Holland, U.S. Game Warden,* 252 U.S. 416 (1920) and *United States* v. *Oregon,* 295 U.S. 1 (1935). Without treaty support, Congress previously had been unable to get a similar act past the courts. See also Black, Forrest R., "*Missouri* v. *Holland:* A Judicial Milestone in the Road to Absolutism," *Illinois Law Review,* April, 1931, pp. 911–928.

State Failures to Observe Treaty Obligations

Significant instances of Federal embarrassment because of the failure of the States to cooperate in the enforcement of treaty obligations include numerous controversies with foreign governments over repudiated State debts, the Italian Mafia incident in Louisiana in 1891, the California School Case in 1906, and the *Bremen* incident in New York in 1935.

Repudiated State Debts. The controversies over repudiated State debts grew out of extensive loans negotiated abroad for internal improvements in the period following the War of 1812, and out of loans made in the Reconstruction period following the Civil War. There were numerous State defaults with respect to these loans in the 1840's and between 1870 and 1890; for almost a century, those in the first group have been a subject of international controversy. They raise in pointed fashion the question of the international responsibility of States (in the technical sense) for the acts of their political subdivisions—a basic question of international law which the United States was long able to evade. The issue was squarely presented to the Supreme Court in 1934, when the principality of Monaco brought suit against Mississippi on bonds issued by that State. The motion was denied by the Court in an opinion written by Chief Justice Hughes, holding that Article III, Section 2, Clause 1 of the Constitution gives the Supreme Court jurisdiction of such suits only in the event of the State's consent to be sued; otherwise a State is immune from suits brought against it by a foreign state.[18]

The Italian Mafia Incident. The Italian Mafia incident arose from the murder of the Chief of Police of New Orleans, John C. Hennessey. Investigation revealed that certain Italian residents of the city, members of the Black Hand or Mafia Society, were guilty of the crime. These persons were arrested and confined in the parish jail. One morning, prior to the date of their trial, one of the local papers announced that there would be a meeting of citizens on the plaza in front of the jail at four o'clock that afternoon. The crowd assembled, and after a series of harangues descended upon the jail, battered down the gates, seized five of

---

[18] *Monaco* v. *Mississippi*, 292 U.S. 313 (1934). See McGrane, Reginald C., *Foreign Bondholders and American State Debts* (New York: The Macmillan Co., 1935) and "Some Aspects of American State Debts in the Forties," *American Historical Review*, July, 1933, pp. 673–686; see also Ratchford, B. U., "An International Debt Settlement: The North Carolina Debt to France," *ibid.*, October, 1934, pp. 63–69, and *American State Debts* (Durham: Duke University Press, 1941).

the accused persons, and carried them off and lynched them. Since some of these persons were citizens of Italy, the Italian government protested.

Although the identity of the mob leaders was known, both the Governor and the local authorities were in sympathy with the lynchers and refused to take any effective action toward their arrest and conviction. Secretary of State Blaine was placed in the painful and embarrassing position of having to explain to the Italian government that reprehensible as the crime was and much as the Federal authorities regretted its occurrence, there was nothing they could do about it, since under our federal system the matter fell entirely within the authority of the State government. Even though Blaine literally begged the State authorities to take action for the purpose of avoiding complications between the United States and Italy, they obdurately refused. Italy severed diplomatic relations and recalled its ambassador, and for some time there was serious danger of war between the two countries.[19]

California School Case. In the California School case, a controversy between the United States and Japan developed through California's refusal to comply with certain treaty arrangements existing between Japan and the United States under the Treaty of 1894, in which the United States had agreed to accord Japanese citizens equality of treatment. The San Francisco Board of Education passed in October, 1906, and attempted to enforce a race segregation ordinance in its public schools, under which all Chinese, Japanese, and Korean children would attend an Oriental school. The complaints of the Japanese government raised numerous and complicated questions, and because the controversy was eventually terminated by negotiations between the President and the municipal government of San Francisco, none of them reached an authoritative settlement.

President Roosevelt was deeply concerned about the whole affair; the day after the school board order was issued, he wrote:

> I am being horribly bothered about the Japanese business. The infernal fools in California insult the Japanese recklessly and, in the event of war, it will be the Nation as a whole which will pay the consequences.[20]

[19] This account is based upon a study of the *State Papers,* a government publication, made by the author a number of years ago; for a fuller account, see Curtis, William E., *The United States and Foreign Powers* (New York: Charles Scribner's Sons, 1900), Chapter 16.

[20] Quoted in Bailey, Thomas A., *Theodore Roosevelt and the Japanese-American Crisis* (Stanford: Stanford University Press, 1934), p. 46; see also Root, Elihu, "The Real Question Under the Japanese Treaty and the San Francisco School Board Resolution," *American Journal of International Law,* April, 1907, pp. 274–283. For a valuable discussion of the background and the

Through negotiation, the President was able to persuade the board members to rescind the order, but they continued to press for restrictive legislation against the Japanese, as in the past they had done against the Chinese. After a mob attack on a Japanese bathhouse, relations with Japan became still more difficult. From 1909 to 1913, Presidents Roosevelt and Taft were able to prevent California from passing more restrictive local legislation, but by the latter date, when alien land bills were enacted by the California legislature, the general international situation was becoming serious. Japan protested this legislation, but because of the outbreak of World War I, the questions involved were never settled. California was finally able to get its exclusion laws through Congress in 1923 when, under the leadership of Senator Hiram Johnson, the bill was passed and signed into law by President Coolidge.

The general issues involved were widely discussed, from many angles and with a variety of bias, so that the results remained quite inconclusive. Again, as in the Mafia incident, the Secretary of State—this time, Elihu Root—was obliged to explain to a foreign power the impotence of the Federal government under the circumstances, and to plead with the California officials for such modification of the resolution as would enable the United States to honor its treaty obligations, thereby avoiding a possible conflict with Japan.

The treatment accorded Orientals on the West Coast before and after the enactment of the Chinese Exclusion Act, as illustrated by the San Francisco School Case and by the placing of all Japanese (including those who were American citizens) in "relocation camps" during World War II, can now be seen to have definitely harmed the United States' position as a world leader. Non-white peoples in the underdeveloped countries of Asia and Africa are apt to believe, despite our protestations to the contrary, that prejudice, bigotry, and intolerance are more characteristic of Americans than the liberty, justice, and democracy in which we profess to believe. This was pointed out forty years ago when Mary Roberts Coolidge noted that the treatment of the Chinese by Western State officials was one of the main reasons why the United States was included with other "hated foreigners." [21] Although the Federal government may have the constitutional power to act for the protection of aliens and the enforcement of their rights, it is obvious that it often lacks the political power effectively to implement its constitutional obligations.

---

constitutional aspects of the race problem in California, see Swisher, Carl B., *Motivation and Political Technique in the California Constitutional Convention, 1878–1879* (Claremont, Cal.: doctoral dissertations, Pomona College, 1930), Chapter 6.

[21] Coolidge, Mary Roberts, *Chinese Immigration* (New York: Henry Holt & Co., 1909) and quoted by Palumbo, p. 162.

The Bremen Incident. Even more embarrassing to the Federal government was an incident which occurred in New York City in the summer and fall of 1935. The German liner *Bremen* arrived in New York harbor on July 26 flying the new flag of the Nazi government. A riot occurred, in the course of which the flag was hauled down and treated with disrespect. The German government filed a vigorous protest with the Department of State, and relations between the two governments became somewhat strained. In due course, six prisoners charged with participation in the riot were brought for a hearing before Magistrate Louis B. Brodsky. Five of them he discharged, commenting as he did so upon the Nazi regime in language "offensive to another government with which we have official relations," as Secretary of State Hull said shortly thereafter in an official apology to the German government, whose protest at the words of the magistrate were even more vigorous than before. Three paragraphs from Secretary Hull's statement to the Counselor of the German Embassy are worthy of quotation:

> The complaint of the German government is specifically directed at the statements made by the magistrate in rendering his decision which that Government interprets as an unwarranted reflection upon it.
>
> The Department is constrained to feel that the magistrate, in restating contentions of the defendants in the case and in commenting upon the incident, unfortunately so worded his opinion as to give the reasonable and definite impression that he was going out of his way adversely to criticize the government, which criticism was not a relevant or legitimate part of his judicial decision.
>
> I may explain that State and municipal officials are not instrumentalities of the Federal government. Although in this country the right of freedom of speech is well recognized by our fundamental law, it is to be regretted that an official having no responsibility for maintaining relations between the United States and other countries should, regardless of what he may personally think of the laws and policies of other governments, thus indulge in expressions offensive to another government with which we have official relations.

It is a serious weakness of the federal system that it should be possible for a State so to conduct its affairs as to involve the Federal government in diplomatic difficulties with other nations. The question has often been discussed, but no remedial measures have ever been adopted. Perhaps the most promising solution is one proposed by Attorney General Daugherty in 1922; he suggested that Congress should by law provide that all cases involving questions arising under the treaty obligations of the United States, regardless of the subject with which they might deal, should be taken immediately and automatically into the Federal courts for adjudication. This proposal has the merit of being simple and effective and of not requiring any modification of the Constitution. Its adoption would seem to be both wise and reasonable.

Any other attempt to cope with the basic problem of localism would be far more difficult to accomplish. That localism has frequently erected barriers to the proper conduct of American foreign relations is obvious, as is the fact that the subjects of controversy have been traditionally domestic matters under State and local control. The cause of the friction cannot be reduced or eliminated unless, at least when disputes arise, the national government is free to exercise greater control over domestic matters. The problem is to find means of preserving as much local autonomy as possible, while at the same time curbing the power of a noncooperative State to create an international crisis.

The Bricker Amendment

Since the United States signed the United Nations Charter, it is bound to encourage and promote respect for and observance of human rights and freedoms. It is also required by the Universal Declaration of Human Rights to promote respect for human rights through education and teaching. To date, however, the United States has not ratified the Genocide Convention, although enough nations have done so to put it into effect; the Covenant of Human Rights has yet to be approved by the United States.

From a constitutional standpoint, American obligations under these documents raise difficult questions. Issues involving human rights are to a large extent, though not exclusively, the responsibility of the States. Since valid treaties are a part of the law of the land, however, could not Congress implement them, and could not the courts restrain violations of them with or without Congressional authorization? If the courts were to take the position that the Charter of the United Nations is part of the supreme law of the land, as one or two minor courts have done, the Charter could even now be effective without implementing legislation passed by Congress. If not, the courts could grant relief only after Congress had enacted appropriate legislation, but in either event, the Federal government would have a much clearer mandate for guarding civil rights, especially against violations by private individuals, than is now generally supposed.

On the basis of this possibly serious threat to States' rights, Senator John W. Bricker of Ohio and a coalition of Senators proposed a constitutional amendment which would have limited the authority of the President to make treaties and executive agreements. The proposal would have nullified any provision of a treaty which conflicted with the Constitution, and would have prevented a treaty or executive agreement from becoming effective as internal law unless it would have been valid in the absence of a treaty (or agreement). Its purpose was to establish Congressional control over the President's exercise of the treaty-making powers conferred upon him by the Constitution.

President Eisenhower fully appreciated this fact, as is evident in the following letter to Senator Knowland:

> I am unalterably opposed to the Bricker amendment as reported by the Senate Judiciary Committee. It would so restrict the conduct of foreign affairs that our country could not negotiate the agreements necessary for the handling of our business with the rest of the world. Such an amendment would make it impossible for us to deal effectively with friendly nations for our mutual defense and common interests.[22]

This view was shared by most informed people, regardless of party affiliation. In February, 1954, the 50 to 42 vote fell considerably short of the two-thirds vote required to submit proposed constitutional amendments, and a milder substitute proposed by Senator Walter F. George the following day also failed of adoption. While the matter has occasionally been mentioned since, there now appears to be little danger that it will be revived and given favorable consideration.

The Bricker amendment is obviously not the right answer to a problem which confronts all federal states, our own included. Robert E. Looper notes in a recent article that:

> There are, or may be, matters of genuine international concern which fall within the constitutionally reserved powers of the constituent units in every federation. . . . Can a federate state operate to meet these problems without destroying the essence of federalism itself? The international law rule is that a federation cannot plead its constitutional division of powers as a means of avoiding international obligations. Yet, in some federations—notably Canada—internationally valid treaties can be violated through the negligence or adverse action of any of the component states. The Bricker Amendment would extend this result to the United States. Obviously such a situation puts a federal state at a disadvantage in its dealings with other states. The one thing modern conditions now demand of federal government is that it provide the same effectiveness in the conduct of foreign relations as that provided

[22] Letter from the President to Senator Knowland, January 25, 1954. See Schubert, Glendon A., Jr., "Politics and the Constitution: The Bricker Amendment During 1953," Journal of Politics, May, 1954, pp. 257–298; Wright, Quincy, "Congress and the Treaty-Making Power," American Society of International Law, Proceedings, 1952, pp. 43–69; and Commager, Henry S., "The Perilous Folly of Senator Bricker," Reporter, October 13, 1953, pp. 12–27.

by a unitary state. Yet it is equally obvious that, with the expansion of the area of what may legitimately be made the subject of international negotiation, the treaty power contains the seeds for the virtual destruction of the federation's constituent units. This is the dilemma of the federal government in the international community today.[23]

ADVERSE EFFECTS OF STATE DOMESTIC POLICIES

When the laws or the administrative practices of the States interfere with the observance of the treaty obligations of the Federal government, the obligation of the Federal authorities to act is quite clear, whether or not they are always able to act effectively. There is another type of situation, however, in which no question of treaty obligation is involved but in which the laws (or the lack of them) and the policies of the States in dealing with purely domestic matters serve to embarrass the United States in its relations with other nations and to create ill will toward the United States. This section will cover a few interesting and significant illustrations, such as American degree mills, property holding by aliens, state barriers to foreign commerce, and the effect of an occasional failure in the process of judicial administration.

Many years ago Professor Corwin pointed out that "It has not a few times come about that something done by a State in the supposed exercise of its police powers has fallen athwart something done by the National Government in the supposed exercise of its power to make treaties." [24] The supreme law clause in Article VI of the Constitution seems to provide a clear and definite answer to this impasse. Unquestionably, a treaty made "under the authority of the United States" overrides all conflicting provisions of State constitutions or State statutes. Although this power appears to be almost unlimited, the dangers may be far less than have sometimes been imagined. They might conceivably be rather negligible, since as Corwin observes, "the actual check imposed upon the treaty power by the method prescribed in the Constitution for its exercise—in other words, the political check—should be not a little efficacious in practice."

It is significant to observe that while the members of the Constitutional Convention found themselves divided by the most fundamental differences of motive and opinion on many issues, on this they were

[23] Looper, Robert E., "Limitations on the Treaty Power in Federal States," *New York University Law Review,* June, 1959, pp. 1045–1066.
[24] Corwin, *National Supremacy,* p. 3.

unanimous. Whether from large States or small, whether of States' rights or nationalistic predilections, whether from North or South, they were in unanimous agreement that the national authority, whatever the range of powers to be assigned to it, must with respect to such powers be absolutely assured of supremacy over State authority—a supremacy which under the Articles of Confederation, owing to the fact of their ratification by the State legislatures, was thought by some to be at least conjectural.[25]

Such questions as arise in this area involve matters which, under our federal system, fall within the area of State responsibility. The use which the States make (or fail to make) of their police powers may not only affect their own citizens, but the citizens of other States and other nations as well. If American citizens choose to be swindled because their State governments fail to provide effective measures for their protection, that is bad enough; such a situation takes on a different connotation, however, when innocent people from other lands become the victims.

The powers of the Federal government in the field of foreign affairs are very broad. There is every reason to believe that the Founding Fathers intended that they should be, and certainly the course of developments in our government over the years has provided no basis for a modification of that view. But are they broad enough to protect American interests abroad from the ill effects of the failures of the States at home properly to exercise their unquestioned powers? In such situations, can and should the Federal government impose regulations which the States themselves could and should have adopted long ago?

American Degree Mills

Situations involving these questions are not numerous, but a few of them are important enough to have serious consequences. The facts with respect to one such situation have once again been brought to public attention by a study of American degree mills, sponsored by the American Council on Education.[26] The neglect of this problem is the more inexcusable because it is so old. As far back as 1924, a Subcommittee of the Senate Committee on Education and Labor (commonly known as the Copeland Subcommittee) held hearings on diploma mills in medical education.[27] Dr. George F. Zook, then Assistant Commissioner and

[25] Corwin, *National Supremacy*, p. 33.

[26] Reid, Robert H., *American Degree Mills* (Washington: American Council on Education, 1959).

[27] *Hearings: Pursuant to Senate Resolution No. 61, January-March, 1924,* 68th Cong., 1st Sess. (Washington, 1924).

later Commissioner on Education, was unable to appear in person, but sent written testimony in which he emphasized the importance of the problem and suggested means of dealing with it:

> I cannot emphasize too strongly the ill effects on the reputation of American higher education abroad which have been caused by the traffic in university and college degrees, including medical degrees. If something can be done to put a stop to this miserable business in foreign countries, it will relieve this country of a very unsavory reputation abroad. . . .
> [There are] two possible ways of accomplishing this end: (1) By action of the several States through their laws governing the incorporation of higher institutions; and (2) amending the postal laws so as to make illegal the solicitation of students and the granting of degrees in course for work done wholly by correspondence.[28]

This was a quarter of a century ago. The nature of the problem was as clear then as it is now. What has been done about it in the meantime? The following excerpt from a 1956 report states concisely the problems and dangers of American degree mills:

> The lax provisions for the issuance of institutional charters, and the virtual absence of supervision over the quality of the programs maintained in existing institutions in most States, have led to the operation of many fraudulent institutions, often known as "diploma mills," which sell degrees, diplomas, and credentials at a price to unwary or unscrupulous customers. From time to time, the Federal Trade Commission or the Post Office Department is able to obtain sufficient evidence to put some of these fraudulent institutions out of business. In many instances, however, the enterprising managers of such institutions peddle their bogus degrees and credentials to persons in foreign countries who are unfamiliar with the fact that the control over higher education in so many of the States in the United States is lax enough to permit such fraudulent operation.[29]

The current report finds that there have been a number of serious attempts to control American degree mills, but that, with certain exceptions, these attempts have not curbed the malpractices which harm the reputation of American higher education abroad. Major difficulties, so far as the role of the States is concerned, arise from a number of sources.

[28] Copeland Subcommittee *Hearings*, and quoted by Reid, p. 57.
[29] Blauch, Lloyd, in *American Universities and Colleges 1956*, Irwin, Mary, ed. (Washington: American Council on Education, 1956), pp. 21–22, and quoted by Reid, p. 1.

First is the shackles which bind the States in the issuance of charters which, under the decision of the Supreme Court in the Dartmouth College Case,[30] are practically irrevocable.

While there is good legal authority for forcing dissolution of an institution for abuse of its degree-granting privilege, the State must have evidence "of flagrant and continued abuse," and, moreover, dissolution in one State does not prevent reincorporation in another State under the same name or in the same State under a different name. A second problem arises from the fact that "nowhere is the diversity of State law more apparent than in legislation regulating the operation of correspondence schools or the offering of correspondence study—the most fertile field for diploma mill activity." [31]

Eighteen States and the District of Columbia have laws regarding the right to confer degrees, but this means that there are still thirty-two States lacking such legislation. The only new legislation prompted by the extensive activity of the diploma mills was enacted in California in 1958, after four years of study and investigation which brought astounding numbers and types of abuses to light. Estimates of the number of institutions selling bogus degrees in the Los Angeles area alone ranged from fifty to one hundred. One correspondence school offered a B.A. degree for $90, another a Ph.D. in psychology for $250. The Council of State Governments has indicated its interest in the problem and its willingness to cooperate in developing a solution.

The American Council on Education report urges the basic need for concerted action on the part of the States in the adoption of uniform legislation setting minimum standards for the licensing and operation of all institutions of higher education, with special reference to their degree-granting privileges. A model act for this purpose, sponsored by the National Education Association, has been in existence since 1953. The American Council report concludes that "even if all the States do pass satisfactory statutes, the need for supplementary Federal legislation is apparent, for there will still be loopholes in interstate and international control." [32] As of 1961, it appeared that little progress had been made.[33]

Property Holding by Aliens

The Federal government must certainly share the blame for such friction as has developed in this aspect of Federal-State relations, because

[30] *Trustees of Dartmouth College* v. *William H. Woodward*, 4 Wheaton 518 (1819).

[31] Reid, pp. 65–66.   [32] Reid, pp. 77–78.

[33] See Hechinger, Fred M., " 'Diploma Mills' Hit in U.S. Action," *The New York Times*, August 4, 1961, p. 23.

it has never adopted or adhered to any consistent policy. With almost pendulum-like regularity, the central government has first shown deference to the position of the States, then made loud protestations when the States asserted powers which had at other times been freely recognized. As regards property holding by aliens, the emphasis has tended to shift from the enforcement of treaty obligations to emphasis upon the rights of man. Examples may be noted at many points in the history of the nation.

The early constitutional doctrine on this type of case was well illustrated by an 1840 opinion of Chief Justice Taney, several provisions included in a treaty between the United States and Switzerland in 1850 which led to an important court decision, and a consular convention with France in 1853. In 1840, in *Holmes* v. *Jennison*,[34] Chief Justice Taney took the position that the Framers of the Constitution had intended that the power to make treaties should extend to all those objects which, in the normal intercourse of nations, had been regarded as proper subjects of negotiation and treaty—provided, of course, that they were not inconsistent with the nature of our government or with the established patterns in the relations between the States and the United States.

Only a little more than a decade after this, but still more than a century prior to the time these lines were written, the State Department had, in a consular convention with France in 1853, included a provision that:

> In all the States of the Union, *whose existing laws permit it,* so long and to the same extent as the said laws shall remain in force, Frenchmen shall enjoy the right of possessing personal and real property by the same title and in the same manner as the citizens of the United States. . . . As to the States of the Union, by whose existing laws aliens are not permitted to hold real estate, the President engages to recommend to them the passage of such laws as may be necessary for the purpose of conferring this right.[35]

Though the Swiss Treaty had been adopted in 1850, the case involving the right of a Swiss citizen to recover the estate of a relative dying intestate in Virginia, to sell the same, and to export the proceeds of the sale did not arise until 1879.[36] Justice Swayne, speaking for a unanimous Court, used a vague expression to the effect that "there are doubtless limitations on this power as there are to all others arising under such

---

[34] 14 Peters 540 (1840).

[35] *Treaties and Conventions*, Article VIII, p. 352, and Moore, John Bassett, *A Digest of Federal Law*, 8 vols. (Washington: Government Printing Office, 1906), V, 177.

[36] *Hauenstein* v. *Lynham*, 100 U.S. 483 (1879).

instruments" as the Constitution. He quotes extensively and with general approval from the decision of Justice Chase in *Ware* v. *Hylton.*

At this same time, evidences of the shift in the basic reasoning of the Court were appearing. The chief force behind this shift was Mr. Justice Field. It was, in fact, a double shift, involving both a change in the constitutional basis for protecting the rights of the alien from treaty obligation to the Fourteenth Amendment, and a change in the reason for providing protection at all from enforcement of a treaty obligation to recognition of humanitarian considerations. The Field thesis was that the final clause of Section 1 of the Fourteenth Amendment guaranteed "to all persons *whether native or foreign, high or low,* whilst within the jurisdiction of the United States" essentially the same rights. This humanitarian approach had been presented in the argument of the Slaughter House Cases, but had been curtly rejected by the Court, when it doubted very much "whether any action of a State not directed by way of discrimination against the *Negroes as a class,* or on account of *their* race, will ever be held to come within the purview of this provision."

The change was already under way. Mr. Justice Field, one of the four dissenting justices in the Slaughter House Cases, while on circuit shortly after, undertook to convert his ideas into law. This he did first in the Ah Fong Case, from which the above quotations were taken. Five years later in *Ho Ah Kow* v. *Nunan,*[37] he held void a San Francisco ordinance providing that every person imprisoned in the county jail upon a criminal judgment should immediately have his hair clipped to a uniform length of one inch from the scalp. In this so-called "Queue Case," he more decisively applied the same doctrine, the treaty with China furnishing his argument with merely subordinate support.

Finally, in *Yick Wo* v. *Hopkins,*[38] the Supreme Court itself adopted the same point of view, overturning a municipal ordinance which, though couched in general terms, was intended to and in fact did discriminate against the Chinese. Ostensibly a safety measure under the police power designed to eliminate the fire hazard involved in conducting laundries in frame buildings, exemptions were possible for laundries not conducted by Chinese.

The general effect of this interpretation of the Fourteenth Amendment is obvious, but its specific applicability to the problems of resident aliens is not so obvious. The disabilities involved are not political, nor do they relate to matters, such as the holding of real estate, which are grounded in common law. Even so, a large and valuable class of rights was now established, to be shared by aliens within the jurisdiction of the United States on a basis of equality with citizens, even in the absence

[37] 5 Sawyer 552 (1879).   [38] 118 U.S. 336 (1886).

of treaty provisions assuring their protection. Years of conflict and indecision were yet to come, however, years producing many serious cases involving the property-owning rights of aliens, until the middle of the twentieth century. Most of these cases continued to involve Orientals in the West Coast States.

State Barriers to Foreign Commerce

Under the police power, the States can and often do adopt measures that have a restrictive effect on foreign trade. Sometimes the State regulations are more stringent than the Federal ones, and may be purposely made so under the guise of enforcing Federal law. Health and sanitary regulations may affect plants and animals as well as human beings; it is reported that in the early 1930's, the Northeastern States passed sanitary laws respecting milk and cream that practically excluded Canadian imports. In June, 1937, the Florida legislature provided for an inspection fee to be levied on foreign cement only, a product that was imported chiefly from Belgium; when Belgium protested to the United States, the Governor of Florida vetoed the bill. In 1939, the General Assembly of Ohio imposed discriminatory taxes on all wines imported into the State from foreign countries, but the State Supreme Court declared this act unconstitutional.

Again in 1939, the New York State Assembly passed a bill establishing a more stringent marks-of-origin requirement for goods imported from Germany than that required under Federal law, which prompted Secretary of State Hull to declare that the passage of this bill would be "most unfortunate in view of the efforts being made by the Federal government to restore our foreign commerce by securing the removal of excessive and discriminatory barriers to the sale of American products abroad." [39] Governor Lehman vetoed the legislation, citing Secretary Hull's letter as the principal reason. There are many other illustrations of this general type.

Alabama and South Carolina passed restrictive legislation requiring all stores selling cotton textiles from Japan to display a sign to this effect in a prominent place. Japan protested, since this amounted to a virtual boycott of Japanese textiles in these States. The Department of State took the position that these acts conflicted with the postwar policy of friendliness with Japan, aimed at helping Japan to establish a sound

[39] On these matters, see Bidwell, Percy, *The Invisible Tariff* (New York: Council of Foreign Relations, 1939), p. 229; Palumbo, p. 52; and Rogers, James H., "From States' Rights to State Autarchy," *Harper's Magazine*, November, 1938, pp. 646–650.

economic system, that they might incite leftwing groups in Japan to attack the United States, that they might inspire retaliatory measures in Japan, and that they might impair a very large market for American agricultural products. A compromise was reached in which Japan voluntarily agreed to limit imports to the United States, if no further restrictive action was taken.

The protection of American industry from foreign competition takes many forms. Examples are to be noted in the "Buy American" policy in governmental purchasing and in the constant pressure on the part of States for the protection of domestic industries. The "Buy American" policy, which is re-emphasized from time to time, is one important way in which the States impose restrictions on foreign imports. Very often, this legislation not only restricts State and local purchases to American-made goods, but restricts them to products made within the State as well. Such policies swept the country in 1933; although the trend was temporary, similar legislation has appeared occasionally since then and is believed by some to have left a permanent impression on governmental purchasing policy.

Although the Southern States have traditionally supported free trade, they have been able to be "practical" when their interests were directly affected. In 1961, the Southern Governors moved still further away from their support of free trade when they demanded protection for their domestic industries against foreign imports. Two strongly supported resolutions designed to limit "excessive" imports were up for adoption at the Southern Governors' Conference. One called for "greater protection and assistance for domestic manufacturers and producers imperiled by foreign competition," the other urged the President to curtail textile product imports on national security grounds.[40]

The drive for Philippine independence provides another excellent illustration of the influence of State commercial interests on foreign policy. Americans have always been told, and most of them have been disposed to believe, that the granting of independence to these islands was a generous and magnanimous gesture on the part of the American people, a tangible expression of their belief in freedom and the right of all peoples to self-determination. Although these considerations were involved, the driving force behind the independence movement, which had its inception in the early 1920's, was the American agricultural and commercial interests which adopted this method of eliminating the free importation of competing products from the islands. Thus the most ardent advocates of independence were the cotton seed growers, beet sugar growers, the National Grange, the Farmers' Union, the cordage in-

---

[40] "Governors Ask Limits on Foreign Products," *Washington Star,* September 17, 1961.

dustry, and the National Dairy Association. Their motives were the protection of the American sugar industry, and the desire on the part of California among other States to curtail Filipino immigration into the United States. The act granting independence to the islands was passed by Congress in 1933, vetoed by President Hoover, and promptly passed over his veto.[41]

While all of these incidents arose out of positive action taken by the States themselves, incidents may also arise from the effect upon the States of action taken by a foreign government. It was in this way that a conflict between the State of New York and Germany over insurance companies was touched off in 1885, when Prussia began requiring foreign insurance companies to file exacting statistics if they were to continue to do business in Germany. The German policy was to eliminate foreign companies as a basic step toward consolidation of its domestic companies. The reprisals instigated by New York, Missouri, and a few other States came close to making Germany reverse its policy, and certainly delayed its execution. Following the Bigelow incident, the matter remained unsettled for a number of years, during which time the Senate initiated a study of the limits of the national power over foreign relations.[42]

It may be noted in conclusion that the individual States have considerable jurisdiction over economic matters related to foreign affairs. They can either assist or obstruct national policies in this area. Their trouble-making propensity is such that, in making commercial treaties, both the United States and the second party would do well to bear it in mind as a significant factor. Some foreign nations have been aware of the States' influence and have considered it carefully when negotiating agreements, and the Federal government has on occasion declined to enter into certain treaties because enforcement would fall largely into the hands of various States. On such matters, the States can either act directly or seek to exert influence through Congress, some members of which will, for political reasons, react favorably to this type of local pressure.

Miscarriages in the Administration of Justice

The United States has always espoused high standards in law and the administration of justice, and because our devotion to these standards is widely known, a great deal is expected of America. Consequently, any miscarriage of justice in American courts, any mal-functioning of the courts, is promptly seized upon and heralded throughout the world,

[41] Palumbo, pp. 53–54.   [42] Palumbo, p. 50.

often with detrimental effects upon the prestige and influence of the nation. Such errors mar the "image" of the United States in its relations with other nations. Brief reference to several striking cases will illustrate the point.

In the famous Scottsboro Cases in Alabama in 1932, nine Negroes were indicted and tried for the rape of two white women. All nine were convicted and sentenced to death; an appeal to the Supreme Court was requested, a new trial was ordered, and as a result, only two of the group received the death penalty. Four of them were eventually released, one was sentenced to seventy-five years in prison, one was brutally shot by a guard, and the other trial was adjourned. This miscarriage of justice aroused public opinion around the world, for the Communist Party seized upon the case to show that the United States was not interested in the rights of minorities. As one student has summarized the situation:

> The Communists have not been content to publicize racial injustice to an exclusively American audience; they have carried the message to every corner of the globe through the world propaganda machine of the Kremlin. And the Party has not confined itself to the facts, though they are damaging enough in themselves as anti-American propaganda. . . . This kind of propaganda serves to embarrass the U.S. State Department and compromise its prestige as it seeks to make friends for democracy among foreign racial and ethnic groups.[43]

In connection with another case in Alabama, in which a Negro was sentenced to death for the robbery of $1.95 from a white woman, Secretary of State Dulles sent a letter to Governor Folsom stating that protests were flooding American embassies overseas concerning the sentence. Just as the treatment accorded Orientals on the West Coast alienated China and Japan, racial discrimination in the administration of justice in the South reacts to our disadvantage among the new countries in Asia and Africa. The same detrimental repercussions may result from a case like that of Caryl Chessman, the famous "red light bandit" of California. In this instance, the error was not an actual miscarriage of justice, but an unbelievable and inexcusable bungling in the administration of justice. These were the facts:

On Friday, February 19, 1960, Chessman, a sex fiend and kidnapper who had been condemned to death in the California courts in 1948, had been scheduled to go to the gas chamber in the San Quentin Prison. After a dozen years of dodging his sentence through clever legal maneuvering, he had exhausted all legal remedies and had just lost an eleventh-

[43] Record, Wilson, *The Negro and the Communist Party* (Chapel Hill: University of North Carolina Press, 1951); the case was *Powell* v. *Alabama*, 287 U.S. 45 (1932).

hour appeal. Governor Pat Brown, who had the day before said that he was powerless to act in the case, suddenly granted Chessman a sixty-day reprieve. Specifically, the Governor was prompted to take this action by a telegram from the Department of State, which relayed to him a Uruguayan protest against Chessman's execution. The telegram said that the government of Uruguay "has tonight brought to urgent attention of the State Department grave concern of Council over anticipated hostile demonstrations of student elements and others to Chessman's execution when our President visits Uruguay March 2." In addition, the Governor was literally bombarded with letters and telegrams, not only from Uruguay but from all over the world, all based upon the argument that twelve years in death row was punishment enough for the crimes that Chessman committed, whatever they may have been.

FOREIGN RELATIONS AND THE STATES

Although the Federal Constitution clearly intends that the central government shall have sole responsibility for the conduct of foreign affairs, the States have in practice had a significant impact on many situations involving such relations. Three of these may be briefly considered here: boundary questions, including both land boundaries and the dispute over the tidelands; the responsibility of the States for municipal violations of diplomatic courtesy; and the influence of the actions of individuals and groups within States on the foreign relations of the Nation. Still another type of relationship has evolved from the tremendous growth in Federal-State and interstate compacts and agreements in recent years. Many of the problems with which these agreements deal (urban and metropolitan, public works, water supply, recreational facilities) are no more restrained by international boundaries than they are by State lines, as is clearly evident from experience along the extensive Canadian border where there has been a marked development of cross-border communication. Congress did, in fact, during the postwar years, authorize several agreements between States and Canadian governments, and interlocal cooperation between individual communities along the border is not uncommon.[44]

[44] See Graves, W. Brooke, "State Provision for Federal-State Cooperation," *Annals of the American Academy of Political and Social Science,* September, 1935, pp. 142–148; Zimmermann, Frederick L., and Wendell, Mitchell, "No Positive Barriers," *National Civic Review,* November, 1959, pp. 522–525, 554; and Graves, W. Brooke, ed., *Major Problems in State Constitutional Revision*

Boundary Disputes

Disputes over land boundaries pertinent to the present discussion take one back to the days of the Founding; the tidelands controversy, on the other hand, occurred in the relatively recent past. The first incident involved General Isaac Shelley of Kentucky and the mission of Citizen Genêt in 1793–1794. Since the United States was determined not to become involved in a war against Great Britain, Genêt undertook to exploit the Mississippi River controversy to get the United States into a war with Spain, England's ally against France. General Shelley was to launch an expedition to open the Mississippi for the purpose of forcing the government to take positive steps with Spain aimed at opening the River for navigation. Shelley succeeded, at least to the extent that the United States did negotiate a settlement of the Mississippi problem.

At approximately the same time, the Northeastern Boundary Controversy between Maine and New Brunswick arose over the location of the boundary between the two. The controversy began with the Treaty of 1793, the stipulations of which were unclear. A commission established in 1796 to solve the problem failed to do so. As a matter of fact, a number of border disputes developed; negotiations between the United States and Great Britain collapsed because Maine refused to accept the compromise agreed upon by the two countries. In 1831, under the Treaty of Ghent, the King of the Netherlands, appointed as an impartial arbiter, reached a decision concerning the disputed lands. The United States refused to accept his decision unless it was approved by Maine. Maine refused, however, and the border dispute became so violent that troops were massed on either side of the disputed territory, ready for action. The situation had deteriorated to such an extent that the Senate passed a resolution upholding Maine's contentions, and the House of Representatives authorized $10 million to resist by force of arms any attempt on the part of England to enforce her claims.[45] Obviously, there was still political mileage to be gained from twisting the British lion's tail. A compromise was finally reached in the Webster-Ashburton Treaty, but not until the two nations had almost reached the point of war, due merely to Maine's contention that the United States could not cede land which Maine claimed.

(Chicago: Public Administration Service, 1960), Chapter 16 by Wiltsee, Herbert L., and Wendell, Mitchell. See also Cail, Harold L., "Neighborly Fete: Two Towns on U.S.-Canadian Border to Join in Dual Celebration," *The New York Times*, June 18, 1961.

[45] *Congressional Globe*, 25th Cong., 3rd Sess., VI, 230–232.

The Northeastern Boundary Controversy was only one of several such controversies occurring in the life of the nation; others have involved the Northwest (Oregon), the Southeast (Louisiana), and the Southwest (Texas) boundaries.[46]

A number of years later, in 1837–1838, the *Caroline* Affair occurred. A revolt by the people of lower Canada against the central government evoked much sympathy among the inhabitants of upper New York State and led to the capture by a band of United States citizens of Navy Island in Canadian territory. This island was used as an arsenal by the band, and supplies were ferried across the Niagara River by the ship *Caroline*. The Canadians, resenting this unwarranted interference in their domestic affairs, retaliated by crossing the Niagara at night, burning the ship on the American side, and killing one American. In further retaliation, numerous destructive raids were launched against the Canadians by various "patriotic groups," raids which do not appear to have been at all restrained by the Governors of the States within which the attacks were organized.

Meanwhile, President Van Buren was attempting to enforce the neutrality laws, but with little success. After the *Caroline* Affair, the President issued a proclamation (January 5, 1838) requesting Americans to forbear retaliatory measures. Further complications developed when Alexander McLeod, a Canadian, was arrested by Federal officials for participating in the burning of the *Caroline* and the killing. Great Britain protested, calling the incident a public act of persons in Her Majesty's Service and contending that McLeod could not be held accountable under international law. Secretary of State Forsyth responded that the Federal government was powerless to act because events took place in New York State and were in violation of New York State law. McLeod was held for trial but released on lack of evidence. It is interesting to note that a few years later, in 1842, Congress passed a law providing that henceforth persons in such situations would be tried by Federal courts.[47]

In Chapter IV, some consideration was given to those aspects of the tidelands controversy bearing on internal politics and domestic policy. This discussion must now be supplemented by other aspects of the problem which involve foreign relations and national security. A number of the States made extensive claims to ownership of off-shore lands—claims ranging from one to as many as eighteen nautical miles from shore— which, had they been allowed, would have given other countries an excuse for claiming control over the seas beyond the normally recognized

[46] These controversies are discussed in Mitchell, Nicholas P., *State Interests in American Treaties* (Richmond: Garrett & Massie, Inc., 1936), Chapter 2.

[47] These incidents are discussed at some length in Palumbo, pp. 91–114.

three-mile limit. Attacking these claims, a representative of the State Department wrote:

A change of the traditional position of this Government would be seized upon by other States as justification for broad and extravagant claims over adjacent areas. This is precisely what happened when this Government issued its proclamation of 1945 regarding jurisdiction and control over resources of the continental shelf. It precipitated a chain reaction of claims, going beyond the terms of the U.S. proclamation, including claims to sovereignty extending as much as 200 miles from the shore.[48]

Municipal Violations of Diplomatic Courtesy

Among the factors governing the nature and extent of State participation in foreign relations is the state-based, decentralized character of the American party system. The claim has been made that the States are able to participate in foreign relations as they do, in spite of constitutional doctrine and provisions to the contrary, largely because the highly decentralized party system gives State officials important political power and a large role in the selection and sustenance of national government officials.[49] In some instances, also, the States are drawn into foreign affairs through the action, or failure to act, of their cities. One such instance, involving the German steamship *Bremen*, has already been mentioned. Another also occurring in New York City, took place in January, 1957, at a time when the United States was seeking to support King Saud of Saudi Arabia in connection with the difficult Middle Eastern situation. Both King Saud and Marshal Tito of Yugoslavia were planning visits to this country; as chiefs of state, they were both entitled to the usual diplomatic courtesies.

However, Mayor Robert F. Wagner chose to insult both of them, to the great embarrassment of the Department of State. In a public statement, he characterized King Saud as anti-Jewish, anti-Catholic, and an

---

[48] Tate, Jack B., "Deputy Legal Advisor to the State Department," *The New York Times*, March 6, 1953, quoted by Palumbo, p. 77. For subsequent developments, see *The New York Times*, December 22, 1953, and April 17, 1958. According to S.J. Res. 13, the claims were: Louisiana, nine miles; Alabama, up to eighteen miles; Texas, up to ten and a half miles; Massachusetts, up to ten leagues; California, to three miles; Oregon, to one league. All claims were made under the terms of the Submerged Lands Act. See Shalowitz, Aaron L., "Boundary Problems Raised by the Submerged Lands Act," *Columbia Law Review*, November, 1954, pp. 1021–1048.

[49] Palumbo, p. 32.

advocate of slavery, and Tito as both Communist and anti-Catholic. "Neither," the Mayor asserted, "is the kind of person we want to recognize in New York City." [50] In the emergency situation thus created, the State Department was obliged to dispatch its Chief of Protocol to New York to do the honors when the visiting dignitaries arrived.

Mayor Wagner's hostility to King Saud was based upon the discriminatory policies practiced in Saudi Arabia against American Jews, including the exclusion of Jewish servicemen from Dhahran Air Force Base and from employment at an American oil company situated there. The Government of the United States had acquiesced to Saudi Arabia's request that no Jews be sent to Saudi Arabia on the ground that the American national interest was too vital to be put in jeopardy. The New York State Commission Against Discrimination (SCAD), however, exempted the Arabian American Oil Company (ARAMCO) from the operation of the State's Fair Employment Practices Act. New York, of course, has a very large Jewish population; the Mayor, a popularly elected official, felt impelled to refuse to welcome the King because of the discriminatory practices engaged in by his government. The matter was discussed with the Secretary of State during the King's visit to this country. King Saud refused to modify his position, he said, because of the treatment he had received in New York City, whereupon Mayor Wagner pointed out that the discriminatory practices had been in effect long before the King's visit to this country.

On July 7, 1959, a ruling of the State Supreme Court held that the State Commission must withdraw the ruling which exempted ARAMCO. When the Commission was granted time in which to consult the Department of State, Assistant Secretary of State Macomber stated that the Department was anxious to avoid a ruling that would force ARAMCO to employ Jews.[51] Justice Epstein's opinion, overruling SCAD, was appealed.

Influence of Individual Actions on Foreign Relations

Even the most commonplace actions of individual citizens may occasionally cause repercussions far beyond the borders of the city or State in which they occur. Several such incidents in 1960 and 1961, involving racial discrimination, arose with respect to African diplomats. One, a minister representing one of the new African countries, was refused service at a chain restaurant in Hagerstown, Maryland. Before the incident was settled, the Mayor of the city and the Governor of the State had

[50] *The New York Times*, January 30, 1957, p. 1.
[51] *The New York Times*, April 24 and 25, 1957.

become involved, and the General Assembly of Maryland, under pressure from the Governor and the Federal administration as well, was considering the enactment of antidiscriminatory legislation. The Secretary of State, various members of the State Department, and even the President of the United States became involved, either in the offering of apologies to the minister and his government for a wholly unnecessary and inexcusable affront, or in efforts to make certain that similar incidents would be avoided in the future.

African diplomats found it virtually impossible to obtain suitable housing accommodations in either New York or Washington. In July, 1961, it was reported that thirty of the approximately one hundred African diplomats had been unable to find decent homes for their families and were living in segregated areas some distance from the diplomatic community.[52] In New York, "many African delegates to the United Nations are so outraged over discrimination that they have joined the Russians in demanding that the United Nations headquarters be moved out of the United States." Most Americans would agree that this would be a high price to pay for continuing discriminatory practices which are both offensive to the concept of the dignity of man and contrary to the spirit—if not the letter—of the law of the land.

The housing aspects of the problem can be solved, at least in part. The State Department canvassed 211 better class apartment buildings in Northwest Washington, finding only eight that stated definitely that they would accept African diplomats as tenants. One hundred twenty-eight, accounting for 60 per cent of the rental space, definitely stated that they would not admit the Africans, some because of the racial question, others because they believed that diplomats generally were not desirable tenants. The State Department then called together the prominent real estate men in the city to spell out graphically the pressing problem of finding suitable housing for these diplomats. Thereupon, a number of the apartment house owners and/or managers agreed to change their policy. Important as housing is, it is only one of the racial problems confronting us. Basically, the problem is that of racial discrimination, not only in New York and Washington, but in American life.

The diplomats were finally housed, but incidents like the following still occurred:

An Ambassador's wife, shopping in one of the better stores, is told that she can try on a dress only if she is definitely going to buy it.
A non-white diplomat is turned away by a barber with the remark: "I don't cut your kind of hair."

[52] Pearson, Drew, *Washington Post*, July 4, 1961, p. 23; Lukas, J. Anthony, "Trouble on Route 40," *The Reporter*, October 26, 1961, pp. 41–43.

A secretary in an African embassy picks up the phone and hears a voice say threateningly: "If you don't get out of this neighborhood, we'll get even with you."

African diplomats traveling between the United Nations in New York and their Washington embassies are refused service at gas stations and at coffee counters.

A private secretarial school turns down the daughter of one of the non-white diplomatic families.[53]

Serious or petty, these racial snubs are embarrassing to the dignity of the Africans and embarrassing to the United States as well. They are having a damaging effect upon our foreign relations. "Discrimination has always been immoral and now, as it undermines United States foreign policy, it is a matter of national concern, not of local mores." [54] Angier Biddle Duke, United States Chief of Protocol, explained the consequences of such incidents: "In many cases, the way these diplomats vote in the United Nations is directly affected by their experiences in this country." Chester Bowles expressed the same idea in another way when he said that "racial rebuffs to African diplomats are seriously harming the reputation of the United States abroad." [55] Similarly, Edward R. Murrow is quoted as saying that "the recent racial incidents have damaged America's reputation as a defender of individual rights and have provided America's detractors with the obvious usable material." [56]

WORLD GOVERNMENT AND NEW OBLIGATIONS

In addition to serious problems with international implications in the field of civil rights, the States since World War II have been confronted with a number of new and unusual problems. They were obliged, as a practical matter, to enact legislation to make the securities of the International Bank marketable. New York in 1946 authorized by law the investment of State funds in debentures of this bank, and the Council of State Governments' Committee of State Officials on Suggested State Legislation drafted a model act for the same purpose, submitting it to

[53] White, Jean M., "Help to Envoys No Solution to Race Problems," *Washington Post,* July 9, 1951, p. B2.

[54] Coffin, William Sloane, Jr., quoted in *Life,* June 2, 1961, p. 54.

[55] "Bowles Shows How Snubs to Envoys Harm U.S.," *Washington Post,* September 21, 1961.

[56] "Murrow Reports Bus Test Effects," *The New York Times,* June 25, 1961, p. 1.

the States with recommendations for its adoption in the legislative sessions of 1947.

New York, where the headquarters of the United Nations had been established, was faced with problems even more unusual. After the offer of John D. Rockefeller, Jr. to donate land in New York City as a United Nations site, there still remained the necessity of conferring upon the United Nations by law, limited territorial sovereignty over its head-quarters and diplomatic immunity for its representatives and their employees and staff. The Joint Legislative Committee on Affairs of the United Nations took the position that the Federal government could not, without the consent of New York, cede to any international organization sovereign rights over any territory within the State, and only such sovereign rights should be ceded as were necessary to effectuate the purposes of the United Nations and as were consistent with the moral, political, and economic welfare of the people of the State.[57] The New York Attorney General ruled in 1948 that immunity from arrest and conviction for crimes and traffic infractions within the State must be accorded to members of delegations to the United Nations because they are listed by the Department of State as entitled to diplomatic privileges and immunities in the United States.

Changing Role of the Governors' Conference

Under the heading "The International Dimension," Glenn E. Brooks describes the end of isolationism as a guiding philosophy in the Governors' Conference and as leading toward the emergence of an active leadership role for the Governors in the field of foreign affairs and international relations. Prior to World War II, the Governors eschewed any activity in the field of foreign affairs. They had little to gain politically by acquiescing to national wishes on matters that seemed of little concern to local interests. During the war, however, they were given briefings by top military leaders at their annual conferences. In the postwar years, both the interest and the activity of the Governors in this field have increased. From support of the United Nations Charter, the Marshall Plan, and the North Atlantic Pact (NATO), they have moved into the assessment of world problems. This latter activity began with briefings by the Secretary of State (Marshall in 1951, Acheson in 1953), other top government officials, and leading journalists and news analysts.

More recently, groups of Governors have taken organized tours. (When such trips are taken by legislators, they are characterized as

[57] Legislative Document No. 66 (Albany, 1949).

"junkets.") In 1959, a group of ten Governors made a widely publicized and fully reported trip to Russia, a move which shortly inspired a return visit by a comparable group of Russian officials. In 1960, the Governors turned their attention to Latin America; this time a group of twenty-eight participated in the tour. No one claims that this activity has had anything more than a very modest influence in the determination of foreign policy. Yet the activity is still significant, for it indicates that "the Governors have been willing to break out of the confines of their traditional role to take a part, however minor, in the shaping of international affairs." [58]

The States and Foreign Aid

It is trite but nevertheless true that new thinking and new procedures are necessary to deal effectively with the conditions of the modern world. A recent paper presents a discussion of a possible role for the States in foreign aid.[59] The nation is definitely committed to the idea of assisting underdeveloped countries. So far, the rendering of this assistance has been regarded solely as a national responsibility but the question has been raised as to whether the potential usefulness of State governments and institutions may not have been overlooked. Dale and Fulton point out that "many institutions of our society at the State and local levels are actively involved in the development process both locally and abroad. Research organizations, colleges and universities, private firms, and towns and cities have, in one way or another, been enlisted. The State institutional framework as such, however, has not been tapped as a basis for development assistance overseas, although in many ways it appears to be one of the most logical structures."

In the past, American cities have frequently established cooperative relationships with older European towns of the same name. Dale and Fulton suggest the possibility of extending this approach to the field of foreign aid, with an American State helping an African state, or a city within the American State helping a city within the African state. For example:

> In Africa, there are many new nations. . . . In virtually all of these countries, the problems match those of State governments more closely than they do those of the Federal Government. Thus, we suggest that

[58] Brooks, Chapter 6, p. 126.

[59] Dale, William B., and Fulton, David C., *Do the States Have a Role to Play in Foreign Aid?* (Menlo Park, California: Stanford Research Institute, January, 1961).

logical twin relationships might be formed between the government of an underdeveloped nation and a State government in the United States to provide contact and help on a sustained and continuing basis. . . .

Our problems with the new African nations are well known. We are feared. They find us big, impersonal, and sometimes overpowering. Their attitudes—a matter of vital concern to us in the United States— are frequently uncertain, ambivalent, defiant. But suppose a new African nation, let us say Senegal, for example, could form a special relationship with one State—perhaps Nebraska. And suppose, over a two or three year period, that as a result of aid activities, Senegal's progress became a matter of quite personal concern to the people of the State of Nebraska.

Nebraska could send a mission of experts to Senegal. Its university could undertake a program of cooperation with theirs. Eventually, per- haps, its companies might be interested in Senegal's industrial develop- ment, at least to the point of helping in practical training programs and in corresponding with particular businesses in Senegal to suggest how problems could be approached. The State Development Commission could set up an exchange of ideas and experience on how to attract, encourage and support industry (perhaps learning something in the process). Communities in Nebraska could "adopt" communities in Senegal, and take a special interest in their problems, their people, their progress. This kind of cooperation could extend across the whole spectrum of development needs, involving all kinds of institutions.

The result of all this might well be the development of cordial re- lations between the United States and Senegal. As there were relation- ships between Nebraska and Senegal, the good will might extend to the whole United States. The other side of the coin, of course, as Dale and Fulton point out, might be "a deeper involvement of Nebraska and other States in the overseas development process" which "could contribute to an increased understanding and appreciation at home of the United States aid program, and indeed of foreign policy problems generally."

BIBLIOGRAPHICAL NOTES

Foreign Relations. Most academic and legal writing on American foreign relations has taken the position that the role of the States, if not insignificant, is at least a minor, incidental, or indirect one. The following writers, among others, take this view: Edward S. Corwin, *The President's Control of Foreign Affairs* (Princeton: Princeton University Press, 1917); John M. Mathews, *American Foreign Relations: Conduct and Policies* (New York: The Appleton-Century Company, 1938), Chapter 14; Nicholas P. Mitchell, *State Interests in American Treaties* (Richmond: Garrett & Massie, Inc.,

1936); Elmer Plischke, *Conduct of American Diplomacy* (New York: D. Van Nostrand Co., Inc., 1950); Richard C. Snider and Edgar S. Furniss, *American Foreign Policy* (New York: Rinehart & Company, Inc., 1958); Harold W. Stoke, *Foreign Relations in the Federal State* (Baltimore: Johns Hopkins Press, 1931). See also James M. Hendry, *Treaties and Federal Constitutions* (Washington: Public Affairs Press, 1955) and Quincy Wright, *The Control of American Foreign Relations* (New York: The Macmillan Co., 1922).

Constitutional Aspects. Charles H. Butler, *The Treaty Power of the United States*, 2 vols. (New York: Banks Law Publishing Company, 1902); Edward S. Corwin, *The Constitution and World Organization* (Princeton: Princeton University Press, 1944); Robert T. Devlin, *The Treaty Power Under the Constitution of the United States* (San Francisco: Whitney-Bancroft Company, 1908); Dennis J. Palumbo, *The States and American Foreign Relations* (Chicago: Department of Photoduplication, University of Chicago Library, 1960); John N. Pomeroy, *Introduction to the Constitutional Law of the United States* (New York: Hurd & Houghton, 1870); and Westel W. Willoughby, *Constitutional Law of the United States*, 2 vols. (New York: Baker, Voorhees Company, 1910).

Among the early works in this field, two strongly emphasized the States' rights point of view: Franklin Pierce, *Federal Usurpation* (New York: D. Appleton Company, 1908) and John R. Tucker, *Constitution of the United States: A Critical Discussion of Its Genesis, Development, and Interpretation* (Chicago: Callaghan & Company, 1899). The extreme nationalist position was taken by Edward S. Corwin, *National Supremacy: Treaty Power v. State Power* (New York: Henry Holt & Co., 1913) and George Sutherland, *Constitutional Power and World Affairs* (New York: Columbia University Press, 1919). For comment on Sutherland, see David M. Levitan, "The Foreign Relations Power: An Analysis of Justice Sutherland's Theory," *Yale Law Journal*, April, 1946, pp. 467–497.

CHAPTER XII

National Security:
Increasing State Responsibility

Although the colonies of British North America were planted chiefly by farmers and merchants avid to exploit the riches of the New World, these commercial civilians soon found that they had to be soldiers as well. Not only did they have to fight back the resentful and suspicious aborigines; but also they were from time to time embroiled in small scale colonial wars occasioned by the grander conflicts of Europe. Since the colonists had only a handful of professional soldiers and—in the seventeenth century at least—hardly any garrisons of troops from England, they could not escape military obligations for themselves.

And so very early in the history of each colony, the legislature enacted general draft laws modelled largely on the militia system which they remembered from England. . . . These militia served as the basis of the Revolutionary Army, although once the War was well underway the Congress raised large numbers of troops itself. After the Revolution, however, the United States in 1784 disbanded its entire force . . . ; the military affairs of the nation were for all practical purposes placed entirely in the hands of State governments. . . .

The framers of the Constitution divided up control of the militia in a most unmilitary manner. . . . Believing in the cliché of the eighteenth century, that government consisted of the purse and the sword, all these national legislators preserved a good sword for the States. However absurd from a military point of view, the militia system of the Constitution and the Act of 1792 expresses a coherent theory of federalism; that the functions of government might be thus arbitrarily divided between the Nation and the States.[1]

[1] Riker, William H., *Soldiers of the States: The Role of the National Guard in American Democracy* (Washington: Public Affairs Press, 1957), pp. 11, 20.

Because the role of the States in the national defense has always been recognized as important, its exact limits have at times been a subject of dispute. In every major struggle, when the strength and resources of the nation have been severely taxed, the States have played a significant role. In the late colonial period, it was the colonial legislatures that drafted resolutions of protest against abuses on the part of British authorities. It was the colonial legislatures also that provided for the training and arming of the militia and that levied the taxes that provided a major portion of the financial support for the war for independence—however inadequate that support may have been.

Even before the new nation had been firmly established, however, questions arose regarding the respective roles of States and Nation in the field of national defense. The first such question was presented as early as 1783, when the Nation was confronted with serious difficulty in compelling Great Britain to observe the terms of the Treaty of Paris. Military considerations encouraged the British ministry to withdraw their troops from Charleston, New York, and Savannah, but these considerations did not apply to the various forts in the Northwest which were under the command of a new Governor-General of Canada who had not personally received orders to evacuate them (the orders having been sent to his predecessor), and who steadily refused to surrender to the United States the disputed posts on the Great Lakes until he was ordered to do so. The only way in which evacuation could be secured, therefore, was by the application of military pressure in that part of the country.

General Washington had contemplated detaching a few men from the Continental Army to take charge of these posts, but he was immediately confronted by some very difficult problems. New York objected because the troops were Massachusetts regiments, and some of the particular posts were located within territory then in dispute between New York and Massachusetts. The other posts were in territory claimed by Virginia under her old charter and the expeditions of George Rogers Clark. Furthermore, apprehension was expressed in Congress at the idea of Continental troops taking possession of lands that were within the limits of the several States and which, they felt, should be occupied by State troops. Thus, one observes early signs of friction between State and Nation with respect to the authority for taking steps that were obviously necessary for the enforcement of treaty obligations and the firm establishment of the national boundaries. Under the Articles of Confederation, Congress had no constitutional authority to maintain troops, although the States were under a qualified prohibition not to do so.

In the Constitution, the prohibition was made absolute, the change being approved in the Convention without discussion or opposition on two different occasions. A corollary provision is to be noted in the prohibition against the States' issuing letters of marque and reprisal. Although the States had been free to issue such letters under the Articles, their prohibition in the Constitution is significant, since they were (or soon became) associated with hostilities. Since Congress was given the power to declare war, it was scarcely fitting to leave the States in a position to commit warlike acts and perhaps involve the nation in war. The removal of this danger "serves to underscore the creation of a national sovereignty with exclusive powers over external affairs." [2]

In the War Between the States, the States continued to play a major role. It happened that many of those who served as Governors during this period were men of outstanding ability, men upon whose assistance and support President Lincoln greatly relied. This was true to such an extent that upon one occasion he wrote: "The Governors of the Northern States are the North. What they decide must be carried out." [3]

During two world wars, Presidents Wilson and Roosevelt relied greatly on the cooperation and resources of the States. Cooperation, however, implies mutual action. The central government has long provided financial assistance for the maintenance of the military establishment in times of peace, while in wartime—with rare exceptions—the States have helped the central government solve the manpower problem.

The discussion which follows falls into three main parts. The first part sketches, in broad outline, the historical background in the development of defense policy from earliest times to the present. This is largely the story of the gradual transformation of the State militia from an untrained citizen force into an organized, properly equipped, well trained, and disciplined National Guard, an important component of the national defense establishment. The second part is concerned with the use of troops (both Federal and National Guard) for police

[2] See Murphy, William P., "State Sovereignty and the Drafting of the Constitution," II, *Mississippi Law Journal*, December, 1960, pp. 1–23.
[3] In a letter to N. F. Dixon, June 28, 1862. See also Hesseltine, William B., *Lincoln and the War Governors* (New York: Alfred A. Knopf, Inc., 1948).

duty. The third part, which inevitably involves some of the same considerations as the others, undertakes to show how, conflict by conflict throughout the Nation's history, the States have played a vitally important role in national defense.

MAINTENANCE OF THE ARMED FORCES

The concept of the citizen-soldier has been recognized in this country from the earliest colonial times. It comes as no surprise, then, that the National Guard, with the longest continuous history of any military organization in the country, is actually older than the nation in whose history it has played such a prominent part. The distinction of being the oldest National Guard units in the United States with unbroken lineages is shared by the 101st Engineer Battalion and the 182nd Infantry Regiment, both of the Massachusetts National Guard, which were originally organized on October 7, 1636, when the Central Court at Boston ordered that all eligible men be ranked into militia regiments. Another historic regiment, the 176th Infantry of the Virginia National Guard, descends from the Charles City–Henrico Counties Regiment of militia organized in 1652. Elements of this regiment were reorganized with other county militia in 1754 to form the Virginia Regiment, which in turn was expanded a few years later to form the 1st and 2nd Regiments of Virginia, commanded successively by Colonels George Washington, William Byrd, Patrick Henry, and John Marshall.[4]

Before 1789, questions involving national defense had been left to the States, even including the building and arming of forts. An organized militia was, from the beginning, regarded as essential for the protection of the lives, property, and liberties of the people. In a frontier economy where every able-bodied man was needed for productive labor, there was no professional army; citizens could ill afford to set aside periods of time from their normal activities for military training. The war for independence had, to a large extent, been carried on by the militiamen of the thirteen colonies, and President Washington paid tribute to the indispensable role which the militia had played in the Revolutionary War when, in "Sentiments on a Peace Establishment," he emphasized the obligation of every citizen of a free government to serve, when needed, in its defense and the need for the establishment of "a well-regulated militia" as a basis for the nation's defense.

Following Washington's suggestion, Congress passed the Militia Act of 1792, laying the basis for a national militia and completely disbanding

[4] Young, Gordon R., ed., *Army Almanac*, 2nd ed. (Harrisburg: Stackpole Co., 1959), pp. 117–118.

the small regular army then existing.[5] This system endured for more than 100 years, until the passage of the Dick Act of 1903. Under this legislation, the militia operated under the dual controls existing in a federal system, each State being empowered to enroll every free, able-bodied, male citizen between the ages of eighteen and forty-five years into a State militia which was to be ready to serve in times of State or national emergency. Although the militia was originally organized and supported entirely by the State, both early legislation and early court decisions recognized the necessity for presidential control over it, particularly when the government was faced with an emergency situation.

The first test case arose when a militiaman refused to obey the orders of the President calling him into service. In *Martin* v. *Mott*,[6] the Supreme Court decided that: (1) the case could be tried under the fifth section of the Act of 1795; and (2) the President has full authority to make decisions respecting the need for men in a period of emergency. On the latter point, the Court declared: "The authority to decide whether the exigencies contemplated in the Constitution of the United States, and the act of Congress of 1798, in which the President has the authority to call forth the militia, to execute the laws of the Union, suppress insurrection and repel invasions, have arisen, is exclusively vested in the President, and his decision is exclusive upon all other persons."

Whenever, in the early years of the government, the question of financial support for the national defense was broached to the Members of Congress, the magnitude and the costliness of this undertaking appalled them. The problem of coastal defenses had troubled the Federal authorities for years, and in November, 1804, and again in February, 1807, President Jefferson had placed the whole subject of national defense before Congress, speaking, in the latter message, of land batteries, movable artillery, floating batteries, and gunboats. Probably largely as a result of these efforts, the Federal government began to provide assistance as early as 1808,[7] appropriating $200,000 annually to assist the States in arming and equipping their militia. This was the first grant-in-aid in history, and for that reason is notable in the history of American federalism. The payments were felt to be necessary, particularly in the newer States which, unlike the older ones, had no military tradition and no funds with which to maintain a militia. In fact, it was all they could do

[5] Mahon, John K., *The American Militia: Decade of Decision, 1789–1800* (Gainesville: University of Florida Press, 1962).

[6] 12 Wheaton 19 (1827).

[7] Act of April 23, 1808. 2 Stat. 490–491. Even earlier than this, the central government had recognized its obligation to assist veterans and the families of veterans, in return for their services to their country; see the concluding paragraph of the Land Ordinance of 1785 and the Congressional controversy regarding obligations to veterans under the Articles of Confederation.

to get new State governments organized and to maintain a minimum of the normal governmental services. No attempt was made at this time to impose conditions or to exercise control in return for these modest grants.

Although it is clear from the record that the State militias had always been regarded as an important element in the nation's armed forces, they did not in practice function very well. One student who made a careful survey of the whole problem characterizes the period 1792–1860 as one of degeneration of the militia; he writes:

> The militia of the early Nineteenth Century could hardly be described as an effective military force. After 1814 not even its strongest supporters dared to describe it thus. Indeed the demonstration of its unreliability in the War of 1812 is what led the national government to ignore the militia and to develop a military force wholly under its own control. It seems likely also that it was this war-time failure that led even those State militias that had inherited glory from the Revolution to lose confidence in themselves and to neglect their constitutional duties.[8]

The term "National Guard" was first employed on August 18, 1824, when, as a compliment to the visiting Lafayette, New York applied it to the units of its State militia. At the opening of the Civil War, the State militias were the creations of State law; their officers were appointed under State authority and their services were under the command of the Governor while, at the same time, they constituted a definite part of the national system of defense.[9] The militia system soon proved inadequate; organization had been left primarily to the States, and they had neglected the job. In Lincoln's second call for troops, volunteers rather than militiamen were requested, and they were asked to serve for a term of three years. On July 17, 1862, Congress passed a law authorizing the President to call the militia into Federal service for fixed periods of time (not to exceed nine months) and to "issue rules to cover defects in State laws to provide for enrolling the militia and putting the act into execution." All male citizens between the ages of eighteen and forty-five were included, and the total number needed was to be apportioned among the various States. Three hundred thousand men were called under this "draft" on August 4, 1862. Its defect was that it was "a conscription law without a conscription clause" since the decision as to who was called was left to the States.[10]

Finally, on March 3, 1863, a comprehensive draft law was enacted

[8] Riker, p. 113.

[9] Randall, James G., *Constitutional Problems Under Lincoln*, 2nd ed. (Urbana: University of Illinois Press, 1951), pp. 241–242.

[10] Randall, pp. 245–247.

which was to be administered by the central government. This act did not mention the militia, and the men drafted were to be assigned to the national army. Until long after the Civil War, the States continued to maintain control over their militia, although the process of transforming the militia into the National Guard began at a fairly early date. A revival of the militia began in 1876–1877, when Congress made its first serious attempt to establish some control over it. At that time, the Federal grants established in 1808 were doubled, but it was required that a State, in order to be eligible to participate in the program, must have 100 militiamen for each of its Senators and Representatives in Congress.

Although this requirement was not very strictly enforced, it marked the beginning of the use of modern grant-in-aid techniques in the development of the National Guard. In addition to the manpower requirements for intermittent wars, there was also a constant need for armed forces to protect the lives of the settlers as they pushed farther into the Western country and the lifelines of trade on the frontier. To meet these needs, the central government soon began to develop a small standing army. The need for such a force, and the important service rendered by it, are well illustrated by the experience of Kansas, where for the half-century from 1818 to 1879, the territory that was to become a State was protected by Federal military forces. More than thirty military installations, including forts and posts, were established in an effort to guarantee safe passage and protect settlement.[11]

Although the post-Reconstruction period has been characterized as one of the revival of the militia, the militia system was still operating under very serious handicaps. There was widespread hostility in many quarters toward militia service, resulting in a "constant increase in the number of exemptions, outright evasion of service, passive disobedience, and positive displays of contempt."[12] In addition, the militia acquired a very unsavory reputation as a strike-breaking organization before and after the turn of the century. In an alarming number of instances, troops were called out in strike situations, either by the President (see tables, pages 412–413 or by the Governor of the State concerned.

The building of armories became a significant characteristic of this period of expansion. At first reluctant to provide building funds, the State legislatures grew highly competitive as the Guard became better organized and able to exert real political pressure. Indeed, it has been said that armories became to many State legislatures what rivers and harbors were to Congress—a device for distributing the pork, if not to every district, at least to as many districts as possible. Whenever they

[11] Murphy, Anna M., "Guardians of the Plains," *Kansas Teacher*, March, 1961, pp. 28–33.

[12] Riker, p. 27.

could, says Riker, "the National Guard officials took full advantage of the pork barrel. Thus in the two decades, 1891–1910, New York built armories in forty legislative districts at a cost of nearly $20,000,000." [13]

During much of the nineteenth century, both National and State forces were rather weak. The standing army was very small and engaged for the most part in Indian fighting in the West. During the first 100 years under the present Constitution, the State militias were rarely used for national defense; instead, forces were raised either on a voluntary basis or by conscription, as in the War of 1812, the Mexican War, the Civil War, and the Spanish-American War. By 1896, only three States still retained the word "militia" in their official designations. Financial assistance from the central government was increased in amount, as was the number of purposes for which assistance was available. Armories to house the equipment and training operations of the National Guard were erected with Federal funds in cities throughout the country, to a total of many millions of dollars, and additional funds were provided for uniforms, equipment, and training. Nevertheless, Riker finds that even the revived militia of the late nineteenth and early twentieth century was not particularly efficient.

> The most telling argument . . . that General Wood and Secretaries Stimson and Garrison had against the militia pay bills was that the militia did not live up to the military standards of the Regular Army. The ineffectiveness of the militia in this era is not particularly surprising, however, because it received very little instruction from professional soldiers at a time when warfare was becoming increasingly technical.

On a number of occasions, the Guard has been reorganized and the financial arrangements for its support revised. One such occasion came at the end of the Spanish-American War. Until that time, the regular army had been smaller than the National Guard, and both had been ill equipped and poorly manned. After the distressing experiences of the American Army in Cuba, Secretary of War Elihu Root instituted a general program to reorganize the military establishment. This was accomplished under the provisions of the Dick Act of 1903, one portion of which called for joint support of the National Guard by the Federal government and the States. In order to qualify for their respective shares of the funds provided, each State was required to comply with the provisions of the Act. Each had to maintain a force of 100 men, properly armed, equipped, and disciplined, for each Senator and Representative in Congress. With Federal financial assistance, the Guard was developed

[13] Riker, p. 60. See also annual reports of the Adjutant General of New York and of the State Armory Board, therein cited.

into comparatively well organized and adequately trained regiments, in all important respects conforming—for the first time—to standards established by Congress. The units were divided into two classes, the Organized Militia to be known as the National Guard of each State or Territory, and the Reserve militia which was to be composed of the remainder of the men of eligible age. In 1908, limitations were lifted on the length of time for which the President could activate the National Guard, and Guard service was no longer restricted to duty within the United States.

Although George Washington had stressed the need for a strong reserve force to supplement the regular army, little had been done prior to 1916 to make such a force a reality. The Reserve Officer Training Corps (ROTC) program, first proposed by Allen Partridge in 1819, had been established and functioning in the land-grant colleges since 1862, but had seldom been taken very seriously. The first steps toward the organization and training of a real reserve force, separate from both the regular army and the National Guard, were taken in 1915–1916 under

NATIONAL GUARD INFANTRY DIVISIONS PARTICIPATING IN WORLD WARS I AND II *

Division	Composed of Men From	Division	Composed of Men From
26	Massachusetts	36	Texas
28	Pennsylvania	37	Ohio
29	Virginia and Maryland	38	Indiana
30	North Carolina	39 †	Arkansas and Louisiana
31	Alabama and Mississippi	41	Oregon and Washington
32	Wisconsin	42	New York
33	Illinois	43 ‡	Connecticut and Rhode Island
34	Iowa and Nebraska	45 ‡	Oklahoma
35	Missouri		

* Source: Young, Gordon R., ed., *Army Almanac*, 2nd ed. (Harrisburg: Stackpole Co., 1959), pp. 659–669.

† World War I only.   ‡ World War II only.

the leadership of General Leonard Wood. It became possible, under the provisions of the National Defense Act of June 3, 1916, for him to establish a special training camp at Plattsburgh to turn professional men into reserve officers. Much was heard of the "Plattsburgh plan."

Another important effect of the 1916 legislation was that it brought the National Guard into the armed forces of the nation. Some 380,000 men were brought into Federal service in this way in World War I; two-fifths of the divisions of the Army Expeditionary Force (AEF) were National Guard divisions. These men, many of them having had some previous training on the Mexican border, distinguished themselves at Château-Thierry, St. Mihiel, Meuse-Argonne, and elsewhere. All of these same divisions served again in World War II, from Bataan to Okinawa, as is shown in the table on page 408.

The 1916 Act included another important step toward greater Federal control and a more efficient fighting force. Whereas, at the beginning of World War I, members of the National Guard had individually to signify their willingness to shift from State to Federal control, the new legislation provided that in any period of emergency, the shift for the entire Guard organization would take place automatically. As amended again in 1920, the organized militia was officially re-established as the National Guard and was made to conform with Regular Army standards. Thus the Guard became a component part of the organized peacetime establishment.

Under new legislation adopted in 1933, further effort was made to establish the National Guard as, in fact, a component of the Army. As stated by the Department of Defense, the National Guard of the United States, identical in personnel and organization with the National Guard of the States, "is the designation used to indicate the Guard's Federal mission for the defense and security of the United States." By joint resolution of Congress in 1940, the Guard was ordered into active military service, and induction was completed the following year. In the words of Robert P. Patterson, Secretary of War:

> The National Guard took to the field eighteen infantry divisions— 300,000 men. Those State troops doubled the strength of the Army at once, and their presence in the field gave the country a sense that it had passed the lowest ebb of its weakness. . . . Nine of these divisions crossed the Atlantic to Europe and Africa and nine went to the far reaches of the Pacific. The soldiers of the Guard fought in every action in which the Army participated from Bataan to Okinawa. They made a brilliant record on every fighting front. They proved once more the value of the trained citizen-soldier.

Riker concludes that "although the Guard has retained and assured itself a permanent and unequivocal role in the defense system," it is administratively rather weak; although largely financed by the Federal government, it is, except in periods of emergency, under State control. The Federal agencies which supervise the Guard within the States are the National Guard State Headquarters and Headquarters Detachments. Their task is to assist State authorities in the administration, training, and operation of the Guard as an instrument in the national defense establishment.

Legislation adopted in 1955, recognizing the existing deficiency in

State forces, provided for additional State military forces, but it did nothing toward solving the administrative problem. The weakness is due to a wide variation in quality, and this in turn is due to the fact that control of the Guard is divided among some fifty-one separate administrations. This defect, Riker concludes, is ineradicable so long—and only so long—as the command is divided between the Nation and the States.[14] The dual status of the Guard as a component of the national defense establishment and as a military force under State control has long been an object of Congressional and military concern. The desire for a more centralized and presumably more efficient military establishment, on the one hand, is set off, on the other, against a lurking fear that centralization of military power might open the way for a military dictatorship.

Another area of Federal-State cooperation involves manpower. The one exception was the draft riots which took place in New York City in 1863. Because of traditional hostility to compulsory military service, the nation had always, up to that time, found it possible to meet its manpower needs under a system of voluntary enlistment. When this system failed to provide sufficient personnel during the trying days of the Civil War, and Congress enacted a draft law on March 3, 1863, serious disorder broke out in New York City.

The March 3 legislation, known as the Enrollment Act, imposed liability for military service on virtually all able-bodied males between the ages of twenty and forty-five. After serious disorders on July 14 and 15 (incited by opponents of conscription and by persons sympathetic to the Confederate cause) a temporary suspension of the draft was announced; by July 16, law and order was restored and the operation of the draft was resumed. Estimated fatalities during the three days of violence totaled more than 1,000; more than fifty large buildings were destroyed by fire, and property damage approximated $2 million.

Although draft laws have never been and probably never will be popular, the necessity for them under modern conditions has been so well recognized that no repetition of the draft riots of Civil War days has occurred during the twentieth century. Both citizens and States have in both world wars accepted the draft as fair and equitable and a necessary solution of the problem of military manpower. States have also accepted the burden and responsibility of administering it.

[14] Riker, Chapter 6 on Federalism and the Militia.

USE OF FEDERAL TROOPS FOR POLICE PURPOSES

Americans pride themselves on being a law-abiding, peace-loving people. In general, they are, but when aroused about an issue that seems vitally to affect their interests, they can also be stubborn and determined. Several instances of this type have caused serious trouble. Most such instances have involved difficult questions of Federal-State relations, and on a number of occasions, local resistance has been so intense that the President has felt obliged to call out Federal troops to protect life and property and restore order. The Founding Fathers foresaw this possibility, which Hamilton discussed at some length in Number 29 of *The Federalist Papers*. Due to the long established separation of civil and military affairs in this country, such action has always been taken with extreme reluctance; nevertheless, it has been taken on numerous occasions, as is evident from the table on page 412 and the following discussion.

The widespread tendency in the post-Reconstruction period to use troops for domestic police purposes may be seen in the left-hand column of the table on page 412, and the men were ruthless and hardboiled about their duty. For instance, the Adjutant General of Pennsylvania, speaking before a convention of the National Guard Association of the United States in Philadelphia in 1881, used these words: ". . . there can be no question of the efficiency of the artillery of the National Guard in putting down riots . . . a battery loaded with grape and cannister has a most discouraging effect upon a body of rioters. . . ."

The extent to which the Guard has been used for strike-breaking and the preservation of peace and order has sharply declined in recent years; instead, the Guard has been pressed into a variety of forms of community service, and with this change has come increased prestige for the Guard organization. The character of the Guards' service has altered markedly since World War II, and the frequency of its use has considerably increased. The two columns in the second table on page 413 allow a comparison of the old and new activities of the Guard.

The first use of Federal troops for police purposes was during the Whiskey Rebellion that confronted President Washington before the infant Republic was even five years old. While there were other instances of State objection to Federal policy, such as the South Carolina nullification controversy, few disputes prior to the Civil War actually involved the use of troops, but in the years following the Civil War, there were many. Toward the close of the nineteenth century, the famous Pullman

Strike occurred in Chicago, and in the middle of the twentieth century, the nation was confronted with Little Rock. Every one of these instances involved, if it did not center around, issues in the field of Federal-State relations.

THE PRESIDENT, FEDERAL TROOPS, AND THE STATES:

A CHRONOLOGY OF SIGNIFICANT EVENTS, 1789–1961 *

Date	Incident or Action	President
1792	Act of May 2, providing for organization of militia	Washington
1794	Use of troops to suppress Whiskey Rebellion	Washington
1812	Militia called to serve in War of 1812	Madison
1832–1833	South Carolina nullification controversy	Jackson
1842	Dorr Rebellion in Rhode Island	Tyler
1844–1845	Use of troops to protect Texas from invasion	Tyler-Polk
1861	Troops called to serve in Civil War	Lincoln
1861	Blockage of the Confederacy	Lincoln
1861	Draft of the Militia	Lincoln
1862	Emancipation Proclamation issued	Lincoln
1863–	Reconstruction	Lincoln-Johnson
1866	End of insurrection in Southern States	Johnson
1867	Reconstruction	Johnson
1867	Presidential authority limited by law	Johnson
1877	Railroad strike	Hayes
1894	Pullman strike	Cleveland
1899	Idaho mining strike	McKinley
1902	Pennsylvania coal strike	T. Roosevelt
1907	Nevada mining strike	T. Roosevelt
1914	Colorado coal strike	Wilson
1919	Indiana steel strike	Wilson
1921	West Virginia coal strike	Harding
1941	Martial law in Hawaii	F. D. Roosevelt
1955	Little Rock school integration	Eisenhower

* Based mainly on Schaffter, Dorothy, and Mathews, Dorothy M., *The Powers of the President as Commander-in-Chief of the Army and Navy of the United States,* House Document No. 443, 84th Cong., 2nd Sess. (Washington, 1956).

The Whiskey Rebellion

The so-called Whiskey Rebellion occurred in Western Pennsylvania and surrounding counties in 1791–1794. This conflict between the Fed-

OCCASIONS FOR THE USE OF MILITIA *

1877–1892		*1947–1953*	
Type of Service	*Instances*	*Type of Service*	*Instances*
Labor troubles	33	Floods	115
Guarding jails and assistance		Windstorms	59
in making arrests	24	Search for lost persons	55
Suppression of riots	14	Fires and explosions in cities	24
Preservation of peace and order	12	Forest fires	23
Repression of a mob	11	Transportation of ill or injured	
Prevention of lynchings	9	persons and medical supplies	23
Natural disasters	4	Snowstorms	20
Indian troubles	2	Traffic and crowd control	15
Election riots	2	Aircraft and train wrecks	14
Other	1	Strike duty	8
Total	112	Search for escaped prisoners	
		and prison riot control	6
		Other	25
		Total	387

* House Report No. 754, 52nd Cong., 1st Sess. (Washington, 1892), pp. 16–20, quoted in Riker, p. 52; and Rich, Bennett M., and Burch, P. H., Jr., "The Changing Role of the National Guard," *American Political Science Review*, September, 1956, pp. 702–706.

eral authorities and a State grew out of popular dissatisfaction with the excise regulations applied to liquor, and in the summer of 1794 it culminated in open riot and the destruction of property.[15] Lacking transportation facilities, the Scotch-Irish farmers of the area found it easier to ship their grain to market in the form of whiskey rather than in bulk. The excise tax levied on domestic distilled liquors, therefore, caused great discontent in the settlements beyond the Alleghenies. The State protested against the 1791 excise law, and conventions were held at which strong resolutions of protest were adopted.

Whether any real hardship was inflicted by the excise law may be questioned, but the inquisitorial methods employed in its enforcement were foreign to the peoples' ideas of liberty, especially those of frontiersmen. Groups of rebels held meetings, mobbed Federal officials, tarred and feathered tax collectors, and in general showed a disposition to nullify the enforcement of the law. Although the Federal government, in an effort to appease the discontent, modified the law in 1792, the disorder persisted. Among the earlier acts passed by Congress was one authorizing

[15] See Baldwin, Leland D., *Whiskey Rebels: The Story of a Frontier Uprising* (Pittsburgh: University of Pittsburgh Press, 1939).

the President to call out State militias to repel invasion or suppress insurrection whenever a Federal judge certified that the courts were unable to enforce the law. Such a certificate was issued by the judge of the Federal District Court in Pennsylvania; although Governor Mifflin denied the necessity for Federal action, he did nothing himself to insure the enforcement of the law. President Washington therefore issued a proclamation calling upon all citizens to obey the law, but when the disobedience persisted and even grew worse, he dispatched Federal troops to restore order. The insurgents were ordered to retire to their homes, and 15,000 men from New Jersey, Pennsylvania, Maryland, and Virginia were ordered into the area.

At first, there was some hesitancy in Pennsylvania, but it was only temporary. The troops were easily assembled and marched in good order over the mountains to the western country. They met no opposition in the field. The ringleaders were seized and handed over to the law enforcement officers and the courts for trial. Most of the soldiers then returned to their homes, but a few of them passed the winter in the disturbed area. The promptness with which the resistance was put down won respect for the new government and established a precedent with regard to its power and duty, should similar situations arise in the future. There were, of course, those who objected to the measures employed, who thought that Hamilton had seized upon this opportunity to show the strength of the new government and to demonstrate its capacity to raise many troops in a very short time, whether or not they were actually needed.

Disorder During Reconstruction

During the post-Civil War years, there were many civil disturbances in the Southern States which led the President to send Federal troops into the area, in some cases upon the request of the Governors and in others upon his own initiative. In fact, military government prevailed in this area a large part of the time and was not discontinued until Federal troops were withdrawn in 1877. These numerous disturbances were not surprising, since conditions during the Reconstruction period were inextricably linked with the war itself.

A listing of the more important examples will indicate their general nature. Early in the Reconstruction period, serious riots occurred, particularly in Memphis and Mobile. Federal troops were used on numerous occasions to police the conduct of elections: in Nashville in 1867; in Louisiana in 1866–1876; in Alabama in 1874; in Columbia, South Carolina in 1876; in Florida and Virginia in 1876. Serious trouble with the

Ku Klux Klan arose during 1866–1872 in Tennessee, North Carolina, Georgia, Mississippi, Alabama, and South Carolina. Disturbances of a similar nature, but without Klan leadership, occurred in many other States.

In 1877, there were disorders arising from strikes on railroads in fourteen States. In most cases, their respective Governors made formal requests for Federal aid, which were granted. In some instances, the President broke through the legal requirements, and acted on very informal requests from Governors without waiting for assurance that the legislatures of their States could not be convened, as provided by Federal law. Only in five or six places in Indiana were there cases in which a Federal official was responsible for initiating a call for Federal troops in order to protect Federal property or property in Federal receivership.[16]

The Pullman Strike

Many years later, in May, 1894, a wage dispute developed between the Pullman Palace Car Company and its employees. The American Railway Union, headed by Eugene V. Debs, imposed a boycott on the cars of the company. A strike was called for May 10, and a convention of the Union voted on June 26 to cease handling Pullman cars. On July 2, an injunction was issued restraining Debs and others from interfering with trains carrying mail, and 3,000 deputy marshals were sworn in, in Chicago. Great violence followed, and the marshal asked the Attorney General for troops to move the trains and handle 2,000 rioters.

After conferences with officials in Washington, troops were moved in on July 4, and were soon reinforced by additional troops. On July 5, Governor Altgeld of Illinois sent a sharp protest to President Cleveland, challenging his right to send troops into the State. On July 6, the Mayor of Chicago, who had previously made no request for State militia, asked the Governor for five regiments. They arrived that night. On July 8, the President issued a proclamation warning all rioters to return to their homes and stating that those who resisted the laws of the United States "cannot be regarded otherwise than as public enemies."

On July 13, a few trains were running under armed guard; the strike was broken a few days later, and all Federal troops were out of the city by July 20. On July 10, indictments for conspiracy were returned against Debs and other leaders of the American Railway Union, who were tried, found guilty, and sentenced to jail. Their appeal to the Supreme Court

[16] See Pollitt, Daniel H., "Presidential Use of Troops to Execute the Laws: A Brief History," *North Carolina Law Review*, February, 1958, pp. 117–141.

for a writ of habeas corpus was denied, and the President's power to prevent obstructions to the free and uninterrupted flow of the mails and of interstate commerce was fully and completely upheld.[17]

There has always been a good deal of contention regarding the course followed by President Cleveland in this situation. Governor Altgeld had not requested Federal troops; on the contrary, he protested vigorously when they were sent in. A leading historian, Henry Steele Commager, points out that "there is no convincing evidence that the local and State authorities were not fully competent to handle the situation without outside aid. Cleveland's action broke the strike and earned him contemporary applause, but in perspective it appears unwarranted either by circumstances or by law." [18]

School Desegregation in Little Rock

An outstanding instance arose in connection with the school desegregation crisis in Little Rock. On August 15, 1956, the Federal District Court for the Eastern District of Arkansas approved the Little Rock School Board's high school integration plan. The decree, on appeal, was approved by the Eighth Circuit Court of Appeals on April 25, 1957. The School Board prepared to carry out the plan at the beginning of the fall semester on September 3, but on September 2, Governor Orval E. Faubus of Arkansas called out part of the State's National Guard, giving orders to keep the peace and prevent the entrance of Negro children into Central High School.

A series of Federal court actions resulted in an order that the School Board's integration plan go into effect without further delay and that State authorities cease interference with the attendance of Negro students. Governor Faubus withdrew the National Guard, and Little Rock police took over maintenance of law and order. When nine Negro boys and

---

[17] *United States* v. *Debs et al.*, 64 Fed. 724 (1894); and *In re Debs*, 158 U.S. 564 (1895).

[18] Note in Commager, Henry Steele, *Documents in American History*, 6th ed. (New York: Appleton-Century-Crofts, Inc., 1958), p. 159. Out of a voluminous literature, the following are useful for further information: Browne, Waldo R., *Altgeld of Illinois* (New York: B. W. Huebsch, 1924); Cleveland, Grover, *Presidential Problems* (New York: The Century Company, 1904), Chapter 2 on the government and the Chicago strike; Manning, Thomas G., and Potter, David M., *The Chicago Strike of 1894: Industrial Labor in the Late Nineteenth Century* (New York: Henry Holt & Co., 1960); Nevins, Allan, *Grover Cleveland: A Study in Courage* (New York: Dodd, Mead & Co., 1932); Warne, Colston E., ed., *The Pullman Boycott of 1894: The Problem of Federal Intervention* (Boston: D. C. Heath and Co., 1955).

girls arrived at the school for admittance on September 23, violence broke out, and the Negro children were escorted back to their homes. At this stage, President Eisenhower issued Proclamation No. 3204, commanding "all persons engaged in such obstruction of justice to cease and desist therefrom, and to disperse forthwith."

Order was not restored at Little Rock; so the following day, the President issued Executive Order No. 10730, directing the Secretary of Defense to federalize the Arkansas Army and Air National Guard and to carry out the Federal Court's integration orders, using Guard or Federal troops as deemed necessary. The President cited Chapter 15, Title 10 of the United States Code, sections 332–334, as his specific authority. One thousand airborne troops of the regular Army (members of the 101st Airborne Division) were sent into Little Rock, and about 10,000 Arkansas Guardsmen were called into Federal service.

Governors Collins, Hodges, Clement, and McKeldin, of Florida, North Carolina, Tennessee, and Maryland respectively, after discussing the matter with the President, failed in an attempt to get the Arkansas Governor to reconcile State law enforcement with Federal authority. After a few weeks, the regular Army force had been reduced in size, then removed; a small force of federalized National Guardsmen remained on duty until May 28, 1958, the end of the school year when the first Negro student was graduated.

STATE COOPERATION IN WARTIME

Early Experiences

In colonial days, each colony had been more or less responsible for its own defense. Massachusetts had built and maintained a fort in Boston harbor, and New York had, from time to time, fortified positions leading up to the city. During the Revolution, the new States had protected themselves as best they could, and when attacked, had been defended by the armies of the Congress and the Confederation, together with local levies. There was a good deal of criticism of the conduct of the War, but:

> It is easy, looking back from the present, to criticize American conduct of the Revolution—to emphasize the reliance upon paper currency, the faulty organization of the services of supply, the sufferings of the army, and the bickering in the higher levels of the government and the army. It is particularly easy to call attention to the shortcomings of the Continental Congress—to highlight its administrative failures and its apparent indecision and timidity. And many of these indictments

should be noted, because often the mistakes of the past, when known, will prevent repetition of error in the future. But we should not look so hard for the mistakes that we fail to comprehend the full import of the Revolution itself. After all, the Americans, with the help of foreign nations it is true, did win their independence. A careful analysis of the Revolution leads one to wonder not that the Americans did so badly but that they did so well—which is the kind of conclusion, I believe, reached by historians after studying most human experiences.[19]

The thirteen colonies, or States, had challenged one of the great powers of the world, and they had done it successfully. From the end of the Revolution until 1789, there was no obligation of local defense on the part of the central government. The history of the armed services in this country, from Revolutionary times until the present, has been one of oscillation from one extreme to another. A tremendous build-up in time of emergency has regularly been followed by virtually complete demobilization, usually carried out with precipitant haste. This general policy has been due to a popular fear of the military and to a desire to "get the boys home" as soon as possible. These practices began at the time the nation was born. A distinguished military historian has recently written:

> In 1784, when the forces of the Revolution were disbanded, the Congress retained eighty men in military service, caretakers to watch over supplies. As Indian troubles threatened in the West or domestic insurrection flamed in the East (Shays's Rebellion), the Congress called on the States for militia or attempted to enlist volunteers in a national force. When the new government of the Constitution took over in 1789 it found an "army" of 595 men, commanded by Lieutenant Colonel Josiah Harmar, and a military administration, presided over by "Secretary of War" Henry Knox and consisting of three clerks and a messenger. The contingent expenses of Knox's department reached the staggering total of $176 a year.[20]

After the new nation was established, various attempts were made to direct public attention to the problem of national defense, particularly to securing the safety of the leading seaports. What little had been done had been at the smallest possible expenditure of funds, for coastal fortification was an exceedingly costly undertaking. Jefferson had suggested the possibility of developing a system of mobile fortifications, gunboats, and guns that could be transported from place to place so that they could be protected behind earthworks and natural barriers.

[19] Williams, T. Harry, *Americans at War* (Baton Rouge: Louisiana State University Press, 1960), pp. 10–11.
[20] Williams, pp. 17–18.

The War of 1812

There had been a small but not particularly efficient Regular Army ever since the formation of the Union in 1789, but it was quite inadequate in terms of the immense task now placed upon it at the outbreak of the War of 1812. There was then, as now, a prejudice against a large standing army as a threat to democratic institutions. Congress had, nevertheless, authorized the volunteer enlistment of soldiers, but had refused, or at least failed, to provide the funds necessary for equipping them and molding them into an effective organization. The result was that conditions of life in the Army were not such as to attract men who could make a living doing anything else. The size of the Regular Army varied, being originally fixed at 1,216 men and expanded as necessary. At the end of the century, it numbered 5,400 men according to one source, and 6,744 men according to another.

The War of 1812, it has been said, occupies an unhappy place in history books. Madison inherited "a tangled and unsatisfactory military system," but one which remained substantially unchanged down to 1846. While it was not very clear what lessons might be gleaned from the Revolutionary War experience, it was clear that, whatever they were, they had not been learned. When the war began, the strength of the Army stood at about one-fifth of its authorized level of 35,603 men. The Military Academy at West Point had been established in 1802, but in one decade it had provided few graduates for service in the Army. The State militias were asked to make up the difference and to expand the military establishment, but it proved to be impossible to develop any large and reliable militia force. "In between came the curious and ambiguous troops known as volunteers—some 10,110 of them—who were neither regulars nor militia but something of both," and some 3,049 rangers.[21]

Congress requested 30,000 volunteers and 80,000 men from existing militia units to prosecute the war. Many militiamen responded, to be sure, and continued to serve throughout the war. As a matter of fact, the bulk of the armed forces was furnished by the militia, of whom 458,463 (including duplicates) were called into the field. When Jackson won at New Orleans, for instance, many of his troops were militia soldiers from various State units. The results of the drive for mobilization were highly disappointing. The Regular Army was increased from less than 7,000 men in 1812 to 56,032, but despite bounties and land grants, it was never possible to fill the Regular Army ranks during the war. The great majority of the troops served for periods of less than six months. This mobilization

---

[21] Based mainly on May, Ernest R., ed., *The Ultimate Decision* (New York: George Braziller, Inc., 1960), pp. 35–36.

performance may be contrasted, as Williams points out, with that of the harassed Continental Congress, which succeeded in enlisting 231,000 regulars and employed only 164,000 militia soldiers at the time when the total population of the country was considerably smaller. In addition to all this, the States proved to be anything but cooperative in the war effort.

When war was declared, Secretary of War Dearborn, on orders from the President, called upon the Governors of New York and New England to protect their respective borders. The Governor of Massachusetts replied that no invasion existed which justified calling out the militia, while two successive Governors of Connecticut declined to do anything. New York, likewise, was reluctant to take any effective action. The President's authority to decide when an emergency had arisen was challenged, but in a test case,[22] the Supreme Court fully confirmed the President's powers. Although the Governor of New York was of the same party as the national administration, the rank and file of the New York militia appear to have had little heart in the campaigns of 1812. Indeed, the national administration was greatly hampered in its effort to put forces in the field on the Canadian border by the reluctance of the States most affected to cooperate.

As the war progressed, it made little difference to New York and the New England States what the government in Washington did, for it was sure to be wrong. Whether governmental action related to the floating of a new loan, to enlistment policy, or to anything else, it was always construed as prejudicial to State interests. The Governor of Vermont was an exponent of anti-national spirit; when Vermont militiamen had been marched into New York and placed under the command of an Army officer, the Governor issued a proclamation ordering them to return forthwith, and to hold themselves "in constant readiness to march on the shortest notice" to the defense of the frontiers of Vermont or to join with other citizens in repelling invasion. Be it noted to their credit that the officers of the Vermont regiment refused to obey the Governor's orders, declaring that they were not going to desert their fellow citizens in the defense of New York.

The people of Massachusetts and the New England area were prosperous at this time, compared to those in other parts of the Union, but they were far from contented. The restrictive policies of the central government had injured their trade, and the government did nothing to help except try to employ their militiamen, always expecting the State to pay for them. In addition, they were unhappy because a large part of the taxes collected in New England were used elsewhere. The wealthier the New England area became, the louder were the complaints.

[22] *Martin* v. *Mott*, 12 Wheaton 19 (1827).

The War Between the States

In a long period of suspense that preceded secession and the actual outbreak of hostilities, a number of strange events took place. President Buchanan, though a Northerner, was a Democratic politician of the old school and, by this time, infirm in both mind and body. His cabinet was composed of Southern and Southern-sympathizing Democrats who so conducted affairs as to strengthen the military position of the South and weaken that of the North. For example, there was only one naval vessel on hand when President Lincoln took office. Secretary of War Floyd had permitted work to continue on the forts in Charleston harbor, however, and munitions of various sorts were shipped into the South. Channing reports that orders were given to send certain pieces of heavy ordnance from the Pittsburgh arsenal, ostensibly to unfinished fortifications at the mouth of the Mississippi River, but that this was prevented by the action of local residents who refused to permit the guns to be removed until a countermanding order was received from Washington.[23]

In the field of small arms, Channing reports that the greater part of the muskets possessed by the government in 1858 and 1859 were in Northern arsenals. These consisted of three varieties of guns: (1) old Springfield flintlock muskets which the Bureau of Ordnance was anxious to get rid of; (2) old muskets which had been altered to the percussion type; and (3) newly manufactured Springfield percussion muskets. The Bureau was anxious to dispose of the old weapons, which took up much storage space, and actually sold several thousand of them to Southern State governments, as well as several more thousand altered flintlock muskets. Even so, the Federal arsenals in the Southern States contained rather less than their due share of small arms and ammunition. When the war broke out, however, there were arms and ammunition in the Southern States that had not come from the Federal arsenals, especially in South Carolina and Virginia, where an accumulation of ordnance, both small and heavy, was sufficient to enable the Confederacy to carry on for some time until imported munitions became available to them.

In Illinois, the situation was very bad, but typical. When the President's call came on April 15 for 75,000 men, Illinois' quota amounted to 125 officers and 4,458 men from the militia forces of the State. But Illinois had no "available, efficient armed and organized militia companies in the State," and those companies which did exist were described as "composed of active and enterprising young men, whose occupational meetings for drill were held more for exercise and amusement than from any

[23] Channing, Edward, *History of the United States*, 6 vols. (New York: The Macmillan Co., 1905-1925), VI, 285-286.

sense of duty to the State." In the State arsenal at that time, there were only 362 altered muskets, 105 Harpers Ferry and Deniger's rifles, 133 muskatoons, and 297 horse pistols. Illinois, reports the State Historian, "was not at all prepared for war." [24]

On April 13, 1861, the ominous news spread through the capital that Fort Sumter in Charleston harbor had surrendered. The next morning, Governor Alexander Ramsey of Minnesota, who happened to be in Washington at the time, hurried to the office of Secretary of War Simon Cameron, an old friend and colleague of his from Pennsylvania, to offer 1,000 soldiers for national defense. "Cameron was about to leave for a conference with President Lincoln and said that he would present the offer if Ramsey would write it out. Ramsey did so and Lincoln accepted the tender, the first received by the Government. By telegraph, Ramsey put in motion a chain of events at home that soon had ten companies of the First Regiment of Minnesota Volunteers training at Fort Snelling." Originally organized on a ninety-day basis, the 42,000 volunteers changed to a three-year basis in response to President Lincoln's call, and on May 3 were organized as the senior three-year regiment of the war.[25]

On April 15, 1861, President Lincoln issued a proclamation calling for 75,000 militiamen for three months to put down disturbances in the Southern States that were too serious for the government law officers to suppress. The response was immediate and overwhelming, and regiments from Pennsylvania, Massachusetts, and New York, as well as from Minnesota, soon appeared in Washington. Some had arms, some did not. Through-rail connections between the capital and the Northeast were still non-existent, so in order to reach Washington, Northern soldiers had to pass through hostile demonstrations by Southern sympathizers in Baltimore on April 19. Railroad tracks were torn up near Annapolis; communications were re-opened between these cities and the capital only after Baltimore was occupied by Union troops.[26]

The results of the call in the border States were less encouraging, though the loyalty of these States was essential to the success of the North. Tennessee promptly seceded, while Kentucky's Governor attempted to establish a policy of neutrality—an action which has been characterized as "one of the strange anomalies of the War." A similar effort at neutrality was made in Missouri, although this State finally remained loyal.

[24] Walton, Clyde C., *Illinois and the Civil War* (Springfield: Civil War Centennial Commission of Illinois, 1961), p. 3.

[25] Carley, Kenneth, *Minnesota in the Civil War* (Minneapolis: Ross & Haines, Inc., 1961), pp. 15–16.

[26] Manakee, Harold R., *Maryland in the Civil War* (Baltimore: Maryland Historical Society, 1961).

Southern Ohio, Indiana, and Illinois, then regarded as border territory, were not hostile to slavery but were not large slaveholding States. Although their family ties and commercial relationships were in the South, the great railroad expansion of the 1850's in this area had benefited it greatly and had so modified the attitudes of many of its inhabitants that they remained loyal to the Union. Indiana, Illinois, and Wisconsin all responded to the call for troops, furnishing more than had been requested; normally peace-loving people, a martial spirit was instilled in them by stirring appeals to rally to the colors.

In Illinois, for instance, war mass meetings were held in every village and town to encourage enlistments; funds were raised to contribute to the relief of the families of volunteers; county boards of supervisors and city authorities offered bounties in addition to those held out by the general government. For example, after a succession of increases, Rockford volunteers received a bounty of $400 from the city and county authorities. As a result of all these efforts and enticements, by the fall of 1863 the ten extreme Southern counties had exceeded their quotas by nearly 50 per cent. The State, between April 17, 1861, and April 30, 1865, furnished a total of 256,297 men for periods of service that varied from three months to three years; there were 152 regiments and three companies of infantry, seventeen regiments of cavalry, and two regiments and nine battalions of artillery.[27]

After the first burst of enthusiasm for a fight which nobody yet regarded as really serious, both sides experienced great difficulty in recruiting an army. Almost from the outset, bounties had to be paid to those who volunteered. Southern people blamed their politicians for bringing on a war they did not want to fight, describing the fracas as "a rich man's war and the poor man's fight." The difficulties encountered in securing men for the armies were quite as great in the North, where, except for brief moments, the people were never united for war. As the volunteering spirit declined and the need for men increased, the bounties were increased also, until in 1863, over $1,000 was offered for a recruit in Massachusetts. If conscription had been adopted earlier, it might have been accepted by the people, and might have solved the problem. When it did come in 1863, there was widespread opposition, especially in New York and Boston. Draft riots, it will be recalled, took place in New York City. Efforts were even made to recruit immigrant-soldiers and "mercenaries" abroad, in an attempt to solve the critical manpower problem.

Such controversy as developed during the war between the Federal government and the States centered around policies relating to manpower procurement. The early legislation left many of the details of

[27] *Report of the Civil War Centennial Commission of Illinois* (Springfield, March, 1961), pp. 9–15.

execution to the President and the Governors. Federal regulations set the quotas but left the raising of these quotas to the Governors, either under State law or following a procedure contained in the regulations. In a Wisconsin case, it was argued that under the constitutional division of powers, the legislation, which in effect delegated legislative powers to the President, was unconstitutional. The Supreme Court declined to accept this view: "When the militia were once called forth, it was a matter of no vital importance how they should be detached and drafted. Congress indicated an intention of adopting the State laws on the subject, as far as they were applicable. . . . This practice of giving discretionary power to other departments or agencies . . . had its origin in the adoption of the Constitution, and in the action of the First Congress under it." [28]

Although the 1862 Act did not specifically provide for a draft, such a procedure was instituted in some States by presidential order. Randall summarized the situation very well: "The opponents of conscription usually adopted the States' right, strict constructionist line and made the distinction between the militia and the army." The militia is a state institution and can be used by the Federal government only when in the "actual service of the United States." Opponents argued that it was unconstitutional to draft members of the State militia, while the government claimed that since it could declare war and raise and support armies, it must be permitted to select proper means for carrying these powers into effect. The authority of the United States is, they argued, higher than the authority of the States over the militia. The 1862 legislation was tested in the courts, just as more than half a century later, the draft legislation of World War I was to be tested.[29] It was, of course, upheld.

A great deal of time and effort have been expended in attempts to determine how many men were actually enrolled in both armies. This, it appears, is a well-nigh impossible assignment. In the North, the records were carefully kept and are quite complete, though total figures make no allowance for re-enlistments, bounty jumpers, deserters who re-enlisted, etc. In the South, the muster rolls were so imperfect that the State authorities who later awarded State pensions to Confederate veterans or their widows were obliged, in some cases, to rely on the testimony of the applicant. The figure 600,000 for men in Confederate ranks during the war makes no allowance for men contributed from States that did not secede, for home guards and State troops, or for the considerable amount of labor performed by Negro slaves.[30] Losses due to illness often exceeded battle casualties, but medical records were poorly

[28] Randall, p. 254; see also *In re* Griner, 16 Wis. 447, 458 (1863).
[29] *Selective Draft Law Cases*, 245 U.S. 366 (1918).
[30] These questions are discussed at length in Channing, VI, 430–436.

kept. In the absence of modern methods of sanitation, and of medical, surgical, and nursing care, State and local volunteer groups did what they could to aid and comfort the sick and the injured.

On the Northern side, there was a good deal of State action down to the spring of 1863 (a study of the activities of the Governors reveals the vast importance of the functions which devolved upon them); from that point on, however, a good deal of centralization in the hands of the Federal authorities may be observed. Cooperative experience in previous decades provided a basis for the extensive system of Federal-State cooperation that was largely responsible for saving the Union. President Lincoln, architect of the system, was familiar with such early cooperative efforts in Illinois as the Illinois and Michigan Canal and the Illinois Central Railroad. His policy of cooperation with the States met with some resistance (chiefly verbal), but the area of cooperation was considerably expanded and was generally accepted by the nation.[31] Some of this cooperation may have been due to the temporary increase in what Elazar calls the velocity of government, but much of it was due to presidential leadership and insistence on cooperative relationships.[32]

The situation was quite different in the South, where there developed what has been described as the outstanding example of an attempt to implement "classic" dual federalism. Although a wartime situation necessarily imposes strains on any federal system, the fact that Confederate officials at the State level asserted the doctrines of State sovereignty in their administrative actions, and were abetted in their actions by officials of the general government who went out of their way to avoid charges of interference with States' rights, contributed significantly to the defeat of the Confederacy.[33] If the Confederate government could have mobilized the men and material that were available in the individual States during the early days of the war when their armies were consistently winning battles, the course of the war might have been quite different from what it was.

Instead, each State stood on its constitutional rights, as the South had regularly done in the larger sectional struggles of the Union, and refused to do more than the individual Governors thought necessary. When, for instance, the Confederate government resorted to conscription, in a system in which States' rights was supposed to be supreme, they ran into opposition in two of the strongest States—Georgia and North Carolina. Because of the doctrinaire attitude of the Southern

[31] This story is well documented in Hesseltine, William B., *Lincoln and the War Governors* (New York: Alfred A. Knopf, Inc., 1955).

[32] See Elazar, Daniel J., *The American Partnership* (Chicago: University of Chicago Press, 1962).

[33] Elazar, p. 41.

leaders, no real system of cooperation was developed in the South during the entire course of the war.

World War I

Although the United States boasts that it is a peaceful and peace-loving nation, this country has been in wars, large and small, during a major portion of its national existence. In fact, it has been calculated that the nation has been at war more years than it has been at peace. For present purposes, the significance of this is that one military operation has often served as a training school for the next. The National Guard units that were sent to the Mexican border prior to our entry into World War I received training and acquired experience that qualified them for immediate service overseas. While World War I turned out to be a major war, it also provided training for individuals and experience for the nation in the organization of a war effort that stood the United States in good stead when it later became involved in World War II.

Specific procedures developed in World War I proved to be equally effective a quarter of a century later. There had been serious trouble during the Civil War in the administration of a draft law, but the nation learned during World War I how to administer such a law efficiently. In fact, the Selective Service System was better administered in World War I than in World War II. State councils of defense, the pattern for which was developed in 1917, proved to be quite as useful in 1941.[34] Within three months after our entry into the war, the Council of National Defense was established. Since there were no precedents to serve as a guide, there were numerous irritating delays and uncertainties, both in the organization of the State councils, and in the determination of what functions they could best perform.

Consequently, there was no uniformity in the organizational pattern. Despite the preference of the National Council for statutory authorizations in the States, only half of the State councils had been so constituted by the end of the war. In addition to statutory authorization, twenty-one States resorted to various indirect forms. In some instances, action by the Governor rested on special legislation giving emergency war powers to the Governor, while in others, the action creating the council rested upon the presumption of powers inherent in the executive. Three councils were devoid of any visible legal foundations. In practice,

[34] See Carey, William D., "State Councils for Defense: 1917 and 1941 Models," *State Government:* I, May, 1941, pp. 105–108, 117–120, 123; II, June, 1941, pp. 133–135, 145–146, 151.

the councils developed a closer relationship with the Governor than with the legislative branch. The councils were given broad powers, including the power of investigating any matter relating to the national security, and the making of recommendations to the Governor and the legislature. (The later 1941 models emphasized coordination, facilitation, and promotion of Federal-State-local relationships in the defense area, particularly in the field of civil defense.)

Some idea of the scope of the powers of the State councils may be deduced from the duties assigned to the National Council in the National Defense Act of 1916, which directed the advisory commission to consider such questions as the location of railroads, increase of domestic production, mobilization of resources, development of seagoing transportation, defense requirements (production and availability of military supplies), and the maximum utilization of the nation's resources in the war effort.

World War II

The role of the States in World War II was a very significant one. Immediately after Pearl Harbor, plans were launched for the cooperation of the States with the Federal government in the war effort. The contribution which the States made was great, but in turn, the impact of the war upon the States was also great. Two related but quite separate questions are involved here. What the States did in the war effort and what the war effort did to the States.

Early Moves to Encourage Federal-State Cooperation. Within a week after Pearl Harbor, the Council of State Governments issued a statement on Wartime Fiscal Policies for State and Local Governments, drawn up shortly before in a conference with Federal officials. This conference and the issuance of the statement led to a continuing relationship in the form of the Joint National-State-Local Committee on Fiscal Policies and Practices. This body was recognized by the President, and the Bureau of the Budget contributed two of its members, along with ten or twelve from the States.

In November, 1942, a second policy statement was issued on fiscal policies for State and local governments.[35] At this time, the Board of Managers of the Council of State Governments recommended the development of memoranda for the benefit of State legislative and ad-

---

[35] The text of both these statements appears in the Council's *Wartime and Post-War Problems and Policies of the States,* Report and Recommendations of the Interstate Committee on Postwar Reconstruction and Development (Chicago, May, 1944).

ministrative officials in dealing with the wartime and postwar problems of the States. After this recommendation was approved by the General Assembly of the States in Baltimore in 1943, regional conferences of State officials were held for the purpose of promoting interest in the project and developing an effective organization to administer it.

As a result of these conferences, the Interstate Commission on Postwar Reconstruction and Development was created to work for the accomplishment of three major objectives: (1) to assist the States in putting their fiscal and financial affairs in order; (2) to promote the organization of an effective reconstruction and development agency in each State; and (3) to develop an outline of principles and policies relative to postwar problems. The Commission's report centered largely on the third of these objectives, but included the text of important documents relating to the other two.

A movement to eliminate State impediments to the war effort was initiated at the Federal-State Conference on War Restrictions, called by President Roosevelt and held in Washington, May 5–7, 1942. Following the Conference, a committee was appointed to consider the motor vehicle trade barrier problem; this committee met with the Executive Committee of the Governors' Conference. At this meeting, it was agreed that uniform standards for motor transportation, developed by a number of States in cooperation with the Public Roads Administration and approved by the War Department, were satisfactory standards for the duration of the emergency. By June 1, 1942, all of the States had accepted the program which, unfortunately, included no understanding regarding truck and bus registration taxes.[36]

Vital Services Rendered by the State. The States performed many functions that were highly essential to the successful prosecution of the war effort. Particularly vital were their services with respect to manpower. As in World War I, National Guard organizations were transferred to the Federal Service, constituting a major part of the military forces serving in the various theaters of what became an almost global war. In addition, the States were responsible for the administration of the Selective Service System. Administrative authority was vested in the Governor, who normally delegated it either to the adjutant general or to a state director of selective service. The Governor appointed State and local draft boards and was charged with responsibility for the efficient and equitable administration of the law.

[36] See Treasury Department, Special Committee Designated to Conduct a Study of Intergovernmental Fiscal Relations in the United States, *Federal-State-Local Government Fiscal Relations,* Senate Document No. 69, 78th Cong., 1st Sess. (Washington, 1943).

Whereas in World War I, local draft boards had been governed by explicit instructions as to what they should and should not do under various conditions, they were left in World War II with a considerable area for the exercise of their own discretion. Actually, the only binding instructions they had were their quotas. Experience showed that the World War I system of administration was far preferable to that developed in World War II. Due to inevitable variations among boards and board members, some local boards developed a reputation for being "tough," others for being "easy." This lack of uniformity not only did not make sense, but it resulted in many cases in gross unfairness and injustice to individuals and to families.

On the home front also, the States performed many functions. Since an army lacking proper food, clothing, and equipment is no army at all, cooperation in supplying these necessities was very vital. Since many factors contributed to the scarcity of various necessary items, as compared with normal needs, it was necessary to set up an administered price system as a means of controlling inflation, and to ration among the people the amounts of scarce and/or especially desirable items available for domestic consumption. While the legislation governing these matters, and housing and rent control as well, was Federal legislation, the States rendered important assistance in the administration of these programs. The voluntary cooperation of State gasoline tax officers, for instance, in the administration of the gasoline regulations pertaining to the mileage rationing program, was described as a unique development in Federal-State cooperation. Many of these officials assumed greatly increased burdens in both expense and effort in order to pass on to the public all the information necessary for compliance with rationing regulations. Similar efforts were made in connection with the tire rationing program.

State and local officials performed a tremendous service in the conservation of war transportation. A State administrator was appointed to consult with local officials in the effort to control war traffic by spreading peak loads, by staggering working hours, creating car pools and share-the-ride arrangements, and in many other ways curtailing unnecessary travel to insure that the limited resources available could be used for travel necessary in the interests of the war effort. A survey of Federal war agencies made by the Office of War Information in 1943 revealed that the Federal government was receiving full and wholehearted cooperation in the war effort from State and local governments.

Citizens with no official connection whatsoever likewise performed yeoman service in furthering the war effort, through participation in State and local defense councils somewhat similar to those that functioned during World War I, and through membership in a variety of special organizations and committees which sometimes worked independently, sometimes in cooperation with State and National groups in the effort to find solutions to all manner of problems. Bar associations established facilities through which servicemen and women could obtain free legal advice. Women organized and maintained army leagues, navy leagues, and relief services to aid the stricken peoples of many lands. Civilians carried on the Red Cross Blood Donor Service, Red Cross Canteens, USO entertainment centers and gave assistance in war bond drives, hospital work, preparation of bandages, served as aircraft spotters, and performed many other services. All citizens aided in drives for salvage of metals and papers and for books for service personnel.

Impact of the War Effort Upon the States. Although by any standard of measurement the contribution of the State and local governments to the war effort was tremendous, the impact of the war effort upon them was just as great. Some of the effects were temporary, while others had a more or less permanent impact. Five specific effects may be briefly noted here. First, there was a drastic curtailment of governmental services at the State and local levels, even in the case of essential services. Many services were temporarily discontinued, others were skeletonized. Virtually none were added. These curtailments were not due to a lack of funds, as will presently be clear. Both manpower and materials were scarce, and it was felt that available supplies of either should not be utilized for needs that could be at least temporarily postponed, but for the all-important goal of winning the war.

A second effect was an indefinite postponement of even the discussion of ordinary problems of governmental improvement. The virtual suspension of all effort to improve the structure and functioning of the democratic process in this country was described by one contemporary as "a moratorium on civic progress." Thus, the war effort provided people with a convenient and plausible excuse for not doing things which, in normal times, they would have opposed anyway. Only a few were bold enough to wonder how democracy could be strengthened and extended to remote places if it was permitted to languish and function in a desultory manner here at home. That question was never answered.

A third effect of the war effort on State and local government involved crippling losses in the personnel engaged in the performance of governmental services, for which there were a number of more or less obvious reasons. Many—and in time, virtually all—of the able-bodied men of draft age were inducted into the service. A large portion of those who remained soon left State and local positions to accept jobs at higher pay, either in the Federal Service or in war industry. Serious losses would doubtless have occurred in any event, but the grossly inadequate pay scales characteristic of State and local governments up to that time made critical losses inevitable. Turnover rates exceeding 100 per cent in a year's time were common, especially among institutional and other types of lower grade employees.

Still another effect was the considerably improved financial condition of State and local government, both during the war and for a short time following the termination of hostilities. As part of the overall national program of economic controls, State and local governments maintained existing tax levels, even though they did not at the time have need for all the revenues their taxes would produce. These so-called surplus funds were used to reduce existing debt and to build up reserves for use in meeting postwar needs. Although some of the reserves were committed in most States before the war was over, the States came out of the war in better financial condition than when they entered. The accumulation of postwar needs was so great, however, and the needs so urgent, that the wartime surpluses were soon dissipated.

The fifth effect was the seemingly inevitable shift of power from State to Nation, a trend which was accentuated in many fields during the war. The Federal Employment Service, functioning under the War Manpower Commission, took over in their entirety the placement services formerly operated under State authority (see Chapter XII). Paralleling this move affecting placements in private employment was the move to control public employment at the State and local levels. The Civil Service Commission, also functioning under the War Manpower Commission, was made responsible for the general supervision of matters of government employment at all levels, although this power of supervision was very little used. There was much complaint from State and local officials because so many clerical and stenographic employees resigned to take positions in the Federal Service. Actually, these employees made the change of their own accord, because of the salary differential. The Commission scrupulously refrained from recruiting among the employees of other governmental units.

Of similar centralizing effect was the control exercised over labor disputes. Whereas, in the past, such problems had been controlled by State law and handled by the State departments of labor, virtually all control over them shifted to the Federal government during the decade following the enactment of the National Labor Relations (Wagner) Act. The move started under the National Labor Relations Board in the prewar years and continued with renewed energy during the war. Most of the disputes which arose—no matter how local they appeared to be—involved, or could be reasonably claimed to involve, the war effort.

Under these conditions, local controls, while theoretically continuing, practically ceased to exist.

BIBLIOGRAPHICAL NOTES

General Works (including National Guard). On the powers of the President, and Federal-State relations in the field of national defense, the following titles should be helpful: Clarence A. Berdahl, *War Powers of the Executive in the United States* (Urbana: University of Illinois Press, 1921); Harold B. Davis, *The Adjutant General and the National Guard* (Madison: Wisconsin Legislative Reference Library, October, 1953); Ernest R. May, ed., *The Ultimate Decision: The President as Commander-in-Chief* (New York: George Braziller, Inc., 1960); William H. Riker, *Soldiers of the States: The Role of the National Guard in American Democracy* (Washington: Public Affairs Press, 1957); Dorothy Schaffter and Dorothy M. Mathews, *The Powers of the President as Commander-in-Chief,* House Document No. 443. 84th Cong., 2nd Sess. (Washington, 1956); Headquarters, Department of the Army, *American Military History, 1607–1958* (Washington, 1959); T. Harry Williams, *Americans at War* (Baton Rouge: Louisiana State University Press, 1961); Gordon R. Young, ed., *The Army Almanac,* 2nd ed. (Harrisburg: Stackpole Company, 1956); and William B. Weeden, *War Government, Federal and State* (Boston: Houghton Mifflin Co., 1906). See also the following articles: Edmund J. Beckwith, "Laws Relating to State Military Power," *State Government,* March, 1943, pp. 57–58, 74, and Bennett M. Rich and P. H. Burch, Jr., "The Changing Role of the National Guard," *American Political Science Review,* September, 1956, pp. 702–706.

On American military policy, see Edgar S. Furniss, *American Military Policy* (New York: Rinehart & Company, Inc., 1959); John K. Mahon, *The American Militia: Decade of Decision, 1789–1800* (Gainesville: University of Florida Press, 1962); Francis W. Laurent, *Organization for Military Defense of the United States, 1789–1959* (Madison: National Security Studies Group, University of Wisconsin, 1960); Dale O. Smith, *United States Military Policy: A Study and Appraisal* (New York: Duell, Sloan & Pearce, Inc., 1955); Timothy E. Stanley, *American Defense and National Security* (Washington: Public Affairs Press, 1956); and Emory Upton, *The Military Policy of the United States* (Washington: Government Printing Office, 1911).

The President and Civil Disorders. General works in this field include: Robert S. Rankin, *When Civil Law Fails* (Durham: Duke University Press, 1939); Bennett M. Rich, *The President and Civil Disorders* (Washington: Brookings Institution, 1941); Clinton L. Rossiter, *Constitutional Dictatorship: Crisis Government in the Modern Democracies* (Princeton: Princeton University Press, 1948); and J. Malcolm Smith and Cornelius P. Cotter, *Powers of the President During Crises* (Washington: Public Affairs Press, 1960).

On the use of troops to quell specific disturbances, see Leland D. Baldwin, *Whiskey Rebels: The Story of a Frontier Uprising* (Pittsburgh: University of Pittsburgh Press, 1939); Grover Cleveland, *Presidential Problems* (New York: The Century Company, 1904) containing a chapter on the Pullman strike; Thomas G. Manning and David M. Potter, *The Chicago Strike of 1894: Industrial Labor in the Late Nineteenth Century* (New York: Henry Holt & Co., 1960); Colston E. Warne, ed., *The Pullman Boycott of 1894: The Problem of Federal Intervention* (Boston: D. C. Heath and Co.

1955); and Daniel H. Pollitt, "Presidential Use of Troops to Execute the Laws: A Brief History," *North Carolina Law Review*, February, 1958, pp. 117–141.

Civil-Military Relations. In this area, see Arthur A. Ekirch, Jr., *The Civilian and the Military* (New York: Oxford University Press, 1956); Samuel P. Huntington, *The Soldier and the State: The Theory and Politics of Civil-Military Relations* (Cambridge: Harvard University Press, 1957); and Walter Millis, *Arms and the State: Civil-Military Elements in National Policy* (New York: Twentieth Century Fund, 1958).

Manpower Problems. Manpower problems in wartime, both military and civilian, have always been difficult and troublesome: see Robert P. Brooks, *Conscription in the Confederate States of America, 1862–1865* (Athens: University of Georgia Bulletin, 1917); Walter Millis, *Arms and Men: A Study in American Military History* (New York: G. P. Putnam's Sons, 1956); Michigan Unemployment Compensation Commission, *Mobilizing Michigan Manpower for Defense* (Detroit, 1941); Albert B. Moore, *Conscription and Conflict in the Confederacy* (New York: The Macmillan Co., 1924); Fred A. Shannon, *The Organization and Administration of the Union Army, 1861–1865*, 2 vols. (Cleveland: Clark Publishing Co., 1928); Mulford Q. Sibley and Philip E. Jacob, *Conscription and Conscience: The American State and the Conscientious Objector, 1940–1947* (Ithaca: Cornell University Press, 1952); U.S. Department of Labor, *Impact of the War on Employment in 181 Centers of War Activity* (Washington, Bulletin No. 826, 1945); U.S. War Manpower Commission, *Personnel Survey of the U.S. Employment Service: Three Wartime Years Under the U.S. Civil Service Commission* (Washington, 1945).

Civil War. William B. Hesseltine, *Lincoln and the War Governors* (New York: Alfred A. Knopf, Inc., 1948); James G. Randall, *Constitutional Problems Under Lincoln*, rev. ed. (Urbana: University of Illinois Press, 1951). The following titles deal with the war effort in specific States: Kenneth Carley, *Minnesota and the Civil War* (Minneapolis: Ross & Haines, Inc., 1961); Harold R. Manakee, *Maryland in the Civil War* (Baltimore: Maryland Historical Society, 1961); and Clyde C. Walton, *Illinois and the Civil War* (Springfield: Civil War Centennial Commission, 1961).

World War II. Out of a voluminous literature, the following titles are especially helpful: Eric H. Biddle, *Mobilization of the Home Front* (Chicago: Public Administration Service, 1942); Bureau of Public Administration, University of California, *State Councils of Defense*, rev. ed. (Berkeley, December, 1942); Council for Democracy, *Defense on Main Street* (New York, 1941); Council of State Governments, *Wartime and Postwar Problems and Policies of the States* (Chicago, May, 1944); Hallie Farmer, ed., *War Comes to Alabama* (University, Ala.: Bureau of Public Administration, University of Alabama, 1943); W. Brooke Graves, *American State Government*, 3rd ed. (Boston: D. C. Heath and Co., 1946), Chapter 24; L. Vaughan Howard and Hugh A. Bone, *Current American Government: Wartime Developments* (New York: The Appleton-Century Co., 1943); Illinois State Planning Commission, *U.S. War Department Activities in Illinois* (Chicago, 1939); Roscoe C. Martin, ed., *National Defense and State Finance* (University, Ala.: Bureau of Public Administration, University of Alabama, 1941); New England Council, *New England and National Defense: The First Year* (Boston, 1941); New York State Department of Commerce, *Handbook of War Agencies* (Albany, 1942); New York State War Council, *New York State War Emergency Act and Other War Emergency Laws, 1941, 1942, 1943* (Albany, 1943); A. Arthur Schiller, *Military Law and Defense Legislation* (St. Paul: West Publishing Company, 1941); S. K. Stevens *et. al.*, *Pennsylvania's First Year at War, 1941–1942*, and *Pennsylvania's Second Year at War, 1942–1943* (Harrisburg, 1944 and 1945 respectively); Earl Stratham, ed., *South Dakota's Contribution to National Defense* (Vermillion: Bureau of Governmental Research, University of South Dakota, 1941); Tax Institute, *Wartime Problems of State and Local Finance* (New York, 1943); and U.S. Department of Commerce, *Federal-State Conferences on War Restrictions* (Washington, 1942). See also the following articles: William H. Draper, "The Role of the States in Registration Under the Selective Service Law," *State Government*, October, 1940, pp. 203, 206; Daniel W. Hoan, "States and Cities in the Defense Program," *National Municipal Review*, March, 1941, pp. 141–146, 159; Herbert H. Lehman, "The States and the Present Emergency," *State Government*, March, 1941, pp. 55–57, 71; Harold E. Stassen, "Duties of the States in National Defense," *State Government*, March, 1941, pp. 53–54, 72, and "State Participation in the War Effort," *State Government*, June, 1942, pp. 3–5, 24.

PART IV

Since no activity, either public or private, can function for long without financial support, it is essential that some consideration be given to the fiscal aspects of intergovernmental relations. The first of four chapters on this subject is concerned with taxation, covering conflict, overlapping, and duplication, on the one hand, and coordination and cooperation on the other, as well as the rise and decline of intergovernmental immunities.

Three chapters are devoted to the origin and development of the grants-in-aid system—its beginnings in the late eighteenth century, its expansion during the nineteenth century, and its gradual transformation during the twentieth into the familiar forms now existing. The use of substantial cash grants on a continuing basis became possible in the World War I era, when the adoption of the Sixteenth (Income Tax) Amendment provided the Federal government with an assured and expanding source of income. Other periods of development and growth were the Roosevelt era, when experiences of the Great Depression inspired and fostered many new grant programs, some temporary, others on a permanent basis, and more recently, the period of postwar adjustment which followed World War II.

CHAPTER XIII

Tax Conflicts and the Balance of Power

American public finance has generally been more concerned with the *economics of taxation* than with the *government of a tax system*. . . . The primary difficulty about administering—let alone planning—American public revenues is the fact that the American tax dollar is split three ways, among the Federal Government, fifty States, and 91,236 local governments. No single level of government may be called the controlling revenue authority of the country. . . . Because of our comparatively decentralized system of government, tax planning, even if it should prove desirable, is going to be difficult on a national scale.

Many in the United States resent the continued increase of the Federal Government's slice of the tax dollar at the expense of the States and the local authorities, but strangely enough, Americans still look to Uncle Sam for the solution of their tax problems just as they depend on him for their general fiscal salvation and for economic recovery. This is the paradox of American public administration. In ordinary times, we resist centralization of government; but when we are in a pinch, we look to the Federal Government for the solution of our ills. At the same time, we are grudging about giving it powers, particularly over the public purse, commensurate with the demands we make upon it; and when things change for either the better or the worse, we are inclined to upset the newer centralizing trends by sudden shifts in governmental powers and fiscal policies.[1]

[1] Lepawsky, Albert, "America's Tax Dollar: A Key Problem in Governmental Reconstruction," *Annals of the American Academy of Political and Social Science,* January, 1940, pp. 185–193, on pp. 185–186.

THE POWER TO TAX

When the Constitution states (Article I, Section 8) that "The Congress shall have power to lay and collect taxes, duties, imposts, and excises," it confers a power that appears to be virtually unlimited, but there are a few limitations, some imposed by other provisions of the Constitution itself, others by interpretation. Property may not be confiscated under the guise of taxation. A "taking" of property is accomplished under the power of eminent domain, for which "just compensation" must be paid, not under the power of taxation. If the power to tax is, theoretically, the power to destroy (as Chief Justice Marshall suggested that it might be), the courts are not likely to sanction taxation which is so oppressive as to destroy the benefits associated with the ownership of property.

Such restrictions as the Constitution itself contains are found in Article I, Section 9. While the provision that "No capitation, or other direct, tax shall be laid, unless in proportion to the census or enumeration herein before directed to be taken" was originally interpreted to make a progressive tax law invalid, this interpretation was reversed when the Sixteenth (Income Tax) Amendment was adopted. The other limitation, that "No tax or duty shall be laid on articles exported from any State," still stands. If there are few limitations in the Constitution on the taxing powers of the Federal government, those applicable to the State governments are more numerous and far more restrictive. In Article I, Section 10, it is provided that:

> No State shall, without the consent of the Congress, lay any imposts or duties on imports or exports, except what may be absolutely necessary for executing its inspection laws; and the net produce of all duties and imposts, laid by any State on imports or exports, shall be for the use of the treasury of the United States; and all such laws shall be subject to the revision and control of the Congress.
>
> No State shall, without the consent of Congress, lay any duty of tonnage. . . .

Some of the many other restrictions are explicit, such as no State shall pass any "law impairing the obligation of contracts" (Article I, Section 9), and others must be interpreted, such as the prohibition (Article IV, Section 2) on discrimination against nonresidents or that implied from the commerce clause (Article I, Section 8) that no State tax shall burden interstate commerce. Congress could be repressive in its attitude toward State powers of taxation, but in fact, its attitude has been one of genuine liberality. This, it has been observed, "is a matter of policy and not of Constitutional law, but it is of great practical importance to the States."

Some Borderline Cases

Over the years, there have been many questions as to what Congress may tax and for what purposes. Many of these questions involve what has been called the regulatory use of the tax power—instances in which Congress has, by taxation or in other ways, sought to establish a national policy over a matter falling within the jurisdiction of the States. These matters have normally been of national concern, at least temporarily, matters with respect to which a uniform rule was deemed to be desirable if not necessary. Invariably, controversy arose either because the States had previously adopted contrary or conflicting policies with respect to these matters or because they had failed to act at all. Certainly they had failed to use the devices at their disposal for establishing and administering a uniform policy. In an effort to protect what was believed to be the national interest, Congress has intervened.

In almost all of these instances, each approaching "the fair limits of constitutionality," the Supreme Court has scrupulously sought to abstain from restricting Congressional choice of policies. Cases in point have involved oleomargarine, child labor (discussed in Chapter X), narcotics, firearms, and the tax on wagering. The decisions in all of these areas seem to permit what otherwise is excluded from Congressional authority to be brought within that authority by casting the legislation in a form that offers an easy way for the legislative imagination to control "any one of the great number of subjects of public interest, jurisdiction of which the States have never parted with. . . ." [2]

Oleomargarine. The manufacture, distribution, and sale of oleomargarine was for many years a subject of intense controversy, for the farmers feared its effect in competition with butter. Being well organized and legislatively powerful, they sought to restrict its sale and use in a number of different ways, one of which was the use of the tax power. The original oleomargarine tax act was passed in 1886 and amended in 1902; the following paragraph is from the Preamble to the 1902 act:

An act to make oleomargarine and other imitation dairy products subject to the laws of any State or Territory or the District of Columbia

[2] *Bailey* v. *Drexel Furniture Company,* 259 U.S. 20 (1921), p. 38.

into which they are transported, and to change the tax on oleomargarine, and to impose a tax, provide for the inspection and regulate the manufacture and sale of certain dairy products.[3]

When their constitutionality was challenged in *McCray* v. *United States*,[4] the Supreme Court declared that "the motive or purpose of Congress in adopting the acts in question may not be inquired into," and that "it was within the authority conferred on Congress to select the objects upon which an excise should be laid." Moreover, "the judiciary is without authority to void an act of Congress which exerts the taxing power, even when it seems to the judicial mind that Congress has, in putting such power in motion, abused its lawful authority by levying a tax which is unwise, oppressive, or the result of the enforcement of which might be to affect indirectly subjects not within the powers delegated to Congress."

Narcotic Drugs. It is generally agreed in this country that the medicinal use of narcotic drugs is the only legitimate use, and that their manufacture, distribution, and sale should be restricted to that purpose alone. Since there is no specific grant of power in the Constitution which enables Congress to control this field, Federal authorities found it difficult to establish control. The Harrison Narcotics Act of 1914[5] requires registration and payment of a special tax by all who deal in opium derivatives. It makes the sale of such drugs unlawful, except to persons having orders on forms issued by the Commissioner of Internal Revenue. The regulatory effect of these provisions upon the peddling of narcotics is obvious.

Nevertheless, the Supreme Court in *United States* v. *Doremus*[6] declared that while Congress may not exert authority which is wholly reserved to the States, the power conferred on Congress by the Constitution to levy excise taxes, uniform throughout the United States, is to be exercised at the discretion of that body. The fact that other motives than the raising of revenue may provoke the exercise of the taxing power does not authorize the courts to inquire into that subject. "If the legislation enacted has some reasonable relation to the exercise of the taxing authority conferred by the Constitution, it cannot be invalidated because of the supposed motives which induced it . . . [nor] because its effect may be to accomplish another purpose as well as the raising of revenue."

This legislation was supplemented in 1937 by the passage of the

[3] 24 Stat. 209 (1886); 32 Stat. 193 (1902).

[4] 195 U.S. 27 (1904), pp. 59, 61, 62–63.

[5] 38 Stat. 785 (1914); later provisions are found in the Jones-Miller Act, 42 Stat. 596 (1922) and the Marihuana Tax Act, 50 Stat. 551 (1937).

[6] 249 U.S. 86 (1918), p. 93.

Marihuana Tax Act. When the validity of this legislation was attacked in 1950, the Supreme Court commented on its regulatory effect but, nevertheless, sustained it:

> It is obvious that Sec. 2590, by imposing a severe burden on transfers to unregistered persons, implements this congressional purpose of restricting traffic in marihuana to accepted industrial and medicinal channels. Hence the attack here rests on the regulatory character and prohibitive burden of the section as well as the penal nature of the imposition. But despite the regulatory effect and the close resemblance to a penalty, it does not follow that the levy is invalid.
>
> *First.* It is beyond question that a tax does not cease to be valid merely because it regulates, discourages, or even definitely deters the activities taxed.* The principle applies even though the revenue obtained is obviously negligible, or the revenue purpose of the tax may be secondary.† Nor does a tax statute necessarily fail because it touches on activities which Congress might not otherwise regulate.‡
>
> These principles are controlling here. The tax in question is a legitimate exercise of the taxing power despite its collateral regulatory purpose and effect.[7]
>
> * *Sonsinsky* v. *United States*, 300 U.S. 506 (1937), pp. 513–514.
>
> † *Hampton & Company* v. *United States*, 276 U.S. 394 (1928).
>
> ‡ As was pointed out in *Manano Company* v. *Hamilton*, 292 U.S. 40 (1934), p. 47, "From the beginning of our government, the courts have sustained taxes although imposed with the collateral intent of effecting ulterior ends which, considered apart, were beyond the constitutional power of the lawmakers to realize by legislation directly addressed to their accomplishment."

Control of Firearms. The National Firearms Act of 1934,[8] one of the enactments in the crime field which followed the Lindbergh kidnapping, required every dealer in firearms, as defined in the Act, to register and pay an annual occupation tax of $200 and an additional tax of $200 on each transfer of any firearm. The definition of "firearms" clearly shows the act to have been aimed at "sawed-off" shotguns, machine guns, and silencers. In sustaining the Sonzinsky Case, previously cited, the Supreme Court said:

> On its face it is only a taxing measure, and we are asked to say that the tax, by virtue of its deterrent effect on the activities taxed, operates as a regulation which is beyond the congressional power.
>
> Every tax is in some measure regulatory. To some extent it interposes an economic impediment to the activity taxed. But a tax is not any

[7] *United States* v. *Sanchez et al.*, 340 U.S. 42 (1950), pp. 44–45.
[8] 48 Stat. 1236 (1934).

the less a tax because it has a regulatory effect. . . . Inquiry into the hidden motives which may move Congress to exercise a power constitutionally conferred upon it is beyond the competency of courts. . . .

Here the annual tax of $200 is productive of some revenue. We are not free to speculate as to the motives which moved Congress to impose it, or as to the extent to which it may operate to restrict the activities taxed. As it is not attended by an offensive regulation, and since it operates as a tax, it is within the national taxing power.[9]

Wagering. The Revenue Act of 1951 [10] levied a tax on all persons engaged in the business of accepting wagers, and required such persons to register with the Collector of Internal Revenue. The information was made available to the public which could, of course, include State law enforcement officers. Although the Act obviously had a regulatory motive, the Supreme Court upheld it.[11]

Taxing for the General Welfare

The general welfare clause of the Constitution is so broad as not to be susceptible to clear and precise definition. It provides the basis for what Professor Corwin has called "the spending power," but if money is to be spent, it must first be raised by taxes or other means. The Supreme Court has taken the position that the power of the Federal government to spend for the general welfare is broad enough to allow, for instance, spending to alleviate the distress of the unemployed and the aged, since these problems are "plainly national in area and dimensions." The decision as to what is for the general welfare is largely one for Congress, not the courts, to make:

> The discretion, however, is not confided to the courts. The discretion belongs to Congress, unless the choice is clearly wrong, a display of arbitrary power, not an exercise of judgment. This is now familiar law. "When such a contention comes here we naturally require a showing that by no reasonable possibility can the challenged legislation fall within the wide range of discretion permitted to Congress." [Cases omitted] Nor is the concept of the general welfare static. Needs that were narrow or parochial a century ago may be interwoven in our day with the well-being of the Nation. What is critical or urgent changes with the times.[12]

[9] *Alston* v. *United States*, 274 U.S. 289 (1926), p. 294.
[10] 65 Stat. 529 (1951).
[11] *United States* v. *Kahriger*, 345 U.S. 23 (1952).
[12] *Helvering* v. *Davis*, 301 U.S. 619 (1937), pp. 641–642.

Both the unemployment compensation features of the Social Security Act of 1935 [13] and the old age benefits provision were challenged, the former in *Steward Machine Company* v. *Davis*,[14] the latter in the *Helvering* v. *Davis* decision. Both were sustained; in the Steward Case, the Court upheld both the tax imposed on employers to provide unemployment benefits and the credit allowed for similar taxes paid to a State. To the argument that the tax and credit in combination were weapons of coercion, destroying or impairing the autonomy of the States, the Court replied that relief of unemployment was a legitimate object of Federal expenditure under the general welfare clause; that the Social Security Act represented a legitimate attempt to solve the problem by the cooperation of State and Federal governments; and that the credit allowed for State taxes bore a reasonable relation "to the fiscal need subserved by the tax in its normal operation," since State unemployment compensation payments would relieve the burden for direct relief borne by the national treasury.

Enforcement Problems

The tax collector has never been popular anywhere, at any time in history. To this general statement, the United States is no exception. Although most citizens normally comply with the requirements of the tax laws—even if somewhat grudgingly—there have been a few instances of open revolt. One such was the Whiskey Rebellion in western Pennsylvania in 1791–1794, during President Washington's first term, when, as discussed in Chapter XIII, it was deemed necessary to use Federal troops to enforce the law and to restore order. Some years later, the South Carolina Nullification controversy, discussed in Chapter IV, presented a new problem, one not present either in the Whiskey Rebellion or in the Fries Incident, which also took place in Pennsylvania five years later. Whereas the Pennsylvania incidents both involved scattered citizen resistance to Federal authority, the South Carolina controversy involved the formal resistance of a State government and its duly elected officers. Whereas troops were requested in the previous incidents, they were ordered directly by the President over the strongest possible objection of the South Carolina authorities.

Enforcement problems may arise, however, in the normal course of affairs when no question of resistance is involved. There are questions of jurisdiction between States and between the different levels of government, of the applicability of particular tax laws in specific situations, of

---

[13] 49 Stat. 620 (1935).   [14] 301 U.S. 548 (1937).

methods and procedures of tax collection, and many others. Of particular concern to the student of intergovernmental relations are the numerous instances of multiple taxation and the overlapping and duplication of tax laws and tax collecting machinery. The results are sometimes fantastic as well as very unjust in their application to individual taxpayers.

For example, suppose a man domiciled in Connecticut holds stock in an Illinois corporation. The stock had been placed, for safekeeping, in a safe deposit box in a New York bank. While visiting a relative in Ohio, he is stricken with what proves to be a fatal illness. When his estate is settled, half a dozen States claim the right to tax his stock, each for different but quite legitimate reasons: Connecticut, because he was a citizen of that State; Illinois, because the stock was that of an Illinois corporation; New York, because the stock was property within the borders of the State; and Ohio, because one of the heirs was the relative he was visiting at the time of his death. Other heirs lived in Minnesota and Louisiana, both of whom received their share; if there had been additional heirs in still other States, they too would have claimed a taxable share. While the claims of the individual States were legitimate, their cumulative effect results in an obviously excessive tax burden to one individual or group of individuals. It is to prevent such excesses that cooperative arrangements in both tax legislation and enforcement procedures have become necessary.

THE RISE AND FALL OF INTERGOVERNMENTAL IMMUNITIES

The Immunities Doctrine: Its Origin and Growth

The constitutional doctrine of intergovernmental immunity had its origin in the famous *McCulloch* v. *Maryland* case,[15] although it had been clearly written into Article IV of the Northwest Ordinance that no State should impose a tax on lands which are United States property. Chief Justice Marshall declared in the McCulloch decision that a State could not tax a national bank which was chartered by Congress. The States have no power, he said,

> by taxation or otherwise, to retard, impede, burden or in any manner control the operations of the constitutional laws enacted by Congress to carry into execution the powers vested in the general government. This is, we think, the unavoidable consequence of that supremacy

[15] 4 Wheaton 315 (1819).

which the Constitution has declared. The framers of our Constitution foresaw this state of things and provided for it, by declaring the supremacy not only of itself, but of the laws made in pursuance of it. The nullity of any act, inconsistent with the Constitution, is produced by the declaration that the Constitution is the supreme law. The appropriate application of that part of the clause which confers the same supremacy on laws and treaties, is to such acts of the State Legislatures as do not transcend their powers, but, though enacted in the execution of acknowledged State powers, interfere with, or are contrary to the laws of Congress, made in pursuance of the Constitution, or some treaty made under the authority of the United States. In every such case, the act of Congress, or the treaty, is supreme; and the law of the State, though enacted in the exercise of powers not controverted, must yield to it.

Under this doctrine, Federal powers and instrumentalities were protected from State interference or impairment for the next hundred years. As a matter of fact, the interpretation of this doctrine was extended so that it worked both ways, and for many years it was the prevailing rule of law that neither the Federal government nor the States could tax the officers, agencies, or instrumentalities of the other.

The first significant extension of the doctrine of immunity of Federal instrumentalities from State taxation came in *Weston* v. *Charleston*,[16] in which Chief Justice Marshall found in the supremacy clause a bar to State taxation of the obligation of the United States. The question of the right of States to tax Federal contractors made an early appearance and has been a subject of controversy ever since. In his opinion in *Osborn* v. *Bank of the United States,* the Chief Justice asked, "Can a contractor for supplying a military post with provisions be restrained from making purchases within any State, or from transporting the provisions to the place at which the troops were stationed, or could he be fined or taxed for doing so? We have not yet heard these questions answered in the affirmative." [17] One hundred thirteen years later, however, the Court did answer the last part of his inquiry in the affirmative.[18]

The immunity doctrine did not reach immediate maturity; in fact, it was a century in the making. Although property owned by the United States was wholly immune from State (and local) taxation, as property owned by a State is immune from Federal taxation and property owned by local units is immune from both Federal and State taxation, it was conceded from the beginning that property owned by a federally char-

---

[16] 2 Peters 449 (1829). [17] 9 Wheaton 738 (1824).
[18] See the numerous cases dealing with the subject beginning in 1931 and culminating in *Alabama* v. *King & Boozer,* 314 U.S. 1 (1941), which overruled earlier cases.

tered corporation engaged in private business was subject to State and local ad valorem taxes.[19] No State, however, could regulate by the imposition of an inspection fee any activity carried on by the United States directly through its own officers and employees,[20] and even a nondiscriminatory income tax applied to the salary of a Federal judge was held to violate the immunity doctrine.[21] Similarly, a Federal income tax could not be imposed on income which a municipal corporation derived from its investments.[22] A far-reaching extension of private immunity was granted when it was held that interest received by a private investor in State and municipal bonds was exempt from Federal income taxation.[23]

Waning of the Immunity Doctrine Since 1938

By 1938, the doctrine of intergovernmental immunity from taxation was nearly all-pervasive, having been extended to all government property and instrumentalities, officers and employees, and even to private individuals deriving income from government securities. Federal officers, for instance, were exempted on the ground that a tax would be an unconstitutional diminution of their salaries during their term of office, and a tax on the salaries of government employees was regarded as an improper invasion of the prerogatives of one governmental jurisdiction by another. Such immunities may have appeared necessary in former times, but they had grown to such proportions by 1938 that the three branches of the Federal government joined in a concerted attack upon the whole system.

There had been some earlier criticism of the exemptions, but in 1938 and 1939, President Roosevelt urged Congress to eliminate them completely, taking the position that government employees should pay taxes like other citizens. The Supreme Court had, as a matter of fact, been gradually narrowing the tax immunity of State and local salaries,

[19] McCulloch v. Maryland, confirmed half a century later with respect to railroads incorporated by Congress. See Thompson v. Union Pacific Railroad Company, 9 Wallace 579, 588 (1870) and Railroad Company v. Peniston, 18 Wallace 5, 31 (1873).

[20] Mayo v. United States, 319 U.S. 441 (1943).

[21] Tax Collector v. Day, 11 Wallace 113 (1871); this decision was later overruled.

[22] United States v. Baltimore & Ohio Railroad Company, 17 Wallace 322 (1873).

[23] Pollock v. Farmers Loan & Trust Company, 157 U.S. 429 (1895); for a review of the constitutional doctrines involved from the beginning down to the Gerhardt and other cases, see Konefsky, Samuel J., Chief Justice Stone and the Supreme Court (New York: The Macmillan Co., 1945).

overruling a long line of earlier decisions. Congress passed and the Supreme Court upheld the constitutionality of the Public Salary Tax Act of 1939 and the Buck Act of 1940, which authorized the States to extend sales, use, and income taxes to persons residing or doing business in Federal areas, and to transactions occurring in such areas. The Federal Government was thus free to tax State and local salaries, and the States were reciprocally free to tax Federal salaries. State and local authorities, however, remain generally free from Federal excise taxes, the States are without power to tax the income from Federal bonds or the bonds as property, and the United States cannot yet tax State and local bonds.[24]

In spite of sharp differences of opinion about what has been happening to intergovernmental tax immunities, even among members of the Supreme Court itself, one thing seems quite clear: as compared with former times, the number has been drastically curtailed, and if recent trends continue, what few remain will similarly disappear.

Taxation of Nonresident Income

The constitutional assault on the taxation of nonresident income was made in two cases which came before the Supreme Court in 1920. In the first of these, *Shaffer* v. *Carter*,[25] the taxpayer was an Illinois resident engaged in oil and gas operations in Oklahoma. The Court held that Oklahoma had jurisdiction, in a due process sense, to tax a nonresident on net income derived from sources within the State. The contention that the Oklahoma tax imposed an undue burden on interstate commerce was summarily dismissed by the Court. In the second case, *Travis* v. *Yale & Towne Manufacturing Company*,[26] a Connecticut corporation doing business in New York employed residents of Connecticut and New Jersey against whom New York sought to impose a net income

[24] See *Graves* v. *People of the State of New York ex rel. O'Keefe*, 306 U.S. 466 (1939) and *Helvering* v. *Gerhardt*, 304 U.S. 405 (1938). An excellent analysis of these and other pertinent decisions is found in Corwin, Edward S., ed., "Article VI, Miscellaneous Provisions," *Constitution of the United States: Analysis and Interpretation*, pp. 721–739, and in a series of articles by the late Professor Thomas Reed Powell: "Intergovernmental Tax Immunities," *George Washington Law Review*, June, 1940, pp. 1213–1220; "The Waning of Intergovernmental Tax Immunities," *Harvard Law Review*, May, 1945, pp. 633–674; "The Remnant of Intergovernmental Tax Immunities," *ibid.*, July, 1945, pp. 757–805.

[25] 252 U.S. 37 (1920).

[26] 252 U.S. 60 (1920); both of these cases, and others as well, are discussed in Solomon, Michael B., "Nonresident Personal Income Taxes: A Comparative Study in Eight States," *Fordham Law Review*, October, 1960, pp. 105–142.

tax. The company, acting in the interests of its employees, sought to enjoin the enforcement of the tax. The Court, following the Shaffer Case, affirmed the two basic propositions emerging from that case: (1) a State may constitutionally tax nonresidents, and (2) it may limit the deductions of nonresidents to those related to the production of taxable income. Now, since such taxes are in effect in a majority of the States and an ever-increasing number of municipalities, the problem is one of striking a balance between the continuing need for more revenues and the demand of nonresidents for fair treatment.

The question came in for widespread attention again in the early 1940's after the City of Philadelphia adopted its widely publicized, flat-rate wage tax and attempted to collect it from nonresidents in surrounding counties in both Pennsylvania and New Jersey.[27] In fact, they attempted to collect it from all who were paid salaries or wages by employers within the city limits, including in one instance a West Coast representative of the Curtis Publishing Company who was stationed in Portland, Oregon, and who had never been in Philadelphia for more than a few days in his entire life, and then only to attend a staff meeting in the company's home offices. This Philadelphia ordinance, later widely copied elsewhere, marked the beginning of the metropolitan problem of the taxation of nonresidents.

New legislation and interstate compacts have recently been developed, affecting several of the larger metropolitan areas, in an effort to solve these problems. In addition to tax problems affecting mass transit, it is necessary to consider the tax liabilities of large numbers of commuters who live in one jurisdiction and work in another. The ill effects of excessive tax duplication and overlapping, which may be a very serious matter, have been summarized as follows:

1. They may result in undue concentration of tax charges on a narrow range of economic activity. This may distort the whole pattern of investment and employment.

2. They limit the degree to which State governments have freedom in securing revenue sources to meet their needs.

3. They increase the cost of administration of collecting the taxes.

4. They irritate and annoy the taxpayer who is already heavily burdened by the obligation to pay. He has to face double or triple tax-reporting systems.

5. They reduce efficiency in the operation of State governments due to a duplication of administration and responsibility.[28]

---

[27] The tax had to be flat-rate because under Pennsylvania law, a progressive income tax is not only unconstitutional, but is regarded as un-American.

[28] Caruso, Laurence R., "State Taxation of the Income of Nonresidents," *Rutgers Law Review,* Winter, 1961, pp. 311–325.

The next question naturally is: What can be done to remedy this situation? Many remedies have been proposed, and a few have actually been adopted. At the Federal level, Congress in the 1961 session adopted a piece of legislation which is probably more significant as an indication of a complete reversal of Congressional opinion on the subject than for any real consequences that may be expected to flow from it. After 1942, when the Philadelphia wage tax ordinance was adopted, efforts were made to collect the tax from all federally employed persons in the area. The Philadelphia authorities received no cooperation whatsoever from either Congress or the executive departments responsible for the many Federal field offices and installations in the area. Twenty years later, however, Congress by law authorized Federal departments and agencies to withhold municipal income taxes from the salaries of Federal government employees. Other constitutional and statutory proposals at the Federal level fall within four general categories:

1. Prohibit States or their political subdivisions from levying taxes on income from whatever source except from residents of the taxing States.*

2. Prohibit States or their political subdivisions from levying income tax that discriminates between a resident and nonresident of the such as wages, salaries, professional fees, or for personal services rendered.†

3. Forbid States or their political subdivisions from levying an income tax that discriminates between a resident and nonresident of the taxing State.‡

4. Prevent States or their political subdivisions from imposing taxes upon amounts receivable by natural persons as compensation for personal services rendered within the taxing State unless such persons are domiciled within the State at any time during the taxing period, or reside in the State for at least one-half of the taxing period. This proposal, however, would authorize a uniform application of income tax upon personal services rendered notwithstanding residence and domicile if the revenues derived from the tax are devoted to providing benefits for all persons as distinguished from a specific class comprising residents of the taxing State.§ [29]

* H.J. Res. 68 sponsored by Representative Rodino of New Jersey.

† H.J. Res. 33, 119, 121, 251, and 288, by Representatives Addonizio, Osmers, Cahill, Widnall, and Dwyer, all of New Jersey; S.J. Res. 29, by Senators Bridges and Cotton of New Hampshire; H.J. Res. 203, by Representative Bass of New Hampshire; and H.J. Res. 163, by Representative Libonati of Illinois.

‡ H.J. Res. 118, by Representative Osmers of New Jersey.

§ S.J. Res. 67, by Senator Case of New Jersey.

[29] National Legislative Conference, Committee on Nonresident Income Taxation, *Nonresident Personal Income Taxation in the States* (Chicago: Council of State Governments, August, 1960).

At the State level, forms of reciprocity or even of outright retaliation have been proposed. An interesting example of cooperation is to be noted in the New York metropolitan area, where in 1959, Governor Rocke-feller sponsored legislation designed to assure more equitable treatment for nonresidents who pay New York State income taxes. It is not easy to secure legislative approval for such concessions in any State, and as interstate negotiations continued, powerful opposition developed de-manding that the State's unincorporated business levy must either end or be cut as a price for acceptance of tax concessions to nonresidents. Not-ing that New York would give up $6 million in revenue under the terms of the agreement, the opposition said, "Before we start giving away $6 million to people outside the State, let's take care of our own people in the State who are being discriminated against just as much. Why not reduce the unincorporated business tax? [which the Governor had spon-sored]. That tax amounts to double taxation for a lot of people." [30] As finally adopted after a certain amount of haggling, the law will save 200,000 out-of-State residents a total of more than $5 million a year, if other States in which more than 5,000 New Yorkers are employed adopt reciprocal legislation.[31]

Status of State and Municipal Bonds

The wording of the heading of this section would suggest that inter-governmental tax immunities are a thing of the past, which to a large extent they are, but not entirely. There remain a few remnants of the old system, some of which are distressing because they are so grossly and obviously unfair. There is little basis for objection to Federal income tax exemption for State and municipal bonds issued for legitimate gov-ernmental purposes, but when they are issued to provide facilities for private business, and when these facilities are used to lure business from one location to another with unfair concessions, it is time to call a halt. When, in addition, the taxpayers in the very area from which the indus-try was "stolen" have to help foot the bill, injury is compounded with insult.

This is precisely what happens when a municipality issues tax-exempt bonds to finance construction of industrial facilities which are in turn offered to a company on a lease basis. The company gets a new

[30] The New York Times, September 10, 1959, and March 2, 1961.

[31] Caruso, "State Taxation," Rutgers Law Review, Winter, 1961; the re-ciprocal credit arrangement for income and unemployment insurance taxes is found in such widely separated parts of the country as California, North Carolina, and New York.

plant, with little or no capital outlay. It is surely no mere coincidence that such arrangements are usually made in areas with substandard wage rates. Since the municipality retains title to the plant, the company frequently pays no property taxes; further, the company may itself buy a large portion of the tax-exempt bonds, thus obtaining a double tax advantage. As of 1961, at least fifteen States permitted municipalities to issue such bonds and the practice appeared to be spreading, creating what one Senator called "a serious abuse of an already questionable tax advantage." Here are some examples:

—A $25 million industrial bond issue by Cherokee, Alabama, under which Armour & Company will acquire a new chemical plant with twenty-six years to pay.

—The Norge Division of Borg-Warner Corporation is moving from Michigan to Greenwood, Arkansas, into a new plant financed by a $7 million bond issue, tax exempt. The real tragedy here is that the company will leave behind 1,400 workers who have been given no opportunity to move with the plant, though these very workers, as taxpayers, are helping to subsidize the company's move.

—The Gemmer Manufacturing Company, which has been doing business in Detroit since 1907, is moving to Lebanon, Tennessee, which has floated a $2.4 million bond issue to build a plant for the company. In this situation, 750 employees whose average age is forty-eight and who have spent an average of twenty years with the company, were not even given an opportunity to move with the firm.[32]

TAX COORDINATION

It has long been customary to talk about overlapping jurisdiction and conflict between the Federal government and the States in the tax field. Both have caused problems, to be sure, but the available solutions are generally regarded as either impractical or unacceptable. This section of the chapter is concerned with tax coordination, the first of two possible solutions. Tax coordination means the assignment of sources and/or the allocation of the revenues derived therefrom in such a manner as to accomplish an equitable distribution of the yield and to eliminate competition, overlapping, and duplication. This, it is often contended, is impractical and unrealistic. The second solution of the problem would centralize collection, at least of certain taxes—the Federal govern-

[32] Comments by Senator Pat McNamara, introducing S. 2042, *Congressional Record*, June 8, 1961, pp. 9139–9140.

ment for the States, the States for their political subdivisions. This proposal, which will be considered in the following section, is usually regarded as politically unacceptable, however desirable it might be on theoretical grounds.

Shifts in Control of Revenue Sources

There is not a single major function of government in which governmental units at all three levels are not actively concerned. Parallel with this fact—or perhaps because of it—there is today only one major source of revenue for which the Federal government and the States are not competing: the general property tax which the States themselves have abandoned or are in process of abandoning to the local units. In fiscal matters, a high degree of Federal-State interdependence has developed. This was not always so.

In the beginning, the Federal government obtained its revenues largely from customs, the States and local units from the general property tax. As the needs for revenue increased, each unit began to reach out for every known tax source. The Federal Income Tax Amendment was adopted in 1913; a few States were already using this tax form, many more adopted it, and scores of income tax and wage tax ordinances were imposed in the cities. All of the States had adopted gasoline taxes by 1929, and the Federal government imposed an emergency levy on gasoline to pay for relief during the Great Depression. This tax has been continued until the present, based on the mistaken belief that it has something to do with Federal aid for roads. Moreover, some local units also impose levies on gasoline, until the total taxes in many jurisdictions exceed the cost of the product.

Similar duplication developed with regard to other types of taxes: sales taxes, excise taxes, admissions taxes, and many more. Indeed, the Federal government every year collects more money from specialized sales taxes than all of the States combined collect from theirs. In addition to this unfortunate element of competition, there has been over the last quarter of a century an enormous shift in the distribution of tax receipts among the levels of government. As the graph on page 453 shows, the Federal government collected only about one-fourth of the government revenues in 1932, but it collected almost three-fourths of them in 1946, a ratio which continued through 1957. The States, which collected one-fifth in 1932, collected only one-tenth in 1946 and one-seventh in 1957. The percentage decline of the local units has been even greater.

In terms of dollars, the figures are indeed striking. The figure for the

SHIFTS IN TAX COLLECTIONS
IN THE UNITED STATES

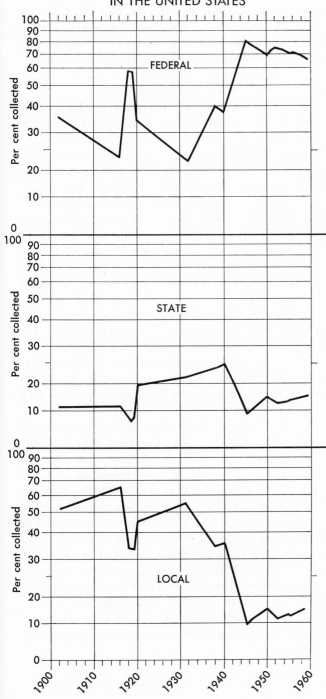

* From *PAR Analysis,*
November, 1960, p. 2.
Because of rounding,
percentages may not
total exactly 100.

Federal government in 1957 was approximately forty-four times that for 1932; at the State level, the increase was only approximately ten times what it had been twenty-five years before. The amount of the increase is important, but the vital question is the significance of these changes upon the nature of the governmental system.[33] The shifts which have taken place are clearly evident from the lines on the graph.

Inevitably connected with these shifts in control over revenue sources is the question of competition for tax dollars. Fiscal statistics tend to highlight what has been called a headlong race between State and Nation. State revenues in 1960 were close to 50 per cent of Federal revenues for the same year; the States collected nearly $33 billion from one source or another, while the receipts of the Federal government were nearly $78 billion. Expenditures of both the Federal government and the States have been steadily rising, but those of the States appear to be increasing at a faster rate than those of the Federal government—at a rate of 4.7 per cent as against 1.7 per cent. State expenditures in 1960 rose in all categories of spending, averaging some $152.49 per capita. Of this amount, $49.60 went for education, $40.98 for highways, and $20.98 for public welfare.

The figures in the tables on page 455 may help the reader to visualize what has been happening with respect to governmental costs. The first table gives figures on total collections for Federal, State, and local governments, and for all three combined, for selected years between 1932–1957. The second table gives total revenue and expenditure figures for selected States and for all States for 1960, the latest year for which final figures are available.

Despite the increase in State expenditures, the State governments are under increasing pressures to spend more for education, more for highways, and more for State hospitals, particularly for State mental institutions. How to raise the revenues to meet these ever mounting costs is a question for which the hard-pressed Governors have long sought an answer, for while costs have increased, the Federal government has encroached upon the areas of taxation available to the States. About the only form of tax which the Federal government has left to the States is the general sales tax. Until a few years ago, most excise taxes were reserved to the States, but the Federal government continues the "emergency" taxes on gasoline, jewelry, and other commodities. In self-defense, one might say, the States have been forced to encroach upon at least one Federal area of taxation, the income tax. Although the States now make extensive use of both income and sales taxes, most of them are confronting serious financial problems.

[33] For a discussion of these changes, see Graves, W. Brooke, "What Is Happening to Our Federal System?" *State Government,* November, 1949, pp. 255–259, 270.

FEDERAL, STATE, AND LOCAL TAX COLLECTIONS IN
SELECTED YEARS, 1932–1957 (In thousands) *

	Federal		State		All Other		Total	
Year	Amount	Per cent	Amount	Per cent	Amount	Per cent	Amount	Per cent
1932	$ 1,809,000	24	$ 1,890,000	23	$ 4,468,000	53	$ 8,167,000	100
1937	4,771,000	39	3,013,000	23	4,481,000	38	12,265,000	100
1942	12,296,000	60	3,903,000	12	4,624,000	22	20,823,000	100
1947	35,160,000	75	5,721,000	13	5,833,000	12	46,714,000	100
1952	59,650,585	75	9,838,000	13	9,400,000	12	78,888,000	100
1957	88,400,000	70	20,200,000	16	18,000,000	14	126,600,000	100

*U.S. Bureau of the Census figures.

TOTAL REVENUES AND EXPENDITURES OF SELECTED
STATES IN 1960 (In thousands) *

State	Revenues	Expenditures
Three largest budgets:		
California	$ 3,752,919	$ 3,583,197
New York	3,303,310	2,317,205
Pennsylvania	2,065,941	2,131,883
Three smallest budgets:		
Vermont	92,315	81,040
Nevada	87,239	68,314
Alaska	74,646	69,871
Total		
All States	$29,163,981	$31,124,932

* U.S. Bureau of the Census, *State Government Finances in 1960* (Washington, 1961).

It is virtually impossible to generalize regarding the extent of the existing overlapping and duplication because all of the tax systems involved are not only different from each other, but they change almost constantly as rates are increased (or decreased) and as new taxes are added or (as rarely happens) abandoned. The table on page 456 illustrates the situation in terms of one State, Minnesota, for the year 1957. One must keep in mind the fact that the details of this picture do not apply to any other State, or even to Minnesota in any year other than the one specified.

To many people, the overlapping and duplication between the two levels of government seems a serious and highly unfortunate matter.

STATE OF MINNESOTA—1957
NATIONAL AND STATE TAX DUPLICATION AND SEPARATION *

Taxes Involving Complete or Substantial Duplication	Federal Taxes Practically Unduplicated	State Taxes Practically Unduplicated by the National Government
Income Taxes Individual	Tariff on imported goods	Property taxes
Corporate income and profits	Retailers excises on furs, jewelry, luggage, toilet goods	Gross earnings taxes on railroads, express and sleeping car companies, telephone and telegraph companies, etc., in lieu of property taxes
Excise Taxes Gasoline and diesel fuel Alcoholic beverages Cigarette and tobacco taxes Processed vegetable oils	Manufacturers excises on lubricating oil; tires and inner tubes; auto, truck, and other automobile chassis and bodies, and motor-cycles; electric, gas, and oil	
Estate and inheritance taxes	appliances; electric light bulbs; radio sets and com-ponents; phonographs and	Iron mining occupation and royalty taxes
Gift taxes	records; musical instru-ments; mechanical refrig-	Bank excise taxes
Unemployment compensa-tion (payroll taxes)	erators; air conditioners, etc.; matches; business and store machines; photo-graphic apparatus and films; sporting goods; fire-arms, shells, and cartridges; fountain pens, mechanical pencils, and lighters	Hunting and fishing li-censes Vessel tonnage tax (a property tax) Corporation licenses Occupational licenses

Other Federal levies:
employment tax (O.A.S.I.); sugar; telephone, telegraph, cable, radio, leased wires, etc.; local telephone service; transportation of oil by pipeline; transportation of persons and property; safety deposit boxes; club dues and initiation fees; bowling alleys; pool tables; coin-operated devices; wagering; narcotics; admissions.

* Adapted from Anderson, William, *Intergovernmental Fiscal Relations* (Minne-apolis: University of Minnesota Press, 1957), p. 60.

These persons feel that determined efforts should be made to eliminate the problem through allocation of sources or through cooperation in the collection and distribution of the receipts from at least some taxes. Others, like Professor William Anderson, regard a certain amount of overlapping and duplication as inevitable in a federal system in which "both Federal and the State Governments are autonomous or relatively independent to make their own choices and policies on a wide range of public questions." [34] While Professor Anderson recognizes, as one must, the numerous disadvantages of overlapping (such as tax encroachments, high administrative costs, high compliance costs, inconvenience to taxpayers, and overburdening of some tax sources, among others), he regards the overlapping as "a minor irritant, and an evidence of a certain disorderliness in the system, such as is found in any society where men and groups have freedom and the initiative to express their differences and to act upon them."

Efforts to Achieve Tax Coordination

The fundamental problem of tax coordination may be stated in the terms of Lasswell's famous question: Who gets what, when, and how? Roger A. Freeman, who has written extensively on tax and fiscal matters, states in picturesque language the various aspects of the problem most frequently discussed: How big a pie for government? How to slice the pie? Who gets the filling, who the crust? How can we minimize jurisdictional conflicts? How far does mutual immunity extend? [35]

In 1943, the Treasury Department's Special Committee to Study Intergovernmental Fiscal Relations opened its report with this sentence: "Coordination and cooperation rather than subordination and coercion is the answer to intergovernmental fiscal relations in the United States." Fifteen years later, Congress proclaimed in the preamble to the act establishing the Advisory Commission on Intergovernmental Relations that "The complexity of modern life intensified the need in a federal form of government for the fullest cooperation and coordination of activities between the levels of government; population growth and scientific developments portend for future years an increasingly complex society in which it is essential that appropriate agencies be established to give continuing attention to intergovernmental problems."

When one surveys the efforts that have been made to solve the problems of tax conflict and tax coordination, he finds that little attention was given to them prior to the Great Depression, but that in the last quarter of a century, numerous attempts have been made to discover workable solutions. From the very beginning, the Council of State Governments has done much work in this field, promoting both interstate

[34] Anderson, William, *Intergovernmental Fiscal Relations* (Minneapolis: University of Minnesota Press, 1957), p. 66.
[35] Freeman, Roger A., "Intergovernmental Tax Relations," *Municipal Finance*, August, 1961, pp. 13-23.

and Federal-State cooperation. In 1933, it established a Committee on Conflicting Taxation and published an extensive report on the subject.[36]

Another early effort to find a solution to interjurisdictional tax conflicts was that of the Tax Policy League, whose first symposium on tax coordination in 1937 was followed by another in 1953. The Treasury Department established in June, 1941, under authority of a Senate resolution,[37] its Committee on Intergovernmental Fiscal Relations, often referred to by the names of its members as the Newcomer-Groves-Gulick Committee, which was instructed to make a thorough study of the whole field. Its excellent report covered events through October, 1942, and contained an enormous amount of valuable information not previously available in a single source.[38] For present purposes, its most important recommendation was the proposal that a Federal-State Fiscal Authority be created to perform such functions as the following:

1. Promote close collaboration among State and Federal administrators with the objective of joint administration of selected overlapping taxes.

2. Facilitate interstate cooperation.

3. Act as a clearinghouse for proposals relating to Federal payments in lieu of property taxes on federally owned property.

4. Conduct research.

5. Create public interest in intergovernmental relations.

6. Disseminate among the States information on Federal taxes and economic trends as they affect the States.

7. Promote better governmental reporting, accounting, and statistics.[39]

When once again no constructive action followed the publication of an impressive report, the Council of State Governments created a Joint Conference on Federal-State Tax Relations, which functioned in 1947 and 1948. At its 1947 meeting in Salt Lake City, the Governors' Confer-

[36] Council of State Governments, *Conflicting Taxation* (Chicago, 1935).

[37] S. Res. No. 160, 77th Cong., 2nd Sess.

[38] *Intergovernmental Fiscal Relations*, 2 vols. (Washington, 1943; also published as Senate Document No. 69, 78th Cong., 1st Sess. (Washington, May, 1943). See also Newcomer, Mabel, *Intergovernmental Fiscal Relations in the United States: A Selected Bibliography* (Washington: Committee on Intergovernmental Fiscal Relations, Treasury Department, 1942).

[39] *Intergovernmental Fiscal Relations*, pp. 5–8. It is to be noted that a quarter of a century later, in 1959, this recommendation was in substance carried out when the Advisory Commission on Intergovernmental Relations was established. Although the responsibilities of the Advisory Commission are by no means limited to fiscal matters, these are most assuredly an important part of its assignment.

ence had again reaffirmed its conviction that there was great need for the States to assume their own responsibilities, had urged the gradual elimination of tax competition between the Federal and State governments, and had resolved to continue a Special Committee on Tax and Fiscal Policy which it had established for the study of intergovernmental tax coordination. The Governors recommended that future Federal aid legislation require Federal administrative agencies to confer with and secure approval from the Executive Committee of the Governors' Conference in the preparation of rules and regulations governing the administration of grants to the States.

The Joint Conference was composed of Members of Congress and representatives of the States, the latter being the members of the above-mentioned Special Committee. This was the first time that top-level Federal and State officials had met together in an attempt to find solutions to common fiscal problems. Meeting in Chicago in 1948 for a two-day conference, the members undertook to study and make recommendations regarding the Federal-State aspects of tax and fiscal policy. A number of further meetings were held, at the conclusion of which a joint statement of general principles and immediate objectives was unanimously adopted. The final report set forth a five-point program for immediate action:

1. The Federal government should reduce Federal excise taxes as soon as practicable.

2. The Federal government should amend inheritance and estate tax laws to provide a more equitable division of this revenue as between the Federal Government and the States.

3. The Federal government should relinquish to the States the Federal tax on employers levied to cover the administrative expenses of State employment security programs and the States would assume the responsibility for the administration of these programs.

4. The Congress should take the earliest possible action to correct inequities existing between the community property and non-community property States.

5. The States should avoid encroachment upon tax fields peculiarly adaptable to Federal uses.[40]

Also in 1948, a Conference on Federal-State-Local Fiscal Relations was held in Washington to develop cooperative arrangements for the drafting of an in lieu payments bill. This project, as a matter of fact,

[40] Council of State Governments, *Federal-State Tax and Fiscal Program* (Chicago, 1948) and symposium, "Taxes, Federal-State-Local," *State Government,* November, 1947, entire issue. The report was also printed as Senate Document No. 4, 81st Cong., 1st Sess. (Washington, 1949).

had been so long under way that it is difficult to establish terminal dates. As early as 1939, a Federal Real Estate Board had been established by Executive Order to study the problem. The recommendations of this Board were not, however, widely endorsed in State and local government councils. In April, 1948, the problem again came to the fore when the above-mentioned conference was held. The Bureau of the Budget was asked to draft an in lieu payments bill, the Treasury Department to draft amendments to or a revision of the Buck Act of October, 1940.[41] The Bureau of the Budget took its assignment seriously, and in cooperation with many Federal and State officials, drafted the first comprehensive in lieu payments bill. This bill was referred to with approval in the Report of the Commission on Intergovernmental Relations (Kestnbaum), and it has been under continuous study by the staff of the Senate Committee on Government Operations for the past several years. The questions involved are so complicated, and the interests involved so diverse, that it has thus far been impossible to obtain sufficient agreement to insure enactment of this legislation.

Chronologically, the report of the Commission on Organization of the Executive Branch of the Government (the first Hoover Commission) came next. Established in 1947 by an act of Congress, this Commission included in its 1949 reports a study of Federal-State relations in which major attention was given to fiscal relationships. Specifically, the Commission made five recommendations:

1. That the functions and activities of government be appraised to determine which can be most advantageously operated by each level of government, and which require joint policy making, financing, and administration.

2. That our tax systems—National, State and local—be revised and that in this revision every effort be made to leave to localities and States adequate resources from which to raise revenues to meet their debts and responsibilities of local and State governments.

3. That all grants-in-aid given to State governments be directly allocated in detail at the Federal and State levels.

4. That the grants-in-aid plan program be clarified and systematized.

5. That a continuing agency of Federal-State relations be created with the primary responsibility, for study, information, and guidance in the field of Federal-State relations.

It is appropriate to mention also the establishment of the House Subcommittee on Coordination of Federal, State, and Local Taxes on October 25, 1951. This action was taken pursuant to the terms of a House

[41] Public Law No. 819, 76th Cong.

Resolution.[42] A few months later, on March 12, 1952, a conference was held with a committee of Governors and representatives of city and county organizations, plus some officials from the Treasury Department.

This effort to find a means of achieving some cooperation between the Federal government and the States in the fiscal field, and some co-ordination between them with respect to governmental functions or services on one hand, and revenues on the other, continued through the 1950's. The Commission on Intergovernmental Relations (Kestnbaum) was established in 1953 in hopes that it might be able to find ways and means of accomplishing this objective; it reported in 1955 without making any very specific recommendations in this area, however. Then, in 1957, in his Williamsburg address before the Governors' Conference, President Eisenhower proposed that a task force be established to designate functions which the States were ready and willing to assume and finance; to recommend Federal and State revenue adjustments necessary to enable the States to carry out these functions; to identify functions and responsibilities likely to require State or Federal attention in the future; and to recommend the level of State effort, or Federal effort, or both, that would be needed to insure effective action.

This series of recommendations was adopted, resulting in the establishment of the Joint Federal-State Action Committee of seventeen members, including nine Governors and seven top-ranking Federal officials. The chairman of the Executive Committee of the Governors' Conference was a member ex officio. The group held a number of meetings during 1957 and 1958, submitting in December, 1957, its *Progress Report No. 1* [43] containing specific recommendations on six subjects: vocational education, waste treatment, disaster relief, atomic energy, urban renewal, and local telephone tax.

The purpose and intent of these recommendations were three-fold: (1) to turn over to the States full responsibility for the performance of certain specific functions; (2) to cut off the Federal financial assistance heretofore provided for the support of these functions; (3) to provide the States with revenues and/or revenue sources adequate to support the transferred functions or services. It was generally recognized that this was a very small beginning on a problem of tremendous proportions.

The recommendations were nowhere accorded a reception that could

[42] See House Report No. 2519, 82nd Cong., 2nd Sess. (Washington, 1951). This report includes, in Appendix A, "A Study of Federal-State-Local Tax Coordination," prepared by the Tax Advisory Staff of the Treasury Department.

[43] *Report of the Joint Federal-State Action Committee to the President of the United States and to the Chairman of the Governors' Conference* (Washington, 1958).

possibly have been mistaken for enthusiastic approval. They were discussed but not acted upon at a meeting of the Board of Managers of the Council of State Governments at Hot Springs in December, 1957. In May, 1958, the Governors' Conference, meeting at Bal Harbour, voted to continue the Joint Action Committee and to broaden its scope, but did not approve its specific proposals relative to the transfer of program responsibilities and the release of a portion of the Federal telephone tax receipts. The President transmitted a letter, accompanied by draft legislation, to the Speaker of the House of Representatives, urging that Congress promptly enact legislation consistent with the recommendations of the Joint Action Committee, but no such action was taken either then or later.

The latest attempt to attain some degree of cooperation and coordination in this field was the establishment in 1959 of the Advisory Commission on Intergovernmental Relations, one of the major purposes of which was to try once again to find a workable solution for this much discussed problem. Meanwhile, as the problem steadily becomes more difficult, its solution becomes more urgent. In a memorandum issued in January, 1960, the National Planning Committee summarized the situation as follows:

> A conflict is developing between the traditional division of functions on the one hand and the traditional division of revenue sources, on the other. The traditional functions of State and local governments are likely to expand more rapidly than their traditional sources of revenue. If we assume no change in the allocation of functions, then serious consideration should be given to possible adjustments or changes in the traditional methods of allocating and utilizing available revenue sources.
>
> One basic approach to such a revenue re-adjustment would be designed to maintain the present division of tax resources but to supplement State-local revenues by grant-in-aid programs or by a tax sharing arrangement. Another approach would induce the States by the tax credit device to make increasing use of income taxes and thereby reduce the predominant reliance of States on indirect taxes. There are political, economic and administrative arguments pro and con for each of these approaches.[44]

The Commission has tackled its assignment intelligently and vigorously, but it is much too soon to evaluate its accomplishments. In 1960 and 1961, it issued several reports dealing with various aspects of this problem, including:

[44] *Joint Statement on Federal-State-Local Financial Relationships* (Washington, January 18, 1960), p. 8.

Coordination of State and Federal Inheritance, Estate, and Gift Taxes
Intergovernmental Cooperation in Tax Administration
Local Nonproperty Taxes and the Coordinating Role of the State
State and Local Taxation of Privately Owned Property Located in
    Federal Areas

In addition, it has in progress, under contract, the most extensive survey ever undertaken of the general property tax, its use and its limitations as a source for the support of governmental operations.

Virtually all of these efforts have been based upon the assumption that a solution could be developed on a broad scale, that some grand strategy of nationwide application is possible, although it has not been found so far. It may be that too much has been attempted, or that it has been undertaken in the wrong way. The Commission study involving the role of the States in the coordination of local nonproperty taxes clearly indicates that the States can do much, not only to prevent abuses and correct inequities, but to establish affirmative policies fostering cooperation and coordination.

Congress and State Taxation of Interstate Commerce

The problem of State taxation of interstate income has long been troublesome; the Council of State Governments characterizes its history as "a stormy one." In response to constant pressure for additional revenues, the States have shown considerable ingenuity in developing techniques for taxing the income from interstate commerce, and the more effective the techniques, the more certainly they impose a burden upon such commerce. Meanwhile, as one State denounced the practices of its neighbors, Congress became so concerned about these barriers to the free flow of interstate trade that in 1959 it passed legislation designed to establish standards and, for the first time in history, to impose some controls.[45]

First of all, the Act specifies the type of activities a multi-state business corporation must conduct within a State before that State may impose a net income tax on the corporation's income. This was the first instance in which Congress had, in general legislation, prescribed limits on the taxing powers of the States. The most significant part of the statute is that contained in Title II, which directs the appropriate Congressional committees to "make full and complete studies of all matters pertaining to the taxation by the States of income derived within the

---

[45] Public Law 86–272. For a good discussion of this legislation, and of the court cases and administrative actions pertaining to it, see Council of State Governments, *Washington Legislative Bulletin,* November, 1960, entire issue.

State from the conduct of business activities which are exclusively in furtherance of interstate commerce." Three of the many important problems involved are: (1) As a policy matter, should uniform standards be adopted by the States themselves rather than by Congress? (2) What would be the economic impact on the revenues of the respective States of such standards as Congress might adopt? (3) Would the standards be administratively feasible?

The question of uniformity is paramount; the issue is largely one of determining how it shall be attained. As far back as 1953, a committee of the Governors' Conference recommended, and the Conference approved, proposals looking toward a uniform apportionment formula, based on definitions of each factor in a three-factor formula—sales, payrolls, and tangible property—adopted and uniformly applied by all States. The Council study was completed and published in 1956.[46] One writer, however, contends that the inclusion of the sales factor is based upon one or the other of two fallacious arguments. He argues for a uniform apportionment formula to spread the net business income of multi-state businesses for purposes of State net income taxation, excluding the sales factor completely and relying upon tangible property and payrolls.[47]

The existing situation in State law with respect to this matter was summarized in 1960 as follows:

> Thirty-six States, including the District of Columbia, use an apportionment formula in levying their corporate income taxes. In determining the apportionment formula, thirty-three States use the property, thirty-six States use receipts (sales), twenty-four States use payrolls (an additional seven States use payrolls in figuring cost factors), and twenty States include other factors (usually relating to items of income that are to be specifically allocated). Unfortunately the diversity among the States does not end here. All thirty-six States use receipts in their tax formulas, but seventy-five items or definitions are used, either singly or in combination, to determine receipts in the appointment formulas.
>
> The disparity in the receipts factor would be further emphasized if one were to consider specific statutory language and court interpretation. While the above picture appears bleak, a pattern of similarity can be observed. Twenty-three States use a three-factor formula of property, receipts and payrolls as the cornerstone of their corporate income tax structure. In addition, if we include those States which consider payroll

---

[46] Council of State Governments, *Report of Survey of Effects on State Revenues of Various Proposed Uniform Apportionment Formulas* (Chicago, 1956).

[47] Barber, Arthur B., "A Suggested Shot at a Gordian Knot of Income Apportionment," *National Tax Journal,* September, 1960, pp. 243–251.

as a factor in costs, we find twenty-nine out of the thirty-six States use the three factors which are used in the NCCUSL model act.[48]

COOPERATION IN TAX ADMINISTRATION

That there is a sizable amount of duplication and waste in the tax collection process when two or more governments collect the same type of tax from the same citizens within the same territory, no one will deny. Recognizing the problem, however, is far easier than agreeing upon an appropriate solution. Such obvious solutions as central collection, joint collection, tax sharing, grants-in-aid, tax credits, and other devices could do much to eliminate duplication and hold down collection costs.

Although central collection under existing laws with no increase in rates and at a minimum cost of collection would produce more revenue, pleas for the adoption of such a plan have never received any appreciable amount of support. The States have been fearful that under such a system not all of the money due them would be turned over (which sounds a little absurd), or that if turned over, unwanted conditions might be imposed upon them. To illustrate their fears, the States point to the famous Hayden-Cartwright Act of 1934, under the terms of which the States permitting diversion of their highway funds were penalized by the withholding of one-third of the Federal highway aid to which they would otherwise have been entitled. Local units have similarly feared that a system of central collection would preclude their financial independence.

Cooperation in tax administration offers a solution to the problem that is far more acceptable to State and local units. Such cooperative relationships became increasingly common after World War I. Although the States have much more to gain from cooperation than has the Federal government, the latter has in many ways shown its willingness to assist the States and cooperate fully with their tax collecting officials by placing an extensive array of services at their disposal. Such cooperation has gone further in the income tax field than in any other. It has recently been pointed out that "by fully exploiting the facilities now available and by broadening the scope of cooperation, States can overcome many of the disadvantages of limited jurisdiction, appropriations, and staff from which they chronically suffer.[49]

In answer to the question of what can be done to make cooperation

[48] *Washington Legislative Bulletin,* p. 4.

[49] Penniman, Clara, and Heller, Walter W., *State Income Tax Administration* (Chicago: Public Administration Service, 1959), p. 215.

effective, the Advisory Commission on Intergovernmental Relations has suggested some principles and possibilities and made four specific recommendations:

1. The enactment by the States of legislation authorizing the exchange of tax records and information among States and with the Federal Internal Revenue Service;

2. Joint action by the Treasury Department, the Council of State Governments and the Advisory Commission's staff to identify those State and local records and types of information that are potentially useful for the administration of Federal income and other taxes;

3. Development by the States for submission to the Treasury Department and the Congress of a proposal for the admission of State and local tax enforcement personnel to training programs conducted by the Internal Revenue Service;

4. Favorable consideration by the Congress of pending legislation to authorize the Internal Revenue Service to perform statistical and related services for State tax agencies on a reimbursement basis.[50]

Income Tax Cooperation

An income tax law which had been enacted by Congress in 1861 to finance the Civil War remained in effect until it was repealed in 1872. It applied to incomes over $800 and allowed a $600 personal exemption, as at present. It had a rate of 3 per cent, and records show that President Lincoln paid it on his $25,000 annual salary. The provisions of this law had been upheld by the Supreme Court in a unanimous decision,[51] but the income tax provision of an act passed in 1894 was declared unconstitutional on the ground that a tax on the income derived from land was indistinguishable from a tax on the land itself and was therefore a direct tax which must be apportioned among the several States according to population.[52] Because the Springer Case had been only recently decided, the Court had considerable difficulty in reaching a decision on this one. Joseph H. Choate said in his argument before the Court that the tax was "communistic, socialistic and popularistic," and inquired, "where would this march of communism end?" At that time, he could only have known of communism by reading Karl Marx's books, because Lenin was then a young lawyer in Samara, Stalin was a fifteen-year-old attending a religious seminary, and the Czar was still in power.

[50] *Intergovernmental Relations in Tax Administration* (Washington, June, 1961).

[51] *Springer* v. *United States*, 102 U.S. 586 (1880).

[52] *Pollock* v. *Farmers Loan & Trust Company*, 158 U.S. 601 (1895).

The Sixteenth Amendment, proposed and adopted to overcome the effects of the Pollock decision and proclaimed in 1913, empowered Congress to lay and collect taxes on incomes "from whatever source derived." Under the legislation that was soon adopted, all citizens were taxed 1 per cent on all income up to $20,000, with a $4,000 exemption for married persons. Net tax for that sum was $160, although today a married person may pay that amount of tax on an income of $2,250. Various amendments were passed through the years, changing exemptions from $4,000 to $2,500 for married persons and allowing in addition an "earned income credit," but rates remained low until 1942 when exemptions were reduced to $500 and rates were sharply increased. At one time, the names of taxpayers had been exhibited on posters in post offices, but this requirement caused such a furor that it was soon abandoned.

When the Sixteenth Amendment was framed and adopted, it was generally assumed that the States would, when the Amendment became effective, stay out of the income tax field, but this has not proved to be the case; some thirty-two of the States have individual income taxes, one-fourth have corporate income taxes, and the number of both types continues steadily to increase. During and since World Wars I and II, the Federal income tax, levied at steeply progressive rates, has been the most important single source of revenue for the Federal government and is becoming an increasingly important source for the States. In 1953, only nine States derived 25 per cent or more of their total tax revenues from income taxes, but in 1959, there were thirteen such States. It is highly significant, also, that the Sixteenth Amendment assured sufficient Federal income, annually and on a continuing basis, to finance extensive Federal grant-in-aid programs in the States, and later in municipalities as well.

Cooperative relationships between Federal and State governments began at an early date. Both Federal and State sources agree that State tax men began to visit the Bureau of Internal Revenue as early as 1920 to examine Federal returns. Thus, it appears that informal administrative aid to States levying income taxes preceded the original Congressional acts and Executive Orders which established more formal channels for the transmission of information. The first explicit provision by Congress for State access to Federal returns appeared in the Revenue Act of 1926, under the terms of which returns were to be open to State officers upon request of the Governor of the State. This provision was carried forward in essentially the same form in the Revenue Acts of 1928 and 1932, and was supplemented in 1931 by an Executive Order of the President and regulations by the Secretary of the Treasury which made individual returns available to State income tax officials. The Costigan Amendments of 1934 and 1935 were widely publicized, but added little to the already established privileges of State officials.[53]

Since the grant of Congressional authority to give the States access to Federal tax returns, administrative cooperation has passed through two phases and is now well into a third. After the 1931 Executive Order and on through the 1940's, a number of States either ordered audit transcripts of individual returns on a service charge basis or sent members of their own staffs to Washington to abstract Federal audit reports. This type of cooperation proved to be highly beneficial to the States, enabling them to discover taxpayers who had filed no return and to increase receipts from those who had.

The expanding interest of the States in obtaining information on taxpayers from Federal returns created certain problems for the Internal Revenue Service, without giving compensating benefits in return. Space and facilities were required to service the incoming State officials, and even when service was covered by service charges, the money went into the Treasury and could not be used by the Internal Revenue Service. Following a conference in 1949, a not too successful effort was made to make the benefits reciprocal. Then, in the 1950's, the endorsement of administrative cooperation in tax administration in the *Report of the Commission on Intergovernmental Relations* (Kestnbaum), and the efforts of the Eisenhower administration to implement the Commission's recommendations both helped to somewhat equalize the expenses and benefits of cooperative efforts.

More important was the decentralization of most Federal income tax activities to the field, which resulted in a tremendous increase in the extent to which State authorities exercised their right to utilize Federal income tax returns. Several States microfilmed or photostated selected Federal returns for one or more years, and since World War II, at least half a dozen States have so reproduced Federal returns in quantity. One State (Wisconsin) which has a generally effective State income tax enforcement program found that an expenditure of $85,000 for photostating and audit follow-up yielded a return of approximately $500,000. In 1956, this State continued to microfilm the first page of all Federal individual income tax returns filed by its residents. To show that cooperation can work both ways (as it should), the Internal Revenue Service requested that it be furnished a list of all taxpayers for whom the State had a return but for which it found no matching Federal microfilm.

A variety of other cooperative devices has been developed and used, at first on an experimental basis, later on a more permanent basis. These include the Federal-State Audit Information Exchange Program, begun

[53] This summary is based on Penniman and Heller, Chapter 9, and the Advisory Commission's report.

in 1950, under which audit information was exchanged as part of the administrative routine of each agency (Federal and an increasing number of States), under formal agreements, without charge, and without separate official requests.[54] In fiscal 1957, when this program was reactivated, three of these States reported additional assessments of nearly $500,000 each from the use of the Federal audit reports.

It is reported that fifteen States make systematic comparison with Federal records; audit adjustments are used by thirty-six States and the District of Columbia; checking of specific taxpayers is reported from twenty-seven States and the District; and taxpayer lists are matched with Federal rolls in three States and the District. Other cooperative devices include information returns under the Public Salary Tax Act of 1939, conforming State with Federal laws, tax supplement and joint administration—precedents for which are found in State-local tax supplements in California, Illinois, Mississippi, and New Mexico—tax credits and tax sharing. In addition, there are significant opportunities for interstate cooperation, particularly when taxpayers are liable for taxes in more than one State.

The slowly spreading trend, started in Vermont in 1947, toward the "federalization" of State income tax laws is another type of cooperation. By the end of 1961, in more than one-third of the States, income taxes were tied explicitly to the Federal income tax.[55] Under the New Mexico act, more or less typical of the type, the "base income" of the taxpayer is defined as "Federal taxable income and upon which the Federal income tax is calculated less the Federal income tax payable for the taxable year." "Net income" is defined as "base income" with several adjustments, among them the following: amounts taxed by the State or allowed as a deduction by the State in a previous year may not be taxed or deducted again; the full amount of the Federal capital gains deduction for the taxable year shall be subject to the State income tax. All persons required to file a Federal income tax return must file a State return as well.[56]

[54] These include North Carolina and Wisconsin (1950); Colorado, Kentucky, and Montana (1951); Minnesota (1957); Kansas (1960); California, Indiana, Ohio, Oregon, and Utah (1961). Data from *Tax Administrators News*, June, 1961, and Leon Rothenberg, *Federal-State Exchange of Tax Information* (Chicago: Federation of Tax Administrators, 1962), pp. 23–24.

[55] These include Vermont (1947); Alaska (1949); Kentucky (1954); Iowa and Montana (1955); Hawaii (1957); Idaho and North Dakota (1959); New York (1960); and Minnesota, West Virginia, and New Mexico (1961). Wisconsin considered but did not adopt such a measure in 1959, and Georgia and South Carolina once adopted and later repealed income tax laws based on the Federal Internal Revenue Code.

[56] Besides the New Mexico act, see *Simplifying the State Income Tax by Gearing It to the Federal Income* (Madison: Wisconsin Legislative Reference

The Advisory Commission's report concludes that, in view of the compelling arguments for reciprocity between Federal and State tax administrators, "the performance after thirty years of effort leaves much to be desired." In spite of the known benefits and the absence of detrimental effects to any State, there are still many obstacles to cooperation to be overcome. There is the usual preoccupation of officials with day to day problems, not to mention occasional ignorance, apathy, or indifference. In some States, statutory authority for the exchange of information is limited. In others, staffing is inadequate, and because the return per dollar of enforcement effort is likely to be greater from consumer taxes than from income taxes, emphasis is apt to be upon the former. The States are notably lacking in anything approaching uniformity in the quality of their enforcement efforts and in their methods. Consequently, their records differ significantly in potential usefulness to the Federal government or to other States. The Advisory Commission recommends a four-point program for the immediate future, as shown on p. 466.

Tax Credit on Inheritance, Estate, and Gift Taxes

A chronological survey of Federal-State death tax developments shows that questions of how death taxes should be used and by which level of government have been controversial for more than half a century. Property bequests at death are now taxed by the Federal government and all States except Nevada. Gifts are taxed by the Federal government and twelve States. This group of taxes annually contributes revenues of about $2 billion—$1.6 billion to the Federal government, and $400 million to the States.

A wartime Federal inheritance tax was repealed in 1902. President Roosevelt recommended its re-enactment in 1906, as did the Progressive Party in 1912, the latter accompanied by a proposal for distributing part of the proceeds to the States. Shortly after the law was re-enacted in 1916, President Wilson recommended its permanent retention but proposed that the Federal-State relationship should be re-examined. The tax credit feature was adopted by Congress in 1924 at 25 per cent, then increased in 1926 to 80 per cent, where it now stands. The exemptions were reduced in 1932, and a gift tax, lacking the credit device, was enacted. In the intervening years, a tremendous number of studies of the problem have been made under Federal, State, and intergovernmental auspices.

Library, December, 1960). This publication, Information Bulletin 200, discusses the principles and practices involved in such efforts in Wisconsin and other States.

The National Tax Association has consistently taken the position that these taxes should be reserved for State use. The arguments for exclusive State use and against Federal withdrawal from this field are summarized in the following table.

SEPARATION OF REVENUE SOURCES: INHERITANCE,
ESTATE AND GIFT TAXES *

Arguments for Exclusive State Use	*Arguments Against Federal Withdrawal*
1. The States were first to develop this tax area and have a proprietary interest in it.	1. Since taxpayers tend to migrate from States with high death taxes, interstate competition would soon dissipate the yield from these taxes.
2. The transfer of property from the deceased to his heirs is a privilege controlled by State law, and in the absence of an heir the property reverts to the State.	2. Federal taxation prevents an unfair concentration of the yield from taxes on activities conducted nationally by a relatively few more highly industrialized States.
3. The States have lesser financial resources and relatively greater need for tax revenues than has the National Government.	3. Exclusive State taxation would increase multiple taxation and interstate jurisdictional conflicts.
	4. The States are ill-equipped to absorb the revenue fluctuations characteristic of such an unstable revenue source.

5. State death tax administration is frequently divided between legal and lay authority and between State and local responsibility with the result that its quality is not uniformly good.

* Advisory Commission on Intergovernmental Relations, *Coordination of State and Federal Inheritance, Estate, and Gift Taxes* (Washington, January, 1961), pp. 84-85.

Currently, the estate-inheritance taxes are characterized by overlapping and complexity, heavy tax compliance burdens for taxpayers, occasional multiple taxation, and relatively high administrative costs which are out of all proportion to the small contribution which these taxes normally make to most State revenues. On the basis of a study made by the Advisory Commission on Intergovernmental Relations, bills are now before Congress to remedy these inequities, facilitate Federal-State cooperation, and strengthen the operation of both Federal and State revenue systems.[57] This legislation could ultimately represent the loss of several millions of dollars in Federal revenues through relinquishing these revenues to the States. The loss would not begin for several years, however, because the States would need time to bring their tax laws into conformity.

Specifically, the Commission recommends amendment of the Internal Revenue Code to increase the credit against the Federal estate tax for inheritance and estate taxes paid to the States, such amendment to be effective with respect to any given State only after (1) State legislative action which shifts the State tax from an "inheritance base" to an "estate base" and (2) legislative action which adjusts State tax rates to assure that the effect of the increased credit would redound to the benefit of the State treasury rather than to individual Federal taxpayers.

Employment Security Tax Offset

The national employment security program was an outgrowth of the Great Depression. It was established through the legislative cooperation of Congress and the State legislatures, and has since been administered cooperatively by the two levels of government. Particularly significant at this point are the cooperative arrangements regarding taxes which provide funds for the support of the system of public employment offices and unemployment compensation benefits. A Federal-State system of public employment offices was provided for in the Wagner-Peyser Act of 1933, and the program was enlarged and strengthened by the unemployment insurance features of the Social Security Act of 1935.

The major objectives of the system are three-fold: to promote employment opportunities, to encourage efforts to stabilize employment, and to minimize the effects of unemployment. A nationwide network of public employment offices, where job seekers and job openings can be quickly and efficiently matched, is maintained to accomplish the first of these objectives, and the unemployment insurance aspects of the program seek to accomplish the other two objectives. The cooperative arrangements between the two levels of government are as complex as they are unusual. Because this is the only major grant program where the total cost of administration is borne by one level of government (the

---

[57] *Coordination of State and Federal Inheritance, Estate, and Gift Taxes* (Washington, January, 1961). The bills are S. 1344 (86th Cong.), by Senator Muskie of Maine, H.R. 6207 by Mrs. Dwyer of New Jersey, and H.R. 6206 by Mr. Fountain of North Carolina, and H.R. 5039 by Mr. Keogh of New York. See also Maxwell, James A., "A New Proposal for Coordination of Death Taxation," *National Tax Journal,* December, 1961, pp. 382–387.

National) and the actual administration is carried on by another (the States), it is necessary to describe briefly both the legislative basis and the administrative arrangements under which the system operates.

The system is supported by both Federal and State taxes on earnings. The Federal government levies a 3 per cent tax on the annual wages of each covered worker up to $3,000. This tax is paid exclusively by the employer, but the employer can offset up to 90 per cent of the sum as a credit for what he has paid to the State. The 10 per cent retained by the Federal government goes into the general funds, but Congress has annually appropriated 100 per cent grants to pay the costs of administration. The actual functioning of these arrangements has been described as follows:

> The funds collected by the Federal Government under this tax have usually exceeded the costs of administration, the excess since the program started amounting to $570 million upwards to $1 billion depending upon whether or not certain administrative costs were charged against the funds. Under the provisions of Public Law 567, recently passed by Congress, future collections from this tax will be earmarked, a reserve of $200 million will be accumulated from the excess of collections over costs of administration, after which, further excess will be credited to the unemployment reserve funds of the respective States where it may be used for benefit payment purposes or to pay costs of administration. Furthermore, the States may qualify for repayable loans.[58]

The existence of the tax offset provision virtually assures prompt action on the part of the State legislatures, since if they fail to act, employers in such States must pay the full 3 per cent tax to the Federal government. All of the States acted promptly to establish State systems, and in an incredibly short time a nationwide program was established without setting up an exclusively Federal system. The Social Security Act prescribes half a dozen conditions which State unemployment compensation laws must meet if employers within the State are to be eligible for the tax offset:

1. All funds collected by the State must be used for payment of benefits through a federally approved State agency.

2. Tax receipts must be deposited immediately to the credit of the State in the Unemployment Trust Fund.

3. No benefits should be paid until two years after the collection of taxes begins.

4. Compensation may not be denied to a worker, otherwise eligi-

[58] Commission on Intergovernmental Relations (Kestnbaum), *Unemployment Compensation and Employment Service* (Washington, June, 1955), p. 15.

ble, who refuses to accept new work under certain specified conditions.

5. States must meet certain administrative standards established by the Social Security Administration.

6. A minimum range of protection was established for State laws; States do not have to provide coverage for these groups, although many of them have provided coverage broader than that required by Federal law.

In addition, several methods are provided for maintaining national control over various aspects of State legislation and administration of the program. These include the tax offset device itself, the fact that the Federal government pays 100 per cent of their administrative costs, and that it could withhold further funds for noncompliance. While these pressures toward conformity have rarely been needed, much less used, their very existence is an ever-present pressure upon the States against deviation from Federal requirements.

BIBLIOGRAPHICAL NOTES

General Works. William Anderson and Waite D. Durfee, *Intergovernmental Fiscal Relations* (Minneapolis: University of Minnesota Press, 1956) is one of ten volumes resulting from the University of Minnesota project. The following titles are also significant: Roy Blough, *Tax Relations Among Governmental Units* (New York: Tax Policy League, 1938); Alvin H. Hansen and Harvey S. Perloff, *State and Local Finance in the National Economy* (New York: W. W. Norton & Co., Inc., 1944); James A. Maxwell, *Fiscal Impact of Federalism in the United States* (Cambridge: Harvard University Press, 1946); Selma J. Mushkin, *Statistical Materials on the Distribution of Federal Expenditures Among the States,* and with Beatrice Crowther, *Federal Taxes and the Measurement of Fiscal Capacity* (Washington: Public Health Service, 1956 and 1954 respectively); Thomas H. Reed, ed., *Federal-State-Local Fiscal Relations* (Chicago: Municipal Finance Officers Association, 1942); G. Findley Shirras, *Federal Finance in Peace and War* (New York: The Macmillan Co., 1944); Tax Foundation, *Allocating the Federal Tax Burden Among the States* (New York, 1957); and Treasury Department, Committee on Intergovernmental Fiscal Relations (the Newcomer-Groves-Gulick Committee), *Intergovernmental Fiscal Relations,* 2 vols. (Washington, 1943). As a by-product of the work of this Committee, Dr. Newcomer compiled and the Department issued *Intergovernmental Fiscal Relations in the United States: A Selected Bibliography* (Washington, 1942).

William H. Jones, *Federal Taxes and State Expenses* (New York: G. P. Putnam's Sons, 1887), the first known published analysis of Federal-State fiscal relations, has the following interesting and rather curious subtitle: "or the Decay of Separate State Power of Excise Under the Federal Constitution, and the Compensation Therein Provided for It; and the Relation of the General Civil Administration Under Separate State Authority, to 'The General Welfare of the United States' Under the Federal Authority." Some years later, Mr. Jones published another work, *The "General Welfare*

Clause" and Senate Amendments to House Revenue Bills (Fort Wayne: Archer Printing Company, 1896), again with a most unusual subtitle: "Romances in Politics, and Novels in the Constitution."

Intergovernmental Tax Immunities. A. Miller Hillhouse, "Intergovernmental Tax Exemption," *Municipal Year Book, 1939,* pp. 345–381; George E. Lent, *The Ownership of Tax Exempt Securities* (New York: National Bureau of Economic Research, 1955); Cushman McGee, *Statement Concerning Immunity From Federal Taxation of Interest on Bonds of States and Municipalities* (New York: R. W. Pressprich & Company, 1959); Municipal Finance Officers Association, *Examination of Current Proposals to Tax State and Local Government Bonds* (Chicago, December, 1962); Alden L. Powell, *National Taxation of State Instrumentalities* (Urbana: University of Illinois Press, 1936). Of special value is a series of articles by Professor Thomas Reed Powell: "Intergovernmental Tax Immunities," *George Washington Law Review,* June, 1940, pp. 1213–1220; "The Waning of Intergovernmental Tax Immunities," and "The Remnants of Intergovernmental Tax Immunities," *Harvard Law Review,* May, 1945, pp. 633–674, and July, 1945, pp. 757–805.

Multiple and Conflicting Taxation. Federation of Tax Administrators, *Provisions Limiting Double Taxation of Income by States* (Chicago, September, 1956); Arthur L. Harding, *Double Taxation of Property and Income* (Cambridge: Harvard University Press, 1933); Interstate Commission on Conflicting Taxation, *Conflicting Taxation* (Chicago: Council of State Governments, 1935); Charles E. Ratliff, *Interstate Apportionment of Business Income for State Income Tax Purposes* (Chapel Hill: University of North Carolina Press, 1962); Advisory Commission on Intergovernmental Relations, *Tax Overlapping in the United States* (Washington, September, 1961); House Committee on Ways and Means, *Double Taxation* (Washington: House Committee Print, 72nd Cong., 2nd Sess., 1933); Treasury Department, Tax Division Analysis Staff, *Overlapping Taxes in the United States* (Washington, January, 1954).

Tax Coordination. In this field, in which the literature is voluminous but accomplishments relatively minor in comparison, the following titles are of special interest: American Bar Association *et al.*, *The Coordination of Federal, State, and Local Taxation* (Chicago: Joint Committee on Coordination, 1957); Council of State Governments, *Federal-State Tax and Fiscal Program* (Chicago, 1948); Empire State Chamber of Commerce, *Reallocation of Federal-State Functions and Tax Sources: A Staff Report* (Albany, 1953); Kenneth W. Gemmill *et al.*, a symposium on *Federal-State-Local Tax Correlation* (Princeton: Tax Institute, 1954); Clarence Heer, *Coordination of Federal and State Tobacco Taxes* and *Fiscal Coordination Through Intergovernmental Agreement* (both Chicago: American Legislators' Association, April, 1934, and November, 1933, respectively); *Proceedings of the Joint Conference on Federal-State Tax Relations,* (Chicago: Council of State Governments, September, 1947); James A. Maxwell, *Tax Credits and Intergovernmental Fiscal Relations* (Washington: Brookings Institution, 1962); House Committee on Ways and Means, *Coordination of Federal, State, and Local Taxes* (Washington: Report No. 2519, 82nd Cong., 2nd Sess., 1953); Joint Committee on Internal Revenue Taxation, *The Taxing Power of Federal and State Governments* (Washington: 75th Cong., 1st Sess., 1937); Senate Committee on Expenditures in the Executive Departments, *Coordination of Federal and State Taxes* (Washington: Senate Report No. 1054, 80th Cong., 2nd Sess., 1948).

Cooperative Administration. Significant titles in this field include: Boris I. Bittker, *Federal Income, Estate, and Gift Taxation,* 2nd ed. (Boston: Little, Brown and Co., 1958); Charles F. Conlon, "Harmonizing Federal, State, and Local Income Tax Administration," in Tax Institute, *Income Tax Administration* (New York, 1948), pp. 350–358; Clara Penniman and Walter W. Heller, *State Income Tax Administration*

(Chicago: Public Administration Service, 1959); Edwin S. Reno *et al.*, *Interdependent Taxes* (Chicago: Commerce Clearing House, on corporate income taxes, 1937); Leon Rothenberg, *Federal-State Exchange of Tax Information* (Chicago: Federation of Tax Administrators, January, 1962); Advisory Commission on Intergovernmental Relations, *Coordination of State and Federal Inheritance, Estate, and Gift Taxes* and *Intergovernmental Cooperation in Tax Administration* (both, Washington, 1961).

CHAPTER XIV

The Grant-in-Aid System: Origin and Development

Federal aid has become one of the most important aspects of governmental finance in this country. During recent years it has greatly increased in size, and the prospect is for an even greater use of Federal aid in the future. It is time to examine critically the existing Federal aid policies and administration, the significant trends, and the defects indicated by experience, to see what changes are needed. Federal aid in this country has developed without a well-considered, consistent, national policy. It has been guided principally by the advocates of particular forms of aid to the States, with little attention to national interest. . . .

The expansion of Federal aid in this country is by no means exceptional to the trend in other countries. Every industrialized country has faced the problem of a growing disparity between local governmental tax resources and the demands for services, and has been forced to resort to central financial aid to local governments. The grant-in-aid is only one of several devices which may be used. Other means include the assumption by the central government of expensive activities formerly conducted by the local governments, the sharing of centrally collected taxes with the local units, and the use of "block" or unconditional subsidies, permitting the local governments to expend them for whatever purpose they may determine.

Although little attention has been paid to State aid to local units, it has greatly exceeded in amount Federal aid to the States (except emergency expenditures for unemployment relief), and within recent years has been increasing at a very fast rate, particularly for education and relief.[1]

[1] Harris, Joseph P., "The Future of Federal Grants-in-Aid," *Annals of the American Academy of Political and Social Science,* January, 1940, pp. 14–26, on pp. 14, 16.

ANTECEDENTS OF THE GRANT-IN-AID SYSTEM

At the risk of over-simplification, one may say that there were four major problems in nineteenth-century America—disposition of the public domain, internal improvements, education, and slavery. Each of these has its counterpart in the twentieth century—resource conservation and utilization, highways, education, and civil rights and race relations. The first three in both lists involve Federal grants-in-aid.

The system whereby the central government gives monetary or cash grants to the States and local units has become so familiar in modern America that one tends to assume that it has always existed, as in a sense it has. The principle of assistance was early established; the early grants were, with few exceptions, land grants. Land grants for education date back to the eighteenth century, and extensive land grants for internal improvements, education, and agriculture were given during the nineteenth century. In the twentieth century, grants have been given mainly for highways, health and welfare, and education. Thus the grant-in-aid system has evolved from land grants to cash grants, and from "single shot" to annual payments. Federal control has increased, and financial participation by States and municipalities has been encouraged through the development of matching formulae.

Development of a National Land Policy

Since the story begins with the early acquisition by Congress of the western lands for the United States, the nation's land policy is a matter of primary importance in any study of the origins and growth of the grant-in-aid system. Many of the colonies were, by their charters, entitled to land beyond the Appalachian Mountains. Although the western lands had been closed to settlement by the Proclamation of 1763, the States, with the outbreak of the Revolution, resumed their titles to them. Many of these titles were conflicting and uncertain; especially among the States that did not have title to such lands, there was a widespread feeling that they should be surrendered to the central government. In a resolution adopted on October 10, 1780, Congress stated the policy that it intended to follow regarding any lands ceded to it by the States. Briefly, this policy included three important points: (1) that the States should be reimbursed for expenses incurred in the defense of such lands; (2) that the lands should be developed with a view to eventual statehood; and (3) that the lands should be "disposed of for the common benefit of the United States."

This resolution and the attitude of Maryland toward ratification of the Articles of Confederation gave a powerful impulse to the cession of the land claims of the States to the central government. New York and Connecticut indicated their willingness to cede their claims as early as 1781, and Congress accepted the New York cession the following year. The claims of Virginia were most extensive and were stronger than those of any other State, since they were based not only on charter rights but on the achievements of Clark in the Northwest. Virginia's first cession in 1781 was accompanied by conditions that were not acceptable to Congress, but the cession of 1783 was promptly accepted and the deed signed on March 1, 1784. Cessions from other States followed in due course, as shown in the table on page 480.

Having acquired extensive Western lands for the United States, Congress was faced anew with the problem of administering them. Shortly after Virginia's cession had been formally completed, Jefferson introduced in Congress a plan for the governmental organization of the western territory. His proposal included two interesting and important provisions that were not retained in the measure as finally approved on April 23, 1784, although both were approved in substance shortly thereafter in the Northwest Ordinance in 1787: (1) that ten States be created from the territory between the Ohio and Mississippi Rivers, and (2) that after 1800, slavery be excluded from any of the said States. The language used in the latter connection was identical with that appearing later in the Wilmot Proviso and with that which was ultimately incorporated in the Constitution in the Thirteenth Amendment. In the following year, on May 20, 1785, Congress adopted a land ordinance which laid the foundations for the public land system that was to be followed in most essentials until 1862.

The Western public lands were looked upon as prospective producers of wealth for the States, and the idea that the lands were a valuable financial asset to the older settled part of the country continued during the constitutional period, as evidenced by the Land Act of 1796. Included in the 1785 legislation was the famous surveying plan under which the territory was to be divided into townships six miles square, which in turn were divided into thirty-six sections. Two extremely significant provisions on the disposition of the land provided for the sale of some lots and the allocation of others for public school purposes:

> The commissioners of the loan office of the several States shall proceed to sell the townships or fractional parts of townships, at public

CESSIONS OF THE WESTERN LANDS *

1780	February 19	Act of New York Legislature
	March 7	Laid before Congress
	October 10	Act of Connecticut Legislature
		Congress establishes policy, with respect to ceded lands
1781	February 2	Act of Virginia Legislature
	March 1	New York deed of cession executed in Congress
1782	October 29	New York cession accepted by Congress
1783	September 13	Virginia cession rejected
	October 20	Second Virginia Act
1784	March 1	Virginia cession completed
	June 2	Act of North Carolina Legislature
	November 13	Act of Massachusetts Legislature
	November 20	Act of North Carolina Legislature repealed
1785	April 19	Massachusetts cession completed
1786	May 11	Second Act of Connecticut Legislature
	May 28	Connecticut cession completed
1787	March 8	Act of South Carolina Legislature
	August 9	South Carolina cession completed
1788	February 1	First Act of Georgia Legislature
	July 15	Georgia offer rejected
1789	December 22	Act of North Carolina Legislature
1790	February 25	North Carolina cession completed
1802	April 24	Articles of Agreement and Cession entered into between the Commissioners of the United States and of Georgia
	June 16	Ratified by the Georgia Legislature

* Adapted from Treat, Payson J., *National Land System* (New York: E. B. Treat & Company, 1910), p. 14, and reproduced in Channing, Edward, *History of the United States,* 6 vols. (New York: the Macmillan Co., 1905–1925), III, 457–458.

TOTAL FEDERAL LAND GRANTS BY PURPOSE *

Purpose of Grant	Number of Million Acres
Homesteads	285
Sites for Schools and Other Purposes	185
Railroad Construction	111
Military Bounties and Private Claims	95
Timber and Stone Grants	35
Cash and Miscellaneous	300
Total	1,011

* From Clawson, Marion, *Uncle Sam's Acres* (New York: Dodd, Mead & Company, 1951), p. 46.

vendue, in the following manner, viz.: The township or fractional part of a township No. 1, in the first range, shall be sold entire; and No. 2, in the same range, by lots; and thus in alternate order through the whole of the first range . . . provided, that none of the lands, within the said territory, be sold under the price of one dollar the acre, to be paid in specie, or loan-office certificates, reduced to specie value, by the scale of depreciation. . . .

There shall be reserved for the United States out of every township the four lots, being numbered 8, 11, 26, 29, and out of every fractional part of a township, so many lots of the same numbers as shall be found thereon, for future sale. There shall be reserved the lot No. 16 of every township, for the maintenance of public schools within the said township; also one-third part of all gold, silver, lead and copper mines, to be sold, or otherwise disposed of as Congress shall hereafter direct. . . .

It has been said that one of the basic principles of federalism is that the superior resources of the central government shall be used to initiate and support national programs, largely administered by the political subdivisions. If this be true, it is clear that American federalism early passed the test. Even before the present government was established, land grants had been made for many worthy purposes, while cash grants for "common schools" and other purposes followed, sporadically at first but later on a regular basis as a matter of permanent policy, during a period that lasted more than a century until, in fact, the amount of desirable land available for grants was largely depleted. The total amount of these grants (estimated at 1,011 million acres) and the purposes for which they were made, are shown in the preceding table.

Until the close of the nineteenth century, grants of the public domain to the States constituted the usual form of Federal aid. In all, the

Federal government conferred upon the States approximately 15 per cent of its total land holdings; any precise calculation of the financial value of these grants is impossible. Although the data are somewhat incomplete, it is clear that the lion's share was devoted to the field of education.

Early Land Grants for Schools

In the preceding paragraph of the Land Ordinance of 1785, one may observe what was probably the first attempt to make specific provision for the financial support of public education. Within twenty years, two more provisions, equally significant, recorded indelibly the intent of the people under their new government to make proper provision for the support of education. The first of these was made before the present Constitution was framed and adopted, in the Northwest Ordinance of 1787, while the second came after the Constitution in the Enabling Act which admitted Ohio into the Union in 1803. Thus, at an early date, a pattern for the support of public education was firmly established.

The Northwest Ordinance did not mention the earlier Land Ordinance, but its provisions were affirmed in two places. At the beginning of Article III, it is declared that "Religion, morality, and knowledge, being necessary to good government and the happiness of mankind, schools and the means of education shall forever be encouraged," and Article IV provides: "The legislatures of those districts or new States, shall never interfere with the primary disposal of the soil by the United States in Congress assembled, nor with any regulations Congress may find necessary for securing the title in such soil to the bona fide purchasers."

Under the terms of the Enabling Act admitting Ohio into the Union as a State, one section of land in each township (or its equivalent) was reserved for school purposes. In later years—after 1848—and in other States, two sections were so reserved, and the land itself or the proceeds from its sale were devoted to the maintenance and support of common schools. In Arizona, New Mexico, and Utah, four sections were reserved. In most States, a trust fund was established for the administration of school lands and funds.

Early Financial Assistance to the States

Significant financial assistance from the central government to the States was provided at a fairly early date, and proposals for other forms of aid were not long in coming. The first forms of grants to the States were the assumption of the State debts in 1790, Federal aid for railroads and canals in the early 1800's, for support of the militia, and distribution of the surplus in 1838. While in a sense these grants established a precedent, it was not a precedent that took hold immediately or that served as a pattern for future action until more than a century later.

Assumption of State Debts. In the course of the Revolution, the States had incurred a heavy burden of debt, in part because they were fairly strong and self-reliant at the time, and partly because the central government was weak and ineffective. These debts became almost immediately a cause of serious concern. As far back as the period of the war, Congress had recognized that the interests of the States and of the Nation were inextricably bound together. Commissioners had been appointed to settle the accounts between the United States and the several States, and in 1784 elaborate rules had been drawn up for their guidance. The matter had been considered by the Federal Convention, where it had been proposed that the general government should provide for the State debts as well as for those of the Union. This proposition was opposed by some because it did not go far enough, by others because it went too far. The commissioners had continued working over the problem without arriving at any satisfactory solution.

Alexander Hamilton proposed that the central government assume the whole debt, including the State debts, believing that this was essential to the establishment of the national credit. The assumption would cover whatever portion of the State debts should be converted into United States securities, such sums to be charged in the final settlement against the respective States. He contended that since the central government was taking possession of the duties on imported goods, it was only right that it assume responsibility for the State debts. If this were not done, the States would compete with one another and with the United States in search of new sources of revenue with which these obligations might be met. Such competition, he believed, would not only injure the credit of the national government, but that of the States as well.

This proposal, though no new idea, aroused much opposition, largely on a sectional basis. The States that had the largest unpaid debts were Massachusetts and South Carolina, while Virginia and New York had already made provision for a large part of theirs and only very small debts remained unpaid. The Pennsylvania debt was not large, but since the Pennsylvanians estimated that they would receive about as much as they would be obliged to pay out, they took little interest in the matter. It seemed to New York and Virginia, however, that if the State debts were assumed, they would be taxed to pay a part of the interest and, ultimately, a part of the principal on the debts of Massachusetts and South Carolina and other States that had balances to their credit against the United States as a whole.

Congress had already in the first session provided for the continuance of the commission established to settle the accounts between the National government and the States. Some wanted to wait until this commission had completed its work before taking action; others contended that any postponement of assumption would keep down the price of State securities and encourage their movement into the hands of foreign capitalists who could easily afford to buy them at a low rate and hold them until they should appreciate in value. Supporters of early action won, but not without some intrigue and a bargain to locate the capital on the banks of the Potomac. Congress passed the legislation necessary to the assumption of State debts in 1790, whereupon the Virginia House of Delegates (even though the assumption as passed removed almost the whole of Virginia's outstanding debt) protested a few months later that the action was not justified on grounds of justice, policy, or the Constitution. The gross claims of Massachusetts amounted to $26 million, although a large part of this sum disappeared in the process of reducing it from a paper currency to a specie basis.

Owing to the slowness with which the new government machinery was organized and the delays necessarily involved in converting the old debt into the new, payments of interest on the new obligations did not begin for some time. The revenue was small, which made little difference at the moment, but it was plain that more funds would have to be provided in 1792 when payment of interest on the assumed State debts was scheduled to begin. The passage of the first tariff act on August 10, 1790, gave promise of more revenue. This measure, establishing a national custom service, had been adopted as the only available means of avoiding the irregularities that had characterized the State services. On March 3, 1791, Congress further bolstered the revenues when it adopted Hamilton's plan for the assessment and collection of internal revenue duties on distilled spirits and additional duties on imported spirits. Long familiar in England, this was a new tax form in America, one which, in its original form, proved to be impossible to execute. Following the Whiskey Rebellion in western Pennsylvania and western Virginia, the law was given a more workable form by a 1792 revision.

Federal Aid for Roads and Canals. Transportation facilities in America had been of a rather primitive sort. Some improvements had been undertaken in colonial times at the general expense or at the expense of one or two colonies, as when a passable route from Portsmouth, New Hampshire, southward to Baltimore was opened. With the establishment of the new government under the Constitution, the demand for improvement was greatly stimulated by considerations of defense and by recognition of the need for better transportation for economic growth and social welfare. Later, after years of trade embargoes and of war, the demand for improved transportation became increasingly insistent. Before the problem was solved, however, it developed into one of the bitterest controversies in the history of American politics.

Since no State or community, with the crude methods of taxation then prevailing, could finance construction of an extensive system of roads, private corporations, with some aid from the States, took on the job. They obtained the rest of their capital from lotteries, which were in those days generally permitted, and also charged tolls for the use of their facilities, which came to be known as turnpikes or toll roads. It is reported that between 1800 and 1821, some 1,200 miles of such roads were built, nearly all of it of approved construction.

Soon canals and railroads began to attract public attention. The turnpikes failed as profitable investments and had to be taken over by the government. During this period, the Commonwealth of Pennsylvania subscribed nearly $2 million to the capital stock of the road companies within her borders, in addition to contributions that had been made by counties and towns. The construction of bridges on these roads was usually undertaken by other companies which were also often aided by public authorities and by the tolls which they collected. Most of the bridges were of timber, often with stone abutments, which were constantly being damaged or destroyed by ice, flood, or fire.

The Erie Canal is particularly noteworthy for its role in building up the industries of the East, peopling the farms of the West, and providing the laboring masses of large portions of Europe with food. Credit for constructing the canal is attributed to the powerful and continuing support of DeWitt Clinton. The digging of the canal was authorized by the New York legislature in 1817 at the expense of the State, since application for national assistance had been made in vain. Many difficult engineering problems were met and successfully solved in the course of construction; in order to avoid expensive cuttings or embankments, the canal ascended and descended. As first constructed, it was 363 miles long, and the highest point was at Lake Erie, 568 feet above the Hudson River at Albany. By 1825, when it was opened for its full length, the cost of transporting one ton of merchandise from Buffalo to New York City had been reduced from $100 to less than $8.00. Had the canal not been completed, the development of the Western country would have been delayed for twenty or thirty years until the railroads reduced transportation costs. In the years which followed, while most of the canals went out of use in competition with the railroads, only the Erie Canal retained its vitality.

Internal improvements in the nineteenth century involved a multitude of problems—roads, canals, harbors, public buildings and institutions, river improvements, land reclamation, agricultural developments, railroads, and the creation of a national banking system to finance them. They created most of the problems of intergovernmental relations mainly because they accounted for a major portion of governmental activity. But there were constitutional problems as well. Alexander Hamilton is believed to have thought that an amendment to the Constitution would be necessary to authorize the central government to develop improvements in the territory of two or more States. Albert Gallatin, longtime Secretary of the Treasury who did not share this view, is supposed to have first suggested giving Federal aid for the building of roads.

On February 13, 1802, Gallatin wrote to William B. Giles, chairman of the committee that was considering the admission of Ohio into the Union, proposing that one-tenth of the proceeds of the land thereafter sold by the National government within the borders of the State should be applied to the building of roads from the Atlantic seaboard to the Ohio valley, and later to the Mississippi. Giles followed Gallatin's recommendation, and Ohio was admitted to the Union with such a condition in the Act of Congress passed in 1803.

Jefferson accepted Gallatin's plan for internal improvements by the national government, including the construction of national roads, the surveying and protection of the coasts, and the deepening and improvement of rivers and harbors, and became jointly responsible with him for the policy of internal improvements by Federal action. Nevertheless, he still questioned, as did Hamilton, the constitutionality of such a program without specific authorization by a constitutional amendment. In his annual message in December, 1806, Jefferson asked that such an amendment be considered by Congress as an appropriate means of using the surplus revenues that were then anticipated.

When Jefferson signed the bill for the admission of Ohio into law, the Cumberland Road had its origin, and the first decade of the nineteenth century was marked as the beginning of an era of national projects in internal improvement. In 1806, Congress authorized the President to appoint three commissioners to survey a road from Cumberland, Maryland, to the Ohio River, and appropriated $30,000 for that purpose. The President signed the appropriation bill on January 31, 1807. It is extremely interesting to note that, in this case, the consent of the States through which the road was to pass had to be obtained before the actual work of construction could begin.

During the next few years, the road was constructed from Cumberland to Wheeling. The eastern portion, known as the National Road, followed generally the course of an Indian path. Later, the National Road was continued west through Ohio and Indiana to central Illinois, and it was proposed to build a connecting line southward from Zanesville to Maysville, Kentucky, then to Lexington, and finally southwest to the lower Mississippi. During the ten or fifteen years after 1816, the eastern and middle portions of the Cumberland Road were crowded with emigrants and their families moving westward in wagons laden with household goods; in later years, it was equally crowded with wagons bringing the products of Western farms to the markets of the East.

The discussions over the Cumberland Road project and the growing interest in canals culminated in a Senate resolution requesting Gallatin to prepare and report a plan for "the application of such means as are within the power of Congress, to the purposes of opening roads, and making canals." The Secretary of the Treasury replied on April 4, 1808, with a remarkable report in which he proposed the construction of a line of canals along the Atlantic coast and another system connecting the seaboard with the Mississippi Valley and the St. Lawrence River.[2] Several important constitutional issues came up in these discussions. The first involved the power of the central government to spend for internal improvements. Constitutionalists at that time saw, or professed to see, some strange difference between spending on the actual construction of such improvements and spending for surveys looking toward future construction. There was also prevalent at the time an idea that the consent of the States concerned must first be obtained before any public works might be constructed within their borders.

President Madison recognized the need for internal improvements, but resolutely refused to approve measures providing for such expenditures on the ground that there was no power given Congress in the Contitution to provide for them. President Monroe vetoed every bill providing for Federal construction within a State for the same reason. Jackson, whose name must be added to the list of presidential opponents, based at least part of his opposition upon a view which now sounds strange indeed, a desire to keep business out of government and government out of business.

President Polk's views on the problem of constitutionality coincided with those of Hamilton, Jefferson, Madison, Monroe, and Jackson; he recognized somewhat grudgingly the need to aid navigation for purposes of foreign commerce and for the protection and security of American naval vessels, but he could see no difference between river and harbor improvements and canal digging or road building by the Federal government. Like his predecessors, he vetoed every measure of this type that came to his desk, explaining that what is convenient is not always either

[2] *Report of the Secretary of the Treasury, on the Subject of Public Roads and Canals; Made in Pursuance of a Resolution of Senate of March 2, 1807, April 12, 1808.* Printed by Order of the Senate, Washington, 1808.

"necessary and proper" or constitutional. Polk believed—not at all inaccurately, as subsequent experience has shown—that once such a policy is established, there is practically no end to the raids upon the public treasury.

In marked contrast to the other great national leaders of their time, Henry Clay and John Quincy Adams promoted internal improvements as part of the so-called American system and taxed luxuries to get funds to pay for them. In 1837, nearly ten years after he left the Presidency, Adams wrote to a friend bemoaning the fall of "the system of internal improvements by means of national energies." He believed that had the system continued, within ten years, "the surface of the whole Union would have been checkered over with railroads and canals." He concluded with the very interesting observation that "It may still be done half a century later and with the limping gait of State legislatures and private adventure." [3]

The real issue in this whole controversy, as Professor Carter Goodrich has pointed out,

> was between national and state action. This was clear in the constitutional debates which filled so many pages in the *Annals of Congress* and in the works of later historians. In these the issue turned solely on the powers given by the Constitution to the Federal and State governments respectively and not at all on the rights of private individuals and corporations. Advocates of Federal action made elaborate attempts to find justification in various powers enumerated in the document, and on many occasions Presidents or legislators professed themselves to be in sympathy with the purposes of the measures proposed but unable to accept the arguments for their constitutionality.[4]

Joint action for internal improvements in those early days was undertaken for much the same reasons that it is today. The assumption that the States act first in areas in which they have jurisdiction has not always been supported by fact, though it was in the case of the Erie Canal. Usually when the need for action is agreed upon, the decision is reached more or less simultaneously at all levels; certain individual units may move first and thus acquire earlier experience in a field. The Virginia Board of Public Works was established in 1816, at least in part as a result of Federal activities; a development of this type in one State or section of the country may normally be regarded as an indication that the

[3] Quoted by Goodrich, Carter, *Government Promotion of American Canals and Railroads, 1800–1890* (New York: Columbia University Press, 1960), p. 17.
[4] Goodrich, p. 44.

same or a similar problem exists in other sections.[5] Congress formalized previously existing programs by establishing a Board of Internal Improvements in 1824.

Transportation developments provide a fine illustration of the manner in which one invention supplants another. For a time, the cry was for roads, roads, and more roads. The Nation, the States, and private companies as well, with the aid of various local units, undertook their construction and operation, usually in return for tolls which were levied on all traffic using them. Then the canals rendered partially useless the stagecoach and the wagon, and also the stone road except for purely local purposes. In turn, the canal systems were hardly complete when the steamboat and the railway usurped their business. In our own day, the automobile, the motor truck and bus, and the airplane have to a large extent displaced railroads and trolley cars.

During these years of change, capital was in scant supply; both promoters and the general public naturally turned to public authorities for aid, and Congress, the State legislatures, and the cities responded to their demands. As noted, the Erie Canal was constructed by New York State. Both States and cities subscribed to the stock of road companies, and legislatures gave promoters the right to hold lotteries. When the railroads came, therefore, the people were accustomed to public contribution, especially in the Western country, and such contributions were made on a grand scale. In fact, this financial assistance was necessary because roads, canals, and railroads could not be expected to earn any return on the money invested until the country they served had been opened up and developed. The result was a mass of public debt—socially, politically, and economically justified, but still burdensome. Under these circumstances, a number of States went into the banking business, not too successfully, for the most part, although State banks in Virginia and South Carolina were well managed and profitable.

Distribution of the Surplus. Years later, toward the end of the Jacksonian era, the famous incident of the distribution of the surplus took place. A surplus may be defined as the amount of ordinary revenues in the treasury in excess of expenditure requirements. The government had paid off the final installment of its debt in 1835, but not until 1842 could it reduce revenues to the level of requirements for current expenses. There was likely to be a large surplus in 1837, and a still larger one in 1838 amounting to $27 million. The disposition of these funds presented a difficult and troublesome problem. A governmental surplus is a curse which almost invariably opens the way to a type of political manipula-

[5] These aspects of the time sequence of actions in the field of intergovernmental relations are discussed in Elazar, Daniel J., *The American Partnership* (Chicago: University of Chicago Press, 1962), pp. 54–58.

tion which, under other circumstances, is intolerable; governments simply are not organized to be able to cope effectively with such situations.

Before 1837, the surplus funds could have been used to retire the debt, or to make internal improvements, but in that year there was no debt and the President had just recently vetoed the Maysville Bill, so the only things that could be done with the surplus were deposit it with the pet banks or distribute it to the States. No one seems to have advocated the former, so in spite of doubts regarding the constitutional authority of the Federal government to collect money to pay over to the States, the latter course was decided upon. In the end, the constitutional objection was evaded by loaning the money to the States or depositing it with them, with the mutual understanding that they would never be asked to repay it.

This distribution was significant, not so much because of the amount involved as because it marked the first instance in history in which substantial cash payments were made by the Federal government to the States. Such payments are today called unconditional grants, meaning that the States are free to use the money for any proper governmental purpose. Cash grants for specific programs on an annual basis did not begin until the late nineteenth century. For the most part, the States did not make good use of the money; if they had, further grants might have been made in a period of less than a century.

As a matter of fact, the whole operation was badly handled by both parties. The financial situation in the country, already disturbed by the failure to renew the charter of the Second Bank, was in 1837 made even worse by the panic of that year. Three of the four installments of the distribution had already been made; because a procedure for gradually transferring Federal funds as they became available from the so-called pet banks to the States had not been established, the depositing banks were obliged to curtail credits and hold inactive in their vaults funds which could have been usefully employed outside. Actually, until the independent treasury legislation was enacted, there was no place in which receipts could be deposited. Since the Van Buren administration could scarcely be expected to use either the Biddle Bank in Philadelphia or the undemocratic banks in the Northeast, the only thing that could be done at the moment was to instruct the receivers of public funds to care for them as best they could—as in fact they did.

GRANTS FOR AGRICULTURAL EDUCATION AND RESEARCH

Legislation in the broad field of agricultural education falls into one of four main categories, as follows:

1. Land-grant college legislation.
2. Supporting research on agricultural problems at agricultural experiment stations.
3. Making basic information on farm and home problems available to the people, through the Agricultural Extension Service.
4. Providing vocational training on agricultural problems, home economics and industrial subjects, including distributive education.

The legislative record is impressive for a number of reasons, first of all for the number of important enactments—approximately three dozen major laws. Although the foundations of the present system were firmly established in each of the four major categories by the turn of the cen-

GRANTS-IN-AID FOR AGRICULTURAL RESEARCH AND EDUCATION *

Year Enacted	Program and Statutory Citation		Appropriation for Selected Years
1862	Colleges for Agriculture and Mechanic Arts		
	Statutory Basis:	1930	$ 2,550,000
	Morrill Land Grant Act of July 2, 1862. 12 Stat. 503	1940	5,030,000
	Morrill Land Grant Act of August 30, 1890. 26 Stat. 417	1950	5,030,000
		1960	5,051,500
1887	Agricultural Experiment Stations		
	Statutory Basis:	1930	$ 4,335,000
	Hatch Experiment Station Act of March 2, 1887. 54 Stat. 440	1940	8,848,148
	Adams Act of March 16, 1906. 34 Stat. 63	1950	12,243,522
	Purnell Act of February 24, 1925. 43 Stat. 970	1960	31,084,540
	Bankhead-Jones Act of June 29, 1935. 49 Stat. 436–439		
	Act of August 14, 1946. 60 Stat. 1082		
1914	Cooperative Agricultural Extension Work		
	Statutory Basis:	1930	$ 7,561,550
	Smith-Lever Act of May 9, 1914. 38 Stat. 372–374	1940	18,458,267
	Clarke-McNary Act of June 7, 1924. 43 Stat. 653	1950	31,025,919
	Capper-Ketcham Act of May 22, 1928. 45 Stat. 711	1960	61,302,594
	Bankhead-Jones Act of June 29, 1935. 49 Stat. 436–439		
	Cooperative Farm Forestry Act of May 8, 1937. 50 Stat. 188		
	Additional Extension Act of April 24, 1939. 53 Stat. 589		
	Department of Agriculture Organic Act of September 21, 1944. 58 Stat. 742		
	Bankhead-Flanagan Act of June 8, 1945. 59 Stat. 231–233		
	Act of August 11, 1955. 69 Stat. 683–684		

* Source: Annual Reports of the Secretary of the Treasury.

tury, there has been since World War I a continuous stream of new and amendatory legislation in all four categories which has consistently provided for (1) the enlargement and extension of the services offered and (2) the authorization of steadily increasing amounts for financial support.

An effort has been made to present a broad outline of this legislative history in text and tables. The text is concerned with significant legislation in each major category; the chart presents an overall view of 100 years of legislative history by arranging the significant enactments chronologically, according to type. One cannot examine this record of accomplishment without being impressed. The present organization for the administration of these programs is large, the investment in plant is extensive, and the results are noteworthy, both to the agricultural industry and to the nation as a whole. If one wonders at the general scope and effectiveness of the present operation of these programs, it is well to remember that they did not spring into existence overnight. They have grown because the people, who found the services useful and were willing to put up local money to have them expanded, wanted them to grow.

Another characteristic of this group of programs is deserving of more than passing comment. All of them are operated on the basis of interlevel and interjurisdictional cooperation. They are not only Federal, State, or local, but all three together. Units of all three levels of government share in the costs (roughly one-third each) and in the administration. Nowhere is there to be found a better illustration of what has in recent years come to be known as "cooperative federalism."

Colleges of Agriculture and Mechanic Arts

The first Morrill Land Grant Act for Colleges of Agriculture and Mechanic Arts was passed in 1862, the second in 1890. (See table on page 491.) Though sponsored by Senator Justin S. Morrill of Vermont, the real "father" of the act was Professor Jonathan B. Turner of what was then called Illinois College. Existing professions, he pointed out, constituted 1 per cent of the population and had their colleges which would provide a liberal education. He wanted colleges which would provide a similar education suited to the needs of the rest of the people— the farmer, manufacturer, businessman, the ambitious and intelligent worker who, with the aid of science, might transform a trade into a profession or at least a technology. His plan, first presented around 1850, has been called the "common man's educational Bill of Rights." His vision of "a University for the Industrial Classes in each of the States with their consequent subordinate institutes, lyceums and high schools in each of the counties and towns" met with widespread public approval.[6]

The sentiment for agricultural schools was greatly strengthened by local and county agricultural societies, some 900 of which, all more or less active, existed by the eve of the Civil War. Many of these societies were extremely interested in the problem of agricultural education. It is reported that in February, 1853, Daniel Lee insisted that "we should have agricultural schools to teach our youth the principles of soil-building science" and urged Congress to take action.[7] The name of Senator Morrill is inseparably linked with the land-grant college legislation. In 1857, while still a Member of the House of Representatives, he first introduced the bill. It was finally passed by both houses but was vetoed by President Buchanan in 1859. He reintroduced the bill late in 1861. Again it passed both houses, but this time it was signed by President Lincoln in 1862. This legislation established a pattern for Federal support of higher education without Federal control.

The original act appropriated to each State a quantity of public land equal to 30,000 acres for each Senator or Representative in Congress to which the State was entitled under the 1860 census, mineral lands being excluded from either grant or purchase. States not having public lands equalling their distributive share received land scrip "to be sold by said States and the proceeds thereof applied to the use and purposes" prescribed in the Act and for no other. It was also provided that all moneys derived from the sale of land or land scrip "shall be invested in stocks of the United States, or of the States, or some other safe stocks, yielding not less than 5 per centum upon the par value of said stock," and that all income so derived must inviolably be appropriated for the endowment, maintenance, and support of at least one agricultural and mechanical college.

While the Act specifically referred to the teaching of "such branches of learning as are related to agriculture and the mechanic arts," it also indicated its purpose "to promote the liberal and practical education of the industrial classes in the several pursuits and professions of life." These were to be schools of science, rather than classical colleges, but not mere trade schools. The second Morrill Act sought to provide a more adequate endowment of the land-grant colleges by appropriating to each State and Territory for their benefit the proceeds of 500,000 acres of public land, estimated at $1.25 per acre, or a total of $625,000. The Secre-

[6] See Thackrey, Russell I., and Richter, Jay, "The Land-Grant Colleges and Universities, 1862–1962: An American Institution," *Higher Education*, November, 1959, pp. 3–8.

[7] Department of Agriculture, *Some Landmarks of Department of Agriculture History* (Washington, June, 1953), p. 7.

STATE UNIVERSI

WASH.

MONT.

Washington
State University
Pullman • Moscow

ORE.

Corvallis
Oregon State
University

University of Idaho

Montana State College
Bozeman

WYO.

N. DAK.

North Dakota
State University
Fargo

S.DAK.

South Dakota
State College
College Station

CAL.

NEV.

IDAHO

Utah State
University
• *Logan*

University of Wyoming
Laramie •

NEBR.

University of Nevada
• *Reno*

UTAH   COL.

University of Nebras
Linco

Berkeley
University of
California

Fort Collins
Colorado State
University

KANS.

Manha
Kansas
State Univ

ARIZ.

N. MEX.

Langston
University   *La*

OKLA.

TEXAS

St
Oklaho
State Univ

University of
Arizona
• *Tucson*

New Mexico
State University
• *University Park*

ALASKA

University of
Alaska
• *College*

Honolulu
University of
Hawaii

Texas Agricultural
& Mechanical College S
College Station •

Prairie View •

Prairie View Agri
& Mechanical C

HAWAII

494

LAND-GRANT COLLEGES

ME.

University of Maine
Orono

MINN.

WIS.

MICH.

University of Vermont
Burlington

V.T. N.H.

University of N.H.
Durham

Massachusetts Institute
of Technology

Cambridge

University of Minnesota
Minneapolis

University of Wisconsin
Madison

Michigan State University
East Lansing

Cornell University
Ithaca

N.Y.

Amherst

University of Mass.

MASS.

New Haven

Storrs

Kingston University of Rhode Island

IOWA

Iowa State University
Ames

ILL.

IND.

OHIO

PENN.

Pennsylvania State University
University Park

Rutgers University
New Brunswick

University of Connecticut

The Connecticut Agricultural
Experiment Station

University of Illinois
Urbana

Purdue University
Lafayette

Ohio State University
Columbus

N.J.

University of Delaware
Newark

Dover Delaware State College

ersity of Missouri
Columbia

Kentucky State Coll.
Frankfort

Morgantown
W. Va. University

MD.

College Park

DEL.

Princess Anne Maryland State College

Jefferson City

ncoln niversity

University of Kentucky
Lexington

W.VA.

Blacksburg

Virginia Polytechnic Institute

VA.

Petersburg

University of Maryland

MO.

KY.

University of Tenn.
Nashville
Knoxville

TENN.

Greensboro

Virginia State College

Raleigh

etteville iversity of kansas

ARK.

Tenn. Agricultural & Industrial State University

Agricultural & Technical College

N.C.
State College

MISS.

Normal
Alabama Agric. & Mech. College

Athens

Clemson
Clemson Agric. College

N.C.

Pine Bluff

Orangeburg

ricultural Mechanical Normal College

State College

University of Georgia

S.C.State College

S.C.

LA.

Mississippi State U.

Auburn
Alabama Polytechnic Institute

Fort Valley
Fort Valley State College

Alcorn

Alcorn Agric. & Mech. College

ALA.

GA.

Southern University

Baton Rouge

Tallahassee

Florida Agricultural & Mechanical University

Louisiana State University

Gainesville
University of Florida

FLA.

Rio Piedras

University of Puerto Rico

PUERTO RICO

495

tary of the Treasury was required annually to ascertain the net proceeds of the sales of public lands for the preceding year, and to invest the same, insofar as they came under the terms of this Act, in 5 per cent registered United States bonds, or to issue such bonds to the colleges, keeping them in the Treasury but paying the interest semiannually to the trustees of the colleges. It is to be noted that this Act represents a departure from the original one in that it makes a grant of the proceeds from the sale of a specified number of acres of land, rather than the land itself. In view of the fact that some of the States squandered their land, it would appear that this change was made none too soon.

In all the years since the passage of the two Morrill Acts, there has been only one important piece of legislation dealing with the land-grant college system thereby established. This, the Bankhead-Jones Act of June 29, 1935, was a most unusual piece of legislation in that, unlike all other legislation affecting agricultural education, it dealt with more than one of the four major phases of the subject. In fact, it dealt with three phases, including provisions which affected all but the vocational education aspects of the field. For the more adequate endowment of the land-grant colleges, the Bankhead-Jones Act provided for $960,000 annually, plus $1,500,000 annually after three years. A further increase in the amount of the annual grants was made in 1952.

The constitutionality of the provisions of the Morrill Acts has never been questioned in the courts. This, in the words of the late Dean Burdick, "would seem to make it clear that public lands or their proceeds may be given or appropriated for use in the States for purposes which will be for 'the common benefit,' although they are purposes with regard to which Congress could not legislate directly." [8] The Morrill Acts were, however, interpreted by the Supreme Court in two important cases, the first of which related to a private bequest to Cornell University, the second to Wyoming's method of setting up an agricultural and mechanical college.[9]

Since these grants were on a continuing basis, and have from time to time been increased in amount, they may be regarded as the prototype of many modern grants-in-aid. They were the first conditional grants of a now very familiar type. The distinguished historian, Henry Steele Commager, has said of this legislation that, with the exception of the Act of 1785, it was "the most important piece of legislation on behalf of education ever passed." [10] Under its terms some 13 million acres of the public

[8] Burdick, Charles K., *The Law of the American Constitution: Its Origin and Development* (New York: G. P. Putnam's Sons, 1922), p. 327.

[9] *Cornell University* v. *Fiske*, 136 U.S. 152 (1890); *Wyoming* v. *Irvine*, 206 U.S. 278 (1907).

[10] Note in Commager, Henry Steele, *Documents of American History*, 6th ed. (New York: Appleton-Century-Crofts, Inc., 1958), pp. 412–413.

domain have been given to the States for the establishment and maintenance of agricultural and mechanical colleges. This legislation became the keystone of all higher education in many States, giving tremendous impetus to the movement for the establishment of State universities, particularly in the Midwest and Far West where privately endowed colleges and universities, familiar in the East, were lacking.

In the years since their establishment, the land-grant colleges have become the focal points of the whole program of scientific research, collegiate training, and adult education in agriculture in the several States. One may surmise that such institutions might have developed by State action, even if there had been no Morrill Act, but such development would most certainly have been much slower, less uniform, and less widespread. Even with the Act, several of the older Eastern States did not officially establish a State university for nearly 100 years. The action of the Federal government has given funds, stimulus, and some degree of leadership to the movement.

While in many jurisdictions the State universities and the agricultural and mechanical colleges were located on the same or adjoining campuses, as in Illinois, Minnesota, and Wisconsin, the practice in others was to establish separate institutions more or less remote from each other, as in Colorado, Indiana, and Iowa. The tendency in later years has been to transform the agricultural and mechanical colleges into second full-fledged State universities which offer instruction in all fields.[11] Some of the older States along the Atlantic seaboard, having no public lands within their own borders, received grants of western lands or land scrip to the amount in acres for the deficiency of their distributive share; thus, New York received a grant of 939,920 acres of land scrip in Wisconsin, all but a small portion of which were purchased by Ezra Cornell and given as endowment to the new university.[12] New York, whose State College of Agriculture has long been associated with and a part of Cornell University, is only now in the process of establishing a State university, while Massachusetts, New Jersey, and Pennsylvania are each engaged in expanding long existing institutions into State universities.

[11] For example, Michigan State University now has a student body of some 20,000 students and includes nine schools—Agriculture, Business and Public Service, Education, Engineering, Home Economics, Science and Arts, Veterinary Medicine, Graduate Studies, and the Basic College, which is a two-year program of general education. Through continuing programs, both on and off its campus, it serves more than 300,000 additional residents of the State. In addition, it has established educational projects on the Ryuku Islands and in Colombia, Brazil, and India which carry on the land-grant college philosophy of serving people by helping them to improve their conditions of life and living.

[12] For the history of these lands, see Gates, Paul W., *The Wisconsin Pine Lands of Cornell University* (Ithaca: Cornell University Press, 1943).

Development of Agricultural Research

The agricultural societies of Europe and America had long been interested in agricultural research, and they had faith in the beneficial results that its systematic development might have. Scattered attempts to establish research units were reported from 1821 on, and agricultural experiment stations were set up in many of the land-grant colleges prior to the passage of the Hatch Act in 1887, which was the second official step in the development of a nationwide system of agricultural education and research agencies. An Association of American Agricultural Colleges and Experiment Stations was formally organized the same year the Act was passed. Bills providing for the establishment of a nationwide program in this area had been first introduced in Congress in 1883 by Representatives Carpenter of Iowa, Cullen of Illinois, and Hatch of Missouri.

The original Act was one of the early indications of a changing philosophy with respect to Federal grants; it provided a grant of $15,000 annually to each State and Territory, and authorized the use of this money for the purpose of testing, research and publication, and dissemination of scientific information under cooperative arrangements between the States and the Department of Agriculture. The independent experiment stations became associated with the State colleges of agriculture. Under the Hatch Act, stations were soon established in all jurisdictions, although in Connecticut and New York the fund was divided between two stations. Numerous additional stations, branch stations, and experimental farms have since been established with State support, while the national government established experiment stations in each of the Territories. The stations are governed by the laws of the respective States; the central government exercises no control over them beyond an annual audit of financial records to assure that the funds appropriated by Congress are expended for the purposes designated by Federal law.

The Hatch Act was in time supplanted, first by the Adams Act of 1906, under which an additional $15,000 per year was made available to each State for work in agricultural research, and by the Purnell Act of 1925. The first two were almost exclusively concerned with the production phases of agriculture, but the Purnell Act extended the research program to include marketing, rural sociology, agricultural economics, and the broad field of home economics. This shift in emphasis may be ascribed to low prices for farm products in the early 1920's, which developed into a serious agricultural depression. The Purnell Act not only provided more adequate financial support for the work of the agricultural experiment stations on technical production problems, but opened the way for a greatly expanded program of research on the sociological and economic problems of agriculture. This approach, once begun, was further emphasized a decade later in the provisions of the Bankhead-Jones Act which authorized an annual appropriation of $1 million for research for the first five years, and $5 million for each year thereafter. Research was not limited to economic and sociological relationships, but the emphasis had definitely shifted to these aspects of the farm problem.

Another important extension of this program was made in 1946 by the Agricultural Research and Marketing Act, which provided for a comprehensive program of research in which the traditional types were expanded and new types were established. It was anticipated that if the authorizations provided were fully implemented by appropriations, the amount of publicly supported agricultural research in the country would be more than doubled within a few years. This legislation was intended as a major step in providing agricultural research facilities comparable to those available to other types of industry by authorizing additional funds for the support of general research in the following categories: marketing, uses of agricultural products, and cooperative projects in these areas.[13]

Cooperative Agricultural Extension Work

As the land-grant college system developed and was supplemented by the work of the agricultural experiment stations, it became apparent that there was need for a mechanism that would "bring the campus to the people," as it was sometimes expressed. Thus was evolved the agricultural extension system with its county agent and county home demonstration agent. The legislation under which this system developed and the growth in appropriations since 1930 are shown in the table on page 491.

Agricultural extension work, officially inaugurated by the passage of the Smith-Lever Act of May 9, 1914, originally included (1) the farmers' institutes and similar activities and (2) farm demonstration work and experimental farms. The institutes evolved at an early date. The duties of the secretary of the Massachusetts State Board of Agriculture, established in 1852, included visiting the various agricultural districts of the State and delivering lectures on the practice and science of agriculture. The idea was to hold meetings similar to teachers' institutes, but upon agricultural subjects. The purpose of these early group meetings was to

[13] See *The Agricultural Marketing Act of 1946* (Washington: Agriculture Committee on National Policy, National Planning Association, 1948); and Hardin, C. M., "Political Influence and Agricultural Research," *American Political Science Review*, August, 1947, pp. 673–686.

discuss agricultural matters; establish a series of lectures on agriculture, agricultural chemistry, and geology; conduct classes, especially for young farmers and women; and purchase agricultural books, to be read and commented on at the meetings. This was an interesting period which has been characterized as "one of modest beginnings but fecund with ideas foreshadowing much that was to come later."

Farm demonstration experiments began about 1900 on selected farms in various communities, usually one or two per county, to show the value of using scientific production methods. This work was mainly carried on in two areas—in the South by Dr. Seaman A. Knapp and David F. Houston (who became Secretary of Agriculture under President Wilson) and in the West by two Iowans, James Wilson and Henry A. Wallace (both of whom became Secretary of Agriculture). In its early stages, this work was not, for the most part, closely related to that of the State colleges and experiment stations. Many farmers, particularly those of the North, were inclined to regard it with extreme skepticism if not with open hostility, and ridiculed the idea that "book farmers" could be useful to them.

Gradually, however, "the plan gained a foothold in scattered counties, usually under auspices other than those of working farmers." [14] Sentiment for a nationwide system of publicly supported agricultural extension grew; as early as 1908, there was an increasing demand for Federal appropriations for extension work. A bill for this purpose was introduced in the House in 1909 by Representative J. C. McLaughlin of Michigan, and other bills followed. The proposal engendered an enormous amount of controversy, in which even the agricultural colleges were by no means united. "They wanted the money but were fearful of Federal domination." Even eight years later, when the Smith-Lever bill was before Congress, the controversy continued, sometimes over the nature of the program (some regarded it as undesirable, as class legislation, or even as socialistic), sometimes on what groups of farmers were to be included (Southern opposition to inclusion of Negro farmers resulted in the operation of two separate offices for a number of years: South, and North and West).

As finally adopted, the Smith-Lever Act provided for an annual base allotment of $10,000 to each State plus an initial Federal input of $600,-000 to be allocated in proportion to the size of the rural population. There was to be an annual step-up of $500,000 for seven years, bringing the total, aside from the flat $10,000 per State, to $4,100,000. This $3,500,-000 increment above the first year's appropriation was to be matched by funds from the States or other sources. Thus the third major phase came

[14] Benedict, Murray R., *Farm Policies in the United States, 1790–1950* (New York: Twentieth Century Fund, 1953).

into being, fifty-two years after the original founding of the agricultural colleges. Out of it, according to Benedict, "has grown not only a vast educational mechanism but a related organization of farmers that has had much to do with the course of agricultural policy in the decades since 1920." [15]

The agricultural extension program was new and something of an innovation when the Smith-Lever Act was passed in 1914; since then it has developed into a major program of substantial size and of literally inestimable value to the nation's farm population. On August 11, 1916, President Wilson wrote a letter to Representative A. F. Lever, Chairman of the House Committee on Agriculture, congratulating him upon an impressive record of accomplishment in new agricultural legislation during his (the President's) first administration, and presenting a summary so succinct that it would be difficult to improve:

> Greatly increased provision has been made, through the enactment of the cooperative agricultural extension act, for conveying agricultural information to farmers, and for inducing them to apply for it. This piece of legislation is one of the most significant and far-reaching measures for the education of adults ever adopted by any Government. It provides for cooperation between the States and the Federal Government. This is a highly important and significant principle. When the Act is in full operation, there will be expended annually under its terms, from Federal and State sources alone, a total of over $8,600,000 in the direct education of the farmer; this amount is being and will be increasingly supplemented by contributions from local sources. It will permit the placing in each of the 2,850 counties of the Nation two farm demonstrators and specialists, who will assist the demonstrators in the more difficult problems confronting them.[16]

Legislatively, however, the Smith-Lever Act was only the beginning. Agricultural extension became the subject of more pieces of important legislation in the next twenty years than the other three phases of the agricultural education program combined. In 1928 came the enactment of the Capper-Ketcham Act of May 22, 1928, an amendment to the original law authorizing an appropriation of $980,000 each year, plus an annual appropriation of $500,000 starting one year after the $980,000 became available. Two years later, when effects of the Great Depression were being felt even in the Federal Treasury, the 1928 Act was amended by extending the time for the payment of installments (upon the assent of the Governors of the several States) to January 1, 1932.

---

[15] Benedict, p. 154.
[16] *Congressional Record*, 64th Cong., 1st Sess., Appendix, pp. 1762–1763, and reprinted in Commager, pp. 294–296.

In 1935, as has been noted in other connections, Congress enacted the Bankhead-Jones Act of June 29. This Act came closer to being comprehensive legislation covering the whole field of agricultural education than any other single piece of legislation in the history of the program. In addition to provisions relating to the more adequate endowment of the agricultural colleges and to research, it contained important provisions designed to further the development of the agricultural extension system; specifically, $8 million was authorized for this work during the first year, with $1 million to be added each successive year until a total of $12 million was reached, which amount was to be appropriated annually thereafter.

To continue with the story of the development of the statutory basis for the present vast extension program, it may be noted that the Cooperative Farm Forestry Act of May 18, 1937, authorized Federal cooperation in the development of farm forestry in the States and Territories. Two years later the Bankhead-Jones Act was amended by what has been called the Additional Extension Act of April 24, 1939, which made financial provision for the further growth and development of the cooperative extension system inaugurated under the Smith-Lever Act by authorizing $300,000 annually to be allotted to the States by the Secretary of Agriculture. Only a few years later, in the Department of Agriculture Organic Act of September 21, 1944, additional funds were authorized, the $300,000 figure in the 1939 law now being increased to $555,000.

In order to complete the story, mention must be made of one more important enactment. The Bankhead-Flanagan Act of June 8, 1945, authorized additional appropriations for cooperative extension work—$4.5 million for 1946 and each subsequent year, with an additional $4 million for 1947 and each year thereafter, and $4 million in 1948 and each year thereafter. Thus, the financial support of extension work has grown from year to year in response to the demands of farm people throughout the country by the increase of old authorizations and the addition of new ones.

One cannot fail to be impressed with one aspect of the story, as the pattern of this legislation unfolds over the years. In one act after another, "authorizations" were provided for, with increased authorizations for specified periods of time—three, four, or five years—in the future. The technique used is interesting because the authorizations, in and of themselves, are worth nothing. They are no more than declarations of policy by the subject-matter committee which are endorsed by Congress, but they do not make any funds available for expenditure. Funds can be made available only by the process of appropriation, *i.e.*, favorable action of the two appropriation committees, the two houses, and the President's signature. The authorizations have no legal effect; in no way do they bind either of the Appropriation Committees or either House of Congress. Nor can one Congress bind a succeeding Congress in a matter concerning the appropriation of funds—or in any other matter. This is one of the basic rules of the legislative process. The advantage, presumably, is largely psychological, but the history of this type of legislation clearly shows that its supporters have apparently been able to use it to good advantage.

While the legislative structure of the extension system was slowly built, progress was made administratively in carrying out the programs provided for by law. The number of demonstration projects increased. In some areas, agents were appointed who served the farmers in several counties. Local demand developed for more demonstrations and information than could be given by agents whose territory included several counties. Thus it was that in November, 1916, the first county agent in the South was appointed in Smith County, Texas. Sometime later, at Binghamton in Broome County, New York, the first county agent in the Northern and Western States was permanently established. This was done with funds provided by the Chamber of Commerce; it is interesting to observe that in the early stages of its development, there was a good deal of private financing for the extension movement.

In actual operation, the Extension Service of the Department of Agriculture makes grants to the States for cooperative extension work, in order to make the results of research in agriculture and home economics available to those in a position to put the information to practical use. At the State level, the program is administered through the State agricultural colleges and supported by Federal, State, and county funds. Although the program in any given area is largely determined locally and is based on local needs, there is considerable similarity among the various State and county programs. In all, extension work is carried on in nine areas: agricultural production, marketing, natural resources, management, family, youth, leadership, community, and public affairs. The Council of State Governments well describes the intergovernmental relations aspects of the program:

> Each State has a director of extension who represents jointly the U.S. Department of Agriculture and the State agricultural college. Each State has an administrative and advisory staff, usually located at the agricultural college, and, in addition, there are county agents of various types. Agricultural extension work is an excellent example of intergovernmental cooperation, since the county agent (who is the backbone of the whole program) is at the same time a Federal-State-local official who receives his salary from all three levels of government, and who is governed by the policies and requirements of the Nation, the State, and his own county.[17]

[17] Council of State Governments, *Federal Grants-in-Aid* (Chicago, 1949), p. 53.

The Cooperative Extension Service has a nationwide professional staff of more than 14,000 workers to carry on its educational work. Approximately 11,000 of these are county agricultural, home demonstration, and 4-H Club agents, and others located in the county extension offices, usually the county seat. Some 3,000 are specialists and other professional personnel located at State land-grant colleges, and 100 are members of the Federal Extension Service of the Department of Agriculture in Washington. The county is the key unit in the Extension Service. The local personnel are employed by their State colleges and are responsible both to the college and to the people of the county for the development and conduct of the extension educational program. Extension workers are located in almost every rural county and in some cities, and are supported in their work by State staffs. State specialists in a great variety of subject-matter fields interpret scientific findings that county agents pass on to the people. They help to keep the county staffs informed about national programs and policies, while at the same time they keep experiment stations and the Department of Agriculture advised on local needs for new fields of research.

Extension programs in agriculture deal with all aspects of producing, marketing, processing, utilizing, and consuming agricultural products. Agents and specialists have at their fingertips information on general farm subjects such as crops and soils, dairy, poultry and animal husbandry, farm forestry, farm machinery and buildings, marketing, and soil conservation.[18] The homemaking phase of extension work brings families the latest research and information on food and its preparation, clothing, and homemaking.

Farm women participated in farmers' institutes, particularly in the Eastern and Midwestern States, and in 1898 a few Illinois women decided that special subjects of interest to farmers' wives and daughters ought to be presented at the county institutes. Reading courses on such problems had been set up in New York and a number of other States as early as 1900. Women lecturers on topics in the field of home economics began to be a regular part of the farmers' institute program. In many States, especially in the North, the work done by these lecturers later served as a pattern when home demonstrations were organized. Much of the instruction work was carried on by specialists who served as many as six or seven counties, and their number exceeded the number of county home demonstration agents for a number of years after the law was passed. In the South, on the other hand, the number of county home demonstration agents increased much more rapidly.[19]

[18] The standard work on this subject is Gladys Baker, *The County Agent* (Chicago: University of Chicago Press, 1938).

[19] Based on Department of Agriculture, AIB No. 38, *The Home Demonstration Agent* (Washington, July, 1951).

Vocational Training in Agriculture

The controlling purpose of vocational education has been said to be "to fit persons for useful employment." The needs of two distinct groups of people are served by the programs conducted under the provisions of the Smith-Hughes and George-Barden Acts, which constitute the legislative framework for the whole vocational education program. These groups include those who have entered and those who are preparing to enter work in various occupations in the fields of agriculture, homemaking, distribution, and trades and industry.

The Federal aid acts limit the use of Federal funds to programs that are (1) under public supervision and control, (2) of less than college grade, and (3) for persons over fourteen years of age. The grants are based on the assumption that such training is essential to the national welfare, and that financial aid is necessary to stimulate and assist the States in making adequate provisions for such training. The major objectives of training in the important fields of agriculture and home economics are indicated in the table below.

OBJECTIVES OF VOCATIONAL TRAINING IN AGRICULTURE AND HOME ECONOMICS

Agriculture	*Home Economics*
1. To make a beginning and to advance in farming.	1. To prepare students for homemaking responsibilities and activities necessary to achieve family well-being.
2. To produce farm commodities efficiently.	2. To help family members improve the quality of their home life through more thoughtful and efficient development and utilization of human and material resources.
3. To market farm products advantageously.	
4. To conserve soil and other natural resources.	
5. To manage farm business effectively.	
6. To maintain a favorable environment.	
7. To participate in rural leadership activities.	

The legislation providing for the present system of vocational education is voluminous. It began in 1917 with the passage of the Smith-Hughes Act of February 23, 1917. Since that date there have been four additional significant enactments, with each of which the name of the veteran Senator George was associated: the George-Reed Act of 1929, the George-Ellzey Act of 1934, the George-Deen Act of 1936, and the George-Barden Act of 1946.

The Smith-Hughes Act may be regarded as the basic charter of the

vocational education program, for under it, training in agriculture entered a new and different phase. Whereas the Morrill Acts had made
possible training at the college and university level, this Act was intended
to aid the development of vocational education in secondary schools.
In addition to creating the Federal Board of Vocational Education, with
an annual appropriation to investigate and aid States in establishing
vocational schools and programs, it provided for continuing appropriations to be expended in the States *under State plans* for the promotion
of vocational education. The work has been much expanded and the
appropriations increased by subsequent legislation and by numerous
amendments (1924, 1931, and 1933) to the original statute.

The following summary of the provisions of the Smith-Hughes Act
was prepared by the Council of State Governments:

> . . . The Smith-Hughes Act required that new machinery, both
> Federal and State, be set up for the administration of the program
> outlined in the legislation. This Act gave the Federal government more
> influence over the educational programs of the States than had any
> previous legislation. The obligations that the States must meet in order
> to be eligible to participate in the benefits of the Smith-Hughes Act are
> set forth in detail in the law. Through its legislature the State must
> signify its intention to participate in the program and designate the
> State board of education or some similar educational authority to ad-
> minister the program. Several different funds are established under the
> Act, and the State may elect to participate in any of the funds, all of
> which are designated for specific programs.
>
> State authorities are required to prepare an overall plan for voca-
> tional education in the States, subject to approval by the Federal su-
> pervisory agency. No State may use any of the Federal funds allotted to it
> for the purchase, erection, preservation, or repairs of any building or
> equipment, or for the purchase or rental of lands, or for the support of
> any religious or privately owned or conducted school or college.
>
> Annually the Federal Security Agency must determine whether the
> States are using or are prepared to use the money available to them
> under the Act. Furthermore, the Federal Security Agency may withhold
> any State's allotment if it determines that the State is not meeting the
> requirements as set up under the Act. The State, however, has the right
> to appeal such action to the Congress.
>
> Appropriations under the Smith-Hughes Act fall into a number of
> funds calling for specialized programs and that all such funds be
> matched by State, local, or State and local, money. Allotment of some of
> of the Federal funds is upon the basis of state population while in other
> cases it is upon the proportion of rural population of the State to the
> total rural population of the United States.[20]

[20] Council of State Governments, *Federal Grants-in-Aid* (Chicago, 1949),
pp. 245-246.

First in the series of supplementary acts, each of which has made an important contribution to the development of the program, was the George-Reed Vocational Education Act of 1929, which increased the authorizations, both for the Federal Board of Vocational Education and for the program as a whole. An annual appropriation of $100,000 was authorized for the Board, while for the program as a whole, the sum of $500,000 was authorized and "for each year thereafter, for four years, a sum exceeding by $500,000 the sum appropriated for each preceding year."

The George-Ellzey Vocational Education Act of May 21, 1934, second in the series, again increased the Federal financial contribution by authorizing $3 million each year for the fiscal years 1934, 1936, and 1937. Before this Act had run out, it was to some extent supplanted by the George-Deen Vocational Education Act of June 6, 1936, which authorized additional annual appropriations for allotment among the States in furtherance of vocational education, as follows:

1. For training in agricultural, home economics and industrial subjects, $12 million;
2. For training in distributive occupational subjects, $1,200,000—this amount to be matched by the States progressively, reaching 100 per cent by 1947;
3. For teacher training, $1 million.

To persons interested in government and public affairs, this enactment was significant for another reason, namely, that it opened the way for the establishment of institutes of training for the public service on a State-by-State basis. Such programs still function effectively in a few States, notably in New York, North Carolina, and Pennsylvania. These institutes provide job training for a host of different kinds of local officials and employees—assessors, tax collectors, firemen and policemen, notaries public, inspectors of various kinds (housing, plumbing, food and food processing), and many others. They are located at the State Capitol, but are closely linked with the State college or university and with other higher educational institutions.

Last in the series of enactments was the George-Barden Vocational Education Act of August 1, 1946, which was largely a revision of the 1936 measure. Specifically, it provided for the maintenance of adequate programs in vocational education, with annual appropriations for training in a number of specialized fields as follows:

1. Agriculture, $10 million;
2. Home Economics, $8 million;
3. Trades and Industry, $8 million;
4. Distributive Occupations, $2,500,000.

EVOLUTION OF CASH GRANTS

Grants-in-aid, which have been used by the Federal government in some form from its beginning, are basically a device by which a larger unit of government not only gives financial support to a smaller, component unit, but also assures that certain functions will be performed and certain minimum standards maintained throughout the granting jurisdiction—nationwide or statewide. While the present system of Federal grants is largely a twentieth century phenomenon, precedents for it extend back to the founding of the Republic. These grants have been called "only the most obvious example of sharing functions."

Although grant-in-aid legislation has significant effects on the relations of national and State governments, it has more or less escaped judicial scrutiny. Much has been written about modern grants, but little about their early history. Current studies at the University of Chicago have disclosed both interesting and important information:

> Grants-in-land and grants-in-services from the national government were of first importance in virtually all of the principal functions undertaken by the States and their local subsidiaries. Land grants were made to the States for, among other purposes, elementary schools, colleges, and special educational institutions; roads, canals, rivers, harbors, and railroads; reclamation of desert and swamp lands; and veterans' welfare. In fact whatever was at the focus of State attention became the recipient of national grants. (Then, as today, national grants established State emphasis as well as followed it.) If Connecticut wished to establish a program for the care and education of the deaf and dumb, Federal money in the form of a land grant was found to aid that program. If higher education relating to agriculture became a pressing need, Congress could dip into the public domain and make appropriate grants to States. If the need for swamp drainage and flood control appeared, the Federal Government could supply both grants-in-land and, from the Army's Corps of Engineers, the services of the only trained engineers then available.
>
> . . . The essential continuity of the collaborative system is best illustrated by the history of the grants. The land grant tended to become a cash grant based on the calculated disposable value of the land, and the cash grant tended to become an annual grant based upon the national government's superior tax powers. In 1887, only three years before the frontier was officially closed, thus signalizing the end of the

disposable public domain, Congress enacted the first continuing cash grants.[21]

With the passage of time, the number and size of Federal grants has increased, and the prevailing type of grant has changed from land grants, which were early adopted, to money grants which, until quite recently, were disapproved on the ground that they would undermine the integrity and responsibility of the States. On this important point, Professor Anderson explains:

> Federal *land* grants to the States for public schools and internal improvements were early recognized as a temporary and generally desirable method of aiding the States. The Constitution expressly grants to Congress the power to dispose of national property, and the power to grant lands to the States on such conditions as the States will accept has never been denied by the U.S. Supreme Court. A corresponding power in the States to accept the conditions in Federal land grants is also fully approved. There was, however, considerable opposition from the early days of the Constitution down to the Civil War and later to national grants of *money* to the States for State purposes. In offering such grants, the argument ran, the national government was in effect trying to undermine the sovereignty of the States, while any States foolish enough to accept the grants would be willing participants in the undermining of their own authority. Leaders of the prewar Democratic Party in particular took a strong stand in opposition to such grants—although the same leaders took a wholly different position with reference to national grants of money to the territories to get them started toward statehood.[22]

Grants for Education

Grants-in-aid in the nineteenth century took the form of land grants, distribution of materials, cash grants based upon land sales, and direct cash grants (as in the distribution of the surplus). Grants were made for education, including the common schools, colleges, and special educational institutions, and for a variety of other purposes. The disposition of the public domain provided a means by which many other problems

[21] Grodzins, Morton, "The Federal System," in *Report* of the President's Commission on National Goals, *Goals for Americans* (New York: American Assembly, Columbia University, Prentice-Hall, Inc., 1960), pp. 265–282, on p. 270.

[22] Anderson, William, *Intergovernmental Relations in Review* (Minneapolis: University of Minnesota Press, 1960), p. 22.

might be attacked, land serving in the place of cash as the substance of a grant-in-aid. Over a period of almost two centuries, this grant system has had a phenomenal growth, as may be seen by reference to the following table.

ONE HUNDRED AND EIGHTY-FIVE YEARS
OF FEDERAL AID TO EDUCATION *
Major Educational Enactments

Before 1800:
- 1777—Initiation of program for military personnel
- 1785—Ordinance of 1785
- 1787—Ordinance of 1787
- 1796—Ohio Salt-land Grant Act

1800–1849:
- 1800—First Congressional appropriation for books, which became nucleus of Library of Congress
- 1802—Ohio Enabling Act
  - —Military Academy at West Point established
- 1803—Ohio Enabling Act Amendment
- 1804—Start of Federal provision for education in the District of Columbia
- 1824—First Army special service school established
- 1833—U.S. Deposit Fund Act
- 1836—Surplus Revenue Loan Act
- 1845—Naval Academy at Annapolis established

1850–1900:
- 1850—Swamp-land Grant Act
- 1862—First Morrill Act: Colleges for Agriculture and Mechanic Arts
- 1867—Department of Education Act
- 1874—Aid to State nautical schools
- 1879—Federal school for engraving established, beginning in-service training for civilian personnel
- 1887—Hatch Agricultural Experiment Station Act
- 1890—Second Morrill Act: Colleges for Agriculture and Mechanic Arts

- 1893—Army Medical School established

1900–1909:
- 1901—Army War College established
- 1906—Adams Act †
- 1907—Nelson Amendment to the Morrill Act
- 1908—Federal Forest Reserve Fund Act

1910–1919:
- 1911—State Marine School Act
- 1914—Smith-Lever Agricultural Extension Act
- 1915—Coast Guard Academy established
- 1917—Smith-Hughes Vocational Education Act
- 1918—Vocational Rehabilitation Act
- 1919—Use of Federal surplus property by educational institutions

1920–1929:
- 1920—Graduate School of Department of Agriculture organized
  - —Reserve Officers Training Corps established at universities and colleges
  - —Federal Mineral Royalty Act
  - —Smith-Bankhead Vocational Rehabilitation Act
- 1921—Purnell Act †
  - —Naval Reserve Officers Training Corps established at universities and colleges
- 1927—Federal School Land Act
- 1929—Capper-Ketcham Act ‡
  - —George-Reed Act §

The table lists more than four dozen acts of Congress affecting education. The land grants alone total more than 175 million acres, an area larger than Indiana, Ohio, and West Virginia combined. In addition, beginning in 1802 when Ohio was admitted to the Union, Congress

Major Educational Enactments

1930–1939:

1933—Beginning of school lunch program

—Federal Emergency Relief Administration supported various educational programs

1934—George-Ellzey Act §

1935—Bankhead-Jones Act ‡

—National Youth Administration gave part-time employment aid to college students

1936—George-Deen Act §

—International educational exchanges begun

1937—First U.S. Public Health fellowship granted

—Civilian Conservation Corps provided vocational education

1939—Federal Civilian Pilot Training Act

1940–1949:

1940—Vocational Education for National Defense Act

—Lanham Act: aid to schools in federally impacted areas

1942—Armed Forces Institute established

1944—G.I. Bill of Rights (Servicemen's Readjustment Act)

—Surplus Property Act

1945—Amendment to Bankhead-Jones and Smith-Lever Acts

1946—George-Barden Act §

—Aid to Federally Impacted Areas: school construction, and operation and maintenance

—Atomic Energy Act, offering fellowships

—National School Lunch Program

1948—Smith-Mundt Act for international educational exchanges

1949—Federal Property and Administrative Services Act, handling grants of surplus property

1950–1962:

1950—Amendments to Federally Impacted Areas Legislation: P.L. 815 and P.L. 874

1951—College Housing Loans Act

1952—National Science Foundation, fellowship program

1954—School Milk Program

—Air Force Academy established

1956—Library services in rural areas

—Air Force Institute of Technology, a degree-granting institution

1958—National Defense Education Act

—Educational and cultural exchange agreement with U.S.S.R.

---

* Adapted from *One Hundred and Sixty Years of Federal Aid to Education*, with recent enactments added (Washington: National Education Association, July, 1946), p. 3.

† Amendment to Hatch Act.

‡ Amendment to Smith-Lever Act.

§ Amendment to Smith-Hughes Act.

granted it 5 per cent of the money received from the sales of Federal lands within its borders; since then, twenty-nine other States have received similar grants, varying from 5 to 15 per cent. Sixteen States were required to use this money for education, and three others did so on their own accord. Since 1833, the Federal government has from time to time given outright grants to the States. When the use to be made of these funds was not specified, many States devoted all or part of them to schools. Since 1889, Congress has required that money thus received be spent on the schools.

An internal improvement act of 1841 made money received from the sale of certain public lands available to the States for school purposes. The Morrill Land Grant Act of 1862 marks a definite change in Federal educational policy. Grants for general education with no Federal control over how the money would be spent began to change to grants-in-aid of named programs in education, with the law stating conditions for the use of the money by the States. Early twentieth century legislation gave States title to mineral rights in school sections (Federal School Land Act, 1927) and one-fourth of all money received annually from each Federal forest in each State (Federal Forest Reserve Fund Act, 1908). Similarly, funds received from mineral royalties were to be used for school purposes (Federal Mineral Royalty Act, 1920).

Grants for State Militia and International Expositions

Although the early grants were of land, cash grants have been in use for more than 100 years. Probably the first such grant goes back to 1808, when Congress appropriated $200,000 annually to assist the States in arming and equipping their militia. No attempts were made at this time to impose conditions or to exercise control, but in 1886, when the amount of the grant was doubled, Congress did attempt to establish some control over the State militia. Later on, as grants-in-aid were used in the development of the National Guard, these controls were substantially increased.

Strangely enough, some of the earliest cash grants to the States, after those for the support of the militia, were made in connection with international expositions and world's fairs, such as those in 1876 and 1904 respectively. In 1876, the nation celebrated its one hundredth birthday with an international exposition held at Philadelphia. Both the Federal government and the States joined in organizing and financing the venture. A United States Centennial Commission was formed, composed of one delegate and one alternate from each State, appointed by the President on recommendation of the Governor of the State. The

Commission was charged with generally overseeing the fair and with the preparation of a report on the exposition for use by Congress.

The exposition was financed through creation of one of the earliest government corporations known, the Centennial Board of Finance, in which the States were well represented. Two corporators were to come from each Congressional district and four corporators-at-large from each Territory. These individuals, together with the shareholders, elected an executive committee of twenty-five to handle the affairs of the Board. Although forty-four States and Territories participated in the exposition, many of them constructing large State buildings, only four State legislatures (outside of Pennsylvania, the host State) actually subscribed funds to the project. These were Connecticut, Delaware, New Hampshire, and New Jersey.

Federal assistance to the St. Louis World's Fair in 1904 took another form. One of the earliest records of the use of Federal matching funds is found in the annals of the Louisiana Purchase Exposition of 1904. An Act of Congress, passed in 1901, provided that the Federal government would pay the sum of $5 million to the Louisiana Purchase Exposition Company, provided that the City of St. Louis and said company should match this figure with $10 million in reserves. The matching funds were raised by joint city-company action, and the matching grant was paid into the fair's treasury.

BIBLIOGRAPHICAL NOTES

Land Grants. Among several good volumes which tell the story of American policy with respect to public lands, some are general works and others deal with such special uses of land as land grants for internal improvements or education. Some of both types are included in the following list: Payson J. Treat, *National Land System, 1785–1920* (New York: E. B. Treat & Company, 1910); Benjamin N. Hibbard, *A History of Public Land Policies* (New York: The Macmillan Co., 1924); Marion Clawson, *Uncle Sam's Acres* (New York: Dodd, Mead & Co., 1951); Carter Goodrich, *Canals and American Economic Development* and *American Canals and Railroads* (New York: Columbia University Press, 1961 and 1960 respectively); Paul W. Gates, *The Wisconsin Pine Lands of Cornell University: A Study in Land Policy and Absentee Ownership* and *Fifty Million Acres: Conflicts Over Kansas Land Policy, 1854–1890* (Ithaca: Cornell University Press, 1943 and 1954 respectively). For a complete State-by-State tabulation, see John K. Rose, *Land Grants to the States* (Washington: Legislative Reference Service, Library of Congress, July, 1961).

Land Grant Colleges and Agricultural Education. For a biography of the man who proposed the land-grant college idea, see Mary Carriel, *The Life of Jonathan Baldwin Turner* (Urbana: University of Illinois Press, 1961). Albert C. True gave a lifetime of service to the USDA, and wrote extensively on agricultural education in

"History of the Morrill Land Grant College Act of 1890," Land Grant Colleges and Universities, *Proceedings, 1925* (Burlington, Vt.: Free Press Printing Company, 1926), pp. 90–98; "History of the Hatch Experiment Station Act of 1887," *ibid., 1926* (Northampton: Metcalf Printing & Publishing Company, 1927), pp. 93–108; Department of Agriculture, Miscellaneous Publication No. 36, *A History of Agricultural Education in the United States, 1785–1925* (Washington, July, 1929); Department of Agriculture, Miscellaneous Publication No. 15, *A History of Agricultural Extension Work in the United States, 1785–1923* (Washington, October, 1928).

The tremendous literature in the field can be classified under three categories: general works, studies of specific problems discussed in this chapter, and "impact studies" relating to individual States. In the first two categories, several significant works are R. K. Bliss, *The Spirit and Philosophy of Extension Work* (Washington: Epsilon Sigma Phi and Graduate School, Department of Agriculture, 1952); Fred J. Kelly, *Land Grant Colleges and Universities: A Federal-State Partnership* (Washington: Office of Education, Bulletin 1952, No. 21, 1952); Lincoln D. Kelsey and Cannon C. Hearne, *Cooperative Extension Work*, 2nd ed. (Ithaca: Comstock Publishing Associates, 1955); Arthur J. Klein, *Survey of Land-Grant Colleges and Universities*, 2 vols. (Washington: Office of Education, 1930); Donald E. Larimore and John D. Black, *Extension Education in Marketing in the Cooperative Federal-State Agricultural Extension Service of the United States: An Exploratory Study* (Cambridge: Harvard University Press, 1953); Frederick B. Mumford, *The Land-Grant College Movement* (Columbia: University of Missouri Bulletin, 1940); Earle D. Ross, *Democracy's College: The Land-Grant Movement in the Formative Stage* (Ames: Iowa State College Press, 1942); Whitney H. Shepardson, *Agricultural Education in the United States* (New York: The Macmillan Co., 1929); and George A. Works and Barton Morgan, *The Land-Grant Colleges* (Washington: Advisory Committee on Education, 1939).

There is at least one study of the movement, or of a particular land-grant institution, in many of the States. The following is a short representative list: Dorris D. Giles, *et al.*, *Agricultural Education in Texas State-Supported Institutions of Higher Education* (Austin: Legislative Council, Staff Monograph, 1951); Palmer O. Johnson, *Aspects of Land-Grant College Education, with Special Reference to the University of Minnesota* (Minneapolis: University of Minnesota Press, 1935); Madison Kuhn, *Michigan State: The First Hundred Years, 1855–1955* (East Lansing: Michigan State University Press, 1955); *The University of Missouri: First State University in the Louisiana Purchase* (Columbia: University of Missouri Bulletin, 1953); Robert L. Morlan, *Intergovernmental Relations in Education* (Minneapolis: University of Minnesota Press, 1950), one of the series of Minnesota studies prepared under the direction of Professor William Anderson; Grace J. Penny, *A History of the Extension Division of the University of Oklahoma* (Norman: University of Oklahoma Press, 1953); Wilfred B. Shaw, *The University of Michigan: An Encyclopedic Survey*, 7 vols. (Ann Arbor: University of Michigan Press, 1941–1953); Frank T. Stockton, *The Pioneer Years of University Extension at the University of Kansas* (Lawrence: University of Kansas Bulletin, April, 1956); Mark J. Thompson, *The First Forty Years of the Northeast Agricultural Experiment Station, 1913–1953* (Duluth: Northeast Agricultural Experiment Station, June 1954); Frederick W. Williamson, *Origin and Growth of Agricultural Extension in Louisiana, 1860–1948* (Baton Rouge: Division of Agricultural Extension, Louisiana State University, 1951).

CHAPTER XV

The Grant-in-Aid System: World War I Through the Roosevelt Era

Federal aid has become one of the most important aspects of governmental finance in this country. . . . Prior to 1915 the total grants, not including those for the National Guard, amounted to less than $5 million annually. After the passage of the Highway Act of 1916, Federal aid rose to around $100 million annually, at which point it remained fairly constant from 1918 through 1930. . . . During the 1920's, when Federal aid was the subject of considerable controversy, the only substantial Federal aid was for highways; the other grants totalled less than 1 per cent of the national budget. During these years State aid to local governments for highways and schools was several times larger than all Federal aid and was growing rapidly. By 1930 New York State alone was providing nearly $100 million in State aid, or about the same amount as the total Federal aid to all the States.

Since 1930 Federal aid has increased very rapidly, though it still constitutes only a small part of the national budget—less than 10 per cent. It has become in this country, as elsewhere in the world, an important aspect of government finance. While the increase in Federal aid has been rapid since 1933, it is to be noted that such aid has accounted for only a relatively small part of the increase in national expenditures. The increases in the regular, permanent Federal aid between 1931 and 1938 are to be accounted for largely by the new aids provided under the Social Security Act; and in addition, substantial increases have been made in other Federal aid. . . .[1]

[1] Harris, Joseph P., "The Future of Federal Grants-in-Aid," *Annals of the American Academy of Political and Social Science*, January, 1940, pp. 14–26, on 14–15.

Having traced the origins and development of the grant-in-aid system during the nineteenth century in the preceding chapter, attention is now directed to the astonishing growth of this system in the twentieth century, during which three major periods of development are clearly discernible. At the time of World War I, three important new programs were inaugurated in the fields of agricultural extension, highways, and vocational education. Twenty years later in the Roosevelt era, three more major programs were added—social security, State and local planning, and public housing—all three an outgrowth of the experiences of the Great Depression and of an aroused social consciousness on the part of both the people and their government. Since World War II, there have been constant additions to the list of grant programs, chiefly relating to public health services, public education, and problems of the fast-growing urban and metropolitan areas.

NEW PROGRAMS OF THE WORLD WAR I ERA

As a direct and immediate effect of the adoption of the Sixteenth Amendment, which assured the national government of a substantial annual income, Congress enacted several new grant-in-aid programs which have been continued and expanded over the years, becoming an important part of the nation's domestic policy. The following, each revised and amended many times, should be specifically noted:

Smith-Lever Agricultural Extension Act of May 9, 1914
First Federal Aid Highway Act of July 11, 1916
Smith-Hughes Vocational Education Act of February 23, 1917

Agricultural Extension

The first of these programs, on agricultural extension, has been considered briefly in the preceding chapter in keeping with the policy of discussing each major program or type of program at the point at which it is initiated and becomes a part of national policy.

Federal Aid Highways

The highway program came into being in the early days of the development of the automobile, when public demand for smooth, hard-surfaced roads was just beginning. That the leaders responsible for the establishment of this program were fully aware of its significance is attested to by some observations made by President Wilson in a letter of August 11, 1916, to Representative A. F. Lever, Chairman of the House Committee on Agriculture:

> Of no less importance for agriculture and for national development [than the Agricultural Extension Act] is the Federal Aid road act. This measure will conduce to the establishment of more effective highway machinery in each State, strongly influence the development of good road building along right lines, stimulate larger production and better marketing, promote a fuller and more attractive rural life, add greatly to the convenience and economic welfare of all the people, and strengthen the national foundations. The act embodies sound principles of road legislation and not only will safeguard the expenditure of funds arising under the act, but will also result in the more efficient use of the large additional sums made available by States and localities.[2]

This initial Act of 1916 authorized the Secretary of Agriculture to cooperate with the State highway departments in the construction of rural post roads. Each State was required to assent to the provisions of the Act; the consent of the Governor was acceptable, if the legislature was not in session. The States were also required to establish a department, commission, and an official or officials, with sufficient power under State law to perform the functions ordinarily performed by a State highway department. The apportionment formula provided for a three-part division of funds—one-third each on the basis of area, population, and mileage of rural delivery and star routes in each State relative to the total national mileage of such routes. At the time the Act was passed, only seventeen States had highway departments within the meaning of the Act. By 1921, every State had established such a department, and a total of twenty-eight had made provisions for the matching of Federal funds.[3]

Over the years, the program has been gradually expanded—notably in 1946 and again in 1956—to include both normal and emergency highway needs, and, in addition to through routes (now designated as Interstate Highways), important secondary and feeder roads (including farm-to-market roads, mail routes, and school bus routes), forest roads,

[2] *Congressional Record*, 64th Cong., 1st Sess., Appendix, pp. 1762–1763, and reprinted in Commager, Henry Steele, *Documents of American History*, 6th ed. (New York: Appleton-Century-Crofts, Inc., 1958), pp. 294–296.

[3] For an excellent history of the Federal-aid highway program, see Walter Kurylo, *A Study of the Federal-Aid Highway with Emphasis on Its Major Budgetary and Planning Aspects* (Washington: The American University, March, 1959).

public lands highways, projects within urban areas, and projects to eliminate railroad grade crossings and highway intersections at grade. Except on public lands, the Federal government does not construct or maintain highways. Rather, it makes contributions to the States for approved projects falling within any of the four designated Federal aid systems of highways: (1) the primary highway system; (2) the secondary highway system; (3) extensions of these systems within urban areas; and (4) the interstate highway system.

The original purpose of Federal aid was "to get the farmers out of the mud," while as of the present time, the stated purpose is to promote local and interstate commerce and to serve the needs of national and civil defense. In the case of the Federal Aid Highway Act of 1958, an additional immediate purpose was to counteract the existing economic recession. As of 1955, it was reported that the Federal aid system included approximately 700,000 of the 3,300,000 miles of highways, roads, and streets in the nation. The normal procedure for the distribution of funds begins with authorization by Congress, apportionment among the States approximately two years in advance, State contracting and payment of contractors, and finally, Federal reimbursement to the States.

Federal funds for highways must be matched dollar-for-dollar, be channeled through the State treasuries, and be used for construction purposes only, since maintenance has long been regarded as a State and local responsibility. The amounts appropriated for the highway program have increased at a rapid rate, but perhaps not rapidly enough to keep pace with the needs of a growing population, the ever-increasing number of registered motor vehicles, and the volume of traffic. In addition to the regular highway grants, large sums have been appropriated to meet special highway needs. Some of the figures, at ten-year intervals, are shown in the following table.

FINANCING STATE HIGHWAY CONSTRUCTION, 1914–1964 *
(In thousands)

Year	Federal Grant-in-Aid Funds	State Capital Outlay	Percentage of Cost Borne by Federal Grants
1914	$	$ 53,880	0.0
1924	92,870	397,648	23.4
1934	354,812	580,369	61.1
1944	91,918	210,328	43.7
1954	587,857	2,962,562	19.8
1964 †	3,513,000	6,271,000	56.0

* Bureau of the Census, *Historical Statistics of the United States: Colonial Times to 1957* (Washington, 1960), p. 459.
† Provided by Budget Office, Bureau of Public Roads.

The enactment of highway aid legislation signalled the beginning of a new era in the history of Federal assistance to the States. From this time on, the volume of assistance granted for highway construction far exceeded that extended for other purposes. More than that, particularly when the 1921 amendments were made to this legislation, the Federal government began more carefully to scrutinize the projects on which grant-in-aid funds were applied. As Professor Maxwell has written, "The highway grants were, indeed, the first sort of Federal aid to be thoroughly supervised and administered. Advance examination of projects, detailed progress reports, audit of expenditures, careful examination of the finished work to ensure that plans had been followed and that there was proper maintenance—all the techniques of good administration were utilized." [4]

Much has been written about Federal dictation to State and local units. It is true that Federal legislation and administrative requirements have influenced the States which, as noted, had to set up highway departments or agencies and adhere to established standards in order to be eligible for the Federal grants. Most would agree that these conditions were essential to the proper administration of the program. In spite of these policies, serious irregularities occurred in a few States on the interstate program in 1959 and 1960. One of the rare instances in which conditions were imposed that were objectionable because they interfered with a State's control over its own domestic affairs is the oft-mentioned Hayden-Cartwright Act of June 18, 1934, the annual amendment to and revision of the original Federal Aid Highway Act of 1916. This measure was significant in that it established a precedent for the exercise of important policy controls over federally aided programs. Congress sought to prevent further diversion of State highway user revenues by providing for the withholding of one-third of the Federal aid that would otherwise be available in those States where the policy of diversion was practiced. This provision, or a similar one, has been retained in all subsequent highway legislation. Another illustration is found in the provision designed to encourage the States to bar billboards on the Interstate System, as more than forty States have done.

Regularly each year, since the enactment of the original Road Act of 1916, Congress has enacted a highway measure. Particularly significant among these many enactments was the act adopted in 1946—quite separate and distinct from the annual highway act—providing for the 41,000 mile interstate superhighway system. For many years, the nation's highway system had been failing to keep pace with the need. Due to shortages of men and materials, there had been little or no new construction and only a minimum amount of essential maintenance during

[4] Maxwell, James A., *The Fiscal Impact of Federalism in the United States* (Cambridge: Harvard University Press, 1946), p. 187.

World War II, with the result that at the close of the war, the nation found itself with a completely antiquated and outmoded highway system. The inadequacy of the 1946 program became more and more apparent. Although the situation was critical, the Governors were singularly unimpressed. As late as 1953, with characteristic foresight, the Governors' Conference adopted a resolution suggesting that the Federal government withdraw completely from the highway picture, abolishing the Bureau of Public Roads, and turning over to the States the tax sources that go into highways. The Commission on Intergovernmental Relations (Kestnbaum) started out with this idea, but soon shifted its position. Of course this was not done, but if it had, where would the highway program be now?

President Eisenhower discussed the matter in his Economic Report of January 28, 1954. This, plus a general realization that something had to be done, prompted Congress to provide for an interstate program in the Federal Aid Highway Act of May 6, 1954, which contained a revised formula increasing the Federal share in financing the interstate system from 50/50 to 60/40. This move engendered a tremendous controversy over methods of financing. The Governors' Conference set up a seven-member Highway Committee which reported in December, 1954. A six-member Interagency Committee within the Federal government was established "to consider the matter from the standpoint of Federal interest in roads and their financing." The President appointed an Advisory Committee on a National Highway Program, which came to be known as the Clay Committee, which reported in January, 1955. In his Economic Report of January 20, 1955, the President re-emphasized the highway problem; the administration bill (S. 1160) incorporating the recommendations of the Clay Committee was introduced in February, 1955. The Commission on Intergovernmental Relations' *Report to the President* in June, 1955, devoted a chapter to highways, and two other reports included highways as part of a larger discussion of grants-in-aid.[5]

None of the proposals for highway financing made by these study groups was adopted by Congress. On February 21, 1955, there was a nonpartisan meeting of Congressional leaders at the White House, followed by the introduction of a new bill containing two new and controversial proposals, one to create a Federal Highway Corporation (which ultimately became the Highway Trust Fund), the other to reimburse the States for expenditures for toll roads on the Interstate System which met approved Federal standards. None of the reports had even suggested that the national interest in all primary highways was so great as to justify not only Federal financing, but construction of these highways as well.

[5] See Ransone, Coleman B., Jr., *Recent Trends in Federal-State Highway Relations,* a paper presented at a meeting of the Southern Political Science Association, Atlanta, November, 1955.

While the Federal government's share on other highway programs—primary, secondary, and urban—shall not exceed 50 per cent of the cost of construction, its share on the interstate and defense highways is generally 90 per cent of the total cost of the project.

By the end of March, 1963, the Bureau of Public Roads was able to report that 30 per cent of the 41,000-mile system had been completed in seven years. Actually, 14,543 miles were open to traffic, consisting of 9,136 miles built to 1975 traffic standards, 3,101 miles that were deemed adequate but will need improvement to reach 1975 expectations, and 2,306 miles of toll expressways incorporated into the Interstate System. Further, 30,629 miles of the coast-to-coast system, about 75 per cent of the total, was either completed or in various stages of development from planning to paving.

Conventional primary, secondary, and urban highway programs receiving Federal aid have experienced a tremendous spurt of spending during the same period; Bureau figures show that 100,000 miles of non-interstate road projects, involving $9 billion in combined State and Federal funds, have been completed, and 20,000 more miles are under construction. All revenue for the Federal funds spent on or committed to highway projects since 1956, and most of the money for the States' participation, has come from special taxes on motorists, principally gasoline taxes. In order to put the program on a pay-as-you-go basis, the Federal gasoline tax was increased from two to three cents a gallon in 1956. Nationwide, these levies have risen to an average of ten cents a gallon, two-fifths of which is a Federal tax. The proceeds from this levy, along with revenues from taxes on motor vehicles, tires, tubes, and half the receipts from the tax on new trucks and buses, were earmarked for a special Federal Highway Trust Fund. Bureau figures showed that during the first four years the Federal government collected $14.3 billion from all its taxes on motor vehicle ownership and use, but $6.2 billion of this money did not go into the Trust Fund.

In 1959, when the Fund was headed for a deficit, Congress again increased the Federal gasoline tax to four cents a gallon, effective October 1, but with the proviso that the added cent of tax would expire June 30, 1961. On that date, according to the legislation, the expired cent of gasoline tax would be replaced by allocating to the Trust Fund one-half of the proceeds from the 10 per cent tax on new automobiles plus five-eighths of the receipts from the 8 per cent tax on automotive parts and accessories. The legislation provided that this financing arrangement would remain in effect until June 30, 1964. If Congress adheres to this plan, the result will be an actual increase in funds available to the highway program, according to government estimates.

Vocational Education

Proposals for Federal aid for education began to appear in Congress as early as the 1820's. There were more proposals in the 1830's, as the States moved to establish their systems of common schools. As the years have passed, not only has the number of bills introduced increased from one Congress to the next, but the amounts have also risen. It took eight pages of fine print merely to list and describe briefly some fifteen major proposals between 1949 and 1959.[6] The fear of Federal control has been strong enough for approximately a century and a half to prevent passage of any overall aid to education bill. Meantime, it has been possible to obtain passage of a number of bills aimed at helping with the financial support of individual educational programs—sort of nibbling around the edges, as it were. One of the first of these measures was Federal aid for vocational education, followed by aid for federally affected areas and Federal aid for school construction, maintenance, and operation.

Vocational education was the third major program area in which grants were begun in the World War I era. The statutory basis of this work is found in the Smith-Hughes Act of February 23, 1917, as revised and amended at intervals of about ten years, and the George-Barden Act of August 1, 1946. Some of the details regarding this legislation are given in the table on page 523. Figures for the first three entries under permanent appropriations are as provided in the original act, while those for the others are as provided in the 1946 legislation. The basic programs, together with a number of small supplementary programs since established, are listed in the table.

Administration of the program, long a responsibility of the Federal Board of Vocational Education, has been headed by the Office of Education since 1946. The Commissioner of the Office has delegated certain functions and responsibilities to the Division of Vocational Education, which conducts some of the activities authorized by the George-Barden Act almost entirely. Most of them, however, require close cooperation with the States, and with respect to these, the Division works on the national and interstate levels with both public and private agencies and groups.

Federally aided vocational education programs are administered at the State level by State boards of vocational education, and funds are channeled through the State treasuries. At present, the annual author-

---

[6] Legislative Reference Service, *Major Federal Aid to Education Bills: A Chronological Summary and Description of Selected Major Bills, 1949–59, and Bibliography,* 86th Cong., 2nd Sess. (Washington: Committee Print, February, 1960).

ization is approximately $39 million, all of which must be matched by State and local contributions on a dollar-for-dollar basis. Actually, State-local expenditures greatly exceed, by a ratio of about five State-local dollars to every Federal dollar, the equal matching of Federal funds required by law. Federal funds are used principally for the salaries and travel of vocational teachers, teacher-trainers, supervisors, and directors. The organization chart on pages 524-525 is intended to serve two purposes, first to show the complex of interrelationships under this program, and second to serve as a typical illustration of the maze of interlevel and interjurisdictional relationships common to grant programs in general. In the administration of the vocational education program, the division cooperates with the States in identifying the instruction needs of indi-

FEDERAL AID FOR VOCATIONAL EDUCATION

Statutory Basis:

    Smith-Hughes Act of February 23, 1917. 39 Stat. 929

    George-Reed Act of February 5, 1929. 45 Stat. 1151

    George-Ellzey Act of May 21, 1934. 48 Stat. 792-793

    George-Deen Act of June 8, 1936. 49 Stat. 1188-1490

    George-Barden Act of August 1, 1946. 60 Stat. 776-778

Extensions:

Functional	*Territorial*
Practical Nurse Training—Act of August 2, 1956. 70 Stat. 925-929	Hawaii—P.L. 35, 68th Cong.
	Puerto Rico—P.L. 791, 71st Cong.
Fisheries Occupations—Act of August 8, 1956. 70 Stat. 1126	Virgin Islands—P.L. 462, 81st Cong.
	Guam—P.L. 896, 84th Cong.
Training for Adult Indians—Act of August 3, 1956. 70 Stat. 986	

Permanent Appropriation for Allotment to States:

Vocational Program	*Annual Authorization*	*Basis of Apportionment*	*Minimum Grant per State*
Agriculture	$ 3,000,000	Rural population	$10,000
Home economics, trades and			
industry	3,000,000	Urban population	10,000
Teacher training	1,000,000	Total population	10,000
Agriculture	10,000,000	Farm population	40,000
Home Economics	8,000,000	Rural population	40,000
Trades and Industry	8,000,000	Non-farm population ...	40,000
Distributive occupations ..	2,500,000	Total population	15,000

524

ADMINISTRATIVE STRUCTURE

FOR

VOCATIONAL EDUCATION

1962

PRESIDENT OF THE UNITED STATES

Secretary
U. S. Department of Health,
Education, and Welfare

U. S. Commissioner of Education

Deputy Commissioner

Associate Commissioner
Bureau of Educational
Assistance Programs[1]

Assistant Commissioner[2]
DIVISION OF VOCATIONAL AND TECHNICAL EDUCATION

Agricultural Education Branch

Trade and Industrial Education Branch

Home Economics Education Branch

Distributive Education Branch

Technical Education Branch

Manpower Development and Training Staff

State Board for

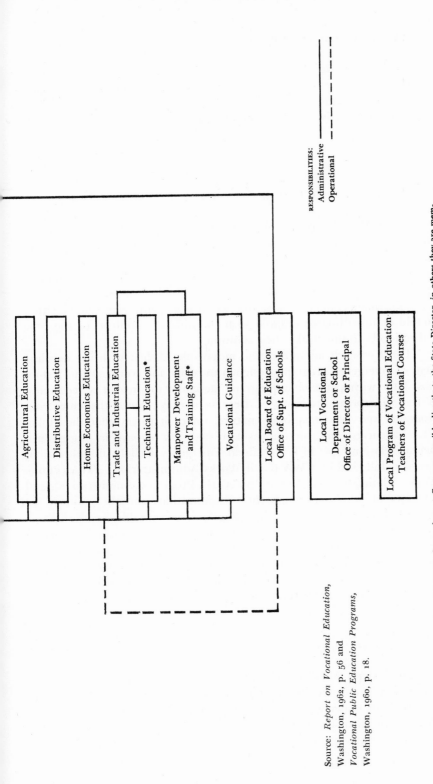

Agricultural Education

Distributive Education

Home Economics Education

Trade and Industrial Education

Technical Education*

Manpower Development and Training Staff*

Vocational Guidance

Local Board of Education
Office of Supt. of Schools

Local Vocational
Department or School
Office of Director or Principal

Local Program of Vocational Education
Teachers of Vocational Courses

RESPONSIBILITIES:
Administrative
Operational

Source: *Report on Vocational Education,*
Washington, 1962, p. 56 and
Vocational Public Education Programs,
Washington, 1960, p. 18.

* In some States these staffs are responsible directly to the State Director, in others they are members of the trade and industrial education staff.

[1] One of three associate commissioners in the Office of Education.
[2] One of three assistant commissioners in the Office of Education.

viduals and communities, on the basis of occupational opportunities and trends. It cooperates in planning, organizing, administering, and supervising the programs, once established, and in the development of instructional materials, suitable standards, and the evaluation of programs.

SIGNIFICANT PROGRAMS OF THE ROOSEVELT ERA

The Roosevelt era was a period during which there occurred an extensive centralization of powers in the hands of the Federal government. Part of this may have been due to the temper of the times, but this in turn may be attributed to the fact that during the Depression era, the prestige of the States was at an exceedingly low ebb. Even those States fortunate enough to have competent leadership seemed to be either unable or unwilling to grapple with the difficult problems of the time and seriously to undertake their solution.

The Roosevelt administration moved ahead, first with the development of emergency programs designed to revive the economy and restore jobs, later with permanent programs designed to prevent a recurrence of the widespread suffering of Depression days. Since the emergency programs were of a temporary nature, suffice it to say that the alphabetical agencies administering them created new patterns in intergovernmental relationships. FERA (Federal Emergency Relief Administration) was soon followed by CWA (Civil Works Administration), PWA (Public Works Administration), and WPA (Works Progress Administration), and a variety of others. Through these organizations and the grants-in-aid connected with their respective programs, a veritable revolution occurred in both the organization and the practice of intergovernmental relations in the United States. Of the permanent programs, the social security program was by far the most important. Other significant programs were established in the fields of housing, airports, conservation, and State and local planning.

Social Security Programs

The Federal Social Security program, based upon the Social Security Act of 1935, as amended, operates on the basis of Federal-State cooperative arrangements under which the Federal government reimburses the States for some or all of the administrative costs incurred and assists with the financial burden of carrying on the program. The several specific programs currently existing in this field fall into three different categories: (1) *Insurance programs*—unemployment compensation, a major aspect of the employment security program (ES), and old age and survivor's insurance (OASI); (2) *Public assistance*—old age assistance (OAA), aid to the blind (AB), aid to dependent children (ADC), aid to the totally and permanently disabled (ATPD), and medical aid for the aged (MAA); (3) *Maternal and child welfare*—grants for maternal and child health services, and services for crippled children. All of these programs were initiated in 1935 with the following exceptions: programs for children begun in 1912 were expanded and enlarged in 1935; aid to dependent children was added in 1939, aid to the totally and permanently disabled in 1950, and medical aid for the aged in 1960. All of these programs require a high degree of cooperation between the several levels and units of government and among the three branches of government at each level.

Insurance Programs. The old age and survivors' insurance program, popularly known as the old age pension system, was designed to prevent suffering by older citizens and to prevent the embarrassment of dependency on relatives. As originally enacted, the Social Security Act provided for the establishment of a system of old-age insurance, federally administered and financed by compulsory contributions from both employer and employee. It was designed to cover about 60 per cent of the working population in the country (employees in commerce and industry), but many subsequent amendments have enlarged the scope of coverage. The 1950 amendments moved far toward a universal plan, covering practically all individuals and families (including the self-employed) dependent upon earnings of any kind. Although the collection of taxes was scheduled to begin in 1937, no benefits were to be paid before 1942, with the exception of lump sum payments to workers who reached the age of sixty-five or to the dependents of those who died without qualifying for benefits.

At its central records center in Baltimore, the Department maintains individual accounts, established between 1937 when the program became effective and mid-1960, for almost 78 million persons. In Old Age and Survivor's Insurance, the only completely Federal program under the Act, monthly payments for some 14 million claimants during fiscal 1960 totalled $10,798,000. The amount of average monthly benefits increased gradually from $22.60 in 1940 to $74.04 in 1960.

Under the Unemployment Compensation program, the cooperating States are required to levy taxes on the payrolls of the employers covered by the law and to set up State agencies to administer the law and disburse money to unemployed workers when valid claims are presented.

In the States that agreed to the plan, the payment by employers of the State payroll tax cancels 90 per cent of the corresponding national tax on payrolls, leaving only 10 per cent to go to the Federal treasury. On the other hand, the whole of the national tax collected in nonparticipating States goes into the national treasury, although workers in such noncooperating States, in the absence of a State law, are not eligible to receive benefits. Of course no State would or did long remain outside of this system.

In a series of cases involving the constitutionality of the Social Security Act, the Supreme Court developed new doctrines concerning the spending power. Professor William Anderson summarized the situation in these words:

> The entire tax collected by each participating State was to go into a special trust fund in the national treasury, to be paid back to the States as needed for payment to the unemployed in accordance with State laws and Federal standards. The 10 per cent of the Federal tax mentioned above was also to go into the Federal treasury but for undefined purposes. However, the national government agreed to pay to each State annually a sum not over the receipts from this 10 per cent, as appropriated annually by Congress, for the administrative expenses of state unemployment compensation systems. Thus a branch of the State government would become dependent upon annual appropriations from the national government and Congress would determine each State's administrative needs under the program. This was a most unusual system of national-state cooperation, especially notable for the strength of the inducements to the States to participate and for the strictness of the Federal controls of expenditures and standards. It was small wonder, therefore, that employers who had to pay the taxes attacked the whole system as an unconstitutional scheme for national invasion of the powers of the States. State laws consenting to the plan were characterized as unconstitutional surrenders of power brought about by coercion and duress.
>
> The Supreme Court decisions in the two leading cases . . . show an almost complete reversal of the attitude of the Court's majority since the AAA decision in 1936 in the face of a somewhat different set of facts.[7] Four justices who were of the majority in the AAA case were not

---

[7] The AAA decision was *United States* v. *Butler*, 297 U.S. 1 (1936), in which the Court by a 6-3 majority held the Agricultural Adjustment Act of 1933 unconstitutional on the ground that the processing taxes were used to coerce farmers in an effort to regulate and control farm production. In the second decision, *Steward Machine Company* v. *Davis*, 301 U.S. 548 (1937), the Court upheld the unemployment insurance taxes, holding that the tax offset device did not unduly coerce the States merely because the law made it to their financial advantage to cooperate.

the dissenting minority. A shift of one vote on the Court had made a significant change.

It was with these decisions and a few related ones that the Supreme Court put behind it practically all ideas of trying to impose limits upon the spending power of the national government. In upholding the provisions of the old-age benefits, administered directly by the national government, the Court justified the program under the power of Congress to tax and spend for "the general welfare." It said that "the line must still be drawn between one welfare and another, between particular and general" but that the decision on this point was not confided to the courts. "The discretion belongs to Congress, unless the choice is clearly wrong, a display of arbitrary powers, not an exercise of judgment." In these decisions also the Court denied that the very strong inducements offered to the States under the Social Security Act amounted to coercion on them, and asserted the right of the States themselves to make agreements with the national government. The charge that the States were thereby abdicating their "sovereignty" was also denied by the Court, and the right of the States under the Constitution to enter into cooperative arrangements with the national government was upheld. "Nowhere in our scheme of government—in the limitations express or implied of our Federal Constitution—do we find she [the State] is prohibited from assenting to conditions that will assure a fair and just requital for benefits received.[8]

Public Assistance Programs. The Social Security Act of 1935 provided for Federal grants-in-aid to assist the States in establishing programs for old-age assistance, aid to dependent children, and aid to the blind. The objective of these programs is that they help needy people in these categories, each person's need determined individually in accordance with each State's standards of assistance. All of the public assistance titles require the State to consider an individual's other income and resources in making that determination. Persons in public domiciliary institutions and in mental and tuberculosis hospitals are excluded. Two other categories of aid have since been added.

Under the old-age assistance program, the Federal government pays four-fifths of the first $30 a month per recipient plus one-half of the balance up to a maximum of $60 per recipient. Thus, if a State pays the maximum of $60, the Federal government pays $24 (four-fifths of the first $30) plus $15 (one-half of the balance), or a total of $39 per recipient. Payments average about $58 monthly.

Aid to dependent children, or mother's assistance, is provided for

[8] Anderson, William, *Intergovernmental Relations in Review* (Minneapolis: University of Minnesota Press, 1960), p. 30.

the mothers of small children when the father has died or, because of illness, is unable to support his family. Originally limited to children under sixteen, the law was amended in 1939 to include children under eighteen if found by the State agency to be regularly attending school, and in 1950 to provide Federal matching for payments to needy parents or certain specified relatives with whom the child or children were living, in addition to payments to children.

In addition to providing reading materials and other benefits for the blind, the Federal government will match State funds, on the same basis as for old-age assistance, up to a total Federal-State monthly grant of $60. To be eligible, blind persons must be sixty-five years of age or older, and needy. They must not be inmates of public institutions, nor may they be receiving other old-age assistance. The 1950 amendments to the Social Security Act made Federal financial aid and other services available to the permanently and totally disabled who are eighteen years of age or older.

The number of recipients and average payments for the four joint Federal-State public assistance programs actually functioning in 1960 are shown in the following table.

PAYMENTS IN PUBLIC ASSISTANCE PROGRAMS, AS OF JULY 1, 1960

Program	Statutory Basis	Number of Recipients	Average Payment
Old-Age Assistance	Title I	2,354,993	$ 68.23
Aid to Dependent Children	Title IV	3,106,344 *	111.28 †
Aid to the Blind	Title X	107,879	72.79
Aid to the Permanently and Totally Disabled	1950 amndts.	364,583	66.21
Medical Aid to the Aged	1960 amndts.	‡	‡

* Number of families, 789,323.   † Amount per family.   ‡ Program established in 1960.

The 1960 amendments to the Social Security Act established a new program of medical assistance for the aged, under which Federal grants are available to States for medical assistance for individuals sixty-five years of age and older. Persons receiving old-age assistance are ineligible, as are those whose income and resources are sufficient to meet the costs of necessary medical care. A State plan must include some institutional and some noninstitutional care and services. The controversy over this program began in 1959 with the introduction of the Forand bill for social security coverage of hospital and medical expenses for the aged. That the problem is a very real one, with constantly mounting costs, no one will deny. The controversy continued into 1960 when, with a presidential election in the offing, both parties agreed that something should be done. The conservative elements of both felt that if government action was to be taken, it should be taken by the States, perhaps with assistance in the form of an annual Federal appropriation. They were opposed to social security coverage, and they were supported in their opposition by the promise of a presidential veto if a social security program was passed by Congress. After prolonged debate, this group won.

No sooner had the Kerr-Mills Act been passed than the Democrats and liberals renewed the drive for a new law with social security coverage. The Democratic platform and Senator Kennedy as the Party candidate supported this approach; early in his administration, the Anderson bill was introduced in the Senate with administration backing. No action on the measure was taken during the 87th Congress, which left it high on the agenda for the 88th. The case for the administration bill was greatly strengthened by the desultory response of the States to the Medical Assistance for the Aged (MAA) program established under the Kerr-Mills Act.[9] As of March 31, 1961, only seven States had programs in operation. A year later the number had doubled, and by January, 1963, there was legislation in twenty-seven States. The drive for a more adequate program was renewed in the 88th Congress.

Maternal and Child Welfare. Services for maternal and child welfare have been mentioned as the third category of programs in the social security field. Grants are made for health services and for services for crippled children, both of which programs are briefly covered in the following chapter dealing with public health services. These services were, with relatively minor exceptions, very late additions to the grant-in-aid program as a whole.

Related Programs. In addition to the cooperative programs considered here, both Federal and State governments carry on other programs which contribute in an important way to the achievement of the ideal that no needy person shall be denied the basic necessities of life. State and local units are responsible for the administration of public assistance under whatever arrangements may be prescribed by State law; the Federal government pays public assistance grants to the States to help them bear the financial burden, and it is highly probable that in the next few years, the amount of these grants will be increased.[10]

A number of States, including California, New Jersey, New York, and Rhode Island, have established and are financing disability insurance programs. While unemployment compensation or employment security

[9] *State Action to Implement Medical Programs for the Aged: A Staff Report,* 87th Cong., 1st Sess. (Washington: Committee Print, June, 1961).

[10] Senator Eugene McCarthy of Minnesota made such a proposal in 1960, in S. 3755; see *Congressional Record,* June 27, 1960, pp. 13413–13421.

(a joint Federal-State program) provides for those who temporarily have no job, and workmen's compensation (a State program) provides for those injured in course of employment, there is, except in the four States noted above, no provision for the assistance of those who are temporarily unable to work because of illness. The close relationship existing between health and welfare matters is further illustrated by some of the programs discussed in the following chapter.

Promotion of State and Local Planning

The planning program initiated during the Roosevelt era, though not a grant-in-aid program in the conventional sense, involved many of the same characteristics. It was one of the major contributions to the general welfare made during this period. Planning represents the attempt of democracy to apply intelligence to the use of natural and human resources in the best interests of all the people. There had been a considerable background of planning in many American cities, but the movement had made little headway in the States until, during the Great Depression, financial and technical assistance was given them for this purpose by the National Resources Board.

As of the 1930's, when thirty-four laws were in effect, some of the boards were more or less inactive. Nearly all were hampered by inadequate support, which in turn meant inadequate staffing. Since then, planning has fallen upon evil times. In 1942, the national agency was abolished when a powerful politician in the Senate suddenly discovered that planning was "socialistic." During the period of its existence, the Board had taken an active interest in urban and regional problems. When it was liquidated, financial aid, technical assistance, and leadership to the States were all cut off, and many of the State agencies were permitted to lapse. Only a few bona fide State planning agencies now remain. After World War II, most of those still in existence degenerated into mere public relations and promotion agencies, operating in response to a great upsurge of interest in industrial promotion and development which is often mistakenly referred to as planning. These agencies are mainly concerned with attracting new industries, with State advertising, and with promoting the tourist trade.

The only encouraging development since World War II has been the inclusion of the community planning and development program which was authorized by Section 701 of the Housing Act of 1954, as amended. This legislation, first applicable to cities rather than to States, serves well to illustrate the circuitous route by which it is often necessary to proceed to meet pressing current needs. Since the scuttling of the earlier planning programs, it had not been proper to admit that State and local matters were a legitimate concern of the central government. It thus became necessary to amend the national housing law in order to make Federal funds available to cities to permit them to undertake planning functions that the States should have been helping them perform.

The Section 701 Program, as it is called, makes funds available to official planning bodies for work in communities with less than 50,000 population, and to States, metropolitan areas, urban regions, disaster areas, and federally impacted areas, *i.e.,* areas experiencing accelerated growth because of Federal installations. The program authorizes Federal grants up to 50 per cent of the cost of the planning work undertaken, with State and local agencies contributing the remainder. The Act, which requires that the program be administered by the State planning agency, permits tailoring of plans to the needs of individual communities, in conformity with the overall State program.[11] In 1960, 493 projects were approved in forty-three States and one Territory to a total of $13.4 million, with $8.9 million being actually disbursed. A major advantage of participation is that technical and professional services essential to comprehensive, coordinated planning are made available to smaller communities which might not otherwise have them because of cost or lack of awareness of their need. Such services can be a distinct benefit to the State as a whole, and in 1961, it was reported that ten States had qualified for modest grants for statewide planning under a 1959 amendment to the Housing Act of 1954 (41 U.S.C. 421b).

The administration of such a program is no easy assignment, either for Federal officials or for those of the States. Federal law requires the development of an overall master plan for the State. The difficulty lies in following a time sequence in the development of such a plan. Many of the States are not "planning oriented" in their thinking, nor do they have the professional staff necessary to proceed at once to develop a master plan. They may have some highway planners, housing planners,

---

[11] A specific example of the nature of the services authorized may be noted in four New Mexico communities which contributed $22,385 in local funds, matched by an equal amount from the Urban Renewal Administration, the total funds to be expended over a two-year period for such items as: (1) base maps, collection of basic data, studies of economic conditions, population, traffic circulation, parking and land use; (2) neighborhood analyses; (3) preparation or revision of plans showing the general location, type, and extent of such elements as major thoroughfares, transportation routes and terminals, community facilities (including schools, parks, recreation areas, and public buildings), and public utilities; (4) public improvements program and capital budget; (5) preparation or revision of zoning and land subdivision, regulations, and other work leading to comprehensive plans for the four communities.

or planners of other types. Should such States be told in a doctrinaire manner that the master plan must come first? If this approach were adopted, many of the States might never develop a master plan. If, on the other hand, these States are encouraged to develop and improve what they have, progress may be made in developing statewide plans in functional areas which can be coordinated and consolidated into a master plan. Involved are some delicate problems in the field of Federal-State relations, the solution of which will require patience and understanding on the part of officials at both levels.

Federal Public Housing Program

The problem of poor and inadequate shelter for some portion of the population has existed in practically all societies through the centuries. Due to changing conditions and changing concepts of adequacy, the exact nature and scope of the problem is usually difficult to define. Here in the United States, as cities continued to grow in size and to become increasingly industrialized, land became scarce and expensive. This resulted in the construction of tenements, with resulting poor facilities, high rents, and serious overcrowding. While there is evidence that these conditions were a matter of concern as early as 1857, it was not until 1901 that the State of New York enacted a Tenement House Law for the cities of New York and Buffalo. By 1917, ten States had enacted such legislation,[12] but State and local governments did little about housing prior to 1933, and the Federal government did virtually nothing because housing was regarded as a purely private matter.

The first venture of the Federal government into the field came in 1892 with an appropriation of $20,000 to finance a survey of slums in cities of 200,000 population or over, but little was accomplished. It was not until the years of the Great Depression that public attention was focused on the smoldering slum problem and that public housing received its first impetus under the National Industrial Recovery Act and the Federal Emergency Administration of Public Works. Even then, accomplishments were rather limited. President Roosevelt followed his

[12] For an excellent historical sketch, see Brown, Robert K., *The Development of the Public Housing Program in the United States* (Atlanta: Georgia State College of Business Administration, June, 1960); see also Wendt, Paul F., *The Role of the Federal Government in Housing* (Washington: American Enterprise Association, 1956). For an excellent brief description of all current housing programs, see Senate Committee on Banking and Currency, *Review of Federal Housing Programs*, Appendix to *Housing Legislation of 1961*, Hearings on various bills to amend the housing laws, April, 1961, 87th Cong., 1st Sess. (Washington, 1961).

oft-quoted statement that one-third of the nation was ill-fed, ill-housed, and ill-clothed with recommendations for a vast public housing program, whereupon in 1937, when Congress enacted the Housing (Wagner-Steagall) Act, public housing actually began to develop. This legislation provided for a Housing Authority in what was then the Federal Works Agency, charged with making long-term loans, up to 80 per cent of the costs involved, to State and local housing authorities for the construction of low-rent housing and for slum clearance.

Under this 1937 legislation, the Federal government was not to engage directly in the work of demolition or construction, but merely to make loans; municipal or other local authorities directly concerned were to plan projects, furnish such additional funds as might be required, and execute the projects. Within four years after the legislation was enacted, all but nine States had qualified for Federal aid by setting up the requisite authorities, sometimes with jurisdiction limited to one or two cities, but often extending to all cities and towns and to rural areas as well.[13]

Space does not permit more than a skeleton outline of developments during and since World War II. Wartime needs necessitated important modifications of the program. Among the numerous pieces of legislation enacted, Public Law 671 of 1940 authorized construction of dwellings for defense workers; the Lanham Act made such construction possible in cities not having housing authorities or low-rent housing programs. An urgent need for better coordination prompted the President in 1942 to establish the National Housing Agency, composed of the Federal Housing Administration, the Federal Home Loan Bank System, and the Federal Public Housing Authority. The over-all adequacy of the war housing program was a great achievement.

Postwar developments began with heated controversy in 1945 over the Wagner-Ellender-Taft bill which, had it passed, would have become the General Housing Act of 1945; when it failed of enactment, President Truman established an Emergency Housing Program for veterans with Wilson Wyatt at its head. Essentially the same bill was introduced again in 1947, under the same sponsorship, providing for additional low-rent housing and a permanent consolidation and enlargement of the housing functions of the Federal government. While the legislation was delayed in Congress, the President by a Reorganization Plan moved another step toward the consolidation of Federal housing agencies.

The effort of the administration to develop a strong public housing program met with strong resistance, particularly from the real estate lobby which succeeded in defeating the proposal in the House in 1948. Following the 1949 election, after five years of frustration and failure, a housing

[13] See Schaffter, Dorothy, *State Housing Agencies* (New York: Columbia University Press, 1942).

act was finally passed, although in spite of increasing need, restrictions on the construction of public housing continued. Still groping for a satisfactory solution of the problem, Congress enacted the Housing Act of 1954, providing for important changes in the existing legislation and in administrative arrangements. Most of the restrictive provisions of this Act were removed by amendments adopted in 1955, but the controversy between the two houses continued in 1956, as the House contended for various "private-use" housing programs and the Senate sought a public housing program of 200,000 additional units for the next three years.

On December 3, 1960, the twenty-fifth anniversary of government-subsidized public housing in the United States was celebrated at a ceremony in the courtyard of First Houses, at Avenue A and East Third Street, on the Lower East Side in New York City. Here Federal, State, and city officials, together with a seven-member group from the United Nations, gathered to mark the occasion. The First Houses project was opened to 123 families on December 3, 1935. Two points in connection with these ceremonies are worthy of note. First, participating in the 1960 ceremony was one of the original tenants, a widow who told a touching story of her situation before and after she moved into the three-room apartment for which she now pays $27.45 a month. Secondly, one should recall the remark, "This is only a beginning," made by Mrs. Franklin D. Roosevelt at the dedication ceremony twenty-five years before. How right she was!

> Public housing in the city has spread to every borough. The New York City Housing Authority now lets apartments to 109,000 families in ninety-two developments, with more to come. Fifty-one projects to house 160,000 people are under construction or on drawing boards now. One-third of the multiple-dwelling units constructed in the city since World War II have been built by the Housing Authority, according to the Authority's department of statistics.[14]

The 1961 amendments to the National Housing Act included provisions for college housing ($1.2 billion in low interest loans for construction of college dormitories); farm homes ($200 million more for direct loans for farm and non-farm housing in rural areas); and home improvement loans (twenty-five year, $10,000 loans insured by the Federal Housing Administration, for housing more than ten years old, primarily). When he signed this legislation, President Kennedy was quoted as saying, "For the communities of the Nation, large and small, it provides an opportunity for a giant step toward better cities and improved housing."

[14] Phillips, McCandlish, "City Marks Birth of Public Housing," *The New York Times,* December 4, 1960.

BIBLIOGRAPHICAL NOTES

General works dealing with grants-in-aid are noted at the conclusion of the following chapter, and references on grant programs in the field of agriculture were given in the preceding bibliographical notes.

Highways. There is an enormous literature on highways, discussions of their history, and technical material on their construction and maintenance, but relatively few general works on questions involving intergovernmental relations. That the Federal government has long been interested in roads is evidenced by the early internal improvements programs; on these programs at midcentury, see William T. Jackson, *Wagon Roads West: A Study of Federal Road Surveys and Construction in the Trans-Mississippi West, 1846–1869* (Berkeley: University of California Press, 1952). For good general works, see Charles L. Deering, *American Highway Policy* (Washington: Brookings Institution, 1941), which is old but still good, and Jean Labatut and Wheaton J. Lane, *Highways in Our National Life* (Princeton: Princeton University Press, 1950). The only historical study of highway grants is Walter Kurylo's excellent doctoral dissertation, *A Study of the Federal-aid Highway Program with Special Emphasis on Its Budget and Planning Aspects* (Washington: American University, 1960).

Other titles of interest include: American Association of State Highway Officials, *History and Accomplishments of Twenty-five Years of Federal Aid for Highways: An Examination of Policies From State and National Viewpoints* (Washington, 1945); B. A. Gomez, *Intergovernmental Relations in Highways* (Minneapolis: University of Minnesota Press, 1950), a volume in the Minnesota series edited by Professor William Anderson; Highway Research Board, *Intergovernmental Relations in State Highway Legislation: An Analysis* (Washington: National Research Council, 1959); G. Donald Kennedy, *The Role of the Federal Government in State Highway Development* (Washington: Bureau of Public Roads, 1944). The National Highway Users Conference publishes a useful pamphlet, *Federal-Aid for Highways: What It Is, How It Works* (Washington, 1959), which is kept up to date by frequent revision. Numerous studies of highway relationships within individual States are concerned solely with State-local relations; for the role of the Federal government, however, see Ralph S. Lewis, *Highway Relationships in Maryland* (Washington: Highway Research Board, 1952); Maine Legislative Research Committee, *Maine Federal Interstate Highway System* (Augusta, January, 1958); and Richard M. Zettel, *Federal Highway Legislation of 1956 and Its Impact on California* (Berkeley: Bureau of Public Administration, University of California, 1957). The Commission on Intergovernmental Relations included in its series of reports, *A Study Committee Report on Federal Aid to Highways* (Washington, June, 1955).

Vocational Education. The American Vocational Association prepared an annotated bibliography of 373 studies in agricultural education, published under the title *Summaries of Studies in Agricultural Education* (Washington: Office of Education, 1935). Shortly after the Smith-Hughes Act was passed, the Carnegie Foundation for the Advancement of Teaching put out a study, *Federal Aid for Vocational Education* (Bulletin No. 10, New York, 1917). Other studies include Herbert M. Hamlin, *Local Policies for Agricultural Education in the Public Schools* (Urbana: College of Education, University of Illinois, 1953) and Rufus W. Stimson and Frank W. Lathrop,

History of Agricultural Education of Less Than College Grade in the United States (Washington: Office of Education, Vocational Bulletin No. 217, 1942). There are, of course, many studies of the problem in individual States, of which the following are representative: Kenneth L. Russell, *Establishing Departments of Vocational Agriculture in Missouri* (Columbia: Department of Agricultural Education, University of Missouri, 1950); Ronald J. Slay, *The Development of the Teaching of Agriculture in Mississippi, with Special Reference on Agriculture as a Part of the School Curricula* (New York: Teachers College, Columbia University, 1928); South Carolina Department of Education, *Vocational Education in South Carolina, 1917–1950* (Columbia, 1951); Texas Legislative Council, *Agriculture Education* and *Home Economics Education* (Austin, 1951).

Social Security. Grace Abbott, *From Relief to Social Security* (Chicago: University of Chicago Press, 1941), tells the story of the origin and establishment of the system; see also the writings of Edwin E. Witte, who drafted the Social Security Act, especially his *Development of the Social Security Act* (Madison: University of Wisconsin Press, 1962) and of Arthur J. Altmeyer, Wilber J. Cohen, and others intimately associated with its early administration. Jane Perry Clark (Carey) did a pioneer study of intergovernmental relations, largely in this field, in *The Rise of a New Federalism: Federal-State Cooperation in the United States* (New York: Columbia University Press, 1938). Eveline M. Burns has written extensively on the social security system and its administration in *The American Social Security System* (Boston: Houghton Mifflin Co., 1949), published with an appendix, *The Social Security Act Amendments of 1950* (1951), and *Social Security and Public Policy* (New York: McGraw-Hill Book Co., Inc., 1956). For other comment and analysis, see American Assembly, *Economic Security for Americans: An Appraisal of the Progress Made During the Last Fifty Years* (New York: Columbia University, 1954) and Brookings Institution, *Functions and Activities of the National Government in the Field of Welfare: A Report with Recommendations* (Washington, 1949), a Task Force report prepared for the first Hoover Commission. See also Domenico Gagliardo, *American Social Security* (New York: Harper & Brothers, 1949) and Department of Health, Education, and Welfare, *Social Security Handbook: Old-Age Survivors and Disability Insurance* (Washington, 1960).

Housing. A few items are included here on the housing program in general, its legislative and legal basis, its financing, and the intergovernmental relationships that have developed in connection with it. For the historical background of public housing in this country, see Jack Levin, *Your Congress and American Housing: The Actions of Congress on Housing from 1892 to 1951*, House Document No. 532. 82nd Cong., 2nd Sess. (Washington, 1952). Catherine Bauer, *A Few Facts About the Housing Program* (Washington: Department of Labor, June, 1938) and Harry C. Bredemeier, *The Federal Public Housing Movement: A Case Study of Social Change* (Ann Arbor: University Microfilms, 1955) are both useful. Miles L. Colean and associates made a study of war housing, *Housing for Defense: A Review of the Role of Housing in Relation to America's Defense* (New York: Twentieth Century Fund, 1940); for postwar housing, see Mary F. Carney, *New Housing in Metropolitan Areas, 1949–1951* (Washington: Bureau of Labor Statistics, 1952). In the early stages of the movement, the National Association of Housing Officials published *A Housing Program for the United States* (Chicago, 1934). Dorothy Schaffter, *State Housing Agencies* (New York: Columbia University Press, 1942) contains a wealth of information on the program in its early stages, as does Nathan Straus in *Seven Myths of Housing* (New York: Alfred A. Knopf, Inc., 1944) and *Two-Thirds of a Nation: A Housing Program* (New York: Alfred A. Knopf, Inc., 1952).

On the legislative and legal background of the housing program, see William

Ebenstein, *The Law of Public Housing* (Madison: University of Wisconsin Press, 1940); Massachusetts Legislative Research Council, *Federal Public Housing Laws* (Boston: Senate Report No. 451, January, 1960); and National Association of Housing Officials, *Legislative History of Certain Aspects of the Housing Act of 1949* (Chicago, 1949). The following works deal with some of the intergovernmental aspects of the housing program: James A. Jarvis, *Intergovernmental Relations in Public Housing* (Ann Arbor: University of Illinois doctoral dissertation, University Microfilms, 1957); Harvey N. Johnson, Jr., *Administration of Federal Public Housing Legislation by Local Authority Personnel in the United States* (Ann Arbor: New York University doctoral dissertation, University Microfilms, 1956); William F. Larsen, *New Homes for Old: Publicly Owned Housing in Tennessee* (Knoxville: Bureau of Public Administration, University of Tennessee, 1948); New York City, Division of Housing, *Housing Law Enforcement and Related Problems* (New York, 1957); New York City, Housing Authority, *Twenty-five Years of Public Housing, 1935–1960* (New York, 1960); New York State Chamber of Commerce, *Public Housing in New York City* (New York, December, 1953).

On the financing and fiscal relations of the housing program, see Robert M. Fisher, *Twenty Years of Public Housing: Economic Aspects of the Federal Program* (New York: Harper & Brothers, 1959); Leo Grebler, *The Role of Federal Credit Aids in Residential Construction* (New York: National Bureau of Economic Research, 1953); and Charles M. Haar, *Federal Credit and Private Housing: The Mass Financing Dilemma* (New York: McGraw-Hill Book Co., Inc., 1960). The following two publications deal with in lieu payments: Municipal Research Bureau, *Payments in Lieu of Taxes on Public Housing in Boston* (Boston, January, 1944) and Illinois Legislative Council, *Payments in Lieu of Taxes Under Housing and Federal Land Purchase Programs* (Springfield, September, 1942). See also Massachusetts Legislative Research Council, *Report Relative to Liquidation of Federally Aided Housing Projects* (Boston: House Report No. 2815, January, 1957); *Statement of the National Association of County Officials in Support of Payments in Lieu of Taxes* (Washington, 1956); National Association of Housing Officials, *State Legislation Providing Funds for Housing* (Chicago, 1948); and Franklin D. Richards, *How F.H.A. Mortgage Insurance Operates* (Washington: Federal Housing Administration, February, 1952).

CHAPTER XVI

The Grant-in-Aid System: Developments Since World War II

"Conflict-of-interest" abuses in the $41,000,000,000 Federal-State highway program "ought to be looked into" further, Representative John A. Blatnik of Minnesota said today [with reference to] contractor practices of charging off sizable gifts to and entertainment for State officials as "business expenses."

Under the 1956 Federal Highway Act, the Federal Bureau of Public Roads has supplied up to 90 per cent of the funds for new interstate road construction. But State highway departments let the contracts and supervise the construction done by private concerns.

The Minnesota Democrat's special public works subcommittee unearthed in hearings last week what it called a "widespread pattern" of contractor payments to State road officials in Florida and six other Southern States engaged in federally aided highway construction. "I'm now convinced," Mr. Blatnik said, "that this practice is quite customary in most of the States." Last week, the hearings brought out the following detailed "pattern" in Florida:

\# Several State engineers admitted doing for contractors technical work that, in their official capacity, they later inspected and approved. Thirty-three of some 250 professional road department officials received a total of $54,000 to $75,000 in gifts and payments from six major contractors since 1956.

\# The contractors involved had Florida road contracts amounting to more than $70,000,000 since 1956. Half the work was federally subsidized.

\# The handouts included $25 weekly cash payments, $500 "loans," gifts of hunting licenses, lumber, whisky, and reimbursement for "services" rendered.

One concern, the W. L. Cobb Construction Company of Atlanta, admitted that in addition to $14,321 in "customary" handouts to Florida officials, it practiced gift-giving in a "very minor way" in Georgia, Mississippi, Tennessee, the Carolinas and Alabama.

In every case, the contractors testified that the handouts were "bad", though customary, and that they were paid to "expedite" construction. Contractors and State officials contended that the payments had not led to relaxation of standards.

"One aspect of this situation we have exposed in Florida," Mr. Blatnik said, "is that a corporation's (taxable) profit is reduced in direct proportion to expenditures made [as gifts to public officials]. Thus the Federal Government is losing tax revenue. . . .[1]

[1] Braestrupe, Peter, "Widened Inquiry on Roads Sought," *The New York Times,* December 11, 1960. Copyright by The New York Times.

The fact that grant-in-aid programs tended to multiply in number and increase in scope after World War I, after the Great Depression, and after World War II has already been noted. It is a generally recognized characteristic of periods of adjustment that new governmental services are desired, and that new programs are instituted to meet them or to meet needs that had necessarily been postponed. Expenditures for grant programs had tapered off significantly while the war was in progress. The total expenditure, which reached a height of $2.9 billion in 1939, declined to $2.4 billion in 1940, $2.1 billion in 1941, and finally to $900 million in 1946—the lowest point since 1933.

This reduction may be generally attributed to the frantic level of economic activity engendered by the war, to the freeze on postponable expenditures during the war, and to a lesser degree, to the assumption by the Federal government of sole responsibility for functions discharged in cooperation with the States under peacetime conditions. The exigencies of war called for the establishment of certain new grant programs on a temporary basis, chiefly for the purpose of assuring an adequate labor supply when and where needed. With this objective, aid was offered for the construction of war housing, for the training of industrial workers, and for the transportation of agricultural workers. The highway program took on a new aspect, since Federal spending for this purpose was governed almost exclusively by the requirements of national defense.

EXPANSION OF PUBLIC HEALTH GRANTS

The postwar situation was, in some respects, a most unusual one. The Hill-Burton Hospital and Medical Facilities Survey and Construction Program and the Federal Airport Program, both initiated in 1946, were the first important enactments of the postwar period. A steep climb in the volume of Federal grants occurred during the next decade. From $900 million in 1946, Federal spending for these programs increased to $2.4 billion in 1952. The closing stages of the war and the postwar period witnessed the establishment of several new programs. Of fifty-one programs listed in a compilation prepared in 1952, twenty-nine had been established since 1944, most of them involving relatively minor expenditures. A few, however, notably airports, school lunch, school construction, and hospital survey and construction grants, were substantial.

The considerable expansion in the number and scope of grant programs during this period was the more remarkable because of the emphasis of the Eisenhower administration on budget balancing and the traditional forms of federalism. Even so, new services and new grant programs were developed and enacted at an astonishing rate. Some, such as the water pollution and depressed areas programs, were vetoed by the President—the latter, in fact, twice. The emphasis during this period centered around the problems of health and welfare, education, and urban and metropolitan area problems, or a combination of these. Air and water pollution, for instance, are health problems as well as urban problems, as are housing and urban renewal. Important programs in each of these three major areas are discussed in the sections which follow, and further consideration is given to the urban and metropolitan area aspects of these programs in Chapter XIX.

General Health Assistance: Categorical Grants and Research

Federal aid for public health, begun very early, made little progress for 100 years, then suddenly began to develop rapidly in many different forms. Irving Brant, noted biographer of Madison, reports that on February 27, 1813, the fourth President signed "An Act to Encourage Vaccination" which provided:

> That the President . . . be . . . authorized to appoint an agent
> to preserve the genuine vaccine matter, and to furnish the same to any

citizen of the United States, whenever it may be applied for, through the medium of the Post Office.

President Madison appointed as agent the doctor who suggested the idea —a point that the American Medical Association might well note—with instructions to spread the benefits as widely as possible throughout the United States. Mr. Brant further points out that "The whole social security and public health system of the United States stems constitutionally from a remark Madison made in the Federal Convention of 1787, that one of the purposes in levying Federal tonnage taxes was 'the support of seamen.'" Within a decade, he continues, "Congress was making deductions from seamen's wages to establish and maintain maritime hospitals. Thomas Jefferson later extended the tax and medical benefits to Mississippi River boatmen."

The initial Federal legislation in the health field in modern times was the famous Sheppard-Towner Infant and Maternity Hygiene Act of 1921, which engendered an enormous amount of controversy. To a present-day American, the story of this legislation is indeed amazing. At the time of its enactment, the death rate of mothers and infants was disgracefully high—the highest, the public was informed, to be found in any important country. The purpose of the legislation was to reduce this needless loss of life by making available proper medical care, both prenatal and postnatal, for mothers and their children. Although the program was well administered and successful in operation, it precipitated a storm of controversy. The program was noteworthy as being one of the first Federal grant programs in the public health field,[2] and because its constitutionality was questioned and upheld by the Supreme Court. Originally set up on a temporary basis, it was actually permitted to lapse in the late 1920's after one extension, but was later revived, in substance, by inclusion with other grant programs in the public health field.

In the attack on the Sheppard-Towner Act on constitutional grounds, two suits were filed, one a taxpayer's suit, the other a challenge by the Commonwealth of Massachusetts that the program served local and not national needs and, in addition, that it invaded the sphere of self-government reserved to the States under the Tenth Amendment. The Supreme Court consolidated the two cases into one decision; while the Court did not specifically affirm the constitutionality of the statute, it brushed aside the Massachusetts contention by pointing out that no State was obliged to accept the grant unless it chose to do so, and set aside the taxpayer's protest on the ground that Massachusetts' share of

---

[2] An earlier related program was initiated in 1918 under the Chamberlain-Kahn Venereal Disease Control Act (40 Stat. 345), revised and amended in 1938 (52 Stat. 439); current provisions in 42 U.S.C. Sec. 246.

the funds granted under the terms of the legislation was too inconsequential to provide reasonable ground for action. Since this decision, national funds in the form of grants-in-aid have flowed into the States and localities in ever-increasing volume under the sanction of an interpretation of the power of Congress, *i.e.*, that Congress may appropriate money for any purpose included within the range of the "common defense and general (or national) welfare." [3]

Major developments in this field have taken place since the passage of the Social Security Act of 1935, but particularly since World War II. Grants for public health programs are more numerous and more highly categorized than those in any other field. As a matter of fact, they have been broken down to an almost ridiculous extent; the main categories are grants for the construction of hospital and health facilities, for research in the health sciences (individual grants being given, disease by disease), for training, and beginning in 1960, for a new category, medical care for the aged. The purposes of a number of other grant programs, such as those relating to water and air pollution, are primarily concerned with health matters. There are also, of course, many Federal laws which involve Federal-State cooperation, such as the Public Health Service Act to protect the public from unsanitary milk and milk products, whose motivation lies in the protection of the public health but which do not provide for grants.

It may be advisable to indicate more exactly the nature and scope of the health grant programs, of which not less than two dozen exist. Half of these programs are earmarked for combatting individually the major causes of illness, disability, or death,[4] while another group of seven programs relates individually to the seven component parts of the National Institutes of Health.[5] Other grant programs function in the training field, providing funds for medical schools and schools of public health, for the training of doctors, nurses, and sanitarians, and for the support of medical research. Although much research is carried on at

[3] *Massachusetts* v. *Mellon* and *Frothingham* v. *Mellon,* 262 U.S. 447 (1923); for comment, see Corwin, Edward S., "The Spending Power of Congress," *Harvard Law Review,* May, 1923, pp. 548–582, and Post, R. L., "The Constitutionality of Spending for the General Welfare," *Virginia Law Review,* November, 1935, pp. 1–30.

[4] These are venereal disease, tuberculosis, mental illness, cancer, heart disease, poliomyelitis, maternal and child health, services to crippled children, children with congenital heart disease, and general grants for health assistance and sanitary engineering.

[5] These are National Arthritis and Metabolic Diseases Institute, National Neurological Disease and Blindness Institute, National Cancer Institute, National Institute of Dental Research, National Institute of Allergy and Infectious Diseases, National Heart Institute, and National Institute of Mental Health.

the National Institutes of Health, there are numerous funds designated for research on particular types of disease and affliction. Construction grants are also numerous, for sanitary engineering activities, hospitals, hospital and medical facilities, health research facilities, and waste treatment works.

In 1960, the Advisory Commission on Intergovernmental Relations studied the methods whereby Federal funds were appropriated, apportioned, and administered for grants-in-aid to the States for eight health categories. They found that although the original purpose of the various categorical grants had been to stimulate increased State and local activity in these particular fields, Congress, by its action in continuing and increasing the sums available, had long since demonstrated an intent that they should serve as a permanent contribution by the national government to the support of the respective State and local activities. At the same time, the States, by providing funds for these categories considerably in excess of matching requirements, have shown that they regard the need for health services in general and in each of the categories as a continuing responsibility of the States.[6] Increased flexibility is needed, however, for the better utilization of these funds.

Hospital and Medical Facilities Survey and Construction Program

The Hospital and Medical Facilities Survey and Construction Program, popularly known as the Hill-Burton Program, was initiated in 1946 for the purpose of making adequate hospital and related medical facilities and services available to all the people by providing Federal aid to assist in the construction of health facilities. Generally speaking, eligibility under the program is dependent upon the type of facility, sponsorship, and proposed construction. Types now eligible, in addition to general facilities, are those for mental, tuberculosis, and chronic disease hospitals, public health centers, diagnostic and treatment centers, rehabilitation centers, nursing homes, State health laboratories, and nurse training. Sponsorship is limited to nonprofit organizations or public agencies, such as cities, counties, or States. Finally, the project must include construction and may be for a new building or for an addition, a renovation, or an alteration of an existing building.

Under the terms of the law, the Public Health Service administers the program through a State agency. The authority and responsibility

[6] *Modification of Federal Grants-in-Aid for Public Health Services* (Washington, January, 1961); see also George C. S. Benson and Harold F. McClelland, *Consolidated Grants: A Means of Maintaining Fiscal Responsibility* (Washington: American Enterprise Association, 1961).

of the latter falls into two broad areas—survey and planning, and construction. Survey and planning includes inventorying existing health facilities, surveying the need for additional facilities and services, developing and annually revising a State plan setting forth these needs, fixing the percentage of Federal funds to go to each project on a variable grant basis (between one-third and two-thirds of the cost), and developing priorities to determine which projects will first receive the Federal funds available in any given fiscal year.

By the end of 1959, over 4,400 projects had been approved under the Hill-Burton Program, at a total cost of approximately $3.8 billion, with a Federal share of nearly $1.2 billion. Approximately 65 per cent of the approved projects were for general hospital construction, 15 per cent for public health center construction, and the remainder for the other types of facilities mentioned above. It is significant that about half of the more than 1,200 completely new general hospitals approved under this Program are located in areas which had no hospitals prior to the beginning of the Program, and an additional 25 per cent are in areas which, in terms of modern standards, had old and obsolete facilities.

The significance of this Program, however, cannot be measured alone in terms of quantity, for it has made important qualitative contributions as well. For example, the introduction of a continuing statewide planning program is a landmark in the field of hospital and medical facility planning and construction, while the utilization of standards of adequacy and the development of patterns for distributing facilities within a State has resulted in important gains in hospital planning and better distribution of health facilities. Another important accomplishment of the program has been the development for the first time of minimum standards of design, construction, and equipment for hospitals and other types of medical health facilities. These standards are now in use throughout the country and have been studied and in some instances adopted in principle by other countries.

It is reported that when this legislation became effective in 1946, only twelve States had licensing laws affecting hospitals. The Hill-Burton requirement that States establish regulations for the maintenance and operation of hospitals receiving Federal aid initiated a drive in most States to adopt licensing laws, so that all States now have licensing laws and standards for nursing homes, and all but four have licensing laws for general hospitals.[7]

[7] Data supplied by Dr. Jack C. Haldeman, Assistant Surgeon General of the United States, and Chief, Division of Hospital and Medical Facilities.

Water Resources and Pollution Control

The problems of water, once regarded as of concern only to arid regions of the West, have of late been recognized as important in all sections of the country. Parching droughts, severe periodic shortages of water in East Coast cities, and devastating floods in many river valleys have impressed upon the minds of all that control of existing water supplies is imperative and that provision must be made to secure additional water supplies for cities in the years ahead. All available evidence points to a fast approaching era of critical water supply when water needs will equal if not exceed the total available supply. An exhaustive study by the Senate Select Committee on National Water Resources, carried on over a two-year period and completed early in 1961, reported that an adequate supply of water is available for present and foreseeable future needs of a growing population, of agriculture, and of industry, provided that it is carefully and wisely used.[8]

Although the States and municipalities have given increasing attention to water development, the results of their efforts have been far from satisfactory. In 1960, President (then candidate) John F. Kennedy described the Potomac as the worst polluted river west of the Ganges. Only a few States have so far entered into the field of construction and operation of water projects, including hydro-electric projects. In a discussion of the emerging responsibilities and problems of the States in the development of water resources, Harvey O. Banks, Director of the Department of Water Resources in California (a State that has done a great deal in this field), expressed the opinion that it is in the best interests of a State, "not to preempt the field but rather to encourage full participation by Federal and local agencies and to supplement their activities where they are inadequate to meet the needs of the State's citizens." [9]

In regard to water pollution, municipalities have blamed industry for existing conditions while industry blamed the cities, neither willing to make the first move to clean up the streams. Federal interest in this area was first asserted when Congress adopted the Water Pollution Control Act of June 30, 1948, which authorized $3 million a year for five years as grants to help State and interstate stream pollution control programs. Although the States showed little interest, Congress extended the

[8] See Senate Report No. 29, 87th Cong., 1st Sess. (Washington, 1961) which summarizes a long series of reports and special studies, all previously published as Committee Prints.

[9] Banks, Harvey O., address before the Fourteenth Biennial Assembly of the States, Chicago, December 4, 1958.

law in 1956, authorizing assistance to any local organization in preparing and carrying out plans for the prevention of erosion, flood water, and sediment damages, or for the conservation, development, and disposal of water in watershed areas. Cost sharing arrangements, under which the State and/or local units are required to pay from one-third to two-thirds of the cost, must be included. The States have expanded their existing programs and initiated many others in research and stream surveys. State appropriations rose sharply during the first three years under the new Federal Act, from $4.2 million in 1956 to $6.5 million in 1959. The 1960 Federal expenditures were $32.7 million, and the program was further extended and expanded in 1961.

The 1948 legislation declares it to be the policy of Congress "to recognize, preserve and protect the primary responsibilities and rights of the States." This policy declaration is not only repeated in the 1956 law, but is strengthened by a further provision that "Nothing in this Act shall be construed as impairing or in any manner affecting any right or jurisdiction of the States with respect to the waters (including boundary waters) of such States." This position, it may be noted, applies not only to the problem of water pollution, but is the basic philosophy of the Public Health Service which, in its long history of working with the States, has found that "the best way of getting a job done is to support and assist the States. The more the State-interstate-Federal working partnership can be strengthened, the more effective it will be." [10]

One major purpose of the legislation is to channel State and municipal tax dollars into pollution control work, including major construction projects, which is indeed important if such construction is to keep pace with the needs of a fast growing urban population. The matching provisions are designed to strengthen State and interstate programs, the benefits of which accrue not only to the States and regions immediately affected, but to the whole country. Under this legislation, the Surgeon General is authorized to make grants-in-aid to public and private agencies and institutions for research, training projects, and demonstrations in this field, and for the construction of treatment works to prevent the discharge of raw or inadequately treated sewage or other waste into any waters.

It is reported that during the first two years of operation of the construction grants program, annual contract awards rose from $351 million in 1957 to nearly $400 million in 1958. In spite of the fact that construction has increased from 40 per cent to 70 per cent of our construction

---

[10] See Hollis, M. D., and McCallum, G. E., "Federal Water Pollution Control Legislation," *Sewage and Industrial Wastes*, March, 1956, pp. 306–310. The laws are P.L. 660, 84th Congress (1956) and P.L. 88, 87th Congress (1961).

needs, the increase must still be doubled if water pollution from municipal waste is to be brought under control.[11] Communities in forty-nine States and the Commonwealth of Puerto Rico have been aided by the construction grants program. On March 1, 1959, 1,403 projects had been approved to receive Federal aid funds; 449 of them had been completed and placed in operation, and an additional 553 projects were under construction. Construction grants to communities through March 1, 1959, totalled approximately $119 million. Every dollar of Federal funds has been matched by more than $4 from local funds. The Chief of the Construction Grants Section reported in 1959 that:

> Grant applications currently being processed or reported in preparation will require an additional $120 million of Federal aid for 916 projects having a total estimated cost of $748 million. Total expenditures approved, in process, or under preparation request Federal grant funds more than 70 per cent in excess of existing appropriations.
>
> The cost of pollution abatement is really quite small when compared to the increased beneficial use of the resulting clean water for municipal and industrial water supply, agriculture, fishing, wildlife and recreation. On the basis of the 1,403 projects approved on March 1, 1959, new and enlarged sewage treatment works being built will provide adequate treatment for an existing population of 19,000,000 people and for industrial waste equivalent to an additional population of 3,800,000. These plants have been designed to serve an ultimate population of 34,000,000. Stated in another way, these plants have been designed to provide adequate treatment for a population 50 per cent in excess of their present load.[12]

For a number of years, a considerable controversy was carried on regarding the proper role of the Federal government in this area and the desirability of continuing the aid program. While the problem of stream pollution prevention and control steadily increases in both size and importance, demanding more effort and larger expenditures and leading to proposals for a permanent Federal control agency or even for the establishment of a Cabinet department, the Eisenhower administration took the position that water pollution is a "uniquely local blight," the primary responsibility for the handling of which rests with State and local governments. President Eisenhower therefore vetoed bills for the expansion of the grant-in-aid program, urging instead that the grants be tapered off and eventually curtailed. He contended, further, that the Federal

[11] Data from Harris, R. R., "Federal Aid Program for Municipal Sewage Treatment Works," *Urban County Congress* (Washington: National Association of County Officials, 1959), pp. 121–122.

[12] Harris, p. 122.

government's role should be to provide research and technical assistance and to deal with interstate problems exceeding the capacity of any single State.

After the 1960 election, the political climate changed. The Federal program was not only continued but strengthened. The 1961 Act increased the authorized $50 million a year grant for construction of sewage treatment facilities to $80 million in fiscal 1962, $90 million in fiscal 1963, and $100 million for each of the years 1964–1967. Individual grants may not exceed 30 per cent of the construction cost or $600,000, whichever is less, and at least 50 per cent of the authorized funds must be used in communities with a population of 125,000 or less. Joint community construction is authorized with a maximum grant of $2.4 million. The Act increased grants to State-administered water pollution control programs from $3 million to $5 million per year and extended the program through June, 1968. Federal pollution abatement authority was extended to all navigable waters, whereas in the past, Federal authority had been limited to some 4,000 bodies of water which cross State lines, and then only where pollution crossed State boundaries. Federal authorities were empowered to initiate court action to secure abatement of pollution on any of the nation's 26,000 lakes and streams, consent of the State being required in writing only in the case of intrastate pollution.

Air Pollution Control

Although most Americans have been accustomed to take the purity of the air more or less for granted, the problem of air pollution actually goes back hundreds of years, and the responsibility of government for its control has long been recognized. Long before Blackstone, the law of nuisance was regarded as providing inadequate protection in an urban community where there were a number of sources of air pollution. As early as 1306, a royal proclamation forbade the burning of coal in London because of the dense smoke it produced. In 1661, John Evelyn wrote a book entitled *Fumifugium: Or the Inconvenience of the Aer and Smoake Over London Dissipated,* concerning the smoke problem of that time. His remedy was quite simple: all industry was to be moved to the leeward side of the city and sweet smelling trees were to be planted in the city.

Air pollution has been broadly defined as the presence in the ambient atmosphere of substances put there by the activities of man in concentrations sufficient to interfere directly or indirectly with his comfort, safety, or health, or with the full use and enjoyment of his property.

There are so many kinds and sources of pollution that, as cities grew and industrial plants multiplied, it became increasingly difficult to prove that any given source was responsible for the nuisance. Awareness of the problem among Americans developed rather recently. The smoke abatement problems in Pittsburgh and St. Louis, smog in Los Angeles, and tragedy in Donora, Pennsylvania, in 1948, when over 1,000 persons were severely affected and twenty died when a blanket of noxious gas suddenly enveloped the whole area, all served to focus public attention upon the seriousness of the air pollution problem.

The Surgeon General of the United States has estimated that more than 10,000 communities throughout the nation are afflicted with air pollution problems of various kinds, problems whose financial costs run into billions of dollars annually. It is estimated that approximately one-third of a billion dollars is spent each year on air pollution prevention, while $4 billion are spent for neglect of air pollution problems in the form of damage to crops, lawsuits, health costs, deterioration of property values, laundry bills, and corrosion. This is not good from a health and welfare standpoint, and it certainly is not good business.

The remarkable progress that has been made in dealing with the problem in Pittsburgh, St. Louis, and Los Angeles is well known, but there is scarcely a city of any size in the country that is not seriously concerned with it. In 1947, California, a pioneer in this field, adopted a statewide air pollution control statute which placed responsibility for actual enforcement in local Air Pollution Control Districts on the county level. The same type of enabling act was adopted in 1952 in Kentucky, and other States followed suit in rapid succession: Massachusetts and New Jersey in 1954; Oregon in 1956; Delaware, Florida, New York, and Washington in 1957. Congress recognized the Federal interest in this problem when it adopted the Air Pollution Control Act of July 14, 1955, providing assistance to State and local governments which bear the primary responsibility for air pollution control.

This legislation authorized the Public Health Service to conduct research on the problems of air pollution and to make grants-in-aid to the States and the District of Columbia, to local air pollution control agencies (including city, county or other local government health authorities), to other public and private agencies and institutions, and to individuals for research, training, and demonstration projects for the prevention and abatement of air pollution. Using appropriations of $8.5 million annually for the first three fiscal years, the Public Health Service has been able to carry on a research program that has already been of much assistance to State and local air pollution authorities.

In addition to research, the Federal program includes basic and advanced training of professional personnel from State and local governments, industry, and other institutions interested in the problem. This training program includes courses at the Taft Sanitary Engineering Center in Cincinnati, field orientation courses, and preparation of manuals used in training other personnel. Grants from the Public Health Service have also supported courses at several universities throughout the nation which study atmospheric contamination.

A new problem has now been injected into the discussion of air pollution control. Smog is injurious to health, and exhaust fumes from motor vehicles help to produce smog. A new device has been invented which controls the exhaust and prevents its discharge into the atmosphere. Several Members of Congress, members of both parties in both houses, have sponsored legislation to require manufacturers to install these devices on all new vehicles and to prohibit the transportation in interstate commerce of vehicles lacking them. Such legislation has been endorsed by both the present Secretary of Health, Education, and Welfare and his predecessor. Although the Automobile Manufacturers Association rejected the proposal as unnecessary, they have indicated their willingness to include the device on new cars sold in California, where its use is now required by State law.

EXPANSION OF SUPPORT FOR EDUCATION

Although the Federal government has not yet made appropriated funds available for the general support of education, it has continuously since 1785 provided lands, and in late years surplus property and funds for the support of a wide variety of specific educational programs.[13] During the Great Depression, the Public Works Administration constructed buildings and provided student aid and funds for research, and the National Youth Administration provided part-time work for students. Two world wars and the Korean Conflict brought literally millions of veterans to the university and college campuses of the nation under programs authorized by Federal law and financed by Federal funds. Since 1958,

[13] The major enactments include: the Survey Ordinance of 1785, the Northwest Ordinance of 1787, the Morrill Act of 1862, the Smith-Hughes Act of 1917 (all of which have been earlier considered), the emergency measures of the 1930's, the Servicemen's Readjustment Act of 1944 (popularly known as the G.I. Bill of Rights), the National School Lunch Act of 1946, the National Science Foundation Act of 1950, the Housing Act of 1950, Public Laws 815 and 874, the Library Services Act of 1956, and the National Defense Education Act of 1958.

funds have been provided for graduate fellowships, graduate and under-graduate loans, school construction, teachers' salaries, and library services.

In the field of higher education, the situation can only be described as chaotic. The Federal government's relationships with institutions of higher education defy description; name or devise any possible scheme and the chances are that such a program already exists. There is no exact count of the Federal programs in this field; estimates of the number of programs run well into the hundreds, if contracts for services are included, and these contracts are completely uncoordinated. There are many Federal policies with respect to higher education, quite separate from each other and oftentimes inconsistent. It might be most accurate to say that the basic policy is expediency:

> There are student aids, fellowships with stipends, and scholarship loans.
> There are foreign student aid and student exchange aid.
> There is veterans aid, regular and disabled, and for off-spring, too, under certain conditions. The veteran must die from a service connected disability.
> The campus Reserve Officer Training Corps programs take the Defense Department right to the campus.
> There are building aids, and loans.
> There is stimulation of particular programs.
> There is payment for contracted training and research needed by the Federal government.
> There is a "back-door" type of persuasion to encourage private corporations and individuals to expend money in a prescribed way for education—to make grants or gifts which are deductible from Federal income taxes.
> Interest on State bonds for these institutions is exempt from Federal taxes.[14]

While general Federal aid has been regarded with apprehension by many, in some cases on constitutional grounds [15] and in others lest it result in Federal control over schools, the Federal government itself conducts schools for the children of armed service personnel at home and abroad. The number and scope of its special programs continues to increase. Other Federal activities in education include aid for vocational education and rehabilitation, education for the mentally retarded, national defense education, and schools in federally impacted areas (Public Laws Nos. 815 and 874 of 1950). Some of these programs, particularly the three which were extended in 1961, will be briefly considered here.

[14] List compiled by Jean M. Flanigan, a graduate student at American University, January, 1961.

[15] See *Constitutionality of Federal Aid to Education in Its Various Aspects*, Senate Document No. 29, 87th Cong., 1st Sess. (Washington, May, 1961).

Fellowships and Loans

After Sputnik in 1957, a wave of hysteria about the condition of our scientific and professional training swept over the land.[16] It was generally recognized even before 1957, however, that there was a manpower shortage in these fields and that the existing scholarships and fellowships were either insufficient in number or were not being distributed in such a manner as to offer reasonable grounds for expecting much improvement.

Surveys showed that the existing financial aid programs supported by the Federal government for education at colleges and universities had been established only for the benefit of special purposes or groups, such as veterans, military science, or agriculture. As of 1955, Federal programs in higher education could be classified as follows:

> Aid for the education of a special group of individuals, such as veterans.
> Aid to individuals for study in special fields, such as military science and medicine.
> Educational activities carried out largely for the promotion of some policy of the Government, such as the development of international goodwill, or building up an officer reserve.
> Annual grants to particular institutions for specific purposes, such as agricultural education.
> Grants and contracts awarded to institutions for research in certain fields, such as the physical sciences.[17]

In an effort to correct this limited situation, Congress in 1958 approved the National Defense Education Act (popularly known as NDEA), with the twofold purpose of making financial aids generally available to able students and of strengthening instruction and improving teaching in subject-matter fields regarded as of prime importance in the defense program of the nation, *i.e.*, science, mathematics, and modern foreign languages.[18] So that no able student should be obliged to discontinue his formal education for reason of lack of funds, the Act established, under the provisions of Title II, a loan program for both undergraduate and graduate study and graduate fellowships.

[16] See, for example, "Hysteria in Education," *National Municipal Review,* June, 1958, pp. 266–270.

[17] Hearings of the Joint Congressional Committee on the Economic Report, *January 1955 Economic Report of the President,* 79th Cong., 1st Sess. (Washington, 1955), pp. 5–6.

[18] Senate Committee on Labor and Public Welfare, *The National Defense Education Act of 1958: A Summary and Analysis of the Act,* 85th Cong., 2nd Sess. (Washington: Committee Print, 1958).

The loan funds for students in institutions of higher education were made available at low interest rates, the Federal government furnishing 90 per cent of the capital, the institutions 10 per cent. Funds were appropriated in an ascending scale for four fiscal years, 1959–1962, with an authorization of the sums needed during the next four years. In the first three years of its existence, 230,000 students received loans totalling $130

THE NATIONAL DEFENSE EDUCATION ACT: WHAT IT HAS ACCOMPLISHED—JUNE, 1961

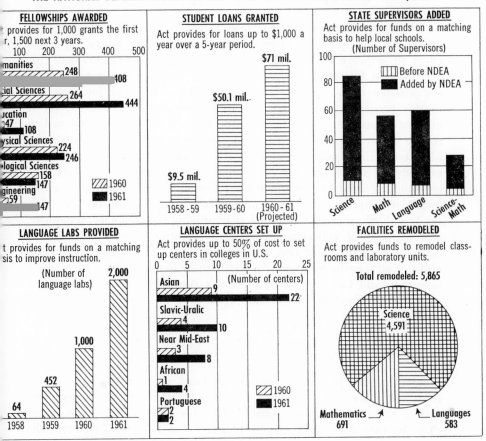

ce: *The New York Times,* June 18, 1961.

In 1958, following the first Soviet sputnik and amid widespread concern over the quality of American education, the National Defense Education Act was passed. Its priority purposes were to strengthen instruction in mathematics, science and foreign languages, to improve pupil guidance and to encourage able students to proceed to higher education. Currently, in the process of revising and extending the act, Congress is reexamining and evaluating its provisions.

million, and $75 million was added for fiscal 1962.[19] No scholarships for undergraduates were provided, but in 1961, President Kennedy proposed an appropriation of $578 million for a national scholarship program.

In the first three years, some 4,000 graduate students were aided by National Defense Fellowships, established under Title IV, at stipends beginning at $2,000 and increasing annually; another 1,500 were expected to receive aid in 1962, at a total cost for the four years of $61.5 million. The fellowships were designed to increase the number of students in graduate programs, particularly those interested in university and college teaching.

Three auxiliary programs were established under Title III, to be administered jointly by the Federal government and the States: (1) In an effort to improve and strengthen instruction in science, mathematics, and modern foreign languages, funds were made available to assist in the purchase of laboratory equipment and materials. The four-year cost of this program (1959–1962) was approximately $44.7 million. (2) A guidance, counseling, and testing program was established, designed to reduce the number of drop-outs in secondary schools and colleges by identifying able students at an early stage, guiding them into the courses of study for which they are best suited, and encouraging students with outstanding ability to complete their formal education. At the end of four years, approximately $74.9 million had been spent on this program. (3) The third program was aimed at improving the adequacy, reliability, and methods of collecting educational statistics in State educational agencies, at a four-year cost of approximately $4.7 million. Dollar-for-dollar matching by State and/or local funds is required in all of these programs, and Congress in 1961 voted a two-year extension of NDEA, thereby insuring their continuation, for a time, at least.

School and College Building Construction

During the 1950's, the nation was faced with an urgent need for classroom space at all levels of education; with mounting school and college enrollments, it is probable that this need will increase rather than decrease during the 1960's. The Office of Education reported the shortage in 1954, first estimating that 340,000 new classrooms would be needed, later increasing its estimate to 370,000. Then the estimate was somewhat reduced—to 336,000 in late 1956, 141,000 in 1958, and 132,400 in the fall of 1959. Realizing that the need was in any case a sizable one,

---

[19] These figures and others cited below were used by Chairman Powell of the Committee on Education and Labor in a speech in the House; see *Congressional Record*, September 6, 1961, pp. 17095-17096.

that it was more likely to increase than to decrease in the future, and that many States either would not or could not meet it adequately, bills providing for Federal aid for school construction began to appear in Congress in 1956 [20] and have been introduced in every Congress since.

Two measures enacted in 1950 had already extended Federal aid for local school construction (P.L. 815) and for teachers' salaries and other operating expenses (P.L. 874) to districts impacted by Federal government activities. These laws were periodically extended until, as a result of an impasse in the House Rules Committee over the administration's general aid for education bill, both were permitted to expire on June 30, 1961. The serious distress that then confronted many school districts and the lack of any alternative funds (due to the failure of the administration bill in the first session of the 87th Congress) made necessary the re-enactment of both measures; the bill providing for the re-enactment was reluctantly signed by President Kennedy on October 3, 1961.

In the first ten years of Public Law 815, Congress appropriated $962.6 million for assistance in the construction of minimum school facilities for federally connected children. For the most part, the funds were expended in school districts having a substantial increase in school attendance as a result of Federal activities, or in districts having a substantial number of pupils residing on tax-exempt Federal properties (chiefly Indian reservations). The greatest activity under this Act took place in the first half of the decade when exceptional effort was required to meet the backlog of school construction needs that had accumulated during World War II.

Some assistance for the construction of buildings for educational purposes has been provided for in other legislation. In the National Defense Education Act of 1958, funds were provided for equipment; loans for student housing and other income-producing university and college facilities became possible under the Housing Act of 1954, as amended. President Kennedy's recommendations, submitted in 1961, 1962 and again in 1963, proposed to continue these programs and to expand the college and university program by establishing a five-year $2.8 billion loan fund for the construction of college residential and classroom facilities in both public and privately supported institutions. The 1961 amendments to the Federal Housing Act provided $1.2 billion in low interest loans for the construction of college dormitories.

---

[20] These were the Kelley bill, H.R. 7535, and the administration bill, S. 2905, in the 84th Cong., 2nd Sess.; the legislative history of this and similar bills, later introduced, can be found in *Federal Aid for Education: A History of Proposals Which Have Received Consideration by the Congress of the United States (1789–1960)*, 87th Cong., 1st Sess. (Washington: House Committee Print, 1961).

Teachers' Salaries and General School Support

It has slowly become possible for Congress to provide financial aid for students and for the construction of buildings for schools and colleges without raising too many serious questions beyond the financial one. However, the use of Federal funds to assist in meeting teachers' salaries and other operating and maintenance expenses—in other words, for general school support—does raise questions that are both difficult and troublesome. Before addressing attention to these problems, it is appropriate to look at Public Law 874 of 1950 which, as mentioned before, was designed to provide financial assistance for school support in federally affected areas. Experience indicates that it may have been a significant step in the direction of general aid for education. The facts with respect to its operation have been well summarized in a recent article:

> Last year—Fiscal Year 1960—3,963 local educational agencies in the fifty States, Guam, and the Virgin Islands applied for Federal funds under Public Law 874 to help them defray current expenditures for their schools. All but 142 were found eligible. The total amount to which they were entitled $177.6 million—was based on their having more than 1½ million federally connected children—15 per cent of their total average daily attendance. But federally connected children were not the only beneficiaries: the recipient districts put the funds under Public Law 874 with their other funds for current expenditures and thereby passed the Federal aid along to all 10,000,000 of their pupils. In other words, one out of every three children in the Nation's public elementary and secondary schools benefited. Ten years earlier, in 1951, only 2.9 million pupils benefited—one out of every eight.
>
> Still other comparisons of 1960 figures with those of a decade earlier indicate how much the program under Public Law 874 has grown in its first decade. Since 1951 the number of districts eligible for payments has more than trebled, and net entitlements under the Act have increased nearly six times [as shown in the table below].

PUBLIC LAW 874: COMPARATIVE DATA ON ITS OPERATION,
1950–51 AND 1959–60

Basic Element Compared	1950–1951	1959–1960
Number of eligible districts	1,172	3,821
Number of federally connected pupils	512,050	1,502,432
Net entitlements of eligible schools	$29,700,000	$177,600,000

There are several reasons for these increases. Federal activities have multiplied. Liberalizing amendments have extended the coverage of the law and increased its benefits: The definition of "federally connected children" has been broadened to include, for instance, Indian children under one subsection of the Act and, under another, children of parents in the Armed Forces; the definition of "Federal property" also had been made more generous; and the average rate of payment per pupil has been raised. Both school population and school expenditures have increased, and local and State school officials have become better informed about the provisions of the law and more interested in taking advantage of the aid they offered.[21]

It thus appears that general aid for education would, in effect, extend the pattern established under Public Law 874, which has been operating with increasing scope and effectiveness. The opposition raises objections that, to them, appear to be of vast importance; to others, these objections seem relatively insignificant when considered in relation to the need to strengthen and improve the quality of the educational program. The first question involves the extent to which, if at all, aid should be extended to private and parochial schools, presenting in an acute form the question of the separation of church and state. Both Catholics and Protestants are sharply divided on the issue. Some Catholics take the position that they should neither ask nor accept public aid in support of their schools, while others see no reason why church supported schools should be discriminated against. Since Protestants rely for the most part on public schools, many of them tend to regard public aid for church schools as something little short of a national calamity.

The second question involves the equally knotty problem of giving (or withholding) aid for segregated schools. This issue presents something of a paradox. The Southern States, which have the greatest need, are most firmly attached to the practice of segregation. The conservative Southern bloc in Congress will not support any form of aid if segregation is barred, while Northern members from both parties tend to oppose aid if segregation is permitted.

The third question, concerning aid for teachers' salaries, is that of control. It is difficult to understand how financial assistance to individual students in the form of loans or grants, scholarships or fellowships, or to school districts for the construction of buildings used for educational purposes could influence the educational curriculum or provide an opportunity for Federal domination or "dictation." Whatever the reason

[21] "Two Billion Dollars in a Decade: Public Laws 815 and 874," *School Life*, April, 1961; reprinted in the remarks of Senator Wayne Morse in *Congressional Record*, September 11, 1961, pp. 17759 ff.

for such an idea may be, it has always been a major obstacle to the passage of legislation which would authorize aid for teachers' salaries.

President Kennedy's omnibus program of 1961 and 1962 included a three-year schedule of grants to States, not only for public elementary and secondary classroom construction but, at the option of the States, for teachers' salaries. For the first year, this portion of his program was estimated at $666 million in Federal funds, and a total of $3.3 billion for the three years. The President sought in 1963 to circumvent the difficulties noted above by leaving to the States the decision as to what portion, if any, of the funds allocated to them should be used for teachers' salaries. In other words, here was a proposal for a block grant, so often recommended in the past, but never before actually attempted for a major purpose and on a large scale.

Library Services

The enactment of the Library Services Act of 1956 serves once more to illustrate a process of evolution in which a governmental function is initiated and developed. In early times, books were both expensive and scarce. The general level of education was low, and few people had either the inclination or the money to buy books. There were few private libraries and no public ones until, in 1700, a municipal public library was established in New York City. During the eighteenth century, the library developed extensively as an independent institution, due chiefly to the establishment of subscription libraries, the first of which was the Library Company of Philadelphia, founded by Benjamin Franklin in 1732. It was decades later before there was any considerable number of libraries, either public or private.

The move toward the establishment of public libraries received great impetus early in the twentieth century from the grants of Andrew Carnegie. Gradually, public libraries increased in number and in quality, as the cities recognized the necessity of contributing to their support and the States not only expanded and improved the State libraries, but established library extension programs and grants-in-aid for both urban and rural libraries.[22] Finally in the sequence of events came the enactment of the Library Services Act of 1956.

The Act was passed because of serious deficiencies, particularly in rural areas where it was estimated that there were 26 million people

[22] On these programs see Morin, Wilfred L., and Cohen, Nathan M., *State Library Extension Services* (Washington: Office of Education, 1960) and by Morin, "American Laws Governing State Aid to Public Libraries," *Library Trends*, July, 1960, pp. 52–82.

without any public library service, and 50 million more with inadequate service. There were 319 rural counties without any public library within their borders. An appropriation of $7.5 million a year for a five-year period was authorized. Matching provisions require State contributions of 33 per cent in the least wealthy States, 66 per cent in those that are better off financially. These funds are used in helping States to develop new library programs and to strengthen others that have proved their worth. Each State that participates must prepare a plan for the development of library services in its rural areas.

By the end of 1960, forty-nine States and three Territories were administering approved plans for the extension and development of public library services in rural areas and Indiana, the fiftieth State, was expected to submit a plan and qualify for participation. The accomplishments during the first three years of the program's operation were impressive. New and improved public library services were made available for some 30 million people as a result of State plans submitted and approved under this legislation. State funds for the development of such programs increased significantly, by 54 per cent. During the same period, local appropriations for rural public libraries increased 45 per cent. County and regional library developments brought public library service for the first time to over 1 million rural children and adults and substantially improved service to 7.6 million more. Several hundred counties and many New England towns formerly without any public libraries are now receiving library service or greatly improved service. The following specific accomplishments may be noted:

Approximately 250 new bookmobiles were placed in operation in rural areas under Library Services Act projects.

More than 5 million books and other informational materials were added to the resources of rural communities.

State library agencies were able to strengthen their staffs by adding some 105 field consultants, an increase of 80 per cent over total field personnel on duty in 1956.

Over 300 separate project activities to extend and develop rural public library service were included in the various State plans in the third year alone.

Large increases in library usage were reported, due to the availability of new books, films, recordings, more library staff, bookmobiles, and additional library branches and stations.

Central purchasing activities increased under State plans, some thirty States having incorporated some activities of this nature under their plans.

California and Delaware are now including scholarship programs under their State plans. Five other States had previously done so, and other States are contemplating adding this project to their future programs.

The evidence shows that, due to greater stress on public library standards, the quality of service is being substantially improved in many communities.[23]

On the basis of these accomplishments, the library people are urging extension of this program on a more or less permanent basis and the inclusion of a new title in the National Defense Education Act to provide assistance in the development of school, college, and university libraries.

A National Policy on Education?

The Public School Assistance bills of 1961, 1962, and 1963 (if the drive to enact the latter is successful) will probably be regarded as the culmination of a long, long struggle to establish an affirmative national policy with respect to education. Some characteristics and milestones of this struggle may well be noted.

There was, in the beginning, no general public support for education, although land grants for common schools, such as the one made by the Continental Congress in 1785, were begun at a very early date. During the Jacksonian era, the States enacted legislation providing for the establishment of a free system of common schools. By 1841, beginnings were made in providing public high schools, and after the Civil War, free public education became fairly general. Since 1882, bills providing Federal aid for the support of elementary and secondary education have appeared in Congress with increasing frequency. In the latter half of the nineteenth century, the principle of public support was extended to higher education, through the Morrill land grant acts and through cash grants beginning in 1887. In the twentieth century, free public school education, supported by the States largely through the localities, became general. Meantime, of course, Federal support for vocational education was provided, and as the financial needs of education increased, the States gradually supplanted the localities as the principal source of financial support for the public schools.

The history of school financing, then, down to the middle of the current century has been a slow evolution from private to local to increasing State support, with sporadic injections of Federal money. As the financial needs of education continued to mount, a beginning was

[23] Compiled from information and reports furnished by John C. Lorenz, Director, Library Services Branch, Office of Education, November 28, 1960.

made in a few jurisdictions in State support of free junior colleges. Many States increased their support of higher education—enormously, in fact, after World War II. The first proposals for the appropriation of Federal funds for the support of education were made singly, later in considerable numbers and with strong support. They have, from the beginning, been highly controversial proposals.

The public schools in this country have always been local institutions, locally administered, and until recently, locally supported. Postwar concerns have evolved from this historical background. The conflict developed between those who fought to preserve the system first against State aid and later against Federal aid, and those who felt that the needs of the schools were too great and too important to be sacrificed while people argued over abstractions in political philosophy.

Those who opposed Federal aid believed that since "he who pays the piper calls the tune," it must inevitably result in some substantial degree of Federal control, and this, to their way of thinking, was an evil to be avoided at all costs. Those who favored Federal aid, with the needs of the schools uppermost in mind, doubted that many of the States could or would provide adequate financial support. Although they had little fear of "Federal control," they were willing to make many concessions designed to prevent it, or at least to minimize its extent. In the course of a long debate, various irrelevant questions were introduced to becloud the issue, questions involving aid to private and parochial schools, the transportation of pupils attending such schools, and questions of segregation and race relations.

This controversy has been before Congress almost continuously since 1933. The supporters of Federal aid have been winning the war one battle at a time, securing aid for vocational education in 1916 and extending aid program by program. There has been, as one writer has said, no demon in the situation. Federal aid for public schools will come, if and when it does, through a natural process of evolution, from land grants to cash grants, from grants for common schools to grants for programs at all levels of education, from grants for specialized programs in the field to general assistance in support of the nation's educational program at all levels. It will come if and when those who realize the need exceed in number and/or influence those who do not. It will come, if and when it does, as a result of a sensible recognition of the fact that many States are either unable or unwilling to meet the need.

AID TO URBAN AND METROPOLITAN AREAS

As the trend toward urbanism has continued at an accelerated pace, more and more Federal grant-in-aid programs have been designed, and existing programs have been redesigned, to include and assist urban areas. Many of these Federal programs have a tremendous impact on urban and metropolitan areas. Some, like air and water pollution, hospital and medical facilities construction, and the school lunch and milk program, directly affect the health of urban citizens. Other important major programs affecting municipalities include housing and urban renewal, civil defense and disaster relief, and such public works as airports and highways.

Federal Airport Program of 1946

The Governors' Conference in 1945 framed and adopted a set of principles of intergovernmental cooperation. These principles were promptly challenged in Congress by legislation to provide for the development of a nationwide airport system. In its original form, this legislation would have authorized the Federal government to deal directly with the thousands of local subdivisions of the States without the cooperation or approval of the State governments. The Governors' Conference urged Congress "in the development of a national airport system to follow the long established and effectively operated pattern of channeling aid to local governments exclusively through the respective State governments." It urged the States to perfect and expand, if necessary, their facilities to provide within themselves the required resources and services "for the development of an adequate and effective national airport system."

On May 13, 1946, Congress enacted the so-called compromise airport bill as the Federal Airport Act, providing for Federal grants to airport development sponsors in order to establish a nationwide system of public airports, in conformity with the national airport plan as prepared and revised by the administrator of the Federal Aviation Agency. The Federal share of the cost of projects, other than costs of installation of high intensity lighting on runways, is 50 per cent of the allowable project costs, except that in States having unappropriated and unreserved public lands exceeding 5 per cent of the total area of all lands therein, the Federal share shall be increased to between 51.65 and 62.50 per cent. This legislation permitted the Federal government to deal directly with certain classes of cities to the extent permitted under State law.

The Governors' Conference promptly urged the States to adopt "channeling legislation," requiring the Federal funds for airport development to be expended in the State only with the approval of the State aviation agency. This requirement resulted in hotly contested efforts to enact this legislation in many States, causing divisions along the familiar urban-rural lines. The cities generally opposed the legislation, preferring to deal directly with Federal authorities; although many legislatures are rural-dominated, the cities were able in a number of instances to muster sufficient voting strength to prevent the passage of the legislation.

The Governors' Conference continued to urge Congress to maintain the pattern of Federal-State-local cooperation which had characterized the successful administration of programs in highway construction, social security, education, and agriculture. At its meeting in Oklahoma City in 1946, it recommended that Congress "examine the field of Federal, State and local government to the end that State and local responsibilities be left to and assumed by the State and local units of government."

Slum Clearance, Urban Renewal, and Community Development

The problems of our cities daily increase in number and complexity. Many of the programs that have been developed to deal with these problems involve grants-in-aid, but the financial assistance aspect of the issues is neither the only nor the most important characteristic. Many of the problems are in Federal-municipal relations (see Chapter XIX); others involve housing and planning programs for which grants-in-aid have been established.

Civil Defense and Disaster Relief

Grants for civil defense were an outgrowth of wartime experience, while those for disaster relief are a relatively recent development. The Federal Civil Defense Act of 1951 provided for the Federal Civil Defense Administration (transferred in 1961 to the Department of Defense), defining its powers and duties, chief among which, despite a confusing series of organizational changes, remains the organization of non-military defense against attack. The administration's program provides assistance to the States and their political subdivisions, on an equal matching basis, in obtaining and operating civil defense facilities. Perhaps because of public apathy, because so many people either took a fatalistic attitude or assumed that there would never be an atomic attack, the civil defense program has never made any very substantial progress.

The program for disaster relief has done far better. Emergency aid had long been provided for stricken areas on a case by case basis, but the appropriation of funds for disaster relief, allocated and expended at the discretion of the President, was new. When disaster strikes, the need for help is urgent and often exceeds the resources immediately available to State and local governments, which supply relief and assistance within the limits of their capacity.

Under the Surplus Property Disaster Act of 1947, the Federal government steps in when need exceeds local resources. Disasters do occur frequently enough, and over a period of time, the number of disasters causing loss of life and heavy property damage is considerable. For example, the Federal Civil Defense Administration reported in 1956 that disaster aid totalled $90 million and affected ninety areas over a three-year period. Included were the regions of sixteen floods, ten hurricanes, nine tornadoes, and an assortment of droughts, earthquakes, forest fires, and even a volcanic eruption in Hawaii. The largest allotment for a single disaster was the nearly $30 million set aside for those Northeastern States ravaged by floods following Hurricane Diane in August, 1955. Droughts in twenty-three States resulted in the allocation of an even larger sum, $52 million, over the same three-year period.[24]

In January, 1953, the President assigned responsibility for coordinating the activities of all Federal agencies in natural disaster relief to the Federal Civil Defense Administration (FCDA). Funds made available by Congress on a continuing basis could be used at the discretion of the President and on recommendation of FCDA, on either an advance to the States or a reimbursement basis. Funds required by a State to start damage control and repair projects may be made available at low interest rates through the Small Business Administration, on specific request of the Governor. Reimbursements may be arranged when a State presents paid bills or requests on vouchers for eligible relief work. The authorization provides for the performance on public or private lands protective and other work essential to the preservation of life and property; clearing debris and wreckage; and making emergency repairs and temporary replacements of public facilities of local governments which are damaged or destroyed in such major disasters, including provisions for temporary housing or emergency shelter. A State must, however, expend a reasonable amount for disaster relief to establish its eligibility for Federal assistance.

[24] *The New York Times,* January 8, 1956, p. 62; see also Local Government and Education Research, Inc., "The Federal Contributions Program for Civil Defense Equipment," *The County Officer,* August, 1961, insert.

In September, 1960, Congress passed the Federal Disaster Act, authorizing the President on a permanent basis to provide Federal assistance to State and local governments to carry out their responsibilities in alleviating suffering and damage resulting from major disasters. During 1960, twelve major disasters were declared under the authority of the disaster legislation. The President authorized allocations for direct aid to the States in the amount of $13.1 million, not including assistance provided by other Federal agencies under their normal authority.[25] FCDA, in the Northeast flood area, again opened emergency engineering and medical supplies that had been set aside against possible enemy attack, including miles of pipe for water supplies and sanitation, water purifiers, power generators, tanks, and medicines. Even so, there are cases in which misunderstandings develop. A survey of the flooded area revealed that the States were receiving far less Federal aid than they had expected, while Federal officials explained that at least $13.5 million had been set aside for direct grants but that the government had expended more than this amount. They stated that the original damage estimates of $100 million were too high and that many of the relief projects proposed by the States were ineligible for Federal aid under the law.

Other Urban Programs

The 1961 amendments to the National Housing Act provided funds for no less than seven major programs; four are definitely urban, and all but one of the other three (rural housing) may be. The urban programs considered briefly in Chapter XIX are listed below; the other programs in the 1961 legislation provide for college housing, farm homes, and home improvement loans.

Mass Transit. $50 million emergency loans to communities for rail, bus, subway, and other transit equipment and facilities, through December, 1962.

Open Spaces. $50 million in grants to State and local authorities, paying 20–30 per cent of the cost of acquiring vacant land for recreation, conservation, and other purposes as part of an overall regional plan.

Urban Renewal. $2 billion in matching grants for slum rehabilitation, land purchase, and redevelopment for four years.

Community Facilities. $450 million in low interest loans for con-

[25] *President's Report of Activity Under Authority of Public Law 875, 81st Congress,* Washington, March, 1961.

struction of sewers, waterworks, fire houses, etc., particularly in small
cities, towns, and depressed areas.

SOME CONCLUSIONS AND EVALUATIONS

Mention was made earlier of the assumption of the State debts, the
distribution of the surplus, and the early land grants for public education and internal improvements. As one views the evolution of Federal
grants in retrospect, he sees land grants first supplemented and later
supplanted by cash grants. He sees early grants for the State militia, for
such relatively unproductive purposes as international fairs and expositions, and for the familiar functional services of State government given
under rigid 50-50 matching requirements. He notes the influence of the
Great Depression in easing the conditions of the matching requirements
or in eliminating them altogether.

He notes, too, that Federal spending for the purpose of aiding the
States and localities takes one of three forms: grants-in-aid, shared revenues, and loans and repayable advances—of which, of course, the first
is by far the largest. Under only three of the programs classified as shared
revenues does the national government make payments of really significant size. These are the Mineral Leasing Act, the National Forest Fund,
and the Land-Grant Fund Payments to the Counties of California and
Oregon. The total loans, substantial in amount, are made chiefly in connection with the housing program and the procurement of materials
needed for civil defense.

The great increase in the number and size of grants, and in the scope
of the grant-in-aid procedure as a whole, came after World War I and
the adoption of the Income Tax Amendment. At that time began the
transition from sporadic outright grants to the complex procedure of
matched grants that exists today. Another significant increase came in
the early 1930's, but no important new programs were undertaken between 1935 and World War II; in fact, Federal expenditures for grants-in-
aid declined steadily after the outbreak of war. Before 1939, total grants
had been measured in such modest terms as $100 million per year, but
after the war, Federal expenditures for these programs increased rapidly.
By 1958, they had more than doubled the 1949–1952 average and by
1960, the total of such payments—though very slightly less than in the
preceding year—had risen to nearly $10 billion a year.[26]

[26] In November, 1960, the Joint Economic Committee issued a study of
Subsidy and Subsidylike Programs of the U.S. Government, 86th Cong., 2nd

Various sources give quite different figures regarding the number of grant programs in existence. Not a little of this confusion arises out of the difficulty in defining a grant. For present purposes, the term is interpreted to include payments from the Federal government to the States or their political subdivisions for the purpose of accomplishing some nationwide objective in which the Federal government has an interest, such as good roads, soil conservation, or trained personnel for mental hospitals or other health facilities. The payments take many forms—outright grants, matched grants, conditioned grants, in lieu payments, shared taxes, or loans to State and local governments. In some cases, payments are made to the individual beneficiaries of the program, as in connection with the training of specialized personnel.

Several years ago, the author attempted to compile a table showing, in the chronological order of their establishment, exactly how many such programs there actually are. This was no simple matter because grant legislation, like any other, is subject to frequent amendment and revision. Some programs are important ones, others obviously less so. Some are more or less permanent, others temporarily conceived in response to a pressing current need. Altogether, some sixty-eight program areas were identified, a cumulative summary of which appears in the table on page 570. Some interesting and probably significant facts are revealed.

Only nine programs were carried over from the nineteenth century into the twentieth. Little change occurred until after World War I, when the number of programs significantly increased. The increase in the 1930's was much greater than the figures indicate, because many programs of a temporary or emergency nature were established during that decade. The greatest increase has come during the last three administrations; note that almost two-thirds of all the programs now in effect rest upon legislation adopted since 1930. There is no indication that any appreciable number of these programs was regarded as temporary at the time of authorization.

The subject-matter fields in which grant programs were and were not adopted is likewise a matter of some interest. The fields in which such legislation was most frequently adopted were, as measured in terms of the number of programs, education, lands, agriculture, and health. At the bottom of the list, again measured in terms of the number of programs in operation, are highways, fish and game, national defense, veterans, and personnel. All of these have the common characteristic of

---

Sess. (Washington: Committee Print, 1960). After some introductory comment, there is a good discussion of five different types of program: agricultural, maritime, transportation, business, and miscellaneous. For statistical charts showing highlights for 1960, see *Congressional Quarterly Weekly Report,* April 7, 1961, pp. 615–619.

being basic government services which still function largely on the basis of a relatively small number of old, firmly established policies. The essential differences between current grants and the earlier ones are the increase in the amount of aid and the use of aid in areas that affect the individual more personally and directly.

The overall story of the development of the system and the amounts of money involved are indicated in the table on page 571.

The overall effect has been that the number of programs and the amounts involved have steadily increased, and the States and their local units have become more and more dependent upon Federal funds for their support. Although the conditions imposed upon the States are not burdensome, onerous, or unreasonable, there is a good deal of complaint; nevertheless the system still continues to grow. Some would prefer to establish a clear division of revenue sources between the differ-

CUMULATIVE SUMMARY OF EXISTING GRANT-IN-AID PROGRAMS BY
SUBJECT FIELD AND DECADE

Subject Field	Before 1900	1900– 1909	1910– 1919	1920– 1929	1930– 1939	1940– 1949	1950– 1960
Agriculture	2	2	3	4	8	9	9
Commerce & Labor	0	0	2	3	5	7	7
Education	4	4	8	10	11	15	21
Fish & Game	0	0	0	1	2	2	2
Forestry	1	2	2	2	2	3	4
Health (Incl. mental health)	0	0	1	2	4	7	11
Highways	1	2	3	3	3	3	3
Housing	0	0	0	0	1	2	4
Lands (Incl. oil, gas, & mineral)	2	2	3	4	7	8	10
National Defense	1	1	1	1	1	32	3
Personnel	0	0	0	0	0	1	2
Public Works	3	3	3	3	3	6	8
Veterans	1	1	1	1	1	2	2
Water Resources & Power	1	1	1	3	5	7	8
Welfare	1	1	1	1	4	4	7
Cumulative total by decade *	9	10	16	25	40	56	58

* Cumulative and itemized totals do not agree since some of the programs relate to more than one subject field.

ent levels and units of government. Others complain that "the bureaucrats in Washington are foisting socialism on all of us" and that the only solution is to reject Washington as completely as possible. Still others find that Washington is evil, but since their State and local governments do not have ready funds for highway construction or relief to drought-stricken cotton farmers or ranchers, for instance, they always seem to be able to somehow salve their consciences and make peace with the devil.

STATE RECEIPTS FROM FEDERAL AID AND TOTAL STATE
REVENUE RECEIPTS, 1902–1957 *

Year	Federal Intergovernmental Expenditures to State and Local Governments (In millions)	State General Revenue Receipts (In millions)	Percentage Federal Aid to Total State Revenue Receipts
1902	$?	$ 986	.7
1913	12	1,912	.6
1922	118	4,781	2.5
1932	232	7,267	3.2
1942	887	10,418	8.5
1952	2,585	25,181	10.3
1957	3,873	38,164	10.1

* Source: U.S. Bureau of the Census, *Historical Statistics of the United States, Colonial Times to 1957*, Washington, 1960, pp. 724, 726.

Despite all this dissatisfaction with existing policy, the States have not relinquished a single Federal grant-in-aid. The story of what happens in such instances has become completely standardized: A grant is made to get a necessary or desirable service started and, perhaps, to soften the opposition to it in some States. "Then it becomes a going concern, vested interests are created, the controversial becomes customary, and the opposition vanishes. Therefore, grants-in-aid do not diminish; they multiply." [27]

BIBLIOGRAPHICAL NOTES

Grants-in-Aid. Walter Thompson published the first scholarly analysis of problems in the field of Federal-State relations in the twentieth century, *Federal Centralization* (New York: Harcourt, Brace, and Co., 1923). Shortly thereafter, Austin F. Macdonald published the first study of the grant-in-aid system, *Federal Aid* (New York:

[27] Carleton, William G., "Centralization and the Open Society," *Political Science Quarterly*, June, 1960, pp. 244–259.

Thomas Y. Crowell Co., 1928). Both of these studies were originally prepared as doctoral dissertations, Thompson's at Wisconsin, Macdonald's at Pennsylvania; to them were added another analysis of grants-in-aid, Henry J. Bitterman, *State and Federal Grants-in-Aid* (Chicago: Mentzer, Bush and Co., 1938), and a study of grant administration, V. O. Key, Jr., *The Administration of Federal Grants-in-Aid* (Chicago: Public Administration Service, 1937). The 1940's brought the Treasury study (Newcomer-Groves-Gulick Committee), *Intergovernmental Fiscal Relations*, 2 vols. (Washington, 1943), James A. Maxwell, *The Fiscal Impact of Federalism in the United States* (Cambridge: Harvard University Press, 1946), and the Council of State Governments' report, *Federal Grants-in-Aid* (Chicago, 1948).

Impact Studies. A good deal of attention has been given to the impact of grants-in-aid upon the States, particularly by the Commission on Intergovernmental Relations (Kestnbaum). Contracts were made with five research and management consulting firms for impact studies in seven States: Connecticut, Kansas, Michigan, Mississippi, South Carolina, Washington, and Wyoming. Two were of outstanding quality: Public Administration Service, *Survey Report on Michigan*, and Governmental Affairs Institute, *Survey Report on South Carolina*. The findings of all seven reports were summarized in *The Administrative and Fiscal Impact of Federal Grants-in-Aid* (Washington: Commission on Intergovernmental Relations, June, 1955). Significant reports on California, New York, and Pennsylvania, set up along parallel lines, were prepared by State government agencies as follows: Earl C. Segrest and Arthur J. Misner, *The Impact of Federal Grants-in-Aid on California* (Berkeley: Bureau of Public Administration, University of California, September, 1954); New York Legislature, Temporary Commission on the Fiscal Affairs of State Government, *Federal Grants to New York State: Interim Report* (Albany, December, 1954); Pennsylvania Commission on Intergovernmental Relations, *Federal Grant-in-Aid Programs in Pennsylvania, 1941–1953* (Harrisburg, September, 1954). Slightly later came Phillip Monypenny, *The Impact of Federal Grants in Illinois* (Urbana: Institute of Government and Public Affairs, University of Illinois, 1958).

In addition, the Commission contracted with the Governmental Affairs Institute for briefer impact studies to be made by local scholars, in accordance with a uniform plan. This project, directed by Professor Roger H. Wells, resulted in a significant and substantial volume, *The Impact of Federal Grants-in-Aid on the Structure and Functions of State and Local Governments* (Washington: Commission on Intergovernmental Relations, June, 1955). All Commission publications are listed in the *Index to the Reports of the Commission on Intergovernmental Relations*, prepared by the Legislative Reference Service, Library of Congress (Washington: Senate Document No. 111, 84th Cong., 2nd Sess., 1956). Other reports and pertinent materials are listed in W. Brooke Graves, *Intergovernmental Relations in the United States: A Selected Bibliography* (Washington: House Committee Print, Intergovernmental Relations Subcommittee, 84th Cong., 2nd Sess., November, 1956).

Federal Aid for Education. Out of a literature of overwhelming proportions, the following titles are most helpful: Hollis P. Allen, *The Federal Government and Education* (New York: McGraw-Hill Book Co., Inc., 1950), a task force report for the first Hoover Commission; Richard G. Axt, *The Federal Government and Financing Higher Education* (New York: Columbia University Press, 1952), prepared for the Commission on Financing of Higher Education; W. C. Eells and E. V. Hollis, *Student Financial Aid in Higher Education* (Washington: Office of Education, 1961); Dawson Hales, *Federal Control of Public Education* (New York: Columbia University Press, 1954); Alice M. Rivlin, *The Role of the Federal Government in Financing Higher Education* (Washington: Brookings Institution, 1961); and James E. Russell, *Federal Activities in Higher Education After the Second World War* (New York: King's Crown

Press, 1951). Roger A. Freeman has written extensively in this field; see *Federal Aid for Education: Boon or Bane?*, *School Needs in the Decade Ahead*, and *Taxes for the Schools* (Washington: Institute for Social Science Research, 1955, 1958, and 1960 respectively).

Water Resources: Their Use and Control. Clinton P. Anderson discusses the *Congressional Interest in Water Resources* in a memorandum prepared for the Senate Committee on Interior and Insular Affairs (Washington: Committee Print, 86th Cong., 1st Sess., 1959). For general information on water resources, their use and administration, see Mont H. Saunderson, *Western Land and Water Use* (Norman: University of Oklahoma Press, 1950); Yang-ch'eng, *American Water Resources Administration*, 2 vols. (New York: Bookman Associates-Twayne Publishers, 1958); Commission on Organization of the Executive Branch of the Government, *Water Resources and Power: A Report to Congress*, 2 vols. (Washington, 1955); and Select Committee on National Water Resources, a series of 25 Senate reports (Washington, 1961).

The following studies deal with Federal-State and regional relationships: Clyde F. Baker and Hugh G. Hansen, *The Central Valley Project: Federal or State?* (Berkeley: Bureau of Public Administration, University of California, June, 1955); Harvey O. Banks, *Emerging Responsibilities and Problems of the States in the Development of Water Resources* (Chicago, December 4, 1958), an address before the General Assembly of the States; Emanuel R. Fuchs, *Federal-State Relations in River Basin Development: A Case Study of the Missouri Valley* (Cambridge: Harvard University Press, 1956), a doctoral dissertation; Kansas Water Resources Board, *State-Federal Relationships in Water Resources Development Programs* (Topeka, 1956); and Ross R. Rice, *The Politics of Missouri Basin Development* (Chicago: University of Chicago, Department of Photographic Reproduction, 1956).

In the field of flood prevention and control, a number of studies have been made by California State agencies, for example: Department of Public Works, *State Legislation and Federal Regulations Governing the Maintenance and Operation of Flood Control Projects in the Sacramento and San Joaquin Valleys* (Sacramento, 1953); Clarence W. Mayott, *Floods, Flood Control, and Power in New England* (1956); and Gilbert F. White, ed., *Papers on Flood Problems* (Chicago: Department of Geography, University of Chicago, 1961). For surveys of Federal-State relations under Federal legislation in this field, see Kirk M. Sandals and L. M. Adams, *Progress in State Legislation Relating to the Watershed Protection and Flood Prevention Act* and R. Frank Hedges and L. M. Adams, *Status of State Legislation Relating to the Watershed Protection and Flood Prevention Act, as Amended* (Washington: Soil Conservation Service, 1958 and 1961 respectively). In a scanty literature on pollution, see George W. Reid, *Water Requirements for Pollution Abatement* (Washington: Senate Committee Print No. 29, 86th Cong., 2nd Sess., 1960).

PART V

While Federal-State relations are obviously of major importance in a federal system, these are not the only forms of intergovernmental relations. At the risk of perpetuating a compartmentalization which is gradually becoming less significant, the chapters of Part V are devoted to the other forms of intergovernmental and interjurisdictional relations—interstate, regional, Federal-local, State-local, and interlocal.

With the exception of regionalism, the terms are more or less self-explanatory. In regionalism, however, a number of different types are involved: that which occurs in the field administration of the various Federal departments and agencies; subnational or river valley regionalism, both voluntary and compulsory; and metropolitan regionalism.

It is the purpose of the following five chapters to describe the origins and development of particular types of intergovernmental relationships and to show the relation of each type to the overall system of intergovernmental relations in the nation.

CHAPTER XVII

Interstate

Cooperation

Cop. Got a trucking license to do business in this State?

Trucker. Sure. Here.

Cop. All right. Got a driver's license?

Trucker. Would I be driving a truck without one? It's right here on my cap.

Cop. Okay. Got an I.C.C. license?

Trucker. Say, what is this? An international border or something?

Cop. Well, I guess that's all. Say, wait a minute. What's the length of this truck?

Trucker. How do I know? I never measured it.

Cop. Well, we're going to measure it right now. 5, 10, 20, 30, 35, 40, 43, 44, 45—45 feet and 3 inches.

Trucker. How long did you say?

Cop. 45 feet and 3 inches. Okay, buddy, you're a lawbreaker.

Trucker. What do you mean, lawbreaker?

Cop. Trucks over 45 feet long aren't allowed on these highways. The State law says so, and your truck is 3 inches over. Back you go over the State line.

Trucker. But I got green vegetables on this truck. They'll all spoil. I'll lose my job.

Cop. Sorry, buddy, I don't make the law, I just enforce it.

Harry Harper, an Iowa farmer, started out for St. Louis, Missouri, to sell a load of melons he had grown. During his journey he was stopped by the Iowa Highway Patrol at night and required to put three green lights on his truck. After driving across the State line into Missouri, the Missouri police stopped him and told him it was illegal in Missouri to have three green lights on his truck, so he had to take them off.[1]

[1] Reported by Frank Bane, Executive Director of the Council of State Governments.

The amount of material on the historical development of interstate relations is so vast that it is difficult to compress the topic within the limits of a single chapter. Brief comment will be made in this chapter on the constitutional basis of interstate relations, on the early jealousies, frictions, and conflict between the States, and on the evolution of organized machinery for interstate cooperation. Attention is given to specialized types of organizations for State officials in the three branches of government, followed by brief comment on efforts toward uniformity, on cooperation in selected program areas, and on some of the current problems involving interstate compacts at both the State and Federal levels.

EARLY RELATIONSHIPS

Constitutional Basis

The Federal Constitution deals with some of the problems of interstate relations. The erection of trade barriers between the States, in the form of import and export duties or both, were supposedly prohibited in Article I, Section 10. The Supreme Court is given original jurisdiction by Article III, Section 2 over cases to which a State is a party. Most of the provisions bearing on interstate relations are in Article IV: the full faith and credit clause, one of the guarantees of the privileges and immunities of citizens (the other is in Amendment XIV); the provision for rendition of fugitives from justice; and the provisions for the admission of new States. The interstate compact clause is found in Article I, Section 10.

Full Faith and Credit. The Constitution provides that "full faith and credit shall be given in each State to the public acts, records, and judicial proceedings of every other State." This provision is mandatory; yet, like others, it has been weakened by judicial interpretation. The necessity for some such rule is obvious; if none existed, it would be possible for individuals to "beat the law" by moving into another State as soon as the law caught up with them. The Constitution further provides that "the Congress may by general laws prescribe the manner in which such acts, records, and proceedings shall be proved, and the effect thereof." In other words, the constitution and the official records of one State, properly proved and authenticated, shall have the same effect in the courts of another State as they may be presumed to have in their own.

Extradition. The extradition of fugitives from justice rests upon the clause of the Constitution (Article IV, Section 2) that provides that a person charged with crime in one State and found in another shall be delivered up on demand of the Governor of the State from which he fled, so that he may be tried by the State in which the crime was committed. Another clause, no longer in effect, provided that persons held to service or labor in one State who escape to another shall be delivered up "on Claim of the Party to which Service or Labor may be due." The wording is unusual in both instances and leaves specific directions to be provided by Congress and the States. The fleeing criminal was to be delivered up on demand of the Governor of the State from which he fled, but the servant or slave was to be delivered on claim of the party to whom the service or labor might be due. The former led to the process of extradition, while the latter resulted in the slaveholder or his agent personally undertaking the seizure of the slave. The line between securing the return of a runaway slave and the kidnapping of a free Negro was always, for obvious reasons, an exceedingly difficult one to draw.

One of the earliest—possibly the first—cases involving the interpretation of these clauses arose in 1791, when Governor Mifflin of Pennsylvania demanded the surrender of three men who were charged with kidnapping a Negro in Pennsylvania and taking him into Virginia to be sold into slavery. The Virginia Governor refused to comply, so Governor Mifflin appealed to President Washington. Channing reports that "it is generally thought that it was the friction that arose between Pennsylvania and Virginia in this case that led to the passage of the law of 1793 which applied both to fugitives from justice and from service or labor." [2] This Act authorized and directed State officials to carry out both constitutional provisions.

Privileges and Immunities. Interstate comity in the protection of the rights of citizens is provided for in Article IV, Section 2, and in the first section of Amendment XIV: "The citizens of each State shall be entitled to all privileges and immunities of citizens in the several States," and "No State shall make or enforce any law which shall abridge the privileges and immunities of citizens of the United States." An analysis of these clauses reveals that citizens have privileges and immunities under both the Federal government and the States; it is also clear that the two clauses are not the same. The protections of procedural rights apply to all persons, whether citizens or not, and hence are not privileges and immunities. It was the intention of the Framers of the Constitution to protect citizens against the action of the States, not against actions of

[2] Channing, Edward, *History of the United States*, 6 vols. (New York: The Macmillan Co., 1905–1925), VI, 88–89.

other individuals. "A private individual," says Burdick, "cannot deny or abridge a right; he can at most interfere with its exercise." [3]

Interstate Compacts. In Article I, Section 10, the Constitution provides that "no State shall, without the consent of Congress . . . enter into any agreement or compact with another State. . . ." The application of this clause was originally restricted largely to political agreements, the settlement of boundary disputes, and the apportionment of water, but not to important policy matters. Following the publication of the important Frankfurter and Landis article in 1925,[4] interest in the possibility of its use for policy purposes increased, though a survey of past experience gave little basis for hope of success.[5] Fortunately, later experience proved this conclusion wrong, as the Council of State Governments and at least one major Federal department began promoting the use of the interstate compact device and seriously undertook to make it work.

The first successful modern compact was that which established the Port of New York Authority in 1921. This compact, largely the brainchild of Julius Henry Cohen, was an outgrowth of studies and discussions begun four years earlier in 1917. Most of the problems which these pioneers anticipated never materialized, while the major problems that have developed they did not foresee. Since then, the compact device has been adapted to an ever-lengthening list of problems, including oil and gas conservation, river basin development, marine fisheries, parks and forests, education, and—of special significance in connection with the Port of New York Authority—metropolitan area problems.

Jealousies, Frictions, and Conflict

Every American has, on numerous occasions, heard derogatory remarks made by a citizen of one State about another State—a comment by a Pennsylvanian about "Jersey justice," for example, or one by a

---

[3] Burdick, Charles K., *The Law of the American Constitution* (New York: G. P. Putnam's Sons, 1922). While these rights, as pertaining to State citizenship, have never been completely enumerated or defined, Dean Burdick has pointed out that they include "certain rights arising from the very nature of the relationship of a citizen to the State of which he is a member. . . ." The interpretation of this clause was dealt with by the Supreme Court in *Colgate v. Harvey,* 296 U.S. 404 (1935).

[4] Frankfurter, Felix, and Landis, James M., "The Compact Clause of the Constitution," *Yale Law Journal,* May, 1925, pp. 685–750.

[5] This was the conclusion reached at the time by three political scientists, Jane Perry Clark (Carey), James Q. Dealey, Jr., and W. Brooke Graves, who studied the matter independently, and later conferred and compared notes.

Marylander about the practices of Virginia in the centuries old "oyster war" that has to be revived each year. There are grievances in the relations between the States, to be sure, but most of them are not too serious, and most of the slighting remarks one hears are made at least in part in jest.

It may be that the population mobility made possible by modern modes of transportation has contributed to this "easing of tensions," for all evidence indicates that at times during the colonial period and in the days of the formative period as well, interstate jealousies were intense and quite serious. Channing observes that, "in these modern days of interstate commerce commissions, Federal corporation taxation, and a nationwide excise, it is difficult to realize the hostile feelings with which the people of some States looked upon their neighbors." [6] There were friction and ill feeling in New England, in the Middle States, and in the South as well.

Much of the friction developed on the part of the smaller States against the larger ones. This was particularly true in the case of antagonisms involving Virginia. The people of North Carolina had no sympathy with the efforts of Virginia to regulate British commerce, a project in which both Virginia and Maryland had been engaged to their mutual dissatisfaction. There were abundant causes of estrangement between the two States, first due to trade rivalries, later to their attempts to regulate navigation in the Chesapeake Bay which culminated in the Alexandria Conference held in 1785 at Washington's home at Mount Vernon. This Conference, in turn, led to the proposal to extend the use of the interstate conference device to other States with similar problems, and finally to the Annapolis Convention of 1786.

Another cause of friction arose with respect to the control of the shell fisheries; an interstate compact on this subject was concluded between Virginia and Maryland in 1784, but perennial differences continued to arise. The compact remained in effect for nearly 200 years, until in 1957, the Maryland General Assembly sought to terminate it unilaterally. This action led to charges and countercharges, but eventually to further negotiations and the development of a new agreement between the two States. Having been officially approved by both States, the new compact was before the 87th Congress for its consent in 1961, in spite of the unhappiness of many of the Maryland fishermen.

Not only do jealousies and conflicting economic interests cause friction, but such lesser matters as differences in point of view and differences in the operating efficiency of government may lead to annoying and vexatious policy variations. A person living near a State border is often acutely aware of these discrepancies. Suppose that a river divides

[6] Channing, III, 468.

two States and a person wants to swim in it. If the water is polluted, as in many cases it is, it avails little for one State to try to clean up the river if the other State continues to dump sewage into it. A person may also find conflicting traffic rules when he drives his car. He may be lawfully divorced in one State and remarry, only to discover that he can be arrested for bigamy in another, that his children are stigmatized, and that all manner of complications with regard to the disposition of his property are likely to arise when he dies. The list of subject-matter areas in which there is urgent need for interstate cooperation could be extended at length.

ORGANIZATION OF THE STATES

First Proposal for a Council of the States

The sessions of the first National Conference on State and Local Taxation, held in Columbus, Ohio, November 12–15, 1907, were opened by an address by Dr. Charles A. L. Reed, a Professor at the University of Cincinnati, in which he proposed for the first time, as far as is known, the organization of a Council of States. This proposal might be regarded as a forerunner of the plan developed nearly two decades later by Senator Henry W. Toll, which resulted in the establishment of the American Legislators' Association, and ultimately in the Council of State Governments. The underlying philosophy of the Reed proposal appears to have been much the same as that expressed the preceding year by Secretary of State Elihu Root.[7] The following quotation is from the Reed address:

> The object of my remarks is to propose the assembling of a Council of the States. The first purpose of such a council would be to formulate standard bills, not only on taxation, but on all other subjects of pressing importance, and submit them for enactment in uniform terms to the State legislatures. Its next purpose would be to act in an advisory capacity in respect of any and all other subjects, concerning which it is desirable that the States either adopt uniform constitutional provisions, or enact uniform laws, or arrange uniform rules, regulations, procedures and practices for the enforcement of existing laws.
>
> It of course goes without saying that the functions of such a body would be restricted to the consideration of subjects which the nation in the exercise of its sovereignty has placed, for the time being, within the purview of the States, as contra-distinguished from those other subjects which it has similarly placed within the jurisdiction of the Federal

[7] See Chapter XXII.

Government. It likewise goes without saying that such a body, to fulfill the objects for which it would be called into existence, must be made up of men of highest ability, selected geographically and in numbers on a representative basis. And it must meet, as a legislature or the Congress meets, in a session or sessions sufficiently long and deliberate to be productive of sound results. Of these not the least would probably be the purely incidental determination, from the point of view of the States, of the powers, if any, that ought to be shifted by constitutional means from the States to the Federal Government, or from the Federal Government to the States. . . .

It seems to me that the assembling of a Council of States ought to be a matter of no difficulty whatever. The Governor of any State could take the initiative by inviting a conference with the Governors of the other States. This conference could determine four points: first, that a Council of States shall be called, together with the time and place; second, the basis of representation; third, the scope of the proceedings, if not the particular subjects, to be submitted for consideration; fourth, the approximate expense attaching to the movement. Each Governor could thereupon lay the matter before his respective legislature which, by joint resolution, could concur or nonconcur in the proposition. If the resolution to concur should prevail, it could provide for the election by the legislature or the appointment by the Governor of the prescribed number of delegates, and at the same time provide funds for their honoraria and for the pro rata expense of the meeting. All further details ought to be left to the Council itself. . . .

If, now, we pause for a final glance at the situation, we shall discover that an imperative duty of good faith rests upon the States. The nation, by assigning certain subjects and functions to the national government, acted upon the principle that like conditions demand like laws, and that, by assigning certain other subjects and functions to the State governments, the nation, with equal precision and definiteness, acted upon the principle that unlike conditions demand equally unlike laws, and that, through the failure of the States to keep their laws in harmonious touch with the rapidly evolving uniformity of conditions that come at present within our purview, the social, commercial and industrial interests of the whole country are made to suffer by the attempted adaptation of like conditions to unlike laws. We see, furthermore, as a natural result of this anomalous condition, widespread unrest on the one hand and incoordinate efforts at remedial activity on the part of the States on the other hand, with the Federal Government, the natural focus of popular appeal, forced to extend to the utmost limits of constitutional interpretation in an effort to protect the welfare, not alone of distinct interests, but of all the people of all the States.

We see, likewise, what it requires no prophetic vision to discern; namely, that if the present assignment of powers as between the Federal and State governments shall continue as at present to annoy the people and embarrass progress, the nation, in the exercise of its sovereignty, must and will readjust these powers—let us hope, by the open and fair methods of constitutional amendment rather than by the more insidious and less candid method of forced construction of the Constitution as it stands. In an effort to avoid either of these contingencies, in an effort honestly and faithfully to fulfill the obligations imposed upon them in the beginning by the nation itself, the States are obviously in need of some mechanism which, while consultative and advisory in its limitations, could still enable them to act in concert on all questions requiring uniformity of treatment. It has seemed to me that such a mechanism might be realized in a body such as I have described, and which might with propriety be designated as a Council of States.[8]

Council of State Governments Organized

In the early 1920's, Senator Henry W. Toll of Colorado conceived the idea of a national organization of State legislators, with a clearing house for the exchange of information on common problems. After several years of planning and preliminary work, the American Legislators' Association was established in 1925, further details on the organization of which are presented on pages 589–590.

Senator Toll, realizing that some more effective organization and assured means of financial support were absolutely essential if work was to continue, succeeded in bringing about a thorough and complete reorganization. The American Legislators' Association became the Council of State Governments. Under the terms of the charter, all States would become members, but two conditions of membership were prescribed: (1) that each State would establish a State commission on interstate cooperation; (2) that each State should contribute to the annual support of the Council's work, on the basis of an ability-to-pay schedule that would be formulated and adopted by the Council's Board of Managers. The financial condition began to improve when the Governors' Conference, for which it serves as secretariat, became active in its behalf. This occurred under the leadership of Senator Toll and his successor as Executive Director, Frank Bane, and when the regional offices, through which the Council's services could be extended directly to State governments and State officials, were established.

From the very beginning, the Council devoted serious attention to problems of intergovernmental relations in all areas. Its initial efforts were directed toward finding a solution to the continuing problem of tax conflicts among the States, and in 1935 the Interstate Commission on Conflicting Taxation was established. A report, prepared under the

[8] National Tax Association, First National Conference on State and Local Taxation, *Proceedings, 1907* (New York: The Macmillan Co., 1908), pp. 20–35.

direction of Professor Clarence Heer of the University of North Carolina, containing the recommendations of the Commission was published.[9] Further evidence of the serious interest of the Council in the intergovernmental field is found in the extensive treatment given this subject in successive editions of *The Book of the States* and in the Council's impressive list of publications, including such outstanding studies as *State-Local Relations* (Chicago, 1946), *Federal Grants-in-Aid* (Chicago, 1949), and most recently, *The States and the Metropolitan Problem* (Chicago, 1956).

As a part of its extensive program of publication, the magazine *State Government* was published monthly from 1925 to 1958, when it was changed to a quarterly and a new monthly publication, *State Government News*, was established. The research and publications program was significantly expanded in the reconstruction period following World War II. During these years, it issued noteworthy studies on such subjects as education (higher and secondary), highway safety, mental health, and conservation of natural resources.[10]

ORGANIZATION OF STATE EXECUTIVE OFFICERS

President Roosevelt Calls the First Governors' Conference

Ever since President Jefferson had written a letter to the Governor of Massachusetts in 1807 concerning the desirability of "a more intimate correspondence between the executives of the several States, and that of the Union," the need for informal machinery of communication between the President of the United States and the Governors had been recognized. The first such meeting ever held was summoned by President Roosevelt in 1908 for the purpose of considering the conservation of natural resources. Governors Hughes and Wilson addressed the 1910 meeting. Although the conference was generally hailed as an epoch-making event, and although it continued to meet regularly (1917 was the only exception), it accomplished very little during its early years.

In 1919, President Wilson summoned a White House Conference of Governors and Mayors to consider problems of re-employment at the end of World War I. The Governors met with President Coolidge

[9] Interstate Commission on Conflicting Taxation, *Conflicting Taxation* (Chicago: Council of State Governments, 1935).

[10] See *The Forty-eight State School Systems* (1949); *Mental Health Programs of the Forty-eight States* (1950); *Highway Safety—Motor Truck Regulations* (1950); *Higher Education in the Forty-eight States* (1952); and *Occupational Licensing Legislation in the States* (1952).

once, and years later with President Franklin D. Roosevelt once. They met three times with President Eisenhower to consider questions relating to national security, intergovernmental relations, and employment security.[11]

Also in these later years, regional conferences of Governors have been organized in the Southern, Western, and New England regions, in each of which exists a formal organization which holds regular meetings. Special conferences of Governors of selected States are frequently summoned to consider current problems of mutual interest, such as metropolitan area problems, parks and recreation areas, or flood control measures. At the end of half a century, such progress had been made that it was possible to write that "during five decades the Governors have developed a new instrument for perfecting the Union of the States." [12]

Associations of State Administrative Officers

Insurance Commissioners. The organization of the National Convention of Insurance Commissioners in 1871 was a significant event in that it was the first national organization of State administrative officials. Of course, there are many such organizations today, created, as was this one, for the dual purpose of achieving some degree of uniformity in the law in a given subject matter field and of facilitating cooperation between the several States in law enforcement work.[13]

Attorneys General. Although the insurance commissioners had been organized in 1871, the National Association of Attorneys General was the first national organization of the heads of a major department of State government. This group, composed of all State and territorial

[11] See *State Government News,* April, 1959, for a summary.

[12] Prior to the publication of Glenn E. Brooks, *When Governors Convene: The Governors' Conference and National Politics* (Baltimore: Johns Hopkins Press, 1961), there had been no comprehensive study of the organization and work of this body; during the 1950's, however, the Council of State Governments has issued a booklet which contains a worthwhile historical summary; see *Governors of the American States, Commonwealths, and Territories* (Chicago, 1957), pp. 1–19. The proceedings of the annual meetings have been regularly published, prior to 1935 at Live Oak, Florida, the home of former Governor Cary A. Hardee, who served for many years as Executive Secretary, and since 1935 by the Council of State Governments, which has since served as general secretariat for the Conference.

[13] A good deal of information regarding this and the other groups which follow is found in W. Brooke Graves, *Uniform State Action: A Possible Substitute for Centralization* (Chapel Hill: University of North Carolina Press, 1934).

Attorneys General and the Attorney General of the United States, was established to provide clearing house facilities and machinery for cooperation among the chief legal officers of the States and Territories, and to facilitate uniformity in the interpretation of State laws. The Council of State Governments, which serves as secretariat, publishes the proceedings of the association's annual meeting and a weekly digest and an annual index of opinions of the Attorneys General.

State Fiscal Officers. With the encouragement and leadership of the Council of State Governments, two new national associations of State fiscal officers were set up at the close of World War II. The National Association of State Budget Officers, composed of all State and territorial budget officers, was established in 1945 to provide machinery for cooperation among the members of this group, to foster more effective budget administration, and to attain greater efficiency in State administration generally. Similarly, the National Association of State Purchasing Officials, organized in 1947, seeks to promote cooperation for more efficient State purchasing and for greater economy in administration. The Council of State Governments serves as secretariat for both organizations.

Headquarters Building for the "1313 Group" Erected

The building at 1313 East 60th Street, on the campus of the University of Chicago, which has since 1935 served as headquarters for the national organizations which constitute the "1313 Group," was made possible through the planning and foresight of many men, notably Charles E. Merriam, Louis Brownlow, Beardsley Ruml, and Guy Moffat, and through a grant from the Spelman Fund (of which Mr. Moffat was at the time Executive Director) to the Public Administration Clearing House, which functioned for many years under the capable leadership of Mr. Brownlow. The building was conceived as a means of bringing under one roof the headquarters offices of a large number of national organizations functioning in the field of government and administration —official and quasi-official in character—thereby facilitating cooperation among them and coordination of their programs.[14]

The passing years have demonstrated that this was a very significant gathering. At the present time, some twenty or more national organizations maintain their headquarters offices in the building, some independently, others as subsidiary organizations affiliated with larger or related groups. The latter alternative applies, for instance, to approxi-

---

[14] See Brownlow, Louis, *A Passion for Anonymity* (Chicago: University of Chicago Press, 1958), Chapters 22–24. This is the second volume of Mr. Brownlow's autobiography.

mately half a dozen groups affiliated with the Council of State Governments. A list of members appears below.

MEMBERS OF THE "1313 GROUP," SHOWING DATE OF FOUNDING

American Public Welfare Association (1930)
American Public Works Association (1894)
American Society of Planning Officials (1934)
American Society for Public Administration (1939)
Conference of Chief Justices (1949—COSGO affiliate)

Council of State Governments (1933)
Federation of Tax Administrators (1937)
Governors' Conference (1908—COSGO affiliate)
International City Managers Association (1914)
Municipal Finance Officers Association (1906)

National Association of Assessing Officers (1934)
National Association of Attorneys General (1907—COSGO affiliate)
National Association of Housing and Redevelopment Officials (1933)
National Association of Juvenile Compact Administrators (1956—COSGO affiliate)
National Association of State Budget Officers (1945—COSGO affiliate)

National Association of State Purchasing Officials (1947—COSGO affiliate)
National Conference of Court Administrative Officials (1955—COSGO affiliate)
National Conference on Uniform State Laws (1892—COSGO affiliate)
National Institute of Municipal Clerks (1947)
National Legislative Conference (1948—COSGO affiliate)

Parole and Probation Compact Administrators' Association (1945—COSGO affiliate)
Public Administration Service (1933)
Public Personnel Association (1906)

LEGISLATIVE ORGANIZATION: UNIFORMITY AND COOPERATION

National Conference of Commissioners on Uniform State Laws

Agitation for some such organization as the National Conference of Commissioners on Uniform State Laws was begun as early as 1857, but no really significant action was taken toward its establishment until 1889 when the American Bar Association, spurred into action by a resolution adopted by the New York State legislature, summoned a national conference on the subject. Nine States were represented at this conference; since 1912, all the States, the Territories, and the District of Columbia have been officially represented. The organization has always maintained a connection with the American Bar Association and in recent years has also worked in close cooperation with the Council of State Governments.[15]

The Uniform Commercial Code was declared complete and was promulgated at the Conference held in New York City in 1951. This code represents twelve years of effort on the part of the Conference and the American Law Institute which worked jointly to accomplish the monumental project. The act, which covers the entire range of commercial and business law in America, when passed by State legislatures, will supersede many of the most popular uniform acts, such as Negotiable Instruments, Bills of Lading, Sales, etc. It will not only streamline the law, but it will vastly facilitate business and commerce. Pennsylvania was the first State to adopt this new legislation.[16]

American Legislators' Association Organized

The leadership of Senator Henry W. Toll, Denver lawyer and member of the Colorado State Senate, in the establishment of the Council of State Governments has already been mentioned. Finding himself beset by many difficult problems to which he had no answers and often little information, he envisioned a national clearing house for the exchange of information on current legislative problems, an organization which could sponsor meetings at which legislators from many States could come together to discuss common and related problems.

His dream was realized in 1925 when the American Legislators' Association was organized. Through its Interstate Reference Service at the national office in Chicago, it accomplished much, but the organization was beset with constant financial worries. Senators Dr. George Woodward

---

[15] The work of the Conference can be followed, year by year, in the *Handbook* of the National Conference of Commissioners on Uniform State Laws which has been published annually since 1891 in Chicago (title may vary slightly). For an analysis of the Council's work down to 1934, see W. Brooke Graves, *Uniform State Action*, Chapter 3.

[16] See Schnader, William A., "The New Commercial Code: Modernizing Our Uniform Commercial Acts," *American Bar Association Journal*, March, 1950, pp. 179–182, 252–254, and "The Uniform Commercial Code: What Is Accomplished, What Remains," *State Government*, Winter, 1936, pp. 49–53. See also three symposia: "The Commercial Code," *Law and Contemporary Problems*, Winter, 1951; "The Uniform Commercial Code: A Major Step in the Evolution of Commercial Practices," *Business Review*, June, 1953, Supplement; "The Proposed Uniform Commercial Code," *Albany Law Review*, January, 1953.

of Philadelphia and Seabury Mastick of New York made personal annual contributions, as did Mark Graves, New York State Tax Commissioner; the Spelman Fund also provided some assistance, but financial support was unpredictable and very uncertain. The States were extremely slow in recognizing their obligation for the support of the work.

Founding of the American Law Institute

A new realization of the need for practical uniformity and coordination of State laws developed in many quarters after World War I. In 1923, there met in Washington a conference called the Preliminary Committee for the Establishment of a Permanent Organization for the Improvement of the Law, set up by the American Bar Association with Elihu Root as chairman. The American Law Institute, which grew out of this conference, was incorporated under the laws of the District of Columbia for the purpose of promoting "the clarification and simplification of the law, and its better adaptation to social needs, to secure the better administration of justice and to encourage and carry on scholarly and scientific legal research." Its offices were established at the Law School of the University of Pennsylvania, where for many years the late Dr. William Draper Lewis served as its executive director.

The Institute early undertook the enormous task of preparing its *Restatement of the Law* in an "attempt to give orderly expression to the common law," by restating in modern form, upon the basis of exhaustive study and research by the ablest legal scholars in the country, the principles of the law. The first published result of this project was the *Restatement of the Law of Contracts,* published in 1932; others followed at the rate of one or two a year until 1947, when the task was completed. The volumes of the Restatements (twenty in all, with supplements) were accompanied by annotations for each State on each subject covered. This program has had a tremendous impact upon the law and its development in the several States.

National Legislative Conferences

The Assembly of the States. The Council of State Governments organized its biennial conference of State legislators for the discussion of common problems, the first meeting being held in Washington, D.C.; most of the succeeding meetings have been held in Chicago, usually in December of even numbered years, just prior to the opening of most State legislative sessions in January. Originally called the Interstate

Assembly, this gathering has been designated the Assembly of the States since World War II.[17]

National Legislative Conference. At the close of World War II, a small group of men engaged professionally in legislative service work on a full-time basis met and formulated plans for a national organization to provide a forum for the discussion of common problems and the exchange of information. The original group of twelve grew to fifty, then to seventy-five. As legislative service activities were expanded throughout the country, the National Legislative Conference in a period of ten years has had an almost phenomenal growth. Some 600 persons attended the annual meeting in Oklahoma City in 1957, 700 the meeting in Boston in 1958. Not all of them were professional people, to be sure; some members brought their families, and an increasing number of legislators came to participate in the meetings.

This tremendous growth has modified somewhat the original plans regarding the nature and purpose of the Conference, one of whose primary objectives was the exchange of information about research on legislative problems carried on by State legislative service agencies. Toward this end, a quarterly checklist has been issued to members by the Council of State Governments, which serves as secretariat for the Conference, showing for each State studies authorized or requested by the legislature, studies in progress, and studies completed. Mounting costs of publication and distribution necessitated greater care in the circulation of reports. Under the terms of the new agreement, each participating agency agrees to send copies of all of its reports to all member agencies and to preserve and keep available for general use all of the reports it receives from other agencies throughout the country.[18]

Other Groups. The Council of State Governments assists and services whatever groups of State officers desire them to do so. Thus, in 1957, an Association of Legislative Clerks and Secretaries was organized when the National Legislative Conference met in Oklahoma City; this group, which had formerly met as part of the Conference, felt lost in the larger organization and wanted one of its own. Several years later, in late 1959, a new type of national legislative organization made its appearance. The legislative leaders of New York, majority and minority leaders in both houses, issued invitations to their counterparts in the other forty-nine States and the Territories to a conference to be held in Albany and New York early in September. High on the list of objectives was the establishment of a national organization similar to the Governors' Conference,

---

[17] Significant addresses and reports of subject matter sessions have regularly appeared soon after each meeting in *State Government.*

[18] See *Historical Sketch of the National Legislative Conference, 1947–1963* (Chicago: Council of State Governments, 1963).

which would meet annually to discuss common legislative problems. By mid-October, acceptances had been received from thirty-eight jurisdictions. Although there is much to be said in favor of the organization, it raises questions regarding its relations with the National Legislative Conference and its possible duplication of some of the purposes and objectives of that organization. The meeting was held as planned, and later, a formal organization was established.

THE CONFERENCE OF CHIEF JUSTICES

The judiciary was the last of the three branches of State government to organize nationally, but in 1949, the Conference of Chief Justices, composed of the Chief Justices of the State Supreme Courts, came into being. The purpose of this Conference is to facilitate the exchange of

THE CONFERENCE OF CHIEF JUSTICES

ideas and information on the operation of the judiciary in the States, and between their highest courts concerning improvement in the administration of justice. Special committees study and report on procedural practices, and the Council of State Governments, which serves as secretariat for the Conference, undertakes such research as the Conference requests. In general, therefore, the Conference functions for the judicial branch in a manner comparable to that in which the National Legislative Conference functions for the Legislative Branch, and the Governors' Conference and the Council of State Governments for the Executive Branch.

UNIFORMITY AND COOPERATION IN SELECTED FIELDS

In Crime Control and Corrections

In 1929, President Hoover appointed George W. Wickersham, a New York lawyer and former Attorney General of the United States, as chairman of the National Law Enforcement Commission, popularly known as the Wickersham Commission. This body was created to study the causes and means of combatting the widespread wave of crime that developed in the Prohibition era. Significant among the findings set forth in its report was the serious deficiency in crime reporting; by bringing this situation to light, the Commission was instrumental in developing a better and far more uniform system of crime reporting throughout the country.[19]

Federal interest in the interstate compact device for combatting crime began in 1933, when Gordon Dean was appointed to the Department of Justice staff with the specific assignment of promoting the use of interstate compacts for this purpose. The Interstate Crime Compact was approved two years later, followed in 1936 by the organization of the Association of States Signatory to the Interstate Crime Compact, as it was first called. Proceedings of this first annual meeting were published in Washington in 1936. In 1945, the organization became the Parole and Probation Compact Administrators' Association, its purpose being to facilitate cooperation and the exchange of information, and to bring about a more effective implementation of interstate probation and parole supervision. By 1951 all States were cooperative members of what is now an almost completely uniform interstate system.[20]

[19] See *Report of the National Law Enforcement Commission* (Washington, 1930).

[20] See Council of State Governments, *The Handbook on Interstate Crime Control*, rev. ed. (Chicago, 1955). Brevard E. Crihfield has two articles dealing

As an administrative arrangement between and among the States, the Compact serves many practical purposes. It facilitates the capture of criminals who have violated the terms of their freedom and encourages rehabilitation by permitting transfer to a receptive environment. The Compact calls for interstate cooperation along a wide front in the fields of probation and parole. It provides a simple, businesslike, legal, and constitutional method of granting probationers and parolees the privilege of moving outside the State in which they were sentenced into other jurisdictions where they may have better opportunities for adjustment, with full protection to society. Prior to the drafting of this Compact and the passage of enabling legislation by the States, some 10,000 parolees were living without supervision or control outside the States in which their offenses had been committed. Now, with all States operating under the Compact, each Governor appoints an official administrator whose duty it is to administer the Compact for that State and, by conference with his fellow administrators in other compacting States, to provide rules and regulations for carrying out its provisions.

Early in 1959, a Western Corrections Compact was adopted by six Western States: Colorado, Idaho, New Mexico, Utah, Washington, and Wyoming. Under the terms of the Compact, the instrument becomes effective when ratified by two contiguous States among those eligible. Adoption does not bind a party State to any obligation or action but provides a legal foundation for contracts among member States to confine specified kinds of convicted persons of one State in the institutions of another. The contracts are specific on such matters as the number of inmates a State will obligate itself to receive; the number of offenders any State may have the right to confine in a particular receiving State or a given institution; the calculation of charges and items to be included in such calculations; and the exact services to be provided incidental to confinement.[21]

An example of new patterns of interstate-Federal cooperation may be noted in S. 3908 (86th Congress), a bill to provide means for the Federal government to combat interstate crime and to assist the States in enforcing their criminal laws. The measure would prohibit travel in inter-

---

with this work: "Crime Control and Uniformity of Criminal Laws," *Journal of Criminal Law, Criminology, and Police Science*, January–February, 1952, pp. 571–588, and "The Interstate Parole and Probation Compact," *Federal Probation*, June, 1953, pp. 3–7. See also Dean, Gordon, "The Interstate Compact: A Device for Crime Repression," *Law and Contemporary Problems*, October, 1934, pp. 460–471; Ellis, William J., "Interstate Parole and Probation Compact: An Appraisal After Ten Years Operation," *State Government*, March, 1945, pp. 40–42 ff.; and Rubin, Sol, "The Standard Probation and Parole Act: Fifteen Years Later," *Federal Probation*, December, 1955, pp. 9–14.

[21] See *State Government News*, April, 1959.

state commerce to aid racketeering enterprises, interstate transportation of wagering paraphernalia, and the transmission of certain gambling information in interstate commerce. When introduced, it focused public attention on the need for legislation and paved the way for early action in the next Congress.[22]

National Attack on Interstate Trade Barriers

The National Conference on Interstate Trade Barriers, organized by and held under the auspices of the Council of State Governments in Chicago in April, 1939, came as the climax of a carefully planned attack upon discriminatory legislation, policies, and practices which had been dangerously Balkanizing the States, thereby greatly impeding the free flow of interstate commerce. Those who attended the Conference returned home to fight new restrictive proposals and to sponsor the repeal of existing restrictions, with the result, in the words of Hubert R. Gallagher, that "the drive to erect additional trade barriers in the forty-four legislatures meeting in 1939 was stopped in its tracks." About this time, extensive studies of trade barriers were undertaken, in addition to those made in preparation for the Conference, by the Department of Agriculture and the Marketing Laws Survey in the Works Progress Administration; all of these resulted in the publication of important studies,[23] and contributed greatly to the success of the national attack on the interstate trade barrier problem.

Problems have a way of recurring in somewhat different forms. Trade barriers to the free flow of interstate commerce were overcome more or less effectively twenty years ago, but some of them still persist. In addition, it has been reported that "State taxes threaten the U.S. common market." [24] Of course, the tax aspects of the problem are not new, but they appear to be developing along new and rather alarming lines. Until recently, the State corporate income tax was limited to cor-

---

[22] *Congressional Record,* August 29, 1960, pp. 16875–16876.

[23] Much of the preparatory work for the Conference, resulting in a series of reports and special studies, was done by Thomas S. Green, Jr., and F. Eugene Melder; for these and other items on interstate trade barriers, see W. Brooke Graves, *Intergovernmental Relations in the United States: A Selected Bibliography* (Washington: Committee Print, House Committee on Government Operations, Subcommittee on Intergovernmental Relations, 84th Cong., 2nd Sess., November, 1956), pp. 63–66.

[24] See Ayer, Josephine, *Effects of State and Local Regulations on Interstate Movement of Agricultural Products by Highway* (Washington: Agricultural Marketing Service, July, 1961) and on the tax angle, Studenski, Paul, and Glasser, Gerald J., "New Threat in State Business Taxation," *Harvard Business Review,* November–December, 1958, pp. 77–91.

porations maintaining permanent establishments within the State. Following a new trend, however, several States have either altered or reinterpreted their statutes to extend the application of their corporation tax laws to corporations which neither own nor maintain establishments within the State, but merely solicit business there.

Yet the mere solicitation of orders can scarcely be regarded as a sufficient basis for imposing a State corporation income tax on an out-of-State corporation. Even if the Supreme Court should decide that it was, Congress, in the exercise of its constitutional responsibility for the regulation of interstate commerce, could "bar the unwise and nationally harmful extension of State corporation income taxation into the domain of interstate commerce." In 1950, as the problem continued to grow more serious, Professor Studenski warned that unless Federal action is taken to correct the situation, "we may lose many of the advantages of free trade across State lines which we have enjoyed since State tariffs were prohibited by the Constitution 173 years ago."[25]

Uniform Reciprocal Support of Dependents

During 1948 and 1949, a few States, led by New York, embarked on an experiment in the field of family relations. It was designed to provide a workable method of securing support for dependents when the person legally responsible had absconded to another State. This attempt to control "skippers" resulted in the development of reciprocal legislation known as the Uniform Reciprocal Support of Dependents Act, adopted in mid-1952 in three territories and all but five States. By 1958, the coverage was complete, including all States and six other jurisdictions. Thirty-two of the laws followed the provisions of the Uniform Act, which confers civil jurisdiction only, while eleven were patterned after the original New York approach.[26]

The Interstate Conference on Reciprocal Support held its ninth annual meeting in 1960, adopting several resolutions having a bearing

[25] Studenski, Paul, "State Taxes Threaten U.S. Common Market," *Harvard Business Review,* July–August, 1950, pp. 57–66. See also Studenski, "The Need for Federal Curbs on State Taxes on Interstate Commerce: An Economist's Viewpoint," *Virginia Law Review,* October, 1960, pp. 1121–1149; this issue consists of a symposium on the general topic.

[26] See Council of State Governments, *Reciprocal State Legislation to Enforce the Support of Dependents* (Chicago, biennially since 1950). See also Allison, Junius L., "The 'Skippers' Act of 1949," *Public Aid in Illinois,* May, 1951, pp. 1–3, 9; Brockelbank, W. J., "Is the Uniform Reciprocal Enforcement of Support Act Constitutional?" *Missouri Law Review,* January, 1952, pp. 1–15; and Seaman, Grace C., "Making the Reciprocal Support Law Work," *State Government,* June, 1952, pp. 132–135.

on interstate-Federal relations. The Social Security Act now requires that law enforcement officials be notified when aid to dependent children is furnished in cases of abandonment by a parent; the Conference recommended that such notification be mandatory only when there is reason to believe that the parent can furnish support, and that information as to the parents' whereabouts and financial circumstances be furnished to other States on request. They also urged that the Department of Health, Education, and Welfare take action to make the address records of the Bureau of Old Age and Survivor's Insurance readily available to State and local officials as an aid in locating persons in connection with reciprocal support proceedings. All States were urged to adopt the 1958 draft of the Uniform Act, and the publication of a *Handbook of Administrative Procedures* for use under the act was authorized.[27]

INTERSTATE COMPACTS

Background of the Interstate Compact Device

The interstate compact, as Frederick R. Zimmermann has said, presents a new frontier in American government. Aside from the significantly successful Port of New York Authority, the first attempts to extend the use of the compact device in the solution of difficult social and economic questions were quite unsuccessful, particularly the attempt to use it as a means of solving interstate problems in the labor field. The Eastern Interstate Conference on Labor Compacts was initiated by Governors Franklin D. Roosevelt of New York and Gifford Pinchot of Pennsylvania for the purpose of framing agreements acceptable to a number of Northeastern States on such subjects as minimum wages, hours, and other labor matters. About a dozen meetings were held by the representatives of as many States, roughly on a quarterly basis, over a period of about three years. Agreements among the conferees, reached only after prolonged argument and by prodigious effort, proved to be generally unacceptable to the legislatures of the cooperating States. The minimum wage compact was approved by the legislatures of three States, but other agreements won no formal acceptance whatever.[28]

Other efforts, as has been noted, were made at the same time to

[27] *State Government News,* January, 1961.

[28] See Graves, *American State Government,* 3rd ed., p. 908, and a note in the *New England News Letter,* "Seven States Sign Pact to Promote Uniform Minimum Wage Regulations," June, 1934. See also Wilson, Francis C., "Industrial and Labor Adjustments by Interstate Compacts," *Marquette Law Review,* January, 1936, pp. 11–36.

extend the use of the compact device by the Roosevelt administration (Gordon Dean in the field of crime control) and by the Council of State Governments. These efforts were notably successful during the next quarter of a century, during which a significant number of compacts were entered into in such fields as river basin development, higher education, oil conservation, pollution control, marine fisheries, parks and forests, corrections, metropolitan area problems, and others. The use of compacts for agreements among local governments has become a significant development in the compact field.

It is not easy to evaluate the significance of these developments. As compared with earlier times, the record of accomplishment is impressive. Many compacts have been ratified on many subjects, involving many States. At the same time, it is obvious that there are great numbers of problems in the solution of which the compact device might be helpful, where it has either not been tried or has not been used effectively. The early difficulties in negotiation, ratification, and modification continue to occur, nourishing in the minds of some observers a lurking suspicion that what the compacts have accomplished, relative to the magnitude of the need, may have been too little and too late. Professor Carleton thus expresses this point of view:

> The interstate compact remains largely a potentiality rather than an actuality, although there is an encouraging tendency by the States to experiment with it more widely. The truth seems to be that the interstate compact works most successfully in the noncontroversial, that is, the relatively unimportant, areas of activity such as the regional education councils, the return of parolees, and so forth.
>
> In the controversial areas—such as electric power, tapping water supplies, preventing water pollution, conserving soil and other natural resources—it has been less successful, although longer and wider experience may bring greater achievement. At the present time what is most impressive, considering the many possibilities for the use of interstate compacts, is this: how few are attempted; of the few attempted, how many founder in the process of negotiation and ratification; of the very few that materialize, how prolonged and difficult the process of negotiation and ratification. Proposed interstate compacts must be watched closely, for they sometimes contain built-in devices for local vetoes, disguises for obstruction.[29] It is instructive that one of the reasons for calling the Constitutional Convention of 1787, to form a stronger general government, was the failure of the Potomac River States to conclude an interstate compact. In the light of the total situation and

[29] See Leuchtenburg, William E., *Flood Control Politics: The Connecticut River Valley, 1927–1950* (Cambridge: Harvard University Press, 1953), Chapter 2. See also Macmahon, Arthur W., ed., *Federalism: Mature and Emergent* (Garden City: Doubleday & Co., Inc., 1955), pp. 344–347.

the many opportunities for employing this device, the use of the interstate compact is still negligible.[30]

This is a severe indictment, containing some truth, but rather too severe in view of the accomplishments under many compacts.

Current Uses in Important Fields

The Interstate Oil Compact. The Interstate Oil Compact was adopted and the commission which enforces it established in 1934 for the purpose of conserving oil and gas through prevention of waste from any cause by established State agencies. From an initial membership of six States, the Compact now has grown to thirty, in addition to which, under the by-laws of the commission, the Oil and Gas Division of the Department of the Interior, the Federal Power Commission, the United States of Venezuela, and the Canadian Provinces of Alberta and Saskatchewan have been invited to participate in Compact activities as official observers. Although the Compact permits any State to withdraw upon sixty days' notice, no State has ever exercised that right. The Commission, whose headquarters are located in its own building in Oklahoma City, consists of one representative appointed by the Governor in each of the thirty oil-producing States, all such States being included. Under most of the State enabling statutes, the Governor is the official representative; many of the Governors attend the quarterly meetings of the Commission in person, though most of them have authority to appoint a substitute or assistant.[31]

Compacts for River Basin Development. The interstate compact device has in late years been much used in river basin development and in sanitation and pollution control work. For the first of these purposes, it has been used in no less than eighteen major river valleys, for the second purpose in a smaller number. A few instances of each type may be cited for illustrative purposes.

The Interstate Commission on the Delaware River Basin is a joint governmental agency created in 1936 by the four Delaware River Valley States—New York, New Jersey, Pennsylvania, and Delaware—for the purpose of formulating, adopting, and carrying out wise and constructive policies for the most appropriate development and use of the natural resources of this river basin and its tributaries. Each of the member

---

[30] Carleton, William G., "Centralization and the Open Society," *Political Science Quarterly*, June, 1960, pp. 244–259.

[31] See the Commission's publication, *The Interstate Compact to Conserve Oil and Gas: A Summary of the Background, Organization, Purposes, and Functions of the Interstate Oil Commission* (Oklahoma City, 1954). For references, see Graves, *Intergovernmental Relations in the United States*, p. 57.

States, of course, has a commission on interstate cooperation, and these agencies jointly organized INCODEL whose committees and research staff are concerned with problems relating to quantity and quality of water, water research and information, and planning.

Five years later, in 1941, the four States of Maryland, Pennsylvania, Virginia, West Virginia, and the District of Columbia entered into a compact creating the Potomac Valley Conservancy District, later transformed into the Interstate Commission on the Potomac River Basin. Under the terms of the compact, the signatories mutually agreed to faithful cooperation in the abatement and control of stream pollution, to the enactment of adequate and, insofar as practical, uniform legislation for the abatement and control of such pollution, and to the appropriation of funds to finance the operations of the coordinating agency which consists of three members from each signatory body and three appointed by the President of the United States.

The Colorado River Compact provides the earliest conspicuous example of voluntary cooperation in river basin development. This Compact, along with that creating the Port of New York Authority, marks the first use of the compact clause for the settlement of serious problems other than those relating to boundary lines. Negotiated in 1922, it had been approved by six States by 1925, but it was not approved by Congress until 1928 or ratified by Arizona, the last State, until 1944. Arizona had gone to court in 1931 to upset the Compact on grounds of constitutionality, contending that it could not properly be concluded because Arizona refused to ratify. The Supreme Court held, however, that it could become effective, but that it might not function in such manner as to foreclose any rights which Arizona might have in the waters of the river.[32]

The Colorado River situation was an exceedingly complicated one, involving many States and two basin areas, the upper and the lower. In addition to the original but limited Colorado River Compact, there is a separate Upper Basin Compact and a number of bi-state subagreements apportioning the use of the waters of particular streams within the area. This Compact marked a new high in the application of the compact device to the solution of water problems. In the West alone, there are at least ten other water allocation compacts in effect. In the years 1951–1961, fifteen compacts became effective in various parts of the country; most of them dealt with water supply, but a few were concerned with pollution control as well.[33]

---

[32] *Arizona* v. *California,* 283 U.S. 423 (1931). This was reinforced in a decision of June, 1963.

[33] See successive editions of *The Book of the States,* and of Graves, *American State Government;* see also Zimmermann, Frederick L., and Wendell,

The Upper Colorado River Commission is a creature of a compact executed by five States in 1948 and now composed of one representative each from Colorado, New Mexico, Utah, Wyoming, and the United States. It has power, among other things, to construct, operate, and maintain water gauging stations, to carry on studies and research on water problems, and to disseminate information regarding the findings thereof. The Commission works closely with both State and Federal agencies, both executive and legislative, in connection with the formulation and development of water resource policies and in the collection and analysis of water resource data.

At the direction of the Missouri River States Committee, the Council of State Governments published in January, 1953, a tentative draft of a Missouri River Basin Compact for study by interested States. The plan contemplates an interstate agreement among the signatory States and between the States and the National government, creating a joint agency, the Missouri River Commission, whose major purpose would be to integrate and coordinate governmental activities relating to the conservation, development, and utilization of water, land, and related resources. The Commission would have broad power to plan and recommend action and to review agency proposals, but it would not engage in construction or other direct operations.

The Compact would become effective when and if Congress approved it and assumed the obligations imposed by it on the Federal government, and when ratified by the States of Kansas, Missouri, Montana, Nebraska, North Dakota, South Dakota, and Wyoming. Also eligible to full participation if they ratified would be Colorado, Iowa, and Minnesota.

The Ohio River Valley Sanitation Commission was created by an interstate compact signed June 30, 1948, by the States of Illinois, Indiana, Kentucky, New York, Ohio, Pennsylvania, Virginia, and West Virginia. Five years after the signing of this compact, each of the States had, in accordance with its pledge, completely revised or amended its water pollution legislation so that it could curb pollution effectively and aggressively on both intrastate and interstate streams. Out of an Ohio Valley population of more than 9 million, almost half had treatment facilities completed or under construction. At this time, the Commission was able to report that "New pollution has been halted, existing pollution is being decreased and the trend of half a century has been reversed."

The New England Interstate Water Pollution Control Commission began with cooperation between New York and New England. A compact between Connecticut, Massachusetts, and Rhode Island in 1947 was

Mitchell, *The Interstate Compact Since 1925* (Chicago: Council of State Governments, August, 1950).

enlarged in 1949 to include New York and in 1951 to include New Hampshire and Vermont. Maine was the only eligible State not a member in 1954. The Commission is composed of five members from each signatory State, appointed by the respective Governors. A technical advisory board on water pollution control has been set up. The Commission is an agency of the signatory States, coordinating a mutually agreed upon plan to improve and control the quality of the waters. As in the Ohio valley, this Commission has made significant progress.

In 1936, Connecticut, New Jersey, and New York entered into the Tri-State Compact establishing the Interstate Sanitation District and the Interstate Sanitation Commission. The preamble to the Compact recites the growth in population and development of the New York metropolitan area, the serious nature of the health hazards created by the pollution of adjacent waters, and the belief that these problems could best be solved through the cooperation of the interested States "by and through a joint or common agency." The overall program of the Commission has been to eliminate raw or untreated sewage and to provide that steps be taken to improve the treatment by plants which discharge an effluent that does not meet established standards. Much progress has been made from year to year, but progress in any one year is but a reflection of years of preparation; much work still remains to be done.[34]

The Marine Fisheries Compacts. After long years of effort, three important fisheries compacts were accepted and approved by the interested States and by Congress in the 1940's. The Atlantic States Marine Fisheries Commission was organized in 1942 and now has fifteen signatory coastal States from Maine to Florida. The Pacific Marine Fisheries Commission, organized in similar fashion, was approved in 1947, with California, Oregon, and Washington as members. The Gulf States Marine Fisheries Commission was likewise organized in 1947, with Alabama, Florida, Louisiana, and Texas as members. Each was established for the fourfold purpose of: (1) promoting the better utilization of the marine, shell, and anadromous fisheries; (2) developing a joint program for the promotion and protection of such fisheries; (3) preventing waste of the fisheries from any cause; (4) creating an interstate policy determining and enforcement agency. Each Commission maintains an office and publishes an annual report of its activities.

In the Atlantic Commission, each State is represented by three commissioners, including the administrator of fisheries, a member of the legislature appointed by the Commission on interstate cooperation, and a citizen appointed by the Governor "having a knowledge of or an interest in the marine fisheries problem." During the first few years of

---

[34] Brief and up to date descriptive notes on these various programs will be found in the current edition of *The Book of the States.*

its existence (a prior organization having functioned from 1941), the Commission developed eight panels on particular species of fish. These were later supplemented and in time replaced by four sections covering specific portions of the Atlantic Coast—North, Middle, South, and Chesapeake Bay. These proved to be much more effective and helped to produce a greater degree of teamwork among the States. Uniform acts have been generally adopted relative to a number of different species, and other types of cooperative arrangements have been made effective.[35]

Compacts for Parks and Forests. In 1900, the Commissioners of the Palisades Interstate Park, the predecessor of the present Palisades Interstate Park Commission, was formed by the cooperative action of New Jersey and New York. The original board was authorized to preserve and maintain the natural beauty of the Palisades, which was threatened by quarries actually in the process of demolishing them. Later the Commission's authority was extended into New York State as far north as Newburgh and west to the Ramapo Mountains.

In 1937, a compact between the two States, approved by Congress, provided for the creation of the Commission as a joint, corporate, municipal instrumentality of the two States, "with appropriate rights, powers, duties, and immunities; for the transfer to the Commission of certain functions, jurisdiction, rights, powers and duties, together with the properties of the bodies politic created in 1900; and for continuance of the Palisades Interstate Park for public use and enjoyment." There are ten commissioners, five appointed by the Governor and confirmed by the senate of each State. All commissioners serve without pay. Their term is for five years and until a successor is appointed and has qualified.

Since its creation in 1900, the Commission has acquired additional areas in both States, and it now exercises jurisdiction over a chain of eleven parks in the two States. They are the Palisades in New Jersey, including the world famous Palisades of the Hudson River, comprising approximately 1,800 acres, and ten parks in New York State. There are approximately 50,000 acres of the park in New York, which combined with the acreage in New Jersey brings the total in both States to approximately 52,000 acres.

The Northeastern Forest Fire Protection Commission was organized January 19, 1950, under the terms of an interstate compact approved by the legislatures of New York and five New England States and by

[35] See accounts by Heydecker, Wayne D., Secretary-Treasurer, in *The Book of the States,* 1943-1944 and succeeding editions, and his "Exploratory Intercoastal Fisheries Conference," *State Government,* October, 1946, pp. 260-264; see also Zimmermann, Frederick L., "Atlantic States Marine Fisheries Compact," *ibid.,* April, 1941, pp. 81-83, 95, and "Interstate Cooperation and Fisheries," *ibid.,* August, 1941, pp. 159-162, 166.

Congress. Rhode Island passed its enabling act the following year. The compact document, among other things, mandated the Commission to provide for mutual aid in times of catastrophe. The regional plan had been completed and was approved by the Commission at its annual meeting in 1953. Because of the fact that the compact legislation was brought about primarily by the Maine fires of 1947, mutual aid requirements naturally received the greatest emphasis. The gross land area of New York and the six New England States is approximately 70 million acres, of which 44 million acres or 63 per cent are under protection from forest fires. In order uniformly to train the more than 10,000 individual employees involved, a training program was developed in cooperation with the district office of the United States Forest Service. Considerable work has been done in connection with the publication of manuals on fire suppression, fire fighting organization, and other related matters.

Regional Education Compacts. Many of the States are not in a position individually to provide high grade professional training in all fields for all eligible applicants, but they have found that they can do so through cooperation. The facilities and equipment for professional training are so costly that many States would find it difficult to provide them, and some would not have enough eligible candidates to justify the expenditure if they did. Former Governor Millard F. Caldwell of Florida, an early advocate and promoter of the plan, frequently compared it to the action of a group of neighboring farmers who contribute to the purchase of an expensive piece of machinery for their joint use. The underlying philosophy of the plan is equally simple—the members of the group can accomplish through cooperation things which no one of them would be able to do alone.

The Southern Regional Education Compact, before Congress for approval in 1949 but never acted upon, provides for a Board of Control consisting of the Governor and three members from each participating State. Originally planned to include fifteen Southern States, nine Governors signed; by 1952, there were fourteen signatories to this Compact which provides the foundation for a regional system of higher education. It was suggested at the time that the Compact was merely a neat trick to circumvent the decision of the Supreme Court in the Sipuel Case [36] and to perpetuate the system of segregation in higher education by establishing, through the pooled resources of a number of States, professional schools for Negroes who had been excluded by law from the tax-supported institutions of the cooperating States. If such a purpose was involved, it was actually a minor consideration, as subsequent developments in at least three important parts of the country have clearly shown. The Southern region had for years been losing large number of its most able young peo-

[36] *Sipuel* v. *University of Oklahoma*, 332 U.S. 631 (1948), (68 Sup. Ct. 299).

ple who went North or West for professional training and never returned. No region can prosper if its most promising leaders are constantly siphoned off.

Against this background, the Board in 1948 helped to execute contracts between States and selected institutions under which the States pay for the costs of training such of their students as the institutions admit under the program. The cooperating institutions agree to admit qualified graduate students from other States on the same basis as residents of their own. Thus, if Florida sends its medical students to Tulane University, it pays $1,500 per year per student; it pays a similar amount for dental students, and $1,000 each for students of veterinary medicine. Under these contracts, several hundred students and approximately $1 million are channeled across State lines each year.

In 1950, in an extension of the plan, topflight graduate programs were developed in agriculture, social work, engineering, forestry, industrial chemistry, and other fields. Recognizing both the small number of institutions in the region offering work for the doctorate and the urgent need of the region for such trained personnel, inter-university conferences were held to determine which fields should first be developed and where, so that funds to support the program might be sought in the ensuing legislative sessions. The larger number of students for which this cooperative plan provides, together with the reimbursement feature under which each State pays for the number of students it contributes, makes possible the maintenance of the highest scholastic standards in the cooperating institutions.

In 1948, the Governors of the Western States made a beginning in the development of a similar program for their region, for the same purposes and for the same reasons. Thirteen States developed a regional compact; in 1953 six States had given their approval, and by 1959 the number had increased to twelve. The Compact now includes all eligible jurisdictions except Hawaii whose adherence is expected. One of the activities under the Compact is a contract program for out-of-state professional training. It was early agreed that costs to the States per student should be uniform. In the case of medical education, the figure was set at $2,000 per student per year, with dental education at $1,800 and veterinary medicine at $1,200. The Compact provides that the Commission shall "first endeavor to provide adequate facilities in the fields of dentistry, medicine, public health, and veterinary medicine and may undertake similar activities in other professional and graduate fields." In 1958–1959, 244 students were receiving training under this program, and an increase to 327 was expected for 1959–1960.

The experience of Wyoming in medical education will serve to illustrate how the program works. In February, 1950, the Wyoming legislature authorized its State university to contract with out-of-state schools for the training of Wyoming students in certain public health fields— medicine, dentistry, veterinary medicine, and nursing. Under this authorization, the University negotiated a contract with the University of Colorado School of Medicine under the terms of which:

> Colorado agreed to accept a specified number of qualified medical students who are Wyoming residents, and Wyoming agreed to pay Colorado the full cost of their training. Wyoming, in return, can require each student to shoulder a portion of the cost as "tuition." Thus, from one point of view, the University of Wyoming has added a school of medicine "away from home." Colorado, on the other hand, can expand its staff and equipment, thus strengthening the training program for all its students at no additional cost to Colorado taxpayers. This simple bilateral arrangement points the way toward a solution of the West's perplexing dilemma in the field of higher education.[37]

The New England Board of Higher Education was established in 1955 under the New England Higher Education Compact, ten years after a similar organization had been set up in the South and six years after the one in the West. The purposes and structure of the three agencies are alike in many ways, though not identical. In all, thirty-five of the fifty States are now members of one of these interstate regional compacts. The New England Board consists of eighteen members, three from each of the six States which have joined the compact by legislative vote. The administrative costs are met by appropriations from the member States in proportion to their population. The Board also seeks funds from other sources to support its program of educational research. Its purpose is to improve and increase educational opportunities in higher education, both public and private, for the youth of the New England region through the establishment and maintenance of a coordinated educational program.[38]

The Problem of Responsiveness and Responsibility

The rapid multiplication of interstate agencies has not taken place without attracting some attention or without engendering a certain amount of criticism. Although many of the compact agencies have been notably successful and compared with other undertakings, both public

[37] Council of State Governments, *Western Regional Cooperation in Higher Education: A Proposed Program* (Chicago, 1951).

[38] See the Board's annual report for 1959, *Three Years of Regional Cooperation in Higher Education* (Winchester, Mass., 1959).

and private, conspicuously well administered, they have been subjected to a barrage of criticism, much of it based upon sheer ignorance.[39] Those who are connected with the movement and know that the charges are without foundation realize that it may be desirable to modify certain conditions, probably unavoidable in a relatively new development, which seem to provide justification for the charges.

There are numerous different types of compacts in existence, formulated for a wide variety of purposes. A survey made in New York in 1960 disclosed at least four different types. Some were purely technical, some regulatory, some study and advisory, and still others were charged with definite administrative responsibilities. Classifying the findings in another way, it was found that out of thirty compacts to which the State was a party, eight were in the nature of boundary settlements and agreements; nine provided for administrative cooperation in procedural matters, with or without an agency; and thirteen more were engaged in the performance of such specific functions as the allocation of waters, fisheries administration, and forest fire protection, all with an agency. The disturbing thing was that they were not as closely geared into the State governmental structure as might be desirable.

On the basis of these findings, the survey team made recommendations along three lines, and the administration has already met with some measure of success in securing their adoption. The objectives of the new legislation are threefold: (1) to assign responsibility for each interstate agency to the appropriate department in the executive branch of government; (2) to assign the head of that department, when legally possible, as the chairman or leader of the State delegation to the interstate agency in question, for the purpose of achieving a coordination of the interstate and intrastate interests in the functional area and of including the budgetary needs of the agency as an item in the department budget; (3) to make the compact agencies definitely a part of the State government, not an appendage vaguely and uncertainly associated with it.

By arrangement with the chairman of the State Commission on Interstate Cooperation, the State committee for each compact agency will henceforth consist of nine persons—three members from the department to which the agency is attached, three from the assembly, and three from the State senate. The primary purpose of all of these changes has been to achieve better integration of interstate programs within the State, and more effective cooperative relationships with other States.

[39] For an authoritative discussion of these matters, see Leach, Richard H., and Sugg, Redding S., Jr., *The Administration of Interstate Compacts* (Baton Rouge: Louisiana State University Press, 1959) and Professor Leach's address before the Conference on Interstate Agencies, printed in *State Government*, Summer, 1961, pp. 199–204.

Federal Interest in Interstate Compacts

There has always been a recognition of the Federal interest—or of a possible Federal interest—in interstate compacts, but several developments since World War II give new significance to this problem. The constitutional requirement for consent was predicated upon the idea that Congress should have an opportunity to negative any proposed compact in which a proper Federal interest was violated or in which it appeared that a group of States was attempting to "gang up" on the Federal government. Since such cases are actually so rare as to be almost nonexistent, Congress has for many years given its consent in advance to certain compacts or types of compacts, as shown in the table on page 609. There has been some question as to whether Congressional consent is necessary at all for certain types of compacts, the prevailing view being that it should be required only in those instances in which a Federal interest is involved.[40]

There have been occasional questions involving constitutionality, but these have normally been resolved in favor of the compact.[41] Where Federal funds are involved, there has never been any question of the right of the Federal government to ascertain whether or not these funds have been properly used. Although Federal policy regarding compacts has not in the past greatly restricted their use, there are increasing indications that the Federal attitude, and particularly the attitude of Congress, "has become critical, if not actually hostile."[42] There is urgent need not only

[40] Based upon the doctrine of *Virginia* v. *West Virginia,* 11 Wallace 39 (1870). After extended debate on the Southern Regional Education Compact, the Senate took no action on the ground that Congressional approval was not essential in the case of compacts for the accomplishment of purposes which were clearly within the limits of State powers. See Dunbar, Leslie, "Interstate Compacts and Congressional Consent," *Virginia Law Review,* October, 1950, pp. 753–763; Ferguson, Jo M., "The Legal Basis for a Southern University: Interstate Agreements Without Congressional Consent," *Kentucky Law Journal,* March, 1950, pp. 347–359; Zimmermann, Frederick L., and Wendell, Mitchell, "Congressional Consent to the States," *State Government,* April, 1949, pp. 116–119, 125–127; and Leach, Richard H., "The Federal Government and Interstate Compacts," *Fordham Law Review,* February, 1961, pp. 421–446.

[41] The Supreme Court held, for instance, that the provisions of the Waterfront Commission Compact were not in violation of Amendment XIV in *Lineham* v. *Waterfront Commission of New York Harbor,* 74 Sup. Ct. 623 (1954). For other instances of constitutional interpretation, see Zimmermann and Wendell, *State Government,* April, 1949.

[42] Leach, *Fordham Law Review,* February, 1961, p. 433. This view is supported by data presented in the *Report of the New York Joint Legislative Committee on Interstate Cooperation, 1958* (Albany: Legislative Document No. 45, 1958), pp. 35, 42–43.

ADVANCE CONGRESSIONAL APPROVAL FOR INTERSTATE COMPACTS

Year	Subject	Notes
1911	Forest conservation and forest fire protection.	Weeks Act of 1911.
1917	Conservation of boundary waters and pollution control.	Minnesota, North Dakota, and South Dakota.
1936	Development and maintenance of parks and recreational areas.	. . . . .
1938	Apportionment of waters of the Red River of the North.	Minnesota, North Dakota, and South Dakota
	Control of fisheries in the Great Lakes.	Any two or more of eight States: New York, Pennsylvania, Ohio, Indiana, Illinois, Michigan, Wisconsin, and Minnesota.
1942	Mutual assistance in prevention of crime.	. . . . .
1948	Conservation of water and prevention and control of water pollution.	. . . . .

for a clarification of Federal policy but for the development of a more cooperative and understanding attitude on the part of the Federal government than seems presently to prevail, if compacts are to continue to serve as useful tools of the States.

One recent development which raises new and important questions with respect to Federal participation in this field grows out of the amazing proceedings which took place in the House Judiciary Committee and in a Federal District Court in New York in 1960, in connection with the investigation of the Port of New York Authority. The chairman of the Committee and the attorney for the government, in prosecuting the Executive Director of the Authority on a contempt of Congress citation, took the position that the power of Congress under the compact clause was broader than that under the commerce clause, and that Congress was a sort of senior and controlling partner in any and all interstate compacts to which it had given its consent. Such a doctrine, were it to be sanctioned by the courts, would represent an alarming invasion of the powers and prerogatives of the States in the American federal system.

A compact is a device under which two or more States act together as one in dealing with a common problem. The power of the Federal government over the compact is precisely the same as its power would be over any one of the signatory States acting individually in the same situation. As a result of the proceedings involving the Port of New York Authority, there may be an important judicial decision, a decision which hopefully will uphold the position here stated.

A second development has to do with the growing tendency to draw the Federal government into interstate compacts as an equal partner, a development characterized by the Council of State Governments as one of "the two most significant pioneering developments in the compact field at the present time." This is not entirely new, because the central government has been a functioning member of the Potomac River and a few other compacts since their inception, but there now appears to be a significant expansion of this concept of interstate-Federal cooperation. An excellent example is to be noted in the new Interstate-Federal Compact for the Delaware River Basin.[43] The explanation of this development is, of course, that the compacting States want to be able to draw upon the experience of central government personnel and to use its power and authority as an aid in accomplishing the objectives stated in the compact. There is nothing wrong with doing so, but it is a relatively new pattern in the framing of interstate compacts, one which is likely to raise interesting and possibly important questions.

BIBLIOGRAPHICAL NOTES

Interstate Cooperation. In the early 1930's, two significant pioneer works appeared in the field of interstate cooperation. The volume by Professor Emerson D. Fite, *Government by Cooperation* (New York: The Macmillan Co., 1932) was probably the first ever written on the general subject. It deals with the cooperation of the States in forming the national government in 1789, then in turn with Federal-State, interstate, and other forms of cooperation that have since developed, presenting an interesting array of facts and showing widespread tendencies toward cooperation in areas that, up to that time, were largely unexplored by social scientists.

A volume by W. Brooke Graves, *Uniform State Action: A Possible Substitute for Centralization* (Chapel Hill: University of North Carolina Press, 1934) attempts to present a comprehensive picture of the nature, extent, and effectiveness of the various methods of interstate cooperation—executive, legislative, and judicial—then in use, emphasizing the possibilities for the further development and use of such devices as an alternative to further Federal centralization. The book happened to appear at exactly the right time to be of use to Senator Henry W. Toll who was then groping for ways and means of making the American Legislators' Association a stronger and more effective organization. The volume of the *Annals of the American Academy of Social and Political Science* for January, 1940, devoted to Intergovernmental Relations in the United States, also contained a section on interstate cooperation.

[43] Delaware River Basin Advisory Committee, *Interstate-Federal Compact for the Delaware River Basin* (Philadelphia, February, 1961). The text of the Compact and a full analysis appear in a special bulletin, *The Interstate-Federal Compact* (Philadelphia: Water Resources Association of the Delaware River Basin, February, 1961); for an excellent treatment of the whole Delaware River problem, see Roscoe C. Martin, *River Basin Development and the Delaware* (Syracuse: Syracuse University Press, 1960).

COSGO Historical Background. The history and development of the Council of State Governments and its subsidiary and affiliate organizations can be traced in the successive editions of *The Book of the States*, published biennially since 1935. Similarly, W. Brooke Graves, in successive editions of *American State Government* (Boston: D. C. Heath & Co., 1936, 1941, 1946, and 1953), has attempted to summarize significant developments in the growth of this organization. An invaluable source for the early history is Henry W. Toll, *Orientation: COSGO, 1925–1959*, prepared in limited edition for presentation copies (Denver, December, 1958).

Interstate Compacts. In a literature so voluminous, it is most useful to select several outstanding titles dealing with different aspects of the subject. The historical aspects of interstate compacts have been dealt with in three publications by the Council of State Governments: *Interstate Compacts, 1783–1956* (Chicago, July, 1956); *Congressional Consent to Interstate Compacts: State and Federal Statutes Authorizing Compacts* (Chicago, 1936); and Frederick L. Zimmermann and Mitchell Wendell, *The Interstate Compact Since 1925* (Chicago, August, 1950). The legal aspects of the problem are ably discussed in Vincent V. Thursby, *Inter-State Cooperation: A Study of the Interstate Compact* (Washington: Public Affairs Press, 1953) and in Frederick L. Zimmermann and Mitchell Wendell, *The Law and Use of Interstate Compacts* (Chicago: Council of State Governments, 1961). Clifford H. Stone, long secretary of the Colorado Water Conservation Board, edited *Interstate Cooperation* (Denver: Colorado Water Conservation Board, 1946), an excellent compilation of articles on interstate compacts selected from various sources. For the only careful analysis of the problems of administration now existing, see Richard H. Leach and Redding S. Sugg, Jr., *The Administration of Interstate Compacts* (Baton Rouge: Louisiana State University Press, 1959). In February, 1961, the Council of State Governments called a conference of representatives of interstate agencies to meet in Chicago to discuss administrative problems; a summary of the proceedings was put out by the Council.

There are three excellent monographs on particular compact agencies, two on the Port of New York Authority, another on the Southern Regional Education Board; see Erwin W. Bard, *The Port of New York Authority* (New York: Columbia University Press, 1941) and Frederick L. Bird, *A Study of the Port of New York Authority* (New York: Dun & Bradstreet, 1949). The Authority itself prepared and published *Twenty-fifth Anniversary: The Port of New York Authority, 1921–1946* (New York, 1946). See also Redding S. Sugg, Jr. and George H. Jones, *The Southern Regional Education Board: Ten Years of Regional Cooperation in Higher Education* (Baton Rouge: Louisiana State University Press, 1960).

CHAPTER XVIII

The Role of Regionalism in
a Federal System

The leaders demanded by the challenge of regionalism must have two very special attributes. First, they must have the capacity to see society whole, and to view government in proper perspective against its societal backdrop. This means, among other things and specifically, that they must be able to pass by emotional and sentimental attachments in favor of devotion to the "larger concept of community." Second, they must not be fearful of things new and untried, for the times require bold and daring thought. Leonard White has called attention to the fact that the States produced many notable inventions in government during the first third of the century. The time is right for a new series of inventions, this time at the level of the region. Here is a frontier worthy of our very best in public leadership. Here lies a challenge to justify a man in resigning from the United States Senate to seek—and win—a governorship.

The New Regionalism is not new in the sense that regionalism itself is a novel concept, but only in the sense that the two complexes of problems here identified as requiring regional solutions are new, or at any rate newly arrived at the point where regional solutions are mandatory. Regionalism is new because the makeshift measures of the past will no longer suffice, because nothing less than bold action in new directions will prove adequate to the need. "A journey of a thousand miles begins with but a single step." The initial step requires recognition of the impact of the new regionalism on the practice of federalism, and of the necessity of modifying our federal system in deference to the needs of the region.[1]

[1] Martin, Roscoe C., *Federalism and Regionalism* (Houston: The Rice Institute, 1957), pp. 29-30.

A review of the historical background of the States shows that they have often failed in the past and that they are ill-suited to many of the needs of modern government. Whether or not one agrees with the extreme demands of those who see no solution for the shortcomings of the States except their abolition, one must admit that some modification of existing practices must be made unless, as Elihu Root predicted about half a century ago, they are to lose their power.

Of several available solutions of the problem, three will be considered in this chapter. If the States are retained in their present form, they may be supplemented by administrative regions established for purposes for which the States do not appear to be well suited. The Federal government has done this extensively, usually by executive action, in the development of an elaborate system of field administration. Another form of subnational regionalism may be used for river valley development, either of a compulsory form imposed upon the area by act of Congress, as in the case of the Tennessee Valley Authority, or of a voluntary form developed through interstate cooperation under an interstate compact. Finally, this is an age in which metropolitan regionalism already looms large, and in which this form of regionalism is developing with tremendous momentum.

Regionalism has been defined as a means of territorial decentralization of power within a state. Administrative regionalism seeks to reconcile governmental area and function. The quest for accommodation, the search for the optimum in practicality and effectiveness is continuous and never-ending. "New functions," says Professor Roscoe C. Martin, "are sought to be placed in units equipped to discharge them, and old functions are in constant movement in their search for areas more nearly adequate to their needs. On the other hand, governmental areas themselves are in process of continuous, though usually at any particular time quite modest, adaptation to new needs and demands." [2] Examples are to be noted in the steady decline in the number of school districts since World War II and the increase in the number of special districts for a variety of other purposes.

The fact remains, however, that Americans have only rarely been regionally minded, although they have sometimes been sectionally minded. Insofar as they have accepted regionalism at all, they have done so grudgingly and unwillingly. Yet regions are, as Professor Martin has said, *sui generis*. They are partly the result of geography (river valleys), partly the product of our urban-industrial culture. While the times demand a new approach to the problem, Americans, normally a politically inventive people, have failed signally in their efforts to cope with it. There are many reasons for their failure, including various traditional and senti-

[2] Martin, pp. 11–12.

mental deterrents to constructive action, intellectual or human limitations, and legal barriers.[3]

There are many possible approaches to the study of the problems of regionalism. Political scientists have long shown some interest in them, regarding them as one aspect of their discipline. Many still regard regionalism, particularly metropolitan regionalism, as being largely if not exclusively a governmental phenomenon. Recently, representatives of other disciplines have entered the field. Some economists take the position that the problems of the metropolis are almost exclusively economic problems; one, for instance, has been heard to assert that nothing that any governmental body might do would make the least bit of difference in the form, shape, or character of the New York metropolitan district. Then come the behaviorists to assert that the "governmentalists" are so wide of the mark as to be almost totally unrealistic in their approach to and appraisal of metropolitan problems.

There is some logic in each of these approaches, but rather than argue their relative merits,[4] this chapter will deal primarily with the governmental aspects of regionalism in this country, including metropolitan regionalism.

REGIONALISM IN FIELD ADMINISTRATION

The idea of using regions for administrative purposes is not new either in Europe or in America. In many European countries, it has been common for at least a hundred years; historically, it is much older, having existed in Italy under the Romans, in Manchuria under the Chinese, and in Crimea under the Russians. In the United States, regionalism has often been confused with sectionalism, and hence it becomes important to distinguish clearly between the two. No one has better stated the difference than Professor Howard W. Odum when he said that regionalism "envisions the nation first, making the total national culture the final arbiter, while sectionalism seeks the region first and the nation afterward." While sectionalism has long been strong in certain parts of the country, it is only recently that regionalism has been advanced by serious students as an end to be fostered and encouraged.

[3] Discussed in Martin, pp. 17–20.

[4] Their merits are discussed and to some extent evaluated in Martin, Roscoe C., and Price, Douglas, *The Metropolis and Its Problems*, pp. 25–35 (Maxwell Graduate School of Citizenship and Public Affairs, Syracuse University, Syracuse, 1960).

Background of the Problem

The last century was a period of tremendous expansion in the role of government. The central government not only increased the number and expanded the scope of the services it performed, but in addition subsidized the States for the carrying on of many State and local functions. The old-line functions were, prior to 1900, foreign affairs, defense, regulation of commerce, the postal service, promotion of agriculture, veterans' pensions and welfare, river and harbor improvement, and the administration of the public lands. These have now been expanded to include scientific research and development (much of it for defense), atomic energy, conquest of outer space, river basin development, direct payments to farmers for crop controls and soil conservation, and a nationwide system of veterans' hospitals. Many entirely new functions have been added, including social security, railroad retirement, regulation of industrial relations, aeronautics, radio and television, and rural electrification. In addition, a wide range of grants-in-aid has been established for public health and welfare, public education, and a variety of urban and metropolitan area problems such as air and water pollution, housing, slum clearance, and urban redevelopment.

These functional expansions and innovations have brought with them significant new developments in administrative arrangements. With such notable exceptions as the post office, revenue and land offices, and army and navy posts and installations, the operations of the central government were largely confined to Washington. Now, however, of more than 2,500,000 Federal civilian employees in 1962, only 255,000 were stationed in Washington—a ratio of approximately one in ten; the remainder, with the exception of some 160,000 serving outside Continental United States, were scattered in field offices and installations throughout the fifty States. Of these, approximately 184,000 were at duty stations in New York State. The Department of Defense with its three branches and its many installations accounts for approximately half of the civilian employees, the Post Office Department for about one-fourth, and other departments and agencies for the remaining quarter. The Department of Agriculture has over 100,000 employees, and other departments such as Health, Education, and Welfare have representatives in virtually every city and town in the nation.

Departments and agencies with nationwide responsibilities, performing functions requiring contacts with large numbers of citizens and having hundreds of officers and employees to organize and supervise in the field, had to face major decisions on the regional and district organization of their staffs, and had to select suitable centers for area, regional, zone, or district offices. The problems connected with this dispersion of Federal agencies was first studied seriously during the 1930's. At that time, the so-called alphabetical agencies of the New Deal were establishing field offices wherever their duties required them, resulting in confusion to the public and to the agencies themselves. This uncoordinated mapping of separate field office arrangements to suit the needs of each agency led to some consideration of plans to integrate the various schemes.

No one can read the proposals for the establishment of regional government in this country without being impressed by the lack of agreement among the authors either as to the number of regions required or as to the basis upon which they should be established. This, in itself, might tend to some extent to discredit the proposals, but for a good many years the Federal government has utilized a field organization for the administration of many of its programs. While the States have been used for many administrative purposes, especially in the older services, largely as a matter of convenience, there are many newer services for which zones, districts, regions, or areas have been established without much regard for State boundary lines. There are literally dozens of Federal activities and services in the conduct of which an elaborate system of area administration has been developed.

Since there is no uniform basis for reporting data of this kind, it is difficult to determine exactly how many such units actually exist at any given time. An analysis of data such as that presented in any recent edition of the *United States Organization Manual* reveals a total of not less than 1,500 and probably not more than 1,800. Although, as noted, the States form the basis for the field organization for many purposes, a kind of subnational regionalism has been developed for others when a unit smaller than the Nation but larger than the States is desired. Some two dozen departments, agencies, or programs function with a field organization of less than ten zones, districts, or regions, accounting for approximately 160 offices, while a slightly smaller number of departments and agencies in the ten to nineteen range accounted for 246 offices. At the top of the scale, nine agencies with more than fifty field offices each accounted for a total of 505.

Although it might seem reasonable to suppose that most Federal departments and agencies having a field establishment would tend to select the same cities for their offices, this is only partly true. Because of wide variations in the character of the programs to be administered and the clientele to be served, the same cities are chosen, if at all, largely by accident. Although there is no standard pattern and no central unifying or coordinating force, Federal field offices do tend to cluster in cities that are strategically situated to serve as a center for a considerable surrounding area in addition to the city proper and its metropolitan area population.

A significant study along this line was made in 1935 by the National Resources Committee.[5] At that time, it was found that there were seventy-four Federal agencies of bureau status or higher that had sets of regional areas, and that there were 108 separate regional schemes in operation, with numbers of regional field offices ranging from one to 307. Eighty-two regional schemes had 1,300 field offices in 195 cities. When these were plotted on a map of the country, it was found that eight metropolitan centers led by a substantial margin in the frequency of choice by Federal agencies; thirteen cities were regional centers for twenty or more regional schemes. The board showed various plans for establishing multi-purpose regions, ranging in number from eight to twenty, each based upon a different principle such as metropolitan influence or administrative convenience.

Just as there are no established and accepted functional criteria for field organization, there are no criteria relating to the relationships between the central and field offices. In some agencies, authority is actually decentralized to a large extent, while in others the field offices are merely outposts for the execution of decisions made in Washington or for relaying such decisions to interested parties. Specifically, Federal Reserve Banks exercise a great degree of independent judgment in their respective areas, marked out years ago by law, rather than by executive action as is the usual practice. In some instances, these areas are no longer suitable, as in marginal zones which are nearer to a branch bank other than the one in whose area they happened to be included.

This situation may be contrasted with the now liquidated Reconstruction Finance Corporation whose field employees, it used to be said, could not wipe their noses without obtaining permission from Washington. To a certain extent, the nature of each major activity to be administered tends to dictate its own requirements regarding relationships between the central office and the field. A relationship of a still different type may be observed in the district offices of the United States Corps of Engineers which, working in close cooperation with Governors, and Mayors, and Members of Congress, form a type of administrative regionalism of their own, performing a peculiar function and invoking through their procedures profound substantive effects on the public works policy of the United States.

[5] *Regional Factors in National Planning* (Washington, 1935). See also Graves, W. Brooke, *Intergovernmental Relations in the United States: A Selected Bibliography* (Washington, 1956), pp. 32–49.

SUBNATIONAL REGIONALISM

The Compulsory or Authority Type

The Tennessee Valley Authority stems from operations begun during World War I, when Wilson Dam was constructed in the middle Tennessee River to provide power with which to transform rich deposits of nitrate into munitions. At the end of the war, when the national government held some 2,300 acres of land, two nitrate plants, a power house, and Wilson Dam, a heated controversy developed regarding the use or disposition that should be made of this property. The late Senator George W. Norris of Nebraska, often referred to as the father of TVA, for years resisted efforts to turn this property over to private interests, advocating instead the development of a broad regional program for the natural resources of the area under public ownership.

This became possible in 1933, under the leadership of President Roosevelt. The legislation establishing the TVA aimed at improving the navigability of the Tennessee River, promoting flood control in the Tennessee Valley, and providing for the reforestation and the proper use of marginal lands within the valley. Although the project, now more than a quarter of a century old, has been administered with conspicuous success and to the great benefit of the people residing in the area, the controversy regarding this particular pattern of organization for river valley development still rages. The development of good relations with State and local units has from the beginning been an important characteristic of TVA administration.[6]

In the years following the establishment of the TVA, a tremendous number of valley authority bills were introduced in Congress, covering at one time or another virtually every major river in the country. Some of the bills, notably those relating to the Columbia and Missouri Rivers, became the subject of prolonged and heated controversy.[7] None of them were enacted; actually, none of them came even close to enactment due to the great influence of the private power industry whose reasoning ap-

[6] See 48 S.L. 58, and for important amendments, 49 S.L. 1075 (1935); 52 S.L. 1083 (1939); 40 S.L. 626 (1940); Norwood, A. M., comp., *Congressional Hearings, Reports, and Documents Relating to the Tennessee Valley Authority, 1933–1952: A Documentary History* (Knoxville, 1954) and Hubbard, Preston J., *Origins of the TVA: The Muscle Shoals Controversy, 1920–1932* (Nashville: Vanderbilt University Press, 1961).

[7] See Clark, Wesley C., "Proposed 'Valley Authority' Legislation," *American Political Science Review*, February, 1946, pp. 62–70.

pears to be: The TVA is splendid; the TVA has done an outstanding job; the TVA has served the people well; but the TVA idea ought not to be extended into any other areas!

In the 1940's, as a matter of fact, there was a good deal of activity in this field. The multi-purpose nature of water resources development was recognized in 1943 by the establishment of the Federal Interagency River Basin Committee, which in turn established regional interagency committees in the Missouri, Columbia, and Colorado Basins, with provisions for State participation. This burst of activity was undoubtedly induced by hard and cruel facts which, however, were soon largely forgotten, as evidenced by the fact that no serious attempt has been made since to establish adequate programs in these areas.

Briefly, this was the background. In 1927, the Mississippi Valley sustained a property damage estimated at $301,121,000, accompanied by a loss of 327 lives, all resulting from floods of the Mississippi River and its tributaries. A decade later the figure rose to $424,673,000, and 142 persons lost their lives. By 1947, forty more lives had been added to the death toll and property loss for the first half of that year totalled $156 million. Obviously, something needed to be done, and steps were taken to pool the resources of the Federal government and the States concerned in an effort to expand the flood control work which had been undertaken by the Federal government alone in 1927. Taking the TVA system of water storage as an example, plans were made to erect a series of dams and levies along the main tributaries, harnessing the Missouri, Arkansas, Red, Cumberland, and Ohio Rivers, in addition to the Upper Mississippi region.

A conflict soon developed between two schools of thought regarding the proper method of procedure. One approach favored by President Truman urged centralized direction of all activities by a Missouri Valley Authority for the development of the entire basin, as was established in TVA, but President Eisenhower consistently opposed this plan. At any rate, such programs as have been developed in the area have been carried on through a cooperative arrangement that some have regarded as a pattern for the handling of similar problems in other river valleys. Cooperative efforts have resulted in limited progress in a field where urgent needs indicate the desirability of a far more extensive and more energetic attack upon the basic problems involved.

The Commission on Intergovernmental Relations (Kestnbaum) noted in its *Report* in 1955 some encouraging trends, aimed at achieving unity in water resources planning and development at both National and State levels. Recent amendments to the Federal flood control acts provide for some coordination between the Army Engineers, the Department of the Interior, the Department of Agriculture, and the Federal Power Commission. All flood control acts, beginning with the Act of 1944, have provided for State review of and comment upon programs and projects.

Voluntary Cooperation

Examples of regional cooperation on a voluntary basis are to be found in the Interstate Commission on the Delaware River Basin (INCODEL), the Ohio River Sanitary Commission (ORSANCO, superseding the Interstate Commission on the Ohio River Basin, known as INCOHIO), the Interstate Commission on the Potomac River Basin (INCOPOT), and the Missouri Basin Inter-Agency Committee. The first three are joint governmental agencies created by interstate compact, INCODEL in 1936 by the States of New York, New Jersey, Pennsylvania, and Delaware for the purpose of formulating, adopting, and executing policies for the utilization and development of the natural resources of the basin of the Delaware River and its tributaries. Organized under auspices of the Council of State Governments and the four State commissions on interstate cooperation, it represented an attempt on the part of the States concerned to do themselves, voluntarily, some of the things that were obviously needed in the river basin development. Its cooperative relations with the National Resources Committee were unusual at the time of its establishment.[8]

As expected, the organization has had problems and difficulties in its quarter-century of existence, but it has accomplished much. First of these river basin commissions to be established, INCODEL was soon followed by several other similar organizations. The Potomac River agency was established in 1940, composed of four States and the District of Columbia, the Ohio River agency in 1948 by eight States. As shown in the preceding chapter on interstate relations, a sizable number of such compacts have been developed in the last two decades.

The Missouri Basin Inter-Agency Committee had its origin in 1943 when four Federal agencies—the Departments of Agriculture, Interior, Army, and the Federal Power Commission—undertook surveys of the Missouri Valley. Four years later the Department of Commerce was added to the group which then became known by its present name. The Gov-

[8] See Logue, Thomas A., "Regional Machinery for Regional Planning," *State Government*, June, 1937, pp. 109–110; Pitkin, Francis A., "Interstate Cooperation: A Deterrent to Expansion of the Federal Government," *Torch*, July, 1953, pp. 3–7; Pritchett, C. Herman, "Regional Authorities Through Interstate Compacts," *Social Forces*, December, 1935, pp. 200–210; and Robinson, David W., "Voluntary Regionalism in the Control of Water Resources," *Annals of the American Academy of Political and Social Science*, January, 1940, pp. 116–123.

ernors of ten States were included, five on a regular basis (Missouri, Montana, Nebraska, North Dakota, and Wyoming), five on a "sitting in" basis (Colorado, Iowa, Kansas, Minnesota, and South Dakota) at the monthly meetings of the Committee. The Federal members contribute a broad and expert knowledge of the technique required for full and comprehensive utilization of water resources, while the State representatives offer a more intensive knowledge of the desires and interests of the people of the basin, thereby bringing to the engineering problem a blend of human relations so important in popular government.

The Federal Flood Control Act of 1944, under which the Committee functions, enacted the much discussed Pick-Sloan Plan; it provides for the comprehensive and multi-purpose development of the river. Irrigation and domestic consumption uses have priority upstream, while flood control, navigation, and hydroelectric power are all entitled to fair recognition downstream. The latter is particularly important; the dams are useful for flood control purposes, although if far enough downstream they do prevent navigation. Unanimity is sought as a basis for Committee action. Matters that cannot be so resolved are referred to the parent Committee, similarly constituted insofar as Federal agencies are concerned, but having the broader responsibility for the problems of all river valleys in the nation. There is a continuous interchange of correspondence and engineering data between the various Federal and State officials, through which an unusual degree of coordination has been achieved. One hundred and five dams were projected in the Missouri Valley which comprises one-sixth of the United States, and six were under construction in 1947. It was estimated that the entire program for the Missouri River would cost about $1 billion, about half of the estimate for the entire Mississippi Basin.

This type of cooperative effort, like the interstate compact agencies, illustrates a relatively new and interesting form of voluntary regionalism. Neither type has accomplished as much as its supporters hoped it could. The Inter-Agency Committee is obviously weak, and one observer characterized one of the compact agencies as "a grim joke." Conceivably, both could be strengthened, as INCODEL was recently when it was reorganized. The most significant thing about both types of organization is that, at an intermediate level between the individual States and the Nation, they can function with an overall view of the problems of a whole river valley.

METROPOLITAN REGIONALISM

During the period of more than a century that metropolitan area problems have existed in the United States, Professor Paul Studenski reports that there have been five periods of especially concentrated action: (1) the late 1840's and the early 1850's; (2) the late 1860's and the early 1870's; (3) the 1890's and the opening of the new century; (4) the boom of the 1920's; and (5) the present period of post World War II business expansion and population growth. Professor Studenski observes that:

> During the first three periods and the years intervening, metropolitan area problems were solved mostly by annexation to the city of its suburban territory or by consolidation with it of suburban governments. The most spectacular cases were Philadelphia's consolidation of 1854, Pittsburgh's annexations of 1867 and 1907, Chicago's annexations of 1889, and New York City's consolidation of 1898.[9]

As of 1960, there were in California two great cities to which no one had given a name. One stretches from Santa Barbara to the Mexican border and from the Pacific to the edge of the California desert. It is a single, solid complex roughly the size of the State of Maryland. The other covers the triangle from Santa Rosa to Salinas to Sacramento. It occupies an area about the size of the Commonwealth of Massachusetts. On the East Coast, another stretches along the Atlantic seaboard and inland from Portsmouth to Norfolk. As long ago as 1902, H. G. Wells gave us a name for these sprawling cities. "Enough has been said," he wrote, "to demonstrate that 'town' and 'city' will be, in truth, terms as obsolete as 'mailcoach.' For these new areas that will grow out of them, we want a term, and . . . we may for our present purposes call these coming 'urban regions.' " [10]

An urban region—metropolitan region is the term now most frequently used—may be defined as a densely populated area including a principal city and its suburban and/or satellite communities, each politically and administratively distinct, but physically, socially, economically, and culturally part of a common whole. The larger centers of popula-

[9] Studenski, Paul, "Metropolitan Areas 1960," *National Civic Review*, October, 1960, pp. 467–473. For an analysis of developments up to 1930, see his *Government of Metropolitan Areas* (New York: National Municipal League, 1930).

[10] Quoted from Governor Edmund G. Brown, "State-County Cooperation," *Urban County Congress* (Washington: National Association of County Officials, 1959), pp. 16–19.

tion have continued to grow, not only without regard to geographical boundaries of the minor political subdivisions within the States—counties, cities, boroughs, townships—but without regard to the boundaries of the States themselves. These metropolitan areas have problems of their own, quite different and distinct from those of the rural areas which still dominate the legislative bodies. Neither group, urban or rural, shows much interest in, understanding of, or concern for the problems of the other.

The metropolitan area problem is, undoubtedly, the most pressing domestic problem confronting the nation today. In its simplest terms, it is the result of the unprecedented, unregulated, and largely unanticipated growth and concentration of population in and around the 212 SMA's (Standard Metropolitan Areas) established by the Bureau of the Census. Each city or area having a city of 50,000 or more inhabitants constitutes an SMA; in some instances, two or more such cities may be included within a single area. On this basis, there were in 1950 approximately 84,500,000 people, or about half of the total population of the country, living in 168 metropolitan areas. The following statistics of growth since then and of prospective future growth, presented at a conference in Baltimore by a member of the Maryland State League of Municipalities, are almost staggering:

> For the five year period that ended in 1955, the population increase in metropolitan areas was approximately 11,500,000 and that of the rest of the country only 300,000. These 174 metropolitan areas contain 14 per cent of all local governments, nearly 60 per cent of our population and only 7 per cent of our continental area. 100,000,000 of our people make their homes in these areas. And, according to some population experts, there is no end in sight. By 1975 there may be 60,000,000 more metropolitan area residents. By the year 2000, our nation may have some 300,000,000 people with 220,000,000 concentrated in metropolitan areas. . . .
>
> Maryland is part of what some experts refer to as megalopolis, a continuous urban area stretching along the Atlantic Coast from Boston to Richmond. Within Maryland, there are two great metropolitan areas, Baltimore City and the suburban area of Washington, D.C. Separated by a distance of forty miles in a State of nearly 2,275,000 people, the Baltimore metropolitan area accounts for 1,400,000 citizens and suburban Washington, within the boundaries of Maryland, accounts for an additional 700,000 people. In other words, over 2,000,000 of the State's 2,275,000 people reside in these two metropolitan areas. Within a decade, it is expected that these two metropolitan areas will mesh. Within the Maryland portion of metropolitan Washington, D.C., there are forty municipal corporations, two counties, and special districts all too numerous to count.

Area Definitions by Federal Committee on Standard
Metropolitan Statistical Areas under the direction
of U. S. Bureau of the Budget.

Source: U.S. Department of Commerce,
Bureau of the Census

LEWISTON-AUBURN

UTICA-ROME
PORTLAND
ALBANY-
SCHENECTADY-
TROY
FITCHBURG-LEOMINSTER
LOWELL MANCHESTER
LAWRENCE-HAVERHILL
SPRINGFIELD-CHICOPEE-
HOLYOKE
BOSTON
BROCKTON
WORCESTER
FALL RIVER
NEW BEDFORD
PROVIDENCE-PAWTUCKET
NEW LONDON-GROTON-
NORWICH

GREEN BAY
MUSKEGON BAY CITY
BUFFALO ROCHESTER
MILWAUKEE
MUSKEGON
HEIGHTS
SAGINAW
SYRACUSE
PITTSFIELD
MADISON
GRAND
RAPIDS
FLINT
CLEVELAND
BINGHAMTON
HARTFORD
WATERBURY
MERIDEN
DUBUQUE-
WATERLOO
RACINE
LANSING
DETROIT
LORAIN-
ELYRIA
ERIE
ALLENTOWN-BETHLEHEM-
EASTON
SCRANTON
NEW BRITAIN
NEW HAVEN
KENOSHA
KALAMAZOO
YOUNGSTOWN-
WARREN WILKES-BARRE-
HAZLETON
NEW YORK
NORWALK
AR RAPIDS
ROCKFORD
JACKSON ANN ARBOR
TOLEDO
STAMFORD
DES MOINES
CHICAGO
SOUTH BEND
FORT WAYNE
LIMA AKRON
HARRISBURG READING
TRENTON
PATERSON-CLIFTON-PASSAIC
DAVENPORT-
ROCK ISLAND-MOLINE
CHAMPAIGN-
URBANA
GARY-
HAMMOND-
EAST CHICAGO
CANTON
STEUBENVILLE-WEIRTON
JERSEY CITY
NEWARK
PEORIA
MUNCIE
COLUMBUS
WHEELING
YORK
ATLANTIC CITY
SPRINGFIELD
INDIANAPOLIS DAYTON
SPRINGFIELD PITTSBURGH
JOHNSTOWN
ALTOONA
WILMINGTON
PHILADELPHIA
OSEPH
DECATUR
TERRE HAUTE
HAMILTON-
MIDDLETOWN
LANCASTER
ANSAS CITY
CINCINNATI
BALTIMORE
WASHINGTON
ST. LOUIS
EVANSVILLE
HUNTINGTON-
ASHLAND
CHARLESTON
RICHMOND
NEWPORT NEWS-HAMPTON
NORFOLK-PORTSMOUTH
LOUISVILLE LEXINGTON
ROANOKE
LYNCHBURG
SPRINGFIELD
DURHAM
WINSTON-SALEM
RALEIGH
T SMITH
NASHVILLE
KNOXVILLE
GREENSBORO-
HIGH POINT
LITTLE ROCK-
NORTH LITTLE ROCK
MEMPHIS CHATTANOOGA
ASHEVILLE
CHARLOTTE
HUNTSVILLE
GREENVILLE
GADSDEN
ATLANTA
COLUMBIA
BIRMINGHAM
AUGUSTA
SHREVEPORT
TUSCALOOSA
MACON
CHARLESTON
MONROE
JACKSON
MONTGOMERY
COLUMBUS
SAVANNAH
ALBANY
MOBILE
BATON
ROUGE
PENSACOLA
JACKSONVILLE
LAKE
CHARLES
NEW ORLEANS
ORLANDO
BEAUMONT-
RT ARTHUR
TAMPA-ST. PETERSBURG
WEST PALM BEACH
FORT LAUDERDALE-HOLLYWOOD
MIAMI

SCALE

0   100   200   300   400 MILES

NGEN-

This phenomenon of metropolitan growth is by no means peculiar to the United States. A 1960 survey of the problem in the various countries of the world shows that the metropolitan areas "are capturing a very high proportion of the total increase accruing to the industrialized nations." [11] It may well be that the concept of the Standard Metropolitan Area may in the course of time become obsolete, as population growth continues and densely settled urban areas stretch unbroken for hundreds of miles. The essential elements in the definition of the metropolitan complex as presently conceived are large size, high population density, interdependence, fluidity of movement, and fractionated governments.[12]

Major Urban Area Problems

The metropolitan area problem is not a single problem, readily identifiable and easily defined. It is, in fact, like the metropolitan areas themselves, a complex of many problems. It includes questions of population growth and population movement, multiplicity of governmental units, of economic growth and development, of land planning and land utilization, of mass transit and commuter problems, water supply, the disposal of domestic and industrial wastes, and many more. Basic to an attack upon any or all of these problems is the development of organizations and procedures that are capable of effective action on an area-wide basis. The existing hodgepodge of governmental units within these areas makes it difficult if not impossible to develop and administer such programs; the concluding section of this chapter is devoted to the possible solutions of problems of administrative organization.

Political Organization. The problem of the multiplicity of units of local government presents itself again and again, not only in New York, Chicago, Los Angeles, and Philadelphia areas, but in many other metropolitan areas of lesser population. The Council of State Governments notes that "a complex welter of local governments serves the 140 [now 212] metropolitan areas. The total number in 1940 was 15,827 units. These include 1,741 municipalities, 272 counties, 895 townships, 11,822 school districts, and 1,097 special districts. In the New York area, for example, responsibility for public affairs is divided among 1,038 governments, including fourteen counties, seventy-eight townships, 285 municipalities, 520 school districts, and 141 special districts." [13] While it is true

[11] Gibbs, Jack P., and Schnore, Leo F., "Metropolitan Growth: An International Study," American Journal of Sociology, September, 1960, pp. 160–170.

[12] Gulick, Luther H., "Answers Wanted," Proceedings of the National Conference on Metropolitan Problems, 1956 (New York: Government Affairs Foundation, 1957), pp. 37–43.

[13] Council of State Governments, State-Local Relations (Chicago, 1946), pp. 187–188.

that the five counties—Kings, Queens, Bronx, Manhattan, and Richmond —have been consolidated into the Greater City of New York since 1898, it is also true that there are outside the city extensive areas in southeastern New York and on Long Island, in southwestern Connecticut and northern New Jersey, that are to all intents and purposes a part of the greater city—physically, socially, economically, and culturally—but that are politically as separate as it is possible to make them.

Similarly, the Philadelphia metropolitan area includes not only the five counties of southeastern Pennsylvania—Philadelphia, Bucks, Berks, Montgomery, and Delaware—but all of southern New Jersey south of Trenton and all of northern Delaware. Included within these dozen counties are more than 700 towns, townships, boroughs, and special districts of many types. In the Los Angeles area, where there are some thirty different types of local units of government, the number of such units in 1950 was reported to be 828, but by 1957 the number had been reduced to 319. In connection with this analysis, see the following table.

In a survey made in Chicago some thirty years ago, it was reported that there were, within a radius of fifty miles from State and Madison Streets, not less than 15,000 independent governing agencies carrying on the governmental functions incidental to the life of a community of some 3,500,000 people. These agencies have the power to collect taxes, to appropriate and spend money, and to incur debt. Metropolitan Chicago, the survey reported:

> extends into four different States, Illinois, Wisconsin, Indiana, and a corner of Michigan; it includes fifteen counties and an innumerable array of cities, villages, towns, townships, school districts, park districts,

GOVERNMENTAL UNITS IN THE FOUR LARGEST METROPOLITAN AREAS *

Type of Unit	New York–New Jersey–Connecticut	Chicago	Los Angeles–Long Beach	Philadelphia
Counties	17	6	2	7
Municipalities	367	246	95	140
Towns and Townships	182	114	. . .	199
School Districts	560	340	142	331
Special Districts	330	354	110	286
	1,456	1,060	349	963

* Figures from U.S. Bureau of the Census, *Census of Governments, 1962* (Washington, 1963), except for New York for which the following source was used: Davies, Audrey M., *Political Units in the New York Metropolitan Area* (New York: Institute of Public Administration, March, 1959).

drainage districts. . . . It is conservatively estimated that the population of the Chicago area in 1950 will approach 8,000,000.[14]

Although the population turned out to be somewhat less than anticipated, the number of governmental units had by 1962 been reduced to
1,060. These problems of regional organization are present, however, not
only in the centers of population in this country but in the great cities
all over the world.

Land Use Control. American cities today, particularly the older ones
with narrow streets, are struggling against virtual paralysis due to traffic
congestion. The number of registered passenger cars has increased to
more than 61,569,000, trucks and buses to some 12,299,000, making a total
as of 1960 of more than 73,868,000. Narrow streets designed for horse-
drawn vehicles are clogged both by the volume of traffic and by street
space devoted to parking, with or without parking meters. An already
acute situation promises to become steadily worse unless courageous
steps are taken to deal with it. There is, of course, no simple, complete,
and lasting solution, but there are various remedies that are being used
in an effort to cope with the problem.

One may well begin with the simple and obvious fact that parking
on narrow streets should be prohibited. Public ways were established to
carry traffic and to permit people and goods to be moved from one place
to another, not to impede traffic. It goes without saying that when street
parking is eliminated on busy downtown streets, adequate facilities for
off-street parking must be provided. This responsibility the city itself
must assume; citizens cannot be left to the tender mercies of the operators of parking lots and private parking garages. A solution in the smaller
cities may be found in large, well paved, municipal parking lots, conveniently located and operated at a nominal charge, and in the larger
cities, huge parking facilities, either above or below ground. A few cities
have been experimenting with fringe parking lots at nominal charges;
these both discourage private cars in the central business district and
increase the patronage of mass transit facilities.

When the congestion in the central city becomes too oppressive, those
who can stand it financially tend to move out, thereby withdrawing from
their liability for the support of the city government (unless the city
has a wage tax collectable from non-residents), leaving their property in
the hands of the next lower level in the economic scale. When the congestion becomes so objectionable that women no longer shop in town

[14] Merriam, Charles E., "Metropolitan Regions," an address in *University
of Chicago Record*, April, 1928, and in *Introductory General Course in the
Social Sciences* (Chicago: University of Chicago Bookstore, 1933), pp. 427–440,
on p. 428.

if they can avoid it, suburban shopping centers begin to thrive and business begins its exodus from the central city.

In times past, urban residents purchased all their needs at stores and shops in the central city. Now grocery stores, for instance, are rare in the central city area; one wonders where the people who live there purchase food supplies. Shopping areas with ample parking space, for the purchase of necessary personal and household needs, developed in urban residential and suburban areas, but residents of these areas now find it possible to satisfy all their ordinary needs in local stores and specialty shops, making shopping trips into the central city more and more infrequent. Lack of parking facilities, higher transit fares, and waste of time in transit have all had a significant influence in bringing about this change.

Department stores are no longer crowded. These and other central city business establishments were hard hit by the development of suburban shopping centers, built in cooperation with department stores [15] and chain stores on the one hand, and builders of residential properties on the other. Today, new residential properties are virtually unsalable in the absence of conveniently located, sufficiently large and diversified shopping centers. An important characteristic of all of these has been the provision of extensive parking facilities.

The decentralization of business in the urban area has not, however, been confined to department and chain stores. Suburban areas in many cities are also acquiring the headquarters offices of business concerns formerly located in the heart of the city, such as oil companies, insurance companies, contracting firms, and many others. Characteristically, these office buildings are located on campus-like sites, either in the open country or in the outskirts of the city, and they are normally developed individually by different companies for their own use. The activities in these buildings are administrative and clerical; there are no manufacturing, sales, service, or similar commercial operations, which are reserved for

[15] A survey made by the Regional Plan Association of New York in 1953 found fourteen suburban branch stores as of 1939, seventy-two as of 1953. The trend has everywhere been the same, and has continued at an accelerated pace. Wanamaker's, long with central city locations in New York and Philadelphia, abandoned the former after fifty-eight years, and since 1954 has operated suburban stores in Yonkers and Wynnewood. Macy's now operates six stores in the New York area, Hecht's five in the Washington area. Branches have been established by both Hutzler's and Hochschild, Kohn of Baltimore, Dayton's of Minneapolis, Shoeneman's of St. Paul, and many, many more. Fine specialty shops, formerly only in New York, now have numerous branches, not so much in other cities as in the shopping centers surrounding them. For a good discussion of this whole problem, see Staniford, Edward F., *Business Decentralization* (Bureau of Governmental Research, University of California, Los Angeles, 1960).

industrial parks, although a few establishments have small laboratories for testing purposes.

These momentous changes in metropolitan areas create very serious problems, both for the core city and for the satellite communities or fringe areas. Decentralized cities are not doomed, however; it has been demonstrated that when a progressive city with an alert citizenry and good leadership realizes what is happening, faces the situation squarely, and adopts suitable remedies, the downtown area can be preserved as a center of business activity and of culture. When this is done, suburban areas can no longer maintain an attitude of indifference and self-sufficiency, for in fact, the core city and suburban areas are dependent on one another.

The problem of the fringe areas is basically one of governmental organization among multiple units. If public opinion does not support the consolidation of these units or other forms of structural reorganization, they must at least cooperate with one another in the solution of common problems. Under existing conditions, cooperation is a minimum requirement. The assumption that government close to the scrutiny and control of the people is best is generally accepted, but as one writer has observed:

> The complexity of governmental problems and the inability of many small units of government to cope with them adequately defeats the theory of popular control. Local popular control is effective only if the citizenry is adequately served by its unit of government. Inadequate services and continued failure of neighboring governmental units to solve mutual problems jointly will only result in the continual encroachment of higher levels of government into areas which are rightfully functions of local government.[16]

A third aspect of the land use problem is the urgent need for the preservation of open space. Many of our present urban problems are directly attributable to past failures to provide for parks and recreation areas or to control population density. Planning and zoning were too little and too late. As William H. Whyte, Jr. has said, "As land is absorbed for urban purposes, open land areas disappear with finality." Unless a vast program for the preservation of open space is developed and instituted without delay, cities may find themselves confronted with even more tragic consequences in the future than are now evident from past mistakes. Mr. Whyte urges that:

> . . . the purchase by a public agency of rights in land from private owners [may be necessary to] insure the continued integrity of key open

[16] Associated Institutes of Government of Pennsylvania Universities, State College, *Horizons,* September, 1954, p. 2.

areas. . . . [This is essentially] an adaptation of the common law device of easements. So far, this tool has not been applied extensively to the control of urban sprawl. . . . There is one overriding consideration for any open space program. It is, simply, that open space must be sought as a positive benefit. Open space is not the absence of something harmful; it is a public benefit in its own right, now, and should be primarily justified on this basis.[17]

Mass Transit and Commuter Problems. The transit problem has become one of the major headaches of our metropolitan areas. Ever wider suburban areas continue to develop, in part due to the exodus from the central city, in part to the arrival of new residents from farms and rural areas. Each new suburbanite adds to the central city's transit problem, for all must travel in for work each morning and home each evening. Most commuters prefer to drive to work, many of them alone in their own cars, a preference which has several ill effects: (1) it contributes to an ever greater and more vexatious rush hour traffic congestion; (2) it increases the pressure on already inadequate parking facilities, on-street and off-street; and (3) every commuter who drives his own car, thereby withholding his patronage from local transit services, contributes to the financial woes that everywhere beset the transit systems and railroads that have in the past handled the bulk of a large commuter traffic.

In the legislative sessions of 1959, both New Jersey and New York enacted legislation in this field and secured Congressional consent for an interstate compact between the two States. In New Jersey, Governor Meyner signed three bills designed to alleviate the plight of the commuters. The first made it possible for his State to participate in the New York–New Jersey Metropolitan Transit District, providing for the government, powers, and functions of such a district, to become effective upon enactment of identical legislation in New York. The second created a Division of Railroad Transportation in the State Highway Department, charged with examining and studying the facilities of the various commuter and passenger railroads and with seeking agreements between the operators under which facilities can be coordinated to improve service and increase efficiency. The third appropriated $50,000 for the initial operation of the new Division.

At approximately the same time, the New York legislature gave its approval to the interstate compact and passed legislation designed to provide State assistance to railroads operating within the State. One measure provides tax relief for the railways by exempting them from

[17] Whyte, William H., Jr., *Securing Open Space for Urban America: Conservation Easements* (Washington: Urban Land Institute, 1959).

taxation on certain improvements and by changing the basis of local taxation of railroad property. It is estimated that this will reduce the railroad's tax bill in New York by some $5 million in fiscal 1960–1961, and $15 million in fiscal 1962–1963. The State will reimburse local governments for their losses under the same measure. The legislature also approved a State loan of $20 million to the Port of New York Authority to help finance the purchase of 400 new passenger coaches, largely for use on commuter lines, which will be leased to the railroads. A bond issue of $100 million in Port Authority bonds to finance the purchase of railroad equipment was approved, subject to ratification by the 1961 legislature and subsequently by the electorate at a referendum.[18]

While the States in the New York metropolitan area were grappling with their mass transit and commuter problems, New Jersey was concerned with similar problems at the southern end of the State where two transportation studies were under way, one privately financed, the other a long range study publicly financed on a cooperative basis. The former emphasizes the need for overall transportation planning on the State, regional, and local levels,[19] stating that the Penn-Jersey study, if made a continuing program, could fill many of the deficiencies heretofore evident in the area's transportation planning patterns. The report contains a recommendation for a regional agency having the operating and regulatory powers necessary to insure coordinated development of a balanced transportation network for the metropolitan area.

The Penn-Jersey study, still in progress, is carried on under the terms of an agreement between New Jersey, Pennsylvania, and a group of counties—five in Pennsylvania, four in New Jersey—for a joint study of transportation facilities in the Philadelphia-Camden area. Estimated cost of the three-year survey, to be shared by all participating units, is $2,400,000. The study is expected to develop a plan for meeting anticipated transportation needs in 1975 and 1985.

Philadelphia has experimented with cutting fares and improving service to attract more riders, with the result that the number of passengers on one line was tripled within a year and increased by nearly 700,000 on another line in two years. These accomplishments have been achieved through the payment of a subsidy by the city to the two leading commuter carriers in the area. A plan under consideration in San Francisco in late 1960 included a billion dollar rail system for the Bay

[18] State Government News, April, 1959.

[19] Bureau of Municipal Research and Pennsylvania Economy League (Eastern Division), Improved Transportation for Southeastern Pennsylvania (Philadelphia, 1960); see also a symposium, "Rapid Transit Sets More Green Lights," Modern Passenger Transportation, October, 1960, pp. 25–29, covering the situation in Atlanta, New York, Philadelphia, and Toronto.

Area, a system whose proponents argued would be "considerably more than self-supporting." Eventually, it was estimated that this new rail network would carry more than 125,000,000 passenger trips daily. After county officials in the area had approved a definite plan, it was submitted to the voters in 1962 and approved by them.[20]

Tax problems also loom large in the plight of the commuter. Strife developed in the Philadelphia metropolitan area a quarter of a century ago when the Philadelphia wage tax was first enacted, and it has since become acute in New York and many other areas. While some 70,000 New Yorkers work in New Jersey, there are approximately 148,000 Jerseyites who commute daily to work in New York, not to mention a sizable number of Connecticut residents. As pressure from the commuters increased, the Governors of the three States met, and Governor Rockefeller agreed to sponsor legislation designed to assure more equitable treatment for nonresidents liable for New York State income taxes. Since a revenue loss of some $6 million was involved, it was not easy to obtain passage of tax relief legislation for nonresidents when none was provided—at least at that time—for residents, but it was finally accomplished.

In 1960, these problems began to demand the attention of Congress which consented to two interstate compacts dealing with them, and received for consideration the Williams bill to provide Federal aid for commuter transit. The first compact created the New York-New Jersey Transportation Agency, which replaces the Metropolitan Rapid Transit Commission created in 1954 to handle the commuter problems of the New York area, and the second created the National Capital Transportation Agency, involving the States of Maryland and Virginia and the District of Columbia. Senator Harrison Williams of New Jersey and a group of ten cosponsors introduced a bill (S3278) to provide Federal financial assistance to commuter carriers on a nationwide basis. This measure was designed to aid in maintaining a necessary service which the private carriers have been diminishing or abandoning for some time due to considerable financial losses. The bill, amending the Housing Act of 1954, would be administered by the Community Services Administrator. It would encourage and assist State and local units in surveying and developing suitable provisions for mass transit needs. It has strong support from the American Municipal Association on the one hand, and from the major railroads providing commuter service on the other.

In a 1961 report on mass transportation in metropolitan areas, the Advisory Commission on Intergovernmental Relations recommends that States provide financial and technical assistance for the planning of mass

[20] *Public Administration Bulletin*, November, 1960.

transportation in such areas, that they enact legislation authorizing the creation of metropolitan transportation authorities, and that Congress give advance consent to compacts among States creating interstate transportation planning agencies. Finally, it is proposed that the national government provide financial assistance in meeting the mass transportation problem, through grants for planning and for demonstration projects, and through long term low interest loans for the construction and/or modernization of mass transit facilities.[21]

Other Major Problems. Although governmental organization, area, people, and the movement of people and goods are probably the major problems, most all of the normal functions of municipal administration have areawide significance. Germs that endanger health and criminals fleeing from the scene of a crime are singularly unconcerned about local boundary lines. For this reason and because of the costliness of health, welfare, and transit programs, many of them are carried on with Federal aid. Many types of statistics must cover the entire urban region if they are to be of use in developing policy, but one confronts tremendous financial difficulties at every effort toward solution of these problems. Metropolitan areas are not organized to undertake the task, and most of the component units show little disposition to cooperate to get the job done. The States have done very little, and it seems unlikely that they will, for rural dominated legislatures have little interest in urban problems. Hence the constant multiplication of authorities and special districts and the increasing involvement of the Federal government in financing programs which State and local governments should have inaugurated long ago.

Possible Methods of Administrative Organization

Although there is a growing recognition of the fact that many metropolitan problems are areawide, there appears to be relatively little realization of the benefits of cooperative solutions. In some States, notably in California, a good deal of cooperation takes place, but in others there is not even permissive legislation under which communities volunteering to cooperate with neighboring communities may do so. A first step in achieving interunit cooperation would be to make it legally possible.

The need for joint action on the one hand, and the desire of each local unit to preserve both its geographical integrity and its legal powers on the other, present a troublesome dilemma, indeed. Although they are interacting and interdependent, and although there are large areas of

[21] *Intergovernmental Responsibilities for Mass Transportation Facilities and Services* (Washington, 1961).

potential cooperation, the municipalities and counties that comprise metropolitan areas have not yet found a generally acceptable solution for areawide policy determination and uniform enforcement. Responsible groups or individuals have proposed and are trying various possible methods of common action, six of which are discussed in the following paragraphs.

Creating a Metropolitan Government. Dr. Paul Ylvisaker has observed that "We are moving—I think wisely—toward some form of metropolitan government, not because we *know* about the many problems of urban life and the city, but precisely because we do not know." [22] Popular sentiment, once against the concept of metropolitan government, now tends to support it, but Dr. Ylvisaker warns that it is unrealistic to expect that the creation of new machinery will in and of itself solve any problems. No form of governmental organization can develop satisfactory solutions to problems until some reasonably firm decisions are made regarding the type and character of urban development desired and the purposes it is to serve.

The type and purposes decided, there remains the further question of how to achieve such government. Some would have the legislature abolish at one stroke the hundreds of small, weak, and overlapping local units and jurisdictions, and establish in their place an overall metropolitan government for each area. This solution may appeal to one's logic, but politically it would be next to impossible. Local politicians can always present formidable opposition to any plan that threatens their positions and their power, and the experience of decades has shown that the people of an urban area do not take kindly to drastic changes in their familiar institutions of local government. The members of a legislature that attempted to force through sweeping changes at one time would most certainly find themselves in serious trouble when next they came up for re-election. Yet, consolidation and some centralization may be essential for more than just efficiency. As Louis Brownlow has pointed out, if the metropolitan problem is going to be solved, the spirit of the Constitutional Convention of 1787 may have to be revived, with local units yielding some authority to a central government just as the States did in the Convention held in Philadelphia. [23]

A modest but practical proposal in this direction was made by the California Governor's Commission on Metropolitan Problems which urged that each of the State's nine urban areas be permitted to establish a single, multi-purpose agency with taxing and bonding powers to pro-

[22] In Scott, Stanley, ed., *Metropolitan Area Problems* (Berkeley: Bureau of Public Administration, University of California, 1960), p. 61.

[23] "Centralized Urban Rule Held Vital," by Brownlow, Washington *Evening Star*, June 24, 1960.

vide areawide services. Each district would be established by majority vote of the electorate in the area and governed by a council formed by representatives from its cities and counties. Any city or county in the district would be able to contract for any or all of the services provided. These would include metropolitan planning, air pollution control, water, sewage and disposal services, transportation and terminals, parks and parkways, law enforcement, fire protection, urban renewal, and civil defense.[24]

Cooperation Through Regional Councils. Luther H. Gulick said not long ago that "the paramount political need of each metropolitan area is to bring together, from the area not solely the central city, the major leaders to consider the 'state of the nation' locally." [25] This idea is sound, but it is not new; in fact, the proposal has been around for at least twenty years, and something like fifteen years ago a Citizens Regional Planning Council, including portions of two States, five counties, and numerous cities, was organized in the greater Kansas City area.[26]

In the mid-1950's, the movement began to gather momentum. In an effort to grapple with local problems on an areawide basis, approximately a dozen metropolitan areas, large and small, either have established or appear to be in the process of establishing all-purpose organizations in the form of regional councils or conferences. Beginning with Detroit in 1954, these cities followed in the order and at the dates indicated: New York (1956), Washington (1957), Seattle (1958), Salem (Willamette Valley, 1959), Philadelphia and San Francisco (1961). Such organizations were planned or were in the organization stage in Baltimore, Ithaca, Milwaukee, Norfolk, Omaha, and the Twin Cities.

Of those in actual operation in 1961, three had legal recognition and two were in process of obtaining it. None had more than purely advisory powers. New York City was supporting the New York Council and Berkeley the Bay Area Council, but the others were supported by voluntary contributions from all member local governments. Three had their own secretariat, and presumably all will have one. The general deliberative bodies, ranging in size from five (Salem) to fifty-nine (Washington), meet twice a year in New York, Washington, and the Bay Area, monthly in Detroit and Salem. A smaller body, an executive committee,

[24] Reported in *State Government News*, January, 1961.

[25] Gulick, Luther H., "Goals for Metropolis," *National Civic Review*, December, 1960, pp. 586–594, 609. This excellent discussion deals with human, economic, and political goals; among the latter, effective intergovernmental cooperation is especially emphasized.

[26] See Pinney, Harvey F. *et al.*, "Proposals for Organization and Operation of Regional Councils in Metropolitan Areas," *American City*, June, 1943, pp. 79, 81, 83, 85; on the Kansas City experience, see W. M. Symon, "The Disappearing Boundaries," *National Municipal Review*, May, 1946, pp. 224–227.

has been established in all but the Salem area. The structure of subject matter committees varies widely among the several councils.[27]

The first council was established in Detroit in June, 1954. Prior to the formation of the Supervisors Inter-County Committee in the Detroit area, there had been no convenient way for the supervisors of the various counties in the area to acquaint themselves fully with the work and problems of their neighbors, though such knowledge was often important, even vital, to their work. In 1954, therefore, the chairmen of the Boards of Supervisors of Macomb, Oakland, Washtenaw, and Wayne Counties signed letters to their respective boards suggesting the formation, within each board, of a Committee on Inter-County Affairs. St. Clair County subsequently did the same, so that six such committees were established. Legislative authorization for this and similar cooperative efforts was provided in 1957.

The next step was to organize and elect a chairman for the group. The organization, though voluntary, is a closely knit one representing the six counties equally. Each member county is represented by the chairman of its Board of Supervisors and by a five-member committee authorized by its Board. As stated in the preamble to its by-laws, the Committee was organized "for the purpose of meeting at regular intervals to discuss and study community problems of mutual interest and concern to the counties comprising the metropolitan regional area, and to develop recommendations for ratification by the several Boards of Supervisors."

The Committee has no power of its own. It does not concern itself with local problems which can be capably handled by existing local units of government. Its recommendations on problems affecting the area as a whole can be implemented only by the independent action of each parent board. There had originally been a reluctance to superimpose another governmental layer on top of the many existing governments, but it was the purpose and has come to be the unique value of the Committee that it is able to utilize all the inherent strength of existing tools and agencies of government and to devise a means of putting them to work to their fullest capacity on the areawide problems confronting the six counties.

A period of self-education followed organization, so that the Committee's recommendations would be broad and based upon a full knowledge of various problems. A series of standing committees was established, each to specialize in a specific area: General Public Services, Governmental Organization and Structure, Legislative, Taxation, and Water,

[27] Data from a report by Samuel Humes, Executive Secretary of the Washington Metropolitan Council of Governments, based on a questionnaire survey of the five functioning councils. On plans for a council for the Twin Cities area, see *National Civic Review*, December, 1961, pp. 620–621.

Sewage, and Drainage. These committees looked toward the improvement of port facilities and the establishment of port districts, increased recreational areas and opportunities, integrated road systems, adequate sewage and waste disposal, and an abundant supply of water with adequate distribution systems.[28] Committees were also set up for special projects, some of the early ones being: Huron River Watershed Intergovernmental Committee, Inter-County Highway Commission, Southeastern Michigan Metropolitan Area Aviation Study, and the Sanitation Council for Southeastern Michigan.

After Mayor Robert F. Wagner of New York suggested in an address in Miami that a metropolitan regional council be established, he was urged to take the initiative by calling a conference of local officials. The result was an informal organization of thirty-one—later thirty-six—elected officials of local governments in a twenty-one county area in New York, New Jersey, and Connecticut, with Mayor Wagner as chairman. Just to assemble these officials to discuss common problems represented progress, but the group soon discovered that it was difficult to accomplish very much without legal status. In June, 1960, therefore, legislation was drafted to be introduced under bipartisan sponsorship in the legislatures of the three States, to provide for the establishment of what may become the nation's first official interstate federation of elected local officials to deal with the many problems of metropolitan areas.[29]

The bill blueprinted the structure of the proposed agency, authorizing its financing by local government units and public or private grants and outlining its functions in making studies, establishing cooperative arrangements, and making recommendations to local, State, and Federal governments. It did not confer any operational or regulatory powers such as those of the Port of New York Authority or other interstate agencies devoted to specific problems.

Mayor Wagner has said, "If you ask me why our operation has

[28] *This Is the Supervisors Inter-County Committee* (Detroit: Detroit Edison Company, 1960). Annual reports are available, beginning 1959. For excellent discussions of the work of this Committee, see Edward Connor, "The Detroit Metropolitan Area Inter-County Plan," *Urban County Congress* (Washington: National Association of County Officials, 1959), pp. 40–46, and "The Supervisors Inter-County Committee," *County Officer*, June, 1961, pp. 180–181, 202.

[29] *The New York Times*, June 30, 1960; see also a report by the Special Committee on Metropolitan Governmental Affairs for consideration by the Regional Plan Association, *The Future of the Metropolitan Regional Council* (New York, January, 1959) and Schmandt, Henry J., "The Area Council: Approach to Metropolitan Government," *Public Management*, February, 1960, pp. 30–32.

been successful, I think the answer lies in the four principles that were established when we first met together": (1) the organization is voluntary in character, both in composition and basic policy determination; (2) it consists of the top elected public officials of the member communities; (3) it respects the principle of home rule and the integrity of the communities in the region; (4) it is non-political in motivation and action.[30]

The third regional council was established in the Washington metropolitan area when Robert E. McLaughlin, president of the District of Columbia Board of Commissioners, called a meeting of the elected officials of the area in April, 1957. The Washington Metropolitan Council of Governments was formally organized later that year and an executive secretary appointed in 1960. Conceived as an association of local and State governments in the metropolitan area (two States, six counties, and two independent cities) and of certain State and Federal bodies, its purpose is to provide a nonpartisan forum for the discussion of areawide problems, to develop and formalize policies having significance to the region, to promote intergovernmental cooperation, to provide organizational machinery to insure effective communication and coordination among governmental bodies, and to serve as a means for the collection and exchange of information of interest throughout the region.[31]

The table on page 642 presents what might be called a life history of the Intergovernmental Cooperation Council of the Salem area. The governing body of this agency has five members—one each from the city, State, school district, and two counties involved. A council-type organization known as the Association of Bay Area Governments (ABAG, for short, not to be confused with a regional chamber of commerce called the Bay Area Council) has been formed. It began operations in mid-1961 when a majority of the nine counties and eighty-four cities (having a combined population of more than 3,500,000) had signed contracts.

This undertaking grew out of "A Statement of Principles on Metropolitan Problems" put out by the League of California Cities in 1958. Two preliminary meetings were held in 1959, and an "informal" meeting of the General Assembly was held in January, 1961. The General Assembly, the important policy-making body, is composed of one member

[30] "City-County Cooperation," *Urban County Congress,* pp. 32–34.

[31] It may be noted that shortly after this general purpose organization was set up, the Washington Regional Metropolitan Sanitary Board, which includes Washington and eleven Virginia and Maryland cities and counties, was established by the Council as a subordinate organization. The Board engaged two Johns Hopkins University consultants to draw up a preliminary master plan for the area's sanitary sewers and waste disposal facilities. The plan is to anticipate needs over the next fifty years and will be financed by contributions from all the governmental jurisdictions involved. Also in late 1960, a Metropolitan Transit Authority was established by interstate compact.

COMPOSITIOI
METROPOLITAN WASHINGTOI

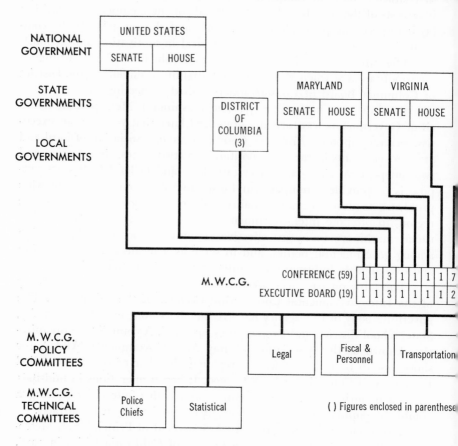

from each city-county and each county board of supervisors. An executive committee has fiscal responsibility. Two votes must be taken on each proposition voted upon, and a majority of both the cities and the counties must be recorded in the affirmative if a proposition is to be adopted. The General Assembly is authorized to review governmental proposals affecting the area and to study and make recommendations with respect to metropolitan area problems.[32]

It has been urged that a regional citizens voice, such as the Alle-

[32] See Fales, James M., Jr., "Bay Area Cities; Counties Organize," *National Civic Review*, October, 1960, pp. 491–493, and Scott, Stanley, "Metropolitan Reorganization in the San Francisco Bay Area: Recent Developments and New Proposals," *Public Affairs Report*, February, 1961, entire issue.

= THE

⊃UNCIL OF GOVERNMENTS

LOCAL GOVERNMENTS

Mont- gomery County (7)	Prince George's County (5)	Arlington County (5)	Fairfax County (7)	Prince William County (6)	Loudoun County (6)	City of Alexandria (7)	City of Falls Church (7)

5	7	6	6	7	7
1	1	1	1	1	1

Publicity	Permanent Organization	Health & Welfare	Water Supply & Pollution Abatement

Regional
Sanitary
Board

⊪icate number in governing body

gheny Conference of Pittsburgh, badly needs to be heard in the decision-making process with respect to such major problems as long-range planning, transportation, and public works. One writer contends that "what evolves from official attempts at regional government is a series of compromises between interests that may not at all conform to the unrepresented regional interest," and he cites a number of illustrations in support of his point.[33]

Metropolitan Federalism. Another solution involves the creation of a new federated government to handle areawide problems, leaving matters of purely local concern to the jurisdiction of existing political subdi-

[33] Albrook, Robert C., "Area Citizens Need Regional Voice," *Washington Post,* November 20, 1960, and Scott, *Public Affairs Report,* February, 1961.

THE SALEM AREA PRESENTS "MASSIVE COOPERATION" *

The Problem—"Web of Governments"

The Location—The Mid-Willamette Valley in Oregon

One Region with 147 Governments; included are Marion and Polk Counties, the City of Salem and 21 smaller cities, 47 special districts, the Metropolitan School District and 47 outside school districts, and various State departments and agencies.

The Answer—"Massive Cooperation"

The Technique

1. *Study*

For one year (1959) by Citizens Conference for Governmental Cooperation, devoting more than 2,400 hours to the undertaking.

2. *Report*

Over 300 pages with 57 maps, organization charts and tables, containing 81 specific recommendations.

3. *Action*

First year (1960), 30 of 81 recommendations acted upon by Intergovernmental Cooperation Council. Eight major programs enacted for improving services or making monetary savings.

Organization

Regional coordination and strengthened counties developed with State support and Federal endorsement in a Region with 147 governments through the Intergovernmental Cooperation Council (ICC), organized in 1959. The committee structure of ICC includes 17 committees, namely:

1. Parks	7. Culture	12. Inspectional Services
2. Stream Pollution	8. Dog Control	13. Maintenance & Repair
3. Building Needs	9. Engineering	14. Personnel Administration
4. Port Development	10. Finance	15. Recreation
5. Purchasing	11. Fire Protection &	16. Social and Health Services
6. Air Pollution	Civil Defense	17. State Buildings

Accomplishments

1. Parks Committee—A regional park system
2. Stream Pollution Committee—A $5,000,000 sewer program
3. Building Needs Committee—Six-year regional building budget
4. Port Development Committee—Regional air-water port agency
5. Purchasing Committee—$20,000 annual savings

---

* Source: Salem Area Chamber of Commerce, "Massive Cooperation" (Salem, 1960). The phrase "Massive Cooperation" attracted favorable attention when, for instance, *The County Officer* devoted its June, 1961, issue to a symposium on the subject.

visions. This plan, which is in effect a partial city-county consolidation, does not require that either city or county surrender its identity and is, therefore, feasible from a political point of view. It was first adopted in Toronto in 1952, in Montreal in 1959, in Winnipeg in 1960, and in this country in the Miami-Dade County plan in 1957. This solution has been much discussed, and the early adoptions have had wide publicity. Aside from Toronto, however, actual experience upon which a sound evaluation could be made is still extremely limited.

The report of the first three years in Miami are, nevertheless, most encouraging. The new plan has modernized an antiquated governmental structure. Although the metropolitan form of government provides the means of cutting across municipal boundary lines for the performance of county-wide services, few decisions have yet been made to determine what services are county-wide in nature or to establish a timetable for their transfer from the municipalities to Metro (popular name for the federated government). In the important changes made in 1957, three specific things were accomplished: home rule was achieved, a manager form of government was established, and a metropolitan government was authorized and established.[34] Students of metropolitan problems at home and abroad will continue to watch its progress with interest.

Creation of Authorities and Special Districts. A third proposal places strong reliance on special purpose authorities created by act of the legislature or, in interstate areas, through interstate compact. Special purpose districts have been used for a long time; in fact, such districts were created in Massachusetts in the last century. Significant as have been the accomplishments of some of these agencies, many of them are limited both by charter and by the credit rating of the bond market from entering areas of critical public need, even though their probable profit is not considerable.

The oldest and best known of the compact agencies is the Port of New York Authority, but more recent examples are to be found in the Philadelphia, St. Louis, and Washington, D.C. metropolitan areas. The Port Authority was created in 1921 by a compact ratified by Congress between the States of New York and New Jersey. This unique corporate municipal instrumentality, a prototype of many others that were to follow, was necessary because of the unusual nature of certain geographical and other factors. It provides a medium through which the two States combine efforts in promoting the commercial development of the Port of New York, with particular attention to the improvement of terminal and transportation facilities. The States authorized it to exercise

---

[34] Government Research Council of the Miami-Dade County Chamber of Commerce, *Metropolitan Dade County—Its First Three Years: A Summary Report* (Miami, November, 1960).

certain corporate powers within the Port District which, roughly speaking, embraces the area within a twenty-mile radius from the Statue of Liberty. The Authority has grown until it now requires a staff of several thousand employees to operate the vast network of airports, bridges, piers, terminals for trucks and buses, tunnels, grain warehouses, and other transit facilities serving the New York metropolitan area.

ATTACKS ON METRO, 1958 – 1961

DADE'S VOTING RECORD ON AMENDING METRO

SEPT. 30, 1958 To change the name of Dade County to Miami County.	**NO**
SEPT. 30, 1958 To give municipalities in Dade more autonomy.	**NO**
NOV. 3, 1959 To make the office of sheriff elective.	**NO**
NOV. 3, 1959 To make the office of tax assessor elective.	**NO**
NOV. 3, 1959 To reduce the commission to nine members at $15,000 salary.	**NO**
NOV. 3, 1959 To reduce the commission to seven members at $15,000 salary.	**NO**
NOV. 3, 1959 To reduce the commission to five members at $15,000 salary.	**NO**
AUG. 15, 1961 To throw out the 1961 deadline on reassessment.	**YES**
OCT. 17, 1961 McLeod Plan for changing county government.	**NO**

This is the ballot as it appeared on the voting machines Tuesday, October 17, 1961

YES   **NO**

Shall the Home Rule Charter of Government for Dade County, Florida, be amended by adoption of an amended Charter, which limits and redefines the powers of the County Commission, reduces the number of County Commissioners to five, fixes Commissioner's salaries at $15,000 per annum, provides for election of new Commissioners, deletes all provisions relating to the County Manager, provides assessments for County and Municipal taxes by Board of Tax Assessors appointed by County Commissioners, eliminates requirement for full-time County Attorney, expands powers of Municipalities, provides for establishment of a County Court, provides Sheriff and Tax Assessor shall be elective offices, limits the tort liability of the County, provides such revised Charter shall become effective immediately upon adoption, prescribes method by which such revised Charter may be abolished, and contains other provisions as set forth in the initiatory petitions on file with Clerk of the County Commission.

A "Yes" vote means:
You favor McLeod's proposed methods for changing county government.

A "No" vote means:
You are against the McLeod plan for amending the Metro charter.

TRANSPORTATION FACILITIES OPERATED BY THE
PORT OF NEW YORK AUTHORITY

Airports
- La Guardia Airport—Queens
- New York International Airport—Idlewild, Queens
- Newark Airport—Newark, New Jersey
- Teterboro Airport—Teterboro, New Jersey
- Heliport Number One—Pier 41, East River, Manhattan
- Heliport Number Two—Pier A, Battery Park, Manhattan
- Port Authority—West 30th Street Heliport, Manhattan

Bridges and Tunnels
- Goethals Bridge—Staten Island–New Jersey
- Outerbridge Crossing—Staten Island–New Jersey
- Bayonne Bridge—Staten Island–New Jersey
- George Washington Bridge—Manhattan–New Jersey
- Holland Tunnel—Manhattan–New Jersey
- Lincoln Tunnel—Manhattan–New Jersey

Piers and Terminals
- Brooklyn—Port Authority Piers, Brooklyn
- Hoboken—Port Authority Piers, Hoboken, New Jersey
- New York Union Motor Truck Terminal—Manhattan
- Newark Union Motor Truck Terminal—Newark, New Jersey
- Port Authority Bus Terminal—Manhattan
- Port Authority Grain Terminal—Brooklyn
- Port Newark Marine Terminal—Newark, New Jersey
- Union Railroad Freight Terminal—Manhattan

Originally, it was provided that the Port Authority would be administered by six commissioners, three from each State appointed by the Governors with the advice and consent of their respective senates. Reorganized and reconstituted in 1930, there have since that date been twelve commissioners, six from each State appointed in the same manner. Commissioners serve for a term of six years, without compensation, in a manner similar to that of a board of directors of a private corporation. They hold frequent regular meetings, a favorable vote by a majority is necessary before any action can be taken, and every action must have the approval of at least three commissioners from each State. The Authority has direct responsibility for the administration of the vast network of transportation facilities and has carried this responsibility with notable success. The corporate form of organization was provided for to enable the Authority to finance self-liquidating public improvements on its own credit, thus avoiding additional taxes or assessments.[35] For a summary of the financial, jurisdictional, and administrative arguments for the use of authorities and special districts, see the table below.

REASONS FOR THE CREATION OF SPECIAL AUTHORITIES *

Financial	Jurisdictional	Administrative
1. To finance public improvements without resort to additional taxes.	1. To facilitate provision of services or improvements that involve more than one regular governmental jurisdiction.	1. To remove the administration of enterprises from direct control of politically responsible officers.
2. To finance improvements through charges upon the users thereof instead of upon the general taxpaying public.	2. To provide for continuity of a program or activity involving more than one department or agency of government.	2. To provide a more flexible administrative instrument to manage commercial type public enterprise.
3. To finance improvements without conflict with constitutional debt limitations.		3. To facilitate the transition from private to public operation of enterprises.

4. To obtain additional revenues and greater financial autonomy for certain activities of regular state agencies.

5. To take advantage of Federal loans and grants.

6. To finance improvements through revenue bonds without earmarking taxes.

7. To facilitate the financing of enterprises taken over from private ownership.

* Source: New York State Temporary Commission on Coordination of State Activities, *Public Authorities Under New York State*, Legislative Document No. 44, Albany, 1956.

The interstate compact device has proved to be advantageous in a number of instances in which more than one State was involved; in fact,

[35] In addition to the authority's annual reports and its numerous other publications (such as *The Port of New York Authority: A Monograph*, 1935, and *Twenty-Fifth Anniversary: The Port of New York Authority: 1921-1946*, 1946), see Bard, Erwin W., *The Port of New York Authority* (New York: Columbia University Press, 1941) and Bird, Frederick L., *A Study of the Port of New York Authority* (New York: Dun & Bradstreet, 1949). The September, 1948, issue of *State Government* was devoted to a symposium on port authorities, State and municipal; see also Crothers, J. A., "Port of Boston Authority," *State Government*, April, 1948, pp. 91-93.

it has sometimes appeared to be easier to secure effective action where this was the case than to get a single State to deal adequately with the problems of a metropolitan area located entirely within its own borders.

The Bi-State Development Agency established on September 20, 1949, in the St. Louis area by the States of Illinois and Missouri is a case in point. By this agreement, the two States were pledged to "faithful cooperation in the future planning and development of the St. Louis–East St. Louis metropolitan district, holding in high trust for the benefit of the people and of the Nation the special blessings and advantages thereof." The signing had been authorized by legislative action of the two States and was later approved by Congress. The agency is administered by a board of ten commissioners, five appointed by the Governor of each State; each commissioner serves for a term of five years, without compensation. No meeting of the board may be held unless a majority of the commissioners from each State is present, and no action is valid unless approved by a majority of those present from each State.

The Agency has two types of functions: (1) to construct, maintain, own, and operate bridges and/or tunnels, airports, and terminal facilities; and (2) to make plans for submission to the communities involved for coordination of streets, highways, parking areas, terminals, water supply and sewage and drainage facilities, recreational facilities, land-use patterns, and other matters in which joint or coordinated action will be generally beneficial. The Agency can charge and collect fees for use of its facilities and issue bonds on the security of the revenues to be derived therefrom. It has no taxing powers and is prohibited from taking any action which will affect the finances of any governmental subdivisions.[36]

To the growing list of compact agencies must be added the Washington Metropolitan Area Transit Regulation Compact, signed in December, 1960, by the chairman of the Board of District Commissioners and the Governors of the two adjacent States, Virginia and Maryland. One observer noted that it marked the first time that the top officials of the three jurisdictions had met to complete action on a matter benefiting the residents of all three. "But even more important," he continued, "it should serve as an example of harmony and common purpose for officials of other metropolitan regions in this country."[37] The Compact places the regulation of privately-owned transit and transportation service in the entire area in the hands of a single agency, replacing the previously existing four separate commissions. The new commission is a three-member board, with one member from each of the regulatory

[36] *The Book of the States, 1954–1955* (Chicago: Council of State Governments, 1954), p. 34.

[37] WTOP editorial, Steve Cushing speaking for WTOP, Washington, December 27, 1960.

commissions of the cooperating jurisdictions, and has an executive director to manage its operations.

There is considerable evidence of interest in the regional solution of common local problems. Legislation is being drafted for the creation of a multi-purpose special district for the Twin Cities area, a district that would have broad powers to assume any municipal function which could no longer be effectively performed by existing jurisdictions. Administration of the district would be assigned to the Minneapolis-St. Paul Sanitary District, with provision for it to assume additional functions as needed. Another multi-purpose district was proposed in Oregon through the joint action of several local chapters of the League of Women Voters. Major objectives would be to provide selected urban services to unincorporated areas of Multnomah, Clackamas, and Washington Counties; to coordinate several services among the cities and counties; and to plan the area's future development.

The Urban County and Services Under Contract. Still another proposal places reliance upon the county to render "municipal type services" to the inhabitants of the unincorporated and fringe areas lying either outside the borders of the core cities or by contract within the core cities themselves. This device, discussed in Chapter XIX, has the advantage of avoiding the establishment of new and additional governmental units or mechanisms.

Territorial Expansion: Consolidation and Annexation. Adjustments in territorial boundaries is another solution for the metropolitan area problem. As far back as 1898, the five counties within the City of New York lost their county status and became boroughs within the greater city. Similar city-county consolidations have taken place in Baton Rouge, Denver, Miami, Newport News, Philadelphia, St. Louis, and San Francisco.

City-county consolidation has been described as one of the most drastic but still most frequently proposed methods of dealing with the metropolitan area problem, but, except in the seven cities noted above, it has usually been defeated in one way or another. The usual methods have been by a vote in the legislature, by a state-wide referendum on a constitutional amendment, or in a local election. The table on page 650 presents some information regarding a large number of these proposals in summary form.

It is possible, of course, though rare, to have boundary adjustments within a county without consolidation, accomplished through the annexation of territory. For a long time there was little activity of this type, but as pressure for some solution for metropolitan area problems has continued to mount, annexations have become more frequent and have often involved considerable territory. Liberal legislation in Texas, Virginia, and Wisconsin has encouraged annexation in these States.[38]

A Consolidated Program. In some areas, the question is not which one approach to choose, but how to combine several of them for coordinated attacks upon their problems. Such an approach was recommended for the Chagrin Falls area in Cleveland in 1960 as a part of the Metro follow-up. Chagrin Falls is not a large area, nor is it one of vast population, yet the program recommended for it "brought into focus four major approaches to achieving stronger local administration, namely, improved management, intergovernmental contracts, boundary adjustments, and selective consolidation."[39] Consolidation is reasonably effective for communities seeking at least a start toward the solution of pressing problems.[40]

Elsewhere it has been suggested that revenue producing services like transit, airports, ports, water and sewer services be administered by one or more authorities, while non-revenue producing services be provided under contract by the governmental unit in the area best equipped to undertake their administration. What the Los Angeles City and County Consolidation Commission said in its report of December, 1916 is still true today: "The thing to be avoided is a stratification in the Constitution of the State and in local charters so as to render needed changes and readjustment impossible. Matters should be left so that changes can be made as experience shall show them to be necessary."

Recognizing the almost insurmountable political obstacles to consolidation of governmental units, Governor Richard J. Hughes of New Jersey proposed instead the concept of "regionalization," or consolidation on a functional basis. This is, in substance, another name for interlocal cooperation, which has in New Jersey and other States been successfully employed in many functional areas such as education, health, fire and police, parks and recreation, and sewer districts.

[38] See Sengstock, Frank S., *Annexation: A Solution to the Metropolitan Area Problem* (Ann Arbor: University of Michigan Law School, 1960); Bain, Chester W., "Recent Developments in the Virginia Annexation System," *Virginia Law Review*, June, 1960, pp. 1023–1035; O'Quinn, Truman, "Annexing New Territory: A Review of Texas Law and the Proposals for Legislative Control of Cities Extending Their Boundaries," *Texas Law Review*, December, 1960, pp. 172–187; and Rabin, Joel J., "Changes in Wisconsin Annexation Proceedings and Remedies," *Wisconsin Law Review*, January, 1961, pp. 123–140.

[39] Cleveland Bureau of Governmental Research, *Intergovernmental Problems in the Chagrin Falls Area: A Case Study* (Cleveland, February, 1960).

[40] See, for instance, Gulick, Luther, "How Do We Get Off Dead Center?" in Scott, Stanley, ed., *Metropolitan Area Problems* (Berkeley: Bureau of Public Administration, University of California, 1960), pp. 69–79.

CITY-COUNTY CONSOLIDATION AND/OR SEPARATION

City	Adopted County	Date	City	Defeated County	Date
Atlanta		1951	Albuquerque	Bernalillo	1933, 1959
Baton Rouge	East Baton Rouge Parish	1949	Austin	Travis	
Boston	Suffolk	1959	Birmingham	Jefferson (CA)	1936, 1948
Buffalo	Erie	1959	Boston	Suffolk	1931
Denver	*	1961	Charlotte	Guilford	
Honolulu	Honolulu	1907	Cleveland	Cuyahoga (L, LE)	1925, 1959
Miami	Dade	1958	Durham	Durham	1961
Newport News	Warwick, Elizabeth City (LE)	1957	Houston	Harris	
New Orleans	Orleans Parish	1813	Jacksonville	Duval	1935
New York	Kings, Queens, Bronx, Manhattan, Richmond	1894–1898	Kansas City, Mo.	Kansas City (L) Mo.	1935
Philadelphia	Philadelphia	1854, 1916, 1951	Kansas City, Kan.	Wyandotte (L)	1937
Seattle	Kings (LE)	1958	Knoxville	Knox (LE)	1959
Syracuse	Onondaga (LE)	1961	Louisville	Jefferson (LE)	1937, 1956
Utica	Oneida (LE)	1961	Macon	Bill (LE)	1937, 1960
			Miami	Dade (CA)	1948
			Milwaukee	Milwaukee (L)	1937
			Nashville	Davidson (LE)	1958
	City-County Separation		Newport News	Warwick, Elizabeth City (LE)	1950, 1956
			Portland	Multnomah (CA)	1927
Baltimore	Baltimore	1850	Richmond	Henrico (LE)	1961
Denver	Denver	1902	St. Louis	St. Louis (LE)	1926, 1959
St. Louis	St. Louis	1876	St.Paul	Ramsey (L)	1924
San Francisco	San Francisco	1850	San Antonio	Bexar	
			Seattle	King	1923
Various Virginia cities			Toledo	Lucas	1959

Key: LE—Local Election L—Legislature CA—Constitutional Amendment

* Metropolitan Capital Improvements District, composed of Adams, Arapahoe, Denver, and Jefferson Counties, authorized by the General Assembly in September, 1961, and declared unconstitutional, February 13, 1962.

BIBLIOGRAPHICAL NOTES

General Works. Prior to 1935, there had been some writing on sectionalism, notably by the distinguished historian Frederick J. Turner, but very little on regionalism; see Turner, *The Significance of Sections in American History*, 2nd ed. (New York: Peter Smith, Publisher, 1950). After publication of a regionalism study by the National Resources Board, however, others began to appear. Donald Davidson wrote extensively on the concept of regionalism; see especially his *Regionalism and Nationalism in the United States* (Chapel Hill: University of North Carolina Press, 1938). In the same year, Howard E. Odum and Harry E. Moore published *American Regionalism: A Cultural-Historical Approach to National Integration* (New York: Henry Holt and Co., 1938), presenting a cultural approach to the problem of finding a basis for unifying the regional interests of the nation. See also Merrill Jensen, ed., *Regionalism in America* (Madison: University of Wisconsin Press, 1951).

Administrative Regionalism. The pioneer study of the basic factors of regionalism in the United States appeared in 1935—National Resources Board, *Regional Factors in National Planning*—and was followed by: David B. Truman, *Administrative Decentralization* (Chicago: University of Chicago Press, 1940); Kurt Wilk, *Decentralizing Governmental Work* (New York: Institute of Public Administration, 1942); Legislative Reference Service, Library of Congress, *Federal Field Offices: A Letter from the Director to Senator Carl Hayden* (Washington: Senate Document No. 22, 78th Cong., 2nd Sess., 1943); and Earl Latham, *The Federal Field Service* (Chicago: Public Administration Service, 1947). In an excellent series of lectures, James W. Fesler, *Area and Administration* (University, Ala.: University of Alabama Press, 1949), discusses the character of natural and administrative areas and the reconciliation of function and area. Current interest in the subject is expressed in an address by William D. Carey, a member of the Bureau of the Budget Staff in 1961, "Regionalizing the Federal Government: Outlook and Prospects," published in William R. Monat, ed., *Public Administration in an Era of Change* (Philadelphia: Pennsylvania Economy League, 1962).

A number of studies have been made of administrative regionalism in specific functional fields: Ladd Haystead and Gilbert C. Fite, *The Agricultural Regions of the United States* (Norman: University of Oklahoma Press, 1955); Norman H. Jones, *The Regional Impact of Federal Fiscal Policy* (Ann Arbor: State University of Iowa, University Microfilms, 1954), a doctoral dissertation; John Hebal, *Field Administration of the Bureau of Indian Affairs in Minnesota and Wisconsin* (Minneapolis: University of Minnesota, 1956), a doctoral dissertation; Karl B. Lohman, *Regional Planning* (Ann Arbor: Edwards Brothers, 1937); Emmette S. Redford, *Field Administration of Wartime Rationing* (Washington: Office of Temporary Controls, 1947); Harry S. Perloff *et al.*, *Regions, Resources and Economic Growth* (Baltimore: Johns Hopkins Press, 1960); University of Wisconsin, *The Regional Approach to the Conservation of Natural Resources* (Madison: University of Wisconsin Press, 1938); John A. Davis, *Regional Organization of the Social Security Administration: A Case Study* (New York: Columbia University Press, 1950); and Charles A. R. Wardwell, *Regional Trends in the United States Economy* (Washington: Bureau of Foreign and Domestic Commerce, 1951).

River Basin Development. A truly voluminous literature has grown up on river basin development; for the more significant items through 1955, see W. Brooke Graves,

Intergovernmental Relations in the United States: A Selected Bibliography (Washington: Committee Print, House Committee on Government Operations, 84th Cong., 2nd Sess., 1956), pp. 32–37. Several of the more important general works, most of them published since that date, include: John V. Krutilla and Otto Eckstein, *Multiple Purpose River Development: Studies in Applied Economic Analysis* (Baltimore: Johns Hopkins Press, 1958); Arthur Maass, *Muddy Waters: The Army Engineers and the Nation's Rivers* (Cambridge: Harvard University Press, 1951); Luna B. Leopold and Thomas Maddock, Jr., *The Flood Control Controversy: Big Dams, Little Dams, and Land Management* (New York: Ronald Press, 1954); Vincent Ostrom, *Water and Politics: A Study of Water Politics in the Development of Los Angeles* (Los Angeles: Haynes Foundation, 1953); Norman Wengert, *Natural Resources and the Political Struggle* (New York: Doubleday and Co., Inc., 1955); and a symposium which appeared in the Spring and Summer, 1957 issues of *Law and Contemporary Problems*. In this symposium, the following articles are of special interest: Ernest A. Engelbert, "Federalism and Water Resources Development," Summer, pp. 325–350; James W. Fesler, "National Water Resources Administration," Summer, pp. 444–471; Irving L. Fox, "National Water Resources Policy Issues," Summer, pp. 474–509; Carl F. Kraenzel, "The Social Consequences of River Basin Development," Spring, pp. 221–236; Robert J. Morgan, "The Small Watershed Program," Summer, pp. 405–432; and Norman Wengert, "The Politics of River Basin Development," Spring, pp. 258–275.

Tennessee Valley Authority. On the Tennessee Valley Authority, the following volumes are most useful: Preston J. Hubbard, *Origins of the TVA: The Muscle Shoals Controversy, 1920–1932* (Nashville: Vanderbilt University Press, 1961); Judson King, *The Conservation Fight: From T.R. to TVA* (Washington: Public Affairs Press, 1959) and his *Legislative History of Muscle Shoals*, 5 vols. (Knoxville: Tennessee Valley Authority, 1936); Roscoe C. Martin, ed., *TVA, the First Twenty Years: A Staff Report* (University, Ala.: University of Alabama Press, 1956) and his "The TVA: A Study of Federal Control," *Law and Contemporary Problems*, Summer, 1957, pp. 351–377; C. Herman Pritchett, *The Tennessee Valley Authority: A Study in Public Administration* (Chapel Hill: University of North Carolina Press, 1943) and his article, "The Development of the Tennessee Valley Authority Act," *Tennessee Law Review*, February, 1938, pp. 128–141; Elliott Roberts, *One River—Seven States* (Knoxville: Bureau of Public Administration, University of Tennessee, 1955), well describes the TVA-State relations in the development of the Tennessee River.

Other River Basins. For works on the Mississippi, the Missouri, and the Delaware, see Arthur D. Frank, *The Development of the Federal Program of Flood Control on the Mississippi River* (New York: Columbia University Studies, 1930), which relates early efforts to control this river; Henry C. Hart, *The Dark Missouri* (Madison: University of Wisconsin Press, 1957); Marion S. Ridgeway, *The Missouri Basin's Pick-Sloan Plan: A Case Study in Congressional Policy Determination* (Urbana: University of Illinois Studies, 1955); and Roscoe C. Martin, *River Basin Administration and the Delaware* (Syracuse: Syracuse University Press, 1960). On another large project in a single state, see Mary Montgomery and Marion Clauson, *History of Legislation and Policy Formulation of the Central Valley Project* (Berkeley: U.S. Bureau of Agricultural Economics, 1946).

Metropolitan Areas. Prior to the Roosevelt era, there had been some text writing on urban problems, but little basic research and little emphasis on metropolitan area problems, which came into prominence in the 1930's. Some of the early works were undertaken by individual scholars, particularly by members of a group centered around the University of Chicago, some by public agencies, and others by private organizations. Most significant among them were Paul Studenski, *The Government of*

Metropolitan Areas in the United States (New York: National Municipal League, 1930); Victor Jones, *Metropolitan Government* (Chicago: University of Chicago Press, 1942); and National Resources Board, *Urban Government*, 2 vols. (Washington, 1939). For a sociological study of rural local government, see Theodore B. Manny, *Rural Muncipalities* (New York: The Century Company, 1930).

As interest in the metropolitan area problem has increased, the literature on the subject has grown in staggering proportions. The following are among the more significant works: John C. Bollens, *The States and the Metropolitan Problem* (Chicago: Council of State Governments, 1956); Scott, Stanley, ed., *Metropolitan Area Problems* (Berkeley: Bureau of Public Administration, University of California, 1960); Martin Myerson *et al.*, eds., "Metropolis in Ferment," *Annals of the American Academy of Political and Social Science*, September, 1957, entire issue; and Robert C. Wood, *Metropolis Against Itself* (New York: Committee for Economic Development, 1960). Of special value is the report of the Advisory Commission on Intergovernmental Relations, *Governmental Structure, Organization, and Planning in Metropolitan Areas* (Washington: Committee Print, House Committee on Government Operations, 87th Cong., 1st Sess., 1961).

Important bibliographical assistance may be found in two publications of the Governmental Affairs Foundation, *Metropolitan Communities: A Bibliography* and *Supplement* (New York, 1956 and 1960 respectively) and *Metropolitan Surveys: A Digest* (New York, 1958). See also Graves, *Intergovernmental Relations*, Chapters V and VI-B.

The New York Metropolitian Region Study (Cambridge: Harvard University Press 1959-1960) was undertaken for the purpose of detecting the main forces shaping economic and population patterns in the area and of projecting probable developments, providing data which might serve as a basis for future planning. Many of the nine volumes have a significance extending far beyond the specific area about which they were written: Benjamin Chinitz, *Freight and the Metropolis*; Max Hall, ed., *Made in New York*; Oscar Handlin, *The Newcomers*; Edgar M. Hoover and Raymond Vernon, *Anatomy of a Metropolis*; Robert M. Lichtenberg *et al.*, *One Tenth of a Nation*; Sidney M. Robbins, *Money Metropolis*; Martin Segal, *Wages in the Metropolis*; Raymond Vernon, *Metropolis, 1985*; Robert C. Wood, *1400 Governments*.

The most important general works on mass transit are by Wilfred Owens: *The Metropolitan Transportation Problem* (Washington: Brookings Institution, 1956) and *Cities in the Automobile Age* (New York: Viking Press, 1959). A substantial number of surveys of this problem have been made in individual metropolitan areas, and a fast growing literature attests to the fact that these facilities are important and must be preserved and developed; for a good short list, see *Selected References on Mass Transit*, rev. ed. (Berkeley: Institute of Transportation and Traffic Engineering, University of California, September, 1959).

CHAPTER XIX

Federal-Local
Relations

Within the past half-century, the United States has been transformed from a predominantly rural to a predominantly urban nation. As late as 1910, fewer than half our people lived in urban areas—and I use the Census definition of urban areas as communities over 2,500 population. Today, the proportion is 70 per cent—and rising. The year 1970 will see 160 million urban residents, and more than our entire national population of ten years ago. By the year 2000 it is estimated that over 300 million Americans will live in urban areas.

This unprecedented growth has brought, and is bringing, enormous problems. Central cities are beset with rising needs and declining tax bases as slums and blight spread and as high-income residents leave and are replaced by families of low-income. Meanwhile, their suburbs struggle with the public service demands of the population explosion.

In 1957, President Eisenhower said, "The needs of our cities are glaringly evident. Unless action is prompt and effective, urban problems will soon almost defy solution."

And four years later, his successor, President Kennedy, said, "Our national household is cluttered with unfinished and neglected tasks. Our cities are engulfed in squalor. Twelve long years after Congress declared our goal to be 'a decent home and a suitable living environment for every American family,' we still have 25 million Americans living in substandard homes." [1]

[1] Senator Joseph S. Clark of Pennsylvania, in his testimony before the Senate Subcommittee on Organization, on his bill, S. 1633, to establish a Federal department of urban affairs and housing, June 21, 1961.

For well over a century after the present system of government was established, important indirect relations between the Federal government and local units were fairly numerous,[2] but direct relations between the two levels were virtually nonexistent. The latter, however, have developed during the past quarter of a century, and now exist between the Federal government and the cities, the counties, and various kinds of special districts.

FEDERAL-MUNICIPAL RELATIONS

Although a considerable number of indirect relationships involving goods and services developed in various fields in the years between World War I and the Great Depression, it was reported as late as 1932 that the American delegation at the International Congress of Cities in London was the only one of more than forty countries having no direct administrative relationships between the central or national government and its cities.[3] The Roosevelt era marked a sharp break with previous practice, and direct relationships involving governmental programs and policies began to develop. The urgent need to distribute relief funds provided the Federal government with an excuse for short-circuiting the States and dealing directly with the cities.

The trend established in the Roosevelt era has continued at an accelerated pace since World War II. In the postwar years, the Federal government began contributing to the financing of airports, hospitals and health facilities, low-rent housing, and urban renewal. Then were added highways, control of air and water pollution, new public assistance programs, and some aspects of education, and in 1961 alone bills were passed establishing new programs of assistance for mass transit, depressed areas, and juvenile delinquency control. To the solution of these national problems—they are no longer only urban problems—the resources of all levels of government must be applied. The pattern of Federal-local cooperation has been firmly established, and it is no longer likely that the trend will or can be reversed.

[2] See Betters, Paul V., *Federal Services to Municipal Government* (New York: Administration Service, 1931) and the more recent Blundred, R. H., and Hanks, Donald W., *Federal Services to Cities and Towns* (Chicago: American Municipal Association, 1950). For a list of such services, see Advisory Committee Report, *Local Government* (Washington: Commission on Intergovernmental Relations, June, 1955), pp. 60–62, and U.S. Office of Area Development, *Federal Activities Helpful to Communities* (Washington, 1958).

[3] Bromage, Arthur W., *Introduction to Municipal Government and Administration* (New York: Appleton-Century-Crofts, Inc., 1950), p. 182.

Constitutional Provisions

Every State has a written constitution with provisions on many matters, including local government. Within each State, provisions with respect to State and local powers and organization take legal precedence over statutes and administrative regulations, as well as over all actions of local governments. Under the supreme law clause in Article VI of the Federal Constitution, any pertinent provision of the latter takes legal precedence over State constitutions, laws, or regulations, whenever these appear to be in conflict with the provisions of the Federal Constitution.

It has always been understood, however, that the States and not the National government have power to create, alter, and abolish local governments and to regulate their affairs. In this respect, it has been pointed out, local government corporations are like private corporations, the great majority of which have been created by the States. Thus it is not strange that there is in the Federal Constitution no mention of local governments within the States. Since the Federal government has no authority over the local and internal concerns of the States, any existing Federal control over such matters must arise more or less indirectly from the application of basic constitutional principles to the actions of State and/or local governments.

Cases involving the status of local governments under the Federal Constitution have arisen under the contract clause and under the due process and equal protection clauses of the Fourteenth Amendment. In *Trenton* v. *New Jersey,* for example, the Supreme Court in 1923, in a suit involving the apportionment of the water of the Delaware River and the water supply of the City of Trenton, held that "a municipality is merely a department of the State, and the State may withhold, grant or withdraw powers and privileges as it sees fit. However great or small its sphere of action, it remains the creature of the State exercising and holding powers and privileges subject to the common will." [4] The only way the city could acquire the right to divert water from a river for the use of its inhabitants was by grant from the State or by authorized purchase or condemnation from one to whom the right had been granted by the State.

The principle of this case has never been overruled, and the decision with respect to cities is equally applicable to any county, town, village, school district, or other local unit. Another case likewise involved

---

[4] 262 U.S. 182 (1923). Both of these cases are discussed in Anderson, William, *Intergovernmental Relations in Review* (Minneapolis: University of Minnesota Press, 1960), pp. 89–91.

a municipal water supply problem. Tacoma was upheld by the Supreme Court in a controversy with the State over water rights in a navigable river. Under the Federal Water Power Act of 1920, the City of Tacoma, a municipal corporation created by the State of Washington, had applied for and received from the Federal Power Commission a license to build several dams on the Cowlitz River and to develop water power at these dams. Since doing so would result in the flooding of some State-owned land and a State fish hatchery, the State in its sovereign capacity opposed the Tacoma power project in one lawsuit after another. State attorneys argued that the city as a creature of the State and subject to the power of the State could not exercise any power not conferred upon it by the State, and that the State had not granted it any power to take State property such as the fish hatchery, even though it was conceded that the State had granted to the city broad powers to engage in the production of electric power by means of dams and other works in streams.

The Supreme Court, overruling a State supreme court decision and affirming the Federal Court of Appeals, rejected the plea of the State: "The Federal Government under the commerce clause of the Constitution . . . has dominion, to the exclusion of the States, over navigable waters of the United States." [5] Congress had enacted the Federal Power Act, and the Federal Power Commission, after full hearings, had licensed the city to do what it was doing; thus the central government had in effect conferred upon the city the Federal power of eminent domain to take and remove properties such as the State fish hatchery. As Professor Anderson has summarized it, "No action of the State was needed to authorize this taking, and no State action could obstruct the Federal licensee in carrying out its power."

Developments in the Roosevelt Era

The Federal alphabetical agencies of the Roosevelt era brought about a veritable revolution in the long-established pattern of Federal-local relations. The Federal Emergency Relief Administration (FERA) was the first to be established; this was soon followed by Civil Works Administration (CWA), Public Works Administration (PWA), Works Progress Administration (WPA), and a variety of others. Through these organizations, and the grants-in-aid included in their respective programs, sweeping changes came about. The change of policy was evident in both executive and legislative actions. New administrative procedures, involving direct relations between the Federal government and the cities, were

[5] *City of Tacoma* v. *Taxpayers*, 357 U.S. 320 (1958).

developed, and Congress authorized the Reconstruction Finance Corporation (RFC) to make loans to States and municipalities and passed municipal bankruptcy legislation, at first unsuccessfully, later successfully.

An extraordinary number of bankruptcies during the Great Depression led to the enactment of numerous debt adjustment and mortgage moratorium laws. Significant among these was the Municipal Bankruptcy Act of 1934. Although the Supreme Court upheld its constitutionality in 1938, it was amended in that year, amended again and reenacted in 1940, extending—provided the legislature of the State approved—to counties, cities, "and other local taxing districts" privileges similar to those that had been conferred on individuals and railroads in 1933,[6] and amended again in 1946.[7]

During this period when the needs of the cities were so great, Mayors and other city officials clamored for more and more Federal aid for relief, public works, housing, and slum clearance. Congress, as noted, came twice to the rescue of defaulting municipalities with debt limitation legislation. The cities, especially the larger ones, enjoyed a high degree of Federal preference as units for the administration of such programs as public housing, urban planning, slum clearance, urban renewal; for the construction and maintenance of port facilities, airports, and Federal office buildings; and for aid in building urban connections with highways in the State and Interstate Highway Systems.[8]

In the late 1930's, a number of steps were taken by the administration to improve Federal-municipal relations. The Federal Works Agency, composed of various alphabetical and old-line agencies, was created by Reorganization Plan No. 1 of 1939.[9] By an Executive Order issued September 9, 1939, providing for White House staff reorganization, the President directed the National Resources Planning Board to consult with Federal, regional, State, local, and private agencies in developing orderly programs of public works, and to act as a clearing house and a means of coordinating activities at the various levels and in the various aspects of planning. An Office of Government Reports in the Executive Office was charged, among other things, with the performance of the following duties:

[6] See U.S. Code, Title 11, pp. 401–404, enacted in 1934 and upheld in *United States* v. *Bekins*, 304 U.S. 27 (1938). For amendments, see 50 Stat. 654 (August 16, 1937) and 54 Stat. 667 (June 28, 1940); see also Chatters, Carl H., and Ray, John S., *The Federal Municipal Debt Adjustment Act: A Guide for Municipalities* (Chicago: Public Administration Service, 1934).

[7] See House Committee on the Judiciary, *Amending Municipal Bankruptcy Act*, Hearings, 79th Cong., 2nd Sess. (Washington, 1946).

[8] Anderson, p. 115.

[9] Reorganization Plan No. 1 of 1939, approved June 7, 1939. Public Resolution No. 2, 76th Cong.

1. To provide a central clearing house through which citizens, State and local governmental bodies, and, where appropriate, agencies of the Federal government might transmit inquiries and complaints and receive advice and information.

2. To assist the President in dealing with special problems requiring the clearance of information between the Federal government and State and local governments and private institutions.

3. To keep the President informed of the opinions, desires, and complaints of citizens and groups of citizens and of State and local governments with respect to the work of Federal agencies.

In addition, a municipal reference bureau was established in the Bureau of the Census, while in the National Resources Planning Board, a special committee was named to discover and make available aids to local planning.[10] Some provision, though not always an adequate one, was made for in lieu payments, offsetting in part the loss of revenue resulting from the withdrawal of valuable properties from the tax rolls.

World War II and After

Whereas Federal-city relations had been a depression-born experiment to deal with unemployment and resulting distress, the exigencies of war shifted them to congested areas and to problems of civil defense and rationing in which local governments and millions of volunteers participated. After World War II, Federal-city relations continued in a complex of direct and indirect administrative relationships.

Cash surpluses accumulated during the war, largely because of wartime restrictions, were quickly dissipated, with the result that cities soon found themselves again in a serious financial plight, ground, as it were, between the upper and the nether millstones. They were faced on one hand with strong pressure for more, better, and more costly services for a constantly increasing population, while on the other hand, their revenue-raising potential was severely restricted by antiquated constitutional and statutory provisions. Only two States acted promptly and effectively to relieve the plight of their cities—Pennsylvania with P.L. 481 of 1947, and New York with its Moore Plan. In other jurisdictions, the situation seemed to give tangible evidence in support of the declara-

---

[10] These developments are discussed in Short, Raymond S., "Municipalities and the Federal Government," *Annals of the American Academy of Political and Social Science*, January, 1940, pp. 44–53. Cooperation of this type received a serious setback when in 1942 Senator Taft and several colleagues brought about the abolition of the NRPB on the ground that planning was "socialistic."

tion of the late Professor Charles E. Merriam, made many years before, that the States would neither govern their cities nor permit the cities to govern themselves. Although there has been some improvement since World War II, Professor Merriam's statement is unfortunately still generally applicable to the situation today.

While the States sought to restore their power over funds by the enactment of "channeling legislation" as applied to Federal grants-in-aid, cities fought to preserve their newly established direct relationships with the Federal government and were largely successful in the effort. While little actual help came from the States, the Federal government provided substantial financial assistance for them in many different ways—in housing, airport development, hospital construction, highway improvement, and other types of public works. Various Federal laws provided numerous exemptions from Federal taxes as applied to municipalities, exemptions ranging from 5 to 7 per cent to as much as 20 per cent of the cost of specified purchases. Further reductions from previous rates became effective in April, 1954.[11]

In the early stages, these developments did not interfere materially with the legal control of the States over their cities, nor did they jeopardize State controls, for the new pattern of relationships was superimposed upon the old. It afforded, as Professor Arthur W. Bromage observed, "a new line of attack on perplexing problems, local in origin but national in effect, without supplanting the basic position of the State in creating and controlling municipalities." [12] These relationships now follow a firmly established pattern, and they have tended to increase steadily both in number and in importance and appear likely to continue to do so. It is highly improbable that the cities now can or would agree to any cutbacks looking toward a restoration of the conditions existing in the pre-Roosevelt era.

FEDERAL RELATIONS WITH COUNTIES AND SPECIAL DISTRICTS

The Federal government is now concerned with the problems of all people—foreign and domestic, national, regional, and local. In the latter category, the problems of rural dwellers are included as well as those of

[11] See Smith, Wilbur E., "Federal Tax Savings for Municipalities," "Municipal Exemptions from Federal Taxes," and similar titles which appeared in many journals of the State leagues of municipalities in January and February, 1958.

[12] Bromage, p. 183.

the increasing numbers of people who live in metropolitan areas. Probably the most significant direct relationships between the Federal government and the counties, the basic unit in rural areas in most States, are found in agriculture. Here, be it remembered, there are county agents,

CHECKLIST OF MAJOR FEDERAL PROGRAMS OF
ASSISTANCE TO COMMUNITIES *

	Grants	Loans	Assistance Technical	Construction Federal	Procurement	Surplus
Community Economic Development	X	X	X		X	X
Community Facilities	X	X	X	X		X
Housing	X	X	X			
Community Welfare	X		X			
Federal Procurement			X	X	X	X
Aids to the Business Community	X	X	X		X	X
Federal Policies		X	X	X		X
Civil Defense	X		X			X

* United States Area Development Administration, Office of Research and Planning, Government Printing Office, Washington, June, 1961.

county home demonstration agents, and representatives of each of the major programs of the Department of Agriculture, in each of the farming counties of the nation,[13] who are an important illustration of the network of cooperative relationships existing between Federal, State, and local

[13] See Baker, Gladys, *The County Agent* (Chicago: University of Chicago Press, 1939); see also Ball, Carleton R., *Federal, State, and Local Administrative Relationships in Agriculture*, 2 vols. (Berkeley: University of California Press, 1938) and a recent article by Fletcher Harrington, "The County Agent as a Member of the Court House Team," *County Officer*, July–August, 1956, pp. 157–162, 183.

governments. These officials are Federal employees, functioning under both Federal and State laws, and selected and paid by the counties in which they serve.

Because the towns and townships of the Northern States have generally been considered too small to be effective as local units for the administration of national programs, the counties have been the units most frequently relied upon in administering rural secondary roads, social security, agricultural extension work, agricultural action programs, rural library work, and others. In part as a result of these Federal preferences, "the financial and administrative importance of the counties has greatly increased nationally in recent years." [14]

In addition, there are relationships between the Federal government and a variety of special districts, some old, some new. Among the former are the school districts. While the Federal government has no direct responsibility for maintaining the public school system, it has made in lieu payments to school districts [15] and given financial assistance for public school construction and maintenance in areas where there has developed acute shortages of classroom space or acute hardship due to an influx of people connected with a Federal installation or project. In agriculture, new districts have frequently been set up for soil conservation purposes and for rural electrification, in instances where county lines seemed unsuited to the needs of the program.[16]

SLUM CLEARANCE AND URBAN RENEWAL

Historical Background

The historical development of urban planning, zoning, and urban redevelopment in American cities during the twentieth century can be characterized by decades, as follows:

1900–1910
> Emphasis on city beautification; creation of civic centers, as in Denver and San Francisco.

[14] Anderson, p. 115.

[15] See Kentucky Legislative Research Commission, *Federal in lieu Payments to School Districts* (Frankfort, January, 1958) and Senate Committee on Labor and Public Welfare, *Operating Expenses of School Districts Affected by Federal Activities*, Report No. 714, to accompany H.R. 6078, 83rd Cong., 1st Sess. (Washington, 1953).

[16] See Parks, William R., *Soil Conservation Districts in Action* (Ames: Iowa State College Press, 1952).

1910–1920
Emphasis on street planning, due to the growing importance of the automobile.
1920–1930
Development of zoning.
1930–1940
Emphasis on housing, probably an over-emphasis, on the basis of the mistaken belief that large scale public housing would retard deterioration of central city areas, and prevent the spread of blight.
1940–1950
Emphasis on highway development, including circumferential roads.
1950–1960
Urban renewal and redevelopment, including the condemnation of large areas, and complete rebuilding, with the needs of the city as a whole in mind, not only for today but for the future.[17]

From this tabulation, it is quite clear that the antecedents of urban renewal go back at least to the 1930's, when the public housing program was first initiated, in part to replace slum housing with decent, safe, and sanitary dwellings, and in part to stimulate the economy. The first federally aided slum clearance program was a limited one under the PWA public housing program. The United States Housing Act of 1937, the first major Federal program dealing with slum clearance on a broad scale, declared it to be the policy of Congress:

. . . to assist the several States and their political subdivisions to alleviate present and recurring unemployment and to remedy the unsafe and insanitary housing conditions and the acute shortage of decent, safe, and sanitary dwellings for families of low income, in rural and urban communities, that are injurious to the health, safety and morals of the citizens of the Nation.[18]

Under this legislation, slum clearance was coupled with low-rent housing, and an "equivalent elimination" requirement assured the upgrading of housing in local communities. Thus, a community could not receive annual contributions for a low-rent housing project unless provision was made to eliminate substantially the same number of substandard dwellings as the number of public housing units to be constructed. The elimination could be accomplished by repair and rehabilitation as well as by complete demolition.

Slum clearance, urban renewal and community development, however, did not become major objectives until a few years later. In 1943, Senator Elbert D. Thomas of Utah introduced a bill to establish a pro-

[17] Bartholomew, Harland, in an address before the Washington Chapter of the American Society for Public Administration, December 14, 1955.
[18] 50 Stat. 896 (1937).

gram of Federal aid to municipalities for urban redevelopment. This pioneer proposal recognized both the need for comprehensive planning in each urban community and the financial limitations confronting urban areas which sought to cope with conditions resulting from the increasing spread of blighted areas and slums. Alfred Bettman of Cincinnati played an important role in the drafting of this bill to provide long-term loans at low interest rates.

Two years later in 1945, the famous Taft-Ellender-Wagner bill was under consideration; passed, it would have become the National Housing Act. It did pass the Senate, but adoption was delayed by four years of controversy in the House. Finally passed in the summer of 1949, the new Act was aimed particularly at slum clearance (urban and rural) and redevelopment, providing for some 810,000 new units for low-income families only. All projects were to be developed, owned, and operated by local housing authorities (usually municipal) established under State statutes. Within a year, 500 such authorities had been set up in forty-two States.

In the 1940's, the State redevelopment statutes accomplished what might be called a bloodless revolution in the law of property rights by permitting public agencies to acquire slum property by eminent domain, to clear and assemble the land, and to dispose of it to a new private owner who agreed to put it to the use determined best for the community as a whole. In order for the land to be sold at a fair market price, a large loss had to be absorbed by public subsidy, and in the Housing Act of 1949, Congress recognized that the task of slum clearance was too costly for cities to accomplish alone. The Federal government undertook to pay two-thirds of the net cost. The 1961 amendments to the National Housing Act provided $2 billion in matching funds for slum rehabilitation, land purchase, and redevelopment, for four years.

Mention should be made of the fact that at least two States, New York and New Jersey, have developed extensive housing programs of their own. The New York program is administered by the Division of Housing in the Executive Department, that of New Jersey by the Department of Conservation and Development. Both States have invested many millions of dollars in these programs. Both include public housing for low-income families and programs designed to meet the needs of the lower-middle income families that earn too much to be eligible for public housing but not enough to afford housing built by the unaided private dollar. In addition, programs are now under way to meet two other rapidly increasing needs—urban renewal and housing for the aged.

In New York, the voters authorized in 1958 a $25 million State fund to help communities finance their share of urban renewal programs carried on under the Federal Housing Act of 1949. Programs are also under way to provide safe, moderate rent apartments for the aged in both the low and middle income groups.[19] That these programs are live and steadily expanding is shown by an announcement, made in November, 1960, that eight new middle income apartments, including 5,862 units, were to be built under the State's limited-profit program.[20]

Conflicting Philosophies and Administrative Difficulties

Two schools of thought developed with regard to the proper procedure for fighting slums. Those who rejected the subsidy method of slum clearance contended that property owners could be induced to rehabilitate the slums themselves, if long ignored housing, health, and sanitation codes were enforced. Eventually it became apparent that neither approach was adequate in itself, "that clearance and redevelopment were too slow and costly to overcome the backlog of slums and at the same time keep pace with the unchecked formation of new blight, and that code enforcement alone cannot save a neighborhood if obvious hazards are not cleared out, and if public facilities are not raised to acceptable modern standards."

These opposing views were reconciled in the Housing Act of August 2, 1954. This program retained the appeal of slum clearance, with its opportunity to bulldoze the most noxious slums, to create large new taxable values, and to create from a clean slate a portion of the city of tomorrow. At the same time, the concept of urban renewal struck a responsive chord in the minds of vast numbers of homeowners who had sunk their savings into aging neighborhoods and who could see the first hope of rescue from the inroads of blight. Now the city could apply " 'spot clearance' to eliminate the obvious hazards and the pockets of decay, while conserving and rehabilitating the values that had made the neighborhood worth while." [21]

Soon after this controversy was settled, others developed over the manner in which urban redevelopment projects were planned and executed. Dissatisfaction developed in many communities because too many projects were started, resulting in dislocaton of persons, disruption of traffic, and general confusion. This became such a problem in Washington, D.C., that in 1960, Representative Louis C. Rabaut of Michigan introduced and the House of Representatives passed by an overwhelming

---

[19] State Division of Housing, *An Action Program for Community Development* (Albany, March, 1960), annual report for 1959–1960.

[20] *The New York Times*, November 2, 1960.

[21] Quoted from Millspaugh, Martin, "Objectives and Criteria of Urban Renewal," *Academy of Political Science Proceedings*, May, 1960, pp. 49–56.

vote a bill prohibiting the starting of new projects until existing projects were completed. The Washington Board of Trade had opposed the initiation of new projects until the tremendous redevelopment of Southwest Washington was at least 70 per cent completed. These solutions may not be the right ones, but the fact that they have been proposed serves to underscore the frustrating effect upon a community of having too many simultaneous projects in varying stages of completion.

A second cause of dissatisfaction arose from poor judgment in approving projects or in determining their exact scope and nature. Urban renewal should concentrate in those areas where it is most needed. It should not demolish properties in good condition merely to satisfy the urge to build anew on a grand scale, as seems to have been done in some cases, nor should it sweep out old and historic structures that are part of a community's historic heritage, as was first attempted in the Lafayette Square area in Washington. Such incidents indicate bad planning and sometimes go so far as to violate comprehensive planning ordinances presumably affording protection to the entire city. Urban renewal, important though it is, should conform to the highest standards of the planning profession and to the provisions of existing law in the community.

Relocation Requirements

One of the requirements for Federal approval of local urban renewal activities is a detailed plan for relocating displaced families. The Housing and Home Finance Agency (HHFA) has compiled a relocation plan which must be followed, including policies and requirements to which each local public agency must adhere. Members of Congress, local officials, and others have voiced concern over the hardships suffered by small businesses which rent or lease their accommodations on a project site. Goodwill payments are not provided, and testimony presented before Congressional committees and at local government meetings has revealed a number of hardship cases for which relocation payments were insufficient to re-establish some of these small businesses.

The Housing Act of 1956 provided for relocation payments of $100 for families and individuals and $2,000 for small business concerns. The 1957 Act increased the latter to $3,500, while the Act of 1959 provided for relocation payments of $200 to families and individuals and $3,000 to business concerns. These payments are intended to cover moving expenses and other direct losses of property resulting from the displacement. Relocation payments are added to the Federal grant for each particular urban renewal project.

The Problem of the Core Cities

Reference has been made to the exodus of great numbers of tax-paying residents of the city proper to the surrounding suburban and/or satellite communities, and to the consequent loss of revenue due to deterioration of their abandoned properties. These properties were taken over by remaining central city residents, whose properties in turn degenerated into slum areas. This process of disintegration went on steadily over a period of years before the effects became fully obvious, but by that time, it had gone so far that rehabilitation was virtually impossible.

The cities were faced with a serious problem of urban reconstruction and redevelopment for which careful planning was necessary to insure that the best utilization was made of disintegrated areas in relation to the future needs of the city. The President's Advisory Committee on Urban Renewal divided the problem into three main parts: (1) clearing and redeveloping areas that were too far gone to be saved; (2) rehabilitating areas that had started to slide but could still be saved; (3) preventing the spread of blight into good areas. When planning had been completed, there remained the problem of financing the desired improvements. Financed they must be, if further disintegration of the central city areas is to be prevented and if once valuable properties are to be either restored to the tax rolls or devoted to the public use.[22]

The Act of 1954 established as a requirement the development of "a workable plan" as a means of establishing eligibility for Federal aid. A workable plan may be defined as one to prevent further spread of the decay which the Federal assistance is designed to eliminate. The Act further provides that each community must develop locally a plan which contains the following seven elements:

1. Codes and ordinances that establish adequate standards for housing.
2. A comprehensive community plan that offers a basis for community development.
3. Neighborhood analysis to identify sources of blight.
4. Administrative organization establishing clear cut authority and responsibility for coordination of the overall program.

[22] See Augur, Tracy B., "Federal Aids for Local Planning," *Public Administration Survey* (University of Mississippi), May, 1955, entire issue; see also Pennsylvania Bureau of Community Development, *Policies and Procedures for the Urban Planning Assistance Program Under the Federal Housing Act of 1959* (Harrisburg, May, 1960) and Bartholomew, Paul C., "A Practical Conservation Program in Urban Renewal," *Illinois Municipal Review*, October, 1960.

5. Financing to support the various activities needed in carrying out the program.

6. Housing for families displaced by improvement projects.

7. Citizen participation by civic organizations, neighborhood groups, and individuals who can help to shape the program.

It may be noted in passing that these same elements may with slight modification be blended into programs in other areas as well—transportation, industrial development, education, community facilities, or any other area of public concern in which community groups and individual citizens may make decisions and guide the overall growth of the community.

Public housing programs carried on with the financial assistance of the Federal government have helped some, but during the Eisenhower years, Federal aid for the purpose, in spite of steadily mounting needs, was sharply curtailed. Urban renewal programs have not kept up with city decay. The Federal Housing Act of 1954 sought to give a new look to municipal slum clearance and urban redevelopment work. Its supporters coined a new catch-phrase, "urban renewal," which may be defined as a community-wide program to eliminate and prevent the spread of blight. This Act outlined a broad program of Federal assistance designed to alert American municipalities, to arm them to deal with the menace of blight in all its manifestations, and to stimulate a broad program of community action.

> As part of this program, the Federal Government now requires every municipality desiring Federal aid to assume new and specific responsibilities. Municipalities are required to map out their problem and develop definite plans for a sound approach to solving it. Some think of "urban renewal" in terms of redevelopment, some rehabilitation and some conservation. Regardless of the terminology the fundamental problem is the saving of our cities, the rescuing of the great, vital urban nerve centers from the spreading paralysis of blight and slums.[23]

Such a program of rehabilitation, reconditioning, conservation, and stricter and more uniform enforcement of building codes and housing laws is possible in areas in which deterioration is not too far advanced. If these measures are to be effective, there must be careful advance planning and a concerted, sustained, and coordinated attack upon all phases of the problem. In a few instances, insurance companies have made

---

[23] From an article appearing under various titles in the journals of the State leagues of municipalities during the summer of 1954; see also Slayton, William L., "The States and Urban Renewal," *State Government,* October, 1954, pp. 203–204, 215.

substantial investments in housing projects. A few blighted areas have been cleared and turned into parks, or used for parking lots or other public purposes. In Philadelphia in 1954, a war on blight was begun by selecting four areas in which to find ways of keeping neighborhoods from running down. This use of "test areas" represents a new approach to the problem of urban disintegration. Generally speaking, however, sporadic efforts in isolated areas or a piecemeal attack upon the problem will not produce satisfactory results.[24]

As in the case of many major problems, urban renewal is not an exclusively Federal-local problem. The States have a large stake in the prosperity and continued good health of their cities. They have a continuing responsibility with respect to urban renewal and should participate actively with other levels of government in clearing up existing blight and preventing a further deterioration of cities. Although the Kestnbaum Commission made recommendations along this line, outlining a program for the States, including such aspects of the problem as organization, legislation, metropolitan areas, finance, personnel, and research, there was, with the exception of programs in New York, New Jersey, and a few other States, little evidence of serious effort on the part of the States to make these recommendations effective.

OTHER MAJOR PROBLEMS

There are many Federal programs that affect urban areas, some directly, others more or less indirectly. Most of them make technical assistance available, many provide grants and/or loans, and some provide Federal construction, procurement, and distribution of surplus commodities, as shown in the table on page 661. Among those having a direct effect are, in addition to the slum clearance and urban renewal program, the community facilities program, the depressed areas program, air and water pollution control, open space, and highways. Other programs affecting cities are low-rent public housing, hospital, school and airport construction, water treatment, and welfare.[25] Perhaps the most striking characteristic of all of these programs is the almost complete

[24] For full discussion of these problems, see Woodbury, Coleman, ed., *Urban Redevelopment: Problems and Practices*, 2 vols. (Chicago: University of Chicago Press, 1953). Vol. I, Part IV is devoted to the specific problems discussed here.

[25] See Gronin, Daniel S., "Impact of Federal Welfare Grants on Municipal Government," *Boston University Law Review*, Fall, 1960, pp. 531–543.

lack of coordination among them. The result is, unfortunately, that very often the beneficial effects of one program are impaired by unforeseen effects of another. Expressways, for example, affect housing, the desirability of housing sites, and recreation areas, and all of these programs affect the transit problem. Overall planning on a community-wide basis is urgently needed.

Community Facilities

Under Title III of the Defense Housing and Community Facilities and Services Act of 1951, the Housing and Home Finance Administrator is authorized to make grants and other payments for community facilities, equipment, or services to "critical defense housing areas." The term community facilities is defined to include waterworks, sewers, garbage and refuse disposal facilities, police and fire protection facilities, public sanitary facilities, works for treatment and purification of water, libraries, hospitals and other places for the care of the sick, recreation facilities, streets and roads, day-care centers, etc. Community service is defined as the maintenance of such facilities. It may be noted that aid for hospitals has been generally available to municipalities under the Hospital Survey and Construction Program instituted in 1946.

As a prerequisite to aid under the Community Facilities Act, the President must declare the area to be a "critical defense housing area"; private enterprise must be afforded full opportunity to provide the necessary housing; and the chief executive officer of the appropriate political subdivision must certify that such community facilities or services cannot otherwise be provided, without the imposition of an increased and excessive tax burden or an excessive increase in the debt limit of the local subdivision. Although it was provided that this program should taper off after July 31, 1954, continued need made reduction impossible. In its revised form it became known as the Section 702 advanced planning program. By 1961, one of the key features of the Housing Act was a community facility loan program for which $450 million makes possible low interest rate financing for small towns and depressed areas up to a population of 150,000. This program is designed not only to meet the needs of a rapidly growing urban population, but to make possible at least a beginning on the tremendous backlog of need for public works construction.[26]

In its report on governmental structure in metropolitan areas, the Advisory Commission on Intergovernmental Relations submitted a num-

[26] For a list of hundreds of such projects for which plans had been completed as of March 31, 1961, see Representative Albert Rains of Alabama in the *Congressional Record*, June 15, 1961, pp. 9729–9733.

ber of recommendations for expanded activity on the part of the Federal government with respect to the problems of such areas: (1) financial support on a continuing basis to metropolitan area planning agencies; (2) expanded Federal technical assistance to State and metropolitan planning agencies; (3) Congressional consent in advance to interstate compacts creating planning agencies in those metropolitan areas crossing State lines; and (4) review by a metropolitan planning agency of applications for Federal grants-in-aid within the area with respect to airport, highway, public housing and hospital construction, waste treatment works, and urban renewal projects.[27]

Depressed Areas

The depressed area problem, long in the process of development but only lately recognized, gave rise to at least five years of legislative conflict. The chronic localized unemployment which characterizes these areas is usually the result of some basic economic change affecting the community's primary source of jobs. The vast majority of these areas fall into one of several categories: single-industry towns whose industry has closed down or migrated; areas affected by automation in some industries; areas in which a natural resource such as coal, iron, or lumber, upon which the town was largely dependent, is exhausted; or areas in which the working force increases at a rate faster than the economy can absorb new workers.

The result was that, in spite of generally high national levels of employment and wages, there had developed early in 1957 seventy-eight pockets of chronic unemployment, mostly small, where the problem is of significant size and considerable duration. Now the number of such communities is much larger. In all of them, the unemployment rate is at least 6 per cent, in some the jobless exceed 12 per cent, and in many small communities, the unemployed are not even counted.[28] These communities need help, and soon.

The question of how they can be helped is easier asked than answered. All agree that some action is necessary; some feel that it is a State and local responsibility, others that State and local governments

[27] *Governmental Structure, Organization, and Planning in Metropolitan Areas: Suggested Action by Local, State, and National Governments* (Washington: House Committee Print, 87th Cong., 1st Sess., 1961).

[28] See American Enterprise Association, *Legislative Analysis: Proposals for Federal Aid to Depressed Areas* (Washington, January, 1961); see also Mooney, Richard E., "Unemployment Rising: High Jobless Figures and Increase in Number of Depressed Areas Spur Search for Solutions," *The New York Times*, December 19, 1960, p. 10E.

cannot do the job. Some want a Federal program, some want such a program if and only if it is clearly demonstrated that the State and local governments have failed, and others do not want one even then. One Member of Congress contended that the plea for Federal aid for such areas was part of a drive "to usurp the rights of free enterprise and the individual States." The fact remains that it will be necessary for some-

PRESIDENT KENNEDY SIGNS THE DEPRESSED AREAS BILL

one, somehow, to rebuild all or large portions of these areas and to train or retrain the people who live in them so that they may again become independent, self-supporting, and self-respecting members of the community.

Opponents of the Democratic proposal to offer grants for community redevelopment and low-interest loans to private enterprise to create new industry and new jobs in these areas argued that public funds should not be used to establish new industries, artificially stimulated, to compete with existing establishments. If these areas were good markets and were suited to industrial development, they contended, such development would have already occurred; if there are no jobs available, the people should be moved to locations in which they can secure employment. They also contend that if local communities showed a greater spirit of self-reliance, they could solve their own problems. Cases in which afflicted communities have tried to help themselves, however, have been the exception rather than the rule, but there are just enough of them reported in the press to lend plausibility to the argument that rehabilitation could be accomplished in this way.[29]

In recognition of the urgency of these conditions, numerous bills were presented in Congress, beginning in 1955. Three of them, sponsored by Senator Paul H. Douglas of Illinois, were passed. The first met with a pocket veto by President Eisenhower in 1958, the second was vetoed by the same President in 1960, and the third (after extensive discussion during the presidential campaign) was passed by Congress and signed by President Kennedy in 1961. It provided $50 million for emergency loans for rail, bus, subway, or other transit equipment and facilities through December, 1962.

Air and Water Pollution Control

Air Pollution Control. The experience of Los Angeles with air pollution control provides a basis for several general conclusions. The complexities of the air pollution problem demand intergovernmental cooperation, as well as provision for expensive specialized technical and scientific services and facilities; the solution is no longer confined to such a simple technique as the organization of a crew of "smoke watchers." [30] Air pollution does not respect artificial political boundary lines and must be dealt with according to physical factors.

An effective air pollution program involves such elements as the following:

[29] Examples: Torrance, California (Sid Ross and Ed Kiester, "We Did It Ourselves," *Parade,* June 18, 1961); Phoenix, Arizona ("Phoenix Scorns U.S. Assistance for Its Slum Clearance Project," *The New York Times,* May 14, 1961); Wilkes-Barre, Pennsylvania (William G. Weart, "Gifts Bring Jobs in Wilkes-Barre," *ibid.,* March 26, 1961).

[30] These comments are based on Dorn, Warren M., "Air Pollution: A Problem for Urban Counties," *Urban County Congress* (Washington: National Association of County Officials, 1959), pp. 126–129. See also U.S. Public Health Service, *The Federal Role in the Community Air Pollution Problem* (Washington, April, 1955).

1. A legislative body armed with power to enact and enforce air pollution control rules and regulations throughout all sections of the areas, whether incorporated or unincorporated.

2. The strict policing of all new industrial construction to assure that all sources capable of emitting significant types or quantities of air contaminants are properly controlled with suitable air pollution control devices and methods. (In Los Angeles two permits must be secured by potential industrial sources of air pollution: a permit to construct, and a permit to operate.)

3. A careful and comprehensive field program of source inspection and law enforcement to assure that potential sources of air pollution are operating in full compliance with prescribed standards.

4. The adoption of rules and regulations which establish specific emission standards, to be observed by all air pollution sources operating within the area. These rules should fit standards regulating the emission of hydrocarbons, sulfur oxides, particulate matter, combustion contaminates, nuisance causing substances, and visible pollution omissions.

5. Sponsorship of such research, survey, and development activities as are necessary to determine the causes of air pollution problems, to fix emission standards capable of eliminating or reducing these problems, and of providing practicable means for meeting the terms prescribed by the standards.

This kind of program has meant, in the Los Angeles area where it has been administered through the County Air Pollution Control District established in 1948, with a population of nearly 6 million, an organization of 367 employees and an annual budget of approximately $3,500,000, at an average per capita cost of about $.60 annually. Although the cost of control is high, the toll reaped annually by air pollution is even higher.

The intergovernmental relations aspects of this problem cannot be too strongly emphasized. In the opinion of experts in the field, increased Federal and State participation must be promoted by every available means: participation in the areas of basic research, establishment of emission standards, public health research, and training. This will result in spreading the costs (those in Los Angeles have admittedly been high, due to the pioneering aspects of the program) and, after all, this is everyone's problem. If research is done at the higher levels of government, it will be possible for local units to concentrate on engineering and enforcement, which are naturally a local responsibility.

Water Control Program. Problems of air and water pollution are alike in that both affect an element essential to human existence. The purity of both is of vital concern to cities, because of their dense concentrations of population. Control efforts in both areas are difficult and costly to administer. The two problems differ in that the sources of air contamination are largely confined to cities, but this is not necessarily true of the sources of water contamination.

Highways

Prior to 1934, the States were prohibited from spending any portion of the regular Federal aid highway funds in municipalities of more than 2,500 population. Although Congress had made available $125 million in 1932 and $400 million in 1933 as outright grants for highway and grade-crossing elimination work in which municipalities were eligible to participate, municipal officials found that in some cases they had to appeal to the Bureau of Public Roads, over the heads of their State highway departments, if they were to get any benefit from these appropriations. The Bureau directed that 25 per cent of the funds should be spent on municipal projects—a provision which was incorporated in both the emergency and regular Federal-aid highway legislation of 1934, the Hayden-Cartwright Act.

It was not until the Federal-aid Highway Act of 1944, however, that the law authorized expenditure of Federal monies in urban areas. Continuously since that time, the Bureau of Public Roads has encouraged cooperation between State highway departments and city and county officials in planning for the location and design of Federal aid highways in urban areas. The Federal government gave weight to this encouragement by making funds available for joint study of the problem and for the construction of the highways determined to be necessary. Under this legislation, the Federal government makes available for research studies 1.5 per cent of all Federal monies apportioned for highway construction, including the development of the basic data needed for analyzing the current urban highway problem and planning for its solution.

The cooperation of the Federal government does not end there; in fact, as a recent Commissioner of the Bureau of Public Roads observed, that is where it begins.[31] The needs having been determined, monies are available under the Interstate Highway and the so-called ABC programs which can be used for construction of arterial highways in urban areas. Since the Interstate System is intended to link major cities and metropolitan areas, it is not surprising that over 40 per cent of its total estimated cost has been allocated for construction of that portion located within urban boundaries. In dollar volume, this represents roughly $17 billion. In addition to the interstate program, the 1958 Highway Act

[31] Armstrong, Ellis L., "Federal Cooperation," *Urban County Congress,* p. 65.

provided $225 million annually for a two-year period for construction in urban areas of extension of the primary and secondary systems.

Additional Federal funds apportioned for the primary system may be spent in urban areas if so programmed by the State highway departments. Experience indicates that over 30 per cent of the total ABC program is expended in urban areas. Thus, the Federal government in cooperation with the State highway departments stands ready to cooperate not only in planning for the solution of urban transportation problems, but is prepared as well to cooperate in carrying the highway portion of these plans to construction. The commissioner expressed the hope that through cooperation with State and local authorities, an expanded and co-ordinated urban arterial highway program may be possible, with highway construction being an integral part of a long-range community development plan.

Other than population growth, one writer has observed, "the most explosive force in our economy is the Federal highway building program. If ever there was a challenge to unified cooperative effort, give-and-take bargaining, and civic leadership, this is it. Once highways are built, they are there for years. We cannot afford mistakes." [32] These are some of the questions that must be answered before a unified highway system is realized:

> 1. Should the interchanges of the new Federal highway program be planned inside or outside of our urban areas?
> 2. How can the great national programs of urban renewal and highways, working simultaneously in many areas, be coordinated so that the local economic usefulness of existing urban centers is enhanced? Certainly these national programs should not be carried out in opposition to one another.
> 3. In our urban redevelopment planning, how can we compensate in both the public and the private sectors for a potentially successful highway program as contrasted with a dismal outlook for mass rapid transit?
> 4. How will communities finance terminal facilities for the vehicles coming off the new highways into urban centers and provide funds for improvements to local streets and roads?
> 5. How can urban areas provide for the housing and commercial relocation of people displaced by the new highways?
> 6. How can we avoid through proper planning, zoning, and subdivision control the undesirable results of land pollution, urban sprawl, and elimination of large areas from the tax rolls with no equivalent tax return possible as a consequence of the highway building?

[32] Palmer, H. Bruce, "National Programs Affecting Local Economic Growth," *The Little Economies* (New York: Committee for Economic Development, May, 1958), pp. 43–53.

A FEDERAL DEPARTMENT OF LOCAL AFFAIRS

The present situation presents a fine opportunity to re-establish, and to develop and expand to meet current needs, the important programs of the Roosevelt era which have, through the influence of war and inertia, been permitted to deteriorate or be lost altogether. Since 1954, when Representative J. Arthur Younger of California introduced a bill calling for the establishment of a "department of urbiculture," there has been increasing pressure for such action. The cities, at first dubious, have come more and more to favor such a department for at least three reasons: (1) the States' historic neglect of their cities; (2) a period of being snubbed at the council table; (3) mounting difficulties encountered with metropolitan area problems.

Historical Background

Long-time Neglect of Urban Problems. First, and fundamental to an understanding of the whole situation, is the fact that for many long years the health of the cities has been no one's concern. With few exceptions, the States have done a woefully inadequate job in dealing with cities and their problems. State legislatures have neither taken the problems of their cities seriously nor even attempted to deal with them in an intelligent manner. Even now, only half a dozen States have created offices or agencies to advise, counsel, and work with local officials in the solution of their problems, although there should not be a single State without such an agency. The grievances of the cities in this situation are manifold. Not only is their every action governed by State law, but in many States cities must apply to and obtain the permission of the legislature before taking action on the most trivial and often purely local matters. On most of these problems, the members of the characteristically rural-dominated State legislatures know little and care less. Financially, also, the cities have been at a serious disadvantage. After the best and most productive tax sources have been pre-empted by either the Nation or the State, the cities must operate under rigid and often outmoded tax and debt limitations, on one hand, and under the ever-increasing demands of a rapidly growing population for more, better, and more costly services, on the other.

The Federal government is just beginning to focus its attention on urban problems in an effective way. The cities can get a sympathetic hearing in Washington, and some legislation designed to aid in the solution of their problems has been enacted. The Executive Branch and the Senate seem much more understanding than the House which, to a lesser degree, suffers from the same malapportionment that afflicts the State legislatures that are responsible for legislative districting. The ability of the cities to help themselves has been limited to such an extent that even those services which are purely local in their effects far exceed the financing abilities of local government.

Being Snubbed at the Council Table. Over a period of years, the municipal people have felt that they were almost habitually treated as poor and not particularly welcome step-children at the council table. When the original bill providing for a commission of inquiry on intergovernmental relations was drawn up by the author and two members of the staff of the Council of State Governments, provision was made for equal representation for the several levels and units of government. When the act came through several years later, it contained no specific provision for the representation of either municipal or county governments. This unnecessary affront was in part compensated by the commission's setting up a strong local government committee under able leadership. But the local people continued to be very sensitive about the manner in which they were treated.

When the Federal-State Joint Action Committee of Governors and Federal Officials was set up in 1957, the cities were again ignored. This time they were not merely sensitive, they were "sore" and said so in no uncertain terms. Some of them went so far as to warn that unless they were accorded the representation to which they were entitled, they would have no part of the Joint Committee or its works. Their attitude was not difficult to understand, and for this kind of bungling in the field of human relations, there can be little excuse.

Mounting Concern Over Metropolitan Problems. A third major ground for municipal dissatisfaction lies in the difficulties encountered in dealing with the fast increasing metropolitan area problem. The feeling of Mayors in facing these problems without help was voiced in 1957 by Mayor Ben West of Nashville, before the annual meeting of the American Municipal Association in San Francisco. In reporting this meeting, *The New York Times* said:

> Municipalities were warned by mayors and other public officials that the Federal Government was planning to "short change" them in some of the Federal aid programs. . . .
>
> The threat of the Federal Government's reducing or cutting off aid to cities in urban renewal, housing, sewage plant construction and other programs was cited by Mayor Ben West of Nashville, the Association President.

He warned his colleagues that unless they continued "vigilant and alert" they might have to face "our changing cities alone, without sharing the resources of our Federal and State governments, who get theirs first from our taxpayers." [33]

Further threats to reduce Federal aid followed, along with presidential vetoes and threats of vetoes during the remainder of the Eisenhower administration. None of these developments contributed anything to the good will of the municipal officials toward either the Federal government or the States. Since these officials have in many instances found more understanding of their problems and needs and have been able to obtain more help in Washington than in their respective State Capitols, they have developed a strong inclination to look to Washington.

Under these circumstances, it is obvious that municipal officials are not going to sit idly by, viewing with restraint and equanimity the development of a national program which, had it been carried out in full, would have reduced the financial assistance they were receiving while needs continued to mount both in urgency and amount, or would have placed them even more at the mercy of State officials who had all too often been unconcerned and unresponsive to their pleas for help. On the contrary, one might expect insistent demands for more Federal activity in the municipal field.

Alternative Solutions

A Department. One proposal for assistance in the solution of the urban problem has been to establish a Federal department of urban affairs. There are no agreed upon criteria for determining the need for a new cabinet department, for in each instance in the past, there has been a recognized need that could not be met, or met as well, in any other way, and there has been a definitely recognizable clientele to be served, such as farmers, labor, or business. In the present instance, it is to be noted that two-thirds of our population lives in urban areas, and the percentage is constantly rising. The Housing and Home Finance Agency now has a larger annual budget than do six of the existing Federal departments. Between 75 and 80 per cent of the productive capacity of the nation is concentrated in the standard metropolitan areas, not to mention the smaller urban areas.

A Study Commission. Although there would seem to be compelling reasons for establishing a department, there has been nothing approaching unanimity of opinion on the question, even among those who are

[33] Lawrence E. Davies, December 3, 1957, p. 41.

completely sympathetic to the problems of the cities. One proposal, frequently made, has been to establish a study commission to explore the whole range of metropolitan area problems and to make recommendations. While bills for establishing a department were appearing with increasing frequency, study commission bills also began to appear in numbers. In the second session of the 85th Congress, there were four, all of which sought to establish a temporary commission for the study and investigation of problems of municipalities and metropolitan expansion.[34] The Ostertag measure was patterned rather closely after the Kestnbaum Commission on Intergovernmental Relations. The Fascell proposal was favorably reported by the House Committee,[35] but no further action was taken on it.

At the same time, the Bureau of the Budget noted with respect to a similar bill that many of its contemplated studies and investigations were already under way by either government or private agencies, with the result that it was not "necessary to create a study commission on metropolitan problems and urban development at this time." [36] In the first session of the 86th Congress, Senator Joseph S. Clark of Pennsylvania introduced another study commission bill which was reported out and passed by the Senate; [37] no action was taken by the House. Similarly, in the first session of the 87th Congress, Representative Adonnazio of New Jersey included in a department bill provision for a commission on metropolitan problems.[38]

An Advisory Council. A third alternative would have Congress establish an advisory council. The distinguished Louis Brownlow, for instance, believes that an advisor or a small advisory council on urban and metropolitan problems in the Executive Office of the President, in a position comparable to that of the Council of Economic Advisors, might be a far better solution than a cabinet department. This view has been accepted in some other quarters. Professors Connery and Leach, well known students in this area, conclude that "A council on metropolitan areas would serve to bring the Federal role in urban areas into focus and enable the Federal Government to provide the kind of leadership the problem requires. Formulation of a philosophy and evolution of a firm policy based thereon should be the first steps. A staff agency in the President's office, not a department of urban affairs, is the proper unit to take

[34] H.R. 2416, Ostertag of New York; H.R. 7282, Bentley of Michigan; H.R. 7398, Mrs. Granahan of Pennsylvania; and H.R. 7465, Fascell of Florida.

[35] House Report No. 940, August 18, 1959.

[36] On August 3, 1959, in considering the Ostertag bill, H.R. 2416.

[37] S. 1431; reported out in Senate Report No. 881; passed by the Senate, September 10, 1959.

[38] H.R. 301.

them." [39] On February 20, 1962, Mrs. Dwyer, Representative from New Jersey, introduced a bill to establish "a small staff operation within the Executive Office of the President for the purpose of achieving this needed coordination and policy direction." The Office of Urban Affairs which she proposed would be an agency for information and research, coordination of Federal programs, and liaison with State and local authorities administering federally aided programs.[40] It has also been suggested that if the Federal government were properly organized to deal with its intergovernmental problems in general, there would be no need for a cabinet department to deal with the problems of municipalities, for existing agencies would be alert to these problems as they developed and would be prepared to cope with them.

Creating the Department

The idea of a cabinet department to deal with urban problems is not new. First advanced in 1912 by Woodrow Wilson and Philip Kates, a less well known contemporary, the idea appears to have been ignored or forgotten for nearly half a century.[41] Congressional interest in the proposal began to develop after a bill for a department of urbiculture was introduced by Representative J. Arthur Younger of California. The clever name, however, probably prevented the proposal from receiving whatever serious consideration it might otherwise have been accorded. This measure, introduced in the 83rd Congress, has been followed by a host of others; the table on pages 682–683 presents a virtually complete listing of urban department bills introduced in the 84th to 87th Congresses.

The question of establishing such a department, which might have dragged on for years, was suddenly catapulted into national politics as a major issue by (1) President Eisenhower's veto of the depressed areas bill as unwise and unnecessary, and (2) events occurring during and after the presidential campaign of 1960. Both of the major party platforms dealt at some length with the problems of the cities; to the provisions of the Democratic platform, Senator Kennedy pledged his full support. He

[39] Connery, Robert H., and Leach, Richard H., "Do We Need a Department of Urban Affairs?" *Western Political Quarterly*, March, 1960, pp. 99–112. The three sentences quoted are from the concluding paragraph.

[40] H.R. 10302; for her comment on the bill, see *Congressional Record*, February 21, 1962, p. 2462, daily edition. Mr. Scranton of Pennsylvania introduced a similar bill on May 9, 1962, H.R. 11674.

[41] Both appeared in *The American City*—Mr. Kates' article, "A National Department of Municipalities," January, 1912, pp. 405–407, Mr. Wilson's comment in the form of a letter to the editor, on a National Department of Municipalities, August, 1912.

83rd Congress, Second Session—1954
 H.R. 10032—Younger of California, Department of Urbiculture

84th Congress, First Session—1955
 H.R. 1864—Younger of California, Department of Urbiculture

84th Congress, Second Session—1956
 H.R. 10295—Davidson of New York, Department of Housing and Urban Affairs

 S. 3159—Lehman of New York, Department of Housing and Urban Affairs

85th Congress, First Session—1957
 H.R. 1019—Younger of California, Department of Urbiculture

 S. 2159—Clark of Pennsylvania, and others, Department of Housing and Urban Affairs

85th Congress, Second Session—1958
 None

86th Congress, First Session—1959
 H.R. 781—Mrs. Griffiths of Michigan, Department of Urban Affairs
 H.R. 984—Younger of California, Department of Urbiculture
 H.R. 2423—Rains of Alabama, Department of Urban Affairs
 H.R. 4481—Addonizio of New Jersey, Department of Urban Affairs

86th Congress, Second Session—1960
 H.R. 11918—Lindsay of New York, Department of Housing and Metropolitan Problems
 H.R. 12508—Halpern of New York, Department of Housing and Metropolitan Affairs
 H.R. 13024—Santangelo of New York, Department of Housing and Metropolitan Affairs

 S. 2397—Keating of New York, Department of Urbiculture
 S. 3292—Clark of Pennsylvania, and others, Department of Housing and Metropolitan Affairs

87th Congress, First Session—1961
 H.R. 301—Bennett of Michigan, Department of Urban Affairs
 H.R. 557—Rodino of New Jersey, Department of Urban Affairs
 H.R. 962—Mrs. Griffiths of Michigan, Department of Urban Affairs
 H.R. 964—Halpern of New York, Department of Urban Affairs
 H.R. 1125—Younger of California, Department of Urbiculture

H.R. 2042—Lindsay of New York, Department of Urban Affairs

H.R. 2389—Addonizio of New Jersey, Department of Urban Affairs

H.R. 6065—Ryan of New York, Department of Urban Affairs

H.R. 6433—Fascell of Florida, Department of Urban Affairs and Housing

H.R. 8429—Fascell of Florida, Department of Urban Affairs and Housing

S. 289—Keating of New York, Department of Urban Affairs

S. 375—Hartke of Indiana, Department of Urban Affairs

S. 609—Bush of Connecticut, Department of Housing and Urban Affairs

S. 1633—Clark of Pennsylvania, and others, Department of Urban Affairs and Housing

87th Congress, Second Session—1962

S. 2861—Boggs of Delaware, Department of Federal-State-Urban Affairs

---

repeatedly discussed the question in the campaign, assuring the people that, if elected, he would use his influence to bring about the establishment of such a department. Early in 1961, he moved to fulfill that pledge by sending a message on the subject to Congress, accompanied by draft legislation, the enactment of which he recommended. What happened to this legislation, and to Reorganization Plan No. 1 of 1962 which followed it, will be considered at the conclusion of this chapter.

On the basis of the record since 1954, it seems fair to assume that a department to deal with urban affairs (or intergovernmental relations on a broader scale) will be created in the near future. Various questions then present themselves, questions to which satisfactory answers will have to be developed. What shall the new department be called? How shall it be established? What principle(s) shall determine assignment of functions to it? What shall be the nature and scope of its functions and responsibilities?

Name of the Department

The question of selecting a suitable name for the department is an important one, in which many considerations are involved. The new department might conceivably and appropriately be called by any one of the names used on the bills listed in the preceding table; other possibilities are intergovernmental relations, State and local relations, community affairs, and local affairs. It is doubtful that any serious consideration would be given to "urbiculture." The name chosen should be short, descriptive, and as accurately as possible, it should reflect the major purpose behind the establishment of the department.

For several reasons, "local affairs" might be a desirable choice. Its adoption would tend to undermine the claim that this proposal is merely a move on the part of the big city people—the big city political machines—to take over the Federal government. The Bureau of the Census classifies as urban all non-farm areas with communities having a population of 2,500 or more. If the name selected makes it clear that these smaller communities are to be served as well as the larger ones, the potential opposition of rural-minded members might easily be converted into active support. For instance, Senator Karl E. Mundt of South Dakota and two co-sponsors presented to the 86th Congress a bill to establish a study commission on the problems of small towns and rural counties; [42] the bill passed the Senate but was not acted upon in the House, and it was introduced again in the 87th Congress. Smaller communities are confronted with many of the same problems that confront the cities, though on a smaller scale, and the name selected should help to make it clear that the new department is to be concerned with the problems of communities of all sizes. This point was emphasized time after time in the hearings before the Senate subcommittee in June, 1961, and was explicitly stated in the revised bill as reported.

Whatever name is finally decided upon, the department will to a very large extent be concerned with intergovernmental relations. This being true, the name used by Senator J. Caleb Boggs of Delaware, Department of Federal-State-Urban Affairs, has a strong appeal. It was his purpose to select a name that would be accurately descriptive, but that would at the same time suggest that the primary objective of the department was to strengthen the federal system.

Need for the Department

Organizationally, the existing situation within the Federal government is a confusion of unrelated and completely uncoordinated urban programs. Lacking a cabinet department to serve the needs of urban dwellers, one program after another has been smuggled into the Housing and Home Finance Agency which has in fact, though not in name, become largely an urban affairs agency. Still the needs of State and local governments for technical assistance on urban problems vastly exceed the capacity of existing sources of information. An overall urban policy, which can best be achieved through departmental status with urban representation, is urgently needed. When the country was rural, a Department of Agriculture was established to aid farmers and later the farm homemaker in the solution of common problems. Even now, when

[42] S. 3140.

ours has become an urban society, the Federal government spends far more money fighting hog cholera and other animal and plant diseases than it spends to provide decent housing for the millions of human beings who live in our cities.

Senator Clark and Mayor West recently summarized the current situation in dramatic language. Said the former, the Department of Agriculture "can tell us what crops have been planted on almost every acre of ground in every county for the last quarter of a century. In contrast, no Federal agency has any data on urban land use. Yet urban land, acre for acre, has many times the value of farmland. We know more about farm buildings than about urban buildings. We spend more on research in the diseases of a single crop—potatoes, hay, or corn—than on research into the causes and cure of the slums and blight which are the diseases of cities affecting scores of millions of people." Mayor West pointed out that the Department of Agriculture in 1960 "spent seventeen times the amount spent by the agencies which would be located in the new department of urban affairs. Think of it! Less than 6 per cent for urban affairs of that spent for agriculture! Out of this 6 per cent comes the Federal share for slum clearance, urban renewal, low income housing, research, and the whole program of community facility construction and urban development and redevelopment." [43] The point is not that less should be spent for agriculture, but that something commensurate with its expense should be spent on urban problems.

Furthermore, the problems of these areas have long since overrun established political boundaries. Cities reach farther and farther into their hinterlands for water. Municipal sewage disposal affects water quality hundreds of miles downstream. Mass transit systems are regional in scope, not local. Since few large communities can be self-sufficient in open space and outdoor recreation, their residents must depend upon what a whole region can provide. City planning must fit within the context of metropolitan regional planning, sometimes in a very large region, for urban areas now blend into one another.

The four major objectives of such a department were well spelled out in the administration bill's declaration of policy: [44] (1) to achieve the best administration of the principal programs of the Federal government which provide assistance for housing and for the development and redevelopment of our urban communities; (2) to give leadership within the Executive Branch in securing the coordination of the various Federal

[43] In testimony before the Senate Subcommittee on Reorganization, on S. 1633 for the establishment of a department of urban affairs, June 22, 1961.

[44] S. 1633, introduced in the 87th Congress by Senator Joseph S. Clark of Pennsylvania. H.R. 6433, superseded by H.R. 8429, introduced by Representative Dante Fascell of Florida.

activities which have a major effect upon urban, suburban, or metropolitan area development and redevelopment; (3) to encourage the solution of urban, suburban, and metropolitan problems through State, local, and private action, including promotion of interstate, regional, and metropolitan cooperation; (4) to provide for full and appropriate consideration, at the national level, of the needs and interests of urban areas and of the people who live and work in them.

Nature and Scope of the Department's Activities

Probably the greatest obstacle to the establishment of a department of local affairs has been the difficulty in defining in any satisfactory manner the nature and scope of its activities. In discussing this question, the fear has often been expressed that such a department might become a huge aggregation of heterogeneous activities encompassing most of the civilian peacetime activities of the Federal government, some twenty-three of the major programs of which are of vital significance to cities. Such a procedure would violate the principle of functional organization which is normally regarded as essential to good administration. Although it should not be necessary to engage in a major reshuffling of the agencies in the Executive Branch of government every time the nation is confronted with a new and difficult problem, this procedure would result in precisely such a reshuffling.

Both a heterogeneous collection of unrelated services and more reshuffling of executive agencies than is absolutely necessary are to be avoided. Stated more positively, the new department should be established with a minimum of disturbance to essential services now existing and with constant regard for the principle of functional classification. Water and air pollution, for example, are problems of major concern to cities. They are also health problems, and their administration should remain in the Public Health Service where it belongs. In such areas, the job of the new department is one of coordination and of establishing working relationships with existing agencies and programs, to the end that the urban interest in these programs may be given full consideration.

On the basis of this reasoning, it is clear that much thought must go into the planning of the new department, lest—as one commentator observed—it cut too wide a swath or be limited to a too narrow field. There is no existing Federal department or major agency that does not have under its jurisdiction problems directly concerned with urban affairs. Some of the functions most frequently proposed for the new department may be sorted out, in line with the principles here discussed, as suggested in the following table.

MAJOR URBAN FUNCTIONS IN THE FEDERAL GOVERNMENT

Proper Functions for a Department of Local Affairs	*Functions Located in and Belonging in Other Departments and Agencies*
1. District of Columbia Government	1. Highways—BPR
2. Housing, Slum Clearance, and Urban Redevelopment	2. Air Pollution—USPHS
3. Depressed Area Program *	3. Water Pollution—USPHS
4. Planning and Community Development	4. Commercial Development—Department of Commerce and SBA
5. Mass Transit	5. Education, Health, and Welfare—HEW
6. Information, Research, and Consulting Center	6. Juvenile Delinquency—Department of Justice
7. Training for State and Local Government Personnel	7. Civil Defense and Disaster Relief—Department of Defense (formerly ODM)
8. Fiscal Needs and Problems	
9. Growth of Metropolitan Centers	

* Established in 1961 and assigned, at least for the time being, to the Department of Commerce.

This analysis and the Clark-Fascell bill suggest some of the duties which should be assigned to the new department, but there are others. The municipal programs of the Roosevelt era, interrupted by World War II and never fully restored, should be revived and enlarged to meet current needs.[45] The "proper functions" are discussed briefly in the paragraphs which follow.

1. *District of Columbia Government.* The new department should have all responsibilities now vested in the Federal government relating to the government of the District, not performed by the District of Columbia government. There are, for instance, a number of agencies, such as the D.C. Redevelopment Land Agency, the National Capital Housing Authority, and the National Capital Planning Commission, pertaining to the government of the District that are simply suspended in space; they are a part neither of the Federal government nor of the District government.

2. *Housing, Slum Clearance, and Urban Redevelopment.* These programs involve a large part of the responsibility of the present Housing and Home Finance Agency, which would be transferred in its entirety to the new department. If, as is suggested, the new department be called

[45] For the best discussions of these problems, see Connery, Robert H., and Leach, Richard H., *The Federal Government and Metropolitan Areas* (Cambridge: Harvard University Press, 1960) and Wheaton, William L. C., "A New Cabinet Post?" *National Civic Review,* December, 1959, pp. 574–578. The book opposes, the article favors establishment of the proposed department.

a department of local affairs, emphasis can be placed on rural housing and rural slums, as well as on these problems as they exist in the larger municipalities.

3. *Depressed Area Problems.* Following the Eisenhower veto of the depressed area bill passed by the 86th Congress during the short session following the national party conventions in the summer of 1960, this legislation became a major issue in the presidential campaign. Mr. Kennedy, as President-elect, appointed a committee to study the problem and make recommendations. This committee reported in mid-December, endorsing a program along the lines of the ill-fated Douglas bill. This measure called for $390 million in Federal loans, grants, and technical assistance for the economic revival of the country's areas of chronic unemployment. In 1961, a similar bill passed by the 87th Congress was signed by President Kennedy. Although the enforcement of this legislation and the development of the program(s) to be administered under it are obviously tasks for the new department, responsibility was assigned for the time being to the Department of Commerce.

4. *Planning and Community Development.* The National Resources Planning Board made important contributions in this field during the Roosevelt era. After many years of neglect, there have been some signs of a revival of interest. In 1938, the Division of Government in the Bureau of the Census was set up. In 1954, a Community Facilities Administration was established in the Housing and Home Finance Agency. There is a program for research in local government and local finance in the Department of Agriculture. These might well be brought together in the new department and given expanded staff and resources, so that professional assistance and guidance might be generally available for American communities, large and small, that are getting a late start or that are faced with unusual or particularly difficult problems.

5. *Mass Transit.* Mass transit in American cities has fallen victim to the age of the automobile, as well as to its own poor and expensive service. Yet mass transit is recognized as essential to modern urban life. Mention has been repeatedly made of the efforts put forth in some major cities to revive and strengthen this essential service; in addition, there is a proposal for Federal participation in the solution of this problem, presented in the form of S. 3278 in the 86th Congress and S. 345 in the 87th Congress by Senator Harrison Williams of New Jersey. It was enacted into law in the 1961 Amendments to the National Housing Act of 1954, and it is obviously a function that properly belongs within the province of the new department.

6. *Information and Research Center.* An information and research center on local problems was set up during the Roosevelt era in the National Resources Planning Board. Such a service is even more needed

now, on a permanent basis. Component elements for such a service are to be found in the Division of Governments in the Bureau of the Census, a small unit in the Department of Agriculture, and the remnants of the old State Law Division which existed in the Library of Congress for approximately a quarter of a century prior to 1947 and 1948. A bill providing for the establishment of an Intergovernmental Reference Service [46] was introduced in the 86th Congress by Senator Vance Hartke of Indiana, and the same provisions were included in a department of urban affairs bill [47] introduced by the same Senator in the 87th Congress. These provisions, if enacted, would provide an adequate statutory basis for such a service within the new department. The language of the department of urban affairs bill, as reported out by the Senate Committee, may be broad enough to permit the establishment of an information, research, and consulting service by administrative action. A statutory basis would, however, be preferable.

7. *Training for State and Local Government Personnel.* A bill introduced in the 88th Congress, by Representative Henry B. Gonzalaz of Texas provides for the establishment of a modest Federal grant-in-aid program to encourage and assist the States in developing and maintaining in-service training programs for State and local government personnel.[48] This proposal is based upon (1) the favorable experience in this field between 1937 and 1945, when Federal assistance was given for such training under the George-Deen Act of 1936, and (2) the belief that there is a national interest in improving the operating efficiency of State and local government and the competence of its personnel. This is especially true when so many functions of government are now conducted on a cooperative basis, and when the Federal government contributes so heavily to their financial support through numerous grant-in-aid programs. Under these circumstances, it would seem to be both logical and proper for the new department to assume responsibility for this activity.

8. *Aid to Small Business.* The problems of small business are most prevalent in, though not confined to, the towns and smaller cities. In an effort to do something more than merely talk about them, it has been proposed that there be established a system of field representatives, professional consultants who could perform for small business a type of service comparable to that long provided for rural folk by the county demonstration agent and the county home demonstration agent.[49] There

---

[46] S. 2495. [47] S. 375.

[48] H.R. 4561 (also in 87th Congress as H.R. 13305).

[49] Former Senator Ralph E. Flanders of Vermont was interested in this idea, and Senator Hubert Humphrey of Minnesota has put in a bill, S. 2467, designed to carry it out.

is much to be said in favor of this idea; the major objection to placing it in the new department is that this is primarily a commercial activity which would normally be placed in the Department of Commerce or in the Small Business Administration. The Department of Commerce already has a large field force, which could be expanded if this service for small business were to be undertaken.

9. *Civil Defense and Disaster Relief.* Since these programs are necessarily a major concern of cities whose dense populations make them a natural target for enemy attack, it would seem proper that they be either administered by the new department or in very close cooperation with it. For many years, they were administered by an independent agency, but were transferred in 1961 to the Department of Defense.

Method of Establishment

It was generally assumed that the new department should be created by act of Congress, and the experiences of 1961 and 1962 tend to indicate that it was a sound assumption. This has, to be sure, long been the established procedure for the creation of new departments, the sole exception being the recently established Department of Health, Education, and Welfare, for which Reorganization Plan procedure was used. Although the Reorganization Act had been permitted to expire in 1959 as the Eisenhower administration drew toward its close, it was promptly re-enacted in 1961 and extended in 1963 upon requests by President Kennedy. The President, however, decided to use the conventional method; his bill was sponsored, as noted, by Senator Clark and by Representative Dante Fascell of Florida.[50]

For practical reasons, the administration and the Congressional leaders decided that the creation of a new department should be effected without establishing any new Federal activities or programs, but rather to provide for the transfer to it of urban programs already authorized and functioning. Once established, new programs could be added from time to time, either by Reorganization Plan or by act of Congress.

Opposition to the bill developed early from all of the expected sources. For example, a spokesman for the National Association of Real Estate Boards (which, it might be assumed, would profit more than most from its enactment) argued at the Senate hearings that "creation of a cabinet-rank department of urban affairs and housing would toll the

[50] Hearings were held by the House Subcommittee in May, by the Senate Subcommittee in June, 1961: House on H.R. 6433, May–June (House Report No. 1053); Senate, on S. 1633, and other bills, in June (Senate Report No. 879). 87th Cong., 1st Sess., Washington, 1961.

bells for our federal system." His opposition and that of the Council of State Governments (seventeen Governors dissenting) was based largely upon the following considerations: (1) that the proposed bill would not accomplish its stated objectives; (2) that it would aggravate the fragmentation of the nation's housing effort, rather than contribute to its coordination; (3) that it presupposes a permanent and expanding role for the Federal government in housing and urban renewal; (4) that it would hasten the erosion of our system of Federal-State-local relations; (5) that it would invite greater pressure on Congress for more Federal aid; (6) that it would aim programs at "physical locations" rather than at working relationships, thus splintering urban administration. In 1962, the Republican leadership added its strong opposition to the proposal.

Both houses held hearings on the administration bill and other similar bills in 1961, and the Committee on Government Operations in each house reported the measure favorably, but it did not come to a vote in either house during the first session of the 87th Congress. In January, 1962, soon after the second session began, the House Rules Committee refused by a substantial majority to grant a rule for this measure so that it might come to a vote on the House floor. At a press conference, President Kennedy promptly announced that he would submit a Reorganization Plan in the near future, and that he would appoint Dr. Robert C. Weaver, a Negro, as the first Secretary, when and if the plan became effective.[51]

Use of the Reorganization Plan procedure assured that it would be possible for either house to vote on the proposal, for the operation of this procedure is not within the jurisdiction of the House Rules Committee. The announcement with respect to the name of the Secretary he intended to appoint was exactly parallel with a procedure followed by President Eisenhower in 1950, when a Reorganization Plan to establish the Department of Health, Education, and Welfare was before Congress.

In jockeying to see which house should vote first on the Plan, the Senate won. The only legislative strategy available under existing circumstances was for the majority leader, Senator Mansfield, to move as he did to discharge the committee to which the Plan had been referred. The motion was lost on February 20 by a vote of 58 to 42, a vote which appears to be a worse defeat for the Plan than it actually was. Legislative procedures being what they are, it is next to impossible to get a majority to repudiate the leadership by voting to discharge a committee. Thus the vote was more an illustration of legislative procedures than an indication of opposition to the Reorganization Plan itself. Because of the Senate

[51] For comment on the role of the House in this matter, see Hacker, Andrew, "Voice of Ninety Million Americans," *The New York Times Magazine*, March 4, 1962, pp. 11, 80–84.

defeat, no action on the part of the House was necessary. It was expected that the effort to establish the department would be renewed in the 88th Congress, but no action was taken during the First Session.

BIBLIOGRAPHICAL NOTES

A substantial two-volume work edited by Coleman Woodbury contains a vast amount of information on metropolitan problems: *The Future of Cities and Urban Redevelopment* and *Urban Redevelopment: Problems and Practices* (Chicago: University of Chicago Press, 1953). Other useful titles include Robert H. Connery and Richard H. Leach, *The Federal Government and Metropolitan Areas* (Cambridge: Harvard University Press, 1960); Theodore M. Hutcheson, *Metropolitan Area Problems* (Ann Arbor: University of Michigan Law School, 1961); and a symposium, *The Federal Government and the Cities* (Washington: George Washington University, 1961).

Federal Services to Cities. At intervals since 1930, there have been several studies of the services available to municipalities from the Federal government. Significant among them are Paul V. Betters, *Federal Services to Municipal Governments* (New York: Municipal Administration Service, 1931); *Municipal Finance Problems and Proposals for Federal Legislation* (Chicago: American Municipal Association, 1933); *Recent Federal-City Relations* (Washington: United States Conference of Mayors, 1936); and Robert H. Blundred and Donah W. Hanks, Jr., *Federal Services to Cities and Towns* (Chicago: American Municipal Association, 1950), an alphabetical listing of services of the United States to cities, towns, boroughs, and villages, and to counties and other local governments. The Area Redevelopment Administration now issues a *Handbook of Federal Aids to Communities* (latest issue, Washington, June, 1963).

Alphabetical Agencies. Out of a tremendous literature on the New Deal, the following are most useful: Charles A. Beard and George H. E. Smith, *The Future Comes: A Study of the New Deal* (New York: The Macmillan Co., 1933); Harold L. Ickes, *Back to Work: The Story of PWA* (New York: The Macmillan Co., 1935); David Lawrence, *Beyond the New Deal* (New York: Whittlesey House, 1935); and Henry C. Wallace, *New Frontiers* (New York: Reynal & Hitchcock, 1934). For a general comment on the effect of these programs on cities, see Clarence E. Ridley and Orin Nolting, eds., *What the Depression Has Done to Cities* (Chicago: International City Managers Association, 1935) and for a study of one important agency in the nation's largest city, see John D. Millett, *The Works Progress Administration in New York City* (Chicago: Public Administration Service, 1938).

Community Services. The National Association of Home Builders has published an extensive list of selected references under the title *Community Facilities* (Washington, August, 1959). Significant government publications in this area include Community Facilities Administration, *Programs of the Community Facilities Administration: Advances for public works planning, college housing loans, public facility loans* (Washington, December, 1959) and Department of Commerce, Office of Technical Services, *Available Federal Assistance for Community Development* (Washington, 1955). The Senate Committee on Banking and Currency held hearings on S. 3497 in March, 1958, *Community Facilities Act of 1958* (Washington: 85th Cong., 2nd Sess., 1958) and on H.R. 5944 in April, 1959 (Washington, 1959).

Highways. The American Municipal Association has published various brief reports on Federal funds available to cities for highway purposes; for example, *The Federal Highway Act of 1952: How municipalities obtain $275,000,000 Federal aid* (Chicago, 1952). For reports on the progress of the program from the point of view of the cities, see C. D. Curtiss and R. W. Kruser, *Progress of the Federal Aid Urban Highway Program* (Chicago: American Municipal Association, April, 1953); John T. Howard, *Community Growth: Impact of the federal highway program* (New York: National Municipal League, November, 1957); David R. Levin, *The Impact of Highway Improvement on Urban Areas* (Washington: Bureau of Public Roads, 1961); an address by Thomas H. Macdonald, *The Federal Aid Highway Program and Its Relation to Cities* (Washington: Chamber of Commerce of the United States, September, 1957); a symposium, *The New Highways: Challenge to the Metropolitan Region* (Washington: Urban Land Institute, 1957); and Wilbur Smith *et al.*, *Future Highways and Urban Growth* (Detroit: Automobile Manufacturers Association, 1961).

Urban Renewal. The literature in this field has become voluminous; the Public Library of the District of Columbia in 1954 provided an excellent guide in *Publications Relating to Urban Renewal* (Washington, 1954), to which an annual supplement has since been issued. See also National Association of Housing and Redevelopment Officials, *Urban Renewal and the Changing Urban Structure* (Chicago, July, 1960), a discussion of research needs; A. H. Schaaf, *Economic Aspects of Urban Renewal: Theory, Policy, and Area Analysis* (Berkeley: Institute of Business and Economic Research, University of California, 1960); and Joseph F. Turley, *Goals in Urban Renewal for New England* (Boston: Federal Reserve Bank of Boston, 1959). An important symposium on urban renewal, edited by Robinson C. Everett, appears in two issues of *Law and Contemporary Problems*, Part I, Autumn, 1960, and Part II, Winter, 1961. Significant government publications in this area include: **House of Representatives:** Committee on Government Operations, Hearings of June–July, 1959, *Metropolitan Problems and Urban Redevelopment*, 86th Cong., 1st Sess. (Washington, 1959); Select Committee on Small Business, Hearings of May, 1956, on H. Res. 114, *Urban Renewal Projects and Slum Clearance*, 84th Cong., 2nd Sess. (Washington, 1956); **Senate:** Committee on Banking and Currency, *Development Corporations and Authorities*, rev. ed., 86th Cong., 1st Sess. (Washington: Committee Print, 1959), reports, statutes, and other materials on state and local development corporations and authorities; Housing and Home Finance Agency, *How Localities Can Develop a Workable Program for Urban Renewal*, rev. ed. (Washington, December, 1956).

Depressed Areas. In a field that has developed within the last few years, the following titles are of interest: American Enterprise Association, *Legislative Analysis: Proposals for Federal Aid to Depressed Areas* (Washington, January, 1961); Committee for Economic Development, *Distressed Areas in a Growing Economy* (New York, June, 1961), of which a summary by Walter H. Wheeler, Jr. was also released; and Donald P. Gilmore, *Survey of Area Development Programs in the United States* (New York: Committee for Economic Development, 1960). See also the following government publications: **House of Representatives:** Committee on Banking and Currency, Hearings of April, 1956, on H.R. 8555, *Area Assistance Act of 1956*, 84th Cong., 2nd Sess. (Washington, 1956); Hearings of March 1959, *Area Redevelopment Act*, 86th Cong., 1st Sess. (Washington, 1959); Hearings on H.R. 4569, *Area Redevelopment Act*, 87th Cong., 1st Sess. (Washington, 1961); Report No. 360, *Area Redevelopment Act*, 86th Cong., 1st Sess. (Washington, 1959); Report No. 186, *Area Redevelopment Act*, 87th Cong., 1st Sess. (Washington, 1961); **Senate:** Committee on Banking and Currency, Hearings of March–May, 1957, on S. 104 and other bills, *Area Redevelopment*, 85th Cong., 1st Sess. (Washington, 1957–1958), two parts; Hearings of February, 1959, on S. 268 and other bills, *Area Redevelopment Act*, 86th Cong., 1st Sess. (Washington,

1959), two parts; Hearings of August, 1960, *Area Redevelopment Legislation,* 86th Cong., 2nd Sess. (Washington, 1960); Report No. 110, *Area Redevelopment Act,* 86th Cong., 1st Sess. (Washington, 1959); Hearings of January–February, 1961, on S. 1, *Area Redevelopment,* 1961, 87th Cong., 1st Sess. (Washington, 1961); Report No. 61, *Area Redevelopment,* 1961, 87th Cong., 1st Sess. (Washington, 1961).

Department of Urban Affairs. In addition to the several books and articles referred to in chapter footnotes, the following Congressional hearings and reports are available: **House of Representatives:** Committee on Government Operations, Report No. 1360, *Approving Reorganization Plan No. 1 of 1962* (Department of Urban Affairs and Housing), 87th Cong., 2nd Sess. (Washington, 1962); Hearings on H.R. 1864, *Creation of a Department of Urbiculture,* 84th Cong., 1st Sess. (Washington, 1955); Hearings of May–June, 1961, on H.R. 6433, *Department of Urban Affairs and Housing,* 87th Cong., 1st Sess. (Washington, 1961); Report No. 1053, *Establishing a Department of Urban Affairs and Housing,* 87th Cong., 1st Sess. (Washington, 1961); Hearings of June–July, 1959, on H.R. 781 and other bills, *Metropolitan Problems and Urban Development,* 86th Cong., 1st Sess. (Washington, 1959); Hearings of February, 1962, *Reorganization Plan No. 1 of 1962,* 87th Cong., 2nd Sess. (Washington, 1962); **Senate:** Committee on Banking and Currency, Report No. 1607, *Department of Housing and Metropolitan Affairs,* 86th Cong., 2nd Sess. (Washington, 1960); Committee on Government Operations, Hearings of June, 1961, on S. 1633, S. 375, and other bills, *Establish a Department of Urban Affairs and Housing,* 87th Cong., 1st Sess. (Washington, 1961); Report No. 879, *The Department of Urban Affairs and Housing,* 87th Cong., 1st Sess. (Washington, 1961).

CHAPTER XX

State-Local
Relations

The State government is the source and central authority for all the local governments within its boundaries, even for those special districts created by the State virtually at the behest of the Federal Government. It has very definite powers of coercion [over these] creatures of the State, "home rule" notwithstanding. The legislature serves as the constituent assembly for local governments, creating and defining them, limiting or extending their powers, even delimiting the possible forms of government they may adopt. In order to amend the local "constitution," it is often necessary to go to the State capitol— unless the legislature has already provided for options which can be exercised locally, as in the choice of municipal governmental forms. The State even functions as a local legislature and executive in a wide variety of fields, sometimes retaining exclusive powers and sometimes sharing them with the city council or county board.

The sum of a State's constitutional and political powers within its boundaries and its constitutional position and political role within the federal system as a whole places the States at the keystone in the governmental area. In its central position, the States serve as a stimulator of local government activities and as mediator between its local governments and Washington and, when necessary, between its local governments and other States. . . . When a State government fails to fulfill its role as mediator, in this sense, the resulting vacuum leads to a serious weakening of the system.[1]

[1] Elazar, Daniel J., "Local Government in Intergovernmental Perspective," in Pelekoudas, Lois M., ed., *Illinois Local Government* (Urbana: Institute of Government and Public Affairs, University of Illinois, May, 1961), pp. 24–35, slightly edited.

INSTITUTIONS OF LOCAL GOVERNMENT

Origin and Development

From the earliest colonial times, local government in this country has been regarded as a matter of vital importance. The two basic forms of local government organization have been the town and the county; the importance of the city developed much later. For a number of reasons, the town form was indigenous to New England. The terrain was for the most part rocky, if not mountainous. The soil was thin and poor, the climate severe. None of these characteristics were conducive to agricultural development, and in addition, the dense forests were a hindrance to agriculture and a place of refuge for Indians and wild animals. These conditions combined to encourage small, compact settlements in which, as a result of an abundance of water power, manufacturing soon began to develop. The town meeting form of government developed early in these communities.

Just as the town, with its town meeting, came to be the prevailing form of local government in New England, so the county form came to predominate in the South. Again, there were definite reasons to account for this development. The South was from the beginning an agricultural area; the crops which early achieved a position of importance—cotton, indigo, rice, and tobacco—all required the cultivation of large areas of land. Under these circumstances the plantation system developed, in sharp contrast to the densely populated communities in the North. The Southern Indians were for the most part more friendly than those in the North, and the danger from wild animals was less. Consequently, a broader and more extensive unit of local government was natural. The county, in which a number of plantations were grouped together into a single unit for purposes of government, came to be the dominant type in the South, as it did later in the West where, similarly, good land was plentiful, agriculture important, and settlement sparse.

Interesting questions arose when these two types of government came in conflict, or at least in contact. In general it may be said that the importance of each of these units varies directly in proportion to the distance from the area of its origin. That is, the county form steadily diminishes in importance as one travels north along the Atlantic coast, while the town form diminishes in importance as one travels south along the coast. The contact of these two major types resulted in the development of hybrid forms in New York, Pennsylvania, and a few other States.

In New York, Michigan, and parts of Illinois, one finds what has been called the North-Central type, in which the town is more important than the county, though both exist. In Pennsylvania, which has the South-Central type, the county is more important than the town, or as it is called in this jurisdiction, the township. As the settlers moved West, they tended to take with them the governmental forms to which they had become accustomed and established them in their new environment with little or no modification. Thus local government in the States carved out of the Northwest Territory tended to resemble that in New York and New England, while that in the States farther south followed either the Pennsylvania plan or that of the Southern States.[2]

State governments exercise such powers as are authorized in their respective constitutions not inconsistent with the provisions of the Federal Constitution and of Federal law. Local governments, on the other hand, are the creatures of the States. They have only such powers as have been conferred upon them by their respective legislatures. The States are supposed to assume a considerable degree of responsibility for the organization and functioning of their local governments, but in practice they have done so in a very indifferent manner when at all. Since the political subdivisions of a State are established by State law and their powers and duties are defined by law, local units may be abolished (in the absence of such protective constitutional provisions as exist in some States) or their powers modified or withdrawn by legislative act. Judge John F. Dillon of the Supreme Court of Iowa well expressed this conventional view when he wrote: "Municipal corporations owe their origin to, and derive their powers and rights wholly from, the legislature. It breathes into them the breath of life, without which they cannot exist. As it creates, so it may destroy. If it may destroy, it may abridge and control." [3]

An appraisal of State-city constitutional relationships made in 1961 notes the conflict between legal theory and the concept of home rule in these words:

> When the façade of the legal entity is removed so that the population and the property of the city can be seen, there arises a theory which conflicts with the creature theory. The opposing force is derived from a belief that the determination of the destinies of the people in a given area resides in the people themselves. Insofar as the constitution is a product of the people of the State as a whole, the various constitutional limitations concerning State-city relations reflect the people's view of what limits should be placed upon the State. Many of these

[2] This classification follows Porter, Kirk H., *County and Township Government in the United States* (New York: The Macmillan Co., 1922), Chapter 4.

[3] In *City of Clinton* v. *Cedar Rapids & Missouri Railroad Company,* 24 Ia. 455 (1868).

limitations are directed to some extent at preserving a degree of local self-determination. Home rule is the outstanding example, but other constitutional provisions reflect the same policy objective. Thus, the counter-theory does run through the State constitutions.[4]

The city, then, is a creature of the legislature. It is a municipal corporation whose government, powers, and size are subject to the legislative will. A county, on the other hand, has often been termed a quasi-municipal corporation which aids in the administration of governmental affairs and exercises such sovereign powers of the State as may be delegated to it. An early Ohio case explains the historical concept of the county and the legal distinction between the two.

> A municipal corporation proper is created mainly for the interest, advantage, and convenience of the locality and its people; a county organization is created almost exclusively with a view to the policy of the State at large, for purposes of political organization and civil administration, in matters of finance, of education, of provision for the poor, of military organization, of the means of travel and transport, and especially for the general administration of justice. With scarcely an exception, all the powers and functions of the county organization have a direct, and exclusive reference to the general policy of the State, and are, in fact, but a branch of the general administration of that policy.
>
> Counties are local subdivisions of a State, created by the sovereign power of a State, of its own sovereign will, without the particular solicitation, consent, or concurrent action of the people who inhabit them. The former organization (municipal corporation) is asked for, or at least assented to by the people it embraces; the latter is superimposed by a sovereign and paramount authority.[5]

Multiplicity of Governmental Units

Until about a quarter of a century ago, nobody knew how many units of local government there were in the United States. The Division of Governments, Bureau of the Census, made the first survey in 1932, reporting a total of 182,651 units. Professor William Anderson in 1934 found approximately 181,000 units of all types. Subsequent surveys have shown a consistent decline; summary figures for surveys at ten-year intervals are shown in the table on page 699, and the table on pages 702–703

[4] Winters, John M., *State Constitutional Limitations on Solutions of Metropolitan Area Problems* (Ann Arbor: Legislative Research Center, University of Michigan Law School, 1961).

[5] *Commissioners of Hamilton County* v. *Mighels,* 7 Ohio St. 109 at 118 (1857). This quotation and the analysis follow Winters, pp. 45–46.

shows the distribution of the various types of units by States for the 1962 survey.

GOVERNMENTAL UNITS IN THE UNITED STATES, 1932, 1942, 1952, AND 1962 *

Type of Unit	1932	1942	1952	1962
United States Government ..	1	1	1	1
States	48	48	48	50
Counties	3,062	3,050	3,049	3,043
Municipalities	16,442	16,220	16,778	17,997
Townships	19,978	18,919	17,202	17,144
School districts	128,548	108,579	56,346	34,678
Special districts	14,572	8,299	12,319	18,823 †
Totals	182,651	155,116	116,743	91,736

* United States Bureau of the Census, *Governmental Units in the United States,* 1932, 1942, 1952, 1962.

† Includes drainage, road, park, sanitary, irrigation, reclamation, fire, lightning, cemetery, navigation, port, waterworks, and other types.

An examination of the figures in this table reveals a number of significant facts. In a quarter of a century, the total number of governmental units has declined by almost 50 per cent. There has been virtually no change in the total number of counties. A slight increase in the total number of municipalities is offset by a corresponding decrease in the number of townships. In spite of a general impression that the number of special districts has been increasing at an alarming rate, the total number remains constant at the beginning and the end of the period covered by these figures, having in the interval declined significantly and gradually climbed back to the starting level. Practically all of the marked decline in the total number of units is attributable to the tremendous reduction in the number of school districts.

In all States except Delaware, local control over public schools became a firmly established American tradition. In colonial days the early settlers built a little log schoolhouse, which in time was replaced by the old-fashioned one-room country school. The people have been exceedingly reluctant to relinquish local control over their schools, even though they have been in no position, either financially or by way of technical training, to maintain them satisfactorily from an educational point of view. Delaware alone maintained complete State control over its schools and during the period of the Great Depression was joined by North Carolina and West Virginia.

North Carolina guarantees a basic school program of eight months from State funds. Its 1933 law establishing this support dissolved all the previously existing 1,200 school districts and established county units headed by boards of education. State agencies prescribe and supply textbooks, allocate teachers on a uniform basis, require teachers to hold State certificates, pass upon county school budgets, and control pupil transportation. West Virginia substituted fifty-five county units for the 450 previously existing, and conferred upon the State Board of School Finance broad powers similar to those provided for in the North Carolina act.

In other jurisdictions, the rise and fall of the local school district has been only slightly less dramatic than in North Carolina and West Virginia. At the close of World War II, the National Education Association created a National Commission on School District Reorganization, spearheading a nationwide drive to bring some semblance of order out of the chaotic organization of school districts that had been evolved over the years, an organization that was expensive to operate and that left much to be desired in view of the results obtained. The eccentricities of the system were amazing to behold. There were school districts with no schools nor even any children to attend school, yet a full set of machinery for the conduct of schools had to be maintained. As a result of this nation-wide drive, tremendous progress was made in reducing the total number of school districts in individual States and in the Nation as a whole, as shown in the previous table.[6]

HOME RULE

Home rule may be defined as the power of local self-government. Communities have the right to select their own form of governmental organization and either draft their own charter or select one to their liking under an optional charter plan. Home rule may be granted by constitutional provision, by legislative act, or by a constitutional provision which becomes effective only upon legislative implementation. As of 1959, constitutional provision for home rule had been adopted in more than half of the States—in twenty-eight as applicable to cities, and in fourteen as applicable to counties. The home rule concept was originally limited to cities but, particularly since 1955, it has been extended to counties in a slowly increasing number of States.

[6] In addition to survey reports prepared in individual States, see Fitz-water, C. O., *School District Reorganization: Policies and Procedure* (Washington: U.S. Office of Education, 1957), Special Series No. 5.

History of Home Rule

The fight for home rule began in the middle of the nineteenth century. The first States to adopt home rule were Iowa, by statute in 1858, and Missouri, by constitutional amendment in 1875. From that point on, the concept was gradually evolved through a process of trial and error. The first grant of power in New York came when a provision was written into the State constitution of 1894 requiring the legislature to submit all bills that affected fewer than all the cities of the State to the Mayors of those cities for their approval or rejection.[7] Another of the earliest States was Ohio which, in 1897, adopted a constitutional amendment requiring the legislature to group the cities of the State into not more than seven classes on the basis of population. This proved to be quite unsatisfactory because the number of classes was so large that the legislature by skillful manipulation could so adjust the population limits of the various classes as to include only one city in each of the first five classes, the remainder being grouped in classes six and seven. It was thus possible for the legislature to continue the very domination of municipal affairs that the amendment had been designed to prevent. With a smaller number of classes, the classification plan is in effect in the majority of States having any considerable number of urban communities.

The New York plan was quite effective in operation but, strangely enough, it neither satisfied the cities nor appealed strongly enough to people in other jurisdictions to be adopted by them. The New York cities continued to demand affirmative legislation as well as the veto power; this they achieved by a constitutional amendment adopted in 1923, giving them the right to act on their own "property, affairs, and government" but reserving to the legislature the right to pass general laws in any field. Also, special laws affecting only one city could be passed by a two-thirds vote after a special request from the Governor. In 1938, this plan was changed to require a petition from the local unit affected specifically requesting the legislature to pass a particular measure. Under these procedures, the evil of local laws has been largely eliminated in the New York legislature.

[7] A Mayor had fifteen days to consider the measure. If he vetoed the bill as it applied to his city, the legislature could override the veto by a simple majority vote. If he approved, the bill became law. Since most bills were passed then, as now, in the last ten days of the session, such vetoes were practically conclusive. See Moscow, Warren, *Politics in the Empire State* (New York: Alfred A. Knopf, Inc., 1948), Chapter 13; see also, for general background, McBain, Howard L., *The Law and Practice of Muncipal Home Rule* (New York: Columbia University Press, 1916) and McGoldrick, Joseph D., same title, *1916–1930* (New York: Columbia University Press, 1933).

NUMBER OF GOVERNMENTAL UNITS, BY TYPE AND BY STATES: 1962 *

State	All Governmental Units [1]	Local Governments Except School Districts					School Districts
		Total	Counties	Municipalities	Townships	Special Districts	
United States, total	91,736	56,507	3,043	17,997	17,144 [2]	18,823	34,678
Alabama	733	618	67	349	—	202	144
Alaska	57	45	—	40	—	6	10
Arizona	379	127	14	61	—	52	251
Arkansas	1,209	791	75	417	—	299	417
California	4,023	2,392	57	373	—	1,962	1,630
Colorado	1,194	881	62	253	—	566	312
Connecticut	399	390	—	34	152	204	8
Delaware	208	117	3	51	—	63	90
District of Columbia	2	2	—	1	—	1	—
Florida	765	697	67	366	—	264	67
Georgia	1,219	1,021	159	561	—	301	197
Hawaii	21	20	3	1	—	16	—
Idaho	835	713	44	200	—	469	121
Illinois	6,453	4,912	102	1,251	1,433	2,126	1,540
Indiana	3,092	2,207	92	565	1,009	560	884
Iowa	2,643	1,306	99	944	—	263	1,336
Kansas	5,411	3,149	105	618	1,546	880	2,261
Kentucky	873	664	120	365	—	179	208
Louisiana	629	561	62	258	—	241	67
Maine	659	632	16	21	470	125	26
Maryland	352	351	23	152	—	176	—
Massachusetts	587	557	12	39	312	194	29
Michigan	3,817	1,950	83	509	1,259	99	1,866
Minnesota	5,213	2,869	87	845	1,822	115	2,343
Mississippi	773	614	82	266	—	266	158
Missouri	3,727	2,077	114	892	329	742	1,649
Montana	1,388	372	56	124	—	192	1,015
Nebraska	5,125	1,860	93	537	478	752	3,264
Nevada	137	119	17	17	—	85	17
New Hampshire	551	329	10	13	221	85	221
New Jersey	1,396	883	21	334	233	295	512
New Mexico	306	214	32	80	—	102	91
New York	3,803	2,571	57	612	932	970	1,231

| State | All Governmental Units [1] | Local Governments Except School Districts | | | | | School Districts |
		Total	Counties	Municipalities	Townships	Special Districts	
North Carolina	676	675	100	449	—	126	—
North Dakota	3,029	2,042	53	356	1,387	246	986
Ohio	3,359	2,525	88	932	1,328	177	833
Oklahoma	1,960	734	77	533	—	124	1,225
Oregon	1,470	985	36	222	—	727	484
Pennsylvania	6,202	4,022	66	1,003	1,555	1,398	2,179
Rhode Island	98	95	—	8	31	56	2
South Carolina	553	443	46	255	—	142	109
South Dakota	4,464	1,523	64	307	1,072	80	2,940
Tennessee	658	643	95	280	—	268	14
Texas	3,328	1,853	254	866	—	733	1,474
Utah	424	383	29	212	—	142	40
Vermont	425	392	14	68	238	72	32
Virginia	381	380	98	236	—	46	—
Washington	1,647	1,235	39	263	66	867	411
West Virginia	390	334	55	224	—	55	55
Wisconsin	3,727	1,974	72	563	1,271	68	1,752
Wyoming	465	257	23	90	—	144	207

* Source: U.S. Bureau of the Census, *Governmental Units in 1962*, Preliminary Report No. 6, December 6, 1962.

[1] Including the Federal government and the 50 States, not shown in distribution by type.

[2] Includes "towns" in the 6 New England States and in New York and Wisconsin.

The next step in the development of the home rule concept also originated in New York. This was the optional charter plan, under which the legislature drew up model charters for each of the more common forms of municipal government. Communities that were dissatisfied with their existing system were authorized to vote on the question of charter revision and to choose a board of freeholders which would study the problems of the community, select whichever optional charter seemed best suited to its needs, and submit it to the electorate with the recommendation that it be adopted. Thus the communities were permitted to determine, in a general way, the form and structure of their local government. In some jurisdictions, the option was settled by the legislature on the basis of population ranges.

By 1915, fifteen States had adopted constitutional amendments providing for municipal home rule; in fact, the movement made such progress that it appeared likely that constitutional home rule would spread rapidly through the remainder of the States. This, however, was not to be the case. A second study in 1930 reported only one additional adoption in the fifteen-year period. The progress of the movement, sharply arrested for a number of years, has been revived since World War II as both cities and counties, long hampered by restrictive constitutional and statutory provisions, have tried to cope with modern urban problems.

Some late developments in this field are worth noting. In a Texas case decided in 1948, a State Supreme Court for the first time interpreted a home rule provision as conferring residual powers upon cities. A home rule city, said the court, acts by authority of its constitutional powers, and not through powers assigned to it by the legislature.[8] In 1953, the American Municipal Association developed its model plan for home rule; later, in 1958, the State of South Dakota became the first to adopt this plan and put it in operation.[9]

In the long battle for home rule, the cry has often been, "Give us home rule and we will solve our problems." The going has never been easy; there have been decades of rejection and rebuff from legislatures, courts, and occasionally from the voters themselves. However, even though the results have left much to be desired in specific instances in which home rule has been adopted and put in operation, the concept has, in a period of transition, served a number of useful purposes. It has provided for variations in the structure of local government. It has helped state legislatures by relieving them of most of the local bills that were a great burden to their predecessors and that still are a burden in many non-home rule jurisdictions. It has sometimes provided a satisfactory solution to the jurisdictional problems which plague many urban centers. Home rule has frequently created a favorable climate for the growth of metropolitan government, encouraging citizen participation and a certain amount of self-reliance in the solution of local problems. The major criticisms of it have been that it represents the wrong emphasis at the wrong time, that there has been too much of the wrong kind of home

[8] *City of El Paso* v. *State, ex rel. Town of Ascarate*, 209 S.W. 2nd 989 (1948).

[9] See Fordham, Jefferson B., *Model Constitutional Provisions for Municipal Home Rule* (Chicago, 1953); Dean Fordham spoke on behalf of the Association's Committee on Home Rule. See also Mott, Rodney L., *Home Rule for America's Cities* (Chicago: American Municipal Association, 1949) and Cassella, William N., Jr., *Metropolitan Government* (Detroit: Citizens Research Council of Michigan, November, 1961).

rule, and that home rule has not produced the results promised by its advocates.[10]

The Current Crisis Situation

Implicit in the home rule idea is the conflict between the right of local self-government, on one hand, and the right and the duty of the State, on the other, to exercise reasonable regulatory and supervisory powers over its political subdivisions. The field of State-local relations reproduces in miniature, in fact, a great many of the same problems encountered in the field of Federal-State relations. The psychology of the two situations is closely parallel. Just as the States protest against what they regard as the centralizing tendencies of the Federal government and talk loudly about States' rights, so the representatives of local units protest against State centralization and talk quite as loudly about home rule. Actually neither argument has much basis in fact; catch-phrases like "States' rights" and "home rule" serve only to arouse emotional responses and to becloud the real issues. The parallel extends also into the field of finance, where State aid and the tendency of the States to monopolize tax sources at the expense of the local units creates problems strikingly similar to those created by Federal aid and the tendency of the Federal government to monopolize tax sources at the expense of the States.

In both situations, two factors are involved. The first is the effect of scientific development and technological progress. Local units which had to be small in the early days are today too small to operate efficiently in some areas or even to function at all in others. The conditions of modern life virtually compel government to function in larger units, if it is to be effective. Such changes are not the result of the diabolical scheming of bureaucrats; they are simply the inevitable result of changed conditions.

The second factor involves the inability and/or unwillingness of governmental units to assume responsibility which rightfully belongs to them. Just as the States have at times lost powers to the Federal government through sheer ineptitude and inertia, so oftentimes have the local units lost to the States. Prompt, vigorous action by governmenal units at each level, based upon intelligent analysis of the problems at hand, would go a long way toward solving many of our present interjurisdictional conflicts.

Local units have often had legitimate grievances in their relations with the States. As the late Professor Charles E. Merriam pointed out

---

[10] These points are discussed in a critical appraisal of home rule by Lyle E. Schaller in *Political Science Quarterly*, September, 1961, pp. 402-415.

many years ago, the States have been unwilling either to govern their municipalities or to permit their municipalities to govern themselves. The grievances, then, have been of two varieties: limitations, requirements, and unwanted restrictions imposed upon the local units, and failure to grant to these units powers they actually need to discharge their responsibilities in a satisfactory manner. The first finds expression in vast quantities of local legislation, the second in the absence of a reasonable and proper degree of self-determination or home rule.

The problem of local legislation has been important in all the States and still is in some of them, particularly in the Southern region. American cities were originally completely under the domination of their legislatures and even today, vast quantities of local bills—bracket bills, the Texans call them—are introduced and passed in session after session. In some States, local and private bills which are enacted (and for obvious political reasons few such bills fail of enactment) constitute a third or a half of the legislative output. Under this system, municipalities have to go to the legislature for authority to pave a street, raise the salary of an official, or even to install a hydrant. Such a system is vicious; the members of the legislature are permitted to make political capital by handling matters in which they have little competence and no real interest, at the expense of valuable legislative time which might otherwise be used constructively. At the same time, local units are denied the opportunity to decide questions purely local in character. Many of the States have brought this problem under control, and the remainder should do so without delay.

It is reported, as a matter of fact, that thirty-nine States have abolished this obnoxious practice, and at least one other attempted but failed to do so.[11] Actually, this figure is misleading, for as previously noted, legislatures have often found it possible to evade a constitutional prohibition by dividing local units into classes. By the skillful planning and manipulation of the dividing lines between these various classes, they have been able to legislate for individual cities as before. Sometimes the formulae become exceedingly complicated, as in Texas where population brackets are mixed in with area or school population, the presence of cities of a certain size, the number of people per square mile, assessed valuation, votes cast at a previous election, and other factors. More than a dozen different combinations of elements were discovered. Thus the classification device is used to impose local laws upon many communities,

---

[11] Mississippi; see *Constitution*, Sections 87–89. Despite these sections, a large number of local and private bills are passed each regular session. For example, in the 1952 session, 213 local and private bills became law while there were only 435 general laws passed.

in clear violation of the constitutional intent of prohibiting enactment of such legislation.[12]

Various protective devices have been tried in a number of States. In Michigan, for example, the constitution prohibits the passing of a local or special act in any instance where a general act can be made applicable. The provisions of a New York law have been mentioned above. A limitation in the Florida constitution and in that of nine other States provides for publication of a proposed measure in the community affected at least thirty days prior to passage. Evidence of such publication must be furnished to the legislature, becomes part of the official record of the bill in the journals, and is filed in the office of the Secretary of State. Publication is not required if the measure includes a referendum provision, either under provisions contained in the bill or as provided by general law.

Not only does local government need more power and freedom from repressive local legislation to do its job efficiently, but it also needs more money. American cities are today facing a serious financial crisis. While demands from their citizens for costly, administratively efficient services increase, their income rises little, certainly not at a rate commensurate with their steadily mounting costs. While the National or the State government (or the two of them together) skims all the cream from the more productive sources of revenue, the local units are hamstrung in their fiscal operations by rigid tax and debt limitations which bear little relation to present-day conditions and which hamper their ability to raise necessary funds.

Extending Home Rule

Although more than half of the States now report that they have granted home rule to their cities (see table on page 709), and one-fourth to their counties, these figures also are misleading. Many of these constitutional provisions require statutory implementation which has never been provided, and without it, the home rule provisions have no substance. The fullest expression of home rule is found in jurisdictions in which cities and/or counties are authorized to create their own charter commissions and to frame and adopt their own charters.

After a long period of inactivity, the home rule movement was revived after World War II by local units long hampered by restrictive constitutional and statutory provisions. Demands for home rule have

---

[12] See Benton, Wilbourn E., *Texas, Its Government and Politics* (Englewood Cliffs, N.J.: Prentice-Hall, Inc., 1961), pp. 228–232.

been actively supported by such national organizations as the National Municipal League, the American Municipal Association, and the United States Conference of Mayors. The AMA clearly stated the case for the strong and self-reliant local government basic to the Anglo-Saxon tradition, when in its National Policy Statement in 1950 it said that local government "should be autonomous as far as practical and consistent with public welfare. While the Federal government and governments of the States may invoke their broad powers and great financial resources to make possible some local government services, still these powers and finances should be delegated for the purpose of administration to the municipal authorities, in a manner consistent with responsible self-government." This philosophy is basic to the American system of government.

There are several conditions essential to the realization of home rule for American local units. They must be permitted to choose their own form of governmental organization and to frame, or at least to select, their own charters. In doing so, they must be free from legislative veto. They must have the power to determine their own policies with regard to local issues and to adopt appropriate means of carrying out these policies. They must be accorded an opportunity to use productive tax sources sufficient to meet the needs for education, city streets, traffic control, social services, and all other important (and often costly) services which the people expect and demand. These things they cannot do as long as they are held in legal bondage, and as long as both the Federal government and the States continue to monopolize virtually all of the productive sources of revenue.[13]

Thus may be summarized the conventional position, but there are suggestions that, under rapidly changing conditions, realization of this position may be neither possible nor even desirable. More and more States are becoming predominately urban in character; "it is inconceivable," writes Schaller, that their legislatures "will surrender control over these clusters of population which account for the largest share of the State's wealth, power and votes." Since many governmental problems formerly regarded as local in nature are now metropolitan or regional in scope, uniform policies are a virtual necessity; uniformity requires State leadership if not actual centralization of authority—the antithesis of home rule. Under such circumstances, home rule may not be an unmixed blessing, for as the Kestnbaum Commission observed, "Self-determination in one isolated unit of a large community often restricts the opportunity for genuine home rule in the whole community."

[13] For a good discussion of these problems, see Cassella, William N., Jr., "Recent Trends in State-Local Relations," Appendix E in National Municipal League, *Intergovernmental Relations as of 1954* (New York, October, 1954).

CONSTITUTIONAL HOME RULE STATES *

States	Cities	Counties	States	Cities	Counties
Alaska	1958	1958[1]	Nevada	1924[3]	
Arizona	1912		New Jersey	1947[8]	
California	1879	1911	New York	1923	1958[9]
Colorado	1902		Ohio	1912	1933
Connecticut	1951		Oklahoma	1907	
Florida		1956[2]	Oregon	1906	1958
Georgia	1954[3]		Pennsylvania	1923[10]	
Hawaii	1959	1959	Rhode Island	1951	
Louisiana	1952[4]	1946–1956[5]	Tennessee	1953	
			Texas	1912[11]	1933[12]
Maryland	1954[6]	1915	Utah	1932	
Michigan	1908		Virginia	1920[3,13]	
Minnesota	1896	1958	Washington	1889	1948
Missouri	1875[7]	1943	West Virginia	1936	
Nebraska	1912		Wisconsin	1924	
Total				28	14

* Table originally appeared in Graves, W. Brooke, *American State Government*, 4th ed. (Boston: D. C. Heath & Co., 1953), p. 801; it has been revised in cooperation with Professor Arthur W. Bromage, University of Michigan, and Miss Patricia Shumate, National Municipal League, for the supplementary volume of the *Dictionary of American History* (New York: Charles Scribner's Sons, 1961).

[1] No counties; for units designated as boroughs.

[2] Applies to Dade County only.

[3] Authorization to the legislature to grant home rule, rather than direct grant of power to the cities.

[4] Amendments in 1946, 1948, and 1950 had previously authorized home rule for individual cities (Baton Rouge, Shreveport, and New Orleans, respectively); in 1952, home rule was granted to any municipality.

[5] Authorized adoption of a charter in Jefferson Parish; an earlier amendment, in 1946, had given similar authorization to East Baton Rouge Parish.

[6] Baltimore had been granted home rule in 1915.

[7] Only to cities of more than 100,000 population; extended in 1945 to all cities of over 10,000 and to counties of over 85,000 population.

[8] Constitution of 1947 authorized a type of "permissive" home rule; a 1950 law, with subsequent amendments, makes available sixteen optional charter plans, with variations.

[9] New York has been moving toward home rule for counties, as evidenced by amendments adopted in 1935 and 1958 and a number of optional laws enacted between 1935 and 1952.

[10] Legislation necessary to carry out the grant was not enacted until 1949, and then only for cities of the first class (Philadelphia).

[11] Amendment has proved unworkable; consideration is being given to simplifying proposals.

[12] Limited to counties of more than 62,000 population; implementing legislation enacted in 1946.

[13] Implementing legislation enacted in 1946.

Municipalities cannot expect to receive the financial help they need so badly, in the form of grants-in-aid or otherwise, without a corresponding limitation on the scope of some of their powers. It may be, however, that experience in State-local cooperation gained in such fields as education, health, welfare, or highways may be useful in developing forms of cooperation suitable to new fields. Most important of all is the fact that with a growing realization of the problems of metropolitan areas, municipal government ceases to be a matter of purely local concern. What happens to its cities is a matter of concern to the whole State and, in some respects, even to the Nation. Schaller concludes, "Acceptance by the State governments of a larger responsibility for the administration and financing of these municipal and intermunicipal functions will spell the end of home rule." [14] This may well prove to be the case.

Proposals for Secession

If the relations between the Federal government and the States have often been difficult and sometimes explosive, State-local relations have also been difficult and for substantially the same reasons. The latter, in fact, provide a reproduction in miniature of the former. Just as secession has been proposed from time to time in periods of stress in Federal-State relations, and on one occasion was actually attempted on a large scale, it has likewise been proposed for major cities in relations with their respective State governments. Such proposals, to be sure, are likely to be made with tongue in cheek and dismissed by jest or ridicule, but they do have their serious side. They are apt to be half-serious protests against abuses and injustices that *are* real and serious.

The earliest such proposal that has come to the attention of the author was made by Mayor Fernando Wood of New York City in a message presented to the Common Council on January 6, 1861. His reasons for proposing so grave a step were related to policies of the Federal government which were seriously prejudicial to the financial and commercial interests of the city because of their heavy investments in the textile industries of the South, and to political and financial injustices against the city attributed to the State legislature. The former are not relevant to the present discussion, but the latter serve to illustrate how present-day grievances of our larger cities against their State governments,

[14] Many of these points are considered in the Schaller article, pp. 414–415; see also Schaller, "The Role of the States in Reorganizing Local Government," *Social Science*, January, 1961, pp. 48–52, and Tollenaar, Kenneth C., "A Home Rule Puzzle," *National Civic Review*, September, 1961, pp. 411–416.

serious as they are, have been in existence in much the same form for approximately a century.

The following paragraphs from Mayor Wood's message could conceivably have appeared in this morning's paper:

> It is, however, folly to disguise the fact that, judging from the past, New York may have more cause of apprehension from the aggressive legislation of our own State than from external dangers. We have already suffered largely from this cause. For the past five years, our interests and corporate rights have been repeatedly trampled upon. Being an integral portion of the State, it has been assumed, and in effect tacitly admitted on our part by nonresistance, that all political and governmental power over us rested in the State Legislature. Even the common right of taxing ourselves for our own government, has been yielded, and we are not permitted to do so without this authority. . . .
>
> Thus it will be seen that the political connection between the people of the city and the State have been used by the latter to our injury. The Legislature, in which the present partisan majority has the power, has become an instrument by which we are plundered to enrich their speculators, lobby agents, and Abolition politicians.

While Mayor Wood proceeded under the mistaken idea that the disruption of the Union was a foregone conclusion and dreamed of a City of New York free from the burden of Federal taxes as well as from the tyranny of a corrupt and hostile legislature, he was not "prepared to recommend the violence implied in these views."

> In stating this argument in favor of freedom "peaceably if we can, forcibly if we must," let me not be misunderstood. The redress can be found only in appeals to the magnaminity of the people of the whole State. . . .

The friction between the city government and the State continues unabated. Part of it is political, for most of the time the city and the State are controlled by opposing political parties. Occasionally friction breaks out in a new demand for secession, as it did in 1959 when the President of the City Council urged secession and a Member of Congress from New York City had an extensive study made of the whole problem of city-State relations, preparatory to the introduction of a bill to make New York City the fifty-first State in the Union. While these events were taking place in New York, the press reported similar demands from Philadelphia and Chicago, whose city leaders were rankled by the unwillingness of the rural-dominated legislatures in Pennsylvania and Illinois to deal in an understanding way with their problems. A member of the Philadelphia City Council wanted to secede and give the rest of the State back to the Indians!

A STATE AGENCY FOR LOCAL GOVERNMENT

Many of the countries of Europe have long had a department of the interior or of internal affairs whose duty it is to supervise and assist their municipalities. Every province in Canada has a department of local government, but few States have until recently taken steps to provide such governmental machinery.

STATE AGENCIES FOR LOCAL GOVERNMENT

State	Executive Agencies	Established	Legislative Agencies	Established
Alaska	Office of Local Government Local Boundary Commission	1959 1959	Local Government Commission	1959
California	Local Allocation Division, and Office of Planning, Department of Finance	1959	Senate Fact Finding Committee on Local Government	1959
Illinois	. . . .		Northeastern Illinois Metropolitan Area Local Governmental Services Commission	1957
Kentucky	Bureau of Community Service, University of Kentucky	1950	. . . .	
Maryland	Municipal Technical Advisory Service, University of Maryland	1959	State Fiscal Bureau, Legislative Council	1948
Michigan	Institute for Community Development and Service, Michigan State University	1958	. . . .	
Minnesota	. . . .		Municipal Commission	1959
Missouri	. . . .		Local Government Commission	1961
New Jersey	Division of Local Government, Department of Taxation and Finance Local Government Board	1917 1931	. . . .	

State	Executive Agencies	Estab- lished	Legislative Agencies	Estab- blished
New York	Office for Local Government	1959	Joint Legislative Committee on Metropolitan Study	1957
	Local Government Advisory Board	1959		
North Carolina	Local Government Commission	1931	. . . .	
Pennsylvania	Bureau of Municipal Affairs, Department of Internal Affairs	1915	Local Government Commission	1935
Rhode Island	Division of Local and Metropolitan Government	1961	. . . .	
Tennessee	Municipal Technical Advisory Service, University of Tennessee	1949	. . . .	
Wisconsin	Bureau of Community Development, University of Wisconsin	1946	. . . .	

Since 1957, State agencies for local government have sprung up in considerable numbers; they are of many different types. The Office of Local Government in Alaska is a constitutional agency, while the others are created by statute. Many are executive agencies, although several permanent legislative commissions have been established. Executive agencies of a variety of types exist in at least a dozen States, legislative agencies in about half that number, and both types of agency exist in Alaska, New York, and Pennsylvania. Originally conceived largely for purposes of fiscal supervision and control, the executive agencies in California and New Jersey, and formerly in New York as well, are located in the Finance Department. The offices in Alaska and New York are part of the Governor's Office, in Pennsylvania, of the Department of Internal Affairs. The North Carolina agency is a commission, that of Tennessee a branch of the State University's Extension Division. Other States, including Kentucky, Michigan, and Wisconsin, have community development agencies connected with the State university.[15]

Permanent legislative commissions on local government are increas-

[15] The best, in fact the only thorough study of this problem is: Grumm, John G., *A State Agency for Local Affairs?* (Berkeley: Bureau of Public Administration, University of California, 1961). This study is digested in *Public Affairs Report*, October, 1961.

ing in number. Pennsylvania's Local Government Commission, established in 1933, is the oldest interim Commission in the State and very likely the oldest in this field in the country. Such bodies have also been established, as shown in the table on pages 712–713, in Alaska, California, Illinois, Maryland, Minnesota, Missouri, and New York.

New Jersey, New York, North Carolina, and Pennsylvania were pioneers in the development of executive agencies. The organization and functions of these agencies may be briefly noted. The New Jersey Division of Local Government, though largely concerned with fiscal controls, is also engaged in important advisory and facilitative activities. It publishes reports, guides, and statistical data that are helpful to local governments, while the Local Government Board, which has been directed to study the whole field of local government, carries on some research work, provides a consulting service, and makes recommendations to the director of the Division on methods for improving local administration.[16]

Since 1927, when North Carolina began state supervision of local finance, every county has been required to appoint an accountant and operate on a budget basis. A few years later, in 1931, the General Assembly created the Local Government Commission. Under this act, no note or bond of any municipality, county, or political subdivision is valid unless approved by the Commission. All notes or bonds are sold by the Commissioner of Revenue at the State Capitol. Securities are delivered to the purchaser by the State Treasurer, who receives the proceeds and remits them to the proper local authorities. In case any local unit defaults in payment on its debt obligations, the Commissioner may appoint an administrator of finances to collect all taxes and disburse all funds. One well-informed writer has evaluated the Commission as "an eminently successful organization [which] has rendered an invaluable service to the State." [17]

The Pennsylvania Bureau of Municipal Affairs is responsible both for some supervisory functions and for a wide range of services to local governments. On the basis of an extensive study of such agencies, Grumm asserts that, "in the breadth and variety of its activities, the Pennsylvania Bureau is probably unique in the United States. Activities are organized into four divisions," the names of which indicate in a general way the character of the work performed: Research and Information, Local Gov-

[16] See Rich, Bennett M., *The Government and Administration of New Jersey* (New York: Thomas Y. Crowell Co., 1957), pp. 355–359.

[17] Rankin, Robert S., *The Government and Administration of North Carolina* (New York: Thomas Y. Crowell Co., 1955), pp. 383–389; see also McMahon, John A., *The North Carolina Local Government Commission* (Chapel Hill: North Carolina Association of County Commissioners, July, 1960).

ernment Financial Statistics, City Planning and Landscape Architecture, and Bond Approval. The Bureau has had good leadership for many years, and by making extensive use of the services of political scientists on the faculties of the universities and colleges of the State, it has been able to accomplish a good deal in improving the quality and effectiveness of local government in the Commonwealth.

A Division of Local Government functioned in New York for many years as a unit within the Department of Audit and Control. In 1959 this activity was expanded and transferred to the already overloaded executive department. Governor Rockefeller had promised during his campaign to establish such an agency, and had repeated the recommendation in his 1959 message to the legislature. Duties and functions of the agency include: coordination of the services of State departments dealing with the localities, keeping the Governor informed on local government problems, serving as a clearing house for information on local governments, encouraging cooperation between such governments, and assisting in the formulation of policy. The new office is headed by a director appointed by the Governor whose first appointee was the former city manager of Rochester. Assisting him is a local government board of nine members also named by the Governor. Members serve without compensation and are scheduled to hold meetings at least four times a year.[18]

The Minnesota Municipal Commission, established in 1959, has a more limited field of operation. It has three members appointed by the Governor for four-year terms. It hears and makes determinations on petitions with respect to the incorporation of villages, annexation, and other municipal boundary changes (in this respect, it resembles the Alaska Boundary Commission). In important proceedings relating to incorporation or the annexation of an existing municipality by an adjacent city, two county officials serve on the Commission in an ex-officio capacity; these are, in each instance, the chairman of the board of county commissioners and the county auditor of the county in which all or a majority of the property to be annexed or incorporated is located.

The statute enumerates factors which are to serve as a general guide to the Commission in incorporation proceedings: "(1) The population of the area within the boundaries of the proposed incorporation; (2) the area of the proposed incorporation; (3) the area of platted land relative to unplatted land; (4) the character of the buildings on both types of land; (5) past expansion in terms of population and construction; (6) prospective future expansion; (7) the assessed value of platted land relative to the assessed value of the unplatted areas; (8) the present

[18] See Office of Local Government, *Annual Report, 1959–1960*, and Moore, Frank C., "New York State's New Office for Local Government," *State Government*, Autumn, 1960, pp. 227–231.

and/or expected necessity or feasibility of providing governmental services such as sewage disposal, water system, zoning, street planning, police and fire protection." Procedures for annexation of unincorporated areas to a municipality may be initiated by the governing body of the annexing municipality or by property owners in the area to be annexed. In this instance also, the statute lays out guides for the Commission in making its determinations, in a list of items roughly parallel to that applicable to incorporation proceedings.[19]

A new angle to this problem has been presented as the States, however belatedly, have begun to recognize their responsibility for metropolitan areas, which was clearly pointed out in a study made several years ago under the auspices of the Council of State Governments.[20] Now the States are beginning to act. In late 1960, the Governor's Commission on Metropolitan Problems in California issued a report recommending establishment of a State planning agency for metropolitan government. It further urged that each of the nine urban areas be permitted to establish a single, multipurpose agency with taxing and bonding powers to provide areawide services.

In its report on governmental structure in metropolitan areas, the Advisory Commission on Intergovernmental Relations submitted a number of recommendations for consideration by State legislatures, including: (1) Simplified statutory requirements for municipal annexation of unincorporated territory; (2) authorization for interlocal contracting or joint performance of urban services; (3) authorization for establishment of metropolitan service corporations for performance of particular governmental services that call for areawide handling; (4) authorization for voluntary transfer of governmental functions from cities to counties and vice versa; (5) authorization for the creation of metropolitan area commissions on local government structure and services; (6) authorization for creation of metropolitan area planning bodies; (7) establishment of a unit of State government for continuing attention, review, and assistance regarding the State's metropolitan areas; (8) inauguration of State programs of financial and technical assistance to metropolitan areas; (9) stricter State standards for new incorporations within metropolitan areas; (10) financial and regulatory action by the State to secure and preserve "open land" in and around metropolitan areas; and (11) assumption by the State of an active role in the resolution of disputes among local units of government within metropolitan areas.[21]

[19] See note in *National Civic Review*, June, 1959, pp. 311–313.

[20] Bollens, John C., *The States and the Metropolitan Problem* (Chicago: Council of State Governments, 1956).

[21] *Governmental Structure, Organization, and Planning in Metropolitan Areas: Suggested Action by Local, State, and National Governments* (Washington: House Committee Print, 87th Cong., 1st Sess., 1961).

ADMINISTRATIVE RELATIONSHIPS

Essentials of Effective State Supervision

This section is concerned with the essentials for State leadership in local administration, and with the techniques by which such leadership may be made effective: administrative organization and procedures, standard setting and enforcement, supervision and control of local fiscal operations, local personnel administration, and the provision of technical assistance and "know-how" in cooperative undertakings.

Administrative Organization and Procedures. Good results in State-local administrative relationships may be expected only when the States, having put their own houses in order, cooperate with local units legislatively and administratively to bring about a similar result at the local level. There must be clear and unobstructed lines of communication within the administrative hierarchy, with the legislature, with the officials of such other levels and units of government as may be concerned with the problem at hand, and with the public. Detailed local legislation should be replaced by broad grants of authority to local governments through general laws.

Effective administration requires both qualified personnel and adequate financial support used in such ways as to assure maximum benefits to the public for the money spent, at both State and local levels. Supervision within a given field should be under a unified command, for diffusion of administrative responsibility can lead only to waste of funds and inefficient operation. The general effectiveness of State efforts will be enhanced if there is a single State agency, such as has been discussed, concerned with local affairs. The intelligent determination of policy as well as its administration is dependent upon full and accurate information. These principles are truisms in the field of public administration.[22]

Standard Setting and Enforcement. Standard setting and enforcement is a major tool of State governments in any effective cooperation with local units. As the senior partner in the enterprise, and the partner possessing major legal responsibility for the organization and conduct of government, it devolves upon the State to determine what shall be done and how it shall be done. The establishment of minimum standards insures adequate performance and frees local units from the hampering effects of a rigid and often undesirable uniformity. By other supervisory methods, local authorities can be encouraged to exceed the minimum within the limits of their resources and their own discretion.

[22] These points are discussed at greater length in the Council of State Governments' report, *State-Local Relations* (Chicago, 1946), Chapter 2.

The purpose of the State is not to dictate nor merely to exercise its superior authority, but to get the job done as well as possible. Local officials are likely to resent "control," but properly led and properly motivated, they are normally willing to do all and more than the minimum requires. As the Council of State Governments' report observes, control "amounts to the absorption of local government by State authorities"; this can be justified only in those extreme cases in which local officials are either unable or unwilling to adhere to the standards. "Where control is chronic, the States' own standards may be at fault. Or the function concerned might better be transferred direct to State administration."

The State may properly set minimum standards regarding the character and adequacy of the service to be provided in various functional fields; this is regularly done in the administration of education, health, welfare, and various other services. It may make mandatory the use of approved fiscal and personnel procedures in the administration of these services.

Supervision of Local Fiscal Operations. The entire fiscal operation of local government is in many States subject to State supervision and control. This includes what has been called the natural history of the tax dollar from the time of assessment to the final accounting and auditing of its expenditure. The essential steps in this cycle in chronological order are: assessment and equalization, control of local tax sources and rates, collection of taxes, custody of funds, financial planning and budgeting, borrowing and debt administration, expenditure control, procurement, property management, disbursement, accounting, auditing, and financial reporting. These steps in the fiscal process may be supervised by the State agency charged with responsibility for this function, but operating departments of the State government can and do oversee the use of funds appropriated for the programs administered by their respective departments.

Supervision of Local Personnel Administration. In the more advanced States, local units are encouraged, and in some they are required by law, to use the merit system. In New York, the State personnel agency supervises, cooperates with, and assists local personnel agencies in the performance of their duties. In this way, minimum standards may be applied to each stage of public employment, beginning with recruitment and continuing in succession through examination, appointment and placement, classification, compensation, training, conditions of work, employee relations, health and safety, changes in status, and finally, separation and retirement.

In addition to establishing minimum standards for and increased general supervision of these several aspects of the personnel function, operating departments, as in the fiscal field, establish and enforce professional standards relating to the personnel employed in their particular programs. Many governmental activities are today so technical in nature that only specially trained persons are useful in their administration. Thus, in many jurisdictions, teacher certification is administered by the State on the basis of State standards, and persons employed in public health administration or welfare are eligible for appointment only if they meet minimum standards established by the State. Because of the shortage of qualified personnel in some fields, or of the rapid rate of change in methods and procedures in others, the States are doing more and more in the training of both State and local personnel.

Technical Assistance and Cooperative Undertakings. There are many functional areas in which local units cannot afford to employ qualified professional personnel on a full time basis, or in which the volume of work is not great enough to justify such employment. The need in such cases can be met by joint employment of such personnel by adjoining units facing the same problem, or through technical assistance provided by the State department concerned. Once the recruitment and training needs of local units have been met, the State can concentrate on supplying other types of assistance, such as the preparation of operations or procedures manuals, the making of administrative surveys and management studies designed to improve the quality of administration, consultation to bring about improved organization at the local level, technical services on difficult problems, or training conferences for demonstration programs and the exchange of information. Cooperation along these lines tends to raise the level of competence of the whole operation.

Administrative Supervision in Important Functional Areas

If space permitted, one might examine State programs in many important functional areas in which important State-local administrative relationships have developed, attempting in each case to note the extent to which the several types of control are being utilized. Major attention would be given not only to education, public health, public welfare, and highways, but also to such other fields as conservation, law enforcement, regulation of public utilities, recreation administration, and mental health. Since State-local relationships developed early and are still important in the field of education, this field will be used as the principal illustration, with brief reference to selected programs in other areas.

Education. There are not many aspects of elementary and secondary education which do not somewhere or somehow come under State control. This control is exercised in a wide variety of ways—through general supervision, teacher certification, control over curriculum, control over textbooks, and control over school buildings, to mention only a few. Under their powers of general supervision, more than half of the States permit State educational authorities to require reports and to prescribe the forms in which the records of the several school districts shall be kept. Eighteen States have the power of making ordinances within the limits established by the State constitution and statutes. In many States, all controversies arising under local school laws are subject to State adjudication.

In 1912, it is reported, high schools were accredited by State departments in fourteen States; in 1922, forty-one State departments carried on this function, while in 1940, the number had increased to forty-four— all States except California, Colorado, Michigan, and Wisconsin. In the first three, the State universities issued lists of accredited schools. In Wisconsin, although there was no accredited list, high schools had to be approved before they were eligible to receive State grants, and they were then commonly accepted as accredited. Every State has established one or more agencies to certify schools for veterans.

Early inspection of secondary schools grew largely out of the concern of Midwestern universities—especially Indiana, Michigan, and Wisconsin—over the caliber of the schools from which their students came. At first, State supervisory officers were chiefly concerned with accrediting programs, and although this is still a function of major importance, State supervision has tended more and more to emphasize adequate educational programs for all high school students, including the non-college group. There has been a growing emphasis on the content of high school courses and on methods of teaching. Even accrediting has taken the form of emphasizing continuous improvement of schools as well as attainment of established standards necessary for an approved rating.

By use of the system of grants-in-aid for training and salaries, it has been possible for States to exercise extensive control over the personnel engaged in public school work. In the matter of salary control, the locality is obliged to either pay its teachers at the rates prescribed by law or lose its appropriation, and of course it can employ only those teachers who are able to meet State certification requirements. Grants have been used in many States to accomplish one or both of these purposes. The qualifications of teachers are controlled by regulations requiring certification for permanent teaching positions in the State school system. With very few exceptions, examinations for teachers are administered by the State, and State certificates are issued upon the passing of these examinations. In half of the States, the supervising authorities have power to establish standards for admission to the teaching profession. Suspension or removal has been placed under the control of the supervising authorities in one-fourth of the States, removal usually being accomplished by revocation of license.

All States to a greater or lesser degree exercise some supervision over public school curricula. State staffs concerned with this problem have increased significantly in the last half century, and definite courses of study have been established in many States. For a great many years, New York, whose controls are now far less rigid than they once were, was the outstanding example of central control over local schools. The State Department of Education not only prescribed the subjects which should be taught, specifying the number of weeks and the number of hours per week, but it outlined in detail, in a series of syllabi, the exact nature of the subject matter to be presented in each course of study.

State supervisory agencies are concerned with curriculum revision and either prepare prescribed courses of study or issue suggested guides and outlines. In some States, the Council of State Governments reports, curriculum planning is a basic factor in the supervision program, often including cooperation with educational associations, teachers, and local administrators.[23] Almost every State supervisory body uses the technique of demonstration classes, and in some jurisdictions, model or "key" schools are maintained for demonstration purposes.

At least two-thirds of the States have, under their general powers of supervision, established control over the selection of textbooks used in the public schools. In some jurisdictions, this has taken the form of prescribing specific books for each subject and grade, while in others a list of books acceptable to the State department is prepared and distributed to the localities, and individual selections may be made from these lists. A few States have undertaken to publish their own texts for many of the courses required.

Many States supervise school buildings, not only as regards their suitability for the educational purposes for which they are intended, but for factors of physical safety as well, including exits, emergency lighting systems for auditoriums, and safety from fire hazards generally. Such controls are usually exercised, not by the Department of Education, but by the State agency responsible for building inspection and fire and panic regulations. Some States also examine and approve school building plans from the point of view of aesthetics and architectural design.

Supervision of school buildings has become a very effective method of control. Some years ago, in a small town in central New York, the high school building was a dilapidated structure that had been condemned for years as unsafe and unsuitable for school purposes. The local authorities paid no attention to repeated pleas from the State Department

---

[23] *The Forty-eight State School Systems* (Chicago, 1949).

of Education for the construction of a new building. In the meantime, the State law was amended, giving the State department authority to act in such situations. The department was then able to tell local authorities that their State funds would be withheld unless they undertook immediately to plan for a new building and that if this was not done, the department would proceed with the construction of the building and assess the cost upon the taxpayers of the community. Needless to say, the local authorities lost no time in selecting plans, making financial arrangements, and advertising for bids to construct the new building.

Highways. Road-building was originally regarded as primarily a local responsibility. The development of the automobile and of the program of Federal aid for highway construction, however, gradually transformed highways into a major activity of the State governments, while the development of the Interstate program made highway construction an important national concern. Even so, in all but the four States of Delaware, North Carolina, Virginia, and West Virginia, in which the responsibility for highways has been completely centralized, State and local governments still retain important responsibilities in this area. The tendency toward centralization in all States has been accelerated by the staggering cost of modern highway construction and the inability of most local units to utilize on a full time basis either the professional staff or the expensive road-building equipment required.

For these reasons, the tendency has been to leave only local streets and roads and country roads or "feeders" to major highways under the jurisdiction and control of local road-building authorities. There are, of course, many miles of these roads, but even with respect to them, where the laws provide for a divided authority, the degree of local control varies widely. A number of States, including among others, Kentucky, Pennsylvania, and Washington, have achieved a high degree of practical centralization. There are occasional conflicts attending grant-in-aid programs. Although local discretion over local roads is definitely limited in some jurisdictions, others appear disposed to permit counties to proceed in their own way without much interference or even a strict audit of the use made of the funds provided.

State regulation tended in the past to be less extensive in urban areas than in rural, but the development of metropolitan areas has led to increased controls in urban communities as well. The State is responsible for seeing that expressways are so designed and constructed as to tie in with local city streets and urban feeder roads. The percentage of financial responsibility from the State level varies of necessity according to the traffic pattern and volume of each area, but responsibility for scientific planning to meet overall needs must rest with the State. In many instances, of which the Port of New York Authority is an example, the problem has both metropolitan area and interstate aspects, and the State must take the initiative in seeing that uniform policies, standard scientific designs, and proper construction methods are followed. The State must, with both local and Federal cooperation, see that construction projects on the Interstate expressway system are selected so as to be usable when completed for both local and interstate needs and adequate not only for present needs but also for the needs of the foreseeable future.

Public Health. Health, like highways, was originally primarily an activity of local government. State controls have been extended because of the unrestricted manner of the spread of disease and because of the highly technical nature of most of the problems. State controls are exercised in a variety of ways, such as, controls over personnel, standard setting and enforcement. Financial help is extended to local units for health work, if not on an across-the-board basis, at least in emergency situations and/or when requested by local authorities. Control over local health ordinances, which must be submitted for State approval in many jurisdictions, is another means of extending State control, as are control over general sanitary conditions and the inspection of local conditions by State authorities.

Federal and State programs relating to air and water pollution illustrate another means by which controls have passed from the hands of local authorities. The States generally have jurisdiction over municipal water supplies and over both the construction and maintenance of sewage disposal systems. In many States, legislation has been enacted extending the regulatory and supervisory powers of the State sanitary engineers to a wide variety of subjects, such as bottling plants for mineral water and soft drinks, the inspection of public bathing places, the abatement of nuisances, housing inspection, inspection of cemeteries and mausoleums, and care of environmental sanitation.

Public Welfare. Public welfare administration has evolved from private alms giving to a concern of governments at all levels. The provisions of the Federal social security laws make it mandatory that federally supported public assistance plans provide for their application in all political subdivisions of the State, that the States participate financially, that a single State agency administer or supervise local administration of a given welfare plan, that States establish methods of administration (including a merit system) that will make possible the efficient operation of the plan, and that the supervising State agency will make periodic reports to the Federal agency as required. The very existence of these requirements makes it necessary for the States either to administer the programs directly or to exercise a large measure of supervision over the administering local government agencies. In either case, specific standards must be established and maintained.

State supervision and control are by no means limited to federally aided programs, however. There may be a division of responsibility with regard to many others as, for instance, inspecting of boarding homes for the aged, nursing and convalescent homes, and child care centers and homes. In one State, the city inspects the food and sanitary facilities in such establishments, while the State retains responsibility for insuring that medical services are adequate, for checking on narcotics control, and for supervising the administration of the institutions. Such agreements often include provision for liaison between city and State inspectors. The amount of State supervision varies considerably from one program to another and from one State to another.

STATE-LOCAL FISCAL RELATIONSHIPS

Historical Background

In the early days, there was little conscious theorizing about such questions as State-local fiscal relations. The tendency was to "play by ear," acting upon the basis of such fundamental assumptions as the following: (1) that government itself was a necessary evil, and the less we had of it, the better; (2) that such government as must be maintained should do as little as possible—"that government is best which governs least"; (3) that in any event, taxes should be held to the absolute, irreducible minimum. This last assumption was predicated upon another, equally fallacious theory—that money spent by government was wasted, while expenditures made through private channels benefited the economic life of the community.

Some changes in these attitudes became noticeable around the turn of the century as government began to expand and assume a more positive role, but by this time, the constitutional and statutory framework, not to mention the psychological climate of the community, had become so fixed and rigid that progress was always difficult and often impossible. Local units found themselves confined in a constitutional and statutory strait-jacket. Limitations applied to the kinds of taxes and the subjects taxed, as well as to the tax rates. Strict limitations were imposed upon the power to contract indebtedness, and no debt could be authorized without approval in a popular referendum, although this is now known to have little or no deterrent effect on the incurring of public debt. These restrictions continued through the end of World War II.

The financial plight of the local units presented something of a paradox. With one hand, the States shackled them with constitutional and statutory restrictions, and with the other they handed over steadily increasing amounts of money to keep locally administered services in operation. State financial aid to local units may take any of several forms or combinations of these forms: (1) shared taxes; (2) in lieu payments; (3) grants-in-aid for special services, with or without matching; (4) outright grants with no matching. The total amount of aid from grants now totals approximately $10 billion annually, one-fourth of the total expenditure. Of this, nearly half goes for education (at present the most costly State and local function), the other half largely for local highway and public welfare services.

Even with this substantial assistance, the situation of the local units was far from good. Both the restrictions and the grants served to illustrate the paternalistic attitude of the States (the "father knows best" attitude), and in part the fact that all of the most productive sources of revenue had been appropriated by the Federal government or the States, leaving the local units almost wholly dependent upon the general property tax.

This was obviously not a good arrangement. The local units found themselves with inadequate revenues that were relatively if not actually declining, on the one hand, while on the other they were confronted by constantly mounting costs and greater demands. Governmental units, like the individual citizen, were seriously affected by inflation; they found that they had to spend far more in order to simply hold their own, or as Lewis Carroll expressed it in *Alice in Wonderland,* they had to run like everything in order to stand still.

Under these circumstances, something sooner or later had to give. The pressure of the local units for State aid increased to the point where the States, which were themselves facing the effects of many of the same factors, were simply unable to provide more. They did not have it to give. The break came in Pennsylvania in 1947, in New York shortly thereafter, and in other States gradually through the years which followed. As a result, many restrictions upon the fiscal powers of local units were either eased or abandoned altogether, and there developed an intensive search for new non-property tax sources of revenue.

The restrictions upon local government in Pennsylvania had been among the worst. Suddenly, in a complete reversal of policy, the General Assembly enacted its famous "tax everything act," Public Law 481 of 1947. Within two years, there had developed the most amazing array of new taxes and tax forms that had ever been seen or heard of. Local units in Pennsylvania for the first time in history had complete home rule with respect to taxation, and they made the most of it. The law was tightened a bit and polished by amendments adopted in the 1949 session, but the basic plan remained unimpaired and has now been in successful operation for more than a decade. Perhaps the most significant thing about this legislation is its refutation of the frequently made assertion that the people are unwilling to pay taxes; they will tax themselves, even heavily, for governmental services that they want and need.

Control Over Local Tax Sources and Rates

While the financial needs of the cities continued to increase, their revenues either declined, comparatively, or remained stationary. The cities, like the States, came out of World War II in good financial condition. They had been able to reduce their debts, and because under war-time restrictions they had not been able to spend all the tax money they took in, they had accumulated considerable surpluses. These, however, were soon dissipated, and the local units, like individuals, were affected by inflation; in order to buy the same amount of goods and services as before, they had to have more income. Wages had risen greatly, as compared with pre-war standards, as had the prices of all materials, equipment, and supplies.

When, in the face of these conditions, local units cast about for additional revenues, they found themselves thwarted at every turn. Not only did the States control rates, but the States and the Federal government controlled all productive tax sources as well. The local units' chief reliance, therefore, had to be upon the ad valorem tax on real estate. Real estate, while a perfectly proper subject of taxation, was already heavily taxed in most communities, and property owners (and the organized real estate dealers) resisted the effort to further increase their burden. Government people, both State and local, soon realized that the effects of the long existing constitutional and statutory restrictions applying to the local units were more serious than ever before. In many jurisdictions, in addition to restrictions and restraints as to what they might tax, other restrictions imposed limits on how much they might tax.

Although tax limitation had been used previously with some degree of moderation, it owed its widespread popularity to the psychology of the period of the Great Depression, when anything that might possibly hold down taxes was seized upon avidly. Since the Federal government had never used the general property tax, and since approximately half of the States had abandoned it, the restrictions apply chiefly to the local units. There is little logic in the limitations imposed, ranging as they do from 1 per cent in one State to as much as 5 per cent in another. The limitations, most of them prescribed by the constitutions, are of several different types: (1) those which state a fixed maximum rate of tax; (2) those which restrict the amount of levy to a state percentage of the amount of some previous year, or average for certain years; (3) those which restrict the amount of revenue to be raised to a fixed amount per capita; (4) those which give the maximum levy permitted in terms of dollars; and (5) those which fix the ratio between revenues from general property taxes and revenues from other sources.

Thus, in many jurisdictions, the local units were handicapped in the use of the one tax source that is unquestionably theirs. In the past, many of the controls were highly restrictive, and some of them still are, although the tendency since World War II has been to ease them somewhat. Opportunity for supplementing receipts from the general property tax by levies upon other sources were limited both by the number of good sources available and by further restrictions imposed by the States upon their use. Pennsylvania law for many years forbade the City of Philadelphia to levy on sources taxed by the Commonwealth. At that time, the State had no sales tax, though it has since adopted one. Philadelphia tried one, but although such taxes seem acceptable to the people in many jurisdictions, the public rebelled and the ordinance was repealed. The State had no income tax, and because the State Supreme Court had ruled that a graded income tax was unconstitutional, Philadelphia was more or less obliged to resort to the horrible flat-rate income tax which still exists in that city. Similar restrictions applicable to tax sources are also found in many other States.

As local revenue requirements continued to mount, local officials had no recourse except to go, hat-in-hand, to the State Capitol for more and larger grants-in-aid. The so-called surpluses accumulated during the war were soon spent or committed to meet pressing postwar needs. Since the States simply did not have the funds to meet large new and continuing liabilities, Pennsylvania by its Act No. 481, and New York by comparable legislation, led the way among the States in relaxing restrictions on the taxing powers of their political subdivisions.[24] The Pennsylvania plan represented a virtually complete reversal of earlier policy.

State Coordination of Local Nonproperty Taxes

In 1960, when civil government in the nation cost $63 billion, more than half of the total expenditures took place at local levels, slightly more than one-quarter at State levels, and less than one-quarter (18 per cent)

[24] For references, see Graves, W. Brooke, *American State Government*, pp. 805–806, and his *Intergovernmental Relations in the United States: A Selected Bibliography* (Washington: Committee Print, 84th Cong., 2nd Sess., 1956), pp. 74–77.

at the Federal level. Local expenditures have increased significantly since World War II—from $6.5 billion in 1940, to $34 billion in 1960, and are in 1963 nearing the $40 billion mark. The Advisory Commission on Intergovernmental Relations, in its first report in the field of State-local tax relations, points out that "the $33 billion of local revenues available for general government came 48 per cent from property taxes, 30 per cent from State and Federal aid, 15 per cent from non-tax sources, and 7 per cent from nonproperty taxes. Despite the record yield of property taxes and despite sharp increases in State grants-in-aid and shared revenues" for every dollar local government spent in 1960, they were still able to raise only $.70 from local revenues.[25]

This being the case, local governments are turning increasingly to consumer, income, and excise taxes, although except in the case of large cities, these taxes are poorly suited to local needs. They tend to distort competitive business relationships between neighboring communities, handicap local business firms in competition with firms beyond the city line, and are costly for taxpayers to comply with and for governments to collect. With all these disadvantages, what do these taxes amount to for the States, individually and collectively? The Commission report provides some interesting answers.

Local sales, income, and other nonproperty taxes now aggregate $2.5 billion annually, and are likely to continue to grow "because more fundamental adjustments in State-local division of responsibility for functions and in financial aid are likely to lag." In Pennsylvania alone, a State which pioneered in easing restrictions on local taxing powers, there are now more than 5,000 separate taxes, including more than 800 income taxes levied by municipalities, counties, and school districts. To a lesser degree, the practice prevails in some other States. It is plain that this situation requires leadership on the part of State governments, and to this end the Commission sets forth a number of general guidelines for the consideration of State Governors and legislatures:

> 1. Provide cities and adjoining jurisdictions in large metropolitan areas with uniform taxing power and authority for cooperative tax enforcement;
> 2. Authorize the addition of local tax supplements to State sales, income, and excise taxes where these are used both by the State and a large number of local governments;
> 3. Permit pooled administration of similar local taxes levied by numerous local governments;
> 4. Limit local governments to the more productive taxes and discourage the smaller jurisdictions from excessive tax diversity;
> 5. Provide State technical assistance to local tax authorities in-

[25] *Local Nonproperty Taxes and the Coordinating Role of the State* (Washington, September, 1961), p. 3.

cluding tax information, training facilities for local personnel, access to State tax records, and where appropriate, use sanctions against State taxpayers who fail to comply with local tax requirements.

Central Administrative Controls

In many ways, the relations of States with their political subdivisions parallel those of the Federal government with the States. Just as the Federal government has repeatedly moved in when the States were either unable or unwilling to make good in a given situation, so the States have again and again been obliged to extend their regulatory and supervisory powers when local government was unable to function effectively— or to function at all. Nowhere has this been demonstrated more clearly than in the field of financial administration.

While there had been a limited amount of regulation of local finance prior to the time of the Great Depression, the utter collapse of local financial operations during this period in many jurisdictions prompted the States to establish and undertake enforcement of standards relating to virtually every phase of financial administration from assessment through final accounting, auditing, and reporting.

Regulation of Assessment. With few exceptions, State constitutions require full value assessment, but this requirement has been honored more in the breach than in the observance. Other requirements attempt to insure uniformity in assessments to the end that there may be equality in the imposition of taxes between individuals, both in the same taxing unit and in different taxing units. These constitutional provisions probably serve a useful purpose as a statement of basic aims, but good assessment administration is absolutely essential to the realization of these aims in practice. In the effort to achieve improvement in this area, States have been aiding their political subdivisions in the preparation of adequate tax maps, supplying assessment manuals and institutes and short term training programs for local assessors.[26] Illinois and New Jersey among the States and Baltimore among the cities, have recently made determined drives to obtain full value assessment and more equitable assessment,[27] and all States have established a considerable degree of

[26] See Girard, Richard A., *The Scope for Uniformity in State Tax Systems* (Albany: New York State Tax Commission, 1935); Hawaii Legislative Reference Bureau, *Fiscal Provisions of State Constitutions* (Honolulu: University of Hawaii, 1947); and Bird, Frederick C., *Constitutional Aspects of State Financial Administration* (Detroit: Citizens Research Council of Michigan, November, 1961).

[27] See Illinois State's Attorneys Association, *The Full-Value Assessment Program* (Springfield, 1946) and Troupis, Christ T., "Full Fair Value Assessment in Illinois," *Illinois Law Review*, May–June, 1949, pp. 160–180.

control over this activity. The supervisory agencies of some States—for example, Alabama, Louisiana, and Maryland—have comparatively more power than others, and Ohio has gone so far as to take over entirely the function of assessing taxable property.

State-Local Relations in Tax Collection. In the past, in most jurisdictions, there was little supervision over the collection of taxes. Taxes were commonly "received" by the treasurer, tax collector, or receiver of taxes for each local unit in a manner which reminded one of the system by which taxes were farmed out in ancient Rome. The law prescribed who should collect taxes and how, but provided for no proper system of supervision. Consequently, many collectors lacking initiative or know-how permitted large delinquent tax rolls to accumulate. No provision was included in the law to prevent this or to govern the disposition of tax-delinquent properties.

In a few States, as in Pennsylvania, the counties collect certain types of taxes for the State under an extensive supervision exercised by the State revenue collecting agency. Illinois was the first State to collect sales taxes for its municipalities on a large scale, beginning in 1955. Since the practice developed in Illinois, California has been collecting sales taxes for its cities and counties on a voluntary basis, and Mississippi also soon adopted the plan. It thus appears that a new pattern of State-local relationships in the tax collection field is in process of development, one in which the States may serve as the collecting agency for certain local taxes.

Local Budget Control. A fourth type of State financial supervision involves State control over how local units spend their money, which most States now require for cities, counties, school districts, and other local units. Originally the controls applied to current operations only but have gradually been extended to include capital outlays and debt transactions as well. Most States prepare and distribute budget forms to their local units and require that these forms be used. This procedure necessarily developed when it was discovered that many local units in financial distress during the Great Depression had nothing that even resembled a budgetary system. Many local officials vigorously resisted the establishment of the new system as another instance of State interference with local self-government, but now that the system is understood and operating successfully, the opposition has completely disappeared.

Control of Local Debt. Although borrowing might appear to be an obvious recourse for local units which cannot raise necessary funds by taxation, the fact is that local units, even if they were willing to condone the unsound fiscal practice of borrowing to meet current operating expenses, frequently have no borrowing power. Under the provisions of State law, they may borrow only in limited amounts, up to a debt limit set at an arbitrary figure or determined by a specified percentage of the assessed valuation of their real property. In addition, when borrowing power is available, it may be utilized only—and this for good and sufficient reason—under the watchful eye of the State authority responsible for the financial supervision of local units of government.

Supervision of local debt constitutes the fifth method of State control over local finances. State laws regulate the purposes, amounts, terms, and forms of local debt, and are supplemented by several different types of administrative supervision. Nearly all of the limitations on amount of debt are defined in terms of percentage of the assessed valuation of property in the unit concerned. These provisions which seem at times to be too restrictive were felt to be necessary after the experience of the "Roaring Twenties," when many municipalities went headlong into debt for so-called "improvements" for which they actually had no need, and for which in time they found it difficult either to pay for or use. The level of integrity and public responsibility in public debt administration has normally been fairly high; it is to prevent serious abuses when sound judgment fails to provide an effective check that these restrictive laws are necessary.

Accounting, Auditing, and Reporting. Another form of State financial supervision provides for the auditing of local accounts and indeed for the supervision of the whole accounting system. Massachusetts and New Jersey did pioneer work in this field, and during recent years, most of the States have undertaken this type of supervision. New York since 1932 has required the State Comptroller to supervise the accounts of its local units through a field force of State examiners. These men, all trained accountants, examine the records of the local agencies in a manner similar to that in which bank examiners go over the records of the banking institutions under their supervision and control, or in which building and loan examiners inspect the records of State building and loan associations.

The laws of New York and Pennsylvania further provide for uniform local accounting systems which must be used by each of the several types of local government agencies. Systems involving uniform classification of the objects of expenditure are provided for each agency and must be used for annual reports submitted to the State Comptroller in New York or the Bureau of Municipal Affairs in Pennsylvania. With the introduction of such a system, it becomes possible for the first time to compare the expenditures of communities of similar size for a particular administrative purpose; unless the items of expenditure are classified in the same way, such figures are meaningless. More than a quarter of a century ago, at least a fourth of the States were exercising complete control in this field, and the tendency in the intervening years has been to strengthen and improve these controls.[28]

Budgeting, accounting, auditing, and reporting should be regarded

[28] See Kilpatrick, Wylie, *State Supervision of Local Finance* (Chicago: Public Administration Service, 1941).

not as separate but closely interrelated parts of the financial process. Any exaggeration of the importance of one to the neglect of the others prevents attaining the goal of efficient financial administration. Uniform reporting is really a by-product of uniform budgeting and accounting and is easily and inexpensively accomplished if the first two steps are done properly. Reporting is the collecting of information concerning local financial transactions and the furnishing of this information to the State and to the public. A quarter of a century ago, about one-fourth of the States were publishing comprehensive reports, while another fourth published no reports at all.[29] Now, of course, the situation is much improved.

Devices for Tax Sharing

All States now distribute funds to their local governments, some to the extent of more than half of their total tax receipts. In eight States—Alabama, Delaware, Louisiana, Mississippi, New Mexico, South Carolina, Washington, and Hawaii—State aid in 1960 constituted from 40 to 50 per cent of local government revenue. Of the national total of nearly $10 billion distributed annually, the largest share ($5.3 billion) was designated for education, $1.5 billion for welfare in States in which public assistance is legally a local responsibility, and $1.2 billion for roads, mostly as a statutory share of highway user taxes. Barely $500 million is distributed to counties, cities, towns, and other local units for use at their discretion.[30] The funds are distributed by grants-in-aid, designating of revenues, tax sharing, and joint collection; the first is by far the most important device.

Grants-in-Aid. State grants-in-aid were begun after World War I as a means of equalizing the financial burden of and benefits derived from selected local government services. When local relief expenditures tripled during the few years of the Great Depression, the growth of the system received a tremendous impetus which continued through the post-depression years. Governments struggled to meet constantly rising costs for education, highways, and health and welfare programs, and in some jurisdictions efforts took the form of permanent designation of tax receipts (as in the case of the Michigan sales tax) as a means of guaranteeing funds for minimum education programs, higher teachers' salaries, and other worthy purposes. Local authorities with limited taxing powers, faced with steadily mounting costs for expanding programs, descended upon their legislatures for more and larger grants-in-aid. The growth of these grant programs has continued at an accelerated pace since World War II.

[29] Kilpatrick, p. 13.   [30] Advisory Commission, *Report,* p. 16.

Response to these demands has greatly helped the local units, to be sure; it has been a means of bringing about a more equitable distribution of the tax burden, utilizing the broader tax base and the more efficient tax collection machinery of the State, and has insured at least a minimum standard of governmental services for those least able to bear the financial burden of supporting them. But these desirable objectives have not been accomplished without at least two detrimental effects upon the States themselves: (1) to the extent that revenues have been designated for certain purposes, they have interfered with sound budgetary procedures and have weakened the control of the legislature over the State's finances; (2) as the grant programs have grown in number and in size, they have taken an ever greater proportion of the State revenues urgently needed for the support of State programs.

Since State aid for education is of major importance, both in terms of the amounts of money involved and the nature of the function itself, this field will be used for purposes of illustration. In the 1950's, minimum education programs were established in many States. State grants to school districts, many of which have been consolidated to insure more adequate educational programs and better administration, have been an important means of making these programs effective and of equalizing educational opportunity for all children throughout the State. At the same time, they have been an important influence in the direction of centralized control over schools. Originally offered in an attempt to equalize the tax burden for educational purposes and to assist school districts in less prosperous areas, subsidies have everywhere become a vital part of the program for financing public schools.

All States now contribute funds to local districts for certain purposes and under certain conditions. By the same token, they regulate many aspects of school administration. Nearly all require regular reports to be submitted to State authorities. The proportion of total school costs paid by the States, however, varies considerably from one jurisdiction to another, but the State contribution has tended to increase in every State, both in dollars spent and in the proportion of the total cost borne by the State. Delaware and New Mexico pay a larger share of school costs than do other States and Nebraska pays the smallest, contributing 86.4, 87.5, and 5.5 per cent respectively.

It is difficult to generalize upon the manner in which these funds are allocated, because many laws have been amended so frequently that it is often difficult to determine exactly what the law is. There are about twenty bases used by States in the distribution of these funds, including population, average daily attendance, number of teaching units, number of pupils enrolled, salaries paid to teachers, and number of school days per year. Nor is there any clear-cut pattern by which appropriated funds are apportioned to the various school levels—elementary, secondary, and junior colleges. Some States appropriate for general school purposes, making little or no distinction between school grades in the matter of school support; others make a distinction, particularly regarding the State's part of such support.

Tax Sharing. In a grant program, the State collects the revenue under its tax laws, allocating such portions to the assistance of local government programs as the legislature sees fit. When taxes are shared, the State collects the revenue but turns over that portion of the receipts provided by law to designated local units. Whereas grant funds are normally given by the State and received by local units for a specified purpose or function, shared tax receipts may become a part of the local unit's general revenue. The occasion for the use of this device normally occurs either when local units feel that they have a legitimate claim to a portion of the receipts, as in the case of liquor license or gasoline tax receipts, or when both State and local units wish to levy a particular type of tax, such as a general sales tax. In this case, the end result is scarcely distinguishable from any State-collected, locally shared tax.

Central or Joint Collection. Although there are obvious advantages in the central collection of taxes, such as reduced collection costs and presumably greater yield, the method has never won acceptance quickly or easily. Not many years ago, each local unit had a separate collector for each type of tax from which revenue was derived, with the result that a citizen might pay, for instance, three separate real estate assessments to different collectors in different, often widely scattered offices, for support of schools, town, village, or city purposes, and county government. Collectors were paid on a costly fee basis, and many of them were inefficient, while the citizen was inconvenienced by having to write several checks and visit several offices to pay his taxes. The system persisted because the collectors liked the fees, and the taxpayers, long accustomed to the inconvenience, did not realize that it was quite unnecessary and costing them money as well.

Although central collection of local taxes on a unit by unit basis has now been achieved, it has been equally as difficult to attain central collection of taxes in larger, county wide or statewide areas. A very promising development of the postwar years, however, is the practice of joint collection whereby the State adds a local levy to its own sales or excise tax and transmits the proceeds to counties and cities. This procedure, begun experimentally in Illinois, proved so successful that it has been adopted on a wider scale in California, Mississippi, and a few other States. It might be noted that there is no good reason why a similar arrangement with respect to alcohol, tobacco, and gasoline taxes could not be worked out between the Federal government and the States.

BIBLIOGRAPHICAL NOTES

The following notes cover general references, titles on centralization, home rule, and fiscal relations. Only in the centralization group have titles relating to individual States been included, and these chiefly because of their historical interest. There are considerable numbers of studies of other aspects of State-local relations in individual States, many of which are listed in Graves, *Intergovernmental Relations in the United States: A Selected Bibliography.*

General Works. On the number of governmental units, see William Anderson, *The Units of Government in the United States,* rev. ed. (Chicago: Public Administration Service, 1945) and the periodic reports of the Bureau of the Census, *Census of Governments, 1932, 1942, 1952, 1957, and 1962.* On the constitutional issues involved, one old and one new title are of interest: Charles C. Binney, *Restrictions Upon Local and Special Legislation in State Constitutions* (Philadelphia: Kay & Brother, 1894) and John M. Winters, *State Constitutional Limitations on Solutions of Metropolitan Area Problems* (Ann Arbor: University of Michigan Law School, 1961). John M. Grumm, *A State Agency for Local Government?* (Berkeley: Bureau of Public Administration, University of California, 1961) is a study emphasizing an important and comparatively recent aspect of State-local relations. The best general treatises are Council of State Governments, *State-Local Relations* (Chicago, 1946), now out of print, and Arthur Maass, *Area and Power: A Theory of Local Government* (Glencoe: Free Press of Glencoe, 1959).

The States and Metropolitan Areas. Because of the mounting importance of metropolitan area problems, they tend to be emphasized in titles published in the last decade. Note particularly John C. Bollens, *The States and the Metropolitan Problem— 1956* (Chicago: Council of State Governments, 1956); William N. Cassella, Jr., *Constitutional Aspects of State-Local Relationships: Metropolitan Government* (Detroit: Citizens Research Council of Michigan, 1961); Neil Littlefield, *Metropolitan Area Problems and Municipal Home Rule* (Ann Arbor: University of Michigan Law School, 1962); Samuel C. May and James M. Fales, Jr., *The State's Interest in Metropolitan Problems* (Berkeley: Bureau of Public Administration, University of California, 1955); and Winters, *State Constitutional Limitations.*

Centralization. The following titles tell the story of centralization in individual States over a period of three quarters of a century: Paul V. Betters, ed., *State Centralization in North Carolina* (Washington: Brookings Institution, 1932); Harold M. Bowman, *The Administration of Iowa: A Study of Centralization* (New York: Columbia University, 1903); John A. Fairlie, *The Centralization of Administration in New York* (New York: Columbia University, 1898); Clarence J. Hein, *State Administrative Supervision of Local Government Functions in Kansas* (Lawrence: Government Research Center, University of Kansas, 1955); Edwin B. McPheron, *A Summary of Indiana Centralization* (Bloomington: Bureau of Government Research, Indiana University, 1938); Norman Meller, *Hawaii: A Study of Centralization* (Chicago: University of Chicago, 1956), a doctoral dissertation; Samuel P. Orth, *Centralization of Administration in Ohio* (New York: Columbia University, 1903); William A. Rawles, *Centralizing Tendencies in the Administration of Indiana* (New York: Columbia University, 1903); and Robert H. Whitten, *Public Administration in Massachusetts: The Relation of Central to Local Authority* (New York: Columbia University, 1898).

Home Rule. The first work on the subject was Frank J. Goodnow, *Municipal Home Rule* (New York: The Macmillan Co., 1895). The standard treatises on home rule since then have been Howard L. McBain, *The Law and Practice of Municipal Home Rule* (New York: Columbia University Press, 1916); Joseph D. McGoldrick's volume of the same title, *1916–1930* (New York: Columbia University Press, 1933); and Rodney L. Mott, *Home Rule for America's Cities* (Chicago: American Municipal Association, 1949). Opposing theories of the nature of home rule and of the legal basis most likely to insure it are exemplified in *Model State Constitution*, 4th ed. (New York: National Municipal League, 1941) and in the writings of Dean Jefferson B. Fordham, whose views have gained wide acceptance. See his *Model Constitutional Provisions for Municipal Home Rule* (Chicago: American Municipal Association, 1953).

Fiscal Relationships. The following general works should be helpful in gaining an understanding of the basic problems involved: American Legislators' Association, *State Supervision of Local Finance* (Chicago, 1933); American Municipal Association, *Financial Relationships Between State Governments and Municipalities* (Chicago, 1933); Henry J. Bitterman, *State and Federal Grants-in-Aid* (Chicago: Mentzer, Bush, 1938); Alvin H. Hansen and Harvey S. Perloff, *State and Local Finance in the National Economy* (New York: W. W. Norton & Co., Inc., 1944); Thomas L. Hinckley, *Legislation Affecting Municipal Finance in Massachusetts, 1906–1945* (Cambridge: Bureau of Research in Municipal Government, Harvard Graduate School of Public Administration, April, 1946); Russell J. Hinkley, *State Grants-in-Aid* (Albany: New York State Tax Commission, 1936); Ruth G. Hutchinson, *335 State-Administered Locally Shared Taxes* (New York: Columbia University Press, 1931); Wylie Kilpatrick, *State Supervision of Local Finance* (Chicago: Public Administration Service, 1941); Paul E. Malone, *The Fiscal Aspects of State and Local Relationships in New York* (Albany: New York State Tax Commission, 1937); Sydney Merlin, *American Taxes Shared and Allocated, 1938* (Chicago: American Municipal Association, 1939); Municipal Finance Officers Association, *Grants-in-Aid and Shared Taxes* (Chicago, March, 1945); Randall S. Stout, *Recent Trends in State Grants-in-Aid and Shared Taxes* (State College: Bureau of Business Research, Pennsylvania State College, 1948); and United States Conference of Mayors, *Municipal and Intergovernmental Finance in the United States, 1932–1942–1952* (Washington, September, 1953).

CHAPTER XXI

Interlocal
Relations

Another problem has arisen to confound us. Many of the functions of government that we had confidently assigned to this government or that government have a way of refusing to stay assigned to that government. Let me name just a few of such problem children: social welfare, health, hospitals, airports, education, civil defense, roads and highways, urban renewal and even planning.

In such cases, we have had to face alternative choices. Each jurisdiction can go on independently doing the best it can . . . or, we can create new jurisdictions and superimpose them over the existing governments. . . . The third alternative is for several jurisdictions to formally or informally enter into cooperative arrangements of different kinds. Fortunately local officials have not only been alert to this alternative but have been quick to use it. . . .

One form of such intergovernmental cooperation is joint ownership and operation. . . . Yet another form of cooperation is that of performing services for each other under contract, . . . another type takes the form of joint use of personnel. . . . These are but a few examples of different types of intergovernmental cooperation in Kansas.[1]

[1] Wall, Hugo, "The Challenge of Intergovernmental Cooperation," *Kansas Government Journal,* July, 1961, pp. 324–325, 344–345.

EVOLUTION OF INTERLOCAL COOPERATION

Some years ago, each local government unit, like each individual citizen, was able to stand independently and be more or less self-sufficient.

But, today the smaller units of government simply cannot employ on a full time, salaried basis the trained professional personnel, and purchase and efficiently utilize the costly plant and equipment required for many modern governmental services. Nor are they in a position adequately to serve the needs of their citizens. The house of one suburbanite may be located in one suburb, his neighbor's house across the street in another. Although the neighbor's house is larger, he pays less taxes. The neighbor can swim, without charge, at the municipal park in his city, but the first suburbanite cannot. One suburb is residential, the other zoned as suitable for commercial development, which is a matter of some concern to the first suburbanite. The street itself attracted him initially as a place to build a home partly because of the beautiful shade trees that lined both sides of the street. One suburb takes care of its trees, while the other neglects theirs, with tragic results. These are but a few of the common problems which arise in urban communities broken up into a large number of separate, independent governmental units.[2]

What Interlocal Cooperation Is

By interlocal cooperation, one writer has said, "is meant any device, formal or informal, legal or extra-legal, by which two or more local units of government attempt to meet a mutual difficulty or need." [3] In connection with another project, the term has been defined to include "all activities which any local government unit or its officials may carry on voluntarily with another local governmental unit or units, or which one unit may agree to administer for both itself and one or more other local units. The key words in this definition are four: governmental, local, activity and voluntary." [4] Both appear to agree that the activity must be carried on by public, not private, agencies. Emphasis on the voluntary aspect of such cooperation in the second definition was designed more to exclude from consideration vertical cooperation arising under the terms of grant-in-aid or other Federal legislation than to suggest that there

[2] This idea is developed by Thomas H. Eliot, *Governing America, State and Local Supplement* (New York: Dodd, Mead & Company, 1961), pp 18–19.

[3] Birkhead, Guthrie S., Jr., *Extent of Interlocal Cooperation in New York State* (Albany: Department of Audit and Control, 1958), p. 5.

[4] Used as a basic definition in a comprehensive study of interlocal cooperation in five States—Alabama, Indiana, Nebraska, Pennsylvania, and Wisconsin—now in progress. The study is being made by Professor John E. Stoner and associates in the Bureau of Government Research, Indiana University, under a contract with the Farm Economics Division, Economic Research Service, U.S. Department of Agriculture.

is anything improper about such cooperation authorized or even required by State law. It does suggest that interlocal cooperation normally takes place on a horizontal basis. The cooperating governments are usually contiguous, although this is not essential. It is obvious that they are not contiguous in a case in which a city sells water to outlying suburbs along its main supply line.

Whatever the precise terms in which the concept of interlocal relations is defined, the fact remains that an ever-increasing number of interlocal contracts and agreements have been coming into existence, both within a single State and between units in different States. The story of these agreements has been very little dealt with in the literature, partly because the basic information is so scattered and difficult to assemble, partly because the whole development is of comparatively recent origin. There were a few statutory authorizations for cooperative arrangements between specified units for specified purposes prior to World War II, but the bulk of these agreements, and the legislation which authorizes them, has been formulated and adopted during the past decade.

Organizationally, interlocal relations are difficult to deal with in a survey of intergovernmental relations. No one seems to be quite sure what to do with them. One writer groups them with Federal-local relations and metropolitan area problems. This may be a reasonable solution, but it is certainly not an ideal one. For one thing, it covers too much ground; for another, it suggests that they are limited in their usefulness to metropolitan areas, which does not happen to be true. Metropolitan area problems have given rise to an increasing number of such arrangements, but they first appeared and are still frequently found among the governmental units in rural areas. As a matter of fact, it has been suggested that in the development of interlocal relations among rural units, there lies hope of attaining a degree of competence in local administration which might otherwise be expected only through a now unattainable widespread consolidation of the many small, struggling, inefficient units of local government. Popular sentiment appears to be as yet unwilling to consolidate other local units as school districts, for instance, have been consolidated since World War II.

Constitutional and Statutory Basis

There is a wide range of possibilities for cooperative relationships for all varieties of local units. The legislatures have dealt with these problems in several ways, ranging from informal exchanges of information to precisely defined contractual agreements or jointly created agencies with a permanent staff and a substantial budget. The oldest, most obvious, and most frequently used method has been to pass legislation authorizing a particular cooperative undertaking between specified units, or giving a blanket authorization for cooperation in specified administrative areas or functional fields. While there have been few instances in which constitutional provisions have presented an actual barrier to interjurisdictional cooperation,[5] there is no doubt that constitutional authorizations do facilitate and encourage cooperation.

California and Missouri early recognized this fact and adopted appropriate constitutional provisions, blanket authorizations for cooperative arrangements by all units in all fields, the former in 1922, the latter in its constitutional revision of 1943. Alaska and Hawaii did the same in new constitutions. The text of these provisions is presented in the table on page 741; they are not merely the oldest, but so far as is known the only provisions of this type now existing. Appropriate legislation has been adopted in Minnesota, Nebraska, New York, Pennsylvania, Virginia, and Wisconsin. In addition, authorization for local units to enter into cooperative arrangements with adjacent units in other States has been adopted constitutionally in Missouri and by legislative enactment in New York.

Outlining the full story of the evolution of legislative provisions on interlocal cooperation would be a major research project of nationwide scope, a project which could be undertaken only with a sizable staff and substantial financial support. In the absence of such a survey, the best available substitute is to try to see what has happened in a few representative States in which significant developments in the field of interlocal cooperation are known to have taken place. The earliest instances occurred many years ago when adjacent communities envisioned the advantages that cooperative arrangements might bring to them in terms of better service to the public at lower cost, through cooperative purchasing or through joint sponsorship of some costly facility such as a sewage treatment plant. Cases of this sort began to arise in Pennsylvania, for instance, in the 1930's and 1940's, and the General Assembly responded to these needs with authorizations adopted in 1943 and the years following.

The Minnesota, New York, and Pennsylvania laws appear to have been first in this field. The Minnesota Joint Powers Act, adopted in 1957,

[5] See Zimmermann, Frederick L., and Wendell, Mitchell, "No Positive Barriers," *National Civic Review*, November, 1959, pp. 522–525, and Wiltsee, Herbert L., and Wendell, Mitchell, "Intergovernmental Relations," in Graves, W. Brooke, ed., *Major Problems in State Constitutional Revision* (Chicago: Public Administration Service, 1960), pp. 253–264.

made possible for the first time joint action with regard to almost any phase of municipal government in that State.[6] In this Act it was provided that two or more governmental units, by agreement entered into through action of their governing bodies, may jointly or cooperatively exercise any power common to the contracting parties of any similar powers, including those which are the same except for the territorial limits within which they may be exercised. The term "governmental unit" as used in this

CONSTITUTIONAL PROVISIONS FOR INTERLOCAL COOPERATION

Alaska	*California*	*Hawaii*	*Missouri*
Article XII, Section 2: The State and its political subdivisions may cooperate with the United States and its territories, and with other States and their political subdivisions on matters of common interest. The respective legislative bodies may make appropriations for this purpose.	Article XI, Section 7½: It shall be competent, in county charters, framed under the authority of this section to provide, in addition to any other provisions allowable by this Constitution, and the same shall provide, for the following matters: Article XI, Section 4½: For the assumption and discharge by	Article XIV, Section 5: The legislature may provide for cooperation by the State and political subdivisions with the United States, or States and territories or their subdivisions, in matters affecting public health, safety and general welfare; funds may be appropriated to effect cooperation.	Article VI, Section 17: Any municipality or political subdivision of the State may contract and cooperate with other municipalities or political subdivisions thereof, or with other States or their political subdivisions, or with the United States, for the planning, development, construction, acquisition, or operation of any public improvement or facility, or for a common service, in the manner provided by law.

county officers certain of the municipal functions of the cities and towns within the county, however, in the case of cities and towns incorporated under the general laws, the discharge by county officers of such municipal functions is authorized by general law, or whenever, in the case of cities and towns organized under Section 8 of this Article, the discharge by county officers of such municipal functions is authorized by provisions of the charters, or by amendments thereto, of such cities and towns.

[6] 1957 Session, Chapter 468; Stat. Ann., Sec. 473. Some planning provisions go back to 1927. The legislation was developed by enactments in 1937, 1945, and 1957, when a broad authorization was extended to political subdivisions within the State.

statute includes every city, village, borough, town, county, school district, or other political subdivision.

The New York statute authorizing cooperation among local units of government was also enacted in 1957, becoming effective January 1, 1958. Under its terms, any "public agency" (including, as in Minnesota, all types of local units and political subdivisions created by law) was authorized to create interlocal agreements or contracts, subject to the necessary approvals between any public agency of the State and any public agency or agencies of other States. In certain cases a referendum is required, and in all cases a public hearing is required before the agreement may be formally entered into. The consent of the State Comptroller is required in all cases and, in certain instances, the consent of other officials as well.

Interlocal agreements may come into existence in still another way, through interstate compacts. This type has received the greatest amount of publicity, due to its extensive use in metropolitan areas in connection with the management of port, harbor, bridge and tunnel, and other transit facilities, as in the case of the Port of New York Authority.

Origin and Development in Selected States

Tennessee. Several types of cooperative agreements had been authorized for Tennessee cities and counties, in the broad grant of power to cities and counties contained in the general law enacted in 1939, which provided:

> The quarterly county court of any county and the chief legislative body of any municipality that lies within the boundaries of said county are authorized to enter into any such agreements, compacts, or contractual relations as may be desirable or necessary for the purpose of permitting said county and said municipality to conduct, operate, maintain either jointly or by one (1) agency or the other, desirable and necessary services or functions under such terms as may be agreed upon by the two (2) agencies.

The earliest survey of interlocal cooperation that has come to the attention of the author was made in Tennessee in 1942, a survey that covered the experience of some sixty-eight cities having a population of 1,000 or more in providing services outside their corporate limits.[7] Nearly

---

[7] Shaw, Gerald W., *Providing Municipal Services Outside Corporate Limits* (Knoxville: Department of Political Science, University of Tennessee, July, 1943).

half of them furnished police protection to adjacent areas on emergency call; no charge was made for this service. Approximately three-fourths provided some fire protection to nearby areas, at charges showing so great a range as to make little sense. Some were too high, probably designed to discourage requests for service, while others were so low that they could not possibly reimburse the city for the cost of the service it was asked to render. Provision of water service to outside areas was so generally provided that cities were urged to explore this as a possible source of additional revenue.

The practice of furnishing services to outside areas, it was noted, raises a number of legal questions. Is the city properly authorized to provide them? Can it collect appropriate charges? Is it liable for damages resulting from accidents arising therefrom? Little was found in the statutes relating to these questions. The general rule is that the city's powers are confined to its own limits, in the absence of specific authorization to the contrary in statute or charter. Only four statutory authorizations were reported as being in effect at the time: a city might, for corporate purposes, hold real estate outside its limits; it might enter into contract to furnish water and/or sewer facilities to other cities, corporations, or individuals; it could sell electric power to any consumer or user; and it might permit its police to function within a range of one mile beyond the city limits "for the suppression of disorderly acts and practices forbidden by the general laws of the State."

The following generalizations regarding the legal situation were presented: (1) Unless power is granted specifically or by implication in the charters or statutes under which municipalities operate, they have no authority to provide service outside corporate limits. (2) Power to hold property and to operate water, sewage disposal, and electric systems beyond corporate limits is granted by general acts in the State—although, of course, most cities operate under special charters. (3) Municipal powers in Tennessee are usually interpreted liberally, so that some power of operation outside the city can probably be implied. (4) Nonetheless, it may be advisable for individual cities, where services to outside areas are being provided, to study the legal basis through which such services are authorized.[8]

Minnesota. Another early survey of interlocal agreements was made by the State League of Municipalities of Minnesota in 1953. In this survey,

---

[8] Shaw, p. 16. For current information and evidence of subsequent progress, see Meisenholder, Edmund W., III, and Lovelace, Robert A., *Laws for City-County Cooperation in Tennessee* (Knoxville: Bureau of Public Administration, University of Tennessee, June, 1960) and Grubbs, David H., "City-County Agreements in Our Four Metropolitan Areas," *Tennessee Municipalities*, August, 1961, pp. 13–16.

it was found that twenty-two cities in the State with a population of 10,000 or over had entered into ninety-one agreements in seventeen different functional areas. Minneapolis and Rochester had ten each. Three small cities had none; the remaining seventeen cities had agreements ranging in number from one to seven. Fifteen cities had agreements relating to roads and streets, thirteen to fire protection, ten on radio communication. The number of agreements on the remaining fourteen subjects ranged from one to seven; the statistical detail developed by this survey is summarized in the table on page 745.

Missouri. In 1954, the Missouri Public Expenditure Survey made a study of opportunities for savings by eliminating duplication in municipal assessing operations. Of Missouri's 233 cities having populations of 1,000 or more, 161 replied to the survey questionnaire. Overlapping and duplication of facilities, services, and operations among political subdivisions and various layers of government are recognized as costly obstacles to economical operation. Widespread duplication in the performance of the assessing function among the State's municipalities and counties had been subject of frequent comment. Ninety-four of those replying were avoiding the cost of maintaining a city assessor by arranging with their counties for copies of the county assessment of city property. Seventy-five of the ninety-four cities having no assessors were fourth class cities, and the remaining nineteen were scattered among several classes of cities. Of the sixty-seven responding cities which maintained assessors, thirty-five were third class cities, twenty-five fourth class, and the remaining seven were scattered among other classes.

New York. In New York, the Joint Legislative Committee on Metropolitan Area Study issued in 1957 a digest of the law of the State permitting intergovernmental service arrangements among the municipalities of the State; this publication was revised and reissued in 1959.[9] Fourteen major subjects were covered, ranging, as in Minnesota, from civil service to water supply, with a concluding chapter on organization of government and administrative acts in general. The number of statutory authorizations for each of these functional areas or functions, both intrastate and interstate, is shown in the table on page 745. What such cooperation means in practice, in relation to such a vital field of public personnel administration, may be judged from the data presented in the table on page 758. The concluding chapter includes the following topics: blanket provision authorizing joint action by municipalities, alteration of boundaries, general provisions relating to transfer of functions between municipalities, general provisions relating to special districts, public lands and other property, building inspection services, and joint purchasing.

Approaching the problem from a different angle, Birkhead reports

[9] *Municipal Cooperation: A Digest of New York State Law* (Albany: December, 1959).

INTERLOCAL COOPERATION IN MINNESOTA IN CITIES
OVER 1,000 POPULATION, 1953 *

City	Number of Agreements of Cooperation	Area or Function	Number of Cities Cooperating
1. Minneapolis	10	1. Airports	7
2. St. Paul	4	2. Band	1
3. Duluth	6	3. Buildings	3
4. Rochester	10	4. Civil Defense	5
5. St. Cloud	2	5. Civil Service	1
6. Winona	7	6. Elections	1
7. Austin	5	7. Fire Protection	13
8. St. Louis Park	6	8. Health	8
9. Mankato	1	9. Library	6
10. Richfield	5	10. Milk Inspection	1
11. Hibbing	3	11. Public Welfare	1
12. Faribault	4	12. Radio	10
13. South St. Paul	3	13. Recreation	7
14. Moorhead	6	14. Sewer and Water Service	9
15. Albert Lea	4		
16. Fergus Falls	1	15. Streets and Roads	15
17. Brainerd	5	16. Utilities	1
18. Virginia	4	17. Veterans	1
19. Robbindale	0	Total	90
20. Red Wing	5		
21. Owatonna	0		
22. Bemidji	0		
Total	91		

* Based on data in League of Minnesota Municipalities, *Inter-Municipal Cooperation in Minnesota* (Minneapolis, February, 1953), p. 13.

STATE OF NEW YORK: TYPES OF INTERLOCAL COOPERATION
AUTHORIZED BY LAW *

Activity or Function	Intrastate	Interstate
General Municipal Services	9	4
Public Education	1	1
Public Health	2	6
Public Safety	11	3
Public Utilities	4	3
Recreational Facilities	3	2
Refuse Disposal	6	5
Youth Activities	1	1

* Based on data in New York State Legislature, Joint Committee on Metropolitan Area Study, *Municipal Cooperation: A Digest of the Law of New York Permitting Intergovernmental Service Arrangements*, rev. ed. (Albany, 1959), p. 171.

that "one can find in the New York law at least eighteen important substantive areas in which cities may cooperate with neighbors; for villages,
thirty-one instances; for towns, thirty-one; and counties, eighteen. Further,
there are many ways such agencies may work together for their common
good without reference to a specific law and without violation even of the
spirit of the law. The technique of interlocal cooperation is one of the
ways home rule may be kept strong and viable in New York localities." [10]

Pennsylvania. A dissertation written at the University of Pennsylvania in 1953 by J. J. Carrell tells the story of an astonishing number of
interlocal agreements in the Philadelphia metropolitan area. He describes
the 756 "written or clearly understood unwritten, compacts between local
units" among the governments of eight counties in Pennsylvania and New
Jersey in the Philadelphia metropolitan area. "Of the 686 governments in
these eight counties, 64 per cent of the cities, towns and boroughs, and 59
per cent of the school districts are involved in these agreements." Dr.
Carrell finds that this device is "the most extensively used device for
integrating the governments of the Philadelphia area and is the one
"considered most promising." [11]

Dillon's rule is strictly enforced by the courts in both States (New
Jersey and Pennsylvania). The law, however, grants express powers for
making interlocal agreements to various kinds of municipalities in the
fields of airports, bridges, collection of garbage and trash, health, purchasing, road construction, and sewage. Purchasing, one of the areas in
which cautious experiments in cooperation were undertaken in Pennsylvania a quarter of a century ago, has since become a major area of cooperation.[12] No powers are given to any units to cooperate in personnel
or civil service matters in Pennsylvania, and only Pennsylvania counties
can coordinate their building codes, planning, zoning, and a few other
matters by interlocal agreements. The 756 agreements in the Philadelphia
metropolitan area mentioned previously include pacts in five major subject-matter fields, as indicated in the table on page 747. The author finds
that "functional integration has been achieved on a limited scale." He
notes that there are many cases in which such cooperation might be em-

---

[10] Birkhead, p. 5.

[11] Carrell, J. J., *Inter-Jurisdictional Agreements as an Integrating Device
in Metropolitan Philadelphia* (Philadelphia, 1953); see also Williams, Oliver
P., *Intergovernmental Cooperation for Disposal of Sewage: Southeastern Pennsylvania* (Philadelphia: Institute of Local and State Government, University
of Pennsylvania, October, 1961).

[12] See Seyler, William C., "Municipal Cooperation in Action in Pennsylvania," *Department of Internal Affairs Monthly Bulletin:* I, August, 1961,
pp. 6–9; II, September, 1961, pp. 8–15. For a general discussion, see Postley,
Maurice G., "The Case for Cooperative or Centralized Purchasing," *The
County Officer,* November, 1961, pp. 394–407 (insert).

ployed, and he terms the total record "modest" when compared with the problems that exist in the metropolitan area.

A survey of cooperative relationships throughout Pennsylvania in 1958 disclosed that such cooperation in that State, directly or through the use of multi-municipality authorities, was at an all time high, 617

MAJOR TYPES OF COOPERATIVE AGREEMENTS:
PHILADELPHIA METROPOLITAN AREA *

Subject Matter Field	Number of Agreements
Road Construction	102
Sewage Disposal	59
Bridges	51
Police Protection	134
(49 units involved in one of these agreements)	
School Districts	389
(Joint school operation, 34; receiving, 304)	
Miscellaneous	21
Total	756

* Based on data in Carrell, J. J., "Learning to Work Together," *National Municipal Review,* November, 1954, pp. 526–533.

agreements linking 1,784 municipal units. The principal advantages of cooperation are said to be financial savings, increased efficiency of service, needed regional action facilitated, and community identity retained.[13] The scope of the program was essentially the same in Pennsylvania as elsewhere, the same numbers of areas, functions, and fields (eighteen) being involved.

More adequate information was available for Pennsylvania than for other States on dates of original enactment of cooperative legislation.[14] The first such measures enacted appear to have authorized local units to cooperate in the construction and maintenance of public buildings during and after World War I, when two acts were passed, one in 1913 limited to certain counties, the other in 1917 applicable to all local units and many different types of public buildings. From 1917 on, there were only a few new enactments until after World War II. A flood control measure applicable to Pittsburgh and Allegheny County was passed in

[13] Kelley, J. Martin, Jr., "617 Agreements Link 1,784 Units in Cooperative Action," *Department of Internal Affairs Monthly Bulletin,* July, 1958, pp. 1–9, 28.

[14] Current code citations are virtually worthless in the effort to obtain a picture of the origin, development, and growth of a particular type of legislation.

1927, and a joint purchasing authorization of general applicability in 1937. (Though presumably a desirable and advantageous type of co-operation, this authorization appears to have been little used.) The General Cooperation Law was adopted in 1943, and amended in 1945; this was not unusual, for most of these laws are frequently amended, probably because interlocal cooperation is still in the experimental and developmental stage.

The legislative sessions of 1947 and 1953 appear to have been banner years in the history of interlocal cooperation, at least in Pennsylvania. In 1947, local units were authorized to cooperate in the construction, maintenance, and operation of airports, armories, fire and police pro-tection programs, garbage collection, sewage disposal, joint hospital and public health programs, recreation programs, and tax collection. In 1953, additions were made in the fields of history, monuments and memorials, utilities cooperation, water, and zoning. This is, indeed, an impressive record of legislative accomplishment in one State for a period of less than a decade.[15]

Two regional organizations have been established in Pennsylvania to promote intergovernmental cooperation on an areawide basis in the State's two largest metropolitan areas. These organizations are the Allegheny Seminar which has brought together local government officials in the Pittsburgh-Allegheny County area, and the Regional Conference of Elected Officials which is open to membership of officials from each of the 389 governmental bodies in the eleven-county Greater Philadelphia area. Both of these organizations are designed to provide forums for discussion and sharing of information on any intergovernmental problem and to encourage joint action to alleviate these problems.

Since these organizations are unofficial bodies (as were similar ones when they started) and membership is voluntary, the Allegheny Seminar and the Regional Conference offer a means of bringing local officials to-gether for the stated purposes without risk of sacrificing the autonomy of the local units they represent. The Conference was sponsored by Penjerdel (Pennsylvania-New Jersey-Delaware Metropolitan Project). Among the sponsoring agencies of the Allegheny Seminar are the University of Pittsburgh's Institute of Local Government, the Pennsylvania Economy League (Western Branch), and the Pittsburgh Regional Planning As-sociation.[16]

[15] Based on Wise, Sidney, *Selected Areas of Intergovernmental Coopera-tion* (Harrisburg: Department of Internal Affairs, 1957).

[16] Based on "Intergovernmental Cooperation in Pennsylvania," *Department of Internal Affairs Monthly Bulletin*, November, 1961, p. 26.

Cooperation Through State and National Associations

Organizations of local governments and of local officials are among the best coordinated and most effective pressure groups at the State Capitols. The number of such groups ranges from ten or a dozen per State to more than twice these figures. In the older States, there are statewide organizations not only for each type of governmental unit, but for each type of elected official in county, township, or municipal government. In order to present a unified front in dealing with the legislature, all of these may be joined together in an overall organization such as the Alliance of Local Government Organizations in Pennsylvania.[17] These organizations and those which follow, originally developed largely on an extra-legal basis, but as the movement progressed, statutory authority was given for payment from public funds of membership dues and expenses incurred in attendance at meetings.

Although formed for the purpose of advancing (or protecting) the interests of local government and local government officials in the legislature, these organizations have developed into important instruments for interlocal cooperation as well. In this respect, the State leagues of municipalities have been particularly effective. The establishment of these organizations began late in the nineteenth century; by 1938, leagues were operating in three-fourths of the States, and are functioning now in forty-five—all but Connecticut, Delaware, Hawaii, Rhode Island, and Vermont. Total league membership includes approximately 14,000 municipalities, large and small, out of a total of 17,000.[18] The leagues are supported primarily from dues paid by member municipalities. They maintain permanent offices, each with a full time executive director and a small staff. Important league activities include the holding of an annual conference or convention for the discussion of current problems; conducting an information, research, and consulting service; sponsoring a legislative program, training programs for municipal employees; and centralized purchasing for small municipalities. More than half of the leagues publish monthly magazines to publicize league activities and to provide information for members.[19]

[17] For a good analysis of the Pennsylvania experience, see Kurtzman, David H., "Influence of Organizations of Local Government Officials," *Annals,* January, 1938, pp. 103–109, and of Connecticut, see Levenson, Rosaline, *Intergovernmental Cooperation Through Municipal Associations* (Storrs: Institute of Public Service, University of Connecticut, June, 1961).

[18] International City Managers Association, *Municipal Year Book, 1962* (Chicago, 1962), pp. 166–172.

[19] A list of the state leagues and their journals regularly appears in the *Municipal Year Book.*

In addition to the State leagues of municipalities, there are two national organizations, the American Municipal Association and the United States Conference of Mayors, and a host of specialized organizations for various types of municipal officials. The American Municipal Association, organized in 1924, is a type of national federation of State leagues, designed to strengthen the league movement. It holds an annual convention, conducts research on municipal problems, and serves as a national clearing house for information on these problems for its member leagues and municipalities. From its main office in Washington, it attempts to safeguard the interests of municipalities in Federal legislation, and publishes a weekly *Washington News Letter*. Financial support is derived mainly from dues from member leagues, supplemented from time to time by funds from foundations or other sources. The association is the American member of the International Union of Local Authorities and of the Pan-American Commission on Intermunicipal Cooperation.

The United States Conference of Mayors held its first meeting in 1932 and was formally organized the following year. Originally conceived as a means of cooperation in dealing with relief problems in the Depression era, the Conference has developed into a strong and effective national organization of individual municipalities. Any city with a population of more than 50,000 is eligible for membership, although smaller cities may be approved for membership by the Executive Committee. The Conference has grown from 150 cities in 1936 to nearly 580 in 1963. The Conference, whose purposes and activities are in many respects similar to those of the American Municipal Association, is supported by membership dues. It is concerned mainly with the problems of larger cities and with those aspects of intergovernmental relations in which cities are involved, *i.e.,* State-local, Federal-local, and interlocal. Like the American Municipal Association, it represents the interests of cities before Congress and before Federal administrative agencies. Also like AMA, it maintains its headquarters office in Washington, from which it organizes an annual meeting and publishes its newsletter, the *United States Municipal News*.

Among the numerous national organizations of municipal officers, the following are of major importance: the International City Managers Association, the Municipal Finance Officers Association, the National Association of Housing and Redevelopment Officials, the American Association of Planning Officials, and the International Association of Chiefs of Police, all of Chicago, and the National Institute of Municipal Law Officers, of Washington.

The National Association of Counties (NACO), organized in 1937, undertakes to perform for the counties services comparable to those provided for the cities by AMA and USCM. From its offices in Washington, this association also organizes an annual convention for county officers, carries on research on county problems, provides a clearing house information service on such problems, publishes a monthly magazine, *The County Officer*, devoted to articles on these problems, policy statements, research reports, and news items. Like its urban counterparts, it represents the counties before Congress and the Federal administrative agencies. It is supported by dues paid by members and member counties, supplemented from time to time by foundation grants or funds from other sources. The membership system is very complicated. Out of slightly more than 3,000 counties, 2,500 are affiliated through forty-two state associations of counties. As of March, 1963, 305 individual counties were members and contributors to the support of the Association, as were some 10,500 county officers scattered in approximately 2,000 counties throughout the country.

TEMPORARY AND AD HOC ARRANGEMENTS

Some cooperative interlocal arrangements are established on a purely temporary basis,[20] or on a basis supposed to be temporary, for the purpose of developing a solution to a pressing current problem. These sometimes develop on a permanent basis, as both the possibility and the desirability of continuing cooperation are clearly established. There are usually ad hoc organizations and sometimes extra-legal committees or machinery established for dealing with the problems common to a number of governmental units in a given geographical area. Several such voluntary organizations have been developed in Michigan, among which the Supervisors Inter-County Committee has been notable. The Penn-Jersey Transportation Survey comes from another geographical area and involves a different subject matter, as do the joint planning arrangement in the Denver area and the parks and open space program in New York.

Penn-Jersey Transportation Study

On January 23, 1959, the State Highway Departments of New Jersey and Pennsylvania, together with the City of Philadelphia and four neigh-

---

[20] Examples: A task force representing hundreds of American cities found a basis for filing a joint suit against the nation's major electrical firms for damages resulting from price-fixing, *Washington Post*, June 22, 1961, p. D8. See also: Cail, Harold L., "Two Towns on U.S.-Canadian Border Join in Dual Celebration," *The New York Times*, June 18, 1961, X, 7.

boring counties [21] in each State, agreed to undertake a comprehensive transportation study which would take advantage of Federal funds for highway planning administered under the auspices of the Bureau of Public Roads.

The scope and objectives of the study were expressed in a Study Outline which had been developed prior to the agreement by a Program Planning Committee consisting of representatives of the principal sponsoring agencies, the elements of which are incorporated by reference in the agreement. These elements recommended a wide variety of subjects to be covered and items of data to be collected, analyzed, and projected into the future. The fundamental objective of the Study is to devise a workable, acceptable, and adaptable plan to guide transportation development in the nine-county metropolitan area to develop an adequate system for moving its people and goods during the next ten to twenty-five years. The immediate objectives were to develop a plan and program for the staged development of facilities to serve the evolving area and to recommend some form of continuing agency to carry on after the initial study period has ended.

Agreement is needed among the governments in the region as well as among the other agencies affecting the area's growth as to the general layout and functioning of the regional transportation system that is to be developed in the future. In order to enable the evolving region to have and maintain a guiding plan, the study was responsible for initiating a comprehensive planning process. The cost of the undertaking was shared by the twelve participants in accordance with the terms of the Agreement. The findings were made available for public discussion from time to time as they are developed, prior to the publication of the final report.

The *Prospectus* outlined an operation of considerable magnitude that would gradually evolve through no less than nine separate phases: organization, detailed design of work, survey of present conditions and trends significant for transportation planning, data processing, analysis of factors affecting future transportation requirements, development of generalized regional alternatives, selection of the generalized transportation system, detailed planning of the resulting transportation system, determination of program for developing and operating the recommended transportation system and keeping the recommendations up-to-date, and transition to the continuous agency.

[21] Burlington, Camden, Gloucester, and Mercer Counties in New Jersey, and Bucks, Chester, Delaware, Montgomery, and Philadelphia in Pennsylvania. The City of Philadelphia and Philadelphia County are coterminous. See Penn-Jersey Transportation Study, *Prospectus* (Philadelphia, September, 1960) and Fagin, Henry, and Sinks, Alfred H., "Penn-Jersey Transportation Study," *Department of Internal Affairs Monthly Bulletin*, August, 1961, pp. 10–11.

Joint Planning in the Denver Area

Evidence of interest in cooperative planning is now appearing in many urban areas. Maryland is moving toward authorizing the establishment of multi-county planning commissions throughout the State for the dual purpose of developing master plans and coordinating the planning activities of Federal, State, county, and town planning bodies. In Westchester County, New York, communities are joining to plan for the expected population influx.[22] In Colorado, both Denver and Pueblo are undertaking regional, cooperative planning in a serious way.

The Denver metropolitan area provides an excellent example of the evolution of joint planning efforts in one large metropolitan community over a period of a quarter of a century. In the mid-1930's a Regional Planning Association was formed under the auspices of the National Resources Planning Board. This has been described as a voluntary, advisory body performing research into the nature of the metropolitan region. Staff services were provided for it by the Bureau of Business Research at the University of Denver. A few years later, the Upper Platte Valley Regional Planning Commission was established by seven counties in the metropolitan area, under legislation passed in 1939, authorizing regional planning bodies. This organization developed to the point at which staffing seemed imperative, but when it was proposed to establish a budget for this purpose, four of the seven counties dropped out. The three remaining counties—Adams, Arapahoe, and Jefferson—thereupon established in 1944 the Tri-County Regional Planning Commission, which continued to function until 1949.

During the next five years, there was no formal intergovernmental body functioning in this field; the Denver Planning Office performed whatever regional action was undertaken, in consultation with authorities in the adjoining counties. Then in 1955, the present Inter-County Regional Planning Commission was established.[23] Its purposes were: (1) to prepare a comprehensive plan for the growth of the Denver region; (2) to coordinate the planning activities of the cities and counties of the region; and (3) to assist in resolving intergovernmental problems pertaining to the region's growth. The Commission was organized by five counties—

[22] On Maryland, see "Multi-County Plan Groups Bill Endorsed," *Washington Post,* September 14, 1961; on Westchester, Folsom, Merrill, "Westchester Communities Join to Plan for Population Influx," *The New York Times,* October 29, 1961.

[23] Data furnished by its Director and from its *Growth Guide for the Denver Region,* Master Plan Report No. 4 (Denver, November, 1958).

Adams, Arapahoe, Denver, Douglas, and Jefferson. It has twenty-two members: two from each county, one from each city of 4,000 or more population, and three representing an associate membership composed of taxing jurisdictions and civic organizations within the region. The Commission is financed by the citizens of the region through county contributions of six cents per capita. These funds, which are matched by a Federal grant, permit the Commission to undertake technical planning studies such as its regional growth guide report.

Parks and Open Spaces in the New York Area

Two regional groups in the New York metropolitan area, the Metropolitan Regional Council and the Regional Plan Association, recommended in 1960 a great expansion of park and other open space areas in a twenty-two county region. The study was carried on jointly by the two organizations over a period of two years; the final report emphasizes the great need for additional open space to meet the recreational needs of an expanding population which has an increasing amount of leisure time.[24] It is essential, the report contends, to acquire the additional land for parks and open space now, before it is developed for housing and other purposes. The acquisition and development of ten major regional park sites is recommended, nine to be acquired by the States and one by the Federal government.

At the time the survey was made, there were 290 square miles of park land in the area, and the report recommended that this be increased to 1,150 square miles and that other types of permanent open space in the region be increased from 290 to 500 square miles. The cost of the proposed program was estimated at $1.9 billion; existing programs would meet about half of this need, and a forty-year bond issue was proposed to finance the remainder.

COOPERATION ON A CONTINUING BASIS

The discussion so far has been concerned with the origins of interlocal cooperation, its constitutional and statutory basis, and the nature and extent of the cooperative arrangements thus far developed within this legal framework. Most of these developments appear to relate to pressing problems of day-to-day administration, but there is also another and more enduring side to the overall problem of interlocal relations. Some

[24] *The Race for Open Space* (New York, 1960).

illustrations of relatively permanent aspects of cooperation in important functional areas are: fire fighting; personnel administration; the construction, maintenance, and operation of public buildings; library administration; contracts for municipal or municipal type services; and the establishment of special districts or authorities to administer joint programs as a means of solving common problems.

Experience in Particular Functional Areas

Fire Protection. Fire protection was probably the first area in which interlocal cooperation was developed. It is reported that "for nearly a century, the City of Bath (Maine) had fire protection agreements with the surrounding towns of Arrowsic, Georgetown, Phippsburg, West Bath and Woolwich," but these agreements were not formalized until a few years ago.[25] In many States today, most paid and most volunteer fire companies are organized for or within a political jurisdiction, but the majority do not restrict their services to the municipality in which they are located and from which they derive all or most of their financial support. Service outside municipal boundaries may be either regular service, mutual aid, or emergency service. In regular service, the recognized territory of a company or department includes another governmental unit, or a part of it, all fire calls in that outside territory being automatically answered by the neighboring fire company. In mutual aid, two or more companies enter into an agreement to help each other when needed or to furnish a kind of service not available to the other organization.

In emergency service, there is no formal mutual aid agreement, but in an emergency, one company or department will go outside its territory, usually only when requested to do so by the fire chief or a responsible official of the municipality or other unit needing help. Some companies perform outside service on more than one basis. For instance, according to the findings of a 1960 Pennsylvania survey, "a borough may regularly serve the township adjoining it on the east; it may also have a mutual aid agreement with the fire company of the borough located five miles north; and it may go anywhere within twenty-five miles in an emergency." [26]

Many of the fire companies and departments serving outside their municipal boundaries do not restrict their activities to one neighboring governmental unit. The number of outside units served, according to the

[25] Wilson, James, "Manager Under Fire," in Frost, Richard T., *Cases in State and Local Government* (Englewood Cliffs, N.J.: Prentice-Hall, Inc., 1961), pp. 17–27, on p. 19.
[26] Smedley, Elizabeth, *Local Fire Administration in Pennsylvania,* rev. ed. (Harrisburg: Department of Internal Affairs, 1960). Chapter 2 deals with the territory served by fire departments and companies.

Pennsylvania survey report, ranged from one to as many as fourteen, and a number of companies reported that they serve "all surrounding territory," "the vicinity," or "neighboring townships" within a radius of from ten to twenty-five miles. A particularly interesting aspect of interlocal cooperation in fire fighting is to be noted in the fact that Pennsylvania fire companies are not deterred by State lines:

> In no other phase of local public service are there so many examples of matter-of-course service to neighboring communities in other States. For example, the Bristol Borough Fire Department goes to Burlington, New Jersey, when called. The Lawrenceville Fire Company also serves the village of Lindley, New York. The Marcus Hook Fire Company works under a mutual aid agreement with several communities, including one in the State of Delaware. The Fountain Dale Volunteer Fire Department goes into Maryland on call. Other companies report service in Ohio and West Virginia, or cooperate with organizations in those States.
>
> The number of boroughs and townships served by the fire departments and companies reporting regular service outside their own municipality is indicated in the following table. It is important to note that there is undoubtedly some duplication, because in a number of instances, one portion of the township is served by one fire company, another portion by a second company. Nevertheless, the number of boroughs and townships depending upon organizations from other communities for fire protection is surprisingly great. This is especially significant since only 139 fire departments or companies report, as a source of revenue, payments from other municipalities or townships

COMMONWEALTH OF PENNSYLVANIA: BOROUGHS AND TOWNSHIPS
SERVED BY OUTSIDE FIRE DEPARTMENTS AND COMPANIES *

Department or Company Furnishing Outside Service	Number of Departments or Companies	Number of Boroughs Served	Number of Townships Served
Full paid	4	5	4
Predominantly paid	4	2	7
Volunteer—Cities of the Third Class	6	1	10
Volunteer—Boroughs Over 5,000	90	33	219
Volunteer—Boroughs Under 5,000	169	42	438
Volunteer—Townships of the First Class	17	4	16
Volunteer—Townships of the Second Class ...	127	4	264

* Source: Smedley, Elizabeth, *Local Fire Administration in Pennsylvania*, rev. ed. (Harrisburg: Department of Internal Affairs, 1960), p. 13.

served by them. Only 110 report payments from individual property owners served outside their municipality.[27]

Personnel Administration. New York State has been selected to illustrate the field of personnel administration because it adopted civil service by statute in 1883, by constitutional provision in 1894, and has long been a leader among the States in this field. Local units have long been encouraged, and under a recent court decision all counties are required, to have a merit system. Thus, it is significant to note the provisions of New York law designed to permit and/or encourage cooperative relationships between units in the personnel field.

As shown in the table on page 758, these provisions are fairly numerous and they are important. Cooperation is extensive, and in many instances it is required by law. The performance of the local civil service function may be carried on, at the option of the local units, by a commission or a personnel officer of its own creation, by another local unit (a county or a city), by a regional commission or personnel officer, or by the State Civil Service Commission. The provisions relating to regional arrangements are most interesting: "Two or more adjoining counties, two or more cities in the same or adjoining counties, or any combination of such counties and cities may, by agreement, establish a regional civil service commission or regional personnel officer to administer the civil service law in all of the participating municipalities. The agreement must provide for the manner of appointment and removal of the personnel officer or commission members, the location of the principal office of the commission, and the apportionment of costs among the participating municipalities."

The county civil service commission or personnel officer *must* administer the civil service law for the civil subdivisions within the county except, under certain circumstances, school districts. Similarly, a city civil service commission *must* administer the civil service law for a city school district within its borders. In villages or special districts located in two or more counties, the civil service law shall be administered, the law states, "under the jurisdiction of the county selected by the governing board of the village or district or, if no such election is made, under the jurisdiction of the county where the greatest territorial area of the village or district is located." Where a function or agency is jointly maintained by two or more municipalities (including school districts) in the same county, the civil service law shall be administered for it by the agency having jurisdiction over county civil service matters.

The provisions for the transfer of civil service employees from one governmental unit to another are both interesting and important, since in many jurisdictions such transfers, if possible at all, can be made only at

[27] Smedley, p. 13.

great risk or with great personal sacrifice (loss of status, etc.) on the part of the employee concerned. The New York law provides:

> The State and municipal civil service commission may adopt rules concerning the transfer of employees between positions within their jurisdiction and may also adopt reciprocal rules concerning transfer between governmental units. No employee may, however, be transferred to a position for which an examination with different or more difficult tests is required nor may an employee be transferred against his will, except in the case of a transfer of functions.[28]

STATE OF NEW YORK: INTERLOCAL COOPERATION IN CIVIL SERVICE AND PUBLIC OFFICERS

1. *Administration of Civil Service by Counties*

Performance of municipal civil service functions by State, county, or regional commission or officer

Applies to: Cities and Counties
Civil Service Law, Sec. 15 (1), 16

Administration of civil service by county on behalf of municipalities

Applies to: Municipalities
Civil Service Law, Sec. 17 (1)

Performance of school district civil service functions by State or city

Applies to: School Districts and Cities
Civil Service Law, Sec. 18 (1)

Performance of village and special district civil service functions by county

Applies to: Villages and special districts located in more than one county
Civil Service Law, Sec. 19

Administration of civil service for joint functions or agencies

Applies to: Joint municipal functions or agencies
Civil Service Law, Sec. 18 (12)

2. *Transfer of Employees Between Governmental Units*

Transfer of civil service employees from one governmental unit to another

Applies to: Cities, Villages, and Towns
Civil Service Law, Sec. 70 (1)

Civil service status of employees in case of transfer of municipal functions

Applies to: Municipalities
Civil Service Law, Sec. 70 (2)

3. *County-Wide Self-Insurance for Workmen's Compensation*

Participation of counties, cities, and other public corporations in county self-insurance plans

Applies to: Municipalities, Public Benefit Corporations
Workmen's Compensation Law, Sec. 50 (4), 60–75

---

[28] Civil Service Law, Section 70 (1).

DETROIT-WAYNE COUNTY BUILDING

Public Works. Cooperation in the public buildings field is one of the oldest forms of interlocal cooperation, and it is a form still in fairly frequent use. One of the first examples of such cooperation occurred in Detroit in 1871, when the first city hall was opened. This was in reality a city-county building, housing both city and county offices, the county leasing space from the city. As the county expanded rapidly in the years which followed, a new county building to house the county courts and offices was decided upon. The cornerstone for this building was laid in 1897 and the building dedicated in 1902. Half a century later, as the community continued to grow, a giant city-county building to serve as a local government center became a necessity.

The preliminary arrangements for the project were completed in 1946, and voter approval followed in 1947. The Detroit-Wayne Building Authority was incorporated in 1948, and the issuance of bonds authorized by the legislature. Ground was broken in 1951, the cornerstone laid in

1953, and the formal dedication observed in 1955. This building, in which city and county occupy equal space, has 10⅔ million cubic feet, 737,000 square feet of floor space, and a net rentable area of 505,000 square feet. It was anticipated when the building was completed that all of the outstanding revenue bonds would be amortized in less than twenty years, after which the only costs for many years to come would be for operation and maintenance.[29]

The first legislation enacted in Pennsylvania on interlocal cooperation dealt with this subject, and no earlier laws have been noted elsewhere. These preceded by a quarter of a century any extensive legislative consideration of the problem of cooperation at the local level. In 1913, it was provided that in each county in which a county seat was located within the limits of a city, the county commissioners and the proper corporate authorities of such city were authorized to agree upon a site within the limits of such city and to erect thereon a joint county-municipal building, to be used by the county for a county court house and for other purposes and by the city for municipal purposes. By further legislation adopted in 1917, 1919, and 1925, this authorization was extended to all types of local units and to buildings for such special purposes as libraries, public auditoriums, memorials, and monuments.[30]

Arrangements similar to those in the Detroit-Wayne County area are to be noted in Denver and San Francisco, in which city-county consolidation was long ago achieved. Also, in the 1950's, several cases of such cooperation were reported in California.[31] In Alaska, the legislature in 1960 approved for submission to the voters in November, six general bond programs for capital improvements, totalling $39.5 million. Two of the projects were State office buildings in Anchorage and Fairbanks, both of which it was hoped locally might become government centers housing State and local government offices in the two cities.

The Washington Suburban Sanitary Commission, established by the Maryland General Assembly in 1918 to serve about 30,000 people in parts of Montgomery and Prince George's Counties, is probably one of the earliest cooperative ventures of its type. Periodic additions by action of the General Assembly have increased the Commission service zone from ninety-five square miles to an area six times larger than the District of Columbia. The population served by the Commission is estimated at 560,000 persons, nineteen times the 1918 total. There are six commission-

[29] Based upon an undated, processed memorandum supplied by the Citizens' Research Council of Michigan: *Our New Seat of Local Government: The City-County Building, Detroit, Michigan.*

[30] See Wise, pp. 10, 19–20.

[31] See Kerstetter, John R., *Joint City-County Occupancy of Public Office Buildings* (Chicago: American Municipal Association, 1952).

ers who serve for four-year terms. All are appointed by the Governor: two from nominations made by the Montgomery County Council, two from nominations made by the Prince George's County Commissioners, and one from each county of the Governor's own selection.

As one of the outstanding water-sewer agencies in the nation, WSSC has received numerous awards in recognition of its service. The Commission operates two impoundment facilities on the Patuxent River, of which one is a beautiful 800-acre lake containing 6.4 billion gallons of water. In its equipment are included sixteen pumping station and thirty-one storage tanks. Similarly, it operates two huge sewage treatment plants, Parkway and Blue Plains. It completed in 1959 the $12.2 million Prince George's Marina and Anacostia River Flood Control Project which is expected to end the costly flooding of the Peace Cross area while, at the same time, it provides an up-to-date pleasure boat facility and recreation area.

Library Administration. Interlocal cooperation in the field of library administration has been flourishing, particularly since the enactment of the Library Services Act by Congress in 1956. A regional library program requires the coordinated effort of the counties and State, and during the life of the Federal Act, of the Federal government as well. For example, in mid-1961 it was reported that fifteen libraries in Suffolk County, New York, had asked the State Education Department to approve the creation of a county cooperative library system, to be financed by a State subsidy of $100,000. The plan, approved by the County Board of Supervisors, would provide service for more than the minimum of 200,000 residents required by State law. It was reported that at the time, 95 per cent of New York State libraries in fifty-eight counties enjoyed the benefits of similar systems. About one library a month had joined the Nassau County system since its establishment in 1959. Suffolk was one of only four counties in the State that had not then established a county library system.[32] In West Virginia, fourteen library systems have been set up in the State, and as of 1959, four regional libraries in three regions were in actual operation, and a fifth (located in another region) was expected to begin operation in 1962. To encourage local citizen groups to undertake the organization of new regional libraries, the State Library Commission has prepared and published a procedures manual.[33]

[32] See Porterfield, Byron, "Fifteen Libraries Seek Cooperation in Suffolk," *The New York Times,* May 7, 1961.

[33] See *Regional Library Development in West Virginia,* rev. ed. (Charleston, March, 1961) and Miller, Helen M., *A Proposed Regional Library for Wood, Pleasants, Tyler and Wetzel Counties* (Charleston: West Virginia Library Commission, 1960).

Services Under Contract

Contrary to the general impression, intergovernmental service under contract is not a new and modern idea. It was a form of voluntary inter-municipal cooperation used in the early days between the central city and some of its suburbs or neighboring smaller cities for the joint construction and operation of bridges, water supply, and sewer systems, for the sharing of necessary expenses, or for the sale of services by the central city to adjacent governmental units. The late Professor Paul Studenski cited, as a notable example, the construction of the Brooklyn Bridge in New York City and Brooklyn during the years 1874–1883.[34]

As was noted earlier in the discussion of metropolitan areas (Chapter XVIII), pressure is being placed upon many urban counties to render what are often called "municipal type services" to the inhabitants of unincorporated and fringe areas lying outside the borders of the core cities, or by contract within the core cities themselves. Out of 125 counties replying to a questionnaire sent out by the National Association of County Officials in 1958, over half were providing health, prison, election, and planning services for their cities on a cooperative basis. Many were co-operating with cities in assessing property and collecting taxes; in operating airports, libraries, and recreation facilities; in supplying water, maintaining streets, and inspecting buildings; in providing services for government personnel; and in law enforcement, fire fighting, and sewage disposal services. Literally dozens of other government services are provided jointly by cities and counties. Los Angeles County, for example, provides forty-two different municipal services for at least one city, and some cities in that county were contracting for all or nearly all of their municipal services. The nature and scope of this program is shown in the table on page 765. "Intergovernmental cooperation . . . was the most notable characteristic of urban county government in 1958," the survey concluded.

The Los Angeles experience is sufficiently important to deserve further comment. If it is a unique experience, it is so chiefly because of the sheer magnitude of its cooperative effort; intermunicipal cooperative arrangements have been developed on such a broad scale as to include 67 per cent of the cities responding in a 1959 survey conducted by the League of California Cities, a survey that revealed seventy-four inter-municipal written agreements and written contracts in which one city

[34] Studenski, Paul, "Metropolitan Areas 1960," *National Civic Review,* October, 1960, pp. 467–473.

provided services to another in one or more of a dozen different service areas.[35]

Los Angeles County is a sprawling area of 4,083 square miles containing a population of nearly 6 million people—the most populous county in the nation—a population exceeding that of each of thirty-nine States. In 1959, 535 new people were added to the population every day, 16,300 every month, 195,000 every year. While most of these people (81 per cent) live in the City of Los Angeles (population about 2.5 million) and the other sixty-nine incorporated places in the county, more than 1 million (19 per cent) of the county's population live in unincorporated areas.

Governmentally, Los Angeles has been a home rule county since 1913, with a civil service system, non-partisan elections, and a short ballot. On the whole, it has had conspicuously good government. It early dropped a rural outlook, and for more than fifty years has provided municipal-type services on an increasingly expanded scale to its vast population. Thus it was that from 1939 to 1954, while the population of the unincorporated areas grew from 445,000 to 1,150,000, or 129 per cent, not one municipal incorporation took place. The county provided all basic and necessary municipal services to this unincorporated "city" of over 1 million people, as well as many basic services in welfare, justice, recording of documents, hospital services, and others to all its citizens regardless of whether they lived in a municipality or not. The Assistant Chief Administrative Officer in 1959 gave the following account of the history of contract services in Los Angeles County:

> The County of Los Angeles, as a highly organized and municipal-type county, has provided contract services covering various municipal-type activities for a period of fifty years. During this time, many problems of functional over-lapping never occurred—because each new city, or incorporation, automatically looked to the County for assessment and tax collection and health services, and many of them looked to the County for building inspection, library and personnel services. As a matter of fact, when Lakewood was incorporated in 1954, the first incorporation in fifteen years, over 400 service agreements existed with various of the forty-five cities that existed at that time.
>
> What was the significance of the Lakewood incorporation in 1954? In the first place, as stated, it was the first incorporation in Los Angeles County in fifteen years. It was a brand new city that had mushroomed within about a three-year period, in an area of seven square miles with

[35] Cited by Gove, Samuel K., *The Lakewood Plan* (Urbana: Commission Papers of the Institute of Government and Public Affairs, University of Illinois, May, 1961), p. 7.

approximately 60,000 people—and, upon its incorporation, became the fifteenth largest city in the State of California.

The second item of significance was that the Lakewood Plan was born. Lakewood's incorporation brought about a change in the philosophy of offering services by the County to cities—in that total municipal services, including police, fire, public works, and others were provided for the first time in one package to a city. Since that time eighteen cities have incorporated, totaling 109 square miles, and over 450,000 people. Two of the cities provide their own municipal services, leaving the County of Los Angeles providing package services for fifteen cities containing some 350,000 people in an area of ninety-one square miles. Thus the County of Los Angeles is providing municipal services to almost 1,500,000 people including both the cities under contract and the unincorporated area. In addition all of the older cities in the County still participate in the many traditional services areas such as health and assessment and collection of taxes as mentioned above. We expect four additional incorporations within the next six months, these also to be under the Lakewood Plan.

The Lakewood Plan basically provides for the performance of all municipal functions by the County of Los Angeles, while local autonomy and control of municipal affairs remains with the locally elected city council. The result is home rule plus economy, a city operation without large capital investments and fixed overhead, grass-roots government. It is decentralized policy with centralized administration.

The Plan is one of municipal partnership with County government. It authorizes the provision of all municipal services by a county at the request of the city—through their own free choice, not legal necessity. It is voluntary—and therein lies its blessing and its curse. The Plan developed because Lakewood's newly elected City Council asked the County if it would continue to provide all services for the City. The County Board of Supervisors said "yes—for a price." The City reimburses the County for all direct costs of each service, plus a share of the general County overhead. These costs result from detailed analyses by accountants in our Auditor's Office and are revised annually to reflect increase in pay scales and costs of operating supplies.[36]

By way of comparison (or contrast) with the Lakewood Plan, attention may be directed to the experience of Atlanta and Fulton County in extending water service to an extensive suburban population surrounding that city. The task was successfully accomplished by a far different but more conventional procedure.[37] After a careful study, including a house-to-house count of improved properties and population trends, the engineers

[36] Leach, John R., "The Lakewood Plan," *Urban County Congress* (Washington, 1959), pp. 26–31; see also Gove, *The Lakewood Plan*.

[37] See Fuller, A. E., "Extension of Water Mains in Unincorporated Urban Areas," *Urban County Congress*, pp. 79–81.

The services listed below are provided by the county to the cities and other local units at their request. Many services of benefit to the cities and their residents have been excluded. The services covered in this table are divided into four categories: (1) contracts for particular services; (2) resolutions requesting services pursuant to the General Services Agreement; (3) other resolutions which appoint or authorize County Departments to perform certain functions; (4) special districts which perform services within a community based on a special tax rate. A total of 887 services are accounted for in the table, most of them—obviously—performed under contract.

Type of Service	(1)	(2)	(3)	(4)
Assessment and Collection of Taxes	60			
Building Inspection Services	23			
County Jail	52			
Election Services			54	
Emergency Ambulance Service	38			
Engineering Services			16	
Fire Protection District Services				16
General Services Agreement	38	24		
Health Services	57		59	
Rodent Control	24			
Industrial Waste Regulation	7			
Law Enforcement Activities	16	24		
Business License Enforcement	6			
Crossing-Guard Service	4			
Traffic Law Enforcement	14			
Library District Services				34
Microfilm Record Storage	9			
Personnel Staff Services		15		
Pound—Animal Regulation	24			
Preservation of Rights	9			
Recreation Services	3	1		6
Sewer Maintenance	3			14
Street Maintenance and Construction	18		16	
Bridge Maintenance	24			
Traffic Signal Maintenance	38			
Lighting and Lighting Maintenance				15
Street Sweeping	12			
Tree Trimming Service		15		
Traffic Striping	18			
Subdivision Final Map Check—				
County Engineer	56	10		
Water Supply—Operation and Mainte-				
nance	1			2
Zoning and Planning Staff Services		15		

* Release from Chief Administrative Office, County-City Services Division, Hall of Records, Los Angeles, March 10, 1959; see also California Contract Cities Association, *Proceedings*, published annually in Lakewood.

submitted a plan in complete detail, covering construction of the system, costs of construction, maintenance and operation, a schedule of fees and charges, and revenue bond financing.

The collection and treatment of sewage is another field which has given rise to a large number of contracts, compacts, and areawide agreements. A recent survey shows how tremendous this development has actually been.[38] Practically every municipality surrounding Philadelphia has entered into an agreement to let the central city receive and treat its sewage.[39] Although large treatment plants such as those in Atlanta, Cleveland, Detroit, Philadelphia, Toledo, and many other cities benefit the smaller cities served through greatly reduced unit costs for sewage treatment, there are important limitations on intermunicipal cooperation for the disposal of sewage. Among these limitations is the tendency to rely on short range planning "which can lead municipalities into severe long range difficulties," and the possibility that at some point the negotiations may founder.

Special Districts and Authorities

It is well known that an increasing number of agreements for cooperation between local units have required implementation in the form of a special district or authority before their provisions could be made effective. These devices have been especially common in metropolitan areas, but have been by no means confined to them. These units have been established because many existing governmental units have been found unsuited to present day needs because of small area, weak financial position, lack of authorization for the performance of the function or service desired, or because of faulty administrative structure or antagonism, resistance, or unresponsiveness on the part of their officials. Other reasons cited in a recent study include a desire for independence, the advocacy of special districts by existing governments, expediency, the desire to "free the service from politics"—as if this would—or "unadorned self-interest." [40]

If the reasons for these units seem compelling, the reasons against

[38] See Foster, William S., a three-part survey of "Metropolitan Sewerage Pacts in 1960," in *The American City:* I, "Inter-city Contracts," October, pp. 87–89; II, "Intermunicipal Sewerage Compacts," November, pp. 169–176; III, "Metropolitan Sewerage Compacts," December, pp. 143–147.

[39] See Williams, *Intergovernmental Cooperation for Disposal of Sewage: Southeastern Pennsylvania.*

[40] For discussion of these points, see Bollens, John C., *Special District Governments in the United States* (Berkeley: University of California Press, 1957).

them are much more so, in view of both immediate and future effects upon the governmental structure. The immediate effect is that new units are added to the existing governmental jurisdictions which are already far too numerous. In the words of Professor Wall, "this alternative makes still more complex a local governmental structure whose greatest need is simplification." [41]

The numerous long range defects are complicated. Established originally as a device for evading constitutional and statutory debt limitations in the Depression era when many existing units had exhausted their borrowing power, these units continue as special public corporations related to but not an integral part of the governmental structure, to operate outside the range of the normal controls to which governmental agencies are normally subject. There was at one time a hope that these single-purpose units might somehow evolve into multi-purpose units, in effect replacing some of the small, ineffective units upon which they had been superimposed. Such has not been the case; the small units still exist along with the new ones, which have in the meantime grown strong and free from normal supervisory controls.

Special Districts. The number of special districts in the United States has increased steadily over the last quarter century. The functions they perform are so numerous and varied that they do not readily lend themselves to classification; Professor Bollens divides them into eleven categories, while the Division of Governments of the Bureau of the Census uses twelve. Both the categories and the numerical distribution are shown in the table on page 768, presenting figures from the 1957 Census of Governments. Out of a total of 14,405 units reported, 660 were classified as large, 1,572 as "other."

It was estimated in 1949 that there were in California more than 4,000 special districts of four major types—agricultural, school, quasi-municipal, and metropolitan—functioning under 100 different laws and carrying on more than thirty different governmental functions. By 1957, this State had seventy-eight large, 1,572 "other" districts. In Pennsylvania, a joint service district bill was presented to the General Assembly for its consideration; although it was not approved, many of its objectives are being accomplished under the provisions of existing law. In 1957, Pennsylvania had thirty-four single-purpose districts, no multi-purpose; by 1962, these numbers had increased to 1,398 and 61 respectively. Significant increases in numbers occurred in other States as well. Illinois had 1,783 single-function and seventeen multi-function districts in 1957, with 2,126 and five, five years later. In New York, the figures were 918 and six in 1957, and 969 and one for 1962.[42]

[41] Wall, p. 325.
[42] See Scott, Stanley, and Bollens, John C., *Special Districts in California*

NUMBER AND CHARACTER OF SPECIAL DISTRICTS IN THE
UNITED STATES—1957 AND 1962 *

Functional Class	Number 1957	Number 1962
Single-Function Districts	13,743	18,323
Natural Resources	5,543	6,158
Fire Protection	2,624	3,229
Cemeteries	1,107	1,283
Housing and Community Development	969	1,099
Urban Water Supply	787	1,502
Highways	782	773
Sanitation	451	. . .
Hospitals	345	418
Libraries	322	349
Parks and Recreation	316	488
Health	223	231
All other single-function districts	662	515
Total	14,405	18,838
Multi-Function Districts †		
Sewerage and Water Supply	144	138
Natural Resources and Water Supply	108	56
Other multiple-function districts	299	116
Total	551	310

* U.S. Bureau of the Census, *Governments in the United States* (Washington, 1959) and *Governmental Units in 1962* (Washington, December, 1962).

† Includes only districts reporting five or more full-time employees or indebtedness of at least $100,000. Smaller units reporting more than a single service are classed in terms of their primary function.

Authorities. Pennsylvania makes far greater use of the authority device than any other State—a somewhat questionable distinction. A municipal authorities act was passed in 1935; as of 1948, there had been 128 authorities created, and thirty-nine more appeared in 1949.[43] More recent information has been summarized as follows:

Local Government (Berkeley: Bureau of Public Administration, University of California, 1949), summarized in an article, "Special Districts in California Local Government," *Western Political Quarterly*, June, 1950, pp. 233–243. On the use of these devices in lieu of consolidation, see Bollens, John C., "When Services Get Too Big," *National Municipal Review*, November, 1949, pp. 498–501.

[43] See Joint State Government Commission, *Municipal Authorities* (Harrisburg, 1945); and Weintraub, Tina V., and Patterson, James D., *The Authority in Pennsylvania: Pro and Con* (Bureau of Municipal Research, Philadelphia, 1949).

Water utilities and sewer and water authorities file reports with the Department of Internal Affairs. Sewer utilities report to the Department of Health. In 1956 a total of 196 municipal water utilities filed reports, and ninety-six of them indicated that the utility had customers in more than one political subdivision. The ninety-six served a total of 257 municipalities. Many of them serve more than two political subdivisions, and one serves as many as eleven. At the same time, 135 water authorities filed reports, and seventy-seven of them had customers in more than one municipality. The seventy-seven served a total of 369 municipalities. The average water authority serves eight to ten municipalities and one serves as many as thirty-one.

There are 465 municipally owned sewer utilities in the Commonwealth, and sixty-eight of them serve more than one municipality. The sixty-eight serve a total of 187 municipalities. Forty-seven of the sixty-eight serve only two political subdivisions, but the Philadelphia utility serves twelve and Pittsburgh's serves ten.

Eighty-two sewer authorities filed reports in 1956, and twenty-six of them had customers in more than one municipality. The twenty-six serve a total of ninety-two municipalities. Only four sewer authorities serve six or more municipalities, and three of the four are in Delaware County.[44]

An illustration of a very different type from another State and another section of the country may be noted in the Huron-Clinton Metropolitan Authority. Established approximately twenty years ago through the cooperation of five Michigan counties—Livingston, Macomb, Oakland, Washtenaw, and Wayne—this Authority has concerned itself primarily with problems relating to recreation, parks, and parkways. It operates six metropolitan parks, a metropolitan beach, and four parkways. The criticisms of the authority device have been much the same as those leveled against the special district, but there have been few studies of the actual operation of such agencies.

Fortunately such a study is available for the Huron-Clinton Metropolitan Authority,[45] the findings of which are interesting and significant. "When an authority has an independent source of revenue and is governed by a board in which each constituent unit, regardless of size, has an equal say, the authority is invulnerable to opposition from a minority of its constituent units." Its work is not carefully scrutinized by constituents, perhaps because constituent bodies tend to appoint representatives in whom they have substantial confidence. Authority operations in this par-

[44] Kelley, p. 9.

[45] Bosworth, Jerry C., *How the Huron-Clinton Metropolitan Authority Responds to Its Public* (Ann Arbor: Institute of Public Administration, University of Michigan, 1961). Its Board of Commissioners publishes a biennial report, the ninth as of December 31, 1959. Its offices are in the Guardian Building, Detroit.

ticular unit rely heavily on expertise and technical judgment. They have not, however, solved the problem of coordination between constituent governmental units.

PROBLEMS OF ORGANIZATION AND ADMINISTRATION

The practice of cooperation between adjacent units of local government may be possible, at least in some cases, without special structural arrangements, but it does raise organizational problems. First, there is the question of the types of service in which the development of cooperative relationships is possible and/or desirable. As indicated earlier, there appear to be no excepted fields. Cooperation is possible and may be advantageous in almost any functional area within which local government units commonly operate. One early writer, as a matter of convenience, grouped the functions in which cooperative arrangements were most frequent as follows:

Emergency Services: Fire, Police
Regular Services: Collection of Refuse, Sewer Systems
Public Utilities: Water, Electric Power [46]

Such information as is available from States like New York and Tennessee, both of which have pioneered in interlocal relations, indicates that a much broader field of operations now exists. By 1960, many reports showed a trend in favor of regional solution of common local problems, even to the extent of establishing multi-purpose authorities instead of the single-purpose units so common in the past.

Obstacles to Cooperation

The currently widespread existence of interlocal cooperation tends, to some extent, to create an unrealistic impression of it. A great deal of cooperation is now legally possible, and much is actually in existence. Although the general tendency is to support—or at least not oppose—

[46] Shaw, p. 6. That American communities have no monopoly on such problems is occasionally illustrated in the literature on local government in other countries; see, for instance, Sarrailh, Eduardo J., "Outline of Inter-municipal Cooperation Between the City of Buenos Aires and Its Adjacent Municipalities for the Purpose of Creating Therein a Planning Area," *Revista Municipal Interamericana*, January–June, 1959, pp. 29–32.

cooperative projects, there are numerous, important difficulties. Anyone disposed to doubt this need only look at the record in the field of school district consolidation. Great progress has been made in this area since World War II, but what has been accomplised is only a small start on what needs to be done.

Why does school district consolidation move so slowly? A New York study provides thirteen answers.[47] By far the most frequently cited factor in resistance to consolidation is public concern over the potential costs of new programs—the fear, if not the certainty, that tax rates would be increased. The study is based upon data from eighty-one out of ninety-seven centralizations between July 1, 1950, and June 30, 1958, since the coverage of each was comparable in scope and depth. The number of centralization campaigns in which each reason was cited is shown in the table on pages 772–773.

Another illustration of a wholly different character but also relating to schools arose in the State of Michigan in the fall of 1960. While an element of financial cost was involved, the main question was one of race relations and the snobbery of the people in some governmental units toward those in another. The problem was to find a school for forty unwanted ninth-graders (who happened to be Negroes) from Royal Oak Township, adjacent to Detroit. Settlement of the problem came only after a series of extraordinary legal maneuvers into which were drawn the Governor, the State Superintendent of Public Instruction, and the County School Superintendent. Damon Stetson, a correspondent for *The New York Times,* gives the facts in the case:

> The complicated plan calls for [placing the Negro students in adjoining school districts, which are predominantly white. It also] calls for resignation of the school board, an abortive election of new members, forced dissolution of the district and eventual merger with another.
>
> The forty ninth-graders registered this week at the George Washington Carver Elementary School in the township (population 8,000). They were part of the class of sixty-four who were graduated from the school last June. The others have moved away or are not planning further schooling. The poverty-stricken community, living in hastily erected World War II barracks and deteriorating homes, has not had a high school. It has sent its upper class pupils in the past to Detroit high schools as tuition students.
>
> Last year, however, Detroit notified the Carver school district board of education that because of crowded conditions in its own schools, it would be unable to accept this year's class of ninth graders. Two adjacent school districts, Oak Park and Ferndale, with predominantly

[47] Sayles, William C., *Recurring Reasons for Resistance to Centralization* (Albany: Division of Research, State Department of Education, April, 1960).

1. Concern with prospect of increased costs 76
   Opposition to potential tax increases

2. Prospective loss of local control 44
   Concern that local voice in school affairs will be considerably weakened by centralization

3. Transportation issue 32
   Parental dissatisfaction with prospective necessity of conveying pupils by bus over comparatively long distances

4. Preference for alternative centralization plan 32
   Local preference for centralization arrangements other than those indicated by the Master Plan

5. Resistance to change (inertia) 27
   Generalized opposition to altering the *status quo*

6. Conflicts among prospective constituent districts 25
   Friction and strained relations among adjoining districts

7. Conflicts within districts; internal controversy 25
   School-community friction, political schisms, other divisive elements that make it difficult to reach local agreement on centralization

8. Local pride 22
   Civic pride and a desire to preserve community distinctiveness

9. Preference for relatively small schools 18
   Belief that larger schools resulting from centralization will be less able to give personal attention to pupils

10. Lack of clear understanding of centralization 17
    Confusion over conflicting claims by proponents and opponents; uncertainty as to just what centralization entails

11. Influence of opposition groups 12
    Intervention by organized groups actively committed against centralization

12. Vested interests 10
    Special opposition of those whose status would be impaired by centralization, *e.g.*, members of a school board who stand to lose their positions if district centralizes

13. Preference for relatively small population center 5
    Distrust of community "expansion" associated with centralization; preference for "small community" life

* From Sayles, William C., *Recurring Reasons for Resistance to Centralization* (Albany: Division of Research, State Department of Education, April, 1960).

white students, also turned down the township's ninth graders. They said their town schools were crowded, and they pointed to previously enunciated policies against admitting tuition students. . . .

The Governor said neighboring school districts must share concern over Royal Oak Township's school problems even though there was no legal responsibility. He said that the Carver school district had a tenuous financial base and was ill equipped for high school training. He noted that the district had fallen $125,000 behind in its tuition payments to Detroit, where tenth, eleventh, and twelfth grade students from the township are continuing to go to school. Another unpromising portent, he said, was the low property value in the Carver district. The average was only $2,000 a child, compared with $14,000 in Michigan generally. The Governor proposed that the Carver school district be dissolved and attached to a neighboring one.[48]

Some months later, it was reported that this solution had been adopted.[49]

Formal and Informal Agreements

There is no uniform pattern in organization for interlocal cooperation. Arrangements are normally developed according to needs, some formally and some informally, some including many activities and others covering only one or a few. Special districts are frequently employed where formal city-county organization is desired. In this context, they are normally referred to as service districts. They are popular because they are adaptable, being readily expanded or adjusted to the varying service requirements of any large urban county. There would probably be many more of these agreements than there are, were it not for the difficulty of agreeing on specific terms.

Needs vary not only from one county to another but also within a given county, because some portions are more highly urbanized than others or because some portions are older than others, having been developed without curbs and gutters, sidewalks, storm sewers, street improvements, and fire hydrants in years when subdivision controls were lax. The search for such districts goes on in urban counties throughout the country, due mainly to the need for differing types and levels of service in urban and rural sections and the need for a tax differential system which will permit areas to pay for urban services when they receive them.

[48] September 11, 1960, p. 4.
[49] Stetson, Damon, "Schools Merged to End a Dispute," *The New York Times*, November 13, 1960, p. 68.

A study made in Oregon in 1956 recommended legislation authorizing the creation of county service districts which could provide up to six urban services, the county court or board of commissioners to serve as governing body.[50] In Sacramento, California, the following year, the Metropolitan Survey Report suggested a city-county metropolitan service area covering minimum countywide services, and an urban service area with boundaries which could be changed by act of the governing body. In Davidson County, Tennessee, the Metropolitan Charter Commission in 1958 proposed two service districts, a general services district to include the entire county, and an urban services district, initially the City of Nashville but to be expanded to provide such additional services as fire and police protection, water, sewer, refuse collection, and similar urban services to the urbanized area as it grows. The Virginia Sanitary District Law, originally set up to provide sewer districts, has been expanded to include many other services in Fairfax and other highly urbanized counties. A sanitary district may be established by petition to the Circuit Court where the boundaries are defined, generally with the concurrence and recommendation of the governing body of the county. The services are then provided and the necessary tax levied by the county governing body. Sanitary district bond issues are permitted by referendum, with an 18 per cent limitation. Similar enabling statutes are available in other States and where not available, could probably be secured with little difficulty.

The Urban County Plan for Fairfax County contemplates division of the county into from five to eleven districts which would serve both electoral and service purposes.[51] The districts would act to determine what services would be brought into each area, at the expense of the residents, and would thus carry out the purposes of the present Virginia sanitary districts. Sub-districts could be created for very special services. The districts would be built on community of interest, size, and the need for services not performed on a countywide basis. They would, as an arm of county government, work with rather than compete with the county. District councils would be elected in each district which would initially act as advisors to the county board and would perform the following services: (1) determine the number, type, and extent of the "metered" services which the county would provide in the district or part thereof, until such time as the service should be provided on a countywide basis; (2) make recommendations in the fields of planning and zoning, which resolutions

<hr>

[50] *Report of the Joint Interim Committee on Local Government and Urban Area Problems* (Salem, 1956).

[51] Public Administration Service, *Report on an Administrative Survey of Fairfax County, Virginia* (Chicago, 1957, as summarized by Anne Wilkins in "County Service Districts," *Urban County Congress* (Washington: National Association of County Officials, 1959), pp. 47–49.

would have a place on the agenda of the Board of County Supervisors, thus giving the area a formal, official voice in these important fields; (3) perform any county function which can better be performed at the community level, such as the control of neighborhood parks and recreation.

To illustrate informal unwritten agreements, one cannot do better than to cite the experience of Forsyth County and the City of Winston-Salem in North Carolina as recorded by a member of the county board. On the basis of nine years' experience as a board member, he listed in 1959 no less than fifteen different functions in which there were informal joint relationships in city-county governmental functions:

1. Joint City-County Tax Collecting Department—operated by the county, the city paying a proportionate share of the cost.

2. Joint City-County Planning Department—office in city hall, under the city budget. County pays approximately 48 per cent of the cost.

3. Joint Civil Defense Office—in the court house, cost shared equally.

4. Joint Bureau of Elections—office in the court house, with the city sharing the cost on city elections.

5. City Electrical Inspection Department—inspects on a county-wide basis, collecting all fees for the operation of the department.

6. Joint City-County Libraries—the county paying about 35 per cent of the cost of operation. Libraries are located inside the city.

7. City-County Court—with county-wide jurisdiction, operated by the city government. Cost of operation is defrayed from court costs collected.

8. Alcoholic Rehabilitation Program—county-wide, with the county paying 25 per cent of its cost; this is in proportion to the amount received from the profits of the A.B.C. Store operations. All stores are located within the city.

9. Fire Departments—The City and County Fire Departments have a mutual aid program, all fire calls being received over a county-wide radio network operated by the City Fire Department. The county pays a small fee on the cost, and the County Fire School Inspectors inspect all schools county-wide.

10. City and County Jail—each operated separately, but the county furnishes meals for city prisoners, the city paying a small meal charge.

11. Domestic Relations Court—operated by the county on a county-wide basis. Since the Court is new, just beginning operation, the city agreed to pay $25,000 a year for two years to help the county establish it.

12. Revaluation Program—county-wide and paid for by the county. During the first revaluation program several years ago, the city paid a part of the cost of the mapping program.

13. National Guard—both the city and the county contributing to a building maintenance fund.

14. Garbage Disposal—the county uses the city french-trench system, and pays a small service fee for this privilege.

15. Hospitals—At the present time, the city operates two hospitals, the county paying for the care of welfare patients under contract with the City Hospital Commission.[52]

Establishment, Extensions, Abandonments

A good many questions regarding interlocal cooperation present themselves. What prompts the inauguration of such cooperation? What, in other words, are the reasons for the original extension of services beyond the local boundaries? In most cases, there are probably two reasons: a desire in each cooperating community for some public service or facility too expensive for cooperators to supply individually, but within the powers of the cooperators through a pooling of their resources. The principle involved is the same as that employed by farmer neighbors who help each other out by "trading works," as it is called, or by jointly purchasing expensive farm machinery which no one of the cooperators could afford or fully utilize by himself.

Then, there is the question of legal authority. Since cooperation is commonly regarded as a virtue, there is normally little disposition to challenge efforts in this direction. The result is that in the past much cooperation took place without specific authorization, as one neighbor helps another, especially in emergency situations. Such authorizations, once rare, are now quite common. There is little information available on the subject of abandonments, their number and their causes, although there are many possible reasons to explain why a collaborator, having started to cooperate, withdraws from such an arrangement. For instance, the situation may have changed so that the cooperative effort is no longer necessary, or friction may have developed between the cooperators over the assessment of the costs of the service or the manner in which it is being administered.

[52] Dunham, Wally G., "Informal City-County Agreements," *Urban County Congress*, pp. 50–51.

Accomplishments and Possibilities

From this brief sketch of the record, two things are obvious: much has been accomplished in a great many of the functional areas of local government, and in view of the extent of the need, much more can and should be done. Intergovernmental cooperation is equally useful in both urban and rural areas. Its usefulness in the former is well illustrated by a report on the first four years of metropolitan government in Dade County, which presents an interesting picture of both past accomplishments and future possibilities. Approximately a dozen areas of cooperation are listed.

Uniformity in Dade County has gained significantly in many fields. A uniform traffic code has been adopted and is being enforced throughout the county by municipal and county officers alike. Uniform standards for motor vehicle inspection have been established. Uniform subdivision regulations and a uniform building code have been adopted. All traffic engineering is now done by the county, the municipal traffic engineering department having been abolished. The countywide reassessment program is now nearing completion, leading to uniform assessment and collection of taxes throughout the county. Municipal budget years are being synchronized with the county fiscal year, preparatory to the county taking over all assessment and collection of taxes for both the county and the twenty-six municipalities.

A metropolitan county planning department has been established. Countywide water and sewer service has been brought a step closer, as has a unified bus system, countywide regulation of gun permits, animal control, dynamiting, and used car parts sales. Central police radio communication is on the way for eight cities, handled on a contract basis by Metro. Central accident records have been established.[53] A metropolitan court, trying all traffic cases in the county, has been created; municipal courts now try only misdemeanor cases arising from violations of municipal law, but transfer of the Miami Municipal Court to the county is being negotiated.

In rural areas, the needs are somewhat different, but no less real. The same multiplicity of governmental units exists in both. According to existing opinion, it is equally impossible to abolish unneeded units or to consolidate them. Just as the widespread use of interlocal agreements provides at least a partially satisfactory substitute for consolidation in Miami, Philadelphia, and other large metropolitan areas, it may be utilized to

[53] Government Research Council of the Miami-Dade County Chamber of Commerce, *Metropolitan Dade County—Its First Three Years, A Summary Report* (Miami, November, 1960); same, *Four Years* (Miami, November, 1961).

accomplish a similar result in rural areas. One observer has expressed the view that interlocal cooperation might be regarded as a prelude to and an erstwhile substitute for county consolidation in many largely rural States that are plagued by a number of counties greatly in excess of present needs.

BIBLIOGRAPHICAL NOTES

Although cooperation between local units is not new, the literature about it is scant, widely scattered, and fragmentary; one must rely to a large extent on reports of particular agencies. The following titles are grouped roughly under three headings: general interlocal cooperation, cooperation in metropolitan areas, and special districts and authorities.

General Interlocal Cooperation. There are several good studies of interlocal cooperation or compilations of laws relating to such cooperation in individual States: Guthrie S. Birkhead, Interlocal Cooperation in New York State (Albany: State Department of Audit and Control, 1958), prepared for the Governor's Committee on Home Rule; Norman N. Gill, Intergovernmental Cooperation (Milwaukee: Milwaukee Metropolitan Study Commission, October, 1960); George Goodwin, Intermunicipal Relations in Massachusetts (Amherst: Bureau of Government Research, University of Massachusetts, 1956); Edmund W. Meisenhelder, III, and Robert A. Lovelace, Laws for City-County Cooperation in Tennessee (Knoxville: Bureau of Public Administration, University of Tennessee, June, 1960); New York Legislature, Joint Legislative Committee on Metropolitan Areas Study, Municipal Cooperation: A Digest of the Law of New York Permitting Intergovernmental Service Arrangements Among Municipalities of the State (Albany, September, 1958); Sidney Wise, ed., Selected Areas of Intergovernmental Cooperation (Harrisburg: Bureau of Municipal Affairs, Department of Internal Affairs, August, 1957); and Paul N. Ylvisaker, Intergovernmental Relations at the Grass Roots (Minneapolis: University of Minnesota Press, 1956).

Howard H. Earle, A Study of Contract Services Provided by the Los Angeles County Sheriff's Department to Municipalities in Los Angeles County (Los Angeles: University of Southern California Bookstore, June, 1960) and Samuel K. Gove, The Lakewood Plan (Urbana: Institute of Government and Public Affairs, University of Illinois, May, 1961) deal with the special problem of contract services.

Cooperation in Metropolitan Areas. Much of the interlocal cooperation takes place in our metropolitan areas; leads to literature in this area may be found in Victor Jones et al., Metropolitan Communities: A Bibliography with Special Emphasis on Government and Politics (Chicago: Public Administration Service, 1956) and the Supplement thereto, covering 1955–1957, by Jones and Barbara Hudson (Chicago: Public Administration Service, 1960). For analysis of these problems in two of our largest cities, see an unpublished doctoral dissertation by J. J. Carrell, Inter-Jurisdictional Agreements as an Intergrating Device in Metropolitan Philadelphia (Philadelphia: University of Pennsylvania, 1953) and Luther H. Gulick, Toward Metropolitan Action in the Tri-State Metropolitan Region (New York: Regional Plan Association, 1959).

Special Districts and Authorities. Stanley Scott and John C. Bollens have done extensive work on these units, both in California and in the United States; see their *Special Districts in California Local Government* (Berkeley: Bureau of Public Administration, University of California, 1949), and Bollens, *Special District Governments in the United States* (Berkeley, University of California Press, 1957). Tina V. Weintraub and James D. Patterson, in *The "Authority" in Pennsylvania: Pro and Con* (Philadelphia: Bureau of Municipal Research, 1949), give an excellent analysis of the strengths and weaknesses of this type of organization. Jerry C. Bosworth, *How the Huron-Clinton Metropolitan Authority Responds to Its Public* (Ann Arbor: Institute of Public Administration, University of Michigan, 1961) gives a clear picture of how one successful authority operates.

Boundary Changes. In the last few years, several titles have appeared on annexation. Stanley Scott is author of one, *Annexation? Incorporation? A Guide for Community Action*, rev. ed. (Berkeley: Bureau of Public Administration, University of California, March, 1954) and editor of another, *Local Government Boundaries and Areas: New Policies for California* (Sacramento: Governor's Commission on Metropolitan Area Problems, 1960). See also Frank S. Sengstock, *Annexation: A Solution to the Metropolitan Problem* (Ann Arbor: University of Michigan Law School, 1960). Two titles on consolidation deal with the two major metropolitan areas in California: John A. Rush, *The City-County Consolidated* (Los Angeles, 1941) and Herbert A. Simon, *Fiscal Aspects of Metropolitan Consolidation* (Berkeley: Bureau of Public Administration, University of California, 1943).

PART VI

ADJUSTMENT AND CHANGE IN
A FEDERAL SYSTEM

Attention is given here to the never-ending problem of adjusting the machinery and procedures of federalism to the needs of an expanding and rapidly changing society. Although there are always dissatisfied or dissident groups and rumblings of discontent, it seems appropriate to inquire who the dissidents have been, why they were unhappy, and what remedies they proposed. In other chapters, emphasis is placed upon the evolution of cooperative federalism and on the way in which, by direct relationships with the political subdivisions of the States, with corporations, and with individuals, the Federal government has repeatedly by-passed the States.

As this study has developed, it has become very clear that Americans have had neither guide lines nor a national policy on intergovernmental relations, nor have they until very recently made any serious effort to develop such a policy. The tendency has always been to hope that with the aid of a kind and generous Providence the nation might somehow manage to survive. On the whole, the nation has fared far better under such a practice than one would expect. In the last few years, however, there has been some evidence of recognition of the unsatisfactory character of the practices prevailing in the past and of a groping toward a more orderly procedure. These suggested changes are discussed in Chapter XXV.

Finally, the concluding chapter presents a program designed to make American federalism work more smoothly and efficiently in the years ahead. The suggested proposals are both possible and practical. As one good friend of the author expressed it, "After all the tribulations of the wilderness through which we have passed, the promised land stretches out before us." One may hope that with proper organization and tools for policy making and administration, it may one day be possible to identify problems in the field of intergovernmental relations and find suitable ways of dealing with them before they develop to the crisis stage, thus helping to make federalism work more efficiently and more effectively in the service of the nation.

CHAPTER XXII

Constant Rumblings of Discontent

Is the State the appropriate instrumentality for the discharge of these sovereign functions? The answer is not a matter of conjecture or delicate appraisal. It is a matter of brutal record. The American State is finished. I do not predict that the States will go, but affirm that they have gone.

And why have they gone? Because they were unable to deal even inefficiently with the imperative, the life and death tasks of the new national economy. . . . In none of these fields affecting economic life [supervision of banks, railroads in distress, regulation of power and the control of utilities, regulation of insurance companies and security sales, destructive business competition, or the development of security through social insurance] was it possible for any State to do anything decisive without driving business out of its jurisdiction into areas where there was no regulation and no control. The same kind of sectional self-interest made it impossible for any State to move forward with public improvement programs to offset industrial contraction. And finally, where have the States landed in the development of their tax systems? . . . The whole system of unfair duplicate taxation, with unnecessary jurisdictional conflicts and wasteful duplicate administration, is on the road to collapse.

The problems are mostly national in scope. It is extremely wasteful, and in most cases impossible, to solve them State by State. There are two reasons for this fundamental impossibility. First, a problem cannot be solved when only a small fragment of it is available, because of the sheer lack of knowledge and power. Second, the solution of a problem is impossible when it is split up among competing entities, thereby introducing conflicting considerations of self-interest. No State can afford to go far in labor regulation, in business stabilization, or in the use of credit or taxation as a social tool when it is part of an economic system including other States that do not take such steps.[1]

[1] Gulick, Luther H., "Reorganization of the State," *Civil Engineering*, August, 1933, pp. 420–422.

No system of government, no matter how good or how generally it may be accepted by the people, is going to please everybody. Some people are bound to be unhappy, and when the system—or significant portions of it—develops serious weaknesses, there is some justification for their displeasure. This chapter presents the story of these protests—who made them and why, and what the critics proposed to do by way of correcting the evils of which they complained.

PERIODIC INDICTMENTS OF THE GOVERNMENTAL SYSTEM

Periodic Indictments of the States

The Founding Fathers wanted a strong central government and did their best to establish one. Sentiment for the States was so strong, however, that acceptance of States as component parts of a federal system was the price they had to pay, if any effective central government was to be established. Contemporary writings, notably *The Federalist Papers,* clearly show that the Founders were apprehensive lest the States should become so strong that the new central government, like the government under the Articles of Confederation, would be reduced to impotence.[2]

The fears of the Founders were not without foundation. Some of the early amendments to the Constitution—notably the Eleventh—did tend to substantiate them. That these fears were not more fully justified in practice may be attributed largely to Chief Justice John Marshall, to his tremendous personal influence over his colleagues, and to his long tenure. Under other circumstances, all of their worst fears might have been substantiated. As conditions developed, however, there was no reason either to fear the States or seriously to question the state system. For

[2] For a contrary interpretation, see Crosskey, William W., *Politics and the Constitution in the History of the United States,* 2 vols. (Chicago: University of Chicago Press, 1953).

approximately a century, the States supplied reasonably well the modest governmental needs of a rural, agricultural society.

As the first 100 years drew to a close, two great national organizations were established in the social sciences—the Academy of Political Science at Columbia University in 1886 and the American Academy of Political and Social Science at the University of Pennsylvania in 1890. Each proceeded promptly to establish a professional journal—the *Political Science Quarterly* and the *Annals of the American Academy of Political and Social Science,* respectively. Both journals carried in Volume I, Number 1, a ringing indictment of the States and the whole state system.[3] The basis of the argument in both cases was much the same. There was neither rhyme nor reason to the establishment of the existing States, whose boundaries were illogical and often unreasonable, having been determined by the surveyor's line, by negotiation of conflicting claims, or by the arbitrary fiat of the courts without much regard to important geographical considerations or to any guiding principle. Many of the boundaries are so drawn as to divide economic entities, such as river valleys, that should obviously be united. No one will deny that if the task were undertaken at the present time, it would be handled quite differently. Modern methods of communication and transportation have made the existing arrangements seem highly unsatisfactory to many people.

Both writers regarded the States as an obstacle to effective local government; States are too small to serve well the need for administrative districts and too large and heterogeneous in composition to serve satisfactorily as local units. Both pointed out that the States often failed to deal adequately with many of the pressing responsibilities with which they were confronted. Their failure to render efficient service and to coordinate their activities with other governmental units has tended to accelerate the breakdown of State control, the drift toward Federal centralization, and the extension of the Federal subsidy system.

Interest in the States and in government generally was greatly stimulated in this country by the publication in 1887 of the first edition of James Bryce's *American Commonwealth.*[4] Although no serious efforts were made to put in practice the recommendations of these distinguished writers, the States did begin to make some progress in the early years of the present century. There arose in many of the States, particularly in the

[3] See Burgess, John W., "The American Commonwealth," *Political Science Quarterly,* March, 1886, pp. 9–35, and Patton, Simon N., "Decay of State and Local Government," *Annals of the American Academy of Political and Social Science,* July, 1890, pp. 26–42.

[4] (New York: The Macmillan Co., 1887; rev., 1919.) For an appraisal of the influence of this work, see Brooks, Robert C., ed., *Bryce's "American Commonwealth": Fiftieth Anniversary* (New York: The Macmillan Co., 1939); see especially Chapter 2 by Frances L. Reinhold (Fussell).

Middle West, a group of strong and effective leaders who were able to rally extensive popular support and who as Governors were able to arouse new interest in State government and to bring new vitality and efficiency to the conduct of its affairs. Notable among these men were Johnson of California, Folk of Missouri, Cummings of Iowa, La Follette of Wisconsin, Hanly of Indiana, Roosevelt and Hughes of New York, and Wilson of New Jersey.

The next decade brought not only World War I, but also some significant developments in State government. The era of the Muckrakers is ordinarily associated with the cities, but the members of this determined group did not overlook the States. As early as 1903, the Folk exposures in Missouri had shaken the State. Lincoln Steffens did a series of articles on Illinois, Missouri, and Wisconsin in 1904, and others on New Jersey, Ohio, and Rhode Island appeared the following year. Beginning in 1910, a number of articles appeared in the magazines on corruption in Colorado, Delaware, Montana, New York, Pennsylvania, and other States.[5] Each of these States had a businessman-turned-politician boss. All appeared to be completely lacking in moral and ethical standards, and in even the slightest concern for the public welfare. These exposés gave added impetus to the reform movement and strengthened the position of the progressive and public spirited Governors.

A second development was the movement for administrative reorganization, a movement which appears to have begun in Oregon in 1909 with a proposal of the People's Power League to concentrate "executive power in the hands of the Governors—checked only by an independent auditor, and to establish vital connections between the Governor and the legislature." Charles E. Hughes, in his inaugural address as Governor of New York in 1910 and later in an address at Yale University, likewise urged a concentration of responsibility with few offices and short ballots. The movement gained further impetus by the report of President Taft's Economy and Efficiency Commission in 1912. Then, in 1917, the first administrative code, designed to strengthen the position of the Governor and to bring some semblance of order into the administrative structure, was enacted in Illinois under the leadership of Governor Frank O. Lowden and began a movement that was to hold an important position in the State field for the next two decades.

The period of two World Wars and the Great Depression subjected the States to many new burdens and responsibilities, few of which they were able to discharge adequately. Their most conspicuous failures during the last half century occurred during the Great Depression, when they were subjected to a new series of indictments and attacks, many of them

---

[5] Regier, Cornelius C., *The Era of the Muckrakers* (Chapel Hill: University of North Carolina Press, 1932), Chapter 7.

at the hands of distinguished political scientists. These attacks were often vigorous and sometimes intemperate, like the one at the opening of this chapter. Like the famous report of the death of Mark Twain, this announcement of the demise of the States was somewhat premature. Not only do the States still exist in a reasonably live and vigorous condition a quarter of a century later, but they are likely to exist long after both the author and the readers of these pages have passed to their reward.

After the Depression, some writers continued to insist that even if the States were not gone, they should be. As late as 1939, Harold J. Laski wrote that:

> federalism is insufficiently positive in character; it does not provide for sufficient rapidity of action; it inhibits the emergence of necessary standards of uniformity; it relies upon compacts and compromises which take insufficient account of the urgent category of time; it leaves the backward areas in restraint, at once parasitic and poisonous, on those which seek to move forward.[6]

One gathers the impression that Mr. Laski was criticizing in the 1930's the federalism of the 1920's which was then unquestionably obsolete and unworkable. To these criticisms, one is justified in answering that under the federal system as it now operates, there is sufficient constitutional power to deal with virtually any problem of national proportions, provided that there is the will to use it.

Of special significance here is a recent discussion of the role of the States by Professor Coleman Woodbury in which he summarizes what the States have done in the present century and, after a consideration of their disabilities, discusses what lies ahead for the States and what the States themselves must do.[7] In his analysis of disabilities, Professor Woodbury mentions six specific items. He points out that, in the first place, the States are non-economic areas. Although this is a familiar objection, it is true that very few of the States correspond "even approximately to a natural unit or region for a significant proportion of their economic enterprises." Secondly, they are in a position of relative fiscal weakness, although many fiscal weaknesses—such as antiquated tax laws, tax rate and debt limitations, designated revenues, and segregated funds—are self-imposed. The unbalanced representation of which he complains may, since the *Baker* v. *Carr* decision (see pp. 154–156), be on the way to substantial improvement.

[6] Laski, Harold J., "The Obsolescence of Federalism," *New Republic*, May 3, 1939, pp. 367–369.

[7] Woodbury, Coleman, *The Role of the States* (New York: National Municipal League, first draft prepared in 1957, to be published in 1963).

Observing that "most State governments show little foresight or vigor of approach," Professor Woodbury concludes that there is a basic weakness in policy formulation. Too often the States "seem officially blind to the clear handwriting on the wall, hide behind differences of opinion expressed by non-official groups, and then, when the accumulated problems are on them in full force, come up with half-hearted measures that are too little, too late, and too short-sighted." The lack of responsible political parties he sees as a serious handicap to effective State government, and finally, he believes that the States have a poor sense of community, which is defined "to mean a common feeling of identification with and shared responsibility for many aspects of the public life and welfare of all those who live within a particular place or area." All six of these weaknesses are serious, and to the extent that they are valid criticisms, impose serious limitations upon the States as units of government.

Indictment of the Cities

In the closing decades of the nineteenth century, standards of integrity in American politics fell to an all-time low. After the Civil War, corruption was rampant in the Executive Branch of the national government, while in Congress, the Radical Republicans held sway. Conditions in many States were comparably bad, and scandal and mismanagement were so common and so widespread in the cities that they came to be accepted as normal conditions. However, the abuses characteristic of the time were felt most acutely at the local level.

The cities and the people who live in them have always been the target of suspicion and distrust on the part of the ruralites, who have never hesitated to heap criticism and abuse upon them. In American cities of the late nineteenth century, there were plenty of abuses to criticize, many of them the product of significant changes in the economic and social life of the nation. The Industrial Revolution had attracted large numbers of both rural folk and immigrants into urban areas that were ill-equipped to absorb them or to provide the services essential to a decent standard of living in an urban environment. As part of this era of change, there developed a new class of fortune hunters—public utility magnates, loan sharks, avaricious landlords, vice kings, and so on. The city government (or the political organization which controlled the city government) became involved in many of these enterprises to such an extent that the city government and the businessman came to be indispensable to each other.

Collusion between businessmen and local officials developed in many areas, particularly in the granting of charters for the establishment of transit facilities, in procurement, and in the letting of contracts for municipal public works. Meanwhile, an apathetic public and an equally apathetic Supreme Court [8] contributed to the deification of business and businessmen by according them a preferred position in society. The development of these conditions made inevitable a barrage of criticism against the cities, the most vigorous of which was published in the period between 1870 and 1914. This criticism emanated from a number of different sources: impartial observers, like Bryce; the civil service reformers who saw in the boss-ridden cities the stronghold of the patronage system that they so thoroughly despised; leading citizens, like those who in 1894 banded together to organize the National Municipal League; and the Muckrakers who early in the twentieth century exploited every shortcoming of the cities in sensational exposures, just as later on the tabloids exploited every human weakness and frailty.

The chief points of criticism centered around the incompetence of local officials, the futility of federalism at the local level, and the constant intervention of the State into the decision-making processes related to matters that were purely local in character. James Bryce, one of the most eminent and certainly one of the most tolerant and understanding commentators on American institutions, pointed out that the attempt to adapt the federal form of organization to the purposes of local government could result only in such fragmentation of power and authority as to make it difficult to assign responsibility for the actions of public officials.[9] In discussing legislative intervention in local affairs, he argued that the legislature had neither the time nor the expertise necessary for the proper handling of the governmental problems of urban areas.

Even if there were good elected officials, State interference tended to make good local government difficult, if not impossible. It encouraged rivalry between city and State officials, State approval of franchises that had been rejected by the city authorities, and most frequently of all, the refusal of State legislatures to permit cities to raise revenues commensurate with their needs.[10] Summarizing the whole disheartening system in his oft-quoted statement, Bryce contended that "There is no denying that the government of cities is the one conspicuous failure of the United States." He continued:

[8] See, for example, Paul, Arnold M., *Conservative Crisis and the Rule of Law: Attitudes of Bar and Bench, 1887–1895* (Ithaca: Cornell University Press, 1960).

[9] Bryce, James, *American Commonwealth*, 2 vols. (London and New York: The Macmillan Co., 1888); see especially, I, 593–619.

[10] For discussion, see Griffith, Ernest S., *Modern Development of City Government*, 2 vols. (New York: Oxford University Press, 1927), I, 131.

The deficiencies of the National government tell but little for good or evil on the welfare of the people. The faults of the State governments are insignificant compared with the extravagance, corruption, and mismanagement which mark the administrations of most of the great cities. For these evils are not confined to one or two cities. The commonest mistake of Europeans who talk about America is to assume that the political vices of New York are found everywhere. The next most common is to assume that they are found nowhere else. In New York they have revealed themselves on the largest scale. They are "gross as a mountain, monstrous, palpable." But there is not a city with a population exceeding 200,000 where the poison germs have not sprung into a vigorous life; and in some of the smaller ones, down to 70,000, it needs a microscope to note the results of their growth. Even in cities of the third rank, similar phenomena may occasionally be discerned, though there, as some one has said, the jet black of New York or San Francisco dies away into a harmless gray.[11]

The last decade of the nineteenth century and the first decade of the twentieth was a period characterized by vigorous denunciation of machine politics and bossism, a period during which the man who could condemn the boss with the loudest voice and in the most vehement language was accounted the most patriotic citizen. Along with oratorical fireworks, there was also a surge of sentiment for reform which expressed itself in various ways. The civil service reformers, most of whom were city dwellers, tended to belabor not the cities themselves so much as their political bosses, whom they regarded as responsible for the iniquitous patronage system.[12] Another aspect of the reform movement involved the group of outstanding citizens who organized the National Municipal League. Locally, the movement for reform expressed itself by the election of reform administrations in a number of the larger cities.

More than a decade after the incorporation of the League, the Muckrakers came upon the scene, renewing the indictment of the cities during the first decade of the twentieth century. Lincoln Steffens in his famous book, *The Shame of the Cities,* examined conditions in some of our leading cities and concluded that anything could be accomplished by a determined individual or business having the money to bribe the "city fathers." In addition to Steffens, the Muckraker group included many famous names: Samuel Hopkins Adams, Ray Stannard Baker, William Hard, Will Irwin, Alfred Henry Lewis, S. S. McClure, Frank A. Munsey, David Graham Phillips, Charles Edward Russell, Upton Sinclair, Mark Sullivan,

---

[11] Bryce, I, 608.
[12] See, for example, Fish, Carl R., *The Civil Service and the Patronage* (New York: Longmans, Green, 1905) and Foulke, William D., *Fighting the Spoilsmen* (New York: G. P. Putnam's Sons, 1919).

Ida M. Tarbell, William English Walling, and William Allen White.[13]

Steffens pointed out that in 1902 a street railway company spent approximately $144,000 in bribing the city council in St. Louis to obtain passage of an ordinance favorable to their interests. Minneapolis represented, in Steffens' view, a different facet of municipal corruption; there, vice was the major revenue producer for the city officials, police protection being granted to any illicit operation which contributed to the support of the Mayor and his organization. In other cities, local governments were prone to blend the operations of business and vice in order to obtain revenue from both sources.[14]

The municipal boss was able to capitalize on the heterogeneous nature of the city's population, the various elements of which were utilized in building an organization that could perpetuate itself and insulate itself from the possibility of criminal prosecution. Immigrants, normally shunned by the established order in these cities, attached themselves to a spokesman-member of the organization for the protection of their interests. The absorption of rural workers presented a more difficult problem. For them, urban life was radically different from that to which they had been accustomed in the relative tranquility of their former environment. It was this situation which led Steffens to his conclusion that leadership was of prime importance: "Whenever anything extraordinary is done in American municipal politics, whether for good or for evil, you can trace it almost invariably to one man. The people cannot do it." [15] Steffens' contention may have had much merit, for during this period the people were for the most part illiterate, badly housed, and poorly paid. Conditions were not conducive to that reflection and contemplation which are so essential to orderly democratic procedures.

In order for the machine to win votes, it was necessary to raise sufficient funds and to insure continuing majorities. Funds were obtained from various sources—business, vice-lords, and assessments made on employees working for the city. Vote fraud was common and in many instances had its humorous aspects. Dogs, children, and fictitious people were voted with regularity. One Philadelphia paper printed a picture of

[13] On this group, see Regier, and for a symposium in which some thirty of the more important articles are reprinted, see Weinberg, Arthur and Lila, eds., *The Muckrakers* (New York: Simon & Schuster, Inc., 1961). See also Savados, Harvey, ed., *Years of Conscience: The Muckrakers, an Anthology of Reform Journalism* (Cleveland: World Publishing Company, 1962) and Ross, Edward A., *Sin and Society* (Boston: Houghton Mifflin Co., 1907).

[14] Steffens, Lincoln, *The Shame of the Cities* (New York: Peter Smith, Publisher, 1948), pp. 69–97, 118.

[15] Steffens, p. 63. See also Cooke, Morris L., *Our Cities Awake* (Garden City: Doubleday, Page, 1918) and Hofstader, Richard, *The Age of Reform: From Bryan to F. D. R.* (New York: Alfred A. Knopf, Inc., 1955).

a dog who was regularly exercising his right to vote. One ward leader, speaking in the ward in which Independence Hall is located, commented on the fact that the signers of the Declaration of Independence had voted and were in fact still voting in his ward.[16] Commenting on the situation in the same city a quarter of a century later, at the conclusion of a Senate committee investigation of the famous Vare-Pepper-Pinchot primary of 1926, Senator James A. Reed of Missouri observed that getting one's name on the registration list in Philadelphia was one sure way of inheriting eternal life.

That the reformers deeply resented these very real abuses is understandable, but the intensity of their aversion to all things political soon began to have—and has to this day—adverse effects upon the political life of the community which they did not foresee. Had they suspected some of the results of their work, they would probably have been among the first to deplore them. Their hostility to parties and party leaders gave strong support to those who were later to plead, "I didn't raise my boy to be a politician." Their attitude encouraged "nice people" to avoid politics as one would the plague. Their attitude lent support to the idea of nonpartisan elections, as if partisanship was an evil always to be shunned. The Muckraker movement, based largely on assumptions that were basically unsound, led to innumerable conflicts between State and local political regimes, to the detriment of both. Many of the governmental gadgets they advocated, instituted in a bygone era, are now frustrating to the concept of cooperative federalism under which three levels must share the burdens of government, and they should be abandoned.

After World War I and continuing through the 1920's, a group of young political scientists, cognizant of these factors, undertook the study of political bossism from a new approach. They reasoned that since bossism as an institution had been denounced for years but the bosses had neither been dislodged nor their power seriously weakened, it might be wise to try to understand the system, to study its natural history, the reasons for its existence, the methods of its operation, and the sources of its power, and thus to gain insight on problems which the Muckrakers had only clouded over with invective. Only with such knowledge and understanding could rational judgments be made. Often criticized at the time for being too friendly with the bosses and condoning their practices, the members of this group contributed much to an understanding of machine organization and procedures.[17]

---

[16] Steffens, pp. 199–200.

[17] Among those who were prominently connected with this group and who published studies dealing with some aspect of the problem, were: Charles E. Merriam and Harold F. Gosnell of the University of Chicago;

Meantime, a new type of leadership was emerging, as educated business and professional men replaced the old-style boss, long caricatured in the public prints and on the stage and screen. Still later, the social legislation of the Roosevelt era modified the role of the political leader, greatly diminishing his power over the voters by making them less dependent upon him and the services which had been the basis of his power. Nevertheless, in spite of these changes and of tremendous improvement in the quality of municipal administration, political bosses still flourished in many cities, even as late as the 1950's. The cities still have their critics, and some writers still profess to see much the same conditions existing in them now as formerly. Robert S. Allen, for instance, in a collection of case studies in selected cities highlights some of the same abuses of power by local officials, abuses which range from the privileged position of business to a type of bossism similar to that in the careers of James M. Curley of Boston and Frank Hague of Jersey City.[18]

Finally, in the 1950's, one observes a period of gradual change during which politics has become if not a preferred profession, at least respected. The result is that a considerable number of capable young people are working in the political parties of their choice, offering themselves as candidates for public office, and in other ways assuming an active role in government and politics. These activities are being encouraged by the work of the National Center for Education in Politics (formerly the Citizenship Clearing House), by a host of internship programs in government and politics, and in other ways. Citizen participation, if it continues, is the best possible assurance against a recurrence of past abuses.

Indictment of Rural Local Government

After World War I, it was the counties and townships whose short-comings were widely exposed and publicized. The attack upon the counties began with a study in which they were referred to as "the dark continent of American politics," [19] and the attack has been continued intermittently ever since. Howard P. Jones pointed out in a very dramatic

---

William B. Munro, E. Pendleton Herring, and Harold Zink of Harvard University; David H. Kurtzman and John T. Salter of the University of Pennsylvania; Peter H. Odegard of Columbia University; Dayton D. McKean of Princeton University; and Roy V. Peel of New York University.

[18] Allen, Robert S., ed., *Our Fair City* (New York: Vanguard Press, Inc., 1947).

[19] Gilbertson, Henry S., *The County: The Dark Continent of American Politics* (New York: National Short Ballot Association, 1917).

way that county government had remained virtually unchanged for at least 200 years. Richard S. Childs described the organization of local government as "a local jungle." Later, Edward S. Weidner characterized the average county as a "patchwork of boards." [20] An examination of published works relating to the subject indicates that counties had few supporters among students of government, but that this appears not to have harmed the counties at all. Except in Connecticut, all of the more than 3,000 American counties still exist.

Attacks upon the smaller units of rural government—towns, townships, villages, boroughs, and districts—have also been vigorous and persistent. It is interesting to observe what some political scientists have written about these units during the past few decades: Professor Kirk H. Porter, State University of Iowa:

> On the whole the township has ceased to be a necessary instrument of government. It serves no important purpose that cannot be more conveniently and effectively served through other agencies. . . . Within a few decades it will be nothing but an empty shell, with very little of importance left to do.[21]

Professor John A. Fairlie, University of Illinois:

> As now functioning, the township is no longer a satisfactory unit of local government.[22]

Professor James T. Young, University of Pennsylvania:

> It is the unanimous verdict of those who have studied the township that it should be abolished. The township, like the horse-drawn carriage, has had its day.[23]

The result of this concerted attack upon the townships has been the same as in the case of the counties. Many political scientists believe that

[20] *The American County: Patchwork of Boards* (New York: National Munipical League, 1946).

[21] Porter, Kirk H., *County and Township Government in the United States* (New York: The Macmillan Co., 1922), pp. 317–318.

[22] Fairlie, John A., "Revamping Local Areas," in *Proceedings of the Virginia Institute of Public Affairs, 1932* (Charlottesville, 1932).

[23] Young, James T., *The New American Government and Its Work,* 3rd ed. (New York: The Macmillan Co., 1933). Within a period of five years in the 1950's, the *National Municipal Review* ran three articles on the decline of the township: Spencer, Richard C., "Iowa Townships Still Here?" September, 1952, pp. 397–399; Wager, Paul W., "Townships on Way Out," October, 1957, pp. 456–460, 475; and Drury, James W., "Townships Lose Ground," January, 1955, pp. 10–13. Drury points out that the duties of the 1,500 townships in Kansas are steadily being reduced.

the townships have outlived their usefulness, but they also still exist. The fact that more than half of the States have never had township government and get along very well without it is proof enough that townships are not indispensable.

There is, nevertheless, a well established need for a general overhauling of the machinery of local government, "*first* to reduce the waste to which uncoordinated action inevitably leads; *second* to add flexibility to the multilevel structure of government; and *third* to equip local units to serve more effectively in the multiple role they must play as instruments of local self-government and as administrative agencies of Nation and State." [24]

Responses at the Local Level

As early as 1871, the quest for good government had one of its beginnings in the organization of local citizen groups. Later, as reform administrations were tried and often found to be inadequate, attention was directed to municipal research as a possible means of ameliorating the problems of city government. The first citizen groups were organized in New York and Philadelphia in 1871—the Council of Political Reform in the former, the Citizens' Municipal Reform Association in the latter. Three years later, the Citizens' Association was established in Chicago. Gaining strength as the century moved to a close, the reform movement led to the creation of the National Civil Service Reform League, the National Municipal League, and numerous local civic groups in all parts of the country. At the National Conference on Good City Government in 1896, it was reported that 245 organizations of this type were functioning.

The National Municipal League is a non-partisan, non-profit corporation which was founded in Philadelphia in 1894. Its founders included many outstanding men of the time, notably Theodore Roosevelt, Charles Evans Hughes, and Carl Schurz.[25] It was essentially an organization of protest, an outgrowth of the widespread dissatisfaction resulting from

[24] Ylvisaker, Paul N., *Intergovernmental Relations at the Grass Roots: A Study of Blue Earth County, Minnesota, to 1946* (Minneapolis: University of Minnesota Press, 1956).

[25] Others: Charles Francis Adams, Charles J. Bonaparte (President, 1903–1910), Louis D. Brandeis, Henry Bruere, James C. Carter (President, 1894–1903), Richard S. Childs, R. Fulton Cutting, Richard H. Dana, Charles W. Eliot, Richard T. Ely, William Dudley Foulke (President, 1910–1915), Clinton Rogers Woodruff, who served for a quarter of a century as executive secretary. Mr. Hughes was President from 1919–1921. Other presidents have been Lawson Purdy, Frank L. Polk, Murray Seasongood, Harold W. Dodds, Charles Edison, George H. Gallup, William Collins, and, currently, Alfred E. Driscoll.

the inefficiency and graft which at the time characterized American municipal government. Its major purpose was to improve municipal organization and administration. After a quarter of a century of experience in this field, the League has since 1920 extended the range of its interest and activity to include county and State government as well. In its more than sixty years of effort, the League has had a long and distinguished list of leaders. Today, it is the oldest and the only national citizen organization concerning itself with the competence and efficiency of State and local government.

Over the years, the League's program has expanded and the influence and effectiveness of its work has increased.[26] Organized for the purpose of "doing something" toward the redemption of municipal government, the League has actively sponsored the city manager plan, the short ballot, and other measures. It has advocated the reconstruction of county government and the substitution of a county medical examiner for the office of coroner. It has sponsored the *Model State Constitution* (now in its Sixth Edition), advocated constitutional revision and modernization, unicameralism, a better executive structure, improved methods in the selection of judges and in the administration of justice. It has, throughout, taken a special interest in the field of intergovernmental relations.

In the early stages of the movement, reform groups frequently sought to improve city government by "turning the rascals out" and electing to office men who were competent and honest, while at the same time they were groping for new forms of organization for municipal government. Illustrative of the reform administrations were those of Carter H. Harrison in Chicago, Seth Low, and some years later, John Purroy Mitchell as Mayor of New York, and Rudolph Blankenburg as Mayor of Philadelphia. Many of the attempts at reform were short-lived, accomplishing little of permanent value, and when it was found that they were unable to accomplish their objectives, civic enthusiasm waned, and the old forces were swept back into power.

As a consequence of the difficulties encountered in achieving lasting progress through the use of the ballot, there was a tendency to look for other possible means of solving the problem. The groping for new forms of municipal organization included experimentation with the commission form in Galveston and Des Moines, and later in other cities; the attempt to develop a strong mayor type of organization; and somewhat later, to promote the adoption of city manager or council-manager government. Plans were developed also for the creation of premanent, nonpartisan research agencies, privately financed and professionally staffed. The establishment of the New York Bureau of Municipal Research in 1904 and

[26] See Stewart, Frank M., *A Half Century of Municipal Reform: The History of the National Municipal League* (Berkeley: University of California Press, 1950).

the Philadelphia Bureau in 1906 represented the first attempts to direct research techniques toward the realization of efficiency and economy in public business. Municipal research bureaus patterned after the early ones soon spread into many cities throughout the country.[27]

The cities also developed effective organizations of their own, both National and State. Notable among the former are the American Municipal Association, the United States Conference of Mayors, and the International City Managers Association, as well as a host of others in finance and in particular functional fields. Most of these organizations are members of the "1313 Group," dedicated to elevating the standards and improving the quality of municipal administration. Significant also are the State leagues of municipalities, the organization of which began in 1898–1900 when six were established. Eleven more were formally organized between 1910 and 1915, twelve between 1934 and 1941, six since 1948. In 1962, forty-five were actively functioning, the States not having such organizations being Connecticut, Delaware, Hawaii, Rhode Island and Vermont. The National Association of Counties seeks to accomplish a similar objective. Initiated in the early 1930's through the efforts of George F. Breitbach who served as Treasurer of Milwaukee County for a quarter of a century, the association had a difficult time existing in its early years. Since World War II, it has expanded its program under new leadership and is fast becoming an effective instrument for the improvement of county government. As in the case of the cities, there are many State associations of counties and county officials.

MOVEMENTS AND PROPOSALS FOR REFORM

At the turn of the century, there were clearly evident signs of some of the changes in American federalism that have taken place during recent decades. Of course, these signs were not widely observed, and few of those who did note them had any clear comprehension of their meaning and significance. Elihu Root was one who did.

Elihu Root's Famous Speech

In an address delivered December 12, 1906, at a dinner of the Pennsylvania Society of New York, Mr. Root made some remarks show-

[27] Gill, Norman N., *Municipal Research Bureaus: A Study of the Nation's Leading Citizen-Supported Agencies* (Washington: American Council on Public Affairs, 1944).

ing great insight into the current trends in Federal-State relations. He attributed the principle cause of these trends to three factors: (1) the impressive growth of a national sentiment, which was at first almost imperceptible; (2) the common interests which tied together the people in once separate communities, through the working of free trade among the States; (3) the tremendous development of facilities for travel and communication made possible by the inventions and discoveries of the past century. Following are some of the more significant portions of Root's address:

> We are surging forward in a development of business and social life which tends more and more to the obliteration of State lines and the decrease of State power as compared with National Power; the relations of the business over which the Federal Government is assuming control, of interstate transportation with State transportation, of interstate commerce with State commerce, are so intimate and the separation of the two is so impracticable, that the tendency is plainly toward the practical control of the National Government over both. New projects of National control are mooted; control of insurance, uniform divorce laws, child labor laws, and many others affecting matters formerly entirely within the cognizance of the State are proposed.
>
> With these changes and tendencies, in what way can the power of the States be preserved?
>
> I submit to your judgment, and I desire to press upon you with all the earnestness I possess, that there is but one way in which the States of the Union can maintain their power and authority under the conditions which are now before us, and that way is by an awakening on the part of the States to a realization of their own duties to the country at large. Under the conditions which now exist, no State can live unto itself alone and regulate its affairs with sole reference to its own treasury, its own convenience, its own special interests.
>
> Every State is bound to frame its legislation and its administration with reference not only to its own special affairs, but with reference to the effect upon all its sister States, as every individual is bound to regulate his conduct with some reference to its effect upon his neighbors. The more populous the community and the closer individuals are brought together the more imperative becomes the necessity which constrains and limits individual conduct. If any State is maintaining laws which afford opportunity and authority for practices condemned by the public sense of the whole country, or laws which, through the operation of our modern system of communications and business, are injurious to the interests of the whole country, that State is violating the conditions upon which alone can its power be preserved. If any State maintains laws which promote and foster the enormous overcapitalization of corporations condemned by the people of the country generally, if any State maintains laws designed to make easy the formation of

trusts and the creation of monopolies, if any State maintains laws which permit conditions of child labor revolting to the sense of mankind, if any State maintains laws of marriage and divorce so far inconsistent with the general standard of the nation as to violently derange the domestic relations, which the majority of the States desire to preserve, that State is promoting the tendency of the people of the country to seek relief through the National Government and to press forward the movement for National control and the extinction of local control.

The intervention of the National Government in many of the matters which it has recently undertaken would have been wholly unnecessary if the States themselves had been alive to their duty toward the general body of the country. It is useless for the advocates of State rights to inveigh against the supremacy of the constitutional laws of the United States or against the extension of National authority in the fields of necessary control where the States themselves fail in the performance of their duty. The instinct for self-government among the people of the United States is too strong to permit them long to respect any one's right to exercise a power which he fails to exercise. The governmental control which they deem just and necessary they will have.

It may be that such control would better be exercised in particular instances by the governments of the States, but the people will have the control they need either from the States or from the National Government; and if the States fail to furnish it in due measure, sooner or later constructions of the Constitution will be found to vest the power where it will be exercised—in the National Government. The true and only way to preserve State authority is to be found in the awakened conscience of the States, their broadened views and higher standard of responsibility to the general public; in effective legislation by the States, in conformity to the general moral sense of the country; and in the vigorous exercise for the general public good of that State authority which is to be preserved.[28]

The Progressives and the New Nationalism

The phrases, "The New Nationalism," used as the title of a book, and "The New Federalism," used in his writing in *The Outlook,* were employed by President Theodore Roosevelt to suggest his philosophy of a strong central government and strong States, so geared together that there would be no hazy areas or governmental no man's land. In an address delivered at Osawatomie, Kansas, August 31, 1910, Mr. Roosevelt said:

[28] *How to Preserve the Local Self-Government of the States: A Brief Study of National Tendencies.* Authorized and correct edition (New York: Brentano's, 1907).

National efficiency has to do, not only with natural resources and men, but it is equally concerned with institutions. The States must be made efficient for the work which concerns only the people of the States; and the nation for that which concerns all the people. There must remain no neutral ground to serve as a refuge for lawbreakers and especially for lawbreakers of great wealth, who can hire the vulpine legal cunning which will teach them how to avoid both jurisdictions. It is a misfortune when the national legislature fails to do its duty in providing a national remedy, so that the only national activity is the purely negative activity of the judiciary in forbidding the States to exercise power in the premises. I do not ask for overcentralization; but I do ask that we work in a spirit of broad and far-reaching nationalism when we work for what concerns our people as a whole.[29]

Herbert Croly, distinguished publicist, was another important member of the Progressive group. "American government," he wrote in his most significant book, "demands more rather than less centralization merely and precisely because of the growing centralization of American activity." [30] He offered an interesting alternative to some of the problems that are encountered today in intergovernmental relations. He felt that the government needed a program of constructive discrimination in which it would favor the weak against the strong in the interests of national efficiency. His plan would have entailed a major redistribution of economic functions. Since he believed that the States were largely artificial political units, he contended that they should be deprived of virtually all control over economic matters. Local utilities should be regulated by the towns and cities, while the rest of the economy should be regulated from Washington. Mr. Croly also advocated a complete overhauling of State governmental machinery, so that the central government would be in a supreme position:

The State governments, either individually or by any practicable methods of cooperation, are not competent to deal effectively in the national interest and spirit with the grave problems created by the aggrandizement of corporate and individual wealth and the increasing classification of the American people. They have, no doubt, an essential part to play in the attempted solution of these problems; and there are certain aspects of the whole situation which the American nation, because of its federal organization, can deal with much more effectively than can a rigidly centralized democracy like France. But the amount of responsibility in respect to fundamental national problems, which, in

[29] Roosevelt, Theodore, *The New Nationalism* (New York: Outlook Publishers, 1910), pp. 26–27.

[30] Croly, Herbert, *The Promise of American Life* (New York: The Macmillan Co., 1912), pp. 274–275.

law almost as much as in practice, is left to the States, exceeds the responsibility which the State governments are capable of efficiently redeeming. They are attempting (or neglecting) a task which they cannot be expected to perform with any efficiency.

The fact that the States fail properly to perform certain essential functions such as maintaining order or administering justice, is no sufficient reason for depriving them thereof. Functions which should be bestowed upon the central government are not those which the States happen to perform badly. They are those which the States, even with the best will in the world, cannot be expected to perform satisfactorily; and among these functions the regulation of commerce, the organization of labor, and the increasing control over property in the public interest are assuredly to be included. The best friends of local government in this country are those who seek to have its activity confined to the limits of possible efficiency, because only in case its activity is so confined can the States continue to remain an essential part of a really efficient and well coordinated national organization.

The Roosevelt and Croly brands of progressivism would both tend to strengthen the national government. Some States moved to counter this approach by adopting programs looking toward more democratic and efficient government at the State level. The two States that were most active in this regard, though in quite different ways, were Oregon and Wisconsin. Both were interested in popular control of government. Oregon approached the problem largely through mechanisms for electoral reform [31] and for improved structuring of the Executive Branch of government. Wisconsin tended to emphasize the importance of enabling the States to do efficiently and well what they are supposed to do as members of our federal system.[32]

It is not easy to define the Wisconsin Idea briefly. Fundamentally, it meant returning the control of government to the people. The latter part of the nineteenth century had seen the emergence of big business, the amassing of huge fortunes, and the worship of wealth. The exploiters of the nation's resources had no conscience and no sense of public responsibility. Doan states that the phrase, the "Wisconsin Idea," came to be used

---

[31] Examples are the Australian ballot, adopted in 1891; the first registration law, adopted in 1899; and the initiative and referendum, from 1902 to 1904. For this story, see Eaton, Allen H., *The Oregon System: The Story of Direct Legislation in Oregon* (Chicago: A. C. McClurg & Company, 1912).

[32] For discussions of Wisconsin federalism, see especially Governor La Follette's autobiography, *A Personal Narrative of Political Experiences* (Madison: published by the Governor, 1913); Doan, Edward N., *The La Follettes and the Wisconsin Idea* (New York: Rinehart and Company, 1947); and Howe, Frederic C., *Wisconsin: An Experiment in Democracy* (New York: Charles Scribner's Sons, 1912).

"to explain a new technique in public administration," a technique based upon such principles as these:

La Follette held that the railroads should be regulated by the State, and not be permitted to use the power of the State to accomplish their own often devious purposes. The public utility commissions should regulate the utilities, not the utilities control the commissions. The forests and other natural resources belong to the people, not to the corporation that could exploit them most quickly and most ruthlessly to its own advantage. The agricultural producer is entitled to protection from exploitation by rigged markets and dishonest middlemen, the consumer by fraud and misrepresentation, and the worker is entitled to an honest enforcement of labor laws enacted for his protection. The reactionaries who considered public controls anathema, viewed this as revolutionary doctrine. All manner of abuse was heaped upon La Follette as it invariably is upon a leader who seeks by word and deed to protect the public interest.

The pattern of rushing to Washington with every problem had yet to be established. Practically, therefore, the La Follette philosophy meant the strengthening of the State government, though not much appears to have been said or written on this specific point. The Wisconsin Progressives regarded the American State as "probably our most conspicuous political failure," although at the same time they regarded the State as important. If the States were corrupt, they reasoned, their corruption would be reflected in the cities and subsequently, through their influence on the legislative process and on the national government as well. Wisconsin, when the Progressives started working on it, was, according to Frederic C. Howe, "not unlike the other States." After an interval of twenty years, the Progressives had raised the State "from the low estate into which it had fallen" and had "converted it into a vital political agency."

> Twenty years ago Wisconsin was not unlike other States. Its legislature was discredited and corrupt. The biennial bartering of legislation, of place and privilege, the boss and machine were not dissimilar from conditions disclosed in other States. All this has passed away. In a few years' time Wisconsin has become the most efficient commonwealth in the Union. Of the honesty of the legislative and administrative departments there is no question. Executive offices are filled with trained men who are animated by enthusiasm for the public service.[33]

What was done in Wisconsin had a profound effect upon developments in the rest of the country, for Wisconsin proceeded to establish an impressive list of "firsts." Although the Wisconsin Legislative Refer-

[33] Howe, p. ix.

ence Library was not the first to be established, it served as the point from which this important legislative improvement spread to other States. Wisconsin passed the first workmen's compensation law; it lead in establishing a reasonable child labor law, in hours legislation, and in many other fields. Its specialists at the State university were brought into active participation in developing new policies and new programs. This interplay between the university and the State Capitol was, in a sense, the heart of the Wisconsin Idea, antedating by a generation the "brain trust" of the early Roosevelt era. The accomplishments in Wisconsin added strength to the efforts of progressive leaders in other jurisdictions to modernize their governments. Repeatedly these leaders visited Wisconsin and borrowed personnel to help them in the solution of their own problems.

Depression Inspired Proposals for Change

No people can live through experiences so severe and nerve-wracking as those which occurred in the period of the Great Depression without having many questions raised regarding the adequacy of the institutional arrangements under which such a catastrophe could occur. There are certain to be at such times many different diagnoses of the causes and many different prescriptions as to the remedy. Neither the diagnoses nor the prescriptions may be the correct ones, but when a patient is in a critical condition, he is apt to be willing—if he is able to think at all—to consider any remedy that may be proposed.

The events leading up to the Great Depression made it unmistakably clear that the States were in a pitifully weak condition. They simply had not been doing their job. In one single metropolitan area, for instance, forty State banks were forced to close as against only two that were members of the Federal Reserve System, and even with respect to these there were extenuating circumstances. After President Roosevelt declared the bank holiday, which included all Federal and State banks, it was clear that the States were not only weak, they were so weak that they did not even have to be considered.

At this point, where their power and prestige had dropped to what was undoubtedly the lowest point in history, two important types of depression-inspired proposals for change were advanced: thoroughly to revise the Federal Constitution; and to supplant the States, in whole or in part, by a new system of subnational regionalism. In some instances, the two proposals were bound together. Either of them or the two of them together, had they been adopted, would have so undermined the States that their later revival would have been virtually impossible.

Constitutional Revision. Between 1935 and 1943, four separate treatises were published, each calling for a thorough revision of the Federal Constitution and a re-evaluation of the existing federal system.[34] The first of these was written by Professor William Y. Elliott of Harvard University to call public attention to some of the glaring defects resulting from continued reliance upon the 1787 Constitution. At this time, the institutions of representative government were under attack in Europe both from the right and from the left. Elliott and many other thoughtful people were concerned that the same thing should not happen here. He attacked the growing concentration of power in the hands of the central government as one factor contributing to a situation in which a "takeover" might be possible.

The answer to this dilemma, he believed, was to be found in a realignment of powers and functions at all levels of government. Only in this way would the people respect the instrumentalities of government at levels lower than the national. He was concerned that unless our administrative machinery was updated, America could go the way of the older countries that had collapsed from sheer inability to govern democratically—or even to govern at all.[35] He saw in regionalism an instrument for achieving administrative efficiency at what had been and still is the State level.

Elliott proposed to abolish the States and consolidate them into regions roughly comparable in population and pertaining, insofar as possible, to the economic and cultural backgrounds of particular areas. This would, he pointed out, put an end to such foolishness as Nevada having two Senators and an elaborate State government for only 90,000 people.[36] Regionalism, he argued, "would revive our drooping federalism and stay the present march of centralization in Washington." [37] These regions would be similar to the Canadian Provinces, with sole powers in local functions but with one set of laws for the whole country. Representation in Congress, at the national level, would be accorded equally to each "province."

Hazlitt contributed much less to the subject. He advocated a cabinet form of government and an increased use of referendum procedures as a means of developing more responsible government. Heymeyer was also interested in regionalism and was more concerned with intergovernmental relations generally. He took the position that each government,

---

[34] Elliott, William Y., *The Need for Constitutional Reform* (New York: McGraw-Hill Book Co., Inc., 1935); Hazlitt, Henry, *A New Constitution Now* (New York: McGraw-Hill Book Co., Inc., 1942); Heymeyer, Alexander, *Time for Change* (New York: Farrar & Rinehart, 1943); and Wallace, William K., *Our Obsolete Constitution* (New York: John Day Co., 1932).

[35] Elliott, pp. 207–208.   [36] Elliott, p. 203.   [37] Elliott, p. 193.

Federal and State, should have exclusive jurisdiction over taxation—the Federal Government over the income tax, the State governments over the general property tax—in order to avoid tax duplication. This, he felt, must be ended, and he proposed that the Supreme Court be given jurisdiction to rule in cases in which a State attempts to tax outside its boundaries. Territorial allocation of tax revenues would go far toward ending interstate squabbles in this field.

Heymeyer, like Elliott, saw the desirability of regions, but felt that the establishment of regions would be difficult to accomplish. His proposal did not go as far as Elliott's, for he wanted the States to continue to function in those areas best suited to State action and the larger regional units to deal only with problems exceeding the capacities of individual States. Under his plan, these regional authorities would have the right "to borrow money, receive grants, own property and issue appropriate rules and regulations." [38]

Subnational Regionalism. Proposals of regionalism were by no means restricted to the advocates of constitutional revision. The elaborate study of regionalism made by the National Resources Planning Board doubtless inspired many of the proposals that were made to wipe out the waste and confusion emanating from the existence of so many State governments. In addition to Luther Gulick, whose views have been cited, the supporters of regionalism included many respected members of the political science profession, first and foremost, Charles E. Merriam of the University of Chicago, who urged the establishment of city-states; James T. Young of the University of Pennsylvania; and Roy V. Peel, then of Indiana University. William K. Wallace proposed nine regional States in place of the forty-eight then existing. Proposals for regionalism by Representative E. J. Jones and others also found their way into Congress.

Centralization Accentuated in the Depression Era

The trend toward centralization was described by Walter Thompson at the end of World War I,[39] and numerous other writers had commented upon it in articles in professional journals and law reviews. However well the trend may have been noted and discussed prior to the Great Depression, it received a tremendous boost during the Depression years. Several reasons for this development are to be noted.

First and foremost was the sheer ineptitude which seemed to paralyze the State governments at the time. They almost literally fiddled while

---

[38] Heymeyer, p. 123.

[39] Thompson, Walter, *Federal Centralization* (New York: Harcourt, Brace & Company, 1920).

Rome burned. In Pennsylvania, for instance, in the legislative session of 1933, the General Assembly wasted two months arguing about a beer bill, a Sunday fishing bill, and a Sunday baseball bill, while suffering among the unemployed was widespread throughout the Commonwealth. Almost daily, delegations of the unemployed descended upon the Capitol. That legislation providing for the establishment of the State Emergency Relief Board was passed when it was, or even that it was passed at all, can be explained only in terms of the extraordinary leadership and tremendous driving power of Governor Gifford Pinchot.

The second reason was the urgency of the need. Neither hungry people nor those who are trying to help them are likely to stand long on ceremony. The situation required that cash (and food) be given to those in need in the shortest possible time. The third reason is that under these circumstances, patterns were established for short-circuiting the States by direct Federal-municipal relationships. Such procedures were inevitable when the States were either unable or unwilling to move and when the cities were anxious to do what they could, if financial assistance was made available to them.

These conditions brought about tremendous changes in what had long been established patterns of American federalism. It was assumed that these changes would be temporary but many of them became permanent, and even those which did not made their contribution to the development of new patterns of thought with respect to Federal relations with State and local governments. Legislatively, the influence of Federal departments and agencies upon the course of State legislation became very great. While any intention of exerting pressure on the legislatures to secure adoption of legislation desired by the departments and agencies concerned was regularly denied by most of them, the intention did exist and pressure was exerted.

Similar pressures were applied for the purpose of establishing administrative cooperation. The National Recovery Administration, in 1935, through its State Relations Division, approached the appropriate State officials and party leaders in and out of the legislature in the hope of advancing its model act and of assuring the cooperation of the States with NRA. The Federal Power Commission and the Interstate Commerce Commission both sought state legislation designed to permit the corresponding State agencies to function cooperatively with the Federal agencies in utility control. The Federal Housing Administration sought and obtained legislation permitting all lending and savings institutions to make loans on obligation either issued or insured by it. The Lindbergh Case triggered a whole series of Federal and State laws designed to facilitate cooperative relationships in the field of crime control.

Most important of all in their significance upon both the legislative and administrative policies of the States were the controls designed to safeguard abuses in the use of Federal funds made available to the States in connection with federally aided programs. These developments of the Depression era were continued and enlarged upon as new fields were opened up during and after World War II. This course of events caused many questions to be raised about the effect that controls of this type, however necessary they may be, were having on the course of American federalism.

The Council of State Governments, at one of its Interstate Assemblies in Detroit in 1948, raised the question: Are we maintaining our federal system?, and devoted a session to a series of papers discussing it. The writer, among other interested observers, undertook to discuss the matter in an article, "What Is Happening to Our Federal System?" [40]

The Impact of Federal Grants-in-Aid

There are many lists of Federal programs involving intergovernmental relations. One is given in Appendix A of this volume; the *Annual Report of the Secretary of the Treasury on the State of the Finances* regularly presents another. In the 1960 issue of this report, sixty-four programs are listed, involving every major department and agency of the Federal government with a domestic program. All together, these expended about $7 billion, 8 per cent of all Federal revenues and 12 per cent of the revenues of the receiving State and local governments. The Bureau of the Census reports that after receiving $7 billion from the Federal government in 1960, some $9.4 billion were paid out by the States to localities, about 30 per cent of the income of these governments. [41]

A good deal has been written about the effect or "impact" of these Federal grants upon State and local governments. Probably the most extensive work in this field was done by the Commission on Intergovernmental Relations (Kestnbaum), and in the Minnesota study carried on under the direction of Professor William Anderson. The concluding and summary volume of the latter reports that, taken as a group, Federal grants-in-aid and certain closely related national measures seem to have brought with them, or were accompanied by, at least a dozen important changes in State governments:

[40] Symposium with answers by John W. Bricker, Roscoe Drummond, John M. Gaus, and William P. Lane, Jr., in supplement to *State Government,* January, 1949. The article was in the November, 1949, issue of the same journal, pp. 255–259, 270.

[41] Bureau of the Census, *Government Finances in 1960* (Washington, September, 1961).

1. New and enlarged State functions.

2. Direct State administration of functions formerly delegated to counties, towns, and municipalities—in short, increased centralization in the State.

3. The creation of new State agencies and the strengthening and enlargement of older ones, with considerable increases in State personnel.

4. The adoption of new State merit systems and the expansion and improvement of old ones, with considerable professionalization of the State services, and some reduction of political party pressures on State agencies. A new State emphasis upon the importance of qualified personnel.

5. New and increased contacts between State administrators and the district and regional administrators of Federal programs.

6. The establishment of new national organizations of State and national officials in the functional fields covered by the grants.

7. Considerable standardization among the States in service levels, methods, and rules under the grant-in-aid programs.

8. A new and increased emphasis upon the planning of State services in the aided fields, and upon adequate reporting of the work done.

9. A new and increased emphasis upon interstate cooperation in the administration of the aided service programs.

10. With general public acceptance of the grant-in-aid programs, a considerable increase in State revenues and expenditures, usually going far beyond the matching requirements of the Federal aids received.

11. Along with their many new contacts and joint responsibilities, an increase also in the points of potential friction between State and national administrators over personnel standards, service regulations, audits and inspections, together with some difficulties in State budgeting of the federally granted funds.

12. Despite these difficulties, no general demand to decrease or eliminate the grants but instead a general and usually successful pressure from State agencies to get increases in the grants and liberalization of the rules controlling expenditures.[42]

The impartial observer must admit that grant funds have helped many States both to inaugurate many new programs and to expand existing programs which would not otherwise have been undertaken. He must admit also that the grant system has had a centralizing influence, which may be good or bad according to one's point of view, and that it has tended to promote uniformity among the States. National grants have es-

[42] See Anderson, William, *Intergovernmental Relations in Review* (Minneapolis: University of Minnesota Press, 1960), pp. 61–62. See also Gilliam, Thomas A., "The Impact of Federal Subsidies Upon State Functions," *Nebraska Law Review*, May, 1960, pp. 528–546, and Bibliographical Notes for this chapter.

tablished national programs which have to be administered in accordance with national standards, which are to a large extent determined and agreed upon by a process of mutual accommodation. Even so, administrative responsibility has remained, to a considerable extent, in the hands of State and local officials who, "acting through their professional organizations, are in considerable part responsible for the very standards that national officers try to persuade all State and local officers to accept."[43]

It should be pointed out that while most of these changes are desirable, or have had desirable effects, the grant-in-aid system is not without its disadvantages. Instead of encouraging State and local responsibility, it does quite the opposite, encouraging State and local governments to believe that if they stall long enough, Uncle Sam will provide the necessary funds as, frequently, he does. Moreover, the very fact that the grant system exists has often had an unfortunate effect upon the States' use of their own available funds; since no Governor wants to admit that he has not qualified for every possible Federal aid dollar allotted to his State, there is a tendency to "skew" State budgets by allotting State money where it is needed to obtain the most Federal funds, not where it is most needed within the State. Thus, since there is little Federal help for schools and a good deal for highways, the latter tend to get the State funds available while the schools suffer. One remedy for this— one in which Congress has never shown the slightest interest—might be to substitute block grants for major purposes instead of categorical grants for very specific purposes. Then the States could allocate their money where it was needed most.

While it is true, as the Supreme Court observed some forty years ago in one of the earliest test cases, that the States do not have to accept Federal grants if they do not wish to do so, it is also true, at least with respect to some grant programs, that they will have to accept a good deal of Federal "intervention" on matters of State concern if they do accept them. For example, the highway people have succeeded in getting an anti-diversion provision written into the Federal law and into the constitutions of more than half (twenty-seven) of the States. In the unemployment compensation and employment security program, for which the central government pays the entire cost of State administration, the single agency rule is in effect. If, for any reason, the Federal officials do not like the State administrative arrangements, the funds for that State can be cut off abruptly. Of course, in practice, this very rarely happens. In some programs, such as the Pittman-Robertson game and wildlife program, Federal controls, though largely indirect, are nevertheless quite extensive.

[43] Grodzins, p. 266.

Although the single agency rule is not required by law, it is required in effect by the earmarking of funds and by the threat of losing Federal aid if any portion of the State's designated funds are used for any purpose not included in the program. The organized hunters and sportsmen have such a stranglehold on National and State legislators that no proposal to modify this vicious designation requirement has even a chance of being given serious consideration. Because of provisions in the Federal law, the States could not if they would correct the situation, and Congress has shown little disposition to resist this powerful lobby. Actually, the States might be better off without the money than with it, in view of the conditions governing its use.[44]

There can be no dissent with the original purpose of grants-in-aid of reducing the economic inequalities existing among the States. No child born in America should be denied equal educational opportunities, standard health and welfare services, or other common advantages, simply by accident of birth, but in practice the system often does not operate to prevent such denials. The States that most need the aid are not necessarily the ones that receive it. Thus, when such measures are under consideration in Congress, the representatives of the large, wealthy, industrial States which could pay their own bills and do not need the help—in fact, are not entitled to it—make certain that they get every cent they can, thereby largely defeating the avowed purpose of the grant-in-aid system. A striking illustration of this may be noted in New York, where a Governor of one party and a Senator of the other have both bitterly bemoaned the fact that New York does not get as much out of the grant-in-aid system as they put into it.[45]

Difficulty has arisen, thus, because the original purpose has been lost sight of and also because the system has been permitted to expand in size and scope with no plan or supervision whatsoever. Members of Congress from the larger and wealthier States have, by and large, only grudgingly admitted their responsibility for those less well off than themselves. Small programs for those in need degenerated into a grab bag from which each attempted to obtain as much as he could. No serious effort has ever been made to survey the whole problem, much less to plan for its

[44] For good discussions of these problems, see two reports of the Commission on Intergovernmental Relations, *Natural Resources and Conservation* and *Unemployment Compensation and Employment Service* (Washington, June, 1955).

[45] Testimony of Governor W. Averill Harriman before the House Subcommittee on Intergovernmental Relations, in New York, *Federal-State-Local Relations: State and Local Officials*, Part I, Hearings, September–October, 1957 (Washington: 85th Cong., 1st Sess., 1958), pp. 143–157, and Keating, Kenneth B., "Federal Grant-in-Aid Programs: New York's Experience," *New York University Law Review*, June, 1959, pp. 1011–1017.

1960 FEDERAL GRANTS: AIDED AND AIDING STATES

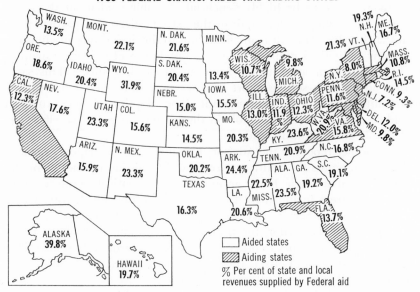

WASH. 13.5%
MONT. 22.1%
ORE. 18.6%
IDAHO 20.4%
WYO. 31.9%
N. DAK. 21.6%
MINN.
S. DAK. 20.4%
WIS. 10.7%
9.8%
MICH.
19.3%
N.H.
ME. 16.7%
21.3% VT.
MASS. 10.8%
N.Y. 8.0%
R.I. 14.5%
CONN. 9.3%
CAL. 12.3%
NEV. 17.6%
UTAH 23.3%
COL. 15.6%
NEBR. 15.0%
IOWA 13.4%
ILL. 13.0%
IND. 11.9%
OHIO 12.3%
PENN. 11.6%
N.J. 7.2%
DEL. 12.0%
MD. 9.8%
15.5%
ARIZ. 15.9%
N. MEX. 23.3%
KANS. 14.5%
MO. 20.3%
KY. 23.6%
VA. 15.8%
N.C. 16.8%
OKLA. 20.2%
ARK. 24.4%
TENN. 20.9%
ALA. 22.5%
GA. 19.2%
S.C. 19.1%
TEXAS 16.3%
LA. 20.6%
MISS. 23.5%
FLA. 13.7%

ALASKA 39.8%
HAWAII 19.7%

☐ Aided states
▨ Aiding states
% Per cent of state and local revenues supplied by Federal aid

solution. The total grants increased from year to year because the amounts approved for old and established grants were increased and new grants were added for various purposes in response to the pressures of well organized groups. The purposes of these grants were laudable enough; each of them individually or all of them together could be defended as being in the public interest. The question is not one of purpose but regards the method of accomplishing the purpose.

Serious attention might well be given to some of the important opportunities for improving the whole grant-in-aid operation. Twenty years ago, Professor Joseph P. Harris called attention to the need, urgent then and far more urgent today, for establishing a national policy on grants-in-aid, better allocation formulae, and better administrative supervision.[46] A number of constructive proposals have been made for improvement including periodic surveys, block grants, and a uniform allotment and matching formula.

In 1961, the Advisory Commission on Intergovernmental Relations published a report in which it was recommended that all individual grant programs be terminated automatically five years after their establishment, unless specifically continued. The appropriate Congressional committees would be required to re-evaluate each program prior to the ex-

---

[46] On the haphazard and planless character of the grant programs, see Harris, Joseph P., "The Future of Federal Grants-in-Aid," *Annals of the American Academy of Political and Social Science*, January, 1940, pp. 14–26.

piration of the five-year period.[47] This proposal makes sense and might very likely prove to be highly beneficial. An able student of the grant system calls attention once more to the extreme degree of particularization that has developed in many fields and to the desirability of eliminating many individual grants through consolidation of existing programs in broad program areas under a system of block grants.[48] This same author advocates a serious effort to make procedures and requirements more uniform among the various grants. The adoption of these proposals would seem to be highly desirable in the interests of economy, efficiency, and simple good administration.

In another report of the Advisory Commission on Intergovernmental Relations on grants for health services, the Commission did not favor the substitution of a single block grant for the categorical grants existing in the eight areas included in its study, and recommended instead that the Public Health Service Act of 1944 be amended to authorize, at the discretion of the Governor, the transfer of up to one-third of the funds in any one grant category to other programs in the group. This flexibility would apply to such grants as those for general health, venereal disease, cancer, heart disease, and tuberculosis control.

The Commission also recommended the establishment of a uniform allotment and matching formula for Federal grants-in-aid to States for general health assistance and for the categorical grants in the health field. To establish such uniformity, the Commission proposed that such formulae provide for the allotment of funds on the basis of State population and financial need as measured by State per capita income (as in the Hill-Burton formula), and that matching requirements be placed on a sliding scale relative to State per capita income.[49]

SUMMARY AND CONCLUSIONS

The American States today are in a position somewhat comparable to that of the automobile several decades ago before the self-starter was

[47] Six identical bills were promptly introduced in the House in the 87th Cong. to carry out this recommendation: Thomas B. Curtis of Missouri, H.R. 7808; Florence P. Dwyer of New Jersey, H.R. 7803; L. H. Fountain of North Carolina, H.R. 7802; Frank Ikard of Texas, H.R. 7804; Thomas M. Pelly of Washington, H.R. 7814; and Neal Smith of Iowa, H.R. 7805.

[48] Mushkin, Selma J., "Barriers to a System of Federal Grants-in-Aid," *National Tax Journal*, September, 1960, pp. 193–218.

[49] *Modification of Federal Grants-in-Aid for Public Health Services* (Washington, January, 1961).

invented. The old cars would go if one could manage to get them started, provided he did not break an arm in the process. The States can move too, but even after 200 years, the self-starter for them has yet to be invented.

The States do many things very well indeed. They have shown themselves to be capable of taking on new functions and of expanding existing programs, with the result that they now perform many more functions and administer them with a higher degree of competence and efficiency than ever before. They collect more revenue, spend more money, and employ more personnel than ever before. In many ways, they have made significant progress. Paradoxically, however, they have repeatedly demonstrated an amazing degree of ineptitude in doing those things which are essential to their own strength and well-being, possibly even their survival, under the different social and economic conditions under which they must operate.

When it comes to protecting civil rights, with a few notable exceptions the States have failed completely. They have not performed their obvious responsibilities in behalf of their growing urban populations, and what is worse, they have either been indifferent to urban needs or taken action that was prejudicial to those needs. Most States have consistently refused to put their own governmental houses in order by revising and modernizing their constitutions or by reorganizing and updating the organization and procedures of the three branches of government and their antiquated and unfair tax systems. In these and many other ways, they have either been unable or unwilling to do the things that must be done if democratic government is to be effective at the State and local levels and if the American federal system of government is to be preserved.

This utter indifference to matters so essential to their own welfare and to the governmental health of the nation is difficult to understand. The people were not paralyzed by apathy in the days of the Founding; they may not all have been in agreement, but they were alert, interested, and active in expressing their views. One of many examples of the amazing lassitude that now afflicts the States is revealed by an analysis of the appearances at the Senate hearings on the Federal Aid for Education bill in 1961.[50] It would be difficult to conceive of any issue more vitally affecting the interests of State and local government, both financially and governmentally. But the representatives of cities, counties, and school districts were present in force to present their views (most of them for the bill), while spokesmen for the States were conspicuous by their

[50] Senate Committee on Labor and Public Welfare, *Public School Assistance Act of 1961*, 2 vols., Hearings, March, 1961 (Washington: 87th Cong., 1st Sess., 1961).

absence. The hearings filled two volumes and ran to 1,329 printed pages, but only one Governor appeared to testify, one who had planned to come was obliged to cancel his appearance, and one sent a telegram!

Some of what appears to be apathy may, of course, be due to ignorance, for a great many supposedly educated people appear to have no understanding of or interest in American political institutions. A growing concern about world politics and international affairs has probably detracted from the interest in State and local problems. Interest in international affairs is good and is to be commended, but it is also well to remember that what happens locally is also important, both domestically and internationally. A rude or thoughtless action by even a private citizen can under certain conditions precipitate an international "incident."

One Member of Congress who represents a district in which interest in foreign and international affairs is paramount reports that little interest in the States or in federalism exists in his district, and that his constituents would be perfectly happy to see the States disappear so that the Federal government could take over completely. What the States need today more than any other one thing is leadership—strong, courageous, and effective leadership capable of awakening them to their opportunities and responsibilities and to the imposing agenda of unfinished business which confronts them.

The problems which confront the States will not be solved by appealing to any of the time-honored and outmoded shibboleths so often relied upon in the past, to concepts that now serve only to arouse emotional responses that becloud and make rational consideration of the real issues more difficult. "States' rights" has long since outlived any usefulness it may once have had as a suitable guide in the determination of public policy. "Home rule" of the conventional variety common in the past is an anachronism in the modern world. The idea that centralization is wicked will not help either, for much of it is necessary, or at least inevitable, under modern conditions. Nor will the idea that bigness is in and of itself improper help, for this is a big country and growing larger. Even State and local government is today big business.

Nor will it help to rely upon the virtues of a balanced budget, as stated in the conventional terms of the past, and to regard every expenditure in the public interest, broadly defined, as some new form of pork-barrel raid upon the Treasury. As for the philosophy that the least government is the best government, and that governmental action is inherently undesirable, a scanning of the daily press or the *Congressional Record* will almost any day turn up such remarks as the following, attributed (without citation) to Jefferson: "To preserve our independence, we must not let our rulers load us with perpetual debt. . . . If we can prevent the Government from wasting the labors of the people, under the pretense of caring for them, they will be happy." One might suspect that the power lobby had something to do with a characterization of TVA "as flowing through four or five States and draining the whole fifty—of tax money, that is."

BIBLIOGRAPHICAL NOTES

Indictment of the States. Two distinguished foreign commentators on American institutions gave some attention to problems discussed here: Alexis de Toqueville, in the Jacksonian Era, *Democracy in America,* Phillips Bradley, ed., 2 vols. (New York: Rinehart and Company, 1948) and James Bryce about three-quarters of a century ago, *American Commonwealth,* 2 vols. (New York: The Macmillan Co., 1887, revised 1910). Two important articles on the shortcomings of the States appeared at approximately the same time as Bryce's first edition: John W. Burgess, "The American Commonwealth," *Political Science Quarterly,* March, 1886, pp. 9–35, and Simon N. Patton, "Decay of State and Local Governments," *Annals of the American Academy of Political and Social Science,* July, 1890, pp. 26–42. For at least three decades Bryce's work remained the accepted treatise on American government; for an evaluation of it fifty years after, see Robert C. Brooks, ed., *Bryce's "American Commonwealth," Fiftieth Anniversary* (New York: The Macmillan Co., 1939). Roy V. Peel, *State Government Today* (Albuquerque: University of New Mexico Press, 1948) and Robert S. Allen, *Our Sovereign State* (New York: Vanguard Press, Inc., 1949) are the most recent critical commentaries on the state system.

There have been a few attempts to deal constructively with the plight of the States. At the time of the Great Depression when the States were in virtual collapse, there were a number of urgent pleas for the revision of the Federal Constitution: William Y. Elliott, *The Need for Constitutional Reform* (New York: McGraw-Hill Book Co., Inc., 1935); Henry Hazlitt, *A New Constitution Now* (New York: McGraw-Hill Book Co., Inc., 1942); Alexander Heymeyer, *Time for a Change: A Proposal for a Second Constitutional Convention* (New York: Rinehart and Company, 1943); and William K. Wallace, *Our Obsolete Constitution* (New York: John Day Co., 1932). Reform in the personnel field affected the States, as it did the Federal government; see Carl R. Fish, *The Civil Service and the Patronage* (New York: Longmans, Green & Co., Inc., 1906) and William D. Foulke, *Fighting the Spoilsmen* (New York: G. P. Putnam's Sons, 1919). Since World War II, the tendency has been to think in terms of increasing the strengths and overcoming the weaknesses of the States; see Commission on Intergovernmental Relations (Kestnbaum), *Report to the President* (Washington, June, 1955); James W. Fesler, ed., *The Forty-eight States: Their Role as Policy Makers and Administrators* (New York: American Assembly, Columbia University, 1955); and Coleman Woodbury, *The Future Role of the States* (New York: National Municipal League, 1963).

Indictment of the Cities. Although Bryce had found the cities the one conspicuous failure in American democracy, it was the Muckrakers whose exposés really brought these failures to public attention. Lincoln Steffens, *The Shame of the Cities* and *The Struggle for Self-Government* (New York: McClure, Phillips & Company, 1904 and 1906 respectively) were undoubtedly the most influential books by a Muckraker, and Cornelius C. Regier, *The Muckrakers* (Chapel Hill: University of North Carolina Press, 1932), was the best book about them. Regier includes an extensive list of the Muckrakers' writings, including a large number of the magazine articles for which they became famous. Two symposia of their writings have recently appeared: Harvey Swados, ed., *Years of Conscience: The Muckrakers; an Anthology of Reform Journalism*

(Cleveland: World Publishing Company, 1962) and Arthur M. and Lila Weinberg, eds., *The Muckrakers: The Era in Journalism That Moved America to Reform—the Most Significant Articles of 1902–1912* (New York: Simon & Schuster, Inc., 1961). Another publication of this general type is Robert S. Allen, ed., *Our Fair City* (New York: Vanguard Press, Inc., 1947).

Some half dozen books, taken together, give a fairly clear idea of the steps that have been taken to correct the conditions set forth in the indictment: Morris L. Cooke, *Our Cities Awake* (Garden City: Doubleday, Page, 1918); on the contribution of research to better municipal government, see Norman N. Gill, *Municipal Research Bureaus: A Study of the Nation's Leading Citizen-supported Agencies* (Washington: American Council on Public Affairs, 1944); on the contribution of improved citizen organization, see Richard S. Childs, *Civic Victories* (New York: Harper & Brothers, 1952) and Frank M. Stewart, *A Half Century of Municipal Reform: The History of the National Municipal League* (Berkeley: University of California Press, 1950); and for the history of city government, see Ernest S. Griffith, *Modern Development of City Government*, 2 vols. (New York: Oxford University Press, 1927).

Indictment of Rural Government. Rural local government never had a group of Muckrakers to dramatize its failures, though Henry S. Gilbertson, *County Government: The Dark Continent of American Politics* (New York: National Short Ballot Association, 1917) created a stereotype of county government so unfavorable to the counties that today county people are still trying to overcome it and to create in its place a more favorable and more accurate image of county government. Other significant titles are: Howard P. Jones, *Constitutional Barriers to Improvement in County Government* (New York: National Municipal League, 1932, originally a supplement to the August, 1932, issue of the *National Municipal Review*) and Edward W. Weidner, *The American County: Patchwork of Boards* (New York: National Municipal League, 1946). What the counties themselves have been doing to improve county organization and procedure is revealed in the Proceedings of the successive annual meetings of the National Association of Counties, particularly in the *Proceedings* of their Urban County Congress (Washington, 1959 and 1963).

The Progressive Movement. Much of the driving power of the Progressive movement was derived from the ardor of its leaders for reform at both the National and State levels. At the national level, the most helpful titles are: Theodore Roosevelt, *The New Nationalism* (New York: Outlook Publishers, 1910); Herbert Croly, *The Promise of American Life* (New York: The Macmillan Co., 1912); Richard Hofstader, *The Age of Reform: From Bryan to Franklin D. Roosevelt* (New York: Alfred A. Knopf, Inc., 1955); Otis A. Pease, ed., *The Progressive Years: The Spirit and Achievement of American Reform* (New York: George Braziller, Inc., 1962); James H. Timberlake, *Prohibition and the Progressive Movement, 1900–1920* (Cambridge: Harvard University Press, 1963); and Walter E. Weyl, *The New Democracy* (New York: The Macmillan Co., 1920).

On what progressivism meant in Wisconsin, see Robert M. La Follette, *Autobiography: A Personal Narrative of Personal Experiences* (Madison: published by the author, 1913). Several good titles on developments in Wisconsin and Oregon are: Allen E. Davis, *Spearheads for Reform: Social Settlements and the Progressive Movement, 1890–1914* (Ann Arbor: University Microfilms, 1960); Edward N. Doan, *The La Follettes and the Wisconsin Idea* (New York: Rinehart and Company, 1947); Allen H. Eaton, *The Oregon System: The Story of Direct Legislation in Oregon* (Chicago: A. C. McClurg & Company, 1912); Edward A. Fitzpatrick, *McCarthy of Wisconsin* (New York: Columbia University Press, 1944); and Frederic C. Howe, *Wisconsin: An Experiment in Democracy* (New York: Charles Scribner's Sons, 1912).

CHAPTER XXIII

Cooperative
Federalism

The American form of government is often, but erroneously, symbolized by a three-layer cake. A far more accurate image is the rainbow or marble cake, characterized by an inseparable mingling of differently colored ingredients, the colors appearing in vertical and diagonal strands and unexpected whirls. As colors are mixed in the marble cake, so functions are mixed in the American federal system. Consider the health officer, styled "sanitarian," in a rural county in a border State. He embodies the whole idea of the marble cake of government.

The sanitarian is appointed by the State under merit standards established by the Federal Government. His base salary comes jointly from State and Federal funds, the county provides him with an office and office amenities and pays a portion of his expenses, and the largest city in the county also contributes to his salary and office by virtue of his appointment as a city plumbing inspector. It is impossible from moment to moment to tell under which governmental hat the sanitarian operates [Federal, State, State-local, or local]. The sanitarian is an extreme case, but he accurately represents an important aspect of the whole range of governmental activities in the United States. . . .

Even in the absence of joint financing, Federal-State-local collaboration is the characteristic mode of action. Federal expertise is available to aid in the building of a local jail (which may later be used to house Federal prisoners), to improve a local water purification system, to step up building inspections, to provide standards for State and local personnel in protecting housewives against dishonest butchers' scales, to prevent gas explosions, or to produce a land use plan. State and localities, on the other hand, take important formal responsibilities in the development of national programs for atomic energy, civil defense, the regulation of commerce, and the protection of purity in foods and drugs; local political weight is always a factor in the operation of even a post office or a military establishment. From abattoirs and accounting, through zoning and zoo administration, any governmental activity is almost certain to involve the influence, if not the formal administration, of all three planes of the federal system.[1]

[1] Grodzins, Morton, "The Federal System," *Report* of the President's Commission on National Goals, *Goals for Americans* (New York: American Assembly, Columbia University, Prentice-Hall, Inc., 1960), pp. 265–282, on pp. 265–266.

THE CONCEPT OF COOPERATIVE FEDERALISM

The pattern of American federalism has changed significantly since the days of the Founding Fathers. One must assume that they, as reasonable men, sought to establish a system in which "peaceful coexistence" between the central government and the States would be possible, not a system which would foment discord, strife, and misunderstanding. Madison, who was at the same time the chief architect of this system and of the check and balance system within it, surely wanted to achieve harmony as a result of his balancing act, not perennial partisan conflict.

In the days of the founding of the present government, the pattern of federalism was quite simple. It was then possible to think in terms of assigning both responsibility for specific governmental functions and tax sources adequate for their financial support exclusively to one or another of the several units or levels of government. Today this "layer cake concept of federalism" is no longer applicable; some contend, in fact, that it never did exist to the extent commonly assumed. Conditions have so changed that two or frequently all three levels of government are involved in the administration of virtually every important governmental function. The long process of transition was accelerated by two world wars, the Great Depression, Korea, and the continuing necessity for an adequate national defense, with the result that the marble cake became a more descriptive symbol of American federalism than the layer cake.

Thus developed the concept of cooperative federalism which Professor John M. Gaus expressed well when he wrote:

No problem of any consequence which affects our local communities or national strength can be solved or seriously attacked in

PIONEERS IN THE MOVEMENT FOR
COOPERATIVE FEDERALISM

ᴇɴʀʏ W. Toʟʟ, Founder
ᴅd First Executive Director,
ᴏuncil of State
ᴏvernments

Fʀᴀɴᴋ Bᴀɴᴇ, Executive
Director of the Council of
State Governments for
20 years; First Chairman,
Advisory Commission on
Intergovernmental Relations

Wɪʟʟɪᴀᴍ Aɴᴅᴇʀsoɴ, Member
of the Kestnbaum Com-
mission, and long-time
student and advocate of
intergovernmental
cooperation

ᴡʀᴇɴᴄᴇ H. Fouɴᴛᴀɪɴ,
ᴇpresentative from North
ʀolina; Member of the
ᴠisory Commission on
ᴇrgovernmental Rela-
ᴬs; Chairman, since 1956,
ᵗhe House Subcommittee
Intergovernmental
ᴬations

Roвᴇʀᴛ F. Wᴀɢɴᴇʀ, Mayor
of the City of New York;
Founder and First Chair-
man, Metropolitan Regional
Conference

Eᴅᴍuɴᴅ S. Muskɪᴇ, U.S.
Senator from Maine,
Member of the Advisory
Commission on Intergovernmental Relations; Chairman,
since 1962, of the Senate Subcommittee on Intergovern-
mental Relations

819

this country unless the resources of every level of government operating in a given area are mobilized to supplement (not supplant) each other.[2]

Thus cooperative federalism has gradually supplemented the original form in which there was a more or less specific assignment of functions at each governmental level. This has been accomplished by modifications made within the existing governmental framework, achieved without constitutional amendment, a fact which is important because it serves to emphasize the informal manner in which changes of far-reaching importance have often been made. More than 100 years ago, de Tocqueville wrote that he was "struck by the good sense and the practical judgment of the Americans . . . in the ingenious devices by which they elude the numberless difficulties resulting from their federal constitution." [3]

Federal-State relations, once the more or less exclusive province of the constitutional lawyer found in every town, have become more and more the concern of the tax and fiscal expert, the welfare administrator, the public works engineer, and other specialists. Changes yet to come may be expected further to modify the existing pattern of federalism. As expressed in the preamble of the act creating the new Advisory Commission on Intergovernmental Relations: "The complexity of modern life intensifies the need in a federal form of government for the fullest cooperation and coordination of activities between the levels of government; population growth and scientific developments portend for future years an increasingly complex society in which it is essential that appropriate agencies be established to give continuing attention to intergovernmental problems."

Its Emergence

Relations among and between the units of government which compose the American federal system have been of ever-increasing importance during this century. In fact, the growing number and importance of these relationships has given rise within one generation to a whole new terminology. Although evidence of such relations can be traced back to

[2] Gaus, John M., *Reflections on Public Administration* (University: University of Alabama Press, 1947), p. 80. Professor Grodzins recognizes the present cooperative nature of American federalism, but contends that it has always been so. "The American federal system," he writes, "has never been a system of separated governmental activities. There has never been a time when it was possible to put neat labels on discrete [sic] 'Federal,' 'State,' and 'local' functions." Grodzins, p. 268.

[3] Tocqueville, Alexis de, *American Institutions and Their Influence* (New York: Allyn & Bacon, 1855), p. 165.

colonial times and through the days of the founding of the Republic, the term "intergovernmental relations" as applied to them is of recent origin. It may very likely have been used for the first time in 1940 in the title, "Intergovernmental Relations in the United States." [4]

Until the beginning of the Roosevelt era, the literature of intergovernmental relations, such as it was, was largely devoted to stories of conflict between the Federal government and the States in taxation and in the administration of various functional programs involving officials at both levels. As an antidote for this conflict, there began to appear a number of studies of successful cooperative efforts and pleas for the extension of the concept of cooperation. One of the earliest articles on the subject called for the framing of such permissive provisions as possible, to be included in our State constitutions, designed to encourage and facilitate Federal-State cooperation.[5]

Professors William Anderson and Roger H. Wells published new texts in which more space and emphasis were given to intergovernmental relations than in previously published works.[6] Significant also was a symposium on cooperative federalism, published in the *Iowa Law Review*,[7] which may be the first use of the phrase in print in this context; the origin of the phrase is not, however, entirely certain.[8] Also at this time, several important studies appeared showing what was actually being done by way of Federal-State cooperation in the field of agriculture and social security.

Constitutional Basis

While it is generally recognized that the provisions of the Constitution embodied a compromise between a unitary state and a confederation, it seems to be less appreciated that the Founders, in enumerating the responsibilities of the Federal and State governments, provided for

[4] "Intergovernmental Relations in the United States," *Annals of the American Academy of Political and Social Science*, January, 1940, entire issue.

[5] Graves, W. Brooke, "State Provisions for Federal-State Cooperation," *Annals of the American Academy of Political and Social Science*, September, 1935, pp. 142–148.

[6] Anderson, William, *American Government* (New York: Henry Holt & Co., 1938), Chapters 14 and 15 in the 1st ed., and Wells, Roger H., *American Local Government* (New York: McGraw-Hill Book Co., Inc., 1939).

[7] "Cooperative Federalism: A Symposium," *Iowa Law Review*, May, 1938, entire issue.

[8] See Graves, W. Brooke, *Intergovernmental Relations in the United States: An Annotated Chronology* (Chicago: Council of State Governments, December, 1958).

joint action in a cooperative fashion in many places. There are numerous specific examples, such as the election of Federal officers, State inspection of imports, election laws, adjudication between two or more States, provision that Congress may prescribe the manner in which full faith and credit shall be given, and constitutional amendments. Both history and the logical necessities of our society depend upon cooperation.

The basic assumptions underlying the concept of cooperative federalism have been well summarized in a paper by Professor Bruce B. Mason:

1. Our Constitution and our political processes have been based on the premise that not only is this a federal system, but a cooperative federal system.

2. Ours has been a cooperative system since its very beginning; those who demarcate divisions between cooperative and uncooperative periods unduly focus upon some particular aspect of the relationship at a specific time in history.

3. The cooperative relationship has always presupposed Federal supremacy in certain areas, and, more importantly, has never been static. There have been periods of increased emphasis on "States' rights" as well as national action, though the long range trend has favored the national government.

4. The division of responsibilities in this cooperative relationship has never been finalized, and may never be. The guidelines and the stimuli for a greater or lesser role by one of the parties result from pragmatic determinations of need and means at any point in history.

5. Needs are determined by political processes which react on policy-making institutions at all levels of government, and means are determined by common sense evaluation of respective governmental abilities and/or willingness to meet the needs which arise.

6. The case for determining the level at which action ought to take place is not (or has not been) a subject for scientific investigation. The question of the impact of Federal versus State action on freedom versus control, for example, is undecided, however much there may be an emotional preference of one over the other.[9]

Use in Day-to-day Administration

There is much available evidence of the daily growth and expansion of cooperative relationships between the several units and levels of American government. However much intergovernmental relations may have been neglected in the past, the subject is today very much in the news. A careful reading of almost any issue of *The New York Times* reveals

[9] Mason, Bruce B., *A Critique of Cooperative Federalism* (Phoenix: National Conference on Government, November, 1960).

at least a dozen items that have important implications in this field. All three levels of government are likely to be involved in all possible combinations and some half dozen different subject matter areas. While civil rights and fiscal relations may presently be subjects of major interest, there are to be found other articles on housing and urban renewal, regulation of commerce, judicial relations, and many more.

Further illustrations are found in the releases issued from time to time by the Governors' offices as, for instance, one from Governor William A. Egan of Alaska in February, 1961. After realizing its years-long ambition to achieve statehood, this State still finds it necessary frequently to consult with the President and the heads of the numerous Federal executive departments and agencies in order to accomplish the governmental job that must be done. In addition to these, the Governor has numerous contacts with Members of Congress from his own and other States. Illustrative excerpts from the Governor's press release are reproduced below and on pages 824–825.

This experience is certainly not unique, but it is interesting to note that the government of one of the newest States illustrates so clearly this important development in American federalism. Cooperative relationships have been or are now being developed in many important functional fields. In the case of such well established functions as agriculture, education, highways, social welfare, and veterans' affairs, cooperative relationships have in most respects worked well, although some difficult and sometimes troublesome aspects do exist. Various problems in these areas periodically attracted public attention, usually of the tempest-in-a-teapot variety. Although not of great significance as individual cases, they served to direct attention to larger and more basic problems, even to the extent of causing in one instance a thorough re-examination of the whole program.

In the case of functional areas that are new both to government and to the techniques of cooperation, such as the peacetime uses of atomic energy, science program coordination, and the drafting of legislation, the question is how, in the absence of hampering precedents and legal barriers, there are significant opportunities for new ways of adapting the mechanisms of federalism to the needs of people and their governments in the new age of science and technology.

STATE OF ALASKA

Governor's Office   February, 1961

YOUR STATE GOVERNMENT

Notwithstanding Statehood, Alaska—as other States—must look to the Nation's capital in meeting many immediate problems. This was evidenced in recent weeks by Governor Egan's direct approach to the

President, Cabinet officers and Federal agencies on widely varying subjects.

Transpacific Route Case: Following earlier personal appeal to the Civil Aeronautics Board and to former President Eisenhower, Governor Egan has twice written to President Kennedy asking that he reconsider the decision of his predecessor and approve the recommendation of the Board granting authority to Pan American World Airways to fly a New York-Tokyo route by way of Fairbanks. As the Governor advised the President, the Pan American application "is of direct concern and importance to the State of Alaska, its people and its economy. . . ."

Housing: As the Governor advised the Legislature, such a step [legislative enactment of a bill to create an Alaska State Mortgage Association, functioning through and staffed by the Alaska State Housing Authority] would be only a start toward meeting the problem. Consequently, he has initiated a new request for a further allocation of Special Assistance funds and last week wrote to Robert Weaver, newly appointed administrator of the Housing and Home Finance Agency, pointing out the threat to the home construction field in Alaska should this fund be depleted and urging his approval of the request.

Alaska Methodist University: Another Washington-bound letter was directed to Secretary of the Interior Stewart L. Udall urging that he grant a hearing to officials of the Alaska Methodist University and review a decision of the Washington Office of the Bureau of Land Management which would deny to the University an opportunity to buy thirty-five acres of public land which it desires for campus expansion. Approval of the University's request had previously been given by the Anchorage BLM office.

Wilderness Bill: Under terms of the so-called Wilderness bill now before the Congress, an estimated 46,000,000 acres of national forests, parks, monuments, wildlife refuges and game ranges in Alaska could be committed to the Wilderness system by administrative action of the Secretaries of Agriculture and Interior, subject only to the enactment by Congress of a concurrent resolution opposing such a recommendation.

Recognizing its possible threat to Alaska's development, Governor Egan urged members of the Alaska Congressional delegation to seek an amendment to the bill providing that the areas considered for inclusion in the system be given cooperative study and classification on the local and State levels prior to recommendations being made to the President and the Congress.

Shipping: While in Washington for the inauguration of President Kennedy, the Governor met with Governor William F. Quinn of Hawaii, Governor Múnoz-Marin of Puerto Rico, and Senators Oren Long of Hawaii and Bob Bartlett and Ernest Gruening of Alaska concerning a mutual approach to shipping problems facing each area.

Interior: Conferences were also held with James Carr, Under

Secretary of the Interior, and John Carver, Jr., Assistant Secretary of the Interior, on Alaska matters under the jurisdiction of that Department.

There is some evidence that many Federal administrators now realize the importance of their relations with the State and local units to a degree that has seldom been true in the past. Consequently, they tend to give intergovernmental relations a place on the agenda when members of the field staff are brought in to the central office for conference and instruction, as the Veterans Administration and other agencies have done, or to include intergovernmental relations as one aspect of a management development program for top administrative personnel in the agency, as has been done in the employment security field.

COOPERATIVE FEDERALISM IN ESTABLISHED FUNCTIONAL AREAS

Agriculture

The promotion of agriculture was originally performed privately by local agricultural societies; later, the States began to assume some responsibility; and in 1862 the Federal government entered the field. For nearly thirty years, the Federal law was administered by a Commissioner of Agriculture. Under legislation enacted in 1889, the powers and duties of the agency were enlarged and it was given status as an executive department. As part of this change, the Commissioner became the Secretary of Agriculture with a seat at the Cabinet table. Very early in the life of the Federal agency, programs were established involving cooperative relationships between the Federal government and the States.

First among these were the Morrill Land Grant Acts of 1862 and 1890 with their generous provisions for the financing of higher education, with particular reference to "agriculture and the mechanic arts." This legislation laid the foundations for the tremendously important system of public higher education in this country. The system is unique; its contribution to the enrichment of American life has been so great that it has often been characterized as being, by any standard of measurement, by far the most important among the many grant-in-aid programs of the Federal government. For the purposes of this discussion, it is significant because it has provided needed financial assistance without imposing the dreaded "Federal controls" upon either the administrations of the aided institutions or their educational programs.

The second major program involving cooperation among Federal, State, and local governments was the animal and poultry diseases control and eradication program instituted by legislation enacted by Congress in 1883. The purpose of the program is to ascertain the prevalence of such diseases and by appropriate measures to prevent the introduction of new diseases from abroad and the spread of diseases already in this country. The original legislation has been amended, revised, and supplemented on innumerable occasions in the three-quarters of a century since the program was initiated. The Department of Agriculture now also administers acts and regulations governing the interstate transportation of livestock and poultry, such as Federal domestic animal quarantines and the twenty-eight hour law requiring the humane treatment of livestock in transit.

Other laws and regulations include the Virus-Serum Toxin Act; the Hog Cholera Serum Marketing Agreement Act; laws to prevent the introduction of a long list of diseases destructive of domestic animals; and laws providing for the certification and free entry of purebred livestock for breeding purposes. State departments of agriculture function in many of these areas. Every effort is made, not only to avoid overlapping and duplication of effort, but to achieve the maximum beneficial results through cooperation and coordination of the efforts of all agricultural agencies and personnel.

In 1887 came a third major agricultural program involving intergovernmental cooperation. Under the Hatch Agricultural Experiment Station Act, in cooperation with the land-grant colleges of the several States, the agricultural experiment stations carry on investigations and experiments designed to promote a permanent and efficient agricultural industry. Grants are made primarily for projects designed to find solutions to specific agricultural problems. In this work, the States contribute about $3.00 for every dollar paid by the Federal government. Because of differences in climate, soil, market outlets, and other local conditions, each State has its own problems in the production and marketing of crops and livestock. It is to the solution of these problems, in each State, that this cooperative effort is dedicated.

Research in agricultural economics began as part of the early work in farm management and was conducted by various organizations within the Department of Agriculture prior to its formal organization in 1905. Marketing research was added under the provisions of legislation adopted in 1939. Major research projects now conducted fall roughly into three categories: broad economic analysis, economic and statistical research on farm problems, and analysis and interpretation of developments affecting both foreign and domestic markets for American farm products. In the marketing and crop reporting services, there is the closest possible cooperation between the corresponding units of the Federal and State departments of agriculture.

The years 1905 and 1906 appear to have been banner years for the establishment of new agricultural programs in which cooperative arrangements between Federal and State agencies have since been developed on an impressive scale. The United States Forest Service first came into being in 1905; its forest and range experiment stations and its forest products laboratories now conduct investigations on a cooperative basis with appropriate State agencies in the entire field of forestry and wild land management; the growth and harvesting of timber, protection of forests from fire, insects and diseases, and many other problems.

Since 1924, the Federal government has granted financial assistance to State governments for forest fire control, to States to encourage reforestation by giving young trees or selling them at low cost to farmers, and since 1949, to private owners of forest lands. An important development occurred in 1950 when Congress enacted the Cooperative Forest Management Act, under which State departments of forestry are given assistance in making professional personnel available to advise and consult with owners of small wood lots, with small sawmill operators, and with other processors of primary forest products. More than 1,000 counties are now served with foresters under this cooperative Federal-State forest management plan.

In legislation originally adopted in 1905, amended in 1912, and thoroughly revised and rewritten in 1947, the Department of Agriculture in cooperation with State and local agencies works for the control and eradication of injurious insects and plant diseases. They regulate disease controlling insecticides, pesticides, and other devices; they administer domestic plant quarantines to control a number of destructive crop pests; and their field men are stationed at all United States land, sea, and air ports of entry to guard against the introduction into this country of foreign plant pests and diseases.

The Food and Drug Administration was established in the Department of Agriculture in 1906, was continued in that department for many years, and was subsequently transferred to the Federal Security Agency in 1940 and the Department of Health, Education, and Welfare in 1953. Probably no Federal agency has a record of more efficient cooperation with its counterpart agencies at the State and local levels than does the Food and Drug Administration. The original Federal Meat Inspection Act was also adopted in 1906, largely in response to public pressure resulting from the disclosure of the shocking conditions then existing in the slaughter houses and meat packing plants in Chicago. Meat inspection is administered at packing plants to insure the wholesomeness of meat and meat food products marketed in interstate and foreign commerce. Although for many years there was less Federal-State cooperation in this area than in many others, conditions are now considerably improved and the dangers arising from inadequate State inspection correspondingly reduced.

The Smith-Lever Act of 1914 together with the many amendments and revisions that have since been adopted mark another significant advance in Federal-State cooperative relationships in the field of agriculture. The Cooperative Agricultural Extension Service is composed of fifty-one State and territorial extension services, each of which operates in conjunction with the land-grant college of its jurisdiction. Work is financed and administered under a three-way partnership between the local people, the land-grant college in the State, and the Department of Agriculture. The details of operation are set forth in a Department memorandum, frequently revised. The basic purpose is to help farm people analyze their problems and utilize the results of agricultural research, practical experience, and the various programs and services administered by the Department. The close coordination of extension work, carried on by the county agent, and the findings of agricultural research have played an important part in motivating farm people to adopt new and improved farm and home management practices. The duties of the county agent relate to the conservation of the soil and other natural resources, work with 4-H clubs, the securing of better livestock and crops, the marketing of farm produce, organization of groups of young farm people, control of disease and pests affecting crops and livestock, poultry raising, feed production, and assistance to the home program.

The Soil Conservation Service was first established in the Department of the Interior in 1933 and transferred to the Department of Agriculture in 1935 when the Soil Conservation Act was adopted. The Department, in cooperation with State agricultural experiment stations, had long been studying soils and investigating soil building and passing the information on to farmers through the Extension Service. The Act made possible a tremendous expansion of this program, spreading the use of soil-erosion-control practices through demonstrations in selected areas and providing assistance to some 2,000 or more soil conservation districts, embracing nearly 4 million farms organized under State laws. The Service aids these farmer-managed districts with technical advice, materials, and equipment. A considerable controversy was engendered in 1953–1954 when the regional offices were abolished and greater responsibility for soil conservation was transferred to the State headquarters and to the land-grant colleges.

Education

Although control over education is, under the doctrine of residuary powers, a responsibility of State and local rather than of national government, the central government has been drawn more and more deeply into educational matters. This is a development quite contrary to the hopes and expectations of the Founders. Thomas Jefferson, for example, said repeatedly that public education was a function of local government. He did not even regard it as a State function. The States were drawn in when the localities faced questions of financial support that they were ill-equipped to solve. In late years, Federal programs in education have increased in number, in total amounts appropriated, and in influence. Thus the Federal government has been drawn into education for precisely the same reasons that the States were drawn in earlier.

The beginnings of Federal participation were the land grants of 1785 made by the Continental Congress, and further land grants made by Congress under the present Constitution upon the admission of new States, beginning with Ohio in 1803. In many jurisdictions, these lands and the proceeds from their sale or use have been set aside in the form of trust funds, the proceeds of which are dedicated exclusively to the support of the public schools. Following these extensive grants in support of "common schools," as they were called, came the Morrill Land Grant Acts with equally generous grants in support of higher education.[10]

Shortly after the first Morrill Act in 1862, the Office of Education was established to collect statistics and facts to show the condition and progress of education, to encourage and assist in the establishment and maintenance of efficient school systems, and otherwise to promote the cause of education. The activities of this Office now include education at all levels—elementary, secondary, higher, and vocational. It has also been assigned responsibility for administering many programs under the National Defense Education Act of 1958.

Although most Americans profess great interest in education and have contributed more or less generously for its support, they have never bothered to formulate anything that even remotely resembles a positive national policy on education. As long as good land was still available, tremendous grants were made for the support of both "common schools" and land-grant colleges; when the supply of desirable lands became largely depleted, cash grants, often in substantial amounts, began to appear. Be-

[10] See Rivlin, Alice M., *The Role of the Federal Government in Financing Higher Education* (Washington: Brookings Institution, 1962) and Nevins, Allan, *The State Universities and Democracy* (Urbana: University of Illinois Press, 1962).

cause Americans have always cherished a belief in the importance of local control over local schools, there has been a constant fear that in spite of all reasonable precautions to prevent it Federal support of education might eventually develop into some form of Federal control over the curriculum and over school personnel, although such a fear seems unfounded in view of the tremendous variety of services performed by the government in other functional fields. Moreover, it seems rather paradoxical in view of the allegiance and support generally given the government in recognition of these services.

The few existing elements of national policy, however, are largely grounded upon this fear. Some seize upon it as a means of preventing all action; in fact, the Senator who most resolutely opposed Federal intervention in education himself invoked the authority of the Federal Government in requiring a loyalty oath as a means of establishing eligibility for a student loan. In general, there has been a willingness to have Federal grants to assist particular school programs such as vocational education, student loans, government contracts for research, and the like. Grants have been authorized for school construction, college dormitories, and other school facilities and equipment, perhaps on the theory that it is safe to allow the government to supply bricks and mortar but not to train teachers. Perhaps these Congressional opponents of Federal intervention in education believe that by agreeing to do a little they can prevent the enactment of any major legislation aimed at financing an adequate program of school support.

It appears to be acceptable for the Federal government to organize and administer schools for the children of American parents stationed abroad, for the children of armed service personnel at defense installations at home, and for Indian children, but quite unacceptable for it to influence public school policy in general. Congress has been willing under certain circumstances to supply funds for school maintenance and operation, but not for teachers' salaries. When legislation could be related to national defense and security, Congress has gone further (as in the National Defense Education Act of 1958) than under normal peacetime conditions. The absence of a national policy or of uniform standards in the field of education results in schools of very uneven quality throughout the nation.

While the so-called population explosion gives warning of unprecedented needs for school support in the years ahead, needs which can be met only by far greater financial outlays than State and local governments seem willing or able to provide, the problem of Federal aid for education assumes increasing importance. For more than a decade, this type of legislation has been a sort of political football. Every extraneous matter that could be pressed into service has been seized upon to confuse the issue, which can be very simply stated: Do the American people honestly want the best schools and the best education that can be provided for the youth of the land? In general up to this time, the division on this question has revealed the same basic attitudes and political cleavages that are apparent on other major issues with important social implications. Strangely enough, the very areas where the opposition is most deeply entrenched are the areas which, on the basis of any apportionment formula that might conceivably be adopted, would gain the most.

Highways

Road building in this country began and for a long period of time continued to be a local responsibility. Actually, judged by modern standards, the roads that were built would never pass inspection, as accounts written by early travelers abundantly testify. City streets were not much better; early accounts indicate that many of them were little better than wallowing mud-holes into which all manner of refuse was indiscriminately thrown. Benjamin Franklin, first in so many things, appears to have been first to urge the paving of city streets.

Some private toll roads were constructed for intercity travel, and the Federal government contributed to the building of roads to the West as part of the internal improvement program. State governments showed no particular interest in road building until the bicycle craze developed late in the nineteenth century and the motor car began to establish itself as an important means of transportation early in the twentieth. Both developments spurred the demand for smooth and, in time, hard-surfaced roads. In the period between 1893 and 1917, many State highway departments were established. All of the twenty-two existing in 1910 were small. Only seven had designated a State highway system. Less than one-half million motor vehicles were in use in 1910; by 1915, the number had increased to nearly 2.5 million; by 1920, it was nine million; and it has continued to increase ever since. The move toward the establishment of State highway departments received great impetus under the first Federal-aid Highway Act of 1916, one of the requirements of which was that each State must have a single department or agency responsible for its road building operations.

The early road building operations of the State departments were concerned to a large degree with the need for getting the farmers "out of the mud"; later they were centered on the development of farm-to-market roads. The experience of Pennsylvania was more or less typical of what happened in many States. The first act creating a highway department in that State was passed in 1903; construction work was under a highway commissioner from then until 1911, when the present department was created. At that time, the State also took over nearly 9,000 miles of township roads, to which mileage additions were made through the intervening years until the system comprised nearly 34,000 miles of road. In 1933, the maintenance of some 48,000 additional miles was undertaken without actually adding this mileage to the State highway system. In other jurisdictions, State grants-in-aid for roads were provided for the local units, in a manner parallel to that in which the Federal government was providing financial assistance to the States.

By 1926, when the Federal grant-in-aid program for highways was ten years old, the Federal government had established standards which State executives found difficult and burdensome. Recalling his experience many years later, Senator Harry F. Byrd observed:

> The standards were so restrictive and so difficult to meet that when I became Governor of Virginia in 1926 I had difficulty in obtaining Federal funds from Washington, to which we were entitled, because of the very high standard which the Federal Department of Roads maintained at that time. I am not challenging it. I think perhaps that department has been as well managed as any other. But the fact remains that during that particular period, before we were entering into the construction of costly roads, there was a time when it was difficult for the States to match by 50 per cent the Federal contribution by reason of the high standard established by the Federal Government.[11]

Grants for highways were continued year by year—with the exception of the war years—in increasing amounts until 1956 when the Interstate Highway System was authorized. By the summer of 1963, one-third of the system was open to traffic, although the Commissioner was careful to emphasize that this mileage had not actually been completed. Of the 14,829 miles open to traffic, some 2,300 miles were toll roads, bridges, and tunnels, and 3,000 miles had been improved only to capacity for the handling of current traffic. Ten thousand miles of the system, however, 70 per cent, had been brought to the 1975 standard that has been established as the goal. Shortly thereafter, the Commissioner stressed four major highway problem areas: nonuniformity, research, cooperation, and integrity. In connection with these, he raised some very blunt questions bearing on intergovernmental relations:

> Is the endless variation among the State highway departments and other highway agencies in structural design criteria, construction specifi-

[11] Remarks on the floor of the Senate, *Congressional Record*, May 5, 1949, p. 5652.

cations, and methods of test really necessary? . . . You may raise an eyebrow at the concept of uniform construction specifications for nation-wide application. Why not? [12]

In the field of research, some States are using their full allotments and are even supplementing them, while others are using little or none of their allocated research and planning funds. Twelve States account for 75 per cent of the available funds that have not been used. The cooperation problem arises particularly in the area of urban transportation. At a series of regional conferences of officials at all levels of government, civic and business leaders, and the press, a pilot city program is to be planned for each State to serve as a demonstration project. This is described as "a long-range effort to undertake the development of transportation plans and programs in every city above 5,000 population in the United States," the objective being "that the Federal-aid system will be developed as an integral part of a soundly based, balanced transportation system for the area involved." After emphasizing the point that "we cannot successfully attack the urban problem in piecemeal fashion," the Commissioner still felt it necessary to assure his audience of State highway officials that "this is not intended as Federal meddling, nor are the provisions unduly restrictive."

The Commissioner's fourth major problem was integrity in the use of the public funds which finance the entire highway program. The few instances in which such funds have been misused have hurt the program and the highway industry as a whole. To those who complain that the Federal law and regulations are too restrictive, a few instances clearly show that occasionally they may not have been restrictive enough.[13] Representative John A. Blatnik, Chairman of a Subcommittee on the Federal Highway Program, in the course of extensive hearings uncovered evidence of widespread irregularities in four States—Florida, Massachusetts, New Mexico, and Oklahoma. The evidence was of such a nature as to create a

[12] See speeches by Whitton, Rex M., "One-third Done, Two-thirds to Go," before Ninth Highway Transportation Congress, Washington, May 10, 1962, and "Four Tigers: Major Highway Problem Areas," before the Western Association of State Highway Officials, Seattle, June 11, 1962. The latter is printed in the *Congressional Record*, June 12, 1962, pp. A4348–A4350.

[13] See, for example, Special Subcommittee on the Federal-aid Highway Program, *Right of Way Acquisition Practices in Massachusetts*, Hearings, Part I, February, 1962 (Washington: 87th Cong., 2nd Sess., 1962). That problems of this character are neither new nor recent is attested by the natural cement case which developed in Minnesota under Governor Stassen in the late 1930's; see Ylvisaker, Paul N., *The Natural Cement Case*, in the Inter-University Case Program, reprinted in Stein, Harold, *Public Administration and Policy Development* (New York: Harcourt, Brace & Company, 1952), pp. 107–141.

strong presumption that similar practices existed in other States, and it was feared that they might even be nationwide. One of the most common abuses involved gifts of cash or items of value by contractors to officials and employees of State highway departments and their families. On one Oklahoma project, the Subcommittee found deficiencies in construction totalling more than half a million dollars:

> Investigation by the staff, and unrefuted testimony adduced at the hearings, disclosed that the contractor did, in fact, ignore the specifications, that substandard materials were used during construction of the bypass, that there was improper weighing of materials, that there was falsification of test reports and test samples, that there was double billing for materials and overpayments for materials and, finally, that there were shortages of materials in the finished highway.

Such moral and ethical problems are not, however, the only illustrations of the problems that develop in the field of intergovernmental relations. The prohibition of signs along the right-of-way on Interstate Highways and the control of over-hanging signs on any highway in the construction of which Federal funds have been spent have had wide publicity. In the case of the former, the law authorizes a small financial inducement to the States, which most of them have been quick to accept, for compliance with Federal policy; as in the case of other federally aided highways, the burden of enforcement is placed upon the State department of highways. If the department has previously approved the erection of signs, the enforcement of compliance with Federal policy can place the department in a difficult position. Thus in Michigan in 1962, the tourist industry was so unhappy about the expense of moving certain signs that appeal was made to the State legislature, which responded by passing a resolution requesting the highway department to re-examine its sign removal policies.[14]

Social Welfare

Social welfare provides an extraordinarily good example of an age-old activity that was originally a purely private concern, later becoming a responsibility of governments at all levels. When haphazard private alms-giving, supplemented by the efforts of churches, fraternal groups, and political organizations, proved unable to meet the need, charities' aid societies were organized and local government began to concern itself with

[14] See Cederberg, Elford A., in the *Congressional Record,* June 5, 1962, pp. 9024–9025.

what was then called "poor relief." After World War I, the States established departments of welfare, and when during the Great Depression private, local, and State resources together proved to be completely inadequate, the national government stepped in to assume responsibility for certain aspects of the program. Although public assistance or welfare programs had historically been a function of State and local government, the pattern established in emergency relief became a permanent part of our governmental system. When the Social Security Act was passed in 1935, it was designed to operate within the State and local government framework.

Public welfare, therefore, in its modern sense—the acceptance by government of a responsibility to provide shelter and a minimum amount of sustenance and medical care for the helpless, the young, the indigent, and the aged—dates back only thirty years to the Roosevelt era. The social welfare program as a whole, as it now exists, is so constructed that there is at least one purely Federal program, a few State programs, and a number of joint Federal-State programs. Social security (OASI), a completely Federal program, is not for the dispensing of charity. It is, on the contrary, a vast program of social insurance under which, through contributions made jointly by the insured and his employer, funds are accumulated for the payment of benefits to those who have retired on age or disability, payments to cover at least in part the costs that result from the hazards of life. In the administration of this enormous program, the Federal government maintains individual accounts for millions of Americans. While the law states who is eligible to draw benefits and under what conditions, it is necessary to apply both the law and the rules and regulations to the specific conditions relating to the status of individual human beings. Thus millions of elderly people are brought into a direct personal relationship with the Federal government.

Workmen's compensation, on the other hand, is an exclusively State program, organized under State law and State financed. Unemployment compensation is a tax supported program, unique in that it is State administered with all administrative costs paid by the Federal government. Other major programs which are also federally aided but State administered lie in the field of public assistance, including aid to the blind (AB), aid for dependent children (ADC), aid for the permanently and totally disabled (APTD), old age assistance (OAA), and medical care for the aged (MCFA). General assistance, which is public relief to needy persons who are not eligible for one of the other assistance programs, is financed by the State and local units without Federal funds. Taken together, these assistance programs provide an outstanding example of cooperative federalism in action.

The Newburgh Incident. As has been noted in connection with programs in other functional fields, a single incident, relatively unimportant in and of itself, can serve to center the spotlight of national publicity upon a particular program. Such an incident occurred in the field of public assistance in the City of Newburgh, New York. It broke into the headlines in the spring of 1961. The basic facts were that in a small upstate New York city, an increasing number of in-migrants was placing a heavy financial burden upon the local government, particularly with respect to housing accommodations and welfare costs. Thus a complex situation developed in which many factors were involved: race relations, pressure group activity, welfare policies and costs, and perhaps most important of all, the political power of a publicity-seeking city manager. From the point of view of intergovernmental relations, public welfare is itself an outstanding example. The developments at Newburgh vividly illustrate the interplay of the Federal, State, and local law and administration in this field. Newburgh was unusual, largely in the amount of publicity it received; its problems in welfare, finance, and intergovernmental relations were quite typical of those faced by many local units in New York and other States.

Although other aspects of the public assistance program were involved, the Newburgh episode centered around aid for dependent children, a program in which provision is made for a large measure of State and local administration. Some degree of uniformity has been achieved through the grant-in-aid technique, the States having cooperated voluntarily in this and other Federal programs because of powerful financial inducements. As Arthur P. Miles has written, "Public welfare administration . . . is a partnership. The chief operating partner is the State with the Federal Government . . . and the localities serving as the administrative agents of the State." [15] In essence, the Federal government has, through the Social Security Act, wrapped itself around the various State and local welfare programs in an effort to achieve national standards in public welfare scope and administration. Under the Act, the States must meet certain general requirements to qualify for public assistance grants-in-aid. The following is a brief summary outline:

1. The law must be in effect in all political subdivisions of the State.
2. There must be a single agency for the administration or supervision of the program.
3. There must be financial participation by the State.
4. The State must provide fair hearings for dissatisfied applicants and recipients.

[15] Miles, Arthur P., *An Introduction to Public Welfare* (Boston: D. C. Heath and Co., 1949), p. 380; see also Friedlander, Walter A., *Introduction to Social Welfare* (Englewood Cliffs, N.J.: Prentice-Hall, Inc., 1961), pp. 260–268.

5. Employees of the State and county public assistance agencies must be selected through a merit system.

6. The States are required to have such methods of administration as are found to be necessary for the efficient operation of the plan.

7. The State agency must make such reports as the Federal authority may find necessary.

8. The State must take into consideration all income and resources in determining eligibility and computing grants.

9. The State and local agencies must keep all records confidential.

10. The Federal government will not provide Federal funds for both old age assistance and aid to the blind grants for the same individuals.

11. Certain eligibility requirements, such as age standards, are imposed upon the States.

At the State level, reference is made to New York because this is the State in which the City of Newburgh is located. Article XVII of the State Constitution contains a basic statement of welfare policy:

> The aid, care and support of the needy are public concerns and shall be provided by the State and such of its subdivisions in such manner and by such means as the legislature may from time to time determine.

The State Board of Social Welfare, which is responsible for the practical application and administration of this policy, has enunciated two basic purposes which guide all State activities relating to the care of the needy: (1) to assure that adequate provision is made for the care of the needy at public expense and (2) to assure that only those who are in need will be so maintained and only for so much of their maintenance as cannot be and is not provided by themselves or other sources. Even before the Newburgh incident brought public assistance policies into the headlines in virtually every newspaper in the country, there were latent signs of doubt and some criticism regarding these policies. These developments were reflected in a New York report on controls and safeguards designed to prevent fraud and waste in the administration of public assistance; to prevent abuses by employables and interstate abuses; to limit or minimize expenditures; and to recover expenditures which were later found to have been unwarranted.

Thus it is a mistake to assume that criticism of New York's welfare program began with the controversy at Newburgh. Dissatisfaction with the program or with the manner in which it was being administered was evident for many months before Newburgh became headline news. The Senate majority leader had spearheaded a drive for a tighter welfare policy in the 1960 legislature. His bill requiring one-year residency as a requisite for relief benefits was vetoed by Governor Rockefeller; in the next session, however, a six-month residence eligibility requirement was enacted and signed by the Governor. Another indication of the lack of confidence in the State's welfare program was illustrated by the Temporary State Commission on Coordination of State Activities, established in 1961 and authorized to study the administration of public welfare. In its report, this Commission called for replacement of the Board of Social Welfare by a board more responsible to the Governor, more professional in character, and policy-making rather than advisory in function.

To a degree, then, Newburgh was an extreme manifestation of some rather widespread notions that the State welfare program was not functioning properly. Upstate leaders had been particularly critical of the program, and had called for improvement in efficiency and effectiveness within the existing organizational framework. There is little evidence that serious consideration was given to such radical alterations in welfare policy as were to be presented so forcefully by the leaders in Newburgh.

The City of Newburgh, with a population of some 31,000, is located sixty miles up the Hudson River from New York City in Orange County. The area is hilly and predominantly rural and agricultural in character. There are a few low-paying textile mills in the city, little heavy industry. Berries and fruit are the major crops. Since the war, migratory workers have been imported to pick berries and work in the orchards. Many of them, when the season is over, continue to live in Newburgh, creating a welfare problem of a type common to many American cities. The non-white population of Newburgh is listed at 5,143 or 16.6 per cent of the whole, as compared to 6.4 per cent of the national population in 1960. With this influx of unskilled, low-income labor came difficult problems in public welfare. There simply were not enough year-round jobs in Newburgh for so large a supply of unskilled labor, and many families were forced to go on relief. The city claimed that 5 per cent of its population was on relief in the spring of 1961 and that it was spending 30 per cent of its total budget of $3.5 million for welfare and public assistance.[16]

A by-product of the population growth of Newburgh was the creation of extensive, spreading slum areas along the city's waterfront which crept across the city and severely reduced real estate values and thus the city's property tax receipts. This development served to stimulate the growth of suburban areas outside the city's corporate limits. Tax increases became necessary, and many residents believed that the welfare program was both the cause and effect of the higher tax rates. Newburgh's problems were unique among comparable cities in upstate New York only because it was one of the five municipalities in the State administering its own welfare

[16] *The New York Times,* June 11, 1961.

program. Welfare programs are generally administered by the county government, but Newburgh has been administering its own since 1853.[17]

Things began to happen when the new city manager declared war on the welfare program. "We've got to do something about welfare here. And I intend to do it."[18] On the first of May, welfare recipients were ordered to police headquarters to pick up their checks; the purpose of the muster, according to Mitchell, the new city manager, was to uncover welfare chiselers. None were found. The action brought the following official comment from the area director of the State Department of Social Welfare:

> You had no right to call a muster which consisted of ordering ambulatory welfare recipients, including the aged, the blind, the disabled, the handicapped, and mothers, to go to the Newburgh police headquarters.

The State also threatened to withdraw State and Federal funds from the city. Mitchell and the city council ignored the State, saying that it was interfering in justified local efforts to reduce welfare expense. Thus the conflict was born.[19]

The city followed this initial action with the adoption of a new welfare code that became the core of the controversy. Adopted on June 19 over the strenuous objections of Mayor Ryan, the code was to become effective on July 15. It was this code and its famous thirteen points that elevated Newburgh's welfare problems to the national level, both legally and editorially:

> 1. All cash payments which can be converted to food, clothing and rent vouchers and the like without basic harm to the intent of the aid shall be issued in voucher form henceforth.
>
> 2. All able-bodied adult males on relief of any kind who are capable of working are to be assigned to the chief of building maintenance for work assignment on a forty-hour week.
>
> 3. All recipients physically capable of and available for private employment who are offered a job but refuse it, regardless of the type of employment involved, are to be denied relief.
>
> 4. All mothers of illegitimate children are to be advised that should they have more children out of wedlock, they shall be denied relief.
>
> 5. All applicants for relief who have left a job voluntarily, i.e., who have not been fired or laid off, shall be denied relief.

[17] *The New York Times*, May 23, 1961, and Greenfield, Meg, "The 'Relief Chiselers' of Newburgh," *The Reporter*, August 17, 1961, pp. 37–40.

[18] Rollins, William B., and Lefkowitz, Bernard, "Welfare à la Newburgh," *The Nation*, September 16, 1961, p. 158.

[19] *The New York Times*, May 19 (for the quotation) and May 23, 1961.

6. The allotment for any one family unit shall not exceed the take-home pay of the lowest paid city employee with a family of comparable size. Also no relief shall be granted to any family whose income is in excess of the latter figure.

7. All files of all Aid to Dependent Children cases are to be brought to the office of the corporation counsel for review monthly. All new cases of any kind shall be referred to the corporation counsel prior to certification of payment.

8. All applicants for relief who are new to the city must show evidence that their plans in coming to the city involved a concrete offer of employment, similar to that required of foreign immigrants. All such persons shall be limited to two weeks of relief. Those who cannot show evidence shall be limited to one week of relief.

9. Aid to persons except the aged, blind and disabled shall be limited to three months in any one year—this is a feature similar to present employment benefits policy.

10. All recipients who are not disabled, blind, ambulatory or otherwise incapacitated shall report to the Department of Welfare monthly for a conference regarding the status of their case.

11. Once the budget for the fiscal year is approved by the council, it shall not be exceeded by the Welfare Department unless approved by council for a supplementary appropriation.

12. There shall be a monthly expenditure limit on all categories of welfare aid. This monthly expenditure limit shall be established by the Department of Welfare at the time of presenting the budget, and shall take into account seasonable variations.

13. Prior to certifying or continuing any more Aid to Dependent Children cases, a determination shall be made as to home environment. If the home environment is not satisfactory, the children in that home shall be placed in foster care in lieu of welfare aid to the family adults.

Reaction to the new code was immediate and vocal, as many groups hastened to go on record in opposition to the plan. Major objections were concentrated on the points dealing with Aid to Dependent Children, the provision limiting relief to not more than three months in any one year, and the provision requiring able-bodied men to accept work on city work-relief projects. The following editorial from *The New York Times* fairly summarizes the opposition to the code and stresses the importance of State governmental responsibility in the situation:

The State and Federal governments, supplying a considerable percentage of the money, have a legal as well as a moral interest in standards. Albany has always been timid in asserting its disciplinary power to correct local deficiencies. . . . The State has a duty to help Newburgh as well as to forbid cruel and unusual punishment for the crime of being poor. Newburgh . . . must be made by the State to realize that it is not a law unto itself.[20]

The State Board of Social Welfare held a special meeting in New York City on June 26 to discuss the Newburgh program. A special five-member committee was appointed to investigate the problem. The Board was, of course, conscious of the critical feeling generated by the Newburgh code, but even without this interest group pressure, it would have been compelled to challenge the program. Several of the provisions of the code appeared to be in direct conflict with the basic Federal public assistance regulations listed previously; as such, they constituted a threat to the State's Federal grant program. The State's interest in the administration of local welfare in Newburgh went beyond the New York law governing State-local welfare relations. The Board's concern was, to a great degree, the reflection of the indirect power of a third governmental unit—the Federal government.

Federal power in State public assistance programs had been strengthened by recent Congressional action. During the winter, Congress had, as an anti-recession measure, authorized aid to dependent children in families where the father was unemployed. Prior to this action, aid of this type was granted only to families where the father was absent, incapacitated, or dead. It was estimated that New York would receive between $16 and $20 million in additional Federal aid as a result of this legislation. However, the Federal program did not appear to permit localities to force fathers receiving aid to work on relief projects. Work relief was a major part of the Newburgh program; this factor alone could have cost the State millions of dollars in Federal funds. There was also the possibility that the Newburgh code would jeopardize the entire $150 million Federal assistance program in New York.[21]

When the special committee held a hearing on the Newburgh program in Albany, Mr. Mitchell, the City Council, and Newburgh welfare officials were asked to appear. After only limited testimony by Newburgh officials, the committee held that the code violated both Federal and State welfare law, pointing out also that as a result of its investigation, it found welfare problems in Newburgh to be less severe than they had been pictured by the city. It recommended that the State Board forbid Newburgh to carry out its proposed welfare program.

The position of Mr. John J. O'Donnell, Newburgh's welfare director, clearly illustrates the basic intergovernmental aspect of the controversy. Mr. O'Donnell, who was a State civil service employee receiving 80 per

[20] *The New York Times,* June 29, 1961; for report on statements of opposition, see June 27.

[21] *The New York Times,* June 29, 1961.

cent of his salary from the State, testified at the hearing that he could not legally enforce eleven of the thirteen points in the Newburgh code. He was in the peculiar position of having two masters who viewed his role from completely opposite points of view. After the hearing, he was branded a "turncoat" by the Newburgh officials. Three days later he resigned, and the city lost the services of an official who had more than twenty years' experience in welfare administration.[22]

Disregarding the decision of the State committee, the city manager said that the new code would go into effect as planned on July 15. As a means of enforcing compliance, the State could cut off welfare funds to Newburgh or request court action to halt the program. The city manager said that the city would welcome a court test of its code. As the conflict deepened, other elements of the State government were drawn into the fray. On July 11, Mayor Ryan sent the following telegram to Governor Rockefeller: "As Mayor of the City of Newburgh, I respectfully call upon you to speak out and use Executive powers to direct the State Board of Welfare to enjoin the enactment of the illegal thirteen point welfare program." [23]

At a news conference, Governor Rockefeller declined to take action until Newburgh violated State and Federal law by actually implementing its code. In response to a question concerning his ultimate authority in the Newburgh situation, he said, "I have the power to remove local government officials from office." [24] The Governor's authority was an additional means of enforcing compliance with State and Federal law, but this type of coercive action could scarcely be expected to contribute to long-run, positive State-local cooperation. Hence he did not openly offer it as a means of solving the problem.

Early in July the State Board had accepted the findings of its special committee and held the Newburgh code illegal. Commissioner Houston on July 13 ordered Newburgh not to carry out the provisions of the code and sent five State welfare officials to Newburgh to investigate the city's welfare records. Mitchell, the city manager, again refusing to comply with the State agency's directions, said:

> Mr. Houston is not the boss of the City of Newburgh even if he would like to think he is. The regulations are going into effect on July 15 as scheduled. Houston's actions merely prove the point we have been making that the State Board of Social Welfare attempts to dictate policy in local government without recognizing the need of such government.[25]

[22] *The New York Times,* June 29, 1961.
[23] *The New York Times,* June 29, 1961; also July 12, 1961.
[24] *The New York Times,* July 14, 1961.
[25] *The New York Times,* July 13, 1961.

Newburgh's code went into effect as planned on July 15. Mitchell said that the city would seek court action if the State welfare agency attempted to cut off State and Federal welfare funds. These funds, amounting to $500 thousand, comprise 55 per cent of the city's welfare budget.[26] At this point, the city had successfully thwarted every effort of the State welfare agency to direct welfare policy in Newburgh.

On July 19, the Board asked Attorney General Lefkowitz to seek a court injunction to halt the program. Solicitor General Paxton Blair was assigned to investigate the case. On August 2, the Attorney General sought an injunction before the State Supreme Court. Justice Joseph P. Donohue granted a temporary injunction on August 19 [27] which was made permanent on December 21. The court then ruled that twelve of the thirteen points were illegal.[28] Newburgh complied with the ruling of the court and halted this phase of its welfare program. However, the city continued with welfare "reforms" that were not a part of the basic code. City welfare workers were replaced with non-professionals; a former Newburgh high school physical education teacher was made director of city welfare. All welfare recipients were photographed and efforts were begun to publish names of such recipients in the press. Mitchell continued to pursue a "tough" welfare policy in Newburgh.

In the end the State was able to suppress the welfare rebellion at Newburgh and protect the State welfare program. Suppression, however, can hardly be termed a triumph in intergovernmental relations. Newburgh was, to some degree, symptomatic of general dissatisfaction with the State's program, and the Governor was quick to realize that cooperative rather than coercive relationships were necessary if State and local units were to solve their joint welfare problems. With this in mind, he appointed an eleven-member study group to make a broad survey of welfare in the State. He took this action under the authority of New York's well-known Moreland Act which permits him to investigate State and local government.[29] Newburgh's effect on the establishment of this study may be considered as its sole contribution to constructive intergovernmental relations.

National Impact. Newburgh's attempt to establish welfare policy apart from the State and Federal governments engendered an enormous amount of public discussion, favorable and unfavorable. Support for

[26] *The New York Times,* July 16, 1961.

[27] *The New York Times,* August 19, 1961.

[28] *The New York Times,* December 23, 1961.

[29] *The New York Times,* August 31, 1961; this report led to legislation establishing a Bureau of Registry and Location of Deserting Parents. See Infausto, Felix, and Rosenblatt, Nathan, "New York State Services for Locating Deserting Parents," *State Government,* Winter, 1963, pp. 45-48.

Newburgh's position came from conservative elements, often anti-welfare, who have never accepted the welfare reforms of the Roosevelt era. Some may be attributed to the frustrations that many areas had experienced in administering their welfare programs. The issues presented by the Newburgh incident were discussed on the editorial pages of both the major national papers and the smallest rural ones.[30] Conservative leaders such as Senators Goldwater and Tower and Representative St. George enthusiastically supported Newburgh. Mrs. St. George, who said she was "tired of professional chiselers walking up and down the streets," asserted that she "would like to see every city in the country adopt the plan." [31]

The attitude of Senators Javits and Keating illustrates a more constructive approach to the problem, particularly with respect to work relief. In July, these Senators met with Secretary of Health, Education, and Welfare Ribicoff to discuss the work relief provisions of the modified aid to dependent children legislation that Congress had passed in the winter. Many in New York felt that work relief was a necessary part of an effective welfare program, but the new Federal law appeared to disallow work relief projects. The Newburgh crisis had stimulated interest in a work relief program, and the Senators sought a clarification of the law. Several days after the meeting, Secretary Ribicoff issued a statement approving work relief and giving local units the option to apply work relief programs.

The national impact of the Newburgh controversy was evident at the August meeting of the County Officers Conference in Chicago. Newburgh was a main topic at the meeting, and both Mr. Mitchell and Governor Rockefeller were speakers.[32] The one aspect of the Newburgh controversy on which both proponents and opponents of public welfare agreed was that Newburgh had served to illustrate the need for welfare reform. Positive reform by definition requires improvement in intergovernmental relations. Most of the abuses in the program were traceable to defects in intergovernmental administration. In December, Secretary Ribicoff introduced a new ten-point welfare reform plan. Several points in this plan, such as the requirement of special units in the States for locating deserting parents, are directly aimed at improving intergovernmental welfare administration. Although the Secretary said "that 'his hackles were raised' by the suggestion that his program was stimulated by the Newburgh code," the discussion of welfare policy raised by Newburgh

[30] Examples: Editorial in *The Wall Street Journal,* July 10, 1961; Editorial in the *Milford Chronicle* (Delaware), November 10, 1961.

[31] *The New York Times,* July 19, 1961.

[32] *The New York Times,* July 20, 1961.

certainly will not detract from the Federal government's efforts to shape welfare policy with a "hard head and compassionate heart." [33]

In January, 1962, a conference of over 100 welfare officials met in Washington at the request of Secretary Ribicoff to discuss his plan for improvements in the nation's welfare program. "There was unanimous support for the goals and objectives of both the administrative directives and the overall legislative measures, and a majority of the State welfare directors specifically approved recommendations in line with the suggestions made by the Secretary. While some recommendations looked toward a tightening up of the rules, other jurisdictions took action to make it easier for needy persons to obtain assistance. Delaware, New York, Rhode Island, and a citizen's welfare committee in the District of Columbia, recommended dropping the one-year residence requirement for eligibility.

After Newburgh put public welfare in the headlines, it was evident that a new symbol of unrest had been found. A whole rash of studies and investigations was launched. In addition to the Governor's investigation under the Moreland Act, the New York State Board of Social Welfare, having "been concerned over the years with the many problems that have stemmed from Federal-State relationships in the public welfare field, especially with the steadily increasing domination by Federal authorities and the consequent loss of State and local autonomy," found it necessary to express "its very real alarm" over the latest welfare proposals from the Federal Department of Health, Education, and Welfare. Investigations of welfare chiseling were launched amidst great publicity in the District of Columbia and other jurisdictions. A new emphasis on work relief projects appears in reports from many areas. Public welfare, especially the aid for dependent children program and general assistance, appeared to be in for a period of intensive public scrutiny.

Veterans Administration

An awareness of the importance of intergovernmental relations has recently appeared in a number of Federal agencies, most of which have paid little attention to such relationships in the past. Each of them is now trying to develop suitable procedures for dealing in an effective manner with such problems as arise in this field. Of these agencies, the Veterans Administration is a good illustration. The V.A., as it is known throughout

---

[33] *Washington Post*, December 12, 1961; see also Burns, Eveline M., "What's Wrong With Public Welfare?" *Welfare Reporter*, January, 1962, pp. 6–16.

the country, held a conference of its district office managers in the fall of 1960, in the course of which an effort was made to create in the minds of the managers an awareness of their responsibility for coordination with related State and local agencies, public and private, in the interests of more effective service to their veteran clientele. They were told that total service to veterans, their dependents, and survivors requires communication, cooperation, and coordination within the V.A. and between V.A. and all levels of government in the States. The lines of action in intergovernmental relations required to accomplish this purpose were presented to them in graphic form, as shown in the following chart. Those attending the conference were given the following succinct statement of V.A. policy on intergovernmental relations:

> Managers must take the initiative.
> Regional Office Manager of jurisdiction is responsible in some cases.
> Common solution to problems preferred where possible.
> Independent station action appropriate in many cases.
> Central Office may occasionally designate managers to coordinate relations.
> Goal of effective relations which will:
>   a. Avoid duplication of effort.
>   b. Eliminate overlapping functions.
>   c. Improve service to veterans.

VETERANS ADMINISTRATION
LINES OF ACTION IN INTERGOVERNMENTAL RELATIONS

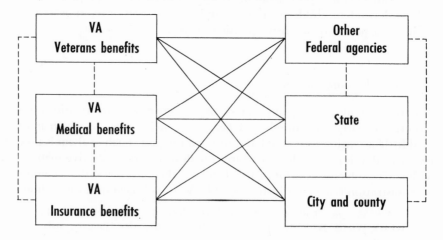

COOPERATIVE FEDERALISM IN NEW AREAS

Not only has the pattern of cooperation been firmly established in a variety of programs and agencies, but it has fortunately become so much accepted as a normal procedure for getting things done that it is being utilized in some areas in which governmental activity at any level is itself something new. The following section is devoted to developments in two such areas: cooperation in the development of peaceful uses of atomic energy, and coordination and cooperation in the development of programs in the field of science.

A third area, the drafting of legislation, might also serve as an appropriate illustration. Significant as the work of the Committee on Suggested State Legislation has been, it is but a part of the cooperative effort in the drafting of legislation. In Chapter V, attention was given to new techniques in the drafting of both Federal and State legislation on pleasure boating. This may not be a vitally important legislative subject, but the techniques developed while the work on it was in progress may readily be applied to other legislative subjects.

Control of Atomic Energy Development

The atomic age began in Chicago on December 2, 1942, when scientists first released energy from the uranium atom in a controlled reactor (atomic furnace). The story of intergovernmental relations in the control of this new source of energy is somewhat unique in that it reverses what has come to be regarded as the normal line of development. There was virtually no regulation existing in this field prior to 1946 when the Atomic Energy Act, sponsored by the late Senator Brian McMahon of Connecticut, was enacted into law. Atomic development has taken place so rapidly that in the 1960's atomic energy is playing a vital role in the life of every man, woman, and child in the country.

Federal Legislation. The Atomic Energy Act of 1946 was enacted during a period of popular excitement following important discoveries in the field of nuclear science. When it was passed, American scientists seemed, for the time being at least, to have a monopoly in the field. Since attention was almost exclusively on the national defense aspects of atomic development, the possible peacetime uses of atomic energy were largely ignored. Because of this concentration on the defense aspects of the problem, it was believed that atomic information was of a highly secret character. Under these circumstances, it seemed natural to vest exclusive control over its development and utilization in the Federal government which, under the terms of the Act, pre-empted the field.

It was not until nearly a decade later that it became apparent that important changes in the law were desirable and perhaps even necessary. The principles of atomic science had become so widely known among the peoples of the world that continued secrecy was absurd if not impossible. Furthermore, when the vast possibilities of the peacetime uses of atomic energy came to be realized, it was apparent that the States had a large, important interest in atomic development. With the passage of the second Atomic Energy Act in 1954 (amended in 1959), a new era in atomic energy regulation began as the Federal government relinquished its monopoly in atomic activities. Local interest in some aspects of the problem such as those relating to health and safety, is both considerable and legitimate. Such problems do not necessarily require a uniform rule; the 1954 Act recognized this but left open the question of the scope of State authority and the manner in which it was to be exercised. It also prepared the way for private investment and development of atomic energy.

The new law not only recognized the interests of the States in the peaceful uses of atomic energy, but the need for clarification of the respective responsibilities of the Federal government and the States. Specific procedures were provided for the Atomic Energy Commission to relinquish and the State governments to assume responsibility for the exercise of control over atomic materials. Under this plan, the Governor of the State certifies that his State has a program for the control of radiation hazards which is adequate to protect public health and safety with respect to the materials covered by the agreement and that it is the desire of the State to assume regulatory responsibility. The AEC then evaluates the State program; if found to be adequate, a formal agreement may be drawn and executed for the official transfer of regulatory responsibility.[34] On February 8, 1962, Kentucky became the first State in the Nation to assume control of nuclear energy materials under these provisions.

Increasing State Interest in Atomic Energy. The interest of the States in atomic energy development has been stimulated by a number of considerations. In the first place, the States are interested in the possibility of cheap power for industrial development and economic growth, but they are interested as well in knowing more about the effects of atomic radiation on problems of industrial health, occupational disease, and work-

[34] The 1954 Act was amended in 1959 by Public Law 86-373; for analysis of its provisions with respect to Federal-State relations, see Neel, James N., Jr., "The States' New Role in Atomic Energy," *Kentucky Law Journal,* Spring, 1961, pp. 351-362.

men's compensation. State agencies most directly concerned with these problems are the public utility commissions, health departments, and labor and industrial safety divisions. Others involved may include departments of conservation, insurance, highways, and agriculture; natural resource agencies; planning and development agencies; commissions regulating the sale of securities; and workmen's compensation boards.

Evidence of this mounting interest on the part of the States has been indicated in a number of ways. States have adopted legislation covering the establishment and organization of appropriate administrative agencies, making possible the development of atomic power, and regulatory measures required in the interests of public health and safety.

As of November, 1958, there was not a single State that had not established either some sort of administrative agency or study committee looking toward a State agency.[35] Some States chose coordinators, others a coordinating commission. Only nine States had not had one or more study commissions charged with study of the problems involved and recommending needed legislation. California had had two such commissions; New York, four. All of this activity had taken place since 1955, following the Congressional legislation of 1954, and seemed to indicate the readiness of the States to assume the larger role in the task of controlling radiation hazards that they had long been requesting.

The experience of New York has been unique in some respects, but in others more or less typical of the States in their desire to succeed in their new role. In a special message to the legislature in February, 1959,[36] Governor Rockefeller pointed out that New York was losing its lead in the field to California and asked the legislature to create a State Office of Atomic Energy Development. This was done, and under this authorization the Governor promptly appointed the first State atomic energy officer in the country, who was charged with the organization of the new agency and the administration of its program.

In the field of atomic development, ambitious programs are under way in a number of States. Georgia has allocated $2.5 million for the construction of a high-powered research and training reactor; Pennsylvania, $2 million for nuclear research and training facilities; California, $1.8 million for nuclear projects; New York, $1 million for a nuclear research

[35] Council of State Governments, *Roster of State Atomic Energy Coordinators, Coordinating Commissions, and Current Study Committees* (Chicago, November, 1958).

[36] *The New York Times*, February 18, 1959, gives the text of the message in full, as does the Office of Atomic Development, *An Atomic Development Plan for the State of New York* (Albany, December, 1959); see also Rockefeller, Nelson A., *The Future of Federalism* (Cambridge: Harvard University Press, 1962), pp. 39–41.

center, including a nuclear reactor. Both New Jersey and New York have established atomic service parks, and many other States have contributed lesser amounts to atomic energy research and development. The largest potential use of energy produced by nuclear reactions is the generation of electricity. The first full-scale atomic power plant in the country, an AEC project, was located in Pennsylvania; four more were in an advanced stage of construction in late 1959, one each in Illinois, Massachusetts, Michigan, and New York, and six more were already under way in California, Florida, Michigan, Nebraska, Pennsylvania, and South Dakota.

In the exercise of their regulatory powers, the States have been advised by the Council of State Governments to adopt measures based on their police powers, having as their objective the protection of public health, safety, and welfare.[37] Many of the agencies, like the one in New York, serve more in the nature of coordinators for existing regulatory agencies than as regulatory agencies in their own right. Radiation protection regulations had been adopted in more than half of the States in 1960; eight were comprehensive, while the others covered aspects not under Federal control. The mere registration of users of radiation sources in California already numbers close to 10,000 professional men and some institutions (mostly hospitals).

Interstate Cooperation. Interstate activity in the atomic energy field has been steadily increasing in both extent and significance. There have been numerous interstate conferences of Governors and other top level officials, and these meetings have frequently developed into interstate compacts or agreements. Delaware, New Jersey, Pennsylvania (through an interstate agency), and New York are carrying on surveys of radioactivity in water, vegetables, soil, fish, and animals. The Governors of the New England and Southern States have each established continuing committees and hold regional conferences for the purpose of exploring the possibilities of State promotion of atomic development, what the problems are, and what steps the States can and should take to meet them. The Southern group, known as the Southern Regional Advisory Council on Nuclear Energy, was created by the Southern Governors' Conference in 1956. In 1960, it proposed the Southern Interstate Nuclear Compact for

[37] See *Suggested State Legislation: Program for 1959* which contains the draft of a model law. See also Massachusetts Department of Public Health, *Regulatory and Protective Measures Pertaining to Radioactive Materials* (Boston: House Report No. 2650, 1959); Adams, George B., Jr., "Regulation of Health and Safety in Private Atomic Energy Activities: A Problem in Federal-State Relationships," *George Washington Law Review*, December, 1958, pp. 163–204; and Cavers, David F., "Legislative Readjustments in Federal and State Regulatory Powers Over Atomic Energy," *California Law Review*, March, 1958, pp. 22–39.

submission to sixteen Southern States, to provide for the coordination of atomic development. This Compact was ratified and became effective July 31, 1962.[38]

Science Program Coordination

In the years since World War II, there has been a tremendous increase of interest in and financial support for work in the field of science. Among the first tangible evidences of this was the establishment in 1950 of the National Science Foundation to promote the progress of science; advance national health, prosperity, and welfare; and secure the national defense. Support for this work received an important impetus after Sputnik in 1957, an event which spurred Congress into the passage of the National Defense Education Act of 1958.

Developments in this field have been broad in scope and far-reaching in their effects. They create problems, the social implications of which affect public policy. As science reaches further into outer space, penetrates deeper into the nature of matter, and probes toward the origin of life itself, one can foresee more significant consequences for society and an even closer relationship between affairs of state and those of science. In an address before the American Association for the Advancement of Science on December 27, 1960, Dr. E. Pendleton Herring declared:

> The polity has a greater stake in the advancement of science than ever before and science receives more support from the state today than in all of history. It is clear that governmental and scientific affairs are joined, for better or worse; for better, the clearer the mutual understanding between the two and on the part of the rest of society.

The major needs are for funds in very substantial amounts, for more highly trained professional personnel than are now or seem likely to be available, and for public understanding and support. As the Director of

[38] See House Committee on the Judiciary, *Southern Interstate Nuclear Compact*, Hearings on H.R. 7498 and H.R. 7466, July 13, 1961 (Washington: 87th Cong., 1st Sess., 1962). See also House Report No. 1723, to accompany H.R. 10618, a later version of the bill to approve the Compact (Washington: House Judiciary Committee, May, 1962); the Act became P.L. 87-563; and Virginia General Assembly, Advisory Legislative Council, *The State's Role in Control and Development of Radiation and Nuclear Energy* (Richmond: Senate Document No. 18, 1962) and Solomons, Richard H., III, "The Southern Interstate Nuclear Compact and Board," *State Government*, Winter, 1963, pp. 40–44.

the National Science Foundation said in a public statement issued September 3, 1958:

> Under our democratic system, no segment of Government, whether Federal, State or local can succeed in securing necessary action programs or funds to carry them out unless our citizens understand, actively endorse, and indeed participate in the steps that need to be taken. In short, the wholehearted cooperation of the people of the country is necessary to achieve the goals which the President has pointed out so clearly. Most important here is a realization that this is not a single emergency but a continuing—possibly a permanent—one. In this modern world there can be no relaxation of our determination to compete successfully and continuously.

A beginning was made when the Foundation was established. Some improvements have since been made in education. More adequate Federal support for basic research has been provided. A new agency, the National Aeronautics and Space Administration, was established. Military research and technology have received increasing emphasis in planning for national defense. These steps are all to the good, but in this discussion, the major concern is with the intergovernmental relations aspects of the effort to achieve maximum progress in the field of science and technology.

Beginning in 1951, the Foundation made a survey of State activity in science. All States were investigated, and detailed studies were made of the programs in a selected group of six: California, Connecticut, New Mexico, New York, North Carolina and Wisconsin. Six monographs covering the activities of these States were published for the Foundation by the University of North Carolina Press, and Professor Frederic N. Cleaveland later used this material as the basis for a book which includes an excellent chapter on intergovernmental relations; [39] the comments which follow are based primarily upon these works.

The field of scientific research and development provides good opportunity for the study of Federal-State relations because the agencies in this field have utilized many different types of intergovernmental relationships. Illustrations of most of the common forms of cooperation can be found in the field of science.

The exchange of information is an obvious, elementary form of cooperation. Such agencies as the agricultural experiment stations, both through the Washington Office in the Department of Agriculture and the stations in the field, and through the Fish and Wildlife Service in the

---

[39] Cleaveland, Frederic N., *Science and State Government* (Chapel Hill: University of North Carolina Press, 1959); the government summary of the reports was *Scientific Activities in Six State Governments* (Washington: National Science Foundation, 1958).

Department of the Interior, serve as interstate clearing houses providing the means for exchange of information among State research agencies in their respective fields. Similarly, it is reported that in public works there are often agreements providing for an informal division of labor in gathering basic physical data, each of the cooperators supplying different segments of the data for the use of all, as the Public Health Service and the corresponding State agencies work together and exchange information in the field of water pollution control.

All six of the States studied, and probably most of the other States as well, engage in many cooperative projects with the Federal government and with neighboring States. The Department of Agriculture, for example, may be given responsibility by Congress to coordinate the development of a cooperative research program through the experiment stations, focusing on a particular agricultural problem which is regional in scope. Other areas of cooperation include various phases of conservation—geological survey, water supply, and forestry. In certain forestry projects, "personnel from State and Federal agencies may work side by side, some work parties supervised by Federal foresters and others by State foresters. Equipment may be furnished by one or both agencies involved; there may be a pooling of funds to finance a particular project, or one or more parties may contribute personnel and equipment rather than funds."

Professional associations of government officials may and very often do perform an important coordinating role. Some associations engage in occasional research and data collection activities but, on the whole, these groups are probably better equipped to provide supplemental assistance and informal clearinghouse services than to assume major responsibilities in a systematic effort at research coordination.

No less than five different forms of financial aid are in use for the support of scientific research. Some grants-in-aid are designated for a specific type of scientific activity, as in the support of the agricultural experiment stations; other grants are authorized without such specific designation, as in the case of grants for unemployment compensation; a third type of grant may be made available to the States under conditions designed to require the expansion of research activity. Grants for highways are an excellent example of the last type of grant, the basic highway program providing that 1.5 per cent of the total Federal grant shall be used to finance highway research, as long as the State has matched these Federal funds in accordance with the prescribed formula. A fourth type is the categorical grant to support research, a device that has been used increasingly since World War II for the Public Health Service and the National Institutes of Health. The fifth and last form of assistance involves funds for the training of scientific manpower, frequently used in the Federal health agencies and in the Children's Bureau. Professor

Cleaveland concludes that "the authors of the six State reports are in substantial agreement that Federal grants have generally stimulated the growth of State scientific programs." [40]

BIBLIOGRAPHICAL NOTES

General Works. In the 1940's a number of publications appeared dealing with and emphasizing the importance of intergovernmental relations. George C. S. Benson published his survey of the field, and W. Brooke Graves edited a symposium surveying the field and first proposing the establishment of a national study commission. Phillips Bradley, editor of the series in which the Benson volume appeared, observed in the Foreword: "The literature of politics has been one of the major forces in our national life." This book, *The New Centralization: A Study of Intergovernmental Relationships in the United States* (New York: Farrar & Rinehart, 1941), another "first" in the literature of the field, is a good illustration of the truth of Bradley's statement. In compact form, it surveys several of the major types of interlevel relationship.

W. Brooke Graves' symposium, *Intergovernmental Relations in the United States,* in *Annals of the American Academy of Political and Social Science,* January, 1940, contained twenty-five articles written by leading political scientists. It presented, for the first time in a single volume, a comprehensive survey of the problems of interlevel and interjurisdictional relations. In a concluding piece called "Readjusting Governmental Areas and Functions," a proposal was made, also for the first time, to establish a national study commission to survey the whole field of intergovernmental relations and to make recommendations.

At approximately the same time, the fourth edition of *Model State Constitution* appeared. This document, first published by the National Municipal League in 1921, had been revised and reissued a number of times. The fourth edition, published in 1941, was significant for present purposes because it contained a new article on intergovernmental relations, designed to eliminate road-blocks, insofar as possible, to encourage and facilitate cooperative relationships between the different levels and units of government.

An article by Professor William Anderson, "Federalism: Then and Now," *State Government,* May, 1943, pp. 107–112, dealt with the changes that could be discerned in an evolving federal system. His analysis displeased some and stirred up a considerable amount of controversy. Oswald D. Heck, a State legislator, Harold L. Dodds, a political scientist turned university president, and William L. Chenery, a journalist, took occasion to reply to the article in a later issue of the magazine (June, 1943, pp. 141–144). Not long thereafter, Professor Anderson was responsible for another important addition to the literature of the field. The Social Science Research Council had for many years maintained a Committee on Public Administration which carried on some projects itself, promoted and assisted others. At this time, under the leadership of Professor Anderson, the Committee formulated and published a plan for research in the field of intergovernmental relations: *Federalism and Intergovernmental Relations: A Budget of Suggestions for Research* (Chicago: Public Administration Service, 1946).

For a more up-to-date sequel to the Anderson suggestions for research, see Emil

[40] Cleaveland, p. 125.

Sady, *Research in Federal-State Relations: A Report on Recent Developments and Problems Requiring Further Study* (Washington: Brookings Institution, 1957). For two good American comments and one English, the following titles are of interest: Nelson A. Rockefeller, *The Future of Federalism* (Cambridge: Harvard University Press, 1962); Leonard D. White, *The States and the Nation* (Baton Rouge: Louisiana State University Press, 1950); and M. J. C. Vile, *The Structure of American Federalism* (New York: Oxford University Press, 1962).

Cooperation in Atomic Energy and Science. On atomic energy, the following general titles are helpful: American Assembly, *Atoms for Power* (New York: Columbia University, 1957); William H. Berman and Lee M. Hydeman, *Federal and State Responsibilities for Radiation Protection: The Need for Federal Legislation* (Ann Arbor: University of Michigan Law School, 1959); Robert A. Dahl, ed., "The Impact of Atomic Energy," *Annals of the American Academy of Political and Social Science*, November, 1953, entire issue; E. Blythe Stason, *et al.*, eds., *Atoms and the Law* (Ann Arbor: University of Michigan Law School, 1959); Symposium, "Federal-State Cooperation in the Atomic Energy Field," *Kentucky Law Journal*, Fall, 1961, entire issue; Joint Congressional Committee on Atomic Energy, *Atomic Energy Through the 85th Congress, 1st Session* (Washington: Joint Committee Print, 85th Cong., 1st Sess., 1957).

On government and science, the most useful title for present purposes is Frederic N. Cleaveland, *Science and State Government* (Chapel Hill: University of North Carolina Press, 1959); much of the contents of this work also appeared as a government document, *Scientific Activities in Six States* (Washington: National Science Foundation, 1958). See also Bureau of Labor Statistics, *Scientific and Technical Personnel in State Government Agencies* (Washington: National Science Foundation, 1961). The following items are more general in nature: Carl F. Stover, *The Government and Science* (Santa Barbara: Center for the Study of Democratic Institutions, 1961); House Committee on Appropriations, Subcommittee on Independent Offices, *Highlights of Science in the United States* (Washington: National Science Foundation Hearings, 87th Cong., 2nd Sess., 1962); Dael Wolfle, *Science and Public Policy* (Lincoln: University of Nebraska Press, 1959); and Norman Wengert, ed., "Perspectives on Government and Science," *Annals of the American Academy of Political and Social Science*, January, 1960, entire issue.

CHAPTER XXIV

The Federal Government
Bypasses the States

A very controversial example of cooperative federalism involves relations between national and local governments that bypass the States. According to the traditional theory of American federalism, the national government should deal with local governments only through the States, [because] in a constitutional sense local governments are creatures of the States. . . . Although sooner or later everything the national government does affects the operations of local governments, it was not until the Great Depression that the national government began to deal directly with city officials. Today cities receive Federal aid for building streets and airports, for civil defense, for slum clearance and housing, urban renewal, and other projects.

State officials have sharply criticized this bypassing of the States; on the other hand, of course, city officials favor direct Federal help. Many large cities—actually "city-states" in many respects—fail to receive sympathetic treatment from State legislatures dominated by rural representatives who not only have little sympathy or understanding of city problems but are often downright hostile to city politicians. As a result, as President Eisenhower told the Conference of State Governors, "Today, for help in urban problems, committees of Mayors are far more likely to journey to Washington than to their own State capitals." [1]

The difference of opinion between State and city officials over Federal assistance reflects a more general conflict. City people often contribute most of the tax money to support State

[1] Text of an address by President Eisenhower at the State Dinner of the 1957 Governors' Conference, June 24, 1957, in *Report of the Joint Federal-State Action Committee* (Washington, 1957), p. 20.

activities, but because they are underrepresented in the State legislatures they have a proportionately small voice in its allotment. Since urban populations are likely to have more influence with the national than with their own State governments, it is not surprising that States sometimes get caught in the squeeze between national and city officials. Probably the best way to correct this situation, if correction appears to be called for, would be to reorganize State governments to improve their operations, and give city people a greater voice in State affairs so that the States could serve as more effective intermediaries between national and local governments.[2]

Clearly, intergovernmental relations can be cooperative as well as competitive, and cooperative federalism is a going business. And yet cooperative federalism means all things to all men. To some it is a midway station on the road to greater power for the national government; to others it is a way to strengthening the States; but above all it is an example of what de Tocqueville noticed over a hundred years ago: "I have never been more struck by the good sense and the practical judgment of the Americans than in the manner in which they elude the numberless difficulties resulting from their Federal Constitution."[3]

[2] *Report of the Commission on Intergovernmental Relations* (Washington, June, 1955), p. 40.

[3] Burns, James M., and Peltason, Jack W., *Government by the People*, 4th ed. (Englewood Cliffs, N.J.: Prentice-Hall, Inc., 1960), pp. 125–126.

———

As was stated at the beginning of Part VI, one of the most striking aspects of the development of American federalism has been its increasing tendency to bypass the States, either in favor of direct relations with local units of government or, particularly in recent years, with institutions or individuals.

EARLY FEDERAL-INDIVIDUAL RELATIONSHIPS

The origins of direct relationships between the Federal government and its individual citizens, as of most governmental problems, lie deep in the records of the past. Every American school boy learns that a very critical weakness of the government under the Articles of Confederation was its inability to raise the revenues essential to its effective operation or to recruit the military manpower essential to its defense. The story of its futile efforts in these two fields is an interesting one.

GROWTH OF THE BYPASSING TENDENCY: SOME SIGNIFICANT
ILLUSTRATIONS, CHRONOLOGICALLY ARRANGED

Year	Federal-Municipal Relations	Federal-Institutional Relations	Federal-Individual Relations
1933	Emergency programs of Depression era Beginnings of public housing		Agricultural contracts and direct payments
1935			Social security payments
1937		Contracts with housing authorities; loan program	Public Health Service fellowships inaugurated
1944		Veterans affairs; education program	Veterans benefits
1946	Federal airport program		
1947	Surplus Property Disaster Act		
1950			Technical services to private forest landowners
1951			Accelerated amortization for defense plants in industrial dispersion program
1954	Funds to develop a reserve of planned public works projects Air pollution abatement control		Tax depreciation write-offs on defense production facilities
1958		Grants for scientific research at universities	Defense education; loans
1959			Senior housing loans
1961	Effort to establish a department of urban affairs		

In both areas, the central government was completely at the mercy of the States, which with callous disregard for the welfare of the rest of their fellow countrymen refused—with a few very notable exceptions—to honor the requests of the central government for either men or money. In so doing they were, of course, taking a very short-sighted view of their own welfare. When for these and other reasons it became apparent to all that the central government had failed and that it could not under existing conditions be expected to function effectively, the representatives of these States were confronted by the responsibility of devising a governmental structure that would be able to function, adequately serving the national interest, and that at the same time would protect the power and integrity of the States.

The Founders' answers to these problems in terms of specific provisions of the new Constitution which they framed and adopted are as familiar as they are direct. In Article I, Section 8, they provided that Congress should have power:

With respect to taxation:

1. To *lay and collect* taxes, duties, imposts, and excises, to pay the debts and provide for the common defense and general welfare of the United States.

With respect to the national defense:

11. To *raise and support* armies.

12. To *provide and maintain* a navy.

13. To *make rules for the government* and regulation of the land and naval forces.

14. To *provide for calling forth* the militia to execute the laws of the Union, suppress insurrections, and repel invasions.

The significance of these clauses is that they abandoned the old concept of central government dependence upon the States by providing instead for a direct relationship between the new central government and the individual. One cannot help but wonder whether the Framers fully realized the tremendous significance of the change they were making. Whether they did or not, the States, by their policy of non-cooperation, had condemned themselves, and a very basic change in the structure of the governmental system had come into being.

Important as was the original change with respect to the tax power, the Federal-individual relationship principle was significantly strengthened well over a hundred years later when the Income Tax Amendment was adopted. Similarly, in the field of defense, the effect of the change was momentous. Although the national policy has always been to rely to the greatest possible extent on volunteers to fill the ranks of the armed forces, experience has repeatedly demonstrated that sooner or later the volunteer system breaks down. So, first in the Civil War and successively in World War I, World War II, the Korean conflict, and the unsteady peace that marked the period of the Cold War, it has been necessary to resort to conscription. (See Chapters XII and XIII.)

The Indians provide another early and very interesting example of direct relationships between the Federal government and individuals. Although the Fourteenth Amendment states that "all persons born or naturalized in the United States are citizens of the United States and of the States wherein they reside," Indians living in tribal relations, although born in the United States, were long regarded as subject to the jurisdiction of their tribes. Until 1924, they could become citizens only by naturalization, as in the case of other "aliens." As of that date, however, when one-third of the Indian population of the country still lacked citizen status, an act of Congress conferred citizenship on all native-born Indians. Their position is still unique; in some respects they are subject to the jurisdiction of their tribe and in others to that of the Federal government which tends to deal largely with the tribes, while the States deal with individual Indians.

There are in the United States over 200 Indian reservations, scattered over twenty-five States, including 52,495,353 acres (1961) and a population of 285,000 (1961). The gradual establishment of these segregated areas marked a relatively late stage in the long and troubled relations between the white man and the Indian. Reservations were not necessarily permanent because when the inhabitants became capable of owning their own land and managing their own affairs, a reservation could be terminated and absorbed into the State in which it was located. Although the Constitution gives only to Congress the power "to regulate commerce . . . with the Indian tribes," authority has been found on one basis or another both for gathering most surviving Indians into reservations and for full Federal control over all such areas, supervising the inhabitants in their exercise of such rights of local self-government as may appear to be justified under the circumstances and the stage of their development.

In such situations, the Bureau of Indian Affairs acts in the capacity of a trustee, in charge of Indian lands and monies, and provides a wide range of personal services in education, vocational training, and health and welfare services not otherwise available. In its trusteeship capacity, it leases lands, forests, water power sites, mineral lands, and other resources, and turns over the proceeds to the Indians. Under policies adopted during the Eisenhower administration, the Federal government sought early termination of the trusteeship and the disposition of Indian property. Pending accomplishment of this objective, Indian lands require much assistance in soil and water conservation, mineral development, and forest management. The States have historically given the Indian as much freedom as some of the Southern States have given to the Negro. Few States with large Indian populations (Arizona, New Mexico, and Oklahoma have the largest) are in a position to offer Indians the full range of public services available to other citizens.

The administration of the extensive Indian Affairs program requires a large amount of field work which is carried on by a staff of local superintendents, agents, and other officials under the regional supervision of five district superintendents. Where the States cannot or will not assume responsibility for meeting the needs of their Indian population, the Federal government must continue to meet them, whatever the effect upon the States. To some degree, public assistance and employment security services are rendered by the States, and categorical assistance is provided entirely on this basis. Indian reservations are partly a direct Federal responsibility; their residents may participate to some extent in all the rights and obligations of other citizens of the individual States. In general, the Federal government deals with the individual Indian who lives on a reservation through the tribal organization; this is true both of the Bureau of Indian Affairs and the Indian Division of the Public Health Service. By contrast, the FBI has direct supervision over the individual Indian with respect to cases involving the so-called "ten major crimes."

DIRECT FEDERAL-MUNICIPAL RELATIONS

Chapter XIX discussed the late origin and development of direct relations between the Federal government and the local units, chiefly the municipalities. Several different categories of aid to such governments (including air and water pollution control programs; planning, research, training, and demonstration projects; public works; airport construction; and disaster relief) may be direct without any State action involved.[4] In some programs, Federal-municipal contracts which not only bypass the States but which are vigorously opposed by them have been upheld, as in the Tacoma Case discussed in Chapter XIX. This section considers three aspects of the problem—the emergency programs of the Depression era, the channeling of funds controversy, and current moves to establish a Federal department of urban affairs.

[4] See Hutchinson, Theodore M., *Metropolitan Area Problems: The Role of the Federal Government* (Ann Arbor: Legislative Research Center, University of Michigan Law School, 1961), Chapter 3.

Emergency Programs of the Great Depression

For many years prior to the Great Depression, a wide variety of indirect Federal services to municipal governments had been developing.[5] The pattern of direct Federal-municipal relationships, however, was established during the Depression era when the pressure to relieve widespread suffering was very great. Although under such conditions the maximum of speed consistent with ordinary care to prevent fraud was urgently necessary, the States again proved to be either uncooperative or ineffective or both, with the result that the Federal emergency agencies were practically forced to seek municipal cooperation if they were to act. The cities welcomed this release from State domination; the States resented it, but being either unable or unwilling to do the job themselves, they were not in a position to offer any effective protest or resistance.

The Federal Airport Act and Channeling Legislation

There appears to have been practically no Federal or State financial participation in airport development prior to 1933. The expenditures from 1911 to 1933 were about equally divided between municipal and private or commercial airports. Federal activity was limited to airfields on the original transcontinent–air mail routes and to military installations. State development of airports was negligible. Between 1933 and World War II, the work relief programs were responsible for the bulk of airport development.

The channeling controversy developed in connection with the Federal Airport Act of 1946. The cities wanted to continue to deal directly with the Federal agency administering the program, but as the years had passed the resentment of the States at being cut out of relationships between the Federal government and their own cities had continued to mount. State officials, in fact, found themselves in an embarrassing position. Whenever the cities did not get what they wanted at the State Capitol, they took their requests to Washington where usually the climate was more favorable and funds more abundant. The cities proceeded to take full advantage of the new relationship.

When the Airport Act was under consideration, the Council of State

[5] For example, see Betters, Paul V., *Federal Services to Municipal Governments* (New York: Municipal Administration Service, 1931), and for subsequent developments, see Blundred, Robert H., and Hanks, Donoh W., Jr., *Federal Services to Cities and Towns: An Alphabetical Listing* (Chicago: American Municipal Association, 1950).

Governments, as spokesman for the States, requested that Congress provide that the funds allocated for municipal airports be channeled through the States. The cities fought this proposal; Congress therefore did what it so often does and adopted a compromise solution in the form of a permissive provision. In those States which might by law so provide, Federal funds would be channeled through the State treasury; where no such legislation was on the books, funds would go directly to the municipality. This ruling set off a tremendous controversy in many of the States. The Council of State Governments drafted and submitted to the States for their approval a model channeling law. Many of the legislatures adopted it, while in others the effort to enact it precipitated an intense conflict along conventional urban-rural lines.

State approval of individual projects may be regarded as a face-saving technique for States in which the law does not require channeling. In 1955, it was reported that the laws of twenty-nine States required such approval; in twenty States, channeling of funds was required; and in twenty-one, the State government participated in financial aid. Such participation is a significant means of spreading costs to suburban dwellers living outside the sponsoring municipality.[6]

A Federal Department of Urban Affairs

Virtually no one had advocated or probably even seriously considered establishing a department of urban affairs until after World War II. Certainly there was no legislation introduced in Congress prior to 1954. By 1960, however, the creation of such a department became a campaign issue, and by 1961 the new department appeared for a time to be on the way to becoming a reality.

These developments in so short a time can be explained only by the great increase in population, the greater mobility of population, and the growth of urbanism. In times past these same changes, impressive though they are, would not have brought about the establishment of a new Federal department, nor would they have done so now if the States had been interested in and responsive to the problems of their urban and metropolitan areas. In 1862, when our society was rural and agricultural, a Federal Commissioner of Agriculture was established because the States were not providing adequate assistance for the farmer, and in 1889 this agency was converted into a department with a Secretary of Cabinet rank.

Essentially the same thing happened again 100 years later. The

[6] Commission on Intergovernmental Relations, *Federal Aid to Airports* (Washington, June, 1955), pp. 87–88, and cited by Hutchinson, p. 12.

society had greatly increased in size and had become predominantly urban and industrial. The failure of the States to deal in a realistic manner with the problems of their cities drew the Federal government deeply into a relatively new area and caused the establishment of new and direct lines of communication in the field of Federal-municipal relations. Once again the States stood by, viewing what was happening with disapproval, but still not taking the required action which would have made the establishment of a new Federal department quite unnecessary.

DIRECT FEDERAL RELATIONS WITH INSTITUTIONS

The increasing direct relationships between the Federal government and institutions, public and private, have developed primarily in three fields, which could but do not involve contacts with the States. All three involve Federal-individual relationships through the medium of an agency or institution other than the State. In housing, for example, the individual obtains the benefits of Veterans Administration or Federal Housing and Home Finance Agency programs by making arrangements with a municipal housing authority established under State law as a municipal, not a State agency. In education, beginnings made in the form of payments to institutions for veterans have been expanded into a long list of grants for scientific research for both defense and peacetime activities and for the training of doctors, nurses, sanitarians, and other types of professional personnel.

Education

The size and scope of Federal relationships with the great universities of the nation have expanded in recent years to such an extent as to become a matter of some concern. The government-sponsored projects in which the universities are engaged have become so numerous and so costly that they now constitute a major item in the annual budget of even the largest, most adequately financed institutions. The arrangements may become highly complicated even within a single State, as in Virginia in 1962 when the General Assembly authorized the University of Virginia, Virginia Polytechnic Institute, and the College of William and Mary to enter into a joint agreement to operate and manage the proposed space radiation effects laboratory of the National Aeronautics and Space Administration, to be located in the Hampton Roads area.[7] The questions that have been raised involve the possible effect of this activity upon the integrity of the institutions as centers of teaching and research. Having become dependent upon Federal funds, one wonders what would happen to the universities if the funds were suddenly terminated or drastically reduced.

These programs had their start during World War II when the Federal government entered into specific contracts with specific institutions for the performance of research required in connection with the war effort. These projects were most willingly undertaken and there is no objection to them now, per se, but a situation that was assumed to be temporary has taken on more or less permanent characteristics, as war has been followed by a prolonged period of international tension during which problems of national security continue to hold a high priority.

Between 1954 and 1958, a National Science Foundation study showed that American universities and colleges increased their expenditures for scientific research and development by 80 per cent, from $409.7 million in 1954 to $735.8 million in 1958, in which year more than half of the total expenditures, or $408.3 million, was spent by agricultural experiment stations and Federal contract research centers administered by educational institutions, while the expenditures for these institutions proper accounted for the remaining $327.5 million. The latter were oriented toward basic rather than applied research, expending 74 per cent of their funds for this purpose, while experiment stations and contract centers were more mission-minded, reporting only 35 per cent and 24 per cent respectively for basic research.[8]

It was in this environment that the Rand Corporation, pioneer in corporate research organization, was established. This was a non-profit institution devoted to research in those aspects of science that are of special interest to the Air Force. It took the name Rand from the identifying phrase "research and development." Although many university scientists are employed in this undertaking, the Corporation itself has no specific university connections. In 1956, with the aid of a substantial grant from the Ford Foundation, a group of universities (now numbering nine) deeply involved in government work formed an Institute of Defense Analysis (IDA) whose purpose is to help the government solve its security problems. This organization describes itself as a "scientific servant to the Government." It is institutionalizing the role of those university scientists who divide their time between secret government projects and their campuses.

[7] M. M. Chambers, *Grapevine*, June, 1962, p. 296.
[8] *Review of Data on Research and Development* (Washington, March, 1962).

IDA, it is reported, performs some experiments on its own, but more typically it acts as a bridge between the academic world and the government, providing consultants and keeping informed about men who can be called into government service. It operates in a gray area between the government and the campus, sometimes paying the salaries of scientists who are working in government offices. It is flexible; it can cut red tape and avoid cumbersome civil service rules and salary schedules. In short, it makes it possible for the government to get the services of experts who might be reluctant to leave their campuses for full-time government employment and is therefore one answer to the government's scientific manpower problem. The basic theory is that national security is closely tied to scientific research and that a new tool was needed to enable the government to benefit from the knowledge existing in the universities. Much of the work, which covers a broad scope, is highly classified.

This type of project has not been developed without serious problems. A significant segment of the costs of such federally sponsored research and development imposes considerable "indirect expenses" or "overhead" upon the universities and colleges. In Fiscal 1962, the total indirect costs were estimated at $175 million. "Approximately 47 per cent or $83 million of the estimated $175 million represents the indirect costs of federally sponsored research grants; the balance covers indirect costs of R & D contracts. Under current Federal practices, $7 million of the $83 million in indirect costs of research grants will come from the Government and an additional $36 million represents the necessary contributions of the colleges and universities." [9] At present there is no uniform policy, since the policy relating to grants is more restrictive than that applied to research done under contract. The universities are glad to be of assistance to the government and to serve the public, but the substantial overhead costs impose a financial burden upon them which can be met only by using income from endowment or from other sources that, in a period of tremendous expansion in higher education, is sorely needed for other purposes.

[9] *Review of Data on Research and Development*, pp. 1–6. See also *Government-University Relationships in Federally Sponsored Scientific Research and Development* (Washington: National Science Foundation, 1958); House Committee on Government Operations, *The Administration of Grants by the National Institutes of Health*, Hearings, March, 1962 (Washington: 87th Cong., 2nd Sess., 1962); and *Payment of Indirect Costs of Research and Development by College and University Contractors*, Hearings, March, 1962 (Washington: 87th Cong., 2nd Sess., 1962). This problem is considered at some length in the 1961 "Annual Report of the President of Harvard University" and in a statement on "Cost Reimbursement for University Research Sponsored by the Federal Government," by the Massachusetts Institute of Technology, in *Congressional Record*, June 5, 1962, pp. A4092–A4094.

While no attempt has been made to make across-the-board grants in addition to those for research because of the controversy over aid to church-connected institutions, the Federal government has given financial assistance to higher education by providing, for example, substantial loan funds for the construction and equipment of many different types of buildings, including dormitories, libraries, and student union buildings. (See Chapter XIV.) Much more of this type of assistance may be expected in the 1960's as the universities and colleges race against time in the effort to expand their facilities to meet expected increases in enrollment.

The persistent refusal of many States to modernize their laws with respect to church-state relations is responsible for another type of procedure by which the Federal government short-circuits the States, not because it wants to but because this is the only means by which, in view of existing provisions of State law, it can accomplish the job assigned to it by Congress. Examples in the field of education are to be found under two programs—the school lunch program established in 1946 and the testing program established in 1958 under the National Defense Education Act.[10]

Under the school lunch program, grant funds and food are made available to State and territorial departments of education to develop and administer, in cooperation with local school authorities, programs for serving several kinds of lunches to elementary and secondary school children. Every Federal dollar advanced under this program must be matched by $3.00 from a State or local source. Private and parochial schools are included in the State program in twenty-five States and Territories, but in twenty-nine they cannot be included. In these jurisdictions, contracts are made directly between such schools and the Department of Agriculture, the State playing no part whatsoever. The student testing program under the NDEA operates in a similar manner, but dollar for dollar matching is required. The Office of Education contracts with the schools for the testing and pays half of the cost in those jurisdictions where State law prohibits participation in such a program.

Public Health

The functioning of cooperative federalism in the public health field may either stimulate or bypass normal Federal-State relationships. In order to qualify for certain kinds of grants, a particular State health agency must prepare a formal and detailed program plan covering a

[10] Both of these instances are discussed in Peterson, Walfred H., *The American Federal System and Church-State Relations*, a report prepared during the summer of 1961. Professor Peterson is a member of the faculty at Bethel College, St. Paul, Minnesota.

specified period of time. In those State health departments where there has been no earlier tradition of program planning, this Federal requirement has had the effect of stimulating the establishment of at least the rudiments of a program planning function. Since, however, public health involves matters which affect the individual intimately, as well as the community in which he lives, it is not surprising that bypassing procedures have become highly developed in this field.

Local units can, as a matter of fact, solve some of their own problems by interlocal cooperation, without much regard for either of the higher echelons in the governmental setup. In the Philadelphia metropolitan area, for instance, it is reported that the Regional Conference of Elected Officials is beginning to tackle the problem of air pollution on an intergovernmental basis. In the New England area, communities too small to support needed professional service have long been able, by joining together, to develop tax bases of sufficient size to support adequate local health services on a full time basis.[11]

These two points, the planning of health services and interlocal cooperation, are more closely related than may have at first appeared. Discussing public health in a metropolitan setting, Dr. Herbert B. Domke, a distinguished authority in public health administration, makes three suggestions: (1) that the health services for metropolitan areas be provided with adequate recording and reporting systems; (2) that local officials be required to coordinate planning and programming before applying for State or Federal grants-in-aid, a requirement which might stimulate more rapid development of areawide planning for other functions; and (3) that local agencies be involved in the program and that areawide responsibilities be delegated to them. In this connection, he continues:

> In many instances State responsibility is delegated to local health departments as a matter of regular policy; extension or modification of such arrangements could insure that the delegated service is performed metropolitanwide. Formal contractual agreements between various governmental units of the metropolises and between municipal jurisdictions and the State or Federal Government might facilitate such a process. Such formal contracts have been effective in Los Angeles County, Calif., and in St. Louis County, Mo. The contract, as an administrative device, makes possible a flexibility of arrangement incomparably greater than a political change by charter amendment.[12]

[11] Penjerdel (Pennsylvania-New Jersey-Delaware Transportation Study), *The Penjerdel Region: A Portrait* (Philadelphia, 1962). See also Dr. Henry C. Huntley, *Intergovernmental Responsibilities for Public Health* (Kingston: Bureau of Government Research, University of Rhode Island, March, 1962), pp. 16–18, on the implementation of local health services in Rhode Island.

[12] Domke, Herbert B., "Public Health in the Metropolitan Setting," *Public Health Reports*, May, 1962, pp. 383–387.

It is true in public health, as has been noted in other functional areas, that the working of cooperative federalism is thwarted in some States by constitutions and laws forbidding a State agency from aiding private religious organizations. Under the Hill-Burton Hospital and Public Health Facilities Program enacted in 1946, approved construction can be aided by from one-third to two-thirds of the cost, the Federal funds being channeled through the appropriate State agency. In eight States and three Territories, it is impossible for a State agency to give any funds to private or religiously affiliated hospitals or medical facilities. In these jurisdictions, arrangements are made directly with the hospital or facility involved only after the State has approved the plans. In these instances, cooperative federalism is limited by the provisions of State law affecting church-state relations. These laws thwart cooperation and encourage more centralization than was contemplated by Federal law or than would otherwise exist. It might be argued that these bypassing arrangements are a kind of subterfuge, yet they were not intended that way. As Dr. Peterson concludes, "The State agency involved determines the eligibility of the private hospital for the Federal grant, then the agency is bypassed in the transfer of funds to satisfy State law on church-State separation."

DIRECT FEDERAL RELATIONS WITH INDIVIDUALS

Prior to the twentieth century, any direct relationships that the individual citizen might have with the central government were few in number and relatively unimportant. If he resided in the West, he might have contact with the Federal Land Office. He would send and receive mail through the local post office, and if he happened to be liable for a Federal tax, he would have some contact with the Collector of Internal Revenue. This situation no longer prevails. Today most citizens have direct personal contacts or relationships with a variety of Federal departments and agencies. The outlook for the future indicates the probability of a continuing increase in the number and scope of these relationships.

By way of illustration, note the following items involving three different aspects of Federal-individual relations quoted from a weekly newsletter of a Senator to his constituents (dated January 31, 1961; headings supplied):

> *Taxation.* Secretary Dillon stated that, if the Administration decides to cut taxes to stimulate the economy, my plan of raising personal exemptions is the best way to do it. That way everyone will receive

immediate benefit. I have proposed raising the exemption for the taxpayer and his dependents from $600 to $1,000, a more realistic figure.

Education. In the field of education, I have introduced a bill to provide a program of government-insured loans to college students. This is similar to FHA insurance on home loans and would not involve any government spending. I have also proposed giving double exemption for income taxes for every dependent in college.

Social Security. In the Social Security field, I have again proposed allowing men to retire at age sixty-two if they wish at reduced benefits. This too will not cost any money because the retirement will be at reduced benefits. I have again offered a bill to remove the earning limit for those on Social Security. Now people who get income from rents and stock dividends, for instance, can earn any amount. But people who earn wages are limited in the amount they may earn.

Obviously a large portion of these new relationships involve some form of payments—loans, grants, or benefits established under social security programs. With the exception of grants to veterans, there has been a trend of late toward loans, the funds for which may be raised either by taxation and appropriation in the usual manner or by borrowing. Low interest bearing loans from the Treasury to individuals, in situations in which risk capital was not generally available through normal channels, have been made extensively as a means of providing funds needed promptly for program operation for at least as long as forty years.[13] With the establishment of the Reconstruction Finance Corporation in 1932, the practice was significantly extended. The Corporation continued in existence for a quarter of a century until, in 1957, it was abolished and such of its functions as were retained were transferred to other agencies.

During this period, the basic idea became so firmly established that its use was extended into several new functional areas. The list of activities of the Veterans Administration includes loans of several types—for homes, for funds with which to establish the veteran as a farm operator or in a business undertaking, and various others. Housing loans have been common since the Housing Act was passed in 1937. The Small Business Administration was established in 1933, primarily for the purpose of providing financial assistance for such legitimate business purposes as construction, conversion, expansion, plant equipment, and so on. All of these practices and organizations involve types of Federal-individual relationships that were uncommon, if not unknown, prior to

[13] This matter was discussed by Senator Paul H. Douglas of Illinois during the debate on the depressed areas bill in 1961; see *Congressional Record*, March 14, 1961, pp. 3635–3636.

the Great Depression. Many of them affect local government and metropolitan area problems.[14]

Following are examples of the ways in which Federal contacts with individuals work in specific subject matter fields, and of the types of problems they sometimes create as they occur in agriculture, education, social welfare, and veterans affairs.

Agriculture

Chronologically, the change began with agriculture, when Congress on May 16, 1862, established the office which was in time to become the Department of Agriculture. It was extended many years later when the extension service established a direct personal relationship between the county agent and the individual farmer, between the county home demonstration agent and the farmer's wife. Although neither States nor counties were excluded from this program, a pattern of direct Federal-individual relationships was established which made such exclusion a natural development. The establishment of marketing and crop reporting services brought each farmer into the data collecting process as he provided figures on acreage planted, estimates of yield and reports of actual yield, prevailing prices in the local market, and other information.

Once a precedent has been established, developments of this sort are often accelerated when a crisis situation occurs, and the twentieth century has been a period during which one crisis has followed quickly on the heels of another. At the close of World War I, the farmers of the Midwest were in serious straits as a result of a prolonged period of drought. How the Federal government moved to meet this situation is clearly described in a nearly contemporary newspaper account. Charles Curtis, then a Senator from Kansas was, as his successors have been, a strong supporter of legislation deemed beneficial to the farmers of his State. A biography of Curtis reports that:

> In 1918, he joined with other members of the House and Senate and actively and vigorously aided in securing loans by the Government to farmers in drought stricken districts in Kansas and elsewhere to buy seed wheat. The sum of over $4 million was loaned for this purpose. Under the provisions of the law, a crop of less than five bushels an acre was to be considered a failure and the borrower was to be released from

[14] For instance, certain tax depreciation allowances, certain war contracts, and such Federal lending programs as the FHA for encouragement of construction outside city limits; these are discussed in Hutchinson, and in the *Report of the Commission on Intergovernmental Relations' Committee on Local Government* (Washington, June, 1955), pp. 45–53.

repayment, but those who raised more than six bushels to the acre were to contribute to a fund which was to be used to settle the loans of those whose wheat crop for 1918 was a failure. A number of loans were made in Kansas and did not have to be repaid because of this provision of the law regarding crop failures. The Senator proposed and had adopted an amendment to the agricultural bill which produced the same relief in 1919.[15]

Still another crisis developed during the period of the Great Depression. As Federal activities in the field of agriculture expanded during these trying times, the number of direct contacts between the individual farmer and the Federal government began to multiply. The Soil Conservation Service, established in 1935, was not the first of these programs, but it was one of the most interesting, its principal purpose being to develop and administer a permanent national soil and water conservation program. In performing this function, the Service assists farmers and ranchers in locally organized, farmer-directed soil conservation districts, through its planning technicians and other soil and water conservation specialists who live and work in the districts. As of January 1, 1961, there were 2,879 such districts.

The program is administered by a staff composed of many types of agricultural specialists. In assisting farmers and ranchers in the solution of their soil and water conservation problems, the Service goes through four principal steps: (1) it makes a detailed, acre-by-acre soil survey of the farm or ranch; (2) the landowner and the technicians together draw up a conservation farm plan; at the beginning of Fiscal 1961, Service technicians had helped more than 1.8 million farmers and ranchers whose farms and ranches totalled more than 571 million acres; (3) the practices called for in the plan are applied; and (4) the farm conservation system is maintained after the practices have been applied to the land. The Service provides the guidance needed for properly executing and maintaining the program.

The early payments to farmers in the Depression era were more or less parallel with the public assistance payments made to the needy unemployed urban dweller and his family. Commodity price supports were established by law as a basis for these payments, the early payments providing the differential between what the farmer received for his crop and the established price. Later the established (or parity) price served as a basis for advancing loans to individual farmers. If a farmer's crop was covered by a price support program, he was eligible for a govern-

[15] Ewy, Martin, *Charles Curtis of Kansas: Vice-President of the United States, 1929–1933* (Emporia: State Teachers College, 1961), p. 33. Ewy credits the quote to the *Topeka Daily Capitol*, August 8, 1926.

ment loan not exceeding the parity value of his crop. Under this plan, if the market price for a commodity went higher than the parity price, the farmer might sell his crop and repay the loan; if the market price stayed below parity, the farmer delivered his crop to the government in payment for the loan.

The next move was an attempt to restrict production, in an effort to hold down the costs of the price support program and to prevent a further increase in the amount of government-owned surplus commodities in storage. Individual farms made contracts with the Department of Agriculture, under the terms of which each farmer agreed to limit the acreage that he would plant in each major crop. In return for his participation in the crop control program, he received direct payments from the department. Thus it was often said by those who were opposed to the program that farmers were being paid not for producing the maximum amount that their land and their unrestricted efforts might produce, but for deliberately curtailing production.

When, with price supports and crop restrictions both in effect, the surplus still continued to mount, a third device, the soil bank plan, was brought into existence. Under this plan, the individual farmer received annual payments for withholding from cultivation some specified portion of the total arable land in his farm. The theory was that these measures were necessary for at least three reasons: (1) to maintain the family farm; (2) to insure a decent standard of living for the farm family; and (3) to prevent a still further increase in the vast store of surplus commodities. Under these programs, there were two basic types of Federal subsidies to farmers: the direct payment typified by the conservation and soil bank programs, and the price support program under which the farmer became eligible for a government loan, the amount of which depended upon the parity value of his crop. The amounts of the payments to farmers vary widely, but farming is by no means the only area in the economy that receives subsidies. As a matter of fact, the history of such grants goes back to the protective tariff of 1789, and over the years has included in one way or another virtually every important element in the nation's economic structure.[16]

It is probably an utter impossibility to administer a program of such vast proportions, involving so many individual commodities and so many individual farmers in so many States, without having some abuses develop and without having charges of abuses where none actually exist. In what appears to be a perfect example of "bureaucracy" run

[16] See House Committee on Agriculture, *Government Subsidy Historical Review* (Washington: Committee Print, 86th Cong., 2nd Sess., 1960), a summary of the use of subsidies to advance the aims and purposes of government from the first Congress to the present time, revised.

riot, one Congressman reported that a dairy farmer in his district in central New York not only had his producer-handler exemption taken away from him but was faced with a fine of $20,899.90 because, over a period of three months four years earlier, he bought cream in twenty-quart cans rather than in small containers. It was quite legal to buy twenty quarts of cream in twenty containers, but not in one.[17] The Supreme Court in 1962 voided the compensatory payments feature of the Federal milk-marketing program.

A nineteen-year-old Arkansas recruit at a Naval Training Center, who had exceeded his five-acre cotton allotment by a fraction of an acre, was sued by the government to collect a penalty of $52.28 for over-planting. At the time the incident was reported, the government had already spent $61.10 to serve court papers on the violator, this amount being listed as official expenses for deputy marshals who made two trips of 300 miles each from Little Rock to Portland to serve the papers.[18]

One widely publicized case was that of a Chemung County, New York, farmer who bought himself a new $6,100 Cadillac with the money the government was paying him to keep 104 acres out of production. The man drove his Cadillac to Washington, saying that he hoped to make the taxpayers angry; apparently he was quite different from other farmers who have been described as "so anaesthetized by subsidies that they welcome supervision and the resulting controls." [19]

Possible future relationships between the Federal government and individual farmers might be predicted on the basis of two available sources of information—the farmers themselves and the Department of Agriculture. To ascertain the views of all farmers in all commodity programs would involve an investigation of gigantic proportions, but by the use of approved sampling techniques it is possible to study the views of the farmers in a single State. This was attempted in a Southern State whose interests are centered chiefly in the programs for cotton and cottonseed, peanuts, tobacco, and corn.

> Not one Georgia farmer expressed opposition to Government participation in agriculture. On the contrary, the consensus was that more government in agriculture would be desirable provided the farmers could more effectively communicate their ideas to personnel at the policy making level. The farmers accepted as a premise that the administration of the programs would be such that the intent of Congress would not be lost before reaching the individual farmer. The statement

[17] Riehlman, R. Walter, *Congressional Record*, March 22, 1962, pp. 4385–4386.

[18] Wilson, Robert, *Congressional Record*, March 15, 1962, Appendix.

[19] Byrd, Harry F., *Congressional Record*, March 28, 1962, pp. 4805–4808, from a speech by Judge Sterling Hutcheson.

is often made by farmers that, "The farmer should be protected by the Federal Government." [20]

In the course of the debate on the Food and Agriculture Act of 1962, Secretary of Agriculture Freeman was quoted as saying, "I don't think there's any alternative except that between price supports and supply management, or no price supports and unlimited production." [21] In briefing the editors of farm magazines on the administration farm plans, the Secretary and his economic advisor indicated that under the proposed program of mandatory controls and production quotas, farmers would need a "franchise" to operate a farm. This was compared to the situation of the automobile dealership which operates under a franchise, not from the government but from the manufacturer of the line of cars the dealer desires to handle.

Education

Education has always been a highly personal matter. When children were taught by private tutors, only those of the wealthy received instruction. Then came the era of the private school, which also was costly. The English colonists, believing that "schooling" should be available to all, built their school house along with the church in each new settlement they established. This, however, was a purely local matter. The States did not become active participants in public education until in the Jacksonian era State departments of education were established and laws providing for the operation and maintenance of a system of free "common schools" were passed. For at least 100 years, the schools themselves remained purely local institutions, locally administered and locally financed from the proceeds of the general property tax.

After World War I, the local school districts, finding themselves hard pressed financially, began to beg for help from the State. Costs mounted as standards were raised and the school population increased, while the general property tax, often badly administered, provided an uncertain and inadequate basis for financial support. The intervening years have witnessed an ever-increasing amount of State aid for schools, some progress in the reorganization of school districts to achieve a more efficient use of the tax dollar for school support, and the opening up of new and

[20] Harper, W. W., *Agricultural Policy and Programs as Viewed by Individual Cotton Farmers in Georgia* (Athens: Georgia Agricultural Experiment Stations, University of Georgia, June, 1961), p. 15.

[21] *Congressional Record*, June 20, 1962, p. 10375.

more adequate revenue sources for support of the schools. Although the Federal government has developed many educational programs of its own and has become involved in educational problems to a great degree, the administration of the public schools, in spite of early land grants for school support and of urgent pleas for Federal grants-in-aid, has remained the responsibility of State and local governments.

Federal involvement in the educational problems of individuals appears to have begun in the field of higher education, when at the close of World War I the Federal Board program was established. "Training" was one of the benefits made available to veterans, hundreds of whom, most of them wholly unprepared for college or university work, descended upon the campuses of the nation with results that were distressing to all concerned. A few of the more capable remained to complete their courses, but great numbers dropped out when, as one of them expressed it, "the professors couldn't learn me no more."

With these unhappy experiences in mind, it was with fear and apprehension that the campuses received the flood of GI's at the end of World War II. This time, however, things were different. These veterans were better prepared. Many of them were able, alert, and anxious to learn, and quite in contrast with the Federal Board men, they were willing to work. Many were married and anxious to make up for the time "lost" while in service. They wanted to start their business or professional careers as soon as possible. The legislation under which the new program functioned was far more effective than before. Each veteran was entitled to "training," but of whatever kind and at whatever level he was qualified to pursue. No attempt was made to force colleges and universities to enroll as students men who had never even been to high school.

The veteran had to meet the entrance requirements of the institution he desired to attend and once accepted, he had to keep up his work. Regular reports on his attendance and the quality of his work were required by the Veterans Administration, from which he received his subsistence allowance. His tuition and fees were not paid to him, however, but to the institution in which he was enrolled—tuition up to $500, and subsistence varying in amount according to marital status, number of dependents, and full-time or part-time school program. Similar arrangements were continued for veterans of the Korean conflict, except that the law reverted to the World War I pattern for the payment of tuition and fees.

The later procedures, those of World War II and after, represented an expansion of the earlier type of relationship between the individual veteran and the government. It represented also the initiation of a new type of relationship between the institution and the government that was destined to develop on a vastly expanded scale during the 1950's, particularly in the research arrangements between the Federal government and the institutions for higher education.

Subsequent developments have brought a multiplicity of fellowships and scholarships, grants and loans, mostly under the National Defense Education Act of 1958. These aids are made available to individuals for the two-fold purpose of aiding their pursuit of professional and/or technical training, and of contributing to the solution of the urgent national manpower problem in the field of scientific and technical personnel. The loan provisions of the Act are considered liberal and even make it impossible for private banks to compete. The plan relieves the student of interest charges while he is in school and allows him up to eleven years after graduation to repay the loan. Only half of the loan must be repaid by those students who become teachers.

This legislation, hailed as a significant and imaginative attempt on the part of the government to provide financial assistance to the cause of higher education, included within its provisions an eligibility clause and the famous loyalty oath, both of which from the very beginning engendered a vast amount of controversy. The eligibility clause stipulates that the applicant must be an outstanding student in science or modern languages and must be "needy." The definition of "needy" is left to the discretion of the college officials. Since this type of loan is made on a national basis, students may attend the college or institution of their choice, thus defeating attempts to hold students within their own States for their higher education.[22]

Many States have recognized the need for long-term, low interest rate loans and have made some provision for them. At least four States—Maine, Massachusetts, New York, and Virginia—have, for example, introduced guaranty funds to support broad educational loan programs through commercial banks. These funds are administered by Higher Education Assistance Corporations, created for the purpose of guaranteeing 80 per cent of the educational loans made by a bank. Such Corporations do not make loans themselves, but administer aid through a fund which is donated by foundations, trusts, industry, and contributions from individuals. These corporations may underwrite loans amounting to $12\frac{1}{2}$ times the size of the accumulated guaranty funds; for example, a fund with capital of $100,000 could make loans up to a total of $1,250,000.[23]

[22] See Department of Health, Education, and Welfare, *National Defense Student Loan Program* (Washington, March, 1962), p. 5, and Virginia Bankers Association, *Report of the Credit Policy Committee on Educational Loans* (Richmond, 1962), p. 2. Even so, 2,575 Virginia students received $1,078,044 in loans during 1960–1961.

[23] See Virginia Bankers Association, p. 1, and Harmon, Dudley, *Massachusetts Higher Education Assistance Corporation* (Boston, November, 1961), p. 1.

Thus a few progressive States have augmented or supplemented the Federal program with programs of their own. The Virginia plan, in fact, goes much further than the other three; in 1958, Virginia started a pilot program of direct loans and scholarships. Two years later, this program was broadened by $500,000 in direct appropriations for loans and scholarships. At the same time, the General Assembly established a State Education Assistance Authority (SEAA) "to encourage, foster and facilitate the industrial and economic development of the Commonwealth by promoting the education at institutions of higher learning of residents of this State. . . ." [24] This Authority was patterned after the guaranty plans in Massachusetts and New York with the hope of encouraging private lenders to make loans, thus decreasing the necessity for direct Federal and State loans.

There has long been an "Idea Exchange Program" between the States and the Federal government—if a State has a good idea the Federal government may adopt it, and vice versa. Hence it may be that the Federal government may in the future adapt this State-devised program to national needs, creating a Higher Education Loan Program on a national basis or expanding the existing NDEA program to encompass the advantages of such a program.

The second major criticism of the NDEA loan program centered around the requirement of a loyalty affidavit disclaiming subversive affiliation in addition to an oath of allegiance, an affirmative protestation of patriotic fealty and support of the United States, its Constitution, and its laws. There was considerable opposition to the inclusion of these provisions when the legislation was under consideration in Congress, but as a concession designed to further the passage of an otherwise constructive measure, the loyalty oath provisions were permitted to remain as the bill moved toward final passage on September 2, 1958. It was apparent at the time that these provisions were quite unnecessary, for the questions of communism, subversion, and disloyalty were already fully covered in existing provisions of law.

This requirement early aroused a storm of protest in the colleges and universities. A few institutions—Oberlin College and the three Quaker colleges in the Philadelphia area (Bryn Mawr, Haverford, and Swarthmore)—refused to participate in the program; soon an increasing number of other institutions were added to the list.[25] A few voiced objections

---

[24] State Education Assistance Authority Act, *Virginia Acts of Assembly of 1960*, p. 1.

[25] Amherst, Antioch, Barnard, Beloit, Bennington, Brandeis, Cornell, Grinnell, Harvard, Mills, Mt. Holyoke, Princeton, Radcliffe, Reed, Sarah Lawrence, St. John's (of Maryland), Vassar, Wellesley, Wesleyan, Wilmington, and Yale. Data summarized from Constanzo, Joseph F., "Loyalty Oath Affidavit," *University of Detroit Law Journal*, June, 1960, pp. 718–728.

but continued to administer the government student loan program.[26] It is reported that the overwhelming majority of institutions—1370, with a total student body comprising more than 85 per cent of the total—accepted the program with some misgivings, but without criticism. Spokesmen for a few institutions even expressed bewilderment as to what the criticism was all about.

The movement for repeal of the disclaimer affidavit actually began within three months after the Act was passed, when Secretary of Health, Education, and Welfare Arthur S. Flemming urged its repeal. In July, 1959, after hearings on the question, the Senate voted down the Kennedy-Clark bill which would have accomplished repeal. On January 28, 1960, Senator Kennedy re-introduced his bill in modified form (S. 2929); this time the committee reported it favorably and the Senate passed it. The argument was long and loud. Supporters of the provision regarded it as quite appropriate, on the ground that those who borrowed money from the Federal government should be required to support the Constitution and to swear that they were not members of any organization striving to overthrow the government. They pointed out that a similar requirement was contained in the National Science Foundation Act of 1950, and that such oaths were required of all applicants for and appointees to Federal civilian offices, employees and members of the Armed Forces, defense contractors, and others. Opponents charged that the requirement was discriminatory in that it singled out students alone in the total population —and, among students, the neediest—as subjects of special distrust.

Veterans Affairs

The veteran population of this country now totals some 22 million. The task of administering veterans affairs is big business, so big that it exceeds in size such business giants as United States Steel or the American Telephone and Telegraph Company. The services performed by the V.A. are not only of many types, ranging from protecting orphans to supplying flags for caskets, but many of them are highly personal in character. Veterans have received bonuses representing pay differentials, hospitalization and out-patient medical and dental care, education at public expense, loans for homes, farms, or business undertakings, and pensions for service-connected disabilities.

Probably no more striking illustrations of the bypassing technique can be found than in the closely related and relatively recent ones involving grants for education and to veterans. In March, 1961, when the means

[26] Bates, Bowdoin, Colby, Smith College, and the University of Chicago.

of financing the depressed areas bill were being debated in the Senate, Senator Paul H. Douglas of Illinois introduced two lists, the first of which showed twenty-eight instances from 1932 to date in which Congress had given to the agency administering the program in question authority to use funds borrowed from the Federal Treasury. A significant item in this list was the Veterans Administration, which was authorized to finance in this manner direct loans to veterans for housing.[27] Important as this was, the second list was even more significant in terms of Federal-individual relationships; it enumerated twenty-eight instances in which Congress has authorized direct payments to or for individual veterans:

1. Grants for specially equipped automobiles for disabled veterans.

2. Compensation for service-connected disabilities for veterans of the Spanish-American War, World War I, World War II, the Korean conflict, and peacetime service.

3. Compensation for non-service-connected disabilities for veterans of World War I, World War II, and the Korean conflict.

4. Hospitalization service for certain veterans of any war or peacetime service.

5. Domiciliary car service for certain veterans of any war or peacetime service.

6. Outpatient medical treatment for veterans of any war or peacetime service.

7. Outpatient dental treatment.

8. Feeding or treatment in the use of prosthetics for veterans of any war or peacetime service.

9. Free medical examination in connection with applications for other Federal benefits.

10. Furnishing, repairing, or replacing certain aids for blind veterans entitled to service-connected benefits.

11. GI bill education and training benefits for veterans of World War II and the Korean conflict.

12. Vocational rehabilitation for disabled veterans.

13. War orphan education assistance program for children of certain disabled veterans.

14. GI loan program.

15. Direct loan program.

16. Grants of assistance for specially adapted wheelchair homes.

17. Unemployment compensation benefits furnished veterans of World War II and the Korean conflict, administered by the Department of Labor.

18. Mustering out payment of World War II and Korean veterans, administered by the Service Department.

19. Guarantee of premiums of commercial life insurance for any person now on active duty.

[27] 64 Stat. 77 (April 20, 1950).

20. GI life insurance for veterans.

21. Dependency and indemnity compensation for service-connected debts on or after January, 1957.

22. Compensation for service-connected debts prior to January, 1957.

23. Compensation for non-service-connected debts of wives and children of veterans.

24. Reimbursement of burial expenses not to exceed $150.

25. Furnishing burial flags to the veteran's survivor.

26. Six months' death gratuity for survivors who died on active duty, administered by Service Department.

27. Furnishing the headstone or grave marker, administered by Department of the Army.

28. Burial of veterans and immediate members of their families in national cemeteries, administered by Department of the Army and Department of the Interior.[28]

Perhaps the most significant thing about the list is not the number and variety of the benefits provided for the nation's veterans, but the concept of government that it suggests, the pattern of thought that is established and strengthened in the minds of millions of Americans. While State and local units have borne tremendous responsibilities in time of national emergency and have discharged them well, while the States have a continually important role in the organization and training of the National Guard, and while all the States and some cities maintain programs and services of benefit to veterans, there is not in the whole list even one reference to State services. Its result, however unintentional, is to strengthen the idea in the popular mind that "the government" in this country is "the national government." As this pattern of thought is deeply imbedded in the minds of the millions of veterans who have served in the nation's armed forces, it is readily transferred to and applied in other fields, to the continuing disadvantage of the States, their influence, and their prestige.

It appears to be generally assumed that the Federal government, by establishing these broad programs for the benefit of veterans under the GI Bill of Rights and other legislation, had in effect pre-empted the field. Such an assumption is far from true, for State laws provide a wide variety of additional and supplementary rights and benefits. While each State has an administrative agency that is roughly a counterpart of the Veterans Administration, there is such a wide variety of services offered as to require a close working relationship between many Federal, State, and local governmental agencies. These programs may be grouped in eight categories: (1) civic recognition of the contribution of the serviceman;

[28] *Congressional Record,* March 14, 1961, pp. 3635-3636.

(2) recognition of veteran organization; (3) specific grants or benefits such as bonuses and pensions, educational benefits, and health benefits; (4) exemptions and exceptions during and after service, particularly with regard to tax liability; (5) consideration in employment relationships, both public and private; (6) legal considerations or benefits; (7) provisions with regard to war records; (8) provisions for burial or burial assistance.

Educational benefits belong in the third category. There are well over 100 pieces of State legislation, some general, others specifically applying to veterans of a particular war or to the children of such veterans. Some laws provide for tuition payments, others for scholarships. Where there are so many laws and types of laws, it becomes important that every effort be made to assure cooperation and coordination between agencies and levels of government if overlapping and waste are to be avoided. This is precisely what the Veterans Administration, in cooperation with the heads of the State veteran agencies, has been trying to accomplish.

BIBLIOGRAPHICAL NOTES

Because so little has been written on the subject of this chapter, it is necessary to rely on such published works as are available in specific areas, when these illustrate the direct relationships of the Federal government with institutions or individuals, rather than with States. A number of such works are available, particularly in the fields of higher education, science, and research.

Higher Education: Undergraduate. Among numerous items dealing with government loans and scholarships for individual students, and to institutions for facilities for use by such students, the following are of interest: College Entrance Examination Board, *Student Financial Aid and National Purpose: A Colloquium on Financial Aid* (Los Angeles, 1962); Robert C. Hall, *The National Defense Student Loan Program: A Two-year Report* (Washington: Office of Education, 1961); Illinois General Assembly, *Adequacy of Federal Loans for Illinois College Students* (Springfield: Legislative Council, October, 1961); Harold C. Riker and Frank G. Lopez, *College Students Live Here: A Study of College Housing* (New York: Educational Facilities Laboratories, 1961); Clarence H. Steinberger, ed., *Scholarships, Loans, and Financial Aids: A Functional Reference and Guidance Tool National in Scope* (Boston: Research Publishing Company, 1949–); Sidney C. Sufrin, *Administering the N.D.E.A.* (Syracuse: Syracuse University Press, 1963); *College Academic Facilities and Student Assistance Act: Conference Report to Accompany H.R. 8900* (Washington: House Report No. 2435, 87th Cong., 2nd Sess., 1962); and House Committee on Education and Labor, *A Directory of Federally Financed Student Loans, Fellowships, and Career Training Programs in the Field of Higher Education in the United States* (Washington: 87th Cong., 2nd Sess., 1962).

Higher Education: Graduate. Comparable titles in the field of graduate study include: John L. Chase, *Doctoral Study, Fellowships, and Capacity of Graduate Schools* (Washington: Office of Education, 1961); Herman A. Estrin, ed., *Higher Education in Engineering and Science* (New York: McGraw-Hill Book Co., Inc., 1963); Harvard

University, *Annual Report of the President* (Cambridge, 1962); Paul E. Marsh and Ross A. Gortner, *Federal Aid to Science Education* (Syracuse: Syracuse University Press, 1963) on high school physics and N.D.E.A.; Harold Orlans, *The Effects of Federal Programs on Higher Education: A Study of 36 Universities and Colleges* (Washington: Brookings Institution, 1962); Sufrin, *Administering the N.D.E.A.;* House Committee on Government Operations, *Payment of Indirect Costs of Research and Development by College and University Contractors* (Washington: Hearing on H.R. 6984, March 8, 1962. 87th Cong., 2nd Sess., 1962).

    Science and Research. A growing literature has been developing on contractual relationships in the research and development field, including: Daniel S. Cheever, *Harvard and the Federal Government* (Cambridge: Publications Office, Harvard University, September, 1961), a summary of a larger Report; George Washington University, National Law Center, *Conference on United States Government Research and Development Contracts, Summary of Proceedings* (Washington, 1962); Charles V. Kidd, *American Universities and Federal Research* (Cambridge: Harvard University Press, 1959); Haldon A. Leedy, *The Role of the Independent Not-for-profit Contract Research Laboratory* (Chicago: Armour Research Laboratory, 1962); Daniel O. Price, *University Research Administration Policies* (Atlanta: Southern Regional Education Board, 1962); and Bureau of the Budget, *Report to the President on Government Contracting for Research and Development* (Washington: Senate Document No. 94, 87th Cong., 2nd Sess., 1962), which contains an annotated bibliography, pp. 69–92. Among items previously cited, see Estrin, Marsh and Gortner, and the Hearings of the House Committee on Government Operations.

    Agriculture, Business, Health and Welfare. In the field of agricultural policy, see Raymond P. Christensen and Donald O. Aines, *Economic Effects of Acreage Control Programs in the 1950's* (Washington: Economic Research Service, Department of Agriculture, 1962); Walton W. Harper, *Agricultural Policy and Programs as Viewed by Individual Cotton Farmers in Georgia* (Athens, Agricultural Experiment Station, University of Georgia, 1961); Edward Steichen, ed., *The Bitter Years: 1935–1941; Rural America as Seen by the Photographers of the Farm Security Administration* (Garden City: Doubleday & Co., Inc., 1962); House Committee on Agriculture, *Government Subsidy Historical Review* (Washington: Committee Print, 86th Cong., 2nd Sess., 1960).

    In the field of business, most of the pertinent material involves small business. See, for instance, Roland Stucki and Roger H. Nelson, *Evaluation of the Use and Impact of the Small Business Administration,* Financial Assistance Program, State of Utah, 1954 through June 30, 1960 (Salt Lake City: Bureau of Business and Economic Research, University of Utah, 1962); House Committee on Banking and Currency, *Small Business Act Amendment* (Washington: Hearing on H.R. 11020, June 7, 1962, 87th Cong., 2nd Sess., 1962).

    The following items are of interest in the health and welfare area: Roger L. Robertson and Eli A. Rubenstein, *Training Grant Program: Fiscal Years 1948–1961* (Washington: National Institute of Mental Health, 1962); House Committee on Government Operations, *The Administration of Grants by the National Health Institutes* (Washington: Hearings, March, 1962, 87th Cong., 2nd Sess., 1962), and Report on same (Washington: House Report No. 1958, 87th Cong., 2nd Sess., 1962); also by the same Committee, see *Health Research and Training* (Washington: Hearings, August, 1961, 87th Cong., 1st Sess., 1961).

CHAPTER XXV

The Search for an Acceptable
Policy

Changes in institutional forms and relationships are not made overnight. Institutions of all kinds are tough and resist sudden breaks, although they respond constantly, if slowly, to external conditions and internal forces. It is this inherent capacity for adjustment that makes it reasonable to talk about some reorientation in Federal-State relations. They were established in the first instance by a collective act of will, and they can be refashioned by taking thought as well as by drift. One thing is certain. The position of the States within the federal system will be different at the end of the next quarter century than it is today. If deliberate planning and action are not forthcoming, there is grave danger that the authority and usefulness of the States will be still further diminished, the congestion of power in Washington still further increased, and the possibility of effective citizen influence progressively decreased.

To prevent this outcome, several lines of action are open for exploration. I say exploration advisedly, because the task of unraveling the complex threads of present Federal-State relations is a delicate one, involving established economic, social, and political interests that deserve careful consideration. In making the specific suggestions that follow I do not wish to be understood as committing myself to their immediate practicability or wisdom, although I believe they are ready for early consideration. Some of them might appear on further study to be impractical or unwise, and all of them are doubtless controversial. They are samples of the kind of action that would be conducive to an improvement of the standing of the States in the federal system. There may well be other and better roads to this goal, and, as I have already stated, the direction of the

884

road and the nature of the ultimate goal are more important
than the specific highways that may be chosen to reach it.[1]

[1] White, Leonard D., *The States and the Nation* (Baton Rouge:
Louisiana State University Press, 1953), pp. 70–71.

While the people have been more conscious of problems in the
field of intergovernmental relations at some times than at others, little
or no attention was ever given to them unless something went wrong.
Then for a time there would be argument and heated discussion. When
the crisis passed, argument and discussion subsided, and intergovernmental relations returned to their normal process of development without guidance or direction.

Aside from the Civil War period when questions of Federal-State
relations loomed large among the issues involved, the nation has been
fortunate in managing better than might be expected under this policy
of blundering through. In the modern world, however, when so much
depends upon the strength and the leadership of the United States, such
reliance upon chance and good luck is no longer—if indeed it ever was
—a defensible policy.

As has been shown in earlier chapters, the pattern of American
federalism has changed significantly since the days of the Founding
Fathers. Gradually, it became apparent that a more positive and pur-
poseful approach to governmental problems was needed. This chapter
traces developments through the years preceding and following World
War II and the Commission on Intergovernmental Relations (Kestnbaum). During these years, there were numerous attempts to study, reform, or reorganize the federal system, or as Professor Grodzins has expressed it, to "unwind" it. At least four of the major efforts were government sponsored, while others were undertaken by private organizations.
Since the Kestnbaum Commission was by far the most important, the
various efforts will be discussed chronologically in relation to the publication of the Commission's report.

EARLY EFFORTS TO PROMOTE COOPERATION

The fifteen-year period from 1938 to 1953 was one of groping toward
an acceptable solution of the growing problems in the field of inter-

governmental relations. Evidence of this appeared both in the publications of the period and in the words and actions of men in their capacity as Federal and State government officials. Some of these efforts were obvious attempts to eliminate causes of tension. Such, for example, was the motivation behind the warfare waged by both the Federal government and the States against interstate trade barriers. Such, also, was the goal reflected in the impressive list of efforts to cope with problems of conflicting and overlapping taxation, beginning with the Treasury Department's establishment of its Committee on Intergovernmental Fiscal Relations.

Undertakings like the Pacific Coast Board of Intergovernmental Relations and the Legislative Drafting Committee (first located in the Department of Justice but currently under the auspices of the Council of State Governments) represented attempts to solve war and postwar problems. On the other hand, the proposal for a national study commission on problems in the field of intergovernmental relations looked toward the possibility of developing a long-range program that would bring some degree of order and stability into a situation in which these characteristics had been conspicuously absent.

President Roosevelt Attempts Coordination of Federal Programs

In the years preceding World War II, the administration made two attempts to coordinate Federal programs involving intergovernmental relations. In the first, James McReynolds of the White House staff was assigned the task, while in the second the assignment went to Guy Moffatt. No official record of either attempt has been located but both were short lived, partly because the administration did not back the efforts of the coordinators and partly because of the almost unlimited ingenuity of department and agency administrators in finding means of resisting any attempt to develop uniform policies and procedures and to coordinate programs. This resistance, incidentally, is the root of much of the present difficulty, and it is not unreasonable to assume that it will continue to be a problem far into the future.

Council on Intergovernmental Relations Organized

The Council on Intergovernmental Relations was a quasi-public venture, inspired and led by Harold D. Smith, Director of the Bureau of the Budget, but privately financed. The members of the Council included the heads of five important Federal agencies that had considerable involvement in intergovernmental relations and four other persons: Luther H. Gulick, Earl D. Mallory, Frank Bane, and William Anderson. Its purpose was, first, to find out what actually goes on in intergovernmental relations at the "grass roots" level, and second, to determine what steps might be taken to facilitate and encourage cooperative relations between the several levels and units of government. Counties in different States and in different sections of the country were selected for research and experimentation.[2]

Governors' Conference Enunciates Principles of Intergovernmental Cooperation

At its meeting at Mackinac Island, Michigan, in 1945, the Governors' Conference set forth five principles which it declared should prevail in the administration of peacetime public services involving the cooperation of National, State, and local governments, as follows:

1. Policies and programs should be developed cooperatively.

2. General policies and overall programs should be set forth explicitly in the statutes after due consideration by Congress, so that the respective parts of the programs to be performed by the several levels of government are clearly defined, and due recognition is given to the rights and duties of each.

3. The immediate supervision and direction of such cooperative programs should be in the hands of the States.

4. Responsibility for the local operation thereof should be given to the subordinate units of government.

5. Necessary authority should be commensurate with responsibility, and lines of direction should be scrupulously followed.

Pacific Coast Board of Intergovernmental Relations

The development of the Pacific Coast Board of Intergovernmental Relations (frequently referred to as PACBIR) provides a striking example

[2] The selected States and counties were: California, Santa Clara County; Georgia, Colquitt County; Indiana, Henry County; Minnesota, Blue Earth County; and Washington, Skagit County. The publications resulting from the work in these counties are listed in Graves, W. Brooke, *Intergovernmental Relations in the United States: A Selected Bibliography* (Washington: Committee Print, House Intergovernmental Relations Subcommittee, 84th Cong., 2nd Sess., November, 1956), pp. 6–9. For a general comment, see Walker, John A., *Grass Roots: A Report and an Evaluation* (Washington: U.S. Council on Intergovernmental Relations, 1947).

of a successful effort to coordinate the activities of all three levels of government in a given area. Although initiated for the accomplishment of certain wartime purposes, it later proved to be quite as useful for other purposes during the period of reconstruction. In the early 1940's, the Bureau of the Budget had established a small number of field offices to serve as contact points not only with Federal offices and installations, but with State and local agencies having direct relations with and/or responsibilities in the administration of Federal programs. One of these developed into an office of outstanding significance.

PACBIR was organized and developed under the capable leadership of James W. Rupley, Chief Field Representative in the San Francisco office, and the late Professor Samuel C. May of the University of California. On an experimental basis, the Board was set up in 1945 during the closing days of World War II with representatives from California, Oregon, and Washington. It was continued during the postwar period as an agency for the discussion of governmental problems by officials at all levels. A grant was obtained from one of the foundations for a small staff and incidental expenses. Its purposes were clearly stated in its "Principles of Organization":

> This Board is created purely on a voluntary cooperative basis for the purpose of mutual discussion and cooperation in administrative efforts to solve problems affecting people, and most especially such problems as are the responsibility of governments during the postwar readjustment period. Such mutual discussion and cooperation will strive for the elimination of duplication in the execution of local, State, and Federal laws and regulations, the pooling of facts regarding economic and social conditions, especially those due to industrialization, and the planning of local, State, and Federal governments for dealing with these matters constructively.

Membership, on a purely voluntary basis, was confined to local, State, and Federal governments, care being taken that no one level should be over-represented in relation to the others:

> From each State the membership shall be the Governor of the State, the Chairman of the State Commission on Interstate Cooperation, an official representative of the League or Association of Cities or Municipalities, and an official representative of the State Association of County Supervisors or Commissioners.
> From the Federal government membership shall be Field Chiefs of Federal agencies, selected by the Pacific Coast Federal Regional Council, and shall be less in number than the combined total of representatives of the other jurisdictions.

Frequent regular meetings were held, usually at the capitals of the participating States, with the Governor of the host State presiding.

At the close of the war, much attention was given to helping States and local units obtain surplus war materials useful in their departments and institutions. At a meeting in mid-1950, the major items on the agenda were community programs to create jobs, and the problem of organized crime with a view to stressing the success of intercity cooperation and the extent of the total crime problem confronting the coast area. Although the conclusions of the Board were purely advisory, participants reported that ways and means for cutting through red tape and obtaining effective action through the cooperative efforts of all levels of government were developed in the discussions. Uniform policies on many problems were also developed.[3] The organization continued to function until, with a change of administration and in the interests of "economy," the field offices of the Bureau of the Budget were discontinued in 1953.

First Hoover Commission Report on Federal-State Relations

The First Commission on the Organization of the Executive Branch of the Government, commonly known from the name of its chairman as the Hoover Commission, set up both a Committee and a Task Force on Federal-State relations. The Committee report was practically suppressed, although the Commission did publish a brief report. The Commission did not publish the excellent Task Force Report prepared for it by the staff of the Council of State Governments. Arrangements were made later to have this report published as a Senate Document. It was a significant report, not only because of its analysis of the problems in the field of intergovernmental relations, but also for its forthright comments on some of the weaknesses of State government and the means for their correction.[4]

Council of State Governments Focuses Attention Upon Our Federal System

In the period following World War II, the Council of State Governments took new and aggressive steps to focus attention on problems in

[3] Two articles on this Board were published: Rohrer, Miriam, "Coast States Try Cooperation," *National Municipal Review*, November, 1945, pp. 484-487, and Crook, Stanley K., "The Pacific Coast Board of Intergovernmental Relations," *Public Administration Review*, Spring, 1951, pp. 103-108.

[4] See Commission on Organization of the Executive Branch of the Government, *Federal-State Relations: A Report to the Congress* (Washington, 1949) and Council of State Governments, *Federal-State Relations* (Washington: Senate Document No. 81, 81st Cong., 1st Sess., 1949).

the field of Federal-State relations. The work that the Council had done for the first Hoover Commission was only one aspect of the campaign. Another aspect that attracted much attention was a program arranged for a session of the Assembly of the States, held in Detroit late in 1948. The program revolved around the question: Are We Maintaining Our Federal System? Two addresses were presented by Governors or former Governors, one by a university professor, and one by a journalist. All four, later published as a supplement to the magazine *State Government*, had wide distribution in pamphlet form.[5]

Minnesota Study of Intergovernmental Relations

A comprehensive and detailed study of intergovernmental relations in the United States, as illustrated by the experience of one State, was carried on during the decade following World War II. Financed by a grant from the Rockefeller Foundation, plus supplements from the University of Minnesota and Michigan State University, the study was organized and directed by Professor William Anderson, assisted by Professor Edward W. Weidner. It resulted in a series of ten volumes published by the University of Minnesota Press between 1950 and 1958, as follows:

> Courts—Talbott, Forrest, *Intergovernmental Relations and the Courts,* 1950.
> Education—Morlan, Robert L., *Intergovernmental Relations in Education,* 1950.
> Finance—Anderson, William, *Intergovernmental Fiscal Relations,* 1956.
> General—Weidner, Edward W., *Intergovernmental Relations as Seen Through Official Eyes,* 1958.
>   Ylvisaker, Paul N., *Intergovernmental Relations at the Grass Roots: A Study of Blue Earth County, Minnesota, to 1940,* 1956.
> Health—Wyatt, Laurence, *Intergovernmental Relations in Public Health,* 1951.
> Highways—Gomez, R. A., *Intergovernmental Relations in Highways,* 1950.
> Labor—Rourke, Francis E., *Intergovernmental Relations in Employment Security,* 1952.
> Welfare—Raup, Ruth M., *Intergovernmental Relations in Social Welfare,* 1952.

[5] "Symposium: Are We Maintaining Our Federal System?" *State Government,* January, 1949, supplement. The four answers were: Bricker, John W., pp. 9–14; Drummond, Roscoe, pp. 1–4; Gaus, John M., pp. 5–9; and Lane, William P., Jr., pp. 15–19. See also Graves, W. Brooke, "What Is Happening to Our Federal System?" *State Government,* November, 1949, pp. 255–259, 270.

Summary and Conclusion—Anderson, William, *Intergovernmental Relations in Review,* 1960.

Intergovernmental Relations in the 1952 Presidential Campaign

Specific problems in the field of intergovernmental relations have been discussed in presidential campaigns in the past, but prior to 1952 there had been little if any discussion of general intergovernmental relationships. In the course of the 1952 campaign, the subject was commented upon by the candidates of both major political parties. The following were illustrative comments:

Adlai E. Stevenson as Governor of Illinois had shown a growing awareness of the problems of federalism. Writing on "The States, the Federal System, and the People," he said in 1950:

> Our great task is to make the 155,000 governing units of this country work, all the way from the mosquito abatement districts to the national government in Washington. Forty-eight of the 155,000 governments are States; the rest are subdivisions of States. That is where the decisions mostly lie. Here is where I suggest we concentrate more attention. . . .
>
> We can make democracy work at all levels. We can get better government. We can do away with graft and corruption. These are today's problems in "States' rights." Solution of these problems, not bitter recriminations, is the answer to those who fear the centralization of power in Washington.[6]

Two years later, as a presidential candidate, writing on "crime and local government," he said:

> I suggest that it is time to explore every possible alternative before we embark upon a course of funneling power over law enforcement to the State level. Once that level is reached, the pressures will build up —as they have already begun to do—to effect a further transfer to the Federal Government.
>
> I think we should travel that inviting but hazardous road very slowly. In this instance I don't think we need travel it at all if we cultivate more positively the sense of community responsibility—if we stop preaching so much about the virtues of local government and begin to practice them.[7]

[6] Stevenson, Adlai E., in *State Government,* February, 1950, pp. 24–27, 40.
[7] Stevenson, Adlai E., "Who Runs the Gambling Machines?" *Atlantic Monthly,* February, 1952, pp. 35–38.

Dwight D. Eisenhower as candidate for the Presidency said at Des Moines, Iowa, on September 18, 1952:

> Next I want to see maintained the constitutional relationship between the Federal and State governments. My oath of office [as President] would demand that. My convictions would require it.
> The Federal Government did not create the States in this republic. The States created the Federal Government.
> . . . if the States lose their meaning, our entire system of government loses its meaning. And the next step is the rise of the centralized national state in which the seeds of autocracy can take root and grow.

After his election, Mr. Eisenhower continued his interest in intergovernmental relations. As one indication of the importance he attached to the problems in this field, he appeared before the Governors' Conference in Seattle during his first year in office to emphasize the importance of "working together"; "Unless we are partners in these things, they cannot be done. When we are partners—the Federal Government and the States —working together—there is no limit to the possibilities for progress that are open to the American people." The address was couched in very general terms and contained no specific recommendations. It may, therefore, be appropriate to observe that the spirit of what the President said, and the fact that he traveled way across the country to say it, was more important than the actual words spoken.[8]

THE COMMISSION ON INTERGOVERNMENTAL RELATIONS

Establishment

The proposal to establish a national study commission in the field of intergovernmental relations had first been made in 1940,[9] but at that time no one in a position of authority appeared to be interested. The first bills introduced in Congress calling for such a commission appeared in 1947; Senator Herbert R. O'Conor of Maryland introduced a bill to authorize a study aimed at clarifying and improving fiscal relationships

[8] Eisenhower, Dwight D., "The Duties of State Government: We Must Work Together," *Vital Speeches*, September 1, 1953, pp. 696–698.

[9] Graves, W. Brooke, "Readjusting Governmental Areas and Functions," *Annals of the American Academy of Political and Social Science*, January, 1940, pp. 203–209. This was the concluding piece in a symposium consisting of twenty-two articles dealing with many aspects of intergovernmental relations in the United States.

between the Federal government and the States, and Senator John W. Bricker of Ohio also introduced a bill at this time. A veritable flood of such bills and resolutions appeared in 1949 in the first session of the 81st Congress. Most of the bills were limited in scope to Federal-State relationships and to the fiscal aspects of such relations. One was restricted to relationships in the field of education.

Most significant of these bills was H.R. 2389, introduced February 7, 1949, by Representative (now Senator) J. Caleb Boggs of Delaware, and S. 810, introduced on the same date by Senator Robert C. Hendrickson of New Jersey and cosponsored by seven other Senators, including members of both parties from all sections of the country. Since House rules do not permit multiple sponsorship, at least four identical bills were introduced in the House.[10] The Boggs-Hendrickson bill, drafted by the author and two members of the staff of the Council of State Governments (Theodore G. Driscoll and Newton Edwards), provided for representation of all three levels of government and for a comprehensive study of all aspects of intergovernmental relations in this country. Joint hearings were held on these bills.[11]

Finally, in 1953, five years after the original Boggs-Hendrickson bill had been introduced, the Senate Majority Leader, acting under strong pressure from the White House, introduced and pressed for passage a new bill;[12] instead of using the earlier bill which had been carefully drawn and on which hearings had been held, the new bill was very hastily and poorly drafted. Passed by the Senate, it was considerably revised and improved by the House, necessitating a conference committee. The con-

[10] These were, in addition to the Boggs bill: H.R. 4184, Harvey of Indiana; H.R. 3944, Secrest of Ohio; and H.R. 4507, Bonner of North Carolina. Other House bills and resolutions included:

H. Res. 383, Bolling of Missouri, Federal-State fiscal relations; H.R. 1838, Latham of New York, tax coordination; and H. J. Res. 48, Hand of New York, directing the Committee on Ways and Means to study intergovernmental relations, with special reference to education. Other Senate bills and resolutions included: S. 1846, Taylor of Idaho and others, A Commission on Intergovernmental Relations; S. 3147, Humphrey of Minnesota and others, A Commission on Intergovernmental Relations; S. 767, Bricker of Ohio, and O'Conor of Maryland (see text above); and S.J. Res. 41, O'Conor of Maryland, fiscal relations.

[11] See Senate and House Committees on Expenditures in the Executive Departments, Joint Hearings on a *National Commission on Intergovernmental Relations,* May, 1949 (Washington: 81st Cong., 1st Sess., 1949). For citations of later Congressional hearings and reports on similar bills, see Graves, W. Brooke, *Intergovernmental Relations in the United States: A Selected Bibliography* (Washington: Committee Print, House Subcommittee on Intergovernmental Relations, 85th Cong., 2nd Sess., November, 1956), p. 7.

[12] S. 1514; when signed by the President, this measure became Public Law 109 on June 27, 1953.

ference report was agreed upon. The measure called for a membership of twenty-five persons, of which fifteen were to be appointed by the President, five by the President of the Senate, and five by the Speaker of the House of Representatives. Appointments were not completed until late in August, so it was impossible to organize the Commission before fall, when an incredibly bad start delayed its work still further.[13]

The first chairman was Clarence E. Manion of Indiana, who was succeeded after a few months by Meyer Kestnbaum of Illinois, under whose leadership the work of the Commission moved forward to a significant conclusion. As the Commission itself pointed out, its study was "the first official undertaking of its kind since the Constitutional Convention in 1787." Originally given one year in which to complete its task, extension necessitated both by the slow start and the normal difficulties encountered in completing so vast an undertaking on a tight schedule was authorized to June 30, 1955, when the *Report to the President,* with supporting documents, was filed and the Commission itself passed out of existence.

Although the creation of the Commission marked the successful culmination of several years of effort, the Act in its final form had three weaknesses which made the work of the Commission much more difficult than it would have been under any circumstances: (1) no provision was made for the representation of local units—an affront which they deeply resented; (2) too much emphasis was placed on fiscal problems—which are important, to be sure, but which are still only one aspect of the problem as a whole; (3) the language of the Act limited the study almost exclusively to Federal-State relationships. These defects were unfortunate, the more so when they could easily have been avoided if the work previously done on this type of legislation had been utilized.

As soon as it became certain that a national commission on intergovernmental relations was to function, there sprang up around the country a sizable number of State commissions intended to study and report on local problems and otherwise to cooperate with the national Commission whenever possible. Many of these State commissions were official bodies, while others were set up by chambers of commerce, taxpayers associations, and other private groups. Official bodies functioned in Delaware, Idaho, Illinois, Indiana, Kansas, Michigan, New Jersey, New York, Pennsylvania, South Carolina, Tennessee, Utah, and Wisconsin.[14]

---

[13] When it appeared that the bring-the-government-back-home group was about to take over, Professor William Anderson began work on a statement of the basic principles of American federalism; this work was later published, in greatly revised form, under the title, *The Nation and the States: Rivals or Partners?* (Minneapolis: University of Minnesota Press, 1955).

[14] The published reports of these agencies are cited in Graves, *Bibliography.*

The Report

The Report, when completed, was divided into two parts, the first of which dealt with the American federal system, emphasizing the role of the States, the importance of strong State and local governments, national responsibilities and cooperative responsibilities, the fiscal aspects of federalism (including the grant-in-aid system), and the second of which discussed intergovernmental responsibilities in twelve different functional fields. In spite of many diverse backgrounds, interests, and points of view among the members, they were able to agree on a surprising number of difficult questions. Recognizing that the conditions of the mid-twentieth century are not and cannot again be those of an earlier age, they did not attempt to turn the clock back. They sought rather to determine what, based on existing conditions, should be our goals in developing for the future a form of federalism that would preserve the best of our heritage from the past, while at the same time making adequate provision for the needs of our people in a new era in the history of our country and of the world.

The following passage, the summary of Chapter I on the evolution of the American federal system, well illustrates the general attitude and point of view from which the Commission approached its task:

> Our federal system is a unique phenomenon, without an earlier model and bearing only a general resemblance to later federal systems established elsewhere. It is the product partly of human purpose, partly of unconscious adaptation to the circumstances and the felt needs of our people. It has survived the vicissitudes of over a century and a half of our history to become now the oldest federal system. It has met the test of civil war. It has accommodated vast territorial expansion to the significant principle that the new States shall enjoy constitutional equality with the old. It has furnished a governmental environment compatible with unparalleled economic growth and social advances. It has shouldered an increased degree of responsibility for social security and welfare. It has enabled the mustering of resources for waging two world wars and developing atomic energy.

> At the same time, it has preserved a degree of local autonomy unmatched among the world's other great powers. The States make their own constitutions, and the laws that govern elections, crimes, property, contracts, torts, domestic relations, and the like. Most States in their turn have tended in practice to establish a virtually federal division of powers and responsibilities between themselves, their counties, and their municipalities. This autonomy has kept under local controls most of the schools, the police, the ordinary administration of criminal and civil justice, the local taxes, and the provision of most municipal services. It has kept in local hands also the machinery of elections and

with it, in the main, the control of the party system. It has enabled local option to prevail on a wide range of domestic concerns. It has furnished local bases of power and refuge for political leaders, parties, and policies in opposition to those for the time being dominant in Washington. It has made possible a large degree of popular participation and consent.

These are results—most citizens would call them achievements in keeping with the original purposes, as set forth in the Preamble to the Constitution. With the passage of the years, the federal division of powers has involved a highly complex distribution of governmental tasks and responsibilities. Because the results are generally approved, the system itself enjoys high prestige. But approval in general should not necessarily imply endorsement of all the details of a going system. Where the problem of our federal system once appeared to be one of creating sufficient strength and authority in the National Government, today contrary concerns have aroused anxiety. The National Government now has within its reach authority well beyond what it requires for ordinary use; forebearance in the exercise of this authority is essential if the federal balance is to be maintained.

Yet prudent limitation of National responsibilities is not likely by itself to prevent overcentralization. A realistic program of decentralization in our contemporary society depends too on the readiness and ability of the States and their subdivisions to assume their full share of the total task of government.[15]

There is little to criticize about what the Commission did. The fact that its studies were made and its report published did much to clear the atmosphere and develop a climate within which further progress could be made. Supporters of the move to establish a commission had hoped, however, that it would develop the historical background, analyze current problems, and present a blueprint which might serve as a guide for future development. The Commission's one failure was that it did not enunciate a national policy or suggest a means of developing and implementing one.

[15] *Report to the President for Transmittal to the Congress*, pp. 33–35. In addition, the Commission published a series of sixteen special reports and supporting documents which are listed in the Bibliographical Notes. See also: Senate Reports Nos. 215 (Washington: 83rd Cong., 1st Sess., 1953) and 1966 (Washington: 83rd Cong., 2nd Sess., 1954); and Anderson, William, "The Commission on Intergovernmental Relations and the United States Federal System," *Journal of Politics*, May, 1956, pp. 211–231.

DEVELOPMENTS INSPIRED BY THE KESTNBAUM
COMMISSION REPORT

What has happened since the Report of the Commission on Intergovernmental Relations was filed? The groping for a policy has continued as various efforts have been made to find solutions to problems that were more or less in harmony with the spirit and intent of the Report.

Many officers and agencies of government have given their cooperation in moving toward a workable solution for problems in intergovernmental relations. Two steps were taken by the President and two by Congress, while the President and the Governors shared in the establishment of the Federal-State Joint Action Committee. In addition, a number of different types of proposals are to be found in bills introduced by Members of Congress.

Actions by the President

President Eisenhower promptly took steps to staff the executive office for the improvement of intergovernmental relations, and a little later, at his second appearance before the Governors' Conference, he made suggestions that resulted in the establishment of the Federal-State Joint Action Committee.

As has been noted elsewhere, two attempts had been made around 1940 to establish among the departments and agencies administering joint programs some coordination in the field of Federal-State relationships. The year 1956 saw a new and significant attempt to accomplish this objective when the President made two appointments to his staff in the executive office. Meyer Kestnbaum, formerly chairman of the Commission on Intergovernmental Relations, was appointed to follow through on the recommendations of both the Second Hoover Commission and the Commission on Intergovernmental Relations. At the same time, former Governor Howard Pyle of Arizona was appointed deputy assistant to the President for intergovernmental relations, being specifically directed:

> to maintain liaison with organizations of officials in the field of Government; to establish *ad hoc* working committees among Federal officials; to grapple with problems concerning State and local governments; to follow through on the findings and recommendations of the Commission

on Intergovernmental Relations; to explore the feasibility of establishing regional boards of intergovernmental relations; to develop periodic reports on the National Government's relations with, and proposed actions involving, State and local governments, and to make such studies as may be required.

The Bureau of the Budget was given the responsibility of assisting in carrying out these duties.[16]

Actions by Congress

In both the Senate and the House of Representatives, the Committees on Government Operations have made a sustained effort to cope with problems in the field of intergovernmental relations. The House had established a Subcommittee on Intergovernmental Relations as far back as the 81st Congress, pursuant to the provision of the Legislative Reorganization Act of 1946 which requires the Committee on Government Operations to study "intergovernmental relationships between the United States and the States and municipalities." Mr. Bonner of North Carolina was chairman during the 82nd Congress, Mrs. Cecil Hardin of Indiana during the 83rd, and Mr. Fountain of North Carolina during the 84th and succeeding Congresses.

Beginning in 1955, the Subcommittee undertook a comprehensive study of Federal-State-local relationships. In December of that year, detailed questionnaires were sent to each Federal department and agency, to every State government, and to a large number of cities and counties. The Subcommittee sought to obtain a description of each Federal program involving intergovernmental relationships, information on official action taken to implement the Kestnbaum Commission recommendations, and each agency's views on the desirability of implementing those Commission recommendations relating to its programs. The State and local officials were asked whether intergovernmental programs would be improved by giving more responsibility to State and local governments and if Federal supervision in these programs was satisfactory.

The questionnaire surveys were followed in the fall of 1957 by regional hearings in which officials of State and local governments, including State legislative leaders, were invited to present their views on

[16] See Merriam, Robert E., "Partners or Rivals?" *National Municipal Review*, December, 1956, pp. 532–536, an address given before the National Conference on Government in Memphis in November. See also Pyle, Howard, "Federal Role in Intergovernmental Relations," in *Proceedings of the National Legislative Conference, 1956* (Chicago: Council of State Governments, 1957), pp. 38–42.

intergovernmental programs and problems. Public hearings were held in a number of cities across the country from Boston and New York in the East, Denver and San Francisco in the West, and New Orleans, Miami, and Raleigh in the South. This was the first time that this procedure had been utilized in the field of intergovernmental relations. The representatives of private organizations and interested persons were given the opportunity to present their views in public hearings held in Washington during July, 1957, and February, 1958. The officials of a number of Federal departments and agencies appeared before the Subcommittee in a series of hearings held in the spring of 1958; other hearings on the report of the Joint Federal-State Action Committee followed in February, 1958, and on the proposal for a permanent national, nonpartisan Advisory Commission on Intergovernmental Relations in June, 1959.[17]

On the Senate side, a Subcommittee on Intergovernmental Relations was also established, on June 19, 1947, likewise pursuant to the requirement of the Legislative Reorganization Act of the preceding year. The original members included Senators Bricker of Ohio, Chairman,

[17] See House of Representatives, Committee on Government Operations:

Recommendations and Major Statements of Commission on Intergovernmental Relations, Annotated to Show Method of Implementation and Federal Agency and Affected (Washington: Committee Print, 84th Cong., 2nd Sess., August, 1956);

Staff Report on Replies from Federal Agencies to Questionnaire on Intergovernmental Relations (Washington: Committee Print, 84th Cong., 2nd Sess., August, 1956);

Replies From State and Local Governments to Questionnaire on Intergovernmental Relations (Washington: Union Calendar No. 200, H.R. 575, 85th Cong., 1st Sess., June, 1957), sixth committee report;

Federal-State-Local Relations, Hearings before a subcommittee, July 29-31, 1957 (Washington: 85th Cong., 1st Sess., 1957);

Federal-State-Local Relations, State and Local Officials, Hearings before a subcommittee (Washington: 85th Cong., 1st Sess., 1957):

Part I—Boston, Mass., and New York, N.Y., September 30, October 1-4 and 7, 1957;

Part II—Chicago, Ill., and Kansas City, Mo., October 16-18, 21-22, 1957;

Part III—Denver, Colo., and San Francisco, Calif., October 24-25, 28-30, 1957;

Part IV—New Orleans, La., and Raleigh, N.C., November 18-19, December 10-11, 1957.

Federal-State-Local Relations: Dade County (Florida) Metropolitan Government, Hearings before a subcommittee, November 21-22, 1957 (Washington: 85th Cong., 1st Sess., 1957).

Federal-State-Local Relations: Joint Federal-State Action Committee, Hearings before a subcommittee, February 18, 1958 (Washington: 85th Cong., 2nd Sess., 1958).

Hickenlooper of Iowa, Hoey of North Carolina, O'Conor of Maryland, and Thye of Minnesota. When its funds ran out in 1951, the Subcommittee was permitted to lapse and the full Committee took over its work.[18] In June, 1962, a new Subcommittee on Intergovernmental Relations was authorized, under the chairmanship of Senator Edmund S. Muskie of Maine.

During these years, while there was no subcommittee, the full Committee continued its effort to perfect and obtain passage of a bill to authorize payments to local governments in lieu of taxes and special assessments, with respect to certain Federal property. In the 85th Congress, this was S. 967, in the 86th, S. 910; both were sponsored by Senator Humphrey of Minnesota and others. This turned out to be an extremely technical subject regarding which it has been most difficult to reconcile the many different interests and points of view—a fact which explains the long delay in the enactment of this needed legislation.

The Joint Federal-State Action Committee

On June 21, 1957, President Eisenhower made his second appearance before the Governors' Conference, this time at Williamsburg, Virginia, suggesting "that this Conference join with the Federal Administration in creating a task force for action—a joint committee—charged with three responsibilities:

> 1. To designate functions which the States are ready and willing to assume and finance that are now performed or financed wholly or in part by the Federal Government;
> 2. To recommend the Federal and State revenue adjustments required to enable the States to assume these functions; and
> 3. To identify functions and responsibilities likely to require State or Federal attention in the future and to recommend the level of State effort, or Federal effort, or both, that will be needed to assure effective action."

In its concluding business session, the Conference voted to go ahead with this proposal and authorized its chairman to name a group "to develop ways and means of attaining a sound relationship of functions and finances between the Federal Government and the States." The

---

[18] See *Activities of the Senate Committee on Expenditures in the Executive Departments, 80th Congress* (Washington: Senate Document No. 4, 81st Cong., 1st Sess., 1949) and *Coordination of Federal and State Taxes* (Washington: Senate Report No. 1054, 80th Cong., 2nd Sess., 1948).

joint committee was promptly organized, with the Secretary of the Treasury and the Governor of New Hampshire as co-chairmen. The seventeen members included nine Governors and seven top-ranking Federal officials. The Chairman of the Executive Committee of the Governors' Conference was a member ex officio. The group held a number of meetings during 1957 and 1958, and in December of the former year submitted its *Progress Report No. 1* [19] in which specific recommendations were made on six subjects. A number of other matters, including both functions and plans for financial support, were listed as "pending items." The recommendations were that:

1. *Vocational Education.* The States assume full responsibility for financial support of the older programs in this field, practical nurse training, and the training program for the fisheries trade and industry.

2. *Waste Treatment.* The States provide financial assistance for waste treatment facilities and for water pollution control, and that they improve municipal capacity to raise funds to finance water treatment works.

3. *Disaster Relief.* The States take steps to insure that necessary resources are available to meet the minimum financial obligations agreed upon for each State, before applying for disaster relief from the Federal Government.

4. *Atomic Energy.* A greater share of the responsibility for the promotion and regulation of the peacetime uses of atomic energy, particularly in the fields of health and safety, be vested in the State governments.

5. *Urban Renewal.* Each State create an agency with specific responsibility for handling problems of urban development, housing, and metropolitan planning.

6. *Local Telephone Service Tax.* By appropriate legislation, the Congress authorize, and the States avail themselves of up to 40 per cent of the Federal Local Telephone Service Tax.

The purpose of the recommendations was three-fold: (1) to turn over to the States full responsibility for the performance of certain specific functions; (2) to cut off the Federal financial assistance heretofore provided for the support of these functions; and (3) to provide the States with revenue and/or revenue sources adequate to support the transferred functions or services. It was generally recognized that this was a very small beginning on a problem of tremendous proportions.

Subsequently, on May 14, 1958, the President transmitted a letter,

[19] *Report of the Joint Federal-State Action Committee to the President of the United States and to the Chairman of the Governors' Conference* (Washington: Progress Report No 1, filed December, 1957, published, 1958).

accompanied by draft legislation, to the Speaker of the House of Representatives urging that Congress promptly enact legislation consistent
with the recommendations of the Joint Federal-State Action Committee,
but no such action was taken then or since. The recommendations were
discussed but not acted upon at a meeting of the Board of Managers of
the Council of State Governments at Hot Springs in December, 1957.
In May, 1958, the Governors' Conference, meeting at Bal Harbour,
Florida, voted to continue the Joint Action Committee and to broaden
its scope but did not approve the Committee's specific proposals relative
to the transfer of program responsibilities and the release of a portion
of the Federal telephone tax. The Conference resolution included the
following statements:

> Progress Report No. 1 of the Joint Committee contains specific
> Recommendations for Action. Those three which recommend new or
> increased effort by the States in areas of governmental activity which will
> be for sometime Federal-State-local responsibilities should be imple-
> mented at the State level at the earliest possible date. The recommenda-
> tions which would result in assumption by the States of complete ad-
> ministrative and financial responsibilities for functions now a joint
> Federal-State responsibility should be implemented only on the follow-
> ing bases:
> (1) That adequate time be allowed for adjustment through prac-
> ticable procedure at both levels to insure that there is no impairment of
> the programs; and
> (2) That modification of the tax relinquishment recommendation
> be made by the Joint Committee to insure that the revenue source made
> available to each State is substantially equivalent to the costs of the
> functions to be assumed.[20]

The members of the Committee were unanimous in wanting to
justify the Committee's existence and, if possible, actually to accomplish
something, but in spite of two years of effort in an atmosphere characterized by an absence of partisan disagreement or of conflict along
governmental lines, there was still no significant accomplishment. Professor Morton Grodzins attributes this failure to the unqualified acceptance of the doctrine of separatism by the members of the Committee,
separatism as applied to both functions and revenues. Modest as were

---

[20] See *Report of the Joint Federal-State Action Committee;* see also the
testimony of the Secretary of the Treasury and Governor Lane Dwinell before
the House Subcommittee on Intergovernmental Relations, Hearings, February
18, 1958, *Federal-State-Local Relations: Joint Federal-State Action Committee*
(Washington: 85th Cong., 2nd Sess., 1958).

the recommendations and attractive as were the financial inducements offered, there were no takers. Even if the recommendations had been accepted and adopted *in toto,* they would have been only a slight beginning toward a solution of a problem of staggering magnitude.

Actions by Private Individuals and Groups

Associations of Local Government Officials. In the years following publication of the Kestnbaum Commission Report, several national organizations of local government officials made implementation of the Report a major issue. The American Municipal Association, the National Association of Counties, and other national groups went on record at their 1957 annual meetings in favor of making the implementation of the Report a major item on the agenda for the coming year. This evidence of interest and support was a significant and reassuring development.[21]

Commercial and Industrial Organizations. A number of influential private organizations have consistently taken a strong position in favor of more effective State and local governments and opposed to the increasing centralization of authority in Washington. Among these may be noted the Chamber of Commerce of the United States, the National Association of Manufacturers, and the National Council of State Chambers of Commerce. The United States Chamber in December, 1953, sponsored a conference on Federal-State relations in Washington, just as the Commission on Intergovernmental Relations project was being launched. Again, in December, 1957, the Chamber staged a meeting of the heads of the State Chambers of Commerce devoted largely to a discussion of this problem. Support for the work of the Joint Federal-State Action Committee was formally expressed, both by this gathering and by the National Council of State Chambers at an earlier meeting in Richmond.[22]

The Eighth American Assembly. Early in 1955, the National Policy Board of the American Assembly decided to devote one of the assemblies

[21] See *Federal-State-Local Relations,* Hearings of the House Committee on Government Operations, Subcommittee on Intergovernmental Relations, July, 1957 (Washington: 85th Cong., 2nd Sess., 1958).

[22] See Graves, W. Brooke, *The Coming Challenge in Federal-State Relations* (Washington: Chamber of Commerce of the United States, December, 1957). The National Association of Manufacturers ran a series of articles in their news bulletin, supporting the activities of the Deputy Assistant to the President for Intergovernmental Relations and the work of the Joint Federal-State Action Committee.

to a discussion of the role of the States. In preparation for this meeting, a planning session was held at Arden House on the Harriman Campus of Columbia University in April. This conference was attended by a group of twenty leading students of State government from universities in all parts of the country. The major questions to be discussed at the Assembly were decided upon, and Professor James W. Fesler of Yale University was asked to assume responsibility for the preparation of suitable materials for the briefing of the participants in the Assembly in October.

A representative group of fifty-five or sixty distinguished citizens, from many walks of life and from all parts of the country, responded to the invitation to attend the Assembly which, as usual, formulated a statement of Participants' Findings. In this statement, they took the position that only by putting their houses in order, by making effective use of their powers, and by efficiently discharging their responsibilities could the States maintain their position in the face of constant pressures toward the centralization of authority.[23]

In one significant respect, the Eighth American Assembly differed from others before or since. In view of the importance of the subject matter, one of the foundations made a grant available to the Assembly's National Policy Board, for the purpose of organizing and conducting a series of State and regional assemblies on an experimental basis, thereby extending the influence of the Assembly to a far larger number of people. In connection with this program, the following assemblies were held: Southern Assembly on State Governments in the South, Biloxi, Mississippi (April 17–19, 1956; plans were made to hold similar conferences thereafter, on an annual basis); Pacific Northwest Assembly on State Government, Spokane, Washington (June 21–24, 1956); New Mexico Assembly on State Government, Albuquerque, New Mexico (September 6, 1956); California Conference on State Government, Stanford University, California (September 1956; plans were made to hold similar conferences thereafter, on an annual basis); Wyoming Assembly on State Government, Laramie, Wyoming (October 31–November 2, 1957): Oklahoma Conference on State Government, Norman, Oklahoma (November 7–9, 1957); Illinois Assembly on State Government, Monticello, Illinois (February 21–23, 1958); Georgia Statewide Citizenship Conference, Atlanta, Georgia (April 13–15, 1959).

[23] See Fesler, James W., ed., *The Forty-eight States: Their Tasks as Policy Makers and Administrators*, Final Edition (New York: American Assembly, Columbia University, 1955). Each of the State and regional assemblies prepared and published similar manuals for the information of participants, and some of them published their findings separately in pamphlet form.

LEGISLATIVE PROPOSALS OF THE LATE 1950'S

Legislative proposals affecting intergovernmental relations have in late years been fairly numerous. In general, the proposals seemed to fall into four major categories: (1) a department of urban affairs; (2) a metropolitan area study commission; (3) a national advisory commission on intergovernmental relations; and (4) an intergovernmental reference service.

Department of Urban Affairs

The proposal to establish a Federal department to render for urban residents a type of service comparable to that provided by the Department of Agriculture for farmers and homemakers was first presented to Congress by Representative J. Arthur Younger of California in 1954. This proposal suffered from its author's attempt to be too clever when he called it a Department of Urbiculture. Senator Joseph S. Clark of Pennsylvania, long an advocate of such a department, presented S. 2154 in the 85th Congress, calling for the establishment of a Department of Housing and Urban Affairs to conduct a continuing study of problems peculiar to urban and metropolitan areas and to provide technical assistance to State and local governmental bodies in developing solutions to such problems. While Senator Clark did not again introduce his bill in the 86th Congress, four bills of similar purpose were presented in the House.[24]

Despite the many serious problems in this area, there are grounds for questioning whether the establishment of a new department of urban affairs is the right solution; some, in fact, question whether it is a solution at all. Many of the problems confronting our cities—such as education, health and welfare, and land use and planning—are general problems of government, affecting urban dwellers and rural folk alike. They are

[24] These were: H.R. 4481, by Hugh J. Addonizio of New Jersey; H.R. 7378, by Kathryn E. Granahan of Pennsylvania; H.R. 781 by Martha W. Griffiths of Michigan; and H.R. 984 by J. Arthur Younger of California. The full text of each appears in the hearings, *Metropolitan Problems and Urban Development*, Hearings before a Subcommittee of the Committee on Government Operations, June 3–July 21, 1959 (Washington: 86th Cong., 1st Sess., 1959). Bills on a metropolitan area study commission were included, as well as those relating to a department of urban affairs.

in no sense peculiar to the cities. Consequently, there is among those best informed and most deeply concerned about urban problems a sharp difference of opinion regarding the desirability of a new department of urban affairs. Not only are they divided on this question, but also on the nature of the duties to be assigned, if such a department were to be created.

Still another complicating factor arises concerning the problem of obtaining Congressional support for such a department and the necessary funds. Although the orientation of Congress is slowly changing, there are still far more members with a rural orientation than with an urban one. Under these circumstances, two practical alternatives for a department seem worthy of consideration. One is to establish an interdepartmental coordinating committee with representatives from each of the departments or agencies whose programs and policies have a direct impact on urban and metropolitan problems. This is, to be sure, a far cry from the second alternative, a department with Cabinet status, but such a committee could render useful service and might even serve as a transition device, should it still appear that a department of urban affairs was desirable.[25]

Metropolitan Area Study Commission

For the past several years, Representative Harold C. Ostertag of New York has submitted a bill for the establishment of a national study commission on metropolitan problems and urban development. The bill first appeared in 1956 as H.R. 5565, and in the next Congress as H.R. 2416, calling for a twenty-five member commission constituted along lines similar to those followed in the Commission on Intergovernmental Relations. In its declaration of purpose, mention was made of the country's expanding population and the greatly accelerated trend toward urban growth. Congress, it stated, finds that "there is a national interest in and need for the formulating of suitable and adequate guidelines for the solution of these problems in the interest of insuring balanced, orderly and dynamic growth between and among the States and their subdivisions."

The commission would be charged with the study and investigation of problems of metropolitan expansion, including all important aspects of urban growth but emphasizing adequate governmental structures. The commission would be directed to study existing and developing

---

[25] This approach has been well developed by Connelly, Robert H., and Leach, Richard H., *The Federal Government and Metropolitan Areas* (Cambridge: Harvard University Press, 1960).

efforts to cope with these problems through such devices as cooperative planning, consolidated city-county planning, federative structures, and intergovernmental contracts or compacts, and to make findings and recommendations as to necessary and desirable steps to be initiated at the National, State, and local levels, to insure sound and orderly metropolitan growth and development. In the 1959 session, Senator Clark introduced a similar measure on which hearings were held,[26] while three additional bills of similar purpose were introduced in the House. Hearings were held on these bills also.[27]

Permanent National Advisory Body

The idea of a permanent national advisory council or commission on intergovernmental relations is by no means a new one. For well over a decade, in fact, there has been a growing conviction that some such agency was needed. The Report of the first Hoover Commission on Federal-State relations had contained the proposal "that a continuing agency on Federal-State Relations be created with primary responsibility for study, information and guidance in the field of Federal-State relations." [28]

Similarly, the National Municipal League, in a statement prepared for the Kestnbaum Commission, had recommended that such an agency as that proposed by the Hoover Commission, augmented by local government and public members, be established as "a continuing commission on intergovernmental relations . . . to review and recommend a course of action designed to develop cooperative, dynamic federalism" and to give "guidance for integrating governmental policies, coordinating taxation, eliminating overlapping administrative hierarchies, and protecting the values of local self-government." [29]

The *Report to the President* of the Commission on Intergovernmental Relations (Kestnbaum) served to strengthen the conviction that

[26] S. 1431; Hearings before the Subcommittee on Reorganization and International Organizations of the Senate Committee on Government Operations, 86th Cong., 1st Sess., July 24, 1959 (Washington, 1959).

[27] The bills were: H.R. 7282, by Alvin M. Bentley of Michigan; H.R. 7465, by Dante B. Fascell of Florida; H.R. 7378, by Kathryn E. Granahan of Pennsylvania; and H.R. 2416, by Harold C. Ostertag of New York. The full text of each appears in the Hearings, *Metropolitan Problems and Urban Development*.

[28] Recommendation No. 5, *Federal-State Relations: A Report to the Congress* (Washington, 1949). See also Council of State Governments, *Federal-State Relations* (Washington: Senate Document No. 81, 81st Cong., 1st Sess., 1949).

[29] *American Intergovernmental Relations as of 1954* (New York: National Municipal League, 1954), p. 9.

such a body was urgently needed. The Commission itself had recognized the need but quite naturally had not thought it proper to recommend its own continuance. After extensive staff study and public hearings throughout the country, the House Subcommittee on Intergovernmental Relations came to a definite conclusion in 1958 that such a body was needed, and so reported.[30]

At least four bills designed to carry out this recommendation were introduced into the first session of the 86th Congress. The Subcommittee's bill for the establishment of a permanent national, nonpartisan Advisory Commission on Intergovernmental Relations was introduced in May, 1959. On July 30, too late to be included in the Hearings, the Hechler bill,[31] whose provisions included a proposal for a national advisory council, was presented. Joint hearings on the Subcommittee's bill were held in June; this bill was reported out in both houses, passed in both houses with unprecedented speed, and signed by the President on September 24, 1959.[32]

The purposes of this legislation are stated in broad terms but they emphasize consideration and discussion of common problems by representatives of the three levels of government: the critical consideration of the conditions and controls involved in the administration of Federal grant programs, the making available of technical assistance to government officials, and the identification and study of new problems at an early stage of their development. That Congress has thus indicated an awareness of the problems in the field of intergovernmental relations and a willingness to do something about them is greatly to be commended.

Intergovernmental Reference Service

Finally, a bill introduced by Senator R. Vance Hartke of Indiana (S. 2295) provided for the establishment of an intergovernmental reference service. This proposal is an integral part of the proposed program presented in the concluding chapter and will be discussed at that point.

[30] *Federal-State-Local Relations,* Committee on Government Operations, Thirteenth Report (Washington: House Report No. 2533, 85th Cong., 2nd Sess., 1958), p. 51.

[31] H.R. 8478, by Ken Hechler of West Virginia, 86th Cong., 1st Sess., 1959.

[32] H.R. 6904, H.R. 6905, and S. 2026, known as the Fountain-Dwyer-Muskie bill, *To Establish an Advisory Commission on Intergovernmental Relations,* Joint Hearings before the Intergovernmental Relations Subcommittee of the House Committee on Government Operations and the Senate Committee on Government Operations, June 16–22, 1959 (Washington, 1959). The Committee reports appeared under the same title: House Report No. 742 (Washington, 1959); Senate Report No. 584 (Washington, 1959). The measure became Public Law No. 380, 86th Cong., 1st Sess.

BIBLIOGRAPHICAL NOTES

As part of its bicentennial celebration, Columbia University arranged a conference on federalism, held at Arden House in January, 1954. The program and the resulting volume of proceedings, Arthur W. Macmahon, ed., *Federalism: Mature and Emergent* (Garden City: Doubleday & Company, 1955), were set up in four parts: (1) Federalism: Its Nature and Role; (2) Basic Controls in a Maturing System; (3) Functional Channels of Relationship; and (4) Supranational Union in Western Europe. Twenty-six papers, all by distinguished students in the field, appear in the volume.

The 1950's were in general a period of analysis and appraisal of federalism and of attempted assessments of directions. Thus in 1953, the Leonard D. White lectures on *The States and the Nation* (Baton Rouge: Louisiana State University Press, 1953) were published. Congressional action in 1953, establishing the Commission on Intergovernmental Relations (Kestnbaum), inspired much activity of this nature throughout the country. A second Arden House conference in 1955, this time under the auspices of the American Assembly, resulted in the publication of a series of background papers, James W. Fesler, ed., *The Forty-eight States: Their Role as Policy Makers and Administrators* (New York: American Assembly, Columbia University, 1955).

Professor William Anderson, in connection with discussions concerning the nature of the federal system in the early days of the work of the Commission of Intergovernmental Relations, began the writing of a manuscript which appeared later, in greatly revised form, under the title, *The Nation and the States: Rivals or Partners?* (Minneapolis: University of Minnesota Press, 1955). It contains a significant statement of the basic principles of federalism and emphasizes the importance of cooperative relationships, as does his later summary volume for the Minnesota studies, *Intergovernmental Relations in Review* (Minneapolis: University of Minnesota Press, 1960).

The Commission's *Report to the President for Transmittal to the Congress* appeared in June, 1955; the following is a complete list of the supplementary reports and supporting documents: 1. *A Study Committee Report on Federal Aid to Agriculture.* 2. *A Study Committee Report on Federal Aid to Highways.* 3. *A Study Committee Report on Federal Aid to Public Health.* 4. *A Study Committee Report on Federal Aid to Welfare.* 5. *A Study Committee Report on Federal Responsibility in the Field of Education.* 6. *A Study Committee Report on Unemployment Compensation and Employment Service.* 7. *A Study Committee Report on Natural Resources and Conservation.* 8. *A Study Committee Report on Payments in Lieu of Taxes and Shared Revenues.* 9. *An Advisory Committee Report on Local Government.* 10. *A Staff Report on Civil Defense and Urban Vulnerability.* 11. *A Subcommittee Report on Natural Disaster Relief.* 12. *A Staff Report on Federal Aid to Airports.* 13. *A Description of Twenty-five Federal Grant-in-Aid Programs.* 14. *Summaries of Survey Reports on the Administrative and Fiscal Impact of Federal Grants-in-Aid.* 15. *A Survey Report on the Impact of Federal Grants-in-Aid on the Structure and Functions of State and Local Governments.*

For a time after the publication of the Commission's Report, while its contents were being studied, no additional publications appeared. Those next appearing similarly tended to emphasize the role of the States. The *New York University Law Review* devoted its June, 1959, issue to a symposium on "State Responsibility in a Federal System." Other current publications in the same vein include M. J. C. Vile, *The Structure of American Federalism* (New York: Oxford University Press, 1962) and Coleman Woodbury, *The Future Role of the States* (New York: National Municipal League, 1962).

An extensive bibliography on intergovernmental relations, prepared by W. Brooke Graves, went through four "editions":

Graves, W. Brooke, *Intergovernmental Relations in the United States: A Selected Bibliography* (Washington: Commission on Intergovernmental Relations, November, 1953);

Joint Reference Library, *Federal-State-Local Relations: A Selected Bibliography*, prepared for the American Municipal Association and the Council of State Governments (Chicago, May, 1954);

Graves, W. Brooke, *Intergovernmental Relations in the United States: A Selected Bibliography on Interlevel and Interjurisdictional Relations* (Washington: Commission on Intergovernmental Relations, June, 1955);

House Committee on Government Operations, Subcommittee on Intergovernmental Relations, *Intergovernmental Relations in the United States: A Selected Bibliography* (Washington: Committee Print, 84th Cong., 2nd Sess., November, 1956).

CHAPTER XXVI

Making Federalism
Work

A PROBLEM AND A POINT OF VIEW

Americans in the Sixties live in an atmosphere of crisis. Not only do they face unprecedented problems of national security—possibly even of survival—in a divided world, but they face critical problems at home in the preservation of American federalism, problems which few of them seem to realize. It is quite conceivable that the Nation might survive, and its federal system of government be irretrievably lost.

The American federal system has served the people well for nearly 200 years. It has great elements of strength. It has survived crises in the past and will, in all probability, survive others in the future. But there is no assurance that it will always continue to do so unless statesmanlike solutions are found— and found quickly—to meet new problems arising out of an almost completely different set of social and economic conditions under which it must operate now and in the future.

Chief among these is the preservation, not of States' rights or of home rule in the conventional sense, but of strong and effective State and local governments, as an alternative to an almost unlimited centralization of power. The time may be later than we think. Only by such steps as modernizing our State constitutions, by correcting the significant weaknesses in the electoral system, by overcoming the serious malapportionment of representation in both State and National legislatures, by finding and putting into effect some equitable solution of the problem of financial support, and by developing effective means of intergovernmental cooperation, can the fundamental characteristics of American federalism be preserved.

What we do about these problems *now* will very largely determine the governmental heritage of Americans for generations yet to come.[1]

[1] A statement written by W. Brooke Graves in 1957, not previously published.

Belief in democratic institutions and belief in the federal system of government constitute important items in the American Credo. There is ground for reasonable doubt, however, whether the nation can preserve the one or strengthen the other without strong and effective institutions of State and local government. Many thoughtful persons, in public life or as private citizens, are giving more serious attention to these matters than ever before.

In times past, intergovernmental relations was rarely recognized as a serious problem. When the United States was a sparsely populated country composed of nearly self-sufficient agrarian communities, there was little need for concern. Important decisions affecting such relationships were made wholly on the basis of other considerations. Sometimes the results were salutary, but very often they were not. Far too much was left to chance. Such a haphazard handling of problems vital to the nation's welfare never was a proper procedure; under modern conditions the policy of drift, improvisation, and "make-do" cannot be tolerated. The nation stands in urgent need of a national policy on intergovernmental relations, with appropriate agencies to implement such a policy and make it effective.

The conditions now existing have developed mostly within the present century. The agricultural and rural economy has been transformed into an industrial and business economy in an urban setting. The influx of immigrants to our cities has been supplemented by a migration from both the rural areas and the cities to the suburbs, and in recent years this migration has been accompanied by the so-called population explosion. Urbanization has created a multitude of new problems and aggravated a host of old ones.

New concepts of justice in the field of race relations at home and abroad, a new recognition of the dignity of man, regardless of race, color, creed, or national origin, has necessitated drastic changes in social concepts and practices and in governmental policies. The role of this nation as leader of the Western World imposes important new responsibilities upon all Americans. These are just a few of the more obvious reasons why it is no longer safe to rely on luck and the favor of a benevolent providence in dealing with vital problems of domestic government.

If it is successfully to discharge its international responsibilities, the nation must develop its maximum strength at home—educationally, culturally, economically, and governmentally. One can scarcely hope to succeed in exporting democratic concepts to people in the far corners of the world if domestic institutions are permitted to languish and become ineffective. Luther Gulick states this point very clearly:

I start with the conviction that we are not only justified by world conditions in devoting major efforts and making major investments in the upgrading of American life here at home, but that this course of action is mandated by the critical world situation. We can hardly expect that our attachment to freedom will be contagious internationally unless we can demonstrate its values here at home.[2]

Since American democracy operates within a federal framework, it is essential that means be found and promptly utilized for making its machinery function effectively in all cases in which different levels and units of government are involved.

Because this is a federal system, the problem is infinitely complex. There is, for example, one State 300 times as large in land area as the smallest, one county with a population of 285 and another with over 4 million. The figure of 100,000 units of government in the United States indicates how many different types, sizes, qualities, and interests exist in government throughout the country. The attitude of the Federal government in its role of leadership in this undertaking is a matter of extreme importance. It should be made very clear that the measures taken are designed for the service of State and local governments; at the same time, emphasis should be placed on the responsibilities of these governments for establishing and maintaining parallel programs and agencies. It is essential that all levels and units of government operate effectively in carrying out joint or cooperative programs.

Meyer Kestnbaum, chairman of the Commission on Intergovernmental Relations, wrote that "Our federal system is sound and flexible enough to serve the country indefinitely." [3] This is basically true, but the system cannot function effectively without proper implementation, any more than a carpenter can build a house without his box of tools. A program for "tooling up" to meet the future needs of American federalism is presented in this chapter; its structure follows, in a general way, the lines of H.R. 8478, introduced in the 86th Congress in July, 1959, by Representative Ken Hechler of West Virginia. This bill presented for the first time in one package, so to speak, the basic elements of a national policy on intergovernmental relations and the implementation necessary to carry it out.[4]

[2] Gulick, Luther, *The Metropolitan Problem and American Ideas* (New York: Alfred A. Knopf, Inc., 1962), p. 8.

[3] Kestnbaum, Meyer, "To Strengthen Our Federal System," *State Government*, August, 1955, pp. 170–176.

[4] At least two national organizations have adopted national policy statements in this field, formulated with the problems and needs of their own particular governmental units in mind. Recommendations involving inter-

The program here presented is by intention and design broad and far-reaching in scope, involving all three levels of government and consisting of several elements, each interrelated with the others and each essential to the program as a whole. The elements are: (1) a declaration of national policy; (2) the establishment of a Department of Federal-State Local Relations, including an advisory council; (3) an annual report by the President on intergovernmental relations; (4) an intergovernmental reference service; (5) a joint Congressional committee on intergovernmental relations; and (6) a structuring of State and local government for effective cooperative relationships.

DECLARATION OF NATIONAL POLICY

As the previous discussion has clearly shown, the United States has never had a definite national policy nor even a statement of what the national policy ought to be. The following from the Hechler bill is submitted as a possible statement:

> The Congress hereby affirms its conviction that strong and effective institutions of State and local government are essential both to the preservation of democratic institutions in this country and the strengthening of the American federal system of government. It recognizes its responsibility for providing assistance with respect to those aspects of federalism, and of intergovernmental relations at the national level, which the individual units of government are not in a position, by their own efforts, to supply for themselves.
> . . . The Congress, therefore, declares that it is the continuing policy and responsibility of the Federal Government to use all practicable means consistent with its needs and obligations, and other essential considerations of national policy, to assist and encourage the smooth and effective operation of the American federal system, and to encourage cooperation between and among its several levels and units of government—national, State, and local—and the coordination of programs affecting such levels and units.

---

governmental relations constitute an important part of the programs of the American Municipal Association and the National Association of Counties. The AMA aims are to be found in its *National Municipal Policy*, which may be amended or added to by the organization's national convention, the American Municipal Congress. Similarly, the *American County Platform* is adopted and kept up-to-date by the national convention of NACO.

DEPARTMENT OF FEDERAL-STATE-LOCAL RELATIONS

Central Organization

The proposal for the establishment of a department of urban affairs, it will be recalled, was given wide publicity during the 1960 presidential campaign. Early in 1961, President Kennedy sent up a message, accompanied by a draft of a bill, for the establishment of such a department. Hearings were held in both houses during the first session of the 87th Congress, but no action was taken. In the second session in 1962, after the House Rules Committee, for reasons largely irrelevant to the merits of the proposal, had refused to grant a rule for the bill, President Kennedy sent up Reorganization Plan No. 1 of 1962 to accomplish the same purpose. This Plan was rejected by the House. These actions made it apparent that no such department would be established during the life of the 87th Congress. The problem, however, still remained; steps toward its solution were merely postponed.

Some Members of Congress who are against neither the cities nor the administration felt that neither the administration bill nor the Reorganization Plan provided the right answer. These members realize that a department is needed, not necessarily limited to urban affairs and preferably not so restricted. They realize that the problems of interlevel and interjurisdictional relations are numerous, complex, and pressing for solution, and that the urgency for constructive action increases with every passing day. Granting that the need for a department is well established, they argue that the department should have a range of authority that is broader, yet more clearly defined than in either of the administration proposals. They argue that the department should be constructed to strengthen, not weaken, the American federal system.

Conspicuous among the members of this group has been Senator J. Caleb Boggs of Delaware who in February, 1962, introduced S. 2861 to establish a Department of Federal-State-Urban Affairs as an alternative proposal to both the administration bill and Reorganization Plan No. 1. The basic concept of this bill is sound, and it may well be that the adoption of this proposal would solve the organization problem. Since the urban communities have no monopoly on the problems involved, Federal-State-Local Relations might be a better name for the department than Federal-State-Urban Affairs, but this a matter of detail rather than of principle.

The Boggs bill is significant and worthy of attention for several reasons. In addition to a declaration of policy and a broad general statement of the duties and responsibilities of the new department, it provides specifically for several of the functions essential to any well conceived department in this area, and for the transfer to its Secretary of "all the functions, powers and duties of the Advisory Commission on Intergovernmental Relations." This proposal should be given serious consideration.

It might be well at the same time to revise the legislation establishing the Commission on Intergovernmental Relations which, although there was a decade of historical development behind the movement to establish a permanent national advisory body, was rushed through without attention to some obvious defects. The Commission was established, as one observer expressed it, "in an administrative limbo without attachment to any organizational element of the Federal Government." Attachment to the department would correct this detail. Furthermore, the duties of the Commission were never clearly or specifically defined. Its members have other full-time jobs, which leave them little free time to devote to Commission problems. Also, there are far too many members for an effective working group. Both of these points were made clear by the experience with the Kestnbaum Commission. Too large in the original bill, the number of members was actually increased while the bill was in course of passage.

A more satisfactory arrangement would call for a small and compact council selected to provide—as the present Commission does—for both geographical and governmental representation. The group should have an impartial chairman, an outstanding person who, by reason of training, experience, and attainments, is qualified to assume the difficult role of guiding and directing the activities of such a body. This council would concern itself with broad questions of national policy in the field of intergovernmental relations, affecting all units and levels of government.

It is well to keep in mind, however, that forming policies is not enough; policies must be applied—regionally, or on an interstate and interlocal basis—day by day, to problems in communities where people live and work. In this connection, recalling the success of the Bureau of the Budget field offices and of PACBIR, the question arises as to whether regional or field councils at work at the task of making national policy effective at the grass roots, so to speak, might not make a real contribution. It is no accident that so many Federal departments and agencies have established field organizations or that the Council of State Governments found it essential to maintain field offices in the Eastern, Western, Southern, and Midwestern sections of the country.

Field Coordination

The Boggs bill provides for the establishment of a close working relationship between a new Federal department of intergovernmental relations and an advisory commission or council. Pending the establishment of such a department, attention should be given to the problems of coordination existing in the field, where the bulk of the work which governments at all levels do, is performed. It is here, in the counties, cities, and towns where men and women live and work and carry on the normal activities of life. Two major problems, separable but related, are involved. One has to do with coordination within the Federal field service, the other with the "gearing-in" of governments at all levels in any given function or geographical area.

In the last half century, numerous attempts have been made to achieve the coordination of Federal programs in the field. Most of these, unfortunately, have accomplished little, and the few that have met with some degree of success have been short-lived. The Federal Business Associations, organized after World War I in the centers where there was a significant concentration of Federal employment, evolved into something not much more than luncheon clubs. Nevertheless, they have continued in existence over a period of many years, while other more significant efforts have been permitted to lapse. During World War II, the Federal Personnel Council set up field councils of personnel administration in key cities throughout the country; some of these were very effective. The Bureau of the Budget set up a few field offices on an experimental basis, and these also were effective. With the change of administration in 1953, the Federal Personnel Council and the Bureau of the Budget field offices were abolished, on the specious grounds of "economy." After 1953, such field councils as still remained soon disappeared.

As has been noted earlier, experiments designed to promote intergovernmental cooperation were developed in the Bureau of the Budget under Harold D. Smith in the form of a Commission on Intergovernmental Relations, and through the field offices. The San Francisco Field Office was particularly successful, being instrumental in developing the Pacific Coast Board of Intergovernmental Relations. Both of these pioneer efforts should be revived, revamped to meet current needs, and established on a firm basis. Fortunately, means are at hand for accomplishing this purpose.

In the early days of the Kennedy administration, the Bureau of the Budget, the Civil Service Commission, and the General Services Administration cooperated in establishing Federal Executive Boards on a more or less experimental basis in a dozen key cities throughout the country.

These Boards seem generally to be functioning in an effective manner, and some have been conspicuously successful. The proposal here submitted is that these Boards be enlarged to include representatives of State, county and city governments, after the pattern established by PACBIR, and that they take on—in addition to the duties already assigned to them—something of the form and function of that earlier organization.

The interstate compact, including the interested States and the Federal Government as equal partners, is another new device for achieving coordination of governmental programs in the field. The first example of this type of organization, the Delaware River Basin Compact, became operative in late 1962, and is currently attempting to get its programs under way. While designed in this instance to deal with the problems of a river valley on a regional basis, there is no reason why it could not be adapted to the handling of interlevel and interjurisdictional problems arising in other governmental functions and areas.

It is true that there are two different jobs to be done—coordination of Federal programs in the field, and coordination of Federal-State-local governmental activities—but the two are very closely related. If effective solutions to these problems of coordination are to be found, top management at all three levels must be organized to accomplish it. If, in time, a Federal department of intergovernmental relations is established, the engineering of these types of cooperation and coordination might well become a major part of its assignment.

PRESIDENT'S REPORT ON INTERGOVERNMENTAL RELATIONS

In 1946, Congress passed the Full Employment Act, one important provision of which called for an annual report by the President on the condition of the economy, with appropriate recommendations for legislative action. Since the condition of the government and its major problems are, like the condition of the economy, matters of major importance to the American people, it is proposed that the same procedure be applied in the one case as in the other. All formal pronouncements of the President get nationwide coverage and receive the attention and consideration of citizens throughout the land. The problems of American federalism are likewise important enough to deserve and receive the attention of the nation's Chief Executive and of all citizens.[5]

[5] For an early comment on the functioning of the Council of Economic Advisors, see Clark, J. D., "Council of Economic Advisors," *Nebraska Law Review*, May, 1949, pp. 530–541.

State and Local Documentation

The historians and political scientists of the country have long been guilty of an inexcusable neglect of State and local government and politics. When political science began to emerge as a separate discipline, many were so preoccupied with national institutions and with the study of the Federal Constitution that they gave little attention to State and local affairs. Lord Bryce, although an understanding and sympathetic student of the American scene, called attention to this weakness almost three-quarters of a century ago:

> American publicists have been too much absorbed in the study of the federal system to bestow much time or thought on the State governments. . . . Yet they are full of interest and he who would understand the changes that have passed on American democracy will find far more instruction in a study of State government than in that of the Federal Constitution.[6]

Bryce bemoaned the fact that "the materials for such a study are unfortunately, at least to a European, either inaccessible or unmanageable." Like Professor Herman V. Ames, he concluded that to be able to use the materials, "one must go to the State and devote one's self to these original authorities." Bryce was critical, too, of American scholarship because only antiquarian and genealogical State histories had been written, not political histories. Some progress in the State documents field has been made, to be sure, due to the significant work of Professor William S. Jenkins in the State Documents Microfilming Project, carried on under cooperative arrangements between the University of North Carolina and the Library of Congress, and to the subsequent effort to establish regional document centers.

Despite these advances and some indication of a greater interest in State and local problems on the part of individual scholars, however, there are still some critical lacks. One is the absence of any constructive and consistent Congressional policy. Having established the State Law Section in the Library of Congress in 1914 and supported it for a quarter of a century, Congress proceeded, in one of the waves of "economy" that periodically sweep the country, to kill the program. In the decade before

[6] Bryce, James, *The American Commonwealth*, 2nd ed., rev. (London: The Macmillan Co., Ltd., 1891), I, 399-400.

the Commission on Intergovernmental Relations (Kestnbaum), other State-local oriented agencies, including the National Resources Board and the Governments Division of the Bureau of the Census, were subjected to the same kind of nerve-wracking experiences with regard to the appropriation of funds necessary to the discharge of duties prescribed by law. There appeared, during this period, no recognition of the need for basic research on problems of State and local government, or of the need for the current information essential to the effective operation of these governments.

Nature of the Current Need

There is abundant evidence to the effect that great numbers of State and local government officials are operating under the severe handicap of inadequate information. No matter how sincere and conscientious they may be in their attempt faithfully to perform their duties, they find their efforts thwarted time after time or their work made unnecessarily difficult by the lack of information essential to the making of policy decisions on a sound and defensible basis.

For example, the Veterans Administration, which has many well equipped hospitals and facilities for the treatment of all manner of physical and mental ailments, has recently made a serious effort to improve relations with related State agencies. When top level officials of the VA met with their State counterparts, they frequently found that neither group had any knowledge of the program and work of the other, although both agencies had been functioning within the State for many years, and although there were numerous ways in which cooperation could be helpful to patients and mutually advantageous to the Federal and State agencies concerned. In some cases, this exchange of information seemed so helpful that it was agreed to continue meetings once or twice a year, to the end that every veteran in need should be given assistance. If he was not eligible under Federal law, he could be referred to the appropriate State or local agency and his requirements met by some program administered by these agencies.

In 1959, after a disastrous flood, a Senator returned to his State to talk with State and local officials to obtain a clearer idea of the nature and extent of the damage. Although several forms of Federal assistance are available in such situations under legislation enacted by Congress, the officials had no idea of what assistance they were entitled to or of how to get it. Still worse, no one in Washington or in the field took the trouble to contact or inform them.

Every telephone directory gives in a conspicuous place a number to call in case of fire or if the police are needed. In similar fashion, every State and local official should have a point of contact with the Federal government to assist him in case of need to utilize such of the vast government resources as are appropriate to his situation. Such a service would not result in a greater centralization of power or in a weakening of State and local government; rather, it would be a practical recognition of the unity of the country, of the fact that disaster or other emergencies in one area are the concern of all.

To meet this need, Senator Vance Hartke of Indiana has proposed the establishment of an Intergovernmental Reference Service which would provide for executive and legislative officers at all levels of government a research and consulting service roughly equivalent to that which the Legislative Reference Service has long provided for Congress on national and international problems. To provide this new service, a great national clearing house for documents, research, and information on questions relating to State and local government, law, and administration would be established. The service would be responsible for the performance of three separate but closely related types of activity: collection and servicing of materials, supplementing the already extensive collections of State materials in the Library of Congress, and of local materials in the Division of Governments, Bureau of the Census; research and consulting work; fostering cooperation and coordination among existing governmental programs.[7]

Consideration might well be given also to a new Local Government Documents Microfilming Project, similar to and parallel with the earlier State project, to be carried out on a cooperative basis between the Federal Government and the States. This program would correct the almost unbelievable indifference that has long existed in this country to the collection and preservation of important local governmental records. At present there is no single place where such a collection is available, with the result that government people and scholars who desire information must visit a number of small, widely scattered collections at a great waste of time, money, and effort. While it is important that such materials be collected, as Senator Hartke pointed out when his bill was introduced in June, 1959, it is equally important that there be a professional staff to work with them after they are collected to make analyses, discern trends and new developments, and identify emerging problems and possible sources of difficulty in the future. The staff would include a group of top-level specialists in various phases of State and local government,

---

[7] S. 2295; the same provisions were incorporated in the Hechler bill, H.R. 8478, in the 86th Congress, and in S. 375 (Senator Hartke's bill for a Department of Urban Affairs), and in substance, in the Boggs bill, S. 2861 (for a Department of Federal-State-Urban Affairs) in the 87th Congress.

such as administrative organization and management; taxation and finance; intergovernmental fiscal relations; judicial organization and procedure; community development; planning, zoning, and land use; and metropolitan area problems.

Staff members would be available as consultants to State and local officials seeking advice on improvement in their agency operations or in their relations with other units of government. Specialists or teams of specialists could be assigned to field offices in the manner used by the Bureau of the Budget during and after World War II. With this decentralized organization, the service would be better able to function as an advisor to the various State and local agencies both on policy questions and on problems in the field of intergovernmental relations. One anticipated effect of these procedures would be the creation of an atmosphere in which cooperative effort would be natural and normal. The specialists would not in any way supplant existing State and local research agencies, which would continue to be responsible for the work they have been performing. Rather, the new agency would undertake studies of national scope which local research agencies cannot be expected to perform.

Finally, the new agency would seek to promote cooperation and coordination among the various levels and units of government, working with both public and private agencies in the performance of this important function. As Senator Hartke said at the conclusion of his remarks when he introduced the bill:

> When so much of the effectiveness of present-day government is dependent upon up-to-date and authentic information and good staff work, and upon the maintenance of smooth working relationships among the various levels and units of government, I feel that this bill has much to commend it to the serious and careful consideration of the Congress.

The Problem of Organization

The establishment of such an agency raises many difficult questions. Where in the Federal structure should it be located? Should it be set up as an independent agency? Should it be located in the Division of Governments in the Bureau of the Census, which already possesses an important collection of local government materials, or in the Library of Congress, which has an extensive collection of State documents? The last solution was the one adopted in the Hartke and Hechler bills, but under the Boggs bill the service is included as a major function of the department of Federal-State-local affairs, which is, perhaps, a satisfactory solution.

There are still other questions that need to be answered. What should be the relations of this agency with specialized libraries in the operating departments and agencies? How shall the use of the new service be safeguarded against possible abuse through requests for types of assistance that local people themselves should provide? Such questions are troublesome, but no more so than those that have been solved in connection with the establishment of other new governmental activities.

JOINT COMMITTEE ON INTERGOVERNMENTAL RELATIONS

It would avail little to adopt the several elements in the proposed program—the annual report by the President; the council to consider and discuss problems in the field and make policy recommendations; and an agency to collect materials and provide a research and consulting service—if there were no certain means of getting the findings of the research and the recommendations of the President and council before the elected representatives of the people for their consideration and for such action as they might find necessary or desirable.

Again, following the precedent established in the Full Employment Act and other legislation, and in accordance with the current thinking of many people and a number of interested national organizations, it is proposed that there be established in Congress a Joint Committee on Intergovernmental Relations to make a continuing study of matters relating to the President's Report. Such a committee could concern itself with means of coordinating programs in order to further the policies set forth in the Declaration of Policy. It could serve as a guide to the several Congressional committees dealing with legislation relating to or involving the Intergovernmental Relations Report, by making its findings and recommendations available for the use of such committees, the need for which was emphasized by several witnesses at the Senate hearings on the Clark bill (the administration bill) for the establishment of a Federal department of urban affairs in June, 1961.

Although there are reasons for questioning the desirability of adding to the number of joint committees, it may be noted that abundant precedent exists in other subject matter areas of major importance or of great current interest, such as the Joint Committee on the Economic Report, the Joint Committee on Atomic Energy, the Joint Committee on Internal Revenue Taxation, and the Joint Committee on Space and Astronautics. Certainly the governmental problems of the nation are no less important or less deserving of the continuing attention of a joint committee of Congress.

Since the Legislative Reorganization Act of 1946 gives the Government Operations Committees of the Senate and House jurisdiction over intergovernmental relations, it may be necessary to amend that Act in order to clear the way for establishing the proposed joint committee. Inasmuch as the present subcommittee chairmen would presumably become alternate chairman and vice-chairman, respectively, of the newly established joint committee, amendment should not be too difficult.

STRUCTURING FOR STATE AND LOCAL COOPERATION

Up to this point, all of the elements in the intergovernmental program have been dependent upon Federal leadership and Federal action, but the Federal government alone cannot do the job. No program to strengthen American federalism and improve its effectiveness can succeed unless State and local governments move with efficiency and dispatch to discharge their responsibilities. If the Federal government offers real cooperation with State and local governments and establishes a mechanism through which such cooperation may be made effective, State and local governments must offer full cooperation in return.

Structuring State Cooperation

How shall State and local governments cooperate? The truth of the matter is that at this moment, the States are no better prepared to give full cooperation in such a program than is the Federal government.[8] The first and basic need of State and local government lies in the field of personnel. The need for able leaders is very serious now and may be expected to become critical in the next few years. While the national government has a great attraction for those with proven qualities of leadership, State and local governments lack a certain glamour and do not, therefore, attract and retain the services of men of similar caliber. The current emphasis on scholarship in the national government serves to underscore the relatively small number of men of similar attainments serving in State and local governments.

Great as is the need for leadership, the need for qualified personnel to perform the scientific and technical functions of State and local governments is also approaching alarming proportions, and to structure

[8] For a discussion of what the States have done and of what remains to be done, See Crihfield, Brevard, and Smothers, Frank, "The States in the Federal System," *New York University Law Review*, June, 1959, pp. 1018–1036.

these governments for effective performance in the area of intergovernmental relations, a determined effort should be made to overcome this
deficiency as well. It may be that Federal assistance in some such form
as that proposed in the Gonzalez bill for the training of State and local
government personnel may be required if the problem is to be met in
any adequate manner.[9]

Under the terms of their membership and participation in the Council of State Governments, the States established in 1935 and have since
maintained State commissions on interstate cooperation. In most cases,
these commissions are composed of fifteen members—five each from the
Senate, the House, and from the Executive Branch, appointed by the
President of the Senate, the Speaker, and the Governor, respectively.
Few of these commissions have seriously attempted to do the job they
were established to perform. In only a few States, particularly in New
York, have both adequate funds and effective leadership been provided.[10]

The commissions should be reorganized and rejuvenated so that they
might be in a position to cooperate effectively with the new Federal advisory council. A few have enlarged their outlook and the scope of their
activities to include the whole field of intergovernmental relations, not
just interstate relations. All of them should do so as promptly as the
schedule of legislative sessions will permit. Competent leadership and
financial support, sufficient to permit employment of a staff to perform
at the State level the same type of research and coordination on State and
local problems that the proposed Federal agencies would undertake at
the national level, should be provided for them. That the Council of
State Governments is aware of this need is attested by the fact that early
in 1962 it issued a report containing "sound and specific recommendations for making the commissions active and useful components of our
intergovernmental structure." [11]

[9] H.R. 4561, 88th Cong.; see also Municipal Manpower Commission,
Governmental Manpower for Tomorrow's Cities, a Report (New York,
McGraw-Hill Book Company, 1962) and Brookings Institution, *Higher Skills
for the City of New York* (Washington, 1963), prepared for The Mayor's
Committee on Professional, Technical and Managerial Manpower of the City
of New York.

[10] See Gallagher, Hubert R., "The Development of Interstate Government," *National Municipal Review*, July, 1937, pp. 345–351, and "Work of
Commissions on Interstate Cooperation," *Annals of the American Academy
of Political and Social Science*, January, 1940, pp. 103–110. For a more current
view, see Zimmermann, Frederick L., and Leach, Richard H., "The Commissions on Interstate Cooperation," *State Government*, Autumn, 1960, pp.
233–242.

[11] *To Improve Cooperation Among the States* (Chicago, 1962). This report
of the Committee on Strengthening Interstate Cooperation Commissions
stresses the obvious needs for organization, leadership, and staff.

A few States—notably Alaska, New Jersey, New York, North Carolina, and Pennsylvania—have departments or other agencies responsible
for performing functions of supervision and assistance to their local units.
In 1959, the New York legislature adopted new legislation designed to
strengthen this activity, thus providing for that State an adequate organization for intergovernmental cooperation, with suitable agencies in
both the Executive and Legislative Branches of government. No State can
rightly plead for exemption from such a program, for every State from
the largest to the smallest in area, population, and wealth and resources,
whether primarily agricultural or industrial, has pressing problems in the
field of intergovernmental relations.

Two other somewhat similar developments are worthy of note, probably also of praise and emulation. A recent study of problems of local
government boundaries and areas, undertaken with a view to developing new policies for California, brings to light some little-known devices
for making boundary adjustments and solving boundary conflicts involving local units. The study includes five States—Alaska, Minnesota, North
Carolina, Virginia, and Wisconsin—and three foreign jurisdictions—
England and Wales, New Zealand, and Ontario, Canada.[12] The inclusion
of these foreign jurisdictions serves to emphasize the universality of the
problem.

Both Alaska and Minnesota have State boundary commissions, the
former subject to legislative veto of its proposals but not a referendum,
the latter with a referendum but also with the possibility of judicial review. North Carolina has legislative authorization for unilateral annexation, without referendum but subject to judicial review. Both Virginia
and Wisconsin have liberal statutory provisions on annexation, and both
provide for judicial determination of local boundary changes. The significance of these developments, all of them quite recent, is to show that
there *are* proper methods of breaking the impasse which hampers the
growth of so many cities and of accomplishing needed boundary changes.

Structuring Local Cooperation

Various tools short of the politically hazardous task of creating new
layers of governmental authority, such as those suggested by Luther Gulick[13] or the type of metropolitan federalism illustrated by the Dade

[12] Scott, Stanley *et al.*, *Local Governmental Boundaries and Areas: New
Policies for California* (Berkeley: Bureau of Public Administration, University of California, February, 1961).

[13] Gulick, Luther, "Metropolitan Organization," *Annals of the American
Academy of Political and Social Science*, November, 1957, pp. 57–65.

County, Florida, experiment, are available for cooperation at the local level. Machinery to encourage more rational management of areawide problems can extend from simple exchanges of information to the establishment of uniform regulations, to contracts between governing bodies to supply services for each other, to joint ownership and operation of facilities. In other words, methods may run the whole gamut of interlocal cooperation.

Planning for cooperation, however, cannot be left exclusively to the good intentions of interested citizens or even to administrative officials in the affected areas. Rather, the politically elected officials who alone are empowered to make the necessary decisions must be encouraged to provide leadership. There is need for the kind of blanket authorization for such cooperation as has been provided for by law in an increasing number of States. State and local governments can provide financial assistance in the form of staff and headquarters facilities for a permanent regional conference. Local governments may themselves provide structurally for the kind of cooperation that is so urgently needed. One possible means of facilitating such cooperation is illustrated in a 1961 report of the New York State Commission on Governmental Cooperation in the City of New York. As part of a program for strengthening the position of the Mayor in the new City Charter, it was proposed that there be established, under the Deputy Mayor, in the executive office, a Director of Intergovernmental Relations who "will advise and represent the Mayor in dealing with Federal, State, regional, and local agencies." [14] In support of this proposal, the Commission says:

> With the swift growth of Federal and State participation in urban affairs, as well as the rapidly expanding problems of the metropolitan region, it is essential that the City be equipped to cooperate effectively in well-planned, well-coordinated ways with the other agencies of government. The Division of Intergovernmental Relations will be the focal point for the development of this major function of the City.

CONCLUSIONS

The American citizen of today is involved in intergovernmental relations, whether he knows it or not. The basic problems in this field are just about universal among governments, whether federally organized or unitary in structure. Intergovernmental relations are not a sporadic

[14] *A New Charter for the City of New York* (Albany, January, 1961), p. 14.

or a specialized type of activity, they are part and parcel of the every-day operation of government. American government is not a three-layer cake; involvement is widespread and interpenetrating. It is useless to attempt to "unwind" the federal system, as some recent attempts to solve intergovernmental problems have advocated.

Many governments have recognized the basic nature of these problems, and long ago established central departments of interior or of internal affairs to deal with them. Although such machinery is also much needed in this country, efforts to obtain it have, so far, been largely unsuccessful. It may be argued that the broad program outlined in this chapter will cost too much money. Of course, it will require financial support, but when considered in relation to the size of the country, the size of the population, and the total annual output of the economy, the outlay will be extremely small. The question is not whether the nation can afford to pay the bill; rather, the question is whether, if the established form of government is to be retained, it can afford *not* to pay it. Unquestionably, the nation's resources are more than ample to provide whatever governmental programs and services are needed for the adequate discharge of its responsibilities both at home and abroad, and in an expanding economy this should certainly continue to be possible.

The late Professor Charles E. Merriam, writing nearly twenty years ago on postwar planning, observed that the new city would "not be built by timid tinkering with old models but will be part of a new streamlined civilization built on a modern model." [15] He concluded with the words of Daniel H. Burnham, the pioneer planner: "Make no small plans. They have no magic in them to stir men's blood." In the field of intergovernmental relations today, there have been enough "small plans" and enough "timid tinkering with old models." The time has come for a broad plan, conceived with foresight and imagination, in keeping with present and foreseeable future needs, and implemented, insofar as possible, to insure its effectiveness.

BIBLIOGRAPHICAL NOTES

The problem of selecting suitable references for this chapter is complicated both by the scarcity of materials on the specific proposals here discussed, and the desire to avoid, insofar as possible, repetition of titles earlier cited. A few items are presented in each of four categories: Federal-State relations, interstate relations, policy statements and proposals, and general works.

[15] Merriam, Charles E., "Make No Small Plans," *National Municipal Review*, February, 1943, pp. 63–67.

Federal-State Relations. Four significant works emphasize the trend toward centralization and the role of grants-in-aid: George C. S. Benson, *The New Centralization: A Study of Intergovernmental Relationships in the United States* (New York: Farrar & Rinehart, 1941); Council of State Governments, *Federal Grants-in-Aid* (Chicago, 1948); and Walter Thompson, *Federal Centralization* (New York: Harcourt, Brace & Company, 1923). Daniel J. Elazar, *The American Partnership* (Chicago: University of Chicago Press, 1962) argues that cooperative federalism, usually considered a twentieth-century characteristic, actually developed during the nineteenth century.

Interstate Relations. W. Brooke Graves, *Uniform State Action: A Possible Substitute for Centralization* (Chapel Hill: University of North Carolina Press, 1934) gives much of the early history of interstate cooperation. Two articles by Hubert R. Gallagher, "The Development of Interstate Government," *National Municipal Review*, July, 1937, pp. 345–351, and "The Work of Commissions on Interstate Cooperation," *Annals of the American Academy of Political and Social Science*, January, 1940, pp. 103–110, cover later developments. For current proposals for the improvement of these relationships, see Council of State Governments, *To Improve Cooperation Among the States* (Chicago, 1962) and Frederick L. Zimmermann and Richard H. Leach, "The Commissions on Interstate Cooperation," *State Government*, Autumn, 1960, pp. 233–242.

Policy Statements and Proposals. The several major national organizations of State and local governments—the Council of State Governments, the American Municipal Association, the United States Conference of Mayors, and the National Association of Counties—each has a policy statement, amended, revised, and reprinted frequently, to keep it up-to-date. Each devotes much attention to intergovernmental relations. The following articles have a definite bearing upon proposed structural arrangements: J. D. Clark, "Council of Economic Advisers," *Nebraska Law Review*, May, 1949, pp. 530–541, and Robert W. Connery and Richard H. Leach, "U.S. Council on Metro," *National Civic Review*, June, 1959, pp. 292–297.

General Works. W. Brooke Graves has compiled or edited three publications, all appearing under the title *Intergovernmental Relations in the United States*, as follows: (1) "A Selected Bibliography" (Washington: House Committee Print, 84th Cong., 2nd Sess., 1956); (2) "An Annotated Chronology," (Chicago: Council of State Governments, December, 1958); and (3) a symposium of twenty-five articles by leading political scientists, *Annals of the American Academy of Political and Social Science*, January, 1940. William Anderson is the author of two important works: *The Nation and the States: Rivals or Partners?* (Minneapolis: University of Minnesota Press, 1955) and *Intergovernmental Relations in Review* (Minneapolis: University of Minnesota Press, 1960), the summary volume for the study of intergovernmental relations in Minnesota which he directed. James W. Fesler edited a series of papers for the Eighth American Assembly, *The Forty-eight States: Their Tasks as Policy Makers and Administrators* (New York: Columbia University, 1955). The symposium edited by Arthur W. Macmahon, *Federalism: Mature and Emergent* (Garden City: Doubleday & Co., Inc., 1955) is one of the major titles available, as is the *Report of the Commission on Intergovernmental Relations* (Washington, June, 1955), the Kestnbaum Commission. Briefer commentaries on recent or current developments are to be found in Roy V. Peel, *State Government Today* (Albuquerque: University of New Mexico Press, 1948); Nelson A. Rockefeller, *The Future of Federalism* (Cambridge: Harvard University Press, 1962); and Leonard D. White, *The States and the Nation* (Baton Rouge: Louisiana State University Press, 1953). Many of the reports published by the Advisory Commission on Intergovernmental Relations have a direct bearing on problems discussed in this chapter.

APPENDICES

APPENDIX A

FEDERAL GRANT-IN-AID PROGRAMS
1803–1962

Although a great deal has been written and published on Federal grants-in-aid, it appears that no one—including the Commission on Intergovernmental Relations (Kestnbaum)—has ever brought together in one place, in a form convenient for reference, the basic data showing the origin, growth, and development of the grant-in-aid system.

Grants-in-aid in some form were used by the Federal government as early as 1785. The early grants were of land, but annual money grants for specified purposes have been in use since 1808. The great increase in the number and size of grant programs came after World War I and the adoption of the Income Tax Amendment. Another increase began in the 1930's; grants then totalled about $100 million, but had risen in the early 1960's to more than $10 billion annually. This is not an inconsiderable sum, even though the total Federal budget is now expressed in figures of fantastic size.

Varying figures have been given regarding the number of grant programs in existence. Some sources give one figure; others give another. Not a little of this confusion arises out of the difficulty encountered in defining what a grant is. For the purposes of this compilation the term has been interpreted to include payments from the Federal government to the States or their political subdivisions, for the purpose of accomplishing some nationwide objective in which the Federal government has an interest, such as good roads, soil conservation, or trained personnel for mental hospitals or other health facilities. These payments take many forms—outright grants, conditional grants, in lieu payments, shared taxes, or loans to State and local governments. In some cases, payments have been authorized to the individual beneficiaries of the program, as in connection with the training of specialized personnel.

This compilation grew out of an effort to determine—insofar as possible—exactly how many such programs there actually are. This is not a simple matter, either, because there are often many amendments to an original piece of legislation, with two or more programs in a given subject matter field. We have tried to determine, in each case, when grants or payments for a given purpose were first made available, arranging all grant programs chronologically according to the date on which Congress first made funds available for each given purpose.

This table was originally based on data on Federal aid payments presented in the Annual Report of the Secretary of the Treasury; in subsequent revisions, the form of presentation has been improved, and some additional information has been added. Programs of a temporary nature, such as the emergency programs of the 1930's, unless consolidated with other programs or later revived, have not been included.

Since grant legislation, like any other, is subject to frequent amendment and revision, it has seemed desirable to list subsequent enactments affecting each given program area. These lists are not all-inclusive; on the contrary, they have deliberately been kept short through the inclusion of *major* enactments only. On this basis, we have identified 50 program areas, involving almost two hundred separate pieces of legislation. By grouping enactments on a subject matter basis, the number of programs or program areas listed here is not much more than half the number listed in the original edition of this tabulation.

The effort has been made to show not only how many program areas there are, but when they were first established and for what purpose. These programs obviously vary greatly in size and importance. Some are large, while some are very small. Some deal with public questions of major importance, while others appear to have come into existence as a result of pressures exerted at the right time and in the right place for help on some relatively minor problem. All of the programs listed involve grants or some form of financial assistance.

A cumulative summary reveals some interesting and probably significant facts. Only nine programs were carried over from the nineteenth century into the twentieth. Little change occurred until after World War I, when a significant increase in the number of programs began to appear. The increase during the decade of the 1930's was much greater than our figures indicate because many programs of a temporary or emergency nature—not listed here—were established during this decade. The great increases have come during the last four administrations; here, it will be noted that almost two-thirds of all the programs now in effect rest upon legislation adopted since 1930. There is no indication that any appreciable number of these were regarded as of a temporary nature at the time of their authorization.

It is also important to note the subject fields in which legislation of this character has been most frequently adopted. These are, in the order of their importance—as measured in terms of the numbers of programs—education, lands, agriculture, and health. At the bottom of the list, again measured in terms of the number of programs in operation, are highways, fish, game and wildlife, national defense, veterans, and personnel. All of these have the common characteristic of being basic government services which still function largely on the basis of a relatively small number of old and firmly established policies.

FEDERAL GRANT-IN-AID PROGRAMS 1803–1962

Arranged in the Order of the Date of Original Enactment and Including both Grants to States and Local Units and Payments to Individuals Within the States, other than Direct Grants and Loans.

Year	Program and Original Act	Citation	Department or Agency
1803	1. *Public Lands for Schools and Internal Improvements* [1]		
	Proceeds from the sale of public lands—3% or 5% of proceeds for roads, schools, canals, irrigation, and internal improvements	2 Stat. 225–226	
1808	2. *Grants-in-Aid for the State Militia*		Defense
	Assistance in arming and equipping the militia		
	Act of April 23, 1808	2 Stat. 490–491	
	Act of February 12, 1887	24 Stat. 401–402	[War]
	Dick Act of January 21, 1903	32 Stat. 775–780	
	National Defense Act of June 3, 1916	39 Stat. 166–217	
	Act of June 4, 1920	41 Stat. 759–812	National Guard (Army)
	Act of June 15, 1933	48 Stat. 153–162	
	Act of July 7, 1952	66 Stat. 440–441	
	State Armories, Storage Facilities, etc.		
	National Defense Facilities Act of August 9, 1950	64 Stat. 829–832	
1826	3. *Rivers and Harbors Improvement*—including flood control, navigable streams, etc.		U.S. Corps of Engineers
	An Act for Improving Certain Harbors and the Navigation of Certain Rivers and Creeks [2]	4 Stat. 175–176	
	Act of March 1, 1893, as amended and supplemented	27 Stat. 511–513	
	Act of May 15, 1928, as amended	45 Stat. 534–537	

		Stat.	Agency
	Water Storage and Utilization Facilities Act of August 28, 1937	50 Stat. 869–870	Agriculture
	Receipts from Flood Control Lands Flood Control Act of January 28, 1938	52 Stat. 1215–1226	Defense
	Alteration of Bridges Over Navigable Streams, Act of June 21, 1940, as amended	54 Stat. 498–502	
	Flood Control Act of August 18, 1941, as amended	55 Stat. 638–651	
	Flood Control Act of December 22, 1944	58 Stat. 887–907	
	Watershed Protection and Flood Prevention Act of August 4, 1954	68 Stat. 666–668	Agriculture
1862	*4. Colleges for Agriculture and Mechanic Arts*		
	Colleges for Agriculture and Mechanic Arts—Regular Grants		Health, Education, and Welfare U. S. Office of Education
	Morrill Land Grant Act of July 2, 1862	12 Stat. 503–505	
	Morrill Land Grant Act of August 30, 1890. Title I.	26 Stat. 417–419	
	Act of June 29, 1935. Title II.	49 Stat. 438–439	
1879	*5. Assistance to the Blind*		
	American Printing House for the Blind—Regular Grants		
	Act of March 3, 1879, as amended	20 Stat. 467–469	

[1] A precedent for these grants was established earlier, in the Northwest Ordinance of 1787.

[2] These appropriations are not grants in the usual and conventional sense, since no funds are paid to the States or their political subdivisions. The expenditures are made by the Federal government in the State for the benefit of the State or the region. Other so-called "pork-barrel" legislation passed at about the same time, and establishing precedent for later legislation of similar character, included: (1) Appropriation of $150 for the removal of obstructions in the Thames River, Connecticut (1821); (2) Provision for the construction of piers on the Delaware River (1822); (3) Establishing post roads and providing that waterways should be considered post roads (1823); (4) Authorizing improvement of the Ohio and Mississippi Rivers for navigation, by the removal of sand bars and other obstructions (1824).

FEDERAL GRANT-IN-AID PROGRAMS 1803–1962 (continued)

Year	Program and Original Act	Citation	Department or Agency
	Aid to the Blind—Regular Grants		
	Social Security Act of August 14, 1935, as amended	49 Stat. 645–647	
	Vending Stands for the Blind in Public Buildings		
	Act of June 20, 1936	49 Stat. 1559–1561	Agriculture
1887	6. *Agricultural Experiment Stations*		
	Hatch Experiment Station Act of March 2, 1887—	24 Stat. 440–442	
	Regular Grants		
	Adams Act of March 16, 1906	34 Stat. 63	
	Purnell Act of February 24, 1925	43 Stat. 970–972	
	Bankhead-Jones Act of June 29, 1935	49 Stat. 436–439	
	Act of August 14, 1946	60 Stat. 1082–1091	
	Act of August 11, 1955	69 Stat. 671–675	
1888	7. *Veterans' Affairs*		Veterans Administration
	State and Territorial Homes for Disabled Soldiers—		
	Regular Grants		
	Act of August 27, 1888, as amended	25 Stat. 975	
	Automobiles for Disabled Veterans		
	Act of September 2, 1958	72 Stat. 1215	
	Vocational Rehabilitation		
	Veterans of World War II Act of March 24, 1943	57 Stat. 43–45	

			Administered by
	Supervision of On-the-job Training—Regular Grants		Agriculture
	G.I. Bill of Rights of June 22, 1944	58 Stat. 287–291	U.S. Forest Service
	Veterans of Korean Conflict Act of December 28, 1950, as amended	64 Stat. 1121	
	Veterans Readjustment Assistance Act of July 16, 1952	66 Stat. 663–691	
	War Orphans Educational Assistance Act of June 29, 1956	70 Stat. 411–412	
	State Supervision of Schools and Training Establishments Act of September 2, 1958	72 Stat. 1182–1183	
1897	8. *Forest Management*		
	Forest Fire Protection		Commerce
	Act of February 24, 1897, as amended	29 Stat. 594	U.S. Bureau of
	National Forest Fund—Shared Revenues Act of May 23, 1908, as amended [3]	35 Stat. 260	Public Roads
	Forest Highways		
	Agricultural Department Appropriation Act of May 23, 1908	35 Stat. 260	
	Weeks Act of March 1, 1911	36 Stat. 961–963	Agriculture
	Reforestation		U.S. Forest Service
	Clarke-McNary Act of June 7, 1924, as amended and supplemented	43 Stat. 653	
	Experiments in Reforestation Act of May 22, 1928	45 Stat. 699–702	
	Forest Land Administration Act of August 29, 1935	49 Stat. 963–965	

[3] Legislation passed in 1910 (36 Stat. 562, 573) applies to Arizona and New Mexico, and in 1950 (16 USC 577 g) to Minnesota.

FEDERAL GRANT-IN-AID PROGRAMS 1803–1962 (continued)

Year	Program and Original Act	Citation	Department or Agency
	Cooperative Forest Management		
	Cooperative Farm Forestry Act of May 8, 1937	50 Stat. 188	
	Cooperative Forest Management Act of August 24, 1950	64 Stat. 473	
	Agricultural Act of May 28, 1956	70 Stat. 207–208	
	Forest Diseases		
	White Pine Blister Rust Control Act of April 26, 1940	54 Stat. 168–169	
	Forest Pest Control Act of June 25, 1947	61 Stat. 177–178	
1911	9. *Maritime Activities*		
	State Maritime Schools—Regular Grants	36 Stat. 1353–1354	Commerce Maritime Administration
1914	10. *Cooperative Agricultural Extension Work*		Agriculture Federal Extension Service
	Smith-Lever Act of May 8, 1914, as amended—Regular Grants	38 Stat. 372–374	
	Clarke-McNary Act of June 7, 1924	43 Stat. 653	
	Capper-Ketcham Act of May 22, 1928	45 Stat. 711	
	Bankhead-Jones Act of June 29, 1935	49 Stat. 436–439	
	Cooperative Farm Forestry Act of May 8, 1937	50 Stat. 188	
	Additional Extension Act of April 24, 1939	53 Stat. 589	
	Bankhead-Flanagan Act of June 6, 1945	59 Stat. 231–233	
	Department of Agriculture Organic Act of September 21, 1944	58 Stat. 737–738	
	Act of June 26, 1953	67 Stat. 83–85	

1916

11. Highway Construction — Commerce, U.S. Bureau of Public Roads

Act of August 11, 1955	69 Stat. 683–684
Federal Aid Road Act of July 11, 1916, as amended—Regular Grants	
Act of February 26, 1919, as amended	39 Stat. 355–359
Federal Highway Act of November 9, 1921	40 Stat. 1180–1181
Hayden-Cartwright Federal Aid Highway Act of June 18, 1934, as amended	42 Stat. 212–219
Federal Aid Highway (Trust Fund) Act of June 16, 1936	48 Stat. 993–996
Federal Aid Road Act—Emergency Grants	49 Stat. 1519–1522
Federal Aid Highway Act of September 7, 1950	64 Stat. 785–789
Coos Bay Wagon Road Grant Fund *(Interior, Bureau of Land Management)*	
Federal Aid Highway Act of June 29, 1956	70 Stat. 374–402

1917

12. Cooperative Vocational Education — Health, Education, and Welfare, U.S. Office of Education

Smith-Hughes Act of February 23, 1917, as amended—Regular Grants	39 Stat. 929–936
George-Reed Vocational Education Act of February 5, 1929	45 Stat. 1151
George-Ellzey Act of May 21, 1934	48 Stat. 792–793
George-Deen Vocational Education Act of June 8, 1936	49 Stat. 1488–1490
George-Barden Vocational Education Act of August 1, 1946. Title I.	60 Stat. 776–778
Act of June 29, 1956. Title II.	70 Stat. 428–430
Vocational Education for Practical Nurse Training Act of August 2, 1956	70 Stat. 925–929

FEDERAL GRANT-IN-AID PROGRAMS 1803–1962 (continued)

Year	Program and Original Act	Citation	Department or Agency
	Vocational Education for the Fishing Industry Act of August 8, 1956	70 Stat. 1126	
	Vocational Training for Adult Indians Act of August 3, 1956	70 Stat. 986	
1918	13. *Education for Children of Federal Employees*		
	Teachers for Children of Lighthouse Keepers Act of June 20, 1918, as amended	40 Stat. 608	Treasury Coast Guard
	Schools for Children of Naval Establishment Personnel Act of August 2, 1946	60 Stat. 854	Defense Navy
	Schools for Dependents of Personnel on Military and Naval Installations Department of Defense Appropriations Act of 1955	68 Stat. 351	Defense
	14. *Venereal Disease Control*		
	Act of July 9, 1918, as amended—Regular Grants	40 Stat. 886–887	Health, Education, and Welfare U.S. Public Health Service
	Public Health Service Act of July 1, 1944 (supersedes above Act of 1918)	58 Stat. 693–695	
1920	15. *Vocational Rehabilitation*		
	Office of Vocational Rehabilitation—Regular Grants Act of June 21, 1920, as amended	41 Stat. 735–737	U.S. Office of Vocational Rehabilitation
	Vocational Rehabilitation Amendments of 1954 (supersedes above Act of 1920)	68 Stat. 652–662	

Program	Statute	Administering Agency
16. Payments to States Under Federal Water Power Act		
Payments to States Under Federal Water Power Act of June 10, 1920, as amended	41 Stat. 1072–1073	Federal Power Commission
17. Leasing of Mineral Lands, Oil and Gas Lands		
Mineral Lands Leasing Receipts—Shared Revenues		
Mineral Lands Leasing Act of February 25, 1920, as amended	41 Stat. 437–438	Interior Bureau of Land Management
Mineral Leasing Act for Acquired Lands Act of August 7, 1947	61 Stat. 913–915	
Oil and Gas Production, Osage County, Oklahoma Act of March 3, 1921	41 Stat. 1250–1251	Office of Oil and Gas
Oil Lands, South Half of Red River in Oklahoma Joint Resolution of June 12, 1926	44 Stat. 740–741	
1921		
18. Maternal and Child Health Services		
Sheppard-Towner Infant and Maternity Hygiene Act of November 23, 1921	42 Stat. 224–226 [4]	Health, Education, and Welfare Children's Bureau
Social Security Act of August 14, 1935, as amended—Regular Grants	49 Stat. 633	
1925		
19. Territories of the United States—Miscellaneous Programs		
Alaska School Land Receipts		
School Land Act of March 4, 1915, as amended	38 Stat. 1215	U.S. Office of Education
Alaska Game Law Receipts		
Alaska Game Law of January 13, 1925, as amended	43 Stat. 746	Interior U.S. Fish and Wildlife Service

[4] Repealed, January 22, 1927 (44 Stat. 1024).

Year	Program and Original Act	Citation	Department or Agency
	Alaska Public Works		
	Alaska Public Works Act of August 24, 1949, as amended	63 Stat. 627–629	Health, Education, and Welfare
	District of Columbia Hospital Grants		
	Act of August 7, 1946	60 Stat. 896–897	
	Act of October 25, 1951	65 Stat. 657	Interior
	National Capital Land Acquisition for Parks, Playgrounds, Recreation		
	Act of May 29, 1930	46 Stat. 482–485	
	Federal Payment to the District of Columbia		Treasury
	Act of July 5, 1955	69 Stat. 246–263	Internal Revenue Service
	Internal Revenue Collections for Puerto Rico		
	Internal Revenue Code of 1954	68A Stat. 907	
	Internal Revenue Collections for the Virgin Islands		
	Internal Revenue Code of 1954	68A Stat. 907–908	
	Payment to Samoa for Taxes Collected on Coconut and Palm Oil		
	Internal Revenue Code of 1954	68A Stat. 909	
	Grants-in-Aid to Guam		
	Act of August 1, 1956	70 Stat. 910–911	
1927	20. *Plant and Animal Diseases: Eradication and Control*		Agriculture
	Plant Diseases		Agricultural Research Service
	European Corn Borer Eradication Act of February 9, 1927, as amended	44 Stat. 1065	

Control of Insect Pests and Plant Diseases
Act of April 6, 1937 — 50 Stat. 57–58

Golden Nematode Eradication
The Golden Nematode Act of June 15, 1948 — 62 Stat. 442–443 — Interior and Agriculture

Halogeton Glomeratus Eradication
Halogeton Glomeratus Control Act of July 14, 1952 — 66 Stat. 597–599

Barberry Eradication
Department of Agriculture Appropriation Act of 1957 — 70 Stat. 230 — Agricultural Research Service

Animal Diseases
Act for Establishment of a Bureau of Animal Industry and . . . of May 29, 1884 (Bovine Tuberculosis) — 23 Stat. 31

Act to Amend the Agricultural Adjustment Act and for other purposes.
Act of August 24, 1935 (Hog Cholera) — 49 Stat. 781

Control and Eradication of Animal Diseases
Department of Agriculture Organic Act of September 21, 1944 — 58 Stat. 734–735

Vesicular Exanthema: Destruction of Swine Infected with
Acts of June 1 and July 27, 1955 — 68 Stat. 563, and 69 Stat. 80

1928   21. *Indians: Grants to States Involving*

Anthropological Research Among American Indians
Act of April 10, 1928, as amended — 45 Stat. 413–414 — Smithsonian Institution

Public Lands for Indians
Johnson-O'Malley Act of April 16, 1934, as amended — 49 Stat. 1458–1459 — Interior Bureau of Indian Affairs

943

FEDERAL GRANT-IN-AID PROGRAMS 1803–1962 (continued)

Year	Program and Original Act	Citation	Department or Agency
	22. *Grants Involving Major Public Power Projects*		Interior
	Revenues from Boulder Canyon Project		
	Boulder Canyon Project Act of December 21, 1928, as amended	45 Stat. 1059	
	Upper Colorado River Basin Fund Act of April 11, 1956	70 Stat. 106–110	
	Tennessee Valley Authority		Tennessee Valley Authority
	In lieu payments under TVA Act of May 18, 1933, as amended; superseded by:	48 Stat. 61–66	
	Act of June 26, 1940	54 Stat. 626	
	Grand Coulee Dam Project—*in lieu* payments		Interior
	Columbia River Project Act of March 10, 1943, as amended	57 Stat. 19, and 71 Stat. 524	Bonneville Power Administration
1930	23. *Shore Erosion Protection and Control*		Army
	Shore Erosion Investigations		Beach Control Board
	Act of July 3, 1930	46 Stat. 945–946	
	Shore Erosion Protection		U.S. Corps of Engineers
	Act of August 13, 1946	70 Stat. 702–703	
	Rio Grande Bank Protection Project		International Boundary and Water Commission
	First Deficiency Appropriation Act of April 25, 1945	59 Stat. 89	
1933	24. *Employment Security System*		Labor
	System of Public Employment Offices		Bureau of Employment Security
	Wagner-Peyser Act of June 6, 1933, as amended—		
	Regular Grants	48 Stat. 113–117	

Social Security Act of August 14, 1935, as amended	49 Stat. 626–627	
Unemployment Compensation for Veterans Act of July 16, 1952	66 Stat. 684–688	
Employment Security Funds Social Security Act Amendments of August 5, 1954	68 Stat. 668–671	
Unemployment Compensation for Federal Employees Act of September 1, 1954	68 Stat. 1130–1135	
25. *Surplus Agricultural Commodities*—Distribution		Agriculture
Commodity Credit Corporation [5]— Value of Commodities Denoted Act of January 31, 1935	49 Stat. 4	Commodity Credit Corporation
Act of June 28, 1950	64 Stat. 261	
Removal of Surplus Agricultural Commodities Surplus Property Act of October 3, 1944	58 Stat. 765–784, especially 775–776	Agricultural Marketing Service
School Lunch Program—Regular Grants National School Lunch Act of June 4, 1946	60 Stat. 230–234	
Special School Milk Program Agricultural Act of August 28, 1954	68 Stat. 900	
Federal Charter for the Commodity Credit Corporation, June 29, 1948	62 Stat. 1070–1074	
26. *Wildlife Conservation*		Interior
Wildlife Restoration—Regular Grants Act of March 10, 1934	48 Stat. 401–402	U.S. Fish and Wildlife Service

[5] Originally organized October 17, 1933, under the laws of the State of Delaware, pursuant to Executive Order No. 6340 of October 16, 1933.

FEDERAL GRANT-IN-AID PROGRAMS 1803–1962 (continued)

Year	Program and Original Act	Citation	Department or Agency
	Pittman-Robertson Act of September 2, 1937, as amended	50 Stat. 917–919	
	Dingell-Johnson Act of July 1, 1951, as amended	64 Stat. 430–434	
	Payments Under Migratory Bird Conservation Act and Alaska Game Law Conservation Act of June 15, 1935	49 Stat. 383	
	Alaska Game Law of July 1, 1943	57 Stat. 309–310	
27.	*Grazing Land and Other Special Fund Receipts*		Bureau of
	Taylor Grazing Act of June 28, 1934—Shared Revenues [6]	48 Stat. 1273	Land Management
28.	*Agricultural Conservation Program*		Agriculture
	Soil Conservation and Domestic Allotment		Soil Conservation Service
	Act of April 27, 1935, as amended	49 Stat. 163–164	
	Soil Bank Programs		
	Act of February 16, 1938	52 Stat. 68–69	
	Retired Submarginal Land Program: Payment to		
	Counties—Shared Revenues	50 Stat. 526	
	Bankhead-Jones Farm Tenant Act of July 22, 1937		
29.	*Children: Health and Welfare Services*		Health, Education,
	Child Welfare Services		and Welfare
	Social Security Act of August 14, 1935, as amended—		Social Security
	Regular Grants	49 Stat. 633	Administration
	Services for Crippled Children		
	Social Security Act of August 14, 1935, as amended—		
	Regular Grants	49 Stat. 631–633	

Aid to Dependent Children			
	Social Security Act of August 14, 1935, as amended—Regular Grants	49 Stat. 627–629	U.S. Public Health Service
	Children with Congenital Heart Disease Act of June 16, 1948	62 Stat. 468–469	
30.	*Mental Health Activities*		
	Social Security Act of August 14, 1935, as amended—Regular Grants	49 Stat. 620	
	Public Health Service Act of July 1, 1944	58 Stat. 682	
	National Mental Health Act of July 3, 1946	60 Stat. 421–426	
	Amendment to Mental Health Act of July 3, 1946 Act of August 2, 1956	70 Stat. 929	
	Alaska Mental Health Act of July 28, 1956	70 Stat. 709–714	
31.	*Old Age Assistance*		Social Security Administration
	Social Security Act of August 14, 1935, as amended—Regular Grants	49 Stat. 620–622	
1936	32. *Federal Housing Program*		Housing and Home Finance Agency
	Low-Rent Housing and Slum Clearance Projects Act of June 29, 1936	49 Stat. 2025–2026	
	Public Housing: Annual Contributions—Regular Grants United States Housing Act of September 1, 1937, as amended	50 Stat. 888–899	Public Housing Administration

a Under separate acts, payments are made to particular States, as follows: Alaska, income and proceeds from school lands: 38 Stat. 1214—1915; Arizona and Nevada, *in lieu* payments, Boulder Dam project: 45 Stat. 1058—1059—1928; Oklahoma, from royalties: 42 Stat. 1448—1450—1923; Oregon, from grant lands: 39 Stat. 218—1916; Oregon and California, from grant lands: 39 Stat. 222—1916; Revested Oregon and California land grants: 44 Stat. 915–916—1927.

FEDERAL GRANT-IN-AID PROGRAMS 1803–1962 (continued)

Year	Program and Original Act	Citation	Department or Agency
	Defense Housing		
	Lanham Act of October 14, 1940	54 Stat. 1127	Housing and Home Finance Agency
	Housing Act of July 15, 1949	63 Stat. 414–431	
	Housing for Educational Institutions		
	Housing Act of July 20, 1950	64 Stat. 79	
	Housing Act of August 2, 1954	68 Stat. 622–633	
	Housing Act of August 7, 1956	70 Stat. 1097–1104	
	Housing Act of July 12, 1957	71 Stat. 294–305	
1938	33. *Agricultural Marketing Services*		Agriculture
	Agricultural Adjustment Act of February 16, 1938 (cooperative projects)	52 Stat. 37	Agricultural Marketing Service
	Agricultural Marketing Services Act of August 14, 1946	60 Stat. 1087–1091	
1940	34. *Assistance in State Personnel Programs*		Health, Education, and Welfare
	Contributions to State Retirement Systems Act of March 4, 1940	54 Stat. 39–40	U.S. Office of Education
	Social Security Coverage Extended to State and Local Government Personnel Social Security Act Amendments of 1950 Act of August 28, 1950.	64 Stat. 558	Social Security Administration
1941	35. *Aid for Community Facilities and Schools in Federally Affected Areas*		Housing and Home Finance Agency
	Defense Housing and Community Facilities Act of September 1, 1941, as amended	68 Stat. 294–295	

		Stat.	Agency
	Other Projects		
	Act of June 3, 1948	62 Stat. 297	Army
	Act of June 29, 1948	62 Stat. 1108	Interior
	School Construction and Survey—Emergency Grants		
	Act of September 23, 1950 (P.L. 815), as amended by:	64 Stat. 967–978	Health, Education, and Welfare U.S. Office of Education
	Act of September 30, 1950—Emergency Grants	64 Stat. 1100–1109	
	Maintenance and Operation of Schools		
	Act of August 12, 1958 (P.L. 874), as amended by:	72 Stat. 555	
	Act of August 12, 1958	72 Stat. 548–549	
1942	36. *Aid for Specific Agricultural Crops*		Agriculture
	Planting of Guayule		
	Act of March 5, 1942	56 Stat. 126–128	
	Sugar Act Program		Commodity Stabilization Service
	Act of August 8, 1947	61 Stat. 929–932	
1944	37. *Public Health Grants: Research on Major Causes of Death and Disability*		Health, Education, and Welfare U.S. Public Health Service
	Cancer Control—Regular Grants		
	Act of July 1, 1944	58 Stat. 707–708	
	Act of September 6, 1950	64 Stat. 650	
	Tuberculosis Control—Regular Grants		
	Act of July 1, 1944, as amended	58 Stat. 693–695	
	Dental Research—Regular Grants		
	National Dental Research Act of June 24, 1948	62 Stat. 598–602	

Year	Program and Original Act	Citation	Department or Agency
	Heart Disease Control—Regular Grants		
	National Heart Act of June 16, 1948	62 Stat. 464–469	
	Research on Neurological Diseases, including Arthritis, Rheumatism, and Blindness		
	Act of August 15, 1950	64 Stat. 443–447	
	Care of Lepers in Hawaiian Hospitals		
	Act of June 25, 1952	66 Stat. 157–158	
	Poliomyelitis Vaccination Program—Emergency Grants		
	Poliomyelitis Vaccination Assistance Act of August 12, 1955 [7]	69 Stat. 704–707	
	38. *General Health Assistance*		
	Act of July 1, 1944, as amended—Regular Grants	58 Stat. 694–695	
	Medical Care Payments		
	Social Security Act Amendments of July 24, 1957	71 Stat. 308–309	
	Aid to the Permanently and Totally Disabled		
	Social Security Act Amendments of August 28, 1950— Regular Grants	64 Stat. 555–558	
1946	39. *Atomic Energy Programs* [8]		Atomic Energy Commission
	Atomic Energy Commission Property—*in lieu* Payments for		
	Atomic Energy Act of August 1, 1946	60 Stat. 765–766	
	Construction of Atomic Reactors		
	Atomic Energy Act of August 30, 1954	68 Stat. 927	
	Training of Personnel for Atomic Energy Installations		
	Atomic Energy Act of August 30, 1954, as amended	68 Stat. 919	

Program / Act	Statute	Administration
Federal Airport Act of May 13, 1946, as amended—Regular Grants	60 Stat. 170–180	State
41. *International Education Programs*		
Cooperating with Foreign Service Institute Foreign Service Act of August 13, 1946	60 Stat. 1018–1019	
International Education Exchange U.S. Information and Education Exchange Act of January 27, 1948	62 Stat. 7	
42. *Hospital Survey and Construction Program* [9]		Health, Education, and Welfare U.S. Public Health Service
Hospital Survey and Construction—Regular Grants Hospital Survey and Construction Act of August 13, 1946, as amended	60 Stat. 1041–1049	
Health Research Facilities Act of July 30, 1956	70 Stat. 717–721	
43. *Water Pollution Control*		
Water Pollution Control Act of June 30, 1948, as amended	62 Stat. 1155–1161	
Federal Water Pollution Control Act of July 9, 1956	70 Stat. 498–507	
Waste Treatment Works Act of July 9, 1956	70 Stat. 502–503	
44. *Paleontology, Geology and Mining*		Smithsonian Institution
Paleontological Investigations Act of August 15, 1949	63 Stat. 606	
Fire Control in Coal Formations Act of July 31, 1953	67 Stat. 269–270	Interior U.S. Geological Survey

[7] Program discontinued on expiration of Act on June 30, 1957.
[8] Grants made to public and private institutions within States.
[9] Grants for National Institutes of Health included under No. 36.

951

FEDERAL GRANT-IN-AID PROGRAMS 1803–1962 (continued)

Year	Program and Original Act	Citation	Department or Agency
	Coal Mine Drainage (Anthracite) Act of July 15, 1955	69 Stat. 352–353	Bureau of Mines
	Geological Survey: surveys for States Interior Department Appropriation Act of 1957	71 Stat. 261	U.S. Geological Survey
1949	45. *Slum Clearance, Urban Renewal and Community Development*		Housing and Home Finance Agency
	Housing Act of July 15, 1949, as amended	63 Stat. 418	
	Territorial Enabling Act of July 18, 1950	64 Stat. 344–347	
	Urban Planning Assistance—Regular Grants Housing Act of August 2, 1954, as amended	68 Stat. 640	
1950	46. *Civil Defense and Disaster Relief*		Defense
	Natural Disaster Relief Act of September 30, 1950	64 Stat. 1109–1111	
	Civil Defense: Funds for Equipment and Shelters Federal Civil Defense Act of January 12, 1951	64 Stat. 1245–1257	
1954	47. *Cooperative Research and Training in Health, Welfare, and Education*		Health, Education, and Welfare
	In Education—Cooperative Research in Education Act of July 26, 1954	68 Stat. 533	U.S. Office of Education
	Teacher training for the mentally retarded Act of September 6, 1958	72 Stat. 1777	
	In Public Health—Traineeships for Public Health Personnel Health Act Amendments of August 2, 1956	70 Stat. 923–925	U.S. Public Health Service
	In Public Welfare—Social Security Act Amendments of August 1, 1956	70 Stat. 850–851	Social Security Administration

Year	Title	Statute	Agency
1955	Traineeships for Public Welfare Personnel Social Security Act Amendments of August 1, 1956	70 Stat. 851–852	U.S. Public Health Service
	48. *Air Pollution Control* Air Pollution Control Act of July 14, 1955	69 Stat. 322–323	
1956	49. *Great Plains Conservation Program* Aid in Reclamation Projects Small Reclamation Projects Act of August 6, 1956	70 Stat. 1044–1047	Interior U.S. Bureau of Reclamation
	Soil Conservation Program Act of August 7, 1956	70 Stat. 1115–1117	
	Investigations by the Bureau of Reclamation Public Works Appropriation Act of 1957	70 Stat. 475	
	50. *Public Library Services* Library Services Act of June 19, 1956	70 Stat. 293–296	Health, Education, and Welfare U.S. Office of Education
1961	51. *Depressed Areas* Area Redevelopment Act of 1961	75 Stat. 47	Commerce Area Redevelopment Administration
	52. *Mass Transit Loans and Demonstration Grants* Housing Act of 1961	75 Stat. 149	Housing and Home Finance Agency Office of the Administrator
1962	53. *Manpower Development* Manpower Development and Training Act of 1962	76 Stat. 23	Labor Bureau of Apprenticeship & Training

APPENDIX B

ALLOCATION FORMULAS AND MATCHING REQUIREMENTS FOR THIRTY-FIVE CURRENTLY EXISTING FEDERAL GRANT-IN-AID PROGRAMS *

Program I. Agricultural Extension Work (Cooperative)

ALLOCATION FORMULA

The Smith Lever Act of 1914 and supplementary acts have provided funds, allocated as follows:

1. Allotments for the 1953 fiscal year as a "base." If appropriations for any given fiscal year fall below the 1953 total, the U.S. Department of Agriculture would reduce allotments to individual States by the appropriate uniform flat percentage.

2. If appropriations for any given fiscal year exceed the 1953 total, the additional sum would be apportioned by the U. S. Department of Agriculture on the following basis:

   (a) First $100,000 to Puerto Rico until maximum allowed Puerto Rico under the Bankhead-Jones Act is reached;

   (b) 48 per cent in the proportion of State rural population to total U.S. rural population;

   (c) 48 per cent in the proportion of State farm population to total U.S. farm population;

   (d) 4 per cent on the basis of special needs as determined by the Secretary.

MATCHING REQUIREMENTS

"Old money" (1953 or below) must be matched in the same minimum ratio as prevailed prior to the enactment of Public Law 83 (approximately $.54 non-Federal to $1.00 Federal).

"New money" (amount over 1953 total) presently must be matched dollar for dollar. (Technically, the matching requirement for "new money" is set each year by Congress, but it is assumed that the 100 per cent current matching requirement will be continued).

Program II. Agricultural Marketing Services

ALLOCATION FORMULA

Funds not allocated to States by formula under this program. Complete discretion

MATCHING REQUIREMENTS

Each Federal dollar must be matched with one State dollar, a condition of a project

* Adapted from two sources: Commission on Intergovernmental Relations, *A Description of Twenty-five Federal Grant-in-Aid Programs* (Washington, June 1955); Advisory Commission on Intergovernmental Relations, *Periodic Congressional Reassessment of Federal Grants-in-Aid to State and Local Governments* (Washington, June 1961).

ALLOCATION FORMULA

rests with the U.S. Department of Agriculture as to which projects from which States will be Federally supported.

MATCHING REQUIREMENTS

agreement being that the State will contribute an amount toward the project at least equal to the Federal contribution.

Program III. Agricultural Research

ALLOCATION FORMULA

Allotments to States are made in three categories, based upon the five pieces of authorizing legislation, as shown in the table below.

MATCHING REQUIREMENTS

Grants under the Hatch, Adams, and Purnell Acts ($90,000 to each State) need not be matched. Grants under the Bankhead-Jones Act, Title I, Section 5, must be matched dollar for dollar; under Section 9, excluding those for regional research and administration, must be matched in full (i.e., 72 per cent in direct allotments must be matched, 28 per cent need not be matched).

Act	Legislative Authorization	1963 Appropriations	Basis of Distribution
Hatch, Adams, and Purnell	$ 4,530,000		Equal amount to each State ($90,000)
Bankhead-Jones Title I, Sec. 5	3,000,000		Principally on basis of rural population
Bankhead-Jones Title I, Sec. 9	20,000,000		(a) 20 per cent in equal amounts.
Consolidated in Act of August 11, 1955	none specified		(b) Not less than 52 per cent by following formula: one-half according to relative rural population; one-half according
Agricultural Research		36,723,000	to relative farm population.
Federal administration		1,290,000	(c) Not more than 25 per cent for regional research.
Penalty Mail Payments		250,000	(d) 3 per cent for administration.
Total		38,263,000	

Program IV. Airport Construction

ALLOCATION FORMULA

(a) 75 per cent of the annual appropriations available for projects is apportioned among the States, one-half on the basis of population, one-half on the basis of area. Sums appropriated to a State are, during the fiscal year

MATCHING REQUIREMENTS

The Federal cash grant is 50 per cent of development costs for smaller airports, a discretionary amount not to exceed 50 per cent for development costs for larger airports.

These maximum limitations are increased

ALLOCATION FORMULA

MATCHING REQUIREMENTS

for which appropriated, available only for projects in the State. Unexpended-sums thereafter are reapportioned among the States on the same basis as new appropriations.

(b) 25 per cent of the annual appropriations constitutes a discretionary fund available to pay costs of projects throughout the States as the Civil Aeronautics Administration determines, regardless of project locations. This fund is the only source of U.S. aid under the airport program for projects serving national parks, monuments, forests, and recreation areas.

in States where unappropriated and un-reserved public lands and nontaxable Indian lands exceed 5 per cent of the total land area of the State. For such States the U.S. share of the costs is increased. . . .

Program V. Blind: Distribution of Educational Materials for

ALLOCATION FORMULA

MATCHING REQUIREMENTS

Federal support for the manufacture and distribution of books and teaching materials for the education of the blind was instituted in 1879. Until 1956 these materials were available only to students enrolled in special public school classes for the blind; under the recent amendment, all blind children attending public schools are eligible to receive these aids. The American Printing House for the Blind, a private nonprofit corporation, operates the program under the supervision of the U.S. Department of Health, Education, and Welfare. Funds are credited to public schools for the blind and to State departments of education in proportion to the number of blind students registered in the public schools; books and materials are shipped by the Printing House in the amount of the funds credited.

Matching of Federal funds is not required.

Program VI. Child Welfare Services

ALLOCATION FORMULA

MATCHING REQUIREMENTS

Section 5, Part 5 of the Social Security Act stipulates that of the sum appropriated by Congress, allotment shall be made

Federal grants to the States under this program are not required to be matched. However, Federal funds are intended to

ALLOCATION FORMULA

to the States on the basis of plans developed jointly by the State agencies and the Administrator in the amount of $40,000 to each State and the remainder to each State on the basis of such plans "not to exceed such part of the remainder as the rural population of such State under the age of eighteen years bears to the total rural population under such age. The Act also provides that the allotment to any State for any fiscal year remaining unpaid to such State at the end thereof shall be available for payment until the end of the second succeeding fiscal year, and that no payment to a State shall be made out of the allotment for any fiscal year until its allotment for the preceding fiscal year has been exhausted or has ceased to be available."

MATCHING REQUIREMENTS

cover only a part of the total cost of these services to the States.

Program VII. Civil Defense Equipment and Supplies

ALLOCATION FORMULA

Allotment of Federal Civil Defense funds is made by the Administrator of Federal Civil Defense, usually on the basis of the ratio which the population of such State bears to the total population of all States. If a State does not present approved requests for all funds allocated to it, any balance may be utilized by States that have matching funds available and which meet legal and administrative requirements for aid.

MATCHING REQUIREMENTS

Federal contributions to States for civil defense supplies and equipment may not exceed 50 per cent of the cost thereof. In other words, one Federal dollar must be matched by at least one State dollar.

Program VIII. Crippled Children's Services

ALLOCATION FORMULA

Funds appropriated for crippled children's services are split into two funds of equal size, "CC Fund A" and "CC Fund B." Fund A includes a flat amount for each State, with the remainder prorated according to the number of children under twenty-one years in each State. 25 per cent of Fund B is reserved for special crippled children's projects of regional or national

MATCHING REQUIREMENTS

Fund A must be matched on the basis of one State dollar for every Federal dollar. Matching is not required for Fund B.

ALLOCATION FORMULA

MATCHING REQUIREMENTS

significance, the remainder being apportioned so that each State receives an
amount which varies directly with the
number of children under twenty-one
years in urban and rural areas (with rural
given double weighting) and varies inversely with State per capita income.

Program IX. Defense Educational Activities

ALLOCATION FORMULA

MATCHING REQUIREMENTS

The National Defense Education Act of
1958 authorized a number of programs of
Federal financial assistance to education,
both at the elementary and secondary
level and for higher education, designed
to meet critical national needs, especially
in the areas of science, technology and
foreign languages. The Act also added
certain technician classifications to the
coverage of the vocational education grant
programs. Grants are authorized for: (a)
purchase of equipment and improvement
of State supervision to strengthen elementary and secondary school instruction
in science, mathematics and foreign languages; (b) the initiation and conduct of
programs to strengthen guidance, counseling and testing in secondary schools
and (c) the improvement of statistical services of State educational agencies. In addition to grants-in-aid to States, direct
loans to college students and private
schools, fellowships for graduate students
and grants and contracts with private institutions of higher education are also authorized. For certain programs allotments
to States take account of school age, population, and per capita income.

Currently, matching is required on a 50-50
basis.

Program X. Disaster Relief

ALLOCATION FORMULA

MATCHING REQUIREMENTS

Allotments to individual States are completely variable according to the impact
of the disaster upon the States.

Public Law 875 states only that the State
or local governments shall expend a reasonable amount of funds in any catastrophe. No formal matching is required.

Program XI. Employment Security and Unemployment Compensation

ALLOCATION FORMULA

Under the Social Security Act of 1935, the States were encouraged by the enactment of a tax credit plan to establish unemployment compensation programs conforming to certain broad Federal standards. A Federal unemployment tax of 3 per cent was levied, with certain exceptions, on the payrolls of employers of eight or more persons (now four or more), and a credit of up to 90 per cent of this tax was allowed employers covered by State laws meeting the requirements of the Federal Act. Each State pays benefits to eligible unemployed workers from a special State trust fund in which payroll taxes contributed by employers (and also by employees in two States) are deposited. The Secretary of Labor apportions the funds appropriated on the basis of the needs of each State for the proper and efficient administration of the program.

MATCHING REQUIREMENTS

The cost of operating each State's employment security agency, which administers both the unemployment compensation and employment security functions, is paid entirely by the grant financed from the Federal Government's .3 of 1 per cent share of the payroll tax. The program is administered by the Bureau of Employment Security in the U.S. Department of Labor.

Program XII. Fish and Wildlife Restoration and Management

ALLOCATION FORMULA

Although administration of the Pittman-Robertson and Dingell-Johnson Acts is merged, funds for each are derived from different sources and allocated to the States by different, yet related methods. Funds for the Federal Aid in Wildlife Restoration (P-R) Act are set apart in the Treasury as a special fund authorized to be appropriated and made available for obligation with a two-year period for carrying out the purposes of the Act. This fund is an amount equal to the revenue accruing during the fiscal year from the tax imposed on firearms, shells, and cartridges. Unexpended appropriations to any State for any fiscal year is authorized to be made available to that State until the close of the succeeding fiscal year. Unexpended or unobligated funds remaining at the end of the period of availability are authorized for expenditure in carrying out the provisions of the Migratory Bird Act.

MATCHING REQUIREMENTS

As soon as a project is approved and the agreement executed, the U.S. Secretary of the Treasury is requested to set aside from the sum apportioned to the State the funds necessary to meet the Federal share of the project cost. When the project is completed, or from time to time as the work progresses, reimbursement to the extent of 75 per cent of actual expenditures is paid to the State for work satisfactorily accomplished.

Program XIII. Flood Prevention and Watershed Protection

ALLOCATION FORMULA

Under the Watershed Protection and Flood Prevention Act of 1954, the Federal Government cooperates with the States and their political subdivisions such as soil conservation districts, flood control districts, counties and municipalities, for the purpose of making full use of water resources, preventing erosion, and reducing damages from floodwater and sediment in small watersheds. The program is intended to be an integral part of the total soil and water conservation program of the Nation and to round out the flood-control program by applying water control measures on upstream watershed lands where the water first falls. The Federal Government shares the cost of installing works of improvement in accordance with a work plan developed for each watershed project.

MATCHING REQUIREMENTS

The amount of the Federal share varies with the nature of the improvement project, and the nature of the benefits. The program is administered by the Soil Conservation Service of the U.S. Department of Agriculture.

Program XIV. Forestry Cooperation—State and Private

ALLOCATION FORMULA

Funds are allotted to States through a formula under which one-half of the Federal appropriation available to the States is distributed on the basis of a percentage determined by the ratio of the amount available to the total estimated cost of protection. This is termed the regular item. The other half is distributed on the basis of a percentage determined by the ratio of the amount available to the excess fiscal year expenditure of State and private funds in the program over the amount required to match the Federal grant. This is termed the extra item.

In practice the determination of the extra item varies in accordance with guidelines mutually agreed upon between the Federal Government and the Association of State Foresters. These to date have included: a 50-50 matching of total State-private program expenditures up to $25,-000; a maximum reduction not to exceed

MATCHING REQUIREMENTS

States must match dollar for dollar all Federal funds supplied. The U.S. Forest Service is prohibited from contributing more than the State.

ALLOCATION FORMULA

3½ per cent of previous year's allotment; no allotment to exceed one-half of the estimated cost of protection.

The sum of the regular and extra items for each State is its allotment, and each State is given the estimate for the next year's allotment in May. Under the forest planting section of the Clarke-McNary Act, a flat sum of $9,500 is allotted each participating State. Under the Forest Pest Control Act and the Blister Rust section, allotments are on a project rather than a formula basis.

MATCHING REQUIREMENTS

Program XV. Highway Construction

ALLOCATION FORMULA

Authorized funds for Federal aid to highways are apportioned among the State by statutory formula, as follows:

1. *Primary System of Highways:* one-third land area; one-third total population; one-third mileage of rural delivery and star routes. However, no State gets less than one-half of 1 per cent of the available funds in this category.
2. *Urban System:* population in municipalities and other urban places of 5,000 or more.
3. *Secondary System:* one-third land area; one-third rural population; and one-third mileage of rural delivery and star routes. However, no State gets less than one-half of 1 per cent of the Federal funds available in this category.
4. *Interstate Highway System:* one-half of the funds on the basis of population; the other half on the same basis as primary highways. (Prior to Act of 1954, all had been allocated on the same basis as for the primary system).

MATCHING REQUIREMENTS

Prior to the 1954 Act, in most States, dollar for dollar matching was required. The exceptions were those States where more than 5 per cent of the total area was unappropriated and unreserved public lands and nontaxable Indian lands. In those States, the Federal share of the cost of Federal-aid projects is determined by a formula set forth in the law which became effective on February 1, 1954.

Program XVI. Hospital and Medical Facilities Survey and Construction

ALLOCATION FORMULA

Section 624 of the Act provides that the share of the total Federal grant going to each individual State shall be computed by:

1. Squaring the allotment percentage, on the basis that per capita income represents both need for the service and financial ability and must be counted twice.
2. Multiplying the percentage thus obtained by the population of the respective States. The result is the weighted population for each State.
3. Making a percentage distribution from the weighted population data and apportioning the Federal grant money on the basis of this percentage distribution.

MATCHING REQUIREMENTS

The Federal share of approved project costs is defined in Section 631, which originally restricted the Federal share to one-third in all States. In 1949, the Act was amended to provide two alternative methods in establishing the Federal share:

1. A uniform percentage for all projects within the State, not less than one-third and not more than two-thirds of the State's "allotment percentage," whichever is the lesser.
2. A variable scale based on economic ability and the need for additional facilities in communities within the State, with a minimum of one-third and a maximum of two-thirds.

Program XVII. Land Grant Colleges

ALLOCATION FORMULA

The 1890 and 1907 acts are "continuing" appropriations requiring no Congressional action each year. The 1935 Act authorizes appropriations upon which Congress must act each year.

The continuing appropriations total $50,000 per year for each State. The 1935 Act, as amended in June 1952, provides an additional $20,000 to each State, plus variable amounts from a total of $1,501,500 distributed on the basis of population. Thus each State automatically is entitled to a total of $70,000 annually, plus an amount relative to population.

MATCHING REQUIREMENTS

Funds granted under this program carry no matching requirements.

Program XVIII. Library Services

ALLOCATION FORMULA

This program, authorized by the Library Services Act of 1956, is intended to stimulate the States to expand public library services to rural areas without such services or with inadequate services. Each State is required to submit a plan of operation for approval by the Commissioner

MATCHING REQUIREMENTS

Federal grants must be matched by State and local funds in amounts varying with a State's fiscal ability.

ALLOCATION FORMULA

of Education, U.S. Department of Health, Education, and Welfare.

MATCHING REQUIREMENTS

Program XIX. Marine Schools: Assistance to States

ALLOCATION FORMULA

The Marine Administration of the U.S. Department of Commerce, in addition to administering financial aid, is authorized to furnish and repair suitable training vessels and to pay certain maintenance allowances and fees for students.

MATCHING REQUIREMENTS

Annual grants are made to California, Maine, Massachusetts, and New York to assist in maintaining academies for training officers to serve in the American merchant marine.

Program XX. Maternal and Child Health Services

ALLOCATION FORMULA

The statute requires that the funds appropriated shall be split into halves termed "MCH Fund A" and "MCH Fund B." Fund A is apportioned among the States partially by a flat grant to each State and the remainder on the basis of live births. From Fund B, a sum is set aside for special programs of national or regional significance to improve service and to meet emergencies. The reserved amount, under present regulations, is 25 per cent of Fund B. The remaining 75 per cent is apportioned among the States according to the financial need of each State for help in carrying out its approved plan. The index of need for such funds is based on live births and average per capita income.

MATCHING REQUIREMENTS

Fund A must be matched on the basis of one State dollar for each Federal dollar. Fund B does not have to be matched.

Program XXI. Public Assistance

ALLOCATION FORMULA

Under the categorical programs for the aged (old age assistance), the blind (aid to the blind), and the disabled (aid to the permanently and totally disabled), the States are eligible to receive Federal grants for each recipient amounting to $20 of the first $25 paid monthly by the State, plus one-half of the remainder of the State's payment up to a maximum Federal grant of $35.

MATCHING REQUIREMENTS

Under approved State programs of aid to dependent children, the Federal Government will match State and local payments at the rate of $12 of the first $15 for each child, and one-half of the remainder up to a monthly total Federal grant of $19.50 for the first child and $15 for each succeeding child in a family. In addition, the Federal Government pays one-half of certain administrative expenses incurred by the States in all of the categories.

Program XXII. Public Health Services

ALLOCATION FORMULA

The Surgeon General allots appropriated funds available to the States on the basis of: (1) population; (2) extent of the health problem generally and within the particular State; (3) financial need. This is the basis for allotment of all grant programs with the exception of venereal disease control, which is on a project basis at the discretion of the Surgeon General. Specific weightings for population, financial need and extent of problem have been established for mental health, cancer control, and heart disease control programs.

MATCHING REQUIREMENTS

Grants for public health, heart disease, tuberculosis control, cancer control, and mental health must be matched on the basis of one dollar from sources within the State for every two Federal dollars. Project grants for venereal disease control do not require matching.

Program XXIII. Public Housing—Low Rent

ALLOCATION FORMULA

The Act provides that no more than 10 per cent of the funds shall be made available in any one State. The Federal Government approves projects on the basis of need for low rent housing as demonstrated by the local unit's compliance with Federal requirements. In general, this results in States with large or numerous cities receiving most of the projects.

MATCHING REQUIREMENTS

While there is no State matching of Federal funds, the local government contributes to the objective of low rents by exempting housing projects from all local taxation. The law permits local authorities to make payments in lieu of taxes up to 10 percent of the shelter rents. On a long-range basis, it is estimated that the local contributions plus the local contributions toward debt payments will equal 50 per cent of Federal contributions.

Program XXIV. School Construction in Federally Impacted Areas

ALLOCATION FORMULA

Eligibility for Federal assistance for school construction is based upon the number of school children whose attendance results from a Federal activity. . . .

MATCHING REQUIREMENTS

"Matching," as such, in terms of individual projects, is not required. Formula assumes that school districts may wish to add such local funds as are needed to complete a desired project, but the project itself might be built entirely with Federal funds. With respect to "C" children, a finding that construction of additional school facilities constitutes an undue financial burden upon the applicant is an additional requirement of Federal assistance.

Program XXV. School Operation and Maintenance in Federally Impacted Areas

ALLOCATION FORMULA

Entitlement to Federal payment to a particular district is based upon the number of school children whose attendance results from a Federal activity. . . .

MATCHING REQUIREMENTS

Federal funds granted under this program do not have to be specifically and separately matched. With respect to children under Section 4 (sudden attendance increase due to Federal activity in the area), a tax effort comparable to other areas and utilization of all possible funds within the State are conditions of eligibility for Federal assistance to any district. The descending scale of Federal payments after the year of initial increase in average daily attendance because of Federal activity insures that, on the whole, all Federal payments are more than matched by State and local finances.

Program XXVI. School Lunches

ALLOCATION FORMULA

The cash allotment is distributed among the States by a formula under which the share of a State varies directly with the number of children of school age (5–17) within its borders and inversely with its per capita income. Commodities acquired under other statutes are distributed at the discretion of the U.S. Secretary of Agriculture to States for distribution to all schools serving non-profit lunches.

MATCHING REQUIREMENTS

The National School Lunch Act provides that Federal cash grants should be matched from sources within the State at the ratio of 1:1 from 1946 through 1950, at the ratio of 1½ from 1951 through 1955, and at the ratio of 1:3 from 1956 on.

Program XXVII. Special Milk Program

ALLOCATION FORMULA

Established by the Agricultural Act of 1953, the program is intended both to expand the market for fluid milk and to increase its consumption by children in non-profit schools of high school grade and under and in non-profit institutions devoted to the care and training of children. The program is administered by agencies of the various States operating under an agreement with the U.S. Department of Agriculture, except where legal or other barriers make it necessary for the Department to administer the program directly.

MATCHING REQUIREMENTS

The amount of funds reserved to each State is based upon previous participation plus an allowance for program expansion.

Program XXVIII. Slum Clearance and Urban Renewal

ALLOCATION FORMULA

Title I provides that not more than 10 per cent of the funds authorized under the Act shall be made available in any one State, with the exception that within an aggregate limitation of $35,000,000 and subject to the overall capital grant authorization, additional capital grant funds may be made available in any State, if two-thirds of the amount permissible under the 10 per cent limitation have been obligated under contract with the local public agency in such State. The practical effect of this exception is to permit more than $50,000,000 (10 per cent of $500,000,000) to be obligated in a State whenever capital grant contracts have been executed with local public agencies in such State in excess of $33,500,000. Actual allocations are determined by the Administrator.

MATCHING REQUIREMENTS

Federal capital grants may finance up to two-thirds of the net project cost, or deficit, of projects undertaken by any local public agency. At least one-third of the net grants-in-aid may consist of cash, donations of land, or the provision of site clearance and site improvement work, or certain types of public facilities such as parks, playgrounds, schools, public buildings, and other public improvements which are of direct benefit to the projects. Such local grants-in-aid may be provided by a State, municipality, or public body, or any other entity.

Program XXIX. State Soldiers' Homes

ALLOCATION FORMULA

An act of 1888, as amended, authorizes payment to the States of $700 a year, or one-half of the per capita cost of maintenance if this amount is less than $700, for each veteran cared for in a State soldiers' home who is eligible for hospital treatment or domiciliary care by the Veterans' Administration.

MATCHING REQUIREMENTS

One-half of the per capita cost of maintenance.

Program XXX. Surplus Agricultural Commodities

ALLOCATION FORMULA

Within the total amount requested by a State, discretion rests with the U.S. Department of Agriculture as to the amount of commodities to be donated to a particular State. Such determination is based upon a balancing of the State's needs and utilization history and availability at a given time of a given commodity.

MATCHING REQUIREMENTS

None.

Program XXXI. *Urban Planning*

ALLOCATION FORMULA

The U.S. Housing and Home Finance Administrator is authorized under the Housing Act of 1954, as amended, to make grants to State planning agencies for planning assistance to municipalities of less than 25,000 population. The Administrator may also make grants to authorized State, metropolitan, or regional agencies for planning work in metropolitan and regional areas, and to municipalities and counties of at least 25,000 population which have suffered substantial damage as a result of a major disaster. Official planning agencies may also receive grants to plan for areas facing rapid urbanization as a result of Federal installations. In addition, grants may be made to State planning agencies to plan for localities affected by major disasters or by Federal installations.

MATCHING REQUIREMENTS

A grant may not exceed 50 per cent of the estimated planning costs.

Program XXXII. *Vocational Education*

ALLOCATION FORMULA

Allotment criteria:
Salaries of teachers of agriculture—rural population.
Salaries of teachers of trades and industry, and home economics—urban population.
Teacher training—total population.
Education in agriculture—farm population.
Education in trades and industry—nonfarm population.
Education in home economics—rural population.
Education in distributive occupations—total population.

MATCHING REQUIREMENTS

One Federal dollar must be matched by one dollar from State and local sources.

Program XXXIII. *Vocational Rehabilitation*

ALLOCATION FORMULA

Allotments for basic services are made on a variable grant basis, *i.e.*, according to the State's population weighted by the square of its allotment percentage (as determined

MATCHING REQUIREMENTS

Under the matching provisions of the formula for establishing the Federal share, it is stated that this share shall range between 50 and 70 per cent (it is fixed at 60

ALLOCATION FORMULA

by an equalization formula). The allotment percentage is squared because per capita income represents both need for the service and financial ability. To insure the uninterrupted operation of each State program under the new formula, the act provides a permanent "base allotment" equal to the State's grant for the fiscal year 1954.

MATCHING REQUIREMENTS

per cent where State per capita income exactly equals the corresponding U.S. figure) in 1963 and after. Each State matched its base allotment through 1959. During Fiscal years 1960 to 1962, adjustments were made so that grants for extension and improvements now carry a fixed Federal share of 75 per cent, Federal participation in a particular project not to exceed three years. Determination of State matching requirements is left to administrative determination, except that the State contribution shall not be less than one dollar for each two Federal dollars provided.

Program XXXIV. Waste Treatment Facilities

ALLOCATION FORMULA

Under the Federal Water Pollution Control Act of 1956, as amended, the Surgeon General of the U.S. Public Health Service is authorized to make grants to any State, interstate, municipal or intermunicipal agency for the construction of necessary treatment works to prevent the discharge of untreated or inadequately treated sewage or other waste into any waters. Such grants must be approved by the State pollution control agency and the Surgeon General. Funds are allotted to the States on the basis of population and per capita income.

MATCHING REQUIREMENTS

Grants are not to exceed 30 per cent of the estimated reasonable cost of the project, as determined by the Surgeon General, or in an amount exceeding $250,000, whichever is the smaller, and at least 50 per cent of the funds are to be used for projects serving municipalities of 125,000 population or under.

Program XXXV. Water Pollution Control

ALLOCATION FORMULA

Grants to State and interstate agencies to assist them in meeting the costs of establishing and maintaining adequate measures for the prevention and control of water pollution were authorized by the Federal Water Pollution Control Act of 1956. Federal grants had previously been authorized from 1950 through 1952 for studies and investigation of water pollution caused by industrial wastes. Funds are allocated to the States on the basis of population, the extent of the water pollution problem, and financial need.

MATCHING REQUIREMENTS

Matching requirements are related to each State's per capita income level. The program is administered by the U.S. Public Health Service, Department of Health, Education, and Welfare.

INDEX